A SELECT LIBRARY

OF THE

NICENE AND POST-NICENE FATHERS

OF

THE CHRISTIAN CHURCH

EDITED BY

PHILIP SCHAFF, D.D., LL.D.,

PROFESSOR OF CHURCH HISTORY IN THE UNION THEOLOGICAL SEMINARY, NEW YORK.

IN CONNECTION WITH A NUMBER OF PATRISTIC SCHOLARS OF EUROPE
AND AMERICA

VOLUME XII

SAINT CHRYSOSTOM:

HOMILIES ON THE EPISTLES OF PAUL TO THE CORINTHIANS

T&T CLARK
EDINBURGH

WM. B. EERDMANS PUBLISHING COMPANY
GRAND RAPIDS, MICHIGAN

British Library Cataloguing in Publication Data
Nicene & Post-Nicene Fathers. — 1st series
1. Fathers of the church
I. Title   II. Schaff, Philip
230'.11   BR60.A62

T&T Clark ISBN 0 567 09401 4

Eerdmans ISBN 0-8028-8110-6

Reprinted, May 1989

PHOTOLITHOPRINTED BY EERDMANS PRINTING COMPANY
GRAND RAPIDS, MICHIGAN, UNITED STATES OF AMERICA

THE HOMILIES OF SAINT JOHN CHRYSOSTOM

ARCHBISHOP OF CONSTANTINOPLE,

ON THE

EPISTLES OF PAUL TO THE CORINTHIANS

THE OXFORD TRANSLATION

REVISED WITH ADDITIONAL NOTES

BY

REV. TALBOT W. CHAMBERS, D. D.,

PASTOR OF THE COLLEGIATE REFORMED DUTCH CHURCH, NEW YORK.

PREFACE.

The British edition of this translation has a preface in which is given a short "sketch" of Chrysostom's history. As a fuller outline has been given in the course of the present re-production of the Homilies, it is considered advisable to omit this sketch here. (See Vol. ix. pp. 3–23.) The remainder of the English editor's preface is as follows:

"The history and remains of St. Chrysostom are in one respect more interesting perhaps to the modern reader, than most of the monuments of those who are technically called the Fathers. At the time when he was raised up, and in those parts of the Christian world to which he was sent, the Patriarchates, namely, of Antioch and Constantinople, the Church was neither agitated by persecution from without, nor by any particular doctrinal controversy within, sufficient to attract his main attention, and connect his name with its history, as the name of St. Asthanasius, e. g., is connected with the Arian, or that of St. Augustine with the Pelagian, controversy. The labours of St. Athanasius and St. Basil, and their friends and disciples, had come to a happy issue at the second Œcumenical Council; the civil power favoured orthodox doctrine, and upheld Episcopal authority. The Church seemed for the time free to try the force of her morals and discipline against the ordinary vices and errors of all ages and all nations. This is one reason why the Homilies of St. Chrysostom have always been considered as eminently likely among the relics of Antiquity, to be useful as models for preaching, and as containing hints for the application of Scripture to common life, and the consciences of persons around us.

Another reason undoubtedly is the remarkable energy and fruitfulness of the writer's mind, that command of language and of topics, and above all, that depth of charitable and religious feeling, which enabled him, to a very remarkable extent, to carry his hearers along with him, even when the things he recommended were most distasteful to their natures and prejudices. It is obvious how much of the expression of this quality must vanish in translation: the elegance and fluency of his Greek style, the flow of his periods, the quickness and ingenuity of his turns, all the excellencies to which more especially his surname was owing, must in the nature of things be sacrificed, except in cases of very rare felicity, on passing into a modern language. His dramatic manner indeed, which was one of the great charms of his oratory among the Greeks, and his rapid and ingenious selection and variation of topics, these may in some measure be retained, and may serve to give even English readers some faint notion of the eloquence which produced so powerful effects on the susceptible people of the East.

"However, it is not of course as compositions that we desire to call attention to these or any other of the remains of the Fathers. Nor would this topic have been so expressly adverted to, but for the two following reasons. First, it is in such particulars as these, that the parallel mainly subsists, which has more than once been observed, between St. Chrysostom and our own

Bishop Taylor : and it is good for the Church in general, and encouraging for our own Church in particular, to notice such providential revivals of ancient graces in modern times.

"Again, this profusion of literary talent, and eloquence and vehemence and skill in moral teaching, is of itself, as human nature now exists, a matter of much jealousy to considerate persons, who are aware how hardly and how seldom the lives of such speakers and writers have been found answerable to the profession implied in their works. And therefore it was desirable to dwell on it in this instance, for the purpose of pointing out afterwards how completely his life gave evidence that he meant and practiced what he taught.

"The Homilies on the First Epistle to the Corinthians have ever been considered by learned and devout men as among the most perfect specimens of his mind and teaching. They are of that mixed form, between exposition and exhortation, which serves perhaps better than any other, first, to secure attention, and then to convey to an attentive hearer the full purport of the holy words as they stand in the Bible, and to communicate to him the very impression which the preacher himself had received from the text. Accordingly they come in not unfitly in this series, by way of specimen of the hortatory Sermons of the ancients, as St. Cyril's, of their Catechetical Lectures, and St. Cyprian's, of the Pastoral Letters, which were circulated among them.

"The date of these Homilies is not exactly known : but it is certain that they were delivered at Antioch, were it only from Hom. xxi. §. 9. ad fin. Antioch was at that time, in a temporal sense, a flourishing Church, maintaining 3,000 widows and virgins[1], maimed persons, prisoners, and ministers of the altar; although, St. Chrysostom adds, its income was but that of one of the lowest class of wealthy individuals. It was indeed in a state of division, on account of the disputed succession in the Episcopate between the followers of Paulinus and Meletius since the year 362 : but this separation affected not immediately any point of doctrine ; and was in a way to be gradually worn out, partly by the labors of St. Chrysostom himself, whose discourse concerning the Anathema seems to have been occasioned by the too severe way in which the partisans on both sides allowed themselves to speak of each other. It may be that he had an eye to this schism in his way of handling those parts of the Epistles to the Corinthians, which so earnestly deprecate the spirit of schism and of party, and the calling ourselves by human names.

"The Text which has been used in this Translation is the Benedictine, corrected however in many places by that of Savile. The Benedictine Sections are marked in the margin thus, (2.) For the Translation, the Editors are indebted to the Reverend HUBERT KESTELL CORNISH, M. A., late Fellow of Exeter College, and to the Reverend JOHN MEDLEY, M. A., of Wadham College, Vicar of St. Thomas, in the city of Exeter."　　　　　　　　J. K[eble].

The Homilies on the Second Epistle were issued four years later than those on the First, and were preceded by the following note :

" The present Volume completes the set of St. Chrysostom's Commentaries on the Epistles of St. Paul, with the exception of that to the Hebrews, the Translation of which is preparing for the press. The edition of the original by MR. FIELD has afforded the advantage of an improved text, in fact of one as good as we can hope to see constructed from existing MSS.

---

[1] Hom. 66. on St. Matt. t. ii. p. 422. ed. Savil.

" These Homilies were delivered at Antioch in the opinion of the Benedictine Editors, though Savile doubted it. The question depends on the interpretation of a passage near the end of Hom. xxvi., in which St. Chrysostom speaks of Constantinople, and presently says 'here.' This, it has been rightly argued, he might say in the sense of 'in the place I am speaking of,' while he was not likely to say, 'in Constantinople,' if he were speaking there.

" For the Translation the Editors are indebted to the Rev. J. ASHWORTH, M. A., of Brasenose College."

S. Clement, 1848.

C. M. M[ARRIOTT.]

This volume of the Nicene and Post-Nicene Fathers, embraces both volumes of the original London issue, one of which appeared in 1844, the other in 1848. The author of the latter had, as appears from his statement above, the advantage of using the recension of the Greek text which was prepared by the late FREDERICK FIELD, M. A., LL. D., an eminent textual critic whose labors leave nothing to be desired so far as concerns the materials at his command. The translators of the First Epistle did not have this advantage. Hence the present editor has made a diligent comparison throughout their work with Dr. FIELD's text, and whenever it was necessary has silently conformed the rendering to that text, in a few instances omitting a note which was made needless or inappropriate by the change. In both Epistles he has occasionally amended the translation to gain perspicuity and smoothness. The work of the English authors has been performed with great care and fidelity, and is literal almost to a fault, it apparently being their endeavour to reproduce the form as well as the spirit of the original. This has given to their pages a stiffness and constraint not altogether agreeable, yet it is a compensation to the reader to know that he has before him the precise thought of the great pulpit orator of the Greek Church. The American Editor's notes have been enclosed in square brackets and marked with his initial.

The English text of the Epistles has been sedulously conformed to that of the Revised Version of 1881, except in cases in which the Greek text used by Chrysostom varied from that adopted by recent Editors. All peculiarities of Chrysostom's text have been faithfully preserved.

In these days when expository preaching is so loudly and generally demanded, it cannot but be of use to the rising ministry to see how this service was performed by the most eloquent and effective of the Fathers, John of the Golden-Mouth.

T. W. CHAMBERS.

NEW YORK, June, 1889.

CONTENTS

FIRST CORINTHIANS

PAGE

SECOND CORINTHIANS.

HOMILIES OF ST. JOHN CHRYSOSTOM,

ARCHBISHOP OF CONSTANTINOPLE,

ON THE

FIRST EPISTLE OF ST. PAUL THE APOSTLE.

TO THE

CORINTHIANS.

ARGUMENT.

[1.] As Corinth is now the first city of Greece, so of old it prided itself on many temporal advantages, and more than all the rest, on excess of wealth. And on this account one of the heathen writers entitled the place "the rich[1]." For it lies on the isthmus of the Peloponnesus, and had great facilities for traffic. The city was also full of numerous orators, and philosophers, and one[2]." I think, of the seven called wise men, was of this city. Now these things we have mentioned, not for ostentation's sake, nor to make, a display of great learning: (for indeed what is there in knowing these things?) but they are of use to us in the argument of the Epistle.

Paul also himself suffered many things in this city; and Christ, too, in this city appears to him and says, (Act. xviii. 10), "Be not silent, but speak; for I have much people in this city:" and he remained there two years. In this city [Acts xix. 16. Corinth put here, by lapse of memory, for Ephesus]. also the devil went out, whom the Jews endeavoring to exorcise, suffered so grievously. In this city did those of the magicians, who repented, collect together their books and burn them, and there appeared to be fifty thousand. (Acts xix. 18. ἀργυρίου omitted.) In this city also, in the time of Gallio the Proconsul, Paul was beaten before the judgment seat[3].

[2] The devil, therefore, seeing that a great and populous city had laid hold of the truth, a city admired for wealth and wisdom, and the head of Greece; (for Athens and Lacedæmon were then and since in a miserable state, the dominion having long ago fallen away from them;) and seeing that with great readiness they had received the word of God; what doth he? He divides the men. For he knew that even the strongest kingdom of all, divided against itself, shall not stand. He had a vantage ground too, for this device in the wealth, the wisdom of the inhabitants. Hence certain men, having made parties of their own, and having become self-elected made themselves leaders of the people, and some sided with these, and some with those; with one sort, as being rich; with another, as wise and able to teach something out of the common. Who on their part, receiving them, set themselves up forsooth to teach more than the Apostle did :[4] at which he was hinting, when he said, "I was not able to speak unto you as unto spiritual " (ch. iii. 1.); evidently not his inability, but their infirmity, was the cause of their not having been abundantly instructed. And this, (ch. iv. 8.) "Ye are become rich without us," is the remark of one pointing that way. And this was no small matter, but of all things most pernicious; that the Church should be torn asunder.

---

[1] Homer, *Il.* ii. 570; Thucyd. i. 13; Strabo, viii. 20.
[2] Periander; but vid. Plutarch. *in Solon*. tom. i. p. 185. ed. Bryan.
[3] This is said of Sosthenes, Acts xviii. 17. But the context makes it probable that St. Paul was beaten also. [Hardly.]

[4] St. Irenæus,*Adv. Hræ.* iii. v. 1, points out this as a main topic of heretical teaching. " These most futile of Sophisters affirm that the Apostles taught feignedly, after the capacity of the hearers, and gave answer after the prejudices of those who enquired of them, discoursing with the blind blindly according to their blindness, with the feeble according to their feebleness, and with the erring according to their error."

And another sin, too, besides these, was openly committed there : namely, a person who had had intercourse with his step-mother not only escaped rebuke, but was even a leader of the multitude, and gave occasion to his followers to be conceited. Wherefore he saith, (ch. 5. 2.) "And ye are puffed up, and have not rather mourned." And after this again, certain of those who as they pretended were of the more perfect sort, and who for gluttony's sake used to eat of things offered unto idols, and sit at meat in the temples, were bringing all to ruin. Others again, having contentions and strifes about money, committed unto the heathen courts (τοῖς ἔξωθεν σιχαδτηρίοις) all matters of that kind. Many persons also wearing long hair used to go about among them; whom he ordereth to be shorn. There was another fault besides, no trifling one; their eating in the churches apart by themselves, and giving no share to the needy.

And again, they were erring in another point, being puffed up with the gifts; and hence jealous of one another; which was also the chief cause of the distraction of the Church. The doctrine of the Resurrection, too, was lame (ἐχώλευε) among them : for some of them had no strong belief that there is any resurrection of bodies, having still on them the disease of Grecian foolishness. For indeed all these things were the progeny of the madness which belongs to Heathen Philosophy, and she was the mother of all mischief. Hence, likewise, they had become divided; in this respect also having learned of the philosophers. For these latter were no less at mutual variance, always, through love of rule and vain glory contradicting one another's opinions, and bent upon making some new discovery in addition to all that was before. And the cause of this was, their having begun to trust themselves to reasonings.

[3.] They had written accordingly to him by the hand of Fortunatus and Stephanas and Achaicus, by whom also he himself writes; and this he has indicated in the end of the Epistle : not however upon all these subjects, but about marriage and virginity; wherefore also he said,

(ch. vii. 1.) "Now concerning the things whereof ye wrote" &c. And he proceeds to give injunctions, both on the points about which they had written, and those about which they had not written; having learnt with accuracy all their failings. Timothy, too, he sends with the letters, knowing that letters indeed have great force, yet that not a little would be added to them by the presence of the disciple also.

Now whereas those who had divided the Church among themselves, from a feeling of shame lest they should seem to have done so for ambition's sake, contrived cloaks for what had happened, their teaching (forsooth) more perfect doctrines, and being wiser than all others; Paul sets himself first against the disease itself, plucking up the root of the evils, and its offshoot, the spirit of separation. And he uses great boldness of speech : for these were his own disciples, more than all others. Wherefore he saith (ch. ix. 2.) "If to others I be not an Apostle, yet at least I am unto you; for the seal of my apostleship are ye." Moreover they were in a weaker condition (to say the least of it) than the others. Wherefore he saith, (ch. iii. 1, 2. οὐδὲ for οὔτε). "For I have not spoken unto you as unto spiritual; for hitherto ye were not able, neither yet even now are ye able." (This he saith, that they might not suppose that he speaks thus in regard of the time past alone.)

However, it was utterly improbable that all should have been corrupted; rather there were some among them who were very holy. And this he signified[1] in the middle of the Epistle, where he says, (ch. iv. 3, 6.) "To me it is a very small thing that I should be judged of you :" and adds, "these things I have in a figure transferred unto myself and Apollos."

Since then from arrogance all these evils were springing, and from men's thinking that they knew something out of the common, this he purgeth away first of all, and in beginning saith,

---

[1] It appears by the subsequent commentary on these verses, that S. Chrysostom understood the Apostle to be alluding in them to persons among the Corinthians, who had suffered from unjust censure and party spirit. See Hom. ii, §. 1; xi, near the end; and the opening of Hom. xii.

HOMILY I.

Paul, called to be an Apostle of Jesus Christ, through the will of God, and Sosthenes our brother, unto the Church of God which is at Corinth, even them that are sanctified in Christ Jesus, called to be Saints, with all that call upon the name of our Lord Jesus Christ in every place, their Lord and ours: Grace unto you and peace from God our Father and the Lord Jesus Christ.

[1.] SEE how immediately, from the very beginning, he casts down their pride, and dashes to the ground all their fond imagination, in that he speaks of himself as "called." For what I have learnt, saith he, I discovered not myself, nor acquired by my own wisdom, but while I was persecuting and laying waste the Church I was called. Now here of Him that calleth is everything : of him that is called, nothing, (so to speak,) but only to obey.

"Of Jesus Christ." Your teacher is Christ ; and do you register the names of men, as patrons of your doctrine?

"Through the will of God." For it was God who willed that you should be saved in this way. We ourselves have wrought no good thing, but by the will of God we have attained to this salvation; and because it seemed good to him, we were called, not because we were worthy.

"And Sosthenes our brother." Another instance of his modesty ; he puts in the same rank with himself one inferior to Apollos; for great was the interval between Paul and Sosthenes. Now if where the interval was so wide he stations with himself one far beneath him, what can they have to say who despise their equals?

"Unto the Church of God." Not "of this or of that man," but of God.

"Which is at Corinth." Seest thou how at each word he puts down their swelling pride ; training their thoughts in every way for heaven? He calls it, too, the Church "of God ; " shewing that it ought to be united. For if it be "of God, " it is united, and it is one, not in Corinth only, but also in all the world : for the Church's name (ἐκκλησία: properly an assembly) is not a name of separation, but of unity and concord.

"To the sanctified in Christ Jesus." Again the name of Jesus ; the names of men he findeth no place for. But what is Sanctification? The Laver, the Purification. For he reminds them of their own uncleanness, from which he had freed them ; and so persuades them to lowliness of mind ; for not by their own good deeds, but by the loving-kindness of God, had they been sanctified.

"Called to be Saints." For even this, to be saved by faith, is not saith he, of yourselves ; for ye did not first draw near, but were called ; so that not even this small matter is yours altogether. However, though you had drawn near, accountable as you are for innumerable wickednesses, not even so would the grace be yours, but God's. Hence also, writing to the Ephesians, he said, (Eph. ii. 8.) "By grace have ye been saved through faith, and this not of yourselves ; " not even the faith is yours altogether ; for ye were not first with your belief, but obeyed a call.

"With all who call upon the Name of our Lord Jesus Christ." Not "of this or that man," but "the Name of the Lord."

[2.] "In every place, both theirs and ours." For although the letter be written to the Corinthians only, yet he makes mention of all the faithful that are in all the earth ; showing that the Church throughout the world must be one, however separate in divers places ; and much more, that in Corinth. And though the place separate, the Lord binds them together, being common to all. Wherefore also uniting them he adds, "both theirs and ours." And this is far more powerful [to unite], than the other [to separate]. For as men in one place, having many and contrary masters, become distracted, and their one place helps them not to be of one mind, their masters giving orders at variance with each other, and drawing each their own way, according to what Christ says, (St. Matt. vi. 24.) "Ye cannot serve God and Mammon ; " so those in different places, if they have not different lords but one only, are not by the places injured in respect of unanimity, the One Lord binding them together. "I say not then, (so he speaks,) that with Corinthians only, you being Corinthians ought to be of one mind, but with all that are in the whole world, inasmuch as you have a common Master." This is also why he hath a second

3

time added "our;" for since he had said, "the Name of Jesus Christ our Lord," lest he should appear to the inconsiderate to be making a distinction, he subjoins again, "both our Lord and theirs."

[3.] That my meaning may be clearer, I will read it according to its sense thus: "Paul and Sosthenes to the Church of God which is in Corinth and to all who call upon the Name of Him who is both our Lord and theirs in every place, whether in Rome or wheresoever else they may be: grace unto you and peace from God our Father and the Lord Jesus Christ."

Or again thus; which I also believe to be rather more correct: "Paul and Sosthenes to those that are at Corinth, who have been sanctified, called to be Saints, together with all who call upon the Name of our Lord Jesus Christ in place, both theirs and ours; " that is to say, "grace unto you, and peace unto you, who are at Corinth, who have been sanctified and called; " not to you alone, but " with all who in every place call upon the Name of Jesus Christ, our Lord and theirs."

Now if our peace be of grace, why hast thou high thoughts? Why art Thou so puffed up, being saved by grace? And if thou hast peace with God, why wish to assign thyself to others? since this is what separation comes to. For what if you be at " peace " with this man, and with the other even find " grace? " My prayer is that both these may be yours from God ; both from Him I say, and towards Him. For neither do they abide (μένει, Savile in marg.) secure except they enjoy the influence from above ; nor unless God be their object will they aught avail you : for it profiteth us nothing, though we be peaceful towards all men, if we be at war with God ; even as it is no harm to us, although by all men we are held as enemies, if with God we are at peace. And again it is no gain to us, if all men approve, and the Lord be offended; neither is there any danger, though all shun and hate us, if with God we have acceptance and love. For that which is verily grace, and verily peace, cometh of God, since he who finds grace in God's sight, though he suffer ten thousand horrors, feareth no one; I say not only, no man, but not even the devil himself; but he that hath offended God suspects all men, though he seem to be in security. For human nature is unstable, and not friends only and brethren, but fathers also, before now, have been altogether changed and often for a little thing he whom they begat, the branch of their planting, hath been to them, more than all foes, an object of persecution. Children, too, have cast off their fathers. Thus, if ye will mark it, David was in favor with God, Absalom was in favor with men. What was the end of each, and which of them gained most

honor, ye know. Abraham was in favor with God, Pharaoh with men ; for to gratify him they gave up the just man's wife. (See St. Chrys. on Gen. xii. 17.) Which then of the two was the more illustrious, and the happy man? every one knows. And why speak I of righteous men; The Israelites were in favor with God, but they were hated by men, the Egyptians ; but nevertheless they prevailed against their haters and vanquished them, with how great triumph, is well known to you all.

For this, therefore, let all of us labor earnestly ; whether one be a slave, let him pray for this, that he may find grace with God rather than with his master ; or a wife, let her seek grace from God her Saviour rather than from her husband ; or a soldier, in preference to his king and commander let him seek that favor which cometh from above. For thus among men also wilt thou be an object of love.

[4.] But how shall a man find grace with God? How else, except by lowliness of mind? "For God, "saith one, (St. Jas. iv. 6.) "resisteth the proud, but giveth grace unto the humble ; and, (Ps. li. 17. τεταπεινωμένην.) the sacrifice of God is a broken spirit, and a heart that is brought low God will not despise." For if with men humility is so lovely, much more with God. Thus both they of the Gentiles found grace and the Jews no other way fell from grace ; (Rom. x. 13.) "for they were not subject unto the righteousness of God." The lowly man of whom I am speaking, is pleasing and delightful to all men, and dwells in continual peace, and hath in him no ground for contentions. For though you insult him, though you abuse him, whatsoever you say, he will be silent and will bear it meekly, and will have so great peace towards all men as one cannot even describe. Yea, and with God also. For the commandments of God are to be at peace with men : and thus our whole life is made prosperous, through peace one with another. For no man can injure God: His nature is imperishable, and above all suffering. Nothing makes the Christian so admirable as lowliness of mind. Hear; for instance, Abraham saying, (Gen. xviii. 27.) "But I am but dust and ashes;" and again, God [saying] of Moses, that (Numb. xii. 3.) "he was the meekest of all men." For nothing was ever more humble than he ; who, being leader of so great a people, and having overwhelmed in the sea the king and the host of all the Egytians, as if they had been flies; and having wrought so many wonders both in Egypt and by the Red Sea and in the wilderness, and received such high testimony, yet felt exactly as if he had been an ordinary person, and as a son-in-law was humbler than his father-in-law, (Exodus xviii. 24.) and took advice from him, and was not indignant, nor did he say, "What is this? After such and so great achievements, art thou come to us with thy counsel?" This is what most people feel; though a man bring the best advice, despising it, because of the lowliness of the person. But not so did he: rather through lowliness of mind he wrought all things well. Hence also he despised the courts of kings, (Heb. xi. 24—26.) since he was lowly indeed: for the sound mind and the high spirit are the fruit of humility. For of how great nobleness and magnanimity, thinkest thou, was it a token, to despise the kingly palace and table? since kings among the Egyptians are honored as gods, and enjoy wealth and treasures inexhaustible. But nevertheless, letting go all these and throwing away the very sceptres of Egypt, he hastened to join himself unto captives, and men worn down with toil, whose strength was spent in the clay and the making of bricks, men whom his own slaves abhorred, (for, saith he (ἐβδελύσσοντο, Sept. Ex. i. 2.) "The Egyptians abhorred them;") unto these he ran and preferred them before their masters. From whence it is plain, that whoso is lowly, the same is high and great of soul. For pride cometh from an ordinary mind and an ignoble spirit, but moderation, from greatness of mind and a lofty soul.

[5] And if you please, let us try each by examples. For tell me, what was there ever more exalted than Abraham? And yet it was he that said, "I am but dust and ashes;" it was he who said, (Gen. xiii. 8.) "Let there be no strife between me and thee." But this man, so humble, (Gen. xiv. 21—24.) despised ("Persian," i. e. perhaps, "of Elam.") Persian spoils, and regarded not Barbaric trophies; and this he did of much highmindedness, and of a spirit nobly nurtured. For he is indeed exalted who is truly humble; (not the flatterer nor the dissembler;) for true greatness is one thing, and arrogance another. And this is plain from hence; if one man esteem clay to be clay, and despise it, and another admire the clay as gold, and account it a great thing; which, I ask, is the man of exalted mind? Is it not he who refuses to admire the clay? And which, abject and mean? Is it not he who admires it, and set much store by it? Just so do thou esteem of this case also; that he who calls himself but dust and ashes is exalted, although he say it out of humility; but that he who does not consider himself dust and ashes, but treats himself lovingly and has high thoughts, this man for his part must be counted mean, esteeming little things to be great. Whence it is clear that out of great loftiness of thought the patriarch spoke that saying, "I am but dust and ashes;" from loftiness of thought, not from arrogance.

For as in bodies it is one thing to be healthy and plump, (σφριγῶντα, firm and elastic.) and another thing to be swoln, although both indicate a full habit of flesh, (but in this case of unsound, in that of healthful flesh;) so also here: it is one thing to be arrogant, which is, as it were, to be swoln, and another thing to be high-souled, which is to be in a healthy state. And again, one man is tall from the stature of his person; another, being short, by adding buskins [1]becomes taller; now tell me, which of the two should we call tall and large? Is it not quite plain, him whose height is from himself? For the other has it as something not his own; and stepping upon things low in themselves, turns out a tall person. Such is the case with many men who mount themselves up on wealth and glory; which is not exaltation, for he is exalted who wants none of these things, but despises them, and has his greatness from himself. Let us therefore become humble that we may become exalted; (St. Luke xiv. 11.) "For he that humbleth himself shall be exalted." Now the self-willed man is not such as this; rather he is of all characters the most ordinary. For the bubble, too, is inflated, but the inflation is not sound; wherefore we call these persons "puffed up." Whereas the sober-minded man has no high thoughts, not even in high fortunes, knowing his own low estate; but the vulgar even in his trifling concerns indulges a proud fancy.

[6.] Let us then acquire that height which comes by humility. Let us look into the nature of human things, that we may kindle with the longing desire of the things to come; for in no other way is it possible to become humble, except by the love of what is divine and the contempt of what is present. For just as a man on the point of obtaining a kingdom, if instead of that purple robe one offer him some trivial compliment, will count it to be nothing; so shall we also laugh to scorn all things present, if we desire that other sort of honor. Do ye not see the children, when in their play they make a band of soldiers, and heralds precede them and lictors, and a boy marches in the midst in the general's place, how childish it all is? Just such are all human affairs; yea and more worthless than these: to-day they are, and to-morrow they are not. Let us therefore be above these things; and let us not only not desire them, but even be ashamed if any one hold them forth to us. For thus, casting out the love of these things, we shall possess that other love which is divine, and shall enjoy immortal glory. Which may God grant us all to obtain, through the grace and loving-kindness of our Lord Jesus Christ; with whom be to the Father, together with the holy and good Spirit, the glory and the power for ever and ever. Amen.

---

[1] ἐμβάδας a leathern shoe coming half way up the leg, with high heels of cork; used especially by tragic actors to elevate their size. Æschylus, says Horace, improving tragedy, "docuit magnumque loqui, nitique cothurno." A. P. 280.

HOMILY II.

1 Cor. i. 4, 5.

I thank my God always concerning you, for the Grace of God which was given you in Jesus Christ; that in every thing you were enriched in him.

[1]. THAT which he exhorts others to do, saying, "(Phil. iv. 6.) Let your requests with thanksgiving be made known unto God," the same also he used to do himself: teaching us to begin always from these words, and before all things to give thanks unto God. For nothing is so acceptable to God as that men should be thankful, both for themselves and for others: wherefore also he prefaces almost every Epistle with this. But the occasion for his doing so is even more urgent here than in the other Epistles. For he that gives thanks, does so, both as being well off, and as in acknowledgment of a favor: now a favor is not a debt nor a requital nor a payment: which indeed every where is important to be said, but much more in the case of the Corinthians who were gaping after the dividers of the Church.

[2.] "Unto my God." Out of great affection he seizes on that which is common, and makes it his own; as the prophets also from time to time use to say, (Ps. xliii. 4; lxii. 1.) "O God, my God;" and by way of encouragement he incites them to use the same language also themselves. For such expressions belong to one who is retiring from all secular things, and moving towards Him whom he calls on with so much earnestness: since he alone can truly say this, who from things of this life is ever mounting upwards unto God, and always preferring Him to all, and giving thanks continually, not [only] for the grace already given,[1] but whatever blessing hath been since at any time bestowed, for this also he offereth unto Him the same praise. Wherefore he saith not merely, "I give thanks," but "at all times, concerning you;" instructing them to be thankful both always, and to no one else save God only.

[3.] "For the grace of God." Seest thou how from every quarter he draws topics for correcting them? For where "grace" is, "works" are not; where "works," it is no more "grace." If therefore it be "grace," why are ye high-minded? Whence is it that ye are puffed up?

"Which is given you." And by whom was it given? By me, or by another Apostle? Not at all, but "by Jesus Christ." For the expression, "In Jesus Christ," signifies this. Observe how in divers places he uses the word ἐν, "in," instead of δι' οὗ, "through means of whom;" therefore its sense is no less.*

"That in every thing ye were enriched." Again, by whom? By Him, is the reply. And not merely "ye were enriched," but "in every thing." Since then it is first of all, "riches," then, "riches of God," next, "in every thing," and lastly, "through the Only-Begotten," reflect on the ineffable treasure!

Ver. 5. "In all utterance, and all knowledge." "Word" ["or utterance,"] not such as the heathen, but that of God. For there is knowledge without "word," and there is knowledge with "word." For so there are many who possess knowledge, but have not the power of speech; as those who are uneducated and unable to exhibit clearly what they have in their mind. Ye, saith he, are not such as these, but competent both to understand and to speak.

Ver. 6. "Even as the testimony of Christ was confirmed in you." Under the color of praises and thanksgiving he touches them sharply. "For not by heathen philosophy," saith he, "neither by heathen discipline, but by "the grace of God," and by the "riches," and the "knowledge," and the "word" given by Him, were you enabled to learn the doctrines of the truth, and to be confirmed unto the testimony of the Lord; that is, unto the Gospel. For ye had the benefit of many signs, many wonders, unspeakable grace, to make you receive the Gospel. If therefore ye were established by signs and grace, why do ye waver?" Now these are the words of one both reproving, and at the same time prepossessing them in his favor.

[4.] Ver. 7. "So that ye come behind in no gift." A great question here arises. They who had been "enriched in all utterance," so as in no respect to "come behind in any gift," are they carnal? For if they were such at the

---

[1] This seems to mean the grace given in Baptism once for all.

* [This is true, but modern criticism prefers the literal sense of the preposition; *in Jesus Christ*, i. e., in your fellowship with him. C.]

6

beginning, much more now. How then does he call them "carnal?" For, saith he, (1 Cor. iii. 1.) "I was not able to speak unto you as unto spiritual, but as unto carnal." What must we say then? That having in the beginning believed, and obtained all gifts, (for indeed they sought them earnestly,) they became remiss afterwards. Or, if not so, that not unto all are either these things said or those; but the one to such as were amenable to his censures, the other to such as were adorned with his praises. For as to the fact that they still had gifts; (1 Cor. xiv. 26, 29.) "Each one," saith he, "hath a psalm, hath a revelation, hath a tongue, hath an interpretation; let all things be done unto edifying." And, "Let the prophets speak two or three." Or we may state it somewhat differently; that as it is usual with us to call the greater part the whole, so also he hath spoken in this place. Withal, I think he hints at his own proceedings; for he too had shewn forth signs; even as also he saith in the second Epistle to them, (2 Cor. xii. 12, 13.) "Truly the signs of an Apostle were wrought among you in all patience:" and again, "For what is there wherein you were inferior to other churches?"

Or, as I was saying, he both reminds them of his own miracles and speaks thus with an eye to those who were still approved. For many holy men were there who had "set themselves to minister unto the saints," and had become "the first fruits of Achaia;" as he declareth (ch. xvi. 15.) towards the end.

[5.] In any case, although the praises be not very close to the truth, still however they are inserted by way of precaution, (οἰκονομικῶς) preparing the way beforehand for his discourse. For whoever at the very outset speaks things unpleasant, excludes his words from a hearing among the weaker: since if the hearers be his equals in degree they feel angry; if vastly inferior they will be vexed. To avoid this, he begins with what seem to be praises. I say, seem; for not even did this praise belong to them, but to the grace of God. For that they had remission of sins, and were justified, this was of the Gift from above. Wherefore also he dwells upon these points, which shew the loving-kindness of God, in order that he may the more fully purge out their malady.

[6.] "Waiting for the revelation (ἀποκάλυψιν. of our Lord Jesus Christ." "Why make ye much ado," saith he, "why are ye troubled that Christ is not come? Nay, he is come; and the Day, is henceforth at the doors." And consider his wisdom; how withdrawing them from human considerations he terrifies them by mention of the fearful judgment-seat, and thus implying that not only the beginnings must be good, but the end also. For with all these

gifts, and with all else that is good, we must be mindful of that Day: and there is need of many labors to be able to come unto the end.

"Revelation" is his word; implying that although He be not seen, yet He is, and is present even now, and then shall appear. Therefore there is need of patience: for to this end did ye receive the wonders, that ye may remain firm.

[7.] Ver. 8. "Who shall also confirm you unto the end, that ye may be unreprovable." Here he seems to court them, but the saying is free from all flattery; for he knows also how to press them home; as when he saith, (1 Cor. iv. 18, 21.) "Now some are puffed up as though I would not come to you:" and again, "What will ye? shall I come unto you with a rod, or in love, and in the spirit of meekness?" And, (2 Cor. xiii. 3.) "Since ye seek a proof of Christ speaking in me." But he is also covertly accusing them: for to say, "He shall confirm," and the word "unreprovable" marks them out as still wavering, and liable to reproof.

But do thou consider how he always fasteneth them as with nails to the Name of Christ. And not any man nor teacher, but continually the Desired One Himself is remembered by him: setting himself, as it were to arouse those who were heavy-headed after some debauch. For no where in any other Epistle doth the Name of Christ occur so continually. But here it is, many times in a few verses; and by means of it he weaves together, one may say, the whole of the proem. Look at it from the beginning. "Paul called [to be] an Apostle of Jesus Christ, to them that have been sanctified in Jesus Christ, who call upon the Name of our Lord Jesus Christ, grace [be] unto you and peace from God the Father, and the Lord Jesus Christ. I thank my God for the grace which hath been given you by·Jesus Christ, even as the testimony of Christ hath been confirmed in you, waiting for the revelation of our Lord Jesus Christ, who shall confirm you unreprovable in the day of our Lord Jesus Christ. God is faithful, by whom ye have been called into the fellowship of His Son Jesus Christ our Lord. And I beseech you by the Name of our Lord Jesus Christ." Seest thou the constant repetition of the Name of Christ? From whence it is plain even to the most unobservant, that not by chance nor unwittingly he doeth this, but in order that by incessant application[1] of that glorious Name he may foment* their inflammation, and purge out the corruption of the disease.

---

[1] The image here seems to be taken from the vulgar use, in medicine, of a charm or amulet.

* [Dr. Field's text reads ἐπαντλῶν.]

[8.] Ver. 9. "God is faithful, by whom ye were called unto the fellowship of His Son." Wonderful! How great a thing saith he here! How vast in the magnitude of the gift which he declares! Into the fellowship of the Only-Begotten have ye been called, and do ye addict yourselves unto men? What can be worse than this wretchedness? And how have ye been called? By the Father. For since "through Him," and "in Him," were phrases which he was constantly employing in regard of the Son, lest men might suppose that he so mentioneth Him as being less, he ascribeth the same to the Father. For not by this one and that one, saith he, but "by the Father" have ye been called; by Him also have ye been "enriched." Again, "ye have been called;" ye did not yourselves approach. But what means, "into the fellowship of His Son?" Hear him declaring this very thing more clearly elsewhere. (2 Tim. ii. 12.) If we suffer, we shall also reign with Him; if we die with Him, we shall also live with Him. Then, because it was a great thing which He had said, he adds an argument fraught with unanswerable conviction; for, saith he, "God is faithful," i. e. "true." Now if "true," what things He hath promised He will also perform. And He hath promised that He will make us partakers of His only-begotten Son; for to this end also did He call us. For (Rom. xi. 29.) "His gifts, and the calling of God," are without repentance.

These things, by a kind of divine art he inserts thus early, lest after the vehemence of the reproofs they might fall into despair. For assuredly God's part will ensue, if we be not quite impatient of His rein. (ἀφηνιάσωμεν.) As the Jews, being called, would not receive the blessings; but this was no longer of Him that called, but of their lack of sense. For He indeed was willing to give, but they, by refusing to receive, cast themselves away. For, had He called to a painful and toilsome undertaking, not even in that case were they pardonable in making excuse; however, they would have been able to say that so it was: but if the call be unto cleansing, (Comp. i. 4—7.) and righteousness, and sanctification, and redemption, and grace, and a free gift, and the good things in store, which eye hath not seen, nor ear heard; and it be God that calls, and calls by Himself; what pardon can they deserve, who come not running to Him? Let no one therefore accuse God; for unbelief cometh not of Him that calleth, but of those who start away (ἀποπηδῶντας) from Him.

[9.] But some man will say, "He ought to

bring men in, even against their will." Away with this. He doth not use violence, nor compel[1]; for who that bids to honors, and crowns, and banquets, and festivals, drags people, unwilling and bound? No one. For this is the part of one inflicting an insult. Unto hell He sends men against their will, but unto the kingdom He calls willing minds. To the fire He brings men bound and bewailing themselves: to the endless state of blessings not so. Else it is a reproach to the very blessings themselves, if their nature be not such as that men should run to them of their own accord and with many thanks.

"Whence it is then," say you, "that all men do not choose them?" From their own infirmity. "And wherefore doth He not cut off their infirmity?" And how tell me—in what way—ought He to cut it off? Hath He not made a world that teacheth His loving-kindness and His power? For (Ps. xix. 1.) "the heavens," saith one, "declare the glory of God." Hath He not also sent prophets? Hath He not both called and honored us? Hath He not done wonders? Hath He not given a law both written and natural? Hath He not sent His Son? Hath he not commissioned Apostles? Hath He not wrought sins? Hath He not threatened hell? Hath He not promised the kingdom? Doth He not every day make His sun to rise? Are not the things which He hath enjoined so simple and easy, that many transcend His commandments in the greatness of their self-denial[2]? "What was there to do unto the vineyard and I have not done it?" (Is. v. 4.)

[10.] "And why," say you, "did He not make knowledge and virtue natural to us?" Who speaketh thus? The Greek or the Christian? Both of them, indeed, but not about the same things: for the one raises his objection with a view to knowledge, the other with a view to conduct. First, then, we will reply to him who is on our side; for I do not so much regard those without, as our own members.

What then saith the Christian? "It were

---

[1] Yet in St. Luke xiv. 23. it is, "*compel* them to come in." But our Lord is there speaking of the kingdom of heaven, S. Chrysostom here, of heaven itself. [A better answer is that the words denote not physical violence or literal compulsion but intense moral earnestness.]

[2] [τῇ περιουσίᾳ τῆς φιλοσοφίας. Lit. "by the excess of philosophy." The term *philosophy* came to be used by the early Christian writers to denote a contemplative, self-denying life. The reference in the text is to the so-called "counsels of perfection," such as voluntary poverty, voluntary celibacy, etc., which as they exceed what is enjoined in the Gospel were supposed to establish a peculiar merit and secure a higher degree of blessedness. This two-fold standard of moral excellence may be traced back as far as the middle of the second century. See *Pastor Hermae Simil.* v. 3. C.]

meet to have implanted in us the knowledge itself of virtue." He hath implanted it; for if he had not done so, whence should we have known what things are to be done, what left undone? Whence are the laws and the tribunals? But "God should have imparted not [merely] knowledge, but also the very doing of it [virtue]. For what then wouldest thou have to be rewarded, if the whole were of God? For tell me, doth God punish in the same manner thee and the Greek upon committing sin[1]? Surely not. For up to a certain point thou hast confidence, viz. that which ariseth from the true knowledge. What then, if any one should now say that on the score of knowledge thou and the Greek will be accounted of like desert? Would it not disgust thee? I think so, indeed. For thou wouldest say that the Greek, having of his own wherewith to attain knowledge, was not willing. If then the latter also should say that God ought to have implanted knowledge in us naturally, wilt thou not laugh him to scorn, and say to him, "But why didst thou not seek for it? why wast thou not in earnest even as I?" And thou wilt stand firm with much confidence, and say that it was extreme folly to blame God for not implanting knowledge by nature. And this thou wilt say, because thou hast obtained what appertains to knowledge. So also hadst thou performed what appertains to practice, thou wouldest not have raised these questions: but thou art tired of virtuous practice, therefore thou shelterest thyself with these inconsiderate words. But how could it be at all right to cause that by necessity one should become good? Then shall we next have the brute beasts contending with us about virtue, seeing that some of them are more temperate than ourselves.

But thou sayest, "I had rather have been good by necessity, and so forfeited all rewards, than evil by deliberate choice, to be punished and suffer vengeance." But it is impossible that one should ever be good by necessity. If therefore thou knowest not what ought to be done, shew it, and then we will tell you what is right to say. But if thou knowest that uncleanness is wicked, wherefore dost thou not fly from the evil thing?

"I cannot," thou sayest. But others who have done greater things than this will plead against thee, and will more than prevail to stop thy mouth. For thou, perhaps, though living with a wife, art not chaste; but another even without a wife keeps his chastity inviolate. Now what excuse hast thou for not keeping the rule,

while another even leaps beyond the lines[2] that have been drawn to mark it?

But thou sayest, "I am not of this sort in my bodily frame, or my turn of mind." That is for want, not of power, but of will. For thus I prove that all have a certain aptness towards virtue: That which a man cannot do, neither will he be able to do though necessity be laid upon him; but, if, necessity being laid upon him, he is able, he that leaveth it undone, leaveth it undone out of choice. The kind of thing I mean is this: to fly up and be borne towards heaven, having a heavy body, is even simply impossible. What then, if a king should command one to do this, and threaten death, saying," Those men who do not fly, I decree that they lose their heads, or be burnt, or some other such punishment:" would any one obey him? Surely not. For nature is not capable of it. But if in the case of chastity this same thing were done, and he were to lay down laws that the unclean should be punished, be burnt, be scourged, should suffer the extremity of torture, would not many obey the law? "No," thou wilt say: "for there is appointed, even now, a law forbidding to commit adultery[3] and all do not obey it." Not because the fear looses its power, but because the greater part expect to be unobserved. So that if when they were on the point of committing an unclean action the legislator and the judge came before them, the fear would be strong enough to cast out the lust. Nay, were I to apply another kind of force inferior to this; were I to take the man and remove him from the beloved person, and shut him up close in chains, he will be able to bear it, without suffering any great harm. Let us not say then that such an one is by nature good, and such an one is by nature evil: for if a man were by nature good, he could never at any time become evil; and if he were by nature evil, he could never be good. But now we see that changes take place rapidly, and that men quickly shift from this side to the other, and from that fall back again into this. And these things we may see not in the Scriptures only, for instance, that publicans have become apostles; and disciples, traitors; and harlots, chaste; and robbers, men of good repute; and magicians have worshipped; and ungodly men passed over unto godliness, both in the New Testament and in the Old; but even every day a man may see many such things occurring. Now if things were natural, they could not change. For so we, being by nature susceptible, could never by any exertions become void

---

[1] The meaning seems to be, "Whatever other sins you commit, you have not the sin of unbelief to answer for; and would, I suppose, think it hard, if *cæteris paribus* you were counted as guilty as an unbeliever. Now this your instinctive judgment confutes any hope you may have that nature and circumstances may excuse you in any other sin."

[2] Τὰ σκάμματα. The image is borrowed from the gymnastic exercise of leaping.
[3] From the time of Constantine to that of Justinian it was a capital offence. Gibbon, c. 44. note 197.

of feeling. For that which is whatever it is by nature, can never fall away from such its natural condition. No one, for example, ever changed from sleeping to not sleeping: no one from a state of corruption unto incorruption: no one from hunger to the perpetual absence of that sensation. Wherefore neither are these things matters of accusation, nor do we reproach ourselves for them; nor ever did any one, meaning to blame another, say to him, "O thou, corruptible and subject to passion:" but either adultery or fornication, or something of that kind, we always lay to the charge of those who are responsible; and we bring them before judges, who blame and punish, and in the contrary cases award honors.

[11.] Since then both from our conduct towards one another, and from others' conduct to us when judged, and from the things about which we have written laws, and from the things wherein we condemn ourselves, though there be no one to accuse us; and from the instances of our becoming worse through indolence, and better through fear; and from the cases wherein we see others doing well and arriving at the height of self-command, (φιλοσοφίας) it is quite clear that we also have it in our power to do well:

why do we, the most part, deceive ourselves in vain with heartless pretexts and excuses, bringing not only no pardon, but even punishment intolerable? When we ought to keep before our eyes that fearful day, and to give heed to virtue; and after a little labor, obtain the incorruptible crowns? For these words will be no defence to us; rather our fellow-servants, and those who have practised the contrary virtues, will condemn all who continue in sin: the cruel man will be condemned by the merciful; the evil, by the good; the fierce, by the gentle; the grudging, by the courteous; the vain-glorious, by the self-denying; the indolent, by the serious; the intemperate, by the sober-minded. Thus will God pass judgment upon us, and will set in their place both companies; on one bestowing praise, on the other punishment. But God forbid that any of those present should be among the punished and dishonored, but rather among those who are crowned and the winners of the kingdom. Which may God grant us all to obtain through the grace and loving-kindness of our Lord Jesus Christ; with Whom unto the Father and the Holy Ghost be glory, power, honor, now and ever, and unto everlasting ages. Amen.

HOMILY III.

1 COR. i. 10.

Now I beseech you, brethren, through the name of our Lord Jesus Christ, that ye all speak of the same thing, and that there be no divisions among you; but that ye be perfected together in the same mind and in the same judgment.

WHAT I have continually been saying, that we must frame our rebukes gently and gradually, this Paul doth here also; in that, being about to enter upon a subject full of many dangers and enough to tear up the Church from her foundations he uses very mild language. His word is that he "beseeches" them, and beseeches them "through Christ;" as though not even he were sufficient alone to make this supplication, and to prevail.

But what is this, "I beseech you through Christ?" "I take Christ to fight on my side, and to aid me, His injured and insulted Name." An awful way of speaking indeed! lest they should prove hard and shameless: for sin makes men restless. Wherefore if at once(ἂν μὲν εὐθέως ἐπιπλήξῃς Savil. ἂν μὴ Ben.) you sharply rebuke

you make a man fierce and impudent: but if you put him to shame, you bow down his neck, you check his confidence, you make him hang down his head. Which object being Paul's also, he is content for a while to beseech them through the Name of Christ. And what, of all things, is the object of his request?

"That ye may all speak the same thing, and that there be no divisions [schisms] among you." The emphatic force of the word "schism," I mean the name itself, was a sufficient accusation. For it was not that they had become many parts, each entire within itself, but rather the One [Body which originally existed] had perished. For had they[1] been entire Churches, there might be many of them; but if they were divisions, then that first One was gone. For that which is entire within itself not only does not become many by division into many parts, but even the original One is lost. Such is the nature of divisions.

---

[1] i. e. the bodies formed by separation.

[2.] In the next place, because he had sharply dealt with them by using the word "schism," he again softens and soothes them, saying, "That ye may be perfectly joined together in the same mind and in the same judgment." That is; since he had said, "That ye may all speak the same thing;" "do not suppose," he adds, "that I said concord should be only in words; I seek for that harmony which is of the mind." But since there is such a thing as agreement in words, and that hearty, not however on all subjects, therefore he added this, "That ye may be perfected together." For he that is united in one thing, but in another dissents, is no longer "perfected," nor fitted in to complete accordance. There is also such a thing as harmony of opinions, where there is not yet harmony of sentiment; for instance, when having the same faith we are not joined together in love: for thus, in opinions we are one, (for we think the same things,) but in sentiment not so. And such was the case at that time; this person choosing one [leader], and that, another. For this reason he saith it is necessary to agree both in "mind" and in "judgment." For it was not from any difference in faith that the schisms arose, but from the division of their judgment through human contentiousness.

[3.] But seeing that whoso is blamed is unabashed so long as he hath no witnesses, observe how, not permitting them to deny the fact, he adduces some to bear witness.

Ver. 11. "For it hath been signified unto me concerning you, my brethren, by them which are of the household of Chloe." Neither did he say this at the very beginning, but first he brought forward his charge; as one who put confidence in his informants. Because, had it not been so, he would not have found fault: for Paul was not a person to believe lightly. Neither then did he immediately say, "it hath been signified," lest he might seem to blame on their authority: neither does he omit all mention of them, lest he should seem to speak only from himself. And again, he styles them "brethren;" for although the fault be plain, there is nothing against calling people brethren still. Consider also his prudence in not speaking of any distinct person, but of the entire family; so as not to make them hostile towards the informer: for in this way he both protects him, and fearlessly opens the accusation. For he had an eye to the benefit not of the one side only, but of the other also. Wherefore he saith not, "It hath been declared to me by certain," but he indicates also the household, lest they might suppose that he was inventing.

[4.] What was "declared?" "That there are contentions among you." Thus, when he is rebuking them, he saith, "That there be no divisions among you;" but when he is reporting the statements of others, he doth it more gently; saying, "For it hath been declared unto me . . . that there are contentions among you; in order that he might not bring trouble upon the informants.

Next he declares also the kind of contention.

Ver. 12. "That each one of you saith, I am of Paul, and I of Apollos, and I of Cephas." "I say, contentions," saith he, "I mean, not about private matters, but of the more grievous sort." "That each one of you saith;" for the corruption pervaded not a part, but the whole of the Church. And yet they were not speaking about himself, nor about Peter, nor about Apollos; but he signifies that if these were not to be leaned on, much less others. For that they had not spoken about them, he saith further on: "And these things I have transferred in a figure unto myself and Apollos, that ye may learn in us not to go beyond the things which are written." For if it were not right for them to call themselves by the name of Paul, and of Apollos, and of Cephas, much less of any others. If under the Teacher and the first of the Apostles, and one that had instructed so much people, it were not right to enroll themselves, much less under those who were nothing. By way of hyperbole then, seeking to withdraw them from their disease, he sets down these names. Besides, he makes his argument less severe, not mentioning by name the rude dividers of the Church, but concealing them, as behind a sort of masks, with the names of the Apostles.

"I am of Paul, and I of Apollos, and I of Cephas. Not esteeming himself before Peter hath he set his name last, but preferring Peter to himself, and that greatly. He arranged his statement in the way of climax, (κατὰ αὔξησιν) that he might not be supposed to do this for envy; or, from jealousy, to be detracting from the honor of others. Wherefore also he put his own name first. For he who puts himself foremost to be rejected, doth so not for love of honor, but for extreme contempt of this sort of reputation. He puts himself, you see, in the way of the whole attack, and then mentions Apollos, and then Cephas. Not therefore to magnify himself did he do this, but in speaking of wrong things he administers the requisite correction in his own person first.

[5.] But that those who addicted themselves to this or that man were in error, is evident. And rightly he rebukes them, saying, "Ye do not well in that ye say, 'I am of Paul, and I of Apollos, and I of Cephas.'" But why did he add, "And I of Christ?" For although those who addicted themselves to men were in error, not surely (οὐδὲ που Bened. οὐ δήπου Savil.) those who dedicated themselves unto Christ. But this was not his charge, that they called themselves by the Name of Christ, but that they did not all call themselves by that Name alone. And I think that he added this of himself, wishing to make the accusation more grievous, and to point out that by this rule Christ must be considered as belonging to one party only : although they were not so using the Name themselves. For that this was what he hinted at he declared in the sequel, saying,

Ver. 3. " Is Christ divided" What he saith comes to this: " Ye have cut in pieces Christ, and distributed His body." Here is anger ! here is chiding ! here are words full of indignation ! For whenever instead of arguing he interrogates only, his doing so implies a confessed absurdity.

But some say that he glanced at something else, in saying, " Christ is divided:" as if he had said, "He hath distributed to men and parted the Church, and taken one share Himself, giving them the other." Then in what follows, he labors to overthrow this absurdity, saying, " Was Paul crucified for you, or were ye baptized into the name of Paul ? " Observe his Christ-loving mind; how thenceforth he brings the whole matter to a point in his own name, shewing, and more than shewing, that this honor belongs to no one. And that no one might think it was envy which moved him to say these things, therefore he is constantly putting himself forward. Observe, too, his considerate way, in that he saith not, " Did Paul make the world? did Paul from nothing produce you into being ? " But only those things which belonged as choice treasures to the faithful, and were regarded with great solicitude —those he specifies, the Cross, and Baptism, and the blessings following on these. For the loving-kindness of God towards men is shewn by the creation of the world also : in nothing, however, so much as by the (τῆς συγκαταβάσεως) condescension through the Cross. And he said not, " did Paul die for you ? " but, " was Paul crucified ? " setting down also the kind of death.

" Or were ye baptized into the name of Paul ? " Again, he saith not, " did Paul baptize you ? " For he did baptize many : but this was not the question, by whom they had been baptized, but, into whose name they had been baptized ! For since this also was a cause of schisms, their being called after the name of those who baptized them, he corrects this error likewise, saying, " Were ye baptized into the name of Paul ? " " Tell me not, " saith he, "who baptized, but into whose name. For not he that baptizeth, but he who is invoked in the

Baptism, is the subject of enquiry. For this is He who forgives our sins[1] "

And at this point he stays the discourse, and does not pursue the subject any further. For he saith not, " Did Paul declare to you the good things to come ? Did Paul promise you the kingdom of heaven ? " Why, then, I ask, doth he not add these questions also ? Because it is not all as one, to promise a kingdom and to be crucified. For the former neither had danger nor brought shame ; but the latter, all these. Moreover, he proves the former from the latter : for having said, (Rom. viii. 32.) " He that spared not His own Son," he adds, " How shall He not with Him also freely give us all things ? And again, (Rom. v. 10.) " For if when we were enemies we were reconciled unto God by the death of His Son, much more being reconciled, we shall be saved." This was one reason for his not adding what I just mentioned : and also because the one they had not as yet, but of the other they had already made trial. The one were in promise; the other had already come to pass.

[6.] Ver. 14. " I thank God that I baptized none of you but Crispus and Gaius." " Why are you elate at having baptized, when I for my part even give thanks that I have not done so ! " Thus saying, by a kind of divine art (οἰκονομικῶς) he does away with their swelling pride upon this point; not with the efficacy of the baptism, (God forbid,) but with the folly of those who were puffed up at having been baptizers: first, by showing that the Gift is not theirs ; and, secondly, by thanking God therefore. For Baptism truly is a great thing : but its greatness is not the work of the person baptizing, but of Him who is invoked in the Baptism : since to baptize is nothing as regards man's labor, but is much less than preaching the Gospel. Yea, again I say, great indeed is Baptism, and without baptism it is impossible to obtain the kingdom. Still a man of no singular excellence is able to baptize, but to preach the Gospel there is need of great labor.

Ver. 15. He states also the reason, why he giveth thanks that he had baptized no one. What then is this reason ? " Lest anyone should say that ye were baptized into my own name." Why, did he mean that they said this in those other cases ? Not at all ; but, " I fear," saith he, " lest the disease should proceed even to that. For if, when insignificant persons and of little worth baptize, a heresy ariseth, had I, the first announcer of Baptism, baptized many, it was likely that they forming a party, would not

---

[1] This seems to allude to the words of the ancient Oriental Creed, as preserved by S. Cyril of Jerusalem, " I believe in one Baptism of Repentance, for the Remission of Sins ;" (see Bp. Bull, *Jud. Eccl. Cath.* c. vi. §. 4. &c.) into which Creed, in all probability, the people of Antioch had been baptized.

only call themselves by my name, but also ascribe the Baptism to me." For if from the inferiors so great an evil arose, from those of higher order it would perhaps have gone on to something far more grievous.

Ver. 16. Then, having abashed those who were unsound in this respect and subjoining, "I baptized also the house of Stephanas," he again drags down their pride, saying besides, "I know not whether I baptized any other." For by this he signifies that neither did he seek much to enjoy the honor accruing hereby from the multitude, nor did he set about this work for glory's sake.

Ver. 17. And not by these only, but also by the next words, he greatly represses their pride, saying, "Christ sent me not to baptize, but to preach the Gospel:" for the more laborious part, and that which needed much toil and a soul of iron, and that on which all depended, was this. And therefore it was that Paul had it put into his hand.

And why, not being sent to baptize, did he baptize? Not in contention with Him that sent him, but in this instance laboring beyond his task. For he saith not, "I am forbidden," but, "I was not sent for this, but for that which was of the greatest necessity." For preaching the Gospel is a work perhaps for one or two; but baptizing, for everyone endowed with the priesthood. For a man being instructed and convinced, to take and baptize him is what any one whatever might do: for the rest, it is all effected by the will of the person drawing near, and the grace of God. But when unbelievers are to be instructed, there must be great labor, great wisdom. And at that time there was danger also annexed. In the former case the whole thing is done, and he is convinced, who is on the point of initiation: and it is no great thing when a man is convinced, to baptize him. But in the latter case the labor is great, to change the deliberate will, to alter the turn of mind, and to tear up error by the roots, and to plant the truth in its place.

Not that he speaks out all this, neither doth he argue in so many words that Baptism has no labor, but that preaching has. For he knows how always to subdue his tone, whereas in the comparison with heathen wisdom he is very earnest, the subject enabling him to use more vehemency of language.

Not therefore in opposition to Him that sent him did he baptize; but, as in the case of the widows[1], though the apostles had said, (Acts. vi. 2.) "it is not fit that we should leave the Word of God and serve tables," he discharged the office (Acts xii. 25. τὴν διακονίαν) of a dea-

con, not in opposition to them, but as something beyond his task : so also here. For even now, we commit this matter to the simpler sort of presbyters, but the word of doctrine unto the wiser : for there is the labor and the sweat. Wherefore he saith himself, (1 Tim. v. 17.) "Let the Elders who rule well be counted worthy of double honor, especially they who labor in the word and in teaching." For as to teach the wrestlers in the games is the part of a spirited and skilful trainer, but to place the crown on the conqueror's head may be that of one who cannot even wrestle, (although it be the crown which adds splendor to the conqueror,) so also in Baptism. It is impossible to be saved without it, yet it is no great thing which the baptizer doth, finding the will ready prepared.

[7.] "Not in wisdom of words, lest the Cross of Christ should be made of none effect."

Having brought down the swelling pride of those who were arrogant because of their baptizing, he changes his ground afterwards to meet those who boasted about heathen wisdom, and against them he puts on his armor with more vehemency. For to those who were puffed up with baptizing he said, "I give thanks that I baptized no one;" and, "for Christ sent me not to baptize." He speaks neither vehemently nor argumentatively, but, having just hinted his meaning in a few words, passeth on quickly. But here at the very outset he gives a severe blow, saying, "Lest the Cross of Christ be made void." Why then pride thyself on a thing which ought to make thee hide thy face? Since, if this wisdom is at war with the Cross and fights with the Gospel, it is not meet to boast about it, but to retire with shame. For this was the cause why the Apostles were not wise; not through any weakness of the Gift, but lest the Gospel preached suffer harm. The sort of people therefore above mentioned were not those employed in advocating the Word: rather they were among its defamers. The unlearned men were the establishers of it. This was able to check vain glory, this to repress arrogance, this to enforce moderation.

"But if it was 'not by wisdom of speech,' why did they send Apollos who was eloquent?" It was not, he replies, through confidence in his power of speech, but because he was (Acts xviii. 24, 29.) "mighty in the Scriptures," and "confuted the Jews." And besides the point in question was that the leaders and first dissemina-tors of the word were not eloquent; since these were the very persons to require some great power, for the expulsion of error in the first instance ; and then, namely, at the very outset, was the abundant strength needed. Now He who could do without educated persons at first, if afterwards some being eloquent were admitted

---

[1] Perhaps the allusion is to such places as Acts ii. 30; 24. 17; 1 Cor. 16. 4; &c.

by Him, He did so not because He wanted them, but because He would make no distinctions. For as he needed not wise men to effect whatever He would, so neither, if any were afterwards found such, did He reject them on that account.

[8.] But prove to me that Peter and Paul were eloquent. Thou canst not: for they were "unlearned and ignorant men!"[1] As therefore Christ, when He was sending out His disciples into the world, having shewn unto them His power in Palestine first, and said, (St. Luke xxii. 35. ὑποδήμάτος, rec. text ὑποδήματων.) "When I sent you forth without purse and wallet and shoe, lacked ye any thing?" permitted them from that time forward to possess both a wallet and a purse; so also He hath done here: for the point was the manifestation of Christ's power, not the rejection of persons from the Faith on account of their Gentile wisdom, if they were drawing nigh. When the Greeks then charge the disciples with being uneducated, let us be even more forward in the charge than they. Nor let any one say, "Paul was wise;" but while we exalt those among them who were great in wisdom and admired for their excellency of speech, let us allow that all on our side were uneducated; for it will be no slight overthrow which they will sustain from us in that respect also: and so the victory will be brilliant indeed.

I have said these things, because I once heard a Christian disputing in a ridiculous manner with a Greek, and both parties in their mutual fray ruining themselves. For what things the Christian ought to have said, these the Greek asserted; and what things it was natural to expect the Greek would say, these the Christian pleaded for himself. As thus: the dispute being about Paul and Plato, the Greek endeavord to show that Paul was unlearned and ignorant; but the Christian, from simplicity, was anxious to prove that Paul was more eloquent than Plato. And so the victory was on the side of the Greek, this argument being allowed to prevail. For if Paul was a more considerable person than Plato, many probably would object that it was not by grace, but by excellency of speech that he prevailed; so that the Christian's assertion made for the Greek. And what the Greek said made for the Christian's; for if Paul was uneducated and yet overcame Plato, the victory, as I was saying, was brilliant; the disciples of the latter, in a body, having been attracted by the former, unlearned as he was, and convinced, and brought over to his side. From whence it is plain that the Gospel was a result not of human wisdom, but of the grace of God.

Wherefore, lest we fall into the same error, and be laughed to scorn, arguing thus with Greeks whenever we have a controversy with them; let us charge the Apostles with want of learning; for this same charge is praise. And when they say that the Apostles were rude, let us follow up the remark and say that they were also untaught, and unlettered, and poor, and vile, and stupid, and obscure. It is not a slander on the Apostles to say so, but it is even a glory that, being such, they should have outshone the whole world. For these untrained, and rude, and illiterate men, as completely vanquished the wise, and powerful, and the tyrants, and those who flourished in wealth and glory and all outward good things, as though they had not been men at all: from whence it is manifest that great is the power of the Cross; and that these things were done by no human strength. For the results do not keep the course of nature, rather what was done was above all nature. Now when any thing takes place above nature, and exceedingly above it, on the side of rectitude and utility; it is quite plain that these things are done by some Divine power and co-operation. And observe; the fisherman, the tentmaker, the publican, the ignorant, the unlettered, coming from the far distant country of Palestine, and having beaten off their own ground the philosophers, the masters of oratory, the skilful debaters, alone prevailed against them in a short space of time; in the midst of many perils; the opposition of peoples and kings, the striving of nature herself, length of time, the vehement resistance of inveterate custom, demons in arms, the devil in battle array and stirring up all, kings, rulers, peoples, nations, cities, barbarians, Greeks, philosophers, orators, sophists, historians, laws, tribunals, divers kinds of punishments, deaths innumerable and of all sorts. But nevertheless all these were confuted and gave way when the fisherman spake; just like the light dust which cannot bear the rush of violent winds. Now what I say is, let us learn thus to dispute with the Greeks; that we be not like beasts and cattle, but prepared concerning "the hope which is in us." (1 St. Pet. iii. 15.) And let us pause for a while to work out this topic, no unimportant one; and let us say to them, How did the weak overcome the strong; the twelve, the world? Not by using the same armor, but in nakedness contending with men in arms.

For say, if twelve men, unskilled in matters of war, were to leap into an immense and armed host of soldiers, themselves not only unarmed but of weak frame also; and to receive no harm from them, nor yet be wounded, though assailed with ten thousand weapons; if while the darts were striking them, with

---

[1] ἀγράμματοι καὶ ἰδιῶται. Acts iv. 13: there spoken of St. Peter and St. John, and by St. Chrysostom here quoted from memory as of St. Peter and St. Paul.

bare naked body they overthrew all their foes, using no weapons but striking with the hand, and in conclusion killed some, and others took captive and led away, themselves receiving not so much as a wound; would anyone have ever said that the thing was of man? And yet the trophy of the Apostles is much more wonderful than that. For a naked man's escaping a wound is not so wonderful by far as that the ordinary and unlettered person—that a fisherman—should overcome such a degree of talent: (δεινότητος) and neither for fewness, nor for poverty, nor for dangers, nor for prepossession of habit, nor for so great austerity of the precepts enjoined, nor for the daily deaths, nor for the multitude of those who were deceived, nor for the great reputation of the deceivers, be turned from his purpose.

[9.] Let this, I say, be our way of overpowering them, and of conducting our warfare against them; and let us astound them by our way of life rather than by words. For this is the main battle, this is the unanswerable arguments the argument from conduct. For though we give ten thousand precepts of philosophy in words, if we do not exhibit a life better than theirs, the gain is nothing. For it is not what is said that draws their attention, but their enquiry is, what we do; and they say, "Do thou first obey thine own words, and then admonish others. But if while thou sayest, 'infinite are the blessings in the world to come,' thou seem thyself nailed down to this world, just as if no such things existed, thy works to me are more credible than thy words. For when I see thee seizing other men's goods, weeping immoderately over the departed, doing ill in many other things, how shall I believe thee that there is a resurrection?" And what if men utter not this in words? they think it and turn it often in their minds. And this is what stays the unbelievers from becoming Christians.

Let us win them therefore by our life. Many, even among the untaught, have in that way astounded the minds of philosophers, as having exhibited in themselves also that philosophy which lies in deeds, and uttered a voice clearer than a trumpet by their mode of life and self-denial. For this is stronger than the tongue. But when I say, "one ought not to bear malice," and then do all manner of evils to the Greek, how shall I be able by words to win him, while by my deeds I am frightening him away? Let us catch them then by our mode of life; and by these souls let us build up the Church, and of these let us amass our wealth. There is nothing to weigh against a soul, not even the whole world. So that although thou give countless treasure unto the poor, thou wilt do no such work as he who converteth one soul. (Jer. xv. 19.) "For he that taketh forth the precious from the vile shall be as my mouth:" so He speaks. A great good it is, I grant, to have pity on the poor; but it is nothing equal to the withdrawing them from error. For he that doth this resembles Paul and Peter: we being permitted to take up their Gospel, not with perils such as theirs;—with endurance of famines and pestilences, and all other evils, (for the present is a season of peace;)—but so as to display that diligence which cometh of zeal. For even while we sit at home we may practice this kind of fishery. Who hath a friend or relation or inmate of his house, these things let him say, these do; and he shall be like Peter and Paul. And why do I say Peter and Paul? He shall be the mouth of Christ. For He saith, "He that taketh forth the precious from the vile shall be as My mouth." And though thou persuade not to-day, to-morrow thou shalt persuade. And though thou never persuade, thou shalt have thine own reward in full. And though thou persuade not all, a few out of many thou mayest; since neither did the Apostles persuade all men; but still they discoursed with all, and for all they have their reward. For not according to the result of the things that are well done, but according to the intention of the doers, is God wont to assign the crowns; though thou pay down but two farthings, He receiveth them; and what He did in the case of the widow, the same will He do also in the case of those who teach. Do not thou then, because thou canst not save the world, despise the few; nor through longing after great things, withdraw thyself from the lesser. If thou canst not an hundred, take thou charge of ten; if thou canst not ten, despise not even five; if thou canst not five, do not overlook one; and if thou canst not one, neither so despair, nor keep back what may be done by thee. Seest thou not how, in matters of trade, they who are so employed make their profit not only of gold but of silver also? For if we do not slight the little things, we shall keep hold also of the great. But if we despise the small, neither shall we easily lay hand upon the other. Thus individuals become rich, gathering both small things and great. And so let us act; that in all things enriched, we may obtain the kingdom of heaven; through the grace and loving-kindness of our Lord Jesus Christ, through Whom and with Whom unto the Father together with the Holy Spirit be glory, power, honor, now and henceforth and for evermore. Amen.

HOMILY IV.

1 COR. i. 18—20.

For the word of the cross is to them that perish. foolishness; but to us which are saved it is the power of God. For it is written, I will destroy the wisdom of the wise, and the prudence of the prudent will I reject. Where is the Wise? Where is the Scribe? Where is the Disputer of the World?

To the sick and gasping even wholesome meats are unpleasant, friends and relations burdensome; who are often times not even recognized, but are rather accounted intruders. Much like this often is the case of those who are perishing in their souls. For the things which tend to salvation they know not; and those who are careful about them they consider to be troublesome. Now this ensues not from the nature of the thing, but from their disease. And just what the insane do, hating those who take care of them, and besides reviling them, the same is the case with unbelievers also. But as in the case of the former, they who are insulted then more than ever compassionate them, and weep, taking this as the worst symptom of the disease in its intense form, when they know not their best friends; so also in the case of the Gentiles let us act; yea more than for our wives let us wail over them, because they know not the common salvation. For not so dearly ought a man to love his wife as we should love all men, and draw them over unto salvation; be a man a Gentile, or be he what he may. For these then let us weep; for "the word of the Cross is to them foolishness," being itself Wisdom and Power. For, saith he, "the word of the Cross to them that perish is foolishness."

For since it was likely that they, the Cross being derided by the Greeks, would resist and contend by aid of that wisdom, which came (forsooth) of themselves, as being disturbed by the expression of the Greeks; Paul comforting them saith, think it not strange and unaccountable, which is taking place. This is the nature of the thing, that its power is not recognized by them that perish. For they are beside themselves, and behave as madmen; and so they rail and are disgusted at the medicines which bring health.

[2.] But what sayest thou, O man? Christ became a slave for thee, "having taken the form of a slave," (Phil. ii. 7.) and was crucified, and rose again. And when thou oughtest for this reason to adore Him risen and admire His loving kindness; because what neither father, nor friend, nor son, did for thee, all this the Lord wrought for thee, the enemy and offender—when, I say, thou oughtest to admire Him for these things, callest thou that foolishness, which is full of so great wisdom? Well, it is nothing wonderful; for it is a mark of them that perish not to recognize the things which lead to salvation. Be not troubled, therefore, for it is no strange nor unaccountable event, that things truly great are mocked at by those who are beside themselves. Now such as are in this mind you cannot convince by human wisdom. Nay, if you want so to convince them, you do but the contrary. For the things which transcend reasoning require faith alone. Thus, should we set about convincing men by reasonings, how God became man, and entered into the Virgin's womb, and not commit the matter unto faith, they will but deride the more. Therefore they who inquire by reasonings, it is they who perish.

And why speak I of God? for in regard of created things, should we do this, great derision will ensue. For suppose a man, wishing to make out all things by reasoning; and let him try by thy discourse to convince himself how we see the light; and do thou try to convince him by reasoning. Nay, thou canst not: for if thou sayest that it suffices to see by opening the eyes, thou hast not expressed the manner, but the fact. For "why see we not," one will say, "by our hearing, and with our eyes hear? And why hear we not with the nostril, and with the hearing smell?" If then, he being in doubt about these things, and we unable to give the explanation of them, he is to begin laughing, shall not we rather laugh him to scorn? "For since both have their origin from one brain, since the two members are near neighbors to each other, why can they not do the same work?" Now we shall not be able to state the cause, nor the method of the unspeakable and curious operation; and should we make the attempt, we should be laughed to scorn. Wherefore, leaving this unto God's power and boundless wisdom, let us be silent.

Just so with regard to the things of God; should we desire to explain them by the wisdom which is from without, great derision will ensue, not from their infirmity, but from the folly of men. For the great things of all no language can explain.

[3.] Now observe: when I say, "He was crucified;" the Greek saith, "And how can this be reasonable? Himself He helped not when undergoing crucifixion and sore trial at the moment of the Cross: how then after these things did He rise again and help others? For if He had been able, before death was the proper time." (For this the Jews actually said.) (St. Matt. xxvii. 41, 42.) "But He who helped not Himself, how helped he others? There is no reason in it," saith he. True, O man, for indeed it is above reason; and unspeakable is the power of the Cross. For that being actually in the midst of horrors, He should have shewn Himself above all horrors; and being in the enemy's hold should have overcome; this cometh of Infinite Power. For as in the case of the Three Children, their not entering the furnace would not have been so astonishing, as that having entered in they trampled upon the fire;—and in the case of Jonah, it was a greater thing by far, after he had been swallowed by the fish, to suffer no harm from the monster, than if he had not been swallowed at all;—so also in regard of Christ; His not dying would not have been so inconceivable, as that having died He should loose the bands of death. Say not then, "why did He not help Himself on the Cross?" for he was hastening on to close conflict with death himself. (See Hooker, E. P. v. 48. 9.) He descended not from the Cross, not because He could not, but because He would not. For Him Whom the tyranny of death restrained not, how could the nails of the Cross restrain?

[4.] But these things, though known to us, are not so as yet to the unbelievers. Wherefore he said that "the word of the Cross is to them that perish foolishness; but to us who are saved it is the power of God. For it is written, I will destroy the wisdom of the wise, and the prudence of the prudent will I reject." Nothing from himself which might give offence, does he advance up to this point; but first he comes to the testimony of the Scripture, and then furnished with boldness from thence, adopts more vehement words, and saith,

Ver. 20, 21. "Hath not God made foolish the wisdom of this world? Where is the wise? Where the Scribe? Where the disputer of this world? Hath not God made foolish the wisdom of this world? For seeing that in the wisdom of God the world through its wisdom knew God, it was God's good pleasure through the fool-ishness of the preaching to save them that believe." Having said, "It is written, I will destroy the wisdom of the wise," He subjoins demonstration from facts, saying, "Where is the wise? where the Scribe?" at the same time glancing at both Gentiles and Jews. For what sort of philosopher, which among those who have studied logic, which of those knowing in Jewish matters, hath saved us and made known the truth? Not one. It was the fisherman's work, the whole of it.

Having then drawn the conclusion which he had in view, and brought down their pride, and said, "Hath not God made foolish the wisdom of this world?" he states also the reason why these things were so done. "For seeing that in the wisdom of God," saith he, "the world through its wisdom knew not God," the Cross appeared. Now what means, "in the wisdom of God?" The wisdom apparent in those works whereby it was His will to make Himself known. For to this end did he frame them, and frame them such as they are, that by a sort of proportion, (ἀναλόγως) from the things which are seen admiration of the Maker might be learned. Is the heaven great, and the earth boundless? Wonder then at Him who made them. For this heaven, great as it is, not only was made by Him, but made with ease; and that boundless earth, too, was brought into being even as if it had been nothing. Wherefore of the former He saith, (Ps. cii. 25. τῶν χειρῶν LXX.) "The works of Thy fingers are the heavens," and concerning the earth, (Is. xl. 23. LXX.) "Who hath made the earth as it were nothing." Since then by this wisdom the world was unwilling to discover God, He employed what seemed to be foolishness, i. e. the Gospel, to persuade men; not by reasoning, but by faith. It remains that where God's wisdom is, there is no longer need of man's. For before, to infer that He who made the world such and so great, must in all reason be a God possessed of a certain uncontrollable, unspeakable power; and by these means to apprehend Him;—this was the part of human wisdom. But now we need no more reasonings, but faith alone. For to believe on Him that was crucified and buried, and to be fully persuaded that this Person Himself both rose again and sat down on high; this needeth not wisdom, nor reasonings, but faith. For the Apostles themselves came in not by wisdom, but by faith, and surpassed the heathen wise men in wisdom and loftiness, and that so much the more, as to raise disputings is less than to receive by faith the things of God. For this transcends all human understanding.

But how did He "destroy wisdom?" Being made known to us by Paul and others like him, He shewed it to be unprofitable. For towards receiving the evangelical proclamation, neither is the wise profited at all by wisdom, nor the unlearned injured at all by ignorance. But if one may speak somewhat even wonderful, ignorance rather than wisdom is a condition suitable for that impression, and more easily dealt with. For the shepherd and the rustic will more quickly receive this, once for all both repressing all doubting thoughts and delivering himself to the Lord. In this way then He destroyed wisdom. For since she first cast herself down, she is ever after useful for nothing. Thus when she ought to have displayed her proper powers, and by the works to have seen the Lord, she would not. Wherefore though she were now willing to introduce herself, she is not able. For the matter is not of that kind; this way of knowing God being far greater than the other. You see then, faith and simplicity are needed, and this we should seek every where, and prefer it before the wisdom which is from without. For "God," saith he, "hath made wisdom foolish."

But what is, "He hath made foolish?" He hath shewn it foolish in regard of receiving the faith. For since they prided themselves on it, He lost no time in exposing it. For what sort of wisdom is it, when it cannot discover the chief of things that are good? He caused her therefore to appear foolish, after she had first convicted herself. For if when discoveries might have been made by reasoning, she proved nothing, now when things proceed on a larger scale, how will she be able to accomplish aught? now when there is need of faith alone, and not of acuteness? You see then, God hath shewn her to be foolish.

It was His good pleasure, too, by the foolishness of the Gospel to save; foolishness, I say, not real, but appearing to be such. For that which is more wonderful yet is His having prevailed by bringing in, not another such wisdom more excellent than the first, but what seemed to be foolishness. He cast out Plato for example, not by means of another philosopher of more skill, but by an unlearned fisherman. For thus the defeat became greater, and the victory more splendid.

[5.] Ver. 22–24. Next, to shew the power of the Cross, he saith, "For Jews ask for signs and Greeks seek after wisdom: but we preach Christ crucified, unto Jews a stumbling-block, and unto Greeks foolishness; but unto them that are called, both Jews and Greeks, Christ the Power of God, and the Wisdom of God."

Vast is the import of the things here spoken! For he means to say how by contraries God hath overcome, and how the Gospel is not of man. What he saith is something of this sort. When, saith he, we say unto the Jews, Believe; they answer, Raise the dead, Heal the demoniacs, Shew unto us signs. But instead thereof what say we? That He was crucified, and died, who is preached. And this is enough, not only to fail in drawing over the unwilling, but even to drive away those even who are willing. Nevertheless, it drives not away, but attracts and holds fast and overcomes.

Again; the Greeks demand of us a rhetorical style, and the acuteness of sophistry. But preach we to these also the Cross: and that which, in the case of the Jews seemed to be weakness, this in the case of the Greeks is foolishness. Wherefore, when we not only fail in producing what they demand, but also produce the very opposites of their demand; (for the Cross has not merely no appearance of being a sign sought out by reasoning, but even the very annihilation of a sign;—is not merely deemed no proof of power, but a conviction of weakness;—not merely no display of wisdom, but a suggestion of foolishness;)—when therefore they who seek for signs and wisdom not only receive not the things which they ask, but even hear the contrary to what they desire, and then by means of contraries are persuaded;—how is not the power of Him that is preached unspeakable? As if to some one tempest-tost and longing for a haven, you were to shew not a haven but another wilder portion of the sea, and so could make him follow with thankfulness? Or as if a physician could attract to himself the man that was wounded and in need of remedies, by promising to cure him not with drugs, but with burning of him again! For this is a result of great power indeed. So also the Apostles prevailed, not simply without a sign, but even by a thing which seemed contrary to all the known signs. Which thing also Christ did in the case of the blind man. For when He would heal him, He took away the blindness by a thing that increased it: i. e. He put on clay. (St. John ix. 6.) As then by means of clay He healed the blind man, so also by means of the Cross He brought the world to Himself. That certainly was adding an offence, not taking an offence away. So did He also in creation, working out things by their contraries. With sand, for instance, He walled in the sea, having made the weak a bridle to the strong. He placed the earth upon water, having taken order that the heavy and the dense should be borne on the soft and fluid. By means of the prophets again with a small piece of wood He raised up iron from the bottom. (2 Kings vi. 5—7.) In like manner also with the Cross He hath drawn the world to Himself. For as the water beareth up the earth, so also the Cross beareth up the world. You see now, it is proof of great power and wisdom, to convince by means of the things which tell directly against us. Thus the Cross seems to be matter of offence; and yet far from offending, it even attracts.

[6.] Ver. 25. All these things, therefore, Paul bearing in mind, and being struck with astonishment, said that "the foolishness of God is wiser than men, and the weakness of God is stronger than men;" in relation to the Cross, speaking of a folly and weakness, not real but apparent. For he is answering with respect unto the other party's opinion. For that which philosophers were not able by means of reasoning to accomplish, this, what seemed to be foolishness did excellently well. Which then is the wiser, he that persuadeth the many, or he that persuadeth few, or rather no one? He who persuadeth concerning the greatest points, or about matters which are nothing? (μηδὲν ὄντων Reg. MS. μὴ δεόντων Bened.) What great labors did Plato endure, and his followers, discoursing to us about a line, and an angle, and a point, and about numbers even and odd, and equal unto one another and unequal, and such-like spiderwebs; (for indeed those webs are not more useless to man's life than were these subjects;) and without doing good to any one great or small by their means, so he made an end of his life. How greatly did he labor, endeavoring to show that the soul was immortal! and even as he came he went away, having spoken nothing with certainty, nor persuaded any hearer. But the Cross wrought persuasion by means of unlearned men; yea it persuaded even the whole world: and not about common things, but in discourse of God, and the godliness which is according to truth, and the evangelical way of life, and the judgment of the things to come. And of all men it made philosophers: the very rustics, the utterly unlearned. Behold how "the foolishness of God is wiser than men," and "the weakness stronger?" How "stronger?" Because it overran the whole world, and took all by main force, and while men were endeavoring by ten thousands to extinguish the name of the Crucified, the contrary came to pass: that flourished and increased more and more, but they perished and wasted away; and the living at war with the dead, had no power. So that when the Greek calls me foolish, he shows himself above measure foolish: since I who am esteemed by him a fool, evidently appear wiser than the wise. When he calls me weak, then he shows himself to be weaker. For the noble things which publicans and fishermen were able to effect by the grace of God, these, philosophers, and rhetoricians, and tyrants, and in short the whole world, running ten thousand ways here and there, could not even form a notion of. For what did not the Cross introduce? The doctrine concerning the Immortality of the Soul; that concerning the Resurrection of the Body; that concerning the contempt of things present; that concerning the desire of things future. Yea, angels it hath made of men, and all, every where, practice self-denial, (φιλοσοφοῦσι) and show forth all kinds of fortitude.

[7.] But among them also, it will be said, many have been found contemners of death. Tell me who? was it he who drank the hemlock? But if thou wilt, I can bring forward ten thousand such from within the Church. For had it been lawful when prosecution befel them to drink hemlock and depart, all had become more famous than he. And besides, he drank when he was not at liberty to drink or not to drink; but willing or against his will he must have undergone it: no effect surely of fortitude, but of necessity, and nothing more. For even robbers and man-slayers, having fallen under the condemnation of their judges, have suffered things more grievous. But with us it is all quite the contrary. For not against their will did the martyrs endure, but of their will, and being at liberty not to suffer; shewing forth fortitude harder than all adamant. This then you see is no great wonder, that he whom I was mentioning drank hemlock; it being no longer in his power not to drink, and also when he had arrived at a very great age. For when he despised life he stated himself to be seventy years old; if this can be called despising. For I for my part could not affirm it: nor, what is more, can anyone else. But show me some one enduring firm in torments for godliness' sake, as I shew thee ten thousand every where in the world. Who, while his nails were tearing out, nobly endured? Who, while his joints were wrenching (ἀνασχαπτομένων) asunder? Who, while his body was cut in pieces, (τοῦ σώματος κατὰ μέρος πορθουμένου; τῆς κεφαλῆς;) member by member? or his head? Who, while his bones were forced out by levers? (ἀναμοχλευομένων) Who, while placed without intermission upon frying-pans? Who, when thrown into a caldron? Show me these instances. For to die by hemlock is all as one with a man's continuing in a state of sleep. Nay even sweeter than sleep is this sort of death, if report say true. But if certain [of them] did endure torments, yet of these, too, the praise is gone to nothing. For on some disgraceful occasion they perished; some for revealing mysteries; some for aspiring to dominion; others detected in the foulest crimes; others again rashly, and fruitlessly, and foolishly, there being no reason for it, made away with themselves. But not so with us. Wherefore of the deeds of those nothing is said; but these flourish and daily increase. Which Paul having in mind said, " The weakness of God is stronger than all men."

[8.] For that the Gospel is divine, even from hence is evident; namely, whence could it have occurred to twelve ignorant men to attempt such great things? who sojourned in marshes, in rivers, in deserts; who never at any time perhaps had entered into a city nor into a forum;—whence did it occur, to set themselves in array against the whole world? For that they were timid and unmanly, he shews who wrote of them, not apologizing, nor enduring to throw their failings into the shade: which indeed of itself is a very great token of the truth. What then doth he say about them? That when Christ was apprehended, after ten thousand wonders, they fled; and he who remained, being the leader of the rest, denied. Whence was it then that they who when Christ was alive endured not the attack of the Jews; now that He was dead and buried, and as ye say, had not risen again, nor had any talk with them, nor infused courage into them—whence did they set themselves in array against so great a world? Would they not have said among themselves, "what meaneth this? Himself He was not able to save, and will He protect us? Himself He defended not when alive, and will He stretch out the hand unto us now that he is dead? Himself, when alive, subdued not even one nation; and are we to convince the whole world by uttering His Name?" How, I ask, could all this be reasonable, I will not say, as something to be done, but even as something to be imagined? From whence it is plain that had they not seen Him after He was risen, and received most ample proof of his power, they would not have ventured so great a cast.

[9.] For suppose they had possessed friends innumerable; would they not presently have made them all enemies, disturbing ancient customs, and removing their father's landmarks? (ὅρια Ms. Reg. ἔθη Ben.) But as it was, they had them for enemies, all, both their own countrymen and foreigners. For although they had been recommended to veneration by everything external, would not all men have abhorred them, introducing a new polity? But now they were even destitute of everything; and it was likely that even on that account all would hate and scorn them at once. For whom will you name? The Jews? Nay, they had against them an inexpressible hatred on account of the things which had been done unto the Master. The Greeks then? Why, first of all, these had rejected one not inferior to them; and no man knew this so well as the Greeks. For Plato, who wished to strike out a new form of government, or rather a part of government; and that

not by changing the customs relating to the gods, but merely by substituting one line of conduct for another; was cast out of Sicily, and went near to lose his life.[1] This however did not ensue: so that he lost his liberty alone. And had not a certain Barbarian been more gentle than the tyrant of Sicily, nothing could have rescued the philosopher from slavery throughout life in a foreign land. And yet it is not all one to innovate in affairs of the kingdom, and in matters of religious worship. For the latter more than any thing else causes disturbance and troubles men. For to say, " let such and such an one marry such a woman, and let the guardians[2] [of the commonwealth] exercise their guardianship so and so," is not enough to cause any great disturbance: and especially when all this is lodged in a book, and no great anxiety on the part of the legislator to carry the proposals into practice. On the other hand, to say, "they be no gods which men worship, but demons; He who was crucified is God;" ye well know how great wrath it kindled, how severely men must have paid for it, what a flame of war it fanned.

For Protagoras, who was one of them, having dared to say, " I know of no gods," not going round the world and proclaiming it, but in a single city, was in the most imminent peril of his life[3]. And Diagoras[4] the Milesian[5], and Theodorus, who was called Atheist,[6] although they had friends, and that influence which comes from eloquence, and were held in admiration because of their philosophy; yet nevertheless none of these profited them. And

[1] Plutarch. in *Dion.* t. v. p. 162. ed. Bryan. "Plato having been introduced to Dionysius, they discoursed in general about human virtue; when Plato maintained that any thing might be credible rather than for tyrants to be truly brave. Then changing the subject, he argued concerning Justice, that the life of the just is blessed, of the unjust miserable. The tyrant was not well pleased with the discourse, understanding it as a reproof: and he was vexed with the bystanders, who mightily approved the man, and were taken with his remarks. At last, in anger and bitterness, he asked him what was his object in coming to Sicily. He said, To look for a good man. By heaven, he replied, it is clear you have not found him. Now Dion's friends thought this had been the end of his anger, and as Plato was anxious to go, they provided him with a passage in a galley, in which Pollis the Spartan was sailing to Greece. But Dionysius secretly besought Pollis, if possible, to kill him at sea, but at any rate to sell him for a slave, for that he would never be the worse for it, but just as happy, in that Justice of his, though he became a slave. Upon which it is said that Pollis took Plato to Ægina and sold him there, the Æginetæ being at war with Athens, and having made a decree, that any Athenian coming there should be sold."
[2] φύλακες, Plato's word in the *Republic* for citizens.
[3] Cic. *de Nat. Deor.* i. 23. Protagoras of Abdera, a distinguished Sophist of his time, having opened a certain treatise with these words, "Concerning the Gods, I cannot speak of them either as being or as not being;" the Athenians banished him from Athens and Attica, and burned his books in the Assembly. He flourished about B. C. 444. Clinton, *Fasti Hellenici,* i. 53.
[4] B. C. 466. Clinton, F. H. i. 39. The Scholiast on Aristophanes calls him "a writer of songs, called an Atheist; a bringer in of strange gods. Whereupon the Athenians condemned him, voting a talent of silver to whoever should kill him, and two talents to any one who should bring him alive: and prevailed on the Peloponnesians to join with them." Of Theodorus, Cicero says that he was threatened with death by Lysimachus, but he does not say that it was for his "atheism:" this must have been between B. C. 306—281. Clinton, F. H. i. 174, 184.
[5] ὁ Μήλιος.   Schol. in Aristoph. *Ran.* 323.
[6] Cic. *de. N. D.* i. 23; *Tusc. Disp.* i. 43.

the great Socrates, too, he who surpassed in philosophy all among them, for this reason drank hemlock, because in his discourses concerning the gods he was suspected of moving things a little aside. Now if the suspicion alone of innovation brought so great danger on philosophers and wise men, and on those who had attained boundless popularity; and if they were not only unable to do what they wished, but were themselves also driven from life and country; how canst thou choose but be in admiration and astonishment, when thou seest that the fisherman hath produced such an effect upon the world, and accomplished his purposes; hath overcome all both Barbarians and Greeks.

[10.] But they did not, you will say, introduce strange gods as the others did. Well, and in that you are naming the very point most to be wondered at; that the innovation is twofold, both to pull down those which are, and to announce the Crucified. For from whence came it into their minds to proclaim such things? whence, to be confident about their event? Whom of those before them could they perceive to have prospered in any such attempt? Were not all men worshipping demons? Were not all used to make gods of the elements? Was not the difference [but] in the mode of impiety? But nevertheless they attacked all, and overthrew all, and overran in a short time the whole world, like a sort of winged beings; making no account of dangers, of deaths, of the difficulty of the thing, of their own fewness, of the multitude of the opponents, of the authority, the power, the wisdom of those at war with them. For they had an ally greater than all these, the power of Him that had been crucified and was risen again. It would not have been so wondrous, had they chosen to wage war with the world in the literal sense, (πόλεμον αἰσθητόν) as this which in fact has taken place. For according to the law of battle they might have stood over against the enemies, and occupying some adverse ground, have arrayed themselves accordingly to meet their foes, and have taken their time for attack and close conflict. But in this case it is not so. For they had no camp of their own, but were mingled with their enemies, and thus overcame them. Even in the midst of their enemies as they went about, they eluded their grasp, (λαβὰς Reg. βλαβὰς Bened.) and became superior, and achieved a splendid victory; a victory which fulfils the prophecy that saith, "Even in the midst of thine enemies thou shalt have dominion." (Ps. cx. 2) For this it was, which was full of all astonishment, that their enemies having them in their power, and casting them into prison and chains, not only did not vanquish them, but themselves also eventually had to bow down to them: the scourgers to the scourged, the binders in chains to those who were bound, the persecutors to the fugitives. All these things then we could say unto the Greeks, yea much more than these; for the truth has enough and greatly to spare. (πολλή τῆς ἀληθείας ἡ περιουσία.) And if ye will follow the argument, we will teach you the whole method of fighting against them. In the meanwhile let us here hold fast two heads; How did the weak overcome the strong? and, From whence came it into their thoughts, being such as they were, to form such plans, unless they enjoyed Divine aid?

[11.] So far then as to what we have to say. But let us shew forth by our actions all excellencies of conduct, and kindle abuntantly the fire of virtue. For "ye are lights," saith he, "shining in the midst of the world." (Phil. 11. 15) And unto each of us God hath committed a greater function than He hath to the sun: greater than heaven, and earth, and sea; and by so much greater, as spiritual things be more excellent than things sensible. When then we look unto the solar orb, and admire the beauty, and the body and the brightness of the luminary, let us consider again that greater and better is the light which is in us, as indeed the darkness also is more dreadful unless we take heed. And in fact a deep night oppresses the whole world. This is what we have to dispel and dissolve. It is night not among heretics and among Greeks only, but also in the multitude on our side, in respect of doctrines and of life. For many entirely disbelieve the resurrection; many fortify themselves with their horoscope; (γένεσιν ἑαυτοῖς ἐπιτειχίζουσι) many adhere to superstitious observances, and to omens, and auguries, and presages. And some likewise employ amulets and charms. But to these also we will speak afterwards, when we have finished what we have to say to the Greeks.

In the meanwhile hold fast the things which have been said, and be ye fellow-helpers with me in the battle; by your way of life attracting them to us and changing them. For, as I am always saying, He that teaches high morality (περὶ φιλοσοφίας) ought first to teach it in his own person, and be such as his hearers cannot do without. Let us therefore become such, and make the Greeks feel kindly towards us. And this will come to pass if we make up our minds not only not to do ill, but also to suffer ill. Do we not see when little children being borne in their father's arms give him that carries them blows on the cheek, how sweetly the father lets the boy have his fill of wrath, and when he sees that he has spent his passion, how his countenance brightens up? In like manner let us also act; and as fathers with children, so let us discourse with the Greeks.

For all the Greeks are children. And this, some of their own writers have said, that "that people are children always, and no Greek is an old man." Now children cannot bear to take thought for any thing useful; so also the Greeks would be for ever at play; and they lie on the ground, grovelling in posture and in affections. Moreover, children oftentimes, when we are discoursing about important things, give no heed to anything that is said, but will even be laughing all the time: such also are the Greeks. When we discourse of the Kingdom, they laugh. And as spittle dropping in abundance from an infant's mouth, which oftentimes spoils its meat and drink, such also are the words flowing from the mouth of the Greeks, vain and unclean. Even if thou art giving children their necessary food, they keep on vexing those who furnish it with evil speech, and we must bear with them all the while. (διαβαστάζεσθαι) Again, children, when they see a robber entering and taking away the furniture, far from resisting, even smile on the designing fellow; but shouldest thou take away the little basket or the rattle (σεῖστρα) or any other of their playthings, they take it to heart and fret, tear themselves, and stamp on the floor; just so do the Greeks also: when they behold the devil pilfering all their patrimony, and even the things which support their life, they laugh, and run to him as to a friend: but should any one take away any possession, be it wealth or any childish thing whatsoever of that kind, they cry, they tear themselves. And as children expose their limbs unconsciously, and blush not for shame; so the Greeks, wallowing in whoredoms and adulteries, and laying bare the laws of nature, and introducing unlawful intercourses, are not abashed.

Ye have given me vehement applause and acclamation[2], but with all your applause have a care lest you be among those of whom these things are said. Wherefore I beseech you all to become men: since, so long as we are children, how shall we teach them manliness? How shall we restrain them from childish folly? Let us, therefore, become men; that we may arrive at the measure of the stature which hath been marked out for us by Christ, and may obtain the good things to come: through the grace and loving-kindness, etc. etc.

HOMILY V.

I COR. i. 26, 27.

For behold[1] your calling, brethren, that not many wise men after the flesh, not many mighty, not many noble, [are called;] but God chose the foolish things of the world, that he might put to shame them that are wise.

HE hath said that "the foolishness of God is wiser than men;" he hath shewed that human wisdom is cast out, both by the testimony of the Scriptures and by the issue of events; by the testimony, where he says, "I will destroy the wisdom of the wise;" by the event, putting his argument in the form of a question, and saying, "Where is the wise? Where the Scribe?" Again; he proved at the same time that the thing is not new, but ancient, as it was presignified and foretold from the beginning. For, "It is written," saith he, "I will destroy the wisdom of the wise." Withal he shews that it was neither inexpedient nor unaccountable for things to take this course: (for, "seeing that in the wisdom of God the world," saith he, "knew not God, God was well pleased through the foolishness of preaching to save them which believe:") and that the Cross is a demonstration of ineffable power and wisdom, and that the foolishness of God is far mightier than the wisdom of man. And this again he proves not by means of the teachers, but by means of the disciples themselves. For, "Behold your calling," saith he: that not only teachers of an untrained sort, but disciples also of the like class, were objects of His choice; that He chose "not many wise men" (that is his word) "according to the flesh." And so that of which he is

---

[2] This custom is referred to by St. Chrysostom in many places as also by St. Augustin and others: the earliest mention of it appears to be the censure passed on Paul of Samosata in the synod of Antioch, A. D 272, for demanding and encouraging such applause. Vid. Euseb. E. H. vii. 30. St. Chrysostom in his 30th Hom. on the Acts says, "When I am applauded in my speaking, for the moment I feel as an infirm human being, (for why should not one confess the truth?)....but when I am come home, and consider that those who have been applauding are no wise profited, but rather by their applause and acclamation have lost what good they might have attained, I......feel as if I had said all to no purpose......And often I have thought of making a law to forbid all signs of applause, and to enforce listening in silence and with becoming order......Yea, if you please, let us even now pass such a law......Why do you applaud at the very moment that I am making a rule to check that practice? &c." iv. 784. Ed. Savil. Vid. Bingham Antiquit. xiv. 4. 27; Suicer, v. κρότος.

speaking is proved to surpass both in strength and wisdom, in that it convinces both the many and the unwise: it being extremely hard to convince an ignorant person, especially when the discourse is concerning great and necessary things. However, they did work conviction. And of this he calls the Corinthians themselves as witnesses. For, "behold your calling, brethren," saith he: consider; examine: for that doctrines so wise, yea, wiser than all, should be received by ordinary men, testifies the greatest wisdom in the teacher.

[2.] But what means, "according to the flesh?" According to what is in sight; according to the life that now is; according to the discipline of the Gentiles. Then, lest he should seem to be at variance with himself, (for he had convinced both the Proconsul, (Acts xiii. 12.) and the Areopagite, (Acts xvii. 34.) and Apollos; (Acts xviii. 26: through Aquila and Priscilla) and other wise men, too, we have seen coming over to the Gospel;) he said not, No wise man, but, "Not many wise men." For he did not designedly (ἀποκεκληρωμένως) call the ignorant and pass by the wise, but these also he received, yet the others in much larger number. And why? Because the wise man according to the flesh is full of extreme folly; and it is he who especially answers to the term "foolish," when he will not cast away his corrupt doctrine. And as in the case of a physician who might wish to teach certain persons the secrets of his art, those who know a few things, having a bad and perverse mode of practicing the art which they make a point of retaining, would not endure to learn quietly, but they who knew nothing would most readily embrace what was said: even so it was here. The unlearned were more open to conviction, for they were free from the extreme madness of accounting themselves wise. For indeed the excess of folly is in these more than any, these, I say, who commit unto reasoning things which cannot be ascertained except by faith. Thus, suppose the smith by means of the tongs drawing out the red-hot iron; if any one should insist on doing it with his hand, we should vote him guilty of extreme folly: so in like manner the philosophers who insisted on finding out these things for themselves disparaged the faith. And it was owing to this that they found none of the things they sought for.

"Not many mighty, not many noble;" for these also are filled with pride. And nothing is so useless towards an accurate knowledge of God as arrogance, and being nailed down (προσηλῶσθαι) to wealth: for these dispose a man to admire things present, and make no account of the future; and they stop up the ears through the multitude of cares: but "the foolish things

of the world God chose:" which thing is the greatest sign of victory, that they were uneducated by whom He conquers. For the Greeks feel not so much shame when they are defeated by means of the "wise," but are then confounded, when they see the artisan and the sort of person one meets in the market more of a philosopher than themselves. Wherefore also he said himself, "That He might put to shame the wise." And not in this instance alone hath he done this, also in the case of the other advantages of life. For, to proceed, "the weak things of the world He chose that He might put to shame the strong." For not unlearned persons only, but needy also, and contemptible and obscure He called, that He might humble those who were in high places.

V. 18. "And the base things of the world, and the things that are despised, and the things that are not, that he might bring to naught the things that are." Now what doth He call things "that are not?" Those persons who are considered to be nothing because of their great insignificance. Thus hath He shown forth His great power, casting down the great by those who seem to be nothing. The same elsewhere he thus expresses, (2 Cor. xii. 9.) "For my strength is made perfect in weakness." For a great power it is, to teach outcasts and such as never applied themselves to any branch of learning, how all at once to discourse wisely on the things which are above the heavens. For suppose a physician, an orator, or any one else: we then most admire him, when he convinces and instructs those completely uneducated. Now, if to instil into an uneducated man the rules of art be a very wonderful thing, much more things which pertain to so high philosophy.

[3.] But not for the wonder's sake only, neither to shew His own power, hath He done this, but to check also the arrogant. And therefore he both said before, "That he might confound the wise and the strong, that He might bring to nought the things which are," and here again,

V. 29. "That no flesh should glory in the presence of God." For God doeth all things to this end, to repress vainglory and pride, to pull down boasting." "Do you, too," saith he, "employ yourselves in that work." He doth all, that we may put nothing to our own account; that we may ascribe all unto God. And have ye given yourselves over unto this person or to that? And what pardon will ye obtain?"

For God Himself hath shown that it is not possible we should be saved only by ourselves: and this He did from the beginning. For neither then could men be saved by themselves;

but it required their compassing the beauty of the heaven, and the extent of the earth, and the mass of creation besides; if so they might be led by the hand to the great artificer of all the works. And He did this, repressing beforehand the self-conceit which was after to arise. Just as if a master who had given his scholar charge to follow wheresoever he might lead, when he sees him forestalling, and desiring to learn all things of himself, should permit him to go quite astray; and when he hath proved him incompetent to acquire the knowledge, should thereupon at length introduce to him what himself has to teach: so God also commanded in the beginning to trace Him by the idea which the creation gives; but since they would not, He, after showing by the experiment that they are not sufficient for themselves, conducts them again unto Him by another way. He gave for a tablet, the world; but the philosophers studied not in those things, neither were willing to obey Him, nor to approach unto Him by that way which Himself commanded. He introduces another way more evident than the former; one that might bring conviction that man is not of himself alone sufficient unto himself. For then scruples of reasoning might be started, and the Gentile wisdom employed, on their part whom He through the creation was leading by the hand; but now, unless a man become a fool, that is, unless he dismiss all reasoning and all wisdom, and deliver up himself unto the faith, it is impossible to be saved. You see that besides making the way easy, he hath rooted up hereby no trifling disease, namely, in forbidding to boast, and have high thoughts: "that no flesh should glory:" for hence came the sin, that men insisted on being wiser than the laws of God; not willing so to obtain knowledge as He had enacted: and therefore they did not obtain it at all. So also was it from the beginning. He said unto Adam, "Do such a thing, and such another thou must not do." He, as thinking to find out something more, disobeyed; and even what he had, he lost. He spake unto those that came after, "Rest not in the creature; but by means of it contemplate the Creator." They, forsooth, as if making out something wiser than what had been commanded, set in motion windings innumerable. Hence they kept dashing against themselves and one another, and neither found God, nor concerning the creature had any distinct knowledge; nor had any meet and true opinion about it. Wherefore again, with a very high hand, (ἐκ πολλοῦ τοῦ περίοντος) lowering their conceit. He admitted the uneducated first, showing thereby that all men need the wisdom from above. And not only in the matter of knowledge, but also in all other things, both men and all other creatures He hath constituted so as to be in great need of Him; that they might have this also as a most forcible motive of submission and attachment, lest turning away they should perish. For this cause He did not suffer them to be sufficient unto themselves. For if even now many, for all their indigency, despise Him, were the case not so, whither would they not have wandered in haughtiness? So that He stayed them from boasting as they did, not from any grudge to them, but to draw them away from the destruction thence ensuing.

[4.] V. 30 "But of Him are ye in Christ Jesus, who was made unto us wisdom from God, and righteousness, and sanctification, and redemption."

The expression "of Him," I suppose he uses here, not of our introduction into being, but with reference to the faith: that is, to our having become children of God, "not of blood, nor of the will of the flesh." (St. John i. 13.) "Think not then, that having taken away our glorying, He left us so: for there is another, a greater glorying, His gift. For ye are the children of Him in whose presence it is not meet to glory, having become so through Christ." And since he has said, " The foolish things of the world He chose, and the base," he signifies that they are nobler than all, having God for their Father. And of this nobility of ours, not this person or that, but Christ is the cause, having made us wise, and righteous, and holy. For so mean the words, "He was made unto us wisdom."

Who then is wiser than we are who have not the wisdom of Plato, but Christ Himself, God having so willed.

But what means, "of God?" Whenever he speaks great things concerning the Only-Begotten, he adds mention of the Father, lest any one should think that the Son is unbegotten. Since therefore he had affirmed His power to be so great, and had referred the whole unto the Son, saying that He had "become wisdom unto us, and righteousness, and sanctification and redemption;"—through the Son again referring the whole to the Father, he saith, "of God."

But why said he not, He hath made us wise, but "was made unto us wisdom?" To show the copiousness of the gift. As if he had said, He gave unto us Himself. And observe how he goes on in order. For first He made us wise by delivering from error, and then righteous and holy, by giving us the Spirit; and He hath so delivered us from all our evils as to be "of Him." and this is not meant to express communication of being, (οὐσιώσεως) but is spoken concerning the faith. Elsewhere we find him saying, "We were made righteousness in Him;" in these words, "Him who knew no sin He made to be sin for us that we might be made the righteousness of God in Him;" (2 Cor. v. 21.) but now he saith, "He hath been made righteousness unto us; so that whosoever will may partake plentifully." For it is not this man or that who hath made us wise, but Christ. "He that glorieth," therefore, "let him glory in Him," not in such or such an one. From Christ have proceeded all things. Wherefore, having said, "Who was made unto us wisdom, and righteousness, and sanctification, and redemption," he added, "that, according as it is written, he that glorieth, let him glory in the Lord."

For this cause also he had vehemently inveighed against the wisdom of the Greeks, to teach men this lesson, (τοῦτο αὐτὸ Savile; τούτῳ αὐτῷ Bened.) and no other: that (as indeed is no more than just) they should boast themselves in the Lord. For when of ourselves we seek the things which are above us, nothing is more foolish, nothing weaker than we are. In such case, a tongue well whetted we may have; but stability of doctrine we cannot have. Rather, reasonings, being alone, are like the webs of spiders. For unto such a point of madness have some advanced as to say that there is nothing real in the whole of being: yea, they maintain positively that all things are contrary to what appears.

Say not therefore that anything is from thyself, but in all things glory in God. Impute unto no man anything at any time. For if unto Paul nothing ought to be imputed much less unto any others. For, saith he, (ch. iii. 6.) "I planted, Apollos watered, but God gave the increase." He that hath learnt to make his boast in the Lord, will never be elated, but will be moderate at all times, and thankful under all circumstances. But not such is the mind of the Greeks; they refer all to themselves; wherefore even of men they make gods. In so great shame hath desperate arrogance plunged them. (ἐξετραχήλισεν)

[5.] It is time then, in what remains, to go forth to battle against these. Recollect where we left our discourse on the former day. We were saying that it was not possible according to human cause and effect that fishermen should get the better of philosophers. But nevertheless it became possible: from whence it is clear that by grace it became so. We were saying that it was not possible for them even to conceive such great exploits: and we shewed that they not only conceived, but brought them to a conclusion with great ease. Let us handle, to-day, the same head of our argument: viz. From whence did it enter their thoughts to expect to overcome the world, unless they had seen Christ after He was risen? What? Were they beside

themselves, to reckon upon any such thing inconsiderately and at random? For it goes even beyond all madness, to look, without Divine grace, for success in so great an undertaking. How did they succeed in it, if they were insane and frenzied? But if they were in their sober senses, as indeed the events shewed, how, but on receiving credible pledges from the heavens and enjoying the influence which is from above, did they undertake to go forth to so great wars, and to make their venture against earth and sea, and to strip and stand their ground so nobly, for a change in the customs of the whole world which had been so long time fixed, they being but twelve men?

And, what is more, what made them expect to convince their hearers, by inviting them to heaven and the mansions above? Even had they been brought up in honor, and wealth, and power, and erudition, not even so would it have been at all likely that they should be roused to so burthensome an undertaking. However, there would have been somewhat more of reason in their expectation. But as the case now stands, some of them had been occupied about lakes, some about hides[1], some about the customs: than which pursuits nothing is more unprofitable towards philosophy, and the persuading men to have high imaginations: and especially when one hath no example to shew. Nay, they had not only no examples to make their success likely, but they had examples against all likelihood of success, and those within their own doors.* (ἔναυλα) For many for attempting innovations had been utterly extinguished, I say not among the Greeks, for all that was nothing, but among the Jews themselves at that very time; who not with twelve men, but with great numbers had applied themselves to the work. Thus both Theudas and Judas, having great bodies of men, perished together with their disciples. And the fear arising from their examples was enough to control these, had they not been strongly persuaded that victory without divine power was out of the question.

Yea, even if they did expect to prevail, with what sort of hopes undertook they such great dangers, except they had an eye to the world to come? But let us suppose that they hoped for no less than victory; what did they expect to gain from the bringing all men unto Him, "who is not risen again," as ye say? For if now, men who believe concerning the kingdom of heaven and blessings unnumbered with reluctance encounter dangers, how could they have undergone so many for nothing, yea rather, for evil? For if the things which were done did

---

[1] That is, some were fishers in the sea or lake of Tiberias, some, as St. Paul, engaged in making tents out of hides.
* [Dr. Field prefers the reading, *and these recent.*]

not take place, if Christ did not ascend into heaven; surely in their obstinate zeal to invent these things, and convince all the world of them, they were offending God, and must expect ten thousand thunderbolts from on high.

[6.] Or, in another point of view; if they had felt this great zeal while Christ was living, yet on His death they would have let it go out. For He would have seemed to them, had He not risen, as a sort of deceiver and pretender. Know ye not that armies while the general and king is alive, even though they be weak, keep together; but when those in such office have departed, however strong they may be, they are broken up?

Tell me then, what were the enticing arguments whereupon they acted, when about to take hold of the Gospel, and to go forth unto all the world? Was there any kind of impediment wanting to restrain them? If they had been mad, (for I will not cease repeating it,) they could not have succeded at all; for no one follows the advice of madmen. But if they succeeded as in truth they did succeed, and the event proves, then none so wise as they. Now if none were so wise as they, it is quite plain, they would not lightly have entered upon the preaching. Had they not seen Him after He was risen, what was there sufficient to draw them out unto this war? What which would not have turned them away from it? He said unto them, "After three days I will rise again," and He made promises concerning the kingdom of heaven. He said, they should master the whole world, after they had received the Holy Spirit; and ten thousand other things besides these, surpassing all nature. So that if none of these things had come to pass, although they believed in Him while alive, after His death they would not have believed in Him, unless they had seen Him after He was risen. For they have said, " 'After three days,' He said, 'I will rise again,' and He hath not arisen. He promised that He would give the Spirit, and He hath not sent Him. How then shall His sayings about the other world find credit with us, when His sayings about this are tried and found wanting?"

And why, if He rose not again, did they preach that He was risen? "Because they loved Him," you will say. But surely, it was likely that they would hate Him afterwards, for deceiving and betraying them; and because, having lifted them up with innumerable hopes, and divorced them from house, and parents, and all things, and set in hostility against them the entire nation of Jews, He had betrayed them after all. And if indeed the thing were of weakness, they might have pardoned it; but now it would be deemed a result of exceeding malice. For He ought to have spoken the truth, and not have promised heaven, being a mortal man, as ye say. So that the very opposite was the likely line for them to take; to proclaim the deception, and declare Him a pretender and imposter. Thus again would they have been rid of all their perils; thus have put an end to the war. Moreover, seeing that the Jews gave money unto the soldiers to say that they stole the body, if the disciples had come forward and said, "We stole Him, He is not risen again," what honor would they not have enjoyed? Thus it was in their power to be honored, nay, crowned. Why then did they for insults and dangers barter away these things, if it was not some Divine power which influenced them, and proved mightier than all these?

[7.] But if we do not yet convince, take this also into consideration; that had this not been so, though they were ever so well disposed, they would not have preached this Gospel in His name, but would have treated Him with abhorrence. For ye know that not even the names of those who deceive us in this sort are we willing to hear. But for what reason preached they also His name? Expecting to gain the mastery through Him? Truly the contrary was natural for them to expect; that even if they had been on the point of prevailing, they were ruining themselves by bringing forward the name of a deceiver. But if they wished to throw into the shade former events, their line was to be silent; at any rate, to contend for them earnestly was to excite more and more both of serious hostility and of ridicule. From whence then did it enter their thoughts to invent such things? I say, " invent: " for what they had heard, they had forgotten. But if, when there was no fear, they forgot many things, and some did not even understand, (as also the Evangelist himself saith,) now that so great a danger came upon them, how could it be otherwise than that all should fleet away from them? Why speak I of words? when even their love towards their Master Himself began gradually to fade away, through fear of what was coming: wherewith also He upraided them. For since, before this, they hung upon him, and were asking continually, "Whither goest Thou," but afterwards on His drawing out His discourse to so great length, and declaring the terrors which at the very time of the Cross, and after the Cross should befal them, they just continued speechless and frozen through fear;—hear how He alleges to them this very point saying, "None of you asketh Me, Whither goest Thou? But because I have said these things unto you, sorrow hath filled your heart." (St. John xvi. 5—6.) Now if the expectation that He would die and rise again was such a grief to them, had they failed to see Him after He was risen, how could it be less than annihilation? Yea, they would have been fain to sink into the depths of the earth, what with dejection at being so deceived, and what with dread of the future, feeling themselves sorely straightened.

Again: from whence came their high doctrines? for the higher points, He said, they should hear afterwards. For, saith He, (St. John xvi. 12.) "I have many things to speak unto you, but ye cannot bear them now." So that the things not spoken were higher. And one of the disciples was not even willing to depart with Him into Judea, when he heard of dangers, but said, "Let us also go that we may die with Him," (St. John xi. 16.) taking it hardly[1] because he expected that he should die. Now if that disciple, while he was with Him, expected to die and shrunk back on that account, what must he not have expected afterwards, when parted from Him and the other disciples, and when the exposure of their shameless conduct was so complete?

[8.] Besides, what had they to say when they went forth? For the passion indeed all the world knew: for He had been hanged on high, upon the frame of wood, (ἰχρίου) and in mid-day, and in a chief city, and at a principal feast and that from which it was least permitted that any should be absent. But the resurrection no man saw of those who were without: which was no small impediment to them in working conviction. Again, that He was buried, was the common talk of all: and that His disciples stole His body, the soldiers and all the Jews declared: but that He had risen again, no one of them who were without knew by sight. Upon what ground then did they expect to convince the world? For if, while miracles were taking place, certain soldiers were persuaded to testify the contrary, upon what ground did these expect without miracles to do the work of preachers, and without having a farthing to convince land and sea concerning the resurrection? Again, if through desire of glory they attempted this, so much the rather would they have ascribed doctrines each one to himself, and not to Him that was dead and gone. Will it be said, men would not have believed them? And which of the two was the likelier, being preached, to win their belief? He that was apprehended and crucified, or those who had escaped the hands of the Jews?

[1] St. Chrys. Hom. 62. on St. John. "All feared the violence of the Jews, but Thomas more than the rest. Wherefore also he said, *Let us also &c.* Some indeed say that he desired to share our Lord's death: but it is not so: for it is the saying rather of a coward. Yet he was not reproved. For as yet He went on bearing their weakness. Afterwards, however, he (St. Thomas) became stronger than any, and irreproachable: this being the great wonder, that one so weak before the time of the Cross, after the Cross and faith in the Resurrection should be seen more zealous than all. So great is the power of Christ."

[9.] Next, tell me with what view were they to take such a course? They did not immediately, leaving Judæa, go into the Gentile cities, but went up and down within its limit. But how, unless they worked miracles, did they convince? For if such they really wrought, (and work them they did,) it was the result of God's power. If on the other hand they wrought none and prevailed, much more wonderful was the event. Knew they not the Jews —tell me—and their evil practice, and their soul full of grudgings? For they stoned even Moses, (Numb. xiv. 10. comp. Exod. xvii. 4.) after the sea which they had crossed on foot; after the victory, and that marvellous trophy which they raised without blood, by means of his hands, over the Egyptians who had enslaved them; after the manna; after the rocks, and the fountains of rivers which break out thence; after ten thousand miracles in the land of Egypt and the Red Sea and the wilderness. Jeremiah they cast into a pit, and many of the prophets they slew. Here, for example, what saith Elias, after that fearful famine, and the marvellous rain, and the torch which he brought down from heaven, and the strange holocaust; driven, as he was, to the very extreme edge of their country: "Lord, thy prophets they have killed, thine altars they have digged down, and I am left alone, and they seek my life." (1 Kings xix. 10.) Yet were not those (who were so persecuted) disturbing any of the established rules. Tell me then, what ground had men for attending to these of whom we are speaking? For, on one hand, they were meaner persons than any of the prophets; on the other, they were introducing just such novelties as had caused the Jews to nail even their Master to the Cross.

And in another way, too, it seemed less unaccountable for Christ to utter such things than for them; for He, they might suppose, acted thus to acquire glory for himself; but these they would have hated even the more, as waging war with them in behalf of another.

[10.] But did the laws of the Romans help them? Nay, by these they were more involved in difficulties. For their language was, (St. John xix. 12.) "Whosoever maketh himself a king is not Cæsar's friend." So that this alone was a sufficient impediment to them, that of Him who was accounted an usurper they were first disciples, and afterwards desirous to strengthen His cause. What in the world then set them upon rushing into such great dangers? And by what statements about Him would they be likely to gain credit? that He was crucified? That He was born of a poor Jewish woman who had been betrothed to a Jewish carpenter? That He was of a nation hated by the world? Nay, all these things were enough not only to fail of persuading and attracting the hearers, but also to disgust every one; and especially when affirmed by the tent-maker and the fisherman. Would not the disciples then bear all these things in mind? Timid nature can imagine more than the reality, and such were their natures. Upon what ground then did they hope to succeed? Nay, rather, they had no hope, there being things innumerable to draw them aside, if so be that Christ had not risen. Is it not quite plain even unto the most thoughtless that unless they had enjoyed a copious and mighty grace, and had received pledges of the resurrection, they would have been unable, I say not, to do and undertake these things, but even so much as to have them in their minds? For if when there were so great hinderances, in the way of their planning, I say not of their succeeding, they yet both planned and brought to effect and accomplishing things greater than all expectation, every one, I suppose, can see that not by human power but by divine grace they wrought all things.

Now these arguments we ought to practice, not by ourselves only, but one with another; and thus also the discovery of what remains will be easier to us.

[11.] And do not, because thou art an artisan, suppose that this sort of exercise is out of your province; for even Paul was a tent-maker. "Yes," saith some one, "but at that time he was also filled with abundant grace, and out of that he spake all things." Well; but before this grace, he was at the feet of Gamaliel; yea, moreover, and he received the grace, because of this, that he shewed a mind worthy of the grace; and after these things he again put his hand to his craft. Let no, one, therefore, of those who have trades be ashamed; but those, who are brought up to nothing and are idle, who employ many attendants, and are served by an immense retinue. For to be supported by continual hard work is a sort of asceticism. (φιλοσοφίας εἶδος comp. Hooker, E. P. V. lxxii. 18.) The souls of such men are clearer, and their minds better strung. For the man who has nothing to do is apter to say many things at random, and do many things at random; and he is busy all day long about nothing, a huge lethargy taking him up entirely. But he that is employed will not lightly entertain in himself any thing useless,

in deeds, in words, or in thoughts; for his whole soul is altogether intent upon his laborious way of livelihood. Let us not therefore despise those who support themselves by the labor of their own hands; but let us rather call them happy on this account. For tell me, what thanks are due unto thee, when after having received thy portion from thy father, thou goest on not in any calling, but lavishing away the whole of it at random? Knowest thou not that we shall not all have to render the same account, but those who have enjoyed greater licence here, a more exact one; those who were afflicted with labor, or poverty, or any thing else of this kind, one not so severe? And this is plain from Lazarus and the rich man. For as thou, for neglecting the right use of thy leisure, art justly accused; so the poor man, who having full employment hath spent his remnant of time upon right objects, great will be the crowns which he shall receive. But dost thou urge that a soldier's duties should at least excuse thee; and dost thou charge them with thy want of leisure? The excuse cannot be founded in reason. For Cornelius was a centurion, yet in no way did the soldier's belt impair his strict rule of life. But thou, when thou art keeping holiday with dancers and players, and making entire waste of thy life upon the stage, never thinkest of excusing thyself from such engagements by the necessity of military service or the fear of rulers: but when it is the Church to which we call you, then occur these endless impediments.

And what wilt thou say in the day, when thou seest the flame, and the rivers of fire, and the chains never to be broken; and shalt hear the gnashing of teeth? Who shall stand up for thee in that day, when thou shalt see him that hath labored with his own hand and hath lived uprightly, enjoying all glory; but thyself, who art now in soft raiment and redolent of perfumes, in incurable woe? What good will thy wealth and superfluity do thee? And the artisan—what harm will his poverty do him?

Therefore that we may not suffer then, let us fear what is said now, and let all our time be spent in employment on things which are really indispensable. For so, having propitiated God in regard of our past sins, and adding good deeds for the future, we shall be able to attain unto the kingdom of heaven: through the favor and loving-kindness, etc., etc.

HOMILY VI.

1 COR. ii. 1, 2.

And I, brethren, when I came to you, came not with excellency of speech or of wisdom, declaring unto you the testimony of God. For I determined not to know any thing among you, save Jesus Christ, and Him crucified.

Nothing was ever more prepared for combat than the spirit of Paul; or rather, I should say, not his spirit, (for he was not himself the inventor of these things,) but, nothing was ever equal to the grace working within him, which overcometh all things. For sufficient indeed is what had been said before to cast down the pride of the boasters about wisdom; nay, even a part of it had been enough. But to enhance the splendor of the victory, he contends anew for the points which he had been affirming; trampling upon the prostrate foe. Look at it in this way. He had brought forward the prophecy which saith, "I will destroy the wisdom of the wise." He had shewn the wisdom of God, in that by means of what seemed to be foolishness, He destroyed the philosophy of the Gentiles; he had shewn that the "foolishness of God is wiser than men;" he had shewn that not only did He teach by untaught persons, but also chose untaught persons to learn of Him. Now he sheweth that both the thing itself which was preached, and the manner of preaching it, were enough to stagger people; and yet did not stagger them. As thus: "not only," saith he, "are the disciples uneducated, but I myself also, who am the preacher."

Therefore he saith, "And I, brethren, "(again he useth the word "brethren," to smooth down the harshness of the utterance,)" came not with excellency of speech, declaring unto you the testimony of God." "What then? tell me, hadst thou chosen to come 'with excellency,' wouldest thou have been able?" "I, indeed, had I chosen, should not have been able; but Christ, if He had chosen, was able. But He would not, in order that He might render His trophy more brilliant." Wherefore also in a former passage, shewing that it was His work which had been done, His will that the word should be preached in an unlearned manner, he said, "For Christ sent me not to baptize, but to preach the Gospel; not with wisdom of words." But far greater, yea, infinitely greater, than Paul's willing this, is the fact that Christ willed it.

"Not therefore," saith he, "by display of eloquence, neither armed with arguments from without, do I declare the testimony of God." He saith not "the preaching," but "the testimony[1] of God;" which word was itself sufficient to withhold him. For he went about preaching death: and for this reason he added, "for I determined not to know anything among you, save Jesus Christ, and Him crucified." This was the meaning he meant to convey, that he is altogether destitute of the wisdom which is without; as indeed he was saying above, "I came not with excellency of speech:" for that he might have possessed this also is plain; for he whose garments raised the dead and whose shadow expelled diseases,[2] much more was his soul capable of receiving eloquence. For this is a thing which may be taught: but the former transcendeth all art. He then who knows things beyond the reach of art, much more must he have had strength for lesser things. But Christ permitted not; for it was not expedient. Rightly therefore he saith, "For I determined not to know any thing:" "for I, too, for my part have just the same will as Christ."

And to me it seems that he speaks to them in a lower tone even than to any others, in order to repress their pride. Thus, the expression, " I determined to know nothing," was spoken in contradistinction to the wisdom which is without. "For I came not weaving syllogisms nor sophisms, nor saying unto you anything else than "Christ was crucified." They indeed have ten thousand things to say, and concerning ten thousand things they speak, winding out long courses of words, framing arguments and syllogisms, compounding sophisms without end. But I came unto you saying no other thing than "Christ was crucified," and all of them I outstripped: which is a sign such as no words can express of the power of Him whom I preach."

---

[1] τὸ μαρτύριον, the martyrdom, or testimony by death: see 1 Tim. ii. 6.
[2] Here again what is written of St. Peter is taken as if written of St. Paul: see Acts xix. 12; v. 5.

[2.] Ver. 3. "And I was with you in weakness, and in fear, and in much trembling."

This again is another topic: for not only are the believers unlearned persons; not only is he that speaketh unlearned; not only is the manner of the teaching of an unlearned cast throughout; not only was the thing preached of itself enough to stagger people; (for the cross and death were the message brought;) but together with these there were also other hindrances, the dangers, and the plots, and the daily fear, and the being hunted about. For the word "weakness," with him in many places stands for the persecutions: as also elsewhere. "My weakness which I had in my flesh ye did not set at nought:" (Gal. iv. 13, 14.) and again, "If I must needs glory, I will glory of the things which concern my weakness." (2 Cor. xi. 30.) What [weakness]? "The governor under Aretas the king guarded the city of the Damascenes, desirous to apprehend me." (2 Cor. v. 32.) And again, "Wherefore I take pleasure in weakness:" (2 Cor. 12 10.) then, saying in what, he added, "In injuries, in necessities, in distresses." And here he makes the same statement; for having said, "And I was in weakness," etc. he did not stop at this point, but explaining the word "weakness," makes mention of his dangers. He adds again, "and in fear, and in much trembling, I was with you."

"How sayest thou? Did Paul also fear dangers?" He did fear, and dreaded them excessively; for though he was Paul, yet he was a man. But this is no charge against Paul, but infirmity of human nature; and it is to the praise of his fixed purpose of mind that when he even dreaded death and stripes, he did nothing wrong because of this fear. So that they who assert that he feared not stripes, not only do not honor him, but rather abridge greatly his praises. For if he feared not, what endurance or what self-restraint was there in bearing the dangers? I, for my part, on this account admire him; because being in fear, and not simply in "fear," but even in "trembling," at his perils, he so ran as ever to keep his crown; and gave not in for any danger, in his task of purging out[1] the world, and everywhere both by sea and land sowing the Gospel.

[3.] Ver. 4. "And my speech and my preaching was not in persuasive words of wisdom:" that is, had not the wisdom from without. Now if the doctrine preached had nothing subtle, and they that were called were unlearned, and he that preached was of the same description, and thereto was added persecution, and trembling, and fear; tell me, how did they overcome without Divine power? And

this is why, having said, "My speech and my preaching was not in persuasive words of wisdom," he added, "but in demonstration of the Spirit and of power."

Dost thou perceive how "the foolishness of God is wiser than men, and the weakness stronger?" They for their part, being unlearned and preaching such a Gospel, in their chains and persecution overcame their persecutors. Whereby? was it not by their furnishing that evidence which is of the Spirit? For this indeed is confessed demonstration. For who, tell me, after he had seen dead men rising to life and devils cast out, could have helped admitting it?

But seeing that there are also deceiving wonders, such as those of sorcerers, he removes this suspicion also. For he said not simply "of power," but first, "of the Spirit," and then, "of power:" signifying that the things done were spiritual.

It is no disparagement, therefore, that the Gospel was not declared by means of wisdom; rather it is a very great ornament. For this, it will be allowed, is the clearest token of its being divine and having its roots from above, out of the heavens. Wherefore he added also,

Ver. 5. "That your faith should not stand in the wisdom of men, but in the power of God."

Seest thou how clearly in every way he hath set forth the vast gain of this "ignorance," and the great loss of this "wisdom?" For the latter made void the Cross, but the former proclaimed the power of God: the latter, besides their failing to discover any of those things which they most needed, set them also upon boasting of themselves; the former, besides their receiving the truth, led them also to pride themselves in God. Again, wisdom would have persuaded many to suspect that the doctrine was of man: this clearly demonstrated it to be divine, and to have come down from heaven. Now when demonstration is made by wisdom of words, even the worse oftentimes overcome the better, having more skill in words; and falsehood outstrips the truth. But in this case it is not so: for neither doth the Spirit enter into an unclean soul, nor, having entered in, can it ever be subdued; even though all possible cleverness of speech assail it. For the demonstration by works and signs is far more evident than that by words.

[4.] But some one may say perhaps, "If the Gospel is to prevail and hath no need of words, lest the Cross be made of none effect; for what reason are signs withholden now?" For what reason? Speakest thou in unbelief and not allowing that they were done even in the times of the Apostles, or dost thou truly seek to know? If in unbelief, I will first make my stand against

---

[1] ἐκκαθαίρων: there seems to be an allusion to the classical fable about Hercules, who is represented as "purging the world" of monsters and oppressors; Soph. *Trach.* 1078. ed Musgrave.

this. I say then, If signs were not done at that time, how did they, chased, and persecuted, and trembling, and in chains, and having become the common enemies of the world, and exposed to all as a mark for ill usage, and with nothing of their own to allure, neither speech, nor show, nor wealth, nor city, nor nation, nor family, nor pursuit (ἐπιτήδευμα,) nor glory, nor any such like thing; but with all things contrary, ignorance, meanness, poverty, hatred, enmity, and setting themselves against whole commonwealths, and with such a message to declare; how, I say, did they work conviction? For both the precepts brought much labor, and the doctrines many dangers. And they that heard and were to obey, had been brought up in luxury and drunkenness, and in great wickedness. Tell me then, how did they convince? Whence had they their credibility? For, as I have just said, If without signs they wrought conviction, far greater does the wonder appear. Do not then urge the fact that signs are not done now, as a proof that they were not done then. For as then they were usefully wrought; so now are they no longer so wrought.

Nor doth it necessarily follow from discourse being the only instrument of conviction, that now the "preaching" is in "wisdom." For both they who from the beginning sowed the word were unprofessional (ἰδιῶται) and unlearned, and spake nothing of themselves; but what things they received from God, these they distributed to the world: and we ourselves at this time introduce no inventions of our own; but the things which from them we have received, we speak unto all. And not even now persuade we by argumentation; but from the Divine Scriptures and from the miracles done at that time we produce the proof of what we say. On the other hand, even they at that time persuaded not by signs alone, but also by discoursing. And the signs and the testimonies out of the Old Scriptures, not the cleverness of the things said, made their words appear more powerful.

[5.] How then, you will say, is it that signs were expedient then, and now inexpedient? Let us suppose a case; (for as yet I am contending against the Greek, and therefore I speak hypothetically of what must certainly come to pass,) let us, I say, suppose a case; and let the unbeliever consent to believe our affirmations, though it be only by way of concession: (κἂν κατὰ συνδρομήν) for instance, That Christ will come. When then Christ shall come and all the angels with Him, and be manifested as God, and all things made subject unto Him; will not even the Greek believe? It is quite plain that he will also fall down and worship, and confess Him

God, though his stubbornness exceed all reckoning. For who, at sight of the heavens opened and Him coming upon the clouds, and all the congregation of the powers above spread around Him, and rivers of fire coming on, and all standing by and trembling, will not fall down before Him, and believe Him God? Tell me, then; shall that adoration and knowledge be accounted unto the Greek for faith? No, on no account. And why not? Because this is not faith. For necessity hath done this, and the evidence of the things seen; and it is not of choice, but by the vastness of the spectacle the powers of the mind are dragged along. It follows that by how much the more evident and overpowering the course of events, by so much is the part of faith abridged. For this reason miracles are not done now.

And that this is the truth, hear what He saith unto Thomas (St. John xx. 29) "Blessed are they who have not seen, and yet have believed." Therefore, in proportion to the evidence wherewith the miracle is set forth is the reward of faith lessened. So that if now also miracles were wrought, the same thing would ensue. For that then we shall no longer know Him by faith, Paul hath shewn, saying, "For now we walk by faith, not by sight." (2 Cor. v., 7. νῦν not in the received text.) As at that time, although thou believe, it shall not be imputed unto thee, because the thing is so palpable; so also now, supposing that such miracles were done as were formerly. For when we admit things which in no degree and in no way can be made out by reasoning, then it is faith. It is for this that hell is threatened, but is not shewn: for if it were shewn, the same would again ensue.

[6.] Besides, if signs be what thou seekest after, even now thou mayest see signs, although not of the same kind; the numberless predictions and on an endless variety of subjects: the conversion of the world, the self-denying (φιλοσοφίαν) course of the Barbarians, the change from savage customs, the greater intenseness of piety. "What predictions?" you will say. "For all the things just mentioned were written after the present state of things had begun." When? Where? By whom? Tell me. How many years ago? Will you have fifty, or an hundred? They had not then, a hundred years ago, anything written at all. How then did the world retain the doctrines and all the rest, since memory would not be sufficient? How knew they that Peter was crucified? (ἀνεσχολοπίσθη) How could it have entered the minds of men who came after the events had taken place to foretell, for instance, that the Gospel should be preached in every part of the whole world? that the Jewish institutions should cease, and never return again? And they who gave up their lives for the Gospel, how would they have endured to see the Gospel adulterated? And how would the writers have won credit, miracles having ceased? And how could the writings have penetrated to the region of Barbarians, and of Indians, and unto the very bounds of the ocean, if the relators had not been worthy of credit? The writers, too, who were they? When, how, and why, did they write at all? Was it to gain glory to themselves? Why then inscribed they the books with other men's names? "Why, from a wish to recommend the doctrine." As true, or as false? For if you say, they stuck to it, as being false; their joining it at all was out of all likelihood: but if as being truth, there was no need of inventions such as you speak of. And besides, the prophecies are of such a kind, as that even until now time has been unable to force aside the predicted course of things: (ὡς μὴ δύνασθαι βιάζεσθαι χρόνῳ τὰ εἰρημένα) for the destruction indeed of Jerusalem took place many years ago; but there are also other predictions which extend along from that time until His coming; which examine as you please: for instance, this, "I am with you alway, even unto the end of the world: (St. Matt. xxviii. 20.) and, "Upon this Rock I will build My Church, and the gates of hell shall not prevail against it:" (St. Matt. xvi. 18.) and, "This Gospel shall be preached unto all nations:" (St. Matt. xxiv. 14.) and that which the woman which was an an harlot did[1]: and many others more than these. Whence then the truth of this prediction if indeed it were a forgery? How did "the gates of hell" not "prevail" against "the Church?" How is Christ always "with us?" For had He not been "with us," the Church would not have been victorious. How was the Gospel spread abroad in every part of the world? They also who have spoken against us are enough to testify the antiquity of the books; I mean, such as Celsus[2] and he of Batanea[3], who came after him. For they, I suppose, were not speaking against books composed after there time.

[7] And besides, there is the whole world which with one consent hath received the Gospel. Now there could not have been so great

agreement from one end of the earth to the other, unless it had been the Grace of the Spirit; but the authors of the forgery would have been quickly found out. Neither could so great excellencies have originated from inventions and falsehoods. Dost thou not see the whole world coming in; error extinguished; the austere wisdom (φιλοσοφίαν) of the old monks shining brighter than the sun; the choirs of the virgins; the piety among Barbarians; all men serving under one yoke? For neither by us alone were these things foretold, but also from the beginning, by the Prophets. For you will not, I trow, cavil at their predictions also: for the books are with their enemies, and through the zeal of certain Greeks they have been transferred into the Greek tongue. Many things then do these also foretell concerning these matters, shewing that it was God who should come among us.

[8] Why then do not all believe now? Because things have degenerated: and for this we are to blame. (For from hence the discourse is addressed unto us also.) For surely not even then did they trust to signs alone, but by the mode of life also many of the converts were attracted. For, "Let your light so shine before men," saith He, "that they may see your good works, and glorify your Father which is in heaven." (St. Matt. v. 16.) And, "They were all of one heart and one soul, neither said any man that aught of the things which he possessed was his own, but they had all things common; and distribution was made unto every man, according as he had need."; (Acts iv. 32, 35.) and they lived an angelic life. And if the same were done now, we should convert the whole world, even without miracles. But in the meanwhile, let those who will be saved attend to the Scriptures; for they shall find there both these noble doings, and those which are greater than these. For it may be added that the Teachers themselves surpassed the deeds of the others; living in hunger, in thirst, and nakedness. But we are desirous of enjoying great luxury, and rest, and ease; not so they: they cried aloud, "Even unto the present hour we both hunger, and thirst, and are naked, and are buffeted, and have no certain dwelling place. (I Cor. iv. 11.) And some ran from Jerusalem unto Illyricum, (Rom. xv. 19.) and another unto the country of the Indians, and another unto that of the Moors, and this to one part of the world, that to another. Whereas we have not the courage to depart even out of our own country; but seek for luxurious living and splendid houses and all other superfluities. For which of us ever was famished for the word of God's sake? Which ever abode in a wilderness? Which ever

---

1 Vid. St. Matt. xxvi. 13. and comp. St. Luke vii. 37. which two texts St. Chrys. apparently considers as relating to the same person: but in his commentary on St. Matthew xxvi. 6. he distinctly says they were not the same. The Fathers are divided on this point. Tertullian (*de Pudic.* 11.) and, St. Augustin (*de Consensu Evangelist* ii. 79.) consider them as the same, St. Augustin adding, that she was led to repeat the action with circumstances that shewed her increased perfection: Ambrosiaster (*in loc.*) leaves the matter doubtful.

2 Celsus, the Epicurean philosopher, against whom Origen wrote about A. D. 170.

3 Porphyry; so called also by St. Jerome, in the Preface to his *Commentary on Galatians* where the Editor's conjecture is, that the name was that of Porphyry's residence or birth, but that it was also a term of reproach, alluding to the fat bulls of Basan, Ps. xxii. 12. He is commonly called a Tyrian, but they suppose that Batanea, which is in Syria, was a colony of Tyre.

set out on a distant peregrination? Which of our teachers lived by the labor of his hands to assist others? Which endured death daily? Hence it is that they also who are with us have become slothful. For suppose that one saw soldiers and generals struggling with hunger, and thirst, and death, and with all dreadful things, and bearing cold and dangers and all like lions, and so prospering; then afterwards, relaxing that strictness, and becoming enervated, and fond of wealth, and addicted to business and bargains, and then overcome by their enemies, it were extreme folly to seek for the cause of all this. Now let us reason thus in our own case and that of our ancestors; for we too have become weaker than all, and are nailed down unto this present life.

And if one be found having a vestige of the ancient wisdom, leaving the cities and the market-places, and the society of the world, and the ordering of others, he betakes himself to the mountains: and if one ask the reason of that retirement, he invents a plea which cannot meet with allowance. For, saith he, " lest I perish too, and the edge of my goodness be taken off, I start aside." Now how much better were it for thee to become less keen, and to gain others, than abiding on high to neglect thy perishing brethren?

When, however, the one sort are careless about virtue, and those who do regard it withdraw themselves far from our ranks, how are we to subdue our enemies? For even if miracles were wrought now, who would be persuaded? Or who of those without would give heed unto us, our iniquity being thus prevalent? For so it is, that our upright living seems unto the many the more trustworthy argument of the two: miracles admitting of a bad construction on the part of obstinate bad men: whereas a pure life will have abundant power to stop the mouth of the devil himself.

[9.] These things I say, both to governors and governed; and, before all others, unto myself; to the end that the way of life shown forth in us may be truly admirable, that taking our appropriate stations, we may look down on all things present; may despise wealth, and not despise hell; overlook glory, and not overlook salvation; endure toil and labor here, lest we fall into punishment there. Thus let us wage war with the Greeks; thus let us take them captive with a captivity better than liberty.

But while we say these things without intermission, over and over, they occur very seldom. Howbeit, be they done or not, it is right to remind you of them continually. For if some are engaged in deceiving by their fair speech, so much more is it the duty of those who allure back unto the truth, not to grow weary of speaking what is profitable. Again: if the deceivers make use of so many contrivances—spending as they do money, and applying arguments, and undergoing dangers, and making a parade of their patronage—much more should we, who are winning men from deceit, endure both dangers and deaths, and all things; that we may both gain ourselves and others, and become to our enemies irresistible, and so obtain the promised blessings, through the grace and loving-kindness, etc.

HOMILY VII.

1 COR. ii. 6, 7.

Howbeit we speak wisdom among the perfect, yet a wisdom not of this world, nor of the rulers of this world, which are coming to naught; but we speak God's wisdom in a mystery, even the wisdom that hath been hidden, which God fore-ordained before the worlds unto our glory.

DARKNESS seems to be more suitable than light to those that are diseased in their eyesight: wherefore they betake themselves by preference to some room that is thoroughly shaded over. This also is the case with the wisdom which is spiritual. As the wisdom which is of God seemed to be foolishness unto those without: so their own wisdom, being foolishness indeed, was accounted by them wisdom. The result has been just as if a man having skill in navigation were to promise that without a ship or sails he would pass over a boundless tract of sea, and then endeavor by reasonings to prove that the thing is possible; but some other person, ignorant of it all, committing himself to a ship and a steersman and sailors, were thus to sail in safety. For the seeming ignorance of this man is wiser than the wisdom of the other. For excellent is the art of managing a ship; but when it makes too great professions it is a kind of folly. And so is every art which is not contented with its own proper limits. Just so the wisdom which is without [were wisdom indeed[1]]

---

[1] There seems to be a word or two wanting in the text here, which has been supplied by conjecture in the translation. [But they are found in Codex C. Aretinus].

if it had had the benefit of the spirit. But since it trusted all to itself and supposed that it wanted none of that help, it became foolishness, although it seemed to be wisdom. Wherefore having first exposed it by the facts, then and not till then he calls it foolishness; and having first called the wisdom of God folly, according to their reckoning, then and not till then he shews it to be wisdom. (For after our proofs, not before, we are best able to abash the gainsayers.)

His words then are, " Howbeit we speak wisdom among the perfect :" for when I, accounted foolish and a preacher of follies, get the better of the wise, I overcome wisdom, not by foollishness but by a more perfect wisdom ; a wisdom, too, so ample and so much greater, that the other appears foolishness. Wherefore having before called it by a name such as they named it at that time, and having both proved his victory from the facts, and shewn the extreme foolishness of the other side : he thenceforth bestows upon it its right name, saying, " Howbeit we speak wisdom among the perfect." " Wisdom" is the name he gives to the Gospel, to the method of salvation, the being saved by the Cross. " The perfect," are those who believe. For indeed they are "perfect," who know all human things to be utterly helpless, and who overlook them from the conviction that by such they are profited nothing : such were the true believers.

" But not a wisdom of this world." For where is the use of the wisdom which is without, terminating here and proceeding no further, and not even here able to profit its possessors ?

Now by the " rulers of the world," here, he means not certain demons, as some suspect[1], but those in authority, those in power, those who esteem the thing worth contending about, philosophers, rhetoricians and writers of speeches (λογογράφους). For these were the dominant sort and often became leaders of the people.

" Rulers of the world" he calls them, because beyond the present world their dominion extends not. Wherefore, he adds further, "which are coming to nought ;" disparaging it both on its own account, and from those who wield it. For having shewn that it is false, that it is foolish, that it can discover nothing, that it is weak, he shews moreover that it is but of short duration.

[2.] " But we speak God's wisdom in a mystery." What mystery ? For surely Christ saith, (St. Matt. x. 27. ἠκούσατε rec. text ἀκούετε.) " What ye have heard in the ear, proclaim upon the housetops." How then does he call it " a mystery?" Because that neither angel nor archangel, nor any other created power knew of it before it actually took place. Wherefore he saith, (Ephes. iii. 10.) " That now unto the principalities and powers in heavenly places might be known by the Church the manifold wisdom of God." And this hath God done in honor to us, so that they not without us should hear the mysteries. For we, too, ourselves, whomsoever we make our friends, use to speak of this as a sure proof of friendship towards them, that we tell our secrets to no one in preference to them. Let those hear who expose to shame[2] the secrets of the Gospel, and unto all indiscriminately display the "pearls" and the doctrine, and who cast "the holy things" unto "dogs," and "swine," and useless reasonings. For the Mystery wants no argumentation ; but just what it is, that only is to be declared. Since it will not be a mystery, divine and whole in all its parts, when thou addest any thing to it of thyself also.

And in another sense, too, a mystery is so called ; because we do not behold the things which we see, but some things we see and others we believe. For such is the nature of our Mysteries. I, for instance, feel differently upon these subjects from an unbeliever. I hear, " Christ was crucified ;" and forthwith I admire His loving-kindness unto men : the other hears, and esteems it weakness. I hear, " He became a servant ;" and I wonder at his care for us : the other hears, and counts it dishonor. I hear, " He died ;" and am astonished at His might, that being in death He was not holden, but even broke the bands of death : the other hears, and surmises it to be helplessness. He hearing of the resurrection, saith, the thing is a legend ; I, aware of the facts which demonstrate it, fall down and worship the dispensation of God. He hearing of a laver, counts it merely as water : but I behold not simply the thing which is seen, but the purification of the soul which is by the Spirit. He considers only that my body hath been washed ; but I have believed that the soul also hath become both pure and holy ; and I count it the sepulchre, the resurrection, the sanctification, the righteousness, the redemption, the adoption, the inheritance, the kingdom of heaven, the plenary effusion (χορηγίαν) of the Spirit. For not by the sight do I judge of the things that appear, but by the eyes of the mind. I hear of the " Body of Christ :" in one sense I understand the expression, in another sense the unbeliever.

And just as children, looking on their books, know not the meaning of the letters, neither know what they see ; yea more, if even a grown man be unskilful in letters, the same thing will befall him ; but the skilful will find

---

[1] e. g. Origen, in *Lament.* iv. 11 ; in Ezek. *Hom.* xiii. §. 1 ; *Com. in St. Matt.* §. 125 ; St. Athanasius on Ps. cviii. (cix. Heb.) v. 15. t. i. 1194. Ed. Bened. The author of the Questions and Answers published with St. Justin Martyr's works agrees with St. Chrysostom ; see qu. cviii, clxx. Why may not both be right ?

[2] ἐκπομπεύοντες. vid. Conc. Ant. A. D. 270. ap. E. H. vii. 30.

much meaning stored up in the letters, even complete lives and histories: and an epistle in the hands of one that is unskilful will be accounted but paper and ink; but he that knows how to read will both hear a voice, and hold converse with the absent, and will reply whatsoever he chooses by means of writing: so it is also in regard of the Mystery. Unbelievers albeit they hear, seem not to hear: but the faithful, having the skill which is by the Spirit, behold the meaning of the things stored therein. For instance, it is this very thing that Paul signified, when he said that even now the word preached is hidden: for "unto them that perish," he saith, "it is hidden." (2 Cor. iv. 3.)

In another point of view, the word indicates also the Gospel's being contrary to all expectation. By no other name is Scripture wont to call what happens beyond all hope and above all thought of men. Wherefore also in another place, "My mystery is for Me[1]," and for Mine. And Paul again, (2 Cor. xv. 51.) "Behold, I shew you a mystery: we shall not all sleep, but we shall all be changed."

[3.] And though it be everywhere preached, still is it a mystery; for as we have been commanded, "what things we have heard in the ear, to speak upon the house tops," so have we been also charged, "not to give the holy things unto dogs nor yet to cast our pearls before swine." (St. Matt. vii. 9.) For some are carnal and do not understand: others have a veil upon their hearts and do not see: wherefore that is above all things a mystery, which everywhere is preached, but is not known of those who have not a right mind; and is revealed not by wisdom but by the Holy Ghost, so far as is possible for us to receive it. And for this cause a man would not err, who in this respect also should entitle it a mystery, the utterance whereof is forbidden. (ἀπόρρητον) For not even unto us, the faithful, hath been committed entire certainty and exactness. Wherefore Paul also said, (ch. xiii. 9.) "We know in part, and we prophesy in part: for now we see in a mirror darkly; but then face to face."

[4.] For this cause he saith, "We speak wisdom in a mystery, the hidden wisdom which God fore-ordained before the worlds unto our glory. Hidden:" that is, that no one of the powers above hath learnt it before us; neither do the many know it now.

"Which he fore-ordained unto our glory"

and yet, elsewhere he saith, "unto his own glory," for he considereth our salvation to be His own glory: even as also He calleth it His own riches, (vid. Ephes. iii. 8,) though He be Himself rich in good and need nothing in order that He may be rich.

"Fore-ordained," he saith, pointing out the care had of us. For so those are accounted most both to honor and to love us, whosoever shall have laid themselves out to do us good from the very beginning: which indeed is what fathers do in the case of children. For although they give not their goods until afterwards, yet at first and from the beginning they had predetermined this. And this is what Paul is earnest to point out now; that God always loved us even from the beginning and when as yet we were not. For unless He had loved us, He would not have fore-ordained our riches. Consider not then the enmity which hath come between; for more ancient than that was the friendship.

As to the words, "before the worlds," (πρὸ τῶν αἰώνων) they mean eternal. For in another place also He saith thus, "Who is before the worlds." The Son also, if you mark it, will be found to be eternal in the same sense. For concerning Him he saith, (Heb. i. 2.) "By Him He made the worlds;" which is equivalent to subsistence before the worlds; for it is plain that the maker is before the things which are made.

[5.] Ver. 8. "Which none of the rulers of this world knew; for had they known, they would not have crucified the Lord of Glory."

Now if they knew not, how said He unto them, (St. John vii. 28.) "Ye both know Me, and ye know whence I am?" Indeed, concerning Pilate the Scripture saith, he knew not. (vid. St. John xix, 9.) It is likely also that neither did Herod know. These, one might say, are called rulers of this world: but if a man were to say that this is spoken concerning the Jews also and the Priests, he would not err. For to these also He saith, (St. John viii. 19.) "Ye know neither Me nor My Father." How then saith He a little before, "Ye both know Me, and ye know whence I am?" However, the manner of this way of knowledge and of that hath already been declared in the Gospel; (Hom. 49. on St. John,) and, not to be continually handling the same topic, thither do we refer our readers.

What then? was their sin in the matter of the Cross forgiven them? For He surely did say, "Forgive them." (Luke xxiii. 34.) If they repented, it was forgiven. For even he who set countless assailants on Stephen and persecuted the Church, even Paul, became the champion of the Church. Just so then, those others also who

---

[1] This is the rendering, in some old Greek version, though not in the LXX, of the clause in Isaiah XXIV. 16. which in our authorized version runs, "My leanness, my leanness; woe unto me!" "Mystery" stands for the Chaldee "a secret:" which meaning the Targum of Jonathan gives to the word in this place: as do the Vulgate, and the Syriac according to Walton. The received reading of the LXX may be explained as a pharaphrase of this rendering. The words, "*and for mine,*" seem added by St. Chrysostom.

chose to repent, had forgiveness: and this indeed Paul himself meant, when he exclaims, (Rom. xi. 11, 1, 2). "I say then, have they stumbled that they should fall? God forbid." "I say then, hath God cast away His people whom He foreknew? God forbid." Then, to shew that their repentance was not precluded, he brought forward as a decisive proof his own conversion, saying, "For I also am an Israelite."

As to the words, "They knew not;" they seem to me to be said here not concerning Christ's Person, but only concerning the dispensation hidden in that event: (περὶ αὐτῆς τοῦ πράγματος τῆς οἰκονομίας,) as if he had said, what meant "the death," and the "Cross," they knew not. For in that passage also He said not, "They know not Me," but, "They know not what they do;" that is, the dispensation which is being accomplished, and the mystery, they are ignorant of. For they knew not that the Cross is to shine forth so brightly; that it is made the salvation of the world, and the reconciliation of God unto men; that their city should be taken; and that they should suffer the extreme of wretchedness.

By the name of "wisdom," he calls both Christ, and the Cross and the Gospel. Opportunely also he called Him, "The Lord of glory." For seeing that the Cross is counted a matter of ignominy, he signifies that the Cross was great glory: but that there was need of great wisdom in order not only to know God but also to learn this dispensation of God: and the wisdom which was without turned out an obstacle, not to the former only, but to the latter also.

[6.] Ver. 9. "But as it is written, Things which eye saw not and ear heard not, and which entered not into the heart of man, whatsoever things God prepared for them that love Him."

Where are these words written? Why, it is said to have been "written," then also, when it is set down, not in words, but in actual events, as in the historical books[1]; or when the same meaning is expressed, but not in the very same words, as in this place: for the words, "They to whom it was not told about Him shall see, and they who have not heard shall understand," (Is. lii. 15; Sept. Comp. Rom. xv. 21.; Is. lxiv. 4.) are the same with "the things which eye hath not seen, nor ear heard." Either then this is his meaning, or probably it was actually written in some books, and the copies have perished. For indeed many books were destroyed, and few were preserved entire even in the first captivity. And this is plain, in those which

remain to us.* For the Apostle saith (Acts iii. 24.) "From Samuel and the Prophets which follow after they have all spoken concerning Him:" and these their words are not entirely extant. Paul, however, as being learned in the law and speaking by the Spirit, would of course know all with accuracy. And why speak I of the captivity? Even before the captivity many books had disappeared; the Jews having rushed headlong to the last degree of impiety: and this is plain from the end of the fourth book of Kings, (2 Kings xxii. 8. 2 Chron. xxxiv. 14.) for the book of Deuteronomy could hardly be found, having been buried somewhere in a dunghill[2].

And besides, there are in many places double prophecies, easy to be apprehended by the wiser sort; from which we may find out many of the things which are obscure.

[7.] What then, hath "eye not seen what God prepared?" No. For who among men saw the things which were about to be dispensed? Neither then hath "the ear heard, nor hath it entered into the heart of man." How is this? For if the Prophets spoke of it, how saith he, "Ear hath not heard, neither hath it entered into the heart of man?" It did not enter; for not of himself alone is he speaking, but of the whole human race. What then? The Prophets, did not they hear? Yes, they heard; but the prophetic ear was not the ear "of man:" for not as men heard they, but as Prophets. Wherefore he said, (Is. l. 4. Sept.) "He hath added unto me an ear to hear," meaning by "addition" that which was from the Spirit. From whence it was plain that before hearing it had not entered into the heart of man. For after the gift of the Spirit the heart of the Prophets was not the heart of man, but a spiritual heart; as also he saith himself, "We have the mind of Christ" (v. 16.) as if he would say, "Before we had the blessing of the Spirit and learnt the things which no man can speak, no one of us nor yet of the Prophets conceived them in his mind. How should we? since not even angels know them. For what need is there to speak," saith he, "concerning 'the rulers of this world,' seeing that no man knew them, nor yet the powers above?"

What kind of things then are these? That by what is esteemed to be the foolishness of preaching He shall overcome the world, and the nations shall be brought in, and there shall be reconciliation of God with men, and so great blessings shall come upon us!

How then have we "known? Unto us," he saith, "God hath revealed them by His Spirit;"

---

[1] Of which, perhaps, *He shall be called a Nazarene*, St. Matt. ii. 23. is an instance: although that indeed is not said to be "written," but *spoken by the Prophets*.

* [Dr. Field prints the original with a capital letter, making it= Paraleipomena, the LXX. name for the books of Chronicles, and refers to II. Chron. ix. 29, xii. 5, xiii. 22. C.]

[2] Two circumstances in this account appear to be traditional: that the book found was that of Deuteronomy; and that the place where it was found was a dunghill.

not by the wisdom which is without; for this like some dishonored handmaid hath not been permitted to enter in, and stoop down and look into (see St. John xx. 5.) the mysteries pertaining to the Lord. Seest thou how great is the difference between this wisdom and that? The things which angels knew not, these are what she hath taught us: but she that is without, hath done the contrary. Not only hath she failed to instruct, but she hindered and obstructed, and after the event sought to obscure His doings, making the Cross of none effect. Not then simply by our receiving the knowledge, does he describe the honor vouchsafed to us, nor by our receiving it with angels, but, what is more, by His Spirit conveying it to us.

[7.] Then to show its greatness, he saith, If the Spirit which knoweth the secret things of God had not revealed them, we should not have learned them. Such an object of care was this whole subject to God, as to be among His secrets. Wherefore we needed also that Teacher who knoweth these things perfectly; for "the Spirit," (v. 10, 11, 12.) saith he, "searcheth all things, even the deep things of God." For the word "to search" is here indicative not of ignorance, but of accurate knowledge: it is the very same mode of speaking which he used even of God, saying, "He that searcheth the hearts knoweth what is the mind of the Spirit." (Rom. viii. 27.) Then having spoken with exactness concerning the knowledge of the Spirit, and having pointed out that it is as fully equal to God's knowledge, as the knowledge of a man itself to itself; and also, that we have learned all things from it and necessarily from it; he added, "which things also we speak, not in words which man's wisdom teacheth, but which the Holy Ghost teacheth; comparing spiritual things with spiritual." Seest thou to what point he exalted us because of the Teacher's dignity? For so much are we wiser than they as there is difference between Plato and the Holy Spirit; they having for masters the heathen rhetoricians; but we, the Holy Spirit.

[8.] But what is this, "comparing spiritual things with spiritual?" When a thing is spiritual and of dubious meaning, we adduce testimonies from the things which are spiritual. For instance, I say, Christ rose again—was born of a Virgin; I adduce testimonies and types and demonstrations; the abode of Jonah in the whale and his deliverance afterwards; the child-bearing of the barren, Sarah, Rebecca, and the rest; the springing up of the trees which took place in paradise (Gen. ii. 5.) when there had been no seeds sown, no rains sent down, no furrow drawn along. For the things to come were fashioned out and figured forth, as in shadow, by the former things, that these

which are now might be believed when they came in. And again we shew, how of the earth was man, and how of man alone the woman; and this without any intercourse whatever; how the earth itself of nothing, the power of the Great Artificer being every where sufficient for all things. Thus "with spiritual things" do I "compare spiritual," and in no instance have I need of the wisdom which is without—neither its reasonings nor its embellishments. For such persons do but agitate the weak understanding and confuse it; and are not able to demonstrate clearly any one of the things which they affirm, but even have the contrary effect. They rather disturb the mind and fill it with darkness and much perplexity. Wherefore he saith, "with spiritual things comparing spiritual."[1] Seest thou how superfluous he sheweth it to be? and not only superfluous, but even hostile and injurious: for this is meant by the expressions, "lest the Cross of Christ be made of none effect," and, "that our ('your faith,' rec. text) faith should not stand in the wisdom of men." And he points out here, that it is impossible for those who confidently entrust every thing to it, to learn any useful thing: for

[9.] Ver. 14. "The natural man receiveth not the things of the Spirit."

It is necessary then to lay it aside first. "What then," some man will say; "is the wisdom from without stigmatized? And yet it is the work of God." How is this clear? since He made it not, but it was an invention of thine. For in this place he calls by the term "wisdom" curious research and superfluous elegance of words. But should any one say that he means the human understanding; even in this sense the fault is thine. For thou bringest a bad name upon it, who makest a bad use of it; who to the injury and thwarting of God demandest from it things which indeed it never had. Since then thou boastest therein and fightest with God, He hath exposed its weakness. For strength of body also is an excellent thing, but when Cain used it not as he ought, God disabled him and made him tremble (Gen. iv. 12, 14. Sept. "sighing and trembling," rec. ver. "fugitive and vagabond.") Wine also is a good thing; but because the Jews indulged in it immoderately, God prohibited the priests entirely from the use of the fruit.[2] And since thou also hast abused wisdom unto the rejecting of God, and hast demanded of it more than it can do of its own strength; in order to withdraw thee from human hope, he hath shewed thee its weakness.

---

[1] [Principal Edwards explains the phrase adopting the A. V., as "combining revealed truths so as to form a consistent and well-proportioned system" Com. *in lo.*]

[2] i. e. when they were in course of attendance on the tabernacle. Levit. x. 8. 9.

For (to proceed) he is "a natural man, who attributes every thing to reasonings of the mind and considers not that he needs help from above; which is a mark of sheer folly. For God bestowed it that it might learn and receive help from Him, not that it should consider itself sufficient unto itself. For eyes are beautiful and useful, but should they choose to see without light, their beauty profits them nothing; nor yet their natural force, but even doth harm. So if you mark it, any soul also, if it choose to see without the Spirit, becomes even an impediment unto itself.

"How then, before this," it will be said, "did she see all things of herself?" Never at any time did she this of herself but she had creation for a book set before her in open view. But when men having left off to walk in the way which God commanded them, and by the beauty of visible objects to know the Great Artificer, had entrusted to disputations the leading-staff of knowledge; they became weak and sank in a sea of ungodliness; for they presently brought in that which was the abyss of all evil, asserting that nothing was produced from things which were not, but from uncreated matter; and from this source they became the parents of ten thousand heresies.

Moreover, in their extreme absurdities they agreed; but in those things wherein they seemed to dream out something wholesome, though it were only as in shadows, they fell out with one another; that on both sides they might be laughed to scorn. For that out of things which are not nothing is produced, nearly all with one accord have asserted and written; and this with great zeal. In these absurdities then they were urged on by the Devil. But in their profitable sayings, wherein they seemed, though it were but darkly, (ἐν αἰνίγματι,) to find some part of what they sought, in these they waged war with one another: for instance, that the soul is immortal; that virtue needs nothing external; and that the being good or the contrary is not of necessity nor of fate.

Dost thou see the craft of the Devil? If any where he saw men speaking any thing corrupt, he made all to be of one mind; but if any where speaking any thing sound, he raised up others against them; so that the absurdities did not fail, being confirmed by the general consent, and the profitable parts died away, being variously understood. Observe how in every respect the soul is unstrung, (ἄτονος) and is not sufficient unto herself. And this fell out as one might expect. For if, being such as she is, she aspire to have need of nothing and withdraw herself from God; suppose her not fallen into that condition, and into what extreme madness would she not have insensibly sunk? If,

endowed with a mortal body, she expected greater things from the false promise of the Devil— (for, "Ye shall be," said he, "as gods" Gen. iii. 4)—to what extent would she not have cast herself away, had she received her body also, from the beginning, immortal. For, even after that, she asserted herself to be unbegotten and of the essence of God, through the corrupt mouth of the Manicheans[1], and it was this distemperature which gave occasion to her invention of the Grecian gods. On this account, as it seems to me, God made virtue laborious, with a view to bow down the soul and to bring it to moderation. And that thou mayest convince thyself that this is true, (as far as from trifles one may guess at any thing great,) let us learn it from the Israelites. They, it is well known, when they led not a life of toil but indulged in relaxation, not being able to bear prosperity, fell away into ungodliness. What then did God upon this? He laid upon them a multitude of laws with a view to restrain their licence. And to convince you that these laws contribute not to any virtue, but were given to them as a sort of curb, providing them with an occasion of perpetual labor; hear what saith the prophet concerning them; "I gave them statutes which were not good." Ezek. xx. 25. What means, "not good?" Such as did not much contribute towards virtue. Wherefore he adds also, "and ordinances whereby they shall not live."

[10.] "But the natural man receiveth not the things of the Spirit."

For as with these eyes no man could learn the things in the heavens; so neither the soul unaided the things of the Spirit. And why speak I of the things in heaven? It receives not even those in earth, all of them. For beholding afar off a square tower, we think it to be round; but such an opinion is mere deception of the eyes: so also we may be sure, when a man by means of his understanding alone examines the things which are afar off much ridicule will ensue. For not only will he not see them such as indeed they are, but will even account them the contraries of what they are. Wherefore he added, "for they are foolishness unto him" But this comes not of the nature of the things, but of his infirmity, unable as he is to attain to their greatness through the eyes of his soul.

[11.] Next, pursuing his contrast, he states the cause of this, saying, "he knoweth not because they are spiritually discerned:" i. e. the things asserted require faith, and to apprehend them by reasonings is not possible, for their

---

[1] 'Manes opposed to each other two diverse and adverse principles, alike eternal and coeternal: and fancied two natures and substances, Good and Bad; in this following elder heretics;" (some of the Gnostics, see S. Aug. above, §. 6, 14, 16, 21, 22) . . . . "Hence they are compelled to affirm that good souls are of the same nature with God." S. Aug. de Hæresibus, §. 46.

magnitude exceeds by a great deal the meanness of our understanding. Wherefore he saith, "but he that is spiritual judgeth all things, yet he himself is judged of no man." For he that has sight, beholds himself all things that appertain to the man that has no sight; but no sightless person discerns what the other is about. So also in the case before us, our own matters and those of unbelievers, all of them we for our part know; but ours, they know not henceforth any more. We know what is the nature of things present, what the dignity of things to come; and what some day shall become of the world when this state of things shall be no more, and what sinners shall suffer, and the righteous shall enjoy. And that things present are nothing worth, we both know, and their meanness we expose; (for to "discern" is also to expose;) (ἀναχρίνειν, ἐλέγχειν) and that the things to come are immortal and immoveable. All these things are known to the spiritual man; and what the natural man shall suffer when he is departed into that world; and what the faithful shall enjoy when he hath fulfilled his journey from this: none of which are known to the natural man.

[12.] Wherefore also, subjoining a plain demonstration of what had been affirmed, he saith, "For who hath known the mind of the Lord, that he may instruct Him? But we have the mind of Christ." That is to say, the things which are in the mind of Christ, these we know, even the very things which He willeth and hath revealed. For since he had said, "the Spirit had revealed them;" lest any one should set aside the Son, he subjoins that Christ also shewed us these things. Not meaning this, that all the things which He knoweth, we know; but that all the things which we know are not human so as to be open to suspicion, but of His mind and spiritual.

For the mind which we have about these things we have of Christ; that is, the knowledge which we have concerning the things of the faith is spiritual; so that with reason we are "judged of no man." For it is not possible that a natural man should know divine things. Wherefore also he said, "For who hath known the mind of the Lord?" implying that our own mind which we have about these things, is His mind. And this, "that he may instruct Him," he hath not added without reason, but with reference to what he had just now said, "the spiritual man no one discerneth." For if no man is able to know the mind of God, much less can he teach and correct it. For this is the meaning of, "that he may instruct Him."

Seest thou how from every quarter he repels the wisdom which is without, and shews that the spiritual man knoweth more things and

greater? For seeing that those reasons, "That no flesh should glory;" and, "For this cause hath He chosen the foolish things, that He might confound the wise men;" and, "Lest the Cross of Christ should be made void:" seemed not to the unbelievers greatly worthy of credit, nor yet attractive, or necessary, or useful, he finishes by laying down the principal reason; because in this way we most easily see from Whom we may have the means of learning even high things, and things secret, and things which are above us. For reason was absolutely made of none effect by our inability to apprehend through Gentile wisdom the things above us.

You may observe, too, that it was more advantageous to learn in this way from the Spirit. For that is the easiest and clearest of all teaching.

"But we have the mind of Christ." That is, spiritual, divine, that which hath nothing human. For it is not of Plato, nor of Pythagoras, but it is Christ Himself, putting His own things into our mind.

This then, if naught else, let us revere, O beloved, and let our life shine forth as most excellent; since He also Himself maketh this a sure proof of great friendship, viz. the revealing His secrets unto us: where He saith, (St. John xv. 15.) "Henceforth I call you not servants, for all ye are My friends; for all things which I have heard from My Father I have told unto you:" that is, I have had confidence towards you. Now if this by itself is a proof of friendship, namely, to have confidence: when it appears that He has not only confided to us the mysteries conveyed by words, (τὰ διὰ ῥημάτων μυστηρία) but also imparted to us the same conveyed by works, (διὰ τῶν ἔργων, i. e. sacramental actions) consider how vast the love of which this is the fruit. This, if nothing else, let us revere; even though we will not make any such great account of hell, yet let it be more fearful than hell to be thankless and ungrateful to such a friend and benefactor. And not as hired servants, but as sons and freemen, let us do all things for the love of our Father; and let us at last cease from adhering to the world that we may put the Greeks also to shame. For even now desiring to put out my strength against them, I shrink from so doing, lest haply, surpass them as we may by our arguments and the truth of what we teach, we bring upon ourselves much derision from the comparison of our way of life; seeing that they indeed, cleaving unto error and having no such conviction, abide by philosophy, but we do just the contrary. However, I will say it. For it may be, it may be that in practising how to contend against them, we shall long as rivals to become better than they in our mode of life also.

[14.] I was saying not long ago, that it would not have entered the Apostles' thoughts to preach what they did preach, had they not enjoyed Divine Grace; and that so far from succeeding, they would not even have devised such a thing. Well then, let us also to-day prosecute the same subject in our discourse; and let us shew that it was a thing impossible so much as to be chosen or thought of by them, if they had not had Christ among them: not because they were arrayed, the weak against the strong, not because few against many, not because poor against rich, not because unlearned against wise, but because the strength of their prejudice, too, was great. For ye know that nothing is so strong with men as the tyranny of ancient custom. So that although they had not been twelve only, and not so contemptible, and such as they really were, but another world as large as this, and with an equivalent number arrayed on their side, or even much greater; even in this case the result would have been hard to achieve. For the other party had custom on their side, but to these their novelty was an obstacle. For nothing so much disturbs the mind, though it be done for some beneficial purpose, as to innovate and introduce strange things, and most of all when this is done in matters relating to divine worship and the glory of God. And how great force there is in this circumstance I will now make plain; first having made the following statement that there was added also another difficulty with regard to the Jews. For in the case of the Greeks, they destroyed both their gods and their doctrines altogether; but not so did they dispute with the Jews, but many of their doctrines they abolished, while the God who had enacted the same they bade them worship. And affirming that men should honor the legislator, they said, "obey not in all respects the law which is of Him;" for instance, in the keeping the Sabbath, or observing circumcision, or offering sacrifices, or doing any other like thing. So that not only was custom an impediment, but also the fact, that when they bade men worship God, they bade them break many of His laws.

[15.] But in the case of the Greeks great was the tyranny of custom. For if it had been a custom of ten years only, I say not of such a length of time, and if it had preoccupied but a few men, I say not the whole world, when these persons made their approaches; even in this case the revolution would have been hard to effect. But now sophists, and orators, and fathers, and grandfathers, and many more ancient than all these, had been preoccupied by the error: the very earth and sea, and mountains and groves, and all nations of Barbarians, and all tribes of the Greeks, and wise men and ignorant, rulers and subjects, women and men, young and old, masters and slaves, artificers and husbandmen, dwellers in cities and in the country; all of them. And those who were instructed would naturally say, "What in the world is this? Have all that dwell in the world been deceived? both sophists and orators, philosophers and historians, the present generation and they who were before this, Pythagoreans, Platonists, generals, consuls, kings, they who in all cities from the beginning were citizens and colonists, both Barbarians and Greeks? And are the twelve fishermen and tent-makers and publicans wiser than all these? Why, who could endure such a statement?" However, they spake not so, nor had it in their mind, but did endure them, and owned that they *were* wiser than all. Wherefore they overcame even all. And custom was no impediment to this, though accounted invincible when she hath acquired her full swing by course of time.

And that thou mayest learn how great is the strength of custom, it hath oftentimes prevailed over the commands of God. And why do I say, commands? Even over very blessings. For so the Jews when they had manna, required garlic; enjoying liberty they were mindful of their slavery; and they were continually longing for Egypt, because they were accustomed to it. Such a tyrannical thing is custom.

If thou desire to hear of it from the heathens also; it is said that Plato, although well aware that all about the gods was a sort of imposture, condescended to all the feasts and all the rest of it, as being unable to contend with custom; and as having in fact learnt this from his master. For he, too, being suspected of some such innovation, was so far from succeeding in what he desired that he even lost his life; and this, too, after making his defence. And how many men do we see now by prejudice held in idolatry, and having nothing plausible to say, when they are charged with being Greeks, but alleging the fathers, and grandfathers, and great grandfathers. For no other reason did some of the heathens call custom, second nature. But when doctrines are the subject-matter of the custom, it becomes yet more deeply rooted. For a man would change all things more easily than those pertaining to religion. The feeling of shame, too, coupled with custom, was enough to raise an obstacle; and the seeming to learn a new lesson in extreme old age, and that of those who were not so intelligent. And why wonder, should this happen in regard of the soul, seeing that even in the body custom hath great force?

[16.] In the Apostles' case, however, there was yet another obstacle, more powerful than these; it was not merely changing custom so ancient and primitive, but there were perils also under which the change was effected. For they were not simply drawing men from one custom to another, but from a custom wherein was no fear to an undertaking which held out threats of danger. For the believer must immediately incur confiscation, persecution, exile from his country; must suffer the worst ills, be hated of all men, be a common enemy both to his own people and to strangers. So that even if they had invited men to a customary thing out of novelty, even in this case it would have been a difficult matter. But when it was from a custom to an innovation, and with all these terrors to boot, consider how vast was the obstacle!

And again, another thing, not less than those mentioned, was added to make the change difficult. For besides the custom and the dangers, these precepts were both more burdensome, and those from which they withdrew men were easy and light. For their call was from fornication unto chastity; from love of life unto sundry kinds of death; from drunkenness unto fasting; from laughter unto tears and compunction; from covetousness unto utter indigence; from safety unto dangers: and throughout all they required the strictest circumspection. For, "Filthiness," (Ephes. v. 4.) saith he, "and foolish talking, and jesting, let it not proceed out of your mouth." And these things they spake unto those who knew nothing else than how to be drunken and serve their bellies; who celebrated feasts made up of nothing but of "filthiness" and laughter and all manner of revellings (κωμῳδίας ἁπάσης.) So that not only from the matter pertaining to severity of life were the doctrines burthensome, but also from their being spoken unto men who had been brought up in careless ease, and "filthiness," and "foolish talking," and laughter and revellings. For who among those who had lived in these things, when he heard, (Matt. x. 38) "If a man take not up his cross and follow Me, he is not worthy of Me;" and, (Ibid. 34) "I came not to send peace but a sword, and to set a man at variance with his father, and the daughter at variance with her mother," would not have felt himself chilled all over (ἐνάρχησε)? And who, when he heard, "If a man bid not farewell to home and country and possessions, he is not worthy of Me," would not have hesitated, would not have refused? And yet there were men, who not only felt no chill, neither shrunk away when they heard these things, but ran to meet them and rushed upon the hardships, and eagerly caught at the precepts enjoined. Again, to be told, "For every idle word we shall give account;" (Matt. xii. 36) and, "whosoever looketh upon a woman to lust after her, hath committed adultery with her as soon as seen;" (Matt. v. 28, 25) and, "whosoever is angry

without cause shall fall into hell;"—which of the men of that day would not these things have frightened off? And yet all came running in, and many even leaped over the boundaries of the course. What then was their attraction? Was it not, plainly, the power of Him who was preached? For suppose that the case were not as it is, but just contrary[1], that this side was the other, and the other this; would it have been easy, let me ask, to hold fast and to drag on those who resisted? We cannot say so. So that in every way that power is proved divine which wrought so excellently. Else how, tell me, did they prevail with the frivolous and the dissolute, urging them toward the severe and rough course of life?

[17.] Well; such was the nature of the precepts. But let us see whether the doctrine was attractive. Nay, in this respect also there was enough to frighten away the unbelievers. For what said the preachers? That we must worship the crucified, and count Him as God, who was born of a Jewish woman. Now who would have been persuaded by these words, unless divine power had led the way? That indeed He had been crucified and buried, all men knew; but that He had risen again and ascended, no one save the Apostles had seen.

But, you will say, they excited them by promises and deceived them by an empty sound of words. Nay, this very topic most particularly shews (even apart from all that has been said) that our doctrines are no deceit. For all its hardships took place here, but its consolations they were to promise after the resurrection. This very thing then, for I repeat it, shews that our Gospel is divine. For why did no one of the believers say, "I close not with this, neither do I endure it? Thou threatenest me with hardships here, and the good things thou promisest after the resurrection. Why, how is it plain that there will be a resurrection? Which of the departed hath returned? Which of those at rest hath risen again? Which of these hath said what shall be after our departure hence?" But none of these things entered into their minds; rather they gave up their very lives for the Crucified. So that this bare fact was more than anything a proof of great power; first, their working conviction at once, touching matters so important, in persons that had never in their lives before heard of any such thing; secondly, that they prevailed on them to take the difficulties upon trial, and to account the blessings as matter of hope. Now if they had been deceivers they would have done the contrary: their good things they would have promised as of this world (ἐντεῦθεν, so St. John xviii. 36.); the

---

[1] i. e. suppose miracles and the attempt to convert had been the other way, from strictness to ease and pleasure.

fearful things they would not have mentioned, whether they related to the present life or the future. For so deceivers and flatterers act. Nothing harsh, nor galling, nor burdensome, do they hold out, but altogether the contrary. For this is the nature of deceit.

[18.] But "the folly," it will be said, "of the greater part caused them to believe what they were told." How sayest thou? When they were under Greeks, they were not foolish; but when they came over to us, did their folly then begin? And yet they were not men of another sort nor out of another world, that the Apostles took and persuaded: they were men too who simply held the opinions of the Greeks, but ours they received with the accompaniment of dangers. So that if with better reason they had maintained the former, they would not have swerved from them, now that they had so long time been educated therein; and especially as not without danger was it possible to swerve. But when they came to know from the very nature of the things that all on that side was mockery and delusion, upon this, even under menaces of sundry deaths, they sprang off (ἀπεπήδησαν) from their customary ways, and came over voluntarily unto the new; inasmuch as the latter doctrine was according to nature, but the other contrary to nature.

But " the persons convinced," it is said, "were slaves, and woman, and nurses, and midwives, and eunuchs." Now in the first place, not of these alone doth our Church consist; and this is plain unto all. But be it of these; this is what especially makes the Gospel worthy of admiration; that such doctrines as Plato and his followers could not apprehend, the fishermen had power on a sudden to persuade the most ignorant sort of all to receive. For if they had persuaded wise men only, the result would not have been so wonderful; but in advancing slaves, and nurses, and eunuchs unto such great severity of life as to make them rivals to angels, they offered the greatest proof of their divine inspiration. Again; had they enjoined I know not what trifling matters, it were reasonable perhaps to bring forward the conviction wrought in these persons, to show the trifling nature of the things which were spoken: but if things great, and high, and almost transcending human nature, and requiring high thoughts, were the matter of their lessons of wisdom; the more foolishness thou showest in those who were convinced, by so much the more dost thou shew clearly that they who wrought the conviction were wise and filled with divine grace.

But, you will say, they prevailed on them through the excessive greatness of the promises. But tell me, is not this very thing a wonder to thee, how they persuaded men to expect prizes and recompenses after death? For this, were there nothing else, is to me matter of amazement. But this, too, it will be said, came of folly. Inform me wherein is the folly of these things: that the soul is immortal; that an impartial tribunal will receive us after the present life; that we shall render an account of our deeds and words and thoughts unto God that knoweth all secrets; that we shall see the evil undergoing punishment, and the good with crowns on their heads. Nay, these things are not of folly, but the highest instruction of wisdom. The folly is in the contrary opinions to these.

[19.] Were this then the only thing, the despising of things present, the setting much by virtue, the not seeking rewards here, but advancing far beyond in hopes, and the keeping the soul so intent and faithful as by no present terror to be hindered in respect of the hope of what shall be; tell me, to what high philosophy must this belong? But would you also learn the force of the promises and predictions in themselves, and the truth of those uttered both before and after this present state of things? Behold, I shew you a golden chain, woven cunningly from the beginning! He spake some things to them about Himself, and about the churches, and about the things to come; and as He spake, He wrought mighty works. By the fulfilment therefore of what He said, it is plain that both the wonders wrought were real, and the future and promised things also.

But that my meaning may be yet plainer, let me illustrate it from the actual case. He raised up Lazarus by a single word merely, and shewed him alive. Again, He said, "The gates of Hades shall not prevail against the Church (St. Matt. xvi. 18.) and, " He that forsaketh father or mother, shall receive an hundred-fold in this life, and shall inherit everlasting life." (ib. 19. 29.) The miracle then is one, the raising of Lazarus; but the predictions are two; made evident, the one here, the other in the world to come. Consider now, how they are all proved by one another. For if a man disbelieve the resurrection of Lazarus, from the prophecy uttered about the Church let him learn to believe the miracle. For the word spoken so many years before, came to pass then, and received accomplishment: for " the gates of Hades prevailed not against the Church." You see that He who spake truth in the prophecy, it is clear that he also wrought the miracle: and He who both wrought the miracle and brings to accomplishment the words which He spake, it is clear that He speaks the truth also in the predictions of things yet to come, when He saith, " He who despiseth things present shall receive an hundred-fold, and shall inherit everlasting life." For the things which have been already done and spoken, He hath given as the surest pledges of those which shall hereafter come to pass.

Of all these things then, and the like to these, collecting them together out of the Gospels, let us tell them, and so stop their mouths. But if any one say, Why then was not error completely extinguished? this may be our answer: Ye yourselves are to blame, who rebel against your own salvation. For God hath so ordered this matter (ῲκονόμησεν,) that not even a remnant of the old impiety need be left.

[20.] Now, briefly to recount what has been said: What is the natural course of things? That the weak should be overcome by the strong, or the contrary? Those who speak things easy, or things of the harsher sort? those who attract men with dangers, or with security? innovators, or those who strengthen custom? those who lead into a rough, or into a smooth way? those who withdraw men from the institutions of their fathers, or those who lay down no strange laws? those who promise all their good things after our departure from this world, or those who flatter in the present life? the few to overcome the many, or the many the few?

But you, too, saith one, gave promises pertaining to this life. What then have we promised in this life? The forgiveness of sins and the laver of regeneration. Now in the first place, baptism itself hath its chief part in things to come; and Paul exclaims, saying, (Col. iii. 4.) "For ye died, and your life is hid with Christ in God: when your life shall be manifested, then shall ye also with Him be manifested in glory." But if in this life also it hath advantages, as indeed it hath, this also is more than all a matter of great wonder, that they had power to persuade men who had done innumerable evil deeds, yea such as no one else had done, that they should wash themselves clean of all, and they should give account of none of their offences. So that on this very account it were most of all meet to wonder that they persuaded Barbarians to embrace such a faith as this, and to have good hopes concerning things to come; and having thrown off the former burden of their sins, to apply themselves with the greatest zeal for the time to come to those toils which virtue requires, and not to gape after any object of sense, but rising to a height above all bodily things, to receive gifts purely spiritual: yea, that the Persian, the Sarmatian, the Moor, and the Indian should be acquainted with the purification of the soul, and the power of God, and His unspeakable mercy to men, and the severe discipline of faith, and the visitation of the Holy Spirit, and the resurrection of bodies, and the doctrines of life eternal. For in all these things, and in whatever is more than these, the fishermen, initiating by Baptism divers races of Barbarians, persuaded them (φιλοσοφεῖν) to live on high principles.

Of all these things then, having observed them accurately, let us speak unto the Gentiles, and again, let us shew them the evidence of our lives: that by both means we ourselves may be saved and they drawn over by our means unto the glory of God. For unto Him be the glory for ever. Amen.

HOMILY VIII.

1 Cor. iii. 1—3.

And I, brethren, could not speak unto you as unto spiritual, but as unto Carnal, as unto babes in Christ. I fed you with milk, and not with meat: for ye were not yet able to bear it; nay, not even now are ye able. For ye are yet carnal.

AFTER having overturned the philosophy which is from without, and cast down all its arrogance, he comes unto another argument. For it was likely that they would say, "If we were putting forth the opinions of Plato, or of Pythagoras, or any other of the philosophers, reason were thou shouldest draw out such a long discourse against us. But if we announce the things of the Spirit, for what reason dost thou turn and toss up and down (ἄνω καὶ κάτω στρέφεις) the wisdom which is from without?"

Hear then how he makes his stand against this. "And I, brethren, could not speak unto you as unto spiritual." Why, in the first place, says he, though you had been perfect in spiritual things also, not even so ought you to be elated; for what you preach is not your own, nor such as yourselves have found from your own means. But now even these things ye know not as ye ought to know them, but ye are learners, and the last of all. Whether therefore the Gentile wisdom be the occasion of your high imaginations; that hath been proved to be nothing, nay, in regard to spiritual things to be even contrary unto us: or if it be on account of things spiritual, in these, too, ye come short and have your place among the hindmost. Wherefore he saith, "I could not speak unto you as unto spiritual." He·said not, "I did not speak," lest the thing might seem to proceed from his grudging them somewhat; but in two ways he brings down their high spirit; first, because they knew not the things that are perfect; next, because their ignorance was owing to themselves: yea, in a third way besides these, by pointing out that "not even now are they able [to bear it]." For as to their want of ability at first, that perhaps arose from the nature of the case. In fact, however, he does not leave them even this excuse. For not through any inability on their part to receive high doctrines, doth he say they received them not, but because they were "carnal." However, in the beginning this was not so blameworthy; but that after so long a time, they had not yet arrived at the more perfect knowledge, this was a symptom of most utter dulness.

It may be observed, that he brings the same charge against the Hebrews, not however, with so much vehemence. For those, he saith, are such, partly because of tribulation: but these, because of some appetite for wickedness. Now the two things are not the same. He implies too, that in the one case he was intending rebuke, in the other rather stirring them up, when he spake these words of truth. For to these Corinthians he saith, "Neither yet now are ye able;" but unto the others (Heb. vi 1.) "Wherefore let us cease to speak of the first principles of Christ, and press on unto perfection:" and again, (Ib. v. 9.) "we are persuaded better things concerning you, and things which accompany salvation, though we thus speak."

[2.] And how calleth he those "carnal," who had attained so large a measure of the Spirit; and into whose praises, at the beginning he had entered so much at large? Because they also were carnal, unto whom the Lord saith, (St. Matt. vii. 22, 23.) "Depart from Me, ye workers of iniquity, I know you not;" and yet they both cast out devils, and raised the dead, and uttered prophecies. So that it is possible even for one who wrought miracles to be carnal. For so God wrought by Balaam, and unto Pharaoh He revealed things to come, and unto Nebuchadnezzar; and Caiaphas prophesied, not knowing what he said; yea, and some others cast out devils in His name, though they were (Luke ix. 49.) "not with Him;" since not for the doers' sake are these things done, but for others' sake: nor is it seldom, that those who were positively unworthy have been made instrumental to them. Now why wonder, if in the case of unworthy men these things are done for others' sake, see-

ing that so it is, even when they are wrought by saints? For Paul saith, (1 Cor. iii. 22.) "All things are yours; whether Paul, or Apollos, or Cephas, or life, or death:" and again, (Eph. iv. 11, 12) "He gave some Apostles, and some Prophets, and some Pastors and Teachers, for the perfecting of the saints, unto the work of ministering." For if it were not so, there would have been no security against universal corruption. For it may be that rulers are wicked and polluted, and their subjects good and virtuous; that laymen may live in piety, and· priests in wickedness; and there could not have been either baptism, or the body of Christ, or oblation, through such, if in every instance grace required merit. But as it is, God uses to work even by unworthy persons, and in no respect is the grace of baptism damaged by the conduct of the priest: else would the receiver suffer loss. Accordingly, though such things happen rarely, still, it must be owned, they do happen. Now these things I say, lest any one of the bystanders busying himself about the life of the priest, should be offended as concerning the things solemnized (τὰ τελούμενα). "For man introduceth nothing into the things which are set before us[1], but the whole is a work of the power of God, and He it is who initiates (ὁ μυσταγωγῶν) you into the mysteries."

[3.] "And I, brethren, could not speak unto you as unto spiritual, but as unto carnal. I fed you with milk, and not with meat. For ye were not able [to bear it.]"

For lest he should seem to have spoken ambitiously (φιλοτιμίας ἕνεκα, to obtain favor) these things which he hath just spoken; "the spiritual man judgeth all things," and, "he himself is judged of no man," and, "we have the mind of Christ;" with a view also to repress their pride: observe what he saith. "Not on this account," saith he, "was I silent, because I was not able to tell you more, but because ' ye are carnal: neither yet now are ye able.' "

Why said he not, "ye are not willing," but "ye are not able?" Even because he put the latter for the former. For as to the want of ability, it arises from the want of will. Which to them indeed is a matter of accusation, but to their teacher, of excuse. For if they had been unable by nature, one might perhaps have been forgiven them· but since it was frcm choice, they were bereft of all excuse. He then speaks of the particular point also which makes them carnal. "For whereas there is among you strife, and jealousy, and division, are ye not carnal and walk as men?" Although he had fornications also and uncleannesses of theirs to speak of, he sets down rather that offence which

[1] τὰ προκείμενα, a liturgical word; the Sacred Elements; vid. St. Basil's Liturgy, and St. Chrysostom's.

he had been a good while endeavoring to correct. Now if "jealousy" makes men carnal, it is high time for us to bewail bitterly, and to clothe ourselves with sackcloth and lie in ashes. For who is pure from this passion? Except indeed I am but conjecturing the case of others from myself. If "jealousy" maketh men "carnal," and suffereth them not to be "spiritual," although they prophesy and show forth other wonderful works; now, when not even so much grace is with us, what place shall we find for our own doings; when not in this matter alone, but also in others of greater moment, we are convicted.

[4.] From this place we learn that Christ had good reason for saying, (St. John iii. 20.) "He that doeth evil cometh not to light;" and that unclean life is an obstacle to high doctrines, not suffering the clear-sightedness of the understanding to shew itself. As then it is not in any case possible for a person in error, but living uprightly, to remain in error; so it is not easy for one brought up in iniquity, speedily to look up to the height of the doctrines delivered to us, but he must be clean from all the passions who is to hunt after the truth : for whoso is freed from these shall be freed also from his error and attain unto the truth. For do not, I beseech you, think that abstinence merely from covetousness or fornication may suffice thee for this purpose. Not so. All must concur in him that seeketh the truth. Wherefore saith Peter, (Acts x. 34, 35.) "Of a truth I perceive that God is no respecter of persons; but in every nation he that feareth Him, and worketh righteousness, is acceptable to Him:" that is, He calls and attracts him unto the truth. Seest thou not Paul, that he was more vehement than any one in warring and persecuting? yet because he led an irreproachable life, and did these things not through human passion, he was both received, and reached a mark beyond all. But if any one should say, "How doth such a one, a Greek, who is kind, and good, and humane, continue in error?" this would be my answer: He hath some other passion, vainglory, or indolence of mind, or want of carefulness about his own salvation, accounting that all things which concern him are drifted along loosely and at random. [1]Peter calls the man irreproachable in all things one that "worketh righteousness," [and Paul says] "touching the righteousness which is in the law found blameless." Again, "I give thanks to God, whom I serve from my forefathers with a pure conscience,"(2 Tim. i. 3.) How then, you will say, were unclean persons considered worthy of the Gospel? Because they wished and longed for it. Thus the one sort, though in error, are attracted by Him, because they are clean from passions; the others, of

[1 The version of this sentence follows Dr. Field's text. C.]

their own accord approaching, are not thrust back. Many also even from their ancestors have received the true religion.

[5.] Ver. 3. "For whereas there is among you jealousy and strife."

At this point he prepares himself to wrestle with those whose part was obedience: for in what went before he hath been casting down the rulers of the Church, where he said that wisdom of speech is nothing worth. But here he strikes at those in subjection, in the words,

Ver. 4. "For when one saith, I am Paul, and I of Apollos, are ye not carnal?"

And he points out that this, so far from helping them at all or causing them to acquire any thing, had even become an obstacle to their profiting in the greater things. For this it was which brought forth jealousy, and jealousy had made them "carnal;" and the having become "carnal" left them not at liberty to hear truths of the sublimer sort.

Ver. 5. "Who then is Paul, and who is Apollos?"

In this way, after producing and proving his facts, he makes his accusation henceforth more openly. Moreover, he employs his own name, doing away all harshness and not suffering them to be angry at what it is said. For if Paul is nothing and murmur not, much less ought they to think themselves ill used. Two ways, you see, he has of soothing them; first by bringing forward his own person, then by not robbing them of all as if they contributed nothing. Rather he allows them some small portion : small though it be, he does allow it. For having said, "Who is Paul, and who Apollos," he adds, "but ministers by whom ye believed." Now this in itself is a great thing, and deserving of great rewards: although in regard of the archetype and the root of all good, it is nothing. (For not he that "ministers" to our blessings, but he that provides and gives them, he is our Benefactor.) And he said not, "Evangelists," but "Ministers," which is more. For they had not merely preached the Gospel, but had also ministered unto us; the one being a matter of word only, while the other hath deed also. And so, if even Christ be a minister only of good things, and not the root Himself and the fountain, (I mean, of course, in that He is a Son,) observe to what an issue this matter is brought. (ποῦ τὸ πρᾶγμα κατάγεται. "how deep and high it is made to go.") How then, you will ask, doth he say that He "was made a Minister of Circumcision? (Rom. xv. 8.) He is speaking in that place of His secret dispensation in the Flesh, and not in the same sense which we have now mentioned. For there, by "Minister," he means "Fulfiller," (πληρωτὴν, i. e. of types), and not one that of his own store gives out the blessings.

Further, he said not, "Those who guide you into the Faith," but "those by whom ye believed;" again attributing the greater share to themselves, and indicating by this also the subordinate class of ministers (τοὺς διακόνους κἀντεῦθεν δηλῶν). Now if they were ministering to another, how come they to seize the authority for themselves? But I would have you consider how in no wise he lays the blame on them as seizing it for themselves, but on those who endow them with it. For the ground-work of the error lay in the multitude; since, had the one fallen away, the other would have been broken up. Here are two points which he has skilfully provided for: in that first he hath prepared, as by mining(ὑπορύξας,) in the quarter where it was necessary to overthrow the mischief; and next, on their side, in not attracting ill-will, nor yet making them more contentious.

Ver. 5. "Even as Christ (ὁ Κύριος, rec. text.) gave to every man."

For not even this small thing itself was of themselves, but of God, who put it into their hands. For lest they might say, What then? are we not to love those that minister unto us? Yea, saith he; but you should know to what extent. For not even this thing itself is of them, but of God who gave it.

Ver. 6. "I planted, Apollos watered, but God gave the increase."

That is, I first cast the word into the ground; but, in order that the seeds might not wither away through temptations, Apollos added his own part. But the whole was of God.

[6.] Ver. 7. "So then, neither is he that planteth any thing, neither he that watereth, but God that giveth the increase."

Do you observe the manner in which he soothes them, so that they should not be too much irritated, on hearing, "Who is this person," and "Who is that?" "Nay, both are invidious, namely, both the saying, 'Who is this person? Who the other,'" and the saying, that "neither he that planteth nor he that watereth is any thing." How then does he soften these expressions? First, By attaching the contempt to his own person, "Who is Paul, and who Apollos?" and next, by referring the whole to God who gave all things. For after he had said, "Such a person planted," and added, "He that planteth is nothing," he subjoined, "but God that giveth the increase." Nor does he stop even here, but applies again another healing clause, in the words.

Ver. 8. "He that planteth and he that watereth, are one."

For by means of this he establishes another point also, viz. that they should not be exalted one against another. His assertion, that they are one, refers to their inability to do any thing without "God that giveth the increase." And thus saying, he permitted not either those who labored much to lift themselves up against those who had contributed less; nor these again to envy the former. In the next place, since this had a tendency to make men more indolent, I mean, all being esteemed as one, whether they have labored much or little; observe how he sets this right, saying, "But each shall receive his own reward according to his own labor." As if he said, "Fear not, because I said, Ye are one; for, compared with the work of God, they are one; howbeit, in regard to labors, they are not so, but "each shall receive his own reward."

Then he smooths it still more, having succeeded in what he wished; and gratifies them, where it is allowed, with liberality.

Ver. 9. For we are God's fellow-workers: "ye are God's husbandry, God's building."

Seest thou how to them also he hath assigned no small work, having before laid it down that the whole is of God? For since he is always persuading them to obey those that have the rule over them, on this account he abstains from making very light of their teachers.

"Ye are God's husbandry."

For because he had said, "I planted," he kept to the metaphor. Now if ye be God's husbandry, it is right that you should be called not from those who cultivate you, but from God. For the field is not called the husbandman's, but the householder's.

"Ye are God's building."

Again, the building is not the workman's, but the master's. Now if ye be a building, ye must not be forced asunder: since this were no building. If ye be a farm, ye must not be divided, but be walled in with a single fence, namely, unanimity.

Ver. 10. "According to the Grace of God which was given unto me, as a wise master-builder I laid a foundation."

In this place he calls himself wise, not exalting himself, but to give them an ensample, and to point out that this is a wise man's part, to lay a foundation. You may observe as one instance of his modest bearing, that in speaking of himself as wise, he allowed not this to stand as though it were something of his own; but first attributing himself entirely unto God, then and not till then calls himself by that name. For, "according to the Grace of God," saith he, "which was given unto me." Thus, at once he signifies both that the whole is of God; and that this most of all is Grace, viz. the not being divided, but resting on One Foundation.

[7.] "Another buildeth thereon; but let each man take heed how he buildeth thereon."

Here, I think, and in what follows, he puts them upon their trial concerning practice, after that he had once for all knit them together and made them one.

Ver. 11. "For other foundation can no man lay than that is laid, which is Jesus Christ."

I say, no man can lay it so long as he is a master-builder; but if he lay it, (τιθη conj. for τεθη. *Dounæus ap. Savil. viii. not. p. 261.*) he ceases to be a master-builder.

See how even from men's common notions he proves the whole of his proposition. His meaning is this: "I have preached Christ, I have delivered unto you the foundation. Take heed how you build thereon, lest haply it be in vainglory, lest haply so as to draw away the disciples unto men." Let us not then give heed unto the heresies. "For other foundation can no man lay than that which is laid." Upon this then let us build, and as a foundation let us cleave to it, as a branch to a vine; and let there be no interval between us and Christ. For if there be any interval, immediately we perish. For the branch by its adherence draws in the fatness, and the building stands because it is cemented together. Since, if it stand apart it perishes, having nothing whereon to support itself. Let us not then merely keep hold of Christ, but let us be cemented to Him, for if we stand apart, we perish. "For they who withdraw themselves far from Thee, shall perish;" (Ps. lxxiii. 27. Sept.) so it is said. Let us cleave then unto Him, and let us cleave by our works. "For he that keepeth my commandments, the same abideth in Me" (John xiv. 21. in substance.) And accordingly, there are many images whereby He brings us into union. Thus, if you mark it, He is "the Head," we are "the body:" can there be any empty interval between the head and body? He is "a Foundation," we "a building:" He "a Vine," we "branches:" He "the Bridegroom," we "the bride:" He "the Shepherd," we "the sheep;" He is "the Way," we "they who walk therein." Again, we are "a temple," He "the Indweller:" He "the First-Begotten," we "the brethren:" He "the Heir," we "the heirs together with Him:" He "the Life," we "the living:" He "the Resurrection," we "those who rise again:" He "the Light," we "the enlightened." All these things indicate unity; and they allow no void interval, not even the smallest. For he that removes but to a little distance will go on till he has become very far distant. For so the body, receiving though it be but a small cut by a sword, perishes: and the building, though there be but a small chink, falls to decay: and the branch, though it be but a little while cut off from the root, becomes useless. So that this trifle is no trifle, but is even almost the whole. Whensoever then we commit some little fault or even negligence, let us not overlook that little; since this, being disregarded, quickly becomes great. So also when a garment hath begun to be torn and is neglected, it is apt to prolong its rent all throughout; and a roof, when a few tiles have fallen, being disregarded, brings down the whole house.

[8.] These things then let us bear in mind, and never slight the small things, lest we fall into those which are great. But if so be that we have slighted them and are come into the abyss of evils, not even when we are come there let us despond, lest we fall into recklessness (χαρηβαρίαν). For to emerge from thence is hard ever after, for one who is not extremely watchful; not because of the distance alone, but of the very position, too, wherein we find ourselves. For sin also is a deep, and is wont to bear down and crush. And just as those who have fallen into a well cannot with ease get out, but will want others to draw them up; so also is he that is come into any depth of sins. To such then we must lower ropes and draw them up. Nay rather, we need not others only, but ourselves also, that we for our part may fasten on ourselves and ascend, I say not so much as we have descended, but much further, if we be willing: for why? God also helpeth: for He willeth not the death of a sinner so much as his conversion. Let no one then despair; let no one have the feeling of the ungodly; for to them properly belongs this kind of sin: "an ungodly man having come into any depth of evils, makes light of it[1]." So that it is not the multitude of men's sins which causes their despair, but their ungodly mind.

Shouldest thou then have gone all lengths in wickedness, yet say unto thyself, God is loving unto men and he desires our salvation: for "though your sins be as scarlet, I will whiten you as snow,"(Is. i. 10. Sept.) saith He; and unto the contrary habit I will change you. Let us not therefore give up in despair; for to fall is not so grievous, as to lie where we have fallen; nor to be wounded so dreadful, as after wounds to refuse healing. "For who shall boast that he has his heart chaste? or who shall say confidently that he is pure from sin?" (Prov. xx. 9. Sept.) These things I say not to make you more negligent, but to prevent your despairing.

Wouldest thou know how good our Master is? The Publican went up full of ten thousand wickednesses, and saying only, "Be merciful unto me," went down justified. (St. Luke xviii.

---

[1] [This is an exact quotation from the Sept. version of Prov. xviii. 3.]

13, 14.) Yea, God saith by the prophet, "Because of sin for some little season I grieved him, (Is. lvii. 17, 18. Sept.) and I saw that (εἶδον ὅτι not in Sept.) he was grieved and went sorrowful, and I healed his ways" (ἰασάμην αὐτὸν, Sept.) What is there equal to this loving-kindness? On condition (ἵνα στυγνάσῃ. See St. John viii. 56. ἵνα ἴδη τὴν ἡμέραν) of his "being but sorrowful," so he speaks, "I forgave him his sins." But we do not even this: wherefore we especially provoke God to wrath. (For he, who by little things even is made propitious, when He meets not with so much as these, is of course indignant and exacts of us the last penalty; for this comes of exceeding contempt.) Who is there, for instance, that hath ever become melancholy for his sins? Who hath bemoaned himself? Who hath beaten his breast? Who hath taken anxious thought? Not one, to my thinking. But days without number do men weep for dead servants; for the loss of money: while as to the soul which we are ruining day by day, we give it not a thought. How then wilt thou be able to render God propitious, when thou knowest not even that thou hast sinned?

"Yea," saith some one, "I have sinned." "Yea," is thy word to me with the tongue: say it to me with thy mind, and with the word mourn heavily, that thou mayest have continual cheerfulness. Since, if we did grieve for our sins, if we mourned heavily over our offences, nothing else could give us sorrow, this one pang would expel all kinds of dejection. Here then is another thing also which we should gain by our thorough confession; namely, the not being overwhelmed (βαπτίζεσθαι) with the pains of the present life, nor puffed up with its splendors. And in this way, again, we should more entirely propitiate God; just as by our present conduct we provoke Him to anger. For tell me, if thou hast a servant, and he, after suffering much evil at the hands of his fellow-servants, takes no account of any one of the rest, but is only anxious not to provoke his master; is he not able by this alone to do away thine anger? But what, if his offenses against thee are no manner of care to him, while on those against his fellow-servants he is full of thought; wilt thou not lay on him the heavier punishment? So also God doeth: when we neglect His wrath, He brings it upon us more heavily; but when we regard it, more gently. Yea, rather, He lays it on us no more at all. He wills that we should exact vengeance of ourselves for our offences, and thenceforth He doth not exact it Himself. For this is why He at all threatens punishment; that by fear He may destroy contempt; and when the threat alone is sufficient to cause fear in us, He doth not suffer us to undergo the actual trial. See, for instance, what He saith unto Jeremiah, (Jer. vii. 17, 18. Sept. transposing the first and second clauses.) "Seest thou not what they do? Their fathers light a fire, their children gather sticks together, their women knead dough." It is to be feared lest the same kind of thing be said also concerning us. "Seest thou not what they do? No one seeketh the things of Christ, but all their own. Their children run into uncleanness, their fathers into covetousness and rapine, their wives so far from keeping back their husbands from the pomps and vanities of life, do rather sharpen their appetites for them." Just take your stand in the market place; question the comers and goers, and not one wilt thou see hastening upon a spiritual errand, but all running after carnal things. How long ere we awake from our surfeiting? How long are we to keep sinking down into deep slumber? Have we not had our fill of evils?

[9.] And yet one might think that even without words experience itself is sufficient to teach you the nothingness of things present, and their utter meanness. At all events, there have been men, who, exercising mere heathen wisdom and knowing nothing of the future, because they had proved the great worthlessness of present things, have left them on this account alone. What pardon then canst thou expect to obtain, grovelling on the ground and not despising the little things and transient for the sake of the great and everlasting: who also hearest God Himself declaring and revealing these things unto thee, and hast such promises from Him? For that things here have no sufficient power to detain a man, those have shewn who even without any promise of things greater have kept away from them. For what wealth did they expect that they came to poverty? There was none. But it was from their knowing full well that such poverty is better than wealth. What sort of life did they hope for that they forsook luxury, and gave themselves up unto severe discipline? Not any. But they had become aware of the very nature of things; and perceived that this of the two is more suitable, both for the strict training of the soul, and for the health of the body.

These things then duly estimating, and revolving with ourselves continually the future blessings, let us withdraw from this present world that we may obtain that other which is to come; through the favor and loving kindness of our Lord Jesus Christ, with Whom to the Father and the Holy Ghost &c., &c.

HOMILY IX.

1 Cor. iii., 12—15.

If any man build upon this foundation gold, silver, costly stones, wood, hay, stubble; each man's work shall be made manifest: for the day shall declare it, because it is revealed in fire; and the fire shall prove each man's work of what sort it is. If any man's work abide which he built thereon, he shall receive a reward. If any man's work shall be burned, he shall suffer loss: but he himself shall be saved; yet so as through fire.

THIS is no small subject of enquiry which we propose, but rather about things which are of the first necessity and which all men enquire about; namely, whether hell fire have any end. For that it hath no end Christ indeed declared when he said, "Their fire shall not be quenched, and their worm shall not die. [Mark viii. 44, 46, 48.]

Well: I know that a chill comes over you (ναρκᾶτε) on hearing these things; but what am I to do? For this is God's own command, continually to sound these things in your ears, where He says, "Charge this people; (Fors. Exod. xix. 10. 20. διαμαρτύραι, Sept. here διάστειλαι,) and ordained as we have been unto the ministry of the word, we must give pain to our hearers, not willingly but on compulsion. Nay rather, if you will, we shall avoid giving you pain. For saith He, (Rom. xiii. 3, in substance.) "if thou do that which is good, fear not:" so that it is possible for you to hear me not only without ill-will, but even with pleasure.

As I said then; that it hath no end, Christ has declared. Paul also saith, in pointing out the eternity of the punishment, that the sinners "shall pay the penalty of destruction, and that for ever" (2, Thes. i. 9.) And again, (i Cor. vi. 9.) "Be not deceived; neither fornicators, nor adulterers, nor effeminate, shall inherit the the kingdom of God." And also unto the Hebrews he saith, (Heb. xii. 14.) "Follow peace with all men, and the sanctification without which no man shall see the Lord." And Christ also, to those who said, "In thy Name we have done many wonderful works," saith, "Depart from Me, I know you not, ye workers of iniquity" (St. Matt. vii. 22.) And the virgins too who were shut out, entered in no more. And also about those who gave Him no food, He saith, (St. Matt. xxv. 46.)

"They shall go away into everlasting punishment."

[2.] And say not unto me, "where is the rule of justice preserved entire, if the punishment hath no end?" Rather, when God doeth any thing, obey His decisions and submit not what is said to human reasonings. But moreover, how can it be any thing else than just for one who hath experienced innumerable blessings from the beginning, and then committed deeds worthy of punishment, and neither by threat nor benefit improved at all, to suffer punishment? For if thou enquire what is absolute justice; it was meet that we should have perished immediately from the beginning, according to the definition of strict justice. Rather not even then according to the rule of justice only; for the result would have had in it kindness too, if we had suffered this also. For when any one insults him that hath done him no wrong, according to the rule of justice he suffers punishment: but when it is his benefactor, who, bound by no previous favor, bestowed innumerable kindnesses, who alone is the Author of his being, who is God, who breathed his soul into him, who gave ten thousand gifts of grace, whose will is to take him up into heaven;— when, I say, such an one, after so great blessings, is met by insult, daily insult, in the conduct of the other party; how can that other be thought worthy of pardon? Dost thou not see how He punished Adam for one single sin?

"Yes," you will say; "but He had given him Paradise and caused him to enjoy much favor." Nay, surely it is not all as one, for a man to sin in the enjoyment of security and ease, and in a state of great affliction. In fact, this is the dreadful circumstance that thy sins are the sins of one not in any Paradise but amid the innumerable evils of this life; that thou art not sobered even by affliction, as though one in prison should still practise his crime. However, unto thee He hath promised things yet greater than Paradise. But neither hath He given them now, least He should unnerve thee in the season of conflicts; nor hath He been silent about them, lest He should quite cast thee down with thy labors. As for Adam, he committed but one sin and brought on himself certain death; whereas we commit ten thousand transgressions daily. Now if he by that one act brought on himself so great an evil and introduced death; what shall not we suffer who continually live in sins, and instead of Paradise, have the expectation of heaven?

The argument is irksome and pains the hearer: were it only by my own feelings, I know this. For indeed my heart is troubled and throbs; and the more I see the account of hell confirmed, the more do I tremble and shrink through fear. But it is necessary to say these things lest we fall into hell. What thou didst receive was not paradise, nor trees and plants, but heaven and the good things in the heavens. Now if he that had received less was comdemned, and no consideration exempted him, much more shall we who have sinned more abundantly, and have been called unto greater things, endure the woes without remedy.

Consider, for example, how long a time, but for one single sin, our race abides in death. Five thousand years[1] and more have passed, and death hath not yet been done away, on account of one single sin. And we cannot even say that Adam had heard prophets, that he had seen others punished for sins, and it was meet that he should have been terrified thereby and corrected, were it only by the example. For he was at that time first, and alone; but nevertheless he was punished. But thou canst not have anything of this sort to advance, who after so many examples art become worse; to whom so excellent a Spirit hath been vouchsafed, and yet thou drawest upon thyself not one sin, nor two, nor three, but sins without number! For do not, because the sin is committed in a small moment, calculate that therefore the punishment also must be a matter of a moment. Seest thou not those men, who for a single theft or a single act of adultery, committed in a small moment of time, oftentimes have spent their whole life in prisons, and in mines, struggling with continual hunger and every kind of death? And there was no one to set them at liberty, or to say, "The offence took place in a small moment of time; the punishment too should have its time equivalent to that of the sin."

[3.] But, "They are men," some one will say, "who do these things; as for God, He is loving unto men." Now, first of all, not even men do these things in cruelty, but in humanity. And God Himself, as He is loving unto men," in the same character doth He punish sins.

(Sirac. xvi. 12.) "For as His mercy is great, so also is His reproof." When therefore thou sayest unto me, "God is loving unto men," then thou tellest me of so much the greater reason for punishing: namely, our sinning against such a Being. Hence also Paul said, (Heb. x. 31.) "It is a fearful thing to fall into the hands of the living God." Endure I beseech you, the fiery force of the words, for perhaps—perhaps you will have some consolation from hence! Who among men can punish as God has punished? when He caused a deluge and entire destruction of a race so numerous; and again, when, a little while after, He rained fire from above, and utterly destroyed them all? What punishment from men can be like that? Seest thou not that the punishment even in this world is almost eternal? Four thousand years have passed away, and the punishment of the Sodomites abideth at its height. For as His mercy is great, so also is His punishment.

Again: if He had imposed any burdensome or impossible things, one might perhaps have been able to urge difficulty of the laws: but if they be extremely easy, what can we say for our not regarding even these? Suppose thou art unable to fast or to practice virginity; although thou art able if thou wilt, and they who have been able are a condemnation to us. But, however, God hath not used this strictness towards us; neither hath He enjoined these things nor laid them down as laws, but left the choice to be at the discretion of the hearers. Nevertheless, thou art able to be chaste in marriage; and thou art able to abstain from drunkenness. Art thou unable to empty thyself of all thy goods? Nay surely thou art able; and they who have done so prove it. But nevertheless He hath not enjoined this, but hath commanded not to be rapacious, and of our means to assist those who are in want. But if a man say, I cannot even be content with a wife only, he deceiveth himself and reasoneth falsely; and they condemn him who without a wife lives in chastity. But how, tell me, canst thou help using abusive words? canst thou not help cursing? Why, the doing these things is irksome, not the refraining from them. What excuse then have we for not observing precepts so easy and light? We cannot name any at all. That the punishment then is eternal is plain from all that hath been said.

[4.] But since Paul's saying appears to some to tell the other way, come let us bring it forward also and search it out thoroughly. For having said, "If any man's work abide which he hath built thereon, he shall receive a reward; and if any man's work shall be burned, he shall suffer loss," he adds, "but himself shall be saved, yet so as through fire." What shall we

---

[1] According to the reckoning of the LXX, in Gen. 5. which adding 100 years to the five first generations, and also to the seventh, and making some slight difference in the lives of Methuselah and Lamech, brings the date of the flood to A. M. 2242, and that of our Lord's birth to 5500.

say then to this? Let us consider first what is "the Foundation," and what "the gold," and what "the precious stones," and what "the hay," and what the "stubble."

"The Foundation," then, he hath himself plainly signified to be Christ, saying, "For other foundation can no man lay than that which is laid, which," he saith "is Jesus Christ." •

Next, the building seems to me to be actions. Although some maintain that this also is spoken concerning teachers and disciples and concerning corrupt heresies: but the reasoning doth not admit it. For if this be it, in what sense, while "the work is destroyed," is the "builder" to be "saved," though it be "through fire?" Of right, the author ought rather of the two to perish; but now it will be found that the severer penalty is assigned to him who hath been built into the work. For if the teacher was the cause of the wickedness, he is worthy to suffer severer punishment: how then shall he be "saved?" If, on the contrary, he was not the cause but the disciples became such through their own perverseness, he is no whit deserving of punishment, no, nor yet of sustaining loss: he, I say, who builded so well. In what sense then doth he say, "he shall suffer loss?"

From this it is plain that the discourse is about actions. For since he means next in course to put out his strength against the man who had committed fornication, he begins high up and long beforehand to lay down the preliminaries. For he knew how while discussing one subject, in the very discourse about that thing to prepare the grounds of another to which he intends to pass on. For so in his rebuke for not awaiting one another at their meals, he laid the grounds of his discourse concerning the mysteries. And also because now he is hastening on towards the fornicator, while speaking about the "Foundation," he adds, "Know ye not that ye are the Temple of God? and that the Spirit of God dwelleth in you? If any man destroy ($\Phi\theta\epsilon\iota\rho\eta$, rec. version, "defile.") the Temple of God, him will God destroy." Now these things, he said, as beginning now to agitate with fears the soul of him that had been unchaste.

[5.] Ver. 12. "If any man build upon this foundation, gold, silver, costly stones, wood, hay, stubble." For after the faith there is need of edification: and therefore he saith elsewhere, "Edify one another with these words." (perhaps 1 Thess. v. 11; iv. 5.) For both the artificer and the learner contribute to the edifying. Wherefore he saith, "But let every man take heed how he buildeth thereon." (1 Cor. iii. 10.) But if faith had been the subject of

these sayings, the thing affirmed is not reasonable. For in the faith all ought to be equal, since "there is but one faith;" (Eph. iv. 5.) but in goodness of life it is not possible that all should be the same. Because the faith is not in one case less, in another more excellent, but the same in all those who truly believe. But in life there is room for some to be more diligent, others more slothful; some stricter, and others more ordinary; that some should have done well in greater things, others in less; that the errors of some should have been more grievous, of others less notable. On this account he saith, "Gold, silver, costly stones, wood, hay, stubble,—every man's work shall be made manifest:"—his conduct; that is what he speaks of here:—"If any man's work abide which he built thereupon, he shall receive a reward; if any man's work shall be burned, he shall suffer loss." Whereas, if the saying related to disciples and teachers, he ought not to "suffer loss" for disciples refusing to hear. And therefore he saith, "Every man shall receive his own reward according to his own labor" not according to the result, but according to "the labor." For what if the hearers gave no heed? Wherefore this passage also proves that the saying is about actions.

Now his meaning is this: If any man have an ill life with a right faith, his faith shall not shelter him from punishment, his work being burnt up. The phrase, "shall be burned up," means, "shall not endure the violence of the fire." But just as if a man having golden armor on were to pass through a river of fire, he comes from crossing it all the brighter; but if he were to pass through it with hay, so far from profiting, he destroys himself besides; so also is the case in regard of men's works. For he doth not say this as if he were discoursing of material things being burnt up, but with a view of making their fear more intense, and of shewing how naked of all defence he is who abides in wickedness. Wherefore he said, "He shall suffer loss:" lo, here is one punishment: "but he himself shall be saved, but so as by fire;" lo, again, here is a second. And his meaning is, "He himself shall not perish in the same way as his works, passing into nought, but he shall abide in the fire.[1]

[6.] "He calleth it, however, "Salvation," you will say; why, that is the cause of his adding, "so as by fire:" since we also used to say, "It is preserved in the fire," when we speak of those substances which do not immediately burn up and become ashes. For do not at sound of the word fire imagine that

---

[1] [Few accept this singular explanation. The common view of the clause is that it means that the man is saved, but as if through the very flames, i. e., with the greatest difficulty. 1 Pet. iv. 18. c.]

those who are burning pass into annihilation. And though he call such punishment Salvation, be not astonished. For his custom is in things which have an ill sound to use fair expressions, and in good things the contrary. For example, the word "Captivity" seems to be the name of an evil thing, but Paul has applied it in a good sense, when he says, " Bringing into captivity every thought to the obedience of Christ." (2 Cor. x. 5.) And again, to an evil thing he hath applied a good word, saying, "Sin reigned," (Rom. v. 21.) here surely the term "reigning" is rather of auspicious sound. And so here in saying, " he shall be saved," he hath but darkly hinted at the intensity of the penalty : as if he had said, " But himself shall remain forever in punishment."

He then makes an inference, saying,

[7.] Ver. 16. " Know ye not that ye are the Temple of God ? " For since he had discoursed in the section before, concerning those who were dividing the Church, he thenceforward attacks him also who had been guilty of uncleanness ; not indeed as yet in plain terms but in a general way ; hinting at his corrupt mode of life and enhancing the sin, by the Gift which had been already given to him. Then also he puts all the rest to shame, arguing from these very blessings which they had already : for this is what he is ever doing, either from the future or from the past, whether grievous or encouraging. First, from things future; " For the day shall declare it, because it is revealed by fire." Again, from things already come to pass ; " Know ye not that ye are the Temple of God, and the Spirit of God dwelleth in you ? "

Ver. 17. " If any man destroy the Temple of God, him will God destroy." Dost thou mark the sweeping vehemence of his words ? However, so long as the person is unknown, what is spoken is not so invidious, all dividing among themselves the fear of rebuke.

" Him will God destroy, " that is, will cause him to perish. And this is not the word of one denouncing a curse, but of one that prophesieth.

" For the Temple of God is holy :" but he that hath committed fornication is profane.

Then, in order that he might not seem to spend his earnestness upon that one, in saying, " for the Temple of God is holy," he addeth, " which ye are."

[8.] Ver. 18. " Let no man deceive himself." This also is in reference to that person, as thinking himself to be somewhat and flattering himself on wisdom. But that he might not seem to press on him at great length in a mere digression ; he first throws him into a kind of agony and delivers him over unto fear, and then

brings back his discourse to the common fault, saying, " If any man among you seemeth to be wise in this world, let him become a fool, that he may become ($\gamma \acute{\epsilon} \nu \eta \tau a \iota$. rec. vers. " be.") wise." And this [1] he doth afterwards with great boldness of speech, as having sufficiently beaten them down[2], and shaken with that fear the mind not of that unclean person only, but of all the hearers also : so accurately does he measure the reach of what he has to say. For what if a man be rich, what if he be noble ; he is viler than all the vile, when made captive by sin. For as if a man were a king and enslaved to barbarians, he is of all men most wretched, so also is it in regard to sin : since sin is a barbarian, and the soul which hath been once taken captive she knoweth not how to spare, but plays the tyrant to the ruin of all those who admit her.

[9.] For nothing is so inconsiderate as sin : nothing so senseless, so utterly foolish and outrageous. All is overturned and confounded and destroyed by it, wheresoever it may alight. Unsightly to behold, disgusting and grievous. And should a painter draw her picture[3], he would not, methinks, err in fashioning her after this sort. A woman with the form of a beast, savage, breathing flames, hideous, black ; such as the heathen poets depict their Scyllas. For with ten thousand hands she lays hold of our thoughts, and comes on unexpected, and tears everything in pieces, like those dogs that bite slily.

But rather, what need of the painter's art, when we should rather bring forward those who are made after sin's likeness ?

Whom then will ye that we should portray first ? The covetous and rapacious ? And what more shameless than those eyes ? What more immodest, more like a greedy dog ? For no dog keeps his ground with such shameless impudence as he when he is grasping at all men's goods. What more polluted than those hands ? What more audacious than that mouth, swallowing all down and not satisfied ? Nay, look not on the countenance and the eyes as being a a man's. For such looks belong not to the eyes of men. He seeth not men as men ; he seeth not the heaven as heaven. He does not even lift up his head unto the Lord ; but all is money in his account. The eyes of men are wont to look upon poor persons in affliction, and to be softened ; but these of the rapacious man, at sight of the poor, glare like wild beasts'. The eyes of men do not behold other men's goods as if they were their own, but rather their

---

[1] i. e. "reproving them for their common fault."
[2] From this to the end of the sentence is not in Benedictine, but in Savile's margin, evidently from some MS. It seems to complete the connection of the sentences. [But Dr. Field omits it.]
[3] Compare G. Herbert, *Remains*, p. 110. ed. 1824.

own as others; and they covet not the things given to others, but rather exhaust upon others their own means: but these are not content unless they take all men's property. For it is not a man's eye which they have, but a wild beast's. The eyes of men endure not to see their own body stripped of clothing, (for it is their own, though in person it belong to others,) but these, unless they strip every one and lodge all men's property in their own home, are never cloyed; yea rather they never have enough. Insomuch that one might say that their hands are not wild beasts' only, but even far more savage and cruel than these. For bears and wolves when they are satiated leave off their kind of eating: but these know not any satiety. And yet for this cause God made us hands, to assist others, not to plot against them. And if we were to use them for that purpose, better had they been cut off and we left without them. But thou, if a wild beast rend a sheep, art grieved; but when doing the same unto one of thine own flesh and blood, thinkest thou that thy deed is nothing atrocious? How then canst thou be a man? Seest thou not that we call a thing humane, when it is full of mercy and loving-kindness? But when a man doth any thing cruel or savage, inhuman is the title we give to such a one. You see then that the stamp of man as we portray him is his showing mercy; of a beast the contrary; according to constant saying, "Why, is a man a wild beast, or a dog?" (vid. 2 Kings viii. 13.) For men relieve poverty; they do not aggravate it. Again these men's mouths are the mouths of wild beasts; yea rather these are the fiercer of the two. For the words also, which they utter, emit poison, more than the wild beasts' teeth, working slaughter. And if one were to go through all particulars, one should then see clearly how inhumanity turns those who practise it from men into beasts.

[10.] But were he to search out the mind also of that sort of people, he would no longer call them beasts only, but demons. For first, they are full of great cruelty and of hatred against their "fellow-servant: (St. Mat. xviii. 33.) and neither is love of the kingdom there, nor fear of hell; no reverence for men, no pity, no sympathy: but shamelessness and audacity, and contempt of all things to come. And unto them the words of God concerning punishment seem to be a fable, and His threats mirth. For such is the mind of the covetous man. Since then within they are demons, and without, wild beasts; yea, worse than wild beasts; where are we to place such as they are? For that they are worse even than wild beasts, is plain from this. The beasts are such as they are by nature: but these, endowed by nature with gentleness, forcibly strive against nature to train themselves to that which is savage. The demons too have the plotters among men to help them, to such an extent that if they had no such aid, the greater part of their wiles against us would be done away: but these, when such as they have spitefully entreated are vying with them, still try to be more spiteful then they. Again, the devil wages war with man, not with the demons of his own kind: but he of whom we speak is urgent in all ways to do harm to his own kindred and family, and doth not even reverence nature.

I know that many hate us because of these words; but I feel no hatred towards them; rather I pity and bewail those who are so disposed. Even should they choose to strike, I would gladly endure it, if they would but abstain from this their savage mind. For not I alone, but the prophet also with me, banisheth all such from the family of men saying, (Ps. xlix. 20. Sept. τοῖς ἀνοήτοις) "Man being in honor hath no understanding, but is like unto the senseless beasts."

Let us then become men at last, and let us look up unto heaven; and that which is according to His image, (Colos. iii. 10.) let us receive and recover: that we may obtain also the blessings to come through the grace and loving-kindness of our Lord Jesus Christ, with Whom to the Father and the Holy Spirit be glory, power, honor, now and always, and unto everlasting ages. Amen.

HOMILY X.

1 Cor. iii. 18, 19.

Let no man deceive himself. If any man (ἐν ὑμῖν omitted.) thinketh that he is wise in this world, let him become a fool, that he may become wise. For the wisdom of this world is foolishness with God.

As I said before, having launched out before the proper time into accusation of the fornicator, and having half opened it obscurely in a few words, and made the man's conscience to quail, he hastens again to the battle with heathen wisdom, and to his accusations of those who were puffed up there-with, and who were dividing the Church: in order that having added what remained and completed the whole topic with accuracy, he might thenceforth suffer his tongue to be carried away with vehement impulse against the unclean person, having had but a preliminary skirmishing with him in what he had said before. For this, "Let no man deceive himself," is the expression of one aiming chiefly at him and quelling him beforehand by fear: and the saying about the "stubble," suits best with one hinting at him. And so does the phrase, "Know ye not that ye are the Temple of God, and the Spirit of God dwelleth in you?" For these two things are most apt to withdraw us from sin; when we have in mind the punishment appointed for the sin; and when we reckon up the amount of our true dignity. By bringing forward then "the hay" and "the stubble," he terrifies; but by speaking of the dignity of that noble birth which was theirs, he puts them to shame; by the former striving to amend the more insensible kind, by the latter the more considerate.

[2.] "Let no man deceive himself; if any man thinketh that he is wise in this world, let him become a fool."

As he bids one become, as it were, dead unto the world ;—and this deadness harms not at all, but rather profits, being made a cause of life :— so also he bids him become foolish unto this world, introducing to us hereby the true wisdom. Now he becomes a fool unto the world, who slights the wisdom from without, and is persuaded that it contributes nothing towards his comprehension of the faith. As then that poverty which is according to God is the cause of wealth, and lowliness, of exaltation, and to

despise glory is the cause of glory; so also the becoming a fool maketh a man wiser than all. For all, with us, goes by contraries.

Further: why said he not, "Let him put off wisdom," but, "Let him become a fool?" That he might most exceedingly disparage the heathen instruction. For it was not the same thing to say, "Lay aside thy wisdom," and, "become a fool." And besides, he is also training people not to be ashamed at the want of refinement among us; for he quite laughs to scorn all heathen things. And for the same sort of reason he shrinks not from the names, trusting as he does to the power of the things [which he speaks of].

Wherefore, as the Cross, though counted ignominious, became the author of innumerable blessings, and the foundation and root of glory unspeakable ; so also that which was accounted to be foolishness became unto us the cause of wisdom. For as he who hath learned anything ill, unless he put away the whole, and make his soul level and clear, and so offer it to him who is to write on it, will know no wholesome truth for certain; so also in regard of the wisdom from without. Unless thou turn out the whole and sweep thy mind clear, and like one that is ignorant yield up thyself unto the faith, thou wilt know accurately nothing excellent. For so those also who see imperfectly if they will not shut their eyes and commit themselves unto others, but will be trusting their own matters to their own faulty eyesight, they will commit many more mistakes than those who see not.

But how, you will say, are men to put off this wisdom? By not acting on its precepts.

[3.] Then, seeing that he bade men so urgently withdraw themselves from it, he adds the cause, saying, "For the wisdom of this world is foolishness with God." For not only it contributes nothing, but it even hinders. We must then withdraw ourselves from it, as doing harm. Dost thou mark with what a high hand he carries off the spoils of victory, having proved that so far from profiting us at all, it is even an opponent?

And he is not content with his own arguments, but he has also adduced testimony again, saying, "For it is written, (Job v. 13.) He taketh the wise in their own craftiness." By "craftiness," i. e. by their own arms getting the better of them.   For seeing that they made use of their wisdom to the doing away of all need of God, by it and no other thing He refuted them, shewing that they were specially in need of God.   How and by what method? Because having by it become fools, by it, as was meet, they were taken.   For they who supposed that they needed not God, were reduced to so great a strait as to appear inferior to fishermen and unlettered persons; and from that time forth to be unable to do without them.   Wherefore he saith, "In their own craftiness" He took them.   For the saying "I will destroy their wisdom," was spoken in regard to its introducing nothing useful; but this, "who taketh the wise in their own craftiness, with a view of shewing the power of God."

Next, he declares also the mode in which God took them, adding another testimony:

Ver. 20. "For the Lord," saith he, "know-eth the reasonings of men (Ps. xciv. 11. ἀνθρώπων Sept.) that they are vain."   Now when the Wisdom which is boundless pronounces this edict concerning them, and declares them to be such, what other proof dost thou seek of their extreme folly?   For men's judgments, it is true, in many instances fail; but the decree of God is unexceptionable and uncorrupt in every case.

[4.] Thus having set up so splendid a trophy of the judgment from on high, he employs in what follows a certain vehemence of style, turning it against those who were under his ministry, (ἀρχομένους) and speaking thus:

Ver. 21. "Wherefore let no man glory in men; for all things are yours."   He comes again to the former topic, pointing out that not even for their spiritual things ought they to be highminded, as having nothing of themselves. "Since then the wisdom from without is hurtful, and the spiritual gifts were not given by you, what hast thou wherein to boast?"   And in regard to the wisdom from without, "Let no man deceive himself," saith he, because they were conceited about a thing which in truth did more harm than good.   But here, inasmuch as the thing spoken of was really advantageous, "Let no man glory."   And he orders his speech more gently: "for all things are yours."

Ver. 22. "Whether Paul, or Apollos, or Cephas, or the world, or life, or death, or things present, or things to come, all are yours; and ye are Christ's and Christ is God's."   For because he had handled them sharply, he refreshes them again.   And as above he had said, (I. Cor. iii. 9.) "We are fellow-workers with God;" and by many other expressions had soothed them: so here too he saith, "All things are yours;

taking down the pride of the teachers, and signifying that so far from bestowing any favor on them, they themselves ought to be grateful to the others.   Since for their sake they were made such as they were, yea, moreover, had received grace.   But seeing that these also were sure to boast, on this account he cuts out beforehand this disease too, saying, "As God gave to every man," (Supr. vi. 5. 6.) and, "God gave the increase:" to the end that neither the one party might be puffed up as bestowers of good ; nor the others, on their hearing a second time, "All things are yours," be again elated.   "For, indeed, though it were for your sakes, yet the whole was God's doing."   And I wish you to observe how he hath kept on throughout, making suppositions in his own name and that of Peter.

But what is, "or death?" That even though they die, for your sakes they die, encountering dangers for your salvation.   Dost thou mark how he again takes down the high spirit of the disciples, and raises the spirit of the teachers? In fact, he talks with them as with children of high birth, who have preceptors, and who are to be heirs of all.

We may say also, in another sense, that both the death of Adam was for our sakes, that we might be corrected ; and the death of Christ, that we might be saved.

"And ye are Christ's ; and Christ is God's." In one sense "we are Christ's, and in another sense "Christ is God's," and in a third sense is "the world ours."   For we indeed are Christ's, as his work : "Christ is God's, as a genuine Offspring, not as a work : in which sense neither is the world ours.   So that though he saying is the same, yet the meaning is different. For "the world is ours," as being a thing made for our sakes : but "Christ is God's," as having Him the Author of his being, in that He is Father.   And "we are Christ's," as having been formed by Him.   Now "if they are yours," saith he, "why have ye done what is just contrary to this, in calling yourselves after their name, and not after Christ, and God?"

[5.] C. iv. ver. 1.   "Let a man so account of us, as of ministers of Christ, and stewards of the mysteries of God."   After he had cast down their spirit, mark how again he refreshes it, saying, "as ministers of Christ."   Do not then, letting go the Master, receive a name from the servants and ministers.   "Stewards," saith he, indicating that we ought not to give these things unto all, but unto whom it is due, and to whom it is fitting we should minister.

Ver. 2. "Moreover it is required in stewards, that a man be found faithful:" that is, that he do not appropriate to himself his master's goods, that he do not as a master lay claim for himself but administer as a steward. For a steward's part is to administer well the things committed to his charge : not to say that his master's things are his own ; but, on the contrary, that his own are his master's. Let every one think on these things, both he that hath power in speech and he that possesses wealth, namely, that he hath been entrusted with a master's goods and that they are not his own ; let him not keep them with himself, nor set them down to his own account ; .but let him impute them unto God who gave them all. Wouldest thou see faithful stewards? Hear what saith Peter, " Why look ye so earnestly on us, as though by our own power or godliness we had made this man to walk ? " (Acts iii. 12.) Unto[1] Cornelius also he saith, "We also are men of like passions with you : " and unto Christ Himself, " Lo, we have left all, and followed Thee." (St. Matt. xix. 27.) And Paul, no less, when he had said, "I labored more abundantly than they all," (I Cor. xv. 10.) added, " yet not I, but the grace of God which was with me." Elsewhere also, setting himself strongly against the same persons, he said, " For what hast thou which thou didst not receive ? " (C. iv. 7.) " For thou hast nothing of thine own, neither wealth, nor speech, nor life itself ; for this also is surely the Lord's. Wherefore, when necessity calls, do thou lay down this also. But if thou doatest on life, and being ordered to lay it down refusest, thou art no longer a faithful steward."

" And how is it possible, when God calls, to resist ? " Well, that is just what I say too : and on this account do I chiefly admire the loving-kindness of God, that the things which He is able, even against thy will, to take from thee, these He willeth not to be paid in ($\varepsilon\grave{\iota}\sigma\varepsilon\nu\varepsilon\chi\theta\tilde{\eta}\nu\alpha\iota$) by thee unwillingly, that thou mayest have a reward besides. For instance, He can take away life without thy consent ; but His will is to do so with thy consent, that thou mayest say with Paul, " I die daily," (1 Cor. xv. 31.) He can take away thy glory without thy consent, and bring thee low: but He will have it from thee with thine own goodwill, that thou mayest have a recompense. He can make thee poor, though unwilling, but He will have thee willing-ly become such, that He may weave crowns for thee. Seest thou God's mercy to man? Seest thou ·our own brutish stupidity?

What if thou art come to great dignity, and hast at any time obtained some office of Church government? Be not high-minded. Thou hast not acquired the glory, but God hath put it on thee. As if it were another's, therefore, use it sparingly ; neither abusing it nor using it upon

unsuitable things, nor puffed up, nor appropri-ating it unto thyself ; but esteem thyself to be poor and inglorious. For never,—hadst thou been entrusted with a king's purple to keep,—never would it have become thee to abuse the robe and spoil it, but with the more exactness to keep it for the giver. Is utterance given thee? Be not puffed up ; be not arrogant ; for the gracious gift is not thine. Be not grudging about thy Master's good, but distribute them among thy fellow-servants ; and neither be thou elated with these things as if they were thine own, nor be sparing as to the distribution of them. Again, if thou hast children, they are God's which thou hast. If such be thy thought, thou wilt both be thankful for having them, and if bereft thou wilt not take it hard. Such was Job when he said, (Job i. 21.) "The Lord gave, the Lord hath taken away."

For we have all things from Christ. Both existence itself we have through Him, and life, and breath, and light, and air, and earth. And if He were to exclude us from any one of these, we are lost and undone. For (1 S.Pet. ii. 11.) " we are sojourners and pilgrims" And all this about "mine," and "thine," is bare words only, and doth not stand for things. For if thou do but say the house is thine, it is a word without a reality : since the very air, earth, matter, are the Creator's ; and so art thou too thyself, who hast framed it ; and all other things also. But supposing the use to be thine, even this is uncertain, not on account of death alone, but also before death, because of the instability of things.

[6.] These things then continually picturing to ourselves, let us lead strict lives ; and we shall gain two of the greatest advantages. For first, we shall be thankful both when we have and when we are bereaved ; and we shall not be enslaved to things which are fleeting by, and things not our own. For whether it be wealth that He taketh, He hath taken but His own ; or honor, or glory, or the body, or the life itself : be it that He taketh away thy son, it is not thy son that He hath taken, but His own servant. For thou formedst him not, but He made him. Thou didst but minister to his appearing ; the whole was God's own work. Let us give thanks therefore that we have been counted worthy to be His ministers in this matter. But what? Wouldest thou have had him for ever? This again proves thee grudging, and ignorant that it was another's child which thou hadst, and not thine own. As therefore those who part resignedly are but aware that they have what was not theirs ; so whoever gives way to grief is in fact counting the King's property his own. For, if we are not our own, how can they be ours? I say, we: for in two ways we are His, both on

---

[1] These words were addressed by St. Paul and St. Barnabas, to the men of Lystra when they were about to offer sacrifices to them. Acts xiv. 15. [The words of Peter which Chrysostom seems to have had in mind were "Stand up, I myself also am a man." Acts x. 26—C.]

account of our creation, and also on account of the faith. Wherefore David saith, "My substance is with Thee:" (Ps. xxxix. 7. ὑπόστασις Sept. "hope" rec. vers. of. ver. 6; Ps. cxxxix. 14.) and Paul too, "For in Him we live and move and have our being:" (Acts xvii. 28.) and plying the argument about the faith, he says, (1 Cor. vi. 19, 20.) "Ye are not your own," and "ye were bought with a price." For all things are God's. When then He calls and chooses to take, let us not, like grudging servants, fly from the reckoning, nor purloin our Master's goods. Thy soul is not thine; and how can thy wealth be thine? How is it then that thou spendest on what is unnecessary the things which are not thine? Knowest thou not that for this we are soon to be put on our trial, that is, if we have used them badly? But seeing that they are not our's but our Master's, it were right to expend them upon our fellow-servants. It is worth considering that the omission of this was the charge brought against that rich man: and against those also who had not given food to the Lord. (St. Luke xvi. 21. St. Matt. xxv. 42.)

[7.] Say not then, "I am but spending mine own, and of mine own I live delicately." It is not of thine own, but of other men's. Other men's, I say, because such is thine own choice: for God's will is that those things should be thine, which have been entrusted unto thee on behalf of thy brethren. Now the things which are not thine own become thine, if thou spend them upon others: but if thou spend on thyself unsparingly, thine own things become no longer thine. For since thou usest them cruelly, and sayest, "That my own things should be altogether spent on my own enjoyment is fair:" therefore I call them not thine own. For they are common to thee and thy fellow-servants; just as the sun is common, the air, the earth, and all the rest. For as in the case of the body, each ministration belongs both to the whole body and to each several member; but when it is applied to one single member only, it destroys the proper function of that very member: so also it comes to pass in the case of wealth. And that what I say may be made plainer; the food of the body which is given in common to the members, should it pass into one member, even to that it turns out alien in the end. For when it cannot be digested nor afford nourishment, even to that part, I say, it turns out alien. But if it be made common, both that part and all the rest have it as their own.

So also in regard of wealth. If you enjoy it alone, you too have lost it: for you will not reap its reward. But if you possess it jointly with the rest, then will it be more your own,

and then will you reap the benefit of it. Seest thou not that the hands minister, and the mouth softens, and the stomach receives? Doth the stomach say, Since I have received, I ought to keep it all? Then do not thou I pray, in regard to riches, use this language. For it belongs to the receiver to impart. As then it is a vice in the stomach to retain the food and not to distribute it, (for it is injurious to the whole body,) so it is a vice in those that are rich to keep to themselves what they have. For this destroys both themselves and others. Again, the eye receives all the light: but it doth not itself alone retain it, but enlightens the entire body. For it is not its nature to keep it to itself, so long as it is an eye. Again, the nostrils are sensible of perfume; but they do not keep it all to themselves, but transmit it to the brain, and affect the stomach with a sweet savor, and by their means refresh the entire man. The feet alone walk; but they move not away themselves only, but transfer also the whole body. In like manner do thou, whatsoever thou hast been entrusted withal, keep it not to thyself alone, since thou art doing harm to the whole and to thyself more than all.

And not in the case of the limbs only may one see this occuring: for the smith also, if he chose to impart of his craft to no one, ruins both himself and all other crafts. Likewise the cordwainer, the husbandman, the baker, and everyone of those who pursue any necessary calling; if he chose not to communicate to anyone of the results of his art, will ruin not the others only but himself also with them.

And why do I say, "the rich?" For the poor too, if they followed after the wickedness of you who are covetous and rich, would injure you very greatly and soon make you poor; yea rather, they would quite destroy you, were they in your want unwilling to impart of their own: the tiller of the ground, (for instance,) of the labor of his hands; the sailor, of the gain from his voyages; the soldier, of his distinction won in the wars.

Wherefore if nothing else can, yet let this at least put you to shame, and do you imitate their benevolence. Dost thou impart none of thy wealth unto any? Then shouldest thou not receive any thing from another: in which case, the world will be turned upside down. For in every thing to give and receive is the principle of numerous blessings: in seeds, in scholars, in arts. For if any one desire to keep his art to himself, he subverts both himself and the whole course of things. And the husbandman, if he bury and keep the seeds in his house, will bring about a grievous famine. So also the rich man, if he act thus in regard of his wealth, will destroy himself before the poor, heaping up the fire of hell more grievous upon his own head.

[8.] Therefore as teachers, however many scholars they have, impart some of their lore unto each; so let thy possession be, many to whom thou hast done good. And let all say, " such an one he freed from poverty, such an one from dangers. Such an one would have perished, had he not, next to the grace of God, enjoyed thy patronage. This man's disease thou didst cure, another thou didst rid of false accusation, another being a stranger you took in, another being naked you clothed." Wealth inexhaustible and many treasures are not so good as such sayings. They draw all men's gaze more powerfully than your golden vestments, and horses, and slaves. For these make a man appear even odious: (φορτικόν, a conj. of Saville's for φορτικά) they cause him to be hated as a common foe; but the former proclaim him as a common father and benefactor. And, what is greatest of all, Favor from God waits on thee in every part of thy proceedings. What I mean is, let one man say, He helped to portion out my daughter:

another, And he afforded my son the means of taking his station among men: (εἰς ἄνδρας ἐμφανῆναι) another, He made my calamity to cease: another, He delivered me from dangers. Better than golden crowns are words such as these, that a man should have in his city innumerable persons to proclaim his beneficence. Voices such as these are pleasanter far, and sweeter than the voices of the heralds marching before the archons; to be called saviour, benefactor, defender, (the very names of God ;) and not, covetous, proud, insatiate, and mean. Let us not, I beseech you, let us not have a fancy for any of these titles, but the contrary. For if these, spoken on earth, make one so splendid and illustrious; when they are written in heaven, and God proclaims them on the day that shall come, think what renown, what splendor thou shalt enjoy! Which may it be the lot of us all to obtain, through the grace and lovingkindness of our Lord Jesus Christ; with Whom unto the Father and the Holy Spirit, be glory, power, honor, now and always and unto everlasting ages. Amen.

HOMILY XI.

1 Cor. iv. 3, 4.

But with me it is a very small thing that I should be judged of you, or of man's judgment: yea I judge not mine own self. For I know nothing against myself, yet am I not hereby justified: but He that judgeth me is the Lord.

TOGETHER with all other ills, I know not how, there hath come upon man's nature the disease of restless prying and of unseasonable curiosity, which Christ Himself chastised, saying, (S. Matt. vii, 1.) "Judge not, that ye be not judged." A kind of thing, which hath no pleasure as all other sins have, but only punishment and vengeance. For though we are ourselves full of ten thousand evils, and bearing the "beams" in our own eyes, we become exact inquisitors of the offences of our neighbor which are not at all bigger than "motes." And so this matter at Corinth was falling out. Religious men and dear to God were ridiculed and cast out for their want of learning; while others, brimful of evils innumerable, were classed highly because of their fluent speech. Then like persons sitting in public to try causes, these were the sort of votes they kept rashly passing: " such an one is worthy: such an one is better than

such another; this man is inferior to that; that, better than this." And, leaving off to mourn for their own bad ways, they were become judges of others; and in this way again were kindling grievous warfare.

Mark then, how wisely Paul corrects them, doing away with this disease. For since he had said, " Moreover, it is required in stewards that a man be found faithful," and it seemed as if he were giving them an opening to judge and pry into each man's life, and this was aggravating the party feeling; lest such should be the effect on them, he draws them away from that kind of petty disputation, saying, "With me it is a very small thing that I should be judged of you;" again in his own person carrying on the discourse.

[2.] But what means, "With me it is a very small thing that I should be judged of you or of man's day?" (ἡμέρας) "I judge myself unworthy," saith he, " of being judged by you." And why say I, " by you?" I will add, " by (καὶ τὸ [τοῦ?]) any one else." Howbeit, let no one condemn Paul of arrogance; though he saith that no man is worthy to pass sentence concerning him. For first, he saith these things not for his own sake, but wishing to rescue others from the odium which they had incurred from the Corinthians. And in the next place, he limits not the matter to the Corinthians merely, but himself also he deposes from this right of judging; saying, that to decree such things was a matter beyond his decision. At least he adds, "I judge not mine own self."

But besides what has been said, we must search out the ground upon which these expressions were uttered. For he knew well in many cases how to speak with high spirit: and that, not of pride or arrogance, but of a certain excellent management [οἰκονομίας ἀρίστης] seeing that in the present case also he saith this, not as lifting up himself, but as taking down other men's sails, and earnestly seeking to invest the saints with due honor. For in proof that he was one of the very humble, hear what he saith, bringing forward the testimony of his enemies on this point; "His bodily presence is weak, and his speech of no account; (2 Cor. x. 10.) and again, "Last of all, as to one born out of due time, He appeared unto me also." (2 Cor. xv. 8.) But notwithstanding, see this lowly man, when the time called on him, to what a pitch he raises the spirit of the disciples, not teaching pride but instilling a wholesome courage. For with these same discoursing he saith, "And if the world shall be judged by you, are ye unworthy to judge the smallest matters? 1 Cor. vi. 2. For as the Christian ought to be far removed from arrogance, so also from flattery and a mean spirit. Thus, if any one says, " I count money as nothing, but all things here are to me as a shadow, and a dream, and child's play;" we are not at all to charge him as arrogant; since in this way we shall have to to accuse Solomon himself of arrogance, for speaking austerely (φιλοσοφοῦντα) on these things, saying "Vanity of vanities (Eccles. i. 2.) all is vanity." But God forbid that we should call the strict rule of life by the name of arrogance. Wherefore to despise these things is not haughtiness, but greatness of soul; albeit we see kings, and rulers, and potentates, making much of them. But many a poor man, leading a strict life despises them; and we are not therefore to call him arrogant but highminded: just as, on the other hand, if any be extremely addicted to them, we do not call him lowly of heart and moderate, but weak, and poor spirited, and ignoble. For so, should a son despise the pursuits which become his father and affect slavish ways, we should not commend him as lowly of heart, but as base and servile we should reproach him. What we should admire in him would be, his despising those meaner things and making much account of what came to him from his father. For this is arrogance, to think one's self better than one's fellow-servants: but to pass the true sentence on things cometh not of boasting, but of strictness of life.

On this account Paul also, not to exalt himself, but to humble others, and to keep down those who were rising up out of their places, and to persuade them to be modest, said, " With me it is a very small thing that I should be judged of you or of man's day." Observe how he soothes the other party also. For whosoever is told that he looks down on all alike, and deigns not to be judged of any one, will not thenceforth any more feel pain, as though himself were the only one excluded. For if he had said, "Of you," only, and so held his peace; this were enough to gall them as if treated contemptuously. But now, by introducing, "nor yet of man's day," he brought alleviation to the blow; giving them partners in the contempt. Nay, he even softens this point again, saying, "not even do I judge myself." Mark the expression, how entirely free from arrogance: in that not even he himself, he saith, is capable of so great exactness.

[3.] Then because this saying also seemed to be that of one extolling himself greatly, this too he corrects, saying, " Yet am I not hereby justified." What then? Ought we not to judge ourselves and our own misdeeds? Yes surely: there is great need to do this when we sin. But Paul said not this, " For I know nothing," saith he, "against myself." What misdeed then was he to judge, when he "knew nothing against himself?' Yet, saith he, " he was not justified." (1 Cor. vi. 3.) We then who have our conscience filled with ten thousand wounds, and are conscious to ourselves of nothing good, but quite the contrary; what can we say?

And how could it be, if he knew nothing against himself that he was not justified? Because it was possible for him to have committed certain sins, not however, knowing that they were sins. From this make thine estimate how great shall be the strictness of the future judgment. It is not, you see, as considering himself unblameable that he saith it is so unmeet for him to be judged by them, but to stop the mouths of those who were doing so unreasonably. At least in another place, even though men's sins be notorious, he permits not judgment unto others, because the occasion required it. " For why dost thou judge thy brother," saith he, (Rom. xiv. 10.) or, "thou, why dost thou set at nought thy brother?" For thou wert not enjoined, O man, to judge others, but to test thine own doings. Why then dost thou seize upon the office of the Lord? Judgment is His, not thine.

To which effect, he adds, " Therefore judge

nothing before the time, until the Lord come; who will both bring to light the hidden things of darkness, and make manifest the counsels of the hearts, and then shall each man have his praise from God." What then? Is it not right that our teachers should do this? It is right in the case of open and confessed sins, and that with fitting opportunity, and even then with pain and inward vexation: not as these were acting at that time, of vain-glory and arrogance. For neither in this instance is he speaking of those sins which all own to be such, but about preferring one before another, and making comparisons of modes of life. For these things He alone knows how to judge with accuracy, who is to judge our secret doings, which of these be worthy of greater and which of less punishment and honor. But we do all this according to what meets our eye. "For if in mine own errors," saith he, "I know nothing clearly, how can I be worthy to pass sentence on other men? And how shall I who know not my own case with accuracy, be able to judge the state of others?" Now if Paul felt this, much more we. For (to proceed) he spake these things, not to exhibit himself as faultless, but to shew that even should there be among them some such person, free from transgression, not even he would be worthy to judge the lives of others: and that if he, though conscious to himself of nothing declare himself guilty, much more they who have ten thousand sins to be conscious of in themselves.

[4.] Having thus, you see, stopped the mouths of those who pass such sentences, he travails next with strong feeling ready to break out and come upon the unclean person. And like as when a storm is coming on, some clouds fraught with darkness run before it; afterwards, when the crash of the thunders ariseth and works the whole heavens into one black cloud, then all at once the rain bursts down upon the earth: so also did it then happen. For though he might in deep indignation have dealt with the fornicator, he doth not so; but with fearful words he first represses the swelling pride of the man, since in truth, what had occurred was a twofold sin, fornication, and, that which is worse than fornication, the not grieving over the sin committed. For not so much does he bewail the sin, as him that committed it and did not as yet repent. Thus, "I shall bewail many of those," saith he, not simply "who have sinned heretofore," but he adds, "who have not repented of the uncleanness and impurity which they wrought." (2 Cor. xii. 21.) For he who after sinning hath practised repentance, is a worthy object not of grief but of gratulations, having passed over into the choir of the righteous. For, (Is. xliii, 26.) "declare thou thine iniquities first, that thou

mayest be justified:" but if after sinning one is void of shame, he is not so much to be pitied for falling as for lying where he is fallen.

Now if it be a grievous fault not to repent after sins; to be puffed up because of sins, what sort of punishment doth it deserve? For if he who is elate for his good deeds is unclean, what pardon shall he meet with who has that feeling with regard to his sins?

Since then the fornicator was of this sort, and had rendered his mind so headstrong and unyielding through his sin, he of course begins by casting down his pride. And he neither puts the charge first, for fear of making him hardened, as singled out for accusation before the rest; nor yet later, lest he should suppose that what related to him was but incidental. But, having first excited great alarm in him by his plain speaking towards others, then, and not till then, he goes on to him, in the course of his rebuke to others giving the man's wilfulness a share beforehand.

For these same words, viz. "I know nothing against myself, yet am I not hereby justified," and this, "He that judgeth me is the Lord, who will both bring to light the hidden things of darkness, and make manifest the counsels of the hearts," glance not lightly both upon that person, and upon such as act in concert with him and despise the saints. "For what," saith he, "if any outwardly appear to be virtuous and admirable persons? He, the Judge, is not a discerner of externals only, but also brings to light all secrets."

[5.] On two accounts you see, or rather on three, correct judgement belongs not to us. One, because, though we be conscious to ourselves of nothing, still we need one to reprove our sins with strictness. Another, because the most part of the things which are done escape us and are concealed. And for a third besides these, because many things which are done by others seem to us indeed fair, but they come not of a right mind. Why say ye then, that no sin hath been committed by this or that person? That such an one is better than such another? Seeing that this we are not to pronounce, not even concerning him who knows nothing against himself. For He who discerns secrets, He it is who with certainty judges. Behold, for example; I for my part know nothing against myself: yet neither so am I justified, that is, I am not quit of accounts to be given, nor of charges to be answered. For he doth not say this, "I rank not among the righteous;" but "I am not pure from sin." For elsewhere he saith also, (Rom. vi. 7, δεδικαίωται, τουτεστιν ἀπήλλακται.) "He that hath died is justified from sin," that is, "is liberated."

Again, many things we do, good indeed, but

not of a right mind. For so we commend many, not from a wish to render them conspicuous, but to wound others by means of them. And the thing done indeed is right for the well-doer is praised; but the intention is corrupt: for it is done of a satanical purpose. For this one hath often done, not rejoicing with his brother, but desiring to wound the other party.

Again, a man hath committed a great error; some other person, wishing to supplant him, says that he hath done nothing, and comforts him forsooth in his error by recurring to the common frailty of nature. But oftentimes he doth this from no mind to sympathize, but to make him more easy in his faults.

Again, a man rebukes oftentimes not so much to reprove and admonish, as publicly to (ἐκπομπεῦσαι καὶ ἐκτραγῳδῆσαι) display and exaggerate his neighbor's sin. Our counsels however themselves men do not know; but, (Rom. viii, 27.) "He that searcheth the hearts," knows them perfectly; and He will bring all such things into view at that time. Wherefore he saith, "Who will bring to light the secret things of darkness and make manifest the counsels of the hearts."

[6.] Seeing then that not even where we "know nothing against ourselves," can we be clean from accusations, and where we do any thing good, but do it not of a right mind, we are liable to punishment; consider how vastly men are deceived in their judgments. For all these matters are not be come at by men, but by the unsleeping Eye alone: and though we may deceive men, our sophistry will never avail against Him. Say not then, darkness is around me and walls; who seeth me? For He who by Himself formed our hearts, Himself knoweth all things. (Ps. cxxxix, 12.) "For darkness is no darkness with Him." And yet he who is committing sin, well saith, "Darkness is around me and walls;" for were there not a darkness in his mind he would not have cast out the fear of God and acted as he pleased. For unless the ruling principle be first darkened, the entrance of sin without fear is a thing impossible. Say not then, who seeth me? For there is that (Heb. iv, 12.) "pierceth even unto soul and spirit, joints and marrow;" but thou seest not thyself nor canst thou pierce the cloud; but as if thou hadst a wall on all sides surrounding thee, thou art without power to look up unto the heaven.

For whatsoever sin thou wilt, first let us examine, and thou shalt see that so it is engendered. For as robbers and they who dig through walls when they desire to carry off any valuable thing, put out the candle and then do their work; so also doth men's perverse reasoning in the case of those who are committing sin. Since in us

also surely there is a light, the light of reason, ever burning. But if the spirit of wickedness coming eagerly on with its strong blast quench that flame, it straightway darkens the soul and prevails against it, and despoils it straightway of all that is laid up therein. For when by unclean desire the soul is made captive, even as a cloud and mist the eyes of the body, so that desire intercepts the foresight of the mind, and suffers it to see nothing at any distance, either precipice, or hell, or fear; but thenceforth, having that deceit as a tyrant over him, he comes to be easily vanquished by sin; and there is raised up before his eyes as it were a wall without windows, which suffers not the ray of righteousness to shine in upon the mind, the absurd conceits of lust enclosing it as with a rampart on all sides. And from that time forward the unchaste woman is everywhere meeting him: standing present before his eyes, before his mind, before his thoughts. And as the blind, although they stand at high noon beneath the very central point of the heaven, receive not the light, their eyes being fast closed up; just so these also, though ten thousand doctrines of salvation sound in their ears from all quarters, having their soul preoccupied with this passion stop their ears against such discourses. And they know it well who have made the trial. But God forbid that you should know it from actual experience.

[7.] And not only this sin hath these effects, but every misplaced affection as well. For let us transfer, if you please, the argument from the unchaste woman unto money, and we shall see here also thick and unbroken darkness. For in the former case, inasmuch as the beloved object is one and shut up in one place, the feeling is not so violent; but in the case of money which sheweth itself every where, in silversmiths' shops, in taverns, in foundries for gold, in the houses of the wealthy, the passion blows a vehement gale. For when servants swaggering in the market place, horses with golden trappings, men decked with costly garments, are seen with desire by him who has that distemper, the darkness becomes intense which envelopes him. And why speak of houses and silversmiths' shops? for my part I think that such persons, though it be but in a picture and image that they see the wealth, are convulsed, and grow wild, and rave. So that from all quarters the darkness gathers around them. And if they chance to behold a portraiture of a King, they admire not the beauty of the precious stones, nor yet the gold, nor the purple robe, but they pine away. And as the wretched lover before mentioned, though he see but the image of the woman beloved, cleaveth unto the lifeless thing; so this man also, beholding a lifeless image of wealth, is more strongly affected in the same way, as being holden of a more tyrannical passion. And he must henceforth either abide at home, or if he venture into the Forum, return home with innumerable hurts. For many are the objects which grieve his eyes. And just as the former seeth nothing else save the woman, even so the latter hastens by poor persons, and all things else, that he may not obtain so much as a slight alleviation. But upon the wealthy he steadily fixeth his eyes; by the sight of them introducing the fire into his own soul mightily and vehemently. For it is a fire that miserably devours the person that falls into it; and if no hell were threatened nor yet punishment, this condition were itself punishment; to be continually tormented and never able to find an end to the malady.

[8.] Well: these things alone might suffice to recommend our fleeing from this distemper. But there is no greater evil than inconsideration which causes men to be rivetted unto things that bring sorrow of heart and no advantage. Wherefore I exhort that you cut off the passion at its beginning: for just as a fever on its first attack, does not violently burn up the patients with thirst, but on its increase and the heightening of its fire causes from that time incurable thirst; and though one should let them fill themselves full of drink, it puts not out the furnace but makes it burn fiercer: so also it happens in regard to this passion; unless when it first invadeth our soul we stop it and shut the doors; having got in, from that time it makes the disease of those who have admitted it incurable. For so both good things and bad, the longer they abide in us, the more powerful they become.

And in all other things too, any one may see that this cometh to pass. For so a plant but lately set in the ground is easily pulled up; but no more so when rooted for a long time; it then requires great strength in the lever. And a building newly put together is easily thrown down by those who push against it; but once well fixed, it gives great trouble to those who attempt to pull it down. And a wild beast that hath made his accustomed haunt in certain places for a long time is with difficulty driven away.

Those therefore who are not yet possessed by the passion in question, I exhort not to be taken captive. For it is more easy to guard against falling into it, than having fallen to get away.

[9.] But unto those who are seized by it and broken down, if they will consent to put themselves into the hands of the WORD of healing, I promise large hope of salvation, by the Grace of God. For if they will consider those who have suffered and fallen into that distemper and have recovered, they will have good hopes respecting the removal of the disease. Who then

ever fell into this disease, and was easily rid of it? That well-known Zacchæus. For 'who could be more fond of money than a publican? But all at once he became a man of strict life, (Φιλόσοφος) and put out all that blaze. Matthew in like manner: for he too was a publican, living in continual rapine. But he likewise all at once stripped himself of the mischief, and quenched his thirst, and followed after spiritual gain. Considering therefore these, and the like to them, despair not even thou. For if thou wilt, quickly thou shalt be able to recover. And if you please, according to the rule of physicians, we will prescribe accurately what thou shouldest do.

It is necessary then, before all other things, to be right in this, that we never despond, nor despair of our salvation. Next, we must look not only upon the examples of those who have done well, but also upon the sufferings of those who have persisted in sin. For as we have considered Zacchæus, and Matthew, even so ought we also to take account of Judas, and Gehazi, and Ahar, [perhaps Achan, Josh. vii.] and Ahab, and Ananias, and Sapphira, in order that by the one, we may cast out all despair, and by the other cut off all indolence; and that the soul become not reckless of the remedies suggested. And let us teach them of themselves to say what the Jews said on that day, approaching unto Peter, (Acts ii, 37, cf. xvi, 30.) "What must we do to be saved?" And let them hear what they must do.

[10.] What then must we do? We must know how worthless the things in question are, and that wealth is a run-away slave, and heartless, and encompasseth its possessors with ills innumerable. And such words, like charms, let us sound in their ears continually. And as physicians soothe their patients when they ask for cold water, by saying that they will give it, making excuses about the spring, and the vessel, and the fit time, and many more such, (for should they refuse at once, they make them wild with phrensy,) so let us also act towards the lovers of money. When they say we desire to be rich, let us not say immediately that wealth is an evil thing; but let us assent, and say that we also desire it; but in due time; yea, true wealth; yea, that which hath undying pleasure: yea, that which is gathered for thyself, and not for others, and those often our enemies. And let us produce the lessons of true wisdom, and say, we forbid not riches, but ill-gotten riches. For it is lawful to be rich, but without covetousness, without rapine and violence, and an ill report from all men. With these arguments let us first smooth them down, and not as yet discourse of hell. For the sick man endures not yet such sayings. Wherefore let us go to this world for all our arguments upon these matters; and say, "Why is it thy choice to be rich through covetousness? That the gold and the silver may be laid up for others, but for thee, curses and accusations innumerable? That he whom you have defrauded may be stung by want of the very necessaries of life, and bewail himself, and draw down upon thee the censure of thousands; and may go at fall of evening about the market place, encountering every one in the alleys, and in utter perplexity, and not knowing what to trust to even for that one night? For how is he to sleep after all, with pangs of the belly, restless famine besetting him, and that often while it is freezing, and the rain coming down on him? And while thou, having washed, returnest home from the bath, in a glow with soft raiment, merry of heart and rejoicing, and hastening unto a banquet prepared and costly: he, driven every where about the market place by cold and hunger, takes his round, stooping low and stretching out his hands; nor hath he even spirit without trembling to make his suit for his necessary food to one so full fed and so bent on taking his ease; nay, often he has to retire with insult. When therefore thou hast returned home, when thou liest down on thy couch, when the lights round thine house shine bright, when the table is prepared and plentiful, at that time call to rememberance that poor miserable man wandering about, like the dogs in the alleys, in darkness and in mire; except indeed when, as is often the case, he has to depart thence, not unto house, nor wife, nor bed, but unto a pallet of straw; even as we see the dogs baying all through the night. And thou, if thou seest but a little drop falling from the roof, throwest the whole house into confusion, calling thy slaves and disturbing every thing: while he, laid in rags, and straw, and dirt, has to bear all the cold.

What wild beast would not be softened by these things? Who is there so savage and inhuman that these things should not make him mild? and yet there are some who are arrived at such a pitch of cruelty as even to say that they deserve what they suffer. Yea, when they ought to pity, and weep, and help to alleviate men's calamities, they on the contrary visit them with savage and inhuman censures. Of these I should be glad to ask, Tell me, why do they deserve what they suffer? Is it because they would be fed and not starve?

No, you will reply; but because they would be fed in idleness. And thou, dost not thou wanton in idleness? What say I? Art thou not oft-times toiling in an occupation more grievous than any idleness, grasping, and oppressing, and coveting? Better were it if thou too wert idle after this sort; for it is better to be idle in this way, than to be covetous. But now thou even tramplest on the calamities of others, not only idling, not only pursuing an occupation worse than idleness, but also maligning those who spend their days in misery.

And let us farther narrate to them the disasters of others; the untimely bereavements, the dwellers in prison, those who are torn to pieces before tribunals, those who are trembling for life; the unlooked for widowhood of women; the sudden reverse of the rich: and with this let us soften their minds. For by our narrations concerning others, we shall induce them by all means to fear these evils in their own case too. For when they hear that the son of such an one who was a covetous and grasping man, or ($\dot{\eta}$ $\tau o\hat{v}$ $\delta\epsilon\hat{\iota}\nu o\varsigma$ instead of $\dot{\eta}\nu$; $\tau o\hat{v}$ $\delta\epsilon\hat{\iota}\nu o\varsigma$) the wife of such an one who did many tyrannical actions, after the death of her husband endured afflictions without end; the injured persons setting upon the wife and the children, and a general war being raised from all quarters against his house; although a man be the most senseless of beings, yet expecting himself also to suffer the same, and fearing for his own lest they undergo the same fate, he will become more moderate. Now we find life full of many such histories, and we shall not be at a loss for correctives of this kind.

But when we speak these things, let us not speak them as giving advice or counsel, lest our discourse become too irksome: but as in the order of the narrative and by association with something else, let us proceed in each case unto that kind of conversation, and let us be constantly putting them upon stories of the kind, permitting them to speak of no subject except these which follow: How such an one's splendid and famous mansion fell down; How it is so entirely desolate that all things that were in it have come into the hands of others; How many trials have taken place daily about this same property, what a stir; How many of that man's relations ($o\check{\iota}\kappa\epsilon\tau\alpha\iota$, probably $o\check{\iota}\kappa\epsilon\hat{\iota}o\iota$) have died either beggars, or inhabitants of a prison.

All these things let us speak as in pity for the deceased, and as depreciating things present; in order that by fear and by pity we may soften the cruel mind. And when we see men shrinking into themselves at these narrations, then and not till then let us introduce to their notice also the doctrine of hell, not as terrifying these, but in compassion for others. And let us say, But why speak of things present? For far, indeed, will our concern be from ending with these; a yet more grievous punishment will await all such persons: even a river of fire, and a poisonous worm, and darkness interminable, and undying tortures. If with such addresses we succeed in throwing a spell over them, we shall correct both ourselves and them, and quickly get the better of our infirmity.

And on that day we shall have God to praise us: as also Paul saith, "And then shall each man have praise from God." For that which cometh from men, is both fleeting, and sometimes it proceeds from no good intentions. But that which cometh from God both abideth continually, and shines out clearly. For when He who knew all things before their creation, and

who is free from all passion, gives praise, then also the demonstration of our virtue is even unquestionable.

Knowing these things therefore, let us act so as to be praised of God, and to acquire the greatest blessings; which God grant us all to obtain, through the grace and loving-kindness of our Lord Jesus Christ, with Whom to the Father and the Holy Spirit be glory, power, honor, now and always, and unto all the ages of eternity. Amen.

HOMILY XII.

1 COR. iv. 6.

Now these things, brethren, I have in a figure transferred to myself and Apollos for your sakes; that in us ye might learn not to think of men above that which is written.*

So long as there was need of expressions as harsh as these, he refrained from drawing up the curtain, and went on arguing as if he were himself the person to whom they were addressed; in order that the dignity of the persons censured tending to counteract the censurers, no room might be left for flying out in wrath at the charges. But when the time came for a gentler process, then he strips it off, and removes the mask, and shows the persons concealed by the appellation of Paul and Apollos. And on this account he said, "These things, brethren, I have transferred in a figure unto myself and Apollos."

And as in the case of the sick, when the child being out of health kicks and turns away from the food offered by the physicians, the attendants call the father or the tutor, and bid them take the food from the physician's hands and bring it, so that out of fear towards them he may take it and be quiet: so also Paul, intending to censure them about certain other persons, of whom some, he thought, were injured, others honored above measure, did not set down the persons themselves, but conducted the argument in his own name and that of Apollos, in order that reverencing these they might receive his mode of cure. But that once received, he presently makes known in whose behalf he was so expressing himself.

Now this was not hypocrisy, but condescension (συγκατάβασις) and tact (οἰκονομία). For if he had said openly, "As for you, the men whom

ye are judging are saints, and worthy of all admiration;" they might have taken it ill and (κἂν ἀπεπήδησαν) started back. But now in saying, "But to me it is a very small thing that I should be judged of you:" and again, "Who is Paul, and who is Apollos?" he rendered his speech easy of reception.

This, if you mark it, is the reason why he says here, "These things have I transferred in a figure unto myself for your sakes, that in us ye may learn not to be wise above what is written," signifying that if he had applied his argument in their persons, they would not have learnt all that they needed to learn, nor would have admitted the correction, being vexed at what was said. But as it was, revering Paul, they bore the rebuke well.

[2.] But what is the meaning of, "not to be wise above what is written?" It is written, (St. Matt. vii. 3.) "Why beholdest thou the mote that is in thy brothers's eye, but considerest not the beam that is in thine own eye?" and "Judge not, that ye be not judged." For if we are one and are mutually bound together, it behooveth us not to rise up against one another. For "he that humbleth himself shall be exalted," saith he. And (St. Matt. xx, 26, 27; St. Mark x, 43; not *verbatim*.) "He that will be first of all, let him be the servant of all." These are the things which "are written."

"That no one of you be puffed up for one against another." Again, having dismissed the teachers, he rebukes the disciples. For it was they who caused the former to be elated.

And besides, the leaders would not quietly receive that kind of speech because of their desire of outward glory: for they were even blinded with that passion. Whereas the disciples, as not reaping themselves the fruits of the

---

* [The true text of this clause is well given in the Revised Version, "not to go beyond the things which are written."]

glory, but procuring it for others, would both endure the chiding with more temper, and had it more in their power than the leading men to distroy the disease.

It seems then, that this also is a symptom of being " puffed up," to be elated on another's account, even though a man have no such feeling in regard of what is his own. For as he who is proud of another's wealth, is so out of arrogance; so also in the case of another's glory.

And he hath well called it " being puffed up." For when one particular member rises up over the rest, it is nothing else but inflammation and disease; since in no other way doth one member become higher than another, except when a swelling takes place. (So in English " proud flesh.") And so in the body of the Church also; whoever is inflamed and puffed up, he must be the diseased one; for he is swollen above the proportion of the rest. For this [disproportion] is what we mean by " swelling." And so comes it to pass in the body, when some spurious and evil humor gathers, instead of the wonted nourishment. So also arrogance is born; notions to which we have no right coming over us. And mark with what literal propriety he saith, be not " puffed up:" for that which is puffed up hath a certain tumor of spirit, from being filled with corrupt humor.

These things, however, he saith, not to preclude all soothing, but such soothing as leads to harm. " Wouldest thou wait upon this or that person? I forbid thee not: but do it not to the injury of another," For not that we might array ourselves one against another were teachers given us, but that we might all be mutually united. For so the general to this end is set over the host, that of those who are separate he may make one body. But if he is to break up the army, he stands in the place of an enemy rather than of a general.

[3.] Ver. 7. " For who maketh thee to differ? For what hast thou which thou didst not receive?"

From this point, dismissing the governed, he turns to the governors. What he saith comes to this: From whence is evident that thou art worthy of being praised? Why, hath any judgment taken place? any inquiry proceeded? any essay? any severe testing? Nay, thou canst not say it: and if men give their votes, their judgment is not upright. But let us suppose that thou really art worthy of praise and hast indeed the gracious gift, and that the judgment of men is not corrupt: yet not even in this case were it right to be high-minded; for thou hast nothing of thyself but from God didst receive it. Why then dost thou pretend to have that which thou hast not? Thou wilt say, " thou hast it:" and others have it with thee: well then, thou

hast it upon receiving it: not merely this thing or that, but all things whatsoever thou hast.

For not to thee belong these excellencies, but to the grace of God. Whether you name faith, it came of His calling; or whether it be the forgiveness of sins which you speak of, or spiritual gifts, or the word of teaching, or the miracles; thou didst receive all from thence. Now what hast thou, tell me, which thou hast not received, but hast rather achieved of thine own self? Thou hast nothing to say. Well: thou hast received; and does that make thee highminded? Nay, it ought to make thee shrink back into thyself. For it is not thine, what hath been given, but the giver's. What if thou didst receive it? thou receivedst it of him. And if thou receivedst of him, it was not thine which thou receivedst: and if thou didst but receive what was not thine own, why art thou exalted as if thou hadst something of thine own? Wherefore he added also, " Now if thou didst receive it, why dost thou glory, as if thou hadst not received it?

[4.] Thus having, you see, made good his argument by concession,[1] (κατὰ συνδρομὴν.) he indicates that they have their deficiencies; and those not a few: and saith, " In the first place, though ye had received all things, it were not meet to glory, for nothing is your own; but as the case really stands there are many things of which ye are destitute." And in the beginning he did but hint at this, saying, " I could not speak unto you as unto spiritual:" and, " I determined to know nothing among you, save Jesus Christ and Him crucified." But here he doth it in a way to abash them, saying,

Ver. 8. " Already ye are filled, already ye are rich:" that is, ye want nothing henceforth; ye are become perfect; ye have attained the very summit; ye stand, as ye think, in need of no one, either among Apostles or teachers.

" Already ye are filled." And well saith he " already;" pointing out, from the time, the incredibility of their statements and their unreasonable notion of themselves. It was therefore in mockery that he said to them, " So quickly have ye come to the end;" which thing was impossible in the time: for all the more perfect things wait long in futurity: but to be " full " with a little betokens a feeble soul; and from a little to imagine one's self " rich," a sick and miserable one. For piety is an insatiable thing; and it argues a childish mind to imagine from just the beginnings that you have obtained the whole: and for men who are not yet even in the prelude of a matter, to be high-minded as if they had laid hold of the end.

Then also by means of what followeth he puts

---

[1] [That is, conceding that they had the gifts which they claimed. C.]

them yet more out of countenance; for having said, "Already ye are full," he added, "ye are become rich, ye have reigned without us: yea and I would to God ye did reign, that we also might reign with you." Full of great austerity is the speech: which is why it comes last, being introduced by him after that abundance of reproof. For then is our admonition respected and easily received, when after our accusations we introduce our humiliating expressions, (τὰ ἐυτρεπτικὰ ῥήματα.) For this were enough to repress even the shameless soul and strike it more sharply than direct accusation, and correct the bitterness and hardened feeling likely to arise from the charge brought. It being certain that this more than anything else is the admirable quality of those arguments which appeal to our sense of shame, that they possess two contrary advantages. On the one hand, one cuts deeper than by open invective: on the other hand, it causes the person reprimanded to bear that severer stab with more entire patience.

[5.] "Ye have reigned without us." Herein there is great force, as concerns both the teachers and the disciples: and their ignorance, too, of themselves (τὸ ἀσυνείδητον.) is pointed out, and their great inconsideration. For what he saith is this: "In labors indeed," saith he, "all things are common both to us and to you, but in the rewards and the crowns ye are first. Not that I say this in vexation:" wherefore he added also, "I would indeed that ye did reign:" then, lest there should seem to be some irony, he added, "that we also might reign with you;" for, saith he, we also should be in possession (ἐπιτύχοιμεν, MS. Reg., ἐπιτύχωμεν Edd.) of these blessings. Dost thou see how he shews in himself all at once his severity and his care over them and his self-denying mind? Dost thou see how he takes down their pride?

Ver. 9. "For I think that God hath set forth us the Apostles last of all, as men doomed to death."

There is great depth of meaning and severity implied again in his saying, "us:" and not even with this was he satisfied, but added also his dignity, hitting them vehemently: "us the Apostles;" who are enduring such innumerable ills; who are sowing the word of Godliness; who are leading you unto this severe rule of life. These "He hath set forth last, as doomed to death," that is, as condemned. For since he had said, "That we also might reign with you," and by that expression had relaxed his vehemency in order not to dispirit them; he takes it up again with greater gravity, and saith, "For I think that God hath set forth us the Apostles last, as men doomed to death." "For according to what I see," saith he, "and from what

ye say, the most abject of all men and emphatically the condemned, are we who are put forward for continual suffering. But ye have already a kingdom and honors and great rewards in your fancy." And wishing to carry out their reasoning to still greater absurdity, and to exhibit it as incredible in the highest degree, he said not merely, "We are 'last,'" but, "God made us last;" nor was he satisfied with saying, "last," but he added also, "doomed to death:" to the end that even one quite void of understanding might feel the statement to be quite incredible, and his words to be the words of one vexed and vehemently abashing them.

Observe too the good sense of Paul. The topics by which, when it is the proper time, he exalts and shews himself honorable and makes himself great; by these he now puts them to shame, calling himself "condemned." Of so great consequence is it to do all things at the befitting season. By "doomed to death," in this place he means "condemned," and deserving of ten thousand deaths.

[6.] "For we are made a spectacle unto the world, and to angels, and to men."

What means, "We are become a spectacle unto the world?" "Not in a single corner nor yet in a small part of the world suffer we these things," saith he; "but every where and before all." But what means, "unto angels?" It is possible to "become a spectacle unto men," but not so unto angels, when the things done are ordinary. But our wrestlings are such as to be worthy even of angelic contemplation. Behold from the things by which he vilifies himself, how again he shows himself great; and from the things about which they are proud, how he displays their meanness. For since to be fools was accounted a meaner thing than to appear wise; to be weak, than to be made strong; and unhonored, than glorious and distinguished; and that he is about to cast on them the one set of epithets, while he himself accepted the other; he signifies that the latter are better than the former; if at least because of them he turned the throng I say not of men only, but also of the very angels unto the contemplation of themselves. For not with men only is our wrestling but also with incorporeal powers. Therefore also a mighty theatre is set (μέγα θέατρον κάθηται.)

Ver. 10. "We are fools for Christ's sake, but ye are wise in Christ."

Again, this also he spake in a way to abash them; implying that it is impossible for these contraries to agree, neither can things so distant from one another concur. "For how can it be," saith he, "that you should be wise, but we fools in the things relating to Christ?" That is: the one sort beaten and despised and dishonored and esteemed as nothing; the others enjoying honor and looked up to by many as a wise and prudent kind of people; it gives him occasion to speak thus: as if he had said, " How can it be that they who preach such things should be looked upon as practically engaged in their contraries?"

"We are weak, but ye are strong." That is, we are driven about and persecuted; but ye enjoy security and are much waited upon; howbeit the nature of the Gospel endureth it not.

"We are despised, but ye are honorable." Here he setteth himself against the noble and those who plumed themselves upon external advantages.

"Even unto this present hour we both hunger, and thirst, and are naked, and are buffeted, and have no certain dwelling place; and we toil, working with our own hands." That is, " It is not an old story that I am telling but just what the very time present bears me witness of: that of human things we take no account nor yet of any outward pomp; but we look unto God only." Which thing we too have need to practice in every place. For not only are angels looking on, but even more than they He that presides over the spectacle.

[7.] Let us not then desire any others to applaud us. For this is to insult Him; hastening by Him, as if insufficient to admire us, we make the best of our way to our fellow servants. For just as they who contend in a small theatre seek a large one, as if this were insufficient for their display; so also do they, who contending in the sight of God afterwards seek the applause of men; giving up the greater praise and eager for the less, they draw upon themselves severe punishment. What but this hath turned every thing upside down? this puts the whole world into confusion, that we do all things with an eye to men, and even for our good things, we esteem it nothing to have God as an admirer, but seek the approbation which cometh from our fellow-servants: and for the contrary things again, despising Him we fear men. And yet surely they shall stand with us before that tribunal, doing us no good. But God whom we despise now shall Himself pass the sentence upon us.

But yet, though we know these things, we still gape after men, which is the first of sins. Thus were a man looking on no one would choose to commit fornication; but even though he be ten thousand times on fire with that plague, the tyranny of the passion is conquered by his reverence for men. But in God's sight men not only commit adultery and fornication; but other things also much more dreadful many have dared and still dare to do. This then alone, is it not enough to bring down from above ten thousand thunderbolts? Adulteries,

did I say, and fornications? Nay, things even far less than these we fear to do before men: but in God's sight we fear no longer. From hence, in fact, all the world's evils have originated; because in things really bad we reverence not God but men.

On this account, you see, both things which are truly good, not accounted such by the generality, become objects of our aversion, we not investigating the nature of the things, but having respect unto the opinon of the many: and again, in the case of evil things, acting on this same principle. Certain things therefore not really good, but seeming fair unto the many, we pursue, as goods, through the same habit. So that on either side we go to destruction.

[8.] Perhaps many may find this remark somewhat obscure. Wherefore we must express it more clearly. When we commit uncleanness, (for we must begin from the instances alleged,) we fear men more than God. When therefore we have thus subjected ourselves unto them and made them lords over us; there are many other things also which seem unto these our lords to be evil, not being such; these also we flee for our part in like manner. For instance; To live in poverty, many account disgraceful: and we flee poverty, not because it is disgraceful nor because we are so persuaded, but because our masters count it disgraceful; and we fear them. Again, to be unhonored and contemptible, and void of all authority seems likewise unto the most part a matter of great shame and vileness. This again we flee; not condemning the thing itself, but because of the sentence of our masters.

Again on the contrary side also we undergo the same mischief. As wealth is counted a good thing, and pride, and pomp, and to be conspicuous. Accordingly this again we pursue, not either in this case from considering the nature of the things as good, but persuaded by the opinion of our masters. For the people is our master and the great mob (δ $\pi o \lambda \dot{v} \varsigma$ $\delta \chi \lambda o \varsigma$); a savage master and a severe tyrant: not so much as a command being needed in order to make us listen to him; it is enough that we just know what he wills, and without a command we submit: so great good will do we bear towards him. Again, God threatening and admonishing day by day is not heard; but the common people, full of disorder, made up of all manner of dregs, has no occasion for one word of command; enough for it only to signify with what it is well pleased, and in all things we obey immediately.

[9.] "But how," says some one, "is a man to flee from these masters?" By getting a mind greater than their's; by looking into the nature of things; by condemning the voice of the multitude; before all, by training himself in things really disgraceful to fear not men, but the unsleeping Eye ; and again, in all good things, to seek the crowns which come from Him. For thus neither in other sort of things shall we be able to tolerate them. For whoso when he doeth right judges them unworthy to know his good deeds, and contents himself with the suffrage of God ; neither will he take account of them in matters of the contrary sort.

" And how can this be ? " you will say. Consider what man is, what God ; whom thou desertest, and unto whom thou fliest for refuge ; and thou wilt soon be right altogether. Man lieth under the same sin as thyself, and the same condemnation, and the same punishment. " Man is like to vanity," (Psalm cxliv. 4. LXX,) and hath not correct judgment, and needs the correction from above. " Man is dust and ashes," and if he bestow praise, he will often bestow it at random, or out of favor, or ill will. And if he calumniate and accuse, this again will he do out of the same kind of purpose. But God doeth not so : rather irreprovable in His sentence, and pure His judgment. Wherefore we must always flee to Him for refuge ; and not for these reasons alone, but because He both made, and more than all spares thee, and loves thee better than thou dost thyself.

Why then, neglecting to have so admirable (θαυμαστόν) an approver, betake we ourselves unto man, who is nothing, all rashness, all at random? Doth he call thee wicked and polluted when thou art not so? So much the more do thou pity him, and weep because he is corrupt ; and despise his opinion, because the eyes of his understanding are darkened. For even the Apostles were thus evil reported of ; and they laughed to scorn their calumniators. But doth he call thee good and kind? If such indeed thou art, yet be not at all puffed up by the opinion : but if thou art not such, despise it the more, and esteem the thing to be mockery.

Wouldest thou know the judgments of the greater part of men, how corrupt they are, how useless, and worthy of ridicule ; some of them coming only from raving and distracted persons, others from children at the breast? Hear what hath been from the beginning. I will tell thee of judgments, not of the people only, but also of those who passed for the wisest, of those who were legislators from the earliest period. For who would be counted wiser among the multitude than the person considered worthy of legislating for cities and peoples? But yet to these wise men fornication seems to be nothing evil nor worthy of punishment. At least, no one of the heathen laws makes its penal or brings men to trial on account of it. And should any one bring another into court for things of that kind,

the multitude laughs it to scorn, and the judge will not suffer it. Dice-playing, again, is exempt from all their punishments : nor did any one among them ever incur penalty for it. Drunkenness and gluttony, so far from being a crime, are considered by many even as a fine thing. And in military carousals it is a point of great emulation ; and they who most of all need a sober mind and a strong body, these are mcst of all given over to the tyranny of drunkenness ; both utterly weakening the body and darkening the soul. Yet of the lawgivers not one hath punished this fault. What can be worse than this madness ?

Is then the good word of men so disposed an object of desire to thee, and dost thou not hide thyself in the earth? For even though all such admired thee, oughtest thou not to feel ashamed and cover thy face, at being applauded by men of such corrupt judgment ?

Again, blasphemy by legislators in general is accounted nothing terrible. At any rate, no one for having blasphemed God was ever brought to trial and punishment. But if a man steal another's garment, or cut his purse, his sides are flayed, and he is often given over unto death : while he that blasphemeth God hath nothing laid to his charge by the heathen legislators. And if a man seduce a female servant when he hath a wife, it seems nothing to the heathen laws nor to men in general.

[10.] Wilt thou hear besides of some things of another class which shew their folly? For as they punish not these things, so there are others which they enforce by law. What then are these? They collect crowds to fill theatres, and there they introduce choirs of harlots and prostituted children, yea such as trample on nature herself ; and they make the whole people sit on high, and so they captivate their city ; so they crown thcse mighty kings whom they are perpetually admiring for their trophies and victories. And yet, what can be more insipid than this honor? what more undelightful than this delight? From among these then seekest thou judges to applaud thy deeds? And is it in company with dancers, and effeminate, and buffoons, and harlots, that thou art fain to enjoy the sound of compliment? answer me.

How can these things be other than proofs of extreme infatuation? For I should like to ask them, is it or is it not, a dreadful thing to subvert the laws of nature, and introduce unlawful intercourse? They will surely [1] say, it is dreadful : at any rate, they make a show of inflicting a penalty on that crime. Why then dost thou bring on the stage those abused wretches ; and not only bring them in, but honor them also with honors

---

[1] (πάντες Savile; πάντως Bened.) [Dr. Field adopts the former reading. C.]

innumerable, and gifts not to be told? In other places thou punishest those who dare such things; but here even as on common benefactors of the city, thou spendest money upon them and supportest them at the public expense.

"However," thou wilt say, "they are (ἄτιμοι) infamous[1]." Why then train them up? (παιδοτριβεῖς) Why choose the infamous to pay honor to kings withal? And why ruin our (ἐκτραχηλίζεις, Plutarch, περὶ παίδων ἀγωγῆς, c. 17.) cities[2]? Or why spend so much upon these persons? Since if they be infamous expulsion is properest for the infamous. For why didst thou render them infamous? in praise or in condemnation? Of course in condemnation. Is the next thing to be, that although as after condemnation you make them infamous, yet as if they were honorable you run to see them, and admire and praise and applaud? Why need I speak of the sort of charm[3] which is found in the horse races? or in the contests of the wild beasts? For those places too being full of all senseless excitement train the populace to acquire a merciless and savage and inhuman kind of temper, and practise them in seeing men torn in pieces, and blood flowing, and the ferocity of wild beasts confounding all things. Now all these our wise lawgivers from the beginning introduced, being so many plagues! and our cities applaud and admire.

[11.] But, if thou wilt, dismissing these things which clearly and confessedly are abominable, but seemed (οὐκ ἔδοξεν. perhaps "were not decreed.") not [so] to the heathen legislators, let us proceed to their grave precepts; and thou shalt see these too corrupted through the opinion of the multitude. Thus marriage is accounted an honorable thing (Heb. xiii. 4.) both by us and by those without: and it is honorable. But when marriages are solemnized, such ridiculous things[4] take place as ye shall hear

of immediately: because the most part, possessed and beguiled by custom, are not even aware of their absurdity, but need others to teach them. For dancing, and cymbals, and flutes, and shameful words, and songs, and drunkenness, and revellings, and all the Devil's great heap (πολὺς ὁ τοῦ διαβόλου φορυτός) of garbage is then introduced.

I know indeed that I shall appear ridiculous in finding fault with these things; and shall incur the charge of great folly with the generality, as disturbing the ancient laws: for, as I said before, great is the deceptive power of custom. But nevertheless, I will not cease repeating these things: for there is, there is surely a chance, that although not all, yet some few will receive our saying and will choose to be laughed to scorn with us, rather than we laugh with them such a laughter as deserves tears and overflowing punishment and vengeance.

For how can it be other than worthy of the utmost condemnation that a damsel who hath spent her life entirely at home and been schooled in modesty from earliest childhood, should be compelled on a sudden to cast off all shame, and from the very commencement of her marriage be instructed in imprudence; and find herself put forward in the midst of wanton and rude men, and unchaste, and effeminate? What evil will not be implanted in the bride from that day forth? Immodesty, petulance, insolence, the love of vain glory: since they will naturally go on and desire to have all their days such as these. Hence our women become expensive and profuse; hence are they void of modesty, hence proceed their unnumbered evils.

And tell me not of the custom: for if it be an evil thing, let it not be done even once: but if good, let it be done constantly. For tell me, is not committing fornication evil? Shall we then allow just once this to be done? By no means. Why? Because though it be done only once, it is evil all the same. So also that the bride be entertained in this way, if it be evil, let it not be done even once; but if it be not evil, let it even be done always.

"What then," saith one, "dost thou find fault with marriage? tell me." That be far from me. I am not so senseless: but the things which are so unworthily appended to marriage, the painting the face, the coloring the eyebrows, and all the other niceness of that kind. For indeed from that day she will receive many lovers even before her destined consort.

---

[1] Bingham (b. xvi. c. 4. §. 10.) proves that actors and the like were debarred from the Sacraments, except they renounced their calling, from very early times: from S. Cyprian, Ep. 61, who says, "I think it inconsistent with the majesty of God and the discipline of the Gospel, to allow the chastity and glory of the Church to be defiled with so base contagion:" from Tertullian; *de Spectac.* 4; *de Cor. Mil.* 13; and from the Apostolical Constitutions, viii. 32.

[2] Gibbon, c. 31. from Ammianus, relates, that on occasion of a scarcity, when all strangers were expelled from Rome, an exception was made in favor of the actors, singers, dancers, &c.

[3] μαγγανείας. Compare S. Augustin's account in the Confessions of the way in which some persons were bewitched by the gladiatorial shows; of which his friend Alypius in his youth was a remarkable instance. b. vi. §. 13.

[4] S. Chrys. on Gen. Hom. 48. near the end, speaking of Rebekah's veiling herself at sight of Isaac; "See the noble breeding of the maiden. . . . . . and observe here, I pray you, how there is no place here for these superfluous and useless things; for a diabolical procession, for cymbals and flutes and dances, and those revels, the device of Satan, and invectives full of all indecency; but all wisdom, all gravity, all thoughtfulness. . . . . . Let Rebekah be the pattern of our wives, let our husbands emulate Isaac; be it their endeavor thus to bring home their brides." Then complaining, nearly as in the text, of the Fescennine verses, as they were called, and other bad customs, relics of heathenism, "Rather," says he, "should the maiden be trained in all modesty from the beginning, and priests called, and prayers and blessings be used to rivet fast the concord of their common habitation, that so both the bridegroom's love may increase, and the damsel's purity of soul be heightened. So by all ways shall the deeds of

virtue enter into that house, and all the acts of the devil be far off and they shall pass their life with joy, God's Providence bringing them together." So again Hom. 56. of the marriage of Jacob and Leah: in which place he complains especially of the introduction of people from the stage and orchestra at wedding feasts. See both places in Bingham, xxii. iv. 8: as also the 53d Canon of Laodicea: "It is wrong for Christians attending marriages to practise theatrical gestures or dances, but to take their part soberly in the morning or evening meal, as becometh Christians."

"But many will admire the woman for her beauty." And what of that? Even if discreet, she will hardly avoid evil suspicion; but if careless, she will be quickly overtaken, having got that very day a starting point in dissolute behavior.

Yet though the evils are so great, the omission of these proceedings is called an insult, by certain who are no better than brute beasts, and they are indignant that the woman is not exhibited to a multitude, that she is not set forth as a stage spectacle, common to all beholders: whereas most assuredly they should rather count it insult when these things do take place; and a laughing stock, and a farce. For even now I know that men will condemn me of much folly and make me a laughing stock : but the derision I can bear when any gain accrues from it. For I should indeed be worthy of derision, if while I was exhorting to contempt of the opinion of the many, I myself, of all men, were subdued by that feeling.

Behold then what follows from all this. Not in the day only but also in the evening, they provide on purpose men that have well drunk, besotted, and inflamed with luxurious fare, to look upon the beauty of the damsel's countenance; nor yet in the house only but even through the market-place do they lead her in pomp to make an exhibition; conducting her with torches late in the evening so as that she may be seen of all : by their doings recommending nothing else than that henceforth she put off all modesty. And they do not even stop here; but with shameful words do they conduct her. And this with the multitude is a law. And runaway slaves and convicts, thousands of them and of desperate character, go on with impunity uttering whatever they please, both against her and against him who is going to take her to his home. Nor is there any thing solemn, but all base and full of indecency. Will it not be a fine lesson in chastity for the bride to see and hear such things? [Savile reads this sentence with a question.] And there is a sort of diabolical rivalry among these profligates to outdo one another in their zealous us of reproaches and foul words, whereby they put the whole company out of countenance, and those go away victorious who have found the largest store of railings and the greatest indecencies to throw at their neighbors.

Now I know that I am a troublesome, sort of person and disagreeable, and morose, as though I were curtailing life of some of its pleasure. Why, this is the very cause of my mourning that things so displeasing are esteemed a sort of pleasure. For how, I ask, can it be other than displeasing to be insulted and reviled? to be reproached by all, together with your

bride? If any one in the market-place speak ill of thy wife, thou makest ado without end and countest life not worth living : and can it be that disgracing thyself with thy future consort in the presence of the whole city, thou art pleased and lookest gay on the matter? Why, what strange madness is this!

"But," saith one, "the thing is customary." Nay, for this very reason we ought most to bewail it, because the devil hath hedged in the thing with custom. In fact, since marriage is a solemn thing and that which recruits our race and the cause of numerous blessings ; that evil one, inwardly pining and knowing that it was ordained as a barrier against uncleanness, by a new device introduces into it all kinds of uncleanness. At any rate, in such assemblages many virgins have been even corrupted. And if not so in every case, it is because for the time the devil is content with those words and those songs, so flagitious; with making a show of the bride openly, and leading the bridegroom in triumph through the market-place.

Moreover, because all this takes place in the evening, that not even the darkness may be a veil to these evils, many torches are brought in, suffering not the disgraceful scene to be concealed. For what means the vast throng, and what the wassail, and what the pipes? Most clearly to prevent even those who are in their houses and plunged [βαπτιζόμενοι] in deep sleep from remaining ignorant of these proceedings; that being wakened by the pipe and leaning to look out of the lattices, they may be witnesses of the comedy such as it is.

What can one say of the songs themselves, crammed as they are with all uncleanness, introducing monstrous amours, and unlawful connections, and subversions of houses, and tragic scenes without end; and making continual mention of the titles of "friend and lover," "mistress and beloved?" And, what is still more grievous, that young women are present at these things, having divested themselves of all modesty ; in honor of the bride, rather I should say to insult her, exposing even their own salvation [1], and in the midst of wanton young men acting a shameless part with their disorderly songs, with their foul words, with their devilish harmony. Tell me then : dost thou still enquire, "Whence come adulteries? Whence fornications? Whence violations of marriage?"

[12.] "But they are not noble nor decent women," you will say, "who do these things." Why then laugh me to scorn for this remonstrance, having been thyself aware of this law, before I said any thing. I say, if the proceed-

[1] τῆς ἑαυτῶν προτείνουσαι σωτηρίας. The Benedictine translates as if it were τὰς ἑαυτῶν : which is here followed. [The true reading as given by Field is τὴν ἑαυτῶν προπίνουσαι σωτηρίαν. C.]

ings are right, allow those well-born women also to enact them. For what if these others live in poverty? Are not they also virgins? ought not they also to be careful of chastity? But now here is a virgin dancing in a public theatre of licentious youths; and, I ask, seems she not unto thee more dishonored than a harlot?

But if you say, "Female servants do these things;" neither so do I acquit thee of my charge: for neither to these ought such things to have been permitted. For hence all these evils have their origin, that of our household we make no account. But it is enough in the way of contempt to say, "He is a slave," and, "They are handmaids." And yet, day after day we hear, (Gal. iii. 28.) "In Christ Jesus there is neither bond nor free." Again, were it a horse or an ass, thou dost not overlook it but takest all pains not to have it of an inferior kind; and thy slaves who have souls like thine own dost thou neglect? And why do I say slaves, when I might says sons and daughters? What then must follow? It cannot be but grief (λύπην, qu. λύμην, "mischief.") must immediately enter in, when all these are going to ruin. And often also very great losses must ensue, valuable golden ornaments being lost in the crowd and the confusion.

[13.] Then after the marriage if perchance a child is born, in this case again we shall see the same folly and many practices [σύμβολα] full of absurdity. For when the time is come for giving the infant a name, caring not to call it after the saints as the ancients at first did, they light lamps and give them names, and name the child after that one which continues burning the longest; from thence conjecturing that he will live a long time. After all, should there be many instances of the child's untimely death, (and there are many,) great laughter on the devil's part will ensue, at his having made sport of them as if they were silly children. What shall we say about the amulets and the bells which are hung upon the hand, and the scarlet woof, and the other things full of such extreme folly; when they ought to invest the child with nothing else save the protection of the Cross[1]. But now that is despised which hath converted the whole world and given the sore wound to the devil and overthrown all his power: while the thread, and the woof, and the other amulets of that kind are entrusted with the child's safety.

May I mention another thing yet more ridiculous than this? Only let no one tax us with speaking out of season, should our argument proceed with that instance also. For he that would cleanse an ulcer will not hesitate first to pollute his own hands. What then is this so very ridiculous custom? It is counted indeed as

nothing; (and this is why I grieve;) but it is the beginning of folly and madness in the extreme. The women in the bath, nurses and waiting-maids, take up mud and smearing it with the finger make a mark on the child's forehead; and if one ask, What means the mud, and the clay? the answer is, "It turneth away an evil eye, witchcraft and envy[2]." Astonishing! what power in the mud! what might in the clay! what mighty force is this which it has? It averts all the host of the devil. Tell me, can ye help hiding yourselves for shame? Will ye never come to understand the snares of the devil, how from earliest life he gradually brings in the several evils which he hath devised? For if the mud hath this effect, why dost thou not thyself also do the same to thine own forehead, when thou art a man and thy character is formed; and thou art likelier than the child to have such as envy thee? Why dost thou not as well bemire the whole body? I say, if on the forehead its virtue be so great, why not anoint thyself all over with mud? All this is mirth and stage-play to Satan, not mockery only but hell-fire being the consummation to which these deceived ones are tending.

[14.] Now that among Greeks such things should be done is no wonder: but among the worshippers of the Cross, (τὸν σταυρὸν προσκυνοῦσι) and partakers in unspeakable mysteries, and professors of such high morality, (τοσαῦτα φιλοσοφοῦσιν) that such unseemliness should prevail, this is especially to be deplored again and again. God hath honored thee with spiritual anointing; and dost thou defile thy child with mud? God hath honored thee, and dost thou dishonor thyself? And when thou shouldest inscribe on his forehead the Cross which affords invincible security; dost thou forego this, and cast thyself into the madness of Satan?

If any look on these things as trifles, let them know that they are the source of great evils; and that not even unto Paul did it seem right to overlook the lesser things. For, tell me, what can be less than a man's covering his head? Yet observe how great a matter he makes of this and with how great earnestness he forbids it; saying, among many things, "He dishonoreth his head." (i Cor. xi. 4.) Now if he that covers himself "dishonoreth his head"; he that besmears his child with mud, how can it be less than making it abominable? For how, I want to know, can he bring it to the hands of the priest? How canst thou require that on that forehead the seal[3] should be placed by the hand

---

[1] Compare St. Chrys. on Coloss. Hom viii. near the end.

[2] So on Col. ubi supra. "What is all this folly? Here we have ashes, and soot, and salt, and the silly old woman again brought into play. Truly it is a mockery and a shame. 'Nay,' says she, 'an evil eye has caught hold of the child!' How long will you go on with these diabolical fancies?" &c.

[3] i. e. the sign of the cross in baptism, made with consecrated balm or ointment, and called σφραγίς in the Apostolical Constitu-

of the presbyter, where thou hast been smearing the mud? Nay, my brethren, do not these things, but from earliest life encompass them with spiritual armor and instruct them to seal the forehead with the hand (τῇ χειρὶ παιδεύτε σφραγίζειν τὸ μέτωπον): and before they are able to do this with their own hand[1], do you imprint upon them the Cross.

Why should one speak of the other satanical observances in the case of travail-pangs and childbirths, which the midwives introduce with a mischief on their own heads? Of the outcries which take place at each person's death, and when he is carried to his burial; the irrational wailings, the folly enacted at the funerals; the zeal about men's monuments; the importunate and ridiculous swarm of the mourning women[2]; the observances of days; the days, I mean, of entrance into the world and of departure?

[15.] Are these then, I beseech you, the persons whose good opinion thou followest after? And what can it be but the extreme of folly to seek earnestly the praise of men, so corrupt in their ideas, men whose conduct is all at random? when we ought always to resort to the unsleeping Eye, and look to His sentence in all that we do and speak? For these, even if they approve, will have no power to profit us. But He, should He accept our doings, will both here make us glorious, and in the future day will impart to us of the unspeakable good things: which may it be the lot of us all to obtain, through the grace and loving-kindness of our Lord Jesus Christ; with Whom to the Father and the Holy Spirit be glory, power, honor, now and always, and unto everlasting ages. Amen.

HOMILY XIII.

I COR. iv. 10.

"We are fools for Christ's sake:" (For it is necessary from this point to resume our discourse:) "but ye are wise in Christ: we are weak, but ye are strong: ye have glory, but we have dishonor."

HAVING filled his speech with much severity which conveys a sharper blow than any direct charge and having said, "Ye have reigned without us;" and "God hath set forth us last, as men doomed to death" he shows by what comes next how they are "doomed to death;" saying, We are fools, and weak, and despised, and hunger, and thirst, and are naked, and are buffeted, and have no certain dwelling place, and toil, working with our own hands:" which were very signs of genuine teachers and apostles. Whereas the others prided themselves on the things which are contrary to these, on wisdom, glory, wealth, consideration.

Desiring therefore to take down their self-conceit and to point out that in respect of these things, so far from taking credit to themselves, they ought rather to be ashamed; he first of all mocks them, saying, "Ye have reigned without us." As if he had said, "My sentence is that the present is not a time of honor nor of glory, which kind of things you enjoy, but of persecution and insult, such as we are suffering. If however it be not so; if this rather be the time of remuneration: then as far as I see," (but this he saith in irony,) "ye, the disciples, for your part have become no less than kings: but we the teachers and apostles, and before all entitled to receive the reward, not only have fallen very far behind you, but even, as persons doomed to death, that is, condemned convicts, spend our lives entirely in dishonors, and dangers, and hunger: yea insulted as fools, and driven about, and enduring all intolerable things."

Now these things he said that he might hereby cause them also to consider, that they should zealously seek the condition of the Apostles; their dangers and their indignities, not their honors and glories. For these, not the other, are what the Gospel requires. But to this effect he speaks not directly, not to shew himself disagreeable to them: rather in a way characteristic of himself he takes in hand this rebuke. For if he had introduced his address in a direct manner, he would have spoken thus; "Ye err, and are beguiled, and have swerved far from the apostolical mode of instruction. For every apostle and minister of Christ ought to be esteemed a fool, ought to live in affliction and

---

tions, iii. 17; vid. Bingham xi. 9. 6. St. Chrysostom, it may be remarked, takes for granted, 1. that infants would be brought to baptism; 2. that they would be brought to the priest.

[1] Compare the well-known passages in Tertullian and St. Cyprian: the first, "At all our goings out and comings in, &c. we trace upon the forehead the sign of the cross;" de Cor. Mil. 3.: the other, "Arm your foreheads with all boldness, that the sign of the cross may be safe." Ep. 50: both in Bingham ubi supra.

[2] About this custom, of hiring heathen women as mourners, he speaks very strongly elsewhere; Hom. 32. in Matt, Hom. 4. in Heb. both which are quoted in Bingham, xxxiii. 18.

dishonor ; which indeed is our state : whereas you are in the contrary case."

But thus might his expressions have offended them yet more, as containing but praises of the Apostles ; and might have made them fiercer, censured as they were for indolence and vainglory and luxuriousness. Wherefore he conducts not his statement in this way, but in another, more striking but less offensive ; and this is why he proceeds with his address as follows, saying ironically, "But ye are strong and honorable ;" since, if he had not used irony, he would have spoken to this effect ; "It is not possible that one man should be esteemed foolish, and another wise ; one strong, and another weak ; the Gospel requiring both the one and the other. For if it were in the nature of things that one should be this, and another that, perchance there might be some reason in what you say. But now it is not permitted, either to be counted wise, or honorable, or to be free from dangers. If otherwise, it follows of necessity that you are preferred before us in the sight of God ; you the disciples before us the teachers, and that after our endless hardships." If this be too bad for anyone to say, it remains for you to make our condition your object.

[2.] And "let no one," saith he, "think that I speak only of the past :"

Ver. 11. "Even unto this present hour we both hunger and thirst and are naked." Seest thou that all the life of Christians must be such as this ; and not merely a day or two? For though the wrestler who is victorious in a single contest only, be crowned, he is not crowned again if he suffer a fall.

"And hunger ;" against the luxurious. "And are buffeted ;" against those who are puffed up. "And have no certain dwelling-place ;" for we are driven about. "And are naked ;" against the rich.

Ver. 12. "And labor ;" now against the false apostles who endure neither toil nor peril, while they themselves receive the fruits. "But not so are we," saith he : "but together with our perils from without, we also strain ourselves to the utmost with perpetual labor. And what is still more, no one can say that we fret at these things, for the contrary is our requital to them that so deal with us : this, I say, is the main point, not our suffering evil, for that is common to all, but our suffering without despondency or vexation. But we so far from desponding are full of exultation. And a sure proof of this is our requiting with the contrary those who do us wrong."

Now as to the fact that so they did, hear what follows.

[Ver. 12, 13.] "Being reviled, we bless ; being persecuted, we endure ; being defamed, we entreat ; we are made as the filth of the world." This is the meaning of "fools for Christ's sake." For whoso suffers wrong and avenges not himself nor is vexed, is reckoned a fool by the heathen ; and dishonored and weak. And in order that he might not render his speech too unpalatable by referring the sufferings he was speaking of to their city, what saith he? "We are made the filth," not, "of your city," but, "of the world." And again, "the offscouring of all men ;" not of you alone, but of all. As then when he is discoursing of the providential care of Christ, letting pass the earth, the heaven, the whole creation, the Cross is what he brings forward ; so also when he desires to attract them to himself hurrying by all his miracles, he speaks of his sufferings on their account. So also it is our method when we be injured by any and despised, whatsoever we have endured for them, to bring the same forward.

"The offscouring of all men, even until now." This is a vigorous blow which he gave at the end, "of all men ;" "not of the persecutors only," saith he, "but of those also for whom we suffer these things : Oh greatly am I obliged to them." It is the expression of one seriously concerned ; not in pain himself, but desiring to make them feel, (πλῆξαι) that he who hath innumerable complaints to make should even salute them. And therefore did Christ command us to bear insults meekly that we might both exercise ourselves in a high strain of virtue, and put the other party to the more shame. For that effect one produces not so well by reproach as by silence.

Ver. 14. [3.] Then since he saw that the blow could not well be borne, he speedily heals it ; saying, "I write not these things to shame you, but to admonish you as my beloved children." "For not as abashing you," saith he, "do I speak these things." The very thing which by his words he had done, this he says he had not done : rather he allows that he had done it, not however with an evil and spiteful mind. Why, this mode of soothing is the very best, if we should say what we have to say and add the apology from our motive. For not to speak was impossible, since they would have remained uncorrected : on the other hand, after he had spoken, to leave the wound untended, were hard. Wherefore along with his severity he apologizes : for this so far from destroying the effect of the knife, rather makes it sink deeper in, while it moderates the full pain of the wound. Since when a man is told that not in reproach but in love are these things said, he the more readily receives correction.

However, even here also is great severity, and a strong appeal to their sense of shame, (ἐντροπή) in that he said not, "As a master" nor yet "as an apostle," nor yet "as having you for my disciples; (which had well suited his claims on them;) but, "as my beloved children I admonish you." And not simply, children; but, "longed after." "Forgive me," saith he. "If anything disagreeable has been said, it all proceeds of love." And he said not, "I rebuke," but, "I admonish." Now, who would not bear with a father in grief, and in the act of giving good advice? Wherefore he did not say this before, but after he had given the blow.

"What then?" some might say; "Do not other teachers spare us?" "I say not so, but, they carry not their forbearance so far." This however he spake not out at once, but by their professions and titles gave indication of it; "Tutor" and "Father" being the terms which he employs.

Ver. 15. [4.] "For though," saith he, "ye have ten thousand tutors in Christ, yet have ye not many fathers." He is not here setting forth his dignity, but the exceeding greatness of his love. Thus neither did he wound the other teachers: since he adds the clause, "in Christ:" but rather soothed them, designating not as parasites but as tutors those among them who were zealous and patient of labor: and also manifested his own anxious care of them. On this account he said not, "Yet not many masters," but, "not many fathers." So little was it his object to set down any name of dignity, or to argue that of him they had received the greater benefit: but granting to the others the great pains they had taken for the Corinthians, (for that is the force of the word Tutor,) the superiority in love he reserves for his own portion: for that again is the force of the word Father.

And he saith not merely, No one loves you so much; a statement which admitted not of being called in question; but he also brings forward a real fact. What then is this? "For in Christ Jesus I begat you through the Gospel. In Christ Jesus." Not unto myself do I impute this. Again, he strikes at those who gave their own names to their teaching. For "ye," saith he, "are the seal of mine Apostleship." And again, "I planted:" and in this place, "I begat." He said not, "I preached the word," but, "I begat;" using the words of natural relationship. (τοῖς τῆς φύσεως ὀνόμασι) For his one care at the moment was, to shew forth the love which he had for them. "For they indeed received you from me, and led you on; but that you are believers at all came to pass through me." Thus, because he had said, "as children;" lest you should suppose that the expression was flattery he produces also the matter of fact.

Ver. 16. [5.] "I beseech you, be ye imitators of me, as I also am of Christ." (κάθως κἀγὼ Χριστοῦ, omitted in our version: the Vulgate has it, see c. xi. 1.) Astonishing! How great is our teacher's boldness of speech! How highly finished the image, when he can even exhort others hereunto! Not that in self-exaltation he doth so, but implying that virtue is an easy thing. As if he had said, "Tell me not, 'I am not able to imitate thee. Thou art a Teacher, and a great one.' For the difference between me and you is not so great as between Christ and me: and yet I have imitated Him."

On the other hand, writing to the Ephesians, he interposes no mention of himself, but leads them all straight to the one point, "Be ye imitators of God," is his word. (Eph. v. 1.) But in this place, since his discourse was addressed to weak persons, he puts himself in by the way.

And besides, too, he signifies that it is possible even thus to imitate Christ. For he who copies the perfect impression of the seal, copies the original model.

Let us see then in what way he followed Christ: for this imitation needs not time and art, but a steady purpose alone. Thus if we go into the study of a painter, we shall not be able to copy the portrait, though we see it ten thousand times. But to copy him we are enabled by hearing alone. Will ye then that we bring the tablet before you and sketch out for you Paul's manner of life? Well, let it be produced, that picture far brighter than all the images of Emperors: for its material is not boards glued together, nor canvass stretched out; but the material is the work of God: being as it is a soul and a body: a soul, the work of God, not of men; and a body again in like wise.

Did you utter applause here? Nay, not here is the time for plaudits; but in what follows: for applauding, I say, and for imitating too: for so far we have but the material which is common to all without exception: inasmuch as soul differs not from soul in regard of its being a soul: but the purpose of heart shews the difference. For as one body differs not from another in so far as it is a body, but Paul's body is like every one's else, only dangers make one body more brilliant than another: just so is it in the case of the soul also.

[6.] Suppose then our tablet to be the soul of Paul: this tablet was lately lying covered with soot, full of spider's webs; (for nothing can be worse than blasphemy;) but when He came who transformeth all things, and saw that not through indolence or sluggishness were his lines so drawn but through inexperience and his not having the tints (τὰ ἄνθη) of true piety:

(for zeal indeed he had, but the colors were not there; for he had not "the zeal according to knowledge:") He gives him the tint of the truth, that is, grace: and in a moment he exhibited the imperial image. For having got the colors and learnt what he was ignorant of, he waited no time, but forthwith appeared a most excellent artist. And first he shews the head of the king, preaching Christ; then also the remainder of the body; the body of a perfect Christian life. Now painters we know shut themselves up and execute all their works with great nicety and in quiet; not opening the doors to any one: but this man, setting forth his tablet in the view of the world, in the midst of universal opposition, clamor, disturbance, did under such circumstances work out this Royal Image, and was not hindered. And therefore he said, "We are made a spectacle unto the world;" in the midst of earth, and sea, and the heaven, and the whole habitable globe, and the world both material and intellectual, he was drawing that portrait of his.

Would you like to see the other parts also thereof from the head downwards? Or will ye that from below we carry our description upwards? Contemplate then a statue of gold or rather of something more costly than gold, and such as might stand in heaven; not fixed with lead nor placed in one spot, but hurrying from Jerusalem even unto Illyricum, (Rom. xv. 19.) and setting forth into Spain, and borne as it were on wings over every part of the world. For what could be more "beautiful" than these "feet" which visited the whole earth under the sun? This same "beauty" the prophet also from of old proclaimeth, saying, (Is. LII. 7.) "How beautiful are the feet of them that preach the Gospel of peace!" Hast thou seen how fair are the feet? Wilt thou see the bosom too? Come, let me shew thee this also, and thou shalt behold it far more splendid than these beautiful, yea even than the bosom itself of the ancient lawgiver. For Moses indeed carried tablets of stone: but this man within him had Christ Himself: it was the very image of the King which he bore.

For this cause he was more awful than the Mercy Seat[1] and the Cherubim. For no such voice went out from them as from hence; but from them it talked with men chiefly about things of sense, from the tongue of Paul on the other hand about the things above the heavens. Again, from the Mercy Seat it spake oracles to the Jews alone; but from hence to the whole world: and there it was by things without life; but here by a soul instinct with virtue.

This Mercy Seat was brighter even than heaven, not shining forth with variety of stars nor with rays from the sun, but the very Sun of righteousness was there, and from hence He sent forth His rays. Again, from time to time in this our heaven, any cloud coursing over at times makes it gloomy; but that bosom never had any such storm sweeping across it. Or rather there did sweep over it many storms and oft: but the light they darkened not; rather in the midst of the temptation and dangers the light shone out. Wherefore also he himself when bound with his chain kept exclaiming, (2 Tim. ii. 9.) "The word of God is not bound." Thus continually by means of that tongue was It sending forth its rays. And no fear, no danger made that bosom gloomy. Perhaps the bosom seems to outdo the feet; however, both they as feet are beautiful, and this as a bosom.

Wilt thou see also the belly with its proper beauty? Hear what he saith about it, (ch. viii. 13.) "If meat make my brother to stumble, I will eat no flesh while the world standeth: (Rom. xiv. 21.) It is good neither to eat flesh nor to drink wine, nor anything whereby thy brother stumbleth, or is offended, or is made weak: (ch. vi. 13) Meats for the belly and the belly for meats." What can be more beautiful in its kind than this belly thus instructed to be quiet, and taught all temperance, and knowing how both to hunger and be famished, and also to suffer thirst? For as a well-trained horse with a golden bridle, so also did this walk with measured paces, having vanquished the necessity of nature. For it was Christ walking in it. Now this being so temperate, it is quite plain that the whole body of vice besides was done away.

Wouldst thou see the hands too? those which he now hath? Or wouldest thou rather behold first their former wickedness? (Acts viii. 3.) "Entering (this very man) into the houses, he haled," of late, "men and women," with the hands not of man, but of some fierce wild beast. But as soon as he had received the colors of the Truth and the spiritual experience, no longer were these the hands of a man, but spiritual; day by day being bound with chains. And they never struck any one, but they were stricken times without number. Once even a viper (Acts xxviii. 3, 5.) reverenced those hands: for they were the hands of a human being no longer; and therefore it did not even fasten on them.

And wilt thou see also the back, resembling as it does the other members? Hear what he saith about this also. (2 Cor. xi. 24, 25.) "Five times I received of the Jews forty stripes

---

[1] That is, probably, "of our Lord's Human Nature:" according to Theodoret on Rom. iii. 25. "The true Mercy Seat is the Lord Christ. The name suits Him as man, not as God: for as God, He Himself gives oracles from the Mercy Seat." And Theophylact on the same place: "It meant certainly the Human Nature, which was the Sheath of the Deity, covering It over." See Suicer on the word ἱλαστήριον. [This note is based upon a false reading, which has been corrected according to Field. C.]

save one; thrice was I beaten with rods, once was I stoned, thrice I suffered shipwreck, a night and a day I have been in the deep."

[7.] But lest we too should fall into an interminable deep, and be carried away far and wide, going over each of his members severally; come let us quit the body and look at another sort of beauty, that, namely, which proceeds from his garments; to which even devils shewed reverence; and therefore both they made off, and diseases took flight. And wheresoever Paul happened to shew himself, they all retired and got out of the way, as if the champion of the whole world had appeared. And as they who have been often wounded in war, should they see but some part of the armor of him that wounded them feel a shuddering; much in the same way the devils also, at sight of "handkerchiefs" only were astonied. Where be now the rich, and they that have high thoughts about wealth? Where they who count over their own titles and their costly robes? With these things if they compare themselves, it will be clay in their sight and dirt, all they have of their own. And why speak I of garments and golden ornaments? Why, if one would grant me the whole world in possession, the mere nail of Paul I should esteem more powerful than all that dominion: his poverty than all luxury: his dishonor, than all glory: his nakedness than all riches: no security would I compare with the buffeting of that sacred head: no diadem, with the stones to which he was a mark. This crown let us long for, beloved: and if persecution be not now, let us mean while prepare ourselves. For neither was he of whom we speak glorious by persecutions alone: for he said also, (1 Cor. ix. 27. ὑποπιέζω rec. text, ὑπωπίαζω) "I keep under my body;" now in this one may attain excellence without persecutions. And he exhorted not to (Rom. xiii. 14.) "make provision for the flesh to fulfill the lusts thereof." And again, (1 Tim. vi. 8.) "Having food and covering, let us be therewith content." For to these purposes we have no need of persecutions. And the wealthy too he sought to moderate, saying, (Ibid. 9.) "They that desire to be rich fall into temptation."

If therefore we also thus exercise ourselves, when we enter into the contest we shall be crowned: and though there be no persecution before us, we shall receive for these things many rewards. But if we pamper the body and live the life of a swine, even in peace we shall often sin and bear shame.

Seest thou not with whom we wrestle? With the incorporeal powers. How then, being ourselves flesh, are we to get the better of these? For if wrestling with men one have need to be temperate in diet, much more with evil spirits.

But when together with fulness of flesh we are also bound down to wealth, whence are we to overcome our antagonists? For wealth is a chain, a grievous chain, to those who know not how to use it; a tyrant savage and inhuman, imposing all his commands by way of outrage on those who serve him. Howbeit, if we will, this bitter tyranny we shall depose from its throne, and make it yield to us, instead of commanding. How then shall this be? By distributing our wealth unto all. For so long as it stands against us, each single handed, like any robber in a wilderness it works all its bad ends: but when we bring it forth among others, it will master us no more, holden as it will be in chains, on all sides, by all men.

[8.] And these things I say, not because riches are a sin: the sin is in not distributing them to the poor, and in the wrong use of them. For God made nothing evil but all things very good; so that riches too are good; i. e. if they do not master their owners; if the wants of our neighbors be done away by them. For neither is that light good which instead of dissipating darkness rather makes it intense: nor should I call that wealth, which instead of doing away poverty rather increases it. For the rich man seeks not to take from others but to help others: but he that seeks to receive from others is no longer rich, but is emphatically poor. So that it is not riches that are an evil, but the needy mind which turns wealth into poverty. These are more wretched than those who ask alms in the narrow streets, carrying a wallet and mutilated in body. I say, clothed in rags as they are, not so miserable as those in silks and shining garments. Those who strut in the marketplace are more to be pitied than those who haunt the crossings of the streets, and enter into the courts, and cry from their cellars, and ask charity. For these for their part do utter praises to God, and speak words of mercy and a strict morality. And therefore we pity them, and stretch out the hand, and never find fault with them. But those who are rich to bad purpose; cruelty and inhumanity, ravening and satanical lust, are in the words they belch out. And therefore by all are they detested and laughed to scorn. Do but consider; which of the two among all men is reckoned disgraceful, to beg of the rich or the poor. Every one, I suppose, sees it at once:—of the poor. Now this, if you mark it, is what the rich do; for they durst not apply to those who are richer than themselves: whereas those who beg do so of the wealthy: for one beggar asks not alms of another, but of a rich man; but the rich man tears the poor in pieces.

Again tell me, which is the more dignified, to receive from those who are willing and are obliged to you, or when men are unwilling, to compel and tease them? Clearly not to trouble those who are unwilling. But this also the rich do: for the poor receive from willing hands, and such as are obliged to them; but the rich from persons unwilling and repugnant, which is an indication of greater poverty. For if no one would like so much as to go to a meal, unless the inviter were to feel obliged to the guest, how can it be honorable to take one's share of any property by compulsion? Do we not on this account get out of the way of dogs and fly from their baying, because by their much besetting they fairly force us off? This also our rich men do.

"But, that fear should accompany the gift, is more dignified." Nay, this is of all most disgraceful. For he who moves heaven and earth about his gains, who can be so laughed to scorn as he? For even unto dogs, not seldom, through fear, we throw whatever we had hold of. Which I ask again, is more disgraceful? that one clothed with rags should beg, or one who wears silk? Thus when a rich man pays court to old and poor persons, so as to get possession of their property, and this when there are children, what pardon can he deserve?

Further: If you will, let us examine the very words; what the rich beggars say, and what the poor. What then saith the poor man? " That he who giveth alms will never have to give by measure ($\mu\epsilon\tau\rho\iota\acute{a}\sigma\epsilon\iota$ perhaps corrupt: conj. $\pi\epsilon\iota\nu\acute{a}\sigma\epsilon\iota$, "will never hunger); that he is giving of what is God's: that God is loving unto men, and recompenses more abundantly; all which are words of high morality, and exhortation, and counsel. For he recommends thee to look unto the Lord, and he takes away thy fear of the poverty to come. And one may perceive much instruction in the words of those who ask alms: but of what kind are those of the rich? Why, of swine, and dogs, and wolves, and all other wild beasts. For

some of them discourse perpetually on banquets, and dishes, and delicacies, and wine of all sorts, and ointments, and vestures, and all the rest of that extravagance. And others about the interest of money and loans. And making out accounts and increasing the mass of debts to an intolerable amount, as if it had begun in the time of men's fathers or grandfathers, one they rob of his house, another of his field, and another of his slave, and of all that he has. Why should one speak of their wills, which are written in blood instead of ink? For either by surrounding them with some intolerable danger, or else bewitching them with some paltry promises, whomsoever they may see in possession of some small property, those they persuade to pass by all their relations, and that oftentimes when perishing through poverty, and instead of them to enter their own names. Is there any madness and ferocity of wild beasts of any sort which these things do not throw into the shade?

[8.] Wherefore I beseech you, all such wealth as this let us flee, disgraceful as it is and in deaths abundant; and let us obtain that which is spiritual, and let us seek after the treasures in the heavens. For whoso possess these, they are the rich, they are the wealthy, both here and there enjoying things; even all things. Since whoso will be poor, according to the word of God, has all men's houses opened to him. For unto him that for God's sake has ceased to possess any thing, every one will contribute of his own. But whoso will hold a little with injustice, shutteth the doors of all against him. To the end, then, that we may attain both to the good things here and to those which are there, let us choose the wealth which cannot be removed, that immortal abundance: which may God grant us all to obtain, through the grace and loving-kindness of our Lord Jesus Christ, &c.

HOMILY XIV

1 Cor. iv. 17.

For this cause have I sent unto you Timothy, who is my beloved and faithful child in the Lord, who shall put you in remembrance of my ways which be in Christ Jesus.[1]

Consider here also, I entreat, the noble soul, the soul more glowing and keener than fire: how he was indeed especially desirous to be present himself with the Corinthians, thus distem-

pered and broken into parties. For he knew well what a help to the disciples his presence was and what a mischief his absence. And the former he declared in the Epistle to the Philippians, saying, (Phil. ii. 12. $\kappa\alpha\grave{\iota}$ om. in rec. text.) "Not as in my presence only, but also now much more in my absence, work out your own salvation with fear and trembling." The latter he signifies in this Epistle, saying, (ver.

---

[1] '$I\eta\sigma o\hat{v}$ om. in rec. text, [but retained it Rev. Vers.]

18.) "Now some are puffed up, as though I were not coming to you; but I will come." He was urgent, it seems, and desirous to be present himself. But as this was not possible for a time, he corrects them by the promise of his appearance; and not this only, but also by the sending of his disciple. "For this," he saith, "I have sent unto you Timothy." "For this cause:" how is that? "Because I care for you as for children, and as having begotten you." And the message is accompanied with a recommendation of his person: "Who is my beloved and faithful child in the Lord." Now this he said, both to shew his love of him, and to prepare them to look on him with respect. And not simply "faithful," but, "in the Lord;" that is, in the things pertaining to the Lord. Now if in worldly things it is high praise for a man to be faithful, much more in things spiritual.

If then he was his "beloved child," consider how great was Paul's love, in choosing to be separated from him for the Corinthian's sake, And if "faithful" also, he will be unexceptionable in his ministering to their affairs.

"Who shall put you in remembrance." He said not, "shall teach," lest they should take it ill, as being used to learn from himself. Wherefore also towards the end he saith, (1 Cor. xvi. 10, 11.) "For he worketh the work of the Lord, as I also do. Let no man therefore despise him." For there was no envy among the Apostles, but they had an eye unto one thing, the edification of the Church. And if he that was employed was their inferior, they did as it were support (συνεχρότουν) him with all earnestness. Wherefore neither was he contented with saying, "He shall put you in remembrance;" but purposing to cut out their envy more completely,—for Timothy was young,—with this view, I say, he adds, "my ways;" not "his," but "mine;" that is, his methods, (τὰς οἰκονομίας.) his dangers, his customs, his laws, his ordinances, his Apostolical Canons, and all the rest. For since he had said, "We are naked, and are buffeted, and have no certain dwelling place: all these things," saith he, "he will remind you of;" and also of the laws of Christ; for destroying all heresies. Then, carrying his argument higher, he adds, "which be in Christ;" ascribing all, as was his wont, unto the Lord, and on that ground establishing the credibility of what is to follow. Wherefore he subjoins, "Even as I teach every where in every church." "Nothing new have I spoken unto you: of these my proceedings all the other Churches are cognizant as well as you." Further: he calls them "ways in Christ," to shew that they have in them nothing human,

and that with the aid from that source he doth all things well.

[2.] And having said these things and so soothed them, and being just about to enter on his charge against the unclean person, he again utters words full of anger; not that in himself he felt so but in order to correct them: and giving over the fornicator, he directs his discourse to the rest, as not deeming him worthy even of words from himself; just as we act in regard to our servants when they have given us great offence.

Next, after that he had said, "I send Timothy, lest they should thereupon take things too easily, mark what he saith:

Ver. 18. "Now some are puffed up, as though I were not coming unto you." For there he glances both at them and at certain others, casting down their highmindedness: since the love of preeminence is in fault, when men abuse the absence of their teacher for their own self-will. For when he addresses himself unto the people, observe how he does it by way of appeal to their sense of shame; when unto the originators of the mischief, his manner is more vehement. Thus unto the former he saith, "We are the offscouring of all:" and soothing them he saith, "Not to shame you I write these things;" but to the latter, "Now as though I were not coming to you, some are puffed up;" shewing that their self-will argued a childish turn of mind. For so boys in the absence of their master wax more negligent.

This then is one thing here indicated; and another is that his presence was sufficient for their correction. For as the presence of a lion makes all living creatures shrink away, so also does that of Paul the corrupters of the Church.

Ver. 19. And therefore he goes on, "But I will come to you shortly, if the Lord will." Now to say this only would seem to be mere threatening. But to promise himself and demand from them the requisite proof by actions also; this was a course for a truly high spirit. Accordingly he added this too, saying,

"And I will know, not the word of them which are puffed up, but the power." For not from any excellencies of their own but from their teacher's absence, this self-will arose. Which again itself was a mark of a scornful mind towards him. And this is why, having said, "I have sent Timothy," he did not at once add, "I will come;" but waited until he had brought his charge against them of being "puffed up:" after that he saith, "I will come." Since, had he put it before the charge, it would rather have been an apology for himself as not having been deficient, instead of a threat; nor even so (οὕτως so the King's MS. οὗτος the rec. text.) would the statement have been convincing.

But as it is, placing it after the accusation, he rendered himself such as they would both believe and fear.

Mark also how solid and secure he makes his ground: for he saith not simply, "I will come:" but, "If the Lord will:" and he appoints no set time. For since he might perhaps be tardy in coming, by that uncertainty he would fain keep them anxiously engaged. And, lest they should hereupon fall back again, he added, "shortly,"

[2.] "And I will know, not the word of them that are puffed up, but the power." He said not, "I will know not the wisdom, nor the signs," but what? "not the word:" by the term he employs at the same time depressing the one and exalting the other. And for a while he is setting himself against the generality of them who were countenancing the fornicator. For if he were speaking of him, he would not say, "the power;" but, "the works," the corrupt works which he did.

Now why seekest thou not after "the word?" "Not because I am wanting in word but because all our doings are 'in power.'" As therefore in war success is not for those who talk much but those who effect much; so also in this case, not speakers, but doers have the victory. "Thou," saith he, "art proud of this fine speaking. Well, if it were a contest and a time for orators, thou mightest reasonably be elated thereat: but if of Apostles preaching truth, and by signs confirming the same, why art thou puffed up for a thing superfluous and unreal, and to the present purpose utterly inefficient? For what could a display of words avail towards raising the dead, or expelling evil spirits, or working any other such deed of wonder? But these are what we want now, and by these our cause stands." Whereupon also he adds,

Ver. 20. "For the kingdom of God is not in word, but in power." By signs, saith he, not by fine speaking, we have prevailed: and that our teaching is divine and really announces the Kingdom of Heaven we give the greater proof, namely, our signs which we work by the power of the Spirit. If those who are now puffed up desire to be some great ones; as soon as I am come, let them shew whether they have any such power. And let me not find them sheltering themselves behind a pomp of words: for that kind of art is nothing to us.

[4.] Ver. 21. "What will ye? Shall I come unto you with a rod, or in love and a spirit of meekness?"

There is much both of terrror and of gentleness in this saying. For to say, "I will know," was the language of one as yet withholding himself: but to say, "What will ye? Must I come unto you with a rod?" are the words of one thenceforth ascending the teacher's seat,

and from thence holding discourses with them and taking upon him all his authority.

What means, "with a rod?" With punishment, with vengeance: that is, I will destroy; I will strike with blindness: the kind of thing which Peter did in the case of Sapphira, and himself in the case of Elymas the sorcerer. For henceforth he no longer speaks as bringing himself into a close comparison with the other teachers, but with authority. And in the second Epistle too he appears to say the same, when he writes, "Since ye seek a proof of Christ speaking in me."

"Shall I come with a rod, or in love?" What then? to come with a rod, was it not an instance of love? Of love it was surely[1]. But because through his great love he shrinks back in punishing, therefore he so expresses himself.

Further; when he spoke about punishment, he said not, "in a spirit of meekness, but, [simply,] "with a rod:" and yet of that too the Spirit was author. For there is a spirit of meekness, and a spirit of severity. He doth not, however, choose so to call it, but from its milder aspect (ἀπὸ τῶν χρηστοτέρων.) And for a like reason also, God, although avenging Himself, has it often affirmed of Him that He is "gracious and long-suffering, and rich in mercy and pity:" but that He is apt to punish, once perhaps or twice, and sparingly, and that upon some urgent cause.

[5.] Consider then the wisdom of Paul; holding the authority in his own hands, he leaves both his and that in the power of others, saying. "What will ye?" "The matter is at your disposal."

For we too have depending on us both sides of the alternative; both falling into hell, and obtaining the kingdom: since God hath so willed it. For, "behold," saith he, "fire and water: whichever way thou wilt, thou mayest stretch forth thine hand" (Ecclus. xv. 16.) And, "If ye be willing, and will hearken unto me, ye shall eat the good of the land; (Is, i. 19,) but if ye be not willing, the sword shall devour you."

But perhaps one will say, "I am willing; (and no one is so void of understanding as not to be willing;) but to will is not sufficient for me." Nay, but it is sufficient, if thou be duly willing, and do the deeds of one that is willing, But as it is, thou art not greatly willing.

And let us try this in other things, if it seem good. For tell me, he that would marry a wife, is he content with wishing? By no means; but

---

[1] St. Augustin, "cont. Parmen, iii. 3. "Are we to suppose that "the rod" at all excludes "love," because he has given this turn to his sentence, 'Shall I come unto you with a rod,' or 'in love?' Nay, the following clause, 'And in a spirit of meekness,' hints what was passing in his mind—that the rod also has in it love. But love in severity is one thing, love in meekness another thing. The love is the same, but it works diversely in divers cases."

he looks out for women to advance his suit, and request friends to keep watch with him, and gets together money. Again, the merchant is not content with sitting at home and wishing, but he first hires a vessel, then selects sailors and rowers, then takes up money on interest, and is inquisitive about a market and the price of merchandise. Is it not then strange for men to shew themselves so much in earnest about earthly things, but that when they are to make a venture for heaven, they should be content with wishing only? rather I should say, not even in this do they shew themselves properly in earnest. For he that wills a thing as he ought, puts also his hand unto the means which lead to the object of his desire. Thus, when hunger compels thee to take nourishment, thou waitest not for the viands to come unto thee of their own accord, but omittest nothing to gather victuals together. So in thirst, and cold and all other such things, thou art industrious and duly prepared to take care of the body. Now do this in respect of God's kingdom also, and surely thou shalt obtain it.

For to this end God made thee a free agent, that thou mightest not afterwards accuse God, as though some necessity had bound thee : but thou, in regard of those very things wherein thou hast been honored, dost murmur.

For in fact I have often heard people say. " But why did He then make my goodness depend on me ? " Nay, but how was He to bring thee, slumbering and sleeping, and in love with all iniquity, and living delicately, and pampering thyself; how was He to bring thee up to heaven? If He had, thou wouldest not have abstained from vice. For if now, even in the face of threatening, thou dost not turn aside from thy wickedness; had he added no less than heaven as the end of thy race, when wouldest thou have ceased waxing more careless and worse by far? (χείρων πολλῷ. πολλῶν Bened.)

Neither again wilt thou be able to allege, He hath shewed me indeed what things were good but gave no help, for abundant also is His promise to thee of aid.

[6.] "But," say you, "Virtue is burden-"some and distasteful; while with vice great " pleasure is blended; and the one is wide and "broad, but the other strait and narrow."

Tell me then, are they respectively such throughout, or only from the beginning? For in fact what thou here sayest, thou sayest, not intending it, in behalf of virtue; so potent a thing is truth. For suppose there were two roads, the one leading to a furnace, and the other to a Paradise; and that the one unto the furnace were broad, the other unto Paradise, narrow; which road wouldest thou take in preference? For although you

may now gainsay for contradiction's sake, yet things which are plainly allowed on all hands, however shameless, you will not be able to gainsay. Now that that way is rather to be chosen which hath its beginning difficult but not its end, I will endeavor to teach you from what is quite obvious. And, if you please, let us first take in hand the arts. For these have their beginning full of toil, but the end gainful. "But," say you, "no one applies himself to an art without some one to compel him; for," you add, "so long as the boy is his own master, he will choose rather to take his ease at first, and in the end to endure the evil, how great soever, than to live hardly at the outset, and afterwards reap the fruit of those labors." Well then, to make such a choice comes of a mind left to itself, (ὀρφανικῆς διανοίας) and of childish idleness: but the contrary choice, of sense and manliness. And so it is with us : were we not children in mind, we should not be like the child aforesaid, forsaken (ὀρφάνῳ) as he is and thoughtless, but like him that hath a father. We must cast out then our own child-ish mind, and not find fault with the things themselves; and we must set a charioteer over our conscience, who will not allow us to indulge our appetite, but make us run and strive mightily. For what else but absurdity is it to inure our children with pains at first unto pursuits which have laborious beginnings, but their end good and pleasant; while we ourselves in spirit-ual things take just the contrary turn?

And yet even in those earthly things it is not quite plain that the end will be good and pleas-ant: since before now untimely death, or pov-erty, or false accusation, or reverse of fortune, or other such things, of which there are many, have caused men after their long toil to be deprived of all its fruits. What is more, those who have such pursuits, though they succeed, it is no great gain which they will reap. For with the present life all those things are dissolved. But here, not for such fruitless and perishable things is our race, neither have we fears about the end; but greater and more secure is our hope after our departure hence. What pardon then can there be, what excuse for those who will not strip themselves for the evils to be endured for virtue's sake?

And do they yet ask, "Wherefore is the way narrow?" Why, thou dost not deem it right that any fornicator or lewd or drunken (καὶ τῶν μεθυόντων inserted from the King's MS.) person should enter into the courts of earthly kings; and claimest thou for men to be let into heaven itself with licentiousness, and luxury, and drunk-enness, and covetousness, and all manner of iniquity? And how can these things be par-donable?

[7.] "Nay," you reply, "I say not that, but why has not virtue a "broad way?" In good truth if we be willing, its way is very easy. For whether is easier, tell me; to dig through a wall and take other men's goods and so be cast into prison; or to be content with what you have and freed from all fear? I have not however said all. For whether is easier, tell me; to steal all men's goods and revel in few of them for a short time, and then to be racked and scourged eternally; or having lived in righteous poverty for a short time, to live ever after in delights? (For let us not enquire as yet which is the more profitable, but for the present, which is the more easy.) Whether again is it pleasanter, to see a good dream and to be punished in reality; or after having had a disagreeable dream to be really in enjoyment? Of course the latter. Tell me then, In what sense dost thou call virtue harsh? I grant, it is harsh, tried by comparison with our carelessness. However, that it is really easy and smooth, hear what Christ saith, (S. Mat. xi. 30.) "My yoke is easy, and My burden is light." But if thou perceivest not the lightness, plainly it is for want of courageous zeal; since where that is, even heavy things are light; and by the same rule where it is not, even light things are heavy. For tell me, what could be sweeter and more easily obtained than the banquet of manna? Yet the Jews were discontented, though enjoying such delightful fare. What more bitter than hunger and all the other hardships which Paul endured? Yet he leaped up, and rejoiced, and said, (Col. 1. 24.) "Now I rejoice in my sufferings." What then is the cause? The difference of the mind. If then you frame this as it ought to be, you will see the easiness of virtue.

"What then," say you, "does she only become such through the mind of those who pursue her?" She is such, not from their mind alone, but by nature as well. Which I thus prove: If the one had been throughout a thing painful, the other throughout of the contrary sort, then with some plausibility might some fallen persons have said that the latter was easier than the former. But if they have their beginnings, the one in hardship, the other in pleasure, but their respective ends again just opposite to these; and if those ends be both infinite, in the one the pleasure, in the other the burthen; tell me, which is the more easy to choose?

"Why then do many not choose that which is easy?" Because some disbelieve; and others, who believe, have their judgment corrupt, and would prefer pleasure for a season to that which is everlasting. "Is not this then easy?" Not so: but this cometh of a sick soul. And as the reason why persons in a fever long after cool drink is not upon calculation that the momentary luxury is pleasanter than being burned up from beginning to end, but because they cannot restrain their inordinate desire; so also these. Since if one brought them to their punishment at the very moment of their pleasure, assuredly they never would have chosen it. Thus you see in what sense vice is not an easy thing.

[8.] But if you will, let us try this same point over again by an example in the proper subject matter. Tell me, for instance, which is pleasanter and easier? (only let us not take again the desire of the many for our rule in the matter; since one ought to decide, not by the sick, but by the whole; just as you might show me ten thousand men in a fever, seeking things unwholesome upon choice to suffer for it afterwards; but I should not allow such choice;) which, I repeat, brings more ease, tell me; to desire much wealth, or to be above that desire? For I, for my part, think the latter. If thou disbelieve it, let the argument be brought to the facts themselves.

Let us then suppose one man desiring much, another nothing. Which now is the better state, tell me, and which the more respectable? However, let that pass. For this is agreed upon, that the latter is a finer character than the former. And we are making no enquiry about this at present, but which lives the easier and pleasanter life? Well then: the lover of money will not enjoy even what he has: for that which he loves he cannot choose to spend; but would gladly even carve (χατα χόψειε) himself out, and part with his flesh rather than with his gold. But he that despises wealth, gains this the while, that he enjoys what he has quietly and with great security, and that he values himself more than it. Which then is the pleasanter; to enjoy what one has with freedom, or to live under a master, namely wealth, and not dare to touch a single thing even of one's own? Why, it seemeth to me to be much the same as if any two men, having wives and loving them exceedingly, were not upon the same terms with them; but the one were allowed the presence and intercourse of his wife, the other not even permitted to come near his.

There is another thing which I wish to mention, indicating the pleasure of the one and the discomfort of the other. He that is greedy of gain will never be stayed in that desire, not only because it is impossible, for him to obtain all men's goods, but also because whatever he may have compassed, he counts himself to have nothing. But the despiser of riches will deem it all superfluous, and will not have to punish his soul with endless desires. I say, punish; for nothing so completely answers the definition of punishment as desire deprived of gratification; a thing too which especially marks his perverse mind. Look at it in this way. He that lusts after riches and hath increased his store, he is the sort of person to feel as if he had nothing. I ask then, what more complicated than this disease? And the strange thing is not this only, but that although having, he thinks he has not the very things which are in his hold, and as though he had them not he bewails himself. If he even get all men's goods, his pain is but greater. And should he gain an hundred talents, he is vexed that he hath not received a thousand: and if he received a thousand; he is stung to the quick that it is not ten thousand: and if he receive ten thousand, he utterly bemoans himself (*κατα-κόπτεται*) because it is not ten times as much. And the acquisition of more to him becomes so much more poverty; for the more he receives so much the more he desires. So then, the more he receives, the more he becomes poor: since whoso desires more, is more truly poor. When then he hath an hundred talents, is he not very poor?[1] for he desires a thousand. When he hath got a thousand, then he becomes yet poorer. For it is no longer a thousand as before, but ten thousand that he professes himself to want. Now if you say that to wish and not to obtain is pleasure, you seem to me to be very ignorant of the nature of pleasure.

[9.] To shew that this sort of thing is not pleasure but punishment, take another case, and so let us search it out. When we are thirsty, do we not therefore feel pleasure in drinking because we quench our thirst; and is it not therefore a pleasure to drink because it relieves us from a great torment, the desire, I mean, of drinking? Every one, I suppose, can tell. But were we always to remain in such a state of desire, we should be as badly off as the rich man in the parable of Lazarus for the matter of punishment; for his punishment was just this that vehemently desiring one little drop, he obtained it not. And this very thing all covet-

ous persons seem to me continually to suffer, and to resemble him where he begs that he may obtain that drop, and obtains it not. For their soul is more on fire than his.

Well indeed hath one[2] said, that all lovers of money are in a sort of dropsy; for as they, bearing much water in their bodies, are the more burnt up: so also the covetous, bearing about with them great wealth, are greedy of more. The reason is that neither do the one keep the water in the parts of the body where it should be, nor the other their desire in the limits of becoming thought.

Let us then flee this strange and craving (*ξένην καὶ κενὴν*: a play on the sound of the words,) disease; let us flee the root of all evils; let us flee that which is present hell; for it is a hell, the desire of these things. Only just lay open the soul of each, of him who despises wealth and of him who does not so; and you will see that the one is like the distracted, choosing neither to hear nor see any thing: the other, like a harbor free from waves: and he is the friend of all, as the other is the enemy. For whether one take any thing of his, it gives him no annoyance; or if whether, on the contrary, one give him aught, it puffs him not up; but there is a certain freedom about him with entire security. The one is forced to flatter and feign before all; the other, to no man.

If now to be fond of money is to be both poor and timid and a dissembler and a hypocrite and to be full of fears and and great penal anguish and chastisement: while he that despises wealth has all the contrary enjoyments: is it not quite plain that virtue is the more pleasant?

Now we might have gone through all the other evils also whereby it is shewn that there is no vice which hath pleasure in it, had we not spoken before so much at large.

Wherefore knowing these things, let us choose virtue; to the end that we may both enjoy such pleasure as is here, and may attain unto the blessings which are to come, through the grace and loving-kindness, &c. &c.

---

[1] Savile reads this interrogatively, [as does also Dr. Field. C.]

[2] *Crescit indulgens sibi dirus Hydrops, Nec sitim pellit, nisi causa morbi Fugerit venis, et aquosus albo corpore languor.* HOR. *Carm. ii. 2.*

HOMILY XV

It is actually reported that there is fornication among you, and such fornication as is not even named among the Gentiles, that one of you hath his father's wife. And ye are puffed up, and did not rather mourn, that he that had done this deed might be taken away from among you.

WHEN he was discoursing about their divisions, he did not indeed at once address them vehemently, but more gently at first; and afterwards, he ended in accusation, saying thus, (c. 1. xi.) "For it hath been signified unto me concerning you, my brethren, by them which are of the household of Chloe, that there are contentions among you." But in this place, not so; but he lays about him immediately and makes the reproach of the accusation as general as possible. For he said not, "Why did such an one commit fornication?" but, "It is reported that there is fornication among you;" that they might as persons altogether aloof from his charge take it easily; but might be filled with such anxiety as was natural when the whole body was wounded, and the Church had incurred reproach. "For no one," saith he, "will state it thus, 'such an one hath committed fornication,' but, 'in the Church of Corinthians that sin hath been committed.'"

And he said not, "Fornication is perpetrated," but, "Is reported,—such as is not even named among the Gentiles." For so continually he makes the Gentiles a topic of reproach to the believers. Thus writing to the Thessalonians, he said, (1 Thess. iv. 4, 5, καὶ τιμῇ om. τὰ λοιπὰ inserted.) "Let every one possess himself of his own vessel in sanctification, not in the passion of lust, even as the rest of the Gentiles." And to the Colossians and Ephesians, (Eph. iv. 17. cf Col. iii. 6, 7.) "That you should no longer walk, as the other Gentiles walk." Now if their committing the same sins was unpardonable, when they even outdid the Gentiles, what place can we find for them? tell me: "inasmuch as among the Gentiles," so he speaks, "not only they dare no such thing, but they do not even give it a name." Do you see to what point he aggravated his charge? For when they are convicted of inventing such modes of uncleanness as the unbeliev-ers, so far from venturing on them, do not even know of, the sin must be exceeding great, beyond all words. And the clause, "among you," is spoken also emphatically; that is, "Among you, the faithful, who have been favored with so high mysteries, the partakers of secrets, the guests invited to heaven." Dost thou mark with what indignant feeling his works overflow? with what anger against all? For had it not been for the great wrath of which he was full, had he not been setting himself against them all, he would have spoken thus: "Having heard that such and such a person hath committed fornication, I charge you to punish him." But as it is he doth not so; he rather challenges all at once. And indeed, if they had written first, this is what he probably would have said. Since however so far from writing, they had even thrown the fault into the shade, on this account he orders his discourse more vehemently.

[2.] "That one of you should have his father's wife." Wherefore said he not, "That he should abuse his father's wife?" The extreme foulness of the deed caused him to shrink. He hurries by it accordingly, with a sort of scrupulousness as though it had been explicitly mentioned before. And hereby again he aggravates the charge, implying that such things are ventured on among them as even to speak plainly of was intolerable for Paul. Wherefore also, as he goes on, he uses the same mode of speech, saying, "Him who hath so done this thing:" and is again ashamed and blushes to speak out; which also we are wont to do in regard of matters extremely disgraceful. And he said not, "his step-mother," but, "his father's wife;" so as to strike much more severely. For when the mere terms are sufficient to convey the charge, he proceeds with them simply, adding nothing.

And "tell me not," saith he, "that the fornicator is but one: the charge hath become common to all." Wherefore at once he added, "and ye are puffed up:" he said not, "with the sin;" for this would imply want of all reason: but with the doctrine you have heard from that person[1]. This however he set not

---

[1] S. Aug. *cont. Parm.* iii. 5. gives their "glorying" a different turn; saying, (with especial reference to v. 6.) "To glory, not for

83

down himself, but left it undetermined, that he might inflict a heavier blow.

And mark the good sense of Paul. Having first overthrown the wisdom from without, and signified that it is nothing by itself although no sin were associated with it; then and not till then he discourses about the sin also. For if by way of comparison with the fornicator who perhaps was some wise one, he had maintained the greatness of his own spiritual gift; he had done no great thing: but even when unattended with sin to take down the heathen wisdom and demonstrate it to be nothing, this was indicating its extreme worthlessness indeed. Wherefore first, as I said, having made the comparison, he afterwards mentions the man's sin also.

And with him indeed he condescends not to debate, and thereby signifies the exceeding greatness of his dishonor. But to the others he saith, "You ought to weep and wail, and cover your faces, but now ye do the contrary." And this is the force of the next clause, "And ye are puffed up, and did not rather mourn."

"And why are we to weep?" some might say. Because the reproach hath made its way even unto the whole body of your Church. "And what good are we to get by our weeping?" "That such an one should be taken away from you." Not even here doth he mention his name; rather, I should say, not any where; which in all monstrous things is our usual way.

And he said not, "Ye have not rather cast him out," but, as in the case of any disease or pestilence, "there is need of mourning," saith he, "and of intense supplication, 'that he may be taken away.' And you should have used prayer for this, and left nothing undone that he should be cut off."

Nor yet doth he accuse them for not having given him information, but for not having mourned so that the man should be taken away; implying that even without their Teacher this ought to have been done, because of the notoriety of the offence.

[3.] Ver. 3. "For I verily being absent in body, but present in spirit."

Mark his energy. He suffers them not even to wait for his presence, nor to receive him first and then pass the sentence of binding: but as if on the point of expelling some contagion before that it have spread itself into the rest of the body, he hastens to restrain it. And therefore he subjoins the clause, "I have judged already, as though I were present." These things moreover he said, not only to urge them

unto the declaration of their sentence and to give them no opportunity of contriving something else, but also to frighten them, as one who knew what was to be done and determined there. For this is the meaning of being "present in spirit:" as Elisha was present with Gehazi, and said, "Went not my heart with thee? (2 Kings v. 26.) Wonderful! How great is the power of the gift, in that it makes all to be together and as one; and qualifies them to know the things which are far off. "I have judged already as though I were present."

He permits them not to have any other device. "Now I have uttered my decision as if I were present: let there be no delays and puttings off: for nothing else must be done."

Then lest he should be thought too authoritative and his speech sound rather self-willed, mark how he makes them also partners in the sentence. For having said, "I have judged," he adds, "concerning him that hath so wrought this thing, in the Name of our Lord Jesus Christ, ye being gathered together, and my spirit, with the power of our Lord Jesus Christ, to deliver such an one unto Satan.

Now what means, "In the Name of our Lord Jesus Christ?" "According to God;" "not possessed with any human prejudice."

Some, however, read thus, "Him that hath so wrought this thing in the name of our Lord Jesus Christ," and putting a stop there or a break, then subjoin what follows, saying, "When you are gathered together and my spirit to deliver such an one unto Satan:" and they assert that the sense of this reading is as follows, "Him that hath done this thing in the Name of Christ," saith St. Paul, "deliver ye unto Satan;" that is, "him that hath done insult unto the Name of Christ, him that, after he had become a believer and was called after that appellation, hath dared to do such things, deliver ye unto Satan." But to me the former exposition (ἔκδοσις. It seems to mean "enunciation.") appears the truer.

What then is this? "When ye are gathered together in the Name of the Lord." That is; His Name, in whose behalf ye have met, collecting you together.

"And my spirit." Again he sets himself at their head in order that when they should pass sentence, they might no otherwise cut off the offender than as if he were present; and that no one might dare to judge him pardonable, knowing that Paul would be aware of the proceedings.

[4.] Then making it yet more awful, he saith, "with the power of our Lord Jesus Christ;" that is, either that Christ is able to give you such grace as that you should have power to deliver him to the devil; or that He is

Himself together with you passing that sentence against him.

And he said not, "Give up" such an one to Satan, but "deliver;" opening unto him the doors of repentance, and delivering up such an one as it were to a schoolmaster. And again it is, "such an one:" he no where can endure to make mention of his name.

"For the destruction of the flesh." As was done in the case of the blessed Job, but not upon the same ground. For in that case it was for brighter crowns, but here for loosing of sins; that he might scourge him with a grievous sore or some other disease. True it is that elsewhere he saith, "Of the Lord are we judged, (i Cor. xi. 32.) when we suffer these things." But here, desirous of making them feel it more severely, he "delivereth up unto Satan." And so this too which God had determined ensued, that the man's flesh was chastised. For because inordinate eating and carnal luxuriousness are the parents of desires, it is the flesh which he chastises.

"That the spirit may be saved in the day of the Lord Jesus;" that is the soul. Not as though this were saved alone, but because it was a settled point that if that were saved, without all controversy the body too would partake in its salvation. For as it became mortal because of the soul's sinning: so if this do righteousness, that also on the other hand shall enjoy great glory. But some maintain, that "the Spirit" is the Gracious Gift which is extinguished when we sin. "In order then that this may not happen," saith he, "let him be punished; that thereby becoming better, he may draw down to himself God's grace, and be found having it safe in that day." So that all comes as from one exercising a nurse's or a physician's office, not merely scourging nor punishing rashly and at random. For the gain is greater than the punishment: one being but for a season, the other everlasting.

And he said not simply, "That the spirit may be saved," but "in that day." Well and seasonably doth he remind them of that day in order that both they might more readily apply themselves to the cure, and that the person censured might the rather receive his words, not as it were of anger, but as the forethought of an anxious father. For this cause also he said, "unto the destruction of the flesh:" proceeding to lay down regulations for the devil and not suffering him to go a step too far. As in the instance of Job, God said, (Job ii. 6.) "But touch not his life."

[5.] Then, having ended his sentence, and spoken it in brief without dwelling on it, he brings in again a rebuke, directing himself against them;

Ver. 6. "Your glorying is not good:" signifying that it was they up to the present time who had hindered him from repenting, by taking pride in him. Next he shews that he is taking this step in order to spare not that person only, but also those to whom he writes. To which effect he adds,

"Know ye not, that a little leaven leaveneth the whole lump?" "For," saith he, "though the offence be his, yet if neglected it hath power to waste the rest of the body of the Church also. For when the first transgressor escapes punishment, speedily will others also commit the same faults."

In these words he indicates moreover that their struggle and their danger is for the whole Church, not for any one person. For which purpose he needeth also the similitude of the leaven. For "as that," saith he, "though it be but little, transforms unto its own nature the whole lump; so also this man, if he be let go unpunished and this sin turn out unavenged, will corrupt likewise all the rest."

Ver. 7. "Purge out the old leaven," that is, this evil one. Not that he speaketh concerning this one only; rather he glances at others with him. For, "the old leaven" is not fornication only, but also sin of every kind. And he said not, "purge," but "purge out;" "cleanse with accuracy so that there be not so much as a remnant nor a shadow of that sort." In saying then, "purge out," he signifies that there was still iniquity among them. But in saying, "that ye may be a new lump, even as ye are unleavened," he affirms and declares that not over very many was the wickedness prevailing. But though he saith, "as ye are unleavened," he means it not as a fact that all were clean, but as to what sort of people you ought to be.

[6.] "For our Passover also hath been sacrificed for us, even Christ; wherefore let us keep the feast: not with old leaven, nor with the leaven of malice and wickedness, but with the unleavened bread of sincerity and truth." So also Christ called His doctrine Leaven. And further he himself dwells upon the metaphor, reminding them of an ancient history, and of the Passover and unleavened bread, and of their blessings both then and now, and their punishments and their plagues.

It is festival, therefore, the whole time in which we live. For though he said, "Let us keep the feast," not with a view to the presence of the Passover or of Pentecost did he say it; but as pointing out that the whole of time is a festival unto Christians, because of the excellency of the good things which have been given. For what hath not come to pass that is good? The Son of God was made man for thee; He freed thee from death; and called thee to a kingdom. Thou therefore who hast obtained and art still obtaining such things, how can it be less than thy duty to "keep the feast" all thy life? Let no one then be downcast about poverty, and disease, and craft of enemies. For it is a festival, even the whole of our time. Wherefore saith Paul, (Philip. iv, 4.) "Rejoice in the Lord always; again I say, Rejoice." Upon the festival days no one puts on filthy garments. Neither then let us do so. For a marriage hath been made, a spiritual marriage. For, "the kingdom of Heaven," saith He, "is likened unto a certain king which would make (S. Mat. xxii, 1. ἠθέλησε ποιῆσαι, rec. text ἐποίησε.) a marriage feast for his son." Now where it is a king making a marriage, and a marriage for his son, what can be greater than this feast? Let no one then enter in clad in rags. Not about garments is our discourse but about unclean actions. For if where all wore bright apparel one alone, being found at the marriage in filthy garments, was cast out with dishonor, consider how great strictness and purity the entrance into that marriage feast requires.

[7.] However, not on this account only does he remind them of the "unleavened bread," but also to point out the affinity of the Old Testament with the New; and to point out also that it was impossible, after the "unleavened bread," again to enter into Egypt; but if any one chose to return, he would suffer the same things as did they. For those things were a shadow of these; however obstinate the Jew may be. Wherefore shouldest thou enquire of him, he will speak, no great thing, rather it *is* great which he will speak of, but nothing like what we speak of: because he knows not the truth. For he for his part will say, "the Egyptians who detained us were so changed by the Almighty that they themselves urged and drave us out, who before held us forcibly; they did not suffer us so much as to leaven our dough." But if a man asketh me, he shall hear not of Egypt nor of Pharaoh; but of our deliverance from the deceit of demons and the darkness of the devil: not of Moses but of the Son of God; not of a Red Sea but of a Baptism overflowing with ten thousand blessings, where the "old man" is drowned.

Again, shouldest thou ask the Jew why he expels all leaven from all his borders; here he will even be silent and will not so much as state any reason. And this is because, although some indeed of the circumstances were both types of things to come, and also due to things then happening; yet others were not so, that the Jews might not deal deceitfully; that they might not abide in the shadow. For tell me, what is the meaning of the Lamb's being a "Male," and "Unblemished," and a "year old," and of, "a bone shall not be broken?" and what means the command to call the neigh-

bors also, (Exod. xii, 4.) and that it should be eaten "standing" and "in the evening;" or the fortifying the house with blood? He will have nothing else to say but over and over all about Egypt. But I can tell you the meaning both of the Blood, and of the Evening, and the Eating all together, and of the rule that all should be standing.

[8.] But first let us explain why the leaven is cast out of all their borders. What then is the hidden meaning? The believer must be freed from all iniquity. For as among them he perishes with whomsoever is found old leaven, so also with us wheresoever is found iniquity: since of course the punishment being so great in that which is a shadow, in our case it cannot choose but be much greater. For if they so carefully clear their houses of leaven[1], and pry into mouse-holes; much more ought we to search through the soul so as to cast out every unclean thought.

This however was done by them of late[2]; but now no longer. For every where there is leaven, where a Jew is found. For it is in the midst of cities that the feast of unleavened bread is kept: a thing which is now rather a game at play than a law. For since the Truth is come, the Types have no longer any place.

So that by means of this example also he mightily drives the fornicator out of the Church. For, saith he, so far from his presence profiting, he even doth harm, injuring the common estate of the body. For one knows not whence is the evil savor while the corrupt part is concealed, and so one imputes it to the whole. Wherefore he urges upon them strongly to "purge out the leaven, that ye may be," saith he, "a new lump, even as ye are unleavened."

"For our Passover hath been sacrificed for us even Christ." He said not, hath died, but more in point to the subject in hand, "hath been sacrificed." Seek not then unleavened bread of this kind, since neither hast thou a lamb of the same kind. Seek not leaven of this description, seeing that thine unleavened bread is not such as this.

[9.] Thus, in the case of material leaven,

---

[1] Lightfoot, *Works*, i. 953. "'*Seven days there shall be no leaven found in your houses.*' The Jews to meet this command that was so exceeding strict, and to make sure for its observance soon enough, 'did on the fourteenth day, while yet there was some light, make search for leaven by the light of a candle.' (*Talm. in Pesachim.* no. 1.) Thus is the Tradition; in which by the light of the fourteenth day their glossaries tell us that we must understand the 'thirteenth day at even, when it began to be duskish and candle-light.' The rubric of the Passover in the Hebrew and Spanish tongues renders it, 'At the entrance of the fourteenth day of the month Nisan, they searched for leaven in all the places where they were wont to use leaven, even in holes and crannies; and that not by light of the sun and moon, or torch, but by the light of a wax candle,' . . . because it is the fittest for searching holes and corners, and because the Scripture speaketh of searching Jerusalem with candles." See Zeph. i. 12.

[2] i. e. (as it should seem) it has now become impossible for the Jews to keep this command, since they and their false doctrine are (spiritually) that very leaven, which is to be put away. Compare St. Matt. xvi. 6.

the unleavened might become leavened, but never the reverse; whereas here there is a chance of the direct contrary occuring. This however he has not plainly declared: and observe his good sense. In the former Epistle he gives the fornicator no hope of return, but orders that his whole life should be spent in repentance, lest he should make him less energetic through the promise. For he said not, "Deliver him up to Satan," that having repented he might be commended again unto the Church. But what saith he? "That he may be saved in the last day." For he conducts him on unto that time in order to make him full of anxiety. And what favors he intended him after the repentance, he reveals not, imitating his own Master. For as God saith, (Jonah iii, 4. lxx: rec. text, "forty days.") "Yet three days, and Nineveh shall be overthrown," and added not, "but if she repent she shall be saved:" so also he did not say here, "But if he repent worthily, we will 'confirm our love towards him.'" (ii. Cor. ii. 8.). But he waits for him to do the work that so he may then receive the favor. For if he had said this at the beginning he might have set him free from the fear. Wherefore he not only does not so, but by the instance of leaven allows him not even a hope of return, but reserves him unto that day: "Purge out (so he says) the old leaven;" and, "let us not keep the feast with old leaven." But as soon as he had repented, he brought him in again with all earnestness.

[10.] But why does he call it "old?" Either because our former life was of this sort, or because that which is old is "ready to vanish away," (Heb. viii. 13.) and is unsavory and foul; which is the nature of sin. For He neither simply finds fault with the old, nor simply praises the new, but with reference to the subject matter. And thus elsewhere He saith, (Ecclus. ix. 15.) "New wine is as a new friend: but if it become old, then with pleasure shalt thou drink it:" in the case of friendship bestowing his praise rather upon the old than the new. And again, "The Ancient of days sat," (Dan. vii. 9.) here again, taking the term "ancient" as among those laudatory expressions which confer highest glory. Elsewhere the Scripture takes the term "old" in the sense of blame; for seeing that the things are of various aspect as being composed of many parts, it uses the same words both in a good and an evil import, not according to the same shade of meaning. Of which you may see an instance in the blame cast elsewhere on the old: (Ps. xvii. 46. ap. LXX.) "They waxed old, and they halted from their paths." And again, (Ps. vi. 7. ap. LXX.) "I have become old in the midst of all mine enemies." And again, (Dan. xiii. 52. Hist. Susan.) "O thou that art become old in evil days." So also the "Leaven" is often taken for the kingdom of Heaven, although here found fault with. But in that place it is used with one aspect, and in this with another.

[11.] But I have a strong conviction that the saying about the leaven refers also to the priests who suffer a vast deal of the old leaven to be within, not purging out from their borders, that is, out of the Church, the covetous, the extortioners, and whatsover would exclude from the kingdom of Heaven. For surely covetousness is an "old leaven;" and whenever it lights and into whatsoever house it enters, makes it unclean: and though you may gain but little by your injustice, it leavens the whole of your substance. Wherefore not seldom the dishonest gain being little, hath cast out the stock honestly laid up however abundant. For nothing is more rotten than covetousness. You may fasten up that man's closet with key, and door, and bolt: you do all in vain, whilst you shut up within covetousness, the worst of robbers, and able to carry off all.

"But what," say you, "if there are many covetous who do not experience this?" In the first place, they will experience it, though their experience come not immediately. And should they now escape, then do thou fear it the more: for they are reserved for greater punishment. Add to this, that in the event of themselves escaping, yet those who inherit their wealth will have the same to endure. "But how can this be just," you will say? It is quite just. For he that has succeeded to an inheritance full of injustice, though he have committed no rapine himself, detains nevertheless the property of others; and is perfectly aware of this; and it is fair he should suffer for it. For if this or that person had robbed and you received a thing, and then the owner came and demanded it back; would it avail you in defence to say that you had not seized it? By no means. For what would be your plea when accused! tell me. That it was another who seized it? Well: but you are keeping possession. That it was he who robbed? But you are enjoying it. Why these rules even the laws of the heathen recognise, which acquitting those who have seized and stolen, bid you demand satisfaction from those persons in whose possession you happen to find your things all laid up.

If then you know who are the injured, restore and do what Zacchæus did, with much increase. But if you know not, I offer you another way yet; I do not preclude you from the remedy. Distribute all these things to the poor: and thus you will mitigate the evil.

But if some have transmitted these things even to children and descendants, still in retribution they have suffered other disasters.

[12.] And why speak I of things in this present life? In that day at any rate will none of these things be said, when both appear naked, both the spoiled and the spoilers. Or rather not alike naked. Of riches indeed both will be equally stripped; but the one will be full of the charges to which they gave occasion. What then shall we do on that day, when before the dread tribunal he that hath been evil entreated and lost his all is brought forward into the midst, and you have no one to speak a word for you? What will you say to the Judge? Now indeed you may be able even to corrupt the judgment, being but of men; but in that court and at that time, it will be no longer so: no, nor yet now will you be able. For even at this moment that tribunal is present: since God both seeth our doings and is near unto the injured, though not invoked: it being certain that whoever suffers wrong, however in himself unworthy to obtain any redress, yet nevertheless seeing that what is done pleases not God, he hath most assuredly one to avenge him.

"How then," you will say, "is such an one well off, who is wicked?" Nay, it will not be so unto the end. Hear what saith the Prophet; (Ps. xxxvii. 1, 2.) "Fret not thyself because of the evil doers, because as grass they shall quickly wither away." For where, tell me, where is he who wrought rapine, after his departure hence? Where are his bright hopes! Where his august name? Are they not all passed and gone? Is it not a dream and a shadow, all that was his? And this you must expect in the case of every such person, both in his own person while living, and in that of him who shall come after him. But not such is the state of the saints, nor will it be possible for you to say the same things in their case also, that it is shadow and a dream and a tale, what belongs to them.

[13.] And if you please, he who spake these things, the tent-maker, the Cilician, the man whose very parentage is unknown, let him be the example we produce. You will say, "How is it possible to become such as he was?" Do you then thoroughly desire it? Are you thoroughly anxious to become such? "Yes," you will say. Well then, go the same way as he went and they that were with him. Now what way went he? One saith, (2 Cor. xi. 27.) "In hunger, and thirst, and nakedness." Another, (Acts iii. 6.) "Silver and gold I have none." Thus they "had nothing and yet possessed all things." (2 Cor. vi. 10.) What can be nobler than this saying? what more blessed or more abundant in riches? Others indeed pride themselves on the contrary things, saying, "I have this or that number of talents of gold, and acres of land without end, and houses, and slaves;" but this man on his being naked of all things; and he shrinks not from poverty, (which is the feeling of the unwise,) nor hides his face, but he even wears it as an ornament.

Where now be the rich men, they who count up their interest simple and compound, they who take from all men and are never satisfied? Have ye heard the voice of Peter, that voice which sets forth poverty as the mother of wealth? That voice which has nothing, yet is wealthier than those who wear diadems? For this is that voice, which having nothing, raised the dead, and set upright the lame, and drove away devils, and bestowed such gracious gifts, as those who are clad in the purple robe and lead the mighty and terrible legions never were able to bestow. This is the voice of those who are now removed into heaven, of those who have attained unto that height.

[14.] Thus it is possible that he who hath nothing may possess all men's goods. Thus may he who possesses nothing acquire the goods of all: whereas, were we to get all men's goods, we are bereft of all. Perhaps this saying seems to be a paradox; but it is not. "But," you will say, "how does he who hath nothing possess all men's goods? Doth he not have much more who hath what belongs to all?" By no means: but the contrary. For he who hath nothing commands all, even as they did. And throughout the world all houses were open to them, and they who offered them took their coming as a favor, and they came to them as to friends and kindred. For so they came to the woman who was a seller of purple, (Acts xvi. 14.) and she like a servant set before them what she had. And to the keeper of the prison; and he opened to them all his house. And to innumerable others. Thus they had all things and had nothing: for (Acts iv. 32.) "they said that none of the things which they possessed was their own;" therefore all things were theirs. For he that considers all things to be common, will not only use his own, but also the things of others as if they belonged to him. But he that parts things off and sets himself as master over his own only, will not be master even of these. And this is plain from an example. He who possesses nothing at all, neither house, nor table, nor garment to spare, but for God's sake is bereft of all, uses the things which are in common as his own; and he shall receive from all whatsoever he may desire, and thus he that hath nothing possesses the things of all. But he that hath some things, will not be master even of these. For first, no one will give to him that hath possessions; and, secondly, his property shall belong to robbers and thieves and informers and changing events and be any body's rather than his. Paul, for instance, went up and down throughout all the world, carrying nothing with him, though he went neither unto friends nor kindred. Nay, at first he was a common enemy to all: but nevertheless he had all men's goods after he had made good his entrance. But Ananias and Sapphira, hastening to gain a little more than their own, lost all together with life itself. Withdraw then from thine own, that thou mayest use others' goods as thine own.

[15.] But I must stop: I know not how I have been carried into such a transport in speaking such words as these unto men who think it a great thing to impart but ever so little of their own. Wherefore let these my words have been spoken to the perfect. But to the more imperfect, this is what we may say, Give of what you have unto the needy. Increase your substance. For, saith He, (Prov. xix. 17.) "He that giveth unto the poor, lendeth unto God." But if you are in a hurry and wait not for the time of recompense, think of those who lend money to men: for not even these desire to get their interest immediately; but they are anxious that the principal should remain a good long while in the hands of the borrower,

provided only the repayment be secure and they have no mistrust of the borrower. Let this be done then in the present case also. Leave them with God that He may pay thee thy wages manifold. Seek not to have the whole here; for if you recover it all here, how will you receive it back there? And it is on this account that God stores them up there, inasmuch as this present life is full of decay. But He gives even here also; for, "Seek ye," saith He, "the kingdom of heaven, and all these things shall be added unto you." (S. Mat. vi. 33.) Well then, let us look towards the kingdom, and not be in a hurry for the repayment of the whole, lest we diminish our recompense. But let us wait for the fit season. For the interest in these cases is not of that kind, but is such as is meet to be given to God. This then having collected together in great abundance, so let us depart hence, that we may obtain both the present and the future blessings; through the grace and loving-kindness of our Lord Jesus Christ, with Whom unto the Father and the Holy Spirit be glory, power, honor, now, henceforth, and for evermore. Amen.

HOMILY XVI.

1 Cor. v. 9—11.

I wrote unto you in my epistle to have no company with fornicators: yet not altogether with the fornicators of this world, or with the covetous and extortioners, or with idolaters, for then must ye needs go out of the world: but now I write unto you not to keep company, if any man that is named a brother be a fornicator, or covetous, or an idolater, or a drunkard, or a reviler, or an extortioner; with such an one no not to eat.

FOR since he had said, "Ye have not rather mourned, that such an one should be taken away;" and, "Purge out the old leaven;" and it was likely that they would surmise it to be their duty to avoid all fornicators: for if he that has sinned imparts some of his own mischief to those who have not sinned, much more is it meet to keep one's self away from those without: (for if one ought not to spare a friend on account of such mischief arising from him, much less any others;) and under this impression, it was probable that they would separate themselves from the fornicators among the Greeks also, and the matter thus turning out impossible, they would have taken it more to heart: he used this mode of correction, saying, "I wrote unto you to have no company with

fornicators, yet not altogether with the fornicators of this world:" using the word "altogether," as if it were an acknowledged thing. For that they might not think that he charged not this upon them as being rather imperfect, and should attempt to do it under the erroneous impression that they were perfect, he shews that this were even impossible to be done, though they wished it ever so much. For it would be necessary to seek another world. Wherefore he added, "For ye must needs then go out of the world." Seest thou that he is no hard master, and that in his legislation he constantly regards not only what may be done, but also what may be easily done. For how is it possible, says he, for a man having care of a house and children, and engaged in the affairs of the city, or who is an artisan or a soldier, (the greater part of mankind being Greeks,) to avoid the unclean who are to be found every where? For by "the fornicators of the world," he means those who are among the Greeks. "But now I write unto you, If any brother" be of this kind, "with such an one no not to eat." Here also he glances at others who were living in wickedness.

But how can one "that is a brother" be an idolater? As was the case once in regard to the Samaritans who chose piety but by halves. And besides he is laying down his ground beforehand for the discourse concerning things offered in sacrifice to idols, which after this he intends to handle.

"Or covetous." For with these also he enters into conflict. Wherefore he said also, "Why not rather take wrong? Why not rather be defrauded? Nay, ye yourselves do wrong and defraud."

"Or a drunkard." For this also he lays to their charge further on; as when he says, "One is hungry and another is drunken:" and, "meats for the belly and the belly for meats."

"Or a reviler, or an extortioner:" for these too he had rebuked before.

[2.] Next he adds also the reason why he forbids them not to mix with heathens of that character, implying that it is not only impossible, but also superfluous.

Ver. 12, "For what have I to do with judging them that are without?" Calling the Christians and the Greeks, "those within" and "those without," as also he says elsewhere, (1 Tim. iii. 7.) "He must also have a good report of them that are without." And in the Epistle to the Thessalonians he speaks the same language, saying, (2 Thes. iii. 14.) "Have no intercourse with him to the end that he may be put to shame." And, "Count him not as an enemy, but admonish him as a brother." Here, however, he does not add the reason. Why? Because in the other case he wished to soothe them, but in this, not so. For the fault in this case and in that was not the same, but in the Thessalonians it was less. For there he is reproving indolence; but here fornication and other most grievous sins. And if any one wished to go over to the Greeks, he hinders not him from eating with such persons; this too for the same reason. So also do we act; for our children and our brethren we leave nothing undone, but of strangers we do not make much account. How then? Did not Paul care for them that were without as well? Yes, he cared for them; but it was not till after they received the Gospel and he had made them subject to the doctrine of Christ, that he laid down laws for them. But so long as they despised, it was superfluous to speak the precepts of Christ to those who knew not Christ Himself.

"Do not ye judge them that are within, whereas them that are without, God judgeth?" For since he had said, "What have I to do with judging those without;" lest any one should think that these were left unpunished, there is another tribunal which he sets over them, and that a fearful one. And this he said, both to terrify those, and to console these; intimating

also that this punishment which is for a season snatches them away from that which is undying and perpetual: which also he has plainly declared elsewhere, saying, (1 Cor. xi. 32.) "But now being judged, we are chastened, that we should not be condemned with the world."

[3.] "Put away from among yourselves the wicked person." He used an expression found in the Old Testament, (Deut. xvii. 7.) partly hinting that they too will be very great gainers, in being freed as it were from some grievous plague; and partly to shew that this kind of thing is no innovation, but even from the beginning it seemed good to the legislator that such as these should be cut off. But in that instance it was done with more severity, in this with more gentleness. On which account one might reasonably question, why in that case he conceded that the sinner should be severely punished and stoned, but in the present instance not so; rather he leads him to repentance. Why then were the lines drawn in the former instance one way and in the latter another? For these two causes: one, because these were led into a greater trial and needed greater long-suffering; the other and truer one, because these by their impunity were more easily to be corrected, coming as they might to repentance; but the others were likely to go on to greater wickedness. For if when they saw the first undergoing punishment they persisted in the same things, had none at all been punished, much more would this have been their feeling. For which reason in that dispensation death is immediately inflicted upon the adulterer and the manslayer; but in this, if through repentance they are absolved, they have escaped the punishment. However, both here one may see some instances of heavier punishment, and in the Old Testament some less severe, in order that it may be signified in every way that the covenants are akin to each other, and of one and the same lawgiver: and you may see the punishment following immediately both in that covenant and in this, and in both often after a long interval. Nay, and oftentimes not even after a long interval, repentance alone being taken as satisfaction by the Almighty. Thus in the Old Testament, David, who had committed adultery and murder, was saved by means of repentance; and in the New, Ananias, who withdrew but a small portion of the price of the land, perished together with his wife. Now if these instances are more frequent in the Old Testament, and those of the contrary kind in the New, the difference of the persons produces the difference in the treatment adopted in such matters.

[4.] C. vi. ver. 1. "Dare any one of you, having a matter against his brother, (τὸν ἀδελφὸν, rec. text τὸν ἕτερον.) go to law before the unrighteous, and not before the saints?"

Here also he again makes his complaint upon acknowledged grounds; for in that other place he says, "It is actually reported that there is fornication among you." And in this place, "Dare any one of you?" From the very first outset giving signs of his anger, and implying that the thing spoken of comes of a daring and lawless spirit.

Now wherefore did he bring in by the way that discourse about covetousness and about the duty of not going to law without the Church? In fulfilment of his own rule. For it is a custom with him to set to right things as they fall in his way; just as when speaking about the tables which they used in common, he launched out into the discourse about the mysteries. So here, you see, since he had made mention of covetous brethren, burning with anxiety to correct those in sin, he brooks not exactly to observe order; but he again corrects the sin which had been introduced out of the regular course, and so returns to the former subject.

Let us hear then what he also says about this. "Dare any of you, having a matter, go to law before the unrighteous, and not before the saints?" For a while, he employs those personal terms to expose, discredit, and blame their proceedings: nor does he quite from the beginning subvert the custom of seeking judgment before the believers: but when he had stricken them down by many words, then he even takes away entirely all going to law. "For in the first place," says he, "if one must go to law it were wrong to do so before the unrighteous. But you ought not to go to law at all." This however he adds afterwards. For the present he thoroughly sifts the former subject, namely, that they should not submit matters to external arbitration. "For," says he, "how can it be otherwise than absurd that one who is at variance (μιχροφυχοῦντα) with his friend should take his enemy to be a reconciler between them? And how can you avoid feeling shame and blushing when a Greek sits to judge a Christian? And if about private matters it is not right to go to law before Greeks, how shall we submit to their decisions about other things of greater importance?"

Observe, moreover, how he speaks. He says not, "Before the unbelievers," but, "Before the unrighteous;" using the expression of which he had most particular need for the matter before him, in order to deter and keep them away. For see that his discourse was about going to law, and those who are engaged in suits seek for nothing so much as that the judges should feel great interest about what is just; he takes this as a ground of dissuasion. all but saying, "Where are you going? What are you doing, O man, bringing on yourself the contrary to what you wish, and in order to obtain justice committing yourself to unjust men?" And because it would have been intolerable to be told at once not to go to law, he did not immediately add this, but only changed the judges, bringing the party engaged in the trial from without into the Church.

[5.] Then, since it seemed easily open to contempt, I mean our being judged by those who were within, and especially at that time, (for they were not perhaps competent to comprehend a point, nor were they such as the heathen judges, well skilled in laws and rhetoric, inasmuch as the greater part of them were uneducated men,) mark how he makes them worthy of credit, first calling them "Saints."

But seeing that this bore witness to purity of life, and not to accuracy in hearing a case, observe how he orderly handles this part also, saying thus, "Do ye not know that the saints shall judge the world?" How then canst thou who art in thy day to judge them, endure to be judged by them now? They will not indeed judge, taking their seat in person and demanding account, yet they shall condemn. This at least he plainly said; "And if the world is judged in you, are ye unworthy to judge the smallest matters?" He says not "by you," but "in you:" just as when He said, (S. Mat. xii. 42.) "The queen of the south shall rise up and condemn this generation:" and, "The men of Nineveh shall arise and condemn this generation." For when beholding the same sun and sharing all the same things, we shall be found believers but they unbelievers, they will not be able to take refuge in ignorance. For we shall accuse them, simply by the things which we have done. And many such ways of judgment one will find there.

Then, that no one should think he speaks about other persons, mark how he generalizes his speech. "And if the world is judged in you, are ye unworthy to judge the smallest matters?"

The thing is a disgrace to you, he says, and an unspeakable reproach. For since it was likely that they would be out of countenance at being judged by those that were within; "nay," saith he, "on the contrary, the disgrace is when you are judged by those without: for those are the very small controversies, not these."

Ver. 3. "Know ye not that we shall judge angels? how much more, things which pertain to this life?

Some say that here the priests are hinted at, but away with this. His speech is about demons. For had he been speaking about corrupt priests, he would have meant them above when he said, "the world is judged in you:" (for the Scripture is wont to call evil men also "The world:") and he would not have said the same thing twice, nor would he, as if he was saying something of greater consequence, have put it down afterwards. But he speaks concerning those angels about whom Christ saith, "Depart ye into the fire which is prepared for the devil and his angels." (St. Matt. xxv. 41.) And Paul, "his angels fashion themselves as ministers of righteousness." (2 Cor. xi. 15.) For when the very incorporeal powers shall be found inferior to us who are clothed with flesh, they shall suffer heavier punishment.

But if some should still contend that he speaks of priests, "What sort of priests?" let us ask. Those whose walk in life has been worldly, of course. In what sense then does he say, "We shall judge angels, much more things that relate to this life?" He mentions the angels, in contradistinction to "things relating to this life": likely enough; for they are removed from the need of these things, because of the superior excellence of their nature.

[6.] Ver. 4. "If then ye have to judge things pertaining to this life, set them to judge who are of no account in the Church.[1]

Wishing to instruct us as forcibly as possible that they ought not to commit themselves to those without, whatsoever the matter may be; having raised what seemed to be an objection, he answers it in the first instance. For what he says is something like this: Perhaps some one will say, "No one among you is wise, nor competent to pass sentence; all are contemptible." Now what follows? "Even though none be wise," says he, "I bid you entrust things to those who are of least weight."

Ver. 5. "But this I say to move you to shame." These are the words of one exposing their objection as being an idle pretext: and therefore he adds, "Is it so that there is not a wise man among you, no not even one?" Is the scarcity, says he, so great? so great the want of sensible persons among you? And what he subjoins strikes even still harder. For having said, "Is it so, that there is not a wise man among you, not even one?" he adds, "who shall be able to judge in the case of his brother." For when brother goes to law with brother, there is never any need of understanding and talent in the person who is mediating in the cause, the feeling and relationship contributing greatly to the settlement of such a quarrel.

"But brother goeth to law with brother, and that before unbelievers." Do you observe with what effect he disparaged the judges at first by calling them unrighteous; whereas here, to move shame, he calls them Unbelievers? For surely it is extremely disgraceful if the priest

could not be the author of reconciliation even among brethren, but recourse must be had to those without. So that when he said, "those who are of no account," his chief meaning was not (οὐ τοῦτο εἶπε προηγουμένως.) that the Church's outcasts should be appointed as judges, but to find fault with them. For that it was proper to make reference to those who were able to decide, he has shewn by saying, "Is it so, that there is not a wise man among you, not even one?" And with great impressiveness he stops their mouths, and says, "Even though there were not a single wise man, the hearing ought to have been left to you who are unwise rather than that those without should judge." For what else can it be than absurd, that whereas on a quarrel arising in a house we call in no one from without and feel ashamed if news get abroad among strangers of what is going on within doors; where the Church is, the treasure of the unutterable Mysteries, there all things should be published without?

Ver. 6. "But brother goeth to law with brother, and that before unbelievers."

The charge is twofold; both that he "goeth to law," and "before the unbelievers." For if even the thing by itself, To go to law with a brother, be a fault, to do it also before aliens, what pardon does it admit of?

[7.] Ver. 7. "Nay, already it is altogether a defect in you, that ye have lawsuits one with another."

Do you see for what place he reserved this point? And how he has cleared the discussion of it in good time? For "I talk not yet," saith he, "which injures, or which is injured." Thus far, the act itself of going to law brings each party under his censure, and in that respect one is not at all better than another. But whether one go to law justly or unjustly, that is quite another subject. Say not then, "which did the wrong?" For on this ground I at once condemn thee, even for the act of going to law.

Now if being unable to bear a wrong-doer be a fault, what accusation can come up to the actual wrong? "Why not rather take wrong? Why not rather be defrauded?"

Ver. 8. "Nay, ye yourselves do wrong, and defraud, and that your brethren."

Again, it is a twofold crime, perhaps even threefold or fourfold. One, not to know how to bear being wronged. Another, actually to do wrong. A third, to commit the settlement of these matters even unto the unjust. And yet a fourth, that it should be so done to a brother. For men's offences are not judged by the same rule, when they are committed against any chance person, and towards one's own member. For it must be a greater degree of recklessness to venture upon that. In the other

---

[1] [Most of the modern critics and the Rev. Version make this a question, but Principal Edwards agrees with Chrysostom in considering it a precept. C.]

case, the nature of the thing is alone trampled on; but in this, the quality of the person also.

[8.] Having thus, you see, abashed them from arguments on general principles, and before that, from the rewards proposed[1]; he shuts up the exhortation with a threat, making his speech more peremptory, and saying thus, (ver. 9.) "Know ye not that the unrighteous shall not inherit the kingdom of God? Be not deceived: neither fornicators, nor idolaters, nor adulterers, nor effeminate, nor abusers of themselves with men, (ver. 10.) nor covetous, nor thieves, nor drunkards, nor revilers, nor extortioners, shall inherit the kingdom of God." What sayest thou? When discoursing about covetous persons, have you brought in upon us so vast a crowd of lawless men? "Yes," says he, "but in doing this, I am not confusing my discourse, but going on in regular order." For as when discoursing about the unclean he made mention of all together; so again, on mentioning the covetous he brings forward all, thus making his rebukes familiar to those who have such things on their conscience. For the continual mention of the punishment laid up for others makes the reproof easy to be received, when it comes into conflict with our own sins. And so in the present instance he utters his threat, not at all as being conscious of their doing such things, nor as calling them to account, a thing which has special force to hold the hearer and keep him from starting off; namely, the discourse having no respect unto him, but being spoken indefinitely and so wounding his conscience secretly.

"Be not deceived." Here he glances at certain who maintain (what indeed most men assert now) that God being good and kind to man, takes not vengeance upon our misdeeds: "Let us not then be afraid." For never will he exact justice of any one for any thing. And it is on account of these that he says, "Be not deceived." For it belongs to the extreme of error and delusion, after depending on good to meet with the contrary; and to surmise such things about God as even in man no one would think of. Wherefore saith the Prophet in His person, (Ps. xlix. LXX. l. Heb. ver. 21.)[2] "Thou hast conceived iniquity, that I shall be like unto thee: I will reprove thee and set before thy face thine iniquities." And Paul here, "Be not deceived; neither fornicators," (he puts first the one that was already condemned,) "nor adulterers, nor effeminate, nor drunkards, nor revilers, shall inherit the kingdom of God."

Many have attacked this place as extremely severe, since he places the drunkard and the reviler with the adulterer and the abominable and the abuser of himself with mankind. And yet the offenses are not equal: how then is the award of punishment the same? What shall we say then? First, that drunkenness is no small thing nor reviling, seeing that Christ Himself delivered over to hell him that called his brother Fool. And often that sin has brought forth death. Again, the Jewish people too committed the greatest of their sins through drunkenness. In the next place, it is not of punishment that he is so far discoursing, but of exclusion from the kingdom. Now from the kingdom both one and the other are equally thrust out; but whether in hell they will find any difference, it belongs not to this present occasion to enquire. For that subject is not before us just now.

[9.] Ver. 11. "And such were some of you: but ye were washed, but ye were sanctified."

In a way to abash them exceedingly, he adds this: as if he said, "Consider from what evils God delivered us; how great an experiment and demonstration of loving-kindness He afforded us! He did not limit His redemption to mere deliverance, but greatly extended the benefit: for He also made thee clean. Was this then all? Nay: but He also "sanctified." Nor even is this all: He also "justified." Yet even bare deliverance from our sins were a great gift: but now He also filled thee with countless blessing. And this He hath done, "In the Name of our Lord Jesus Christ;" not in this name or in that: yea also, "In the Spirit of our God."

Knowing therefore these things, beloved, and bearing in mind the greatness of the blessing which hath been wrought, let us both continue to live soberly, being pure from all things that have been enumerated; and let us avoid the tribunals which are in the forums of the Gentiles; and the noble birth which God hath freely given us, the same let us preserve to the end. For think how full of shame it is that a Greek should take his seat and deal out justice to thee.

But you will say, what if he that is within judge contrary to the law? Why should he? tell me. For I would know by what kind of laws the Greek administers justice, and by what the Christian? Is it not quite plain that the laws of men are the rule of the Greek, but those of God, of the Christian? Surely then with the latter there is greater chance of justice, seeing that these laws are even sent from heaven. For in regard to those without, besides what has been said, there are many other things also to suspect; talent in speakers and corruption in magistrates and many other things which are the ruin of justice. But with us, nothing of this sort.

---

[1] i. e. in the clause, *Do ye not know that the Saints shall judge the world?* ver. 2.

[2] τὰς ἀνομίας σου not in rec. text.

" What then," you will say, " if the adversary be one in high place? Well, for this reason more than all one ought to go to law in Christian courts : for in the courts without he will get the better of you at all events. "But what if he acquiesce not, but both despise those within and forcibly drag the course without?" Better were it to submit willingly to what you are likely to endure by compulsion, and not go to law, that thou mayest have also a reward. For, (St. Matt. v. 40.) "If any one will go to law with thee, and take away thy coat, thou shalt let him have thy cloak also:" and, (v. 25.) "Agree with thine adversary quickly, whilst thou art with him in the way." And why need I speak of our rules? For even the pleaders in the heathen courts very often tell us this, saying, " it were better to make up matters out of court." But, O wealth, or rather, O the absurd love of wealth! It subverts all things and casts them down ; and all things are to the many an idle tale and fables because of money! Now that those who give trouble to courts of laws should be worldly men is no marvel : but that many of those who have bid farewell to the world should do the very same, this is a thing from which all pardon is cut off. For if you choose to see how far you should keep from this sort of need, I mean that of the tribunals, by rule of the Scripture, and to learn for whom the laws are appointed, hear what Paul saith ; (1 Tim. i. 9.) " For a righteous man law is not made, but for the lawless, and unruly." And if he saith these things about the Mosaic Law, much more about the laws of the heathen.

[10.] Now then, if you commit injustice, it is plain that you cannot be righteous: but if you are injured and bear it, (for this is a special mark of a righteous man,) you have no need of the laws which are without. "How then," say you, "shall I be able to bear it when injured?" And yet Christ hath commanded something even more than this. For not only hath he commanded you when injured to bear it, but even to give abundantly more to the wrong-doer; and in your zeal for suffering ill to surpass his eagerness for doing it. For he said not, "to him that will sue thee at law, and take away thy coat, give thy coat," but, "together with that give also thy cloak." But I bid you overcome him, saith He, by suffering, not by doing, evil: for this is the certain and splendid victory. Wherefore also Paul goes on to say, " Now then it is altogether a defect in (ἥττημα rec. vers. " a fault.") you that ye have lawsuits one with another." And, " Wherefore do ye not rather take wrong?" For that the injurèd person overcomes, rather than he who cannot endure being injured, this I will make

evident to you. He that cannot endure injury, though he force the other into court and gain the verdict, yet is he then most of all defeated. For that which he would not, he hath suffered ; in that the adversary hath compelled him both to feel pain and to go to law. For what is it to the point that you have prevailed? and what, that you have recovered all the money? You have in the meanwhile borne what you did not desire, having been compelled to decide the matter by law. But if you endure the injustice, you overcome; deprived indeed of the money, but not at all of the victory which is annexed to such self-command. For the other had no power to oblige you to do what you did not like.

And to shew that this is true ; tell me, which conquered at the dunghill? Which was defeated? Job who was stripped of all, or the devil who stripped him of all? Evidently the devil who stripped him of all. Whom do we admire for the victory, the devil that smote, or Job that was smitten? Clearly, Job. And yet he could not retain his perishing wealth nor save his children. Why speak I of riches and children? He could not insure to himself bodily health. Yet nevertheless this is the conqueror, he that lost all that he had. His riches indeed he could not keep; but his piety he kept with all strictness. " But his children when perishing he could not help." And what then? Since what happened both made them more glorious, and besides in this way he protected himself against the despiteful usage. Now had he not have suffered ill and been wronged of the devil, he would not have gained that signal victory. Had it been an evil thing to suffer wrong, God would not have enjoined it upon us: for God enjoineth not evil things. What, know ye not that He is the God of Glory? that it could not be His will to encompass us with shame and ridicule and loss, but to introduce (προξενῆσαι) us to the contrary of these? Therefore He commands us to suffer wrong, and doth all to withdraw us from worldly things, and to convince us what is glory, and what shame; what loss, and what gain.

" But it is hard to suffer wrong and be spitefully entreated." Nay, O man, it is not, it is not hard. How long will thy heart be fluttering about things present? For God, you may be sure, would not have commanded this, had it been hard. Just consider. The wrong-doer goes his way with the money, but with an evil conscience besides : the receiver of the wrong, defrauded indeed of some money, but enriched with confidence towards God; an acquisition more valuable than countless treasures.

[11.] Knowing these things, therefore, let us of our free choice go on strict principles, and not be like the unwise, who think that they are then not wronged, when their suffering wrong is the result of a trial. But, quite on the contrary, that is the greatest harm ; and so in every case when we exercise self-restraint in these matters, not willingly, but after being worsted in that other quarter. For it is no advantage that a man defeated in a trial endures it ; for it becomes thenceforth a matter of necessity. What then is the splendid victory ? When thou lookest down on it : when thou refusest to go to law.

"How say you ? have I been stripped of every thing," saith one, "and do you bid me keep silent ? Have I been shamefully used, and do you exhort me to bear it meekly ? And how shall I be able ?" Nay, but it is most easy if thou wilt look up unto heaven ; if thou wilt behold the beauty that is in sight ; and whither God hath promised to receive thee, if thou bear wrong nobly. Do this then ; and looking up unto the heaven, think that thou art made like unto Him that sitteth there upon the Cherubim. For He also was injured and He bore it ; He was reproached and avenged not Himself ; and was beaten, yet He asserted not His cause. Nay, He made return, in the contrary kind, to those who did such things, even in benefits without number ; and He commanded us to be imitators of Him. Consider that thou camest naked out of thy mother's womb, and that naked both thou and he that hath done thee wrong shall depart ; rather, he for his part, with innumerable wounds, breeding worms. Consider that things present are but for a season ; count over the tombs of thine ancestors ; acquaint thyself accurately with past events ; and thou shalt see that the wrong-doer hath made thee stronger. For his own passion he hath aggravated, his covetousness I mean ; but yours, he hath alleviated, taking away the food of the wild beast. And besides all this, he hath set you free from cares, agony, envy, informers, trouble, worry, perpetual fear ; and the foul mass of evils he hath heaped upon his own head.

"What then," saith one, "if I have to struggle with hunger ?" Thou endurest this with Paul, who saith, (1 Cor. iv. 10.) "Even unto this present hour we both hunger, and thirst, and are naked." But he did it, you will say, "for God's sake :" do thou it also for God's sake. For when thou abstainest from avenging, thou dost so for God's sake.

"But he that wronged me, takes his pleasure with the wealthy." Nay, rather with the devil. But be you crowned with Paul.

Therefore fear not hunger, for (Prov. x. 3.) "the Lord will not kill with hunger the souls of the righteous." And again, another saith, (Ps. lv. 23.) "Cast upon the Lord thy care, and He

will nourish thee." For if the sparrows of the field are nourished by Him, how shall He not nourish thee ? Now let us not be of little faith nor of little soul, O my beloved ! For He who hath promised the kingdom of heaven and such great blessings, how shall He not give things present ? Let us not covet superfluous things, but let us keep to a sufficiency, and we shall always be rich. Let shelter be what we seek and food, and we shall obtain all things ; both these, and such as are far greater.

But if you are still grieving and bowing down, I should like to shew you the soul of the wrong-doer after his victory, how it is become ashes. For truly sin is that kind of thing : while one commits it, it affords a certain pleasure ; but when it is finished, then the trifling pleasure is gone, one knows not how, and in its place comes dejection. And this is our feeling when we do hurt to any : afterwards, at any rate, we condemn ourselves. So also when we over-reach we have pleasure ; but afterwards we are stung by conscience. Seest thou in any one's possession some poor man's home ? Weep not for him that is spoiled, but for the spoiler : for he has not inflicted, but sustained an evil. For he robbed the other of things present ; but himself he cast out of the blessings which cannot be uttered. For if he who giveth not to the poor shall go away into hell ; what shall he suffer who takes the goods of the poor ?

"Yet," saith one, "where is the gain, if I suffer ill ?" Indeed, the gain is great. For not of the punishment of him that hath done thee harm doth God frame a compensation for thee : since that would be no great thing. For what great good is it, if I suffer ill and he suffer ill ? And yet I know of many, who consider this the greatest comfort, and who think they have got all back again, when they see those who had insulted them undergoing punishment. But God doth not limit His recompense to this.

Wouldest thou then desire to know in earnest how great are the blessings which await thee ? He openeth for thee the whole heaven ; He maketh thee a fellow-citizen with the Saints ; He fits thee to bear a part in their choir : from sins He absolveth ; with righteousness He crowneth. For if such as forgive offenders shall obtain forgiveness, those who not only forgive but who also give largely to boot, what blessing shall they not inherit ?

Therefore, bear it not with a poor spirit, but even pray for him that injured thee. It is for thyself that thou dost this. Hath he taken thy money ? Well : he took thy sins too : which was the case with Naaman and Gehazi. How much wealth wouldest thou not give to have thine iniquities forgiven thee ? This, believe me, is the case now. For if thou endure nobly and curse not, thou hast bound on thee a glorious crown. It is not my word, but thou hast heard Christ speaking, "Pray for those that despitefully use you." And consider the reward how great! "That ye may be like your Father which is in the heavens." So then you have been deprived of nothing, yea, you have been a gainer: you have received no wrongs, rather you have been crowned; in that you are become better disciplined in soul; are made like to God; are set free from the care of money; are made possessor of the kingdom of heaven.

All these things therefore taking into account, let us restrain ourselves in injuries, beloved, in order that we may both be freed from the tumult of this present life, and cast out all unprofitable sadness of spirit, and may obtain the joy to come; through the grace and loving-kindness of our Lord Jesus Christ, with Whom to the Father and the Holy Spirit be glory, power, honor, now, henceforth, and for ever and ever. Amen.

HOMILY XVII.

1 COR. VI. 12.

"All things are lawful for me, but not all things are expedient. All things are lawful for me, but I will not be brought into the power of any.

HERE he glances at the gluttons. For since he intends to assail the fornicator again, and fornication arises from luxuriousness and want of moderation, he strongly chastises this passion. It cannot be that he speaks thus with regard to things forbidden, such not being "lawful:" but of things which seem to be indifferent. To illustrate my meaning: "It is lawful," he says, "to eat and to drink; but it is not expedient with excess." And so that marvellous and unexpected turn of his, which he is often wont to adopt; (Cf. Rom. xii. 21; 1 Cor. 7. 23.) bringing his argument clear round to its contrary, this he manages to introduce here also; and he signifies that to do what is in one's power not only is not expedient, but even is not a part of power, but of slavery.

And first, he dissuades them on the ground of the inexpediency of the thing, saying, "they are not expedient:" in the next place, on that of its contrariety to itself, saying, "I will not be brought under the power of any." This is his meaning: "You are at liberty to eat," says he; "well then, remain in liberty, and take heed that you do not become a slave to this appetite: for he who uses it properly, he is master of it; but he that exceeds the proper measure is no longer its master but its slave, since gluttony reigns paramount within him." Do you perceive how, where the man thought he had authority Paul points out that he is under authority? For this is his custom, as I was saying before, to give all objections a turn the contrary way. It is just this which he has done here. For mark; each of them was saying, "I have power to live luxuriously." He replies, "In doing so, thou art not so much acting as one who had power over a thing, but rather as being thyself subject to some such power. For thou hast not power even over thine own belly, so long as thou art dissolute, but it hath power over thee." And the same we may say both of riches and of other things.

Ver. 13. "Meats for the belly." By "the belly" here he means not the stomach, but the stomach's voraciousness. As when he says, (Phil. iii. 19.) "Whose God is their belly:" not speaking about that part of the body, but about greediness. To prove that so it is, hear what follows: "And the belly for meats; but the body is not for fornication, but for the Lord." And yet "the belly" also is of "the body." But he puts down two pairs of things, "meats" and gluttony, (which he terms "the belly;") "Christ," and "the body."

What then is the meaning of, "Meats for the belly?" "Meats," he says, are on good terms with gluttony, and it with them. It cannot therefore lead us unto Christ, but drags towards these. For it is a strong and brutal passion, and makes us slaves, and puts us upon ministering to the belly. Why then art thou excited and gaping after food, O man? For the end of that service is this, and nothing further shall be seen of it: but as one was waiting on some mistress, it abides keeping up this slavery, and advances no further, and has no other employment but this same fruitless one. And the two are connected together and destroyed together; "the belly" with "the meats," and "the meats" with "the belly;" winding out a sort of interminable course; just as from a corrupt body worms may be produced, and again by worms the body consumed; or as it were a wave swoln high and breaking, and having no further effect. But these things he says not concerning food and the body, but it is the passion of greediness and excess in eatables which he is censuring: and what follows shews it. For he proceeds:

"But God shall bring to nought both it and them:" speaking not of the stomach, but of immoderate desire: not of food but of high feeding. For with the former he is not angry, but even lays down rules about them, saying, (1 Tim. vi. 8.) "Having food and covering we shall be therewith content. However, thus he stigmatizes the whole thing; its amendment (after advice given) being left by him to prayer.

But some say that the words are a prophecy, declaring the state which shall be in the life to come, and that there is no eating or drinking there. Now if that which is moderate shall have an end, much more ought we to abstain from excess.

Then lest any one should suppose that the body is the object of his censure, and suspect that from a part he is blaming the whole, and say that the nature of the body was the cause of gluttony or of fornication, hear what follows. "I blame not," he says, "the nature of the body, but the immoderate license of the mind." And therefore he subjoins, "Now the body is not for fornication, but for the Lord;" for it was not formed for this purpose, to live riotously and commit fornication, as neither was the belly to be greedy; but that it might follow Christ as a Head, and that the Lord might be set over the body. Let us be overcome with shame, let us be horror-struck, that after we have been counted worthy of such great honor as to become members of Him that sitteth on high, we defile ourselves with so great evils.

[2.] Having now sufficiently condemned the glutton, he uses also the hope of things to come to divert us from this wickedness: saying,

Ver. 14. And God both raised up the Lord, and will raise up us also through His power.

Do you perceive again his Apostolical wisdom? For he is always establishing the credibility of the Resurrection from Christ, and especially now. For if our body be a member of Christ, and Christ be risen, the body also shall surely follow the Head.

"Through his power." For since he had asserted a thing disbelieved and not to be apprehended by reasonings, he hath left entirely to His incomprehensible power the circumstances of Christ's own Resurrection, producing this too as no small demonstration against them. And concerning the Resurrection of Christ he did not insert this: for he did not say, "And God shall also raise up the Lord;"—for the thing was past and gone;—but how? "And God

both raised up the Lord;" nor was there need of any proof. But concerning our resurrection, since it has not yet come to pass, he spoke not thus, but how? "And will raise up us also through His power:" by the reliance to be placed on the power of the Worker, he stops the mouths of the gainsayers.

Further: if he ascribe unto the Father the Resurrection of Christ, let not this at all disturb thee. For not as though Christ were powerless, hath he put this down, for He it is Himself who saith, (S. John ii. 19.) "Destroy this Temple, and in three days I will raise it up:" and again, (S. John x. 18.) "I have power to lay down My life, and I have power to take it again." And Luke also in the Acts says, (c. i. 3.) "To whom also He shewed Himself alive." Wherefore then does Paul so speak? Because both the acts of the Son are imputed unto the Father, and the Father's unto the Son. For He saith, (S. John v. 19.) "Whatsoever things He doeth, these the Son also doeth in like manner."

And very opportunely he here made mention of the Resurrection, keeping down by those hopes the tyranny of gluttonous desire; and all but saying, Thou hast eaten, hast drunk to excess: and what is the result? Nothing, save only destruction. Thou hast been conjoined unto Christ; and what is the result? A great and marvellous thing: the future Resurrection, that glorious one, and transcending all utterance!

[3.] Let no one therefore go on disbelieving the Resurrection: but if a man disbelieve, let him think how many things He made from nothing, and admit it as a proof also of the other. For the things which are already past are stranger by far, and fraught with overpowering wonder. Just consider. He took earth and mixed it, and made man; earth which existed not before this. How then did the earth become man? And how was it produced from nothing? And, how, all the things that were made from it? the endless sorts of irrational creatures; of seeds; of plants; no pangs of travail having preceded in the one case, no rains having come down upon the others; no tillage seen, no oxen, no plough, nor any thing else contributing to their production? Why, for this cause the lifeless and senseless thing was made to put forth in the beginning so many kinds of plants and irrational creatures, in order that from the very first He might instruct thee in the doctrine of Resurrection. For this is more inexplicable than the Resurrection. For it is not the same thing to rekindle an extinguished lamp, and to shew fire that has never yet appeared. It is not the same thing to raise up again a house which has fallen down, and to produce one which has never at all had an existence. For in the former case, if nothing else, yet the material was given to work with : but in the latter, not even the substance appeared. Wherefore He made first that which seemed to be the more difficult, to the end that hereby thou mightest admit that which is the more easy ; more difficult, I say, not to God, but as far as our reasonings can follow the subject. For with God nothing is difficult : but as the painter who has made one likeness will make ten thousand with ease, so also with God it is easy to make worlds without number and end. Rather, as it is easy for you to conceive a city and worlds without bound, so unto God is it easy to make them ; or rather again it is easier by far. For thou consumest time, brief though it be, in thy conception ; but God not even this, but as much as stones are heavier than any of the lightest things, yea even than our minds ; so much is our mind surpassed by the rapidity of God's work of creation.

Do you marvel at His power on the earth ? Think again how the heaven was made, not yet being ; how the innumerable stars, how the sun, how the moon ; and all these things not yet being. Again, tell me how after they were made they stood fast, and upon what ? What foundation have they ? and what the earth ? What comes next to the earth ? and again, what after that which came next to the earth ? Do you see into what an eddy the eye of your mind is plunged, unless you quickly take refuge in faith and the incomprehensible power of the Maker ?

But if you choose from human things also to make conjecture, you will be able by degrees to find wings for your understanding. "What kind of human things ?" may be asked. Do you not see the potters, how they fashion the vase which had been broken in pieces and become shapeless ? Those who fuse the ore from the mine, how the earth in their hands turns out (τὴν γῆν χρύσιον ἀποφαίνουσι) gold, or silver, or copper ? Others again who work in glass, how they transform the sand into one compact and transparent substance ? Shall I speak of the dressers of leather, the dyers of purple vestments ; how they make that which had received their tint shew as one thing, when it had been another ? Shall I speak of the generation of our own race ? Doth not a small seed, at first without form and impress, enter into the womb which receives it ? Whence then the so intricate formation of the living creature ? What is the wheat ? Is it not cast a naked seed into the earth ? After it has been cast there, doth it not decay ? Whence is the ear, the beard, the stalk, and all the other parts ? Doth not often a little grain of a fig fall into the ground, and produce both root, and branches, and fruit ? And dost thou hereupon admit each of these and make no curious enquiries, and of God alone dost thou demand account, in His work of changing the fashion of our body ? And how can such things be pardonable ?

These things and such like we say to the Greeks. For to those who are obedient to the Scriptures, I have no occasion to speak at all.

I say, if you intend to pry curiously into all His doings, what shall God have more than men ? And yet even of men there are many about whom we do not so enquire. Much more then ought we to abstain from impertinent inquiry about the wisdom of God, and from demanding accounts of it : in the first place, because He is trustworthy who affirmeth : in the second place, because the matter admits not investigation by reasonings. For God is not so abjectly poor as to work such things only as can be apprehended by the weakness of thy reasonings. And if thou comprehendest not the work of an artisan, much less of God, the best of artificers. Disbelieve not then the Resurrection, for very far will ye be from the hope of that which is to come.

But what is the wise argument of the gainsayers ; rather, I should say, their exceeding senseless one ? "Why how, when the body is mixed up with the earth and is become earth, and this again is removed elsewhere, how," say they, "shall it rise again ?" To thee this seems impossible, but not to the unsleeping Eye. For unto that all things are clear. And thou in that confusion seest no distinction of parts ; but He knows them all. Since also the heart of thy neighbor thou knowest not, nor the things in it ; but He knoweth all. If then, because of thy not knowing how God raiseth men up, thou believest not that He doth raise them, wilt thou disbelieve that He knoweth also what is in thy mind ? for neither is that obvious to view. And yet in the body it is visible matter, though it be dissolved : but those thoughts are invisible. Shall He then who knoweth with all certainty the invisible things, not see the things which be visible, and easily distinguish the scattered parts of the body ? I suppose this is plain to every one.

Do not then disbelieve the Resurrection ; for this is a doctrine of the Devil. This is what the Devil is earnest for, not only that the Resurrection may be disbelieved, but good works also may be done away with. For the man who does not expect that he shall rise again and give an account of the things which he has done, will not quickly apply himself to virtue ; will in turn come to disbelieve the Resurrection entirely : for both these are established by each other ; vice by unbelief, and unbelief by vice. For the conscience filled with many wickednesses, fearing and trembling for the recompense to come and not willing to provide itself with comfort by changing to what is most excellent, is fain to repose in unbelief. Thus when thou deniest resurrection and judgment, the other for his part will say, "Then shall I also not have to render account of my bold deeds."

[4.] But why saith Christ? (St. Matt. xxii. 29.) "Ye do err, not knowing the Scriptures, nor the power of God." For God would not have wrought so many things, had He intended not to raise us up again, but to dissolve and blot us out in annihilation. He would not have spread out this heaven, He would not have stretched the earth beneath, He would not have made all the rest of the universe only for this short life. But if all these are for the present, what will He not do for that which is to come? If, on the contrary, there is to be no future life, we are in this respect of far meaner account than the things which have been made for our sakes. For both the heaven, and the earth, and the sea, and the rivers, are more lasting than we are: and some even of the brutes; since the raven, and the race of elephants, and many other creatures, have a longer enjoyment of the present life. To us, moreover, life is both short and toilsome, but not to them. Theirs is both long, and freer from grief and cares.

"What then? tell me: hath he made the slaves better than the masters?" Do not, I beseech thee, do not reason thus, O man, nor be so poverty-stricken in mind, nor be ignorant of the riches of God, having such a Master. For even from the beginning God desired to make thee immortal, but thou wert not willing. Since the things also of that time were dark hints of immortality: the converse with God; the absence of uneasiness from life; the freedom from grief, and cares, and toils, and other things which belong to a temporary existence. For Adam had no need either of a garment or a shelter, or any other provision of this sort; but rather was like to the Angels; and many of the things to come he foreknew, and was filled with great wisdom. Even what God did in secret, he knew, I mean with regard to the woman: wherefore also he said, "This is now bone of my bone, and flesh of my flesh." (Gen. ii. 23.) Labor came into being afterwards: so did sweat, so did shame, and cowardice, and want of confidence. But on that day there was no grief, nor pain, nor lamentation. But he abode not in that dignity.

What then, saith one, am I to do? must I perish on his account? I reply, first, It is not on his account: for neither hast thou remained without sin: though it be not the same sin, at least there is some other which thou hast committed. And again, you have not been injured by his

punishment, but rather have been a gainer. For if you had been to remain altogether mortal, perchance what is said would have had some reason in it. But now thou art immortal, and if thou wilt, thou mayest shine brighter than the sun itself.

[5.] "But," says one, "had I not received a mortal body, I had not sinned." Tell me then, had he a mortal body when he sinned? Surely not: for if it had been mortal before, it would not have undergone death as a punishment afterwards. And that a mortal body is no hindrance to virtue, but that it keeps men in order and is of the greatest service, is plain from what follows. If the expectation of immortality alone so lifted up Adam; had he been even immortal in reality, to what a pitch of arrogance would he not have proceeded? And as things are, after sinning you may do away with your sins, the body being abject, falling away, and subject to dissolution: for these thoughts are sufficient to sober a man. But if you had sinned in an immortal body, your sins were likely to have been more lasting.

Mortality then is not the cause of sin: accuse it not: but the wicked will is the root of all the mischief. For why was not Abel at all the worse for his body? Why are the devils not at all the better for being incorporeal? Wilt thou hear why the body's becoming mortal, so far from hurting, has been positively useful? Mark how much thou gainest thereby, if thou art sober. It drags thee back and pulls thee off from wickedness, by griefs and pains and labors and other such things. "But it tempts men to uncleanness," perhaps you will say. Not the body, but incontinence, doth this. For all these things which I was mentioning certainly do belong to the body: on which account it is impossible that a man who has entered into this life should escape disease and pain and lowness of spirits: but that he commit no uncleanness is possible. Thus it appears that if the affections of vice were part of the nature of the body they would be universal: since all things natural are so; but to commit fornication is not so. Pain indeed cometh of nature: but to commit fornication proceeds from deliberate purpose.

Blame not the body then; let not the Devil take away thine honor, which God hath given thee. For if we choose, the body is an excellent bridle to curb the wanton sallies of the soul, to pull down haughtiness, to repress arrogance, to minister to us in the greatest achievements of virtue. For tell me not of those who have lost their senses; since we often see horses, after they have thrown out their drivers, dashing with their reins over the precipices, and yet we do not blame the rein. For it is not the breaking of that which caused it all, but the driver not holding them in was the ruin of every thing. Just so do thou reason in this case. If thou seest a young person living in orphanhood and doing innumerable evil things, blame not the body, but the charioteer who is dragged on, I mean, the man's faculty of reasoning. For as the reins give no trouble to the charioteer, but the charioteer is the cause of all the mischief through his not holding them properly: (and therefore do they often exact a penalty of him, entangling themselves with him, and dragging him on, and compelling him to partake in their own mishap:) so is it also in the case before us. "I," say the reins, "made bloody the horse's mouth as long as you held me: but since you threw me away, I require satisfaction for your contempt, and I entwine myself about you, and drag you along, so as not to incur the same usage again." Let no one then blame the reins, but himself and his own corrupt mind. For over us too is a charioteer, even reason: and the reins are the body, connecting the horses with the charioteer; if then

these be in good condition, you will suffer no harm: but if you let them go, you have annihilated and ruined every thing. Let us be temperate then, and lay all blame not on the body, but on the evil mind. For this is the Devil's special work, to make foolish men accuse the body and God and their neighbor, rather than their own perverted minds; lest, having discovered the cause, they get free from the root of the evils.

But do ye, being aware of his design, direct your wrath against him: and having set the charioteer upon the car, bend the eye of your minds towards God. For in all other instances he that appoints the games contributes nothing, but only awaits the end. But in this case, He is all in all, who appointed the contest, even God. Him therefore let us render propitious, and surely we shall obtain the blessings in store; through the grace and loving-kindness of our Lord Jesus Christ, to Whom, with the Father and the Holy Spirit, be glory, power, honor, now, henceforth, and for evermore. Amen.

HOMILY XVIII.

1 Cor. vi. 15.

"Know ye not that your bodies are members of Christ? Shall I then take away the members of Christ, and make them members of a harlot? God forbid.

HAVING passed on from the fornicator to the covetous person, he comes back to the former from the latter, no longer henceforth discoursing with him but with the others who had not committed fornication. And in the act of securing them lest they fall into the same sins, he assails him again. For he that has committed sin, though you direct your words to another, is stung even in that way; his conscience being thoroughly awakened and scourging him.

Now the fear of punishment indeed was enough to keep them in chastity. But seeing that he does not wish by fear alone to set these matters right, he uses both threatenings and reasons.

Now upon that other occasion, having stated the sin, and prescribed the punishment, and pointed out the harm which intercourse with the fornicator brought upon all, he left off, and passed to the subject of covetousness: and having threatened the covetous and all the rest whom he mentioned with expulsion from the kingdom, he so concluded his discourse. But

here he takes in hand the work of admonition in a yet more terrific manner. For as he that only punishes a sin and does nothing to point out its most extreme lawlessness, produces no such great effect by his chastisement: so again, he who only abashes and fails to terrify by his mode of punishing, does not very keenly hit men of hardened minds. Wherefore Paul does both: here he abashes, saying, "Know ye not that we shall judge angels?" there again he terrifies, saying, "Know ye not that the covetous shall not inherit the kingdom of God?"

And in regard to the fornicator, he again uses this order of discourse. For having terrified him by what he had said before; first cutting him off and delivering him to Satan, and then reminding him of that day which is coming; he abashes him again by saying, "Know ye not that your bodies are members of Christ?" thenceforth speaking as to children of noble birth. For whereas he had said, "Now the body is for the Lord," he indicates it more plainly now. And in another place as well he does this same thing, saying, (xii. 27.) "Now ye are the body of Christ, and severally members thereof." And the same figure he often employs, not with the same aim, but at one time to shew His love, and at another to increase their fear. But here he has employed it to startle and fill them with alarm. "Shall I then take the members of Christ, and make them members of a harlot? God forbid." Nothing can be apter to strike horror than this expression. He said not, "Shall I take the members of Christ, and join them on to a harlot?" but what? "make them members of a harlot;" which surely would strike more keenly.

Then he makes out how the fornicator becomes this, saying thus, "Know ye not that he that is joined unto a harlot is one body?" How is this evident? "For the twain, saith He, shall become one."

Ver. 17. "But he that is joined unto the Lord is one spirit."

For the conjunction suffers the two no longer to be two, but makes them both one.

[2.] Now mark again, how he proceeds by means of the bare terms, conducting his accusation in the names of the harlot and of Christ.

Ver. 18. "Flee fornication."

He said not, "abstain from fornication," but "Flee:" that is, with all zeal make to yourselves deliverance from that evil. "Every sin that a man doeth is without the body; but he that committeth fornication sinneth against his own body." This is less than what went before; but since he had to speak of fornicators, he amplifies that guilt by topics drawn from all quarters, from greater things and smaller alike, making the charge heinous. And, in fact, that former topic was addressed to the more religious, but this to the weaker sort. For this also is characteristic of the wisdom of Paul, not only to allege the great things wherewith to abash men, but the lesser also, and the consideration of what is disgraceful and unseemly.

"What then," say you, "does not the murderer stain his hand? What, of the covetous person and the extortioner?" I suppose it is plain to every one. But since it was not possible to mention anything worse than the fornicator, he amplifies the crime in another way, by saying that in the fornicator the entire body becomes defiled. For it is as polluted as if it had fallen into a vessel of filth, and been immersed in defilement. And this too is our way. For from covetousness and extortion no one would make haste to go into a bath, but as if nothing had happened returns to his house. Whereas from intercourse with a harlot, as having become altogether unclean, he goes to a bath. To such a degree does the conscience retain from this sin a kind of sense of unusual shame. Both however are bad, both covetous-

ness and fornication; and both cast into hell. But as Paul doeth every thing with good management, so by whatever topics he had he magnified the sin of fornication.

[3.] Ver. 19. "Know ye not that your body is a temple of the Holy Ghost which is in you?"

He did not merely say, "of the Spirit," but, "which is in you;" which was the part of one who also was soothing. And again, explaining himself still further, he added, "which ye have from God." He mentioned Him that gave also, both exalting the hearer and putting him in fear, both by the magnitude of the deposit, and by the munificence of Him that made it.

"And ye are not you own." This is not only to abash, but even to force men towards virtue. "For why," says he; "doest thou what thou wilt? thou art not thine own master." But these things he said, not to take away free-will. For so in saying, "All things are lawful for me, but not all things are expedient," he does not take away our liberty. And here again, writing, "Ye are not your own," he makes no infringement upon freedom of choice, but he leads away from vice and indicates the guardian care of the Lord. And therefore he added, "For ye were bought with a price."

"But if I am not my own, upon what ground do you demand of me duties to be done? And why do you go on to say again, "Glorify God therefore in your body and in your spirit, which are God's?" What then is the meaning of, "ye are not your own?" And what does he wish to prove thereby? To settle them in a state of security against sin, and against following the improper desires of the mind. For indeed we have many improper wishes: but we must repress them, for we can. And if we could not, exhortation would be in vain. Mark, accordingly, how he secures his ground. For having said, "Ye are not your own," he adds not, "But are under compulsion;" but, "Ye were bought with a price." Why sayest thou this? Surely on another ground, one might say perhaps, you should have persuaded men, pointing out that we have a Master. But this is common to the Greeks also together with us: whereas the expression, "Ye were bought with a price," belongs to us peculiarly. For he reminds us of the greatness of the benefit and of the mode of our salvation, signifying that when we were alienated, we were "bought:" and not simply "bought," but, "with a price."

"Glorify then, take up and bear,[1] God in your body, and in your spirit."[2] Now these things

---

[1] ἄρατε om. in rec. text., *portate* Vulg.: so St. Ignatius was called Theophorus.
[2] [The last clause, *and in your spirit, which are God's*, not being found in the uncials, is omitted by all the modern Editors C.]

he says, that we may not only flee fornication in the body, but also in the spirit of our mind abstain from every wicked thought, and from driving away grace.

"Which are God's." For as he had said "your," he added therefore, "which are God's:" continually reminding us that all things belong to the Lord, both body and soul and spirit. For some say, that the words "in the spirit" mean the gracious Gift; for if That be in us, God is glorified. And this will be, if we have a clean heart.

But He has spoken of these things as God's, not only because He brought them into being, but also because, when they were alienated, He won them again a second time, paying as the price, the blood of the Son. Mark how He brought the whole to completion in Christ, how He raised us up into heaven. "Ye are members of Christ," saith he, "ye are a temple of the Spirit." Become not then "members of a harlot:" for it is not your body which is insulted; since it is not your body at all, but Christ's. And these things he spake, both to make manifest His loving-kindness in that our body is His, and to withdraw us from all evil license. For if the body be another's, "you have no authority," says he, "to insult another's body; and especially when it is the Lord's; nor yet to pollute a temple of the Spirit." For if any one who invades a private house and makes his way revelling into it, must answer for it most severely; think what dreadful things he shall endure who makes a temple of the King a robber's lurking place.

Considering these things therefore, reverence thou Him that dwelleth within. For the Paraclete is He. Thrill before Him that is enfolded and cleaves unto thee; for Christ is He. Hast thou indeed made thyself members of Christ? Think thus, and continue chaste; whose members they were, and Whose they have become. Erewhile they were members of an harlot, and Christ hath made them members of His own Body. Thou hast therefore henceforth no authority over them. Serve Him that hath set thee free.

For supposing you had a daughter, and in extreme madness had let her out to a procurer for hire, and made her live a harlot's life, and then a king's son were to pass by, and free her from that slavery, and join her in marriage to himself; you could have no power thenceforth to bring her into the brothel. For you gave her up once for all, and sold her. Such as this is our case also. We let out our own flesh for hire unto the Devil, that grievous procurer: Christ saw and set it free, and withdrew it from that evil tyranny; it is not then ours any more but His who delivered it. If you be willing to use it as a King's bride, there is none to hinder; but if you bring it where it was before, you will suffer just what they ought who are guilty of such outrages. Wherefore you should rather adorn instead of disgracing it. For you have no authority over the flesh in the wicked lusts, but in those things alone which God may enjoin. Let the thought enter your mind at least from what great outrage God hath delivered it. For in truth never did any harlot expose herself so shamefully as our nature before this. For robberies, murders, and every wicked thought entered in and lay with the soul, and for a small and vulgar hire, the present pleasure. For the soul, being mixed up with all wicked devices and deeds, reaped this reward and no other.

However, in the time before this, bad though it were to be such as these, it was not so bad: but after heaven, after the King's courts, after partaking of the tremendous Mysteries, again to be contaminated, what pardon shall this have? Or, dost thou not think that the covetous too, and all those whom he recounted before, have the Devil to lie with them? And dost thou not judge that the women who beautify themselves for pollution have intercourse with him? Why, who shall gainsay this word? But if any be contentious, let him uncover the soul of the women who behave in this unseemly manner, and he will surely see that the wicked demon closely entwined with them. For it is hard, brethren, it is hard, perchance even impossible, when the body is thus beautified, for the soul to be beautified at the same time: but one must needs be neglected, while the other is cared for. For nature does not allow these to take place together.

[4.] Wherefore he saith, "He that is joined to a harlot is one body; but he that is joined to the Lord is one Spirit." For such an one becomes thenceforth Spirit, although a body envelope him. For when nothing corporeal nor gross nor earthly is around him, the body doth but merely envelope him; since the whole government of him is in the soul and the Spirit. In this way God is glorified. Wherefore both in the Prayer we are commanded to say, "Hallowed be Thy Name:" and Christ saith also, "Let your light shine before men, that they may see your good works, and glorify your Father which is in heaven."

So do the heavens also glorify Him, uttering no voice, but by the view of them attracting wonder and referring the glory unto the Great Artificer. So let us glorify Him also, or rather more than they. For we can if we will. For not so much do the heaven nor day nor night glorify God, as a holy soul. For as one that gazeth upon the beauty of the heaven, saith,

" Glory be to Thee, O God! How fair a work hast thou formed!" so too when beholding virtue in any man: nay, and much more so in the latter instance. For from these works of creation all do not glorify God; but many even assert that the things which exist are self-moving: and others impute to demons the workmanship of the world and providence; and these indeed greatly and unpardonably err: but in regard to the virtue of man, no one shall have power to hold these shameless opinions, but shall assuredly glorify God when he seeth him that serveth Him living in goodness. For who shall help being astonished when one being a man, and partaking of our common nature, and living among other men, like adamant yields not at all to the swarm of passions? When being in the midst of fire and iron and wild beasts, he is even harder than adamant and vanquishes all for the Word of godliness' sake? when he is injured, and blesses; when he is evil reported of, and praises; when he is despitefully used, and prays for those who injure him; when he is plotted against, and does good to those that fight with him and lay snares for him? For these things, and such as these, will glorify God far more than the heaven. For the Greeks when they behold the heavens feel no awe; but when they see a holy man exhibiting a severe course of life with all strictness, they shrink away and condemn themselves. Since when he that partakes of the same nature as themselves is so much above them, a great deal more so than the heaven is above the earth, even against their inclination they think that it is a Divine power which works these things. Wherefore He saith, " And glorify your Father which is in heaven."

[5.] Wilt thou learn also from another place how by the life of His servants God is glorified, and how by miracles? Nebuchadnezzar once threw the Three Children into the furnace. Then when he saw that the fire had not prevailed over them, he saith, (Dan. iii. 28. LXX. ἐκ τῆς καμίνου added.) " Blessed be God, who hath sent His Angel, and delivered his servants out of the furnace, because they trusted in Him and have changed the word of the king." " How sayest thou? Hast thou been despised, and dost thou admire those who have spit upon you?" " Yes," saith he, " and for this very reason, that I was despised." And of the marvel he gives this reason. So that not because of the miracle alone was glory given to God at that time, but also because of the purpose of those who have been thrown in. Now if any one would examine this point and the other, as they are in themselves, this will appear not less than that: for to persuade souls to brave a furnace is

not less in respect of the wonder than to deliver from a furnace. For how can it be otherwise than astonishing for the Emperor of the world, with so many arms around him, and legions, and generals, and viceroys, and consuls, and land and sea subject to his sway, to be despised by captive children; for the bound to overcome the binder and conquer all that army? Neither was there any power in the king and his company to do what they would, no, not even with the furnaces for an ally. But they who were naked, and slaves, and strangers, and few, (for what number could be more contemptible than three?) being in chains, vanquished an innumerable army. For already now was death despised, since Christ was henceforth about to sojourn in the world. And as when the sun is on the point of rising, even before his rays appear the light of the day groweth bright; so also when then the Sun of Righteousness was about to come, death henceforth began to withdraw himself. What could be more splendid than that theatre? What more conspicuous than that victory? What more signal than those new trophies of theirs?

The same thing is done in our time also. Even now is there a king of the Babylonish furnace, even now he kindles a flame fiercer than that. There is even now such an image, and one who giveth command to admire it. At his side are satraps and soldiers and bewitching music. And many gaze in admiration upon this image, so varied, so great. For somewhat of the same kind of thing as that image is covetousness, which doth not despise even iron[1], but unlike as the materials are whereof it is composed, it giveth command to admire all, both brass and iron, and things much more ordinary than they.

But as these things are, so also even now are there some who are emulous of these children: who say, " thy gods we serve not, and thine images we worship not;" but both the furnace of poverty we endure and all other distress, for the sake of God's laws." And the wealthy for their part, even as those at that time, oftentimes, worship this image too and are burnt. But those who possess nothing despise even this, and although in poverty, are more in the dew[2] than those who live in affluence. Even as at that time they who cast into the fire were burnt up; but those in the midst of it found themselves in dew as it were rain. Then also that tyrant was more burnt up with the flame, his wrath kindling him violently, than those children. As to them, the fire had no power even to touch the

---

[1] St. Chrysostom evidently considers the image which Nebuchadnezzar set up as intended to represent the image which he had seen in his dream.

[2] Μᾶλλον εἰσὶ ἐν δρόσῳ. Alluding to the words in LXX, ἐποίησε τὸ μέσον τῆς καμίνου ὡς πνεῦμα δρόσου διασύριζον. v. 26.

ends of their hair : but more fiercely than that
fire did wrath burn up his mind.   For consider
what a thing it was that with so many to look
on, he should be scorned by captive children.
And it was a sign that his taking their city also
had not been through his own might, but by
reason of the sin of the multitude among them.
Since if he had not the power to overcome these
men in chains, and that when they were cast
into a furnace, how could he have overcome
the Jews in regular warfare, had they been all
such as these?   From which it is plain that the
sins of the multitude betrayed the city.

[6.] But mark also the children's freedom
from vain-glory.   For they did not leap into the
furnace, but they kept beforehand the commandment of Christ where he says, (St. Matt. xxvi.
41.) "Pray that ye enter not into temptation."
Neither did they shrink when they were brought
to it ; but stood in the midst nobly, neither contending without a summons, nor yet when summoned playing the coward : but ready for everything, and noble, and full of all boldness of
speech.

But let us hear also what they say, that from
this also we may learn their [1] lofty spirit.   (Dan.
iii. 17.)   "There is a God in heaven able to
deliver us :" they take no care for themselves, but
even when about to be burned the glory of God
is all their thought.   For what they say comes to
this, "Lest perchance if we are burnt thou shouldest charge God with weakness, we now declare
unto thee accurately our whole doctrine.   "There
is a God in heaven," not such as this image here
on earth, this lifeless and mute thing, but able to
snatch even from the midst of the burning fiery
furnace.   Condemn him not then of weakness
for permitting us to fall into it.   So powerful is
He that after our fall, He is able to snatch us
out again out of the flame.   "But if not, be it
known unto thee, O king, that we will not serve
thy gods, nor worship the golden image which
thou hast set up."   Observe that they by a
special dispensation are ignorant of the future :
for if they had foreknown, there would have
been nothing wonderful in their doing what
they did.   For what marvel is it if when they
had a guarantee for safety, they defied all terrors?   Then God indeed would have been
glorified in that He was able to deliver from
the furnace : but they would not have been
wondered at, inasmuch as they would not have
cast themselves into any dangers.   For this
cause He suffered them to be ignorant of the
future that He might glorify them the more.
And as they cautioned (ἠσφαλίζοντο) the king
that he was not to condemn God of weakness
though they might be burnt, so God accomplished both purposes ; the shewing forth His

own power and the causing the zeal of the children to appear more conspicuous.

From whence then arose their doubting and
their not feeling confident that they should at
all events be preserved ?   Because they esteemed
themselves assuredly too mean, and unworthy of
such a benefit.   And to prove that I say not
this upon conjecture ; when they fell into the
furnace, they bewailed themselves after this sort,
saying, (Song of the three Children vv. 6, 10.)
"We have sinned, we have done iniquity, we
cannot open our mouth."   And therefore they
said, "But if not."   But if they did not plainly
say this, namely, "God is able to deliver us ;
but if he deliver us not, for our sin's sake He will
not deliver us ;" wonder not at it.   For they
would have seemed to the barbarians to be sheltering the weakness of God under the pretext of
their own sins.   Wherefore His power only is
what they speak of : the reason they allege not.
And besides, they were well disciplined not to
be over-curious about the judgments of God.

With these words then, they entered into the
fire ; and they neither cast insult upon the king,
nor overturned the statue.[2]   For such should
the courageous man be, temperate and mild ;
and that especially in dangers ; that he may not
seem to go forth to such contests in wrath and
vain-glory ; but with fortitude and self-possession.   For whoso deals insolently undergoes the
suspicion of those faults : but he that endures,
and is forced into the struggle, and goes through
the trial with meekness, is not only admired as
brave, but his self-possession also and consideration cause him to be no less extolled.   And this
is what they did at that time ; shewing forth
all fortitude and gentleness, and doing nothing for reward nor for recompense or return.
"'Though He be not willing 'so it stands'
to deliver us, we will not serve thy gods :' for
we have already our recompense in that we are
counted worthy to be kept from all impiety, and
for that end to give our bodies to be burned."

We then also having already our recompense,
(for indeed we have it in that we have been
vouchsafed the full knowledge of Him, vouchsafed to be made members of Christ,) let us
take care that we make them not members of an
harlot.   For with this most tremendous saying
we must conclude our discourse, in order that
having the fear of the threat in full efficacy, we
may remain purer than gold, this fear helping
to make us so.   For so shall we be able, delivered from all fornication, to see Christ.   Whom
God grant us all to behold with boldness at that
day, through the grace and loving-kindness of
our Lord Jesus Christ ; to Whom be the glory,
for evermore.   Amen.

---

[1] MS. Reg. φιλόθεον, "devout." Bened. φιλόσοφον.

[2] This may be a covert allusion to the outrage on the statues of
Theodosius, which had brought Antioch into so great trouble in
the second year of S. Chrysostom's ministry there.

HOMILY XIX.

1 COR. vii. 1, 2.

Now concerning the things whereof ye wrote to me: it is good for a man not to touch a woman. But because of fornications, let each man have his own wife; and let each woman have her own husband.

HAVING corrected the three heaviest things laid to their charge, one, the distraction of the Church, another, about the fornicator, a third, about the covetous person, he thenceforth uses a milder sort of speech. And he interposes some exhortation and advice about marriage and virginity, giving the hearers some respite from more unpleasant subjects. But in the second Epistle he does the contrary; he begins from the milder topics, and ends with the more distressing. And here also, after he has finished his discourse about virginity, he again launches forth into matter more akin to reproof; not setting all down in regular order, but varying his discourse in either kind, as the occasion required and the exigency of the matters in hand.

Wherefore he says, " Now concerning the things whereof ye wrote unto me." For they had written to him, " Whether it was right to abstain from one's wife, or not:" and writing back in answer to this and giving rules about marriage, he introduces also the discourse concerning virginity: " It is good for a man not to touch a woman." " For if," says he, " thou enquire what is the excellent and greatly superior course, it is better not to have any connection whatever with a woman: but if you ask what is safe and helpful to thine own infirmity, be connected by marriage."

But since it was likely, as also happens now, that the husband might be willing but the wife not, or perhaps the reverse, mark how he discusses each case. Some indeed say that this discourse was addressed by him to priests. But I, judging from what follows, could not affirm that it was so: since he would not have given his advice in general terms. For if he were writing these things only for the priests, he would have said, " It is good for the teacher not to touch a woman." But now he has made it of universal application, saying, "It is good for a man;" not for priest only. And again, " Art thou loosed from a wife? Seek not a wife." He said not, " You who are a priest and teacher," but

indefinitely. And the whole of his speech goes on entirely in the same tone. And in saying, " Because of fornications, let every man have his own wife " by the very cause alleged for the concession he guides men to continence.

[2.] Ver. 3. " Let the husband pay the wife the honor[1] due to her: in like manner the wife the husband."

Now what is the meaning of " the due honor? The wife hath not power over her own body;" but is both the slave and the mistress of the husband. And if you decline the service which is due, you have offended God. But if thou wish to withdraw thyself, it must be with the husband's permission, though it be but a for short time. For this is why he calls the matter a debt, to shew that no one is master of himself but that they are servants to each other.

When therefore thou seest an harlot tempting thee, say, " My body is not mine, but my wife's." The same also let the woman say to those who would undermine her chastity, " My body is not mine, but my husband's."

Now if neither husband nor wife hath power even over their own body, much less have they over their property. Hear ye, all that have husbands and all that have wives: that if you must not count your body your own, much less your money

Elsewhere I grant He gives to the husband abundant precedence, both in the New Testament, and the Old saying, (ἡ ἀποστροφή σου, LXX. Gen. iii. 16.) " Thy turning shall be towards thy husband, and he shall rule over thee." Paul doth so too by making a distinction thus, and writing, (Ephes. v. 25, 33.) " Husbands, love your wives; and let the wife see that she reverence her husband." But in this place we hear no more of greater and less, but it is one and the same right. Now why is this? Because his speech was about chastity. " In all other things," says he, " let the husband have the prerogative; but not so where the question is about chastity." " The husband hath no power over his own body, neither the wife." There is great equality of honor, and no prerogative.

---

[1] τιμὴν: rec. text. εὐνοίαν. [The latest editors adopt the reading 'ὀφειλὴν. C.]

[3.] Ver. 5. " Defraud ye not one the other, except it be by consent."

What then can this mean ? " Let not the wife," says he, " exercise continence, if the husband be unwilling ; nor yet the husband without the wife's consent." Why so ? Because great evils spring from this sort of continence. For adulteries and fornications and the ruin of families have often arisen from hence. For if when men have their own wives they commit fornication, much more if yon defraud them of this consolation. And well says he, " Defraud not ; fraud " here, and " debt " above, that he might shew the strictness of the right of dominion in question. For that one should practice continence against the will of the other is " defrauding ; " but not so, with the other's consent : any more than I count myself defrauded, if after persuading me you take away any thing of mine. Since only he defrauds who takes against another's will and by force. A thing which many women do, working sin rather than righteousness, and thereby becoming acountable for the husband's uncleanness, and rending all asunder. Whereas they should value concord above all things, since this is more important than all beside.

We will, if you please, consider it with a view to actual cases. Thus, suppose a wife and husband, and let the wife be continent, without consent of her husband ; well then, if hereupon he commit fornication, or though abstaining from fornication fret and grow restless and be heated and quarrel and give all kind of trouble to his wife ; where is all the gain of the fasting and the continence, a breach being made in love ? There is none. For what strange reproaches, how much trouble, how great a war must of course arise ! since when in an house man and wife are at variance, the house will be no better off than a ship in a storm when the master is upon ill terms with the man at the head. Wherefore he saith, " Defraud not one another, unless it be by consent for a season, that ye may give yourselves unto prayer." It is prayer with unusual earnestness which he here means. For if he is for bidding those who have intercourse with one another to pray, how could " pray without ceasing " have any place ? It is possible then to live with a wife and yet give heed unto prayer. But by continence prayer is made more perfect. For he did not say merely, " That ye may pray ; " but, " That ye may give yourselves unto it ; " as though what he speaks of might cause not uncleanness but much occupation.

" And may be together again, that Satan tempt you not." Thus lest it should seem to be a matter of express enactment, he adds the reason. And what is it ? " That Satan tempt you not." And that you may understand that it is not the devil only who causeth this crime, I mean adultery, he adds, " because of your incontinency."

" But this I say by way of permission, not of commandment. For I would that all men were even as I myself ; in a state of continence." This he doth in many places when he is advising about difficult matters ; he brings forward himself, and says, " Be ye imitators of me."

" Howbeit each man hath his own gift from God, one after this manner, and another after that." Thus since he had heavily charged them saying, " for your incontinence," he again comforteth them by the words, " each one hath his own gift of God ;" not declaring that towards that virtue there is no need of zeal on our part, but, as I was saying before, to comfort them. For if it be a " gift," and man contributes nothing thereunto, how sayest thou, " But (v. 8.) I say to the unmarried and to widows, it is good for them if they abide even as I : (v. 9.) but if they have not continency let them marry ?" Do you see the strong sense of Paul how he both signifies that continence is better, and yet puts no force on the person who cannot attain to it ; fearing lest some offence arise ?

" For it is better to marry than to burn." He indicates how great is the tyranny of concupiscence. What he means is something like this : " If you have to endure much violence and burning desire, withdraw yourself from your pains and toils, lest haply you be subverted."

[4.] Ver. 10. " But to the married I give charge, yet not I, but the Lord."

Because it is a law expressly appointed by Christ which he is about to read to them about the " not putting away a wife without fornication ; "(S. Mat. v. 32 ; xix. 9 ; S. Mark x. 11 ; S. Luke xvi. 18.) therefore he says, " Not I." True it is what was before spoken though it were not expressly stated, yet it also is His decree. But this, you see, He had delivered in express words. So that the words " I and not I " have this difference of meaning. For that you might not imagine even his own words to be human, therefore he added, " For I think that I also have the Spirit of God."

Now what is that which " to the married the Lord commanded ? That the wife depart not from her husband : (v. 11.) but if she depart, let her remain unmarried, or be reconciled unto her husband." Here, seeing that both on the score of continence and other pretexts, and because of infirmities of temper, (μιχροφυχίας.) it fell out that separations took place : it were better, he says, that such things should not be at all; but however if they take place, let the wife remain with her husband, if not to cohabit with him, yet so as not to introduce any other to be her husband.

Ver. 12. "But to the rest speak I, not the Lord. If any brother have a wife that believeth not, and she is content to dwell with him, let him not leave her. And if any woman hath an husband that believeth not, and he is content to dwell with her, let her not leave him."

For as when discoursing about separating from fornicators, he made the matter easy by the correction which he applied to his words, saying, "Howbeit, not altogether with the fornicators of this world;" so also in this case he provideth for the abundant easiness of the duty, saying, "If any wife have a husband, or husband a wife, that believeth not, let him not leave her." What sayest thou? "If he be an unbeliever, let him remain with the wife, but not if he be a fornicator? And yet fornication is a less sin than unbelief." I grant, fornication is a less sin: but God spares thine infirmities extremely. And this is what He doth about the sacrifice, saying, (S. Mat. v. 24.) "Leave the sacrifice, and be reconciled to thy brother." This also in the case of the man who owed ten thousand talents. For him too He did not punish for owing him ten thousand talents, but for demanding back a hundred pence from his fellow-servant He took vengeance on him.

Then lest the woman might fear, as though she became unclean because of intercourse with her husband, he says, "For the unbelieving husband is sanctified in the wife, and the unbelieving wife is sanctified in the husband." And yet, if "he that is joined to an harlot is one body," it is quite clear that the woman also who is joined to an idolater is one body. Well: it is one body; nevertheless she becomes not unclean, but the cleanness of the wife overcomes the uncleanness of the husband; and again, the cleanness of the believing husband overcomes the uncleanness of the unbelieving wife.

How then in this case is the uncleanness overcome, and therefore the intercourse allowed; while in the woman who prostitutes herself, the husband is not condemned in casting her out? Because here there is hope that the lost member may be saved through the marriage; but in the other case the marriage has already been dissolved; and there again both are corrupted; but here the fault is in one only of the two. I mean something like this: she that has been guilty of fornication is utterly abominable: if then "he that is joined to an harlot is one body," he also becomes abomina-

ble by having connection with an harlot; wherefore all the purity flits away. But in the case before us it is not so. But how? The idolater is unclean but the woman is not unclean. For if indeed she were a partner with him in that wherein he is unclean, I mean his impiety, she herself would also become unclean. But now the idolater is unclean in one way, and the wife holds communion with him in another wherein he is not unclean. For marriage and mixture of bodies is that wherein the communion consists.

Again, there is a hope that this man may be reclaimed by his wife for she is made completely his own: but for the other it is not very easy. For how will she who dishonored him in former times and became another's and destroyed the rights of marriage, have power to reclaim him whom she had wronged; him, moreover, who still remains to her as an alien?

Again in that case, after the fornication the husband is not a husband: but here, although the wife be an idolatress, the husband's rights are not destroyed.

However, he doth not simply recommend cohabitation with the unbeliever, but with the qualification that he wills it. Wherefore he said, "And he himself be content to dwell with her." For, tell me, what harm is there when the duties of piety remain unimpaired and there are good hopes about the unbeliever, that those already joined should so abide and not bring in occasions of unnecessary warfare? For the question now is not about those who have never yet come together, but about those who are already joined. He did not say, If any one wish to take an unbelieving wife, but, "If any one hath an unbelieving wife." Which means, If any after marrying or being married have received the word of godliness, and then the other party which had continued in unbelief still yearn for them to dwell together, let not the marriage be broken off. "For," saith he, "the unbelieving husband is sanctified in the wife." So great is the superabundance of thy purity.

What then, is the Greek holy? Certainly not: for he said not, He is holy; but, "He is sanctified in his wife." And this he said, not to signify that he is holy, but to deliver the woman as completely as possible from her fear and lead the man to desire the truth. For the uncleanness is not in the bodies wherein there is communion, but in the mind and the thoughts. And here follows the proof; namely, that if thou continuing unclean have offspring, the child, not being of thee alone, is of course unclean or half clean. But now it is not unclean. To which effect he adds, "else were your children unclean; but now are they holy;"

that is, not unclean. But the Apostle calls them, "holy," by the intensity of the expression again casting out the dread arising from that sort of suspicion.

Ver. 15. "Yet if the unbelieving departeth, let him depart," for in this case the matter is no longer fornication. But what is the meaning of, "if the unbelieving departeth?" For instance, if he bid thee sacrifice and take part in his ungodliness on account of thy marriage, or else part company; it were better the marriage were annulled, and no breach made in godliness. Wherefore he adds, "A brother is not under bondage, nor yet a sister, in such cases." If day by day he buffet thee and keep up combats on this account, it is better to separate. For this is what he glances at, saying, "But God hath called us in peace." For it is the other party who furnished the ground of separation, even as he did who committed uncleanness.

Ver. 16. "For how knowest thou, O wife, whether thou shalt save thine husband?" This again refers to that expression, "let her not leave him." That is, "if he makes no disturbance, remain," saith he, "for there is even profit in this; remain and advise and give counsel and persuade." For no teacher will have such power to prevail (Reg. πεῖσαι. Bened. ἰσχῦσαι.[1]) as a wife. And neither, on one hand, doth he lay any necessity upon her and absolutely demand the point of her, that he may not again do what would be too painful; nor, on the other, doth he tell her to despair: but he leaves the matter in suspense through the uncertainty of the future, saying, "For how knowest thou, O wife, whether thou shalt save thy husband? or how knowest thou, O husband whether thou shalt save thy wife?"

[5.] And again, ver. 17. "Only as God hath distributed to each man, as the Lord hath called each, so let him walk. Was any one called being circumcised? let him not become uncircumcised. Was any called in uncircumcision? let him not be circumcised. Circumcision is nothing, and uncircumcision is nothing; but the keeping of the commandments of God. Let each man abide in that calling wherein he was called. Wast thou called, being a slave? Care not for it." These things contribute nothing unto faith, saith he. Be not then contentious neither be troubled; for the faith hath cast out all these things.

"Let each man abide in that calling wherein he was called. Hast thou been called, having an unbelieving wife? Continue to have her. Cast not out thy wife for the faith's sake. Hast thou been called, being a slave? Care not for it. Continue to be a slave. Hast thou been

called, being in uncircumcision? Remain uncircumcised. Being circumcised, didst thou become a believer? Continue circumcised. For this is the meaning of, "As God hath distributed unto each man." For these are no hindrances to piety. Thou art called, being a slave; another, with an unbelieving wife; another, being circumcised.

Astonishing! where has he put slavery? As circumcision profits not: and uncircumcision does no harm; so neither doth slavery, nor yet liberty. And that he might point out this with surpassing clearness, he says, "But even (Ἀλλ' εἰ καὶ δυνάσαι) if thou canst become free, use it rather:" that is, rather continue a slave. Now upon what possible ground does he tell the person who might be set free to remain a slave? He means to point out that slavery is no harm but rather an advantage.

Now we are not ignorant that some say, the words, "use it rather," are spoken with regard to liberty: interpreting it, "if thou canst become free, become free."[2] But the expression would be very contrary to Paul's manner if he intended this. For he would not, when consoling the slave and signifying that he was in no respect injured, have told him to get free. Since perhaps some one might say, "What then, if I am not able? I am an injured and degraded person." This then is not what he says: but as I said, meaning to point out that a man gets nothing by being made free, he says, "Though thou hast it in thy power to be made free, remain rather in slavery."

Next he adds also the cause; "For he that was called in the Lord being a bondservant, is the Lord's free man: likewise he that was called, being free, is Christ's bondservant." "For," saith he, "in the things that relate to Christ, both are equal: and like as thou art the slave of Christ, so also is thy master. How then is the slave a free man? Because He has freed thee not only from sin, but also from outward slavery while continuing a slave. For he suffers not the slave to be a slave, not even though he be a man abiding in slavery: and this is the great wonder.

But how is the slave a free man while continuing a slave? When he is freed from passions and the diseases of the mind: when he looks down upon riches and wrath and all other the like passions.

Ver. 23. "Ye were bought with a price: become not bondservants of men." This saying is addressed not to slaves only but also to free men. For it is possible for one who is a slave not to be a slave; and for one who is a free man to be

---

[1] [The latter is adopted by Field.]

[2] [This is the view of Calvin, Neander, Hoffmann, etc., but Bengel, De Wette, Meyer, Alford, Stanley, Principal Edwards agree with Chrysostom. The question is a very nice one. C.]

a slave. "And how can one be a slave and not a slave?" When he doeth all for God : when he feigns nothing, and doeth nothing out of eye-service towards men : that is how one that is a slave to men can be free. Or again, how doth one that is free become a slave? When he serves men in any evil service, either for gluttony or desire of wealth or for office' sake. For such an one, though he be free, is more of a slave than any man.

And consider both these points. Joseph was a slave but not a slave to men : wherefore even in slavery he was freer than all that are free. For instance, he yielded not to his mistress; yielded not to the purposes which she who possessed him desired. Again she was free ; yet none ever so like a slave, courting and beseeching her own servant. But she prevailed not on him, who was free, to do what he would not. This then was not slavery ; but it was liberty of the most exalted kind. For what impediment to virtue had he from his slavery? Let men hear, both slaves and free. Which was the slave? He that was entreated or she that did entreat? She that besought or he that despised her supplication ?

In fact, there are limits set to slaves by God Himself ; and up to what point one ought to keep them, has also been determined, and to transgress them is wrong. Namely, when your master commands nothing which is unpleasing to God, it is right to follow and to obey ; but no farther. For thus the slave becomes free. But if you go further, even though you are free you are become a slave. At least he intimates this, saying, "Be not ye the servants of men."

But if this be not the meaning, if he bade them forsake their masters and strive contentiously to become free, in what sense did he exhort them, saying, "Let each one remain in the calling in which he is called?" And in another place, (1 Tim. vi. 1, 2.) "As many servants as are under the yoke, let them count their own masters worthy of all honor ; and those that have believing masters, let them not despise them, because they are brethren who partake of the benefit." And writing to the Ephesians also and to the Colossians, he ordains and exacts the same rules. Whence it is plain that it is not this slavery which he annuls, but that which caused as it is by vice befalls free men also : and this is the worst kind of slavery, though he be a free man who is in bondage to it. For what profit had Joseph's brethren of their freedom? Were they not more servile than all slaves ; both speaking lies to their father, and to the merchants using false pretences, as well as to their brother? But not such was the free man : rather every where and in all things he was true. And nothing had power to enslave him,

neither chain nor bondage nor the love of his mistress nor his being in a strange land. But he abode free every where. For this is liberty in the truest sense when even in bondage it shines through.

[6.] Such a thing is Christianity ; in slavery it bestows freedom. And as that which is by nature an invulnerable body then shews itself to be invulnerable when having received a dart it suffers no harm ; so also he that is strictly free then shows himself, when even under masters he is not enslaved. For this cause his bidding is, "remain a slave." But if it is impossible for one who is a slave to be a Christian such as he ought to be, the Greeks will condemn true religion of great weakness : whereas if they can be taught that slavery in no way impairs godliness, they will admire our doctrine. For if death hurt us not, nor scourges, nor chains, much less slavery. Fire and iron and tyrannies innumerable and diseases and poverty and wild beasts and countless things more dreadful than these, have not been able to injure the faithful ; nay, they have made them even mightier. And how shall slavery be able to hurt? It is not slavery itself, beloved, that hurts ; but the real slavery is that of sin. And if thou be not a slave in this sense, be bold and rejoice. No one shall have power to do thee any wrong, having the temper which cannot be enslaved. But if thou be a slave to sin, even though thou be ten thousand times free thou hast no good of thy freedom.

For, tell me, what profit is it when, though not in bondage to a man, thou liest down in subjection to thy passions? Since men indeed often know how to spare ; but those masters are never satiated with thy destruction. Art thou in bondage to a man? Why, thy master also is slave to thee, in arranging about thy food, in taking care of thy health and in looking after thy shoes and all the other things. And thou dost not fear so much less thou shouldest offend thy master, as he fears lest any of those necessaries should fail thee. "But he sits down, while thou standest." And what of that? Since this may be said of thee as well as of him. Often, at least, when thou art lying down and sleeping sweetly, he is not only standing, but undergoing endless discomforts in the market-place ; and he lies awake more painfully than thou.

For instance ; what did Joseph suffer from his mistress to be compared with what she suffered from her evil desire? For he indeed did not the things which she wished to put upon him ; but she performed every thing which her mistress ordered her, I mean her spirit of unchastity : which left not off until it had put her to open shame. What master commands such things? what savage tyrant? "Intreat thy slave," that is the word: "flatter the person bought with thy money, supplicate the captive; even if he reject thee with disgust, again besiege him: even if thou speakest to him oftentimes, and he consent not, watch for his being alone, and force him, and become an object of derision." What can be more dishonorable, what more shameful, than these words? "And if even by these means you make no progress, why, accuse him falsely and deceive your husband." Mark how mean, how shameful are the commands, how unmerciful and savage and frantic. What command does the master ever lay on his slave, such as those which her wantonness then laid upon that royal woman? And yet she dare not disobey. But Joseph underwent nothing of this sort, but every thing on the contrary which brought glory and honor.

Would you like to see yet another man under severe orders from a hard mistress, and without spirit to disobey any of them? Consider Cain, what commands were laid on him by his envy. She ordered him to slay his brother, to lie unto God, to grieve his father, to cast off shame; and he did it all, and in nothing refused to obey. And why marvel that over a single person so great should be the power of this mistress? She hath often destroyed entire nations. For instance, the Midianitish women took the Jews, and all but bound them in captivity; their own beauty kindling desire, was the means of their vanquishing that whole nation. Paul then to cast out this sort of slavery, said, "Become not servants of men;" that is, "Obey not men commanding unreasonable things: nay, obey not yourselves." Then having raised up their mind and made it mount on high, he says,

[7.] Ver. 25. "Now concerning virgins. I have no commandment of the Lord; but I give my judgment, as one that hath obtained mercy of the Lord to be faithful."

Advancing on his way in regular order, he proceeds next to speak concerning virginity. For after that he had exercised and trained them, in his words concerning continence, he goes forth towards what is greater, saying, "I have no commandment, but I esteem it to be good." For what reason? For the self-same reason as he had mentioned respecting continence.

Ver. 27. "Art thou bound unto a wife? Seek not to be loosed. Art thou loosed from a wife? Seek not a wife."

These words carry no contradiction to what had been said before but rather the most entire agreement with them. For he says in that place also, "Except it be by consent:" as here he says, "Art thou bound unto a wife? Seek

not separation." This is no contradiction. For its being against consent makes a dissolution: but if with consent both live continently, it is no dissolution.

Then, lest this should seem to be laying down a law, he subjoins, (v. 28.) "but if thou marry, thou hast not sinned." He next alleges the existing state of things, "the present distress, the shortness of the time," and "the affliction." For marriage draws along with it many things, which indeed he hath glanced at, as well here as also in the discourse about continence: there, by saying, "the wife hath not power over herself;" and here, by the expression, "Thou art bound."

"But if and thou marry, thou hast not sinned." He is not speaking about her who hath made choice of virginity, for if it comes to that, she hath sinned. Since if the widows[1] are condemned for having to do with second marriages after they have once chosen widowhood, much more the virgins.

"But such shall have trouble in the flesh." "And pleasure too," you will say: but observe how he curtails this by the shortness of the time, saying, (v. 28.) "the time is shortened;" that is, "we are exhorted to depart now and go forth, but thou art running further in." And yet even although marriage had no troubles, even so we ought to press on towards things to come. But when it hath affliction too, what need to draw on one's self an additional burden. What occasion to take up such a load, when even after taking it you must use it as having it not? For "those even that have wives must be," he saith, "as though they had none."

Then, having interposed something about the future, he brings back his speech to the present. For some of his topics are spiritual; as that, "the one careth about the things which be her husband's, the other about those which be God's." Others relate to this present life; as, "I would have you to be free from cares." But still with all this he leaves it to their own choice: inasmuch as he who after proving what is best goes back to compulsion, seems as if he did not trust his own statements. Wherefore he rather attracts them by concession, and checks them as follows:

Ver. 35. "And this I say for your own profit, not that I may cast a snare upon you, but for that which is seemly, and that ye may attend upon the Lord without distraction.

Let the virgins hear that not by that one point is virginity defined; for she that is careful about the things of the world cannot be a virgin, nor seemly. Thus, when he said, "There is difference between a wife and a virgin," he added this as the difference, and that wherein they are distinguished from each other And laying down

---

[1] i. e. the widows whom St. Paul mentions, 1. Tim. v. 11, 12.

the definition of a virgin and her that is not a virgin, he names, not marriage nor continence but leisure from engagements and multiplicity of engagements. For the evil is not in the cohabitation, but in the impediment to the strictness of life.

Ver. 36. "But if any man think that he behaveth himself unseemly toward his virgin."

Here he seems to be talking about marriage; but all that he says relates to virginity; for he allows even a second marriage, saying, "only in the Lord." Now what means, "in the Lord?" With chastity, with honor: for this is needed very where, and must be pursued; for else we cannot see God.

Now if we have passed lightly by what he says of virginity, let no one accuse us of negligence; for indeed an entire book hath been composed by us upon this topic and as we have there with all the accuracy which we could, gone through every branch of the subject, we considered it a waste of words to introduce it again here. Wherefore, referring the hearer to that work as concerns these things, we will say this one thing here: We must follow after continence. For, saith he, "follow after peace, and the sanctification without which no one shall see the Lord." Therefore that we may be accounted worthy to see Him, whether we be in virginity or in the first marriage or the second, let us follow after this that we may obtain the kingdom of heaven, through the grace and loving-kindness of our Lord Jesus Christ ; to Whom with the Father and the Holy Spirit, be glory, power, honor, now, henceforth, and for everlasting ages. Amen.

HOMILY XX.

1 Cor. viii. 1.

Now concerning things sacrificed to idols: we know that we all have knowledge. Knowledge puffeth up, but love edifieth.

IT is necessary first to say what the meaning of this passage is: for so shall we readily comprehend the Apostle's discourse. For he that sees a charge brought against any one, except he first perceive the nature of the offence will not understand what is said. What then is it of which he was then accusing the Corinthians? A heavy charge and the cause of many evils. Well, what is it? Many among them, having learnt that (St. Matt. xv. 11.) "not the things which enter in defile the man, but the things which proceed out," and that idols of wood and stone, and demons, have no power to hurt or help, had made an immoderate use of their perfect knowledge of this to the harm both of others and of themselves. They had both gone in where idols were and had partaken of the tables there, and were producing thereby great and ruinous evil. For, on the one hand, those who still retained the fear of idols and knew not how to contemn them, took part in those meals, because they saw the more perfect sort doing this; and hence they got the greatest injury: since they did not touch what was set before them with the same mind as the others, but as things offered in sacrifice to idols; and the thing was becoming a way to idolatry. On the other hand, these very persons who pretended to be more perfect were injured in no common way, partaking in the tables of demons.

This then was the subject of complaint. Now this blessed man being about to correct it, did not immediately begin to speak vehemently; for that which was done came more of folly than of wickedness: wherefore in the first instance there was need rather of exhortation than of severe rebuke and wrath. Now herein observe his good sense, how he immediately begins to admonish.

"Now concerning things sacrificed to idols, we know that we all have knowledge." Leaving alone the weak, which he always doth, he discourses with the strong first. And this is what he did also in the Epistle to the Romans, saying, (Rom. xiv. 10.) "But thou, why dost thou judge thy brother?" for this is the sort of person that is able to receive rebuke also with readiness. Exactly the same then he doth here also.

And first he makes void their conceit by declaring that this very thing which they considered as peculiar to themselves, the having perfect knowledge, was common to all. Thus, "we know," saith he, "that we all have knowledge." For if allowing them to have high thoughts, he had first pointed out how hurtful the thing was to others, he would not have done them so much good as harm. For the ambitious soul when it plumes itself upon any thing, even though the same do harm to others, yet strongly adheres to it because of the tyranny of vain-glory. Wherefore Paul first examines the matter itself by itself : just as he had done before in the case of the wisdom from without, demolishing it with a high hand. But in that case he did it as we might have expected : for the whole thing was altogether blameworthy and his task was very easy. Wherefore he signifies it to be not only useless, but even contrary to the Gospel. But in the present case it was not possible to do this. For what was done was of knowledge, and perfect knowlege. Nor was it safe to overthrow it, and yet in no other way was it possible to cast out the conceit which had resulted from it. What then doeth he? First, by signifying that it was common, he curbs that swelling pride of theirs. For they who possess something great and excellent are more elated, when they alone have it ; but if it be made out that they possess it in common with others, they no longer have so much of this feeling. First then he makes it common property, because they considered it to belong to themselves alone.

Next, having made it common, he does not make himself singly a sharer in it with them ; for in this way too he would have rather set them up ; for as to be the only possessor elates, so to have one partner or two perhaps among leading persons has this effect just as much. For this reason he does not mention himself but all : he said not, " I too have knowledge," but, " we know that we all have knowledge."

[2.] This then is one way, and the first, by which he cast down their pride ; the next hath greater force. What then is this? In that he shews that not even this thing itself was in all points complete, but imperfect, and extremely so. And not only imperfect, but also injurious, unless there were another thing joined together with it. For having said that " we have knowledge," he added, " Knowledge puffeth up, but love edifieth :" so that when it is without love, it lifts men up to absolute arrogance.

" And yet not even love," you will say, " without knowledge hath any advantage." Well : this he did not say ; but omitting it as a thing allowed by all, he signifies that knowledge stands in extreme need of love. For he who loves, inasmuch as he fulfils the commandment which is most absolute of all, even though he have some defects, will quickly be blest with knowledge because of his love ; as Cornelius and many others. But he that hath knowledge but hath not love, not only shall gain nothing more, but shall also be cast out of that which he hath, in many cases falling into arrogance. It seems then that knowledge is not productive of love, but on the contrary debars from it him

that is not on his guard, puffing him up and elating him. For arrogance is wont to cause divisions : but love both draws together and leads to knowledge. And to make this plain he saith, " But if any man loveth God, the same is known of Him." So that " I forbid not this," saith he, " namely, your having perfect knowledge ; but your having it with love, that I enjoin ; else is it no gain, but rather loss."

Do you see how he already sounds the first note of his discourse concerning love? For since all these evils were springing from the following root, i. e., not from perfect knowledge, but from their not greatly loving nor sparing their neighbors ; whence ensued both their variance and their self-satisfaction, and all the rest which he had charged them with ; both before this and after he is continually providing for love ; so correcting the fountain of all good things. " Now why," saith he, " are ye puffed up about knowledge? For if ye have not love, ye shall even be injured thereby. For what is worse than boasting? But if the other be added, the first also will be in safety. For although you may know something more than your neighbor, if you love him you will not set yourself up but lead him also to the same." Wherefore also having said, " Knowledge puffeth up," he added, " but love edifieth." He did not say, " Behaveth itself modestly," but what is much more, and more gainful. For their knowledge was not only puffing them up but also distracting them. On this account he opposes the one to the other.

[3.] And then he adds a third consideration, which was of force to set them down. What then is this? that although charity be joined with it, yet not even in that case is this our knowledge perfect. And therefore he adds,

Ver. 2. " But if any man think that he knoweth any thing, he knoweth nothing yet as he ought to know." This is a mortal blow. " I dwell not," saith he, " on the knowledge being common to all. I say not that by hating your neighbor and by arrogance, you injure yourself most. But even though you have it by yourself alone, though you be modest, though you love your brother, even in this case you are imperfect in regard of knowledge. " For as yet thou knowest nothing as thou oughtest to know," Now if we possess as yet exact knowledge of nothing, how is it that some have rushed on to such a pitch of frenzy as to say that they know God with all exactness? Whereas, though we had an exact knowledge of all other things, not even so were it possible to possess this knowledge to such an extent. For how far He is apart from all things, it is impossible even to say.

And mark how he pulls down their swelling pride: for he said not, " of the matters before us ye have not the proper knowledge," but, "about every thing." And he did not say, " ye," but, " no one whatever," be it Peter, be it Paul, be it any one else. For by this he both soothed them and carefully kept them under.

Ver. 3. " But if any man love God, the same," he doth not say, " knoweth Him," but, " is known of Him." For we have not known Him, but He hath known us. And therefore did Christ say, " Ye have not chosen Me, but I have chosen you." And Paul elsewhere, " Then shall I know fully,[1] even as also I have been known."

Observe now, I pray, by what means he brings down their high-mindedness. First, he points out that not they alone knew the things which they knew; for " we all," he saith, " have knowledge." Next, that the thing itself was hurtful so long as it was without love; for " knowledge," saith he, " puffeth up." Thirdly, that even joined with love it is not complete nor perfect. " For if any man thinketh that he knoweth any thing, he knoweth nothing as yet as he ought to know," so he speaks. In addition to this, that they have not even this from themselves, but by gift from God. For he said not, " hath known God," but, " is known of Him." Again, that this very thing comes of love which they have not as they ought. For, " if any man," saith he, " love God, the same is known of Him." Having then so much at large allayed their irritation, he begins to speak doctrinally, saying thus.

[4.] Ver. 4. " Concerning therefore the eating of things sacrificed to idols, we know that no idol is anything in the world, and that there is no God but one." Look what a strait he hath fallen into! For indeed his mind is to prove both; that one ought to abstain from this kind of banquet, and that it hath no power to hurt those who partake of it : things which were not greatly in agreement with each other. For when they were told that they had no harm in them, they would naturally run to them as indifferent things. But when forbidden to touch them, they would suspect, on the contrary, that their having power to do hurt occasioned the prohibition. Wherefore, you see, he puts down their opinion about idols, and then states as a first reason for their abstaining the scandals which they place in the way of their brethren ; in these words : " Now concerning the eating of things sacrificed to idols, we know that no idol is anything in the world." Again he makes it common property and doth not allow this to be theirs alone, but extends the knowledge all over the world. For " not among you alone," says he, " but every where on earth this doctrine prevails." What then is it ? " That no idol is anything in the world ; that there is no God

but one." What then ? are there no idols ? no statues ? Indeed there are ; but they have no power : neither are they gods, but stones and demons. For he is now setting himself against both parties ; both the grosser sort among them, and those who were accounted lovers of wisdom. Thus, seeing that the former know of no more than the mere stones, the others assert that certain powers reside in them[2], which they also call gods ; to the former accordingly he says, that " no idol is anything in the world ," to the other, that " there is no God but one."

Do you mark how he writes these things, not simply as laying down doctrine, but in opposition to those without ? A thing indeed which we must at all times narrowly observe, whether he says anything abstractedly, or whether he is opposing any persons. For this contributes in no ordinary way to the accuracy of our doctrinal views, and to the exact understanding of his expressions.

[5.] Ver. 5. " For though there be that are called gods, whether in heaven or on earth, as there are gods many and lords many ; yet to us there is one God, the Father, of Whom are all things, and we unto Him ; and one Lord Jesus Christ, through Whom are all things, and we through Him." Since he had said, that " an idol is nothing " and that " there is no other God ; " and yet there were idols and there were those that were called gods ; that he might not seem to be contradicting plain facts, he goes on to say, " For though there be that are called gods, as indeed there are ; " not absolutely, " there are ; " but, " called," not in reality having this but in name : " be it in heaven or on earth :—in heaven," meaning the sun and the moon and the remainder of the choir of stars ; for these too the Greeks worshipped : but upon the earth demons, and all those who had been made gods of men :—" yet to us there is One God, the Father." In the first instance having expressed it without the word " Father," and said, " there is no God but one," he now adds this also, when he had utterly cast out the others.

Next, he adduces what indeed is the greatest token of divinity ; " of Whom are all things." For this implies also that those others are not gods. For it is said (Jer. x. 11.), " Let the gods who made not the heaven and the earth perish." Then he subjoins what is not less than this, " and we unto Him." For when he saith, " of Whom are all things," he means the creation and the bringing of things out of nothing into existence. But when he saith, " and we unto Him," he speaks of the word of faith and mutual

---

[1] ἐπιγνώσομαι.

[2] Olympius the Sophist, of Alexandria, A. D. 389, thus comforted the people when their idols were destroyed : " Shapes and counterfeits they were, fashioned of matter subject unto corruption, therefore to grind them to dust was easy : but those celestial powers which dwelt and resided in them are ascended to Heaven." Sozom. vii. 15, quoted by Hooker, E. P. v. 65. 15.

appropriation (οἰκειώσεως.), as also he said before (1 Cor. i. 30.), "but of Him are ye also in Christ Jesus." In two ways we are of Him, by being made when we were not, and by being made believers. For this also is a creation: a thing which he also declares elsewhere; (Eph. ii. 15.) "that He might create in Himself of the twain one new man."

"And there is one Lord, Jesus Christ, through Whom are all things, and we through Him." And in regard to Christ again, we must conceive of this in like manner. For through Him the race of men was both produced out of nothing into existence, and returned from error to truth. So that as to the phrase "of Whom," it is not to be understood apart from Christ. For of Him, through Christ, were we created.

[6.] Nor yet, if you observe, hath he distributed the names as if belonging exclusively, assigning to the Son the name Lord, and to the Father, God. For the Scripture useth also often to interchange them; as when it saith, (Psalm cx. 1.) "The Lord saith unto My Lord;" and again, (Psalm xlv. 8.) "Wherefore God Thy God hath appointed Thee;" and, (Rom. ix. 5.) "Of Whom is Christ according to the flesh, Who is God over all." And in many instances you may see these names changing their places. Besides, if they were allotted to each nature severally, and if the Son were not God, and God as the Father, yet continuing a Son: after saying, "but to us there is but One God," it would have been superfluous, his adding the word "Father," with a view to declare the Unbegotten. For the word of God was sufficient to explain this, if it were such as to denote Him only.

And this is not all, but there is another remark to make: that if you say, "Because it is said 'One God,' therefore the word God doth not apply to the Son;" observe that the same holds of the Son also. For the Son also is called "One Lord," yet we do not maintain that therefore the term Lord applies to Him alone. So then, the same force which the expression "One" has, applied to the Son, it has also, applied to the Father. And as the Father is not thrust out from being the Lord, in the same sense as the Son is the Lord, because He, the Son, is spoken of as one Lord; so neither does it cast out the Son from being God, in the same sense as the Father is God, because the Father is styled One God.

[7.] Now if any were to say, "Why did he make no mention of the Spirit?" our answer might be this: His argument was with idolaters, and the contention was about "gods many and lords many." And this is why, having called the Father, God, he calls the Son, Lord. If now he ventured not to call the Father Lord together with the Son, lest they might suspect him to be speaking of two Lords; nor yet the Son, God, with the Father, lest he might be supposed to speak of two Gods: why marvel at his not having mentioned the Spirit? His contest was, so far, with the Gentiles: his point, to signify that with us there is no plurality of Gods. Wherefore he keeps hold continually of this word, "One;" saying, "There is no God but One; and, to us there is One God, and One Lord." From which it is plain, that to spare the weakness of the hearers he used this mode of explanation, and for this reason made no mention at all of the Spirit. For if it be not this, neither ought he to make mention of the Spirit elsewhere, nor to join Him with the Father and the Son. For if He be rejected from the Father and Son, much more ought He not to be put in the same rank with them in the matter of Baptism; where most especially the dignity of the Godhead appears and gifts are bestowed which pertain to God alone to afford. Thus then I have assigned the cause why in this place He is passed over in silence. Now do thou if this be not the true reason, tell me, why He is ranked with Them in Baptism? But thou canst not give any other reason but His being of equal honor. At any rate, when he has no such constraint upon him, he puts Him in the same rank, saying thus: (2 Cor. xiii. 14.) "The grace of our Lord Jesus Christ, and the love of God and the Father,[1] and the fellowship of the Holy Ghost, be with you all:" and again, (ch. xii 4.) "There are diversities of gifts, but the same Spirit: and there are diversities of administrations, but the same Lord; and there are diversities of workings but the same God." But because now his speech was with Greeks and the weaker sort of the converts from among Greeks, for this reason he husbands it (ταμιεύεται) so far. And this is what the prophets do in regard of the Son; no where making mention of Him plainly because of the infirmity of the hearers.

Ver. 7. "But not in all is knowledge," saith he. What knowledge doth he mean? about God, or about things offered in sacrifice to idols? For either he here glances at the Greeks who say that there are many gods and lords, and who know not Him that is truly God; or at the converts from among Greeks who were still rather infirm, such as did not yet know clearly that they ought not to fear idols and that "an idol is nothing in the world." But in saying this, he gently soothes and encourages the latter. For there was no need of mentioning all he had to reprove, particularly as he intended to visit them again with more severity.

[8.] "But some being used to the idol eat as of a thing sacrificed to an idol, and their con-

---

[1] καὶ Πατρός, om. in rec. text.

science being weak is defiled." They still tremble at idols, he saith. For tell me not of the present establishment, and that you have received the true religion from your ancestors. But carry back your thoughts to those times, and consider when the Gospel was just set on foot, and impiety was still at its height, and altars burning, and sacrifices and libations offering up, and the greater part of men were Gentiles; think, I say, of those who from their ancestors had received impiety, and who were the descendants of fathers and grandfathers and great-grandfathers like themselves, and who had suffered great miseries from the demons. How must they have felt after their sudden change! How would they face and tremble at the assaults of the demons! For their sake also he employs some reserve, saying, "But some with conscience of the things sacrificed to an idol.[1]" Thus he neither exposed them openly, not to strike them hard; nor doth he pass by them altogether: but makes mention of them in a vague manner, saying, "Now some with conscience of the idol even until now eat as of a thing sacrificed to an idol; that is, with the same thoughts as they did in former times : 'and their conscience being weak is defiled ; '" not yet being able to despise and once for all laugh them to scorn, but still in some doubt. Just as if a man were to think that by touching a dead body he should pollute himself according to the Jewish custom, and then seeing others touching it with a clear conscience, but not with the same mind touching it himself, would be polluted. This was their state of feeling at that time. "For some," saith he, "with conscience of the idol do it even until now." Not without cause did he add, "even until now;" but to signify that they gained no ground by their refusing to condescend. For this was not the way to bring them in, but in some other way persuading them by word and by teaching.

"And their conscience being weak is defiled." No where as yet doth he state his argument about the nature of the thing, but turns himself this way and that as concerning the conscience of the person partaking. For he was afraid lest in his wish to correct the weak person, he should inflict a heavy blow upon the strong one, and make him also weak. On which account he spares the one no less than the other. Nor doth he allow the thing itself to be thought of any consequence, but makes his argument very full to prevent any suspicion of the kind.

[9.] Ver. 8. "But meat doth not commend us to God. For neither if we eat are we the better, nor if we eat not are we the worse." Do you see how again he takes down their high spirit? in that, after saying that "not only they

but all of us have knowledge," and that "no one knoweth any thing as he ought to know," and that "knowledge puffeth up;" then having soothed them, and said that "this knowledge is not in all," and that "weakness is the cause of these being defiled," in order that they might not say, "And what is it to us, if knowledge be not in all? Why then has not such an one knowledge? Why is he weak?" —I say, in order that they might not rejoin in these terms, he did not proceed immediately to point out clearly that for fear of the other's harm one ought to abstain: but having first made but a sort of skirmish upon mention of him, he points out what is more than this. What then is this ? That although no one were injured nor any perversion of another ensued, not even in this case were it right so to do. For the former topic by itself is laboring in vain. Since he that hears of another being hurt while himself has the gain, is not very apt to abstain; but then rather he doth so, when he finds out that he himself is no way advantaged by the thing. Wherefore he sets this down first, saying, "But meat commendeth us not to God." See how cheap he holds that which was accounted to spring from perfect knowledge! "For neither if we eat are we the better," (that is, stand higher in God's estimation, as if we had done any thing good or great :) "nor if we eat not are we the worse," that is, fall in any way short of others. So far then he hath signified that the thing itself is superfluous, and as nothing. For that which being done profits not, and which being left undone injures not, must be superfluous.

[10.] But as he goes on, he discloses all the harm which was likely to arise from the matter. For the present, however, that which befel the brethren is his subject.

Ver. 9. "For take heed," saith he, "lest by any means this liberty of yours become a stumbling-block to the weak among the brethren." ($\tau\hat{\omega}\nu$ $\dot{\alpha}\delta\epsilon\lambda\phi\hat{\omega}\nu$ not in rec. text.)

He did not say, "Your liberty is become a stumbling-block," nor did he positively affirm it that he might not make them more shameless; but how? "Take heed;" frightening them, and making them ashamed, and leading them to disavow any such conduct. And he said not, "This your knowledge," which would have sounded more like praise; nor "this your perfectness;" but, "your liberty;" a thing which seemed to savor more of rashness and obstinacy and arrogance. Neither said he, "To the brethren," but, "To those of the brethren who are weak;" enhancing his accusation from their not even sparing the weak, and those too their brethren. For let it be so that you correct them not, nor arouse them: yet why trip them up,

---

[1] τοῦ εἰδωλοθύτου. rec. text. εἰδώλου.

and make them to stumble, when you ought to stretch out the hand? but for that you have no mind: well then, at least avoid casting them down. Since if one were wicked, he required punishment; if weak, healing: but now he is not only weak, but also a brother.

Ver. 10. "For if a man see thee who hast knowledge, sitting at meat in an idol's temple, will not his conscience if he is weak, be emboldened[1] to eat things sacrificed to idols?"

After having said, "Take heed lest this your liberty become a stumbling-block," he explains how and in what manner it becomes so: and he continually employs the term "weakness," that the mischief may not be thought to arise from the nature of the thing, nor demons appear formidable. As thus: "At present," saith he, "a man is on the point of withdrawing himself entirely from all idols; but when he sees you fond of loitering about them, he takes the circumstance for a recommendation and abides there himself also. So that not only his weakness, but also your ill-timed behavior, helps to further the plot against him; for it is you who make him weaker."

Ver. 11. "And through thy meat[2] he that is weak perisheth, the brother for whose sake Christ died."

For there are two things which deprive you of excuse in this mischief; one, that he is weak, the other, that he is thy brother: rather, I should say, there is a third also, and one more terrible than all. What then is this? That whereas Christ refused not even to die for him, thou canst not bear even to accommodate thyself to him. By these means, you see, he reminds the perfect man also, what he too was before, and that for him He died. And he said not, "For whom even to die was thy duty;" but what is much stronger, that even Christ died for his sake. "Did thy Lord then not refuse to die for him, and dost thou so make him of none account as not even to abstain from a polluted table for his sake? Yea, dost thou permit him to perish, after the salvation so wrought, and, what is still more grievous, 'for a morsel of meat?'" For he said not, "for thy perfectness," nor "for thy knowledge," but "for thy meat." So that the charges are four, and these extremely heavy: that it was a brother, that he was weak, and one of whom Christ made so much account as even to die for him, and that after all this for a "morsel of meat" he is destroyed.

Ver. 12. "And thus sinning against the brethren, and wounding their weak conscience, ye sin against Christ."

Do you observe how quietly and gradually he

hath brought their offence up to the very summit of iniquity? And again, he makes mention of the infirmity of the other sort: and so, the very thing which these considered to make for them, that he every where turns round upon their own head. And he said not, "Putting stumbling-blocks in their way," but, "wounding;" so as by the force of his expression to indicate their cruelty. For what can be more savage than a man who wounds the sick? and yet no wound is so grievous as making a man to stumble. Often, in fact, is this also the cause of death.

But how do they "sin against Christ?" In one way, because He considers the concerns of His servants as His own; in another, because those who are wounded go to make up His Body and that which is part of Him: in a third way, because that work of His which He built up by His own blood, these are destroying for their ambition's sake.

[11.] Ver. 13. "Wherefore, if meat make my brother to stumble, I will eat no flesh for ever." This is like the best of teachers, to teach in his own person the things which he speaks. Nor did he say whether justly or unjustly; but in any case. "I say not," (such is his tone,) "meat offered in sacrifice to an idol, which is already prohibited for another reason; but if any even of those things which are within license and are permitted causes stumbling, from these also will I abstain: and not one or two days, but all the time of my life." For he saith, "I will eat no flesh for ever." And he said not, "Lest I destroy my brother," but simply, "That I make not my brother to stumble." For indeed it comes of folly in the extreme that what things are greatly cared for by Christ, and such as He should have even chosen to die for them, these we should esteem so entirely beneath our notice as not even to abstain from meats on their account.

Now these things might be seasonably spoken not to them only, but also to us, apt as we are to esteem lightly the salvation of our neighbors and to utter those satanical words. I say, satanical: for the expression, "What care I, though such an one stumble, and such another perish?" savors of his cruelty and inhuman mind. And yet in that instance, the infirmity also of those who were offended had some share in the result: but in our case it is not so, sinning as we do in such a way as to offend even the strong. For when we smite, and raven, and overreach, and use the free as if they were slaves, whom is not this enough to offend? Tell me not of such a man's being a shoemaker, another a dyer, another a brazier: but bear in mind that he is a believer and a brother. Why these are they whose disciples we are; the fishermen,

---

[1] οἰκοδομηθήσεται, "established," "edified."
[2] βρώσει, rec. text γνώσει, Comp. Rom. xiv. 15.

the publicans, the tent-makers, of Him who was brought up in the house of a carpenter ; and who deigned to have the carpenter's betrothed wife for a mother ; and who was laid, after His swaddling clothes, in a manger ; and who had not where to lay His head ;—of Him whose journeys were so long that His very journeying was enough to tire Him down ; of Him who was supported by others.

[12.] Think on these things, and esteem the pride of man to be nothing. But count the tent-maker as well as thy brother, as him that is borne upon a chariot and hath innumerable servants and struts in the market-place : nay, rather the former than the latter ; since the term brother would more naturally be used where there is the greater resemblance. Which then resembles the fisherman ? He who is supported by daily labor and hath neither servant nor dwelling, but is quite beset with privations ; or that other who is surrounded with such vast pomp, and who acts contrary to the laws of God ? Despise not then him that is more of the two thy brother, for he comes nearer to the Apostolic pattern.

"Not however," say you, "of his own accord, but by compulsion ; for he doeth not this of his own mind." How comes this ? Hast thou not heard, "Judge not, that ye be not judged ? " But, to convince thyself that he doeth it not against his inclination, approach and give him ten thousand talents of gold, and thou shalt see him putting it away from him. And thus, even though he have received no wealth by inheritance from his ancestors, yet when it is in his power to take it, and he lets it not come near him neither adds to his goods, he exhibits a mighty proof of his contempt of wealth. For so John was the son of Zebedee that extremely poor man : yet I suppose we are not therefore to say that his poverty was forced upon him.

Whensoever then thou seest one driving nails, smiting with a hammer, covered with soot, do not therefore hold him cheap, but rather for that reason admire him. Since even Peter girded himself, and handled the drag-net, and went a fishing after the Resurrection of the Lord. And why say I Peter ? For this same Paul himself, after his incessant runnings to and fro and all those vast miracles, standing in a tent-maker's shop, sewed hides together : while angels were reverencing him and demons trembling. And he was not ashamed to say, (Acts xx. 34.) " Unto my necessities, and to those who were with me, these hands ministered." What say I, that he was not ashamed ? Yea, he gloried in this very thing.

But you will say, " Who is there now to be compared with the virtue of Paul ? " I too am aware that there is no one, yet not on this account are those who live now to be despised : for if for Christ's sake thou give honor, though one be last of all, yet if he be a believer he shall justly be honored. For suppose a general and a common soldier both present themselves before you, being friends of the king, and you open your house to both : in which of their persons would you seem to pay most honor to the king ? Plainly in that of a soldier. For there were in the general, beside his loyalty to the king, many other things apt to win such a mark of respect from you : but the soldier had nothing else but his loyalty to the king.

Wherefore God bade us call to our suppers and our feasts the lame, and the maimed, and those who cannot repay us ; for these are most of all properly called good deeds which are done for God's sake. Whereas if thou entertain some great and distinguished man, it is not such pure mercy, what thou doest : but some portion many times is assigned to thyself also,[1] both by vain-glory, and by the return of the favor, and by thy rising in many men's estimation on account of thy guest. At any rate, I think I could point out many who with this view pay court to the more distinguished among the saints, namely, that by their means they may enjoy a greater intimacy with rulers, and that they may find them thenceforth more useful in their own affairs and to their families. And many such favors do they ask in recompense from those saints ; a thing which mars the repayment of their hospitality, they seeking it with such a mind.

And why need I say this about the saints ? Since he who seeks, even from God, the reward of his labors in the present life and follows after virtue for this world's good, is sure to diminish his recompense. But he that asks for all his crowns wholly there, is found far more admirable ; like that Lazarus, who even now is " receiving" (St. Luke xvi. 25.) there all " his good things ; " like those Three Children, who when they were on the point of being thrown into the furnace said, (Dan. iii. 17, 18.) " There is a God in heaven able to deliver us ; and if not, be it known unto thee, O king, that we serve not thy gods, nor worship the golden image which thou hast set up : " like Abraham, who even offered[2] his son and slew him ; and this he did, not for any reward, but esteeming this one thing the greatest recompense, to obey the Lord.

These let us also imitate. For so shall we be visited with a return of all our good deeds and that abundantly, because we do all with such a mind as this : so shall we obtain also the

---

[1] μερίζεταί τι πρὸς σε.
[2] ἀνήγαγε.

brighter crowns. And God grant that we may all obtain them, through the grace and loving-kindness of our Lord Jesus Christ, with Whom, to the Father and the Holy Spirit, be glory, power, honor, now, henceforth, and for ever-lasting ages. Amen.

HOMILY XXI

1 Cor. ix. 1.

Am I not an Apostle? am I not free? have I not seen Jesus Christ our Lord? are not ye my work in the Lord?

INASMUCH as he had said, "If meat make my brother to stumble I will eat no flesh forever;" a thing which he had not yet done, but professed he would do if need require: lest any man should say, "Thou vauntest thyself at random, and art severe in discourse, and utterest words of promise, a thing easy to me or to any body; but if these sayings come from thy heart, shew by deeds something which thou hast slighted in order to avoid making thy brother stumble:" for this cause, I say, in what follows he is compelled to enter on the proof of this also, and to point out how he was used to forego even things permitted that he might not give offence, although without any law to enforce his doing so.

And we are not yet come to the admirable part of the matter: though it be admirable that he abstain even from things lawful to avoid offence: but it is his habit of doing so at the cost of so much trouble and danger[1]. "For why," saith he, "speak of the idol sacrifices? Since although Christ had enjoined that those who preach the Gospel should live at the charge of their disciples, I did not so, but chose, if need were, to end my life with famine and die the most grievous of deaths, so I might avoid receiving of those whom I instruct."

Not because they would otherwise be made to stumble, but because his not receiving would edify them[2]: a much greater thing for him to do. And to witness this he summons themselves, among whom he was used to live in toil and in hunger, nourished by others, and put to straits, in order not to offend them. And yet there was no ground for their taking offence, for it would but have been a law which he was fulfilling. But for all this, by a sort of supereroga-tion[3] he used to spare them.

Now if he did more than was enacted lest they should take offence, and abstained from permitted things to edify others; what must they deserve who abstain not from idol sacri-fices? and that, when many perish thereby? a thing which, even apart from all scandal one ought to shrink from, as being "the table of demons."

The sum therefore of this whole topic is this which he works out in many verses. But we must resume it and make a fresh entrance on what he hath alleged. For neither hath he set it down thus expressly as I have worded it; nor doth he leap at once upon it; but begins from another topic, thus speaking;

[2.] "Am I not an Apostle?" For besides all that hath been said, this also makes no small difference that Paul himself is the person thus conducting himself. As thus: To prevent their alleging, "You may taste of the sacrifices, sealing[4] at the same time:" for a while he withstands not that statement, but argues, "Though it were lawful, your brethren's harm should keep you from doing so;" and after-wards he proves that it is not even lawful. In this particular place, however, he establishes the former point from circumstances relating to himself. And intending presently to say that he had received nothing from them, he sets it not down at once, but his own dignity is what he first affirms: "Am I not an Apostle? am I not free?"

Thus, to hinder their saying, "True; thou didst not receive, but the reason thou didst not was its not being lawful;" he sets down there-fore first the causes why he might reasonably have received, had he been willing to do so.

Further: that there might not seem to be any thing invidious in regard of Peter and such as Peter, in his saying these things, (for they did not use to decline receiving;) he first shows that they had authority to receive, and then that no one might say, "Peter had authority to receive but thou hadst not," he possesses the hearer beforehand with these encomiums of himself. And perceiving that he must praise

---

[1] The reading here adopted is Savile's.
[2] A slight transposition has been made here: the sense seeming to require it.
[3] ἐκ περιουσίας.

[4] i. e. making the sign of the Cross: σφραγίζοντι.

himself, (for that was the way to correct the Corinthians,) yet disliking to say any great thing of himself, see how he hath tempered both feelings as the occasion required: limiting his own panegyric, not by what he knew of himself, but by what the subject of necessity required. For he might have said, "I most of all had a right to receive, even more than they, because 'I labored more abundantly than they.'" But this he omits, being a point wherein he surpassed them; and those points wherein they were great and which were just grounds for their receiving, those only he sets down: as follows:

"Am I not an Apostle? am I not free?" i. e. "have I not authority over myself? am I under any, to overrule me and forbid my receiving?"

"But they have an advantage over you, in having been with Christ."

"Nay, neither is this denied me." With a view to which he saith,

"Have I not seen Jesus Christ our Lord?" For "last of all," (c. xv. 8.) saith he, "as unto one born out of due time, He appeared unto me also." Now this likewise was no small dignity: since "many Prophets," (S. Mat. xiii. 17.) saith He, "and righteous men have desired to see the things which ye see, and have not seen them:" and, "Days will come when ye shall desire to see one of these days." (S. Luke xvii. 22.)

"What then, though thou be 'an Apostle,' and 'free,' and hast 'seen Christ,' if thou hast not exhibited any work of an Apostle; how then can it be right for thee to receive?" Wherefore after this he adds,

"Are not ye my work in the Lord?" For this is the great thing; and those others avail nothing, apart from this. Even Judas himself was "an Apostle," and "free," and "saw Christ;" but because he had not "the work of an Apostle," all those things profited him not. You see then why he adds this also, and calls themselves to be witnesses of it.

Moreover, because it was a great thing which he had uttered, see how he chastens it, adding, "In the Lord:" i.e., "the work is God's, not mine."

Ver. 2. "If to others I am not an Apostle, yet at least I am to you."

Do you see how far he is from enlarging here without necessity? And yet he had the whole world to speak of, and barbarous nations, and sea and land. However, he mentions none of these things, but carries his point by concession, and even granting more than he need. As if he had said, "Why need I dwell on things over and above, since these even alone are enough for my present purpose? I speak not, you will observe, of my achievements in other quarters,

but of those which have you for witnesses. Upon which it follows that if from no other quarter, yet from you I have a right to receive. Nevertheless, from whom I had most right to receive, even you whose teacher I was, from those I received not."

"If to others I am not an Apostle, yet at least I am to you." Again, he states his point by concession. For the whole world had him for its Apostle. "However," saith he, "I say not that, I am not contending nor disputing, but what concerns you I lay down. 'For the seal of mine Apostleship are ye:'" i.e., its proof. "Should any one, moreover, desire to learn whence I am an Apostle, you are the persons whom I bring forward: for all the signs of an Apostle have I exhibited among you, and not one have I failed in." As also he speaks in the Second Epistle, saying, (2 Cor. xii. 12.) "Though I am nothing, truly the signs of an Apostle were wrought among you in all patience, by signs and wonders and mighty works. For what is there wherein ye were made inferior to the rest of the Churches?" Wherefore he saith, "The seal of mine Apostleship are ye." "For I both exhibited miracles, and taught by word, and underwent dangers, and shewed forth a blameless life." And these topics you may see fully set forth by these two Epistles, how he lays before them the demonstration of each with all exactness.

[3.] Ver. 3. "My defence to them that examine me is this." What is, "My defence to them that examine me is this?" "To those whe seek to know whereby I am proved to be an Apostle, or who accuse me as receiving money, or inquire the cause of my not receiving, or would fain shew that I am not an Apostle: to all such, my instruction given to you and these things which I am about to say, may stand for a full explanation and defence." What then are these?

Ver. 4, 5. "Have we no right to eat and to drink? Have we no right to lead about a wife that is a believer?" Why, how are these sayings a defence? "Because, when it appears that I abstain even from things which are allowed, it cannot be just to look suspiciously on me as a deceiver or one acting for gain."

Wherefore, from what was before alleged and from my having instructed you and from this which I have now said, I have matter sufficient to make my defence to you: and all who examine me I meet upon this ground, alleging both what has gone before and this which follows: "Have we no right to eat and to drink? have we no right to lead about a wife that is a believer?" "Yet for all this, having it I abstain?"

What then? did he not use to eat or to drink?

It were most true to say that in many places he really did not eat nor drink: for (c. iv. 11.) "in hunger," saith he, "and in thirst, and in nakedness" we were abiding." Here, however, this is not his meaning; but what? "We eat not nor drink, receiving of those whom we instruct, though we have a right so to receive."

"Have we no right to lead about a wife that is a believer, even as the rest of the Apostles, and the brethren of the Lord, and Cephas?" Observe his skilfulness. The leader of the choir stands last in his arrangement: since that is the time for laying down the strongest of all one's topics. Nor was it so wonderful for one to be able to point out examples of this conduct in the rest, as in the foremost champion and in him who was entrusted with the keys of heaven. But neither does he mention Peter alone, but all of them: as if he had said, Whether you seek the inferior sort or the more eminent, in all you find patterns of this sort.

For the brethren too of the Lord, being freed from their first unbelief (vid. S. John vii. 5.), had come to be among those who were approved, although they attained not to the Apostles. And accordingly the middle place is that which he hath assigned to them, setting down those who were in the extremes before and after.

Ver. 6. "Or I only and Barnabas, have we not a right to forbear working?"

(See his humility of mind and his soul pure from envy, how he takes care not to conceal him whom he knew to be a partaker with himself in this perfection.) For if the other things be common, how is not this common? Both they and we are apostles and are free, and have seen Christ, and have exhibited the works of Apostles. Therefore we likewise have a right both to live without working and to be supported by our disciples.

[4.] Ver. 7. "What soldier ever serveth at his own charges?" For since, which was the strongest point, he had proved from the Apostles that it is lawful to do so, he next comes to examples and to the common practice, as he uses to do: "What soldier serveth at his own charges?" saith he. But do thou consider, I pray, how very suitable are the examples to his proposed subject, and how he mentions first that which is accompanied with danger; viz. soldiership and arms and wars. For such a kind of thing was the Apostolate, nay rather much more hazardous than these. For not with men alone was their warfare, but with demons also, and against the prince of those beings was their battle array. What he saith therefore is this: "Not even do heathen governors, cruel and unjust as they are, require their soldiers to endure service and peril and live on their own means. How then could Christ ever have required this?"

Nor is he satisfied with one example. For to him who is rather simple and dull, this also is wont to come as a great refreshment, viz. their seeing the common custom also going along with the laws of God. Wherefore he proceeds to another topic also and says, "Who planteth a vineyard, and eateth not of the fruit thereof?" For as by the former he indicated his dangers, so by this his labor and abundant travail and care.

He adds likewise a third example, saying, "Who feedeth a flock, and eateth not of the milk thereof?" He is exhibiting the great concern which it becomes a teacher to show for those who are under his rule. For, in fact, the Apostles were both soldiers and husbandmen and shepherds, not of the earth nor of irrational animals, nor in such wars as are perceptible by sense; but of reasonable souls and in battle array with the demons.

It also must be remarked how every where he preserves moderation, seeking the useful only, not the extraordinary. For he said not, "What soldier serveth and is not enriched?" but, "What soldier ever serveth at his own charges?" Neither did he say, "Who planteth a vineyard, and gathereth not gold, or spareth to collect the whole fruit?" but, "Who eateth not of the fruit thereof?" Neither did he say, "Who feedeth a flock, and maketh not merchandize of the lambs?" But what? "And eateth not of the milk thereof?" Not of the lambs, but of the milk; signifying, that a little relief should be enough for the teacher, even his necessary food alone. (This refers to those who would devour all and gather the whole of the fruit.) "So likewise the Lord ordained," saying, "The laborer is worthy of his food." (St. Mat. x. 10.)

And not this only doth he establish by his illustrations, but he shows also what kind of man a priest ought to be. For he ought to possess both the courage of a soldier and the diligence of a husbandman and the carefulness of a shepherd, and after all these, to seek nothing more than necessaries.

[5.] Having shewn, as you see, both from the Apostles, that it is not forbidden the teacher to receive, and from illustrations found in common life, he proceeds also to a third head, thus saying,

Ver. 8. "Do I speak these things after the manner of men? or saith not the law also the same?"

For since he had hitherto alleged nothing out of the Scriptures, but put forward the common custom; "think not," saith he, "that I am confident in these alone, nor that I go to the opinions of men for the ground of these enactments. For I can shew that these things are also well-pleasing to God, and I read an ancient law enjoining them." Wherefore also he carries on his discourse in the form of a question, which is apt to be done in things fully acknowledged; thus saying, "Say I these things after the manner of men?" i. e. "do I strengthen myself only by human examples?" "or saith not the law also the same?"

Ver. 9. "For it is written in the law of Moses, Thou shalt not muzzle the ox when he treadeth out the corn."

And on what account hath he mentioned this, having the example of the priests? Wishing to establish it far beyond what the case required. Further, lest any should say, "And what have we to do with the saying about the oxen?" he works it out more exactly, saying, "Is it for the oxen that God careth;" Doth God then, tell me, take no care for oxen? Well, He doth take care of them, but not so as to make a law concerning such a thing as this. So that had he not been hinting at something important, training the Jews to mercy in the case of the brutes, and through these, discoursing with them of the teachers also; he would not have taken so much interest as even to make a law to forbid the muzzling of oxen.

Wherein he points out another thing likewise, that the labor of teachers both is and ought to be great.

And again another thing. What then is this? That whatever is said by the Old Testament respecting care for brutes, in its principal meaning bears on the instruction of human beings: as in fact do all the rest: the precepts, for example, concerning various garments; and those concerning vineyards and seeds and not making the ground bear divers crops,[1] and those concerning leprosy; and, in a word, all the rest: for they being of a duller sort He was discoursing with them from these topics, advancing them by little and little.

And see how in what follows he doth not even confirm it, as being clear and self-evident. For having said, "Is it for the oxen that God careth?" he added, "or saith he it altogether for our sake?" Not adding even the "altogether" at random, but that he might not leave the hearer any thing whatever to reply.

And he dwells upon the metaphor, saying and declaring, "Yea for our sakes it was written, because he who ploweth ought to plow in hope;" i. e., the teacher ought to enjoy the returns of his labors; "and he that thresheth ought to thresh in hope of partaking." And observe his wisdom in that from the seed he transferred the matter to the threshing floor; herein also again manifesting the many toils of the teachers, that

they in their own persons both plough and tread the floor. And of the ploughing, because there was nothing to reap, but labor only, he used the word, "hope;" but of treading the floor he presently allows the fruit, saying, "He that thresheth is a partaker of his hope."

Further, lest any should say, "Is this then the return for so many toils," he adds, "in hope," i. e., "which is to come." No other thing therefore doth the mouth of this animal being unmuzzled declare than this; that the teachers who labor ought also to enjoy some return.

[6.] Ver. 11. "If we sowed unto you spiritual things, is it a great matter if we shall reap your carnal things?"

Lo, he adds also a fourth argument for the duty of yielding support. For since he had said, "What soldier ever serveth at his own charges?" and, "who planteth a vineyard?" and, "who feedeth a flock?" and introduced the ox that treadeth the corn; he points out likewise another most reasonable cause on account of which they might justly receive; viz. having bestowed much greater gifts, no more as having labored only. What is it then? "if we sowed unto you spiritual things, is it a great matter if we shall reap your carnal things?" Seest thou a most just allegation and fuller of reason than all the former? for "in those instances," says he, "carnal is the seed, carnal also is the fruit; but here not so, but the seed is spiritual, the return carnal." Thus, to prevent high thoughts in those who contribute to their teachers, he signified that they receive more than they give. As if he had said, "Husbandmen, whatsoever they sow, this also do they receive; but we, sowing in your souls spiritual things, do reap carnal." For such is the kind of support given by them. Further, and still more to put them to the blush.

Ver. 12. "If others partake of this right over you, do not we yet more?"

See also again another argument, and this too from examples though not of the same kind. For it is not Peter whom he mentions here nor the Apostles, but certain other spurious ones, with whom he afterwards enters into combat, and concerning whom he says, (2 Cor. xi. 20.) "If a man devour you, if he take you captive, if he exalt himself, if he smite you on the face," and already he is sounding the prelude[2] to the fight with them. Wherefore neither did he say, "If others take of you," but pointing out their insolence and tyranny and trafficking, he says, "if others partake of this right over you," i. e., "rule you, exercise authority, use you as servants, not taking you captive only, but with much authority." Wherefore he added "do not we yet more?" which he would not have said if

---

[1] διάφορον ποιεῖν τὴν γῆν. See Deut. xxii. 9. LXX.

[2] προανακρούεται.

the discourse were concerning the Apostles. But it is evident that he hints at certain pestilent men, and deceivers of them. "So that besides the law of Moses even ye yourselves have made a law in behalf of the duty of contribution."

And having said, "do not we yet more?" he does not prove why yet more, but leaves it to their consciences to convince them of that, wishing at the same time both to alarm and to abash them more thoroughly.

[7.] "Nevertheless, we did not use this right;" i.e., "did not receive." Do you see, when he had by so many reasons before proved that receiving is not unlawful, how he next says, "we receive not," that he might not seem to abstain as from a thing forbidden? "For not because it is unlawful," saith he, "do I not receive; for it is lawful and this we have many ways shown : from the Apostles; from the affairs of life, the soldier, the husbandman, and the shepherd; from the law of Moses; from the very nature of the case, in that we have sown unto you spiritual things; from what yourselves have done to others." But as he had laid down these things, lest he should seem to put to shame the Apostles who were in the habit of receiving; abashing them and signifying that not as from a forbidden thing doth he abstain from it : so again, lest by his large store of proof and the examples and reasonings by which he had pointed out the propriety of receiving, he should seem to be anxious to receive himself and therefore to say these things ; he now corrects it. And afterwards he laid it down more clearly where he says, "And I wrote not these things, that it may be so done in my case;" but here his words are, "we did not use this right."

And what is a still greater thing, neither could any have this to say, that being in abundance we declined using it ; rather, when necessity pressed upon us we would not yield to the necessity. Which also in the second Epistle he says; "I robbed other Churches, taking wages of them that I might minister unto you; and when I was present with you, and was in want, I was not a burden on any man." (2 Cor. xi. 8, 9.) And in this Epistle again, "We both hunger, and thirst, and are naked, and are buffeted." (1 Cor. iv. 11.) And here again he hints the same thing, saying, "But we bear all things." For by saying, "we bear all things," he intimates both hunger and great straits and all the other things. "But not even thus have we been compelled," saith he, "to break the law which we laid down for ourselves. Wherefore? "that we may cause no hinderance to the Gospel of Christ." For since the Corinthians were rather weak-minded, "lest we should wound you," saith he "by receiving, we

chose to do even more than was commanded rather than hinder the Gospel," i.e., your instruction. Now if we in a matter left free to us, and when we were both enduring much hardship and having Apostles for our pattern, used abstinence lest we should give hindrance, (and he did not say, "subversion," but "hindrance;" nor simply "hindrance," but "any" hindrance,) that we might not, so to speak, cause so much as the slightest suspense and delay to the course of the Word : "If now," saith he, "we used so great care, how much more ought you to abstain, who both come far short of the Apostles and have no law to mention, giving you permission : but contrariwise are both putting your hand to things forbidden and things which tend to the great injury of the Gospel, not to its hindrance only[1]; and not even having any pressing necessity in view." For all this discussion he had moved on account of these Corinthians, who were making their weaker brethren to stumble by eating of things sacrificed to idols.

[8.] These things also let us listen to, beloved ; that we may not despise those who are offended, nor, "cause any hindrance to the Gospel of Christ;" that we may not betray our own salvation. And say not thou to me when thy brother is offended, "this or that, whereby he is offended, hath not been forbidden; it is permitted." For I have something greater to say to thee : "although Christ Himself have permitted it, yet if thou seest any injured, stop and do not use the permission." For this also did Paul ; when he might have received, Christ having granted permission, he received not. Thus hath our Lord in His mercy mingled much gentleness with His precepts that it might not be all merely of commandment, but that we might do much also of our own mind. Since it was in His power, had He not been so minded, to extend the commandments further and to say, "he who fasts not continually, let him be chastised; he who keeps not his virginity, let him be punished; he that doth not strip himself of all that he hath, let him suffer the severest penalty." But he did not so, giving thee occasion, if thou wilt, to be forward in doing more. Wherefore both when He was discoursing about virginity, He said, "He that is able to receive, let him receive it:" and in the case of the rich man, some things He commanded, but some He left to the determination of his mind. For He said not, "Sell what thou hast," but, "If thou wilt be perfect, sell."

But we are not only not forward to do more, and to go beyond the precepts, but we fall very short even of the measure of things commanded.

---

[1] The reading seems imperfect, and unintelligible: it is rendered as if it were, οὐκ ἐπὶ τῷ ἐγκοπὴν μόνον δοῦναι.

And whereas Paul suffered hunger that he might not hinder the Gospel; we have not the heart even to touch what is in our own stores, though we see innumerable souls overthrown. "Yea," saith one, "let the moth eat, and let not the poor eat; let the worm devour, and let not the naked be clothed; let all be wasted away with time, and let not Christ be fed; and this when He hungereth." "Why, who said this?" it will be asked. Nay, this is the very grievance, that not in words but in deeds these things are said: for it were less grievous uttered in words than done in deeds. For is not this the cry, day by day, of the inhuman and cruel tyrant, Covetousness, to those who are led captive by her? "Let your goods be set before informers and robbers and traitors for luxury, and not before the hungry and needy for their sustenance." Is it not ye then who make robbers? Is it not ye who minister fuel to the fire of the envious? Is it not ye who make vagabonds and traitors, putting your wealth before them for a bait? What madness is this? (for a madness it is, and plain distraction,) to fill your chests with apparel, and overlook him that is made after God's image and similitude, naked and trembling with cold, and with difficulty keeping himself upright.

"But he pretends," saith one, "this tremor and weakness." And dost thou not fear lest a thunderbolt from heaven, kindled by this word, should fall upon thee? (For I am bursting with wrath: bear with me.) Thou, I say, pampering and fattening thyself and extending thy potations to the dead of night and comforting thyself in soft coverlets, dost not deem thyself liable to judgment, so lawlessly using the gifts of God: (for wine was not made that we should be drunken; nor food, that we should pamper our appetites; nor meats, that we should distend the belly.) But from the poor, the wretched, from him that is as good as dead, from him demandest thou strict accounts, and dost thou not fear Christ's tribunal, so full of all awfulness and terror? Why, if he do play the hypocrite, he doth it of necessity and want, because of thy cruelty and inhumanity, requiring the use of such masks and refusing all inclination to mercy. For who is so wretched and miserable as without urgent necessity, for one loaf of bread, to submit to such disgrace, and to bewail himself and endure so severe a punishment? So that this hypocrisy of his goeth about, the herald of thine inhumanity. For since by supplicating and beseeching and uttering piteous expressions and lamenting and weeping and going about all day, he doth not obtain even necessary food, he devised perhaps even this contrivance also, the disgrace and blame whereof falls not so much on himself as on

thee: for he indeed is meet to be pitied because he hath fallen into so great necessity; but we are worthy of innumerable punishments because we compel the poor to suffer such things. For if we would easily give way, never would he have chosen to endure such things.

And why speak I of nakedness and trembling? For I will tell a thing yet more to be shuddered at, that some have been compelled even to deprive their children of sight at an early age in order that they might touch our insensibility. For since when they could see and went about naked, neither by their age nor by their misfortunes could they win favor of the unpitying, they added to so great evils another yet sterner tragedy, that they might remove their hunger; thinking it to be a lighter thing to be deprived of this common light and that sunshine which is given to all, than to struggle with continual famine and endure the most miserable of deaths. Thus, since you have not learned to pity poverty, but delight yourselves in misfortunes, they satisfy your insatiable desire, and both for themselves and for us kindle a fiercer flame in hell.

[9.] And to convince you that this is the reason why these and such like things are done, I will tell you of an acknowledged proof which no man can gainsay. There are other poor men, of light and unsteady minds and not knowing how to bear hunger, but rather enduring every thing than it. These having often tried to deal with us by piteous gestures and words and finding that they availed nothing, have left off those supplications and thenceforward our very wonder-workers are surpassed by them, some chewing the skins of worn-out shoes, and some fixing sharp nails into their heads, others lying about in frozen pools with naked stomachs, and others enduring different things yet more horrid than these, that they may draw around them the ungodly spectators. And thou, while these things are going on, standest laughing and wondering the while and making a fine show of other men's miseries, our common nature disgracing itself. And what could a fierce demon do more? Next, you give him money in abundance that he may do these things more promptly. And to him that prays and calls on God and approaches with modesty, you vouchsafe neither an answer nor a look: rather you utter to him, continually teazing you, those disgusting expressions, "Ought this fellow to live? or at all to breathe and see this sun?" whereas to the other sort you are both cheerful and liberal, as though you were appointed to dispense the prize of that ridiculous and Satanic unseemliness. Wherefore with more propriety to those who appoint these sports and bestow nothing till they see others punishing themselves, might these words be addressed, "Ought these men to live, to breathe at all, or see the sun, who trangress against our common nature, who insult God?" For whereas God saith, "Give alms, and I give thee the kingdom of heaven," thou hearest not: but when the Devil shews thee a head pierced with nails, on a sudden thou hast become liberal. And the contrivance of the evil spirit pregnant with so much mischief, hath wrought upon thee more than the promise of God bringing innumerable blessings. If gold were to be laid down to prevent the doing of these things or the looking upon them when done, there is nothing which thou oughtest not to practise and endure, to get rid of so excessive madness; but ye contrive every thing to have them done, and look on the doing of them. Still askest thou then, tell me, to what end is hell-fire? Nay, ask not that any more, but how is there one hell only? For of how many punishments are not they worthy, who get up this cruel and merciless spectacle and laugh at what both they and yourselves ought to weep over; yea, rather of the two, ye who compel them to such unseemly doings.

"But I do not compel them," say you. What else but compelling is it, I should like to know? Those who are more modest and shed tears and invoke God, thou art impatient even of listening to; but for these thou both findest silver in abundance and bringest around thee many to admire them.

"Well, let us leave off," say you, "pitying them. And dost thou too enjoin this?" Nay, it is not pity, O man, to demand so severe a punishment for a few pence, to order men to maim themselves for necessary food and cut into many pieces the skin of their head so mercilessly and pitifully. "Gently," say you, "for it is not we who pierce those heads." Would it were thou, and the horror would not be so horrible. For he that slays a man does a much more grievous[1] thing than he who bids him slay himself, which indeed happens in the case of these persons. For they endure more bitter pains when they are bidden to be themselves the executors of these wicked commands.

And all this in Antioch, where men were first called Christians, wherein are bred the most civilized of mankind, where in old time the fruit of charity flourished so abundantly. For not only to those at hand but also to those very far off, they used to send, and this when famine was expected.

[10.] What then ought we to do? say you. To cease from this savage practice: and to convince all that are in need that by doing these things they will gain nothing, but if they modestly approach they shall find your liberal-

ity great. Let them be once aware of this, even though they be of all men most miserable, they will never choose to punish themselves so severely, I pledge myself; nay, they will even give you thanks for delivering them both from the mockery and the pain of that way of life. But as it is, for charioteers you would let out even your own children, and for dancers you would throw away your very souls, while for Christ an hungered you spare not the smallest portion of your substance. But if you give a little silver, you think as much of it as if you had laid out all you have, not knowing that not the giving but the giving liberally, this is true almsgiving. Wherefore also it is not those simply who give whom the prophet proclaims and calls happy, but those who bestow liberally. For he doth not say simply, He hath given, but what? (Ps. cxii. 8.) "he hath dispersed abroad, he hath given to the poor." For what profit is it, when out of it thou givest as it were a glass of water out of the sea, and even a widow's magnanimity is beyond thy emulation? And how wilt thou say, "Pity me, O Lord, according to thy great pity, and according to the multitude of thy mercies blot out my transgression," thyself not pitying according to any great pity, nay, haply not according to any little. For I am greatly ashamed, I own, when I see many of the rich riding upon their golden-bitted chargers with a train of domestics clad in gold, and having couches of silver and other and more pomp, and yet when there is need to give to a poor man, becoming more beggarly than the very poorest.

[11.] But what is their constant talk? "He hath," they say, "the common church-allowance." And what is that to thee? For thou wilt not be saved because I give; nor if the Church bestow hast thou blotted out thine own sins. For this cause givest thou not, because the Church ought to give to the needy? Because the priests pray, wilt thou never pray thyself? And because others fast, wilt thou be continually drunken? Knowest thou not that God enacted not almsgiving so much for the sake of the poor as for the sake of the persons themselves who bestow?

But dost thou suspect the priest? Why this thing itself, to begin with, is a grievous sin. However, I will not examine the matter too nicely. Do thou it all in thine own person, and so shalt thou reap a double reward. Since in fact, what we say in behalf of almsgiving, we say not, that thou shouldest offer to us, but that thou shouldest thyself minister by thine own hands. For if thou bringest thine alms to me, perhaps thou mayest even be led captive by vain-glory, and oftentimes likewise thou shalt go away offended through suspicion of something

---

[1] χαλεπώτερον; the sense seems to require "*less* grievous:" perhaps the negative has slipped out of the text.

evil: but if ye do all things by yourselves, ye shall both be rid of offences and of unreasonable suspicion, and greater is your reward. Not therefore to compel you to bring your money hither, do I say these things; nor from indignation on account of the priests being ill-reported of. For if one must be indignant and grieve, for you should be our grief, who say this ill. Since to them who are spoken ill of falsely and vainly the reward is greater, but to the speakers the condemnation and punishment is heavier. I say not these things therefore in their behalf, but in solicitude and care for you. For what marvel is it if some in our generation are suspected, when in the case of those holy men who imitated the angels, who possessed nothing of their own, I mean the Apostles, there was a murmuring in the ministration to the widows (Acts vi. 1.) that the poor were overlooked? when "not one said that aught of the things he possessed was his own, but they had all things common?" (Acts iv. 32.)

Let us not then put forward these pretexts, nor account it an excuse that the Church is wealthy. But when you see the greatness of her substance, bear in mind also the crowds of poor who are on her list, the multitudes of her sick, her occasions of endless expenses. Investigate, scrutinize, there is none to forbid, nay, they are even ready to give you an account. But I wish to go much farther. Namely, when we have given in our accounts and proved that our expenditure is no less than our income, nay, sometimes more, I would gladly ask you this further question: When we depart hence and shall hear Christ saying, "Ye saw me hungry, and gave me no meat; naked, and ye clothed me not;" what shall we say? what apology shall we make? Shall we bring forward such and such a person who disobeyed these commands? or some of the priests who were suspected? "Nay, what is this to thee? for I accuse thee," saith He, "of those things wherein thou hast thyself sinned. And the apology for these would be, to have washed away thine own offences, not to point to others whose errors have been the same as thine."

In fact, the Church through your meanness is compelled to have such property as it has now. Since, if men did all things according to the apostolical laws, its revenue should have been your good will, which were both a secure chest and an inexhaustible treasury. But now when ye lay up for yourselves treasures upon the earth and shut up all things in your own stores, while the Church is compelled to be at charges with bands of widows, choirs of virgins, sojournings of strangers, distresses of foreigners, the misfortunes of prisoners, the necessities of the sick and

maimed, and other such like causes, what must be done? Turn away from all these, and block up so many ports? Who then could endure the shipwrecks that would ensue; the weepings, the lamentations, the wailings which would reach us from every quarter?

Let us not then speak at random what comes into our mind. For now, as I have just said, we are really prepared to render up our accounts to you. But even if it were the reverse, and ye had corrupt teachers plundering and grasping at every thing, not even so were their wickedness an apology for you. For the Lover of mankind and All-wise, the Only-Begotten Son of God, seeing all things, and knowing the chance that in so great length of time and in so vast a world there would be many corrupt priests; lest the carelessness of those under their rule should increase through their neglect, removing every excuse for indifference; "In Moses' seat," saith He, "sit the Scribes and the Pharisees; all things, therefore, whatsoever they bid you, these do ye, but do not ye after their works:" implying, that even if thou hast a bad teacher, this will not avail thee, shouldest thou not attend to the things which are spoken. For not from what thy teacher hath done but from what thou hast heard and disobeyed, from that, I say, doth God pass his sentence upon thee. So that if thou doest the things commanded, thou shalt then stand with much boldness: but if thou disobey the things spoken, even though thou shouldest show ten thousand corrupt priests, this will not plead for thee at all. Since Judas also was an apostle, but nevertheless this shall never be any apology for the sacrilegious and covetous. Nor will any be able when accused to say, "Why the Apostle was a thief and sacrilegious, and a traitor;" yea, this very thing shall most of all be our punishment and condemnation that not even by the evils of others were we corrected. For this cause also these things were written that we might shun all emulation of such things.

Wherefore, leaving this person and that, let us take heed to ourselves. For "each of us shall give account of himself to God." In order therefore that we may render up this account with a good defence, let us well order our own lives and stretch out a liberal hand to the needy, knowing that this only is our defence, the showing ourselves to have rightly done the things commanded; there is no other whatever. And if we be able to produce this, we shall escape those intolerable pains of hell, and obtain the good things to come; unto which may we all attain, by the grace and mercy of our Lord Jesus Christ, with Whom, to the Father and the Holy Ghost, be glory, power, and honor, now and ever, and world without end. Amen.

HOMILY XXII.

Know ye not that they which minister about sacred things eat of the temple? and they which wait upon the altar have their portion with the altar? Even so did the Lord ordain that they which proclaim the Gospel should live of the Gospel.

HE takes great care to show that the receiving was not forbidden. Whereupon having said so much before, he was not content but proceeds also to the Law, furnishing an example closer to the point than the former. For it was not the same thing to bring forward the oxen and to adduce the law expressly given concerning priests.

But consider, I pray, in this also the wisdom of Paul, how he mentions the matter in a way to give it dignity. For he did not say, "They which minister about sacred things receive of those who offer them." But what? "They eat of the temple:" so that neither they who receive may be blamed nor they who give may be lifted up. Wherefore also what follows he hath set down in the same way.

For neither did he say, "They which wait upon the altar receive of them which sacrifice," but, "have their portion with the altar." For the things offered now no longer belonged to those who offered them, but to the temple and the altar. And he said not, "They receive the holy things," but, they "eat of the temple," indicating again their moderation, and that it behoves them not to make money nor to be rich. And though he say that they have their portion "with the altar," he doth not speak of equal distribution but of relief given them as their due. And yet the case of the Apostles was much stronger. For in the former instance the priesthood was an honor, but in the latter it was dangers and slaughters and violent deaths. Wherefore all the other examples together did not come up to the saying, "If we sowed unto you spiritual things:" since in saying, "we sowed," he points out the storms, the danger, the snares, the unspeakable evils, which they endured in preaching. Nevertheless, though the superiority was so great, he was unwilling either to abase the things of the old law or to exalt the things which belong to himself: nay he even contracts his own, reckoning the superiority not from

the dangers, but from the greatness of the gift. For he said not, "if we have jeoparded ourselves," or "exposed ourselves to snares," but, "if we sowed unto you spiritual things."

And the part of the priests, as far as possible, he exalts, saying, "They which minister about sacred things," and "they that wait upon the altar," thereby intending to point out their continual servitude and patience. Again, as he had spoken of the priests among the Jews, viz. both the Levites and the Chief Priests, so he hath expressed each of the orders, both the inferior and the superior; the one by saying, "they which minister about sacred things," and the other by saying, "they which wait upon the altar." For not to all was one work commanded; but some were entrusted with the coarser, others with the more exalted offices. Comprehending therefore all these, lest any should say, "why talk to us of the old law? knowest thou not that ours is the time of more perfect commandments?" after all those topics he placed that which is strongest of all, saying,

Ver. 14. "Even so did the Lord ordain that they who proclaim the Gospel should live of the Gospel."

Nor doth he even here say that they are supported by men, but as in the case of the priests, of "the temple" and "of the altar," so likewise here, "of the Gospel;" and as there he saith, "eat," so here, "live," not make merchandize nor lay up treasures. "For the laborer," saith He, "is worthy of his hire."

[2.] Ver. 15. "But I have used none of these things:"

What then if thou hast not used them now, saith one, but intendest to use them at a future time, and on this account sayest these things. Far from it; for he speedily corrected the notion, thus saying;

"And I write not these things that it may be so done in my case."

And see with what vehemence he disavows and repels the thing:

"For it were good for me rather to die, than that any man should make my glorying void."

And not once nor twice, but many times he uses this expression. For above he said, "We

126

did not use this right: " and after this again, "that I abuse not my right: " and here, " but I have used none of these things." "These things;" what things? The many examples.[1] That is to say, many things giving me license; the soldier, the husbandman, the shepherd, the Apostles, the law, the things done by us unto you, the things done by you unto the others, the priests, the ordinance of Christ; by none of these have I been induced to abolish my own law, and to receive. And speak not to me of the past: (although I could say, that I have endured much even in past times on this account,) nevertheless I do not rest on it alone, but likewise concerning the future I pledge myself, that I would choose rather to die of hunger than be deprived of these crowns.

"For it were good for me rather to die," saith he, "than that any man should make my glorying void."

He said not, "that any man should abolish my law," but, "my glorying." For lest any should say, "he doth it indeed but not cheerfully, but with lamentation and grief," willing to show the excess of his joy and the abundance of his zeal, he even calls the matter "glorying." So far was he from vexing himself that he even glories, and chooses rather to die than to fall from this "glorying." So much dearer to him even than life itself was that proceeding of his.

[3.] Next, he exalts it from another consideration also, and signifies that it was a great thing, not that he might show himself famous, (for far was he from that disposition,) but to signify that he rejoices, and with a view more abundantly to take away all suspicion. For on this account, as I before said, he also called it a glorying: and what saith he?

Ver. 16, 17, 18. "For if I preach the Gospel, I have nothing to glory of; for necessity is laid upon me; for woe is unto me, if I preach not the Gospel! For if I do this of mine own will, I have a reward: but if not of mine own will, I have a stewardship entrusted to me. What then is my reward? That when I preach the Gospel, I may make the Gospel of Christ without charge, so as not to use to the full my right in the Gospel."

What sayest thou? tell me. "If thou preach the Gospel, it is nothing for thee to glory of, but it is, if thou make the Gospel of Christ without charge?" Is this therefore greater than that? By no means; but in another point of view it hath some advantage, inasmuch as the one is a command, but the other is a good deed of my own free-will: for what things are done

beyond the commandment, have a great reward in this respect: but such as are in pursuance of a commandment, not so great: and so in this respect he says, the one is more than the other; not in the very nature of the thing. For what is equal to preaching; since it maketh men vie even with the angels themselves. Nevertheless since the one is a commandment and a debt, the other a forwardness of free-will, in this respect this is more than that. Wherefore he saith, explaining the same, what I just now mentioned:

"For if I do this of mine own will, I have a reward, but if not of mine own will, a stewardship is entrusted to me;" taking the words of mine own "will" and "not of mine own will," of its being committed or not committed to him. And thus we must understand the expression, "for necessity is laid upon me;" not as though he did aught of these things against his will, God forbid, but as though he were bound by the things commanded, and for contradistinction to the liberty in receiving before mentioned. Wherefore also Christ said to the disciples, (St. Luke xvii. 10.) "When ye have done all, say, We are unprofitable servants; for we have done that which was our duty to do."

"What then is my reward? That when I preach the Gospel, I may make the Gospel without charge." What then, tell me, hath Peter no reward? Nay, who can ever have so great an one as he? And what shall we say of the other Apostles? How then said he, "If I do this of mine own will I have a reward, but if not of mine own will, a stewardship is entrusted to me?" Seest thou here also his wisdom? For he said not, "But if not of mine own will," I have no reward, but, "a stewardship is committed unto me:" implying that even thus he hath a reward, but such as he obtains who hath performed what was commanded, not such as belongs to him who hath of his own resources been generous and exceeded the commandment.

"What then is the reward? That, when I preach the Gospel," saith he, "I may make the Gospel without charge, so as not to use to the full my right in the Gospel." See how throughout he uses the term "right," intimating this, as I have often observed; that neither are they who receive worthy of blame. But he added, "in the Gospel," partly to show the reasonableness of it, partly also to forbid our carrying the matter out into every case. For the teacher ought to receive, but not the mere drone also.[2]

---

[1] [Better, "None of these preogatives," such as freedom from restrictions as to food, freedom to marry, and authority to claim maintenance from the churches. Edwards *in lo.* C.]

[2] [Chrysostom's view of this difficult passage appears to be: "If my preaching the Gospel is an optional thing, I have a reward; if on the other hand it is not optional but obligatory, then reward is out of the question (Luke xvii. 10). But it is obligatory in my case, and yet I have a reward, viz. the privilege of preaching gratuitously." This is one of Paul's felicitous paradoxes. "The consciousness of preaching freely a free Gospel was his pay for declining to be paid." C.]

[4.] Ver. 19. " For though I was free from all men, I brought myself under bondage to all, that I might gain the more."

Here again he introduces another high step in advance. For a great thing it is even not to receive, but this which he is about to mention is much more than that. What then is it that he says? "Not only have I not received," saith he, " not only have I not used this right, but I have even made myself a slave, and in a slavery manifold and universal. For not in money alone, but, which was much more than money, in employments many and various have I made good this same rule: and I have made myself a slave when I was subject to none, having no necessity in any respect, (for this is the meaning of, "though I was free from all men; ") and not to any single person have I been a slave, but to the whole world."

Wherefore also he subjoined, " I brought myself under bondage to all." That is, " To preach the Gospel I was commanded, and to proclaim the things committed to my trust; but the contriving and devising numberless things beside, all that was of my own zeal. For I was only under obligation to invest the money, whereas I did every thing in order to get a return for it, attempting more than was commanded." Thus doing as he did all things of free choice and zeal and love to Christ, he had an insatiable desire for the salvation of mankind. Wherefore also he used to overpass by a very great deal the lines marked out, in every way springing higher than the very heaven.

[5.] Next, having mentioned his servitude, be describes in what follows the various modes of it. And what are these?

Ver. 20. " And I became," says he, " to the Jews as a Jew, that I might gain Jews." And how did this take place? When he circumcised that he might abolish circumcision. Wherefore he said not, "a Jew," but, "as a Jew," which was a wise arrangement. What sayest thou? The herald of the world and he who touched the very heavens and shone so bright in grace, doth he all at once descend so low? Yea. For this is to ascend. For you are not to look to the fact only of his descending, but also to his raising up him that was bowed down and bringing him up to himself.

" To them that are under the law, as under the law, not being myself under the law, that I might gain them that are under the law." Either it is the explanation of what went before, or he hints at some other thing besides the former: calling those Jews, who were such originally and from the first: but "under the law," the proselytes, or those who became be-

lievers and yet adhered to the law. For they were no longer as Jews, yet 'under the law.' And when was he under the law? When he shaved his head; when he offered sacrifice. Now these things were done, not because his mind changed, (since such conduct would have been wickedness,) but because his love condescended. For that he might bring over to this faith those who were really Jews, he became such himself not really, showing himself such only, but not such in fact nor doing these things from a mind so disposed. Indeed, how could he, zealous as he was to convert others also, and doing these things only in order that he might free others who did them from that degradation?

Ver. 21. " To them that are without law, as without law." These were neither Jews, nor Christians, nor Greeks; but 'outside of the Law,' as was Cornelius, and if there were any others like him. For among these also making his appearance, he used to assume many of their ways. But some say that he hints at his discourse with the Athenians from the inscription on the altar, and that so he saith, "to them that are without law, as without law."

Then, lest any should think that the matter was a change of mind, he added, "not being without law to God, but under law to Christ; " i.e., "so far from being without law, I am not simply under the Law, but I have that law which is much more exalted than the older one, viz. that of the Spirit and of grace." Wherefore also he adds, " to Christ." Then again, having made them confident of his judgment, he states also the gain of such condescension, saying, " that I might gain them that are without law." And every where he brings forward the cause of his condescension, and stops not even here, but says,

Ver. 22. "To the weak became I weak, that I might gain the weak : " in this part coming to their case, with a view to which also all these things have been spoken. However, those were much greater things, but this more to the purpose; whence also he hath placed it after them. Indeed he did the same thing likewise in his Epistle to the Romans, when he was finding fault about meats; and so in many other places.

Next, not to waste time by naming all severally, he saith, "I am become all things to all men, that I may by all means save some."

Seest thou how far it is carried? " I am become all things to all men," not expecting, however, to save all, but that I may save though it be but a few. And so great care and service have I undergone, as one naturally would who was about saving all, far however from hoping to gain all: which was truly magnanimous[1]

---

[1] πολὺ μέγα.

and a proof of burning zeal. Since likewise the sower sowed every where, and saved not all the seed, notwithstanding he did his part. And having mentioned the fewness of those who are saved, again, adding, "by all means," he consoled those to whom this was a grief. For though it be not possible that all the seed should be saved, nevertheless it cannot be that all should perish. Wherefore he said, "by all means," because one so ardently zealous must certainly have some success.

Ver. 23. "And I do all things for the Gospel's sake, that I may be a joint partaker thereof."

"That is, that I may seem also myself to have added some contribution of mine own, and may partake of the crowns laid up for the faithful. For as he spake of "living of the Gospel," i.e, of the believers; so also here, "that I may be a joint partaker in the Gospel, that I may be able to partake with them that have believed in the Gospel." Do you perceive his humility, how in the recompense of rewards he places himself as one of the many, though he had exceeded all in his labors? whence it is evident that he would in his reward also. Nevertheless, he claims not to enjoy the first prize, but is content if so be he may partake with the others in the crowns laid up for them. But these things he said, not because he did this for any reward, but that hereby at least he might draw them on, and by these hopes might induce them to do all things for their brethren's sake. Seest thou his wisdom! Seest thou the excellency of his perfection? how he wrought beyond the things commanded, not receiving when it was lawful to receive. Seest thou the exceeding greatness of his condescension? how he that was "under law to Christ," and kept that highest law, "to them that were without law," was "as one without law," to the Jews, as a Jew, in either kind showing himself preeminent, and surpassing all.

[6.] This also do thou, and think not being eminent, that thou lowerest thyself, when for thy brother's sake thou submittest to some abasement. For this is not to fall, but to descend. For he who falls, lies prostrate, hardly to be raised up again; but he who descends shall also rise again with much advantage. As also Paul descended indeed alone, but ascended with the whole world: not acting a part, for he would not have sought the gain of them that are saved had he been acting. Since the hypocrite seeks men's perdition, and feigns, that he may receive, not that he may give. But the apostle not so: as a physician rather, as a teacher, as a father, the one to the sick, the other to the disciple, the third to the son, condescends for his correction, not for his hurt; so likewise did he.

To show that the things which have been stated were not pretence; in a case where he is not compelled to do or say any such thing but means to express his affection and his confidence; hear him saying, (Rom. viii. 39.) "neither life, nor death, nor angels, nor principalities, nor powers, nor things present, nor things to come, nor height, nor depth, nor any other creature, shall be able to separate us from the love of God which is in Christ Jesus our Lord." Seest thou a love more ardent than fire? So let us also love Christ. For indeed it is easy, if we will. For neither was the Apostle such by nature. On this account, you see, his former life was recorded, so contrary to this, that we may learn that the work is one of choice, and that to the willing all things are easy.

Let us not then despair, but even though thou be a reviler, or covetous, or whatsoever thou art, consider that Paul was (1 Tim. i. 13, 16.) "a blasphemer, and persecutor, and injurious, and the chief of sinners," and suddenly rose to the very summit of virtue, and his former life proved no hindrance to him. And yet none with so great frenzy clings to vice as he did to the war against the Church. For at that time he put his very life into it; and because he had not ten thousand hands that he might stone Stephen with all of them, he was vexed. Notwithstanding, even thus he found how he might stone him with more hands, to wit, those of the false witnesses whose clothes he kept. And again, when he entered into houses like a wild beast and no otherwise did he rush in, haling, tearing men and women, filling all things with tumult and confusion and innumerable conflicts. For instance, so terrible was he that the Apostles, (Acts ix. 26.) even after his most glorious change, did not yet venture to join themselves to him. Nevertheless, after all those things he became such as he was: for I need not say more.

[7.] Where now are they who build up the necessity of fate against the freedom of the will? Let them hear these things, and let their mouths be stopped. For there is nothing to hinder him that willeth to become good, even though before he should be one of the vilest. And in fact we are more aptly disposed that way, inasmuch as virtue is agreeable to our nature, and vice contrary to it, even as sickness and health. For God hath given us eyes, not that we may look wantonly, but that, admiring his handi-work, we may worship the Creator. And that this is the use of our eyes is evident from the things which are seen. For the lustre of the sun and of the sky we see from an immeasurable distance, but a woman's beauty one cannot discern so far off. Seest thou that for this end our eye was chiefly given? Again, he made the ear that we should entertain not blasphemous words, but saving doctrines. Wherefore you see, when it receives any thing dissonant, both our soul shudders and our very body also. "For," saith one, (Ecclus. xxvii. 5.) "the talk of him that sweareth much maketh the hair stand upright." And if we hear any thing cruel or merciless, again our flesh creeps; but if any thing decorous and kind, we even exult and rejoice. Again, if our mouth utter base words, it causes us to be ashamed and hide ourselves, but if grave words, it utters them with ease and all freedom. Now for those things which are according to nature no one would blush, but for those which are against nature. And the hands when they steal hide themselves, and seek excuses; but if they give alms, they even glory. So that if we will, we have from every side a great inclination towards virtue. But if thou talk to me of the pleasure which arises from vice, consider that this also is a thing which we reap more of from virtue. For to have a good conscience and to be looked up to by all and to entertain good hopes, is of all things most pleasant to him that hath seen into the nature of pleasure, even as the reverse is of all things the most grievous to him that knows the nature of pain; such as to be reproached by all, to be accused by our own conscience, to tremble and fear both at the future and the present.

And that what I say may become more evident, let us suppose for argument's sake one man having a wife, yet defiling the marriage-bed of his neighbor and taking pleasure in this wicked robbery, enjoying his paramour. Then let us again oppose to him another who loves his own spouse. And that the victory may be greater and more evident, let the man who enjoys his own wife only, have a fancy also for the other, the adulteress, but restrain his passion and do nothing evil: (although neither is this pure chastity.) However, granting more than is necessary, that you may convince yourself how great is the pleasure of virtue, for this cause have we so framed our story.

Now then, having brought them together, let us ask them accordingly, whose is the pleasanter life: and you will hear the one glorying and exulting in the conquest over his lust: but the other—or rather, there is no need to wait to be informed of any thing by him. For thou shalt see him, though he deny it times without number, more wretched than men in a prison. For he fears and suspects all, both his own wife and the husband of the adulteress and the adulteress herself, and domestics, and friends, and kinsmen, and walls, and shadows, and himself, and what is worst of all, he hath his conscience crying out against him, barking aloud every day. But if he should also bring to mind the judg-

ment-seat of God, he will not be able even to stand. And the pleasure is short: but the pain from it unceasing. For both at even, and in the night, in the desert and the city, and every where, the accuser haunts him, pointing to a sharpened sword and the intolerable punishment, and with that terror consuming and wasting him. But the other, the chaste person, is free from all these things, and is at liberty, and with comfort looks upon his wife, his children, his friends, and meets all with unembarrassed eyes. Now if he that is enamored but is master of himself enjoy so great pleasure, he that indulges no such passion but is truly chaste, what harbor, what calm will be so sweet and serene as the mind which he will attain? And on this account you may see few adulterers but many chaste persons. But if the former were the pleasanter, it would be preferred by the greater number. And tell me not of the terror of the laws. For this is not that which restrains them, but the excessive unreasonableness, and the fact that the pains of it are more than the pleasures, and the sentence of conscience.

[8.] Such then is the adulterer. Now, if you please, let us bring before you the covetous, laying bare again another lawless passion. For him too we shall see afraid of the same things and unable to enjoy real pleasure: in that calling to mind both those whom he hath wronged, and those who sympathize with them, and the public sentence of all concerning himself, he hath ten thousand agitations.

And this is not his only vexation, but not even his beloved object can he enjoy. For such is the way of the covetous; not that they may enjoy do they possess, but that they may not enjoy. But if this seem to thee a riddle, hear next what is yet worse than this and more perplexing; that not in this way only are they deprived of the pleasure of their goods, by their not venturing to use them as they would, but also by their never being filled with them but living in a continual thirst: than which what can be more grievous? But the just man is not so, but is delivered both from trembling and hatred and fear and this incurable thirst: and as all men curse the one, even so do all men conspire to bless the other: and as the one hath no friend, so hath the other no enemy.

What now, these things being so acknowledged, can be more unpleasing than vice or more pleasant than virtue? Nay, rather, though we should speak for ever, no one shall be able to represent in discourse either the pain of this, or the pleasure of the other, until we shall experience it. For then shall we find vice more bitter than gall, when we shall have fully tasted the honey of virtue. Not but vice is even now unpleasant, and disgusting, and burdensome, and this not even her very votaries gainsay; but when we withdraw from her, then do we more clearly discern the bitterness of her commands. But if the multitude run to her, it is no marvel; since children also oftentimes, choosing things less pleasant, despise those which are more delightful; and the sick for a momentary gratification lose the perpetual and more certain joy. But this comes of the weakness and folly of those who are possessed with any fondness, not of the nature of the things. For it is the virtuous man who lives in pleasure; he who is rich indeed and free indeed.

But if any one would grant the rest to virtue,—liberty, security freedom from cares, the fearing no man, the suspecting no man,—but would not grant it pleasure; to laugh, and that heartily, occurs to me, I confess, as the only course to be taken. For what else is pleasure, but freedom from care and fear and despondency, and the not being under the power of any? And who is in pleasure, tell me, the man in frenzy and convulsion, who is goaded by divers lusts, and is not even himself; or he who is freed from all these waves, and is settled in the love of wisdom, as it were in a harbor? Is it not evident, the latter? But this would seem to be a thing peculiar to virtue. So that vice hath merely the name of pleasure, but of the substance it is

destitute. And before the enjoyment, it is madness, not pleasure: but after the enjoyment, straightway this also is extinguished. Now then if neither at the beginning nor afterwards can one discern the pleasure of it, when will it appear, and where?

And that thou mayest more clearly understand what I say, let us try the force of the argument in an example. Now consider. One is enamored of a fair and lovely woman: this man as long as he cannot obtain his desire is like unto men beside themselves and frantic; but after that he hath obtained it, he hath quenched his appetite. If therefore neither at the beginning doth he feel pleasure, (for the affair is madness,) nor in the end, (for by the indulgence of his lust he cools down his wild fancy,) where after all are we to find it? But our doings are not such, but both at the beginning they are freed from all disturbance, and to the end the pleasure remains in its bloom: nay rather there is no end of our pleasure, nor have our good things a limit, nor is this pleasure ever done away.

Upon all these considerations, then, if we love pleasure, let us lay hold on virtue that we may win good things both now and hereafter: unto which may we all attain, through the grace and mercy, &c.

HOMILY XXIII.

1 COR. ix. 24.

Know ye not that they which run in a race run all, but one receiveth the prize?

HAVING pointed out the manifold usefulness of condescension and that this is the highest perfectness, and that he himself having risen higher than all towards perfection, or rather having gone beyond it by declining to receive, descended lower than all again; and having made known to us the times for each of these, both for the perfectness and for the condescension; he touches them more sharply in what follows, covertly intimating that this which was done by them and which was counted a mark of perfectness, is a kind of superfluous and useless labor. And he saith it not thus out clearly, lest they should become insolent; but the methods of proof employed by him makes this evident.

And having said that they sin against Christ and destroy the brethren, and are nothing

profited by this perfect knowledge, except charity be added; he again proceeds to a common example, and saith,

"Know ye not that they which run in a race run all, but one receiveth the prize?" Now this he saith, not as though here also one only out of many would be saved; far from it; but to set forth the exceeding diligence which it is our duty to use. For as there, though many descend into the course not many are crowned, but this befalls one only; and it is not enough to descend into the contest, nor to anoint one's self and wrestle: so likewise here it is not sufficient to believe, and to contend in any way; but unless we have so run as unto the end to show ourselves unblameable, and to come near the prize, it will profit us nothing. For even though thou consider thyself to be perfect according to knowledge, thou hast not yet attained the whole; which hinting at, he said, "so run, that ye may obtain." They had not then yet, as it seems, attained. And having said thus, he teaches them also the manner.

Ver. 25. "And every man that striveth in the games is temperate in all things."

What is, "all things?" He doth not abstain from one and err in another, but he masters entirely gluttony and lasciviousness and drunkenness and all his passions. "For this," saith he, "takes place even in the heathen games. For neither is excess of wine permitted to those who contend at the time of the contest, nor wantonness, lest they should weaken their vigor, nor yet so much as to be busied about any thing else, but separating themselves altogether from all things they apply themselves to their exercise only." Now if there these things be so where the crown falls to one, much more here, where the incitement in emulation is more abundant. For here neither is one to be crowned alone, and the rewards also far surpass the labors. Wherefore also he puts it so as to shame them, saying, "Now they do it receive to a corruptible crown, but we an incorruptible."

[2.] Ver. 26. "I therefore so run, as not uncertainly."

Thus having shamed them from those that are without, he next brings forward himself also, which kind of thing is a most excellent method of teaching: and accordingly we find him every where doing so.

But what is, "not uncertainly?" "Looking to some mark," saith he, "not at random and in vain, as ye do. For what profit have ye of entering into idol-temples, and exhibiting forsooth that perfectness? None. But not such am I, but all things whatsoever I do, I do for the salvation of my neighbor. Whether I show forth perfectness, it is for their sake; or condescension, for their sake again: whether I surpass Peter in declining to receive [compensation], it is that they may not be offended; or descend lower than all, being circumcised and shaving my head, it is that they may not be subverted. This is, "not uncertainly." But thou, why dost thou eat in idol-temples, tell me? Nay, thou canst not assign any reasonable cause. For "meat commendeth thee not to God; neither if thou eat art thou the better, nor if thou eat not art thou the worse." (1 Cor. viii. 8.) Plainly then thou runnest at random: for this is, "uncertainly."

"So fight I, as not beating the air." This he saith, again intimating that he acted not at random nor in vain. "For I have one at whom I may strike, i.e., the devil. But thou dost not strike him, but simply throwest away thy strength."

Now so far then, altogether bearing with them,

he thus speaks. For since he had dealt somewhat vehemently with them in the preceding part, he now on the contrary keeps back his rebuke, reserving for the end of the discourse the deep wound of all. Since here he says that they act at random and in vain ; but afterwards signifies that it is at the risk of no less than utter ruin to their own soul, and that even apart from all injury to their brethren, neither are they themselves guiltless in daring so to act.

Ver. 27. "But I buffet my body, and bring it into bondage lest by any means, after that I have preached to others, I myself should be rejected."

Here he implies that they are subject to the lust of the belly and give up the reins to it, and under a pretence of perfection fulfil their own greediness; a thought which before also he was travailing to express, when he said, "meats for the belly, and the belly for meats." (1 Cor. vi. 13.) For since both fornication is caused by luxury, and it also brought forth idolatry, he naturally oftentimes inveighs against this disease ; and pointing out how great things he suffered for the Gospel, he sets this also down among them. "As I went," saith he, "beyond the commands, and this when it was no light matter for me: " ("for we endure all things," it is said,) "so also here I submit to much labor in order to live soberly. Stubborn as appetite is and the tyranny of the belly, nevertheless I bridle it and give not myself up to the passion, but endure all labor not to be drawn aside by it."

"For do not, I pray you, suppose that by taking things easily I arrive at this desirable result. For it is a race and a manifold struggle,[1] and a tyrannical nature continually rising up against me and seeking to free itself. But I bear not with it but keep it down, and bring it into subjection with many struggles." Now this he saith that none may despairingly withdraw from the conflicts in behalf of virtue because the undertaking is laborious. Wherefore he saith, "I buffet and bring into bondage." He said not, "I kill:" nor, "I punish" for the flesh is not to be hated, but, "I buffet and bring into bondage ;" which is the part of a master not of an enemy, of a teacher not of a foe, of a gymnastic master not of an adversary.

"Lest by any means, having preached to others, I myself should be a rejected."

Now if Paul feared this who had taught so many, and feared it after his preaching and becoming an angel and undertaking the leadership of the whole world ; what can we say?

For, "think not," saith he, "because ye have believed, that this is sufficient for your salvation : since if to me neither preaching nor

---

[1] παγκράτιον.

teaching nor bringing over innumerable persons, is enough for salvation unless I exhibit my own conduct also unblameable, much less to you."

[3.] Then he comes to other illustrations again. And as above he alleged the examples of the Apostles and those of common custom and those of the priests, and his own, so also here having set forth those of the Olympic games and those of his own course, he again proceeds to the histories of the Old Testament. And because what he has to say will be somewhat unpleasing he makes his exhortation general, and discourses not only concerning the subject before him, but also generally concerning all the evils among the Corinthians. And in the case of the heathen games, "Know ye not?" saith he: but here,

Chap. x. ver. 1. "For I would not, brethren, have you ignorant."

Now this he said, implying that they were not very well instructed in these things. And what is this which thou wouldest not have us ignorant of?

Ver. 1—5. "That our fathers," saith he, "were all under the cloud, and all passed through the sea; and were all baptized unto Moses in the cloud and in the sea; and did all eat the same spiritual meat; and did all drink the same spiritual drink; for they drank of a spiritual Rock that followed them: and the Rock was Christ. Howbeit with most of them God was not well pleased."

And wherefore saith he these things? To point out that as they were nothing profited by the enjoyment of so great a gift, so neither these by obtaining Baptism and partaking of spiritual Mysteries, except they go on and show forth a life worthy of this grace. Wherefore also he introduces the types both of Baptism and of the Mysteries.

But what is, "They were baptized into Moses?" Like as we, on our belief in Christ and His resurrection, are baptized, as being destined in our own persons to partake in the same mysteries; for, "we are baptized," saith he, "for the dead," i.e., for our own bodies; even so they putting confidence in Moses, i.e., having seen him cross first, ventured also themselves into the waters. But because he wishes to bring the Type near the Truth; he speaks it not thus, but uses the terms of the Truth even concerning the Type.

Further: this was a symbol of the Font, and that which follows, of the Holy Table. For as thou eatest the Lord's Body, so they the manna: and as thou drinkest the Blood, so they water from a rock. For though they were things of sense which were produced, yet were they spiritually exhibited, not according to the order of nature, but according to the gracious intention of the gift, and together with the body nourished also the soul, leading it unto faith. On this account, you see, touching the food he made no remark, for it was entirely different, not in mode only but in nature also; (for it was manna;) but respecting the drink, since the manner only of the supply was extraordinary and required proof, therefore having said that "they drank the same spiritual drink," he added, "for they drank of a spiritual Rock that followed them," and he subjoined, "and the Rock was Christ." For it was not the nature of the rock which sent forth the water, (such is his meaning,) else would it as well have gushed out before this time: but another sort of Rock, a spiritual One, performed the whole, even Christ who was every where with them and wrought all the wonders. For on this account he said, "that followed them"

Perceivest thou the wisdom of Paul, how in both cases he points out Him as the Giver, and thereby brings the Type nigh to the Truth? "For He who set those things before them," saith he, "the same also hath prepared this our Table: and the same Person both brought them through the sea and thee through Baptism; and before them set manna, but before thee His Body and Blood."

[4.] As touching His gift then, such is the case: now let us observe also what follows, and consider, whether when they showed themselves unworthy of the gift, He spared them. Nay, this thou canst not say. Wherefore also he added, "Howbeit with most of them God was not well-pleased;" although He had honored them with so great honor. Yea, it profited them nothing, but most of them perished. The truth is, they all perished, but that he might not seem to prophesy total destruction to these also, therefore he said, "most of them." And yet they were innumerable, but their number profited them nothing: and these were all so many tokens of love; but not even did this profit them, inasmuch as they did not themselves show forth the fruits of love.

Thus, since most men disbelieve the things said of hell, as not being present nor in sight; he alleges the things heretofore done as a proof that God doth punish all who sin, even though He have bestowed innumerable benefits upon them: "for if ye disbelieve the things to come," so he speaks, "yet surely the things that are past ye will not disbelieve." Consider, for example, how great benefits He bestowed on them: from Egypt and the slavery there He set them free, the sea He made their path, from heaven he brought down manna, from beneath He sent forth strange and marvellous fountains of waters; He was with them every where, doing wonders and fencing them in on every side: nevertheless since they showed forth nothing worthy of this gift, He spared them not, but destroyed them all.

Ver. 5. "For they were overthrown," saith he, "in the wilderness." Declaring by this word both the sweeping destruction, and the punishments and the vengeance inflicted by God, and that they did not so much as attain to the rewards proposed to them. Neither were they in the land of promise when He did these things unto them, but without and afar somewhere, and wide of that country; He thus visiting them with a double vengeance, both by not permitting them to see the land, and this too though promised unto them, and also by actual severe punishment.

And what are these things to us? say you. To thee surely they belong. Wherefore also he adds,

Ver. 6. "Now these things were figures of us[1]."

For as the gifts are figures, even so are the punishments figures: and as Baptism and the Table were sketched out prophetically, so also by what ensued, the certainty of punishment coming on those who are unworthy of this gift was proclaimed beforehand for our sake that we by these examples might learn soberness. Wherefore also he adds,

"To the intent we should not lust after evil things, as they also lusted." For as in the benefits the types went before and the substance followed, such shall be the order also in the punishments. Seest thou how he signifies not only the fact that these shall be punished, but also the degree, more severely than those ancients? For if the one be type, and the other substance, it must needs be that the punishments should as far exceed as the gifts.

And see whom he handles first: those who eat in the idol-temples. For having said, "that we should not lust after evil things," which was general, he subjoins that which is particular, implying that each of their sins arose from evil lusting. And first he said this,

Ver. 7. "Neither be ye idolaters, as were some of them; as it is written, 'the people sat down to eat and to drink, and rose up to play.'"

Do you hear how he even calls them "idolaters?" here indeed making the declaration, but afterwards bringing the proof. And he assigned the cause too wherefore they ran to those tables; and this was gluttony. Wherefore having said, "to the intent that we should not lust after evil things," and having added, nor "be idolaters," he names the cause of such transgression; and this was gluttony. "For the people sat

down," saith he, "to eat and to drink," and he adds the end thereof, "they rose up to play." "For even as they," saith he, "from sensuality passed into idolatry; so there is a fear lest ye also may fall from the one into the other." Do you see how he signifies that these, perfect men forsooth, were more imperfect than the others whom they censured? Not in this respect only, their not bearing with their brethren throughout, but also in that the one sin from ignorance, but the others from gluttony. And from the ruin of the former he reckons the punishment to these, but allows not these to lay upon another the cause of their own sin but pronounces them responsible both for their injury, and for their own.

"Neither let us commit fornication, as some of them committed." Wherefore doth he here make mention of fornication again, having so largely discoursed concerning it before? It is ever Paul's custom when he brings a charge of many sins, both to set them forth in order and separately to proceed with his proposed topics, and again in his discourses concerning other things to make mention also of the former: which thing God also used to do in the Old Testament, in reference to each several transgression, reminding the Jews of the calf and bringing that sin before them. This then Paul also does here, at the same time both reminding them of that sin, and teaching that the parent of this evil also was luxury and gluttony. Wherefore also he adds, "Neither let us commit fornication, as some of them committed, and fell in one day three and twenty thousand."

And wherefore names he not likewise the punishment for their idolatry? Either because it was clear and more notorious, or because the plague was not so great at that time, as in the matter of Balaam, when they joined themselves to Baalpeor, the Midianitish women appearing in the camp and alluring them to wantonness according to the counsel of Balaam. For that this evil counsel was Balaam's Moses sheweth after this, in the following statement at the end of the Book of Numbers. (Numb. xxxi. 8, 11, 15, 16. in our translation.) "Balaam also the son of Beor they slew in the war of Midian with the sword and they brought the spoils. . . . And Moses was wroth, and said, Wherefore have ye saved all the women alive? For these were to the children of Israel for a stumbling-block, according to the word of Balaam, to cause them to depart from and despise the word of the Lord for Peor's sake."

Ver. 9. "Neither let us tempt Christ, as some of them also tempted, and perished by serpents."

By this he again hints at another charge which he likewise states at the end, blaming them because they contended about signs. And indeed

---

[1] τύποι ἡμῶν, rec. vers. *our examples.*

they were destroyed on account of trials, saying, "when will the good things come? when the rewards?" Wherefore also he adds, on this account correcting and alarming them,

Ver. 10. "Neither murmur ye, as some of them murmured, and perished by the destroyer."

For what is required is not only to suffer for Christ, but also nobly to bear the things that come on us, and with all gladness: since this is the nature of every crown. Yea, and unless this be so, punishment rather will attend men who take calamity with a bad grace. Wherefore, both the Apostles when they were beaten rejoiced, and Paul gloried in his sufferings.

[5.] Ver. 11. "Now all these things happened unto them by way of example; and they were written for our admonition, upon whom the ends of the ages are come."

Again he terrifies them speaking of the "ends," and prepares them to expect things greater than had already taken place. "For that we shall suffer punishment is manifest," saith he, "from what hath been said, even to those who disbelieve the statements concerning hell-fire; but that the punishment also will be most severe, is evident, from the more numerous blessings which we have enjoyed, and from the things of which those were but figures. Since, if in the gifts one go beyond the other, it is most evident that so it will be in the punishment likewise." For this cause he both called them types, and said that they were "written for us," and made mention of an "end," that he might remind them of the consummation of all things. For not such will be the penalties then as to admit of a termination and be done away, but the punishment will be eternal; for even as the punishments in this world are ended with the present life, so those in the next continually remain. But when he said, "the ends of the ages," he means nothing else than that the fearful judgment is henceforth nigh at hand.

Ver. 12. "Wherefore let him that thinketh he standeth take heed lest he fall."

Again, he casts down their pride who thought highly of their knowledge. For if they who had so great privileges suffered such things; and some for murmuring alone were visited with such punishment, and others for tempting, and neither their multitude moved God to repent[1], nor their having attained to such things; much more shall it be so in our case, except we be sober. And well said he, "he that thinketh he standeth:" for this is not even standing as one ought to stand, to rely on yourself: for quickly will such an one fall: since they too, had they not been high-minded and self-confident, but of a subdued frame of mind, would not have

suffered these things. Whence it is evident, that chiefly pride, and carelessness from which comes gluttony also, are the sources of these evils. Wherefore even though thou stand, yet take heed lest thou fall. For our standing here is not secure standing, no not until we be delivered out of the waves of this present life and have sailed into the tranquil haven. Be not therefore high-minded at thy standing, but guard against thy falling; for if Paul feared who was firmer than all, much more ought we to fear.

[6.] Now the Apostle's word, as we have seen, was, "Wherefore let him that thinketh he standeth take heed lest he fall;" but we cannot say even this; all of us, so to speak, having fallen, and lying prostrate on the ground. For to whom am I to say this? To him that committeth extortion every day? Nay, he lies prostrate with a mighty fall. To the fornicator? He too is cast down to the ground. To the drunkard? He also is fallen, and knoweth not even that he is fallen. So that it is not the season for this word, but for that saying of the prophet which he spake even to the Jews, (Jer. viii. 4.). "He that falleth, doth he not rise again?" For all are fallen, and to rise again they have no mind. So that our exhortation is not concerning the not falling, but concerning the ability of them that are fallen to arise. Let us rise again then, late though it be, beloved, let us rise again, and let us stand nobly. How long do we lie prostrate? How long are we drunken, besotted with the excessive desire of the things of this life? It is a meet opportunity now to say, (Jer. vi. 10.) "To whom shall I speak and testify?" So deaf are all men become even to the very instruction of virtue, and thence filled with abundance of evils. And were it possible to discern their souls naked; as in armies when the battle is ended one may behold some dead, and some wounded, so also in the Church we might see. Wherefore I beseech and implore you, let us stretch out a hand to each other and thoroughly raise ourselves up. For I myself am of them that are smitten, and require one to apply some remedies.

Do not however despair on this account. For what if the wounds be severe? yet are they not incurable; such is our physician: only let us feel our wounds. Although we be arrived at the very extreme of wickedness, many are the ways of safety which He strikes out for us. Thus, if thou forbear to be angry with thy neighbor, thine own sins shall be forgiven. "For if ye forgive men," saith He, "your heavenly Father will also forgive you." (Mat. vi. 14.) And if thou give alms, He will remit thee thy sins; for, "break off thy sins," saith He, "by alms." (Dan. iv. 24.) And if thou

---

[1] ἐδυσώπησε.

pray earnestly, thou shalt enjoy forgiveness: and this the widow signifieth who prevailed upon that cruel judge by the importunity of her prayer. And if thou accuse thine own sins, thou hast relief: for "declare thou thine iniquities first, that thou mayest be justified:" (Is. xlvii. 26.) and if thou art sorrowful on account of these things, this too will be to thee a powerful remedy: "for I saw," saith He, "that he was grieved and went sorrowful, and I healed his ways." (Is. lvii. 17.) And if, when thou sufferest any evil, thou bear it nobly, thou hast put away the whole. For this also did Abraham say to the rich man, that "Lazarus received his evil things, and here he is comforted." And if thou hast pity on the widow, thy sins are washed away. For, "Judge," saith He, "the orphan, and plead for the widow, and come and let us reason together, saith the Lord. And if your sins be as scarlet, I will make them white as snow; and if they be as crimson, I will make them white as wool." (Is. i. 17.) For not even a single scar of the wounds doth He suffer to appear. Yea, and though we be come to that depth of misery into which he fell, who devoured his father's substance and fed upon husks, and should repent, we are undoubtedly saved. And though we owe ten thousand talents, if we fall down before God and bear no malice, all things are forgiven us. Although we have wandered away to that place whither the sheep strayed from his keeper, even thence He recovers us again: only let us be willing, beloved. For God is merciful. Wherefore both in the case of him that owed ten thousand talents, He was content with His falling down before Him; and in the case of him who had devoured his father's goods, with his return only; and in the case of the sheep, with its willingness to be borne.

[7.] Considering therefore the greatness of His mercy, let us here make Him propitious unto us, and "let us come before His face by a full confession," (Ps. xcv. 2. LXX.) that we may not depart hence without excuse, and have to endure the extreme punishment. For if in the present life we exhibit even an ordinary diligence, we shall gain the greatest rewards: but if we depart having become nothing better here, even though we repent ever so earnestly there it will do us no good. For it was our duty to strive while yet remaining within the lists, not after the assembly was broken up idly to lament and weep: as that rich man did, bewailing and deploring himself, but to no purpose and in vain, since he overlooked the time in which he ought to have done these things. And not he alone, but many others there are like him now among the rich; not willing to despise wealth, but despising their own souls for wealth's sake:

at whom I cannot but wonder, when I see men continually interceding with God for mercy, whilst they are doing themselves incurable harm, and unsparing of their very soul as if it were an enemy. Let us not then trifle, beloved, let us not trifle nor delude ourselves, beseeching God to have mercy upon us, whilst we ourselves prefer both money and luxury, and, in fact, all things to this mercy. For neither, if any one brought before thee a case and said in accusation of such an one, that being to suffer ten thousand deaths and having it in his power to rid himself of the sentence by a little money, he chose rather to die than to give up any of his property, would you say that he was worthy of any mercy or compassion. Now in this same way do thou also reason touching thyself. For we too act in this way, and making light of our own salvation, we are sparing of our money. How then dost thou beseech God to spare thee, when thou thyself art so unsparing of thyself, and honorest money above thy soul?

Wherefore also I am greatly astonished to see, how great witchery lies hid in wealth, or rather not in wealth, but in the souls of those that are beguiled. For there are, there are those that utterly derided this sorcery[1]. For which among the things therein is really capable of bewitching us? Is it not inanimate matter? is it not transitory? is not the possession thereof unworthy of trust? is it not full of fears and dangers? nay, of murders and conspiracy? of enmity and hatred? of carelessness and much vice? is it not dust and ashes? what madness have we here? what disease?

"But," say you, "we ought not merely to bring such accusations against those that are so diseased, but also to destroy the passion." And in what other way shall we destroy it, except by pointing out its baseness and how full it is of innumerable evils?

But of this it is not easy to persuade a lover concerning the objects of his love. Well then, we must set before him another sort of beauty. But incorporeal beauty he sees not, being yet in his disease. Well then, let us show him some beauty of a corporeal kind, and say to him, Consider the meadows and the flowers therein, which are more sparkling than any gold, and more elegant and transparent than all kinds of precious stones. Consider the limpid streams from their fountains, the rivers which like oil flow noiselessly out of the earth. Ascend to heaven and behold the lustre of the sun, the beauty of the moon, the stars that cluster like flowers[2]. "Why, what is this," say you, "since we do not, I suppose, make use of them as of wealth?" Nay, we use them more than

---

[1] μαγγανείας.
[2] τῶν ἀστρων ἀ ἄνθη.

wealth, inasmuch as the use thereof is more needful, the enjoyment more secure. For thou hast no fear, lest, like money, any one should take them and go off: but you may be ever confident of having them, and that without anxiety or care. But if thou grieve because thou enjoyest them in common with others, and dost not possess them alone like money; it is not money, but mere covetousness, which thou seemest to me to be in love with: nor would even the money be an object of thy desire, if it had been placed within reach of all in common.

[8.] Therefore, since we have found the beloved object, I mean Covetousness, come let me show thee how she hates and abhors thee, how many swords she sharpens against thee, how many pits she digs, how many nooses she ties, how many precipices she prepares; that thus at any rate thou mayest do away with the charm. Whence then are we to obtain this knowledge? From the highways, from the wars, from the sea, from the courts of justice. For she hath both filled the sea with blood, and the swords of the judges she often reddens contrary to law, and arms those who on the highway lie in wait day and night, and persuades men to forget nature, and makes parricides and matricides, and introduces all sorts of evils into man's life. Which is the reason why Paul entitles her "a root of these things." (1 Tim. vi. 10.) She suffers not her lovers to be in any better condition than those who work in the mines. For as they, perpetually shut up in darkness and in chains, labor unprofitably; so also these buried in the caves of avarice, no one using any force with them, voluntarily draw on their punishment, binding on themselves fetters that cannot be broken. And those condemned to the mines. at least when even comes on, are released from their toils; but these both by day and night are digging in these wretched mines. And to those there is a definite limit of that hard labor, but these know no limit, but the more they dig so much the greater hardship do they desire. And what if those do it unwillingly, but these of their own will? in that thou tellest me of the grievous part of the disease, that it is even impossible for them to be rid of it, since they do not so much as hate their wretchedness. But as a swine in mud, so also do these delight to wallow in the noisome mire of avarice, suffering worse things than those condemned ones. As to the fact that they are in a worse condition, hear the circumstances of the one, and then thou wilt know the state of the other.

Now it is said that that soil which is impregnated with gold has certain clefts and recesses in those gloomy caverns. The malefactor then condemned to labor in that place, taking for that purpose a lamp and a mattock, so, we are told,

enters within, and carries with him a cruse to drop oil from thence into the lamp, because there is darkness even by day, without a ray of light, as I said before. Then when the time of day calls him to his wretched meal, himself, they say, is ignorant of the time, but his jailor from above striking violently on the cave, by that clattering sound declares to those who are at work below the end of the day.

Do ye not shudder when ye hear all this? Let us see now, whether there be not things more grievous than these in the case of the covetous. For these too, in the first place, have a severer jailor, viz. avarice, and so much severer, as that besides their body he chains also their soul. And this darkness also is more awful than that. For it is not subject to sense, but they producing it within, whithersoever they go, carry it about with themselves. For the eye of their soul is put out: which is the reason why more than all Christ calls them wretched, saying, "But if the light that is in thee be darkness, how great is that darkness." (S. Mat. vi. 23.) And they for their part have at least a lamp shining, but these are deprived even of this beam of light; and therefore every day they fall into countless pitfalls. And the condemned when night overtakes them have a respite, sailing into that calm port which is common to all the unfortunate, I mean the night: but against the covetous even this harbor is blocked up by their own avarice: such grievous thoughts have they even at night, since then, without disturbance from any one, at full leisure they cut themselves to pieces.

Such are their circumstances in this world; but those in the next, what discourse shall exhibit? the intolerable furnaces, the rivers burning with fire, the gnashing of teeth, the chains never to be loosed, the envenomed worm, the rayless gloom, the never-ending miseries. Let us fear them, beloved, let us fear the fountain of so great punishments, the insatiate madness, the destroyer of our salvation. For it is impossible at the same time to love both money and your soul. Let us be convinced that wealth is dust and ashes, that it leaves us when we depart hence, or rather that even before our departure it oftentimes darts away from us, and injures us both in regard of the future and in respect of the present life. For before hell fire, and before that punishment, even here it surrounds us with innumerable wars, and stirs up strifes and contests. For nothing is so apt to cause war as avarice: nothing so apt to produce beggary, whether it show itself in wealth or in poverty. For in the souls of poor men also this grievous disease ariseth, and aggravates their poverty the more. And if there be found a poor covetous man, such an one suffers not punishment in money, but in hunger. For he allows not himself to enjoy his moderate means with comfort, but both racks his belly with hunger and punishes his whole body with nakedness and cold, and every where appears more squalid and filthy than any prisoners ; and is always wailing and lamenting as though he were more wretched than all, though there be ten thousand poorer than he. This man, whether he go into the market-place, goes away with many a stripe ; or into the bath, or into the theatre, he will still be receiving more wounds, not only from the spectators, but also from those upon the stage, where he beholds not a few of the unchaste women glittering in gold. This man again, whether he sail upon the sea, regarding the merchants and their richly-freighted ships and their enormous profits, will not even count himself to live : or whether he travel by land, reckoning up the fields, the suburban farms, the inns, the baths, the revenues arising out of them, will count his own life thenceforth not worth living ; or whether thou shut him up at home, he will but rub and fret the wounds received in

the market, and so do greater despite to his own soul : and he knows only one consolation for the evils which oppress him ; death and deliverance from this life.

And these things not the poor man only, but the rich also, will suffer, who falls into this disease, and so much more than the poor, inasmuch as the tyranny presses more vehemently on him, and the intoxication is greater. Wherefore also he will account himself poorer than all ; or rather, he is poorer. For riches and poverty are determined not by the measure of the substance, but by the disposition of the mind : and he rather is the poorest of all, who is always hangering after more and is never able to stay this wicked lust.

On all these accounts then let us flee covetousness, the maker of beggars, the destroyer of souls, the friend of hell, the enemy of the kingdom of heaven, the mother of all evils together ; and let us despise wealth that we may enjoy wealth, and with wealth may enjoy also the good things laid up for us ; unto which may we all attain, &c.

HOMILY XXIV

1 COR. X. 13.

There hath no temptation taken you, but such as man can bear : but God is faithful, Who will not suffer you to be tempted above that ye are able ; but will with the temptation make also the way of escape, that ye may be able to endure it.

THUS, because he terrified them greatly, relating the ancient examples, and threw them into an agony, saying, "Let him that thinketh he standeth take heed lest he fall ; " though they had borne many temptations, and had exercised themselves many times therein ; for "I was with you," saith he, "in weakness, and in fear, and in much trembling : " (1 Cor. ii. 3.) lest they should say, "Why terrify and alarm us ? we are not unexercised in these troubles, for we have been both driven and persecuted, and many and continual dangers have we endured : " repressing again their pride, he says, "there hath no temptation taken you but such as man can bear," i.e., small, brief, moderate. For he uses the expression "man can bear[2]," in respect of what is small ; as when he says, "I speak after the manner of men because of the infirmity of your flesh."

(Rom. vi. 19.) "Think not then great things," saith he, "as though ye had overcome the storm. For never have ye seen a danger threatening death nor a temptation intending slaughter : " which also he said to the Hebrews, "ye have not yet resisted unto blood, striving against sin." (Heb. xii. 4.)

Then, because he terrified them, see how again he raises them up, at the same time recommending moderation ; in the words, "God is faithful, Who will not suffer you to be tempted above that ye are able." There are therefore temptations which we are not able to bear. And what are these? All, so to speak. For the ability lies in God's gracious influence ; a power which we draw down by our own will. Wherefore that thou mayest know and see that not only those which exceed our power, but not even these which are "common to man" is it possible without assistance from God easily to bear, he added,

"But will with the temptation also make the way of escape, that ye may be able to endure it."

For, saith he, not even those moderate temptations, as I was remarking, may we bear by our

---

[2] ἀνθρώπινον.

own power: but even in them we require aid from Him in our warfare that we may pass through them, and until we have passed, bear them. For He gives patience and brings on a speedy release; so that in this way also the temptation becomes bearable. This he covertly imtimates, saying, "will also make the way of escape, that ye may be able to bear it:" and all things he refers to Him.

[2.] Ver. 14. "Wherefore, my brethren[1], flee from idolatry."

Again he courts them by the name of kindred, and urges them to be rid of this sin with all speed. For he did not say, simply, depart, but "flee;" and he calls the matter "idolatry," and no longer bids them quit it merely on account of the injury to their neighbor, but signifies that the very thing of itself is sufficient to bring a great destruction.

Ver. 15. "I speak as to wise men: judge ye what I say."

Because he hath cried out aloud and heightened the accusation, calling it idolatry; that he might not seem to exasperate them and to make his speech disgusting, in what follows he refers the decision to them, and sets his judges down on their tribunal with an encomium. "For I speak as to wise men," saith he: which is the mark of one very confident of his own rights, that he should make the accused himself the judge of his allegations.

Thus also he more elevates the hearer, when he discourses not as commanding nor as laying down the law, but as advising with them and as actually pleading before them. For with the Jews, as more foolishly and childishly disposed, God did not so discourse, nor did He in every instance acquaint them with the reasons of the commands, but merely enjoined them; but here, because we have the privilege of great liberty, we are even admitted to be counsellors. And he discourses as with friends, and says, "I need no other judges, do ye yourselves pass this sentence upon me, I take you for arbiters."

[3.] Ver. 16. "The cup of blessing which we bless, is it not a communion of the Blood of Christ?"

What sayest thou, O blessed Paul? When thou wouldest appeal to the hearer's reverence, when thou art making mention of awful mysteries, dost thou give the title of "cup of blessing" to that fearful and most tremendous cup? "Yea," saith he; "and no mean title is that which was spoken. For when I call it 'blessing,' I mean thanksgiving, and when I call it thanksgiving I unfold all the treasure of God's goodness, and call to mind those mighty gifts." Since we too, recounting over the cup the unspeakable mercies of God and all that we have been made partakers of, so draw near to Him, and communicate; giving Him thanks that He hath delivered from error the whole race of mankind[2]; that being afar off, He made them nigh; that when they had no hope and were without God in the world, He constituted them His own brethren and fellow-heirs. For these and all such things, giving thanks, thus we approach. "How then are not your doings inconsistent," saith he, "O ye Corinthians; blessing God for delivering you from idols, yet running again to their tables?"

"The cup of blessing which we bless, is it not a communion of the Blood of Christ?" Very persuasively spake he, and awfully. For what he says is this: "This which is in the cup is that which flowed from His side, and of that do we partake." But he called it a cup of blessing, because holding it in our hands, we so exalt Him in our hymn, wondering, astonished at His unspeakable gift, blessing Him, among other things, for the pouring out of this self-same draught that we might not abide in error: and not only for the pouring it out, but also for the imparting thereof to us all. "Wherefore if thou desire blood," saith He, "redden not the altar of idols with the slaughter of brute beasts, but My altar with My blood." Tell me, what can be more tremendous than this? What more tenderly kind? This also lovers do. When they see those whom they love desiring what belongs to strangers and despising their own, they give what belongs to themselves, and so persuade them to withdraw themselves from the gifts of those others. Lovers, however, display this liberality in goods and money and garments, but in blood none ever did so. Whereas Christ even herein exhibited His care and fervent love for us. And in the old covenant, because they were in an imperfect state, the blood which they used to offer to idols He Himself submitted to receive, that He might separate them from those idols; which very thing again was a proof of His unspeakable affection: but here He transferred the service to that which is far more awful and glorious, changing the very sacrifice itself, and instead of the slaughter of irrational creatures, commanding to offer up Himself.

[4.] "The bread which we break, is it not a communion of the Body of Christ?" Wherefore said he not, the participation? Because he intended to express something more and to

---

[1] ἀδελφοὶ, rec. text ἀγαπητοί, [which is well sustained. C.]

[2] "When we had fallen away, Thou didst raise us again, and didst not cease doing all things, until Thou hadst brought us up to Heaven, and given unto us freely Thy future Kingdom." Liturgy of St. Chrysostom. Ed. Savile. vi. 996. "When we had fallen from our eternal life and were exiled from the Paradise of delight: Thou didst not cast us off to the end, but did, visit us continually," &c. Lit. of St. Basil, t. ii. 677: and so in all the old Liturgies, vid. Brett's Collection.

point out how close was the union: in that we communicate not only by participating and partaking, but also by being united. For as that body is united to Christ, so also are we united to him by this bread.

But why adds he also, "which we break?" For although in the Eucharist one may see this done, yet on the cross not so, but the very contrary. For, "A bone of Him," saith one, "shall not be broken." But that which He suffered not on the cross, this He suffers in the oblation for thy sake, and submits to be broken, that he may fill all men.

Further, because he said, "a communion of the Body," and that which communicates is another thing from that whereof it communicates; even this which seemeth to be but a small difference, he took away. For having said, "a communion of the Body," he sought again to express something nearer. Wherefore also he added,

Ver. 17. "For we, who are many, are one bread, one body." "For why speak I of communion?" saith he, "we are that self-same body." For what is the bread? The Body of Christ. And what do they become who partake of it? The Body of Christ: not many bodies, but one body. For as the bread consisting of many grains is made one, so that the grains no where appear; they exist indeed, but their difference is not seen by reason of their conjunction; so are we conjoined both with each other and with Christ: there not being one body for thee, and another for thy neighbor to be nourished by, but the very same for all. Wherefore also he adds,

"For we all partake of the one bread." Now if we are all nourished of the same and all become the same, why do we not also show forth the same love, and become also in this respect one? For this was the old way too in the time of our forefathers: "for the multitude of them that believed," saith the text, "were of one heart and soul." (Acts iv. 32.) Not so, however, now, but altogether the reverse. Many and various are the contests betwixt all, and worse than wild beasts are we affected towards each other's members. And Christ indeed made thee so far remote, one with himself: but thou dost not deign to be united even to thy brother with due exactness, but separatest thyself, having had the privilege of so great love and life from the Lord. For he gave not simply even His own body; but because the former nature of the flesh which was framed out of earth, had first become deadened by sin and destitute of life; He brought in, as one may say, another sort of dough and leaven, His own flesh, by nature indeed the same, but free from sin and full of life; and gave to all to partake thereof, that being nourished by this and laying aside the old dead material, we might be blended together unto that which is living and eternal, by means of this table.

[5.] Ver. 18. "Behold Israel after the flesh: have not they which eat the sacrifices communion with the altar?"

Again, from the old covenant he leads them unto this point also. For because they were far beneath the greatness of the things which had been spoken, he persuades them both from former things and from those to which they were accustomed. And he says well, "according to the flesh," as though they themselves were according to the Spirit. And what he says is of this nature: "even from persons of the grosser sort ye may be instructed that they who eat the sacrifices, have communion with the altar." Dost thou see how he intimates that they who seemed to be perfect have not perfect knowledge, if they know not even this, that the result of these sacrifices to many oftentimes is a certain communion and friendship with devils, the practice drawing them on by degrees? For if among men the fellowship of salt[1] and the table becomes an occasion and token of friendship, it is possible that this may happen also in the case of devils.

But do thou, I pray, consider, how with regard to the Jews he said not, "they are partakers with God," but, "they have communion with the altar;" for what was placed thereon was burnt: but in respect to the Body of Christ, not so. But how? It is "a Communion of the Lord's Body." For not with the altar, but with Christ Himself, do we have communion.

But having said that they have "communion with the altar," afterwards fearing lest he should seem to discourse as if the idols had any power and could do some injury, see again how he overthrows them, saying,

Ver. 19. "What say I then? That an idol is any thing? or that a thing sacrificed to idols is any thing?"

As if he had said, "Now these things I affirm, and try to withdraw you from the idols, not as though they could do any injury or had any power: for an idol is nothing; but I wish you to despise them." "And if thou wilt have us despise them," saith one, "wherefore dost thou carefully withdraw us from them?" Because they are not offered to thy Lord.

Ver. 20.[2] "For that which the Gentiles sacrifice," saith he, "they sacrifice to demons, and not to God."

---

[1] Cf. Lev. ii. 13; Numbers xviii. 19; 2 Chron. xiii, 5. Theodoret on the latter place says, "By *a covenant of salt for ever*, he expresses the stability of the Kingdom, since even Barbarians oftentimes upon eating with their enemies keep the peace entire, *remembering the salt* thereof."

[2] ὁ γὰρ θύει. rec. text ἀλλ ὅτι ἃ θύει. [which is correct. C.]

Do not then run to the contrary things. For neither if thou wert a king's son, and having the privilege of thy father's table, shouldest leave it and choose to partake of the table of the condemned and the prisoners in the dungeon, would thy father permit it, but with great vehemence he would withdraw thee; not as though the table could harm thee, but because it disgraces thy nobility and the royal table. For verily these too are servants who have offended; dishonored, condemned, prisoners reserved for intolerable punishment, accountable for ten thousand crimes. How then art thou not ashamed to imitate the gluttonous and vulgar crew, in that when these condemned persons set out a table, thou runnest thither and partakest of the viands? Here is the cause why I seek to withdraw thee. For the intention of the sacrificers, and the person of the receivers, maketh the things set before thee unclean.

"And I would not that ye should have communion with demon." Perceivest thou the kindness of a careful father? Perceivest thou also the very word, what force it hath to express his feeling? "For it is my wish," saith he, "that you have nothing in common with them."

[6.] Next, because he brought in the saying by way of exhortation, lest any of the grosser sort should make light of it as having license, because he said, "I would not," and, "judge ye;" he positively affirms in what follows and lays down the law, saying,

Ver. 21. "Ye cannot drink the cup of the Lord, and the cup of demons: ye cannot partake of the Lord's table, and of the table of demons."

And he contents himself with the mere terms, for the purpose of keeping them away.

Then, speaking also to their sense of shame,

Ver. 22. "Do we provoke the Lord to jealousy?[1] are we stronger than He?" i. e., "Are we tempting Him, whether He is able to punish us, and irritating Him by going over to the adversaries and taking our stand with His enemies?" And this he said, reminding them of an ancient history and of their fathers' transgression. Wherefore also he makes use of this expression, which Moses likewise of old used against the Jews, accusing them of idolatry in the person of God. "For they," saith He, "moved Me to jealousy[2] with that which is not God; they provoked Me to anger with their idols." (Deut. xxxii. 21.)

"Are we stronger than He?" Dost thou see how terribly, how awfully he rebukes them, thoroughly shaking their very nerves, and by his way of reducing them to an absurdity, touching them to the quick and bringing down their pride? "Well, but why," some one will say, "did he not set down these things at first, which would be most effectual to withdraw them?" Because it is his custom to prove his point by many particulars, and to place the strongest last, and to prevail by proving more than was necessary. On this account then, he began from the lesser topics, and so made his way to that which is the sum of all evils: since thus that last point also became more easily admitted, their mind having been smoothed down by the things said before.

Ver. 23, 24. "All things are lawful for me, but all things are not expedient: all things are lawful for me, but all things edify not. Let no man seek his own, but each his neighbor's good."

Seest thou his exact wisdom? Because it was likely that they might say, "I am perfect and master of myself, and it does me no harm to partake of what is set before me;" "Even so," saith he, "perfect thou art and master of thyself; do not however look to this, but whether the result involve not injury, nay subversion." For both these he mentioned, saying, "All things are not expedient, all things edify not;" and using the former with reference to one's self, the latter, to one's brother: since the clause, "are not expedient," is a covert intimation of the ruin of the person to whom he speaks; but the clause, "edify not," of the stumbling block to the brother.

Wherefore also he adds, "Let no man seek his own;" which he every where through the whole Epistle insists upon and in that to the Romans; when he says, "For even Christ pleased not Himself:" (Rom. xv. 3.) and again, "Even as I please all men in all things, not seeking mine own profit." (Cor. x. 33.) And again in this place; he does not, however, fully work it out here. That is, since in what had gone before he had established it at length, and shown that he no where "seeks his own," but both "to the Jews became as a Jew and to them that are without law as without law," and used not his own "liberty" and "right" at random, but to the profit of all, serving all; he here broke off, content with a few words, by these few guiding them to the remembrance of all which had been said.

[7.] These things therefore knowing, let us also, beloved, consult for the good of the brethren and preserve unity with them. For to this that fearful and tremendous sacrifice leads us, warning us above all things to approach it with one mind and fervent love, and thereby becoming eagles, so to mount up to the very heaven, nay, even beyond the heaven. "For wheresoever the carcase is," saith He, "there also will be the eagles," (St. Mat. xxiv. 28.) calling His

---

[1] παραζηλοῦμεν.
[2] παρεζήλωσαν.

body a carcase by reason of His death. For unless He had fallen, we should not have risen again. But He calls us eagles, implying that he who draws nigh to this Body must be on high and have nothing common with the earth, nor wind himself downwards and creep along; but must ever be soaring heavenwards, and look on the Sun of Righteousness, and have the eye of his mind quick-sighted. For eagles, not daws, have a right to this table.[1] Those also shall then meet Him descending from heaven, who now worthily have this privilege, even as they who do so unworthily, shall suffer the extremest torments.

For if one would not inconsiderately receive a king—(why say I a king? nay were, it but a royal robe, one would not inconsiderately touch it with unclean hands;)—though he should be in solitude, though alone, though no man were at hand: and yet the robe is nought but certain threads spun by worms: and if thou admirest the dye, this too is the blood of a dead fish; nevertheless, one would not choose to venture on it with polluted hands: I say now, if even a man's garment be what one would not venture inconsiderately to touch, what shall we say of the Body of Him Who is God over all, spotless, pure, associate with the Divine Nature, the Body whereby we are, and live; whereby the gates of hell were broken down and the sanctuaries[1] of heaven opened? how shall we receive this with so great insolence? Let us not, I pray you, let us not slay ourselves by our irreverence, but with all awfulness and purity draw nigh to It; and when thou seest It set before thee, say thou to thyself, "Because of this Body am I no longer earth and ashes, no longer a prisoner, but free: because of this I hope for heaven, and to receive the good things therein,

immortal life, the portion of angels, converse with Christ; this Body, nailed and scourged, was more than death could stand against; this Body the very sun saw sacrificed, and turned aside his beams; for this both the veil was rent in that moment, and rocks were burst asunder, and all the earth was shaken. This is even that Body, the blood-stained, the pierced, and that out of which gushed the saving fountains, the one of blood, the other of water, for all the world."

Wouldest thou from another source also learn its power? Ask of her diseased with an issue of blood, who laid hold not of Itself, but of the garment with which It was clad; nay not of the whole of this, but of the hem: ask of the sea, which bare It on its back: ask even of the Devil himself, and say, "Whence hast thou that incurable stroke? whence hast thou no longer any power? Whence art thou captive? By whom hast thou been seized in thy flight?" And he will give no other answer than this, "The Body that was crucified." By this were his goads broken in pieces; by this was his head crushed; by this were the powers and the principalities made a show of. "For," saith he, "having put off from himself principalities and powers, He made a show of them openly, triumphing over them in it." (Col. ii. 15.)

Ask also Death, and say, "whence is it that thy sting hath been taken away? thy victory abolished? thy sinews cut out? and thou become the laughing-stock of girls and children, who wast before a terror even to kings and to all righteous men?" And he will ascribe it to this Body. For when this was crucified, then were the dead raised up, then was that prison burst, and the gates of brass were broken, and the dead were loosed,[1] and the keepers of hell-gate all cowered in fear. And yet, had He been one of the many, death on the contrary should have become more mighty; but it was not so. For He was not one of the many. Therefore was death dissolved. And as they who take food which they are unable to retain, on account of that vomit up also what was before lodged in them; so also it happened unto death. That Body, which he could not digest, he received: and therefore had to cast forth that which he had within him. Yea, he travailed in pain, whilst he held Him, and was straitened until He vomited Him up. Wherefore saith the Apostle, "Having loosed the pains of death." (Acts xi. 24.) For never woman labouring of child was so full of anguish as he was torn and racked in sunder, while he held the Body of the Lord. And that which happened to the Babylonian dragon, when, having taken the food it burst asunder in the midst,[2]

---

[1] "This Table is not, saith Chrysostom, for chattering jays, but for eagles, who fly thither where the dead body lieth." Hom. Of the worthy receiving of the Sacrament, &c. This interpretation seems to be generally recognised by the Fathers, See S. Iren. iv. 14; Orig. on S. Matt. §. 47; S. Ambr. on S. Luke xvii. 7. "The souls of the righteous are compared unto eagles, because they seek what is on high, leave the low places, are accounted to lead a long life. Wherefore also David saith to his own soul, *Thy youth shall be renewed as of an eagle.* [Ps. ciii. 5.] If then we have come to know what the *eagles* are, we can no longer doubt about the *Body;* especially if we recollect that Body which Joseph once received from Pilate. Seem they not unto thee as eagles around a Body, I mean Mary the wife of Cleopas, and Mary Magdelene and Mary the Mother of the Lord, and the gathering of the Apostles around the Lord's entombing? Doth it not seem to thee as eagles around a body, when the Son of Man shall come with the mystical clouds, *and every eye shall see Him, and they also which pierced Him?*

"There is also the Body concerning which it was said, *My Flesh is meat indeed, and My Blood is drink indeed.* Around this Body are certain eagles, which hover over It with spiritual wings. They are also eagles round the Body, which believe that Jesus is come in the Flesh: since *every spirit which confesseth that Jesus Christ is come in the flesh, is of God.* Wheresoever then faith is, there is the Sacrament, there the resting place of holiness. Again, this Body is the Church, wherein by the grace of Baptism we are renovated in spirit, and whatever tends to decay through old age is refreshed, for ages of new life."

Comp. also Theodoret on *Providence* Orat. 5. t. iv. 550. Ed· Schultze; S. Jerome, *Ep.* xlvi. 11; S. Aug. *Quæst. Evangel.* i. 42.

[1] ἀψίδες, originally "arches," afterwards "the vaults of the sanctuary or choir in a church."

[1] ἀφείθησαν, Ms. Reg. Bened. ἀνίστησαν.
[2] Bel and the Dragon, v. 27.

this also happened unto him. For Christ came not forth again by the mouth of death, but having burst asunder and ripped up in the very midst, the belly of the dragon, thus from His secret chambers (Psalm xix. 5.) right gloriously He issued forth and flung abroad His beams not to this heaven alone, but to the very throne most high. For even thither did He carry it up.

This Body hath He given to us both to hold and to eat; a thing appropriate to intense love. For those whom we kiss vehemently, we ofttimes even bite with our teeth. Wherefore also Job, indicating the love of his servants towards him, said, that they ofttimes, out of their great affection towards him, said, "Oh! that we were filled with his flesh!" (Job xxxi. 31.) Even so Christ hath given to us to be filled with His flesh, drawing us on to greater love.

[8.] Let us draw nigh to Him then with fervency and with inflamed love, that we may not have to endure punishment. For in proportion to the greatness of the benefits bestowed on us, so much the more exceedingly are we chastised when we show ourselves unworthy of the bountifulness. This Body, even lying in a manger, Magi reverenced. Yea, men profane and barbarous, leaving their country and their home, both set out on a long journey, and when they came, with fear and great trembling worshipped Him. Let us, then, at least imitate those Barbarians, we who are citizens of heaven. For they indeed when they saw Him but in a manger, and in a hut, and no such thing was in sight as thou beholdest now, drew nigh with great awe; but thou beholdest Him not in the manger but on the altar, not a woman holding Him in her arms, but the priest standing by, and the Spirit with exceeding bounty hovering over the gifts set before us. Thou dost not see merely this Body itself as they did, but thou knowest also Its power, and the whole economy, and art ignorant of none of the holy things which are brought to pass by It, having been exactly initiated into all.

Let us therefore rouse ourselves up and be filled with horror, and let us show forth a reverence far beyond that of those Barbarians; that we may not by random and careless approaches heap fire upon our own heads. But these things I say, not to keep us from approaching, but to keep us from approaching without consideration. For as the approaching at random is dangerous, so the not communicating in those mystical suppers is famine and death. For this Table is the sinews of our soul, the bond of our mind, the foundation of our confidence, our hope, our salvation, our light, our life. When with this sacrifice we depart into the outer world, with much confidence we shall tread the sacred threshold, fenced round on every side as with a kind of golden armor. And why speak I of the world to come? Since here this mystery makes earth become to thee a heaven. Open only for once the gates of heaven and look in; nay, rather not of heaven, but of the heaven of heavens; and then thou wilt behold what I have been speaking of. For what is there most precious of all, this will I show thee lying upon the earth. For as in royal palaces, what is most glorious of all is not walls, nor golden roofs, but the person of the king sitting on the throne; so likewise in heaven the Body of the King. But this, thou art now permitted to see upon earth. For it is not angels, nor archangels, nor heavens and heavens of heavens, that I show thee, but the very Lord and Owner of these. Perceivest thou how that which is more precious than all things is seen by thee on earth; and not seen only, but also touched; and not only touched, but likewise eaten; and after receiving It thou goest home?

Make thy soul clean then, prepare thy mind for the reception of these mysteries. For if thou wert entrusted to carry a king's child with the robes, the purple, and the diadem, thou wouldest cast away all things which are upon the earth. But now that it is no child of man how royal soever, but the only-begotten Son of God Himself, Whom thou receivedst; dost thou not thrill with awe, tell me, and cast away all the love of all worldly things, and have no bravery but that wherewith to adorn thyself? or dost thou still look towards earth, and love money, and pant after gold? What pardon then canst thou have? what excuse? Knowest thou not that all this worldly luxury is loathsome to thy Lord? Was it not for this that on His birth He was laid in a manger, and took to Himself a mother of low estate? Did He not for this say to him that was looking after gain, "But the Son of Man hath not where to lay His head?" (St. Mat. viii. 20.)

And what did the disciples? Did they not observe the same law, being taken to houses of the poor and lodged, one with a tanner, another with a tent-maker, and with the seller of purple? For they inquired not after the splendor of the house, but for the virtues of men's souls.

These therefore let us also emulate, hastening by the beauty of pillars and of marbles, and seeking the mansions which are above; and let us tread under foot all the pride here below with all love of money, and acquire a lofty mind. For if we be sober-minded, not even this whole world is worthy of us, much less porticoes and arcades. Wherefore, I beseech you, let us adorn our souls, let us fit up this house which we are also to have with us when we depart; that we may attain even to the eternal blessings, through the grace and mercy, &c.

HOMILY XXV

1 COR. X. 25.

Whatsoever is sold in the shambles, eat, asking no question for conscience sake.

HAVING said that "they could not drink the cup of the Lord and the cup of the devils," and having once for all led them away from those tables, by Jewish examples, by human reasonings, by the tremendous Mysteries, by the rites solemnized among the idols[1]; and having filled them with great fear; that he might not by this fear drive again to another extreme, and they be forced, exercising a greater scrupulosity than was necessary, to feel alarm, lest possibly even without their knowledge there might come in some such thing either from the market or from some other quarter; to release them from this strait, he saith, "Whatsoever is sold in the shambles, eat, asking no question." "For," saith he, "if thou eat in ignorance and not knowingly, thou art not subject to the punishment: it being thenceforth a matter not of greediness, but of ignorance."

Nor doth he free the man only from this anxiety, but also from another, establishing them in thorough security and liberty. For he doth not even suffer them to "question;" i.e., to search and enquire, whether it be an idol-sacrifice or no such thing; but simply to eat every thing which comes from the market, not even acquainting one's self with so much as this, what it is that is set before us. So that even he that eateth, if in ignorance, may be rid of anxiety. For such is the nature of those things which are not in their essence evil, but through the man's intention make him unclean. Wherefore he saith, "asking no question."

Ver. 26. "For to the Lord belongeth the earth and the fulness thereof." Not to the devils. Now if the earth and the fruits and the beasts be all His, nothing is unclean: but it becomes unclean otherwise, from our intention and our disobedience. Wherefore he not only gave permission, but also,

Ver. 27. "If one of them that believe not bid-deth you," saith he, "to a feast, and you are disposed to go; whatsoever is set before you, eat, asking no question for conscience sake."

See again his moderation. For he did not command and make a law that they should withdraw themselves, yet neither did he forbid it. And again, should they depart, he frees them from all suspicion. Now what may be the account of this? That so great curiousness might not seem to arise from any fear and cowardice. For he who makes scrupulous enquiry doth so as being in dread: but he who, on hearing the fact, abstains, abstains as out of contempt and hatred and aversion. Wherefore Paul, purposing to establish both points, saith, "Whatsoever is set before you, eat."

Ver. 28. "But if any man say unto you, This hath been offered in sacrifice unto idols; eat not, for his sake that showed it."

Thus it is not at all for any power that they have but as accursed, that he bids abstain from them. Neither then, as though they could injure you, fly from them, (for they have no strength;) nor yet, because they have no strength, indifferently partake: for it is the table of beings hostile and degraded. Wherefore he said, "eat not for his sake that showed it, and for conscience sake. For the earth is the Lord's and the fulness thereof." *

Seest thou how both when he bids them eat and when they must abstain, he brings forward the same testimony? "For I do not forbid," saith he, "for this cause as though they belonged to others: ("for the earth is the Lord's:") but for the reason I mentioned, for conscience sake; i.e., that it may not be injured." Ought one therefore to inquire scrupulously? "Nay" saith he · "for I said not thy conscience, but his. For I have already said, 'for his sake that showed it.'" And again, v. 29, "Conscience, I say, not thine own, but the other's."

[2.] But perhaps some one may say, "The brethren indeed, as is natural, thou sparest, and dost not suffer us to taste for their sakes, lest their conscience being weak might be emboldened to eat the idol sacrifices. But if it be some heathen, what is this man to thee? Was it not thine own word, 'What have I to do with judging them that are without?' (1 Cor. v. 12.)

---

[1] Savile conj. εἰδωλείοις, "'in the idol Temples:' but εἰδώλοις is the actual reading.

* [The latest editions omit this clause as unsustained by MS. authority and needless to the argument. C.]

Wherefore then dost thou on the contrary care for them?" "Not for him is my care," he replies, "but in this case also for thee." To which effect also he adds,

"For why is my liberty judged by another conscience?" meaning by "liberty," that which is left without caution or prohibition. For this is liberty, freed from Jewish bondage. And what he means is this: "God hath made me free and above all reach of injury, but the Gentile knoweth not how to judge of my rule of life, nor to see into the liberality of my Master, but will condemn and say to himself, 'Christianity is a fable; they abstain from the idols, they shun demons, and yet cleave to the things offered to them: great is their gluttony.'" "And what then?" it may be said. "What harm is it to us, should he judge us unfairly?" But how much better to give him no room to judge at all! For if thou abstain, he will not even say this. "How," say you, "will he not say it? For when he seeth me not making these inquiries, either in the shambles or in the banquet; what should hinder him from using this language and condemning me, as one who partakes without discrimination?" It is not so at all. For thou partakest, not as of idol-sacrifices, but as of things clean. And if thou makest no nice enquiry, it is that thou mayest signify that thou fearest not the things set before thee; this being the reason why, whether thou enterest a house of Gentiles or goest into the market, I suffer thee not to ask questions; viz. lest thou become timid[1] and perplexed,[2] and occasion thyself needless trouble.

Ver. 30. "If I by grace partake, why am I evil spoken of for that for which I give thanks?" "Of what dost thou 'by grace partake?' tell me." Of the gifts of God. For His grace is so great, as to render my soul unstained and above all pollution. For as the sun sending down his beams upon many spots of pollution, withdraws them again pure; so likewise and much more, we, living in the midst of the world remain pure, if we will, by how much the power we have is even greater than his. "Why then abstain?" say you. Not as though I should become unclean, far from it; but for my brother's sake, and that I may not become a partaker with devils, and that I may not be judged by the unbeliever. For in this case it is no longer now the nature of the thing, but the disobedience and the friendship with devils which maketh me unclean, and the purpose of heart worketh the pollution.

But what is, "why am I evil spoken of for that for which I give thanks?" "I, for my part," saith he, "give thanks to God that He hath thus set me on high, and above the low

estate of the Jews, so that from no quarter am I injured. But the Gentiles not knowing my high rule of life will suspect the contrary, and will say, 'Here are Christians indulging a taste for our customs; they are a kind of hypocrites, abusing the demons and loathing them, yet running to their tables; than which what can be more senseless? We conclude that not for truth's sake, but through ambition and love of power they have betaken themselves to this doctrine.' What folly then would it be that in respect of those things whereby I have been so benefited as even to give solemn thanks, in respect of these I should become the cause of evil-speaking?" "But these things, even as it is," say you, "will the Gentile allege, when he seeth me not making enquiry." In no wise. For all things are not full of idol-sacrifices so that he should suspect this: nor dost thou thyself taste of them as idol-sacrifices. But not then scrupulous overmuch, nor again, on the other hand, when any say that it is an idol-sacrifice, do thou partake. For Christ gave thee grace and set thee on high and above all injury from that quarter, not that thou mightest be evil spoken of, nor that the circumstance which hath been such a gain to thee as to be matter of special thanksgiving, should so injure others as to make them even blaspheme. "Nay, why," saith he, "do I not say to the Gentile, 'I eat, I am no wise injured, and I do not this as one in friendship with the demons'?" Because thou canst not persuade him, even though thou shouldst say it ten thousand times: weak as he is and hostile. For if thy brother hath not yet been persuaded by thee, much less the enemy and the Gentile. If he is possessed by his consciousness of the idol-sacrifice, much more the unbeliever. And besides, what occasion have we for so great trouble?

"What then? whereas we have known Christ and give thanks, while they blaspheme, shall we therefore abandon this custom also?" Far from it. For the thing is not the same. For in the one case, great is our gain from bearing the reproach; but in the other, there will be no advantage. Wherefore also he said before, "for neither if we eat, are we the better; nor if we eat not, are we the worse." (c. viii. 8.) And besides this too he showed that the thing was to be avoided, so that even on another ground ought they to be abstained from, not on this account only but also for the other reasons which he assigned.

[3.] Ver. 31. "Whether therefore ye eat, or drink, or whatsoever ye do, do all to the glory of God."

Perceivest thou how from the subject before him, he carried out the exhortation to what was general, giving us one, the most excellent of all

---

[1] ψοφοδεής.
[2] λινοπλήξ.

aims, that God in all things should be glorified?

Ver. 32. "Give no occasion of stumbling, either to Jews, or to Greeks, or to the Church of God:" i. e., give no handle to anyone: since in the case supposed, both thy brother is offended, and the Jew will the more hate and condemn thee, and the Gentile in like manner deride thee even as a gluttonous man and a hypocrite.

Not only, however, should the brethren receive no hurt from us, but to the utmost of our power not even those that are without. For if we are "light," and "leaven," and "luminaries," and "salt," we ought to enlighten, not to darken; to bind, not to loosen; to draw to ourselves the unbelievers, not to drive them away. Why then puttest thou to flight those whom thou oughtest to draw to thee?· Since even Gentiles are hurt, when they see us reverting to such things: for they know not our mind nor that our soul hath come to be above all pollution of sense. And the Jews too, and the weaker brethren, will suffer the same.

Seest thou how many reasons he hath assigned for which we ought to abstain from the idol-sacrifices? Because of their unprofitableness, because of their needlessness, because of the injury to our brother, because of the evil-speaking of the Jew, because of the reviling of the Gentile, because we ought not to be partakers with demons, because the thing is a kind of idolatry.

Further, because he had said, " give no occasion of stumbling," and he made them responsible for the injury done, both to the Gentiles and to the Jews ; and the saying was grievous; see how he renders it acceptable and light, putting himself forward, and saying,

Ver. 33. "Even as I also please all men in all things, not seeking mine own profit, but the profit of the many, that they may be saved."

Chap. xi. ver. 1. "Be ye imitators of me, even as I also am of Christ."

This is a rule of the most perfect Christianity, this is a landmark exactly laid down, this is the point that stands highest of all ; viz. the seeking those things which are for the common profit: which also Paul himself declared, by adding, "even as I also am of Christ." For nothing can so make a man an imitator of Christ as caring for his neighbors. Nay, though thou shouldest fast, though thou shouldest lie upon the ground, and even strangle thyself, but take no thought for thy neighbor; thou hast wrought nothing great, but still standest far from this Image, while so doing.

However, in the case before us, even the very thing itself is naturally useful, viz; the abstaining from idol-sacrifices. But "I," saith he, "have done many of those things which were unprofitable also: e. g., when I used circumcision, when I offered sacrifice; for these, were any one to examine them in themselves, rather destroy those that follow after them and cause them to fall from salvation: nevertheless, I submitted even to these on account of the advantage therefrom : but here is no such thing. For in that case, except there accrue a certain benefit· and except they be done for others' sake, then the thing becomes injurious: but in this, though there be none made to stumble, even so ought one to abstain from the things forbidden.

But not only to things hurtful have I submitted, but also to things toilsome. For, "I robbed other Churches," saith he, "taking wages of them; (2 Cor. xi. 8.) and when it was lawful to eat and not to work, I sought not this, but chose to perish of hunger rather than offend another." This is why he says, " I please all men in all things." "Though it be against the law, though it be laborious and hazardous, which is to be done, I endure all for the profit of others. So then, being above all in perfection, he became beneath all in condescension."

[4.] For no virtuous action can be very exalted, when it doth not distribute its benefit to others also: as is shown by him who brought the one talent safe, and was cut in sunder because he had not made more of it. And thou then, brother, though thou shouldest remain without food, though thou shouldest sleep upon the ground, though thou shouldest eat ashes and be ever wailing, and do good to no other ; thou wilt do no great work. For so also those great and noble persons who were in the beginning made this their chiefest care : examine accurately their life, and thou wilt see clearly that none of them ever looked to his own things, but each one to the things of his neighbor, whence also they shone the brighter. For so Moses (to mention him first) wrought many and great wonders and signs ; but nothing made him so great as that blessed voice which he uttered unto God, saying, " If Thou wilt forgive their sin," forgive ; " but if not, blot me also out." (Exod. xxxii. 32.) Such too was David: wherefore also he said, " I the shepherd have sinned, and I have done wickedly, but these, the flock, what have they done? Let Thine hand be upon me and upon my father's house." (2 Sam. xxiv. 17.) So likewise Abraham sought not his own profit, but the profit of many. Wherefore he both exposed himself to dangers and besought God for those who in no wise belonged to him.

Well: these indeed so became glorious. But as for those who sought their own, consider what harm too they received. The nephew, for instance, of the last mentioned, because he listened to the saying, "If thou wilt go to the right,

I will go to the left;'' (Gen. xiii. 9.) and accepting the choice, sought his own profit, did not even find his own: but this region was burned up, while that remained untouched. Jonah again, not seeking the profit of many, but his own, was in danger even of perishing : and while the city stood fast, he himself was tossed about and overwhelmed in the sea. But when he sought the profit of many, then he also found his own. So likewise Jacob among the flocks, not seeking his own gain, had exceeding riches for his portion. And Joseph also, seeking the profit of his brethren, found his own. At least, being sent by his father, (Gen xxxvii. 14.) he said not, '' What is this? Hast thou not heard that for a vision and certain dreams they even attempted to tear me in pieces, and I was held responsible for my dreams, and suffer punishment for being beloved of thee? What then will they not do when they get me in the midst of them?'' He said none of these things, he thought not of them, but prefers the care of his brethren above all. Therefore he enjoyed also all the good things which followed, which both made him very brilliant and declared him glorious. Thus also Moses,—for nothing hinders that we should a second time make mention of him, and behold how he overlooked his own things and sought the things of others :—I say this Moses, being conversant in a king's court, because he '' counted the reproach of Christ (Heb. xi. 26.) greater riches than the treasures of Egypt;'' and having cast them even all out of his hands, became a partaker of the afflictions of the Hebrews;—so far from being himself enslaved, he liberated them also from bondage.

Well : these surely are great things and worthy of an angelical life. But the conduct of Paul far exceeds this. For all the rest leaving their own blessings chose to be partakers in the afflictions of others: but Paul did a thing much greater. For it was not that he consented to be a partaker in others' misfortunes, but he chose himself to be at all extremities that other men might enjoy blessings. Now it is not the same for one who lives in luxury to cast away his luxury and suffer adversity, as for one himself alone suffering adversity, to cause others to be in security and honor. For in the former case, though it be a great thing to exchange prosperity for affliction for your neighbor's sake, nevertheless it brings some consolation to have partakers in the misfortune. But consenting to be himself alone in the distress that others may enjoy their good things,—this belongs to a much more energetic soul, and to Paul's own spirit.

And not by this only, but by another and greater excellency doth he surpass all those before mentioned. That is, Abraham and all the rest exposed themselves to dangers in the present life, and all these were but asking for this kind of death once for all: but Paul prayed (Rom. ix. 3.,) that he might fall from the glory of the world to come for the sake of others' salvation.*

I may mention also a third point of superiority. And what is this? That some of those, though they interceded for the persons who conspired against them, nevertheless it was for those with whose guidance they had been entrusted : and the same thing happened as if one should stand up for a wild and lawless son, but still a son : whereas Paul wished to be accursed in the stead of those with whose guardianship he was not entrusted. For to the Gentiles was he sent. Dost thou perceive the greatness of his soul and the loftiness of his spirit, transcending the very heaven? This man do thou emulate : but if thou canst not, at least follow those who shone in the old covenant. For thus shalt thou find thine own profit, if thou seekest that of thy neighbor. Wherefore when thou feelest backward to care for thy brother, considering that no otherwise canst thou be saved, at least for thine own sake stand thou up for him and his interests.

[5.] And although what hath been said is sufficient to convince thee that no otherwise is it possible to secure our own benefit: yet if thou wouldst also assure thyself of it by the examples of common life, conceive a fire happening anywhere to be kindled in a house, and then some of the neighbors with a view to their own interest refusing to confront the danger but shutting themselves up and remaining at home, in fear lest some one find his way in and purloin some part of the household goods ; how great punishment will they endure? Since the fire will come on and burn down likewise all that is theirs ; and because they looked not to the profit of their neighbor, they lose even their own besides. For so God, willing to bind us all to each other, hath imposed upon things such a necessity, that in the profit of one neighbor that of the other is bound up; and the whole world is thus constituted. And therefore in a vessel too, if a storm come on, and the steersman, leaving the profit of the many, should seek his own only, he will quickly sink both himself and them. And of each several art too we may say that should it look to its own profit only, life could never stand, nor even the art itself which so seeketh its own. Therefore the husbandman sows not so much corn only as is sufficient for himself, since he would long ago have famished both himself and others; but seeks the profit of the many: and the soldier

---

* [But the Apostle did not say absolutely '' I wish,'' but '' I could wish '' or pray. The difference is great. C.]

takes the field against dangers, not that he may save himself, but that he may also place his cities in security: and the merchant brings not home so much as may be sufficient for himself alone, but for many others also.

Now if any say, "each man doeth this, not looking to my interest, but his own, for he engages in all these things to obtain for himself money and glory and security, so that in seeking my profit he seeks his own:" this also do I say and long since wished to hear from you, and for this have I framed all my discourse; viz. to signify that thy neighbor then seeks his own profit, when he looks to thine. For since men would no otherwise make up their mind to seek the things of their neighbor, except they were reduced to this necessity; therefore God hath thus joined things together, and suffers them not to arrive at their own profit except they first travel through the profit of others.

Well then, this is natural to man, thus to follow after his neighbors' advantage; but one ought to be persuaded not from this reason, but from what pleases God. For it is not possible to be saved, wanting this; but though thou shouldest exercise the highest perfection of the work and neglect others who are perishing, thou wilt gain no confidence towards God. Whence is this evident? From what the blessed Paul declared. "For if I bestow my goods to feed the poor, and give my body to be burned, and have not love, it profiteth me nothing," (1 Cor. xiii. 3.) saith he. Seeth thou how much Paul requireth of us? And yet he that bestowed his goods to feed the poor, sought not his own good, but that of his neighbor. But this alone is not enough, he saith. For he would have it done with sincerity and much sympathy. For therefore also God made it a law that he might bring us into the bond of love. When therefore He demands so large a measure, and we do not render even that which is less, of what indulgence shall we be worthy?[1]

"And how," saith one, "did God say to Lot by the Angels, 'Escape for thy life?'" (Gen. xix. 17.) Say, when, and why. When the punishment was brought near, not when there was an opportunity of correction but when they were condemned and incurably diseased, and old and young had rushed into the same passions, and henceforth they must needs be burned up, and in that day when the thunderbolts were about to be launched. And besides, this was not spoken of vice and virtue but of the chastisement inflicted by God. For what was he to do, tell me? Sit still and await the punishment, and without at all profiting them, be burned up? Nay, this were the extremest folly.

For I do not affirm this, that one ought to bring chastisement on one's self without discrimination and at random, apart from the will of God. But when a man tarries long in sin, then I bid thee push thyself forward and correct him: if thou wilt, for thy neighbor's sake: but if not, at least for thine own profit. It is true, the first is the better course: but if thou reachest not yet unto that height, do it even for this. And let no man seek his own that he may find his own; and bearing in mind that neither voluntary poverty nor martyrdom, nor any other thing, can testify in our favor, unless we have the crowning virtue of love; let us preserve this beyond the rest, that through it we may also obtain all other, both present and promised blessings; at which may we all arrive through the grace and mercy of our Lord Jesus Christ; Whom be the glory world without end. Amen.

HOMILY XXVI.

1 COR. xi. 2.

Now I praise you that ye remember me in all things, and hold fast the traditions, even as I delivered them to you.

HAVING completed the discourse concerning the idol-sacrifices as became him, and having rendered it most perfect in all respects, he proceeds to another thing, which also itself was a complaint, but not so great a one. For that which I said before, this do I also now say, that he doth not set down all the heavy accusations continuously, but after disposing them in due order, he inserts among them the lighter matters, mitigating what the readers would else feel offensive in his discourse on account of his continually reproving.

---

[1] [This passage and others like it show, as Neander says, that while Chrysostom was enthusiastically alive to the ideal of holy temper and holy living in Monachism, yet he was too deeply penetrated by the essence of the Gospel not to be aware that this indeed should pervade *all the relations of life*. C.]

Wherefore also he set the most serious of all last, that relating to the resurrection. But for the present he goes to another, a lighter thing, saying, "Now I praise you that ye remember me in all things." Thus when the offence is admitted, he both accuses vehemently and threatens: but when it is questioned, he first proves it and then rebukes. And what was admitted, he aggravates: but what was likely to be disputed, he shows to be admitted. Their fornication, for instance, was a thing admitted. Wherefore there was no need to show that there was an offence; but in that case he proved the magnitude of the transgression, and conducted his discourse by way of comparison. Again, their going to law before aliens was an offence, but not so great a one. Wherefore he considered by the way, and proved it. The matter of the idol-sacrifices again was questioned. It was however, a most serious evil. Wherefore he both shows it to be an offence, and amplifies it by his discourse. But when he doeth this, he not only withdraws them from the several crimes, but invites them also to their contraries. Thus he said not only that one must not commit fornication, but likewise that one ought to exhibit great holiness. Wherefore he added, "Therefore glorify God in your body, and in your spirit." (c. vi. 20.) And having said again that one ought not to be wise with the wisdom that is without, he is not content with this, but bids him also to "become a fool." (c. iii. 18.) And where he advises them not to go to law before them that are without, and to do no wrong; he goeth further, and takes away even the very going to law, and counsels them not only to do no wrong, but even to suffer wrong. (c. vi. 7, 8.)

And discoursing concerning the idol-sacrifices, he said not that one ought to abstain from things forbidden only, but also from things permitted when offence is given: and not only not to hurt the brethren, but not even Greeks, nor Jews. Thus, "give no occasion of stumbling," saith he, "either to Jews, or to Greeks, or to the Church of God." (c. x. 32.)

[2.] Having finished therefore all the discourses concerning all these things, he next proceeds also to another accusation. And what was this? Their women used both to pray and prophesy unveiled and with their head bare, (for then women also used to prophesy;) but the men went so far as to wear long hair as having spent their time in philosophy[1], and covered their heads when praying and prophesying, each of which was a Grecian custom. Since then he had already admonished them concerning these things when present, and some per-

haps listened to him and others disobeyed; therefore in his letter also again, he foments the place, like a physician, by his mode of addressing them, and so corrects the offence. For that he had heretofore admonished them in person is evident from what he begins with. Why else, having said nothing of this matter any where in the Epistle before, but passing on from other accusations, doth he straightway say, "Now I praise you that ye remember me in all things, and hold fast the traditions, even as I delivered them to you?"

Thou seest that some obeyed, whom he praises; and others disobeyed, whom he corrects by what comes afterwards, saying, "Now if any man seem to be contentious, we have no such custom." (ver. 16.) For if after some had done well but others disobeyed, he had included all in his accusation, he would both have made the one sort bolder, and have caused the others to become more remiss; whereas now by praising and approving the one, and rebuking the other, he both refreshes the one more effectually, and causes the other to shrink before him. For the accusation even by itself was such as might well wound them; but now that it takes place in contrast with others who have done well and are praised, it comes with a sharper sting. However, for the present he begins not with accusation, but with encomiums and great encomiums, saying, "Now I praise you that ye remember me in all things." For such is the character of Paul; though it be but for small matters he weaves a web of high praise; nor is it for flattery that he doth so: far from it; how could he so act to whom neither money was desirable, nor glory, nor any other such thing? but for their salvation he orders all his proceedings. And this is why he amplifies the encomium, saying, "Now I praise you that ye remember me in all things."

All what things? For hitherto his discourse was only concerning their not wearing long hair and not covering their heads; but, as I said, he is very bountiful in his praises, rendering them more forward. Wherefore he saith,

"That ye remember me in all things, and hold fast the traditions, even as I delivered them to you." It appears then that he used at that time to deliver many things also not in writing, which he shows too in many other places. But at that time he only delivered them, whereas now he adds an explanation of their reason: thus both rendering the one sort, the obedient, more steadfast, and pulling down the others' pride, who oppose themselves. Further, he doth not say, "ye have obeyed, whilst others disobeyed," but without exciting suspicion, intimates it by his mode of teaching in what follows, where he saith,

---

[1] To let the hair and beard grow was a token of devotion to any study; as Poetry, Hor. *A. P.* 297; Philosophy, as it is told of Julian the Apostate that it was part of his affectation to let his hair and beard grow.

Ver. 3. " But I would have ye know, that the head of every man is Christ ; and the head of every woman is the man ; and the head of Christ is God."

This is his account of the reason of the thing, and he states it to make the weaker more attentive. He indeed that is faithful, as he ought to be, and steadfast, doth not require any reason or cause of those things which are commanded him, but is content with the ordinance[1] alone. But he that is weaker, when he also learns the cause, then both retains what is said with more care and obeys with much readiness.

Wherefore neither did he state the cause until he saw the commandment transgressed. What then is the cause ? " The head of every man is Christ." Is He then Head of the Gentile also ? In no wise. For if "we are the·Body of Christ, and severally members thereof," (c. xii. 27.) and in this way He is our head, He cannot be the head of them who are not in the Body and rank not among the members. So that when he says, "of every man," one must understand it of the believer. Perceivest thou how every where he appeals to the hearer's shame by arguing from on high ? Thus both when he was discoursing on love, and when on humility, and when on alms-giving, it was from thence that he drew his examples.

[2.] "But the head of the woman is the man ; and the head of Christ is God." Here the heretics rush upon us with a certain declaration of inferiority, which out of these words they contrive against the Son. But they stumble against themselves. For if "the man be the head of the woman," and the head be of the same substance with the body, and " the head of Christ is God," the Son is of the same substance with the Father. " Nay," say they, " it is not His being of another substance which we intend to show from hence, but that He is under subjection." What then are we to say to this ? In the first place, when any thing lowly is said of him conjoined as He is with the Flesh, there is no disparagement of the Godhead in what is said, the Economy admitting the expression. However, tell me how thou intendest to prove this from the passage ? "Why, as the man governs the wife," saith he, " so also the Father, Christ." Therefore also as Christ governs the man, so likewise the Father, the Son. " For the head of every man," we read, " is Christ." And who could ever admit this ? For if the superiority of the Son compared with us, be the measure of the Fathers' compared with the Son, consider to what meanness thou wilt bring Him.

So that we must not try[2] all things by like measure in respect of ourselves and of God, though the language used concerning them be similar ; but we must assign to God a certain appropriate excellency, and so great as belongs to God. For should they not grant this, many absurdities will follow. As thus ; "the head of Christ is God :" and, "Christ is the head of the man, and he of the woman." Therefore if we choose to take the term, " head," in the like sense in all the clauses, the Son will be as far removed from the Father as we are from Him. Nay, and the woman will be as far removed from us as we are from the Word of God. And what the Son is to the Father, this both we are to the Son and the woman again to the man. And who will endure this ?

But dost thou understand the term "head" differently in the case of the man and the woman, from what thou dost in the case of Christ ? Therefore in the case of the Father and the Son, must we understand it differently also. " How understand it differently ?" saith the objector. According to the occasion[3]. For had Paul meant to speak of rule and subjection, as thou sayest, he would not have brought forward the instance of a wife, but rather of a slave and a master. For what if the wife be under subjection to us ? it is as a wife, as free, as equal in honor. And the Son also, though He did become obedient to the Father, it was as the Son of God, it was as God. For as the obedience of the Son to the Father is greater than we find in men towards the authors of their being, so also His liberty is greater. Since it will not of course be said that the circumstances of the Son's relation to the Father are greater and more intimate than among men, and of the Father's to the Son, less. For if we admire the Son, that He was obedient so as to come even unto death, and the death of the cross, and reckon this the great wonder concerning Him ; we ought to admire the Father also, that He begat such a son, not as a slave under command, but as free, yielding obedience and giving counsel. For the counsellor is no slave.

But again, when thou hearest of a counsellor, do not understand it as though the Father were in need, but that the Son hath the same honor with Him that begat Him. Do not therefore strain the example of the man and the woman to all particulars.

For with us indeed the woman is reasonably subjected to the man : since equality of honor causeth contention. And not for this cause only, but by reason also of the deceit (1 Tim. ii. 14.) which happened in the beginning. Wherefore you see, she was not subjected as soon as she was made ; nor, when He brought her to the man, did either she hear any such thing from

---

[1] τῇ παραδόσει.
[2] ἐξεταστέον.

[3] τὸ αἴτιον.

God, nor did the man say any such word to her: he said indeed that she was "bone of his bone, and flesh of his flesh:" (Gen. ii. 23.) but of rule or subjection he no where made mention unto her. But when she made an ill use of her privilege and she who had been made a helper was found to be an ensnarer and ruined all, then she is justly told for the future, "thy turning shall be to thy husband." (Gen. iii. 16.)

To account for which; it was likely that this sin would have thrown our race into a state of warfare; (for her having been made out of him would not have contributed any thing to peace, when this had happened, nay, rather this very thing would have made the man even the harsher, that she made as she was out of him should not have spared even him who was a member of herself:) wherefore God, considering the malice of the Devil, raised up the bulwark of this word; and what enmity was likely to arise from his evil device, He took away by means of this sentence and by the desire implanted in us: thus pulling down the partition-wall, i. e, the resentment caused by that sin of hers. But in God and in that undefiled Essence, one must not suppose any such thing.

Do not therefore apply the examples to all, since elsewhere also from this source many grievous errors will occur. For so in the beginning of this very Epistle, he said, (1 Cor. iii. 22, 23.) "All are yours, and ye are Christ's, and Christ is God's." What then? Are all in like manner ours, as "we are Christ's, and Christ is God's?" In no wise, but even to the very simple the difference is evident, although the same expression is used of God, and Christ, and us. And elsewhere also having called the husband "head of the wife," he added, (Eph. v. 23.) "Even as Christ is Head and Saviour and Defender of the Church, so also ought the man to be of his own wife." Are we then to understand in like manner the saying in the text, both this, and all that after this is written to the Ephesians concerning this subject? Far from it. It is impossible. For although the same words are spoken of God and of men, they do not have the same force in respect to God and to men, but in one way those must be understood, and in another these. Not however on the other hand all things diversely: since contrariwise they will seem to have been introduced at random and in vain, we reaping no benefit from them. But as we must not receive all things alike, so neither must we absolutely reject all.

Now that what I say may become clearer, I will endeavor to make it manifest in an example. Christ is called "the Head of the Church." If I am to take nothing from what is human in the idea, why, I would know, is the expression used at all? On the other hand, if I under-

stand all in that way, extreme absurdity will result. For the head is of like passions with the body and liable to the same things. What then ought we to let go, and what to accept? We should let go these particulars which I have mentioned, but accept the notion of a perfect union, and the first principle; and not even these ideas absolutely, but here also we must form a notion, as we may by ourselves, of that which is too high for us and suitable to the Godhead: for both the union is surer and the beginning more honorable.

Again, thou hearest the word "Son;" do not thou in this case admit all particulars; yet neither oughtest thou to reject all: but admitting whatever is meet for God, e. g. that He is of the same essence, that He is of God; the things which are incongruous and belong to human weakness, leave thou upon the earth.

Again, God is called "Light." Shall we then admit all circumstances which belong to natural light? In no wise. For this light yields to darkness, and is circumscribed by space, and is moved by another power, and is overshadowed; none of which it is lawful even to imagine of That Essence. We will not however reject all things on this account, but will reap something useful from the example. The illumination which cometh to us from God, the deliverance from darkness, this will be what we gather from it.

[4.] Thus much in answer to the heretics: but we must also orderly go over the whole passage. For perhaps some one might here have doubt also, questioning with himself, what sort of a crime it was for the woman to be uncovered, or the man covered? What sort of crime it is, learn now from hence.

Symbols many and diverse have been given both to man and woman; to him of rule, to her of subjection: and among them this also, that she should be covered, while he hath his head bare. If now these be symbols, you see that both err when they disturb the proper order, and transgress the disposition of God, and their own proper limits, both the man falling into the woman's inferiory, and the woman rising up against the man by her outward habiliments.

For if exchange of garments be not lawful, so that neither she should be clad with a cloak, nor he with a mantle or a veil: ("for the woman," saith He, "shall not wear that which pertaineth to a man, neither shall a man put on a woman's garments:") much more is it unseemly for these (Deut. xxii. 5.) things to be interchanged. For the former indeed were ordained by men, even although God afterwards ratified them: but this by nature, I mean the being covered or uncovered. But when I say Nature, I mean God. For He it is Who created Nature. When therefore thou overturnest these boundaries, see how great injuries ensue.

And tell me not this, that the error is but small. For first, it is great even of itself: being as it is disobedience. Next, though it were small, it became great because of the greatness of the things whereof it is a sign. However, that it is a great matter, is evident from its ministering so effectually to good order among mankind, the governor and the governed being regularly kept in their several places by it.

So that he who transgresseth disturbs all things, and betrays the gifts of God, and casts to the ground the honor bestowed on him from above; not however the man only, but also the woman. For to her also it is the greatest of honors to preserve her own rank; as indeed of disgraces, the behavior of a rebel. Wherefore he laid it down concerning both, thus saying,

Ver. 4. "Every man praying or prophesying having his head covered, dishonoreth his head. But every woman praying or prophesying with her head unveiled dishonoreth her head."

For there were, as I said, both men who prophesied and women who had this gift at that time, as the daughters of Philip, (Acts. xxi. 9.) as others before them and after them: concerning whom also the prophet spake of old : "your sons shall prophesy, and your daughters shall see visions." (Joel ii. 28. Acts ii. 17.)

Well then : the man he compelleth not to be always uncovered, but only when he prays. "For every man," saith he, "praying or prophesying, having his head covered, dishonoreth his head." But the woman he commands to be at all times covered. Wherefore also having said, "Every woman that prayeth or prophesieth with her head unveiled, dishonoreth her head," he stayed not at this point only, but also proceeded to say, " for it is one and the same thing as if she were shaven." But if to be shaven is always dishonorable, it is plain too that being uncovered is always a reproach. And not even with this only was he content, but added again, saying, "The woman ought to have a sign of authority on her head, because of the angels." He signifies that not at the time of prayer only but also continually, she ought to be covered. But with regard to the man, it is no longer about covering but about wearing long hair, that he so forms his discourse. To be covered he then only forbids, when a man is praying; but the wearing long hair he discourages at all times. Wherefore, as touching the woman, he said, "But if she be not veiled, let her also be shorn ; " so likewise touching the man, "If he have long hair, it is a dishonor unto him." He said not, "if he be covered," but, "if he have long hair," Wherefore also he said at the beginning, "Every man praying

or prophesying, having any thing on his head, dishonoreth his head." He said not, "covered," but "having any thing on his head ; " signifying that even though he pray with the head bare, yet if he have long hair, he is like to one covered. "For the hair," saith he, "is given for a covering."

Ver. 6. "But if a woman is not veiled, let her also be shorn : but if it be a shame for a woman to be shorn or shaven, let her be veiled."

Thus, in the beginning he simply requires that the head be not bare : but as he proceeds he intimates both the continuance of the rule, saying, "for it is one and the same thing as if she were shaven," and the keeping of it with all care and diligence. For he said not merely covered, but "covered over[1]," meaning that she be carefully wrapped up on every side. And by reducing it to an absurdity, he appeals to their shame, saying by way of severe reprimand, "but if she be not covered, let her also be shorn." As if he had said, "If thou cast away the covering appointed by the law of God, cast away likewise that appointed by nature."

But if any say, "Nay, how can this be a shame to the woman, if she mount up to the glory of the man ? " we might make this answer ; "She doth not mount up, but rather falls from her own proper honor." Since not to abide within our own limits and the laws ordained of God, but to go beyond, is not an addition but a diminution. For as he that desireth other men's goods and seizeth what is not his own, hath not gained any thing more, but is diminished, having lost even that which he had, (which kind of thing also happened in paradise :) so likewise the woman acquireth not the man's dignity, but loseth even the woman's decency which she had. And not from hence only is her shame and reproach, but also on account of her covetousness.

Having taken then what was confessedly shameful, and having said, "but if it be a shame for a woman to be shorn or shaven," he states in what follows his own conclusion, saying, "let her be covered." And he said not, "let her have long hair," but, "let her be covered," ordaining both these to be one, and establishing them both ways, from what was customary and from their contraries : in that he both affirms the covering and the hair to be one, and also that she again who is shaven is the same with her whose head is bare. "For it is one and the same thing," saith he, "as if she were shaven." But if any say, "And how is it one, if this woman have the covering of nature, but the other who is shaven have not even this?" we answer, that as far as her will goes, she threw

---

[1] οὐδὲ γὰρ καλύπτεσθαι, ἀλλα κατακαλύπτεσθαι.

that off likewise by having the head bare. And if it be not bare of tresses, that is nature's doing, not her own. So that as she who is shaven hath her head bare, so this woman in like manner. For this cause He left it to nature to provide her with a covering, that even of it she might learn this lesson and veil herself.

Then he states also a cause, as one discoursing with those who are free: a thing which in many places I have remarked. What then is the cause?

Ver. 7. "For a man indeed ought not to have his head veiled, forasmuch as he is the image and glory of God."

This is again another cause. "Not only," so he speaks, "because he hath Christ to be His Head ought he not to cover the head, but because also he rules over the woman." For the ruler when he comes before the king ought to have the symbol of his rule. As therefore no ruler without military girdle and cloak, would venture to appear before him that hath the diadem: so neither do thou without the symbols of thy rule, (one of which is the not being covered,) pray before God, lest thou insult both thyself and Him that hath honored thee.

And the same thing likewise one may say regarding the woman. For to her also is it a reproach, the not having the symbols of her subjection. "But the woman is the glory of the man." Therefore the rule of the man is natural.

[5.] Then, having affirmed his point, he states again other reasons and causes also, leading thee to the first creation, and saying thus:

Ver. 8. "For the man is not of the woman, but the woman of the man."

But if to be of any one, is a glory to him of whom one is, much more the being an image of him.

Ver. 9. "For neither was the man created for the woman, but the woman for the man."

This is again a second superiority, nay, rather also a third, and a fourth, the first being, that Christ is the head of us, and we of the woman; a second, that we are the glory of God, but the woman of us; a third, that we are not of the woman, but she of us; a fourth, that we are not for her, but she for us.

Ver. 10. "For this cause ought the woman to have a sign of authority on her head."

"For this cause:" what cause, tell me? "For all these which have been mentioned," saith he; or rather not for these only, but also "because of the angels." "For although thou despise thine husband," saith he, "yet reverence the angels."

It follows that being covered is a mark of subjection and authority. For it induces her to look down and be ashamed and preserve entire her proper virtue. For the virtue and honor of the governed is to abide in his obedience.

Again: the man is not compelled to do this; for he is the image of his Lord: but the woman is; and that reasonably. Consider then the excess of the transgression when being honored with so high a prerogative, thou puttest thyself to shame, seizing the woman's dress. And thou doest the same as if having received a diadem, thou shouldest cast the diadem from thy head, and instead of it take a slave's garment.

Ver. 11. "Nevertheless, neither is the man without the woman, nor the woman without the man, in the Lord."

Thus, because he had given great superiority to the man, having said that the woman is of him and for him and under him; that he might neither lift up the men more than was due nor depress the women, see how he brings in the correction, saying, "Howbeit neither is the man without the woman, nor the woman without the man, in the Lord." "Examine not, I pray," saith he, "the first things only, and that creation. Since if thou enquire into what comes after, each one of the two is the cause of the other; or rather not even thus each of the other, but God of all." Wherefore he saith, "neither is the man without the woman, nor the woman without the man, in the Lord."

Ver. 12. "For as the woman is of the man, so is the man also by the woman."

He said not, "of the woman," but he repeats the expression, (from v. 7.) "of the man." For still this particular prerogative remains entire with the man. Yet are not these excellencies the property of the man, but of God. Wherefore also he adds, "but all things of God." If therefore all things belong to God, and he commands these things, do thou obey and gainsay not.

Ver. 13. "Judge ye in yourselves: is it seemly that a woman pray unto God veiled?" Again he places them as judges of the things said, which also he did respecting the idol-sacrifices. For as there he saith, "judge ye what I say:" (c. x. 15.) so here, "judge in yourselves:" and he hints something more awful here. For he says that the affront here passes on unto God: although thus indeed he doth not express himself, but in something of a milder and more enigmatical form of speech: "is it seemly that a woman pray unto God unveiled?"

Ver. 14. "Doth not even nature itself teach you, that if a man have long hair, it is a dishonor unto him?"

Ver. 15. "But if a woman have long hair, it is a glory to her; for her hair is given her for a covering."

His constant practice of stating commonly

received reasons he adopts also in this place, betaking himself to the common custom, and greatly abashing those who waited to be taught these things from him, which even from men's ordinary practice they might have learned. For such things are not unknown even to Barbarians: and see how he every where deals in piercing expressions : " every man praying having his head covered dishonoreth his head ; " and again, " but if it be a shame for a woman to be shorn or shaven, let her be veiled : " and here again, " if a man have long hair, it is a shame unto him ; but if a woman have long hair, it is a glory to her, for her hair is given her for a covering."

" And if it be given her for a covering," say you, "wherefore need she add another covering ? " That not nature only, but also her own will may have part in her acknowledgment of subjection. For that thou oughtest to be covered nature herself by anticipation enacted a law. Add now, I pray, thine own part also, that thou mayest not seem to subvert the very laws of nature; a proof of most insolent rashness[1], to buffet not only with us, but with nature also. This is why God accusing the Jews said, (Ezek. xvi. 21, 22.) "Thou hast slain thy sons and thy daughters: this is beyond all thy abominations."[2]

And again, Paul rebuking the unclean among the Romans thus aggravates the accusation, saying, that their usage was not only against the law of God, but even against nature. "For they changed the natural use into that which is against nature." (Rom. i. 26.) For this cause then here also he employs this argument signifying this very thing, both that he is not enacting any strange law and that among Gentiles their inventions would all be reckoned as a kind of novelty against nature.[3] So also Christ, implying the same, said, " Whatsoever ye would that men should do to you, do ye also so them ; " showing that He is not introducing any thing new.

Ver. 16. "But if any man seems to be contentious, we have no such custom, neither the Churches of God."

It is then contentiousness to oppose these things, and not any exercise of reason. Notwithstanding, even thus it is a measured sort of rebuke which he adopts, to fill them the more with self-reproach ; which in truth rendered his saying the more severe. "For we," saith he, "have no such custom," so as to contend and to strive and to oppose ourselves. And he stopped not even here, but also added, "neither the Churches of God;" signifying that they resist and oppose themselves to the whole world by not yielding. However, even if the Corinthians were then contentious, yet now the whole world hath both received and kept this law. So great is the power of the Crucified.

[6.] But I fear lest having assumed the dress, yet in their deeds some of our women should be found immodest and in other ways uncovered. For therefore also writing to Timothy Paul was not content with these things, but added others, saying, "that they adorn themselves in modest apparel, with shamefacedness and sobriety ; not with braided hair, or gold." (1 Tim. ii. 9.) For if one ought not to have the head bare, but everywhere to carry about the token of authority, much more is it becoming to exhibit the same in our deeds. Thus at any rate the former women also used both to call their husbands lords, (1 Pe. iii. 6.) and to yield the precedence to them. "Because they for their part, " you say," used to love their own wives." I know that as well as you : I am not ignorant of it. But when we are exhorting thee concerning thine own duties, let not theirs take all thine attention. For so, when we exhort children to be obedient to parents, saying, that it is written, "honor thy father and thy mother," they reply to us, "mention also what follows, 'and ye fathers, provoke not your children to wrath," (Eph. vi. 1–4.) And servants when we tell them that it is written that they should "obey their masters, and not serve with eye-service," they also again demand of us what follows, bidding us also give the same advice to masters. For Paul bade them also, they saw, "to forbear threatening." But let us not do thus nor enquire into the things enjoined on others, when we are charged with regard to our own : for neither will thy obtaining a partner in the charges free thee from the blame: but look to one thing only, how thou mayest rid thyself of those charges which lie against thyself. Since Adam also laid the blame on the woman, and she again on the serpent, but this did in no wise deliver them. Do not thou, therefore, for thy part, say this to me now, but be careful with all consideration to render what thou owest to thy husband: since also when I am discoursing with thy husband, advising him to love and cherish thee, I suffer him not to bring forward the law that is appointed for the woman, but I require of him that which is written for himself. And do thou therefore busy thyself with those things only which belong to thee, and show thyself tractable to thy consort. And accordingly if it be really for God's sake that thou obeyest thy husband, tell me not of the things which ought to be done by him, but for what things thou hast been made responsible by the lawgiver, those perform with exactness. For this is especially to obey God, not to transgress the law

---

[1] ἰταμότητος.
[2] βδελύγματα. rec. text. πορνείαν.
[3] τὰ τῆς καινοτομίας ἅπαντα τῆς παρὰ φύσιν. Perhaps the text is mutilated.

even when suffering things contrary to it. And by the same rule, he that being beloved loves, is not reckoned to do any great thing. But he that waits upon a person who hateth him, this above all is the man to receive a crown. In the same manner then do thou also reckon that if thy husband give thee disgust, and thou endure it, thou shalt receive a glorious crown : but if he be gentle and mild, what will there be for God to reward in thee? And these things I say, not bidding the husbands be harsh ; but persuading the wives to bear even with harshness in their husbands. Since when each is careful to fulfil his own duty, his neighbor's part also will quickly follow: as when the wife is prepared to bear even with rough behavior in the husband, and the husband refrains from abusing her in her angry mood ; then all is a calm and a harbor free from waves.

[7.] So also was it with those of old time. Each was employed in fulfilling his own duty, not in exacting that of his neighbor. Thus, if you mark it, Abraham took his brother's son : his wife found no fault with him. He commanded her to travel a long journey ; she spake not even against this but followed. Again, after those many miseries and labors and toils having become lord of all, he yielded the precedency to Lot. And so far from Sarah being offended at this, she did not even open her mouth, nor uttered any such thing as many of the women of these days utter, when they see their own husbands coming off inferior in such allotments, and especially in dealing with inferiors ; reproaching them, and calling them fools and senseless and unmanly and traitors and stupid. But no such thing did she say or think, but was pleased with all things that were done by him.

And another thing, and that a greater : after that Lot had the choice put in his power, and had thrown the inferior part upon his uncle, a great danger fell upon him. Whereof the patriarch hearing, armed all his people, and set himself against the whole army of the Persians with his own domestics only, and not even then did she detain him, nor say, as was likely, " O man, whither goest thou, thrusting thyself down precipices, and exposing thyself to so great hazards ; for one who wronged thee and seized on all that was thine, shedding thy blood? Yea, and even if thou make light of thyself, yet have pity on me which have left house and country and friends and kindred, and have followed thee in so long a pilgrimage ; and involve me not in widowhood, and in the miseries of widowhood." None of these things she said : she thought not of them but bore all in silence.

After this, her womb continuing barren, she herself suffers not the grief of women nor laments : but he complains, though not to his wife, but to God. And see how each preserves his own appropriate part : for he neither despised Sarah as childless, nor reproached her with any such thing : and she again was anxious to devise some consolation to him for her childlessness by means of the handmaid. For these things had not yet been forbidden then as now. For now neither is it lawful for women to indulge their husbands in such things, nor for the men, with or without the wife's knowledge, to form such connexions, even though the grief of their childlessness should infinitely harass them : since they also shall hear the sentence, " their worm shall not die, neither shall their fire be quenched." For now it is not permitted, but then it had not been forbidden. Wherefore both his wife commanded this, and he obeyed, yet not even thus for pleasure's sake. But " behold," it will be said, " how he cast Hagar out again at her bidding." Well, this is what I want to point out, that both he obeyed her in all things, and she him. But do not thou give heed to these things only, but examine, thou who urgest this plea, into what had gone before also, Hagar's insulting her, her boasting herself against her mistress ; than which what can be more vexatious to a free and honorable woman?

[8.] Let not then the wife tarry for the virtue of the husband and then show her own, for this is nothing great ; nor, on the other hand, the husband, for the obedience of the wife and then exercise self-command ; for neither would this any more be his own well-doing ; but let each, as I said, furnish his own share first. For if to the Gentiles smiting us on the right, we must turn the other cheek ; much more ought one to bear with harsh behavior in a husband.

And I say not this for a wife to be beaten ; far from it : for this is the extremest affront, not to her that is beaten, but to him who beateth. But even if by some misfortune thou have such a yokefellow allotted thee, take it not ill, O woman, considering the reward which is laid up for such things and their praise too in this present life. And to you husbands also this I say : make it a rule that there can be no such offence as to bring you under the necessity of striking a wife. And why say I a wife? since not even upon his handmaiden could a free man endure to inflict blows and lay violent hands. But if the shame be great for a man to beat a maidservant, much more to stretch forth the right hand against her that is free. And this one might see even from heathen legislatures who no longer compel her that hath been so treated to live with him that beat her, as being unworthy of her fellowship. For surely it comes of extreme lawlessness when thy partner of life, she who in the most intimate relations and in the highest degree, is united with thee; when she, like a base slave, is dishonored by thee. Wherefore also such a man, if indeed one must call him a man and not rather a wild beast, I should say, was like a parricide and a murderer of his mother. For if for a wife's sake we were commanded to leave even father and mother, not wronging them but fulfilling a divine law; and a law so grateful to our parents themselves that even they, the very persons whom we are leaving, are thankful, and bring it about with great eagerness; what but extreme frenzy can it be to insult her for whose sake God bade us leave even our parents?

But we may well ask, Is it only madness? There is the shame too: I would fain know who can endure it. And what description can set it before us; when shrieks and wailings are borne along the alleys, and there is a running to the house of him that is so disgracing himself, both of the neighbors and the passers by, as though some wild beast were ravaging within? Better were it that the earth should gape asunder for one so frantic, than that he should be seen at all in the forum after it.

"But the woman is insolent," saith he. Consider nevertheless that she is a woman, the weaker vessel, whereas thou art a man. For therefore wert thou ordained[1] to be ruler; and wert assigned to her in place of a head, that thou mightest bear with the weakness of her that is set under thee. Make then thy rule glorious. And glorious it will be when the subject of it meets with no dishonor from thee. And as the monarch will appear so much the more dignified, as he manifests more dignity in the officer under him; but if he dishonor and depreciate the greatness of that rank, he is indirectly cutting off no small portion of his own glory likewise: so also thou dishonor her who governs next to thyself, wilt in no common degree mar the honor of thy governance.

Considering therefore all these things, command thyself: and withal think also of that evening on which the father having called thee, delivered thee his daughter as a kind of deposit, and having separated her from all, from her mother, from himself, from the family, intrusted her entire guardianship to thy right hand. Consider that (under God) through her thou hast children and hast become a father, and be thou also on that account gentle towards her.

Seest thou not the husbandmen, how the earth which hath once received the seed, they tend with all various methods of culture, though it have ten thousand disadvantages; e. g., though it be an unkindly soil or bear ill weeds, or though it be vexed with excessive rain through

the nature of its situation? This also do thou. For thus shalt thou be first to enjoy both the fruit and the calm. Since thy wife is to thee both a harbor, and a potent healing charm to rejoice thy heart. Well then: if thou shalt free thy harbor from winds and waves, thou shalt enjoy much tranquility on thy return from the market-place: but if thou fill it with clamor and tumult, thou dost but prepare for thyself a more grievous shipwreck. In order then to prevent this, let what I advise be done: When any thing uncomfortable happens in the household, if she be in the wrong console her and do not aggravate the discomfort. For even if thou shouldest lose all, nothing is more grievous than to have a wife without good-will sharing thine abode. And whatever offence thou canst mention, thou wilt tell me of nothing so very painful as being at strife with her. So that if it were only for such reasons as these, let her love be more precious than all things. For if one another's burdens are to be borne, much more our own wife's.

Though she be poor do not upbraid her: though she be foolish, do not trample on her, but train her rather: because she is a member of thee, and ye are become one flesh. "But she is trifling and drunken and passionate." Thou oughtest then to grieve over these things, not to be angry; and to beseech God, and exhort her and give her advice, and do every thing to remove the evil. But if thou strike her thou dost aggravate the disease: for fierceness is removed by moderation, not by rival fierceness. With these things bear in mind also the reward from God: that when it is permitted thee to cut her off, and thou doest not so for the fear of God, but bearest with so great defects, fearing the law appointed in such matters which forbids to put away a wife whatsoever disease she may have: thou shalt receive an unspeakable reward. Yea, and before the reward thou shalt be a very great gainer, both rendering her more obedient and becoming thyself more gentle thereby. It is said, for instance, that one of the heathen philosophers[2], who had a bad wife, a trifler and a brawler, when asked, "Why, having such a one, he endured her;" made reply, "That he might have in his house a school and training-place of philosophy. For I shall be to all the rest meeker," saith he, "being here disciplined every day." Did you utter a great shout? Why, I at this moment am greatly mourning, when heathens prove better lovers of wisdom than we; we who are commanded to imitate angels, nay rather who are commanded to follow God Himself in respect of gentleness.

But to proceed: it is said that for this reason the philosopher having a bad wife, cast her not

---

[1] ἐχειροτονήθης.

[2] Socrates.

out; and some say that this very thing was the reason of his marrying her. But I, because many men have dispositions not exactly reasonable, advise that at first they do all they can, and be careful that they take a suitable partner and one full of all virtue. Should it happen, however, that they miss their end, and she whom they have brought into the house prove no good or tolerable bride, then I would have them at any rate try to be like this philosopher, and train her in every way, and consider nothing more important than this. Since neither will a merchant, until he have made a compact with his partner capable of procuring peace, launch the vessel into the deep, nor apply himself to the rest of the transaction. And let us then use every effort that she who is partner with us in the business of life and in this our vessel, may be kept in all peace within. For thus shall our other affairs too be all in calm, and with tranquility shall we run our course through the ocean of the present life. Compared with this, let house, and slaves, and money, and lands, and the business itself of the state, be less in our accouut. And let it be more valuable than all in our eyes that she who with us sits at the oars should not be in mutiny and disunion with us. For so shall our other matters proceed with a favoring tide, and in spiritual things also we shall find ourselves much the freer from hindrance, drawing this yoke with one accord; and having done all things well, we shall obtain the blessings laid up in store; unto which may we all attain, through the grace and mercy of our Lord Jesus Christ, with Whom to the Father, with the Holy Ghost, be glory, power, and honor, now and ever, and world without end. Amen.

HOMILY XXVII.

1 COR. XI. 17.

But in giving you this charge, I praise you not, that ye come together not for the better, but for the worse.

IT is necessary in considering the present charge to state also first the occasion of it. For thus again will our discourse be more intelligible. What then is this occasion?

As in the case of the three thousand who believed in the beginning, all had eaten their meals in common and had all things common; such also was the practice at the time when the Apostle wrote this: not such indeed exactly; but as it were a certain outflowing of that communion which abode among them descended also to them that came after. And because of course some were poor, but others rich, they laid not down all their goods in the midst, but made the tables open on stated days, as it should seem; and when the solemn service[1] was completed, after the communion of the Mysteries, they all went to a common entertainment, the rich bringing their provisions with them, and the poor and destitute being invited by them, and all feasting in common. But afterward this custom also became corrupt. And the reason was, their being divided and addicting themselves, some to this party, and others to that, and saying, "I am of such a one," and "I of such a one;" which thing also to correct he said in the beginning of the Epistle, "For it hath been signified unto me concerning you, my brethren, by them which are of the household of Chloe, that there are contentions among you. Now this I mean, that each one of you saith, I am of Paul; and I of Apollos; and I of Cephas." Not that Paul was the person to whom they were attaching themselves; for he would not have borne it: but wishing by concession to tear up this custom from the root, he introduced himself, indicating that if any one had inscribed upon himself even his name when breaking off from the common body, even so the thing done was profane and extreme wickedness. And if in his case it were wickedness, much more in the case of those who were inferior to him.

[2.] Since therefore this custom was broken through, a custom most excellent and most useful; (for it was a foundation of love, and a comfort to poverty, and a corrective of riches, and an occasion of the highest philosophy, and an instruction of humility:) since however he saw so great advantages in a way to be destroyed, he naturally addresses them with severity, thus saying: "But in giving you this charge, I praise you not." For in the former charge, as there were many who kept (the ordinances), he began otherwise, saying thus: "Now I praise you that ye remember me in all things:" but here contrariwise, "But in giving you this charge, I praise you not." And here is the reason why

---

[1] τῆς συνάξεως.

he placed it not after the rebuke of them that eat the idol-sacrifices. But because that was unusually harsh he interposes the discourse about wearing of long hair, that he might not have to pass from one set of vehement reproofs to others again of an invidious kind and so appear too harsh : and then he returns to the more vehement tone, and says, "But in giving you this charge, I praise you not." What is this? That which I am about to tell you of. What is, "giving you this charge, I praise you not?" "I do not approve you," saith he, "because ye have reduced me to the necessity of giving advice : I do not praise you, because ye have required instruction in regard to this, because ye have need of an admonition from me." Dost thou perceive how from his beginning he signifieth that what was done was very profane? For when he that errs ought not to require so much as a hint to prevent his erring, the error would seem to be unpardonable.

And why dost thou not praise? Because "ye come together," saith he, "not for the better but for the worse;" i.e., because ye do not go forward unto virtue. For it were meet that your liberality[1] should increase and become manifold, but ye have taken rather from the custom which already prevailed, and have so taken from it as even to need warning from me, in order that ye may return to the former order.

Further, that he might not seem to say these things on account of the poor only, he doth not at once strike in to the discourse concerning the tables, lest he render his rebuke such as they might easily come to think slightly of, but he searches for an expression most confounding and very fearful. For what saith he?

Ver. 18. "For first of all, when ye come together in the Church, I hear that divisions[2] exist among you.

And he saith not, "For fear that you do not sup together in common;" "for I hear that you feast in private, and not with the poor:" but what was most calculated thoroughly to shake their minds, that he set down, the name of division, which was the cause of this mischief also : and so he reminded them again of that which was said in the beginning of the Epistle, and was "signified by them of the house of Chloe." (c. i. 11.)

"And I partly believe it."

Thus, lest they should say, "But what if the accusers speak falsely?" he neither saith, "I believe it," lest he should rather make them reckless ; nor again, on the other hand, "I disbelieve it," lest he should seem to reprove without cause, but, "I partly believe it," saith he, i. e., "I believe it in a small part;" making them

anxious and inviting them to return to correction.

[3.] Ver. 19. "For there must be also factions among you, that they which are approved may be made manifest among you."

By "factions," here he means those which concern not the doctrines, but these present divisions. But even if he had spoken of the doctrinal heresies, not even thus did he give them any handle. For Christ Himself said, "it must needs be that occasions of stumbling come," (Matt. xviii. 7.) not destroying the liberty of the will nor appointing any necessity and compulsion over man's life, but foretelling what would certainly ensue from the evil mind of men ; which would take place, not because of his prediction, but because the incurably disposed are so minded. For not because he foretold them did these things happen : but because they were certainly about to happen, therefore he foretold them. Since, if the occasions of stumbling were of necessity and not of the mind of them that bring them in, it was superfluous His saying, "Woe to that man by whom the occasion cometh." But these things we discussed more at length when we were upon the passage itself[3]; now we must proceed to what is before us.

Now that he said these things of these factions relating to the tables, and that contention and division, he made manifest also from what follows. For having said, "I hear that there are divisions among you," he stopped not here, but signifying what divisions he means he goes on to say, "each one taketh before other his own supper ;" and again, "What? have ye not houses to eat and to drink in? or despise ye the Church of God?" However, that of these he was speaking is evident. And if he call them divisions, marvel not. For, as I said, he wishes to touch them by the expression : whereas had they been divisions of doctrine, he would not have discoursed with them thus mildly. Hear him, for instance, when he speaks of any such thing, how vehement he is both in assertion and in reproof : in assertion, as when he says, "If even an angel preach any other gospel unto you than that ye have received, let him be accursed ;" (Gal. i. 8.) but in reproof, as when he says, "Whosoever of you would be justified by the law, ye are fallen away from grace." (Gal. v. 4.) And at one time he calls the corrupters "dogs," saying, "Beware of dogs :" (Phil. iii. 2.) at another, "having their consciences seared with a hot iron." (1 Tim. iv. 2.) And again, "angels of Satan :" (2 Cor. xi. 14-15.) but here he said no such thing, but spoke in a gentle and subdued tone.

---

[1] φιλοτιμίαν.
[2] σχίσματα.

[3] vid. S. Chrys. on S. Matth. Hom. 59.

But what is, "that they which are approved may be made manifest among you?" That they may shine the more. And what he intends to say is this, that those who are unchangable and firm are so far from being at all injured hereby, but even shows them the more, and that it makes them more glorious. For the word, "that[1]," is not every where indicative of cause, but frequently also of the event of things. Thus Christ Himself uses it, when He saith, "For judgement I am come into this world; that they which see not may see, and that they which see may be made blind." (John ix. 39.) So likewise Paul in another place, when discoursing of the law, he writes, "And the Law came in beside, that the trespass might abound." (Rom. v. 20.) But neither was the law given to this end that the trespasses of the Jews might be increased: (though this did ensue:) nor did Christ come for this end that they which see might be made blind, but for the contrary; but the result was such. Thus then also here must one understand the expression, "that they which are approved may be made manifest." For not at all with this view came heresies into being, that "they which are approved may be made manifest," but on these heresies taking place such was the result. Now these things he said to console the poor, those of them who nobly bore that sort of contempt. Wherefore he said not, "that they may become approved," but, "that they which are approved may be made manifest; showing that before this also they were such, but they were mixed up with the multitude, and while enjoying such relief as was afforded them by the rich, they were not very conspicuous: but now this strife and contentiousness made them manifest, even as the storm shows the pilot. And he said not, "that ye may appear approved," but, "that they which are approved may be made manifest, those among you who are such." For neither when he is accusing doth he lay them open, that he may not render them more reckless; nor when praising, that he may not make them more boastful; but he leaves both this expression and that in suspense[2], allowing each man's own conscience to make the application of what he saith.

Nor doth he here seem to me to be comforting the poor only, but those also who were not violating the custom. For it was likely that there were among them also those that observed it.

And this is why he said, "I partly believe it." Justly then doth he call these "approved," who not only with the rest observed the custom, but even without them kept this good law undisturbed. And he doth this, studying by such praises to render both others and these persons themselves more forward.

[4.] Then at last he adds the very form of offence. And what is it?

Ver. 20. "When ye assemble yourselves together," saith he, "it is not possible to eat the Lord's Supper."

Seest thou how effectually appealing to their shame, even already by way of narrative he contrives to give them his counsel? "For the appearance of your assembly," saith he, "is different. It is one of love and brotherly affection. At least one place receives you all, and ye are together in one flock. But the Banquet, when you come to that, bears no resemblance to the Assembly of worshippers." And he said not, "When ye come together, this is not to eat in common,' "this is not to feast with one another;" but otherwise again and much more fearfully he reprimands them, saying, "it is not possible to eat the Lord's Supper," sending them away now from this point to that evening on which Christ delivered the awful Mysteries. Therefore also he called the early meal "a supper." For that supper too had them all reclining at meat together: yet surely not so great was the distance between the rich and the poor as between the Teacher and the disciples. For that is infinite. And why say I the Teacher and the disciples? Think of the interval between the Teacher and the traitor: nevertheless, the Lord Himself both sat at meat with them and did not even cast him out, but both gave him his portion of salt and made him partaker of the Mysteries.

Next he explains how "it is not possible to eat the Lord's Supper."

Ver. 21. "For in your eating,[3] each one taketh before other his own supper," saith he, "and one is hungry, and another is drunken."

Perceivest thou how he intimates that they were disgracing themselves rather? For that which is the Lord's, they make a private matter: so that themselves are the first to suffer indignity, depriving their own table of its greatest prerogative. How and in what manner? Because the Lord's Supper, i. e. the Master's, ought to be common. For the property of the master belongs not to this servant without belonging to that, but in common to all. So that by "the Lord's" Supper he expresses this, the "community" of the feast. As if he had said, "If it be thy master's, as assuredly it is, thou oughtest not to withdraw it as private, but as belonging to thy Lord and Master to set it in common before all. For this is the meaning of, 'the Lord's.' But now thou dost not suffer it to be the Lord's, not suffering it to be

---

[1] ἵνα.

[2] εἰς μετέωρον ἀφίησι, "sends it out into the air."

[3] ἐν τῷ φαγεῖν.

common but feasting by thyself." Wherefore also he goes on to say,

"For each one taketh before other his own supper." And he said not, "cutteth off," but "taketh before," tacitly censuring them both for greediness and for precipitancy. This at least the sequel also shows. For having said this, he added again, "and one is hungry, and another is drunken," each of which showed a want of moderation, both the craving and the excess. See also a second fault again whereby those same persons are injured : the first, that they dishonor their supper: the second, that they are greedy and drunken; and what is yet worse, even when the poor are hungry. For what was intended to be set before all in common, that these men fed on alone, and proceeded both to surfeiting and to drunkenness. Wherefore neither did he say, " one is hungry, and another is filled :" but, " is drunken." Now each of these, even by itself, is worthy of censure : for it is a fault to be drunken even without despising the poor; and to despise the poor without being drunken, is an accusation. When both then are joined together at the same time, consider how exceeding great is the transgression.

Next, having pointed out their profaneness, he adds his reprimand in what follows, with much anger, saying,

Ver. 22. " What? have ye not houses to eat and to drink in ? Or despise ye the Church of God, and put them to shame that have not?"

Seest thou how he transferred the charge from the indignity offered to the poor to the Church, that his words might make a deeper impression of disgust? Here now you see is yet a fourth accusation, when not the poor only, but the Church likewise is insulted. For even as thou makest the Lord's Supper a private meal, so also the place again, using the Church as a house. For it was made a Church, not that we who come together might be divided, but that they who are divided might be joined : and this act of assembling shows.

"And put them to shame that have not." He said not, "and kill with hunger them that have not," but so as much more to put them to the blush, "shame them;" to point out that it is not food which he cares for so much as the wrong done unto them. Behold again a fifth accusation, not only to overlook the poor but even to shame them. Now this he said, partly as treating with reverence the concerns of the poor, and intimating that they grieve not so for the belly as for the shame; and partly also drawing the hearer to compassion.

Having therefore pointed out so great impieties, indignity to the Supper, indignity to the Church, the contempt practised towards the poor; he relaxes again the tones of his reproof,

saying, all of a sudden[1], " Shall I praise you? In this I praise you not." Wherein cne might especially marvel at him that when there was need to strike and chide more vehemently after the proof of so great offences, he doeth the contrary rather, gives way, and permits them to recover breath. What then may the cause be? He had touched more painfully than usual in aggravating the charge, and being a most excellent physician, he adapts the incision to the wounds, neither cutting superficially those parts which require a deep stroke; (for thou hast heard him how he cut off among those very persons him that had committed fornication;) nor delivering over to the knife those things which require the milder sort of remedies. For this cause then here also he conducts his address more mildly, and in another point of view likewise, he sought especially to render them gentle to the poor: and this is why he discourses with them rather in a subdued tone.

[5.] Next, wishing also from another topic to shame them yet more, he takes again the points which were most essential and of them weaves his discourse.

Ver. 23. "For I received of the Lord," saith he, "that which also I delivered unto you: how that the Lord Jesus in the night in which He was betrayed, took bread:"

Ver. 24. "And when He had given thanks, He brake it, and said, Take, eat: this is My Body, which is broken for you: this do in remembrance of me."

Wherefore doth he here make mention of the Mysteries? Because that argument was very necessary to his present purpose. As thus: " Thy Master," saith he, "counted all worthy of the same Table, though it be very awful and far exceeding the dignity of all : but thou considerest them to be unworthy even of thine own, small and mean as we see it is; and while they have no advantage over thee in spiritual things, thou robbest them in the temporal things. For neither are these thine own."

However, he doth not express himself thus, to prevent his discourse becoming harsh : but he frames it in a gentler form, saying, that " the Lord Jesus in the night in which He was betrayed, took bread."

And wherefore doth he remind us of the time, and of that evening, and of the betrayal? Not indifferently nor without some reason, but that he might exceedingly fill them with compunction, were it but from consideration of the time. For even if one be a very stone, yet when he considers that night, how He was with His disciples, "very heavy," how He was betrayed, how He was bound, how He was led away, how He was judged, how He suffered all

---

[1] χαλᾷ τὸν τόνον, ἀθρόον λέγων.

the rest in order , he becometh softer than wax, and is withdrawn from earth and all the pomp of this world. Therefore he leads us to the remembrance of all those things, by His time, and His table, and His betrayal, putting us to shame and saying, "Thy Master gave up even Himself for thee : and thou dost not even share a little meat with thy brother for thine own sake."

But how saith he, that "he received it from the Lord?" since certainly he was not present then but was one of the persecutors. That thou mayest know that the first table had no advantage above that which cometh after it. For even to-day also it is He who doeth all, and delivereth it even as then.

And not on this account only doth he remind us of that night, but that he may also in another way bring us to compunction. For as we particularly remember those words which we hear last from those who are departing ; and to their heirs if they should venture to transgress their commands, when we would put them to shame we say, "Consider that this was the last word that your father uttered to you, and until the evening when he was just about to breathe his last he kept repeating these injunctions:" just so Paul, purposing hence also to make his argument full of awfulness; "Remember," saith he, "that this was the last mysterious rite[1] He gave unto you, and in that night on which He was about to be slain for us, He commanded these things, and having delivered to us that Supper after that He added nothing further."

Next also he proceeds to recount the very things that were done, saying, "He took bread, and, when He had given thanks, He brake it, and said, Take, eat: this is My Body, which is broken for you." If therefore thou comest for a sacrifice of thanksgiving,[2] do thou on thy part nothing unworthy of that sacrifice : by no means either dishonor thy brother, or neglect him in his hunger ; be not drunken, insult not the Church. As thou comest giving thanks for what thou hast enjoyed: so do thou thyself accordingly make return, and not cut thyself off from thy neighbor. Since Christ for His part gave equally to all, saying, "Take, eat." He gave His Body equally, but dost not thou give so much as the common bread equally? Yea, it was indeed broken for all alike, and became the Body equally for all.

Ver. 25. "In like manner also the cup after supper, saying, This cup is the New Covenant in My Blood : this do, as oft as ye drink of it, in remembrance of Me."

What sayest thou? Art thou making a remembrance of Christ, and despisest thou the poor and tremblest not? Why, if a son or brother had died and thou wert making a remembrance of him, thou wouldst have been smitten by thy conscience, hadst thou not fulfilled the custom and invited the poor : and when thou art making remembrance of thy Master, dost thou not so much as simply give a portion of the Table?

But what is it which He saith, "This cup is the New Covenant?" Because there was also a cup of the Old Covenant; the libations and the blood of the brute creatures. For after sacrificing, they used to receive the blood in a chalice and bowl and so pour it out. Since then instead of the blood of beasts He brought in His own Blood; lest any should be troubled on hearing this, He reminds them of that ancient sacrifice.

[6.] Next, having spoken concerning that Supper, he connects the things present with the things of that time, that even as on that very evening and reclining on that very couch and receiving from Christ himself this sacrifice, so also now might men be affected; and he saith,

Ver. 26. "For as often as ye eat this bread, and drink this cup, ye proclaim the Lord's death till He come."

For as Christ in regard to the bread and the cup said, "Do this in remembrance of Me," revealing to us the cause of the giving of the Mystery, and besides what else He said, declaring this to be a sufficient cause to ground our religious fear upon :—(for when thou considerest what thy Master hath suffered for thee, thou wilt the better deny thyself :)—so also Paul saith here : "as often as ye eat ye do proclaim His death." And this is that Supper. Then intimating that it abides unto the end, he saith, "till He come."

Ver. 27. "Wherefore whosoever shall eat this bread and drink the cup of the Lord unworthily, shall be guilty of the Body and the Blood of the Lord."

Why so? Because he poured it out, and makes the thing appear a slaughter and no longer a sacrifice. Much therefore as they who then pierced Him, pierced Him not that they might drink but that they might shed His blood : so likewise doth he that cometh for it unworthily and reaps no profit thereby. Seest thou how fearful he makes his discourse, and inveighs against them very exceedingly, signifying that if they are thus to drink, they partake unworthily of the elements[3]? For how can it be other than unworthily when it is he who neglects the hungry? who besides overlooking him puts him to shame? Since if not giving to the poor casteth one out of the kingdom, even though one should be a virgin; or rather, not giving

---

[1] μυσταγωγίαν.
[2] εὐχαριστία.
[3] τῶν προκειμένων.

II

liberally: (for even those virgins too had oil, only they had it not abundantly:) consider how great the evil will prove, to have wrought so many impieties?

"What impieties?" say you. Why sayest thou, what impieties? Thou hast partaken of such a Table and when thou oughtest to be more gentle than any and like the angels, none so cruel as thou art become. Thou hast tasted the Blood of the Lord, and not even thereupon dost thou acknowledge thy brother. Of what indulgence then art thou worthy? Whereas if even before this thou hadst not known him, thou oughtest to have come to the knowledge of him from the Table; but now thou dishonorest the Table itself; he having been deemed worthy to partake of it and thou not judging him worthy of thy meat. Hast thou not heard how much he suffered who 'demanded the hundred pence? how he made void the gift vouchsafed to him[1]? Doth it not come into thy mind what thou wert and what thou hast become? Dost thou not put thyself in remembrance that if this man be poor in possessions, thou wast much more beggarly in good works, being full of ten thousand sins? Notwithstanding, God delivered thee from all those and counted thee worthy of such a Table: but thou art not even thus become more merciful: therefore of course nothing else remaineth but that thou shouldest be "delivered to the tormentors."

[7.] These words let us also listen to, all of us, as many as in this place approach with the poor to this holy Table, but when we go out, do not seem even to have seen them, but are both drunken and pass heedlessly by the hungry; the very things whereof the Corinthians were accused. And when is this done? say you. At all times indeed, but especially at the festivals, where above all times it ought not so to be. Is it not so, that at such times, immediately after Communion, drunkenness succeeds and contempt of the poor? And having partaken of the Blood, when it were a time for thee to fast and watch, thou givest thyself up to wine and revelling. And yet if thou hast by chance made thy morning meal on any thing good, thou keepest thyself lest by any other unsavory viand thou spoil the taste of the former: and now that thou hast been feasting on the Spirit thou bringest in a satanical luxury. Consider, when the Apostles partook of that holy Supper, what they did: did they not betake themselves to prayers and singing of hymns? to sacred vigils? to that long work of teaching, so full of all self-denial? For then He related and delivered to them those great and wonderful things, when Judas had gone out to call them who were about to crucify Him.

Hast thou not heard how the three thousand also who partook of the Communion continued even in prayer and teaching, not in drunken feasts and revellings? But thou before thou hast partaken fastest, that in a certain way thou mayest appear worthy of the Communion: but when thou hast partaken, and thou oughtest to increase thy temperance, thou undoest all. And yet surely it is not the same to fast before this and after it. Since although it is our duty to be temperate at both times, yet most particularly after we have received the Bridegroom. Before, that thou mayest become worthy of receiving: after, that thou mayest not be found unworthy of what thou hast received.

"What then? ought we to fast after receiving?" I say not this, neither do I use any compulsion. This indeed were well: however, I do not enforce this, but I exhort you not to feast to excess. For if one never ought to live luxuriously, and Paul showed this when he said, "she that giveth herself to pleasure is dead while she liveth" (1 Tim. v. 6.); much more will she then be dead. And if luxury be death to a woman, much more to a man: and if this done at another time is fatal, much more after the communion of the Mysteries. And dost thou having taken the bread of life, do an action of death and not shudder? Knowest thou not how great evils are brought in by luxury? Unseasonable laughter, disorderly expressions, buffoonery fraught with perdition, unprofitable trifling, all the other things, which it is not seemly even to name. And these things thou doest when thou hast enjoyed the Table of Christ, on that day on which thou hast been counted worthy to touch His flesh with thy tongue. What then is to be done to prevent these things? Purify thy right hand, thy tongue, thy lips, which have become a threshold for Christ to tread upon. Consider the time in which thou didst draw near and set forth a material table, raise thy mind to that Table, to the Supper of the Lord, to the vigil of the disciples, in that night, that holy night. Nay, rather should one accurately examine, this very present state is night. Let us watch then with the Lord, let us be pricked in our hearts with the disciples. It is the season of prayers, not of drunkenness; ever indeed, but especially during a festival. For a festival is therefore appointed, not that we may behave ourselves unseemly, not that we may accumulate sins, but rather that we may blot out those which exist.

I know, indeed, that I say these things in vain, yet will I not cease to say them. For if ye do not all obey, yet surely ye will not all disobey; or rather, even though ye should all be disobedient, my reward will be greater, though

---

[1] ἐξενεχθεῖσαν, perhaps "officially declared."

yours will be more condemnation. However, that it may not be more, to this end I will not cease to speak. For perchance, perchance, by my perseverance I shall be able to reach you.

Wherefore I beseech you that we do not this to condemnation ; let us nourish Christ, let us give Him drink, let us clothe Him. These things are worthy of that Table. Hast thou heard holy hymns ? Hast thou seen a spiritual marriage ? Hast thou enjoyed a royal Table ? Hast thou been filled with the Holy Ghost ? Hast thou joined in the choir of the Seraphim ? Hast thou become partaker of the powers above ? Cast not away so great a joy, waste not the treasure, bring not in drunkenness, the mother of dejection, the joy of the devil, the parent of ten thousand evils. For hence is a sleep like unto death, and heaviness of head, and disease, and obliviousness, and an image of dead men's condition. Further, if thou wouldst not choose to meet with a friend when intoxicated, when thou hast Christ within, durst thou, tell me, to thrust in upon Him so great an excess ?

But dost thou love enjoyment ? Then, on this very account cease being drunken. For I, too, would have thee enjoy thyself, but with the real enjoyment, that which never fadeth. What then is the real enjoyment, ever blooming ? Invite Christ to sup[1] (Rev. ii. 20.) with thee ; give Him to partake of thine, or rather of His own. This bringeth pleasure without limit, and in its prime everlastingly. But the things cf sense are not such ; rather as soon as they appear they vanish away ; and he that hath enjoyed them will be in no better condition than he who hath not, or rather in a worse. For the one is settled as it were in a harbor, but the other exposes himself to a kind of torrent, a besieging army of distempers, and hath not even any power to endure the first swell of the sea.[2]

That these things be therefore not so, let us follow after moderation. For thus we shall both be in a good state of body, and we shall possess our souls in security, and shall be delivered from evils both present and future : from which may we all be delivered, and attain unto the kingdom, through the grace and mercy of our Lord Jesus Christ, with Whom to the Father, together with the Holy Spirit, be glory, power, and honor, now and ever, and world without end. Amen.

HOMILY XXVIII.

1 COR. xi. 28.

But let a man prove himself, and so let him eat of the bread, and drink of the cup.

WHAT mean these words, when another object is proposed to us ? This is Paul's custom, as also I said before, not only to treat of those things which he had proposed to himself, but also if an argument incidental to his purpose occur, to proceed upon this also with great diligence, and especially when it relates to very necessary and urgent matters. Thus, when he was discoursing with married persons, and the question about the servants fell in his way, he handled it very strenuously and at great length. Again, when he was speaking of the duty of not going to law before those courts, then also having fallen upon the admonition respecting covetousness, he discoursed at length concerning this subject likewise. Now the same thing he hath also done here : in that having once found occasion to remind them of the Mysteries, he judged it necessary to proceed with that subject. For indeed it was no ordinary one. Wherefore also he discoursed very awfully concerning it, providing for that which is the sum of all good things, viz. their approaching those Mysteries with a pure conscience. Whence neither was he content with the things said before alone, but adds these also, saying,

"But let a man prove himself :" which also he saith in the second Epistle : "try your own selves, prove your own selves :" (2 Cor. xiii. 5.) not as we do now, approaching because of the season rather than from any earnestness of mind. For we do not consider how we may approach prepared, with the ills that were within us purged out, and full of compunction, but how we may come at festivals and whenever all do so. But not thus did Paul bid us come : he knoweth only one season of access and communion, the purity of a man's conscience. Since if even that kind of banquet which the senses take cognizance of cannot be partaken of by us when feverish and full of bad humors, without risk of perishing : much more is it unlawful for us to

---

[1] ἐπ᾽ ἄριστον
[2] τὴν ζάλην ταύτην.

touch this Table with profane lusts, which are more grievous than fevers. Now when I say profane lusts, I mean both those of the body, and of money, and of anger, and of malice, and, in a word, all that are profane. And it becomes him that approacheth, first to empty himself of all these things and so to touch that pure sacrifice. And neither if indolently disposed and reluctantly ought he to be compelled to approach by reason of the festival; nor, on the other hand, if penitent and prepared, should any one prevent him because it is not a festival. For a festival is a showing forth of good works, and a reverence of soul, and exactness of deportment. And if thou hast these things, thou mayest at all times keep festival and at all times approach. Wherefore he saith, "But let each man prove himself, and then let him approach." And he bids not one examine another, but each himself, making the tribunal not a public one and the conviction without a witness.

[2.] Ver. 29. "For he that eateth and drinketh unworthily, eateth and drinketh judgment to himself."

What sayest thou, tell me? Is this Table which is the cause of so many blessings and teeming with life, become judgment? Not from its own nature, saith he, but from the will of him that approaches. For as His presence, which conveyed to us those great and unutterable blessings, condemned the more them that received it not: so also the Mysteries become provisions[1] of greater punishment to such as partake unworthily.

But why doth he eat judgment to himself? "Not discerning the Lord's body:" i. e., not searching, not bearing in mind, as he ought, the greatness of the things set before him; not estimating the weight of the gift. For if thou shouldest come to know accurately Who it is that lies before thee, and Who He is that gives Himself, and to whom, thou wilt need no other argument, but this is enough for thee to use all vigilance; unless thou shouldest be altogether fallen.

Ver. 30. "For this cause many among you are weak and sickly, and not a few sleep."

Here he no longer brings his examples from others as he did in the case of the idol-sacrifices, relating the ancient histories and the chastisements in the wilderness, but from the Corinthians themselves; which also made the discourse apt to strike them more keenly. For whereas he was saying, "he eateth judgment to himself," and, "he is guilty;" that he might not seem to speak mere words, he points to deeds also and calls themselves to witness; a kind of thing which comes home to men more than threatening, by showing that the threat has issued in some real fact. He was not however content with

these things alone, but from these he also introduced and confirmed the argument concerning hell-fire, terrifying them in both ways; and solving an inquiry which is handled everywhere. I mean, since many question one with another, "whence arise the untimely deaths, whence the long diseases of men;" he tells them that these unexpected events are many of them conditional upon certain sins. "What then? They who are in continual health," say you, "and come to a green old age, do they not sin?" Nay, who durst say this? "How then," say you, "do they not suffer punishment?" Because there they shall suffer a severer one. But we, if we would, neither here nor there need suffer it.

Ver. 31. "For if we discerned ourselves," saith he, "we should not be judged."

And he said not, "if we punished ourselves, if we were revenged on ourselves," but if we were only willing to acknowledge our offence, to pass sentence on ourselves, to condemn the things done amiss, we should be rid of the punishment both in this world and the next. For he that condemns himself propitiates God in two ways, both by acknowledging his sins, and by being more on his guard for the future. But since we are not willing to do even this light thing, as we ought to do it, not even thus doth He endure to punish us with the world, but even thus spareth us, exacting punishment in this world, where the penalty is for a season and the consolation great; for the result is both deliverance from sins, and a good hope of things to come, alleviating the present evils. And these things he saith, at the same time comforting the sick and rendering the rest more serious. Wherefore he saith,

Ver. 32. "But when we are judged, we are chastened of the Lord."

He said not, we are punished, he said not, we have vengeance taken on us, but, "we are chastened." For what is done belongs rather to admonition than condemnation, to healing than vengeance, to correction than punishment. And not so only but by the threat of a greater evil he makes the present light, saying, "that we may not be condemned with the world." Seest thou how he brings in hell also and that tremendous judgment-seat, and signifies that that trial and punishment is necessary and by all means must be? for if the faithful, and such as God especially cares for, escape not without punishment in whatsoever things they offend, (and this is evident from things present,) much more the unbelieving and they who commit the unpardonable and incurable sins.

[3.] Ver. 33. "Wherefore when ye come together to eat, wait one for another."

Thus, while their fear was yet at its height and the terror of hell remained, he chooses again

---

[1] ἐφόδια, viatica.

to bring in also the exhortation in behalf of the poor, on account of which he said all these things; implying that if they do not this they must partake unworthily. But if the not imparting of our goods excludes from that Table, much more the violently taking away. And he said not, "wherefore, when ye come together, impart to them that need," but, which has a more reverential sound, " wait one for another." For this also prepared the way for and intimated that, and in a becoming form introduced the exhortation. Then further to shame them,

Ver. 34. "And if any man is hungry, let him eat at home."

By permitting, he hinders it, and more strongly than by an absolute prohibition. For he brings him out of the church and sends him to his house, hereby severely reprimanding and ridiculing them, as slaves to the belly and unable to contain themselves. For he said not, "if any despise the poor," but, " if any hunger," discoursing as with impatient children; as with brute beasts which are slaves to appetite. Since it would be indeed very ridiculous, if, because they were hungry they were to eat at home.

Yet he was not content with this, but added also another more fearful thing, saying, "that your coming together be not unto judgment:" that ye come not unto chastisement, unto punishment, insulting the Church, dishonoring your brother. " For for this cause ye come together," saith he, " that ye may love one another, that ye may profit and be profited. But if the contrary happen, it were better for you to feed yourselves at home."

This, however, he said, that he might attract them to him the more. Yea, this was the very purpose both of his pointing out the injury that would arise from hence, and of his saying that condemnation was no trifling one, and terrifying them in every way, by the Mysteries, by the sick, by those that had died, by the other things before mentioned.

Then also he alarms them again in another way, saying, "and the rest will I set in order whensoever I come:" with reference either to some other things, or to this very matter. For since it was likely that they would yet have some reasons to allege, and it was not possible to set all to rights by letter, " the things which I have charged you, let them be observed for the present," saith he ; " but if ye have any thing else to mention, let it be kept for my coming ; " speaking either of this matter, as I said, or of some other things not very urgent. And this he doth that hence too he may render them more serious. For being anxious about his coming, they would correct the error. For the sojourning of Paul in any place was no ordinary thing : and to signify this he said, " some are

puffed up, as though I would not come to you ; " (1 Cor. iv. 18.) and elsewhere again, " not as in my presence only, but now much more in my absence, work out your own salvation with fear and trembling." (Phil. ii. 12.) And therefore neither did he merely promise that he would come, lest they should disbelieve him and become more negligent ; but he also states a necessary cause for his sojourning with them, saying, "the rest I will set in order when I come ; which implies, that the correction of the things that remained, even had he not in any case been desirous, would have drawn him thither.

[4.] Hearing therefore all these things, let us both take great care of the poor, and restrain our appetite, and rid ourselves of drunkenness, and be careful worthily to partake of the Mysteries ; and whatsoever we suffer, let us not take it bitterly, neither for ourselves nor for others ; as when untimely death happen or long diseases. For this is deliverance from punishment, this is correction, this is most excellent admonition. Who saith this ? He that hath Christ speaking in him.

But nevertheless even after this many of our women are so foolishly disposed as even to go beyond the unbelievers in the excess of their grief[1]. And some do this blinded by their passion, but others for ostentation, and to avoid the censures of them that are without : who most of all are deprived of excuse, to my mind. For, "lest such a one accuse me," saith she, " let God be my accuser : lest men more senseless than the brute beasts condemn me, let the law of the King of all be trampled under foot." Why, how many thunderbolts do not these sayings deserve ?

Again ; If any one invite you to a funeral supper[2] after your affliction there is no one to say any thing against it, because there is a law of men which enjoins such things : but when God by His law forbids your mourning, all thus contradict it. Doth not Job come into thy mind, O woman ? Rememberest thou not his words at the misfortune of his children, which adorned that holy head more than ten thousand crowns, and made proclamation louder than many trumpets ? Dost thou make no account of the greatness of his misfortunes, of that unprecedented shipwreck, and that strange and portentous tragedy ? For thou possibly hast lost one, or a second, or third : but he so many sons and daughters : and he that had many children suddenly became childless. And not even by degrees were his bowels wasted away : but at one sweep all the fruit of his body was

---

[1] For the sentiments of Christian antiquity about mourning at funerals, see S. Cyprian, *De Mortalitate*, c. 15, 16.

[2] περίδειπνον.

snatched from him. Nor was it by the common law of nature, when they had come to old age, but by a death both untimely and violent : and all together, and when he was not present nor sitting by them, that at least by hearing their last words he might have some consolation for so bitter an end of theirs: but contrary to all expectation and without his knowing any thing of what took place, they were all at once over-whelmed, and their house became their grave and their snare.

And not only their untimely death, but many things besides there were to grieve him; such as their being all in the flower of their age, all virtuous and loving, all together, that not one of either sex was left, that it befel them not by the common law of nature, that it came after so great a loss, that when he was unconscious of any sin on his own part or on theirs, he suffered these things. For each of these circumstances is enough even by itself to disturb the mind : but when we find them even concurring together, imagine the height of those waves, how great the excess of that storm. And what in particu-lar is greater and worse than his bereavement, he did not even know wherefore all these things happened. On this account then, having no cause to assign for the misfortune, he ascends to the good pleasure of God, and saith, "The Lord gave, the Lord hath taken away : " as it pleased the Lord, even so it happened; "blessed be the name of the Lord for ever." (Job ii. 21.) And these things he said, when he saw himself who had followed after all virtue in the last extremity ; but evil men and impos-tors, prospering, luxurious, revelling on all sides. And he uttered no such word as it is likely that some of the weaker sort would have uttered, " Was it for this that I brought up my children and trained them with all exactness ? For this did I open my house to all that passed by, that after those many courses run in behalf of the needy, the naked, the orphans, I might receive this recompense ? " But instead of these, he offered up those words better than all sacrifice, saying, "Naked came I out of my mother's womb, and naked shall I return thither." If however he rent his clothes and shaved his head, marvel not. For he was a father and a loving father : and it was meet that both the compassion of his nature should be shown, and also the self-com-mand of his spirit. Whereas, had he not done this, perhaps one would have thought this self-command to be of mere insensibility. Therefore he indicates both his natural affection and the exactness of his piety, and in his grief he was not overthrown.

[5.] Yea, and when his trial proceeded fur-ther, he is again adorned with other crowns on account of his reply to his wife, saying, "If we have received good at the hand of the Lord, shall we not endure evil? " (Job ii. 10.) For in fact his wife was by this time the only one left, all his having been clean destroyed, both his children and his possessions and his very body, and she reserved to tempt and to ensnare him. And this indeed was the reason why the devil did not destroy her with the children, nor asked her death, because he expected that she would contribute much towards the ensnaring of that holy man. Therefore he left her as a kind of implement, and a formidable one, for himself. "For if even out of paradise," saith he, "I cast mankind by her means, much more shall I be able to trip him up on the dunghill."

And observe his craft. He did not apply this stratagem when the oxen or the asses or the cam-els were lost, nor even when the house fell and the children were buried under it, but so long looking on the combatant, he suffers her to be silent and quiet. But when the fountain of worms gushed forth, when the skin began to putrify and drop off, and the flesh wasting away to emit most offensive discharge, and the hand of the devil was wearing him out with sharper pain than gridirons and furnaces and any flame, con-suming on every side and eating away his body more grievously than any wild beast, and when a long time had been spent in this misery[1]; then he brings her to him, seasoned and worn down. Whereas if she had approached him at the beginning of his misfortune, neither would she have found him so unnerved, nor would she have had it in her power so to swell out and exaggerate the misfortune by her words. But now when she saw him through the length of time thirsting for release, and desiring the termi-nation of what pressed on him vehemently then doth she come upon him. For to show that he was quite worn down, and by this time had become unable even to draw breath, yea, and desired even to die, hear what he saith; " For I would I could lay hands on myself, or could request another and he should do it for me;" And observe, I pray, the wickedness of his wife, from what topic she at once begins : namely, from the length of time, saying, " How long wilt thou hold out[3]?"

Now, if often even when there were no re-alities words alone have prevailed to unman a person, consider what it was likely he then

<hr />

[1] The LXX begin Job ii.9 with, "After a long time had passed."
[2] τεταριχευμένῳ. Conf. Æsch. Choeph. 294.
[3] Job ii. 9. where, according to the LXX, the speech of Job's wife stands as follows : " How long wilt thou be patient, saying, Lo, let me endure yet a little while, awaiting the hope of my sal-vation ? For behold, thy memorial is vanished from the earth, even sons and daughters, the throes and labors of my womb, for whom I have wearied myself in vain with toils : and thou thyself in corruption of worms sittest all night in the open air, while I am a wanderer and a servant, from place to place, and from house to house, awaiting the sun when it will set, that I may rest from my labors and the pains which now straiten me : but say some word against the Lord, and die."

should feel, when, besides these words, the things themselves also were galling him; and what, as it should seem, was worst of all, it was a wife also who spake thus, and a wife who had sunk down utterly and was giving herself up, and on this account was seeking to cast him also into desperation. However, that we may see more clearly the engine which was brought against that adamantine wall, let us listen to the very words. What then are these? "How long wilt thou hold out? saying, Lo! I wait a short time longer, expecting the hope of my salvation." "Nay," saith she, "the time hath exposed the folly of thy words, while it is protracted, yet shows no mode of escape." And these things she said, not only thrusting him into desperation, but also reproaching and jesting upon him.

For he, ever consoling her as she pressed upon him, and putting her off, would speak as follows: "Wait a little longer, and there will soon be an end of these things." Reproaching him therefore, she speaks: "Wilt thou now again say the same thing? For a long time hath now run by, and no end of these things hath appeared." And observe her malice, that she makes no mention of the oxen, the sheep or the camels, as knowing that he was not very much vexed about these; but she goes at once to nature, and reminds him of his children. For on their death she saw him both rending his clothes and shaving off his hair. And she said not, "thy children are dead," but very pathetically, "thy memorial is perished from the earth," "the thing for which thy children were desirable." For if, even now after that the resurrection hath been made known children are longed for because they preserve the memory of the departed; much more then. Wherefore also her curse becomes from that consideration more bitter. For in that case, he that cursed, said not, "Let his children be utterly rooted out," but, "his memorial from the earth." "Thy sons and thy daughters." Thus whereas she said, "the memorial," she again accurately makes mention of either sex. "But if thou," saith she, "carest not for these, at least consider what is mine." "The pains of my womb, and labors which I have endured in vain with sorrow." Now what she means is this: "I, who endured the more, am wronged for thy sake, and having undergone the toils I am deprived of the fruits."

And see how she neither makes express mention of his loss of property, nor is silent about it and hurries by; but in that point of view in which it also might be most pathetically narrated, in that she covertly refers to it. For when she says, "I too am a vagabond and a slave, going about from place to place, from house to house," she both hints at the loss and

indicates her great distress: these expressions being such as even to enhance that misfortune. "For I come to the doors of others," saith she; "nor do I beg only, but am a wanderer also and serve a strange and unusual servitude, going round everywhere and carrying about the tokens of my calamity, and teaching all men of my woes;" which is most piteous of all, to change house after house. And she stayed not even at these lamentations, but proceeded to say, "Waiting for the sun when it will set, and I shall rest from my miseries and the pains that encompass me, by which I am now straitened. "Thus, that which is sweet to others," saith she, "to behold the light, this to me is grievous: but the night and the darkness is a desirable thing. For this only gives me rest from my toils, this becometh a comfort to my miseries. But speak somewhat against the Lord, and die." Perceivest thou here too her crafty wickedness? how she did not even in the act of advising at once introduce the deadly counsel, but having first pitifully related her misfortunes and having drawn out the tragedy at length, she couches in a few words what she would recommend, and doth not even declare it plainly, but throwing a shade over that, she holds out to him the deliverance which he greatly longed for, and promises death, the thing which he then most of all desired.

And mark from this also the malice of the devil: that because he knew the longing of Job towards God, he suffers not his wife to accuse God, lest he should at once turn away from her as an enemy. For this cause she no where mentions Him, but the actual calamities she is continually harping on.

And do thou, besides what has been said, add the circumstance that it was a woman who gave this counsel, a wonderful orator to beguile the heedless. Many at least even without external accidents have been cast down by the counsel of woman alone.

[6.] What then did the blessed saint, and firmer than adamant? Looking bitterly upon her, by his aspect even before he spake, he repelled her devices: since she no doubt expected to excite fountains of tears; but he became fiercer than a lion, full of wrath and indignation, not on account of his sufferings, but on account of her diabolical suggestions; and having signified his anger by his looks in a subdued tone he gives his rebuke; for even in misfortune he kept his self-command. And what saith he? "Why speakest thou as one of the foolish women?" "I have not so taught thee," saith he, "I did not so nurture thee; and this is why I do not now recognize even mine own consort. For these words are the counsel of a 'foolish woman,' and of one beside herself." Seest thou not here an instance of wounding in moderation, and inflicting a blow just sufficient to cure the disease?

Then, after the infliction, he brings in advice sufficient on the other hand to console her, and very rational, thus speaking: "if we have received our good things at the hand of the Lord, shall we not endure our evils?" "For remember," saith he, "those former things and make account of the Author of them, and thou wilt bear even these nobly." Seest thou the modesty of the man? that he doth not at all impute his patience to his own courage, but saith it was part of the natural result of what happened. "For in return for what did God give us these former things? What recompense did he repay? None, but from mere goodness. For they were a gift, not a recompense; a grace, not a reward. Well then, let us bear these also nobly."

This discourse let us, both men and women, have recorded, and let us engrave the words in our minds, both these and those before them: and by sketching upon our minds as in picture the history of their sufferings,[1] I mean the loss of wealth, the bereavement of children, the disease of body, the reproaches, the mockings, the devices of his wife, the snare of the devil, in a word, all the calamities of that righteous man, and that with exactness, let us provide ourselves with a most ample port of refuge: that, enduring all things nobly and thankfully, we may both in the present life cast off all despondency, and receive the rewards that belong to this good way of taking things;[2] by the grace and mercy of our Lord Jesus Christ, with Whom to the Father, with the Holy Ghost, be glory, power, and honor, now and forever, world without end. Amen.

HOMILY XXIX.

1 COR, XII. 1, 2.

Now concerning spiritual gifts, brethren, I would not have you ignorant. Ye know that when ye were Gentiles, ye were led away unto those dumb idols, howsoever ye might be led.

THIS whole place is very obscure: but the obscurity is produced by our ignorance of the facts referred to and by their cessation, being such as then used to occur but now no longer take place. And why do they not happen now? Why look now, the cause too of the obscurity hath produced us again another question: namely, why did they then happen, and now do so no more?

This however let us defer to another time, but for the present let us state what things were occurring then. Well: what did happen then? Whoever was baptized he straightway spake with tongues and not with tongues only, but many also prophesied, and some also performed many other wonderful works. For since on their coming over from idols, without any clear knowledge or training in the ancient Scriptures, they at once on their baptism received the Spirit, yet the Spirit they saw not, for It is invisible; therefore God's grace bestowed some sensible proof of that energy. And one straightway spake in the Persian, another in the Roman, another in the Indian, another in some other such tongue: and this made manifest to them that were without that it is the Spirit in the

very person speaking. Wherefore also he so calls it, saying, "But to each one the manifestation of the Spirit is given to profit withal;" (v. 7.) calling the gifts "a manifestation of the Spirit." For as the Apostles themselves had received this sign first, so also the faithful went on receiving it, I mean, the gift of tongues; yet not this only but also many others: inasmuch as many used even to raise the dead and to cast out devils and to perform many other such wonders: and they had gifts too, some less, and some more. But more abundant than all was the gift of tongues among them: and this became to them a cause of division; not from its own nature but from the perverseness of them that had received it: in that on the one hand the possessors of the greater gifts were lifted up against them that had the lesser: and these again were grieved, and envied the owners of the greater. And Paul himself as he proceeds intimates this.

Since then herefrom they were receiving a fatal blow in the dissolution of their charity, he takes great care to correct it. For this happened indeed in Rome also, but not in the same way. And this is why in the Epistle to the Romans he moots it indeed, but obscurely and briefly, saying thus: "For even as we have many members in one body, and all the members have not

---

[1] παθημάτων Savile: μαθητῶν Bened.
[2] τῆς εὐφημίας ταύτης, "this way of using well-omened words."

the same office ; so we, who are many, are one body in Christ, and severally members one of another. And having gifts differing according to the grace that was given to us, whether prophecy, let us prophesy according to the proportion of our faith ; or ministry, let us give ourselves to our ministry ; or he that teacheth to his teaching." (Rom. xii. 4 8.) And that the Romans also were falling into wilfulness hereby, this he intimates in the beginning of that discourse, thus saying : " For I say through the grace given unto me, to every man that is among you, not to think of himself more highly than he ought to think ; but so to think as to think soberly, according as God hath dealt to each man a measure of faith." (Rom. xii. 3.) With these, however, (for the disease of division and pride had not proceeded to any length,) he thus discoursed : but here with great anxiety ; for the distemper had greatly spread.

And this was not the only thing to disturb them, but there were also in the place many soothsayers, inasmuch as the city was more than usually addicted to Grecian customs, and this with the rest was tending to offence and disturbance among them. This is the reason why he begins by first stating the difference between soothsaying and prophecy. For this cause also they received discerning of spirits, so as to discern and know which is he that speaketh by a pure spirit, and which by an impure.

For because it was not possible to supply the evidence of the things uttered from within themselves at the moment ; (for prophecy supplies the proof of its own truth not at the time when it is spoken, but at the time of the event ;) and it was not easy to distinguish the true prophesier from the pretender ; (for the devil himself, accursed as he is, had entered into them that prophesied, [See 1 Kings xxii. 23.] bringing in false prophets, as if forsooth they also could foretell things to come ;) and further, men were easily deceived, because the things spoken could not for the present be brought to trial, ere yet the events had come to pass concerning which the prophecy was ; (for it was the end that proved the false prophet and the true :)—in order that the hearers might not be deceived before the end, he gives them a sign which even before the event served to indicate the one and the other. And hence taking his order and beginning, he thus goes on also to the discourse concerning the gifts and corrects the contentiousness that arose from hence likewise. For the present however he begins the discourse concerning the soothsayers, thus saying,

[2.] " Now concerning spiritual gifts, brethren, I would not have you ignorant ; " calling the signs " spiritual," because they are the works of the Spirit alone, human effort contributing nothing to the working such wonders. And intending to discourse concerning them, first, as I said, he lays down the difference between soothsaying and prophecy, thus saying,

" Ye know that when ye were Gentiles, ye were led away[1] unto those dumb idols, howsoever ye might be led." Now what he means is this : " In the idol-temples," saith he, " if any were at any time possessed by an unclean spirit and began to divine, even as one dragged away, so was he drawn by that spirit in chains : knowing nothing of the things which he utters. For this is peculiar to the soothsayer, to be beside himself, to be under compulsion, to be pushed, to be dragged, to be haled as a madman. But the prophet not so, but with sober mind and composed temper and knowing what he is saying, he uttereth all things. Therefore even before the event do thou from this distinguish the soothsayer and the prophet. And consider how he frees his discourse of all suspicion ; calling themselves to witness who had made trial of the matter. As if he had said, " that I lie not nor rashly traduce the religion of the Gentiles, feigning like an enemy, do ye yourselves bear me witness : knowing as ye do, when ye were Gentiles, how ye were pulled and dragged away then."

But if any should say that these too are suspected as believers, come, even from them that are without will I make this manifest to you. Hear, for example, Plato saying thus : (Apol. Soc. c. 7.) " Even as they who deliver oracles and the soothsayers say many and excellent things, but know nothing of what they utter." Hear again another, a poet, giving the same intimation. For whereas by certain mystical rites and witchcrafts a certain person had imprisoned a demon in a man, and the man divined, and in his divination was thrown down and torn, and was unable to endure the violence of the demon, but was on the point of perishing in that convulsion; he saith to the persons who were practicing such mystical arts,[2]

Loose me, I pray you :
The mighty God no longer mortal flesh
Can hold.

And again,

Unbind my wreaths, and bathe my feet in drops
From the pure stream ; erase these mystic lines,[3]
And let me go.

For these and such like things, (for one might

---

[1] ἀπαγόμενοι, properly "dragged to prison or execution."

[2] These verses are taken from an old Oracle, quoted among others by Porphyry in a Treatise *of the Philosophy of Oracles*, and from him again by Theodoret, on *the Remedies for Gentile Errors*, Disp. x. t. iv. p. 957.

[3] Porphyry's note on this verse, as quoted by Hales from Eusebius (Evang. Præp. v.) in Savile's Chrysostom, viii. pt. ii. p. 278, is as follows : " You see, he bids them erase the lines that he may depart : as though these detained him, and not only these, but the other things too about their apparel : because they wore certain portraitures of the deities who were invoked."

mention many more,) point out to us both of these facts which follow; the compulsion which holds dowɒ the demons and makes them slaves; and the violence to which they submit who have once given themselves up to them, so as to swerve even from their natural reason. And the Pythoness too[1]: (for I am compelled now to bring forward and expose another disgraceful custom of theirs, which it were well to pass by, because it is unseemly for us to mention such things; but that you may more clearly know their shame it is necessary to mention it, that hence at least ye may come to know the madness and exceeding mockery of those that make use of the soothsayers:) this same Pythoness then is said, being a female, to sit at times upon the tripod of Apollo astride, and thus the evil spirit ascending from beneath and entering the lower part of her body, fills the woman with madness, and she with dishevelled hair begins to play the bacchanal and to foam at the mouth, and thus being in a frenzy to utter the words of her madness. I know that you are ashamed and blush when you hear these things: but they glory both in the disgrace and in the madness which I have described. These then and all such things Paul was bringing forward when he said, "Ye know that when ye were Gentiles, ye were led away unto those dumb idols, howsoever ye might be led."

And because he was discoursing with those who knew well, he states not all things with exact care, not wishing to be troublesome to them, but having reminded them only and brought all into their recollection, he soon quits the point, hastening to the subject before him.

But what is, "unto those dumb idols?" These soothsayers used to be led and dragged unto them.

But if they be themselves dumb, how did they give responses to others? And wherefore did the demon lead them to the images? As men taken in war, and in chains, and rendering at the same time his deceit plausible. Thus, to keep men from the notion that it was just a dumb stone, they were earnest to rivet the people to the idols that their own style and title might be inscribed upon them. But our rites are not such. He did not however state ours, I mean the prophesyings. For it was well known to them all, and prophecy was exercised among them, as was meet for their condition, with understanding and with entire freedom. Therefore, you see, they had power either to speak or to refrain from speaking. For they were not bound by necessity, but were honored with a privilege. For this cause Jonah fled; (Jonah, i. 3.) for this cause Ezekiel delayed; (Ezek. iii. 15.) for this cause Jeremiah excused

himself. (Jer. i. 6.) And God thrusts them not on by compulsion, but advising, exhorting, threatening; not darkening their mind; for to cause distraction and madness and great darkness, is the proper work of a demon: but it is God's work to illuminate and with consideration to teach things needful.

[3.] This then is the first difference between a soothsayer and a prophet; but a second and a different one is that which he next states, saying,

Ver. 3. "Wherefore I give you to understand, that no man speaking in the Spirit of God calleth Jesus accursed:" and then another: "and that no man can say that Jesus is the Lord, but in the Holy Ghost."

"When thou seest," saith he, "any one not uttering His name, or anathematizing Him, he is a soothsayer. Again, when thou seest another speaking all things with His Name, understand that he is spiritual." "What then," say you, "must we say concerning the Catechumens? For if, no man can say that Jesus is the Lord but by the Holy Ghost, 'what must we say of them who name indeed His Name, but are destitute of His Spirit[2]? But his discourse at this time was not concerning these for there were not at that time Catechumens, but concerning believers and unbelievers.

What then, doth no demon call upon God's Name? Did not the demoniacs say, "We know Thee who Thou art, the Holy One of God? (Mark i. 24.) Did they not say to Paul, "these men are the servants of the Most High God? (Acts xvi. 17.) They did, but upon scourging, upon compulsion; never of their own will and without being scourged.

But here it is proper to enquire, both why the demon uttered these things and why Paul rebuked him. In imitation of his Teacher; for so Christ did also rebuke: since it was not his will to have testimony from them. And wherefore did the devil also practise this? Intending to confound the order of things, and to seize upon the dignity of the Apostles, and to persuade many to pay attention to them[3]: which had it happened, they would easily have made themselves appear from hence worthy of credit, and have brought in their own designs. That these things then might not be, and the deceit might not have a beginning, he stops their mouths even when speaking the truth, so that in their falsehoods men should not at all give heed unto them, but stop their ears altogether against the things said by them.

[4.] Having therefore made manifest the

---

[1] See Strabo, ix. 5.

[2] So St. Austin, Tract 11. on St John: "Inasmuch as the Catechumens have the sign of the Cross in their forehead, they now belong to the Great House: but let them from servants become sons;" alluding to Gal. iv. 6, 7; ap. Bingham, i. 3. 3.

[3] Sav. in marg. reads αὐτοῖς. Bened. αὐτῷ.

soothsayers and the prophets both by the first sign and also by the second, he next discourses of the wonders; not passing without reason to this topic, but so as to remove the dissension which had thence arisen, and to persuade both those that had the less portion not to grieve and those who had the greater not to be elated. Wherefore also he thus began.

Ver. 4. "Now there are diversities of gifts, but the same Spirit."

And first he attends on him that had the lesser gift, and was grieved on this account. "For wherefore," saith he, "art thou dejected? because thou hast not received as much as another? Still, consider that it is a free gift and not a debt, and thou wilt be able to soothe thy pain." For this cause he spake thus in the very beginning: "but there are diversities of gifts." And he said not "of signs," nor "of wonders," but of "gifts," by the name of free gifts prevailing on them not only not to grieve but even to be thankful. "And withal consider this also," saith he, "that even if thou art made inferior in the measure of what is given; in that it hath been vouchsafed thee to receive from the same source as the other who hath received more, thou hast equal honor. For certainly thou canst not say that the Spirit bestowed the gift on him, but an angel on thee: since the Spirit bestowed it both on thee and him. Wherefore he added, "but the same Spirit." So that even if there be a difference in the gift, yet is there no difference in the Giver. For from the same Fountain ye are drawing, both thou and he.

Ver. 5. "And there are diversities of ministrations, but the same Lord."

Thus, enriching the consolation, he adds mention of the Son also, and of the Father. And again, he calls these gifts by another name, designing by this also an increase of consolation. Wherefore also he thus said: "there are diversities of ministrations, but the same Lord." For he that hears of "a gift," and hath received a less share, perhaps might grieve; but when we speak of "a ministration," the case is different. For the thing implies labor and sweat. "Why grievest thou then," saith he, "if he hath bidden another labor more, sparing thee?"

Ver. 6. "And there are diversities of workings, but the same God who worketh all things in all."

Ver. 7. "But to each one is given the manifestation of the Spirit to profit withal."

"And what," saith one, "is a working?" and what "a gift?" and what "a ministration?" They are mere differences of names, since the things are the same. For what "a gift" is, that is "a ministration," that he calls "an operation" also. Thus fulfil thy ministry; (2 Tim. iv. 5. *ministry*.) and, "I magnify my

ministration:" (Rom. xi. 13. *office*.) and writing to Timothy, he says, "Therefore I put thee in remembrance that thou stir up the gift of God, which is in thee. (2 Tim. i. 6.) And again, writing to the Galatians, he said, "for he that wrought in Peter to the Apostleship, the same was mighty in me toward the Gentiles. (Gal. ii. 8.) Seest thou that he implies that there is no difference in the gifts of the Father, and the Son, and the Holy Ghost? Not confounding[1] the Persons, God forbid! but declaring the equal honor of the Essence. For that which the Spirit bestows, this he saith that God also works; this, that the Son likewise ordains and grants. Yet surely if the one were inferior to the other, or the other to it, he would not have thus set it down nor would this have been his way of consoling the person who was vexed.

[5.] Now after this, he comforts him also in another kind of way; by the consideration that the measure vouchsafed is profitable to him, even though it be not so large. For having said, that it is "the same Spirit," and "the same Lord," and "the same God," and having thereby recovered him, he brings in again another consolation, thus saying, "but to each one is given the manifestation of the Spirit to profit withal." For lest one should say, "what if there be the same Lord, the same Spirit, the same God? yet I have received less:" he saith, that thus it was profitable.

But he calls miracles a "manifestation of the Spirit," with evident reason. For to me who am a believer, he that hath the Spirit is manifest from his having been baptized: but to the unbeliever this will in no wise be manifest, except from the miracles: so that hence also again there is no small consolation. For though there be a difference of gifts, yet the evidence is one: since whether thou hast much or little, thou art equally manifest. So that if thou desirest to show this, that thou hast the Spirit, thou hast a sufficient demonstration.

Wherefore, now that both the Giver is one and the thing given a pure favor, and the manifestation takes place thereby, and this is more profitable for thee; grieve not as if despised. For not to dishonor thee hath God done it, nor to declare thee inferior to another, but to spare thee and with a view to thy welfare. To receive more than one has ability to bear, this rather is unprofitable, and injurious, and a fit cause of dejection.

Ver. 8. "For to one is given through the Spirit the word of wisdom; to another the word of knowledge according to the same Spirit;"

Ver. 9. "To another, faith in the same Spirit; to another gifts of healing in the one Spirit."

---

[1] τὰς ὑποστάσεις συναλείφων.

Seest thou how he every where makes this addition, saying, "through the same Spirit, and according to the same Spirit?" For he knew that the comfort from thence was great.

Ver. 10. "To another working of miracles; to another prophecies; to another discernings of spirits; to another divers kind of tongues; to another the interpretation of tongues."

Thus, since they boasted themselves in this, therefore he placed it last, and added,

Ver. 11. "But all these worketh one and the same Spirit."

The universal medicine in which his consolation consists is that out of the same root, out of the same treasures, out of the same streams, they all receive. And accordingly, from time to time dwelling on this expression, he levels the apparent inequality, and consoles them. And above indeed he points out both the Spirit, and the Son, and the Father, as supplying the gifts, but here he was content to make the Spirit, that even hence again thou mayest understand their dignity to be the same.

But what is "the word of wisdom?" That which Paul had, which John had, the son of thunder.

And what is "the word of knowledge?" That which most of the faithful had, possessing indeed knowledge, but not thereupon able to teach nor easily to convey to another what they knew.

"And to another, faith:" not meaning by this faith the faith of doctrines, but the faith of miracles; concerning which Christ saith, "If ye have faith as a grain of mustard-seed, ye shall say to this mountain, Remove, and it shall remove." (S. Mat. xvii. 20.) And the Apostles too concerning this besought Him, saying, "Increase our faith:" (S. Luke xvii. 5.) for this is the mother of the miracles. But to possess the power of working miracles and gifts of healing, is not the same thing: for he that had a gift of healing used only to do cures: but he that possessed powers for working miracles used to punish also. For a miracle is not the healing only, but the punishing also: even as Paul inflicted blindness: as Peter slew.

"To another prophecies; and to another discernings of spirits." What is, "discernings of spirits?" the knowing who is spiritual, and who is not: who is a prophet, and who a deceiver: as he said to the Thessalonians, "despise not prophesyings:" (Thes. v. 20, 21.) but proving[1] all things, hold fast that which is good." For great was at that time the rush[2] of the false prophets, the devil striving underhand to substitute falsehood for the truth.

"To another divers kinds of tongues; to another the interpretation of tongues." For one person knew what he spake himself, but was unable to interpret to another; while another had acquired both these or the other of the two. Now this seemed to be a great gift because both the Apostles received it first, and the most among the Corinthians had obtained it. But the word of teaching not so. Wherefore that he places first, but this last: for this was on account of that, and so indeed were all the rest; both prophecies, and working of miracles, and divers kinds of tongues, and interpretation of tongues. For none is equal to this. Wherefore also he said, "Let the elders that rule well be counted worthy of double honor, especially they who labor in the word and in teaching." (1 Tim. v. 17.) And to Timothy he wrote, saying, "Give attendance to reading, to exhortation, to teaching; neglect not the gift that is in thee." (1 Tim. iv. 13, 14.) Seest thou how he calls it also a gift?

[6.] Next, the comfort which he before gave, when he said, "the same Spirit," this also he here sets before us, saying, "But all these worketh the one and the same Spirit, dividing to each one severally even as he will." And he not only gives consolation but also stops the mouth of the gainsayer, saying here, "dividing to each one severally even as he will." For it was necessary to bind[3] up also, not to heal only, as he doth also in the Epistle to the Romans, when he saith, "But who art thou that repliest against God? (Rom. ix. 20.) So likewise here, "dividing to each one severally as he will."

And that which was of the Father, this he signifieth to be of the Spirit also. For as concerning the Father, he saith, "but it is the same God who worketh all things in all;" so also concerning the Spirit, "but all these things worketh one and the same Spirit." But,[4] it will be said, "He doth it, actuated by God." Nay, he no where said this, but thou feignest it. For when he saith, "who actuateth[5] all things in all," he saith this concerning men: thou wilt hardly say that among those men he numbers also the Spirit, though thou shouldst be ever so manifold in thy doting and madness. For because he had said "through the Spirit," that thou mightest not suppose this word, "through," to denote inferiority or the being actuated, he adds, that "the Spirit worketh," not "is worked,"[6] and worketh "as he will," not as he is bidden. For as concerning the Father, the Son saith that "He raiseth up the dead and quickeneth;" in like manner also, concerning

---

[1] δοκιμάζοντες; rec. text δοκιμάζετε.
[2] Savile reads διαφορὰ, "variety"
[3] ἐπιστύφειν.
[4] In this and other places of this Homily, S. Chrysostom seems to have had in view the controversy, then recent, with the Macedonians, who denied the Divinity of the Holy Spirit.
[5] ἐνεργῶν "worketh."
[6] ἐνεργεῖ, οὐκ ἐνεργεῖται.

Himself, that "He quickeneth whom He will:" (S. John v. 21.) thus also of the Spirit, in another place, that He doeth all things with authority and that there is nothing that hinders Him; (for the expression, "bloweth where it listeth" [S. John iii. 8,] though it be spoken of the wind is apt to establish this;) but here, that "He worketh all things as He will." And from another place to learn that He is not one of the things actuated, but of those that actuate. "For who knoweth," says he, "the things of a man, but the spirit of the man? even so the things of God none knoweth save the Spirit of God." (1. Cor. ii. 11.) Now that "the spirit of a man," i. e., the soul, requires not to be actuated that it may know the things of itself, is, I suppose, evident to every one. Therefore neither doth the Holy Ghost, that he may "know the things of God." For his meaning is like this, "the secret things of God" are known to the Holy Spirit as to the soul of man the secret things of herself." But if this be not actuated for that end, much less would That which knoweth the depths of God and needs no actuation for that knowledge, require any actuating Power in order to the giving gifts to the Apostles.

But besides these things, that also, which I before spake of, I will mention again now. What then is this? That if the Spirit were inferior and of another substance, there would have been no avail in his consolation, nor in our hearing the words, " of the same Spirit." For he who hath received from the king, I grant, may find it a very soothing circumstance, that he himself gave to him; but if it be from the slave, he is then rather vexed, when one reproaches him with it. So that even hence is it evident, that the Holy Spirit is not of the substance of the servant, but of the King.

[7.] Wherefore as he comforted them, when he said, that "there are diversities of ministrations, but the same Lord; and diversities of operations, but the same God;" so also when he said above, "there are diversities of gifts, but the same Spirit;" and after this again when he said, " But all these worketh the one and the same Spirit, dividing to every man severally as he will."

"Let us not, I pray you, be at a loss," saith he; "neither let us grieve, saying, 'Why have I received this and not received that?' neither let us demand an account of the Holy Spirit. For if thou knowest that he vouchsafed it from providential care, consider that from the same care he hath given also the measure of it, and be content and rejoice in what thou hast received: but murmur not at what thou hast not received; yea, rather confess God's favor that thou hast not received things beyond thy power.

[5.] And if in spiritual things one ought not to be over-curious, much more in temporal things; but to be quiet and not nicely enquire why one is rich and another poor. For, first of all, not every single rich man is rich from God, but many even of unrighteousness, and rapine, and avarice. For he that forbade to be rich, how can he have granted that which he forbade to receive?

But that I may, far above what the case requires, stop the mouths of those who concerning these things gainsay us, come, let us carry our discourse higher up, to the time when riches used to be given by God; and answer me. Wherefore was Abraham rich whereas Jacob wanted even bread? Were not both the one and the other righteous? Doth He not say concerning the three alike, " I am the God of Abraham, and of Isaac, and of Jacob?" (Exod. iii. 6.) Wherefore then was the one a rich man, and the other a hired servant? Or rather, why was Esau rich, who was unrighteous and a murderer of his brother, while Jacob was in bondage for so long a time? Wherefore again did Isaac live in ease all his time, but Jacob in toils and miseries? For which cause also he said, " Few and evil are my days." (Gen. xlvii. 9.)

Wherefore did David, who was both a prophet and a king, himself also live all his time in toils? whereas Solomon his son spent forty years in security above all men, in the enjoyment of profound peace, glory, and honor, and going through every kind of deliciousness? What again could be the reason, that among the prophets also one was afflicted more, and another less? Because so it was expedient for each. Wherefore upon each our remark must be, " Thy judgments are a great deep." (Ps. xxxvi. 6.) For if those great and wonderful men were not alike exercised by God, but one by poverty, and another by riches; one by ease, and another by trouble; much more ought we now to bear these things in mind.

[8.] But besides this, it becomes one to consider also that many of the things which happen do not take place according to His mind, but arise from our wickedness. Say not then, " Why is one man rich who is wicked, and another poor who is righteous?" For first of all, one may give an account of these things also, and say that neither doth the righteous receive any harm from his poverty, nay, even a greater addition of honor; and that the bad man in his riches possesseth but a store of punishment on his future road, unless he be changed: and, even before punishment, often-times his riches become to him the cause of many evils, and lead him into ten thousand pitfalls. But God permits it, at the same to signify the free choice of the will, and also to teach all others not to be mad nor rave after money.

" How is it then, when a man being wicked is rich, and suffers nothing dreadful ? " say you. " Since if being good he hath wealth, he hath it justly : but if bad, what shall we say ? " That even therein he is to be pitied. For wealth added to wickedness aggravates the mischief. But is he a good man, and poor ? Yet is he nothing injured. Is he then a bad man, and poor ? This is he so justly and by desert, or rather even with advantage to himself. " But such an one," say you, " received his riches from his ancestors and lavishes it upon harlots and parasites, and suffers no evil." What sayest thou ? Doth he commit whoredom, and sayest thou, " he suffers no evils ? " Is he drunken, and thinkest thou that he is in luxury ? Doth he spend for no good, and judgest thou that he is to be envied ? Nay what can be worse than this wealth which destroys the very soul ? But thou, if the body were distorted and maimed, wouldest say that his was a case for great lamentation ; and seest thou his whole soul mutilated, yet countest him even happy ? " But he doth not perceive it," say you. Well then, for this very reason again is he to be pitied, as all frantic persons are. For he that knows he is sick will of course both seek the physician and submit to remedies ; but he that is ignorant of it will have no chance at all of deliverance. Dost thou call such an one happy, tell me ?

But it is no marvel : for the more part are ignorant of the true love of wisdom. Therefore do we suffer the extremest penalty, being chastised and not even withdrawing ourselves from the punishment. For this cause are angers, dejections, and continual tumults ; because when God hath shown us a life without sorrow, the life of virtue, we leave this and mark out another way, the way of riches and money, full of infinite evils. And we do the same, as if one, not knowing how to discern the beauty of men's bodies but attributing the whole to the clothes and the ornaments worn, when he saw a handsome woman and possessed of natural beauty, should pass quickly by her, but when he beheld one ugly, illshaped, and deformed, but clothed in beautiful garments, should take her for his wife. Now also in some such way are the multitude affected about virtue and vice. They admit the one that is deformed by nature on account of her external ornaments, but turn away from her that is fair and lovely, on account of her unadorned beauty, for which cause they ought especially to choose her.

[9.] Therefore am I ashamed that among the foolish heathen there are those that practise this philosophy, if not in deeds, yet so far at least as judgment goes ; and who know the perish-able nature of things present : whereas amongst us some do not even understand these things, but have their very judgment corrupted : and this while the Scripture is ever and anon sounding in our ears, and saying, " In his sight the vile person is contemned, but he honoreth them that fear the Lord : (Ps. xv. 4.) the fear of the Lord excelleth every thing[1]; fear God, and keep His commandments ; for this is the whole of man : (Eccles. xii. 13 ;) be not thou envious of evil men ; (Ps. xlix. 16 ;) all flesh is grass, and all the glory of man as the flower of grass ;" (Isa. xl. 7.) For these and · such-like things though we hear every day, we are yet nailed to earth. And as ignorant children, who learn their letters continuously, if they be examined concerning their order when they are disarranged, naming one instead of another, make much laughter : so also ye, when here we recount them in order, follow us in a manner ; but when we ask you out of doors and in no set order, what we ought to place first and what next among things, and which after which ; not knowing how to answer, ye become ridiculous. Is it not a matter of great laughter, tell me, that they who expect immortality and the good " things which eye hath not seen, nor ear heard, neither have entered into the heart of man," should strive about things which linger here and count them enviable ? For if thou hast need yet to learn these things that riches are no great thing, that things present are a shadow and a dream, that like smoke they are dissolved and fly away : stand for the present without the sanctuary : abide in the vestibule : since thou art not yet worthy of the entrance to the palace-courts on high. For if thou knowest not to discern their nature which is unstable and continually passing away, when wilt thou be able to despise them ?

But if thou say thou knowest, cease curiously to inquire and busy thyself, what can be the reason why such an one is rich and such an one poor : for thou doest the same when thou askest these questions, as if thou didst go round and enquire, why one is fair and another black, or one hook-nosed and another flat-nosed. For as these things make no difference to us, whether it be thus or thus ; so neither poverty nor riches, and much less than they. But the whole depends upon the way in which we use them. Whether thou art poor, thou mayest live cheerfully denying thyself ; or rich, thou art most miserable of all men if thou fliest from virtue. For these are what really concern us, the things of virtue. And if these things be not added, the rest are useless. For this cause also are those continual questions, because the most think that indifferent things are of importance

---

[1] Or, the love of the Lord.   Sirach xxv. 14.

to them, but of the important things they make no account: since that which is of importance to us is virtue and love of wisdom.

Because then ye stand I know not where, at some far distance from her, therefore is there confusion of thoughts, therefore the many waves, therefore the tempest. For when men have fallen from heavenly glory and the love of heaven, they desire present glory and become slaves and captives. "And how is it that we desire this," say you? From the not greatly desiring that. And this very thing, whence happens it? From negligence. And whence the negligence? From contempt. And whence the contempt? From folly and cleaving to things present and unwillingness to investigate accurately the nature of things. And whence again doth this latter arise? From the neither giving heed to the reading of the Scripture nor conversing with holy men, and from following the assemblies of the wicked.

That this therefore may not always be so, and lest wave after wave receiving us should carry us out into the deep of miseries and altogether drown and destroy us; while there is time, let us bear up and standing upon the rock, I mean of the divine doctrines and words, let us look down upon the surge of this present life. For thus shall we both ourselves escape the same, and having drawn up others who are making shipwreck, we shall obtain the blessings which are to come, through the grace and mercy, &c.

HOMILY XXX.

1 Cor. xii. 12.

For as the body is one, and hath many members, and all the members of the body, being many, are one body; so also is Christ.

After soothing them from the considerations that the thing given was of free favor; that they received all from "one and the self-same Spirit;" that it was given "to profit withal," that even by the lesser gifts a manifestation was made; and withal having also stopped their mouth from the duty of yielding to the authority of the Spirit: ("for all these," saith he, "worketh the one and the same Spirit, dividing to each one severally even as he will;" wherefore it is not right to be over-curious:) he proceeds now to soothe them in like manner from another common example, and betakes himself to nature itself, as was his use to do.

For when he was discoursing about the hair of men and women, after all the rest he drew matter thence also to correct them, saying, "Doth not even nature itself teach you that if a man have long hair, it is a dishonor to him? but if a woman have long hair, it is a glory to her?" (1 Cor. xi. 14, 15.) And when he spake concerning the idol-sacrifices, forbidding to touch them, he drew an argument from the examples also of them that are without, both making mention of the Olympic games, where he saith, "they which run in a race run all, but one receiveth the prize:" (1 Cor. ix. 24.) and confirming these views from shepherds and soldiers and husbandmen. Wherefore he brings forward here also a common example by which he presses on and fights hard to prove that no one was really put in a worse condition: a thing which was marvellous and surprising to be able to show, and calculated to refresh the weaker sort, I mean, the example of the body. For nothing so consoles the person of small spirit and inferior gifts, or so persuades him not to grieve, as the being convinced that he is not left with less than his share. Wherefore also Paul making out this point, thus expresses himself: "for as the body is one and hath many members."

Seest thou his exact consideration? He is pointing out the same thing to be both one and many. Wherefore also he adds, pressing the point more vigorously, "and all the members of the one body, being many, are one body." He said not, "being many, are of one body," but "the one body itself is many:" and those many members are this one thing. If therefore the one is many, and the many are one, where is the difference? where the superiority? where the disadvantage? For all, saith he, are one: and not simply one, but being strictly considered in respect of that even which is principal, i. e., their being a body, they are found all to be one: but when considered as to their particular natures, then the difference comes out, and the difference is in all alike. For none of them by itself can make a body, but each is alike deficient in the making a body, and there is need of a coming together: since when the many become one, then and not till then is there one body. Wherefore also covertly intimating this very thing, he said, "And all the members of the one body, being many, are one body." And he said not, "the superior and the inferior," but "being many," which is common to all.

And how is it possible that they should be one? When throwing out the difference of the members, thou considerest the body. For the same thing which the eye is, this also is the foot, in regard of its being a member and constituting a body. For there is no difference in this respect. Nor canst thou say that one of the members makes a body of itself, but another does not. For they are all equal in this, for the very reason that they are all one body.

But having said this and having shown it clearly from the common judgment of all, he added, "so also is Christ." And when he should have said, "so also is the Church," for this was the natural consequent he doth not say it but instead of it places the name of Christ, carrying the discourse up on high and appealing more and more to the hearer's reverence. But his meaning is this: "So also is the body of Christ, which is the Church." For as the body and the head[1] are one man, so he said that the Church and Christ are one. Wherefore also he placed Christ instead of the Church, giving that name to His body. "As then," saith he, "our body is one thing though it be composed of many: so also in the Church we all are one thing. For though the Church be composed of many members, yet these many form one body."

[2.] Thus having, you see, recovered and raised up by this common example him who thought himself depreciated, again he leaves the topic of common experience, and comes to another, a spiritual one, bringing greater consolation and indicative of great equality of honor. What then is this?

Ver. 13. "For in one Spirit, saith he, were we all baptized into one body, whether Jews or Greeks, whether bond or free."

Now his meaning is this: that which established us to become one body and regenerated us, is one Spirit: for not in one Spirit was one baptized, and another another. And not only is that which hath baptized us one, but also that unto which[2] He baptized us, i. e., for which[2] He baptized us, is one. For we were baptized not that so many several bodies might be formed,

but that we might all preserve one with another the perfect nature of one body: i. e., that we might all be one body, into the same were we baptized.

So that both He who formed it is one, and that into which He formed it is one. And he said not, "that we might all come to be of the same body;" but, "that we might all be one body." For he ever strives to use the more expressive phrases. And well said he, "we all," adding also himself. "For not even I, the Apostle, have any more than thou in this respect," saith he. "For thou art the body even as I, and I even as thou, and we have all the same Head and have passed through[3] the same birth-pains. Wherefore we are also the same body." "And why speak I," saith he, "of the Jews? since even the Gentiles who were so far off from us, He hath brought into the entireness of one body." Wherefore having said, "we all," he stopped not here, but added, "whether Jews or Greeks, whether bond or free." Now if, having before been so far off, we were united and have become one, much more after that we have become one, we can have no right to grieve and be dejected. Yea, the difference, in fact, hath no place. For if to Greeks and Jews, to bond and free, He hath vouchsafed the same blessings, how can it be that after so vouchsafing He divides them, now that He hath bestowed a greater perfection of unity by the supply of His gifts?

"And were all made to drink of one Spirit."

Ver. 14. "For the body is not one member, but many."

i. e., We are come to the same initiation, we enjoy the same Table. And why said he not, "we are nourished by the same body and drink the same blood?" Because by saying "Spirit," he declared them both, as well the flesh as the blood. For through both are we "made to drink of the Spirit."

But to me he appears now to speak of that visitation of the Spirit which takes place in us after Baptism and before the Mysteries. And he said, "We were made to drink," because this metaphorical speech suited him extremely well for his proposed subject: as if he had said respecting plants and a garden, that by the same fountain all the trees are watered, or by the same water; so also here, "we all drank the same Spirit, we enjoyed the same grace," saith he.

If now one Spirit both formed us and gathered us all together into one body; for this is the meaning of, "we were baptized into one body:" and vouchsafed us one table, and gave us all the same watering, (for this is the mean-

---

[1] [The author seems here to imply that the Apostle speaks of Christ simply as the head of the church, the same view which Meyer advocates. It is better to consider the expression as denoting the analogy of the body to Christ, since it is one body yet has many members. Christ is the personal subject, the "Ego" whose body is the church. "Christus non localiter, sed mystice et virtualiter, sive operative et per efficentiam, est corpus, hypostasis, anima et spiritus totius Ecclesiæ." (Cor. a Lap.) Principal Edwards says that the Apostle's meaning if expressed in modern phrase would run thus: "As the Person is one while the members of his body are many, so also Christ is one but the members of his mystical body, the church, are many." C.]

[2] εἰς ὅ—ἐφ' ᾧ.

[3] ἐλύσαμεν.

ing of, "we were made to drink into one Spirit[4],") and united persons so widely separated; and if many things then become a body when they are made one: why, I pray, art thou continually tossing to and fro their difference? But if thou sayest, "Because there are many members and diverse," know that this very thing is the wonder and the peculiar excellency of the body, when the things which are many and diverse make one. But if they were not many, it were not so wonderful and incredible that they should be one body; nay, rather they would not be a body at all.

[3.] This however he states last; but for the present he goes to the members themselves, saying thus:

Ver. 15. "If the foot shall say, Because I am not the hand, I am not of the body; is it therefore not of the body?"

Ver. 16. "And if the ear shall say, Because I am not the eye, I am not of the body; is it therefore not of the body?"

For if the one being made inferior and the other superior, doth not allow their being of the body, the whole is done away. Do not say therefore, "I am not the body, because I am inferior." For the foot also hath the inferior post, yet is it of the body: for the being or not being part of the body, is not from the one lying in this place and the other in that; (which is what constitutes difference of place;) but from the being conjoined or separated. For the being or not being a body, arises from the having been made one or not. But do thou, I pray, mark his considerate way, how he applies their words to our members. For as he said above, "These things have I in a figure transferred to myself and Apollos," (1 Cor. iv. 6.) just so likewise here, to make his argument free from invidiousness and acceptable, he introduces the members speaking: that when they shall hear nature answering them, being thus convicted by experience herself and by the general voice, they may have nothing further to oppose. "For say, if you will," saith he, "this very thing, murmur as you please, you cannot be out of the body. For as the law of nature, so much more doth the power of grace guard all things and preserve them entire." And see how he kept to the rule of having nothing superfluous; not working out his argument on all the members, but on two only and these the extremes; having specified both the most honorable of all, the

eye, and the meanest of all, the feet. And he doth not make the foot to discourse with the eye, but with the hand which is mounted a little above it; and the ear with the eyes. For because we are wont to envy not those who are very far above us, but those who are a little higher, therefore he also conducts his comparison thus.

Ver. 17. "If the whole body were an eye, where were the hearing? If the whole were hearing, where were the smelling?"

Thus, because, having fallen upon the difference of the members, and having mentioned feet, and hands, and eyes, and ears, he led them to the consideration of their own inferiority and superiority: see how again he consoles them, intimating that so it was expedient: and that their being many and diverse, this especially causeth them to be a body. But if they all were some one, they would not be a body. Wherefore, he saith, "If they were all one member, where were the body?" This however, he mentions not till afterwards; but here he points out also something more; that besides the impossibility of any one being a body, it even takes away the being of the rest.

"For if the whole were hearing, where were the smelling," saith he.

[4.] Then because after all they were yet disturbed: that which he had done above, the same he doth also now. For as there he first alleged the expediency to comfort them and afterwards stopped their mouths, vehemently saying, "But all these worketh the one and the same Spirit, dividing to each one man severally even as He will:" so also here having stated reasons for which he showed that it was profitable that all should so be, he refers the whole again to the counsel of God, saying,

Ver. 18. "But now God hath set the members each one of them in the body, even as it pleased Him."

Even as he said of the Spirit, "as He will," so also here, "as it pleased Him." Now do not thou seek further into the cause, why it is thus and why not thus. For though we have ten thousand reasons to give, we shall not be so able to show them that it is well done, as when we say, that as the best Artificer pleased, so it came to pass. For as it is expedient, so He wills it. Now if in this body of ours we do not curiously enquire about the members, much more in the Church. And see his thoughtfulness in that he doth not state the difference which arises from their nature nor that from their operation, but that from their local situation. For "now," saith he, "God hath set the members each one of them in the body even as it pleased Him." And he said well, "each one," pointing out that the use extends to all. For thou canst not say, "This He hath Himself placed but not that:

---

[4][The phrase here "drink into one Spirit" differs from that used in the citation above, where we read "drink of one Spirit." The difference exists in the Greek original. Chrysostom quotes what is now considered to be the correct text, omitting the preposition, but writes afterward, inserting it. There is unusual obscurity in his treatment of the passage. He expressly excludes any reference to the sacraments, saying it is "after baptism and before the mysteries," (i. e. the Lord's Supper), and then speaks of it as if it meant a watering of plants, which however is not natural. Most interpreters refer it baptism. C.]

but every one according to His will, so it is situated." So that to the foot also it is profitable that it should be so stationed, and not to the head only: and if it should invert the order and leaving its own place, should go to another, though it might seem to have bettered its condition, it would be the undoing and ruin of the whole. For it both falls from its own, and reaches not the other station.

[5.] Ver. 19. "And if they were all one member, where were the body?"

Ver. 20. "But now are they many members, but one body."

Thus having silenced them sufficiently by God's own arrangement, again he states reasons. And he neither doth this always nor that, but alternates and varies his discourse. Since on the one hand, he who merely silences, confounds the hearer, and he, on the contrary, who accustoms him to demand reasons for all things, injures him in the matter of faith; for this cause then Paul is continually practising both the one and the other, that they may both believe and may not be confounded; and after silencing them, he again gives a reason likewise. And mark his earnestness in the combat and the completeness of his victory. For from what things they supposed themselves unequal in honor because in them there was great diversity, even from these things he shows that for this very reason they are equal in honor. How, I will tell you.

"If all were one member," saith he, "where were the body?"

Now what he means is, If there were not among you great diversity, ye could not be a body; and not being a body, ye could not be one; and not being one, ye could not be equal in honor. Whence it follows again that if ye were all equal in honor, ye were not a body; and not being a body, ye were not one; and not being one, how could ye be equal in honor? As it is, however, because ye are not all endowed with some one gift, therefore are ye a body; and being a body, ye are all one, and differ nothing from one another in this that ye are a body. So that this very difference is that which chiefly causeth your equality in honor. And accordingly he adds, "But now they are many members, yet one body."

[6.] These things then let us also consider and cast out all envy, and neither grudge against them that have greater gifts nor despise them that possess the lesser. For thus had God willed: let us then not oppose ourselves. But if thou art still disturbed, consider that thy work is oft-times such as thy brother is unable to perform. So that even if thou art inferior, yet in this thou hast the advantage: and though he be greater, he is worse off in this respect; and so equality takes place. For in the body even the little

members seem to contribute no little, but the great ones themselves are often injured by them, I mean by their removal. Thus what in the body is more insignificant than the hair? Yet if thou shouldest remove this, insignificant as it is, from the eyebrows and the eyelids, thou hast destroyed all the grace of the countenance, and the eye will no longer appear equally beautiful. And yet the loss is of a trifle; but notwithstanding even thus all the comeliness is destroyed. And not the comeliness only, but much also of the use of the eyes. The reason is that every one of our members hath both a working of its own and one which is common; and likewise there is in us a beauty which is peculiar and another which is common. And these kinds of beauty appear indeed to be divided, but they are perfectly bound together, and when one is destroyed, the other perishes also along with it. To explain myself: let there be bright eyes, and a smiling cheek, and a red lip, and straight nose, and open brow; nevertheless, if thou mar but the slightest of these, thou hast marred the common beauty of all; all is full of dejection; all will appear foul to look on, which before was so beautiful: thus if thou shouldest crush only the tip of the nose thou hast brought great deformity upon all: and yet it is the maiming of but a single member. And likewise in the hand, if thou shouldest take away the nail from one finger, thou wouldest see the same result. If now thou wouldest see the same taking place in respect of their function[1] also, take away one finger, and thou wilt see the rest less active and no longer performing their part equally.

Since then the loss of a member is a common deformity, and its safety beauty to all, let us not be lifted up nor trample on our neighbors. For through that small member even the great one is fair and beautiful, and by the eyelids, slight as they are, is the eye adorned. So that he who wars with his brother wars with himself: for the injury done reaches not only unto that one, but himself also shall undergo no small loss.

[7.] That this then may not be, let us care for our neighbors as for ourselves, and let us transfer this image of the body now also to the Church, and be careful for all as for our own members. For in the Church also there are members many and diverse: and some are more honorable and some more deficient. For example, there are choirs of virgins, there are assemblies of widows, there are fraternities[2] of those who shine in holy wedlock[3]; in short, many are the

---

[1] ἐπὶ ἐνεργείας.

[2] φρατρίαι.

[3] See Bingham, vii. 2. 6; and as quoted by him, S. Athanas. *ad Dracont*, t. i. p. 263; S. Augustin. *de Hæres*. c. 40; in support of the opinion, that "there was an order of monks which lived in a married state, and enjoyed their own property and possessions as the primitive ascetics were used to do." If the opinion is correct, (the places quoted seem hardly to prove it,) this place of St. Chrysostom may perhaps refer to that order.

degrees of virtue. And in almsgiving again in like manner. For some empty themselves of all their goods: others care for a competency alone and seek nothing more than necessaries; others give of their superfluity: nevertheless, all these adorn one another; and if the greater should set at nought the less, he would in the greatest degree injure himself. Thus, suppose a virgin to deal scornfully with a married woman, she hath cut off no small part of her reward; and he again that emptied himself of all should he upbraid him that hath not done so, hath emptied himself of much of the fruit of his labors. And why speak I of virgins, and widows, and men without possessions? What is meaner than those who beg? and yet even these fulfill a most important office in the Church, clinging to the doors of the sanctuary[1] and supplying one of its greatest ornaments: and without these there could be no perfecting the fulness of the Church. Which thing, as it seems, the Apostles also observing made a law from the beginning, as in regard to all other things, so also that there should be widows: and so great care did they use about the matter as also to set over them seven deacons. For as bishops and presbyters and deacons and virgins and continent persons, enter into my enumeration, where I am reckoning up the members of the Church, so also do widows. Yea, and it is no mean office which they fill. For thou indeed comest here when thou wilt: but these both day and night sing psalms and attend: not for alms only doing this; since if that were their object, they might walk in the market place and beg in the alleys: but there is in them piety also in no small degree. At least, behold in what a furnace of poverty they are; yet never shalt thou hear a blasphemous word from them nor an impatient one, after the manner of many rich men's wives. Yet some of them often lie down to their rest in hunger, and others continue constantly frozen by the cold; nevertheless, they pass their time in thanksgiving and giving glory. Though you give but a penny, they give thanks and implore ten thousand blessings on the giver; and if thou give nothing they do not complain, but even so they bless, and think themselves happy to enjoy their daily food.

"Yes," it is replied, "since whether they will or no, they must bear it." Why, tell me? Wherefore hast thou uttered this bitter expression? Are there not shameful arts which bring gain to the aged, both men and women? Had they not power to support themselves by those means in great abundance, provided they had chosen to cast off all care of upright living? Seest thou not how many persons of that age, by becoming pimps and panders and by other such ministrations, both live, and live in luxury[2]? Not so these, but they choose rather to perish of hunger than to dishonor their own life and betray their salvation; and they sit throughout the whole day, preparing a medicine of salvation for thee.

For no physician stretching out the hand to apply the knife, works so effectually to cut out the corruption from our wounds, as doth a poor man stretching out his right hand and receiving alms, to take away the scars which the wounds have left. And what is truly wonderful, they perform this excellent chirurgery without pain and anguish: and we who are set over the people and give you so much wholesome advice, do not more truly discourse than he doth, who sits before the doors of the church, by his silence and his countenance. For we too sound these things in your ears every day, saying, "Be not high-minded, O man; human nature is a thing that soon declines and is ready to fall away; our youth hastens on to old age, our beauty to deformity, our strength to weakness, our honor to contempt, our health falls away to sickness, our glory to meanness, our riches to poverty; our concerns are like a violent current that never will stand still, but keeps hastening down the steep."

The same advice do they also give and more than this, by their appearance and by their experience itself too, which is a yet plainer kind of advice. How many, for instance, of those who now sit without, were in the bloom of youth and did great things? How many of these loathsome looking persons surpassed many, both in vigor of body and in beauty of countenance? Nay, disbelieve it not nor deride. For surely, life is full of ten thousand such examples. For if from mean and humble persons many have oftentimes become kings, what marvel is it if from being great and glorious, some have been made humble and mean? Since the former is much the more extraordinary: but the latter, of perpetual occurrence. So that one ought not to be incredulous that any of them ever flourished in arts, and arms, and abundance of wealth, but rather to pity them with great compassion and to fear for ourselves, lest we too should sometime suffer the same things. For

---

[1] Bingham, iv. 4. 1. "At the entrance of the interior Narthex," or Choir, "the Poor of the Church placed themselves, both before and after Divine Service, to ask alms of such as came from the Altar." S. Chrys. on I Thess. Hom. xi. near the end. "In the Churches, and in the Chapels of the Martyrs, the poor sit in front of the vestibules. . . When we enter into earthly palaces, there is no such thing to be seen, but grave, splendid, rich, wise men are hastening about on all sides. But at our entrance into the true palaces, the Church, and the houses of prayer of the Martyrs, there are possessed persons, maimed, poor, old, blind, distorted in their limbs." "They are an admirable sort of watch-dogs, keeping guard in the Courts of the Palace. Feed them therefore, for the honor redounds to their king. . . That human things are nought, thou art excellently instructed by the very Porch of the Church: that God delights not in wealth, thou art taught by those who sit before Him." For the custom of the Church of Rome, see the account of St. Lawrence's martyrdom in Prudentius, as quoted by Hooker, E. P. V. lxxix. 14.

[2] τρέφονται καὶ τρυφῶσεν.

we too are men and are subject to this speedy change.

[8.] But perchance some one of the thoughtless, and of those who are accustomed to scoff, will object to what hath been said, and will altogether deride us, saying, "How long wilt thou not cease continually introducing poor men and beggars in thy discourses, and prophesying to us of misfortunes, and denouncing poverty to come, and desiring to make us beggars?" Not from a desire to make beggars of you, O man, do I say these things, but hastening to open unto you the riches of heaven. Since he too, who to the healthy man makes mention of the sick and relates their anguish, saith it not to make him diseased, but to preserve him in health, by the fear of their calamities cutting off his remissness. Poverty seems to you to be a fearful thing and to be dreaded, even to the mere name of it. Yea, and therefore are we poor, because we are afraid of poverty; though we have ten thousand talents. For not he who hath nothing is poor, but he who shudders at poverty. Since in men's calamities also it is not those who suffer great evils whom we lament and account wretched, but those who know not how to bear them, even though they be small. Whereas he that knows how to bear them is, as all know, worthy of praises and crowns. And to prove that this is so, whom do we applaud in the games? Those who are much beaten and do not vex themselves, but hold their head on high; or those who fly after the first strokes? Are not those even crowned by us as manly and noble; while we laugh at these as unmanly and cowards? So then let us do in the affairs of life. Him that bears all easily let us crown, as we do that noble champion[1]; but weep over him that shrinks and trembles at his dangers, and who before he receives the blow is dead with fear. For so in the games; if any before he raised his hands, at the mere sight of his adversary extending his right hand, should fly, though he receive no wound, he will be laughed to scorn as feeble and effeminate and unversed in such struggles. Now this is like what happens to these who fear poverty, and cannot so much as endure the expectation of it.

Evidently then it is not we that make you wretched, but ye yourselves. For how can it be that the devil should not hence-forth make sport of thee, seeing thee even before the stroke afraid and trembling at the menace? Or rather, when thou dost but esteem this a threat, he will have no need so much as to strike thee any more, but leaving thee to keep thy wealth, by the expectation of its being taken away he will render thee softer than any wax. And because it is our nature (so to speak,) not to consider the objects of our dread so fearful after suffering, as before and while yet untried: therefore to prevent thee from acquiring even this virtue, he detains thee in the very height of fear; by the fear of poverty, before all experience of it, melting thee down as wax in the fire. Yea, and such a man is softer than any wax and lives a life more wretched than Cain himself. For the things which he hath in excess, he is in fear: for those which he hath not, in grief; and again, concerning what he hath he trembles, keeping his wealth within as a wilful runaway slave, and beset by I know not what various and unaccountable passions. For unaccountable desire, and manifold fear and anxiety, and trembling on every side, agitate them. And they are like a vessel driven by contrary winds from every quarter, and enduring many heavy seas. And how much better for such a man to depart than to be enduring a continual storm? Since for Cain also it were more tolerable to have died than to be for ever trembling[2].

Lest we then for our part suffer these things, let us laugh to scorn the device of the devil, let us burst his cords asunder, let us sever the point of his terrible spear and fortify every approach. For if thou laugh at money, he hath not where to strike, he hath not where he may lay hold. Then hast thou rooted up the root of evils; and when the root is no more, neither will any evil fruit grow.

[9.] Well: these things we are always saying and never leave off saying them: but whether our sayings do any good, the day will declare, even that day which is revealed by fire, which trieth every man's work, (1 Cor. iii. 13.) which showeth what lamps are bright and what are not so. Then shall he who hath oil, and he who hath it not, be manifest. But may none then be found destitute of the comfort; rather may all, bringing in with them abundance of mercy, and having their lamps bright, enter in together with the Bridegroom.

Since nothing is more fearful and full of anguish than that voice which they who departed without abundant almsgiving shall then hear the Bridegroom, "I know you not." (S. Mat. xxv. 12.) But may we never hear this voice, but rather that most pleasant and desirable one, "Come, ye blessed of My Father, inherit the kingdom prepared for you from the foundation of the world." (S. Mat. xxv. 34) For thus shall we live the happy life, and enjoy all the good things which even pass man's understanding: unto which may we all attain, through the grace and mercy, &c.

---

[1] παγκρατιαστήν.

[2] Gen. iv. 12; vid. supr. Hom. vii. 9.

HOMILY XXXI.

1 Cor. xii. 21.

And the eye cannot say to the hand, I have no need of thee: or again the head to the feet, I have no need of you.

HAVING checked the envy of those in lower rank, and having taken off the dejection which it was likely that they would feel from greater gifts having been vouchsafed to others, he humbles also the pride of these latter who had received the greater gifts. He had done the same indeed in his discourse also with the former. For the statement that it was a gift and not an achievement was intended to declare this. But now he doth it again even more vehemently, dwelling on the same image. For from the body in what follows, and from the unity thence arising, he proceeds to the actual comparison of the members, a thing on which they were especially seeking to be instructed. Since there was not so much power to console them in the circumstance of their being all one body, as in the conviction that in the very things wherewith they were endowed, they were not left greatly behind. And he saith, "The eye cannot say to the hand, I have no need of thee: or again the head to the feet, I have no need of you."

For though the gift be less, yet is it necessary: and as when the one is absent, many functions are impeded, so also without the other there is a maim in the fulness of the Church. And he said not, "will not say," but "cannot say." So that even though it wish it, though it should actually say so, it is out of the question nor is the thing consistent with nature. For this cause having taken the two extremes, he makes trial of his argument in them, first in respect of the hand and the eye, and secondly, in respect of the head and feet, adding force to the example.

For what is meaner than the foot? Or what more honorable and more necessary than the head? For this, the head, more than any thing, is the man. Nevertheless, it is not of itself sufficient nor could it alone perform all things; since if this were so, our feet would be a superfluous addition.

[2.] And neither did he stop here, but seeks also another amplification, a kind of thing which he is always doing, contending not only to be on equal terms but even advancing beyond. Wherefore also he adds, saying,

Ver. 22. "Nay, much rather those members of the body which seem to be more feeble are necessary:"

Ver. 23. "And those parts of the body which we think to be less honorable, upon these we bestow more abundant honor; and our uncomely parts have more abundant comeliness."

In every clause adding the term "body," and thereby both consoling the one and checking the other. "For I affirm not this only,[1]" saith he, "that the greater have need of the less, but that they have also much need. Since if there be any thing weak in us, if any thing dishonorable, this is both necessary and enjoys greater honor." And he well said, "which seem," and, "which we think;" pointing out that the judgment arises not from the nature of the things, but from the opinion of the many. For nothing in us is dishonorable, seeing it is God's work. Thus what in us is esteemed less honorable than our genital members? Nevertheless, they enjoy greater honor. And the very poor, even if they have the rest of the body naked, cannot endure to exhibit those members naked. Yet surely this is not the condition of things dishonorable; but it was natural for them to be despised rather than the rest. For so in a house the servant who is dishonored, so far from enjoying greater attention, hath not even an equal share vouchsafed him. By the same rule likewise, if this member were dishonorable, instead of having greater privileges it ought not even to enjoy the same: whereas now it hath more honor for its portion: and this too the wisdom of God hath effected. For to some parts by their nature He hath given not to need it: but to others, not having granted it by their nature, He hath compelled us to yield it. Yet are they not therefore dishonorable. Since the animals too by their nature have a sufficiency, and need neither clothing nor shoes nor a roof, the greater part

---

[1] The Text of the Editions seems here slightly corrupt. The word μόνον apparently should be transposed, and the second negative omitted.

of them: yet not on this account is our body less honorable than they, because it needs all these things.

Yea rather, were one to consider accurately, these parts in question are even by nature itself both honorable and necessary. Which in truth Paul himself imitated, giving his judgment[1] in their favor not from our care and from their enjoying greater honor, but from the very nature of the things.

Wherefore when he calls them "weak" and "less honorable," he uses the expression, "which seem:" but when he calls them "necessary," he no longer adds "which seem," but himself gives his judgment, saying, "they are necessary;" and very properly. For they are useful to procreation of children and the succession of our race. Wherefore also the Roman legislators punish them that mutilate these members and make men eunuchs, as persons who do injury to our common stock and affront nature herself.

But woe to the dissolute who bring reproach on the handy-works of God. For as many are wont to curse wine on account of the drunken, and womankind on account of the unchaste; so also they account these members base because of those who use them not as they ought. But improperly. For the sin is not allotted to the thing as a portion of its nature, but the transgression is produced by the will of him that ventures on it.

But some suppose that the expressions, "the feeble members," and "less honorable," and "necessary," and "which enjoy more abundant honor," are used by Paul of eyes and feet, and that he speaks of the eye as "more feeble," and "necessary," because though deficient in strength, they have the advantage in utility: but of the feet as the "less honorable:" for these also receive from us great consideration.

[3.] Next, not to work out yet another amplification, he says,

Ver. 24. "But our comely parts have no need:"

That is, lest any should say, "Why what kind of speech is this, to despise the honorable and pay court to the less honored?" "we do not this in contempt," saith he, "but because they 'have no need.'" And see how large a measure of praise he thus sets down in brief, and so hastens on: a thing most conveniently and usefully done. And neither is he content with this, but adds also the cause, saying, "But God tempered the body together, giving more abundant honor unto that part which lacked:"

Ver. 25. "That there should be no schism in the body."

Now if He tempered it together, He did not suffer that which is more uncomely to appear. For that which is mingled becomes one thing, and it doth not appear what it was before: since otherwise we could not say that it was tempered. And see how he continually hastens by the defects, saying, "that which lacked." He said not, "to that which is dishonorable," "to that which is unseemly," but, "to that which lacked, ("that which lacked;" how? by nature,) giving more abundant honor. And wherefore? "That there should be no schism in the body." Thus because, though they enjoyed an endless store of consolation, they nevertheless indulged grief as if they had received less than others, he signifies that they were rather honored. For his phrase is, "Giving more abundant honor to that which lacked."

Next he also adds the reason, showing that with a view to their profit he both caused it to lack and more abundantly honored it. And what is the reason? "That there should be no schism," saith he, "in the body." (And he said not, "in the members," but, "in the body.") For there would indeed be a great and unfair advantage, if some members were cared for both by nature and by our forethought, others not even by either one of these. Then would they be cut off from one another, from inability to endure the connection. And when these were cut off, there would be harm done also to the rest. Seest thou how he points out, that of necessity "greater honor" is given to "that which lacketh?" "For had not this been so, the injury would have become common to all," saith he. And the reason is, that unless these received great consideration on our part, they would have been rudely treated, as not having the help of nature: and this rude treatment would have been their ruin: their ruin would have divided the body; and the body having been divided, the other members also would have perished, which are far greater than these.

Seest thou that the care of these latter is connected with making provision for those? For they have not their being so much in their own nature, as in their being one, by virtue of the body[2]. Wherefore if the body perish, they profit nothing by such health as they have severally. But if the eye remain or the nose, preserving its proper function, yet when the bond of union is broken there will be no use for them ever after; whereas, suppose this remaining, and those injured, they both support themselves through it and speedily return to health.

But perhaps some one may say, "this indeed in the body hath reason, that 'that which lacketh hath received more abundant honor,'

---

[1] ψηφισάμενος.

[2] ὡς ἐν τῷ σώματι εἶναι ἕν.

but among men how may this be made out?" Why, among men most especially thou mayest see this taking place. For so they who came at the eleventh hour first received their hire; and the sheep that had wandered induced the shepherd to leave behind the ninety and nine and run after it, and when it was found, he bore and did not drive it; and the prodigal son obtained more honor than he who was approved; and the thief was crowned and proclaimed before the Apostles. And in the case of the talents also thou mayest see this happen: in that to him that received the five talents, and to him that received two, were vouchsafed the same rewards; yea, by the very circumstance that he received the two, he was the more favored with great providential care. Since had he been entrusted with the five, with his want of ability he would have fallen from the whole: but having received the two and fulfilled his own duty, he was thought worthy of the same with him that had gained the five, having so far the advantage, as with less labor to obtain the same crown. And yet he too was a man as well as the one that traded with the five. Nevertheless, his Master doth not in any wise call him to a strict account, nor compel him to do the same with his fellow-servant, nor doth he say, "Why canst thou not gain the five?" (though he might justly have said so,) but assigned him likewise his crown.

[4.] Knowing these things therefore, ye that are greater, trample not on the less, lest, instead of them, ye injure yourselves. For when they are cut off, the whole body is destroyed. Since, what else is a body than the existence of many members? As also Paul himself saith, that "the body is not one member, but many." If therefore this be the essence of a body, let us take care that the many continue many. Since, unless this be entirely preserved, the stroke is in the vital parts; which is the reason also why the Apostle doth not require this only, their not being separated, but also their being closely united. For instance, having said, "that there be no schism in the body," he was not content with this, but added, "that the members should have the same care one for another." Adding this other cause also of the less enjoying more honor. For not only lest they should be separated one from another hath God so contrived it, but also that there may be abundant love and concord. For if each man's being depends on his neighbor's safety, tell me not of the less and the more: in this case there is no more and less. While the body continues you may see the difference too, but when it perishes, no longer. And perish it will, unless the lesser parts also continue.

If now even the greater members will perish

when the less are broken off, these ought to care in like manner for the less, and so as for themselves, inasmuch as in the safety of these the greater likewise remain. So then, shouldst thou say ten thousand times, "such member is dishonored and inferior," still if thou provide not for it in like manner as for thyself, if thou neglect it as inferior, the injury will pass on to thyself. Wherefore he said not only, that "the members should care one for another," but he added, "that they should have the same care one for another," i. e., in like manner the small should enjoy the same providential care with great.

Say not then, that such is an ordinary person, but consider he is a member of that body which holds together the whole: and as the eye, so also doth he cause the body to be a body. For where the body is builded up, there none hath anything more than his neighbor: since neither does this make a body, there being one part greater and another less, but their being many and diverse. For even as thou, because thou art greater, didst help to make up the body, so also he, because he is less. So that his comparative deficiency, when the body is to be builded up, turns out of equal value with thee unto this noble contribution[1]: yea, he avails as much as thyself. And it is evident from hence. Let there be no member greater or less, nor more and less honorable: but let all be eye or all head: will not the body perish? Every one sees it. Again, if all be inferior, the same thing will happen. So that in this respect also the less are proved equal. Yea, and if one must say something more, the purpose of the less being less is that the body may remain. So that for thy sake he is less, in order that thou mayest continue to be great. And here is the cause of his demanding the same care from all. And having said, "that the members may have the same care one for another," he explains "the same thing" again, by saying,

[5.] Ver. 26. "And whether one member suffereth all the members suffer with it; or one member is honored, all the members rejoice with it."

"Yea, with no other view," saith he, "did He make the care He requires common, establishing unity in so great diversity, but that of all events there might be complete communion. Because, if our care for our neighbor be the common safety, it follows also that our glory and our sadness must be common." Three things therefore he here demands: the not being divided but united in perfection: the having like care for another: and the considering all that happens common. And as above he saith, "He hath given more abundant honor to

---
[1] ἔρανον.

that part which lacked," because it needeth it ; signifying that the very inferiority was become an introduction to greater honor ; so here he equalizes them in respect of the care also which takes place mutually among them. For "therefore did he cause them to partake of greater honor," saith he, "that they might not meet with less care." And not from hence only, but also by all that befalls them, good and painful, are the members bound to one another. Thus often when a thorn is fixed in the heel, the whole body feels it and cares for it : both the back is bent and the belly and thighs are contracted, and the hands coming forth as guards and servants draw out what was so fixed, and the head stoops over it, and the eyes observe it with much care. So that even if the foot hath inferiority from its inability to ascend, yet by its bringing down the head it hath an equality, and is favored with the same honor ; and especially whenever the feet are the cause of the head's coming down, not by favor but by their claim on it. And thus, if by being the more honorable it hath an advantage ; yet in that, being so it owes such honor and care to the lesser and likewise equal sympathy : by this it indicates great equality. Since what is meaner than the heel? what more honorable than the head? Yet this member reaches to that, and moves them all together with itself. Again if anything is the matter with the eyes, all complain and all are idle : and neither do the feet walk nor the hands work, nor doth the stomach enjoy its accustomed food ; and yet the affection is of the eyes. Why dost thou cause the stomach to pine? why keep thy feet still? why bind thy hands? Because they are tied to the feet, and in an unspeakable manner the whole body suffers. For if it shared not in the suffering, it would not endure to partake of the care. Wherefore having said, "that the members may have the same care one for another," he added, "whether one member suffereth, all the members suffer with it ; or one member is honored, all the members rejoice with it." "And how do they rejoice with it ?" say you. The head is crowned, and the whole man is honored. The mouth speaks,. and the eyes laugh and are delighted. Yet the credit belongs not to the beauty of the eyes, but to the tongue. Again if the eyes appear beautiful, the whole woman is embellished : as indeed these also, when a straight nose and upright neck and other members are praised, rejoice and appear cheerful : and again they shed tears in great abundance over their griefs and misfortunes, though themselves continue uninjured.

[6.] Let us all then, considering these things, imitate the love of these members ; let us not in any wise do the contrary, trampling on the miseries of our neighbor and envying his good things. For this is the part of madmen and persons beside themselves. Just as he that digs out his own eye hath displayed a very great proof of senselessness ; and he that devours his own hand exhibits a clear evidence of downright madness.

Now if this be the case with regard to the members, so likewise, when it happeneth among the brethren, it fastens on us the reputation of folly and brings on no common mischief. For as long as he shines, thy comeliness also is apparent and the whole body is beautified. For not at all doth he confine the beauty to himself alone, but permits thee also to glory. But if thou extinguish him, thou bringest a common darkness upon the whole body, and the misfortune thou causest is common to all the members : as indeed if thou preservest him in brightness, thou preservest the bloom of the entire body. For no man saith, "the eye is beautiful : " but what? "such a woman is beautiful." And if it also be praised, it comes after the common encomium. So likewise it happens in the Church. I mean, if there be any celebrated persons, the community reaps the good report of it. For the enemies are not apt to divide the praises, but connect them together. And if any be brilliant in speech, they do not praise him alone but likewise the whole Church. For they do not say only, "such a one is a wonderful man," but what? "the Christians have a wonderful teacher : " and so they make the possession common.

[7.] And now let me ask, do heathens bind together, and dost thou divide and war with thine own body, and withstand thine own members? Knowest thou not that this overturns all? For even a "kingdom," saith he, "divided against itself shall not stand." (S. Mat. xii. 25.)

But nothing so divides and separates as envy and jealousy, that grievous disease, and exempt from all pardon, and in some respect worse than "the root of all evils." (1. Tim. vi. 12.) For the covetous is then pleased when himself hath received : but the envious is then pleased, when another hath failed to receive, not when himself hath received. For he thinks the misfortunes of others a benefit to himself, rather than prosperity ; going about a common enemy of mankind, and smiting the members of Christ, than which what can be more akin to madness? A demon is envious, but of men, not of any demon : but thou being a man enviest men, and withstandest what is of thine own tribe and family, which not even a demon doth. And what pardon shalt thou obtain, what excuse? trembling and turning pale at sight of a brother in prosperity, when thou oughtest to crown thyself and to rejoice and exult.

If indeed thou wishest to emulate him, I forbid not that: emulate, but with a view to be like him who is approved: not in order to depress him but that thou mayest reach the same lofty point, that thou mayest display the same excellence. This is wholesome rivalry, imitation without contention: not to grieve at the good things of others but to be vexed at our own evils: the contrary to which is the result of envy. For neglecting its own evils, it pines away at the good fortune of other men. And thus the poor is not so vexed by his own poverty as by the plenty of his neighbor; than which what can be more grievous? Yea, in this respect the envious, as I before said, is worse than the covetous; the one rejoicing at some acquisition of his own, while the other finds his delight in some one else failing to receive.

Wherefore I beseech you, leaving this evil way, to change to a proper emulation, (for it is a violent thing, this kind of zeal, and hotter than any fire,) and to win thereby mighty blessings. Thus also Paul used to guide those of Jewish origin unto the faith, saying, "If by any means I may provoke to emulation them which are my flesh, and may save some of them." (Rom. xi. 14.) For he whose emulation is like what Paul wished for doth not pine when he sees the other in reputation, but when he sees himself left behind: the envious not so, but at the sight of another's prosperity. And he is a kind of drone, injuring other men's labors; and himself never anxious to rise, but weeping when he sees another rising, and doing every thing to throw him down. To what then might one compare this passion? It seems to me to be like as if a sluggish ass and heavy with abundance of flesh, being yoked with a winged courser, should neither himself be willing to rise, and should attempt to drag the other down by the weight of his carcase. For so this man takes no thought nor anxiety to be himself rid of this deep slumber, but doth every thing to supplant and throw down him that is flying towards heaven, becoming an exact emulator of the devil: since he too, seeing man in paradise, sought not to change his own condition, but to cast him out of paradise. And again, seeing him seated in heaven and the rest hastening thither, he holds to the same plan, supplanting them who are hastening thither and thereby heaping up the furnace more abundantly

for himself. For in every instance this happens: both he that is envied, if he be vigilant, becoming more eminent; and he that is envious, accumulating to himself more evils. Thus also Joseph became eminent, thus Aaron the priest: the conspiracy of the envious caused God once and again to give His suffrage for him, and was the occasion of the rod's budding. Thus Jacob attained his abundant wealth and all those other blessings. Thus the envious pierce themselves through with ten thousand evils. Knowing as we do all these things, let us flee such emulation. For wherefore, tell me, enviest thou? Because thy brother hath received spiritual grace? And from whom did he receive it? answer me. Was it not from God? Clearly then He is the object of the enmity to which thou art committing thyself, He the bestower of the gift. Seest thou which way the evil is tending, and with what sort of a point it is crowning the heap of thy sins; and how deep the pit of vengeance which it is digging for thee?

Let us flee it, then, beloved, and neither envy others, nor fail to pray for our enviers and do all we can to extinguish their passion: neither let us feel as the unthinking do who being minded to exact punishment of them, do all in their power to light up their flame. But let not us do so; rather let us weep for them and lament. For they are the injured persons, having a continual worm gnawing through their heart, and collecting a fountain of poison more bitter than any gall. Come now, let us beseech the merciful God, both to change their state of feeling and that we may never fall into that disease: since heaven is indeed inaccessible to him that hath this wasting sore, and before heaven too, even this present life is not worth living in. For not so thoroughly are timber and wool wont to be eaten through by moth and worm abiding therein, as doth the fever of envy devour the very bones of the envious and destroy all self-command in their soul.

In order then that we may deliver both ourselves and others from these innumerable woes, let us expel from within us this evil fever, this that is more grievous than any gangrene: that having regained spiritual strength, we may both finish the present course and obtain the future crowns; unto which may we all attain, by the grace and mercy of our Lord Jesus Christ, with Whom to the Father, with the Holy Ghost, be glory, power, honor, now and ever, and world without end. Amen.

HOMILY XXXII.

1 COR. xii. 27.

Now ye are the body of Christ and severally members thereof.

For lest any should say, "What is the example of the body to us? since the body is a slave to nature but our good deeds are of choice;" he applies it to our own concerns; and to signify that we ought to have the same concord of design as they have from nature, he saith, "Now ye are the body of Christ." But if our body ought not to be divided, much less the body of Christ, and so much less as grace is more powerful than nature.

"And severally members thereof." That is, "not only," saith he, "are we a body, but members also." For of both these he had before discoursed, bringing the many together into one, and implying that all become some one thing after the image of the body, and that this one thing is made up of the many and is in the many, and that the many by this are held together and are capable of being many.

But what is the expression, "severally?" "So far at least as appertaineth to you; and so far as naturally a part should be built up from you." For because he had said, "the body," whereas the whole body was not the Corinthian Church, but the Church in every part of the world, therefore he said, "severally:" i. e., the Church amongst you is a part of the Church existing every where and of the body which is made up of all the Churches: so that not only with yourselves alone, but also with the whole Church throughout the world, ye ought to be at peace, if at least ye be members of the whole body.

[2.] Ver. 28. "And God hath set some in the Church: first apostles, secondly prophets, thirdly teachers, then miracles, then gifts of healings, helps, governments, divers kinds of tongues."

Thus what I spake of before, this also he now doth. Because they thought highly of themselves in respect of the tongues he sets it last every where. For the terms, "first" and "secondly," are not used by him here at random, but in order by enumeration to point out the more honorable and the inferior. Wherefore also he set the apostles first who had all the gifts in themselves. And he said not, "God hath set certain in the Church, apostles" simply, "or prophets," but he employs "first, second," and "third," signifying that same thing which I told you of.

"Secondly, prophets." For they used to prophesy, as the daughters of Philip, as Agabus, as these very persons among the Corinthians, of whom he saith, "Let the prophets speak, two or three." (c. xiv. 29.) And writing also to Timothy, he said, "Neglect not the gift that is in thee, which was given thee by prophecy." (1. Tim. iv. 14.) And they were much more numerous then than under the old covenant: the gifts not having devolved on some ten, and twenty, and fifty, and an hundred, but this grace was poured out abundantly, and every Church had many that prophesied. And if Christ saith, "The Law and the Prophets prophesied until John," (S. Matt. xi. 13.) He saith it of those prophets who before proclaimed His coming.

"Thirdly, teachers." For he that prophesieth speaks all things from the Spirit; but he that teacheth sometimes discourses also out of his own mind. Wherefore also he said, "Let the elders that rule well be counted worthy of double honor, especially they who labor in the word and in teaching:" (1. Tim. v. 17.) whereas he that speaks all things by the Spirit doth not labor. This accordingly is the reason why he set him after the prophet, because the one is wholly a gift but the other is also man's labor. For he speaks many things of his own mind, agreeing however with the sacred Scriptures.

[3.] "Then miracles, then gifts of healings."

Seest thou how he again divides the healings from the power, which also he did before. For the power is more than the healing: since he that hath power both punishes and heals, but he that hath the gift of healings doeth cures only. And observe how excellent the order he made use of, when he set the prophecy before the miracles and the healings. For above when he said, "To one is given by the Spirit the word of wisdom, and to another the word of knowledge," he spake, not setting them in order, but indifferently. Here, on the other hand, he sets a first and a second rank. Wherefore then doth he set prophecy first? Because even in the old covenant the matter has this order. For example, when Isaiah was discoursing with the Jews, and exhibiting a demonstration of the power of God, and bringing forward the evidence of the worthlessness of the demons, he stated this also as the greatest evidence of his divinity, his foretelling things to come. (Is. xli. 22, 23.) And Christ Himself after working so many signs saith that this was no small sign of His divinity: and continually adds, "But these things have I told you, that when it is come to pass, ye may believe that I am He." (S. John xiii. 19; xiv. 29; xvi. 4.)

"Well then; the gifts of healing are justly inferior to prophecy. But why likewise to teaching?" Because it is not the same thing to declare the word of preaching and sow piety in the hearts of the hearers, as it is to work miracles: since these are done merely for the sake of that. When therefore any one teaches both by word and life, he is greater than all. For those he calls emphatically teachers, who both teach by deeds and instruct in word. For instance: this made the Apostles themselves to become Apostles. And those gifts certain others also, of no great worth, received in the beginning, as they who said, "Lord, did we not prophesy by Thy Name, and do mighty works?" and after this were told, "I never knew you; depart from Me, ye that work inquity." (S. Mat. vii. 22.) But this twofold mode of teaching, I mean that by deeds and by words, no bad man would ever undertake. As to his setting the prophets first marvel not at it. For he is not speaking of prophets simply, but of those who by prophecy do also teach and say every thing to the common benefit: which in proceeding he makes more clear to us.

"Helps, governments." What is, "helps?" To support the weak. Is this then a gift, tell me? In the first place, this too is of the Gift of God, aptness for a patron's office[1]; the dispensing spiritual things; besides which he calls many even of our own good deeds, "gifts," not meaning us to lose heart, but showing that in every case we need God's help, and preparing them to be thankful, and thereby making them more forward and stirring up their minds.

"Divers kinds of tongues." Seest thou where he hath set this gift, and how he every where assigns it the last rank?

[4.] Further, since again by this catalogue he had pointed out a great difference, and stirred up the afore-mentioned distemper of those that had lesser gifts, he darts upon them in what follows with great vehemence, because he had already given them those many proofs of their not being left much inferior. What I mean is; because it was likely that on hearing

[1] προστατικόν εἶναι.

these things they would say, "And why were we not all made Apostles?"—whereas above he had made use of a more soothing tone of discourse, proving at length the necessity of this result, even from the image of the body; for "the body," saith he, "is not one member;" and again, "but if all were one member, where were the body?" and from the fact that they were given for use; for to each one is given "the manifestation of the Spirit," saith he, "to profit withal:" and from all being watered from the same Spirit: and from what is bestowed being a free gift and not a debt; "for there are," saith he, "diversities of gifts, but the same Spirit:" and from the manifestation of the Spirit being made alike through all; for "to each one," saith he, "is given the manifestation through the Spirit:" and from the fact that these things were shaped according to the pleasure of the Spirit and of God; "for all these," saith he, "worketh the one and the same Spirit, dividing to each one severally even as he will:" and, "God hath set the members each one of them in the body, even as it pleased Him:" and from the inferior members also being necessary; "for those which seem," saith he, "to be more feeble are necessary:" from their being alike necessary, in that they constitute the body equally with the greater; "for the body," saith he, "is not one member, but many:" from the greater too needing the less: "for the head," saith he, "cannot say to the feet, I have no need of you:" from these latter enjoying even more honor; for "to that which lacketh," saith he, "He hath given more abundant honor:" from the care of them being common and equal; for "for all the members have the same care one for another:" and from there being one honor and one grief of them all; for "whether," saith he, "one member suffereth, all the members suffer with it; or one member is honored, all the members rejoice with it:"—whereas, I say, he had above exhorted them by these topics, here and henceforth he uses language so as to bear them down and rebuke them. For, as I said, it behoves us neither always to exhort people nor always to silence them. Therefore also Paul himself, because he at length exhorted them, doth henceforth vehemently attack them, saying,

Ver. 29. "Are all apostles? are all prophets? have all gifts of healing?"

And he doth not stop at the first and the second gift, but proceeds to the last, either meaning this that all cannot be all things, (even as he there saith, "if all were one member, where were the body?") or establishing some other point also along with these, which may tell in the way of consolation again. What then is this? His signifying that even the lesser gifts are contended for equally with the greater, from the circumstance that not even these were given absolutely to all ? For " why," saith he, " dost thou grieve that thou hast not gifts of healing? consider that what thou hast, even though it be less, is oftentimes not possessed by him that hath the greater." Wherefore he saith,

Ver. 30. " Do all speak with tongues ? do all interpret ? "

For even as the great gifts God hath not vouchsafed all to all men, but to some this, and to others that, so also did He in respect of the less, not proposing these either to all. And this He did, procuring thereby abundant harmony and love, that each one standing in need of the other might be brought close to his brother. This economy He established also in the arts, this also in the elements, this also in the plants, and in our members, and absolutely in all things.

[5.] Then he subjoins further the most powerful consolation, and sufficient to recover them and quiet their vexed souls. And what is this ?

Ver. 31. " Desire earnestly," saith he, " the better gifts. And a still more excellent way show I unto you."

Now by saying this, he gently hinted that they were the cause of their own receiving the lesser gifts, and had it in their power, if they would, to receive the greater. For when he saith, " desire earnestly," he demands from them all diligence and desire for spiritual things. And he said not, the greater gifts, but " the better," i.e., the more useful, those which would profit. And what he means is this : " continue to desire gifts ; and I point out to you a fountain of gifts." For neither did he say, " a gift," but " a way," that he might the more extol that which he intends to mention. As if he said, It is not one, or two, or three gifts that I point out to you, but one way which leadeth to all these[1]: and not merely a way, but both

" a more excellent way " and one that is open in common to all. For not as the gifts are vouchsafed, to some these, to others those, but not all to all; so also in this case : but it is an universal gift. Wherefore also he invites all to it. " Desire earnestly," saith he, " the better gifts and yet show I unto you a more excellent way ; " meaning love towards our neighbor.

Then intending to proceed to the discourse concerning it and the encomium of this virtue, he first lowereth these by comparison with it, intimating that they are nothing without it ; very considerately. For if he had at once discoursed of love, and having said, " I show unto you a way," had added, " but this is love," and had not conducted his discourse by way of comparison ; some might possibly have scoffed at what was said, not understanding clearly the force of the thing spoken of but still gaping after these. Wherefore he doth not at once unfold it, but first excites the hearer by the promise, and saith, " I show unto you a more excellent way," and so having led him to desire it, he doth not even thus straightway proceed to it, but augmenting still further and extending their desire, he discourses first of these very things, and shows that without it they are nothing; reducing them to the greatest necessity of loving one another ; seeing also that from neglect of it sprang that which caused all their evils. So that in this respect also it might justly appear great, if the gifts not only brought them not together, but divided them even when united : but this, when many were so divided, would reunite them by virtue of its own and make them one body. This however he doth not say at once, but what they chiefly longed for, that he sets down; as that the thing was a gift and a most excellent way to all the gifts. So that, even if thou wilt not love thy brother on the score of friendship, yet for the sake of obtaining a better sign and an abundant gift, cherish love.

[6.] And see whence he first begins ; from that which was marvellous in their eyes and great, the gift of tongues. And in bringing forward that gift, he mentions it not just in the degree they had it in, but far more. For he did not say, " if I speak with tongues," but,

Chap. xiii. ver. 1. " If I speak with the tongues of men,—"

What is, " of men ? " Of all nations in every part of the world. And neither was he content with this amplification, but he likewise uses another much greater, adding the words,

[1] [Chrysostom's view of the text is made more plain by a rendering somewhat different from that of the English translator and of both the Authorized Version and the Revised. " Desire earnestly the better gifts. And furthermore I show you a very excellent way to do it." The contrast is not between the " gifts " on one hand and love on the other, but between eagerness of emulation and the pursuit of love as a means of attaining the gifts. In this the Greek expositor anticipates the conclusions of the best modern critics, such as DeWette, Meyer, Alford, Hodge, Heinrici, etc. The view is sustained by the natural force of the words used and by the connection. It is true that the superiority of love as a means is lost sight of in the beautiful panegyric of love that follows, but that seems due to the ardor of the writer's mind and the attractiveness of the theme. It is not through the pursuit and exercise of gifts that we attain to love ; but it is love that develops the gifts within us, and love is greater than gifts. The reason why the Apostle indulges here in the digression which occupies the thirteenth chapter is thus given by Principal Edwards (in loco). " Partly to rebuke indirectly the dissensions of the Corinthian Church, partly a statement of the peculiarly Christian means to secure possession of the Charismata for the edification of the Church and render them innocuous to their possessor, partly also a glimpse of a moral development different in kind from gifts and greater in moral worth than all other moral virtues, partly a reiteration in a new form of the idea that the Church is an organic body."

In the whole passage the English translator adhered to the rendering of the Authorized Version, " charity," which Wyclif used for the charitas of the Vulgate. I have changed this to " love" which, besides its unambiguousness and its more exact conformity to the original, admits of the deeper meaning and wider application which makes God as well as our brethren the object of the affection. C.]

"and of angels,—and have not love, I am become sounding brass, or a clanging cymbal."

Dost thou see to what point he first exalted the gift, and to what afterwards he lowered and cast it down? For neither did he simply say, "I am nothing," but, "I am become sounding brass," a thing senseless and inanimate But how "sounding brass?" Emitting a sound indeed, but at random and in vain, and for no good end. Since besides my profiting nothing, I am counted by most men as one giving impertinent trouble, an annoying and wearisome kind of person. Seest thou how one void of love is like to things inanimate and senseless?

Now he here speaks of the "tongues of angels," not investing angels with a body, but what he means is this: "should I even so speak as angels are wont to discourse unto each other, without this I am nothing, nay rather a burden and an annoyance." Thus (to mention one other example) where he saith, "To Him every knee shall bow, of things in heaven and things on earth, and things under the earth," (Phil. ii. 10.) he doth not say these things as if he attributed to angels knees and bones, far from it, but it is their intense adoration which he intends to shadow out by the fashion amongst us: so also here he calls it "a tongue," not meaning an instrument of flesh, but intending to indicate their converse with each other by the manner which is known amongst us.

[7.] Then, in order that his discourse may be acceptable, he stops not at the gift of tongues, but proceeds also to the remaining gifts; and having depreciated all in the absence of love, he then depicts her image. And because he preferred to conduct his argument by amplification, he begins from the less and ascends to the greater. For whereas, when he indicated their order, he placed the gift of tongues last, this he now numbers first; by degrees, as I said, ascending to the greater gifts. Thus having spoken of tongues, he proceeds immediately to prophecy; and saith;

Ver. 2. "And if I have the gift of prophecy."

And this gift again with an excellency. For as in that case he mentioned not tongues, but the tongues of all mankind, and as he proceeded, those of angels, and then signified that the gift was nothing without love: so also here he mentions not prophecy alone but the very highest prophecy: in having said, "If I have prophecy," he added, "and know all mysteries and all knowledge;" expressing this gift also with intensity.

Then after this also he proceeds to the other gifts. And again, that he might not seem to weary them, naming each one of the gifts, he sets down the mother and fountain of all, and this again with an excellency, thus saying,

"And if I have all faith." Neither was he content with this, but even that which Christ spake of as greatest, this also he added, saying, "so as to remove mountains and have not love, I am nothing." And consider how again here also he lowers the dignity of the tongues. For whereas in regard of prophecy he signifies the great advantage arising from it, "the understanding mysteries, and having all knowledge;" and in regard of faith, no trifling work, even "the removing mountains;" in respect of tongues, on the other hand, having named the gift itself only, he quits it.

But do thou, I pray, consider this also, how in brief he comprehended all gifts when he named prophecy and faith: for miracles are either in words or deeds. And how doth Christ say, that the least degree of faith is the being able to remove a mountain? For as though he were speaking something very small, did He express Himself when He said, "If ye have faith as a grain of mustard-seed, ye shall say to this mountain, Remove, and it shall remove;" (S. Mat. xvii. 20.) whereas Paul saith that this is "all faith." What then must one say? Since this was a great thing, the removing a mountain, therefore also he mentioned it, not as though "all faith" were only able to do this, but since this seemed to be great to the grosser sort because of the bulk of the outward mass, from this also he extols his subject. And what he saith is this:

"If I have all faith, and can remove mountains, but have not love, I am nothing."

[8.] Ver. 3. "And if I bestow all my goods to feed the poor, and if I give my body to be burned, but have not love, it profiteth me nothing."

Wonderful amplification! For even these things too he states with another addition: in that he said not, "if I give to the poor the half of my goods," or "two or three parts," but, "though I give all my goods." And he said not, "give," but, "distribute in morsels[1]," so that to the expense may be added the administering also with all care.

"And if I give my body to be burned." He said not, "if I die," but this too with an excellency. For he names the most terrible of all deaths, the being burnt alive, and saith that even this without charity is no great thing. Accordingly he subjoins, "it profiteth me nothing."

But not even yet have I pointed out the whole of the excellency, until I bring forward the testimonies of Christ which were spoken concerning almsgiving and death. What then are His testimonies? To the rich man He saith, "If thou wouldest be perfect, sell what thou hast and give to the poor, and come, follow me." (S. Mat. xix. 21.) And discoursing likewise of love to

---

[1] ψωμίσω.

one's neighbor, He saith, "Greater love hath no man than this, that a man may lay down his life for his friends." (S. John xv. 13.) Whence it is evident, that even before God this is greatest of all. But, "I declare," said Paul, "that even if we should lay down life for God's sake, and not merely lay it down, but so as even to be burned, (for this is the meaning of, "if I give my body to be burned,") we shall have no great advantage if we love not our neighbor." Well then, the saying that the gifts are of no great profit without charity is no marvel: since our gifts are a secondary consideration to our way of life. At any rate, many have displayed gifts, and yet on becoming vicious have been punished: as those who "prophesied in His name, and cast out many demons, and wrought many mighty works;" as Judas the traitor: while others, exhibiting as believers a pure life, have needed nothing else in order to their salvation. Wherefore, that the gifts should, as I said, require this, is no marvel: but that an exact life even should avail nothing without it, this is what brings the intensity of expression strongly out and causes great perplexity: especially too when Christ appears to adjudge His great rewards to both these, I mean to the giving up our possessions, and to the perils of martyrdom. For both to the rich man He saith, as I before observed, "If thou wilt be perfect, sell thy goods, and give to the poor, and come, follow me:" and discoursing with the disciples, of martyrdom He saith, "Whosoever shall lose his life for My sake, shall find it;" and, "Whosoever shall confess Me before men, him will will I also confess before My Father which is in heaven." For great indeed is the labor of this achievement, and well nigh surpassing nature itself, and this is well known to such as have had these crowns vouchsafed to them. For no language can set it before us: so noble a soul doth the deed belong to and so exceedingly wonderful is it.

[9.] But nevertheless, this so wonderful thing Paul said was of no great profit without love, even though it have the giving up of one's goods joined with it. Wherefore then hath he thus spoken? This will I now endeavor to explain, first having enquired of this, How is it possible that one who gives all his goods to feed the poor can be wanting in love? I grant, indeed, he that is ready to be burned and hath the gifts, may perhaps possibly not have love: but he who not only gives his goods, but even distributes them in morsels; how hath not he love?[1]

What then are we to say? Either that he supposed an unreal case as real; which kind of thing he is ever wont to do, when he intends to set before us something in excess; as when writing to the Galatians he saith, "If we or an angel from heaven preach any other gospel unto you than that ye received, let him be accursed." (Gal. i. 8.) And yet neither was himself nor an angel about to do so; but to signify that he meant to carry the matter as far as possible, he set down even that which could never by any means happen. And again, when he writes to the Romans, and saith, "Neither angels, nor principalities, nor powers, shall be able to separate us from the love of God;" for neither was this about to be done by any angels: but here too he supposes a thing which was not; as indeed also in what comes next, saying, "nor any other creature," whereas there is no other creature, for he had comprehended the whole creation, having spoken of all things both above and below. Nevertheless here also he mentions that which was not, by way of hypothesis, so as to show his exceeding desire. Now the same thing he doth here also, saying, "If a man give all, and have not love, it profits him nothing."

Either then we may say this, or that his meaning is for those who give to be also joined closely to those who receive, and not merely to give without sympathy, but in pity and condescension, bowing down and grieving with the needy. For therefore also hath almsgiving been enacted by God: since God might have nourished the poor as well without this, but that he might bind us together unto charity and that we might be thoroughly fervent toward each other, he commanded them to be nourished by us. Therefore one saith in another place also; "a good word is better than a gift;" (Ecclus. xviii. 16, 17.) and, "behold, a word is beyond a good gift." (Ecclus. xviii. 16, 17.) And He Himself saith, "I will have mercy, and not sacrifice." (S. Mat. ix. 30; Hos. vi. 6.) For since it is usual, both for men to love those who are benefited by them, and for those who receive benefits to be more kindly affected towards their benefactors; he made this law, constituting it a bond of friendship.

[10.] But the point proposed for enquiry above is, How, after Christ had said that both these belong to perfection, Paul affirms, that

---

[1] [The point which Chrysostom so anxiously discusses is much more readily settled by modern interpreters. Thus one of them says, "All outward acts of beneficence are of no avail without love. A man may give away his whole estate, or sacrifice himself, and be in no sense the gainer. He may do all this from vanity, or from the fear of perdition, or to purchase heaven, and only increase his condemnation. Religion is no such easy thing. Men would gladly compound by external acts of beneficence or by penances for a change of heart; but the thing is impossible.

Thousands indeed are deluded on this point, and think that they can substitute what is outward for what is inward, but God requires the heart, and without holiness the most liberal giver or the most suffering ascetic can never see God." (Hodge) The address of our Saviour to the rich young ruler was not intended to furnish a general rule of action or even to specify a particular kind of perfection. When he told the earnest enquirer to sell all that he had the object was to disclose to him his inordinate love of this world's goods and so lead him to see how far he was from the perfection which he had claimed. Chrysostom's use of this passage is precisely that which was made by Anthony, the first of the Fathers of the Desert, and by St. Francis of Assisi, and which lies at the basis of the whole monastic system. C.]

these without charity are imperfect? Not contradicting Him, God forbid: but harmonizing with Him, and that exactly. For so in the case of the rich man, He said, not merely, " sell thy goods, and give to the poor," but He added, " and come, follow Me." Now not even the following Him proves any man a disciple of Christ so completely as the loving one another. For, " by this shall all men know," saith He, " that ye are My disciples, if ye have love one to another." (S. John xiii. 35.) And also when He saith, " Whosoever loseth his life for My sake, shall find it;" (S. Mat. x. 39, and 35.) and, " whosoever shall confess Me before men, him will I also confess before My Father which is in heaven;" He means not this, that it is not necessary to have love, but He declares the reward which is laid up for these labors. Since that along with martyrdom He requires also this, is what He elsewhere strongly intimates, thus saying, " Ye shall indeed drink of My cup, and be baptized with the baptism that I am baptized with;" (S. Mat. xx. 23.) i. e., ye shall be martyrs, ye shall be slain for My sake; " but to sit on My right hand, and on My left, (not as though any sit on the right hand and the left, but meaning the highest precedency and honor) " is not Mine to give," saith He, " but to those for whom it is prepared." Then signifying for whom it is prepared, He calls them and saith, "whosoever among you will be chief, let him be servant to you all;" (S. Mat. xx. 26.) setting forth humility and love. And the love which He requires is intense; wherefore He stopped not even at this, but added, " even as the Son of Man came not to be ministered unto, but to minister, and to give His life a ransom for many; " pointing out that we ought so to love as even to be slain for our beloved. For this above all is to love Him. Wherefore also He saith to Peter, "If thou lovest Me, feed My sheep." (S. John xxi. 16.)

[11.] And that ye may learn how great a work of virtue it is, let us sketch it out in word, since in deeds we see it no where appearing ; and let us consider, if it were every where in abundance, how great benefits would ensue : how there were no need then of laws, or tribunals, or punishments, or avenging, or any other such things : since if all loved and were beloved, no man would injure another. Yea, murders, and strifes, and wars, and divisions, and rapines, and frauds, and all evils would be removed, and vice be unknown even in name. Miracles, however, would not have effected this ; they rather puff up such as are not on their guard, unto vain-glory and folly.

Again : what is indeed the marvellous part of love ; all the other good things have their evils yoked with them : as he that gives up his poss-

essions is oftentimes puffed up on this account : the eloquent is affected with a wild passion for glory ; the humble-minded, on this very ground, not seldom thinks highly of himself in his conscience. But love is free from every such mischief. For none could ever be lifted up against the person whom he loves. And do not, I pray, suppose one person only loving but all alike ; and then wilt thou see its virtue. Or rather, if thou wilt, first suppose one single person beloved, and one loving ; loving, however, as it is meet to love. Why, he will so live on earth as if it were heaven, every where enjoying a calm and weaving for himself innumerable crowns. For both from envy, and wrath, and jealousy, and pride, and vain-glory, and evil concupiscence, and every profane love, and every distemper, such a man will keep his own soul pure. Yea, even as no one would do himself an injury, so neither would this man his neighbors. And being such, he shall stand with Gabriel himself, even while he walks on earth.

Such then is he that hath love. But he that works miracles and hath perfect knowledge, without this, though he raises ten thousand from the dead, will not be much profited, broken off as he is from all and not enduring to mix himself up with any of his fellow-servants. For no other cause than this did Christ say that the sign of perfect love towards Him is the loving one's neighbors. For, " if thou lovest Me," saith He, " O Peter, more than these, feed My sheep." (S. John xxi. 15.) Dost thou see how hence also He again covertly intimates, in what case this is greater than martyrdom? For if any one had a beloved child in whose behalf he would even give up his life, and some one were to love the father, but pay no regard whatever to the son, he would greatly incense the father ; nor would he feel the love for himself, because of the overlooking his son. Now if this ensue in the case of father and son, much more in the case of God and men : since surely God is more loving than any parents.

Wherefore, having said, " The first and great commandment is, Thou shalt love the Lord thy God," he added, "and the second—(He leaves it not in silence, but sets it down also)—is like unto it, Thou shalt love thy neighbor as thyself." And see how with nearly the same excellency He demands also this. For as concerning God, He saith, "with all thy heart :" so concerning thy neighbor, " as thyself," which is tantamount to, "with all thy heart."

Yea, and if this were duly observed, there would be neither slave nor free, neither ruler nor ruled, neither rich nor poor, neither small nor great; nor would any devil then ever have been known : I say not, Satan only, but whatever other such spirit there be, nay, rather were there a hundred or ten thousand such, they would have no power, while love existed. For sooner would grass endure the application of fire than the devil the flame of love. She is stronger than any wall, she is firmer than any adamant; or if thou canst name any material stronger than this the firmness of love transcends them all. Her, neither wealth nor poverty overcometh: nay, rather there would be no poverty, no unbounded wealth, if there were love, but the good parts only from each estate. For from the one we should reap its abundance, and from the other its freedom from care : and should neither have to undergo the anxieties of riches, nor the dread of poverty.

[12.] And why do I mention the advantages arising from it? Yea, rather consider how great a blessing it is of itself to exercise love; what cheerfulness it produces, in how great grace it establishes the soul ; a thing which above all is a choice quality of it. For the other parts of virtue have each their troubles yoked with them ; as fasting, temperance, watching, have envy, concupiscence, and contempt. But love along with the gain hath great pleasure, too, and no trouble, and like an industrious bee, gathering the sweets from every flower, deposits them in the soul of him who loveth. Though any one be a slave, it renders slavery sweeter than liberty. For he who loveth rejoices not so much in commanding, as in being commanded, although to command is sweet: but love changes the nature of things and presents herself with all blessings in her hands, gentler than any mother, wealthier than any queen, and makes difficulties light and easy, causing our virtues to be facile, but vice very bitter to us. As thus : to expend seems grievous, yet love makes it pleasant: to receive other men's goods, pleasant, but love suffers it not to appear pleasant, but frames our minds to avoid it as an evil. Again, to speak evil seems to be pleasant to all ; but love, while she makes this out to be bitter, causeth speaking well to be pleasant; for nothing is so sweet to us as to be praising one whom we love. Again, anger hath a kind of pleasure ; but in this case no longer, rather all its sinews are taken away. Though he that is beloved should grieve him who loves him, anger no where shows itself: but tears and exhortations, and supplications ; so far is love from being exasperated : and should she behold one in error, she mourns and is in pain ; yet even this pain itself brings pleasure. For the very tears and the grief of love, are sweeter than any mirth and joy. For instance : they that laugh are not so refreshed as they that weep for their friends. And if thou doubt it, stop their tears; and they repine at it not otherwise than as persons intolerably ill-used. "But there is," said one,

"an unbecoming pleasure in love.[1]" Avaunt, and hold thy peace, whoever thou art. For nothing is so pure from such pleasure as genuine love.

For tell me not of this ordinary sort, the vulgar and low-minded, and a disease rather than love, but of this which Paul seeks after, which considers the profit of them that are loved ; and thou shalt see that no fathers are so affectionate as persons of this stamp. And even as they who love money cannot endure to spend money, but would with more pleasure be in straits than see their wealth diminishing : so too, he that is kindly affected towards any one, would choose to suffer ten thousand evils than see his beloved one injured.

[13.] "How then," saith one, "did the Egyptian woman who loved Joseph wish to injure him?" Because she loved with this diabolical love. Joseph however not with this, but with that which Paul requires. Consider then now great a love his words were tokens of, and the action which she was speaking of. "Insult me and make me an adulteress, and wrong my husband, and overthrow all my house, and cast thyself out from thy confidence towards God : " which were expressions of one who so far from loving him did not even love herself. But because he truly loved, he sought to avert her from all these. And to convince you that it was in anxiety for her, learn the nature of it from his advice. For he not only thrust her away, but also introduced an exhortation capable of quenching every flame: namely "if on my account, my master," saith he, "knoweth not any thing which is in his house." He at once reminds her of her husband that he might put her to shame. And he said not, "thy husband," but "my master," which was more apt to restrain her and induce her to consider who she was, and of whom she was enamored,—a mistress, of a slave. "For if he be lord, then art thou mistress. Be ashamed then of familiarity with a servant, and consider whose wife thou art, and with whom thou wouldst be connected, and towards whom thou art becoming thankless and inconsiderate, and that I repay him greater good-will." And see how he extols his benefits. For since that barbarous and abandoned woman could entertain no lofty sentiment, he shames her from human considerations, saying, "He knoweth nothing through me," i. e., "he is a great benefactor to me, and I cannot strike my patron in a vital part. He hath made me a second lord of his house, and no one [2] hath been kept back from me, but thee." Here he endeavors to raise her mind, that so at any rate he might persuade her to be

---

[1] τό φιλεῖν.
[2] οὐδείς, LXX οὐδέν.

ashamed, and might signify the greatness of her honor. Nor did he stop even here, but likewise added a name sufficient to restrain her, saying, "Because thou art his wife; and how shall I do this wickedness? But what sayest thou? That thy husband is not present, nor knoweth that he is wronged? But God will behold it." She however profited nothing by his advice, but still sought to attract him. For desiring to satiate her own frenzy, not through love of Joseph, she did these things; and this is evident from what she did afterwards. As that she institutes a trial, and brings in accusation, and bears false witness, and exposes to a wild beast him that had done no wrong, and casts him into a prison; or rather for her part, she even slew him, in such a manner did she arm the judge against him. What then? Was then Joseph too such as she was? Nay, altogether the contrary, for he neither contradicted nor accused the woman. "Yes," it may be said: "for he would have been disbelieved." And yet he was greatly beloved; and this is evident not only from the beginning but also from the end. For had not his barbarian master loved him greatly, he would even have slain him in his silence, making no defence: being as he was an Egyptian and a ruler, and wronged in his marriage-bed as he supposed, and by a servant, and a servant to whom he had been so great a benefactor. But all these things gave way to his regard for him, and the grace which God poured down upon him. And together with this grace and love, he had also other no small proofs, had he been minded to justify himself; the garments themselves. For if it were she to whom violence was done, her own vest should have been torn, her face lacerated, instead of her retaining his garments. But "he heard," saith she, "that I lifted up my voice, and left his garments, and went out." And wherefore then didst thou take them from him? since unto one suffering violence, the one thing desirable is to be rid of the intruder.

But not from hence alone, but also from the subsequent events, shall I be able to point out his good-will and his love. Yea even when he fell into a necessity of mentioning the cause of his imprisonment, and his remaining there, he did not even then declare the whole course of the story. But what saith he? "I too have done nothing: but indeed I was stolen out of the land of the Hebrews;" and he no where mentioned the adulteress nor doth he plume himself on the matter, which would have been any one's feeling, if not for vain-glory, yet so as not to appear to have been cast into that cell for an evil cause. For if men in the act of doing wrong by no means abstain even so from blaming the same things, although to do so

brings reproach; of what admiration is not he worthy, because, pure as he was he did not mention the woman's passion nor make a show of her sin; nor when he ascended the throne and became ruler of all Egypt, remember the wrong done by the woman nor exact any punishment?

Seest thou how he cared for her? but her's was not love, but madness. For it was not Joseph that she loved, but she sought to fulfil her own lust. And the very words too, if one would examine them accurately, were accompanied with wrath and great blood-thirstiness. For what saith she? "Thou hast brought in a Hebrew servant to mock us:" upbraiding her husband for the kindness; and she exhibited the garments, having become herself more savage than any wild beast: but not so he. And why speak I of his good-will to her, when he was such, we know, towards his brethren who would slay him; and never said one harsh thing of them, either within doors or without?

[14.] Therefore Paul saith, that the love which we are speaking of is the mother of all good things, and prefers it to miracles and all other gifts. For as where there are vests and sandals of gold, we require also some other garments whereby to distinguish the king: but if we see the purple and the diadem, we require not to see any other sign of his royalty: just so here likewise, when the diadem of love is upon our head, it is enough to point out the genuine disciple of Christ, not to ourselves only, but also to the unbelievers. For, "by this," saith He, "shall all men know that ye are My disciples, if ye have love one to another." (S. John xiii. 35.) So that this sign is greater surely than all signs, in that the disciple is recognised by it. For though any should work ten thousand signs, but be at strife one with another, they will be a scorn to the unbelievers. Just as if they do no sign, but love one another exactly, they will continue both reverenced and inviolable by all men. Since Paul himself we admire on this account, not for the dead whom he raised, nor for the lepers whom he cleansed, but because he said, "who is weak, and I am not weak? who is made to stumble, and I burn not?" (2 Cor. xi. 29) For shouldest thou have ten thousand miracles to compare with this, thou wilt have nothing equal to it to say. Since Paul also himself said, that a great reward was laid up for him, not because he wrought miracles, but because "to the weak he became as weak. For what is my reward?" saith he. "That, when I preach the Gospel, I may make the Gospel without charge." (1 Cor. ix. 18.) And when he puts himself before the Apostles, he saith not, "I have wrought miracles more abundant than they," but, "I have labored more abundantly than they." (1 Cor. xv. 10.) And even by famine was he willing to perish for the salvation of the disciples. "For it were better for me to die," saith he, "than that any man should make my glorying void:" (1 Cor. ix. 15.) not because he was glorying, but that he might not seem to reproach them. For he no where is wont to glory in his own achievements, when the season doth not call to it; but even if he be compelled so to do he calleth himself "a fool." But if he ever glory it is "in infirmities," in wrongs, in greatly sympathizing with those who are injured: even as here also he saith, "who is weak, and I am not weak?" These words are greater even than perils. Wherefore also he sets them last, amplifying his discourse.

Of what then must we be worthy compared with him, who neither contemn wealth for our own sake, nor give up the superfluities of our goods? But not so Paul; rather both soul and body did he use to give up, that they who stoned and beat him with rods, might obtain the kingdom. "For thus," saith he, "hath Christ taught me to love;" who left behind Him the new commandment concerning love, which also Himself fulfilled in deed. For being Lord of all, and of that Blessed Nature; from men, whom He created out of nothing and on whom He had bestowed innumerable benefits, from these, insulting and spitting on Him, He turned not away, but even became man for their sakes, and conversed with harlots and publicans, and healed the demoniacs, and promised heaven. And after all these things they apprehended and beat him with rods, bound, scourged, mocked, and at last crucified Him. And not even so did He turn away, but even when He was on high upon the cross, He saith, "Father, forgive them their sin." But the thief who before this reviled Him, He translated into very paradise; and made the persecutor Paul, an Apostle; and gave up His own disciples, who were His intimates and wholly devoted to Him, unto death for the Jews' sake who crucified Him.

Recollecting therefore in our minds all these things, both those of God and of men, let us emulate these high deeds, and possess ourselves of the love which is above all gifts, that we may obtain both the present and the future blessings: the which may we all obtain, through the grace and mercy of our Lord Jesus Christ, with Whom to the Father, with the Holy Ghost, be glory, power, honor, now and ever, and world without end. Amen.

HOMILY XXXIII.

1 Cor. XIII. 4.

Love suffereth long, and is kind; love envieth not; love vaunteth not itself, is not puffed up.

Thus, whereas he had showed, that both faith and knowledge and prophecy and tongues and gifts and healing and a perfect life and martyrdom, if love be absent, are no great advantage; of necessity he next makes an outline of its matchless beauty, adorning its image with the parts of virtue as with a sort of colors, and putting together all its members with exactness. But do not thou hastily pass by, beloved, the things spoken, but examine each one of them with much care, that thou mayest know both the treasure which is in the thing and the art of the painter. Consider, for example, from what point he at once began, and what he set first, as the cause of all its excellence. And what is this? Long-suffering. This is the root of all self-denial. Wherefore also a certain wise man said, "A man that is long-suffering[1] is of great understanding; but he that is hasty of spirit is mightily foolish[2]."

And comparing it too with a strong city, he said that it is more secure than that. For it is both an invincible weapon and a sort of impregnable tower, easily beating off all annoyances. And as a spark falling into the deep doth it no injury, but is itself easily quenched: so upon a long-suffering soul whatever unexpected thing falls, this indeed speedily vanishes, but the soul it disturbs not: for of a truth there is nothing so impenetrable as long-suffering. You may talk of armies, money, horses, walls, arms, or any thing else whatsoever; you will name nothing like long-suffering. For he that is encompassed with those, oftentimes, being overcome by anger, is upset like a worthless child, and fills all with confusion and tempest: but this man, settled as it were in a harbor, enjoys a profound calm. Though thou surround him

---

[1] "He that is slow to wrath," Auth. Vers. Prov. xiv. 31.

[2] "exalteth folly," Auth. Vers.

with loss, thou hast not moved the rock; though thou bring insult upon him, thou hast not shaken the tower: and though thou bruise him with stripes, thou hast not wounded the adamant.

Yea, and therefore is he called long-suffering, because he hath a kind of long and great soul. For that which is long is also called great. But this excellence is born of love, both to them who possess and to them who enjoy it contributing no small advantage. For tell me not of those abandoned wretches, who, doing evil and suffering none, become worse: since here, not from his long-suffering, but from those who abuse it, this result arises. Tell me not therefore of these, but of those gentler persons, who gain great benefit therefrom. For when, having done ill, they suffer none, admiring the meekness of the sufferer, they reap thereby a very great lesson of self command.

But Paul doth not stop here, but adds also the other high achievements of love, saying, "is kind." For since there are some who practise their long-suffering with a view not to their own self-denial, but to the punishment of those who have provoked them, to make them burst with wrath; he saith that neither hath charity this defect. Wherefore also he added, "is kind." For not at all with a view to light up the fire, in those who are inflamed by anger, do they deal more gently [1] with them, but in order to appease and extinguish it: and not only by enduring nobly, but also by soothing and comforting, do they cure the sore and heal the wound of passion.

"Envieth not." For it is possible for one to be both long-suffering and envious, and thereby that excellency is spoiled. But love avoids this also.

"Vaunteth not itself;" i. e., is not rash [2]. For it renders him who loves both considerate, and grave, and steadfast. In truth, one mark of those who love unlawfully is a defect in this point. Whereas he to whom this love is known, is of all men the most entirely freed from these evils. For when there is no anger within, both rashness and insolence are clean taken away. Love, like some excellent husbandman, taking her seat inwardly in the soul and not suffering any of these thorns to spring up.

"Is not puffed up." For so we see many who think highly of themselves on the score of these very excellencies; for example, on not being envious, nor grudging, nor mean-spirited, nor rash: these evils being incidental not to wealth and poverty only, but even to things naturally good. But love perfectly purges out all. And consider: he that is long-suffering is not of course also kind. But if he be not kind, the thing becomes a vice, and he is in danger of falling into malice. Therefore she supplies a medicine, I mean kindness, and preserves the virtue pure. Again, the kind person often becomes over-complaisant; but this also she corrects. For "love," saith he, "vaunteth not itself, is not puffed up:" the kind and long-suffering is often ostentatious; but she takes away this vice also.

And see how he adorns her not only from what she hath, but also from what she hath not. For he saith that she both brings in virtue, and extirpates vice, nay rather she suffers it not to spring up at all [3]. Thus he said not, "She envieth, indeed, but overcometh envy;" nor, "is arrogant, but chastiseth that passion;" but, "envieth not, vaunteth not itself, is not puffed up;" which truly is most to be admired, that even without toil she accomplishes her good things, and without war and battle-array her trophy is set up: she not permitting him that possesseth her to toil and so to attain the crown, but without labor conveying to him her prize. For where there is not passion to contend against sober reason, what labor can there be?

[2.] "Doth not behave itself unseemly.[4]" "Nay, why," saith he, "do I say, she 'is not puffed up,' when she is so far from that feeling, that in suffering the most shameful things for him whom she loves, she doth not even count the thing an unseemliness?" Again, he did not say, "she suffereth unseemliness but beareth the shame nobly," but, "she doth not even entertain any sense at all of the shame." For if the lovers of money endure all manner of reproaches for the sake of that sordid traffic of theirs, and far from hiding their faces, do even exult in it: much more he that hath this praiseworthy love will refuse nothing whatsoever for the safety's sake of those whom he loves: nay, nor will any thing that he can suffer shame him.

And that we may not fetch our example from any thing base, let us examine this same statement in its application to Christ, and then we shall see the force of what hath been said. For our Lord Jesus Christ was both spit upon and beaten with rods by pitiful slaves; and not only did He not count it an unseemliness, but He even exulted and called the thing glory; and bringing in a robber and murderer with Himself before the rest into paradise, and discoursing with a harlot, and this when the standers-by all accused Him, He counted not the thing to

---

[1] ἠθικώτερον.

[2] οὐ προπετεύεται. Theod. in loc. gives the word the same turn. "She inquires not into matters which concern her not, (for that is τὸ περπερεύσθαι,) she feels not about for the measures of the Divine Substance, nor asks questions in His dispensations, as some use to do. He that loveth, cannot endure to do any thing rash."

[3] τὴν ἀρχήν, Saville. τὴν ἀρετήν, Bened.

[4] Or, doth not think herself treated unseemly. Theod. in loc. "There is no mean or lowly thing which for the brethren's sake she refuses to do, under the notion that to do so would be an unseemly thing."

be disgraceful, but both allowed her to kiss His feet, and to bedew His body with her tears, and to wipe them away with her hair, and this amid a company of spectators who were foes and enemies; "for love doeth nothing unseemly."

Therefore also fathers, though they be the first of philosophers and orators, are not ashamed to lisp with their children; and none of those who see them find fault with them, but the thing is esteemed so good and right as to be even worthy of prayer. And again, should they become vicious, the parents keep on correcting, caring for them, abridging the reproaches they incur, and are not ashamed. For love " doth nothing unseemly," but as it were with certain golden wings covereth up all the offences of the beloved.

Thus also Jonathan loved David; and hearing his father say, (1 Sam. xx. 30.) "Thou son of damsels that have run away from their homes[1], thou womanly bred,[2]" he was not ashamed, though the words be full of great reproach. For what he means is this: "Thou son of mean harlots who are mad after men, who run after the passers-by, thou unnerved and effeminate wretch, who hast nothing of a man, but livest to the shame of thyself and the mother who bare thee." What then? Did he grieve at these things, and hide his face, and turn away from his beloved? Nay, quite the contrary; he displayed his fondness as an ornament. And yet the one was at that time a king, and a king's son, even Jonathan; the other a fugitive and a wanderer, I mean, David. But not even thus was he ashamed of his friendship. "For love doth not behave itself unseemly." Yea, this is its wonderful quality that not only it suffers not the injured to grieve and feel galled, but even disposes him to rejoice. Accordingly, he too, of whom we are speaking, after all these things, just as though he had a crown put on him, went away and fell on David's neck. For love knows not what sort of thing shame may be. Therefore it glories in those things for which another hides his face. Since the shame is, not to know how to love; not, when thou lovest, to incur danger and endure all for the beloved.

But when I say, "all," do not suppose I mean things injurious also; for example, assisting a youth in a love affair, or whatsoever hurtful thing any one may beseech another to do for him. For such a person doth not love, and this I showed you lately from the Egyptian woman: since in truth he only is the lover who seeks what is profitable to the beloved: so that if any pursue not this, even what is right and

good, though he make ten thousand professions of love, he is more hostile than any enemies.

So also Rebecca aforetime, because she exceedingly clung to her son, both perpetrated a theft, and was not ashamed of detection, neither was she afraid, though the risk was no common one ; but even when her son raised scruples[3] to her, "upon me be thy curse, my son," she said. Dost thou see even in a woman the soul of the Apostle[4] how, even as Paul chose, (if one may compare a small thing with a great,) to be anathema for the Jews' sake, (Rom. ix. 3.) so also she, that her son might be blessed, chose to be no less than accursed. And the good things she gave up to him, for she was not, it seems, to be blessed with him, but the evils she was prepared to endure herself alone: nevertheless, she rejoiced, and hasted, and this where so great a danger lay before her, and she was grieved at the delay of the business : for she feared lest Esau might anticipate them and render her wisdom vain. Wherefore also she cuts short the conversation and urges on the young man, and just permitting him to answer what had been said, states a

---

[3] ἀκριβολογουμένου, "made some minute objection."

[4] This view of Rebecca's conduct is generally sanctioned by the Fathers : so St. Augustin : " That which Jacob did by direction of his mother so as to appear to deceive his father, if you consider it diligently and faithfully,'non est mendacium sed mysterium.' And if we term that sort of thing a lie, by the same rule we must also account as lies all parables and figures whatsoever." *contr. Mendac. ad Consentium*, c. 24. St. Ambrose, (*de Jacob et vita beata*, ii. 6.) " In the mind of that pious mother the mystery overweighed the tie of affection. She was not so much preferring Jacob to his brother, as offering him to the Lord, who, she knew, had power to preserve the gift presented unto Him." This seems to mean that in consecrating Jacob to be the first-born, she knowingly separated him from herself, and so made a greater sacrifice. S. Chrys. himself says, " Rebecca did this not of her own mind, but in obedience to the divine oracle," (on *Gen*. Hom. liii. 1. 414.) And he proceeds to point out God's hand in certain minute details of the transaction. It appears from St. Jerome, (1. 169.) that Hippolytus, Irenæus' disciple, early in the third century, took the same view. St. Gregory Nazianzen seems to be the only writer who has left a contrary judgment on record : saying, " he pursued a noble object by ignoble means." The general result of the reflections of the Fathers on the subject seems to be, that as where we have God's express command or approbation, we are sure of the rectitude of what would otherwise be wrong, so there may be circumstances rendering such command or approbation more or less "probable," which ought at least to stay us from censure : and that marked providential interference, and mysterious allusion, throughout, are to be considered as such circumstances.
[In the foregoing note the translator has correctly stated the patristic view of Rebecca's conduct, a view which most moderns heartily reject as dishonoring to God and of evil influence upon his people. But while we cannot with Chrysostom cite the wife of Jacob as an example of love, yet there is some extenuation for her. The case is neatly stated by the Bishop of Ely in the *Speaker's Commentary*. "Rebekah had no doubt treasured up the oracle which had assured her, even before their birth, that her younger son Jacob whom she loved should bear rule over Esau, whose wild and reckless life and whose Canaanitish wives had been a bitterness of soul to her. She probably knew that Jacob had bought Esau's birthright. Now believing rightly that the father's benediction would surely bring blessing with it, she fears that these promises and hopes would fail. She believed but not with that faith which can patiently abide till God works out his plans by His providence. So she strove, as it were, to force forward the event by unlawful means ; even, as some have thought that Judas betrayed Christ that he might free Him to declare Himself a king and take the kingdom." Every character in the history comes in for some share of blame, but the greatest seems due to her who originated the whole plot, who swept away the scruples of her favorite son, and taught him to perpetrate the boldest fraud and falsehood upon his venerable father. The overweening idolatrous affection which led to such doings is very different from the love which the Apostle inculcates and praises. C.]

---

[1] κορασίων αὐτομολουσῶν. Auth. " of the perverse and rebellious woman."
[2] LXX, γυναικοτραφές.

reason sufficient to persuade him. For she said not, "thou sayest these things without reason, and in vain thou fearest, thy father having grown old and being deprived of clearness of sight:" but what? "upon me be thy curse, my son. Only do thou not mar the plot, nor lose the object of our chase, nor give up the treasure."

And this very Jacob, served he not for wages with his kinsmen twice seven years? Was he not together with the bondage subject to mockery in respect of that trick? What then? Did he feel the mockery? Did he count it behaving himself unseemly, that being a freeman, and free born, and well brought up, he endured slaves' treatment among his own kinsmen: a thing which is wont to be most vexing, when one receives opprobrious treatment from one's friends? In no wise. And the cause was his love, which made the time, though long, appear short. "For they were," saith he, (Gen. xxix. 20.) "in his sight as a few days." So far was he from being galled and blushing for this his bondage. Justly then said the blessed Paul, "Love doth not behave itself unseemly."

[3.] Ver. 5. "Seeketh not its own, is not provoked."

Thus having said, "doth not behave itself unseemly," he showeth also the temper of mind, on account of which she doth not behave herself unseemly. And what is that temper? That she "seeketh not her own." For the beloved she esteems to be all, and then only "behaveth herself unseemly," when she cannot free him from such unseemliness; so that if it be possible by her own unseemliness to benefit her beloved, she doth not so much as count the thing unseemliness; for the other party thereafter is yourself, when you love [1]: since this is friendship, that the lover and the beloved should no longer be two persons divided, but in a manner one single person; a thing which no how takes place except from love. Seek not therefore thine own, that thou mayest find thine own. For he that seeks his own, finds not his own. Wherefore also Paul said, "Let no man seek his own, but each his neighbor's good." (1 Cor. x. 24.) For your own profit lies in the profit of your neighbor, and his in yours. As therefore one that had his own gold buried in the house of his neighbor, should he refuse to go and there seek and dig it up, will never seek it; so likewise here, he that will not seek his own profit in the advantage of his neighbor, will not attain unto the crowns due to this: God Himself having therefore so disposed of it, in order that we should be mutually bound together: and even as one awakening a slum-

bering child to follow his brother, when he is of himself unwilling, places in the brother's hand that which he desires and longs for, that through desire of obtaining it he may pursue after him that holds it, and accordingly so it takes place: thus also here, each man's own profit hath he given to his neighbor, that hence we may run after one another, and not be torn asunder.

And if thou wilt, see this also in our case who address you. For my profit depends on thee, and thy advantage on me. Thus, on the one hand it profits thee to be taught the things that please God, but with this have I been entrusted, that thou mightest receive it from me, and therefore mightest be compelled to run unto me; and on the other hand it profits me that thou shouldest be made better: for the reward which I shall receive for this will be great; but this again lieth in thee; and therefore am I compelled to follow after thee that thou mayest be better, and that I may receive my profit from thee. Wherefore also Paul saith, "For what is my hope? are not even ye?" And again, "My hope, and my joy, and the crown of my rejoicing." (1 Thes. ii. 19.) So that the joy of Paul was the disciples, and his joy they had. Therefore he even wept when he saw them perishing.

Again their profit depended on Paul: wherefore he said, "For the hope of Israel I am bound with this chain. (Acts xxviii. 20.) And again, "These things I endure for the elect's sakes that they may obtain eternal life. (2 Tim. ii. 10.) And this one may see in worldly things. "For the wife," saith he, "hath not power over her own body, nor yet the husband; but the wife over the husband's, and the husband over the wife's." (1 Cor. vii. 4.) So likewise we, when we wish to bind any together, do this. We leave neither of them in his own power, but extending a chain between them, we cause the one to be holden of the other, and the other of the one.

Wilt thou also see this in the case of governors? He that judges sits not in judgment for himself, but seeking the profit of his neighbor. The governed on the other hand, seek the profit of the governor by their attendance, by their ministry, by all the other things. Soldiers take up their arms for us, for on our account they peril themselves. We for them are in straits; for from us are their supplies.

But if thou sayest, "each one doth this seeking his own," this also say I, but I add, that by the good of another one's own is won. Thus both the soldier, unless he fight for them that support him, hath none that ministers to him for this end: and this same on the other hand, unless he nourish the soldier, hath none to arm himself in his behalf.

[4.] Seest thou love, how it is everywhere ex-

---

[1] ἐκεῖνος γὰρ αὐτός ἐστι λοιπόν.

tended and manages all things? But be not weary, until thou have thoroughly acquainted thyself with this golden chain. For having said, "seeketh not her own," he mentions again the good things produced by this. And what are these?

"Is not easily provoked, thinketh no evil.[1]" See love again not only subduing vice, but not even suffering it to arise at all. For he said not, "though provoked, she overcomes," but, "is not provoked." And he said not, "worketh no evil," but, "not even thinketh;" i. e., so far from contriving any evil, she doth not even suspect it of the beloved. How then could she work any, or how be provoked? who doth not even endure to admit an evil surmise; whence is the fountain of wrath.

Ver. 6. "Rejoiceth not in unrighteousness:" i. e., doth not feel pleasure over those that suffer ill : and not this only, but also, what is much greater, "rejoiceth with the truth." "She feels pleasure," saith he, "with them that are well spoken of," as Paul saith, "Rejoice with them that rejoice, and weep with them that weep." (Rom. xii. 15.)

Hence, she "envieth not," hence she "is not puffed up:" since in fact she accounts the good things[2] of others her own.

Seest thou how by degrees love makes her nursling an angel? For when he is void of anger, and pure from envy, and free from every tyrannical passion, consider that even from the nature of man he is delivered from henceforth, and hath arrived at the very serenity of angels.

Nevertheless, he is not content with these, but hath something even more than these to say : according to his plan of stating the stronger points later. Wherefore he saith, "beareth all things." From her long-suffering, from her goodness; whether they be burdensome, or grievous, or insults, or stripes, or death, or whatsoever else. And this again one may perceive from the case of blessed David. For what could be more intolerable than to see a son rising up against him, and aiming at the usurpation, and thirsting for a father's blood? Yet this did that blessed one endure, nor even so could he bear to throw out one bitter expression against the parricide; but even when he left all the rest to his captains, gave a strong injunction respecting his safety. For strong was the foundation of his love. Wherefore also it "beareth all things."

Now its power the Apostle here intimates, but its goodness, by what follows. For, "it hopeth all things," saith he, "believeth all things, endureth all things." What is, "hopeth all things?" "It doth not despair," saith he, "of the beloved, but even though he be worthless, it continues to correct, to provide, to care for him."

"Believeth all things." "For it doth not merely hope," saith he, "but also believeth from its great affection." And even if these good things should not turn out according to its hope, but the other person should prove yet more intolerable, it bears even these. For, saith he, it "endureth all things."

[5.] Ver. 8. "Love never faileth."

Seest thou when he put the crown on the arch, and what of all things is peculiar to this gift? For what is, "faileth not?" it is not severed, is not dissolved by endurance. For it puts up with everything: since happen what will, he that loves never can hate. This then is the greatest of its excellencies.

Such a person was Paul. Wherefore also he said, "If by any means I may provoke to emulation them which are my flesh;" (Rom. xi. 14.) and he continued hoping. And to Timothy he gave a charge, saying, "And the Lord's servant must not strive, but be gentle towards all....in meekness correcting those that oppose themselves, if God peradventure may give them the knowledge of the truth.[3]" (2 Tim. ii. 24, 25.)

"What then," saith one, "if they be enemies and heathens, must one hate them?" One must hate, not them but their doctrine: not the man, but the wicked conduct, the corrupt mind. For the man is God's work, but the deceit is the devil's work. Do thou not therefore confound the things of God and the things of the devil. Since the Jews were both blasphemers, and persecutors, and injurious, and spake ten thousand evil things of Christ. Did Paul then hate them, he who of all men most loved Christ? In no wise, but he both loved them, and did everything for their sakes: and at one time he saith, "My heart's desire and my supplication to God is for them that they may be saved:" (Rom. x. 1, ix. 3.) and at another, "I could wish that myself were anathema from Christ for their sakes." Thus also Ezekiel seeing them slain saith, "Alas, O Lord, dost Thou blot out the remnant of Israel?" (Ezek. ix. 8.) And Moses, "If Thou wilt forgive their sin, forgive." (Exod. xxxii. 32.)

Why then saith David, "Do not I hate them, O Lord, that hate Thee, and against Thine enemies did I not pine away? I hate them with perfect hatred." (Ps. cxxxix. 21, 22.)

Now, in the first place, not all things spoken in the Psalms by David, are spoken in the person of David. For it is he himself who saith, "I have dwelt in the tents of Kedar;" (Ps. cxx. 5) and, "By the waters of Babylon, there we sat

---

[1 The revised version renders this clause, "taketh not account of evil"—a rendering as old as Theodoret. C.]
[2] Fronto Ducæus reads κακά.

[3] μετάνοιαν εἰς om.

down and wept:" (cxxxvii. 1.) yet he neither saw Babylon, nor the tents of Kedar.

But besides this, we require now a completer self-command. Wherefore also when the disciples besought that fire might come down, even as in the case of Elias, "Ye know not," saith Christ, "what manner of spirit ye are of. (Luke ix. 55.) For at that time not the ungodliness only, but also the ungodly themselves, they were commanded to hate, in order that their friendship might not prove an occasion of transgression unto them. Therefore he severed their connections, both by blood and marriage, and on every side he fenced them off.

But now because he hath brought us to a more entire self-command and set us on high above that mischief, he bids us rather admit and soothe them. For we get no harm from them, but they get good by us. What then doth he say? we must not hate, but pity. Since if thou shalt hate, how wilt thou easily convert him that is in error? how wilt thou pray for the unbeliever? for that one ought to pray, hear what Paul saith: "I exhort therefore, first of all, that supplications, prayer, intercessions, thanksgivings be made for all men." (1 Tim. ii. 1.) But that all were not then believers, is, I suppose, evident unto every one. And again, "for kings and all that are in high place." But that these were ungodly and transgressors, this also is equally manifest. Further, mentioning also the reason for the prayer, he adds, " for this is good and acceptable in the sight of God our Saviour; who willeth that all men should be saved, and come to the knowledge of the truth." Therefore, if he find a Gentile wife consorting with a believer, he dissolves not the marriage. Yet what is more closely joined than a man to his wife? " For they two shall be one flesh," (Gen. ii. 24.) and great in that instance is the charm, and ardent the desire. But if we are to hate ungodly and lawless men, we shall go on to hate also sinners; and thus in regular process thou wilt be broken off from the most even of thy brethren, or rather from all: for there is not one, no, not one, without sin. For if it be our duty to hate the enemies of God, one must not hate the ungodly only, but also sinners: and thus we shall be worse than wild beasts, shunning all, and puffed up with pride; even as that Pharisee. But not thus did Paul command us, but how? " Admonish the disorderly, encourage the faint-hearted, support the weak, be long suffering toward all." (1 Thes. v. 14.)

[6.] What then doth he mean when he saith, "If any obeyeth not our word by this epistle, note that man, that ye have no company with him?" (2 Thes. iii. 14.) In the first place, he saith this of brethren, however not even so without limitation, but this too with gentleness. For do not thou cut off what follows, but subjoin also the next clause: how, having said, "keep no company," he added, "yet count him not as an enemy, but admonish him as a brother." Seest thou how he bade us hate the deed that is evil, and not the man? For indeed it is the work of the devil to tear us asunder from one another, and he hath ever used great diligence to take away love that he may cut off the way of correction, and may retain him in error and thee in enmity, and thus block up the way of his salvation. For when both the physician hates the sick man and flies from him, and the sick man turns away from the physician, when will the distempered person be restored, seeing that neither the one will call in the other's aid, nor will the other go to him?

But wherefore, tell me, dost thou at all turn away from him and avoid him? Because he is ungodly? Truly for this cause oughtest thou to welcome and attend him, that thou mayest raise him up in his sickness. But if he be incurably sick, still thou hast been bidden to do thy part. Since Judas also was incurably diseased, yet God left not off attending upon him. Wherefore, neither do thou grow weary. For even if after much labor thou fail to deliver him from his ungodliness, yet shalt thou receive the deliverer's reward, and wilt cause him to wonder at thy gentleness, and so all this praise will pass on to God. For though thou shouldest work wonders, and raise the dead, and whatsoever work thou doest, the Heathen will never wonder at thee so much, as when they see thee displaying a meek, gentle, mild disposition. And this is no small achievement: since many will even be entirely delivered from their evil way; there being nothing that hath such power to allure men as love. For in respect of the former they will rather be jealous of thee, I mean the signs and wonders; but for this they will both admire and love thee: and if they love, they will also lay hold of the truth in due course. If however he become not all at once a believer, wonder not nor hurry on, neither do thou require all things at once, but suffer him for the present to praise, and love, and unto this in due course he will come.

[7.] And that thou mayest clearly know how great a thing this is, hear how even Paul, going before an unbelieving judge, made his defence. "I think myself happy," saith he, " That I am to make my defence before thee." (Acts xxvi. 2.) And these things he said, not to flatter him, far from it; but wishing to gain him by his gentleness. And he did in part gain him, and he that was till then considered to be condemned took captive his judge, and the victory is confessed by the person himself who was made captive, with a loud voice in the presence of all, saying, "With but little persuasion thou wouldst fain make me a Christian." (Acts xxvi. 28, 29.) What then saith Paul? He spread his net the wider, and saith, "I would to God, that not only thou, but also all that hear me this day, might become such as I am, except these bonds." What sayest thou, O Paul? "except these bonds?" And what confidence remains for thee, if thou art ashamed of these things, and fliest from them, and this before so great a multitude? Dost thou not every where in thy Epistles boast of this matter, and call thyself a prisoner? Dost thou not every where carry about this chain in our sight as a diadem? What then hath happened now that thou deprecatest these bonds? "I myself deprecate them not," saith he, "nor am I ashamed of them, but I condescend to their weakness. For they are not yet able to receive my glorying; and I have learned from my Lord not to put 'a piece of undressed cloth upon an old garment:' (S. Mat. ix. 16.) therefore did I thus speak. For, in fact, unto this time they have heard ill reports of our doctrine, and abhor the cross. If therefore I should add also bonds, their hatred becometh greater; I removed these, therefore, that the other might be made acceptable. So it is, that to them it seems disgraceful to be bound, because they have not as yet tasted of the Glory which is with us. One must therefore condescend: and when they shall have learned of the true life, then will they know the beauty also of this iron, and the lustre which comes of these bonds." Furthermore, discoursing with others, he even calls the thing a free gift, saying, "It hath been granted in the behalf of Christ, not only to believe on Him, but also to suffer in His behalf." (Phil. i. 29.) But for the time then present, it was a great thing for the hearers not to be ashamed of the cross: for which cause he goes on gradually. Thus, neither doth any one introducing a person to a palace, before that he beholds the vestibule, compel him, yet standing without, to survey what is within: since in that way it will not even seem admirable, unless one enter in and so acquaint one's self with all.

So then let us also deal with the heathen sort: with condescension, with love. For love is a great teacher, and able both to withdraw men from error, and to reform the character, and to lead them by the hand unto self-denial, and out of stones to make men.

[8.] And if thou wouldest learn her power, bring me a man timid and fearful of every sound, and trembling at shadows; or passionate, and harsh, and a wild beast rather than a man; or wanton and licentious; or wholly given to wickedness; and deliver him into the hands of love, and introduce him into this school; and thou wilt speedily see that cowardly and timid creature made brave and magnanimous, and venturing upon all things cheerfully. And what is wonderful, not from any change in nature do these things result, but in the coward soul itself love manifests her peculiar power; and it is much the same as if one should cause a leaden sword, not turned into steel but continuing in the nature of lead, to do the work of steel. As thus: Jacob was a "plain man[1], (Gen. xxv. 27.) dwelling in a house[2]," and unpracticed in toils and dangers, living a kind of remiss and easy life, and like a virgin in her chamber, so also he was compelled for the most part to sit within doors and keep the house; withdrawn from the forum and all tumults of the forum, and from all such matters, and even continuing in ease and quietness. What then? After that the torch of love had set him on fire, see how it made this plain and home-keeping man strong to endure and fond of toil. And of this hear not what I say, but what the patriarch himself saith: how finding fault with his kinsman, his words are, "These twenty years am I with thee." (Gen. xxxi. 36.) And how wert thou these twenty years? (For this also he adds,) "Consumed by the heat in the day time, and with the frost by night, and sleep departed from mine eyes," Thus speaks that "plain man, keeping at home," and living that easy life.

Again, that he was timid is evident, in that, expecting to see Esau, he was dead with fear. But see again, how this timid man became bolder than a lion under the influence of love. For putting himself forward like some champion before the rest, he was ready to be first in receiving that savage and slaughter-breathing brother as he supposed him to be, and with his own body to purchase the safety of his wives: and him whom he feared and shuddered at, he desired to behold himself foremost in the array. For this fear was not so strong as his affection for his wives. Seest thou how, being timid, he became suddenly adventurous, not by changing his character, but being invigorated by love? For that after this also he was timid, is evident by his changing from place to place.

But let no man consider what has been said to be a charge against that righteous man: since being timid is no reproach, for this is a man's nature; but the doing any thing unseemly for timidity's sake. For it is possible for one that is timid by nature to become courageous through piety. What did Moses? Did he not, through fear of a single Egyptian, fly, and go away into banishment? Nevertheless, this fugitive who could not endure the menace

---

[1] ἄπλαστος.
[2] οἰκίαν. LXX. rec. vers. "tents."

of a single man, after that he tasted of the honey of love, nobly and without compulsion from any man, was forward to perish together with them whom he loved. "For if thou wilt forgive their sin," saith he, "forgive; and if not, blot me, I pray thee, out of Thy book which thou hast written. (Exod. xxxii. 32.)

[9.] Moreover, that love makes also the fierce moderate, and the wanton chaste, we have no longer need of any examples: this being evident to all men. Though a man be more savage than any wild beast, no sheep so gentle as he is rendered by love. Thus, what could be more savage and frantic than Saul? But when his daughter let his enemy go, he uttered not against her even a bitter word. And he that unsparingly put to the sword all the priests for David's sake, seeing that his daughter had sent him away from the house, was not indignant with her even as far as words; and this when so great a fraud had been contrived against him:

because he was restrained by the stronger bridle of love.

Now as moderation, so chastity, is an ordinary effect of love. If a man love his own wife as he ought to love, even though he be never so much inclined to wantoness, he will not endure to look upon another woman, on account of his affection for her. "For love," (Cant. viii. 5.) saith one, "is strong as death." So that from no other source doth wanton behavior arise than from want of love.

Since then love is the Artificer of all virtue, let us with all exactness implant her in our own souls, that she may produce for us many blessings, and that we may have her fruit continually abounding, the fruit which is ever fresh and never decays. For thus shall we obtain no less than eternal blessings: which may we all obtain, through the grace and mercy of our Lord Jesus Christ, with Whom to the Father, and also the Holy Ghost, be glory, power, and honor, now and for ever, and world without end. Amen.

HOMILY XXXIV.

1 COR. XIII. 8.

But whether there be prophecies, they shall be done away; whether there be tongues, they shall cease; whether there be knowledge, it shall be done away.

HAVING shown the excellency of love from its being requisite both to the spiritual gifts, and to the virtues of life; and from rehearsal of all its good qualities, and by showing it to be the foundation of exact self-denial; from another, a third head, again he points out its worth. And this he doth, first from a wish to persuade those who seemed to be accounted inferior that it is in their power to have the chief of all signs, and that they will be no worse off than the possessors of the gifts, if they have this, but rather much better: secondly, with regard on the other hand to them that had the greater gifts and were lifted up thereby, studying to bring them down and to show that they have nothing unless they have this. For thus they would both love one another, envy as well as pride being hereby taken away; and reciprocally, loving one another, they would still further banish these passions. "For love envieth not, is not puffed up." So that on every side he throws around them an impregnable wall, and a manifold unanimity, which first removes all their disorders, and thereby again

waxes stronger. Therefore also he put forward innumerable reasons which might comfort their dejection. As thus: both "the same Spirit," saith he, is the giver; and He "giveth to profit withal; and divideth as he will," and it is a gift which He divideth, not a debt. Though thou receive but a little, thou dost equally contribute to the body, and even thus thou enjoyest much honor. And he that hath the greater, needs thee who hast the less. And, "Love is the greatest gift, and 'the more excellent way.'"

Now all this he said doubly to bind them to each other, both by their not considering themselves disparaged while they had this; and because, after pursuit and attainment of it, they henceforth would not feel human infirmity; both as having the root of all gifts, and as no longer capable of contentiousness even though they had nothing. For he that is once led captive by love is freed from contentiousness.

And this is why, pointing out to them how great advantages they shall thence reap, he sketched out its fruits; by his praises of it repressing their disorders: inasmuch as each one of the things mentioned by him was a sufficient medicine to heal their wounds. Wherefore also he said, "suffereth long," to them that are at strife one with another; "is kind," to them that stand mutually aloof, and bear a secret grudge; "envieth not," to them that look grudgingly on their superiors; "vaunteth not itself," to them that are separated; "is not puffed up," to them that boast themselves against others; "doth not behave itself unseemly," to them that do not think it their duty to condescend; "seeketh not her own," to them that overlook the rest; "is not provoked, taketh not account of evil," to them that are insolent; "rejoiceth not in unrighteousness, but rejoiceth with the truth," to them again that are envious; "beareth all things," to them that are treacherous; "hopeth all things," to the despairing; "endureth all things, never faileth," to them that easily separate themselves.

[2.] Now then after that in every way he had shown her to be very exceedingly great, again he doth so from another most important head, by a fresh comparison exalting her dignity, and saying thus; "but whether there be prophecies, they shall be done away; whether there be tongues, they shall cease." For if both these were brought in in order to the faith; when that is every where sown abroad, the use of these is henceforth superfluous. But the loving one another shall not cease, rather it shall even advance further, both here and hereafter, and then more than now. For here there are many things that weaken[1] our love; wealth, business, passions of the body, disorders of the soul : but there none of these.

But although it be no marvel that prophecies and tongues should be done away, that knowledge should be done away, this is what may cause some perplexity. For this also he added, "Whether there be knowledge, it shall be done away." What then? are we then to live in ignorance? Far from it. Nay, then specially it is probable that our knowledge is made intense. Wherefore also he said, "Then shall I know, even as also I am known." For this reason, if you mark it, that you might not suppose this to be done away equally with the prophecy and the tongues, having said, "Whether there be knowledge, it shall be done away," he was not silent, but added also the manner of its vanishing away, immediately subjoining the saying,

Ver. 9. 10. "We know in part, and we prophesy in part. But when that which is perfect is come, then that which is in part shall be done away."

It is not therefore knowledge that is done away, but the circumstance that our knowledge is in part. For we shall not only know as much but even a great deal more. But that I may also make it plain by example; now we know

that God is every where, but how, we know not. That He made out of things that are not the things that are we know; but of the manner we are ignorant. That He was born of a virgin, we know; but how, we know not yet. But then shall we know somewhat more and clearer concerning these thing. Next he points out also how great is the distance between the two, and that our deficiency is no small one, saying,

Ver. 11. "When I was a child, I spake as a child, I felt as a child, I thought as a child; but now that I am become a man, I have put away childish things."

And by another example too he manifests the same thing again, saying,

Ver. 12. "For now we see in a mirror."

Further, because the glass sets before us the thing seen indefinitely, he added, "darkly[2]," to show very strongly that the present knowledge is most partial.

"But then face to face." Not as though God hath a face, but to express the notion of greater clearness and perspicuity. Seest thou how we learn all things by gradual addition?

"Now I know in part; but then shall I know even as also I have been known." Seest thou how in two ways he pulls down their pride? Both because their knowledge is in part, and because not even this have they of themselves. "For I knew Him not, but He made Himself known[3] to me," saith he. Wherefore, even as now He first knew me, and Himself hastened towards me, so shall I hasten towards Him then much more than now. For so he that sits in darkness, as long as he sees not the sun doth not of himself hasten to meet the beauty of its beam, which indeed shows itself as soon as it hath begun to shine : but when he perceives its brightness, then also himself at length follows after its light. This then is the meaning of the expression, "even as also I have been known." Not that we shall so know him as He is, but that even as He hastened toward us now, so also shall we cleave unto Him then, and shall know many of the things which are now secret, and shall enjoy that most blessed society and wisdom. For if Paul who knew so much was a child, consider what those things must be. If these be "a glass" and "a riddle," do thou hence again infer, God's open Face, how great a thing It is.

[3.] But that I may open out to thee some small part of this difference, and may impart some faint ray of this thought to thy soul, I would have thee recall to mind things as they were in the Law, now after that grace hath shone forth. For those things too, that came before grace, had a certain great and marvellous

---

[1] χαυνοῦντα.
[2] ἐν αἰνίγματι.
[3] ἐγνώρισε, made me know Him.

appearance: nevertheless, hear what Paul saith of them after grace came: "That which was made glorious had no glory in this respect, by reason of the glory that surpasseth." (2 Cor. iii. 10).

But that what I say may be made yet clearer, let us apply the argument to some one of the rites then performed, and then thou wilt see how great is the difference. And if thou wilt, let us bring forward that passover and this, and then shalt thou be aware of our superiority. For the Jews indeed celebrated it, but they celebrated it "so as in a mirror, and darkly." But these hidden mysteries they never at any time did even conceive in their mind, nor what things they prefigured. They saw a lamb slain, and the blood of a beast, and door-posts sprinkled with it; but that the Son of God incarnate shall be slain, and shall set free the whole world, and shall grant both to Greeks and Barbarians to taste of this Blood, and shall open heaven to all, and shall offer what is there to the whole human race, and having taken His blood-stained flesh shall exalt it above the heaven, and the heaven of heavens, and, in a word, above all the hosts on high, of the angels and archangels and all the other powers, and shall cause it shining in unspeakable glory,—to sit down upon the throne itself of the King, on the right hand of the Father these things, I say, no one, either of them or of the rest of mankind, either foreknew or was able ever to conceive.

[4.] But what say those who shrink from nothing?[1] That the expression, "now I know in part," is spoken in dispensations; for that the Apostle had the perfect knowledge of God. And now he calls himself a child? How sees he "in a mirror?" How "darkly," if he hath the sum of knowledge? And why doth he refer to it as something peculiar to the Spirit, and to no other power in the creation,

saying, "For who among men knoweth the things of a man, save the spirit of the man which is in him? Even so the things of God none knoweth, save the Spirit of God." (1 Cor. ii. 11.) And Christ again sayeth that this belongs to Himself alone, thus saying, "Not that any man hath seen the Father, save He which is from God, He hath seen the Father," (John vi. 46.) giving the name, "sight," to the most clear and perfect knowledge.

And how shall he who knoweth the Essence, be ignorant of the dispensations? since that knowledge is greater than this.

"Are we then," saith he, "ignorant of God?" Far from it. That He is, we know, but what He is, as regards His Essence, we know not yet. And that thou mayst understand that not concerning the dispensations did he speak the words, "now I know in part," hear what follows. He adds then, "but then shall I know, even as also I have been known." He was surely known not by the dispensations, but by God.

Let none therefore consider this to be a small or simple transgression, but twofold, and threefold, yea and manifold. For not only is there this impiety that they boast of knowing those things which belong to the Spirit alone, and to the only-begotten Son of God, but also that when Paul could not acquire even this knowledge "which is in part" without the revelation from above, these men say that they have obtained the whole from their own reasonings. For neither are they able to point out that the Scripture hath any where discoursed to us of these things.

[5.] But however, leaving their madness, let us give heed to the words which follow concerning love. For he was not content with these things, but adds again, saying,

Ver. 13. "And now abideth, faith, hope, love, these three; and the greatest of these is love."

For faith indeed and hope, when the good things believed and hoped for are come, cease. And to show this Paul said, "For hope that is seen is not hope; for who hopeth for that which he seeth." Again, "Now faith is the assurance of things hoped for, the proving of things not seen." (Rom. viii. 24; Heb. xi. 1.) So that these cease when those appear; but love is then most elevated, and becomes more vehement. Another encomium of love. For neither is he content with those before mentioned, but he strives to discover yet another. And observe: he hath said that it is a great gift, and a still more excellent way to these. He hath said, that without it there is no great profit in our gifts; he hath shadowed out its image at length; he intends again and in another manner to exalt

---

[1] The Heretics here referred to were the Eunomians or Anomœans, so called from Eunomius their chief Teacher, (for Aetius first promulgated their opinions,) and from their maintaining not merely the inequality but the dissimilarity (τὸ ἀνόμοιον) of the Son's nature to that of the Father. By this he carried out Arianism, and made it more consistent and more impious. It seems that he arbitrarily selected the term ἀγέννητος, "unbegotten," as setting forth not merely the attribute of the Father, but the very substance of the Godhead, and upon this proceeded, of course, to deny the proper divinity of the Son, because He was confessed to be γεννητὸς, "begotten." And he not only thus implied, but expressly maintained, that knowing thus much of God, we know His whole Nature: whence it followed, that St. Paul's professions of ignorance referred not to the Substance, but to some parts of the Providence of God, called here, "dispensations." Against this result of Eunomius' impiety, St. Chrysostom preached the series of five Homilies, "On the Incomprehensible Nature of God:" in the first of which, (t. vi. 393. ed. Saville,) he argues on this passage almost in the same words. The same fallacy may be seen refuted by St. Basil also, *Ep.* 234, 235; *Epiph. Hær.* 76. p. 989, &c.: Theodoret, ii. 418; and by others. The whole doctrine as grounded on the word ἀγέννητος is exposed at large by St. Basil in his five books against Eunomius, t. i. ed. Bened. In the Appendix to that volume, Eunomius's own treatise is given. The whole forms a melancholy example, how men may deceive themselves by following after simplification and logical consistency, without due reverence for sacred things.

it, and to show that it is great from its abiding. Wherefore also he said, " But now abideth faith, hope, love, these three ; but the greatest of these is love." How then is love the greater ? In that those pass away.

If now so great is the virtue of love, with good reason doth he add and say, " Follow after love. For there is surely need of " following," and a kind of vehement running after her: in such sort doth she fly from us, and so many are the things which trip us up in that direction. Wherefore we have ever need of great earnestness in order to overtake her. And to point out this, Paul said not, " follow love," but, " pursue [1]" her ; stirring us up, and inflaming us to lay hold on her.

For so God from the beginning contrived ten thousand ways for implanting her in us. Thus, first, He granted one head to all, Adam. For why do we not all spring out of the earth? Why not full grown, as he was? In order that both the birth and the bringings up of children, and the being born of another, might bind us mutually together. For this cause neither made He woman out of the earth : and because the thing of the same substance was not equally sufficient to shame us into unanimity, unless we had also the same progenitor, He provided also for this: since, if now, being only separated by place, we consider ourselves alien from one another ; much more would this have happened if our race had had two originals. For this cause therefore, as it were from some one head, he bound together the whole body of the human race. And because from the beginning they seemed to be in a manner two, see how he fastens them together again, and gathers them into one by marriage. For, " therefore," saith He, " shall a man leave his father and his mother, and shall cleave unto his wife; and they shall be for one flesh." (Gen. ii. 24[2].) And he said not, " the woman," but, " the man," because the desire too is stronger in him. Yea, and for this cause He made it also stronger, that it might bow the superior party to the absolute sway of this passion, and might subjugate it to the weaker. And since marriage also must needs be introduced, him from whom she sprang He made husband to the woman. For all things in the eye of God are second to love. And if when things had thus begun, the first man straightway became so frantic, and the devil sowed among them so great warfare and envy; what would he not have done, had they not sprung from one root?

Further, in order that the one might be subject, and the other rule ; (for equality is wont oftentimes to bring in strife ;) he suffered it not to be a democracy, but a monarchy ; and as in an army, this order one may see in every family. In the rank of monarch, for instance, there is the husband; but in the rank of lieutenant and general, the wife; and the children too are allotted a third station in command. Then after these a fourth order, that of the servant. For these also bear rule over their inferiors, and some one of them is oftentimes set over the whole, keeping ever the post of the master, but still as a servant. And together with this again another command, and among the children themselves again another, according to their age and sex; since among the children the female doth not possess equal sway. And every where hath God made governments at small distances and thick together, that all might abide in concord and much good order. Therefore even before the race was increased to a multitude, when the first two only were in being, He bade him govern, and her obey. And in order again that He might not despise her as inferior, and separate from her, see how He honored her, and made them one, even before her creation. For, " Let us make for man," saith He, " a help meet," implying that she was made for his need, and thereby drawing him unto her who was made for his sake : since to all those things are we more kindly disposed, which are done for our sakes. But that she, on the other hand, might not be elated, as being granted him for help, nor might burst this bond, He makes her out of his side, signifying that she is a part of the whole body. And that neither might the man be elated therefore, He no longer permits that to belong to him alone which before was his alone, but effected the contrary to this, by bringing in procreation of children, and herein too giving the chief honor unto the man, not however allowing the whole to be his.

Seest thou how many bonds of love God hath wrought? And these indeed by force of nature He hath lodged in us as pledges of concord. For both our being of the same substance leads to this; (for every animal loves its like;) and the woman being produced from the man, and again the children from both. Whence also many kinds of affection arise. For one we love as a father, another as a grandfather; one as a mother, another as a nurse; and one as a son or grandson or great-grandson again, and another as a daughter, or grand-daughter; and one as a brother, another as a nephew; and one as a sister, another as a niece. And why need one recount all the names of consanguinity?

And He devised also another foundation of affection. For having forbidden the marriage of kindred, he led us out unto strangers and drew them again unto us. For since by this natural kindred it was not possible that they

---

[1] διώκετε.

[2] εἰς σάρκα μίαν.

should be connected with us, he connected us anew by marriage, uniting together whole families by the single person of the bride, and mingling entire races with races.

For, "marry not," saith the Lord, (Levit. xviii. 6.) "thy sister, nor thy father's sister, nor any damsel which hath such consanguinity with thee," as utterly hinders the marriage;" naming the degrees of such relationship. It is enough for thine affection towards them that ye were the fruit of the same birth-pangs, and that the others are in a different relation to thee. Why dost thou narrow the breadth of love? Why dost thou idly throw away a ground of affection towards her, such as that thou mightest thereby provide thyself with distinct source for affection to spring from; I mean, by taking a wife from another family, and through her a chain of kinsmen, both mother, and father, and brethren, and their connexions!

[7.] Seest thou by how many ways He hath bound us together? Nevertheless, not even this sufficed Him, but He likewise made us to stand in need of one another, that thus also He might bring us together, because necessities above all create friendships. For no other reason neither suffered He all things to be produced in every place, that hence also He might compel us to mix with one another. But having set us in need of one another, He on the other hand made the intercourse easy. Since if this were not so, the matter would have turned out painful and difficult in another way. For if one that wanted a physician, or a carpenter, or any other workman, had need to set off on a long foreign sojourn, the whole had come to nought. Here then is why He founded cities also, and brought all into one place. And accordingly that we might easily keep up intercourse with distant countries, He spread the level of the sea between us, and gave us the swiftness of winds, thereby making our voyages easy. And at the beginning He even gathered all men together in one spot, and did not disperse them until they who first received the gift abused their concord unto sin. However, He hath drawn us together in every way; both by nature, and by consanguinity, and by language, and by place; and as he willed not that we should fall from paradise; (for had He willed it, He would not have placed there at all "the man whom He had formed," but he that disobeyed was the cause;) so neither was it His will that men should have divers tongues; since otherwise He would have made it so from the beginning. But now "the whole earth was of one language, and all had one speech." (Gen. xi. 1.)

Here is the reason why, when it was needful that the earth should be destroyed, not even then did He make us of other matter, nor did

He translate the righteous man, but leaving him in the midst of the deluge, like a kind of spark of the world, He rekindled our race from thence, even by the blessed Noah. And from the beginning He made one sovereignty only, setting the man over the woman. But after that our race ran headlong into extreme disorder, He appointed other sovereignties also, those of Masters, and those of Governors, and this too for love's sake. That is, since vice was a thing apt to dissolve and subvert our race, He set those who administer justice in the midst of our cities as a kind of physicians, that driving away vice, as it were a plague to love, they might gather together all in one.

And that not only in cities, but also in each family there might be great unanimity, He honored the man with rule and superiority; the woman on the other hand He armed with desire: and the gift also of procreation of children, He committed in common to both, and withal He furnished also other things apt to conciliate love: neither entrusting all to the man, nor all to the woman; but "dividing these things also severally to each;" to her entrusting the house, and to him the market; to him the work of feeding, for he tills the ground; to her that of clothing, for loom and distaff are the woman's. For it is God Himself who gave to woman-kind skill in woven work. Woe be to covetousness, which suffers not this difference to appear! For the general effeminacy [1] hath gone so far as to introduce our men to the looms, and put shuttles into their hands, and the woof, and threads. Nevertheless, even thus the forethought of the divine economy shines out. For we still greatly need the woman in other more necessary things, and we require the help of our inferiors in those things which keep our life together.

[8.] And so strong is the compulsion of this need that though one be richer than all men, not even thus is he rid of this close conjunction, and of his want of that which is inferior to himself. For it is not, we see, the poor only who need the rich, but the rich also the poor; and these require those more than the others them. And that thou mayest see it more clearly, let us suppose, if it seem good, two cities, the one of rich only, but the other of poor; and neither in that of the rich let there be any poor man, nor in that of the poor any rich; but let us purge out both thoroughly, and see which will be the more able to support itself. For if we find that of the poor able, it is evident that the rich will more stand in need of them.

Now then, in that city of the affluent there will be no manufacturer, no builder, no carpenter, no shoe-maker, no baker, no husband-

---

[1] βλακεία.

man, no brazier, no rope-maker, nor any other such trade. For who among the rich would ever choose to follow these crafts, seeing that the very men who take them in hand, when they become rich, endure no longer the discomfort caused by these works? How then shall this our city stand? "The rich," it is replied, "giving money, will buy these things of the poor." Well then, they will not be sufficient for themselves, their needing the others proves that. But how will they build houses? Will they purchase this too? But the nature of things cannot admit this. Therefore they must needs invite the artificers thither, and destroy the law, which we made at first when we were founding the city. For you remember, that we said, "let there be no poor man within it." But, lo, necessity, even against our will, hath invited and brought them in. Whence it is evident that it is impossible without poor for a city to subsist: since if the city were to continue refusing to admit any of these, it will be no longer a city but will perish. Plainly then it will not support itself, unless it shall collect the poor as a kind of preservers, to be within itself.

But let us look also upon the city of the poor, whether this too will be in a like needy condition, on being deprived of the rich. And first let us in our discourse thoroughly clear the nature of riches, and point them out plainly. What then may riches be? Gold, and silver, and precious stones, and garments silken, purple, and embroidered with gold. Now then that we have seen what riches are, let us drive them away from our city of the poor: and if we are to make it purely a city of poor persons, let not any gold appear there, no not in a dream, nor garments of such quality; and if you will, neither silver, nor vessels of silver. What then? Because of this will that city and its concerns live in want, tell me? Not at all. For suppose first there should be need to build; one does not want gold and silver and pearls, but skill, and hands, and hands not of any kind, but such as are become callous, and fingers hardened, and great strength, and wood, and stones: suppose again one would weave a garment, neither here have we need of gold and silver, but, as before, of hands and skill, and women to work. And what if one require husbandry, and digging the ground? Is it rich men who are wanted, or poor? It is evident to every one, poor. And when iron too is to be wrought, or any such thing to be done, this is the race of men whereof we most stand in need.

What respect then remains wherein we may stand in need of the rich? except the thing required be, to pull down this city. For

should that sort of people make an entrance, and these philosophers, for (for I call them philosophers, who seek after nothing superfluous,) should fall to desiring gold and jewels, giving themselves up to idleness and luxury; they will ruin everything from that day forward.

[9.] "But unless wealth be useful," saith one, "wherefore hath it been given by God?" And whence is it evident, that being rich is from God? "The Scripture saith, 'The silver is Mine, and the gold is Mine,' and to whomsoever I will, I will give it." (Hag. ii. 8.) Here, if I were not doing an unseemly thing, I could at this moment laugh loudly, in derision of those who say these things: because as little children admitted to a King's table, together with that food they thrust into their mouth everything that comes to hand; so also do these together with the divine Scriptures privily bring in their own notions. For this, "the silver is Mine, and the gold is Mine," I know to have been spoken by the Prophet; but that, "to whomsoever I will, I will give it," is not added, but is brought in by these offscourings[1] of the people. And as to the former, why it was said, I will explain. The Prophet Haggai, because he was continually promising to the Jews after their return from Babylon, that he would show the temple in its former appearance, and some doubted of the thing spoken, and considered it to be well nigh impossible that after being reduced to dust and ashes, the house should appear again such as it was;—he, to remove their unbelief, in the person of God saith these things; as if he said, "Why are ye afraid? and why do ye refuse to believe? 'The silver is Mine, and the gold is Mine,' and I need not to borrow from others, and so to beautify the house." And to show that this is the meaning he adds, "and the glory of this house, the latter glory shall be greater than the glory of the former." Let us not then bring in spiders' webs upon the royal robe. For if any person, detected in weaving a counterfeit thread in a purple vest, is to suffer the severest punishment, much more in spiritual things; since neither is it an ordinary sin, which is hereby committed. And why say I, by adding and taking away? By a mere point, and by a mere circumstance of delivery in the reading, many impious thoughts have not seldom been brought into being.

"Whence then the rich," saith one? "for it hath been said, 'Riches and poverty are from the Lord.'" Let us then ask those who object these things against us, whether all riches and all poverty are from the Lord? Nay, who would say this? For we see that both by rapine,

---

1. συρφετῶν.

and by wickedly breaking open of tombs, and by witchcraft, and by other such devices, great wealth is gathered by many, and the possessors are not worthy even to live. What then, tell me, do we say that this wealth is from God? Far from it. Whence then? From sin. For so the harlot by doing indignity to her own body grows rich, and a handsome youth oftentimes selling his bloom with disgrace brings himself gold, and the tomb-spoiler by breaking open men's sepulchres gathers together unjust wealth, and the robber by digging through walls. All wealth therefore is not from God. "What then," saith one, "shall we say to this expression?" Acquaint thyself first with a kind of poverty which proceeds not from God, and then we will proceed to the saying itself. I mean, that when any dissolute youth spends his wealth either on harlots, or on conjurors, or on any other such evil desires, and becomes poor, is it not very evident that this hath not come from God, but from his own profligacy? Again, if any through idleness become poor, if any through folly be brought down to beggary, if any, by taking in hand perilous and unlawful practices; is it not quite evident, that neither hath any one of these and other such persons been brought down to this their poverty by God?

"Doth then the Scripture speak falsely?" God forbid! but they do foolishly, who neglect to examine with due exactness all things written. For if this on the one hand 'be acknowledged, that the Scriptures cannot lie; and this on the other hand proved, that not all wealth is from God; the weakness of inconsiderate readers is the cause of the difficulty.

[10.] Now it were right for us to dismiss you, having herein exculpated the Scripture, that ye may suffer this punishment at our hands for your negligence concerning the Scriptures: but because I greatly spare you and cannot any longer bear to look on you confused and disturbed, let us also add the solution, having first mentioned the speaker, and when it was spoken, and to whom. For not alike to all doth God speak, as neither do we deal alike with children and men. When then was it spoken, and by whom, and to whom? By Solomon in the Old Testament to the Jews, who knew no other than things of sense, and by these proved the power of God. For these are they who say, "Can He give bread also?" and, "What sign showest Thou unto us? Our fathers did eat manna in the desert:—whose God is their belly." (Ps. lxxviii. 24. Mat. xii. 38. John vi. 31. Phil. iii. 19.) Since then they were proving Him by these things, He saith to them, "This is also possible with God to make both rich and poor;" not that it is of course He Himself who maketh them, but that He can, when He will. Just as when he saith, "Who

rebuketh the sea, and maketh it dry, and drieth up all the rivers," (Nahum i. 4.) and yet this was never done. How then doth the prophet say so? Not as though it were a-doing always, but as a thing that was possible for Him to do.

What kind of poverty then doth He give, and what kind of wealth? Remember the patriarch, and thou shalt know the kind of wealth that is given by God. For He made both Abraham rich, and after him Job, even as Job himself saith; "If we have received good from the Lord, shall we not also receive evil?" (Job ii. 10.) And the wealth of Jacob thence had its beginning. There is also a poverty which cometh from Him, that which is commended, such as He once would have introduced to the knowledge of that rich man, saying, "If thou wouldest be perfect, sell thy goods, and give to the poor, and come, follow Me." (Matt. xix. 21.) And to the disciples again, making a law and saying, "Provide neither gold, nor silver, nor two coats." (Matt. ix. 10.) Say not then that all wealth is His gift: seeing that cases have been pointed out of its being collected both by murderers, and by rapine, and by ten thousand other devices.

But again the discourse reverts to our former question: viz. "if the rich are no way useful to us, wherefore are they made rich?" What then must we say? That these are not useful who so make themselves rich; whereas those surely who are made so by God are in the highest degree useful. And do thou learn this from the very things done by those whom we just now mentioned. Thus Abraham possessed wealth for all strangers, and for all in need. For he who on the approach of three men, as he supposed, sacrificed a calf and kneaded three measures of fine flour, and that while sitting in his door in the heat of the day; consider with what liberality and readiness he used to spend his substance on all, together with his goods giving also the service of his body, and this at such an advanced age; being a harbor to strangers, to all who had come to any kind of want, and possessing nothing as his own, not even his son: since at God's command he actually delivered up even him; and along with his son he gave up also himself and all his house, when he hastened to snatch his brother's son out of danger; and this he did not for lucre's sake, but of mere humanity. When, for instance, they who were saved by him would put the spoils at his disposal, he rejected all, even to "a thread and a shoe-latchet." (Gen. xiv. 23.)

Such also was the blessed Job. "For my door," saith, "was open to every one who came:" (Job. xx. 15.) "I was eyes to the blind, and feet to the lame: I was a father of the helpless. the stranger lodged not without, and the helpless, whatever need they had, failed not of it, neither suffered I one helpless man to go out of my door with an empty bosom." And much more too than these, that we may not now recount all, he continued to do, spending all his wealth on the needy.

Wilt thou also look upon those who have become rich but not of God, that thou mayest learn how they employed their wealth? Behold him in the parable of Lazarus, how he imparted not so much as a share of his crumbs. Behold Ahab, how not even the vineyard is free from his extortion: behold Gehazi: behold all such. Thus they on the one hand who make just acquisitions, as having received from God, spend on the commands of God: but they who in act of acquiring offend God, in the expending also do the same: consuming it on harlots and parasites, or burying and shutting it up, but laying out nothing upon the poor.

"And wherefore," saith one, "doth God suffer such men to be rich?" Because He is long-suffering: because He would bring us to repentance; because He hath prepared hell; because "He hath appointed a day in which He is to judge the world." (Acts xvii. 31.) Whereas did He use at once to punish them that are rich and not virtuously, Zacchæus would not have had an appointed time [1] for repentance, so as even to restore fourfold whatever he had unjustly taken, and to add half of his goods; nor Matthew, to be converted and become an Apostle, taken off as he would have been before the due season; nor yet many other such. Therefore doth He bear with them, calling all to repentance. But if they will not, but continue in the same, they shall hear Paul saying that "after their hardness and impenitent heart they treasure up unto themselves wrath against the day of wrath, and revelation, and righteous judgment of God: (Rom. ii. 5.) which wrath that we may escape, let us become rich with the riches of heaven, and follow after the laudable sort of poverty. For thus shall we obtain also the good things to come: the which may we all obtain through the grace and mercy of our Lord Jesus Christ, with Whom to the Father, with the Holy Ghost, be glory, power, and honor, now and for ever, and world without end. Amen.

---

[1] προθεσμίαν.

HOMILY XXXV.

1 Cor. xiv. 1.

Follow after love, yet desire earnestly spiritual gifts; but rather that ye may prophesy.

Thus, inasmuch as he had with exactness rehearsed unto them all the excellence of love, he exhorts them in what follows, with alacrity to lay hold of it. Wherefore also he said, "Follow after:" for he that is in chase beholds that only which is chased, and towards that he strains himself, and leaves not off until he lay hold of it. He that is in chase, when by himself he cannot, by those that are before him he doth overtake the fugitive, beseeching those who are near with much eagerness to seize and keep it so seized for him until he shall come up. This then let us also do. When of ourselves we do not reach unto love, let us bid them that are near her to hold her, till we come up with her, and when we have apprehended, no more let her go, that she may not again escape us. For continually she springs away from us, because we use her not as we ought, but prefer all things unto her. Therefore we ought to make every effort, so as perfectly to retain her. For if this be done, we require not henceforth much labor, nay rather scarce any; but taking our ease, and keeping holiday[1], we shall march on in the narrow path of virtue. Wherefore he saith, "Follow after her."

Then that they might not suppose that for no other end he brought in the discourse of charity, except that he might extinguish the gifts, he subjoins as follows;

Ver. 1. "Yet desire earnestly spiritual gifts; but rather that ye may prophesy."

Ver. 2. "For he that speaketh in a tongue, speaketh not unto men, but unto God: for no man understandeth; but in the Spirit he speaketh mysteries."

Ver. 3. "But he that prophesieth speaketh unto men edification, and exhortation, and comfort."

At this point he makes a comparison between the gifts, and lowers that of the tongues, showing it to be neither altogether useless, nor very profitable by itself. For in fact they were greatly puffed up on account of this, because the gift was considered to be a great one. And

---

[1] πανηγυρίζοντες.

it was thought great because the Apostles received it first, and with so great display ; it was not however therefore to be esteemed above all the others. Wherefore then did the Apostles receive it before the rest ? Because they were to go abroad every where. And as in the time of building the tower the one tongue was divided into many ; so then the many tongues frequently met in one man, and the same person used to discourse both in the Persian, and the Roman, and the Indian, and many other tongues, the Spirit sounding within him : and the gift was called the gift of tongues because he could all at once speak divers languages. See accordingly how he both depresses and elevates it. Thus, by saying, " He that speaketh with tongues, speaketh not unto men, but unto God, for no man understandeth," he depressed it, implying that the profit of it was not great ; but by adding, " but in the Spirit he speaketh mysteries," he again elevated it, that it might not seem to be superfluous and useless and given in vain.

" But he that prophesieth speaketh unto men edification, and exhortation, and comfort."

Seest thou by what he signifies the choice nature of this gift ? i. e., by the common benefit ? and how every where he gives the higher honor to that which tends to the profit of the many ? For do not the former speak unto men also ? tell me. But not so much " edification, and exhortation, and comfort." So that the being possessed by the Spirit is common to both, as well to him that prophesieth, as to him that speaketh with tongues ; but in this, the one (he, I mean, who prophesieth) hath the advantage in that he is also profitable unto the hearers. For they who spake with tongues were not understood by them that had not the gift.

What then ? Did they edify no man ? " Yes," saith he, " themselves alone : " wherefore also he adds,

Ver. 4. " He that speaketh in tongue edifieth himself."

And how, if he know not what he saith ? Why, for the present, he is speaking of them who understand what they say ;—understand it themselves, but know not how to render it unto others.

" But he that prophesieth edifieth the Church." Now as great as is the difference between a single person and the Church, so great is the interval between these two. Seest thou his wisdom, how he doth not thrust out the gift and make nothing of it, but signifies it to have some advantage, small though it be, and such as to suffice the possessor only ?

[2.] Next, lest they should suppose that in envy to them he depresses the tongues, (for the more part had this gift,) to correct their suspicion he saith,

Ver. 5. " I would have you all speak with tongues, but rather that ye should prophesy : for greater is he that prophesieth than he that speaketh with tongues, except he interpret, that the Church may receive edifying."

But " rather " and " greater," do not mark opposition, but superiority. So that hence also it is evident that he is not disparaging the gift, but leading them to better things, displaying both his carefulness on their behalf, and a spirit free from all envy. For neither did he say, " I would that two or three," but, " that ye all spake with tongues " and not this only, but also, " that ye prophesied ; " and this rather than that ; " for greater is he that prophesieth." For since he hath established and proved it, he next proceeds also to assert it ; not however simply, but with a qualification. Accordingly he adds, " except he interpret ; " since if he be able to do this, I mean the interpreting, " he hath become equal unto the prophet," so he speaks, " because then there are many who reap the advantage of it ; " a thing to be especially observed, how this throughout, before all else, is his object.

Ver. 6. " But now, brethren, if I come unto you speaking with tongues, what shall I profit you, unless I speak to you either by way of revelation, or of knowledge, or of prophesying, or of teaching ? "

" And why speak I," saith he, " of the rest ? Nay, let the person who speaketh with tongues be Paul : for not even so will any good come to the hearers." And these things he saith to signify that he is seeking their profit, not bearing any grudge against them that have the gift ; since not even in his own person doth he shrink from pointing out its unprofitableness. And indeed it is his constant way to work out the disagreeable topics in his own person : as in the beginning of the Epistle he said, " Who then is Paul ? and who is Apollos ? and who is Cephas ? " This same then he doth also here, saying, " Not even I shall profit you, except I speak to you either by way of revelation, or of prophesying, or of knowledge, or of teaching." And what he means is, " if I say not somewhat that can be made intelligible to you and that may be clear, but merely make display of my having the gift of tongues ;—tongues which ye do not understand, ye will go away with no sort of profit. For how should you profit by a voice which ye understand not ? "

[3.] Ver. 7. " Even things without life, giving a voice, whether pipe or harp, if they give not a distinction in the sounds, how shall it be known what is piped ? "

" And why do I say," saith he, " that in our

case this is unprofitable, and that only useful which is clear and easy to be apprehended by the hearers? Since even in musical instruments without life one may see this: for whether it be pipe or harp, yet if it be struck or blown confusedly and unskilfully, without proper cadence or harmony, it will captivate none of the hearers. For even in these inarticulate sounds there is need of some distinctness: and if thou strike not or breathe into the pipe according to art, thou hast done nothing. Now if from things without life we require so much distinctness, and harmony, and appropriateness, and into those inarticulate sounds we strive and contend to infuse so much meaning, much more in men indued with life and reason, and in spiritual gifts, ought one to make significancy an object.

Ver. 8. "For if the trumpet give an uncertain voice, who shall prepare himself for war?"

Thus from things merely ornamental he carries on his argument to those which are more necessary and useful; and saith that not in the harp alone, but in the trumpet also one may see this effect produced. For in that also there are certain measures; and they give out at one time a warlike note, and at another one that is not so; and again sometimes it leads out to line of battle and at others recalls from it: and unless one know this, there is great danger. Which is just what he means, and the mischief of it what he is manifesting, when he saith, "who shall prepare himself for war?" So then, if it have not this quality, it is the ruin of all. "And what is this to us," saith one? Truly it concerns you very especially; wherefore also he adds,

Ver. 9. "So also ye, unless ye utter by the tongue speech easy to be understood, ye will be speaking into the air:" i. e., calling to nobody, speaking unto no one. Thus every where he shows its unprofitableness.

[4.] "But if it be unprofitable, why was it given?" saith one. So as to be useful to him that hath received it. But if it is to be so to others also, there must be added interpretation. Now this he saith, bringing them near to one another; that if a person himself have not the gift of interpretation, he may take unto him another that hath it, and make his own gift useful through him. Wherefore he every where points out its imperfection, that so he may bind them together. Any how, he that accounts it to be sufficient for itself, doth not so much commend it as disparage it, not suffering it to shine brightly by the interpretation. For excellent indeed and necessary is the gift, but it is so when it hath one to explain what is spoken. Since the finger too is a necessary thing, but when you separate it from the other members, it will not be equally useful: and the trumpet is

necessary, but when it sounds at random, it is rather an annoyance. Yea, neither shall any art come to light, without matter subject to it; nor is matter put into shape, if no form be assigned to it. Suppose then the voice to be as the subject-matter, but the distinctness as that form, which not being present, there will be no use in the material.

Ver. 10. "There are, it may be, so many kinds of voices in the world, and no kind is without signification:" i. e., so many tongues, so many voices of Scythians, Thracians, Romans, Persians, Moors, Indians, Egyptians, innumerable other nations.

Ver. 11. "If then I know not the meaning of the voice, I shall be to him that speaketh a barbarian." "For suppose not," saith he, "that this happens only in our case; rather in all one may see this taking place: so that I do not say this to disparage the voice, but to signify that to me it is useless, as long as it is not intelligible." Next, that he may not render the accusation unpalatable, he makes his charge alike for the two, saying, "He shall be unto me a barbarian, and I to him." Not from the nature of the voice, but from our ignorance. Seest thou how by little and little he draws men to that which is akin to the subject. Which is his use to do, to fetch his examples from afar, and to end with what more properly belongs to the matter. For having spoken of a pipe and harp, wherein is much that is inferior and unprofitable, he comes to the trumpet, a thing more useful; next, from that he proceeds to the very voice itself. So also before, when he was discoursing to show that it was not forbidden the Apostles to receive, beginning first with husbandmen, and shepherds, and soldiers, then he brought the discourse on to that which is nearer to the subject, the priests in the old covenant.

But do thou, I pray, consider, how every where he hath given diligence to free the gift from censure, and to bring round the charge to the receivers of it. For he said not, "I shall be a barbarian," but, "unto him that speaketh, a barbarian." And again, he did not say, "he that speaketh shall be a barbarian," but "he that speaketh shall be a barbarian unto me[1]."

[5.] "What then must be done?" saith he. Why, so far from disparaging, one ought to recommend and to teach it; as indeed himself also doth. Since after he had accused and rebuked it and shown its unprofitableness, he proceeds to counsel them; saying,

Ver. 12. "So also ye, since as ye are zealous of spiritual gifts, seek that ye may abound unto the edifying of the Church."

---

[1] ὁ ἐμοὶ λαλῶν, he that speaketh unto me.

Seest thou his aim every where, how he looks to one thing continually and in all cases, the general utility, the profiting the Church; laying this down as a kind of rule? And he did not say, "that ye may obtain the gifts," but, "that ye may abound," i. e., that ye may even possess them in great plenitude. Thus, so far am I from wishing you not to possess them, that I even wish you to abound in them, only so that ye handle them with a view to the common advantage. And how is this to be done? This he adds, saying,

Ver. 13. "Wherefore let him that speaketh in a tongue pray that he may interpret."

Ver. 14. "For if I pray in a tongue, my spirit prayeth, but my understanding is unfruitful."

Ver. 15. "What is it then? I will pray with the spirit, and I will pray with the understanding also; I will sing with the spirit, and I will sing with the understanding also."

Here he shows that it is in their power to obtain the gift. For, "let him pray," saith he, i. e., "let him contribute his own part," since if thou ask diligently, thou wilt surely receive. Ask accordingly not to have the gift of tongue only, but also of interpretation, that thou mayest become useful unto all, and not shut up thy gift in thyself alone. "For if I pray in a tongue," saith he, "my spirit prayeth, but my understanding is unfruitful." Seest thou how by degrees bringing his argument to a point, he signifies that not to others only is such an one useless, but also to himself; if at least "his understanding is unfruitful?" For if a a man should speak only in the Persian, or any other foreign tongue, and not understand what he saith, then of course to himself also will he be thenceforth a barbarian, not to another only, from not knowing the meaning of the sound. For there were of old many who had also a gift of prayer, together with a tongue; and they prayed, and the tongue spake, praying either in the Persian or Latin language[1], but their understanding knew not what was spoken. Wherefore also he said, "If I pray in a tongue, my spirit prayeth," i. e., the gift which is given me and which moves my tongue, "but my understanding is unfruitful."

What then may that be which is best in itself, and doth good? And how ought one to act, or what request of God? To pray, "both with the spirit," i. e., the gift, and "with the understanding."[2] Wherefore also he said, "I will pray with the spirit, and I will pray with the understanding also: I will sing with the spirit, and I will sing with the understanding also."

[6.] He signifieth the same thing here also, that both the tongue may speak, and the understanding may not be ignorant of the things spoken. For except this be so, there will also be another confusion.

Ver. 16. "Else," saith he, "if thou bless with the spirit, how shall he that filleth the place of the unlearned say the Amen at thy giving of thanks, seeing he knoweth not what thou sayest?"

Ver. 17. "For thou verily givest thanks well, but the other is not edified."

Observe how again here he brings his stone to the plumb-line,[3] every where seeking the edification of the Church. Now by the "unlearned"[4] he means the laymen, and signifies that he also suffers no little loss when he is unable to say the Amen. And what he saith is this: "if thou shalt bless in a barbarian tongue, not knowing what thou sayest, nor able to interpret, the layman cannot respond the Amen. For not hearing the words, 'forever and ever,' which are at the end[5], he doth not say the Amen." Then again, comforting him concerning this, that he might not seem to hold the gift too cheap; the same kind of remark as he made above, that "he speaketh mysteries," and "speaketh unto God," and "edifieth himself," and "prayeth with the spirit," intending no little comfort from these things, this also he utters here, saying, "for thou indeed givest thanks well," since thou speakest being moved by the Spirit: but the other hearing nothing nor knowing what is said, stands there, receiving no great advantage by it."

[7.] Further, because he had run down the possessors of this gift, as though they had no such great thing; that he might not seem to hold them cheap, as being himself destitute of it, see what he saith:

Ver. 18. "I thank God, speaking[6] with tongues more than ye all."

And this he doth also in another place intending, namely, to take away the advantages of Judaism and to show that henceforth they are nothing, he begins by declaring that himself had been endowed with them, yea, and that in very great excess; and then he calls them "loss," thus saying, "If any man thinketh to have confidence in the flesh, I more: circumcised the eighth day, of the stock of Israel, of the tribe of Benjamin, a Hebrew of Hebrews; as touching the law, a Pharisee; as touching zeal, persecuting the Church; as touching the righteousness which is the law, found blameless." (Philip iii. 4-7.) And then, having

---

[1] [From this phrase—a similar one occurs in the next homily—it seems that Chrysostom held the tongue to mean the power of speaking in a language not before acquired. Most modern expositors understand by it an ecstatic utterance, a view which Tertullian alone of the patristic writers held.—C.]

[2] διανοίᾳ.

[3] πρὸς τὴν σπάρτην τὸν λίθον ἄγει.

[4] ἰδιώτην.

[5] i. e., at the end of the Long Thanksgiving in that part of the Service for the Holy Eucharist, which is called the Anaphora. Vid. Brett's Liturgies, 1838, p. 9, 16, 37, &c.

[6] λαλῶν. Rec. vers. "I speak."

signified himself to have the advantage of all, he saith, "Howbeit what things were gain to me, those have I counted loss for Christ." So also he doth here, saying, "I speak with tongues more than ye all." Do not ye therefore glory as though ye only had the gift. For I also possess it, yea more than ye.

Ver. 19. "Howbeit in the Church I had rather speak five words with my understanding, that I might instruct others also."

What is that, "speak with my understanding, that I might instruct others also?" "Understanding what I say," and "words which I can both interpret to others, and speak intelligently, and teach the hearers." "Than ten thousand words in a tongue." Wherefore? "That I may instruct others," saith he. For the one hath but display only; the other, great utility: this being what he everywhere seeks, I mean the common profit. And yet the gift of tongues was strange, but that of prophecy familiar and ancient and heretofore given to many; this on the contrary then first given: howbeit it was not much cared for by him. Wherefore neither did he employ it; not because he had it not, but because he always sought the more profitable things: being as he was free from all vain-glory, and considering one thing only, how he might render the hearers better.

[8.] And here is the reason of the faculty he had of looking to the expedient both to himself and to others: viz. because he was free from vain-glory. Since he assuredly that is enslaved by it, so far from discerning what is good to others, will not even know his own.

Such was Simon, who, because he looked to vain-glory, did not even see his own advantage. Such also were the Jews, who because of this sacrificed[1] their own salvation to the devil. Hence also did idols spring, and by this madness did the heathen philosophers excite themselves, and make shipwreck in their false doctrines. And observe the perverseness of this passion: how because of it some of them also made themselves poor, others were eager for wealth. So potent is its tyranny that it prevails even in direct contraries. Thus one man is vain of chastity, and contrariwise another of adultery; and this man of justice, and another of injustice; so of luxury and fasting, modesty and rashness, riches and poverty. I say poverty: since some of them that were without, when it was in their power to receive, for admiration's sake forbore to receive. But not so the Apostles: that they were pure from vainglory, they showed by their doings: in that, when some were calling them Gods and were ready to sacrifice unto them oxen with garlands,

they did not merely just forbid what was doing, but they even rent their clothes. (Acts xiv. 13, 14.) And after they had set the lame man upright, when all with open mouths were gazing at them, they said, "Why look ye so earnestly on us, as though by our own power we had made this man to walk[2]?" And those, among men who admired poverty, chose to themselves a state of poverty: but these among persons who despised poverty and gave praise to wealth. And these, if they received aught, ministered to the needy. Thus, not vain-glory but benevolence, was the motive of all they did. But those quite the reverse; as enemies and pests of our common nature, and no otherwise, did they such things. Thus one sunk all his goods in[3] the sea for no good purpose, imitating fools and madmen: and another let all his land go to sheep common.[4] Thus they did every thing for vain-glory. But not so the Apostles; rather they both received what was given them, and distributed to the needy with so great liberality that they even lived in continual hunger. But if they had been enamored of glory, they would not have practiced this, the receiving and distributing, for fear of some suspicion arising against them. For he who throws away his own for glory, will much more refuse to receive the things of others, that he may not be accounted to stand in need of others nor incur any suspicion. But these thou seest both ministering to the poor, and themselves begging for them. So truly were they more loving than any fathers.

[9.] And observe also their laws, how moderate and freed from all vain-glory. Thus: "Having" saith he, "food and covering, let us therewith be content." (1 Tim. vi. 8.) Not like him of Sinope[5], who clothed in rags and living in a cask to no good end, astonished many, but profited none: whereas Paul did none of these things; (for neither had he an eye to ostentation;) but was both clothed in ordinary apparel with all decency, and lived in a house continually, and displayed all exactness in the practice of all other virtue; which the cynic despised, living impurely and publicly disgracing himself, and dragged away by his mad passion for glory. For if any one ask the reason of his living in a cask, he will find no other but vain-glory alone. But Paul also paid rent for the house wherein he abode at Rome. Although he who was able to do things far severer, could much more have had strength for this. But he looked not to glory, that savage monster, that fearful demon, that pest of the world, that

[1] προοίμιον.

[2] Acts iii. 14, ἡ εὐσεβείᾳ om.
[3] Aristippus. See Hor. Sat. ii. 3. 100 ; Cic. de Invent. ii. 58.
[4] Democritus. See Hor. Ep. i. 12.
[5] Diogenes the Cynic.

poisonous viper. Since, as that animal tears through the womb of her parent with her teeth, so also this passion tears in pieces him that begets it.

[10.] By what means then may one find a remedy for this manifold distemper? By bringing forward those that have trodden it under foot, and with an eye to their image so ordering one's own life. For so the patriarch Abraham. —nay, let none accuse me of tautology if I often make mention of him, and on all occasions: this being that which most of all shows him wonderful, and deprives them that refuse to imitate him of all excuse. For, if we exhibit one doing well in this particular, and another in that, some one might say that virtue is hardly to be attained; for that it is scarcely possible to succeed in all those things together, whereof each one of the saints hath performed only a part. But when one and the same person is found to possess all, what excuse will they have, who after the law and grace are not able to attain unto the same measure with them that were before the law and grace? How then did this Patriarch overcome and subdue this monster, when he had a dispute with his nephew? (Gen. xiii. 8.) For so it was, that coming off worst and losing the first share, he was not vexed. But ye know that in such matters the shame is worse than the loss to the vulgar-minded, and particularly when a person having all in his own power, as he had then, and having been the first to give honor, was not honored in return. Nevertheless, none of these things vexed him, but he was content to receive the second place, and when wronged by the young man, himself old, an uncle by a nephew, he was not indignant nor took it ill, but loved him equally and ministered to him. Again, having been victorious in that great and terrible fight, and having mightily put to flight the Barbarians, (Gen. xiv.) he doth not add show to victory, nor erect a trophy. For he wished to save only, not to exhibit himself. Again, he entertained strangers, yet did he not here act vaingloriously, but himself both ran to them and bowed down to them, not as though he were giving, but receiving a benefit, and he calleth them lords, without knowing who they are who are come to him, and presents his wife in the place of a handmaiden. (Gen. xviii.) And in Egypt too before this, when he had appeared so extraordinary a person, and had received back this very woman, his wife, and had enjoyed so great honor (Gen. xii.) he showeth it to no man. And though the inhabitants of the place called him prince, he himself even laid down the price of the sepulchre. (Gen. xxiii. 6.) And when he sent to betroth a wife for his son, he gave no command to speak in high and dignified terms of him, (Gen. xxiv.) but merely to bring the bride.

[11.] Wilt thou examine also the conduct of those under grace, when from every side great was the glory of the teaching flowing round them, and wilt thou see then also this passion cast out? Consider, I pray, this same Apostle who speaks these things, how he ever ascribes the whole to God, how of his sins he makes mention continually, but of his good deeds never, unless perchance it should be needful to correct the disciples; and even if he be compelled to do this, he calls the matter folly, and yields the first place to Peter, and is not ashamed to labor with Priscilla and Aquila, and every where he is eager to show himself lowly, not swaggering in the market place, nor carrying crowds with him, but setting himself down among the obscure. Wherefore also he said, "but his bodily presence is weak." (2 Cor. x: 10.) i. e., easy to be despised, and not at all accompanied with display. And again, "I pray that ye do no evil, not that we may appear approved." And what marvel if he despise this glory? seeing that he despises the glory of heaven, and the kingdom, and hell, for that which was pleasing unto Christ: for he wishes[1] himself to be accursed from Christ for the glory of Christ. For if he saith that he is willing to suffer this for the Jews' sake, he saith it on this account that none of those without understanding might think to take to himself the promises made to them. If therefore he were ready to pass by those things, what marvel is it if he despise human things?

[12.] But the men of our time are overwhelmed by all things, not by desire of glory only, but also, on the other hand, by insult and fear of dishonor. Thus, should any one praise, it would puff thee up, and if he blame, it would cast thee down. And as weak bodies are by common accidents injured, so also souls which grovel on earth. For such not poverty alone, but even wealth destroys, not grief only, but likewise joy, and prosperity more than adversity. For poverty compels to be wise, but wealth leads on oftentimes into some great evil. And as men in a fever are hard to be pleased in any thing, so also they that are depraved in mind on every side receive hurt.

Knowing therefore these things, let us not shun poverty, let us not admire riches: but prepare our soul to be sufficient for all estates. For so any one building an house doth not consider how neither rain may descend, nor sunbeam light on it, (for this were impossible,) but how it may be made capable of enduring all. And he again that builds a ship doth not fashion and design any thing to keep waves from breaking against it, or any tempest from rising in the sea: (for this too were impossible:) but that

---

[1] [Rather he *could* wish, i. e., if it were proper. C.]

the sides of the ship may be ready to meet all. And again, he that cares for the body doth not look to this that there may be no inequality in the temperature, but that the body may easily endure all these things. So accordingly let us act in respect of the soul, and neither be anxious to fly poverty nor to become rich, but to regulate each of them for our own safety.

Wherefore, letting alone these things, let us render our soul meet both for wealth and poverty. For although no calamity, such as man is subject to, befall, which is for the most part impossible, even thus, better is he that seeks not wealth, but knows how to bear all things easily than he that is always rich. And why? First, such an one hath his safety from within, but the other from without. And as he is a better soldier who trusts to his bodily powers and skill in fighting, than he that hath his strength in his armor only; so he that relies on his wealth, compared with him that is fenced in by his virtue, is inferior. Secondly, because even if he do not fall into poverty, it is impossible that he should be without trouble. For wealth hath many storms and troubles; but not so virtue, but pleasure only and safety. Yea, and it puts a man out of the reach of them that lay snares for him, but wealth quite the contrary, rendering him easy to be attacked and taken. And as among animals, stags and hares are of all most easily taken through their natural timidity, but the wild boar, and the bull, and the lion, would not easily fall in the way of the liers-in-wait; just so one may see in the case of the rich, and of them that live voluntarily in poverty. The one is like the lion and the bull, the other like the stag and the hare. For whom doth not the rich man fear? Are there not robbers, potentates, enviers, informers? And why speak I of robbers and informers, in a case where a man suspects his very domestics?

[13.] And why say I, "when he is alive?" Not even when dead is he freed from the villainy of the robbers, nor hath death power to set him in safety, but the evil doers despoil him even when dead, so dangerous a thing is wealth. For not only do they dig into houses, but they even burst open tombs and coffins. What then can be more wretched than this man, since not even death can furnish him with this security, but that wretched body, even when deprived of life, is not freed from the evils of life, those that commit such wickedness hastening to war even with dust and ashes, and much more grievously than when it was alive? For then, it might be, entering his storehouse, they would remove his chests, but abstain from his person, and would not take so much as to strip the body itself; but now the accursed hands of the tomb-breakers do not even abstain from these, but move and turn it about, and with much cruelty insult it. For after it hath been committed to the ground, having stripped it both of its covering of earth and of that which its grave-clothes constitute, they leave it thus to be cast out.

What foe then so deadly as wealth, which destroys both the soul of the living, and insults the body of the dead, not suffering it even to lie buried in the ground, which is common even to the condemned and to them that have been taken in the vilest crimes? For of them the legislators having exacted the punishment of death, inquire no further; but of these, wealth even after death exacts a most bitter punishment, exposing them naked and unburied, a dreadful and pitiable spectacle: since even those who suffer this after sentence and by the anger of their judges, do not suffer so grievously as these. For they indeed remain unburied the first and second day, and so are committed to the ground; but these, when they have been committed to the ground, are then stripped naked and insulted. And if the robbers depart without taking the coffin too, there is still no thanks to their wealth, but in this case also to their poverty. For she it is that guards it. Whereas most assuredly, had we intrusted wealth with even so much as this, and leaving off to form it of stone, had forged it of gold, we should have lost this also.

So faithless a thing is wealth; which belongs not so much to them that have it, as to them that endeavor to seize it. So that it is but a superfluous argument which aims to show that wealth is irresistible, seeing that not even on the day of their death do its possessors obtain security. And yet who is not reconciled with the departed, whether it be wild beast, or demon, or whatever else? The very sight being enough to bend even one who is altogether iron, and quite past feeling. Wherefore, you know, when one sees a corpse, though it be an enemy public or private whom he sees, yet he weeps for him in common with his dearest friends; and his wrath is extinguished with life, and pity is brought in. And it would be impossible, in time of mourning and carrying out of burial, to distinguish an enemy from him who is not such. So greatly do all men revere their common nature, and the customs which have been introduced respecting it. But wealth not even on obtaining this, remits her anger against her possessors; nay, it renders them that have been no way wronged enemies of the dead; if at least to strip the dead body be an act of persons very bitter and hostile. And nature for her part reconciles even his enemies to him then: but wealth makes foes of them that have nothing to accuse him of, and cruelly intreats the body in its utter desolation. And yet in that case there are many things which might lead one to pity, the fact of its being a corpse, its inability to move, and tending to earth and corruption, the absence of any one to help : but none of these things soften those accursed wretches, because of the tyranny they are under from their base cupidity. For the passion of covetousness, like some ruthless tyrant, is at hand, enjoining those inhuman commands, and having made wild beasts of them, so brings them to the tombs. Yea, like wild beasts attacking the dead, they would not even abstain from their flesh, if their limbs were any way useful unto them. Such is our enjoyment of wealth; to be insulted even after death, and deprived of sepulture which even the most desperate criminals obtain.

[14.] Are we still then, tell me, to be fond of so grievous an enemy? Nay, I beseech you, nay, my brethren! but let us fly from it without turning to look : and if it come into our hands, let us not keep it within, but bind it fast by the hands of the poor. For these are the bonds which have more power to hold it, and from those treasuries it will never more escape; and so this faithless one abides for the time to come faithful, tractable, tame, the right hand of Mercy producing this effect on it.

As I have said then, if it ever come to us, let us hand it over to her; but if it come not, let us not seek after it, nor fret ourselves, nor count its possessors happy; for what sort of a notion of happiness is this? Unless thou wouldest also say that those who fight with beasts are to be envied, because those high-priced animals are shut up and reserved by the proposers of such contests for themselves : who however not daring themselves to approach or to touch them, but fearing and trembling because of them, hand over others to them. Something like this, I say, is the case of the wealthy, when they have shut up their wealth in their treasuries as if it were some savage beast, and day by day receive from it innumerable wounds : in this latter unlike to the beasts: since they, when thou leadest them out, then, and not till then, hurt such as meet them : but this, when it is shut up and preserved, then destroys its possessors and hoarders.

But let us make this beast tame. And it will be tame, if we do not shut it up, but give it into the hands of all who are in need. So shall we reap from this quarter the greatest blessings, both living in the present life with safety and a good hope, and in the day that is to come standing with boldness : to which may we all attain, through the grace and mercy, &c. &c.

HOMILY XXXVI.

1 COR. xiv. 20.

Brethren, be not children in mind; howbeit in malice be ye babes, but in mind be men.

As might be expected, after his long argument and demonstration he adopts a more vehement style and abundance of rebuke; and mentions an example suited to the subject. For children too are wont to gape after trifles and to be fluttered, but of things very great they have not so much admiration. Since then these also having the gift of tongues, which was the lowest of all, thought they had the whole; therefore he saith, "Be not children," i. e., be not without understanding where ye ought to be considerate, but there be ye childlike and simple, where unrighteousness is, where vain-glory, where pride. For he that is a babe in wickedness ought also to be wise. Since as wisdom with wickedness would not be wisdom, so also simplicity with folly would not be simplicity, it

being requisite both in simplicity to avoid folly, and in wisdom wickedness. For as neither bitter nor sweet medicines in excess do good, so neither doth simplicity by itself, nor wisdom : and this is why Christ enjoining us to mix both said, "Be ye wise as serpents, and harmless as doves." (Matt. x. 16.)

But what is it to be a babe in wickedness? Not even to know what wickedness is: yea, such he willed them to be. Wherefore also he said, "It is actually reported that there is fornication among you." (1 Cor. v. 1.) He said not, "is done," but is "reported :" as if he said, "ye are not without knowledge of the thing; ye have heard of it some time." I say, he would have them both to be men and children; the one however in wickedness, but the other in wisdom. For so even the man may become a man, if he be also a child: but as long as he is not a child in wickedness, neither will he be a man. For the wicked, instead of being mature, will be but a fool.

Ver. 21. "In the law it is written, By men of strange tongues and by the lips of strangers will I speak unto this people; and not even thus will they hear me, saith the Lord."

Yet surely it is no where written in the Law, but as I said before, he calls always the whole of the Old Testament, the Law: both the prophets and the historical books. And he brings forward his testimony from Esaias the prophet, again covertly detracting from the glory of the gift, for their profit; nevertheless, even thus he states it with praise. For the expression, "not even thus," hath force to point out that the miracle was enough to astonish them; and if they did not believe, the fault was theirs. And wherefore did God work it, if they were not to believe? That He might in every case appear to do His part.

[2.] Having shown then even from the prophecy, that the sign in question is not of great use, he adds,

Ver. 22. "Wherefore tongues are for a sign, not to them that believe, but to the unbelieving: but prophesying is for a sign not to the unbelieving, but to them that believe."

Ver. 23. "If therefore the whole Church be assembled together, and all speak with tongues, and there come in men unlearned or unbelieving, will they not say that ye are mad?"

Ver. 24. "But if all prophesy, and there come in one unbelieving or unlearned, he is reproved by all, he is judged by all: "

Ver. 25. "And thus the secrets of his heart are made manifest; and so he will fall down on his face and worship God, declaring that God is among you indeed."

Great in this place is the difficulty which one seems to find arising from what is said. For if tongues are for a sign to them that believe not, how saith he, if they that believe not should see you speaking with tongues, they will say that "ye are mad?" And if prophecy be "not for the unbelieving, but for them that believe," how shall also the unbelievers gain thereby?

"For if there come in," saith he, "when ye are prophesying, one that believeth not, he is reproved by all, and judged."

And not only this, but also after this another question hence springs up: since the tongue will appear on the contrary greater than the prophecy. For if the tongues are for a sign to the unbelieving, but prophecy to them that believe, that which draws in aliens and makes of the household, is greater than that which regulates those of the household. What then is the meaning of that expression? Nothing difficult nor obscure, nor

contrary to what went before, but rather very agreeable to it, if we give heed: viz., that prophecy is suitable to both, but then tongue not so. Wherefore having said of the tongue, "it is for a sign," he adds, "not to them that believe, but to the unbelievers," and to them "for a sign," i. e., for astonishment, not so much for instruction.

"But in the case of prophecy too," saith some one, "he did the very same thing, saying, 'but prophesying serveth not for the unbelieving, but for them which believe.' For the believer hath no need to see a sign, but requires only teaching and catechizing. How then sayest thou," saith he, "that prophecy is of use to both, when Paul saith 'not to the unbelieving, but to them which believe?'" If thou wilt accurately examine, thou wilt understand what is said. For he said not, "prophecy is not useful to them unbelieving," but, "is not for a sign," as the tongue," i. e., a mere sign without profit: nor is the tongue any way useful to believers; for its only work is to astonish and to confound; the word "sign" being one of those which may be taken two ways: as when he saith, "show me a sign,"(Ps. lxxxvi. 17.) and adds, "for good:" and again, "I am become as a wonder unto many," (Ps. lxxi. 7.) i. e., a sign.

And to show thee that he introduced the term "sign" here, not as a thing which of course did some good, he added that which resulted from it. And what was this? "They will say," saith he, "that ye are mad" This however not from the nature of the sign, but from their folly. But when thou hearest of unbelievers, do not suppose that the same persons are in every case intended, but at one time they which are incurably diseased and abide uncorrected, and at another they which may be changed; such as were they who in the times of the Apostles admire the mighty things of God which they hear of; such as in the case of Cornelius. His meaning accordingly is this; that prophecy avails both among the unbelieving and among them that believe: as to the tongue, when heard by the unbelieving and inconsiderate, instead of profiting by it, they rather deride the utterers as madmen. For, in fact, it is to them but for a sign, i. e., in order to astonish them merely; whereas they who had understanding used also to profit by it: with a view to which the sign was given. Even as then there were not only certain who accused them of drunkenness, but many also admired them as relating the wonderful works of God. It appears then that the mockers were those without understanding. Wherefore also Paul did not simply say, "they will say that ye are mad," but added, "unlearned and unbelievers."

But prophecy is not for a sign merely, but is also suitable and useful for faith and for profit unto both classes. And this, if not directly, yet in the sequel he more clearly explained, saying, "he is reproved by all. For, if all prophesy," saith he, "and there come in one unbelieving or unlearned, he is reproved by all; he is judged by all; and thus are the secrets of his heart made manifest; and so he will fall down on his face and worship God, declaring that God is among you indeed."

So that not in this only is prophecy greater, in its availing with each class[1], but also in its attracting the more shameless of the unbelievers. For it was not the same wonder, when Peter convicted[2] Sapphira, which was a work of prophecy, and when he spake with tongues: but in the former case all shrank into themselves; whereas, when he spake with tongues, he got the credit of being even beside himself.

[3.] Having said then, that a tongue profited not, and having again qualified[3] this statement by turning the charge upon the Jews, he proceeds to signify that it even doth injury. "And wherefore was it given?" That it might go forth with interpretation: since without this, it hath even the contrary effect among them that are without understanding. "For if," saith he, "all speak with tongues, and there come in unbelievers or unlearned, they will say that ye are mad;" as indeed even the Apostles incurred the suspicion of being drunken: for "these men," it saith, "are filled with new wine: (Acts ii. 13.) but it is not the fault of the sign, but of their unskilfulness; therefore he added, "unlearned and unbelievers," to show that the notion belongs to their ignorance and want of faith; for, as I before said, his object is to rank that gift not among things that are disparaged, but among those which do not greatly profit, and this, in order to repress them, and bring them to a necessity of seeking for an interpreter. For since the greater part looked not to this, but made use of it for display and rivalry, this is what he especially withdraws them from, intimating that their credit is injured, they bringing on themselves a suspicion of madness. And this especially is what Paul continually attempts to establish, when he wants to lead men away from any thing: he shows that the person suffers loss in respect of those very things which he desires.

And do thou accordingly likewise: if thou wouldest lead men away from pleasure, show that the thing is bitter: if thou wouldest withdraw them from vain-glory, show that the thing is full of dishonor: thus also was Paul used to do. When he would tear away the rich from

their love of money, he said not merely that wealth is a hurtful thing, but also that it casts into temptations. "For they that desire to be rich," saith he, "fall into a temptation." (1 Tim. vi. 9.) Thus, since it seems to deliver from temptations, he attributes to it the contrary of that which the rich supposed. Others again held fast by the wisdom that is without, as though by it establishing Christ's doctrine; he signifies that not only it gives no aid to the cross, but even makes it void. They held to going to law before strangers, thinking it unmeet to be judged by their own, as if those without were wiser: he points out that going to law before them that are without is shameful. They clave to things offered in sacrifice to idols, as displaying perfect knowledge: he intimates that this is a mark of imperfect knowledge, not to know how to manage in the things which concern our neighbors. So also here, because they were wild[4] about this gift of tongues, through their love of glory, he signifies that this on the other hand more than any thing brings shame upon them, not only depriving them of glory, but also involving them in a suspicion of madness. But he did not at once say this, but having spoken very many things before, when he had made his discourse acceptable, then he brings in that topic so very contrary to their opinion. And this in fact is no more than the common rule; that he who intends thoroughly to shake a deep-rooted opinion and to turn men round to its contrary, must not at once state the opposites: otherwise he will be ridiculous in the eyes of them that are preoccupied by the contrary conviction. Since that which is very much beside expectation cannot be from the beginning easily received, but you must first well undermine by other arguments, and then give it the contrary turn.

Thus for example he did when discoursing of marriage: I mean, since many regarded it as a thing which brings ease, and he wished to intimate that the abstaining from marriage was ease; if he had said this at once he would not so easily have made it acceptable: whereas now, having stated it after much other matter and timing its introduction exactly, he strongly touched the hearers. This also he did in respect of virginity. For before this having said much, and after this again, at last he saith, "I spare you," and, "I would have you to be free from cares." (1 Cor. vii. 28, 32.)

This then he doth in respect of the tongues, showing that they not only deprive of glory, but also bring shame upon those who have them in the eyes of the unbelievers. But prophecy, on the contrary, is both free from reproach among the unbelievers, and hath very great

---

[1] i. e. ἐν ἀπίστοις καὶ πίστοις.
[2] ἤλεγξεν.
[3] ὑποτεμόμενος αὐτὸ τοῦτο.

[4] ἐπτόηντο.

credit and usefulness. For none will say in regard to prophesying, "they are mad;" nor will any one deride them that prophesy; but, on the contrary, will be astonished at and admire them. For "he is reproved by all," i. e., the things which he hath in his heart, are brought forward and shown unto all: now it is not the same thing for any one to come in and see one speaking in Persian and another in Syriac, and to come in and hear the secrets of his own mind; as whether he cometh in as a tempter and with evil mind, or sincerely; or that such and such a thing hath been done by him, and such another designed. For this is much more awful and more profitable than the other. For this cause therefore, whereas of the tongues he saith, "ye are mad;" not however affirming this of himself, but of their judgment: i. e., "they will say," saith he, "that ye are mad;" here, on the contrary, he makes use both of the verdict of the facts[1], and that of those who are the objects of the benefit. "For he is reproved by all," saith he, "he is judged by all; and thus are the secrets of his heart made manifest; and so he will fall down on his face and worship God, declaring that God is around you indeed. Seest thou that this is not capable of two interpretations: how in the former case what is done may be doubted of, and here and there an unbeliever might ascribe it to madness? whereas here there will be no such thing, but he will both wonder and worship, first making a confession by his deeds, and then by his words also. Thus also Nebuchadnezzar worshipped God, saying, "Of a truth, your God, He is the God that revealeth secrets, seeing thou couldest reveal this secret." (Dan. ii. 47.) Seest thou the might of prophecy, how it changed that savage one and brought him under instruction and introduced him to faith?

[4.] Ver. 26. "What is it then, brethren? When ye come together, each one hath a psalm, hath a teaching, hath a tongue, hath a revelation, hath an interpretation. Let all things be done unto edifying."

Seest thou the foundation and the rule of Christianity? how, as it is the artificer's work to build, so it is the Christian's to profit his neighbors in all things.

But since he had vehemently run down the gift; lest it might seem to be superfluous, for with a view to pull down their pride and no more, he did this:—again he reckons it with the other gifts, saying, "hath a psalm, hath a teaching, hath a tongue." For of old they used also to make psalms by a gift and to teach by a gift. Nevertheless, "let all these look to one thing," saith he, "the correction of their neighbor: let nothing be done at random. For if thou comest not to edify thy brother, why dost thou come here at all? In fact, I do not make much account of the difference of the gifts. One thing concerns me, one thing is my desire, to do all things "unto edifying." Thus also he that hath the lesser gift will outrun him that hath the greater, if this be not wanting. Yea, therefore are the gifts bestowed, that each might be edified; since unless this take place, the gift will rather turn to the condemnation of the receiver. For what, tell me, is the use of prophesying? What is the use of raising the dead, when there is none who profits by it? But if this be the end of the gifts, and if it be possible to effect it in another way without gifts, boast not thyself on the score of the signs, nor do thou bewail thyself to whom the gifts are denied.

[5.] Ver. 27. "And if any man speaketh in a tongue, let it be by two, or at the most by three, and that in turn; and let one interpret."

Ver. 28. "But if there be no interpreter, let him keep silence in the Church; and let him speak to himself, and to God."

What sayest thou, tell me? Having spoken so much of tongues, that the gift is a thing unprofitable, a thing superfluous, if it have no interpreter, dost thou command again to speak with tongues? I do not command, saith he, neither do I forbid; as when he saith, "if any of them that believe not bid you to a feast and ye be disposed to go," he saith it not laying down a law for them to go, but not hindering them: so likewise here. "And let him speak to himself and to God." If he endure not to be silent, saith he, but is so ambitious and vain-glorious, "let him speak by himself.[2]" And thus, by the very fact of so permitting, he greatly checked and put them to shame. Which he doth also elsewhere, discoursing of converse with a wife and saying, "But this I say because of your incontinency." But not so did he speak, when he was discoursing of prophecy. How then? In a tone of command and legislation: "Let the prophets speak, two or three." And he no where here seeks the interpreter, nor doth he stop the mouth of him that prophesies as under the former head, saying, "If there be no interpreter, let him keep silence;" because in fact he who speaks in a tongue is not sufficient of himself. Wherefore if any hath both gifts, let him speak. But if he hath not, yet wish to speak, let him do so with the interpreter's aid. For the prophet is an interpreter, but of God; whereas thou art of man. "But if there be no interpreter, let him keep silence:" for nothing ought to be done superfluously, nothing for ambition. Only "let him speak to

---

[1] i. e., the actions of the man's life, and his conscience, which answers to the prophecy.

[2] καθ' ἑαυτόν.

himself and to God;" i. e., mentally, or quietly and without noise: at least, if he will speak. For this is surely not the tone of one making a law, but it may be of one who shames them more even by his permission; as when he saith, "but if any hunger, let him eat at home:" and seeming to give permission, he touches them hereby the more sharply. "For ye come not together for this purpose," saith he, "that ye may show that ye have a gift, but that ye may edify the hearers;" which also he before said, "Let all things be done unto edifying."

[6.] Ver. 29. "Let the prophets speak by two or three, and let the others discern."

No where hath he added, "at the most," as in the case of the tongues. And how is this, one saith? For he makes out that neither is prophesy sufficient in itself, if at least he permitteth the judgment to others. Nay, surely it is quite sufficient; and this is why he did not stop the mouth of the prophet, as of the other, when there is no interpreter; nor, as in his case he said, "if there be no interpreter let him keep silence," so also in the case of the prophet, "if there be none to discern, let him not prophesy;" but he only secured the hearer; since for the satisfaction of the hearers he said this, that no diviner might throw himself in among them. For of this also at the beginning he bade them beware, when he introduced a distinction between divination and prophecy, and now he bids them discriminate and spy out the matter, so that no Satanic teacher might privily enter.

Ver. 30. "But if a revelation be made to another sitting by, let the first keep silence."

Ver. 31. "For ye all can prophesy one by one, that all may learn, and all may be comforted."

What may this be which is spoken? "If when thou prophesiest," saith he, "and art speaking, the spirit of another stir him up, be silent thenceforth." For that which he said in the case of the tongues, this also here he requires, that it should be done "in turn," only in a diviner way here. For he made not use of the very expression, "in turn[1]?" but "if a revlation be made to another." Since what need was there further, that when the second was moved to prophesy the first should speak? Ought they then both? Nay, this were profane and would produce confusion. Ought the first? This too were out of place. For to this end when the one was speaking, the Spirit moved the other, in order that he too might say somewhat.

So then, comforting him that had been silenced, he saith, "For ye all can prophesy one by one, that all may learn, and all may be comforted." Seest thou how again he states the

reason wherefore he doeth all things? For if him that speaks with tongues he altogether forbid to speak, when he hath not an interpreter, because of the unprofitableness; reasonably also he bids restrain prophecy, if it have not this quality, but createth confusion and disturbance and unseasonable tumult.

Ver. 32. "And the spirits of the prophets are subject to the prophets."

Seest thou how he put him to shame earnestly and fearfully? For that the man might not strive nor be factious, he signifies that the gift itself was under subjection. For by "spirit" here, he means its actual working. But if the spirit be subject, much more thou its possessor canst not justly be contentious.

[7.] Then he signifies that this is pleasing also to God, subjoining and saying,

Ver. 33. "For God is not a God of confusion, but of peace, as [I teach] in all the Churches of the saints."[2]

Seest thou by how many reasons he leads him to silence and soothes him, in the act of giving way to the other? By one thing and that the chief, that he was not shut up by such a proceeding; "for ye all can prophesy," saith he, "one by one." By a second, that this seems good to the Spirit Himself; "for the spirits of the prophets are subject to the prophets." Besides these, that this is according to the mind of God; "for God," saith he, "is not a God of confusion, but of peace:" and by a fourth, that in every part of the world this custom prevails, and no strange thing is enjoined upon them. For thus, saith he, "I teach in all the Churches of the saints."

What now can be more awful than these things? For in truth the Church was a heaven then, the Spirit governing all things, and moving each one of the rulers and making him inspired. But now we retain only the symbols of those gifts. For now also we speak two or three, and in turn, and when one is silent, another begins. But these are only signs and memorials of those things. Wherefore when we begin to speak, the people respond, "with thy Spirit[3]," indicating that of old they thus used to speak, not of their own wisdom, but moved by the Spirit. But not so now: (I speak of mine own case so far.) But the present Church is like a woman who hath fallen from her former prosperous days, and in many respects retains the symbols only of that ancient prosperity; displaying indeed the repositories and caskets of

---

[1] ἀνὰ μέρος. v. 7.

[2] [Chrysostom connects this clause with what precedes as do Alford, Tregelles, Edwards and the Rev. Ver. He is doubtless right here, but not in his addition of διδάσκω, for which there is no adequate support. C.]

[3] The "Anaphora," or more solemn part of the Liturgy begins with the Versicle and Response here alluded to, in the Clementine Liturgy, and in those of St. Mark, St. Chrysostom, St. Basil, and the Roman Missal.

her golden ornaments, but bereft of her wealth: such an one doth the present Church resemble. And I say not this in respect of gifts: for it were nothing marvelous if it were this only: but in respect also of life and virtue. Thus the list of her widows, and the choir of her virgins, then gave great ornament to the churches: but now she is made desolate and void, and the tokens only remain. There are indeed widows now, there are also virgins; but they retain not that adornment which women should have who prepare themselves for such wrestlings. For the special distinction of the virgin is the caring for the things of God alone, and the waiting on Him without distraction: and the widow's mark too should be not so much the not engaging in a second marriage, as the other things, charity to the poor, hospitality, continuing instant in prayers, all those other things, which Paul writing to Timothy requires with great exactness. One may see also the married women exhibiting among us great seemliness. But this is not the only thing required, but rather that sedulous attention to the needy, through which those women of old shone out most brightly. Not as the generality now-a-days. For then instead of gold they were clothed with the fair array of almsgiving: but now, having left off this, they are decked out on every side with cords of gold woven of the chain of their sins.

Shall I speak of another repository too emptied of its hereditary splendor? They all met together in old time and sang psalms in common. This we do also now: but then among all was there one soul and one heart: but now not in one single soul can one see that unanimity, rather great is the warfare every where.

"Peace," even now, "to all,"[1] he that presides in the Church prays for, entering as it were into his Father's house: but of this peace the name is frequent, but the reality no where.

[8.] Then the very houses were churches: but now the church itself is a house, or rather worse than any house. For in a house one may see much good order: since both the mistress of the house is seated on her chair with all seemliness, and the maidens weave in silence, and each of the domestics hath his appointed task in hand. But here great is the tumult, great the confusion, and our assemblies differ in nothing from a vintner's shop, so loud is the laughter, so great the disturbance; as in baths, as in markets, the cry and tumult is universal. And these things are here only: since elsewhere it is not permitted even to address one's neighbor in the church, not even if one have received back a long absent friend, but these things are done without, and very properly.

For the church is no barber's or perfumer's shop, nor any other merchant's warehouse in the market-place, but a place of angels, a place of archangels, a palace of God, heaven itself. As therefore if one had parted the heaven and had brought thee in thither, though thou shouldest see thy father or thy brother, thou wouldest not venture to speak; so neither here ought one to utter any other sound but those which are spiritual. For, in truth, the things in this place are also a heaven.

And if thou believest not, look to this table, call to mind for Whose sake it is set, and why: consider Who it is that is coming forth here; tremble with awe even before the time. For so, when one sees the throne only of a king, in heart he rises up, expecting the king's coming forth. And do thou accordingly thrill with awe even before that thrilling moment: raise up thyself, and before thou seest the veils drawn aside and the choir of angels marching forth, ascend thou to the very heaven.

But the uninitiated knows not these things. Well then, it is necessary with a view to him also to introduce other topics. For neither towards him shall we want reasons able to stir him up thoroughly and cause him to soar.

Thou then who knowest not these things, when thou shalt hear the prophet[2] saying, "Thus saith the Lord," quit the earth, ascend thou also unto heaven, consider who it is that by him discourses with thee.

But as things are, for a buffoon who is moving laughter or for a whorish and abandoned woman, so vast an assemblage of spectators is set, listening in entire quietness to what is spoken, and this when none commands silence[3]; and there is neither tumult, nor cry, nor any the least noise: but when God is speaking from heaven on subjects so awful, we behave ourselves more impudently than dogs, and even to the harlot women we pay greater respect than to God.

Doth it make your flesh creep to be told of these things? Nay then, much rather let it creep when ye do them.

[9.] That which Paul said of them that despised the poor and feasted alone, "What, have ye not houses to eat and to drink in? or despise ye the Church of God, and shame them that

---

[1] See Bingham, xiii. 8. 13.; S. Chrys. 3 Hom. in Coloss. t. iv. 106. Ed. Savile.

[2] Because the Catechumens and others, as it seems, were allowed to hear the Lessons read, though not to be present at what was strictly called the Communion Service. See Bingham, xiv. iii. 1.
[3] An allusion to the injunctions for silence used by the Deacon occasionally in the Church: see Bingham, ii. 20. 14: and the Apost. Constit. ii. 57. as quoted by him; " Let the Deacon oversee the people, that none whisper, or doze, or laugh, or nod;" and afterwards in the time of the offering, " Let some of the Deacons observe the people, and make silence among them." Chrys. Hom. 24. on Acts, says, "Prayer is going on, and here are young persons talking and jesting with one another even while on their knees. Do thou who standest by, young or old, rebuke them, if thou seest it; reprimand them more sharply; if he take it not well, call the Deacon."

have not?" (1 Cor. xi. 22.)—the same allow me also to say of those who make a disturbance and hold conversations in this place. "What? have ye not houses to trifle in? or despise ye the Church of God, and corrupt those even who would be modest and quiet?" "But it is sweet and pleasant for you to converse with your friends." I do not forbid this, but let it be done in the house, in the market, in the baths. For the church is not a place of conversation, but of teaching. But now it differs not from the market; nay, if it be not too bold a word, haply, not even from the stage; in such sort do the women who assemble here adorn themselves more wantonly than the unchaste who are to be found there. Accordingly we see that even hither many profligates are enticed by them; and if any one is trying or intending to corrupt a woman, there is no place, I suppose, that seems to him more suitable than the church. And if anything be to be sold or bought, the church appears more convenient than the market. For on such subjects also there is more talk here than in the shops themselves. Or if any wish to say or to hear any scandal, you will find that this too is to be had here more than in the forum without. And if you wish to hear any thing of political matters, or the affairs of private families, or the camp, go not to the judgment-hall, nor sit in the apothecary's shop; for here, here I say are those who report all these things more accurately; and our assemblies are any thing rather than a church.

Can it be that I have touched you to the quick? I for my part think not. For while ye continue in the same practices, how am I to know that you are touched by what hath been said? Therefore I must needs handle the same topics again.

Are these things then to be endured? Are these things to be borne? We weary and distract ourselves every day that ye may not depart without having learned something useful: and none of you go away at all the better, but rather injured the more. Yea, and "ye come together unto judgment," having no longer any cloak for your sin, and ye thrust out the more modest, disturbing them with your fooleries on every side.

But what do the multitude say? "I do not hear what is read," saith one, "nor do I know what the words are which are spoken." Because thou makest a tumult and confusion, because thou comest not with a reverent soul. What sayest thou? "I know not what things are said." Well then, for this very reason oughtest thou to give heed. But if not even the obscurity stir up thy soul, much more if things were clear wouldest thou hurry them by. Yea, this is the reason why neither all things are

clear, lest thou shouldest indulge indolence; nor obscure, lest thou shouldest be in despair.

And whereas that eunuch and barbarian (Acts viii. 20.) said none of these things, but surrounded as he was with a crowd of so important affairs and on his journey, had a book in his hands and was reading: dost thou, both abounding in teachers, and having others to read to thee privately[1], allege to me thine excuses and pretexts? Knowest thou not what is said? Why then pray that thou mayest learn: but sure it is impossible to be ignorant of all things. For many things are of themselves evident and clear. And further, even if thou be ignorant of all, even so oughtest thou to be quiet, not to put out them that are attentive; that God, accepting thy quietness and thy reverence, may make the obscure things also plain. But canst thou not be silent? Well then, go out, not to become a mischief to others also.

For in truth there ought to be but one voice in the church always, even as there is but one body. Therefore both he that reads utters his voice alone, and the Bishop himself is content to sit in silence; and he who chants chants alone; and though all utter the response, the voice is wafted as from one mouth. And he that pronounces a homily pronounces it alone. But when there are many conversing on many and diverse subjects, why do we disturb you for no good? since surely unless ye thought that we are but disturbing you for no good, ye would not in the midst of our speech on such high matters, discourse on things of no consequence.

[10.] Therefore not in your conduct only, but in your very estimation of things, there is great perversion. And ye gape after superfluities, and leaving the truth pursue all sorts of shadows and dreams. Are not all present things a shadow and dreams, and worse than a shadow? For both before they appear, they fly away; and before they are flown, the trouble they give is much, and more than the pleasure. Let one acquire in this world and bury in the earth ever such abundance of wealth, yet when the night is past, naked he shall depart hence, and no wonder. Since they too who are rich but in a dream, on rising from their couch have nothing of what they seemed to have while sleeping. So also are the greedy of gain: or rather not so, but in a much worse condition. For he that dreams of being rich, neither hath the money which he fancied he had, nor is any other mischief found to have accrued to him from this phantasy when he arises, but this man is both deprived of his riches, and hath also to depart, filled with the sins which arise out of them; and in his wealth having but enjoyed a phantasy,

---

[1] ὑπαναγινώσκοντας, perhaps, 'repeating what is read in a lower tone.'

the evils resulting from his wealth he sees not in fancy any more, but in the very truth of things; and his pleasure was in dreams, but the punishment ensuing on his pleasure turns out no more a dream, but is matter of actual experience. Yea rather, even before that punishment, even here he pays the heaviest penalty, in the very collecting of his wealth wearing into himself innumerable sadnesses, anxieties, accusations, calumnies, tumults, perturbations.

In order therefore that we may be delivered both from the dreams and from the evils that are not in dreams, instead of covetuousness let us choose almsgiving, instead of rapine, mercy to mankind. For thus we shall obtain the good things both present and to come, through the grace and mercy of our Lord Jesus Christ, with Whom, to the Father, with the Holy Ghost, be glory, power, honor, now and ever, and world without end. Amen.

HOMILY XXXVII.

1 COR. xiv. 34.

Let your women keep silence in the churches: for it is not permitted unto them to speak; but let them be in subjection, as also saith the law.

HAVING abated the disturbance both from the tongues and from the prophesyings; and having made a law to prevent confusion, that they who speak with tongues should do this in turn, and that they who prophesy should be silent when another begins; he next in course proceeds to the disorder which arose from the women, cutting off their unseasonable boldness of speech: and that very opportunely. For if to them that have the gifts it is not permitted to speak inconsiderately, nor when they will, and this, though they be moved by the Spirit; much less to those women who prate idly and to no purpose. Therefore he represses their babbling with much authority, and taking the law along with him, thus he sews up their mouths; not simply exhorting here or giving counsel, but even laying his commands on them vehemently, by the recitation of an ancient law on that subject. For having said, "Let your women keep silence in the churches;" and, "it is not permitted unto them to speak, but let them be in subjection;" he added, "as also saith the law." And where doth the law say this? "Thy desire shall be to thy husband, and he shall rule over thee." (Gen. iii. 16.) Seest thou the wisdom of Paul, what kind of testimony he adduced, one that not only enjoins on them silence, but silence too with fear; and with as great fear as that wherewith a maid servant ought to keep herself quiet. Wherefore also having himself said, "it is not permitted unto them to speak," he added not, "but to be silent," but instead of "to be silent," he set down what is more, to wit, "the being in subjection." And if this be so in respect of husbands, much more in respect of

teachers, and fathers, and the general assembly of the Church. "But if they are not even to speak," saith one, "nor ask a question, to what end are they to be present?" That they may hear what they ought; but the points which are questioned let them learn at home from their husbands. Wherefore also he added,

Ver. 35. "And if they would learn any thing, let them ask their own husbands at home."

Thus, "not only, as it seems, are they not allowed to speak," saith he, "at random, but not even to ask any question in the church." Now if they ought not to ask questions, much more is their speaking at pleasure contrary to law. And what may be the cause of his setting them under so great subjection? Because the woman is in some sort a weaker being and easily carried away and light minded. Here you see why he set over them their husbands as teachers, for the benefit of both. For so he both rendered the women orderly, and the husbands he made anxious, as having to deliver to their wives very exactly what they heard.

Further, because they supposed this to be an ornament to them, I mean their speaking in public; again he brings round the discourse to the opposite point, saying, "For it is shameful for a woman to speak in the church." That is, first he made this out from the law of God, then from common reason and our received custom; even when he was discoursing with the women about long hair, he said, "Doth not even nature herself teach you?" (c. xi. 14.) And everywhere thou mayest find this to be his manner, not only from the divine Scriptures, but also from the common custom, to put them to shame.

[2.] But besides these things, he also shames them by consideration of what all agreed on, and what was every where prescribed ; which topic also here he hath set down, saying,

Ver. 36. "What ? was it from you that the word of God went forth ? or came it unto you alone ?"

Thus he brings in the other Churches also as holding this law, both abating the disturbance by consideration of the novelty of the thing, and by the general voice making his saying acceptable. Wherefore also elsewhere he said, "Who shall put you in remembrance of my ways which be in Christ, even as I teach everywhere in all the Churches." (1 Cor. iv. 17.) And again, "God is not a God of confusion, but of peace, as in all the Churches of the saints. ' (c. xiv. 33.) And here, "What ? was it from you that the word of God went forth ? or came it unto you alone ?" i. e., "neither first, nor alone are ye believers, but the whole world." Which also writing to the Colossians he said, "even as it is bearing fruit and increasing in all the world," (Coloss. i. 6.) speaking of the Gospel.

But he turns it also at another time to the encouragement of his hearers ; as when he saith that theirs were the first fruits, and were manifest unto all. Thus, writing to the Thessalonians he said, " For from you hath sounded forth the word of God," and, "in every place your faith to God-ward is gone forth." (1 Thes. i. 8.) And again to the Romans, "Your faith is proclaimed throughout the whole world[1]." For both are apt to shame and stir up, as well the being commended of others, as that they have others partakers in their judgment. Wherefore also here he saith ; "What ? was it from you that the word of God went forth ? or came it unto you only ?" "For neither can ye say this," saith he ; "we were made teachers to the rest, and it cannot be right for us to learn of others ; " nor, "the faith remained in this place only, and no precedents from other quarters ought to be received." Seest thou by how many arguments he put them to shame ? He introduced the law, he signified the shamefulness of the thing, he brought forward the other Churches.[2]

[3.] Next, what is strongest of all he puts last, saying, "God ordains these things even at this time by me."

Ver. 37. Thus : "if any man thinketh himself to be a prophet, or spiritual, let him take knowledge of the things which I write unto you that they are the commandments of the Lord.'

Ver. 38. "But if any man is ignorant, let him be ignorant."

And wherefore did he add this ? Intimating that he is not using violence nor contention, which is a sign of them who wish not to set up their own things, but aim at what is profitable to others. Wherefore also in another place he saith, "But if any man seemeth to be contentious, we have no such custom." (1 Cor. xi. 16.) But he doth not this everywhere, but only where the offences are not very great, and then rather as putting them to shame. Since when he discourses of other sins, he speaks not thus. But how ? " Be not deceived : neither fornicators, nor effeminate, shall inherit the kingdom of God." (1 Cor. vi. 9, 10.) And again, " Behold, I Paul say unto you, that if ye receive circumcision, Christ will profit you nothing." (Gal. v. 2.) But here, since his discourse was of silence, he doth not very keenly inveigh against them, by this very thing attracting them the more. Then, as he is ever wont to do, unto the former subject whence he digressed to say these things, he brings back his discourse as follows :

Ver. 39. " Wherefore, brethren, desire earnestly to prophesy, and forbid not to speak with tongues."

For this too is his wont, not only to work out what is before him, but also starting from that to set right whatever seems to him in any way akin to it, and again to return to the former, so as not to appear to wander from the subject. For so when he was discoursing of their concord in their banquets, he digressed to their Communion in the Mysteries, and having thence put them to shame, he returns again to the former, saying, " Wherefore, when ye come together to eat, wait one for another." (1 Cor. xi. 33.)

And here, accordingly, having discoursed of good order in their gifts, and of its being a duty neither to faint in the lesser, nor to be puffed up on account of the greater; then having made an excursion from thence to the sobriety becoming women and having established it, he returns again to his subject, saying, " Wherefore, brethren, desire earnestly to prophesy, and forbid not to speak with tongues." Seest thou how to the end he preserved the difference of these? And how he signifies that the one is very necessary, the other not so? Wherefore of the one he saith, " desire earnestly[3]," but of the other, " forbid not."

[4.] Then, as in brief summary, setting all things right, he adds the words,

Ver. 40. "Let all things be done decently and in order."

---

[1] Rom. i. 8. καταγγέλλεται.

[2] [The sharp rebuke contained in this verse is restricted by Meyer to the regulation laid down respecting women, but it rather refers, as Chrysostom views it, to all the points touched upon in the preceding discussion. As Principal Edwards says, " The Corinthians acted as if they had originated the Gospel or were the only Christian Church ; that is, as if the Gospel took its coloring from local influences and were not broad as humanity itself nor destined to survive nationalities." He thinks too that it is a question whether they asked the Apostle's advice as touching the Spiritual gifts, as the way in which that subject is introduced in the first verse of the twelfth chapter as well as the words of this verse make it doubtful. C.]

[3] ζηλοῦτε.

Again giving a blow to them who chose to behave themselves unseemly without cause, and to incur the imputation of madness; and who keep not their proper rank. For nothing doth so build up as good order, as peace, as love; even as their contraries tend to pull down. And not only in things spiritual, but also in all others one may observe this. Thus whether it be in a dance, or a ship, or in a chariot, or a camp, if thou shouldest confound the order, and casting the greater out of their proper place, shouldest bring in the lesser into their rank, thou destroyest all, and thus things are turned upside down. Neither let us then destroy our order, nor place the head below and the feet above: now this is done when we cast down right reason, and set our lusts, passions, and pleasure, over the rational part: whence violent are the billows, and great the confusion, and intolerable the tempest, all things being wrapt in darkness.

And, if thou wilt, let us first examine the unseemliness which arises herefrom, and then the loss. How then may this be clear to us, and thoroughly known? Let us bring forward a man in that frame of mind; enamoured of a harlot and overcome by a dishonorable passion; and then we shall see the mockery which this comes to. For what can be baser than a man watching the doors before the harlots' chambers, and beaten by a whorish woman, and weeping, and lamenting, and turning his glory into shame? And if thou wilt also see the loss, call to mind, I pray, the expenditure of money, the extreme risks, the contests with rival lovers, the wounds, the stripes received in such affrays.

Such also are they who are holden by the lust of wealth; or rather they behave themselves more unseemly. For whereas these are wholly occupied about one person; the covetous busy themselves about all men's substance alike, both poor and rich, and long for things that are not; a thing which above all denotes the wildness of their passion. For they say not, "I would fain have the substance of such a person or of such another," only, but they want the very mountains to be gold, and the houses and all that they see; and they go forth into another world, and this passion they feel to a boundless degree, and at no point cease from their lusting. What discourse can set before us the tempest of those thoughts, the waves, the darkness? And where the waves and tempest are so great, what pleasure can there be? There is not any; but tumult, and anguish, and black clouds which instead of rain bring great sorrow of heart: the kind of thing which is wont to happen in the case of those who are enamoured of beauty not their own. Wherefore they who have no passionate love at all are in more pleasure than any lovers.

[5.] This however no man would gainsay. But to me even he who loves, but restrains his passion, seems to live more pleasurably than he who continually enjoys his mistress. For though the proof be rather difficult, nevertheless even at that disadvantage the argument must be ventured on: the cause of the increased difficulty not being the nature of the thing, but because of the want of meet hearers for this high morality. Thus: whether is it pleasanter, tell me, to the lover, to be despised by his beloved, or to be honored, and to look down upon her? Evidently the latter. Whom then, tell me, will the harlot value more? Him that is a slave to her and is already led captive at her will, or him that is above her nets and soareth higher than her arrows? Every one must see, the latter. And about whom will she take more thought, the fallen, or him that is not yet so? Him that is not yet so, of course. And which will be more an object of desire, he who is subdued, or he who is not yet taken? He who up to this time is not yet taken. And if ye disbelieve it, I will produce my proof from what takes place within yourselves. As thus: of which woman would a man be more enamored; one that easily submits and gives herself up to him, or one that denies, and gives him trouble? Evidently of this last; since hereby the longing is more vehemently kindled. Of course then in the woman's case also exactly the same thing will happen. And him will they honor and admire more who looks down upon them. But if this be true, so likewise is the other, that he enjoys greater pleasure who is more honored and beloved. Since the general too lets alone the city that hath been once taken, but that which stands out and maintains the struggle he besets with all diligence: and the hunter, when the animal is caught, keeps it shut up in darkness as the harlot doth her lover, but pursues that which flies from him.

But I shall be told, "the one enjoys his desire, the other not so." But freedom from disgrace, and from being a slave under her tyrannical commands, the not being led and dragged about by her as a drudge, beaten, spit upon, pitched head foremost; dost thou consider this to be a small pleasure, tell me? Nay, if one would accurately examine these things, and were able to gather into one their insults, complaints, everlasting quarrels, some arising from their tempers, others from their wantonness, their enmities, and all the rest, such as they only that feel them know;—he will find that there is no war but hath more truces than this wretched life of theirs. What pleasure then meanest thou, tell me? The temporary and brief enjoyment of intercourse? But this speedily doth strife overtake, and storms, and rage, and the same madness again.

[6.] And these things have been said by us, as one would speak discoursing with licentious youths, who do not very patiently submit to hear our discourses of the kingdom and of hell.

And now that we are bringing forward these topics also, it is not even possible to say how great is the pleasure of the continent; if one frame in one's own mind his crowns, his rewards, his converse with the angels, the proclaiming of him before the world, his boldness, those blessed and immortal hopes of his.

"But intercourse hath a certain pleasure:" for this they are continually repeating: "while the continent continually suffers pain contending with the tyranny of nature." Nay, but one shall find just the contrary result. For this violence and tumult is present with the unchaste rather: there being in his body a violent tempest, and no sea in a storm so grievously vexed as he; never withstanding his passion, but ever receiving blows from it; as the possessed and they that are continually rent in the midst by evil spirits. Whereas the temperate like a noble champion continually giving blows to it, reaps the best of pleasures, and sweeter than ten thousand of that kind; and this victory and his good conscience, and those illustrous trophies, are ornaments for him continually to deck himself withal.

As to the other, if after his intercourse he hath a little respite, it must be counted nothing. For again the storm comes on, and again there are waves. But he that commands himself doth not suffer this tumult to lay hold of him at all, nor the sea to arise, nor the wild beast to roar. And even if he endure some violence in restraining such an impulse, yet so doth the other also, continually receiving blows and stabs, and unable to endure the sting: and it is like as if there were a wild horse furious and struggling, and one should check with the bridle, and hold him in with all skill: while another giving him the rein to escape the trouble, were dragged along by him and carried hither and thither.

If I have spoken these things more plainly than is becoming, let no man blame me. For I desire not to make a brave show by a gravity of words, but to make my hearers grave.

Therefore also the prophets spare no such words, wishing to extirpate the licentiousness of the Jews, but do even more nakedly inveigh against them than we do now in the things we have spoken. For so a physician wishing to remove an ulcer doth not consider how he may keep his hands clean, but how he may rid the patient of the ulcer; and he who would raise on high the lowly, first makes himself lowly; and he who seeks to slay the conspirator stains himself with blood as well as the other, and this makes him the more brilliant. Since if one were to see a soldier returning from the war, stained with gore and blood and brains, he will not loathe him nor turn from him on this account, but will even admire him the more. So then let us do, when we see any one returning, covered with blood after the slaughter of his evil desire, let us the more admire him and become partakers of his battle and victory, and say to those who indulge this wild love, "show us the pleasure you derive from lust; for the continent hath that which comes of his victory, but thou none from any quarter. But if ye should mention that which is connected with the criminal act, yet the other is more manifest and satisfactory. For thou hast from the enjoyment something brief and hardly apparent; but he from his conscience, hath both a greater and an enduring and a sweeter joy. The company of a woman hath surely no such power as self-command, to preserve the soul undisturbed and give it wings."

Well then: the continent man, as I said, thus evidently makes his pleasure out to us: but in thy case I see the dejection arising from defeat, but the pleasure, desiring to see, I find not. For what dost thou consider the moment of pleasure? That before the criminal action? Nay, it is not so, for it is a time of madness and delirium and frenzy: to grind the teeth and be beside one's self is not any pleasure: and if it were pleasure, it would not produce the same effects on you which they who are in pain endure. For they who strike with their fists and are stricken grind their teeth, and women in travail distracted with pains do the same. So that this is no pleasure, but frenzy rather, and confusion, and tumult. Shall we say then, the time after the action? Nay, neither is this. For neither could we say that a woman just delivered is in pleasure, but in release from certain pains. But this is by no means pleasure, but weakness rather and falling away: and there is a great difference between these two. What then is the time of pleasure, tell me? There is none. But if there be any, it is so brief as not even to be apparent. At least, having zealously sought in a great many ways to detect and apprehend it, we have not been able. But the time of the chaste man's pleasure is not such, rather it is wider and evident to all. Or rather, all his life is in pleasure, his conscience crowned, the waves laid, no disturbance from any quarter arising within him.

Since then this man's life is more in pleasure, while the life spent in love of pleasure is in dejection and disquiets; let us flee from licentiousness, let us keep hold on continence, that we may also obtain the good things to come, through the grace and mercy, &c., &c.

15

HOMILY XXXVIII.

1 Cor. xv. 1, 2.

Now I make known unto you, brethren, the gospel which I preached unto you, which also ye received, wherein also ye stand; by which also ye are saved: in what words I preached it unto you.[1]

HAVING finished the discourse of spiritual gifts, he passes to that which is of all most necessary, the subject of the resurrection. For in this too they were greatly unsound. And as in men's bodies, when the fever lays actual hold of their solid parts, I mean the nerves and the veins and the primary elements, the mischief becomes incurable unless it receive much attention; just so at that time also it was like to happen. Since to the very elements of godliness the mischief was proceeding. Wherefore also Paul uses great earnestness. For not of morals was his discourse henceforth nor about one man's being a fornicator, another covetous, and another having his head covered; but about the very sum of all good things. For touching the resurrection itself they were at variance. Because this being all our hope, against this point did the devil make a vehement stand, and at one time he was wholly subverting it, at another his word was that it was "past already;" which also Paul writing to Timothy called a gangrene, I mean, this wicked doctrine, and those that brought it in he branded, saying, "Of whom is Hymenæus and Philetus, who concerning the truth have erred, saying that the resurrection is past already, and overthrow the faith of some." (2 Tim. ii. 17, 18.) At one time then they said thus, but at another that the body rises not again but the purification of the soul is the resurrection.

But these things that wicked demon persuaded them to say, not wishing to overturn the resurrection only, but also to show that all the things done for our sakes are a fable. For if they were persuaded that there is no resurrection of bodies, he would have gradually persuaded them that neither was Christ raised. And thereupon he would introduce also this in due course, that He had not come nor had done what He did. For such is the craft of the devil. Wherefore also Paul calls it "cunning craftiness[2]," because he doth not straightway signify what he intends to effect, for fear of being detected, but dressing himself up in a mask of one kind, he fabricates arts of another kind: and like a crafty enemy attacking a city with walls, he secretly undermines it from below: so as thereby to be hardly guarded against and to succeed in his endeavors. Therefore such snares on his part being continually detected, and these his crafty ambushes hunted out by this admirable and mighty man, he said, "For we are not ignorant of his devices." (2 Cor. ii. 11.) So also here he unfolds his whole guile and points out all his stratagems, and whatsoever he would fain effect, Paul puts before us, with much exactness going over all. Yea, and therefore he put this head after the rest, both because it was extremely necessary and because it involves the whole of our condition.

And observe his consideration: how first having secured his own, he then proceeds even beyond in his discourse, and them that are without he doth abundantly reduce to silence. Now he secures his own, not by reasonings, but by things which had already happened and which themselves had received and believed to have taken place: a thing which was most of all apt to shame them, and capable of laying hold on them. Since if they were unwilling to believe after this, it was no longer Paul but themselves they would disbelieve: which thing was a censure on those who had once for all received it and changed their minds. For this cause then he begins also from hence, implying that he needs no other witnesses to prove his speaking truth, but those very persons who were deceived.

[2.] But that what I say may become clearer, we must needs in what follows attend to the very words. What then are these? "I make known unto you, brethren," saith he, "the gospel which I preached unto you." Seest thou with what modesty he commences? Seest thou how from the beginning he points out that he is bringing in no new nor strange thing? For he who "maketh known" that which was already known but afterwards had fallen into oblivion, "maketh known" by recalling it into memory.

---

[1] τίνι λόγῳ εὐηγγελισάμην ὑμῖν.

[2] μεθοδείαν. Eph. iv. 14.

And when he called them " brethren," even from hence he laid the foundation of no mean part of the proof of his assertions. For by no other cause became we " brethren," but by the dispensation of Christ according to the flesh. And this is just the reason why he thus called them, at the same time soothing and courting them, and likewise reminding them of their innumerable blessings.

And what comes next again is demonstrative of the same. What then is this? " The gospel." For the sum of the gospels hath its original hence, from God having become man and having been crucified and having risen again. This gospel also Gabriel preached to the Virgin, this also the prophets to the world, this also the apostles all of them.

" Which I preached unto you, which also ye received, wherein also ye stand. By which also ye are saved, in what word I preached unto you; if ye hold it fast, except ye believed in vain."

Seest thou how he calls themselves to be witnesses of the things spoken? And he saith not, " which ye heard," but, " which ye received," demanding it of them as a kind of deposit, and showing that not in word only, but also by deeds and signs and wonders they received it, and that they should hold it safe.

Next, because he was speaking of the things long past, he referred also to the present time, saying, " wherein also ye stand," taking the vantage ground of them that disavowal might be out of their power, though they wished it never so much. And this is why at the beginning he said not, " I teach you," but, ' I make known unto you' what hath already been made manifest."

And how saith he that they who were so tossed with waves " stand?" He feigns ignorance to profit them; which also he doth in the case of the Galatians, but not in like manner. For inasmuch as he could not in that case affect ignorance, he frames his address in another way, saying, " I have confidence toward you in the Lord, that ye will be none otherwise minded." (Gal. v. 10.) He said not, "that ye were none otherwise minded," because their fault was acknowledged and evident, but he answers for the future; and yet this too was uncertain; but it was to draw them to him more effectually. Here however he doth feign ignorance, saying, " wherein also ye stand."

Then comes the advantage; " by which also ye are saved, in what words I preached it unto you." " So then, this present exposition is for clearness and interpretation. For the doctrine itself ye need not," saith he, " to learn, but to be reminded of it and corrected." And these

things he saith, leaving them no room to plunge into recklessness once for all.

But what is, " in what word I preached it unto you?" " After what manner did I say," saith he, " that the resurrection takes place? For that there is a resurrection I would not say that ye doubt: but ye seek perhaps to obtain a clearer knowledge of that saying. This then will I provide for you: for indeed I am well assured that ye hold the doctrine." Next, because he was directly affirming, " wherein also ye stand;" that he might not thereby make them more remiss, he alarms them again, saying, " If ye hold it fast, except ye believed in vain;" intimating that the stroke is on the chief head, and the contest for no common things but in behalf of the whole of the faith. And for the present he saith it with reserve, but as he goes on and waxes warm, he throws off the veil and proceeds to cry out[1], and say, " But if Christ hath not been raised then is our preaching vain, your faith also is vain: ye are yet in your sins:" but in the beginning not so: for thus it was expedient to proceed, gently and by degrees.

Ver. 3. " For I delivered unto you first of all that which I also received."

Neither here doth he say, " I said unto you," nor, " I taught you," but uses the same expression again, saying, " I delivered unto you that which also I received:" nor again here doth he say, " I was taught," but, " I received:" establishing these two things; first, that one ought to introduce nothing from one's self; next, that by demonstration from his deeds they were fully persuaded, not by bare words: and by degrees while he is rendering his argument credible, he refers the whole to Christ, and signifies that nothing was of man in these doctrines.

But what is this, " For I delivered unto you first of all[2]?" for that is his word. " In the beginning, not now." And thus saying he brings the time for a witness, and that it were the greatest disgrace for those who had so long time been persuaded now to change their minds: and not this only, but also that the doctrine is necessary. Wherefore also it was " delivered " among " the first," and from the beginning straightway. And what didst thou so deliver? tell me. But this he doth not say straightway, but first, " I received." And what didst thou receive? " That Christ died for our sins." He said not immediately that there is a resurrection of our bodies, yet this very thing in truth he doth establish, but afar off and by other topics saying that " Christ died," and laying before a kind of strong base and

---

[1] γυμνῇ λοιπὸν τῇ κεφαλῇ βοᾷ.
[2] ἐν πρώτοις.

irrefragable foundation of the doctrine concerning the resurrection. For neither did he simply say that "Christ died ;" although even this were sufficient to declare the resurrection, but with an addition, "Christ died for our sins."

[3.] But first it is worth while to hear what those who are infected with the Manichæan doctrines say here, who are both enemies to the truth and war against their own salvation. What then do these allege ? By death here, they say, Paul means nothing else than our being in sin ; and by resurrection, our being delivered from our sins. Seest thou how nothing is weaker than error ? And how it is taken by its own wings, and needs not the warfare from without, but by itself it is pierced through ? Consider, for instance, these men, how they too have pierced themselves through by their own statements. Since if this be death, and Christ did not take a body, as ye suppose, and yet died, He was in sin according to you. For I indeed say that He took unto Himself a body and His death, I say, was that of the flesh ; but thou denying this, wilt be compelled to affirm the other. But if He was in sin, how saith He, "Which of you convinceth Me of sin ?" and "The prince of this world cometh, and hath nothing in me ?" (John viii. 46 ; xiv. 30.) and again, "Thus it becometh Us to fulfill all righteousness ?" (Mat. iii. 15.) Nay, how did He at all die for sinners, if Himself were in sin ? For he who dies for sinners ought himself to be without sin. Since if he himself also sin, how shall he die for other sinners ? But if for others' sins He died, He died being without sin : and if being without sin He died, He died—not the death of sin ; for how could He being without sin ?—but the death of the body. Wherefore also Paul did not simply say, "He died," but added, "for our sins :" both forcing these heretics against their will to the confession of His bodily death, and signifying also by this that before death He was without sin : for he that dies for others' sins, it followeth must himself be without sin.

Neither was he content with this, but added, "according to the Scriptures :" hereby both again making his argument credible, and intimating what kind of death he was speaking of : since it is the death of the body which the Scriptures everywhere proclaim. For, "they pierced My hands and My feet," (Ps. xxi. 18.) saith He, and, "they shall look on Him Whom they pierced." (John xix. 37. Zech. xii. 10.) And many other instances, too not to name all one by one, partly in words and partly in types, one may see in them stored up, setting forth His slaughter in the flesh and that He was slain for our sins. For, "for the sins of my peo-

ple," saith one, "is He come[1] to death :" and, the Lord delivered Him up for our sins :" and, "He was wounded for our transgressions." (Is. liii.) But if thou[2] dost not endure the Old Testament, hear John crying out and declaring both, as well His slaughter in the body as the cause of it : thus, "Behold," saith he, "the Lamb of God, Who taketh away the sin of the world :" (John i. 29.) and Paul saying, "For Him Who knew no sin, He made to be sin on our behalf, that we might become the righteousness of God in Him :" (2 Cor. v. 21.) and again, "Christ redeemed us from the curse of the law, having become a curse for us :" (Gal. iii. 13.) and again, "having put off from himself principalities and powers, He made a show of them openly, triumphing over them ;" (Col. ii. 15.) and ten thousand other sayings to show what happened at His death in the body, and because of our sins. Yea, and Christ Himself saith, "for your sakes I sanctify Myself[3]" and, "now the prince of this world hath been condemned[4];" showing that having no sin he was slain.

[4.] Ver. 4. "And that he was buried."

And this also confirms the former topics, for that which is buried is doubtless a body. And here he no longer adds, "according to the Scriptures." He had wherewithal, nevertheless he adds it not. For what cause ? Either because the burial was evident unto all, both then and now, or because the expression, "according to the Scriptures," is set down of both in common. Wherefore then doth he add, "according to the Scriptures," in this place, "and that He rose on the third day according to the Scriptures," and is not content with the former clause, so spoken in common ? Because this also was to most men obscure : wherefore here again he brings in "the Scriptures" by inspiration, having so conceived this thought so wise and divine.

How is it then that he doth the same in regard of His death[5] ? Because in that case too, although the cross was evident unto all and in the sight of all He was stretched upon it ; yet the cause was no longer equally so. The fact indeed of his death all knew, but that He suffered this for the sins of the world was no longer equally known to the multitude. Wherefore he brings in the testimony from the Scriptures.

This however hath been sufficiently proved by what we have said. But where have the Scrip-

---

[1] ἥκει. LXX, ἤχθη.
[2] As a Manichæan.
[3] John xvii. 19. ὑπὲρ αὐτῶν.
[4] John xvi. 11. κατακέκριται. rec. text κέκριται.
[5] The Benedictines insert a negative here, which contradicts the sense, and is not in Savile.

tures said that He was buried, and on the third day shall rise again? By the type of Jonah which which also Himself alleges, saying, "As Jonah was three days and three nights in the whale's belly, so shall also the Son of Man be three days and three nights in the heart of the earth." (Mat. xii. 40.) By the bush in the desert. For even as that burned, yet was not consumed, (Exod. iii. 2.) so also that body died indeed, but was not holden of death continually[1]. And the dragon also in Daniel shadows out this. For as the dragon having taken the food which the prophet gave, burst asunder in the midst;[2] even so Hades having swallowed down that Body, was rent asunder, the Body of itself cutting asunder its womb and rising again.

Now if thou desirest to hear also in words those things which thou hast seen in types, listen to Isaiah, saying, "His life is taken from the earth," (Isa. liii. 8, 10, 11.)[3] and, "it pleaseth the Lord to cleanse Him from His wound...to show unto Him light:" and David before him, "Thou wilt not leave My soul to Hades, nor wilt Thou suffer Thy Holy One to see corruption." (Ps. xvi. 10.)

Therefore Paul also sends thee on to the Scriptures, that thou mayest learn that not without cause nor at random were these things done. For how could they, when so many prophets are describing and proclaiming them beforehand? And no where doth the Scripture mean the death of sin, when it makes mention of our Lord's death, but that of the body, and a burial and resurrection of the same kind.

[5.] Ver. 5. "And that He appeared to Cephas:" he names immediately the most credible of all. "Then to the twelve."

Ver. 6. "Then he appeared to above five hundred brethren at once; of whom the greater part remain until now, but some are fallen asleep."

Ver. 7. "Then he appeared to James; then to all the Apostles."

Ver. 8. "And last of all, as unto one born out of due time, he appeared to me also."

Thus, since he had mentioned the proof from the Scriptures, he adds also that by the events, producing as witnesses of the resurrection, after the prophets, the apostles and other faithful men. Whereas if he meant that other resurrection, the deliverance from sin, it were idle for him to say, He appeared to such and such an one; for this is the argument of one who is establishing the resurrection of the body, not of one obscurely teaching deliverance from sins. Wherefore neither said he once for all, "He appeared," although it were sufficient for him to do so, setting down the expression in common: but now both twice and thrice, and almost in each several case of them that had seen Him he employs it. For "He appeared," saith he, "to Cephas, He appeared to above five hundred brethren, He appeared to me also." Yet surely the Gospel saith the contrary, that He was seen of Mary first. (Mark xvi. 9.) But among men He was seen of him first who did most of all long to see Him.

But of what twelve apostles doth he here speak[4]? For after He was received up, Matthias was taken into the number, not after the resurrection immediately. But it is likely that He appeared even after He was received up. At any rate, this our apostle himself after His ascension was both called, and saw Him. Therefore neither doth he set down the time, but simply and without defining recounts the appearance. For indeed it is probable that many took place; wherefore also John said, "This third time He was manifested." (John xxi. 14.)

"Then He appeared to above five hundred brethren." Some say that "above[5]," is above from heaven; that is, "not walking upon earth, but above and overhead He appeared to them:" adding, that it was Paul's purpose to confirm, not the resurrection only, but also the ascension. Others say that the expression, "above five hundred," means, "more than five hundred."

"Of whom the greater part remain until now." Thus, "though I relate events of old," saith he, "yet have I living witnesses." "But some are fallen asleep." He said not, "are dead," but, "are fallen asleep," by this expression also again confirming the resurrection. "After that, He was seen of James." I suppose, His brother. For the Lord is said to have Himself ordained him and made him Bishop in Jerusalem first. "Then to all the apostles." For there were also other apostles, as the seventy.

"And last of all he appeared unto me also, as unto one born out of due time." This is rather an expression of modesty than any thing

---

[1] This sign is variously yet without contradiction interpreted by the Fathers. St. Augustin considers it a type of the glory of God, inhabiting the Jewish people, yet not consuming the thorny hardness of their heart. t. v. p. 25. St. Cyril (*in Exod.* t. i. p. 263.) of the Divine Nature inhabiting the Human, yet not consuming it, in the person of our Lord. Theodoret (*in loc.*) says, "The power and mercy of God are proclaimed by the circumstance, that the bush being mere brushwood was not consumed by the unquenchable fire: I think however that other intimations are conveyed by this circumstance: as that Israel, plotted against by the Egyptians, should not be consumed, but overcome his enemies; and that the Only-Begotten, being made incarnate and dwelling in the Virgin's Womb, shall keep that virginity inviolate." Tertull. (*adv. Gnost* c. l.) alludes to it, as representing the Church in the fire of persecution.

[2] Bel and the Dragon, v. 27;

[3] LXX. in our vers. " it pleased the Lord to bruise Him...He shall see...and be satisfied."

[4] [It is generally considered that "the twelve " is simply a designation of the Apostolic college. C.]

[5] ἐπάνω. [One wonders that Chrysostom should mention this meaning of the word, yet it has been adopted by Peter Martyr and Seinler. It is certainly far more natural to take it as given in the A. V., especially as it is connected with a numeral. Had the Apostle intended to express the meaning "from above," he would doubtless have used the word ἄνωθεν. C.]

else. For not because he was the least, there-fore did he appear to him after the rest. Since even if He did call him last, yet he appeared more illustrious than many which were before him, yea rather than all. And the five hundred brethren too were not surely better than James, because He appeared to them before him.

Why did He not appear to all at the same time? That He might first sow the seeds of faith. For he that saw Him first and was ex-actly and fully assured, told it unto the residue: then their report coming first placed the hearer in expectation of this great wonder, and made way before for the faith of sight. Therefore neither did He appear to all together, nor in the beginning to many, but to one alone first, and him the leader of the whole company and the most faithful: since indeed there was great need of a most faithful soul to be first to receive this sight. For those who saw him after others had seen him, and heard it from them, had in their testimony what contributed in no small degree to their own faith and tended to prepare their mind beforehand; but he who was first counted worthy to see Him, had need, as I have said, of great faith, not to be confounded by a sight so contrary to expectation. There-fore he appears to Peter first. For he that first confessed Him to be Christ was justly also counted worthy first to behold His resurrection. And not on this account alone doth He appear to him first, but also because he had denied Him, more abundantly to comfort him and to signify that he is not despaired of, before the rest He vouchsafed him even this sight and to him first entrusted His sheep. Therefore also He ap-peared to the women first. Because this sex was made inferior, therefore both in His birth and in His resurrection this first tastes of His grace.

But after Peter, He appears also to each at intervals, and at one time to fewer, at another to more, hereby making them witnesses and teachers of each other, and rendering His apostles trustworthy in all that they said.

[6.] "And last of all, as unto one born out of due time, he appeared to me also." What mean here his expressions of humility, or wherein are they seasonable? For if he wishes to show himself worthy of credit and to enrol himself among the witnesses of the resurrection, he is doing the contrary of what he wishes: since it were meet that he exalt himself and show that he was great, which in many places he doth, the occasion calling for it. Well, the very reason why he here also speaks modestly is his being about to do this. Not straightway, how-ever, but with his own peculiar good sense: in that having first spoken modestly and heaped up against himself many charges, he then magnifies the things concerning himself. What may the

reason be? That, when he comes to utter that great and lofty expression concerning himself, "I labored more abundantly than all," his dis-course may be rendered more acceptable, both hereby, and by its being spoken as a conse-quence of what went before and not as a lead-ing topic. Therefore also writing to Timothy, and intending to say great things concerning himself, he first sets down his charges against himself. For so all persons, when speaking in high terms of others, speak out freely and with boldness: but he that is compelled to praise himself, and especially when he also calls him-self to witness, is disconcerted and blushes. Therefore also this blessed man first declares his own misery, and then utters that lofty expres-sion. This then he doth, partly to abate the offensiveness of speaking about himself, and partly that he might hereby recommend to their belief what he had to say afterwards. For he that truly states what things are discreditable to him and conceals none of them, such as that he persecuted the Church, that he laid waste the faith, doth hereby cause the things that are hon-orable to him also to be above suspicion.

And consider the exceeding greatness of his humility. For having said, "and last of all He appeared to me also," he was not content with this: "For many that are last shall be first," saith He, "and the first last." (Matt. xx. 16.) Therefore he added, "as unto one born out of due time." Neither did he stop here, but adds also his own judgment and with a reason, saying,

Ver. 9. "For I am the least of the apostles, that am not meet to be called an apostle, because I persecuted the Church of God."

And he said not, of the twelve alone, but also of all the other apostles. And all these things he spake, both as one speaking modestly and because he was really so disposed as I said, mak-ing arrangements also beforehand for what was intended to be spoken and rendering it more acceptable. For had he come forward and said, "Ye ought to believe me that Christ rose from the dead; for I saw Him and of all I am the most worthy of credit, inasmuch as I have labored more," the expression might have of-fended the hearers: but now by first dwelling on the humiliating topics and those which in-volve accusation, he both took off what might be grating in such a narrative, and prepared the way for their belief in his testimony.

On this account therefore neither doth he sim-ply, as I said, declare himself to be the last and un-worthy of the appellation of an apostle, but also states the reason, saying, "because I persecuted the Church." And yet all those things were forgiven, but nevertheless he himself never for got them, desiring to signify the greatness of God's favor: wherefore also he goes on to say,

[7.] Ver. 10. "But by the grace of God I am what I am."

Seest thou again another[1] excess of humility? in that the defects he imputes to himself, but of the good deeds nothing; rather he refers all to God. Next, lest he might hereby render his hearer supine, he saith, "And His grace which was bestowed upon me was not found vain." And this again with reserve: in that he said not, "I have displayed a diligence worthy of His grace, " but, "it was not found vain."

"But I labored more abundantly than they all." He said not, "I was honored," but, "I labored;" and when he had perils and deaths to speak of, by the name of labor he again abates his expression.

Then again practicing his wonted humility, this also he speedily passes by and refers the whole to God, saying, "Yet not I, but the grace of God which was with me." What can be more admirable than such a soul? who having in so many ways depressed himself and uttered but one lofty word, not even this doth he call his own; on every side finding ways, both from the former things and from them that follow after, to contract this lofty expression, and that because it was of necessity that he came to it.

But consider how he abounds in the expressions of humility. For so, "to me last of all He appeared," saith he. Wherefore neither doth he with himself mention any other, and saith, "as of one born out of due time," and that himself is "the least of the apostles," and not even worthy of this appellation. And he was not content even with these, but that he might not seem in mere words to be humble-minded, he states both reasons and proofs: of his being "one born out of due time," his seeing Jesus last; and of his being unworthy even of the name of an apostle, "his persecuting the Church." For he that is simply humble-minded doeth not this: but he that also sets down the reasons utters all from a contrite mind. Wherefore also he elsewhere makes mention of these same things, saying, "And I thank him that enabled me ; even Christ Jesus our Lord, for that He counted me faithful, appointing me to his service, though I was before a blasphemer, and a persecutor, and injurious." (1 Tim. i. 12,13.)

But wherefore did he utter at all that same lofty expression, "I labored more abundantly than they?" He saw that the occasion compelled him. For had he not said this, had he only depreciated himself, how could he with boldness call himself to witness, and number himself with the rest, and say,

Ver. 11. "Whether then it be I or they, so we preach."

For the witness ought to be trustworthy, and

a great man. But how he "labored more abundantly than they," he indicated above, saying, "Have we no right to eat and to drink, as also the other Apostles?" And again, "to them that are without law as without law." Thus, both where exactness was to be displayed, he overshot all: and where there was need to condescend, he displayed again the same great superiority.

But some cite his being sent to the Gentiles and his overrunning the larger part of the world. Whence it is evident that he enjoyed more grace. For if he labored more, the grace was also more: but he enjoyed more grace, because he displayed also more diligence. Seest thou how by those particulars whereby he contends and strives to throw into shade the things concerning himself, he is shown to be first of all?

[8.] And these things when we hear, let us also make open show of our defects, but of our excellencies let us say nothing. Or if the opportunity force it upon us, let us speak of them with reserve and impute the whole to God's grace : which accordingly the Apostle also doth, ever and anon putting a bad mark upon his former life, but his after-state imputing to grace, that he might signify the mercy of God from every circumstance : from His having saved him such as he was, and when saved making him again such as he is. Let none accordingly of those who are in sin despair, let none of those in virtue be confident, but let the one be exceeding fearful and the other forward. For neither shall any slothful man be able to abide in virtue, nor one that is diligent be weak to escape from evil. And of both these the blessed David is an example, who after he slumbered a little, had a great downfall : and when he was pricked in his heart, again hastened up to his former height. Since in fact both are alike evils, both despair and slothfulness ; the one quickly casting a man down from the very arch of the heavens; the other not suffering the fallen to rise again. Wherefore with respect to the one, Paul said, "Let him that thinketh he standeth take heed lest he fall :" (1 Cor. x. 12.) but unto the other, "To-day if ye will hear His voice, harden not your hearts: (Heb iv. 7.) and again, "Lift up the hands that hang down and the palsied knees." (Heb. xii. 12.) And him too that had committed fornication but repented, he therefore quickly refreshes, "that such an one might not be swallowed up with his overmuch sorrow?" (2 Cor. ii. 7.)

Why then in regard of other griefs art thou cast down, O man? Since if for sins, where only grief is beneficial, excess works much mischief, much more for all other things. For wherefore grievest thou? That thou hast lost money? Nay, think of those that are not even

---

[1] ἑτέραν conj. Savile. ἑτέρας Bened.

filled with bread, and thou shalt very speedily obtain consolation. And in each of the things that are grievous to thee mourn not the things that have happened, but for the disasters that have not happened give thanks. Hadst thou money and didst thou lose it? Weep not for the loss, but give thanks for the time when thou didst enjoy it. Say like Job, "Have we received good at the hand of the Lord, and shall we not receive evil?" (Job ii. 10.) And together with that use this argument also ; that even if thou didst lose thy money, yet thy body thou hast still sound and hast not with thy poverty to grieve that it also is maimed. But hath thy body too endured some outrage? Yet is not this the bottom of human calamities, but in the middle of the cask thou art as yet carried along. For many along with poverty and maiming, both wrestle with a demon and wander in deserts : others again endure other things more grievous than these. For may it never be our lot to suffer all that it is possible for one to bear.

These things then ever considering, bear in mind them that suffer worse, and be vexed at none of those things : but when thou sinnest, only then sigh, then weep ; I forbid thee not, nay I enjoin thee rather ; though even then with moderation, remembering that there is returning, there is reconciliation. But seest thou others in luxury and thyself in poverty : and another in goodly robes, and in preeminence? Look not however on these things alone, but also on the miseries that arise out of these. And in thy poverty too, consider not the beggary alone, but the pleasure also thence arising do thou take into account. For wealth hath indeed a cheerful mask, but its inward parts are full of gloom; and poverty the reverse. And shouldest thou unfold each man's conscience, in the soul of the poor thou wilt see great security and freedom : but in that of the rich, confusions, disorders, tempests. And if thou grievest, seeing him rich, he too is vexed much more than thou when he beholds one richer than himself. And as thou fearest him, even so doth he another, and he hath no advantage over thee in this. But thou art vexed to see him in office, because thou art in a private station and one of the governed. Recollect however the day of his ceasing to hold office. And even before that day the tumults, the perils, the fatigues, the flatteries, the sleepless nights, and all the miseries.

[9.] And these things we say to those who have no mind for high morality : since if thou knowest this, there are other and greater things whereby we may comfort thee : but for the present we must use the coarser topics to argue with thee. When therefore thou seest one that is rich, think of him that is richer than he, and thou wilt see

him in the same condition with thyself. And after him look also on him that is poorer than thyself, consider how many have gone to bed hungry, and have lost their patrimony, and live in a dungeon, and pray for death every day. For neither doth poverty breed sadness, nor wealth pleasure, but both the one and the other our own thoughts are wont to produce in us. And consider, beginning from beneath : the scavenger grieves and is vexed that he cannot be rid of this his business so wretched and esteemed so disgraceful : but if thou rid him of this, and cause him, with security, to have plenty of the necessaries of life, he will grieve again that he hath not more than he wants : and if thou grant him more, he will wish to double them again, and will therefore vex himself no less than before : and if thou grant him twofold or threefold, he will be out of heart again because he hath no part in the state : and if you provide him with this also, he will count himself wretched because he is not one of the highest officers of state. And when he hath obtained this honor, he will mourn that he is not a ruler ; and when he shall be ruler, that it is not of a, whole nation ; and when of a whole nation, that it is not of many nations ; and when of many nations, that it is not of all. When he becomes a deputy, he will vex himself again that he is not a king ; and if a king, that he is not so alone ; and if alone, that he is not also of barbarous nations ; and if of barbarous nations, that he is not of the whole world even : and if of the whole world, why not likewise of another world? And so his course of thought going on without end does not suffer him ever to be pleased. Seest thou, how even if from being mean and poor thou shouldest make a man a king, thou dost not remove his dejection, without first correcting his turn of thought, enamored as it is of having more?

Come, let me show thee the contrary too, that even if from a higher station thou shouldest bring down to a lower one him that hath consideration, thou wilt not cast him into dejection and grief. And if thou wilt, let us descend the same ladder, and do thou bring down the satrap from his throne and in supposition deprive him of that dignity. I say that he will not on this account vex himself, if he choose to bear in mind the things of which I have spoken. For he will not reckon up the things of which he hath been deprived, but what he hath still, the glory arising from his office. But if thou take away this also, he will reckon up them who are in private stations and have never ascended to such sway, and for consolation his riches will suffice him. And if thou also cast him out again from this, he will look to them that have a moderate estate. And if thou shouldest take away even moderate wealth, and shouldest allow him to partake only of necessary food, he may think upon them that have not even this, but wrestle with incessant hunger and live in prison. And even if thou shouldest bring him into that prison-house, when he reflects on them that lie under incurable diseases and irremediable pains, he will see himself to be in much better circumstances. And as the scavenger before mentioned not even on being made a king will reap any cheerfulness, so neither will this man ever vex himself if he become a prisoner. It is not then wealth that is the foundation of pleasure, nor poverty of sadness, but our own judgment, and the fact, that the eyes of our mind are not pure, nor are fixed anywhere and abide, but without limit flutter abroad. And as healthy bodies, if they be nourished with bread alone, are in good and vigorous condition : but those that are sickly, even if they enjoy a plentiful and varied diet, become so much the weaker ; so also it is wont to happen in regard of the soul. The mean spirited, not even in a diadem and unspeakable honors can be happy : but the self-denying, even in bonds and fetters and poverty, will enjoy a pure pleasure.

[10.] These things then bearing in mind, let us ever look to them that are beneath us. There is indeed, I grant, another consolation, but of a high strain in morality, and mounting above the grossness of the multitude. What is this ? That wealth is naught, poverty is naught, disgrace is naught, honor is naught, but for a brief time and only in words do they differ from each other. And along with this there is another soothing topic also, greater than it ; the consideration of the things to come, both evil and good, the things which are really evil and really good, and the being comforted by them. But since many, as I said, stand aloof from these doctrines, therefore were we compelled to dwell on other topics, that in course we might lead on to them the receivers of what had been said before.

Let us then, taking all these things into account, by every means frame ourselves aright, and we shall never grieve at these unexpected things. For neither if we should see men rich in a picture, should we say they were to be envied, any more than on seeing poor men there depicted we should call them wretched and pitiable : although those are surely more abiding than they whom we reckon wealthy. Since one abides rich in the picture longer than in the nature itself of things. For the one often lasts, appearing such, even to a hundred years, but the other sometimes, not having had so much as a year to live at his ease in his possessions, hath been suddenly stripped of all. Meditating then on all these things, let us from all quarters build up cheerfulness as an outwork against our irrational sorrow, that we may both pass the present life with pleasure, and obtain the good things to come, through the grace and mercy of our Lord Jesus Christ, with Whom to the Father, with the Holy Ghost, be glory, power, honor, now and forever, and world without end. Amen.

HOMILY XXXIX

1 Cor. xv. 11.

Whether then it be I or they, so we preach, and so ye believed.

HAVING exalted the Apostles and abased himself, then again having exalted himself above them that he might make out an equality : (for he did effect an equality, when he showed that he had advantages over them as well as they over him,) and having thereby proved himself worthy of credit ; neither so doth he dismiss them, but again ranks himself with them, pointing out their concord in Christ. Nevertheless he doth it not so as that he should seem to have been tacked on to them,[1] but as himself also to appear in the same rank. For so it was profitable for the Gospel. Wherefore also he

was equally earnest, on the one hand, that he might not seem to overlook them ; on the other, that he might not be on account of the honor paid to them held cheap by those that were under his authority. Therefore he also now makes himself equal again, saying,

"Whether then it be I or they, so we preach." "From whomsoever," saith he, "ye choose to learn, learn ; there is no difference between us." And he said not, "if ye will not believe me, believe them ; " but while he makes himself worthy of credit and saith that he is of himself sufficient, he affirms the same also of them by themselves. For the difference of persons took no effect, their authority being equal. And in the Epistle to the Galatians

---

[1] προσερρίφθαι.

he doth this, taking them with him, not as also standing in need of them, but saying indeed that even himself was sufficient : " For they who were of repute imparted nothing to me : " (Gal. ii. 6.) nevertheless, even so I follow after agreement with them. "For they gave unto me," saith he, "their right hands." (Gal. ii. 9.) For if the credit of Paul were always to depend on others and to be confirmed by testimony from others, the disciples would hence have received infinite injury. It is not therefore to exalt himself that he doeth this, but fearing for the Gospel. Wherefore also he here saith, making himself equal, " Whether it be I or they, so we preach."

Well did he say, " we preach," indicating his great boldness of speech. For we speak not secretly, nor[1] in a corner, but we utter a voice clearer than a trumpet. And he said not, "we preached," but, "even now 'so we preach.'" "And so ye believed." Here he said not, " ye believe," but, "ye believed." Because they were shaken in mind, therefore he ran back to the former times, and proceeds to add the witness from themselves.

[2.] Ver. 12. " Now if Christ is preached that He hath been raised from the dead, how say some among you that there is no resurrection of the dead ? "

Seest thou how excellently he reasons, and proves the resurrection from the fact of Christ's being raised, having first established the former in many ways ? " For both the prophets spake of it," saith he, "and the Lord Himself showed it by His appearing, and we preach, and ye believed ; " weaving thus his fourfold testimony ; the witness of the prophets, the witness of the issue of events, the witness of the apostles, the witness of the disciples ; or rather a fivefold. For this very cause too itself implies the resurrection ; viz. his dying for others' sins. If therefore this hath been proved, it is evident that the other also follows, viz. that the other dead likewise are raised. And this is why, as concerning an admitted fact, he challenges and questions them, saying, "Now if Christ hath been raised, how say some among you that there is no resurrection of the dead ? "

Hereby also again abating the boldness of the gainsayers : in that he said not, "how say ye," but, "how say some among you." And neither doth he bring a charge against all nor declare openly the very persons whom he accuses, in order not to make them more reckless : neither on the other hand doth he con-

ceal it wholly, that he may correct them. For this purpose accordingly, separating them from the multitude, he strips himself for the contest with them, by this both weakening and confounding them, and holding the rest in their conflicts with these firmer to the truth, nor suffering them to desert to those that were busy to destroy them : he being in fact prepared to adopt a vehement mode of speech.

Further, lest they should say, "this indeed is clear and evident unto all that Christ is raised, and none doubts it; this doth not however necessarily imply the other also, to wit, the resurrection of mankind : "—for the one was both before proclaimed and came to pass, and was testified of by his appearing ; the fact, namely, of Christ's resurrection : but the other is yet in hope, i. e., our own part :—see what he doeth ; from the other side again he makes it out : which is a proof of great power. Thus, " why do some say," saith he, "that there is no resurrection of the dead ? " Of course then the former also in its turn is subverted by this, the fact, namely, that Christ is raised. Wherefore also he adds, saying,

Ver. 13. " But if there is no resurrection of the dead, neither hath Christ been raised."

Seest thou Paul's energy, and his spirit for the combat, so invincible ? how not only from what is evident he demonstrates what is doubted, but also from what is doubted, endeavors to demonstrate to gainsayers the former evident proposition ? Not because what had already taken place required demonstration, but that he might signify this to be equally worthy of belief with that.

[3.] " And what kind of consequence is this ? " saith one. "For if Christ be not raised, that then neither should others be raised, doth follow : but that if others be not raised, neither should Christ be raised, what reason can there be in this ? " Since then this doth not appear to be very reasonable, see how he works it out wisely, scattering his seeds beforehand from the beginning, even from the very groundwork of the Gospel : as, that "having died for our sins," He was raised; and that He is " the first-fruits of them that slept." For the first-fruits—of what can He be the first-fruits, except of them that are raised ? And how can He be first-fruits, if they rise not of whom He is first-fruits ? How then are they not raised ?

Again, if they be not raised, wherefore was Christ raised ? Wherefore came He ? Wherefore did He take upon Him flesh, if he were not about to raise flesh again ? For He stood not in need of it Himself but for our sakes. But these things he afterwards set down as he goes on ; for the present he saith, " If the dead be not raised, neither hath Christ been raised," as

---

[1] ἐν παραβύστῳ. The παραβύστον was one of the inferior courts at Athens, so called because it had cognizance only of trivial and obscure matters, and because it was situate ἐν ἀφανεῖ τόπῳ τῆς πόλεως, in an obscure part of the city. Hence the phrase. Pausan. *Attic. c.* 28 ; Demosth. *contr. Timocr. p. 715* Ed. Reiske.

though that were connected with this. For had He not intended to raise Himself, He would not have wrought that other work. Seest thou by degrees the whole economy overthrown by those words of theirs and by their unbelief in the resurrection? But as yet he saith nothing of the incarnation, but of the resurrection. For not His having become incarnate, but His having died, took away death; since while He had flesh, the tyranny of death still had dominion.

Ver. 14. "And if Christ hath not been raised, then is our preaching vain, your faith also is vain."

Although what followed in due course would have been, "but if Christ be not risen, ye fight against things evident, and against so many prophets, and the truth of facts;" nevertheless he states what is much more fearful to them: "then is our preaching vain, your faith also is vain." For he wishes to shake thoroughly their mind: "we have lost all," saith he, "all is over, if He be not risen." Seest thou how great is the mystery of the œconomy? As thus: if after death He could not rise again, neither is sin loosed nor death taken away nor the curse removed. Yea, and not only have we preached in vain, but ye also have believed in vain.

[4.] And not hereby alone doth he show the impiety of these evil doctrines, but he further contends earnestly against them, saying,

Ver. 15. "Yea, and we are found false witnesses of God: because we witnessed of Him that He raised up Christ; whom He raised not up, if so be that the dead are not raised."

But if this be absurd, (for it is a charge against God and a calumny,) and He raised Him not, as ye say, not only this, but other absurdities too will follow.

And again he establishes it all, and takes it up again, saying,

Ver. 16. "For if the dead are not raised, neither hath Christ been raised."

For had He not intended to do this, He would not have come into the world. And he names not this, but the end, to wit, His resurrection; through it drawing all things.

Ver. 17. "And if Christ hath not been raised, your faith is vain."

With whatever is clear and confessed, he keeps on surrounding the resurrection of Christ, by means of the stronger point making even that which seems to be weak and doubtful, strong and clear.

"Ye are yet in your sins." For if He was not raised, neither did He die; and if He died not, neither did He take away sin: His death being the taking away of sin. "For behold," saith one, "the Lamb of God, which taketh away the sin of the world." (John i. 29.) But

how "taketh away?" By His death. Wherefore also he called him a Lamb, as one slain. But if He rose not again, neither was He slain: and if He was not slain, neither was sin taken away: and if it was not taken away, ye are in it: and if ye are in it, we have preached in vain: and if we have preached in vain, ye have believed in vain that ye were reconciled. And besides, death remains immortal, if He did not arise. For if He too was holden of death and loosed not its pains, how released He all others, being as yet Himself holden of it? Wherefore also he adds,

Ver. 18. "Then they also which are fallen asleep in Christ have perished."

"And why speak I of you," saith he, "when all those also are perished, who have done all and are no longer subject to the uncertainty of the future?" But by the expression, "in Christ," he means either "in the faith," or "they who died for His sake, who endured many perils, many miseries, who walked in the narrow way.[1]"

Where are those foul-mouthed Manichees who say that by the resurrection he here means the liberation from sin[2]? For these compact and continuous syllogisms, holding as they do also conversely, indicate nothing of what they say, but what we affirm. It is true, "rising again" is spoken of one who has fallen: and this is why he keeps on explaining, and saith not only that He was raised, but adds this also, "from the dead." And the Corinthians too doubted not of the forgiveness of sins, but of the resurrection of bodies.

But what necessity is there at all, that except mankind be not without sin, neither should Christ Himself be so? Whereas, if He were not to raise men up, it were natural to say, "wherefore came He and took our flesh and rose again?" But on our supposition not so. Yea, and whether men sin or do not sin, there is ever with God an impossibility of sinning, and what happens to us reaches not to Him, nor doth one case answer to the other by way of conversion, as in the matter of the resurrection of the body[3].

[4.] Ver. 19. "If in this life only we have hoped in Christ, we are of all men most pitiable."

What sayest thou, O Paul? How "in this

---

[1] [The author fails to give the full force of this striking phrase. It means "those whose sleep is a sleep in Christ." C.]

[2] The Manichæans say, "that Christ came in the last times, to deliver not bodies but souls." St. Aug. de Hæres. §. 46. They argued against the resurrection of the body from such texts as 1 Cor. v. 5; xv. 50; see Epiph. Hæres. 66. §. 86, 87. They as well as the old Gnostics, of course, took this line, holding as they did the inherent corruption of matter.

[3] His argument may be thus briefly stated. The Apostle had in the former verses made use of the resurrection of Christ and our resurrection as terms implying one another. If (according to the Manichees) the word resurrection means only liberation from sin, the terms no longer imply one another. For Christ by His divine nature cannot sin. It doth not therefore follow, that, if we be not raised, Christ is not risen.

life only have we hope," if our bodies be not raised, the soul abiding and being immortal? Because even if the soul abide, even if it be infinitely immortal, as indeed it is, without the flesh it shall not receive those hidden good things, as neither truly shall it be punished. For all things shall be made manifest before the judgment-seat of Christ, " that every one may receive the things done in the body, according to that he hath done, whether it be good or bad." (2 Cor. v. 10.) Therefore he saith, " if in this life only we have hope in Christ, we are of all men most pitiable." For if the body rise not again, the soul abides uncrowned without that blessedness which is in heaven. And if this be so, we shall enjoy nothing then at all: and if nothing then, in the present life is our recompense. " What then in this respect can be more wretched than we? " saith he.

But these things he said, as well to confirm them in the doctrine of the resurrection of the body, as to persuade them concerning that immortal life, in order that they might not suppose that all our concerns end with the present world. For having sufficiently established what he purposed by the former arguments, and having said, " if the dead are not raised, neither hath Christ been raised ; but if Christ were not raised, we have perished, and we are yet in our sins ; " again he also subjoins this, thoroughly demolishing their arrogance. For so when he intends to introduce any of the necessary doctrines, he first shakes thoroughly their hardness of heart by fear : which accordingly he did here, having both above scattered those seeds, and made them anxious, as those who had fallen from all : and now again after another manner, and so as they should most severely feel it, doing this same thing and saying, " ' we are of all men most pitiable,' if after so great conflicts and deaths and those innumerable evils, we are to fall from so great blessings, and our happiness is limited by the present life." For in fact all depends on the resurrection. So that even hence it is evident that his discourse was not of a resurrection from sins, but of bodies, and of the life present and to come.

[5.] Ver. 20. " But now hath Christ been raised from the dead, the first-fruits of them that are asleep."

Having signified how great mischiefs are bred from not believing the resurrection, he takes up the discourse again, and says, " But now hath Christ been raised from the dead ; " continually adding, " from the dead," so as to stop [1] the mouths of the heretics. " The first-fruits of them that slept." But if their first-fruits, then themselves also, must needs rise again.

Whereas if he were speaking of the resurrection from sins, and none is without sin ;—for even Paul saith, " I know nothing against myself, yet am I not hereby justified [2] ; "—how shall there be any who rise again, according to you? Seest thou that his discourse was of bodies? And that he might make it worthy of credit, he continually brings forward Christ who rose again in the flesh.

Next he also assigns a reason. For, as I said, when one asserts but does not state the reason, his discourse is not easily received by the multitude. What then is the reason?

Ver. 21. " For since by man came death, by man came also the resurrection of the dead."

But if by a man, doubtless by one having a body. And observe his thoughtfulness, how on another ground also he makes his argument inevitable. As thus : " he that is defeated," saith he, " must in his own person also renew the conflict, the nature which was cast down must itself also gain the victory. For so the reproach was wiped away."

But let us see what kind of death he is speaking of.

Ver. 22. " For as in Adam all die, even so in Christ shall all be made alive."

What then? tell me ; did all die in Adam the death of sin [3]? How then was Noah righteous in his generation? and how Abraham? and how Job? and how all the rest? And what, I pray? shall all be made alive in Christ? Where then are those who are led away into hell fire? Thus, if this be said of the body, the doctrine stands : but if of righteousness and sin, it doth so no longer.

Further, lest, on hearing that the making alive is common to all, thou shouldest also suppose that sinners are saved, he adds,

Ver. 23. " But every man in his own order."

For do not, because thou hearest of a resurrection, imagine that all enjoy the same benefits. Since if in the punishment all will not suffer alike but the difference is great ; much more where there are sinners and righteous men shall the separation be yet wider.

---

[1] lit. sew up, ἀπόρραψαι.

[2] οὐδὲν ἐμαυτῷ σύνοιδα. 1 Cor. iv. 4.
[3] This may seem at first sight, especially to the English reader, inconsistent with such texts as Ephes. ii. 1 ; Coloss. ii. 12, &c. But it will be found that the term νεκροὶ used in those texts, is applied rather to each person's actual sin and its effects, than to the general result of Adam's transgression ; and that ἀποθανὼν, when applied to the latter, relates to the death of the body : as in Rom. v. 15. which is so expounded by St. Aug. de Nupt. ii, 46.
[Whatever may be thought of the speaker's view of the former part of this verse, it is clear that he does not make the "all" of the second clause coextensive with the "all" of the first. He expressly excludes sinners. And he is right. Men are connected with Adam by nature, but with Christ by faith and this is the work of grace. Adam and Christ are the two heads of humanity but in a different way. The limitation of the second " all " is further confirmed by the fact that the whole discussion here is about believers. The Apostle says nothing in this chapter about the resurrection of unbelievers. C.]

" Christ the first-fruits, then they that are Christ's ; " i. e., the faithful and the approved.

Ver. 24. " Then cometh the end."

For when these shall have risen again, all things shall have an end, not as now when after Christ's resurrection things abide yet in suspense. Wherefore he added, " at His coming," that thou mayest learn that he is speaking of that time, " when He shall have delivered up the kingdom to God even the Father ; when He shall have abolished all rule and all authority and power."

[6.] Here, give heed to me carefully, and see that no part escape you of what I say. For our contest is with enemies[1] : wherefore we first must practice the *reductio ad absurdum* which also Paul often doeth. Since in this way shall we find what they say most easy of detection. Let us ask them then first, what is the meaning of the saying, " When he shall have delivered up the kingdom to God, even the Father ? " For if we take this just as it stands and not in a sense becoming Deity, He will not after this retain it. For he that hath delivered up to another, ceases any longer to retain a thing himself. And not only will there be this absurdity, but that also the other person who receives it will be found not to be possessor of it before he hath so received it. Therefore, according to them, neither was the Father a King before, governing our affairs : nor will it seem that the Son after these things will be a King. How then, first of all, concerning the Father doth the Son Himself say, " My Father worketh hitherto, and I work : " (John v. 17.) and of Him Daniel, " That His kingdom is an everlasting kingdom, which shall not pass away ? " (Dan. vii. 14.) Seest thou how many absurdities are produced, and repugnant to the Scriptures, when one takes the thing spoken after the manner of men ?

But what " rule," then doth he here say, that Christ " putteth down ? " That of the angels ? Far from it. That of the faithful ? Neither is it this. What rule then ? That of the devils, concerning which he saith, " Our wrestling is not against flesh and blood, but against the principalities, against the powers, against the world-rulers of this darkness." (Ephes. vi. 12.) For now it is not as yet " put down " perfectly, they working in many places, but then shall they cease.

Ver. 25. " For He must reign, till He hath put all enemies under His feet."

Again from hence also another absurdity is produced, unless we take this also in a way becoming Deity. For the expression "until," is one of end and limitation : but in reference to God, this does not exist.

Ver. 26. " The last enemy that shall be abolished is death."

How the last ? After all, after the devil, after all the other things. For so in the beginning also death came in last ; the counsel of the devil having come first, and our disobedience, and then death. Virtually then indeed it is even now abolished : but actually, at that time.

[7.] Ver. 27. " For He hath put all things in subjection under His feet. But when He saith, All things are put in subjection, it is manifest that He is excepted who did subject all things unto Him."

Ver. 28. " And when all things have been subjected unto Him, then shall the Son also Himself be subjected unto Him that did subject all things unto Him."

And yet before he said not that it was the Father who " put things under Him," but He Himself who " abolishes." For " when He shall have abolished," saith he, " all rule and authority : " and again, "for He must reign until He hath put all His enemies under His feet." How then doth he here say, " the Father ? "

And not only is there this apparent perplexity, but also that he is afraid with a very unaccountable fear, and uses a correction, saying, " He is excepted, who did subject all things unto Him," as though some would suspect, whether the Father might Himself not be subject unto the Son ; than which what can be more irrational ? nevertheless, he fears this.

How then is it ? for in truth there are many questions following one upon another. Well, give me then your earnest attention ; since in fact it is necessary for us first to speak of the scope of Paul and his mind, which one may find everywhere shining forth, and then to subjoin our solution : this being itself an ingredient in our solution.

What then is Paul's mind, and what is his custom ? He speaks in one way when he discourses of the Godhead alone, and in another when he falls into the argument of the economy. Thus having once taken hold of our Lord's Flesh, he freely thereafter uses all the sayings that humiliate Him ; without fear as though that were able to bear all such expressions. Let us see therefore here also, whether his discourse is of the simple Godhead, or whether in view of the incarnation he asserts of Him those things which he saith : or rather let us first point out where he did this of which I have spoken. Where then did he this ? Writ-

---

[1] The partisans of Marcellus of Ancyra, who about the middle of the fourth century taught that the Personal Kingdom of the Son, and indeed His Personality, will cease at the last day, He being such an emanation from the Father as shall be again absorbed into the Father. See S. Cyril, *Catech*. xv. 27. and others quoted by Bp. Pearson on the Creed, Art. vi. part 2. This error is supposed to have occasioned the insertion at Constantinople of the words, " Of whose kingdom there shall be no end," in the Nicene Creed. It appears that Marcellus alleged this text.

ing to the Philippians he saith, "Who, being in the form of God, counted it not a prize to be on an equality with God, but emptied Himself of no reputation, taking the form of a servant, being made in the likeness of men : and being found in fashion as a man, He humbled Himself, becoming obedient even unto death, yea, the death of the cross. Wherefore hath God highly exalted Him." (Phil. ii. 6—9.)

Seest thou how when he was discoursing of the Godhead alone, he uttered those great things, that He " was in the form of God " and that He "was equal with " Him that begat Him, and to Him refers the whole ? But when He showed Him to thee made flesh, he lowered again the discourse. For except thou distinguish these things, there is great variance between the things spoken. Since, if He were " equal with God," how did He highly exalt one equal with Himself ? If He were " in the form of God, " how " gave " He Him " a name ? " for he that giveth, giveth to one that hath not, and he that exalteth, exalteth one that is before abased. He will be found then to be imperfect and in need, before He hath received the " exaltation " and " the Name ; " and many other absurd corollaries will hence follow. But if thou shouldest add the incarnation, thou wilt not err in saying these things. These things then here also consider, and with this mind receive thou the expressions.

[8.] Now together with these we will state also other reasons why this pericope of Scripture was thus composed. But at present it is necessary to mention this : first, that Paul's discourse was of the resurrection, a thing counted to be impossible and greatly disbelieved : next, he was writing to Corinthians among whom there were many philosophers who mocked at such things always. For although in other things wrangling one with another, in this they all, as with one mouth, conspired, dogmatically declaring that there is no resurrection. Contending therefore for such a subject so disbelieved and ridiculed, both on account of the prejudice which had been formed, and on account of the difficulty of the thing ; and wishing to demonstrate its possibility, he first effects this from the resurrection of Christ. And having proved it both from the prophets, and from those who had seen, and from those who believed : when he had obtained an admitted *reductio ad absurdum*, he proves in what follows the resurrection of mankind also. " For if the dead rise not," saith he, " neither has Christ been raised."

Further ; having closely urged these converse arguments in the former verses, he tries it again in another way, calling Him the " first-fruits," and pointing to His " abolishing all rule and

authority and power, and death last." " How then should death be put down," saith he, "unless he first loose the bodies which he held ? " Since then he had spoken great things of the Only-Begotten, that He " gives up the kingdom," i.e., that He Himself brings these things to pass, and Himself is victor in the war, and "putteth all things under His feet," he adds, to correct the unbelief of the multitude, " for He must reign till He hath put all His enemies under His feet." Not as putting an end to the kingdom, did he use the expression "until," but to render what was said worthy of credit, and induce them to be confident. For " do not," saith he, " because thou hast heard that He will abolish all rule, and authority and power," to wit, the devil, and the bands of demons, (many as there are,) and the multitudes of unbelievers, and the tyranny of death, and all evils : do not thou fear as though His strength was exhausted. For until He shall have done all these things, " He must reign; " not saying this, that after He hath brought it to pass He doth not reign ; but establishing this other, that even if it be not now, undoubtedly it will be. For His kingdom is not cut off : yea, He rules and prevails and abides until He shall have set to right all things.

And this manner of speech one might find also in the Old Testament ; as when it is said, " But the word of the Lord abideth for ever ; " (Ps. cxix. 89.) and, "Thou art the same, and Thy years shall not fail." (Ps. cii. 27.) Now these and such-like things the Prophet saith, when he is telling of things which a long space of time must achieve and which must by all means come to pass ; casting out the fearfulness of the duller sort of hearers.

But that the expression, " until," spoken of God, and " unto," do not signify an end, hear what one saith : " From everlasting unto everlasting Thou art God : " (Ps. xc. 2.) and again, "I am, I am," and " Even to your old age I am He." (Isa. xlvi. 4.)

For this cause indeed doth he set death last, that from the victory over the rest this also might be easily admitted by the unbeliever. For when He destroys the devil who brought in death, much more will He put an end to His work.

[9.] Since then he referred all to Him, the " abolishing rule and authority," the perfecting of His kingdom, (I mean the salvation of the faithful, the peace of the world, the taking away of evils, for this is to perfect His kingdom,) the putting an end to death ; and he said not, " the Father by Him," but, " Himself shall put down, and Himself shall put under His feet," and he no where mentioned Him that begat Him ; he was afraid afterward, lest on this account among some of the more irrational persons, either the Son might seem to be greater than the Father, or to be a certain distinct principle, unbegotten.[1] And therefore, gently guarding himself, he qualifies the magnitude of his expressions, saying, "for He put all things in subjection under His feet," again referring to the Father these high achievements; not as though the Son were without power. For how could He be, of whom he testified so great things before, and referred to Him all that was said? But it was for the reason which I mentioned, and that he might show all things to be common to Father and Son which were done in our behalf. For that Himself alone was sufficient to "put all things in subjection under Him," hear again Paul saying, (Phil. iii. 21.) "Who shall fashion anew the body of our humiliation that it may be conformed to the body of His glory, according to the working whereby He is able even to subject all things unto Himself."

Then also he uses a correction, saying, "But when He saith, all things are put in subjection, it is evident that He is excepted who did subject all things unto Him," testifying even thence no small glory to the Only-Begotten. For if He were less and much inferior, this fear would never have been entertained by him. Neither is he content with this, but also adds another thing, as follows. I say, lest any should doubtingly ask, "And what if the Father hath not been 'put under Him?' this doth not at all hinder the Son from being the more mighty;" fearing this impious supposition, because that expression was not sufficient to point out this also, he added, going very much beyond it, "But when all things have been subjected unto Him, then shall the Son also Himself be subjected;" showing His great concord with the Father, and that He is the principle of all other good things and the first Cause, who hath begotten One so great in power and in achievements.

[10.] But if he said more than the subject-matter demanded, marvel not. For in imitation of his Master he doeth this: since He too purposing to show His concord with Him that begat Him, and that He hath not come without His mind, descends so far, I say not, as the proof of concord demanded, but as the weakness of the persons present required. For He prays to His Father for no other cause but this; and stating the reason He saith, "that they may believe that Thou hast sent Me." (John xi. 42.) In imitation therefore of Him, Paul here in his manner of speech goes beyond what was required; not that thou mightest have any suspicion of a forced servitude, far from it; but that he might the more entirely cast out those

impious doctrines. For so when he is minded to pull up any thing by the roots, he is wont to do it, and abundantly more with it[2]. Thus too, for example, when he spake of a believing wife and an unbelieving husband, companying with one another by the law of marriage, that the wife might not consider herself defiled by that intercourse and the embraces of the unbeliever, he said not, "the wife is not unclean," nor, "she is no wise harmed by the unbeliever," but, which was much more, "the unbeliever is even 'sanctified' by her," not meaning to signify that the heathen was made holy through her, but by the very great strength of the expression anxious to remove her fear. So also here, his zeal to take away that impious doctrine by a very strong utterance was the cause of his expressing himself as he did. For as to suspect the Son of weakness is extreme impiety : (wherefore he corrects it, saying, "He shall put all enemies under His feet : ") so on the other hand is it more impious to consider the Father inferior to Him. Wherefore he takes it also away with exceeding force. And observe how he puts it. For he said not simply, "He is excepted which put all things under Him," but, "it is manifest," "for even if it be admitted," saith he, "nevertheless I make it sure.[3]"

And that thou mayest learn that this is the reason of the things spoken, I would ask thee this question : Doth an additional "subjection" at that time befal the Son? And how can this be other than impious and unworthy of God? For the greatest subjection and obedience is this, that He who is God took the form of a servant. How then will He be "subjected?" Seest thou, that to take away the impious notion, he used this expression? and this too in a suitable though reserved sense? For he becomes a Son and a divine Person, so He obeys; not humanly, but as one acting freely and having all authority. Otherwise how is he co-enthroned? How, "as the Father raiseth up, even so He, whom He will?" (John v. 21.) How are "all things that the Father hath He," and all that He hath, the Father's? (John xvi. 15.) For these phrases indicate to us an authority exactly measured by[4] that of Him that begat Him.

[11.] But what is this, "When He shall deliver up the kingdom?" The Scripture acknowledges two kingdoms of God, the one by appropriation[5], the other by creation[6]. Thus, He is King over all, both Greeks and Jews and devils and His adversaries, in respect of His

---

[1] ἀρχὴ ἀγέννητος.

[2] πολλῇ κέχρηται τῇ περιουσίᾳ.
[3] ἀσφαλίζομαι.
[4] ἀπηκριβωμένην πρός.
[5] οἰκείωσιν.
[6] This distinction, in these terms, is found elsewhere in St. Chrysostom; as on 47 (48) Psalm, v. 1; on 1 Tim. vi. 11: as quoted by Suicer v. βασιλεία.

creation: but He is King of the faithful and willing and subject, in respect of His making them His own. This is the kingdom which is said also to have a beginning. For concerning this He saith also in the second Psalm, "Ask of Me, and I shall give Thee the heathen for Thine inheritance." (Ps. ii. 8.) Touching this also, He Himself said to His disciples, "All authority hath been given unto Me by My father," (Matt. xxviii. 18.) referring all to Him that begat Him, not as though of Himself He were not sufficient, but to signify that He is a Son, and not unbegotten. This kingdom then He doth " deliver up," i. e., " bring to a right end."

" What then," saith one, "can be the reason why He spake nothing of the Spirit?" Because of Him he was not discoursing now, nor doth he confound all things together. Since also where he saith, "There is one God the Father, and one Lord Jesus," undoubtedly not as allowing the Spirit to be inferior, is he therefore silent, but because for the time it was not urgent, he so expressed himself. For he is wont also to make mention of the Father only, yet we must not therefore cast out the Son: he is wont to speak also of the Son and of the Spirit only, yet not for this are we to deny[1] the Father.

But what is, "that God may be all in all?" That all things may be dependent upon Him, that none may suppose two authorities without a beginning, nor another kingdom separated off; that nothing may exist independent of him. For when the enemies shall be lying under the feet of the Son, and He having them cast under His feet be at no variance with His Father, but at concord with Him in entire perfection, then He shall Himself " be all in all."

But some say that he spake this to declare the removal of wickedness, as though all would yield thenceforth and none would resist nor do iniquity. For when there is no sin, it is evident that "God shall be all in all."

[12.] But if bodies do not rise again, how are these things true? For the worst enemy of all, death, remains, having wrought whatever he listed. "Nay," saith one, " for they shall sin no more." And what of that? For he is not discoursing here of the death of the soul, but of that of the body? How then is he " put down?" For victory is this, the winning of those things which have been carried off and detained. But if men's bodies are to be detained in the earth, it follows that the tyranny of death remains, these bodies for their part being holden, and there being no other body for him to be vanquished in. But if this which Paul spake of, ensue, as undoubtedly it will

ensue, God's victory will appear, and that a glorious one, in His being able to raise again the bodies which were holden thereby. Since an enemy too is then vanquished, when a man takes the spoils, not when he suffers them to remain in the other's possession: but unless one venture to take what is his, how can we say that he is vanquished? After this manner of victory doth Christ Himself say in the Gospels that He hath been victorious, thus speaking, "When he shall bind the strong man, then shall he also spoil his goods." (Matt. xii. 29.) Since if this were not so, it would not be at all a manifest victory. For as in the death of the soul, "he that hath died is justified from sin;" (Rom. vi. 7.) (and yet we cannot say that this is a victory, for he is not the victor who adds no more to his wickedness, but he who hath done away the former captivity of his passions;) just so in this instance also, I should not call death's being stayed from feeding on the bodies of men a splendid victory, but rather that the bodies heretofore holden by him should be snatched away from him.

But if they should still be contentious and should say that these things were spoken of the soul's death, how is this " destroyed last?" since in the case of each one at his Baptism it hath been destroyed perfectly. If however thou speakest of the body, the expression is admissible; I mean, such a saying as that it will be " last destroyed."

But if any should doubt why discoursing of the resurrection, he did not bring forward the bodies which rose again in the time of our Lord, our answer might be the following: that this could not be alleged in behalf of the resurrection. For to point out those who after rising died again, suited not one employed in proving that death is entirely destroyed. Yea, this is the very reason why he said that he is " destroyed last," that thou mightest never more suspect his rising again. For when sin is taken away, much more shall death cease: it being out of all reason when the fountain is dried up, that the stream flowing from it should still subsist; and when the root is annihilated, that the fruit should remain.

[13.] Since then in the last day the enemies of God shall be destroyed, together with death and the devil and the evil spirits, let us not be dejected at the prosperity of the enemies of God. For the enemies of the Lord in the moment of their glory and exaltation fail; "yea, like smoke have they failed away." (Ps. xxxvii. 20.) When thou seest any enemy of God wealthy, with armed attendants and many flatterers, be not cast down, but lament, weep, call upon God, that He may enrol him amongst His friends: and the more he prospers being God's enemy,

---

[1] ἀθετήσομεν.

so much the more do thou mourn for him. For sinners we ought always to bewail, but especially when they enjoy wealth and abundance of good days ; even as one should the sick, when they eat and drink to excess.

But there are some, who when they hear these words are of so unhappy a disposition, as to sigh bitterly thereupon, and say, " Tears are due to me who have nothing." Thou hast well said, "who have nothing," not because thou hast not what another hath, but because thou accountest the thing such as to be called happy ; yea, for this cause art thou worthy of infinite lamentations : even as, if a person living in health should count happy him that is sick and lying on a soft couch, this latter is not near so wretched and miserable as he, because he hath no sense of his own advantages. Just such a result one may observe in these men's case also : nay, and hereby our whole life is confounded and disordered. For these sayings have undone many, and betrayed them to the devil, and made them more pitiable than such as are wasted with famine. Yea, that those who long after more, are more wretched than mendicants, as being possessed with a greater and bitterer sorrow than they, is evident from what follows.

A drought once overtook our city, and all were trembling for the last of evils, and were beseeching God to rid them of this fear. And one might see then that which was spoken of by Moses ; (Deut. xxviii. 23.) " the heavens become brass," and a death, of all deaths the most horrible, waited for every day. But afterwards, when it seemed good to the merciful God, beyond all expectation there was wafted down from heaven a great and plentiful rain, and thenceforth all were in holiday and feasting, as having come up from the very gates of death. But in the midst of so great blessings and the common gladness of all, one of those exceedingly wealthy people went about with a gloomy and downcast countenance, quite dead with sorrow ; and when many enquired the reason, wherefore in the common joy of all men he alone is sorrowful, he could not even keep within him his savage passion, but goaded by the tyranny of the disease, declared before them all the reason. "Why," saith he, "having in my possession ten thousand measures of wheat, I have no means of disposing of them left." Shall we then count him happy, tell me, for these words, for which he deserved to be stoned? Him that was more cruel than any wild beast, the common enemy? What sayest thou, man? Art thou sad because all did not perish, that thou mightest gather gold? Hast thou not heard what Solomon saith, (Prov. xi. 26.) " He that withholdeth[1] corn, the people shall curse

him ?" but goest about a common enemy of the blessings of the world, and a foe to the liberality of the Lord of the world, and a friend of Mammon, or rather his slave? Nay, doth not that tongue deserve to be cut out, and the heart to be quenched, that brought forth these words?

[14.] Seest thou how gold doth not suffer men to be men, but wild beasts and fiends? For what can be more pitiful than this rich man, whose daily prayer is that there may be famine, in order that he may have a little gold ? Yea, and his passion by this time is come round to the contrary of itself : he not even rejoicing in his abundant store of the fruits of the earth, but on this very account grieving the rather, (to such a pass is he come,) that his possessions are infinite. Although one who hath much ought to be joyful : but this man on that very account is dejected. Seest thou that, as I said, the rich do not reap as much pleasure from what is present, as they endure sorrow for what hath not yet been added ? For he that had innumerable quantities of wheat did more grieve and lament than he who suffered hunger. And while the one, on merely having his necessary food, was crowning himself and leaping for joy and giving thanks to God ; the other, who had so much, was fretting and thought he was undone. It is not then the superfluity which causes our pleasure, but a self-controlling mind : since without this, though one obtain and have all, he will feel as one deprived of all and will mourn accordingly : inasmuch as this man too of whom we are now speaking, even if he had sold all he had for as large a sum as he wished, would again have grieved that it was not for more ; and if he could have had more, he would again have sought another advance ; and if he had disposed of the bushel for one pound, he would even then have been distracted for sorrow, that the half bushel could not be sold for as much. And if the price were not set so high at first, marvel not. Since drunkards also are not at first inflamed, but when they have loaded themselves with much wine, then they kindle the flame into greater fierceness : so these men, by how much more they have grasped, in so much the greater poverty do they find themselves, and they who gain more than others, are the very persons to be the most in want.

[15.] But I say these things not only to this man, but also to each one of those who are so diseased : those, I say, who raise the price of their wares and make a traffic of the poverty of their neighbors. For of humanity none any where makes account : but every where the covetous desire brings out many at the time of sale. And oil and wine is sold by one quicker, by another more slowly, but neither out of regard

---

[1] τιμιουλκῶν, Theodotion. συνέχων LXX.

16

to others; rather the one seeks gain, the other to avoid loss by the spoiling of his produce. Thus, because most men not making much account of the laws of God, shut up and keep all in doors, God by other means leading them to humanity,—that were it but of necessity they may do something kind,—hath infused into them the fear of greater loss, not allowing the fruits of the earth to keep any long time, in order that out of mere dread of the damage from their spoiling, they may expose for sale to the needy, even against their will, such things as they wickedly bury at home ·and keep. However, after all this, some are so insatiable as not even thereby to be corrected. Many, for example, have gone so far as to empty whole casks, not giving even a cup-full to the poor man, nor a piece of money to the needy, but after it hath become vinegar, they dash it all upon the ground, and destroy their casks together with the fruit. Others again who would not give a part of a single cake to the hungry, have thrown whole granaries into some river: and because they listened not to God who bade them give to the needy, at the bidding of the moth, even unwillingly, they emptied out all they had in their houses, in utter destruction and waste; drawing down upon their own heads together with this loss much scorn and many a curse.

And such is the course of their affairs here; but the hereafter, what words shall set before us? For as these men in this world cast their moth-eaten grain, become useless, into rivers; even so the doers of such things, on this very account become useless, God casts into the river of fire. Because as the grain by the moth and worm, so are their souls devoured by cruelty and inhumanity. And the reason of these things is their being nailed to things present, and gaping after this life only. Whence also such men are full of infinite sadness; for name whatever pleasure thou wilt, the fear of their end is enough to annihilate all, and such an one "is dead, while he is yet alive." (1 Tim. v. 6.)

Now then that unbelievers should have these feelings, is no marvel; but when they who have partaken of so great mysteries and learned such high rules of self-denial concerning things to come, delight to dwell in things present, what indulgence do they deserve?

[16.] Whence then arises their loving to dwell in present things? From giving their mind to luxury, and fattening their flesh, and making their soul delicate, and rendering their burden heavy, and their darkness great, and their veil thick. For in luxury the better part is enslaved, but the worse prevails; and the former is blinded on every side and dragged on in its maimed condition; while the other draws and leads men about every where, though it

ought to be in the rank of things that are led.

Since great indeed is the bond between the soul and the body; the Maker having contrived this, lest any should induce us to abhor it as alien. For God indeed bade us love our enemies; but the devil hath so far prevailed as to induce some [1] even to hate their own body. Since when a man saith that it is of the devil, he proves nothing else than this; which is the extreme of dotage. For if it be of the devil, what is this so perfect harmony, such as to render it meet in every way for the energies of the self-controlling soul? "Nay," saith one, "if it be meet, how doth the body blind it?" It is not the body which blinds the soul; far from it, O man; but the luxury. But whence do we desire the luxury? Not from our having a body, by no means; but from an evil choice. For the body requires feeding, not high feeding [2], the body needs nourishing, not breaking up and falling apart. You see that not to the soul only, but to the very body also which receives the nourishment, the luxury is hostile. For it becomes weaker instead of strong, and softer instead of firm, and sickly instead of healthful, and heavier instead of light, and slighter instead of compact, and illfavored instead of handsome, and unsavory instead of fragrant, and impure instead of clean, and full of pain instead of being at ease, and useless instead of useful, and old instead of young, and decaying instead of strong, and slow and dull instead of quick, and maimed instead of whole. Whereas if it were of the devil, it ought not to receive injury from the things of the devil, I mean, from sin.

[17.] But neither is the body, nor food, of the devil, but luxury alone. For by means of it that malignant fiend brings to pass his innumerable evils. Thus did he make victims of [3] a whole people. "For the beloved waxed fat," saith one, "and grew thick, and was enlarged, and kicked." (Deut. xxxii. 15.) And thence also was the beginning of those thunderbolts on Sodom. And to declare this, Ezekiel said, "But this was the iniquity of Sodom, in pride and fulness of bread and refinements [4] they waxed wanton." (Ezek. xvi. 4.) Therefore also Paul said, (1 Tim. v. 6.) "She that giveth herself to pleasure [5], is dead while she liveth." How should this be? Because as a sepulchre she bears about her body, bound close to innumerable evils [6]. And if the body so perish, how will the soul be affected; what disorder, what

---

[1] The Manichæans, and Gnostic sects.
[2] τροφῆς οὐ τρυφῆς.
[3] ἐξετραχήλισε.
[4] εὐθηνίαις LXX.
[5] σπαταλῶσα
[6] It is thy own soul, wretched woman, that thou hast lost: the spiritual life gone, thou for a while leadest on a life of thine own, and movest about, wearing thy death upon thee." S. Cypr. *of the Lapsed*, C. 30.

waves, what a tempest will she be filled with? Hereby, you see, she becomes unfitted for every duty, and will have no power easily to speak, or hear, or take counsel, or do anything that is needful. But as a pilot when the storm hath got the better of his skill, is plunged into the deep, vessels and sailors and all: so also the soul together with the body is drowned in the grievous abyss of insensibility.

For, in fact, God hath set the stomach in our bodies as a kind of mill, giving it a proportionate power, and appointing a set measure which it ought to grind every day. If therefore one cast in more, remaining undigested it doth injury to the whole body. Hence diseases and weaknesses and deformities: since in truth luxury makes the beautiful woman not only sickly, but also foul to look upon. For when she is continually sending forth unpleasant exhalations, and breathes fumes of stale wine, and is more florid than she ought to be, and spoils the symmetry that beseems a woman, and loses all her seemliness, and her body becomes flabby, her eyelids bloodshot and distended, and her bulk unduly great, and her flesh an useless load; consider what a disgust it all produces.

Moreover, I have heard a physician say that many have been hindered from reaching their proper height by nothing so much as luxurious living. For the breath being obstructed by the multitude of things which are cast in and being occupied in the digestion of such things, that which ought to serve for growth is spent on this digestion of superfluities. Why need one speak of gout, rheum dispersed every where, the other diseases hence arising, the whole abomination? For nothing is so disgusting as a woman pampering herself with much food. Therefore among the poorer women one may see more of beauty: the superfluities being consumed and not cleaving to them, like some superfluous clay, of no use and benefit. For their daily exercise, and labors, and hardships, and their frugal table, and spare diet, minister unto them much soundness of body, and thence also much bloom.

[18.] But if thou talkest of the pleasure of luxury, thou wilt find it to go no farther than the throat: since as soon as it hath passed the tongue, it is flown away, leaving behind in the body much that is disgusting. For do not I pray look on the voluptuaries at table only, but when you see them rise up, then follow them, and you will see bodies rather of wild beasts and irrational creatures than of human beings. You will see them with headache, distended, bound up, needing a bed and a couch and plenty of rest, and like men who are tossed in a great tempest and require others to save them, and long for that condition in which they were before they were swelled even to bursting[1]: they carrying their bellies about with a burden like that of women with child, and can scarce step forward, and scarce see, and scarce speak, and scarce do any thing. But if it should chance that they sleep a little, they see again strange dreams and full of all manner of fancies.

What should one say of that other madness of theirs? the madness of lust, I mean, for this also hath its fountains from hence. Yea, as horses wild after the female, so they, goaded on by the sting of their drunkenness, leap upon all, more irrational than they, and more frantic in their boundings; and committing many more unseemlinesses which but to name is unlawful. For they know not in fact any longer what they suffer, nor what they do.

But not so he that keeps from luxury: rather he sits in harbor, beholding other men's shipwrecks, and enjoys a pleasure pure and lasting, following after that life which becomes him that is free. Knowing therefore these things, let us flee from the evil banquets of luxury and cleave to a spare table; that being of a good habit both of soul and body, we may both practice all virtue, and attain the good things to come, through the grace and mercy of our Lord Jesus Christ, with Whom to the Father, with the Holy Ghost, be glory, power, and honor, now and ever, and world without end. Amen.

---

[1] πρὶν ἢ διαρραγῆναι.

HOMILY XL.

1 COR. xv. 29.

Else what shall they do which are baptized for the dead? if the dead are not raised at all, why then are they baptized for the dead?

HE takes in hand again another topic, establishing what he said at one time from what God doeth[1], and at another from the very things which they practice[2]. And this also is no small plea for the defence of any cause when a man brings forward the gainsayers themselves as witnessing by their own actions what he affirms. What then is that which he means? Or will ye that I should first mention how they who are infected with the Marcionite heresy pervert this expression? And I know indeed that I shall excite much laughter; nevertheless, even on this account most of all I will mention it that you may the more completely avoid this disease: viz., when any Catechumen departs among them, having concealed the living man under the couch of the dead, they approach the corpse and talk with him, and ask him if he wishes to receive baptism; then when he makes no answer, he that is concealed underneath saith in his stead that of course he should wish to be baptized; and so they baptize him instead of the departed, like men jesting upon the stage[3]. So great power hath the devil over the souls of careless sinners. Then being called to account, they allege this expression, saying that even the Apostle hath said, "They who are baptized for the dead." Seest thou their extreme ridiculousness? Is it meet then to answer these things? I trow not; unless it were

necessary to discourse with madmen of what they in their frenzy utter. But that none of the more exceedingly simple folk may be led captive, one must needs submit to answer even these men. As thus, if this was Paul's meaning wherefore did God threaten him that is not baptized? For it is impossible that any should not be baptized henceforth, this being once devised: and besides, the fault no longer lies with the dead, but with the living. But to whom spake he, "Unless ye eat My flesh, and drink My blood, ye have no life in yourselves?" (John vi. 53.) To the living, or to the dead, tell me? And again, "Unless a man be born again of water and of the Spirit, he cannot see the kingdom of God." (John iii. 5.) For if this be permitted, and there be no need of the mind of the receiver nor of his assent while he lives, what hinders both Greeks and Jews thus to become believers, other men after their decease doing these things in their stead?

But not to prolong fruitless toil in cutting asunder their petty spiders' webs[4], come let us unfold unto you the force of this expression. What then is Paul speaking of?

[2.] But first I wish to remind you who are initiated of the response,[5] which on[6] that evening they who introduce you to the mysteries bid you make; and then I will also explain the saying of Paul: so this likewise will be clearer to you; we after all the other things adding this which Paul now saith. And I desire indeed expressly to utter it, but I dare not on account of the uninitiated; for these add a difficulty to our exposition, compelling us either not to speak clearly or to declare unto them the ineffable mysteries. Nevertheless, as I may be able, I will speak as through a veil[7].

As thus: after the enunciation of those mystical and fearful words, and the awful rules of the doctrines which have come down from heaven, this also we add at the end when we are about to baptize, bidding them say, "I believe in the resurrection of the dead," and upon

---

[1] ποιεῖ.

[2] πράττουσι.

[3] Epiphanius relates the same thing of the followers of Cerinthus, another section of the Gnostics, and says it was continued in his time by a kind of tradition in Asia Minor and in Galatia. Hær. xxviii. § 6.

[The author justly derides this custom and the endeavor to explain the passage as a reference to it. Yet not a few of the soundest expositors hold that the Apostle was referring to the practice of vicarious baptism, not that he approved of it but as an argument ex concessu. See the vindication of it in Hodge (in lo). To the same effect DeWette, Meyer, Stanley, Alford, Heinrici, Beet, and Principal Edwards. On the other hand Canon Evans (in Bible Commentary) contends strenuously for the interpretation of the Greek Fathers, Theophylact, Theodoret, etc., and heartily approves of Chrysostom's scornful repudiation of the monstrous superstition. He insists that vicarious baptism in its legitimate issues must lead to something like salvation by proxy. Then he asks, "Now if such a superstition, even in the germ, had appeared in Corinth before the date of this epistle, would not Paul have come down upon it with all his thunder? Would he not have devoted a whole chapter to its extinction?" To me there seems but one answer to these questions. If so, then the Apostle could not referred to the practice, even in the way of an argumentum ad hominem. C.]

[4] ἀραχνίδια διακόπτοντες.

[5] ῥήσεως.

[6] Probably Easter Eve. Vid. Bingham's Antiquities, ii. 6. s. 7. S. Cyril, Lect. 19, 1

[7] συνεσκιασμένως.

this faith we are baptized. For after we have confessed this together with the rest, then at last are we let down into the fountain of those sacred streams. This therefore Paul recalling to their minds said, "if there be no resurrection, why art thou then baptized for the dead[1]?" i. e., the dead bodies. For in fact with a view to this art thou baptized, the resurrection of thy dead[2] body, believing that it no longer remains dead. And thou indeed in the words makest mention of a resurrection of the dead; but the priest, as in a kind of image, signifies to thee by very deed the things which thou hast believed and confessed in words. When without a sign thou believest, then he gives thee the sign also; when thou hast done thine own part, then also doth God fully assure thee. How and in what manner? By the water. For the being baptized and immersed and then emerging, is a symbol of the descent into Hades and return thence. Wherefore also Paul calls baptism a burial, saying, "Therefore we are buried with Him by baptism into death." (Rom. vi. 4.) By this he makes that also which is to come credible, I mean, the resurrection of our bodies. For the blotting out sins is a much greater thing than the raising up of a body. And this Christ declaring, said, "For whether is easier to say, Thy sins are forgiven, or to say, Take up thy bed, and walk?" (Matt. ix. 5.) "The former is the more difficult," saith He, "but since ye disbelieve it as being hidden, and make the easier instead of the more difficult the demonstration of my power, neither will I refuse to afford you this proof." Then saith He to the paralytic, "Arise, take up thy bed, and go unto thy house."

"And how is this difficult," saith one, "when it is possible to kings also and rulers? For they too forgive adulterers and homicides." Thou art jesting, O man, who sayest these things. For to forgive sins with God only is possible. But rulers and kings, whether it is adulterers whom they forgive or homicides, release them indeed from the present punishment; but their sin they do not purge out. Though they should advance to offices them that have been forgiven, though they should invest them with the purple itself, though they should set the diadem upon their heads, yet so they would only make them kings, but could not free them from their sin. It being God alone who doeth this; which accordingly in the Laver of Regeneration He will bring to pass. For His grace touches the very soul, and thence plucks up the sin by the root. Here is the reason why he that hath been forgiven by the king may be seen with his soul yet impure, but the soul of the baptized no longer so, but

purer than the very sun-beams, and such as it was originally formed, nay rather much better than that. For it is blessed with a Spirit, on every side enkindling it and making its holiness intense. And as when thou art recasting iron or gold thou makest it pure and new once more, just so the Holy Ghost also, recasting the soul in baptism as in a furnace and consuming its sins, causes it to glisten with more purity than all purest gold.

Further, the credibility of the resurrection of our bodies he signifies to thee again from what follows: viz., that since sin brought in death, now that the root is dried up, one must not after that doubt of the destruction of the fruit. Therefore having first mentioned "the forgiveness of sins," thou dost next confess also "the resurrection of the dead;" the one guides thee as by hand on to the other.

Yet again, because the term Resurrection is not sufficient to indicate the whole: for many after rising have again departed, as those in the Old Testament, as Lazarus, as they at the time of the crucifixion: one is bid to say, "and the life everlasting," that none may any longer have a notion of death after that resurrection.

These words therefore Paul recalling to their minds, saith, "What shall they do which are baptized for the dead?" "For if there be no resurrection," saith he, "these words are but scenery. If there be no resurrection, how persuade we them to believe things which we do not bestow?" Just as if a person bidding another to deliver a document to the effect that he had received so much, should never give the sum named therein, yet after the subscription should demand of him the specified monies. What then will remain for the subscriber to do, now that he hath made himself responsible, without having received what he admitted he had received? This then he here saith of those who are baptized also. "What shall they do which are baptized," saith he, "having subscribed to the resurrection of dead bodies, and not receiving it, but suffering fraud? And what need was there at all of this confession, if the fact did not follow?" *

[3.] Ver. 30. "Why do we also stand in jeopardy every hour?"

Ver. 31. "I protest by that glorying in you which I have in Christ Jesus our Lord, I die daily."

See again whence he endeavors to establish the doctrine, from his own suffrage: or rather not from his only, but from that also of the other apostles. And this too is no small thing; that the teachers whom you produce were full

---

[1] See before, Hom. 23. §. 3.
[2] i. e., the very act of immersion and emersion affirms the spiritual death and resurrection of thine own body. cf. Rom. vi. 3—5. as quoted below, and the parallel places.

* [Chrysostom's explanation of this famous *crux*, though followed by Erasmus, Cor. a Lap. and Wordsworth, has not met general acceptance. But I have never seen any that is better. C.]

of vehement conviction and signified the same not by words only, but also by very deeds. Therefore, you see, he doth not say simply, "we are persuaded," for this alone was not sufficient to persuade them, but he also furnishes the proof by facts; as if he should say, "in words to confess these things haply seems to you no marvel; but if we should also produce unto you the voice which deeds send forth, what can ye have to say against that? Hear ye then, how by our perils also day by day we confess these things?" And he said not "I," but "we," taking along with him all the apostles together, and thereby at once speaking modestly and adding credibility to his discourse.

For what can ye have to say? that we are deceiving you when we preach these things, and that our doctrines come of vain-glory? Nay, our perils suffer you not to pass such a sentence. For who would choose to be in continual jeopardy to no purpose and with no effect? Wherefore also he said, "Why do we also stand in jeopardy every hour?" For if one should even choose it through vain-glory, such his choice will be but for once and again, not all his life long, like ours. For we have assigned our whole life to this purpose.

"I protest by that glorying in you which I have in Christ Jesus our Lord, I die daily:" by glorying here, meaning their advancement. Thus since he had intimated that his perils were many, lest he might seem to say this by way of lamentation, "far from grieving," saith he, "I even glory in suffering this for your sake." And doubly, he saith, he takes delight in it, both as being in jeopardy for their sakes and as beholding their proficiency. Then doing what is usual with him, because he had uttered great things, he refers both to Christ.

But how doth he "die daily?" by his readiness and preparation for that event. And wherefore saith he these words? Again by these also to establish the doctrine of the resurrection. "For who would choose," saith he, "to undergo so many deaths, if there be no resurrection nor life after this? Yea, if they who believe in the resurrection would scarcely put themselves in jeopardy for it except they were very noble of heart: much more would not the unbeliever (so he speaks) choose to undergo so many deaths and so terrible." Thus, see by degrees how very high he mounts up. He had said, "we stand in jeopardy," he added, "every hour," then, "daily," then, "I not only 'stand in jeopardy,'" saith he, but "I even 'die:'" he concludes accordingly by pointing out also what kind of deaths they were; thus saying,

Ver. 32. "If after the manner of men I fought with beasts at Ephesus, what doth it profit me?"

What is, "if after the manner of men?" "As far as pertains to men I fought with beasts: for what if God snatched me out of those dangers?[1] So that I am he who ought most to be in care about these things; I, who endure so great dangers and have not yet received any return. For if no time of recompense is at hand, but our reward is shut up in this present world, ours is the greater loss. For ye have believed without jeopardy, but we are slaughtered every day."

But all these things he said, not because he had no advantage even in the very suffering, but on account of the weakness of the many, and to establish them in the doctrine of the resurrection: not because he himself was running for hire; for it was a sufficient recompense to him to do that which was pleasing to God. So that when he adds, "If in this life only we have hoped in Christ, we are of all men most pitiable," it is there again for their sakes, that he might by the fear of this misery overthrow their unbelief of the resurrection. And in condescension to their weakness, he thus speaks. Since in truth, the great reward is to please Christ at all times: and apart from the recompense, it is a very great requital to be in jeopardy for His sake.

[4.] "If the dead are not raised, let us eat and drink for to-morrow we die."

This word, be sure, is spoken in mockery: wherefore neither did he bring it forward of himself, but summoned the prophet of loftiest sound, Isaiah, who discoursing of certain insensible and reprobate persons made use of these words, "Who slay oxen and kill sheep to eat flesh and drink wine; who say, Let us eat and drink, for to-morrow we die. These things are revealed to the ears of the Lord of Hosts,[2] and this iniquity shall not be forgiven you, till ye die." (Is. xxii. 13, 14. LXX.) Now if then they were deprived of pardon who spake thus, much more in the time of Grace.

Then that he might not make his discourse too rough, he dwells not long upon his "*reduc-*

---

[1] [It would seem (although not certainly) from the author's mode of expression as if he supposed that the reference was to an actual conflict in the arena, but the prevailing view is that the phrase is metaphorical, partly because as a Roman citizen the Apostle could not be legally subjected to that punishment, partly because so remarkable a deliverance could hardly fail to be recorded in the book of Acts, and partly because no reference is made to anything of this kind in the long enumeration of his trials in the eleventh chapter of Second Corinthians. The term was often used by the ancients figuratively for contests with enraged men. Its employment by the Apostle gives us a lively picture of the perils to which he was exposed. Ignatius (not Polycarp, as Beet says) in his Epistle to the Romans borrows this phrase, saying "From Syria even unto Rome I am fighting with beasts, both by land and sea, night and day, being bound to ten leopards, i. e., a band of soldiers." C.]

[2] [This is an exact translation of the Greek which Chrysostom quotes accurately. It is a fair specimen of the way in which the translators of the Septuagint not infrequently turn the sense of Holy Writ into nonsense. The Hebrew of the verse as given in the Authorized Version correctly, is, "And it was revealed in mine ears by the Lord of Hosts." And yet it is contended by not a few that the Hebrew text should be amended by the aid of the ancient versions! C.]

tio ad absurdum," but again turns his discourse to exhortation, saying,

Ver. 33. "Be not deceived: evil company doth corrupt good manners."

And this he said, both to rebuke them as without understanding, (for here he by a charitable expression, calls "good" that which is easily deceived,) and also, as far as he could, to make some allowance to them for the past with a view to their return, and to remove from them and transfer to others the greater part of his charges, and so by this way also to allure them to repentance. Which he doth likewise in the Epistle to the Galatians, saying, "But he that troubleth you shall bear his judgment, whosoever he be." (Gal. v. 10.)

Ver. 34. "Awake up righteously[1] and sin not."

As if he were speaking to drunkards and madmen. For suddenly to cast every thing out of their hands, was the part of drunkards and madmen, in not seeing any longer what they saw nor believing what they had before confessed. But what is, "righteously?" with a view to what is profitable and useful. For it is possible to awake up unrighteously, when a man is thoroughly roused up to the injury of his own soul. And well did he add, "sin not," implying that hence were the sins of their unbelief. And in many places he covertly signifies this, that a corrupt life is the parent of evil doctrines; as when he saith, "The love of money is a root of all kinds of evil, which some reaching after, have been led astray from the faith." (1 Tim. vi. 10.) Yea, and many of those who are conscious of wickedness and would fain not pay its penalty are by this fear damaged also in their faith concerning the resurrection: even as they who do very virtuously desire even daily to behold it.

"For some have no knowledge of God; I speak this to move you to shame."

See how again he transfers his accusations to others. For he said not, "Ye have no knowledge," but, "some have no knowledge." Because disbelieving the resurrection is the temper of one not fully aware that the power of God is irresistable and sufficient for all things. For if out of the things which are not He made the things that are, much more will He be able to raise again those which have been dissolved.

And because he had touched them to the quick and exceedingly mocked them, accusing them of gluttony, of folly, of madness; mitigating those expressions, he saith, "I speak to move you to shame," that is, to set upright, to bring back, to make you better, by this shame of yours. For he feared lest if he cut too deep, he should cause them to start away.

[1] δικαίως.

[5.] But let us not consider these things as spoken to them only, but as addressed now also to all who labor under the same disease, and live a corrupt life. Since in truth not they who hold corrupt doctrines only, but they too who are holden of grievous sins, are both drunken and frantic. Wherefore also to them may it be justly said, "Awake," and especially to those who are weighed down by the lethargy of avarice; who rob wickedly. For there is a robbery which is good, the robbery of Heaven, which injures not. And although in respect of money it is impossible for one to become rich, unless another first become poor: yet in spiritual things this is not so, but wholly the reverse: it is impossible that any should become rich without making another's store plentiful. For if thou help no one, thou wilt not be able to grow wealthy. Thus, whereas in temporal things imparting causes diminution: in spiritual things, on the contrary, imparting works increase, and the not imparting, this produces great poverty and brings on extreme punishment. And this is signified by him who buried the talent. Yea, and he too who hath a word of wisdom, by imparting to another increases his own abundance, by making many wise: but he that buries it at home, deprives himself of his abundance by neglecting to win the profit of the many. Again, he that had other gifts, by healing many augmented his own gift: and was neither himself emptied by the imparting, and filled many others with his own spiritual gift. And in all spiritual things this rule abides unshaken. Thus also in the Kingdom, he that makes many partakers with himself of the Kingdom will hereby the more completely have the fruits of it in return: but he that studies not to have any partaker will himself be cast out of those many blessings. For if the wisdom of this world of sense is not spent, though ten thousand are forcibly seizing it; nor doth the artificer by making many artificers lose his own skill; much less doth he who seizes the Kingdom make it less, but then will our riches be increased when we call many to us for that purpose.

Let us seize then the things which cannot be spent but increase whilst we seize them: let us seize the things which admit of none to defraud us of them by false accusation, none to envy us for them. For so, if there were a place which had a fountain of gold gushing forth with continual flood, and flowing the more as more was drawn from it; and there were another place which had a treasure buried in the earth; from which wouldest thou desire to be enriched? Would it not be from the first? Plainly. But that this may not be a mere conception in words, consider the saying in reference to the air and the sun. For these are seized by all, and satisfy all. These, however, whether men enjoy or do not enjoy them, abide the same undiminished: but what I spake of is a much greater thing; for spiritual wisdom abides not the same distributed or not distributed: but it rather increases in the distribution.

But if any endure not what I have said, but still cleave to the poverty of worldly things, snatching at the things which endure diminution: even in respect of those again, let him call to mind the food of manna (Exod. xvi. 20.) and tremble at the example of that punishment. For what happened in that instance, this same result may one now also see in the case of covetous men. But what then happened? worms were bred from their covetousness. This also now happens in their case. For the measure of the food is the same for all; we having but one stomach to fill; only thou who feedest luxuriously hast more to get rid of. And as in that case they who in their houses gathered more than the lawful quantity, gathered not manna, but more worms and rottenness; just so both in luxury and in covetousness, the gluttonous and drunken gather not more dainties but more corruption.

[6.] Nevertheless, so much worse than they are the men of our time, in that they experienced this once for all and received correction; but these every day bringing into their own houses this worm much more grievous than that, neither perceive it nor are satiated. For that these things do resemble those in respect of our useless labor on them: (for in regard of punishment these are much worse:) here is the proof for thee to consider.

Wherein, I ask, differs the rich man from the poor? Hath he not one body to clothe? one belly to feed? In what then hath he the advantage? In cares, in spending himself, in disobeying God, in corrupting the flesh, in wasting the soul. Yea, these are the things in which he hath the advantage of the poor: since if he had many stomachs to fill, perhaps he might have somewhat to say, as that his need was more and the necessity of expense greater. But even "now they may," saith one, "reply, that they fill many bellies, those of their domestics, those of their hand-maidens." But this is done, not through need nor for humanity's sake, but from mere pride: whence one cannot put up with their excuse.

For why hast thou many servants? Since as in our apparel we ought to follow our need only, and in our table, so also in our servants. What need is there then? None at all. For, in fact, one master need only employ one servant; or rather two or three masters one servant. But if this be grievous, consider them that have none

and enjoy more prompt attendance. For God hath made men sufficient to minister unto themselves, or rather unto their neighbor also. And if thou believe it not, hear Paul saying, "These hands ministered unto my necessities, and to them that were with me." (Acts xx. 34.) After that he, the teacher of the world and worthy of heaven, disdained not to serve innumerable others; dost thou think it a disgrace, unless thou carriest about whole herds of slaves, not knowing that this in truth is what most of all brings shame upon thee? For to that end did God grant us both hands and feet, that we might not stand in need of servants. Since not at all for need's sake was the class of slaves introduced, else even along with Adam had a slave been formed; but it is the penalty of sin and the punishment of disobedience. But when Christ came, He put an end also to this. "For in Christ Jesus there is neither bond nor free." (Gal. iii. 28.) So that it is not necessary to have a slave: or if it be at all necessary, let it be about one only, or at the most two. What mean the swarms of servants? For as the sellers of sheep and the slave-dealers, so do our rich men take their round, in the baths and in the forum.

However, I will not be too exact. We will allow you to keep a second servant. But if thou collect many, thou dost it not for humanity's sake, but in self-indulgence. Since if it be in care for them, I bid thee occupy none of them in ministering to thyself, but when thou hast purchased them and hast taught them trades whereby to support themselves, let them go free. But when thou scourgest, when thou puttest them in chains, it is no more a work of humanity.

And I know that I am giving disgust to my hearers. But what must I do? For this I am set, and I shall not cease to say these things, whether any thing come of them or not. For what means thy clearing the way before thee in the market place? Art thou walking then among wild beasts that thou drivest away them that meet thee? Be not afraid; none of these bite who approach thee and walk near thee. But dost thou consider it an insult to walk along side of other men? What madness is this, what prodigious folly, when a horse is following close after thee, to think not of his bringing on thee any insult; but if it be a man, unless he be driven an hundred miles off, to reckon that he disgraces thee. And why hast thou also servants to carry fasces, employing freemen as slaves, or rather thyself living more dishonorably than any slave? For, in truth, meaner than any servant is he who bears about with him so much pride.

Therefore they shall not so much as have a

sight of the real liberty, who have enslaved themselves to this grievous passion. Nay, if thou must drive and clear away, let it not be them that come nigh thee, but thine own pride which thou drivest away; not by thy servant, but by thyself: not with this scourge, but with that which is spiritual. Since now thy servant drives away them that walk by thy side, but thou art thyself driven from thine high place more disgracefully by thine own self-will than any servant can drive thy neighbor. But if, descending from thy horse, thou wilt drive away pride by humility, thou shalt sit higher and place thyself in greater honor, needing no servant to do this. I mean, that when thou art become modest and walkest on the ground, thou wilt be seated on the car of humility which bears thee up to the very heavens, that car which hath winged steeds[1]: but if falling from it, thou pass into that of arrogance, thou wilt be in no better state than the beggars who are drawn along the ground, nay even much more wretched and pitiable than they: since them the imperfection of their bodies compels thus to be drawn, but thee the disease of thine own arrogance. "For every one that exalteth himself," saith He, "shall be abased." (Matt. xxiii. 12.) That we then may not be abased but exalted, let us approach towards that exaltation. For thus also shall we "find rest for our souls" according to the divine oracle, and shall obtain the true and most exalted honor; the which may we all obtain, through the grace and mercy, &c. &c.

HOMILY XLI.

1 Cor. xv. 35, 36.

But some one will say, How are the dead raised? and with what manner of body do they come? Thou foolish one, that which thou thyself sowest is not quickened, except it die.

GENTLE and lowly as the apostle is to a great degree every where, he here adopts a style rather pungent, because of the impiety of the gainsayers. He is not however content with this, but he also employs reasons and examples, subduing thereby even the very contentious. And above he saith, "Since by man came death, by man came also the resurrection of the dead;" but here he solves an objection brought in by the Gentiles. And see how again he abates the vehemence of his censure; in that he said not, "but perhaps ye will say," but he set down the objector indefinitely, in order that, although employing his impetuous style with all freedom, he might not too severely wound his hearers. And he states two difficulties, one touching the manner of the resurrection, the other, the kind of bodies. For of both they on their part made a question, saying, "How is that which hath been dissolved raised up?" and, "with what manner of body do they come?" But what means, "with what manner of body?" It is as if they had said, "with this which hath been wasted, which hath perished, or with some other?"

Then, to point out that the objects of their enquiry are not questionable but admitted points, he at once meets them more sharply, saying, "Thou foolish one, that which thou thyself sowest is not quickened, except it die." Which we also are wont to do in the case of those who gainsay things acknowledged.

[2.] And wherefore did he not at once appeal to the power of God? Because he is discoursing with unbelievers. For when his discourse is addressed to believers, he hath not much need of reasons. Wherefore having said elsewhere, "He shall change the body of your humiliation, that it may be fashioned like to the body of his glory," (Phil. iii. 21.) and having indicated somewhat more than the resurrection, he stated no analogies, but instead of any demonstration, brought forward the power of God, going on to say, "according to the working whereby He is able to subject all things to Himself." But here he also urges reasons. That is, having established it from the Scriptures, he adds also in what comes after, these things over and above, with an eye to them who do not obey the Scriptures; and he saith, "O foolish one, that which THOU sowest:" i. e., "from thyself thou hast the proof of these things, by what thou doest every day, and doubtest thou yet? Therefore do I call thee foolish because of the things daily done by thine own self thou art ignorant, and being thyself an artificer of a resurrection, thou doubtest concerning God." Wherefore very emphatically he said, "what THOU sowest[2]," thou who art mortal and perishing. [3]

---

[1] Alluding perhaps to the story of Bellerophon.
[2] σὺ ὃ σπείρεις.
[3] "Our apostle's inference is as firm and strong, as it is emphatical; *Stulte! Tu quod seminas &c. O fool! That which*

And see how he uses expressions appropriate to the purpose he had in view : thus, "it is not quickened," saith he, "except it die." Leaving, you see, the terms appropriate to seed, as that "it buds," and "grows," and "is dissolved," he adopts those which correspond to our flesh, viz. "it is quickened," and, "except it die ;" which do not properly belong to seeds, but to bodies.

And he said not, "after it is dead it lives," but, which is a greater thing, "therefore it lives, because it dies." Seest thou, what I am always observing, that he continually gives their argument the contrary turn ? Thus what they made a sure sign of our not rising again, the same he makes a demonstration of our rising. For they said, " the body rises not again, because it is dead." What then doth he, retorting their argument, say ? "Nay, but unless it died, it could not rise again : and therefore it rises again, because it died." For as Christ more clearly signifies this very thing, in the words, "Except a grain of wheat fall into the ground and die, it abideth by itself alone : but if it die, it beareth much fruit : " (John xii. 24.) thence also Paul, drawing this example, said not, " it doth not live," but, " it is not quickened ; " again assuming the power of God and showing that not the nature of the ground, but God Himself, brings it all to pass.

And what can be the reason that he did not bring that forward, which was more akin to the subject : I mean, the seed of mankind ? (For our generation too begins from a sort of decay, even as that of the corn.) Because it was not of equal force, but the latter was a more complete instance : for he wants a case of something that perished entirely, whereas this was but a part ; wherefore he rather alleges the other. Besides, that proceeds from a living body and falls into a living womb ; but here it is no flesh, but the earth into which the seed is cast, and into the same it is dissolved, like the body which is dead. Wherefore on this account too the example was more appropriate.

[3.] Ver. 37. "And he who soweth, soweth not that body that shall be[1]."

For the things before spoken meet the question, "how they are raised ;" but this, the doubt, "with what manner of body they come." But what is, "thou sowest not that body which shall be ?" Not an entire ear of corn, nor new grain. For here his discourse no longer

regards the resurrection, but the manner of the resurrection, what is the kind of body which shall rise again ; as whether it be of the same kind, or better and more glorious. And he takes both from the same analogy, intimating that it will be much better.

But the heretics, considering none of these things, dart in upon us and say, "one body falls and another body rises again. How then is there a resurrection ? For the resurrection is of that which was fallen. But where is that wonderful and surprising trophy over death, if one body fall and another rise again ? For he will no longer appear to have given back that which he took captive. And how can the alleged analogy suit the things before mentioned ?" Why, it is not one substance that is sown, and another that is raised, but the same substance improved. Else neither will Christ have resumed the same body when He became the first-fruits of them that rise again : but according to you He threw aside the former body, although it had not sinned, and took another. Whence then is that other ? For this body was from the Virgin, but that, whence was it ? Seest thou to what absurdity the argument hath come round ? For wherefore shows He the very prints of the nails ? Was it not to prove that it is that same body which was crucified, and the same again that rose from the dead ? And what means also His type of Jonah ? For surely it was not one Jonah that was swallowed up and another that was cast out upon dry land. And why did He also say, " Destroy this temple, and in three days I will raise it up ?" For that which was destroyed, the same clearly He raised again. Wherefore also the Evangelist added, that " He spake of the temple of His body." (John ii. 19, 21.)

What is that then which he saith, "Thou sowest not the body that shall be ?" i. e. not the ear of corn: for it is the same, and not the same ; the same, because the substance is the same ; but not the same, because this is more excellent, the substance remaining the same but its beauty becoming greater, and the same body rising up new. Since if this were not so, there were no need of a resurrection, I mean if it were not to rise again improved. For why did He at all pull down His house, except He were about to build it more glorious ?

This now, you see, he said to them who think that it is utter corruption[2]. Next, that none again might suspect from this place that another body is spoken of, he qualifies the dark saying, and himself interprets what he had spoken, not allowing the hearer to turn his thoughts from hence in any other direction. What need is

---

THOU *sowest &c.* The force or emphasis may be gathered thus. If God doth give a body unto that seed which thou sowest for thine own use and benefit, much more will the same God give a body unto the seed which He Himself doth sow, seeing the end why He sows it, is not thy temporal benefit or commodity, but His own immortal glory." Dr. Jackson's Works, vol. iii. 438. See also vol. iii. 433—443.

[1] This seems like a different reading : but it appears afterwards that S. Chrysostom read the verse as it stands. He quotes it therefore here in substance, not *verbatim*.

[2] τὴν αὐτὴν φθοράν. The reading is perhaps corrupt.

there then of our reasonings? Hear himself speaking, and explaining the phrase, "Thou sowest not the body that shall be." For he straightway adds, "but a bare grain, it may chance of wheat, or of some other kind;" i. e., it is not the body that shall be; not so clothed, for instance; not having a stalk and beard, but "a bare grain, it may chance of wheat, or of some other kind."

Ver. 38. "But God giveth it a body even as it pleased Him."

"Yes," saith one, "but in that case it is the work of nature." Of what nature, tell me? For in that case likewise God surely doeth the whole; not nature, nor the earth, nor the rain. Wherefore also he making these things manifest, leaves out both earth and rain, atmosphere, sun, and hands of husbandmen, and subjoins, "God giveth it a body as it pleased Him." Do not thou therefore curiously inquire, nor busy thyself with the how and in what manner, when thou hearest of the power and will of God.

"And to each seed a body of its own." Where then is the alien matter which they speak of? For He giveth to each "his own." So that when he saith, "Thou sowest not that which shall be," he saith not this, that one substance is raised up instead of another, but that it is improved, that it is more glorious. For "to each of the seeds," saith he, "a body of its own."

[4.] From hence in what follows, he introducing also the difference of the resurrection which shall then be. For do not suppose, because grain is sown and all come up ears of corn, that therefore there is also in the resurrection an equality of honor. For in the first place, neither in seeds is there only one rank, but some are more valuable, and some inferior. Wherefore also he added, "to each seed a body of its own."

However, he is not content with this, but seeks another difference greater and more manifest. For that thou mayest not, when hearing, as I said, that all rise again, suppose that all enjoy the same reward; he laid before even in the preceding verses the seeds of this thought, saying, "But each in his own order." But he brings it out here also more clearly, saying,

Ver. 39. "All flesh is not the same flesh." For why speak I, saith he, in respect of seeds? In respect of bodies let us agitate this point, concerning which we are discoursing now. Wherefore also he addeth, and saith,

"But there is one flesh of men, another flesh of beasts, another of birds, and another of fishes."

Ver. 40." There are also celestial bodies, and bodies terrestrial; but the glory of the celestial is one, and the glory of the terrestrial is another."

Ver. 41. "There is one glory of the sun, and another glory of the moon, and another glory of the stars: for one star differeth from another star in glory."

And what means he by these expressions? Wherefore from the resurrection of the body did he throw himself into the discourse of the stars and the sun? He did not throw himself out, neither did he break off from his purpose; far from it: but he still keeps to it. For whereas he had established the doctrine concerning the resurrection, he intimates in what follows that great will be then the difference of glory, though there be but one resurrection. And for the present he divides the whole into two: into "bodies celestial," and "bodies terrestrial." For that the bodies are raised again, he signified by the corn: but that they are not all in the same glory, he signifies by this. For as the disbelief of the resurrection makes men supine, so again it makes them indolent to think that all are vouchsafed the same reward. Wherefore he corrects both. And the one in the preceeding verses he had completed; but this he begins now. And having made two ranks, of the righteous and of sinners, these same two he subdivides again into many parts, signifying that neither righteous nor sinners shall obtain the same; neither righteous men, all of them, alike with other righteous, nor sinners with other sinners.

Now he makes, you see, first, one separation between righteous and sinners, where he says, "bodies celestial, and bodies terrestrial:" by the "terrestrial" intimating the latter, and by the "celestial," the former. Then farther he introduces a difference of sinners from sinners, saying, "All flesh is not the same flesh, but there is one flesh of fishes, another of birds, and another of beasts." And yet all are bodies; but some are in more, and some in lesser vileness. And that in their manner of living too, and in their very constitution.

And having said this, he ascends again to the heaven, saying, "There is one glory of the sun, and another glory of the moon." For as in the earthly bodies there is a difference, so also in the heavenly; and that difference no ordinary one, but reaching even to the uttermost: there being not only a difference between sun and moon, and stars, but also between stars and stars. For what though they be all in the heaven? yet some have a larger, others a less share of glory. What do we learn from hence? That although they be all in God's kingdom, all shall not enjoy the same reward; and though all sinners be in hell, all shall not endure the same punishment. Wherefore he added,

Ver. 42. "So also is the resurrection of the dead."

"So," How? with considerable difference.

Then leaving this doctrine as sufficiently proved, he again comes to the proof itself of the resurrection and the manner of it, saying,

[5.] "It is sown in corruption, it is raised in incorruption." And observe his consideration. As in the case of seeds, he used the term proper to bodies, saying, "it is not quickened, except it die:" so in the case of bodies, the expression belonging to seeds, saying, "it is sown in corruption, it is raised in incorruption." He said not, "is produced[1]," that thou mightest not think it a work of the earth, but is "raised." And by sowing here, he means not our generation in the womb, but the burial in the earth of our dead bodies, their dissolution, their ashes. Wherefore having said, "it is sown in corruption, it is raised in incorruption," he adds,

Ver. 43. "It is sown in dishonor." For what is more unsightly than a corpse in dissolution? "It is raised in glory."

"It is sown in weakness." For before thirty days the whole is gone, and the flesh cannot keep itself together nor hold out for one day. "It is raised in power." For there shall nothing prevail against it for all the future.

Here is why he stood in need of those former analogies, lest many on hearing of these things, that they are "raised in incorruption and glory and power," might suppose that there is no difference among those who rise again. For all indeed rise again, both in power and in incorruption; and in this glory of their incorruption yet are not all in the same state of honor and safety.

Ver. 44. "It is sown a natural body, it is raised a spiritual body. There is a natural body, and there is a spiritual body."

What sayest thou? Is not "this" body spiritual? It is indeed spiritual, but that will be much more so. For now oftentimes both the abundant grace of the Holy Ghost flies away on men's committing great sins; and again, the Spirit continuing present, the life[2] of the flesh depends on the soul: and the result in such a case is a void, without the Spirit[3]. But in that day not so: rather he abides continually in the flesh of the righteous, and the victory shall be His, the natural soul also being present[4].

For either it was some such thing which he

intimated by saying, "a spiritual body," or that it shall be lighter and more subtle and such as even to be wafted upon air; or rather he meant both these. And if thou disbelieve the doctrine, behold the heavenly bodies which are so glorious and (for this time) so durable, and abide in undecaying tranquillity; and believe thou from hence, that God can also make these corruptible bodies incorruptible and much more excellent than those which are visible.

[6.] Ver. 45. "So also it is written, (Gen. ii. 7.) the first man Adam became a living soul: the last Adam became a life-giving Spirit."

And yet the one indeed is written, but the other not written. How then said He, "it is written?" He modified the expression according to the issue of events: as he is wont continually to do: and indeed as it is the way of every prophet. For so Jerusalem, the prophet said, should be "called a city of righteousness;" (Is. i. 26.) yet it was not so called. What then? Did the prophet speak false? By no means. For he is speaking of the issue of events. And that Christ too should be called Immanuel; (Is. vii. 14.) yet was he not so called. But the facts utter this voice; so also here, "the last Adam became a life-giving Spirit."

And these things he said that thou mayest learn that the signs and pledges both of the present life and of that which is to come have already come upon us; to wit, of the present life, Adam, and of the life to come, Christ. For since he sets down the better things as matters of hope, he signifies that their beginning hath already come to pass, and their root and their fountain been brought to light. But if the root and the fountain be evident to all, there is no need to doubt of the fruits. Wherefore he saith, "The last Adam became a life-giving Spirit." And elsewhere too, He "shall quicken your mortal bodies through His Spirit that dwelleth in you." (Rom. vii. 11.) It is the Spirit's work then to quicken.

Further, lest any should say, "why are the worse things the elder? and why hath the one sort, to wit, the natural, come to pass not merely as far as the first-fruits, but altogether; the other as far as the first-fruits only?"—he signifies that the principles also of each were so ordered[5].

Ver. 46. "For that is not first," saith he, "which is spiritual, but that which is natural, then that which is spiritual."

And he saith not, why, but is content with

---

[1] φύεται.

[2] τῆς ψυχῆς ἡ ζωή: "the life of the animal soul:" alluding to the threefold being of the perfect man, in spirit, and soul, and body: cf. 1 Thess. v. 23.

[3] τούτου χωρίς. i. e., the remains, when deprived of the natural life, are an empty vessel without the Holy Ghost, in that Its quickening Power is not put forth in them for the time.

[4] i. e. It is true the body may be called spiritual, because of the Spirit's indwelling: but it is not wholly and entirely so. For sometimes the Spirit leaves men when they sin, and even when the Spirit does not leave them, vitality leaves the body, which then becomes untenanted; whereas at the resurrection the body being quickened, the Spirit remains in them for ever. [This seems to be a satisfactory explanation of a passage difficult in the original, (satis tenebricosa as Dr. Field says,) and quite uncertain as to the text. C.)

[5] i. e. Why does the worst principle come first? Why is the natural principle wholly developed not only in Adam, the first-fruits, but in us and all mankind? And why is the spiritual principal which is to produce the resurrection, not yet developed in us, but only in Christ our first-fruits? The answer is, So is the will of God, by whose ordinance it is that the natural should come first, the spiritual afterwards.

the ordinance of God, having the evidence from the facts testifying to that most excellent œconomy of God, and implying that our state is always going forward to the better ; at the same time by this also adding credibility to his argument. For if the lesser have come to pass, much more ought we to expect the better.

[7.] Since then we are to enjoy so great blessings, let us take our station in this array, and bewail not the departed, but rather those that have ended their life ill. For so the husbandman, when he sees the grain dissolving, doth not mourn ; rather, as long as he beholds it continuing solid in the ground he is in fear and trembling, but when he sees it dissolved rejoices. For the beginning of the future crop is its dissolving. So let us also then rejoice when the corruptible house falls, when the man is sown. And marvel not if he called the burial " a sowing ; " for, in truth, this is the better sowing : inasmuch as that sowing is succeeded by deaths and labors and dangers and cares ; but this, if we lived well, by crowns and rewards ; and that, by corruption and death ; but this by incorruption and immortality, and those infinite blessings. To that kind of sowing there went embraces and pleasures and sleep : but to this, only a voice coming down from heaven, and all is at once brought to perfection. And he that rises again is no more led to a life full of toil, but to a place where anguish and sorrow and sighing are fled away.

If thou requirest protection and therefore mournest thy husband, betake thyself to God, the common Protector and Saviour and Benefactor of all, to that irresistible alliance, to that ready aid, to that abiding shelter which is every where present, and is as a wall unto us on every side.

" But your intercourse was a thing desirable and lovely." I too know it. But if thou wilt trust sound reason with this grief, and wilt consider with thyself who hath taken him away, and that by nobly bearing it thou offerest thy mind as a sacrifice to our God, even this wave will not be too strong for thee to stem. And that which time brings to pass, the same do thou by thy self-command. But if thou shalt yield to weakness, thine emotion will cease indeed in time, but it will bring thee no reward.

And together with these reasons collect also examples, some in the present life, some in the Holy Scriptures. Consider that Abraham slew his own son, and neither shed a tear nor uttered a bitter word. " But he," you say, " was Abraham." Nay, thou surely hast been called to a nobler field of action[1]. And Job grieved indeed, but so much as was proper for a father

who loved his children and was very solicitious for the departed ; whereas what we now do, is surely the part of haters and enemies. For if when a man was taken up to court and crowned, thou wert smiting thyself and lamenting, I I should not say that thou wast a friend of him who was crowned, but a great enemy and adversary. " Nay," say you, " not even as it is do I mourn for him, but for myself." Well, but this is not the part of an affectionate person, to wish for thine own sake that he were still in the conflict and subject to the uncertainty of the future, when he might be crowned and come to anchor ; or that he should be tossed in mid ocean, when he might have been in port.

[8.] " But I know not whither he hath gone," say you. Wherefore knowest thou not, tell me ? For according as he lived well or otherwise, it is evident whither he will go. " Nay, on this very account I lament," say you, " because he departed being a sinner[2]." This is a mere pretext and excuse. For if this were the reason of thy mourning for the departed, thou oughtest to have formed and corrected him, when he was alive. The fact is thou dost every where look to what concerns thyself, not him.

But grant that he departed with sin upon him, even on this account one ought to rejoice, that he was stopped short in his sins and added not to his iniquity ; and help him as far as possible, not by tears, but by prayers and supplications and alms and offerings. For not unmeaningly have these things been devised, nor do we in vain make mention of the departed in the course of the divine mysteries, and approach God in their behalf, beseeching the Lamb Who is before us, Who taketh away the sin of the world ;—not in vain, but that some refreshment may thereby ensue to them. Not in vain doth he that standeth by the altar cry out when the tremendous mysteries are celebrated, " For all that have fallen asleep in Christ, and for those who perform commemorations in their behalf[3]." For if there were no commemorations for them, these things would not have been spoken : since our service is not a mere stage show, God forbid ! yea, it is by

---

[1] μείζονα σκάμματα

[2] Bingham observes, lib. xv. cap. 3. sect. 16. " Another reason for praying for the dead was, they conceived all men to die with some remainders of frailty and corruption, and therefore desired that God would deal with them according to His mercy, and not in strict justice according to their merits." " These prayers," he proceeds to say, see lib. xxiii. cap. 3. sect. 3. and 13. " are not made upon the Romish supposition of the soul's being in purgatory or any place of torment, but on principles that perfectly overthrow it." For they call those for whom they offer, Saints including among them the Blessed Virgin, the Apostles and Prophets : and they represent them as having 'pleased God,' " being at rest," " sleeping in Christ," " departed in His Faith," and other equivalent expressions. *Vid.* Brett's *Liturgies*, p. 270—272. Ed. 1838. See also Bp. Bull, vol. ii. 261. Oxford Ed.

[3] These expressions are not *verbatim* either in St. Chrysostom's or in any other of the Liturgies translated by Brett, but in substance they are in all.

the ordinance of the Spirit that these things are done.

Let us then give them aid and perform commemoration for them. For if the children of Job were purged by the sacrifice of their father, why dost thou doubt that when we too offer for the departed, some consolation arises to them? since God is wont to grant the petitions of those who ask for others. And this Paul signified saying, " that in a manifold Person[1] your gift towards us bestowed by many may be acknowledged with thanksgiving on your behalf." (2. Cor. i. 11.) Let us not then be weary in giving aid to the departed, both by offering on their behalf and obtaining prayers for them: for the common Expiation of the world is even before us. Therefore with boldness do we then intreat for the whole world, and name their names with those of martyrs, of confessors, of priests. For in truth one body are we all, though some members are more glorious than others; and it is possible from every source to gather pardon[2] for them, from our prayers, from our gifts in their behalf, from those whose names are named with theirs. Why therefore dost thou grieve? Why mourn, when it is in thy power to gather so much pardon for the departed?

[9.] Is it then that thou art become desolate and hast lost a protector? Nay, never mention this. For thou hast not surely lost thy God. And so, as long as thou hast Him, He will be better to thee than husband and father and child and kinsman: since even when they were alive, He it was who did all things.

These things therefore think upon, and say with David, "The Lord is my light and my Saviour[3], whom shall I fear? (Ps. xxvii. 1) Say, Thou art a Father of the fatherless, and a Judge of the widows:" (Ps. lxviii. 5.) and draw down His aid, and thou shalt have Him to care for thee now more than before, by how much thou art in a state of greater difficulty.

Or hast thou lost a child? Thou hast not lost it; say not so. This thing is sleep, not death; removal, not destruction; a journeying from the worse unto the better[4]. Do not then provoke

God to anger; but propitiate Him. For if thou bearest it nobly, there will thence accrue some relief both to the departed and to thyself; but if the contrary, thou dost the more kindle God's anger. For if when a servant was chastised by his master, thou didst stand by and complain, thou wouldest the more exasperate the master against thyself. Do not then so; but give thanks, that hereby also this cloud of sadness may be scattered from thee. Say with that blessed one, "the Lord gave, and the Lord hath taken away." (Job i. 21.) Consider how many more well-pleasing in His sight have never received children at all, nor been called fathers. "Nor would I wish to have been so," say you, "for surely it were better not to have had experience than after having tasted the pleasure to fall from it." Nay, I beseech thee, say not so, provoke not thus also the Lord to wrath: but for what thou hast received, give Him thanks; and for what thou hast not to the end, give Him glory. Job said not that which thou sayest unthankfully, "it were better not to have received," but both for the one he gave thanks, saying, "The Lord gave;" and for the other he blessed God, saying, "The Lord hath taken away, blessed be the name of the Lord for ever." And his wife he thus silenced, justifying himself against her, and uttering those admirable words, "Have we received good at the hand of the Lord, and shall we not receive evil?" And yet after this a fiercer temptation befel him: yet was he not even thus unnerved, but in like manner bore it nobly and glorified God.

This also do thou, and consider with thyself that man hath not taken him, but God who made him, who more than thyself cares for him and knows what is good for him: who is no enemy nor lier-in-wait. See how many, living, have made life intolerable to their parents. "But seest thou not the right-hearted ones?" say you. I see these too, but even these are not so safe as thy child is. For though they are now approved, yet it is uncertain what their end will be; but for him thou hast no longer any fear, nor dost thou tremble lest anything should happen to him or he experience any change.

These things also do thou consider respecting a good wife and guardian of thine house, and for all things give thanks unto God. And even if thou shalt lose a wife, give thanks. Perhaps God's will is to lead thee to continence, He calls thee to a nobler field of conflict, He was pleased to set thee free from this bond. If we thus command ourselves, we shall both gain the joy of this life and obtain the crowns which are to come, &c. &c.

---

[1] ἐν πολλῷ προσώπῳ: "in a great Person," "the Person of a manifold Being, i. e., of the whole Church." The common reading is ἐκ πολλῶν προσώπων. St. Chrysostom may have thought that the Apostle was alluding to the Liturgical Service as the voice of the whole mystical Body of Christ. See his comment on the place in Hom. 2. on 2 Cor. §. 3, 4. Ed. Bened. [The singular reading of Chrysostom in this place does not seem to be sustained by any Greek MSS., but is represented in several codices of the old Itala version. On the principle of the *durior lectio* it might claim attention, but surely on no other ground. C.]

[2] συγγνώμην.

[3] σωτήρ LXX.

[4] The same idea is thus expressed by Tertullian. "Why mourn, if thy faith be that he hath not perished? Why bear impatiently *his* being withdrawn for a while, of whom thou believest that he will return? It is but a journey, which thou accountest death. It is not meet to mourn for him who is gone before, but simply to miss him and long for him." *De Patient.* c. 9.

HOMILY XLII.

The first man is of the earth, earthy: the second man is the Lord from heaven.

HAVING said that "the natural was first," and "the spiritual afterward," he again states another difference, speaking of "the earthy" and "the heavenly." For the first difference was between the present life and that which is to come: but this between that before grace and that after grace. And he stated it with a view to the most excellent way of life, saying, —(for to hinder men, as I said, from such confidence in the resurrection as would make them neglectful of their practice and of perfection, from this topic also again he renders them anxious and exhorts to virtue, saying,)—"The first man is of the earth, earthy; the second man is the Lord from heaven:" calling the whole by the name of "man[1]," and naming the one from the better, and the other from the worst part.

Ver. 48. "As is the earthy, such are they also that are earthy:" so shall they perish and have an end. "As is the heavenly, such are they also that are heavenly:" so shall they abide immortal and glorious.

What then? Did not This Man too die? He died indeed, but received no injury therefrom, yea rather by this He put an end to death. Seest thou how on this part of his subject also, he makes use of death to establish the doctrine of the resurrection? "For having, as I said before, the beginning and the head," so he speaks, "doubt not of the whole body."

Moreover also he frames hereby his advice concerning the best way of living, proposing standards of a lofty and severe life and of that which is not such, and bringing forward the principles of both these, of the one Christ, but of the other Adam. Therefore neither did he simply say, "of the earth," but "earthy," i. e., "gross, nailed down to things present:" and again with respect to Christ the reverse, "the Lord from heaven."

[2.] But if any should say, "therefore the Lord hath not a body[2] because He is said to be "from heaven," although what is said before is enough to stop their mouths: yet nothing hinders our silencing them from this consideration also: viz. what is, "the Lord from heaven?" Doth he speak of His nature, or His most perfect life? It is I suppose evident to every one that he speaks of His life. Wherefore also he adds,

Ver. 49. "As we have borne the image of the earthy," i. e., as we have done evil, "let us also bear[3] the image of the heavenly," i. e., let us practise all goodness.

But besides this, I would fain ask thee, is it of nature that it is said, "he that is of the earth, earthy," and, "the Lord from heaven?" "Yea," saith one. What then? Was Adam only "earthy," or had he also another kind of substance congenial with heavenly and incorporeal beings, which the Scripture calls "soul," and "spirit?" Every one sees that he had this also. Therefore neither was the Lord from above only although He is said to be "from heaven," but He had also assumed our flesh. But Paul's meaning is such as this: "as we have borne the image of the earthy," i e., evil deeds, "let us also bear the image of the heavenly," the manner of life which is in the heavens. Whereas if he were speaking of nature, the thing neeeded not exhortation nor advice. So that hence also it is evident that the expression relates to our manner of life.

Wherefore also he introduces the saying in the manner of advice and calls it an "image," here too again showing that he is speaking of conduct, not of nature. For therefore are we become earthy, because we have done evil: not because we were originally formed "earthy," but because we sinned. For sin came first, and then death and then the sentence, "Dust thou

---

[1] i. e., embodying as it were the whole of the two states of being which he is describing in the personal appellation of Man: as in the phrase, Old Man and New Man: &c.

[2] As the Manichees did, and before them the Gnostic sects.

[3] φορέσωμεν. This reading is supported, according to Scholz, by the Alexandrian and six other uncial MSS. It is found in several versions, and has the authority of Irenæus, Origen, Basil, Tertullian, Cyprian, and other Fathers. In favor of the reading in our text, φορέσομεν, is the Vatican MSS. with others of less anthority. Theodoret's words are remarkable; "φορέσομεν, He used the expression prophetically not hortatively." (Chrysostom's reading is adopted by nearly all recent editors, but given only in the margin by the Rev. Ver. The external evidence is decidedly in its favor, but not the internal. C.]

art, and unto dust shalt thou return." (Gen. iii. 19.) Then also entered in the swarm of the passions. For it is not simply the being born "of earth" that makes a man "earthy," (since the Lord also was of this mass and lump[4],) but the doing earthly things, even as also he is made "heavenly" by performing things meet for heaven.

But enough : for why need I labor overmuch in the proof of this, when the apostle himself goes on to unfold the thought to us, thus saying,

Ver. 50. "Now this I say, brethren, that flesh and blood cannot inherit the kingdom of God."

Seest thou how he explains himself again, relieving us of the trouble ? which he often doth : for by flesh he here denotes men's evil deeds, which he hath done also elsewhere ; as when he saith, "But ye are not in the flesh :" and again, "So then they that are in the flesh cannot please God." (Rom. viii. 8, 9.) So that when he saith, "Now this I say," he means nothing else than this : "therefore said I these things that thou mayest learn that evil deeds conduct not to a kingdom." Thus from the resurrection he straightway introduced also the doctrine of the kingdom also ; wherefore also he adds, "neither doth corruption inherit incorruption,[2]" i. e., neither shall wickedness inherit that glory and the enjoyment of the things incorruptible. For in many other places he calls wickedness by this name, saying, "He that soweth to the flesh, shall of the flesh reap corruption." (Gal. vi. 8.) Now if he were speaking of the body and not of evil doing, he would not have said "corruption." For he nowhere calls the body "corruption," since neither is it corruption, but a thing corruptible : wherefore proceeding to discourse also of it, he calls it not "corruption," but "corruptible," saying, "for this corruptible must put on incorruption."

[3.] Next, having completed his advice concerning our manner of life, according to his constant custom blending closely subject with subject, he passes again to the doctrine of the resurrection of the body : as follows :

Ver. 51. "Behold, I tell you a mystery."

It is something awful and ineffable and which all know not, which he is about to speak of : which also indicates the greatness of the honor he confers on them ; I mean, his speaking mysteries to them. But what is this ?

"We shall not all sleep, but we shall all be changed." He means as follows : "we shall not all die, 'but we shall all be changed,'" even those who die not. For they too are mortal. "Do not thou therefore because thou

diest, on this account fear," saith he, "as if thou shouldest not rise again : for there are, there are some who shall even escape this, and yet this suffices them not for that resurrection, but even those bodies which die not must be changed and be transformed into incorruption."

Ver. 52. "In a moment, in the twinkling of an eye, at the last trump."

After he had discoursed much of the resurrection, then opportunely he points out also its very marvellous character. As thus : "not this only," saith he, "is wonderful that our bodies first turn to corruption, and then are raised ; nor that the bodies which rise again after their corruption are better than these present ones ; nor that they pass on to a much better state, nor that each receives back his own and none that of another ; but that things so many and so great, and surpassing all man's reason and conception, are done "in a moment," i. e., in an instant of time : and to show this more clearly, "in the twinkling of an eye," saith he, "while one can wink an eyelid." Further, because he had said a great thing and full of astonishment ; that so many and so great results should take place so quickly ; he alleges, to prove it, the credibility of Him who performs it ; as follows, "For the trumpet shall sound, and the dead shall be raised incorruptible, and we shall be changed." The expression, "we," he uses not of himself, but of them that are then found alive.

Ver. 53. "For this corruptible must put on incorruption."

Thus lest any, hearing that "flesh and blood cannot inherit the kingdom of God," should suppose that our bodies do not rise again ; he adds, "this corruptible must put on incorruption, and this mortal must put on immortality." Now the body is "corruptible," the body is "mortal :" so that the body indeed remains, for it is the body which is put on ; but its mortality and corruption vanish away, when immortality and incorruption come upon it. Do not thou therefore question hereafter how it shall live an endless life, now that thou hast heard of its becoming incorruptible.

[4.] Ver. 54. "But when this corruptible shall have put on incorruption, and this mortal shall have put on immortality, then shall come to pass the saying that is written, Death is swallowed up in victory."

Thus, since he was speaking of great and secret things, he again takes prophecy (Hosea xiii. 14.) to confirm his word. "Death is swallowed up in victory :[3]" i. e., utterly ; not so much as a fragment of it remains nor a hope of returning, incorruption having consumed corruption.

---

[4] μάζης καὶ φυράματος.
[2] κληρονομεῖ rec. text.

[3] εἰς νίκος; i. e. εἰς τέλος.

Ver. 55. " O death, where is thy sting?   O grave, where is thy victory?"

Seest thou his noble soul? how even as one who is offering sacrifices for victory, having become inspired and seeing already things future as things past, he leaps and tramples upon death fallen at his feet, and shouts a cry of triumph over its head where it lies, exclaiming mightily and saying, " O death, where is thy sting?   O grave, where is thy victory?" It is clean gone, it is perished, it is utterly vanished away, and in vain hast thou done all those former things.   For He not only disarmed death and vanquished it, but even destroyed it, and made it quite cease from being.

Ver. 56. " Now the sting of death is sin; and the power of sin is the law."

Seest thou how the discourse is of the death of the body? therefore also of the resurrection of the body.   For if these bodies do not rise again, how is death " swallowed up?"   And not this only, but how is " the law the power of sin?"   For that " sin " indeed is " the sting of death," and more bitter than it, and by it hath its power, is evident; but how is " the law also the power " thereof?   Because without the law sin was weak, being practised indeed, but not able so entirely to condemn : since although the evil took place, it was not so clearly pointed out.   So that it was no small change which the law brought in, first causing us to know sin better, and then enhancing the punishment.   And if meaning to check sin it did but develop it more fearfully, this is no charge against the physician, but against the abuse of the remedy. Since even the presence of Christ made the Jews' burden heavier, yet must we not therefore blame it, but while we the more admire it, we must hate them the more, for having been injured by things which ought to have profited them?   Yea, to show that it was not the law of itself which gives strength to sin, Christ Himself fulfilled it all and was without sin.

But I would have thee consider how from this topic also he confirms the resurrection. For if this were the cause of death, viz. our committing sin, and if Christ came and took away sin, and delivered us from it through baptism, and together with sin put an end also to the law in the transgression of which sin consists, why doubtest thou any more of the resurrection?   For whence, after all this, is death to prevail?   Through the law?   Nay, it is done away.   Through sin?   Nay, it is clean destroyed.

Ver. 57. " But thanks be to God, which giveth us the victory through our Lord Jesus Christ."

For the trophy He Himself erected, but the crowns He hath caused us also to partake of. And this not of debt, but of mere mercy.

[5.] Ver. 58. " Wherefore[1], brethren, be ye steadfast, unmoveable."

Just and seasonable is this exhortation after all that had gone before.   For nothing so disquiets as the thought that we are buffeted without cause or profit.

" Always abounding in the work of the Lord : " i. e., in the pure life.   And he said not, " working that which is good," but " abounding ; " that we might do it abundantly[2], and might overpass the lists.

" Knowing that your labor is not in vain in the Lord."

What sayest thou ?   Labor again ?   But followed by crowns, and those above the heavens. For that former labor on man's expulsion from paradise, was the punishment of his transgressions ; but this is the ground of the rewards to come.   So that it cannot in fact be labor, both on this account and by reason of the great help which it receives from above : which is the cause of his adding also, " in the Lord."   For the purpose of the former was that we might suffer punishment ; but of this, that we might obtain the good things to come.

Let us not therefore sleep, my beloved.   For it cannot, it cannot be that any one by sloth should attain to the kingdom of heaven, nor they that live luxuriously and softly.   Yea it is a great thing, if straining ourselves and " keeping under[3] the body " and enduring innumerable labors, we are able to reach those blessings.   See ye not how vast this distance between heaven and earth?   And how great a conflict is at hand?   And how prone a thing to evil man is?   And how easily sin " besets us ?"   And how many snares are in the way?

Why then do we draw upon ourselves so great cares over and above those of nature, and give ourselves more trouble, and make our burden greater?   Is it not enough, our having to care for our food and clothing and houses ? Is it not enough to take thought for things necessary?   Although even from these Christ withdraws us, saying, " Be not anxious for your life what ye shall eat, neither for your body what ye shall put on." (Matt. vi. 25.) But if one ought not to be anxious for necessary food and clothing, nor for to-morrow ; they who bring on so great a mass of rubbish and bury themselves under it, when shall they shall have power to emerge ?   Hast thou not heard Paul saying, " No soldier on service entangleth himself in the affairs of this life ? " (2 Tim. ii. 4.) But we even live luxuriously and eat and drink to excess and endure buffeting for external

---

[1] μου ἀγαπητοὶ, omitted.
[2] μετὰ περιουσίας.
[3] ὑποπιεζοντας.

things, but in the things of heaven behave ourselves unmanly. Know ye not that the promise is too high for man ? It cannot be that one walking on the ground should ascend the arches of heaven. But we do not even study to live like men, but are become worse than the brutes.

Know ye not before what a tribunal we are to stand ? Do ye not consider that both for our words and thoughts an account is demanded of us, and we take no heed even to our actions. "For whosoever looketh on a woman," saith He, "to lust after her hath already committed adultery with her." (Matt. v. 28.) And yet they who must be accountable for a mere idle look, refuse not even to lie rotting in the sin itself. "Whosoever shall say to his brother, Thou fool, shall be cast into hell fire." (Matt. v. 22.) But we even dishonor them with ten thousand reproaches and plot against them craftily. "He that loveth one that loveth him is no better than the heathen: " (Matt. v. 46, 47.) but we even envy them. What indulgence then shall we have, when commanded as we are to pass over the old lines, we weave ourselves a thread of life by a yet more scanty measure than theirs ? What plea shall deliver us ? Who will stand up and help us when we are punished ? There is no one ; but it must needs be that wailing and weeping and gnashing our teeth, we shall be led away tortured into that rayless gloom, the pangs which no prayer can avert, the punishments which cannot be assuaged.

Wherefore I entreat and beseech, and lay hold of your very knees, that whilst we have this scant viaticum of life, you would be pricked in your hearts by what has been said, that you would be converted, that you would become better men ; that we may not, like that rich man, lament to no purpose in that world after our departure, and continue thenceforth in incurable wailings. For though thou shouldest have father or son or friend or any soever who hath confidence towards God, none of these shall ever deliver thee, thine own works having destroyed thee. For such is that tribunal : it judges by our actions alone, and in no other way is it possible there to be saved.

And these things I say, not to grieve you nor to throw you into despair, but lest nourished by vain and cold hopes, and placing confidence in this person or that, we should neglect our own proper goodness. For if we be slothful, there will be neither righteous man nor prophet nor apostle nor any one to stand by us; but if we have been earnest, having in sufficiency the plea which comes from each man's own works[1], we shall depart with confidence, and shall obtain the good things that are laid up for them that love God ; to which may we all attain, &c. &c.

HOMILY XLIII.

1 COR. XVI. 1.

Now concerning the collection for the saints, as I gave order to the Churches of Galatia, so also do ye.

HAVING completed his discourse concerning doctrines, and being about to enter upon that which belongs rather to morals, he dismisses every thing else and proceeds to the chief of good things, discoursing about alms. Nor does he discuss morals in general, but when he hath treated of this matter alone, he leaves off. A thing however obviously unlike what he did every where else; for of alms and of temperance and of meekness and of long-suffering and of all the rest, he treats in the other Epistles in the conclusion. For what reason then doth he handle here this part only of practical morality? Because the greater part also of what had been spoken before was of an ethical nature : I mean, where he chastised the fornicator ; where he was correcting those who go to law among Gentiles ; where he terrified the drunkards and the gluttons ; where he condemned the seditious, the contentious, and those who loved to have the preeminence ; where those who unworthily approach the Mysteries were delivered over by him unto that intolerable sentence ; where he discoursed concerning love. For this cause, I say, the subject which most pressed on him, viz. the aid required for the saints, this alone he mentions.

And observe his consideration. When he had persuaded them concerning the resurrection, and made them more earnest, then and not till then he discusses this point also.

It is true indeed that on these matters he had spoken to them before, when he said, " If we sowed unto you spiritual things, is it a great matter if we shall reap your carnal things?"

---

[1] τὴν ἀπὸ τῶν ἔργων συνηγορίαν.

And, "Who planteth a vineyard, and eateth not of the fruit thereof?" But because he knew the greatness of this moral achievement, he refuses not to add a fresh mention at the end of his letter.

And he calls the collection λογίαν (a "contribution,") immediately from the very first making out the things to be easy. For when contribution is made by all together, that becomes light which is charged upon each.

But having spoken about the collection, he did not say immediately, "Let every one of you lay up in store with himself;" although this of course was the natural consequence; but having first said, "As I gave order to the Churches of Galatia," he added this, kindling their emulation by the account of the well-doings of others, and putting it in the form of a narration. And this also he did when writing to the Romans; for to them also while appearing to narrate the reason why he was going away to Jerusalem, he introduces thereupon his discourse about alms; "But now I go unto Jerusalem, ministering unto the saints: for it hath been the good pleasure of Macedonia and Achaia to make a certain contribution for the poor among the saints." (Rom. xv. 25.) Only those he stimulates by mention of Macedonians and Corinthians; these of Galatians. For he saith, "As I gave order to the Churches of Galatia, so also do ye:" for they would surely feel ashamed ever afterwards to be found inferior to Galatians. And he saith not, "I advised," and, "I counselled;" but, "I gave order," which is more authoritative. And he doth not bring forward a single city, or two, or three, but an entire nation: which also he doth in his doctrinal instructions, saying, "Even as also in all the Churches of the saints." For if this be potent for conviction of doctrines, much more for imitation of actions.

[2.] "What then, I ask, didst thou give order about?"

Ver. 2. "On the first day of the week," that is, the Lord's day, "let each one of you lay by him in store, as he may prosper." Mark how he exhorts them even from the time: for indeed the day was enough to lead them to almsgiving. Wherefore "call to mind," saith he, "what ye attained to on this day: how all the unutterable blessings, and that which is the root and the beginning of our life took place on this day. But not in this regard only is the season convenient for a zealous benevolence, but also because it hath rest and immunity from toils: the souls when released from labors becoming readier and apter to show pity. Moreover, the communicating also on that day in Mysteries so tremendous and immortal instils great zealousness. On it, accordingly, "let each one of you," not merely this or that individual, but "each one of you," whether poor or rich, woman or man, slave or free, "lay by him in store." He said not, "Let him bring it into the church," lest they might feel ashamed because of the smallness of the sum; but "having by gradual additions swelled his contribution, let him then produce it, when I am come: but for the present lay it up," saith he, "at home, and make thine house a church; thy little box a treasury. Become a guardian of sacred wealth, a self-ordained steward of the poor. Thy benevolent mind assigns to thee this priesthood."

Of this our treasury[1] even now is a sign: but the sign remains, the thing itself no where.

[3.] Now I am aware that many of this congregation will again find fault with me when I treat of these subjects, and say, "Be not, I beseech you, be not harsh and disagreeable to your audience. Make allowances for their disposition; give way to the mind of the hearers. For in this case you really do put us to shame; you make us blush." But I may not endure such words: since neither was Paul ashamed to be continually troublesome upon such points as these and to speak words such as mendicants use. I grant indeed that if I said, "give it me," and "lay it up in my house," there might perchance be something to be ashamed of in what I said: hardly however even in that case; for "they who wait upon the altar," we read, "have their portion with the altar." (c. ix. 13.) However, some one perhaps might find fault as if he were framing an argument for his own interest. But now it is for the poor that I make my supplication; nay, not so much for the poor, as for your sake who bestow the gift. Wherefore also I am bold to speak out. For what shame is it to say, Give unto thy Lord in His hunger: Put raiment on Him going about naked; Receive Him being a stranger? Thy Lord is not ashamed before the whole world to speak thus: "I was an hungred, and ye gave Me not to eat," He who is void of all want and requires nothing. And am I to be ashamed and hesitate? Away with this. This shame is of the snare of the devil. I will not then be ashamed, but will say, and that boldly, "Give

---

[1] το γαζοφυλακίον, Bingham, viii. 7. 11. says, "The Church had her *gazophylacia*, or Treasuries, as well as the Temple; which appears from a Canon of the Fourth Council of Carthage," (93. *ap. Harduin.* i. 984.) "which forbids the offerings of persons at variance with one another to be received *either in the Treasury or the Sanctuary*. So that the Treasury was a distinct place from the Corban in the Sanctuary. . . . Here all such offerings of the people were laid up as were not thought proper to be brought to the Altar." He further refers to the *Apostolical Canons*, 4 and 5, "That beside Bread and Wine, nothing should be brought to the Altar, save only new ears of corn and grapes, and oil for the lamps, and incense for the time of the oblation. But all other fruits should be sent εἰς οἶκον, to the Repository, or Treasury it may be, as first-fruits for the Bishop and Presbyters, and not be brought to the Altar, but be by them divided among the Bishops and Clergy." See Harduin, i. 10.

to the needy;" I will say it with a louder voice than the needy themselves. True it is, if any one can show and prove that in saying these things we are drawing you over unto ourselves, and under the pretence of the poor are ourselves making gain, such a course would be worthy, I say not of shame, but even of ten thousand thunderbolts; and life itself would be more than persons so behaving would deserve. If, on the contrary, by the grace of God, we are in nothing troublesome about ourselves, but "have made the Gospel without charge" to you; laboring indeed in no wise like Paul, but being contented with our own;—with all boldness of speech I will say, "Give unto the needy:" yea, and I will not leave off saying it, and of those who give not I will be a severe accuser. For so, if I were a general and had soldiers, I should not feel ashamed at demanding food for my men : for I vehemently set my heart upon your salvation.

[4.] But that my argument may both be more forcible and more effective, I will take Paul for my comrade, and like him will discourse and say, "Let each one of you lay by him in store, as he may prosper." Now observe also how he avoids being burdensome. He said not, "so much," or "so much," but "as he may prosper," whether much or little. Neither said he, "what any one may have gained," but, "as he may prosper:" signifying that the supply is of God. And not only so, but also by his not enjoining them to deposit all at once, he makes his counsel easy : since the gathering little by little hinders all perception of the burden[1] and the cost. Here you see the reason too for his not enjoining them to produce it immediately, but giving them a long day[2]; whereof adding the cause, he saith. "That there be no gatherings when I come :" which means, that ye may not when the season is come for paying in contributions just then be compelled to collect them. And this too in no ordinary degree encouraged them again : the expectation of Paul being sure to make them more earnest.

Ver. 3. "And when I arrive, whomsoever ye shall approve, them will I send with letters to carry your bounty[3] to Jerusalem."

He said not, "this person," and "that," but, "whomsoever ye shall approve," whomsoever you shall choose, thus freeing his ministration from suspicion. Wherefore to them he leaves the right of voting in the choice of those who are to convey it. He is far enough from saying, "The payment is yours, but the privilege of selecting those who are to carry it is not

yours." Next, that they might not think him quite absent, he adds his letters, saying, "Whomsoever you approve, I will send with letters."[4] As if he had said, I also will be with them and share in the ministration, by my letters. And he said not, "These will I send to bear your alms," but, "your bounty;" to signify that they were doing great deeds ; to mark that they were gainers themselves. And elsewhere he calls it both "a blessing" and "a distribution." (2 Cor. ix. 5, 13.) The one that he might not make them less active, the other that he might not elate them. But in no case whatever hath he called it "alms."

Ver. 4. "And if it be meet for me to go also, they shall go with me."

Here again he exhorts them to liberality. As thus : "if it be so much," saith he, "as to require my presence also, neither will I decline this." But he did not in the first instance promise this, nor say, "When I am come I will carry it." For he would not have made so much of it, if he had so set it down from the first. Afterwards however he adds it well and seasonably. Here then you have the reason why he did not immediately promise, nor yet altogether hold his peace concerning it : but having said, "I will send," then at length he adds himself also. And here too again he leaves it to their own decision; in saying, "If it be meet for me to go also :" whereas this rested with them, namely, to make their collection large ; so large even, as to affect his plans and cause him in person to make the journey.

[5.] Ver. 5. "But I will come to you," saith he, "when I shall have passed through Macedonia." This he had said also above ; then however with anger: at least he added, (c. iv. 19.) "And I will know not the speech of them that are puffed up, but the power :" but here, more mildly ; that they might even long for his coming. Then, that they might not say, "Why is it that you honor the Macedonians above us?" he said not, "When I depart," but, "When I shall have passed through Macedonia ; for I do pass through Macedonia."

Ver. 6. "But with you it may be that I shall abide, or even winter." For I do not at all wish to take you merely in my way, but to continue among you and spend some time. For when he wrote this letter, he was in Ephesus, and it was winter ; as you may know by his saying, "Until Pentecost I will tarry at Ephesus; but after this I shall go away to Macedonia, and after having gone through it, I will be with you in the summer ; and perhaps I shall even spend the winter with you."

And why did he say, "perhaps;" and did

---

[1] λειτουργία.
[2] πολλὴν τὴν προθεσμίαν.
[3] χάριν.

[4] [Chrysostom evidently understood the verse in the sense found in the margin of the Revised Version. C.]

not positively affirm it? Because Paul did not foreknow all things; for good purposes. Wherefore neither doth he absolutely affirm, in order that if it came not to pass, he might have something to resort to; first, his previous mention of it having been indefinite; and next, the power of the Spirit leading him wheresoever It willed, not where he himself desired. And this also he expresses in the second Epistle, when excusing himself on account of his delay, and saying, "Or the things which I purpose, do I purpose according to the flesh, that with me there should be the yea yea and the nay nay?" (2 Cor. i. 17.)

"That ye may set me forward on my journey wheresoever I go." This also is a mark of love, and great strength of affection.

Ver. 7. "For I do not wish to see you now by the way; for I hope to tarry awhile with you, if the Lord permit."

Now these these things he said, both to signify his love and also to terrify the sinners, not however openly, but with outward demonstration of friendship.

Ver. 8. "But I will tarry at Ephesus until Pentecost."

As we should expect, he tells them all exactly, informing them as friends. For this too is a mark of friendship to say the reason why he was not with them, why he delayed, and where he was staying.

Ver. 9. "For a great door and effectual is opened unto me, and there are many adversaries."

Now if it was "great," how could there be "adversaries?" Why on this very account the adversaries were many, because men's faith was great; because the entrance was great and wide. But what means, "A great door?" There are many prepared to receive the faith, many ready to approach and be converted. There is a spacious entrance for me, things being now come to that point that the mind of those approaching is at its prime for the obedience of the faith. On this account, vehement was the blast of the breath of the devil, because he saw many turning away from him.

You see then on both accounts it was needful for him to stay; both because the gain was abundant, and because the struggle was great.

And herewith also he cheered them up, namely, by saying, that henceforth the word works every where and springs up readily. And if there be many who plot against it, this also is a sign of the advance of the Gospel. For at no time doth that evil demon wax fierce, except on seeing his goods made spoil of abundantly. (Matt. xii.)

[6.] Let us then, when we desire to effect any thing great and noble, not regard this, the greatness of the labor which it brings, but let us

rather look to the gain. Mark, for instance, Paul, not therefore lingering, not therefore skrinking back, because "there were many adversaries;" but because "there was a great door," pressing on and persevering. Yea, and as I was saying, this was a sign that the devil was being stripped, for it is not, depend on it, by little and mean achievements that men provoke that evil monster to wrath. And so when thou seest a righteous man performing great and excellent deeds, yet suffering innumerable ills, marvel not; on the contrary, one might well marvel, if the devil receiving so many blows were to keep quiet and bear the wounds meekly. Even as you ought not to be surprised were a serpent, continually goaded, to grow fierce and spring on the person that goaded it. Now no serpent steals on you so fierce as the devil, leaping up against all; and, like a scorpion with its sting raised, he raises himself upright. Let not this then disturb you: since of course he that returns from war and victory and slaughter must needs be bloody, and oftentimes also have received wounds. Do thou, then, for thy part, when thou seest any one doing alms and performing numberless other good works and so curtailing the power of the devil, and then falling into temptations and perils; be not troubled thereupon. This is the very reason why he fell into temptations, because he mightily smote the devil.

"And how did God permit it?" you will say. That he might be crowned more signally: that the other might receive a severer wound. For when after benefits conferred a man suffers, and that grievously, and yet continually gives thanks, it is a blow to the devil. For it is a great thing, even when our affairs are flowing on prosperously, to show mercy and to adhere to virtue: but it is far greater in grievous calamity not to desist from this noble occupation; this is he who may be most truly said to do so for God's sake. So then, though we be in peril, beloved, though we suffer ever so greatly, let us with the greater zeal apply ourselves to our labors for virtue's sake. For this is not at all the season for retribution.

Here then let us not ask for our crowns, lest when the crowns come in their season, we diminish our recompense. For as in the case of artificers, they who support themselves and work receive higher pay; while those who have their maintenance with their employers, are curtailed in no small part of the wages; so also in regard to the saints: he that doth immense good and suffers extreme evil hath his reward unimpaired and a far more abundant recompense, not only for the good things which he hath done, but also for the evil which he hath suffered. But he that enjoys rest and luxury here, hath not such bright crowns there. Let us not then seek for our recompense here. But "then" of all times let us rejoice, when doing well we suffer ill. For God hath in store for us in that world not only the reward of our good deeds, but that of our temptations also.

But to explain myself more clearly: suppose two rich merciful men, and let them give to the poor: then let one continue in his riches and enjoy all prosperity: the other fall into poverty and diseases and calamities, and give God thanks. Now when these are gone away into the other world, which will receive the greater reward? Is it not quite plain that it will be he who is sick and in adversity, seeing that though he did well and suffered ill, he felt not according to human infirmity? I suppose this is plain to every one. And, in truth, this is the adamantine statue, this is the considerate servant. (See S. Mat. xxv. 21.) But if we ought not to do any thing good for the hope of the kingdom, but because it so pleaseth God, which is more than any kingdom; what doth he deserve, who because he doth not receive his recompense here, is become more remiss concerning virtue?

Let us then not be troubled when we see that such an one who invited widows and made continual feasts lost his house by fire, or sustained some other such like disaster. Yea, for this very thing he shall receive his reward. For even Job was not so much admired for his alms-deeds as he was for his sufferings afterwards. For this reason his friends also are little esteemed and deemed of no account; because they sought for the recompenses of the present world, and with a view to this gave sentence against the just man. Let us then not seek for our return here; let us not become poor and needy; since surely it is of extreme meanness, when heaven is proposed, and things which are above the heaven, to be looking round on the things which are here. Let us not by any means do so; but whichsoever of unexpected things come upon us, hold we fast the commands of God continually, and obey the blessed Paul.

[7.] And let us make a little chest for the poor at home; and near the place at which you stand praying, there let it be put: and as often as you enter in to pray, first deposit your alms, and then send up your prayer; and as you would not wish to pray with unwashen hands[1], so neither do so without alms: since

not even the Gospel hanging by our bed[2] is more important than that alms should be laid up for you; for if you hang up the Gospel and do nothing, it will do you no such great good. But if you have this little coffer, you have a defence against the devil, you give wings to your prayer, you make your house holy, having meat for the King (S. Mat. xxv. 34.) there laid up in store. And for this reason let the little coffer be placed also near the bed[3], and the night will not be troubled with fantasies. Only let nothing be cast into it, which is the fruit of injustice. For this thing is charity; and it cannot be that charity should ever spring out of hardheartedness.

Will you have mention also of the resources out of which you should make your deposits, so as in this respect also to make this kind of contribution easy? The handicraft man, for instance, the sandal-maker, or the leather-cutter, or the brass-founder, or any other artificer,—when he sells any article of his trade, let him give the first-fruits of its price unto God: let him cast in a small portion here, and assign something to God out of his portion, though it be rather scanty[4]. For neither do I ask any great thing; but so much as the childish ones among the Jews[5], full as they are of innumerable evils, just so much let us cast in, we who look forward to heaven. And this I say not as laying down a law, neither as forbidding more, but as recommending a deposit of not less than a tenth part. And this also do thou practise not in selling only, but also in buying and receiving a recompense. Let those also who possess land observe this law in regard to their rents: yea, let it be a law for all who gather their incomes in an honest way. For with those who demand usury I have no concern, neither with soldiers who do violence to others and turn to their own advantage their neighbors' calamities. Since from that quarter God will accept nothing. But these things I say to those who gather their substance by righteous labor.

Yea, and if we establish ourselves in this kind of habit, we are ever after stung by our conscience if ever we omit this rule; and after a while we shall not even think it a hard thing; and by degrees we shall arrive at the greater things, and by practising how to despise wealth, and by pulling up the root of evils, we shall both pass the present life in peace, and obtain the life to come; which may it be the portion of us all to attain unto, &c. &c

---

[1] S. Chrys. on St. Matt. xv. Hom. 51. "We see this kind of custom prevailing in the Church with most people; they are anxious to come in with clean garments and to wash their hands, but make no account of presenting their soul clean unto God." *Ed. Sav. t.* ii. 328; *cf. Hom.* 73. p. 861; *in Eph.* 3. p. 778. "Tell me, wouldest thou choose with unwashen hands to approach the Sacrifice? Far from it, to my thinking. Thou wouldest rather not come at all, than with defiled hands. Shall the next thing be, that while thou 'art so scrupulous in that which is but a trifle, thou approachest with a soul defiled, and darest to touch It?"

[2] The custom here alluded to may perhaps explain the traditional wish or invocation.
"Matthew, Mark, Luke, and John,
"Bless the bed that I lie on."

[3] The reading seems corrupt. It is rendered as if it were διὰ τοῦτο καὶ παρὰ τῇ κλίνῃ κείσθω τὸ κιβώτιον.

[4] μεριζέσθω πρὸς τον Θεὸν ἐξ ἐλάττονος μοίρας.

[5] Among whom it was a common saying, "Tithes are the Hedge of the Law." Hooker, *E. P.* v. 79. 8. See S. Luke xviii. 12.

HOMILY XLIV.

1 Cor. xvi. 10.

Now if Timothy come to you[1], see that he be with you without fear.

Perhaps some one may think there is something unworthy of Timothy's courage in this piece of advice. But not on Timothy's account is this said, but for the hearers' sake: lest by their design against him they should hurt themselves: since he for his part had his station always in the way of dangers[2].

"For as a child serveth a father," saith he, "so he served with me in furtherance of the Gospel." (Phil. ii. 22.) But lest from boldness towards the disciple they should proceed also to the teacher, and become worse, he checks them from afar off, saying, "that he may be with you without fear;" that is, that none of those desperate persons rise up against him. For he intended perhaps to rebuke them about the things concerning which Paul also had written: and indeed Paul professed to send him for this very reason. "For I have sent Timothy unto you," saith he, (c. iv. 17.) "who shall put you in remembrance of my ways in Christ even as I teach every where in every Church." In order then that they might not through confidence in their high birth and wealth, and the support of the people, and the wisdom from without, attack him and spit upon him and plot against him, being grieved at the reproofs which came from him; or lest in revenge for the teacher's rebuke they should demand satisfaction of him, so punishing the other; therefore he saith, "that he be without fear with you." As if he had said, "Tell me not of those who are without, the Gentiles and unbelievers. It is your part that I require, you for whom also the whole Epistle was composed," the persons also whom in the beginning and the outset he had frightened. Wherefore he saith, "with you."

Then in virtue of his ministry he sets him forth as a person to be fully trusted; saying "For the work of the Lord he worketh." That is; "look not," saith he, "to this, his not being rich, namely, nor highly educated, nor old: but what commands are laid upon him, what work he is doing. 'For the work of the

Lord he worketh.'" And this serves him instead of all nobility and wealth and age and wisdom.

And he is not content with this, but adds, "Even as I also." And some way above, "Who is my beloved son and faithful in the Lord; he shall put you in remembrance of my ways in Christ." Seeing then that he was both young, and had been singly entrusted with the improvement of so numerous a people, both of which things tended to bring him into contempt, he adds, as we might expect,

Ver. 11. "Let no one therefore despise him."

And not this only doth he demand of them, but also greater honor; wherefore also he saith, "but set him forward in peace;" that is, without fear; causing no fightings or contentions, no enmities or hatreds, but rendering all subjection as to a teacher.

"That he may come unto me: for I expect him with the brethren." This also was the language of one that would alarm them. That is, in order that they might become more considerate, as knowing that all would be told him whatever Timothy's treatment might be, he adds therefore, "for I expect him." And besides, hereby he both shows that Timothy is worthy of their confidence; since being on the point of departing he waits for him; and also signifies the love which he hath towards them, it appearing that for their sakes he sent away one so useful to him.

Ver. 12. "But as touching Apollos the brother, I besought nim much to come unto you with the brethren."

This man appears to have been both well-educated and also older than Timothy. Lest they should say then, "For what possible reason did he not send the man grown, but the youth instead of him?" observe how he softens down this point also, both calling him a brother, and saying that he had besought him much. For lest he should seem to have held Timothy in higher honor than him and to have exalted him more, and on this account not to have sent him, and cause their envy to burst out more abundantly, he adds, "I besought him much to come." What then: did not the other yield nor con-

---

[1] πρὸς ὑμᾶς not in rec. text.
[2] πρός κινδύνους ἦν παρεμβεβλημένος.

263

sent? did he resist and show himself contentious? He saith not this, but that he might not excite prejudice against him, and also might make excuse for himself, he saith, " and it was not at all his will to come now." Then to prevent their saying that all this was an excuse and pretence, he added, " but he will come to you when he shall have opportunity." This was both an excuse for him, and a refreshment to them who desired to see him, by the hope which it gave of his coming.

[2.] Afterwards indicating that not in the teachers but in themselves they ought to have their hopes of salvation, he saith,

Ver. 13. " Watch ye, stand fast in the faith."

Not in the wisdom which is without: for there it is not possible to stand, but to be borne along; even as " in the faith " ye may " stand." " Quit you like men, be strong." " Let all that ye do be done in love." Now in saying these things, he seems indeed to advise; but he is reprimanding them as indolent. Wherefore he saith, " Watch," as though they slept; " Stand," as though they were rocking to and fro: " Quit you like men," as though they were playing the coward: " Let all that ye do be done in love," as though they were in dissensions. And the first caution refers to the deceivers, viz., " Watch," " stand : " the next, to those who plot against us, " Quit you like men : " the third, to those who make parties and endeavor to distract, " Let all that ye do be done in love ; " which thing is " the bond of perfectness," and the root and fountain of all blessings.

But what means, " All things in love?" " Whether any one rebuke," saith he, " or rule or be ruled, or learn or teach, let all be in love :" since in fact all the things which have been mentioned arose from neglect of it. For if this had not been neglected, they would not have been puffed up, they would not have said, " I am of Paul, and I of Apollos." If this had existed, they would not have gone to law before heathens, or rather they would not have gone to law at all. If this had existed, that notorious person would not have taken his father's wife : they would not have despised the weak brethren ; there would have been no factions among them; they would not have been vainglorious about their gifts. Therefore it is that he saith, " Let all things be done in love."

[3.] Ver. 15. " Now I beseech you, brethren ;—ye know the house of Stephanas, that it is the first-fruits of Achaia, and that they have set themselves to minister unto the saints."

In the beginning too he mentions this man, saying, " I baptized also the house of Stephanas : " and now he speaks of him as " the first-

fruits " not of Corinth only, but also of all Greece. And this too is no small encomium that he was the first to come to Christ. Wherefore also in the Epistle to the Romans, praising certain persons on this account, he said, " Who also were in Christ before me." (Rom. xvi. 7.) And he said not, that they were the first who believed, but were the " first-fruits ; " implying that together with their faith they showed forth also a most excellent life, in every way proving themselves worthy, as in the case of fruits. For so the first-fruits ought to be better than the rest of those things whereof they are the first-fruits : a kind of praise which Paul hath attributed to these also by this expression : namely, that they not only had a genuine faith, as I was saying, but also they exhibited great piety, and the climax of virtue, and liberality in alms-giving.

And not from hence only, but from another topic likewise he indicates their piety, i. e., from their having filled their whole house also with godliness.

And that they flourished in good works also, he declares by what follows, saying, " They have set themselves to minister unto the saints." Hear ye, how vast are the praises of their hospitality? For he did not say, " they minister," but, " have set themselves : " this kind of life they have chosen altogether, this is their business in which they are always busy.

" That ye also be in subjection unto such, that is, " that ye take a share with them both in expenditure of money, and in personal service : that ye be partakers with them." For both to them the labor will be light when they have comrades, and the results of their active benevolence will extend to more.

And he said not merely, " be fellow-helpers," but added, " whatsoever directions they give, obey ; " implying the strictest obedience. And that he might not appear to be favoring them, he adds, " and to every one that helpeth in the work and laboreth." " Let this," saith he, " be a general rule : for I do not speak about them individually, but if there be any one like them, let him also have the same advantages." And therefore when he begins to commend, he calls upon themselves as witnesses, saying, " I beseech you, ye know the house of Stephanas." " For ye also yourselves are aware," saith he, " how they labor, and have no need to learn from us."

Ver. 17. " But I was glad of the coming of Stephanas and Fortunatus and Achaicus, for that which was lacking on your part they supplied."

Ver. 18. " For they refreshed my spirit and yours."

Thus, since it was natural for them to be

greatly irritated against these persons, for it was they who had come and showed him all about the division, inasmuch as by them also they had written the questions about the virgins, and about the married persons :—mark how he softened them down ; both in the beginning of his Epistle by saying, " For it hath been signified unto me by them which are of the house of Chloe ; " thus at once concealing these and bringing forward the others : (for it should seem that the latter had given their information by means of the former :) and in this place again, " They have supplied your lack, and refreshed my spirit and yours : " signifying that they had come instead of all, and had chosen to undertake so great a journey on their behalf. How then may this, their peculiar praise, become common ? " If you will solace me for what was wanting on your part by your kindness towards them ; if you will honor, if you will receive, them, if you will communicate with them in doing good." Wherefore he saith, " Acknowledge ye then them that are such." And while praising those that came, he embraces also the others in his praise, the senders together with the sent : where he saith, " ' They refreshed my spirit and yours, therefore acknowledge such as these,' because for your sakes they left country and home." Dost thou perceive his consideration ? He implies that they had obliged not Paul only, but the Corinthians likewise, in that they bore about in themselves the whole city. A thing which both added credit to them, and did not allow the others to sever themselves from them, inasmuch as in their persons they had presented themselves to Paul.

Ver. 19. " All the Churches of Asia salute you." He is continually making the members combine and cleave together in one by means of the salutation.

" Aquila and Priscilla salute you much in the Lord ; "—for with them he was lodging, being a tent-maker—" with the Church which is in their house." This thing too is no small excellency, that they had made their very house a Church.

[4.] Ver. 20. " All the brethren salute you. Salute one another with an holy kiss." This addition of the " holy kiss " he makes only[1]

here. What may the reason be ? They had been widely at variance with one another on account of their saying, " I am of Paul, and I of Apollos, and I of Cephas, and I of Christ ; " on account of " one being hungry, and another drunken ; " on account of their having contentions and jealousies and suits. And from the gifts there was much envying and great pride. Having then knit them together by his exhortation, he naturally bids them use the holy kiss[2] also as a means of union : for this unites, and produces one body. This is holy, when free from deceit and hypocrisy.

Ver. 22. " The salutation of me Paul with mine own hand ; " intimates that the Epistle was composed with great seriousness ; and therefore he added,

Ver. 22. " If any man love not our Lord Jesus Christ, let him be anathema."

By this one word he strikes fear into all : those who made their members the members of an harlot ; those who put stumbling blocks in the way of their brethren by the things offered in sacrifice unto idols ; those who named themselves after men ; those who refuse to believe the resurrection. And he not only strikes fear, but also points out the way of virtue and the fountain of vice, viz. that as when our love towards Him hath become intense, there is no kind of sin but is extinguished and cast out thereby ; so when it is too weak, it causes the same to spring up.

" *Maran atha*."[2] For what reason is this word used ? And wherefore too in the Hebrew tongue ? Seeing that arrogance was the cause of

---

[1] [It seems quite certain that the orator was incorrectly reported here. For this direction is found in the Second Epistle (xiii. 12), and also at the close of First Thessalonians (v. 26) and of Romans (xvi. 16). But his explication of the meaning is correct. Tertullian (*de Oratione*, xviii.) speaks of it as "the kiss of peace," and on this account it was eminently fitting that the distracted Church of Corinth should not omit a salutation so significant. The qualifying epithet "holy" was added, not as Chrysostom says in his Homily on the passage in Second Corinthians, in order to distinguish it from a hollow kiss such as Judas gave to our Lord, but to denote its religious and Christian character. It was not a mere expression of domestic kinship and friendship, but a recognition of the tender relation existing between each believer and all the other members of Christ's mystical person. It required to be free from deceit and hypocrisy, but it also needed to be given and

received as a pledge of mutual forgiveness and love, otherwise the whole object of the salutation failed. C.]

[2] That is, the kiss of peace, constantly used as part of the ceremonial of the holy Eucharist ; as appears by all the Primitive Liturgies.

[3] [Chrysostom gives correctly the object of this solemn utterance. It was surely to strike terror into all who by contentiousness, by profligacy, by covetousness, by litigiousness, by idolatry, by arrogance, or in any other way showed that they were destitute of love to Jesus Christ, our Lord and Saviour. For such there is no outlook in the future but perdition. But the answers to the other questions proposed are not so happy. The use of the East Aramæan term *Maran atha* is hardly to be accounted for by supposing that the Apostle wished to cross the conceit of the Corinthians in their Hellenic language and wisdom, although it is harsh in Meyer to pronounce this "singularly absurd." In the absence of any direct clew to the purpose it is well to accept the opinion of Calvin that the Apostle roused by the gravity of the occasion could not satisfy himself without clothing in the older and more sacred dialect the tremendous truth which gave such solemn weight to the anathema. A similar feeling seems to lie at the root of the use of the corresponding terms, *Abba* in Mark xiv. 36, Rom. viii. 15, Gal. iv. 6, (Compare the Hebrew words *Abaddon* and *Armageddon* in the Apocalypse.)

So in regard to the meaning of the words *Maran atha*. They can just as well bear the rendering "The Lord cometh ' as that which Chrysostom gives, " The Lord has come ' " and the connection renders the latter far more likely, notwithstanding Jerome, Erasmus and Castalio agree with the Greek Fathers. Hence nearly all modern interpreters hold that there is a reference to the final Parousia. It is a solemn warning that the approaching advent of the Son of Man would bring about the execution of the dreadful curse, just as in the 25th chapter of Matthew the sentence of the *cursed* is said to be announced and put in force when " the Son of Man comes in his glory and all the angels with him." The reference to the incarnation has significance as emphasizing the greatness of the sin of those who love not the Lord, but the reference to the Second Advent has much more as it exhibits and enforces the certainty and severity of the doom that awaits all such sinners. C.]

all the evils, and this arrogance the wisdom from without produced, and this was the sum and substance of all the evils, a thing which especially distracted Corinth; in repressing their arrogance he did not even use the Greek tongue, but the Hebrew: signifying that so far from being ashamed of that sort of simplicity, he even embraces it with much warmth.

But what is the meaning of "*Maran atha*?" "Our Lord is come." For what reason then doth he use this phrase in particular? To confirm the doctrine of the Economy: out of which class of topics more than any other he hath put together those arguments which are the seeds of the Resurrection[1]. And not only this, but also to rebuke them; as if he had said, "The common Lord of all hath condescended to come down thus far, and are ye in the same state, and do ye abide in your sins? Are ye not thrilled with the excess of His love, the crown of His blessings? Yea, consider but this one thing," saith he, "and it will suffice thee for progress in all virtue, and thou shalt be able to extinguish all sin."

Ver. 23. "The grace of our Lord Jesus Christ be with you."

This is like a teacher, to help not only with advice, but also with prayers.

Ver. 24. "My love be with you all in Christ Jesus, Amen."

Thus to hinder them from thinking that in flattery to them he so ended, he saith, "In Christ Jesus." It having nothing in it human or carnal, but being of a sort of spiritual nature. Wherefore it is thoroughly genuine. For indeed the expression was that of one who loves deeply. As thus; because he was separated from them as regards place, as it were by the stretching out of a right hand he incloses them with the arms of his love, saying, "My love be with you all;" just as if he said, "With all of you I am." Whereby he intimates that the things written came not of wrath or anger, but of provident care, seeing that after so heavy an accusation he doth not turn himself away, but rather loves them, and embraces them when they are afar off, by these epistles and writings throwing himself into their arms.

[5.] For so ought he that corrects to do: since he at least, who acts merely from anger is but satisfying his own feeling; but he who after correcting the sinner renders also the offices of love, shows that those words also, whatsoever he spake in reproof, were words of fond affection. Just so let us too chasten one another; and let neither the corrector be angry, (for this belongs not to correction, but to passion,) nor let him that is corrected take it ill. For what is done is healing, not despite. Now if physi-

cians use cautery and are not found fault with, and that too, frequently, though they quite miss their object; but even in their pain the subjects of the cautery and amputation esteem as benefactors those who excite this pain; much more ought he who receives reproof to be so disposed, and as to a physician so to give heed to the corrector, and not as to an enemy. And let us also who rebuke approach with great gentleness, with great prudence. And if thou seest a brother committing sin, as Christ commanded, make not your rebuke public, but "between thee and him alone:" (Matt. xviii. 15.) not reproaching nor insulting over him when down, but in pain and with a melting heart[2]. And show thyself ready also to receive reproof, if thou commit error in any thing.

Now that what I say may be plainer, let us put an imaginary case and so try our rule. For God forbid that in very deed we should be provided with such an illustration of it. Suppose any brother dwelling in the same house with a virgin, in honor and chastity, and yet not even so quite escaping evil report.[3] If then you should hear talk of this their dwelling together, be not contemptuous, nor say, "Why, hath he no understanding? Doth he not himself know what is for his good? Get love for nothing, but do not for nothing get hatred. Why, what have I to do with taking up a gratuitous enmity?" These are the doting words of wild beasts, or rather of demons: for it is not so that he is hated for nothing who doth this for his brother's correction, rather it is for great blessings and crowns unutterable.

But if thou sayest, "What? hath he no understanding?" thou shalt hear from me that he hath not: drunken as he is with his passion. For if in the heathen courts of justice, [4]those who are injured must not speak for themselves while glowing with wrath; (although there be no fault in that kind of sympathy;) how much more those whom evil habit holds in subjection. Wherefore I say that manifold as his wisdom may be, he hath not his mind awake. For what can be wiser than David, the man who said, "The dark and the hidden things of Thy wisdom Thou hast made known unto me?" (Ps.

---

[1] ἐξ ὧν μάλιστα τὰ σπέρματα τῆς ἀναστάσεως συντέθεικεν.

[2] τηκόμενος.

[3] St. Chrysostom "attacked in the first instance those ecclesiastics who, under pretence of charity, lived with virgins, whom they treated ¡as adopted sisters, who they called 'subintroductæ' or ἀδελφαὶ ἀγαπηταί. Their excuses were, to assist a maiden left desolate without relations or friends; to take care of her affairs, if rich, and to maintain her in charity, if poor . . . . On the other hand, the clergy said they cast on them the burden of their household, and those trifling cares for which women are most proper, in order to be more at liberty for the offices of their ministry. For the rest, they affirmed that in this intimacy there was no sort of criminal liberty, not at all making the less profession of continence. So Chrysostom maintained the contrary; and we have two whole discourses of his on this subject, which seem to have been written about this time," the time of his promotion to the see of Constantinople. Fleury, *E. H.* b. 20. §. 38.

[4]The Areopagus, and other courts resembling it, which allowed no appeals to the passions.

li. 6. ap. LXX. l. 6.) But when he looked on the wife of the soldier with unjust eyes, then according to what he himself said (Ps. cvii. 27.) of those who sail on the raging sea, "all his wisdom was swallowed up;" and he stood in need of others to correct him, and did not even perceive amidst what evils he was. Wherefore also, bewailing his offences, he said, "As a heavy burden they weighed grievously upon me: my wounds stank and were corrupt because[1] of my folly." (Ps. xxxviii. 5.) He therefore that committeth sin hath no understanding. For he is drunken and is in darkness. Do not then say these things, neither add that other remark, "I care not at all about it. 'For each man shall bear his own burden.'" (Gal. vi. 5.) Nay, against thyself also it grows up into a grievous accusation, that seeing one in error thou dost not restore him. For if it was not right according to the law of the Jews (Exod. xxiii. 4, 5.) to slight the beast of one's enemy; he who despises not the beast of burden nor yet the soul of an enemy perishing, but that of a friend, what pardon shall he obtain?

Yea, neither is it enough for our excuse that he hath understanding: since we too after our many and manifold exhortations have not been sufficient, nor proved useful, unto ourselves. Bear this in mind then in regard to him also that is in error; that it is natural he should receive the best counsel rather from thee than from himself.

And say not, "But what care I about these things?" Fear thou him who first spoke this word; for the saying, "Am I my brother's keeper?" (Gen. iv. 9.) tends to the same point as this. This is the mother of all our evils that we esteem the concerns of our own body as foreign to us. What sayest thou? Thou carest not for thy brother? Who then is to care for him? the unbeliever who rejoices over and reproaches and insults him? or the devil who urges him on and supplants him?

And whence comes this? "How do I know that I shall accomplish anything," saith he, "though I speak and advise what is right." But how is it clear that thou wilt do no good? Why, this again is extreme folly, while the end remains in obscurity to incur the manifold blame of confessed indifference. And yet God who foresees the future often speaks and doth no good; yet doth He not even so give up; and that, knowing that He shall not even persuade men. Now if He who knows beforehand that He shall win no advantage, ceases not from the work of correction, what excuse wilt thou have, who art completely ignorant of the future and yet faintest and art benumbed? Yea, and many have succeeded by frequent attempts:

and when they most of all despaired, then did they most gain their point. And though thou shouldest gain no advantage, thou hast done thine own part.

Be not then inhuman, nor unmerciful, nor careless: for that these words come of cruelty and indifference is plain from what follows: viz. What is the reason that when one of the members of thy body is in pain, thou sayest not, "What care I?" Yet whence is it plain, that if it be taken due care of, it is restored? And yet thou leavest nothing undone, that even although thou profit not, thou mayest not have to blame thyself for the omission of any thing which ought to have been done. Hereupon I ask, are we to take such care for the members of our body and to neglect those of Christ? Nay, how can such things deserve pardon?

For if I make no impression upon thee by saying, "Have a care of thine own member;" in order that thou mayest become better were it only through fear, I put thee in mind of the body of Christ. But how can it be other than a matter of horror to see His flesh putrefying, and neglect it? And if thou hadst a slave or an ass afflicted with a mortifying sore, thou couldest not have the heart to neglect it: but seest thou the Body of Christ full of scurvy[2], and hurriest by? and thinkest not that such things deserve innumerable thunder-bolts? For this cause all things are turned upside down, because of this our inhumanity, because of our indifference. Wherefore now, I beseech you, let this cruelty be cast out from among us.

[6.] Draw near to him whom I speak of, as dwelling with a virgin, and speak some small praise of thy brother, making it up from the other excellencies which he hath. And foment him with thy commendations as it were with warm water, and so mitigate the tumor of his wound. Speak of thyself also as wretched; accuse the common race of mankind; point out that we are all in sins; ask for pardon, saying, that thou art undertaking things too great for thee, but love persuades thee to dare all things. Then in giving thine advice, do it not imperiously, but in a brotherly way. And when by all these means thou hast reduced the swelling and soothed the pain arising from the cutting reproof which is in store for him, and when thou hast again and again deprecated and besought him not to be angry: when thou hast bound him down with these things, then use the knife; neither pressing the matter too close, nor yet undoing it; that he may neither fly off on the one hand, nor on the other think little of it. For if thou strike not to the quick thou hast done no good, and if thy blow be violent, thou makest him start away.

---

[1] ἀπὸ προσώπου, "before the face."

[2] ψώρας.

Wherefore, even after all this, being on the very point of the reproof, mix up again commendation with thy censures. And seeing that this proceeding considered in itself cannot be matter of praise, (for it is not commendable to keep house with a damsel that is a virgin;) let the purpose of him who doth so be thy topic for effecting this; and say, "I know indeed that thou doest it for God's sake, and that the desolation and unprotected state of that poor woman met thine eye, and caused thee to stretch out thine hand to her." And although he may not be doing it with this intention, do thou speak so; and after this add what follows also; again excusing thyself and saying, "These things I speak not to direct but to remind thee. Thou doest it for God's sake; I too know that. But let us see whether another evil be not produced thereby. And if there be none, keep her in thine house, and cling to this excellent purpose. There is no one to hinder thee. But if any mischief arise from hence exceeding the advantage, let us take care, I beseech you, lest while we are earnest to comfort one soul, we put a stumbling-block in the way of ten thousand." And do not add immediately the punishments due to those who give offence, but take his own testimony also, saying, "Thou hast no need to learn these things from me: thou thyself knowest, 'if any one offend one of these little ones,' how great a penalty is threatened. And thus, having sweetened thy speech and smoothed down his wrath, apply the medicine of thy correction. And should he again urge her forlorn condition, do not thou even so expose his pretence, but say to him, "Let nothing of this sort make you afraid: thou wilt have an ample plea, the offence given to others: since not for indifference, but in care towards them, didst thou cease from this thy purpose."

And let the matter of thine advice be brief, for there is no need of much teaching; but let the expressions of forbearance on the other hand be many and close upon one another. And continually have thou recourse to the topic of love; throwing into shade the painfulness of what thou sayest, and giving him his full power, and saying, "This is what I for my part advise and recommend; but about taking the advice thou art only judge: for I do not compel and force thee, but submit the whole thing to thine own discretion."

If we so manage our reproof, we shall easily be able in correct those in error: even as what we now do is surely more like the conduct of wild beasts or irrational creatures than of men. For if any persons now perceive any one committing errors of this kind, with the person himself they do not at all confer, but themselves, like silly old women who have drunk too much,

whisper with another. And the saying, "Get love for nothing, but do not get hatred for nothing," hath not here any place in their opinion. But, when they have a fancy to speak evil, they mind not being "hated for nothing," rather I should say, "being punished;" since it is not hatred alone that is hereby produced, but also punishment. But when there is need of correction, they allege both this, and innumerable other pretexts. Whereas then would be the time to think of these things, when thou speakest evil, when thou calumniatest; I mean the saying, "Be not hated for nothing," and "I can do nothing," and "it is no care of mine." But as things are, in the former case, thou art vehemently and idly curious, and carest not for hatred and ills innumerable; but when thou shouldest be taking thought for the salvation of thy brother, then it is thy pleasure to be a sort of unofficious, inoffensive person. And yet from evil speaking arises hatred both on God's part and on men's; and this is no great care to thee: but by giving advice privately, and reproofs of that kind, both he and God will be made thy friends. And even should he hate thee, God goes on loving thee the rather on this account. Nay, in fact, not even so will he hate thee, as when his hatred came from thine evil speaking: but in that case he will avoid thee as a foe and an enemy, whereas now he will consider thee more venerable than any father. And if he apparently take it ill, inwardly and privately he will feel much obliged to thee.

[7] Bearing in mind these things therefore let us have a care of our own members, and not sharpen the tongue against one another, nor speak words "which may do hurt,[1]" undermining the fame of our neighbor, and as in war and battle, giving and receiving blows. For what after all is the good of fasting or watching, when the tongue is drunken, and feasts itself at a table more unclean than of dog's flesh; when it is grown ravening after blood, and pours out filth, and makes the mouth a channel of a sewer, nay rather something more abominable than that? For that which proceeds from thence pollutes the body: but what comes from the tongue often suffocates the soul.

These things I say, not in anxiety about those who have an ill report falsely: for they are worthy even of crowns, when they bear what is said nobly; but in anxiety for you that so speak. For him that is evil reported of falsely, the Scriptures pronounce "blessed;" but the evil-speaker they expel from the holy Mysteries, nay even from the very precincts. For it is

---

[1] ῥήματα καταποντισμοῦ. Ps. 52. 4. ap. lxx, 51. 4. "Words of swallowing up in the sea;" i. e., as St. Augustin on the place intimates, "words so sinful that they plunge the swimmer again in the deep, and complete his shipwreck, when by repentance he ought to lay hold of the cross."

said, (Ps. ci. 5.) "Him that privily speaketh against his neighbor, this man did I chase out. And he saith too that such a one is unworthy to read the sacred books. For, "Why," saith He, (Ps. l. 16.) "dost thou declare My righteous laws, and takest My covenant in thy mouth?" Then, annexing the cause He saith (v. 20.) "Thou satest and spakest against thy brother." And here indeed he doth not distinctly add whether they be things true or false which he speaks. But elsewhere this too makes part of His prohibition: He implying, that even though thou speak truths, yet such things are not to be uttered by thee. For, "Judge not," saith He, "that ye be not judged:" (Matt. vii. 1.) since he too who spoke evil of the publican was condemned, although it was true which he laid to his neighbor's charge.

"What then," you will say, "if any one be daring and polluted, must we not correct him? must we not expose him?" We must both expose and correct: but in the way which I mentioned before. But if thou do it upbraiding him, take heed lest thine imitation of that Pharisee cause thee to fall into his state. For no advantage accrues from hence; none to thee who speakest, none to him who hears thee, none to the person accused. But the latter, for his part, becomes more reckless: since as long as he is unobserved, he is sensible of shame; but as soon as he becomes manifest and notorious, he casts off the curb also which that feeling imposed on him.

And the hearer will in his turn be yet more injured. For whether he be conscious to himself of good deeds, he becomes puffed and swoln up with the accusation brought against another; or of faults, he then becomes more eager for iniquity.

Thirdly, the speaker too himself will both incur the bad opinion of the hearer, and will provoke God to more anger against himself.

Wherefore, I beseech you, let us cast from us every word that is unsavory. If there be any thing good unto edification, this let us speak.

But hast thou a fancy to avenge thyself on the other person? Why then punish thyself instead of him? Nay, do thou, who art so earnestly seeking redress from those who have annoyed thee, avenge thyself as Paul recommended to take vengeance. "If thine enemy hunger, feed him; if he thirst, give him drink" (Rom. xii. 20.) But if thou do not so, but only plot against him, thou pointest the sword against thyself.

Wherefore if that other speak evil, answer him with praises and commendations. For so wilt thou be able both to take vengeance on him, and wilt deliver thyself from evil surmising. Since he that feels pain at hearing ill of himself, is thought to be so affected because of some consciousness of evil: but he that laughs to scorn what is said, exhibits a most unquestionable token of his not being conscious to himself of any evil thing.[1]

Seeing then that thou profitest neither thine hearer, nor thyself, nor him that is accused, and dost but point thy sword at thine own self, even from such considerations do thou learn more soberness. For one ought indeed to be moved by the thought of the kingdom of heaven, and of what pleases God: but since thou art of grosser disposition and bitest like a wild beast, hereby even be thou instructed; that these arguments having corrected thee, thou mayest be able to order thyself simply from consideration of what pleases God; and having come to be above every passion, mayest obtain the heavenly blessings:—which may God grant us all to obtain, through the grace of our Lord Jesus Christ, and His mercy towards mankind; with Whom, to the Father and the Holy Spirit, be glory, power, honor, now and henceforth, and unto everlasting ages. Amen.

---

[1] [It is impossible to read this Homily without being struck with the consummate skill of the great Christian orator. Nowhere in the literature that preceded or followed him is to be found a better exposition of the duty of reproof or of the manner in which it is to be performed. The disciple must have drunk deeply in the Spirit of the Master to be able to set forth a difficult and delicate obligation in such a wise and winning form. Nothing is overlooked, nothing carelessly stated. C.]

HOMILIES OF ST. JOHN CHRYSOSTOM,

ARCHBISHOP OF CONSTANTINOPLE,

ON THE

SECOND EPISTLE OF ST. PAUL THE APOSTLE.

TO THE

CORINTHIANS

HOMILY I

2 COR. i. 1, 4.

Paul, an Apostle of Jesus Christ through the will of God, and Timothy our brother, unto the Church of God, which is at Corinth, with all the saints which are in the whole of Achaia : grace to you and peace from God our Father and the Lord Jesus Christ. Blessed be the God and Father of our Lord Jesus Christ, the Father of mercies and God of all comfort ; Who comfort us in all our affliction, that we may be able to comfort them that are in any affliction through the comfort wherewith we ourselves are comforted of God.

It is meet to enquire, first, why to the former Epistle he adds a second : and what can be his reason for thus beginning with the mercies and consolation of God.

Why then does he add a second Epistle? Whereas in the first he had said, "I will come to you, and will know not the word of them which are puffed up, but the power ; " (1 Cor. iv. 19.) and again towards the end had promised the same in milder terms, thus, " I will come unto you when I shall have passed through Macedonia ; for I do pass through Macedonia ; and it may be that I shall abide, or even winter with you ;" (1 Cor. xvi. 5, 6.) yet now after a long interval, he came not ; but was still lingering and delaying even though the time appointed had passed away ; the Spirit detaining him in other matters of far greater necessity than these. For this reason he had need to write a second Epistle, which he had not needed had he but a little out-tarried his time.[1]

But not for this reason only, but also because they were amended by the former ; for him that had committed fornication whom before they applauded and were puffed up about, they had cut off and separated altogether. And this he shows where he says, "But if any hath caused sorrow, he hath caused sorrow not to me, but in part (that I press not too heavily) to you all. Sufficient to such a one is this punishment which was inflicted by the many." (2 Cor. ii. 5, 6.) And as he proceeds, he alludes again to the same thing when he says, " For behold that ye were made sorry after a godly sort, what earnest care it wrought in you, yea, what clearing of yourselves, yea, what indignation, yea, what fear, yea, what longing, yea, what zeal, yea, what avenging ! In every thing ye approved yourselves to be pure in this matter." (2 Cor. vii. 11.) Moreover, the collection[2] which he enjoined, they gathered with much forwardness. Wherefore also he says, "For I know your readiness of which I glory on your behalf to them of Macedonia, that Achaia hath been prepared for a year past." (2 Cor. ix. 2.) And Titus too, whom he sent, they received with all kindness, as he shows when he says again, " His inward affection is more abundantly toward you, whilst he remembereth the obedience of you all, how with fear and trembling ye received him." (2 Cor. vii. 15.) For all these reasons he writes the second Epistle. For it was right

---

[1] εἰ παρὰ μικρὸν ὑστέρησεν.

[2] λογίαν, Ben. εὐλογίαν, bounty, as 2 Cor. ix. 5. Engl. Vers.

that, as when they were in fault he rebuked them, so upon their amendment he should approve and commend them. On which account the Epistle is not very severe[1] throughout, but only in a few parts towards the end. For there were even amongst them Jews who thought highly of themselves, and accused Paul as being a boaster and worthy of no regard; whence also that speech of theirs; "His letters are weighty, but his bodily presence is weak, and his speech of no account:" (2 Cor. x. 10.) meaning thereby, when he is present he appears of no account, (for this is the meaning of, "his bodily presence is weak,") but when he is away he boasts greatly in what he writes, (for such is the signification of "his letters are weighty.") Moreover, to enhance their own credit these persons made a pretence of receiving nothing, to which he also alludes where he says, "that wherein they glory, they may be found even as we." (2 Cor. xi. 12.) And besides, possessing also the power of language, they were forthwith greatly elated. Wherefore also he calls himself "rude in speech," (2. Cor. xi. 6.) showing that he is not ashamed thereof; nor deems the contrary any great acquisition. Seeing then it was likely that by these persons some would be seduced, after commending what was right in their conduct, and beating down their senseless[2] pride in the things of Judaism, in that out of season they were contentious to observe them, he administers a gentle[3] rebuke on this subject also.

[2.] Such then, to speak summarily and by the way, appears to me the argument of this Epistle. It remains to consider the introduction, and to say why after his accustomed salutation he begins, as he does, with the mercies of God. But first, it is necessary to speak of the very beginning, and inquire why he here associates Timothy with himself. For, he saith, "Paul an Apostle of Jesus Christ through the will of God, and Timothy our brother." In the first Epistle he promised he would send him; and charged them, saying, "Now if Timothy come, see that he be with you without fear." (1 Cor. xvi. 10.) How then is it that he associates him here in the outset with himself? After he had been amongst them, agreeably to that promise of his teacher, "I have sent unto you Timothy who shall put you in remembrance of my ways which be in Christ," (1 Cor. iv. 17.) and had set everything in order, he had returned back to Paul; who on sending him, had said, "Set him forward on his journey in peace that he may come to me, for I expect him with the brethren." (1 Cor. xvi. 11.)

Since then Timothy was restored to his teacher, and after having with him set in order the things in Asia, (for, says he, "I will tarry at Ephesus until Pentecost," 1 Cor. xvi. 8;) had crossed again into Macedonia; Paul not unreasonably associates him hereafter as abiding with himself. For then he wrote from Asia, but now from Macedonia. Moreover, thus associating him he at once gains increased respect for him, and displays his own exceeding humility[4]: for Timothy was very inferior to himself, yet doth love bring all things together. Whence also he everywhere makes him equal with himself; at one time saying, "as a child serveth a father so he served with me;" (Phil. ii. 22.) at another, "for he worketh the work of the Lord, as I also do;" (1 Cor. xvi. 10.) and here, he even calleth him, "brother;" by all making him an object of respect to the Corinthians amongst whom he had been, as I have said, and given proof of his worth.

"To the Church of God which is at Corinth." Again he calleth them "the Church," to bring and bind them all together in one. For it could not be one Church, while those within her were sundered and stood apart. "With all the saints which are in the whole of Achaia. In thus saluting all through the Epistle addressed to the Corinthians, he would at once honor these, and bring together the whole nation. But he calls them "saints," thereby implying that if any be an impure person, he hath no share in this salutation. But why, writing to the mother city, does he address all through her, since he doth not so everywhere? For instance, in his Epistle to the Thessalonians he addressed not the Macedonians also; and in like manner in that to the Ephesians he doth not include all Asia; neither was that to the Romans written to those also who dwell in Italy. But in this Epistle he doth so; and in that to the Galatians. For there also he writeth not to one city, or two, or three, but to all who are scattered every where, saying, "Paul an Apostle, (not from men neither through man, but through Jesus Christ, and God the Father, Who raised Him from the dead,) and all the brethren which are with me, unto the Churches of Galatia. Grace to you and peace." (Gal. i. 1—3.) To the Hebrews also he writes one Epistle to all collectively; not distinguishing them into their several cities. What can be the reason of this? Because, as I think, in this case all were involved in one common disorder, wherefore also he addresses them in common, as needing one common remedy. For the Galatians were all of them infected. So too were the Hebrews, and so I think these (Achaians) also.

---

[1] καταφορικωτέρα.
[2] ἀπόνοιαν.
[3] συμμέτρως.

[4] σεμνότερον ποιῶν.

[3.] So then having brought the whole nation together in one, and saluted them with his accustomed greeting, for, saith he, "Grace to you and peace from God our Father and the Lord Jesus Christ:" (2 Cor. i. 2.) hear how aptly to the purpose in hand he begins, "Blessed be the God and Father of our Lord Jesus Christ, the Father of mercies and God of all comfort." (ver. 3.) Do you ask, how is this aptly to the purpose in hand? I reply, Very much so; for observe, they were greatly vexed and troubled that the Apostle had not come to them, and that, though he had promised, but had spent the whole time in Macedonia; preferring as it seemed others to themselves. Setting himself then to meet this feeling[1] against him, he declares the cause of his absence; not however directly stating it, as thus; "I know, indeed, I promised to come, but since I was hindered by afflictions forgive me, nor judge me guilty of any sort of contempt or neglect towards you:" but after another manner he invests the subject at once with more dignity and trustworthiness, and gives it greatness by the nature of the consolation[2], so that thereafter they might not so much as ask the reason of his delay. Just as if one, having promised to come to one he longed for, at length arriving after dangers innumerable, should say, ",Glory to Thee, O God, for letting me see the sight so longed for of his dear countenance! Blessed be Thou, O God, from what perils hast Thou delivered me!" for such a doxology is an answer to him who was preparing to find fault, and will not let him so much as complain of the delay; for one that is thanking God for deliverance from such great calamities he cannot for shame drag to the bar, and bid clear himself of loitering. Whence Paul thus begins, "Blessed be the God of mercies," implying by the very words that he had been both brought into and delivered from mighty perils. For as David also doth not address God every where in one way or with the same titles; but when he is upon battle and victory, "I will love Thee, he saith, O Lord my strength; the Lord is my buckler[3]:" when again upon delivery from affliction and the darkness which overwhelmed him, "The Lord is my light and my salvation;" (Ps. xxvii. 1.) and as the immediate occasion suggests, he names Him now from His loving-kindness, now from His justice, now from His righteous judgment:—in like way Paul also here at the beginning describeth Him by His loving-kindness, calling Him "the God of mercies," that is, "Who hath showed me so great mercies as to bring me up from the very gates of death."

And thus to have mercy is the peculiar and excellent attribute of God, and the most inherent in His nature; whence he calleth Him the "God of mercies."

And observe, I pray you, herein also the lowly-mindedness of Paul. For though he were in peril because of the Gospel he preached; yet saith he not, he was saved for his merit, but for the mercies of God. But this he afterwards declareth more clearly, and now goes on to say, "Who comforteth us in all affliction." (2 Cor. i. 4.) He saith not, "Who suffereth us not to come into affliction:" but, "Who comforteth in affliction." For this at once declareth the power of God; and increaseth the patience of those afflicted. For, saith he, "tribulation worketh patience." (Rom. v. 3.) And so also the prophet, "Thou hast set me at large when I was in distress." (Ps. iv. 1.) He doth not say, "Thou hast not suffered me to fall into affliction," nor yet, "Thou hast quickly removed my affliction," but, whilst it continueth, "Thou hast set me at large:" (Dan. iii. 21. &c.) that is, "hast granted me much freedom and refreshment." Which truly happened also in the case of the three children, for neither did He prevent their being cast into the flame, nor when so cast, did He quench it, but while the furnace was burning He gave them liberty. And such is ever God's way of dealing; as Paul also implies when he says, "Who comforteth us in all affliction."

But he teaches something more in these words: Do you ask what? Namely, that God doeth this not once, nor twice, but without intermission. For He doth not one while comfort, another not, but ever and constantly. Wherefore he saith, "Who comforteth," not, "Who hath comforted," and, "in all affliction," not, "in this or that," but, "in all."

"That we may be able to comfort them which are in any affliction through the comfort wherewith we ourselves are comforted of God." See you not how he is beforehand[4] with his defence by suggesting to the hearer the thought of some great affliction; and herein also is his modesty again apparent, that he saith not for their own merits was this mercy showed, but for the sake of those that need their assistance; "for," saith he, "to this end hath He comforted us that we might comfort one another." And hereby also he manifesteth the excellency of the Apostles, shewing that having been comforted and breathed awhile, he lieth not softly down as we, but goeth on his way to anoint[5], to nerve, to rouse others. Some, however, consider this as the Apostle's meaning. "Our consolation is that of others also:" but my opinion is that in

---

[1] τὸ ἀνθορμοῦν.
[2] ἐπαίρων τῇ παραμυθίᾳ τὸ πρᾶγμα.
[3] ὑπερασπιστής Gr.

[4] προανακρούεται.
[5] i. e., for the combat.

this introduction, he is also censuring the false Apostles, those vain boasters who sat at home and lived in luxury; but this covertly and, as it were, incidentally, the leading object being to apologise for his delay. "For," [he would say,] "if for this end we were comforted that we might comfort others also, do not blame us that we came not; for in this was our whole time spent, in providing against the conspiracies, the violence, the terrors which assailed us."

[4.] "For as the sufferings of Christ abound unto us, even so our comfort also aboundeth through Christ." Not to depress the disciples by an aggravated account of his sufferings; he declareth on the other hand that great and superabundant was the consolation also, and lifteth up[1] their heart not hereby alone, but also by putting them in mind of Christ and calling the sufferings "His," and [2]prior to the consolation deriveth a comfort from the very sufferings themselves. For what joy can I have so great as to be partaker with Christ, and for His sake to suffer these things? What consolation can equal this? But not from this source only does he raise the spirits of the afflicted, but from another also. Ask you what other? In that he saith, "abound:" for he doth not say, "As the sufferings of Christ" are "in us," but as they "abound," thereby declaring that they endure not His sufferings only, but even more than these[3]. For, saith he, "not whatsoever He suffered, that have we suffered; "but even more[4]," for, consider, "Christ was cast out, persecuted, scourged, died," but we, saith he, "more than all this," which even of itself were consolation enough. Now let no one condemn this speech of boldness; for he elsewhere saith, "Now I rejoice in my sufferings, and fill up on my part that which is lacking of the afflictions of Christ in my flesh." (Col. i. 24.) Yet neither here nor there is it from boldness or any presumptuousness. For as they wrought greater miracles than He according to that saying of His, "he that believeth on Me shall do

greater works than these," (John xiv. 12.) but all is of Him that worketh in them; so did they suffer also more than He, but all again is of Him that comforteth them, and fitteth them to bear the evils that betide them.

With which respect Paul aware how great a thing he had said, doth again remarkably restrain it by adding, "So our comfort also aboundeth through Christ;" thus at once ascribing all to Him, and proclaiming herein also His loving-kindness; for, he saith not, "As our affliction, such our consolation;" but "far more;" for, he saith not, "our comfort is equal to our sufferings," but, "our comfort aboundeth," so that the season of struggles was the season also of fresh crowns. For, say, what is equal to being scourged for Christ's sake and holding converse with God; and being more than match for all things, and gaining the better of those who cast us out, and being unconquered by the whole world, and expecting hence such good things "as eye hath not seen, nor ear heard, neither have entered into the heart of man!" (1 Cor. ii. 9.) And what is equal to suffering affliction for godliness' sake, and receiving from God consolations infinite, and being rescued from sins so great, and counted worthy of the Spirit, and of being sanctified and justified, and regarding no man with fear and trembling, and in peril itself outshining all.

[5.] Let us then not sink down when tempted. For no self-indulger hath fellowship with Christ, nor sleeper, nor supine [person], nor any of these lax and dissolute livers. But whoso is in affliction and temptation, this man standeth near to Him, whoso is journeying on the narrow way. For He Himself trode this; whence too He saith, "the Son of Man hath not where to lay His head." So then grieve not when thou art in affliction; considering with Whom thou hast fellowship, and how thou art purified by trials; and how great gain is thine. For there is nothing miserable save the offending against God; but this apart, neither afflictions nor conspiracies, nor any other thing hath power to grieve the right-minded soul: but like as a little spark, if thou cast it into a mighty deep, thou presently puttest it out, so doth even a total and excessive sorrow if it light on a good conscience easily die away and disappear.

Such then was the spring of Paul's continual joy: because in whatever was of God he was full of hope; and did not so much as take count of ills so great, but though he grieved as a man yet sank not. So too was that Patriarch encompassed with joy in the midst of much painful suffering; for consider, he forsook his country, underwent journeyings long and hard; when he came into a strange land, had "not so

---

[1] ἀνίστησιν. The word has here probably the double sense, "raiseth up the depressed," and "lifteth upward towards heaven."

[2] πρὸ τῆς παρακλήσεως.

[3] St. Chrysostom does not, of course, mean, for an instant, to compare the sufferings of the Apostles with those of our Lord *in themselves*, but in one point only, their number. His sufferings alone were meritorious and well-pleasing in themselves, their's in Him only; His turned away the Father's wrath, their's were accepted by Him, when reconciled; His were spiritual also, their's bodily only; His were borne by His own power, through His divinity, their's not by their own, but through His indwelling Spirit; but, while of course, beyond all thought inferior in every other respect, S. Chrsostom infers from the Apostle's words, that their bodily sufferings outnumber His, though these also were, (he insists throughout) not their's, but His in these His members, bestowed by Him, borne through Him and acceptable in Him. The whole comment is a development of the word περισσεύει "aboundeth," whence he infers that they were "more abundant," περισσά: (as, plainly, the bodily sufferings of the army of Martyrs have been more *numerous*.) Yet though true, the statement, if repeated by one less reverent and not corrected by the vivid consciousness that these too were His sufferings, would become profane.

[4] περισσά, περισσεύει.

much as to set his foot on." (Acts. vii. 5.) Then again a famine awaited him which made him once more a wanderer; after the famine again came the seizure of his wife, then the fear of death, and child-lessness, and battle, and peril, and conspiracies, and at the last that crowning trial, the slaying of his only-begotten and true[1] son, that grievous irreparable [sacrifice.] For think not, I pray you, that because he readily obeyed, he felt not all the things he underwent. For though his righteousness had been, as indeed it was, ines-timable[2], yet was he a man and felt as nature bade. But yet did none of these things cast him down, but he stood like a noble athlete, and for each one was proclaimed and crowned a victor. So also the blessed Paul, though see-ing trials in very snow-showers assailing him daily, rejoiced and exulted as though in the mid-delights of Paradise. As then he who is gladdened with this joy cannot be a prey to de-spair; so he who maketh not this his own is easily overcome of all; and is as one that hath unsound armor, and is wounded by even a common stroke: but not so he who is well en-cased at all points, and proof against every shaft that cometh upon him. And truly stouter than any armor is joy in God; and whoso hath it, nothing can ever make his head droop or his countenance sad, but he beareth all things nobly. For what is worse to bear than fire? what more painful than continual torture? truly it is more overpowering[3] in pain than the loss of untold wealth, of children, of any thing; for, saith he, "Skin for skin, yea, all that a man hath will he give for his life." (Job ii.4.) So nothing can be harder to bear than bodily pain; nevertheless, because of this joy in God, what even to hear of is intolerable, becomes both tolerable and longed for: and if thou take from the cross or from the gridiron the martyr yet just breathing, thou wilt find such a treasure of joy within him as admits not of being told.

[6.] And doth any one say, What am I to do[4]; for now is no time of martyrdom? What sayest thou? Is now no time of martyrdom? Never is it not a time; but ever is it before our eyes; if we[5] will keep them open. For it is not the hanging on a cross only that makes a Martyr, for were this so, then was Job excluded from this crown; for he neither stood at bar, nor heard Judge's voice, nor looked on execu-tioner; no, nor while hanging on tree aloft had his sides mangled; yet he suffered worse than many martyrs; more sharply than any stroke did the tale of those successive messengers strike

and goad him on every side: and keener the gnawings of the worms which devoured him in every part than thousand executioners.

Against what martyr then may he not worth-ily be set? Surely against ten thousand. For in every kind [of suffering] he both wrestled and was crowned; in goods, and children, and person, and wife, and friends, and enemies, and servants, (for these too even did spit in his face,) in hunger and visions and pains and noisomeness; it was for this I said he might worthily be set, not against one nor two nor three, but against ten thousand Martyrs. For besides what I have mentioned, the time also maketh a great addition to his crown; in that it was before the Law, before Grace, he thus suffered, and that, many months, and each in its worst form; and all these evils assailed him at once. And yet each individual evil by itself intolerable, even that which seemeth most toler-able, the loss of his goods. For many have patiently borne stripes, but could not bear the loss of their goods; but rather than relinquish any part of them were content even to be scourged for their sake and suffer countless ills; and this blow, the loss of goods, appeared to them heavier than all. So then here is another method of martyrdom for one who bears this loss nobly. And doth any ask, How shall we bear it nobly? When thou hast learned that by one word of thanksgiving thou shalt gain more than all thou hast lost. For if at the tidings of our loss we be not troubled, but say, "Bless-ed be God," we have found far more abundant riches. For truly such great fruit thou shalt not reap by expending all thy wealth on the needy, by going about and seeking out the poor, and scattering thy substance to the hungry, as thou shalt gain by the same word. And so neither Job do I admire so much in setting wide his house to the needy, as I am struck with and extol his taking the spoiling of his substance thankfully. The same in the loss of children it happeneth to see. For herein, also, reward no less than his who offered[6] his son and pre-sented him in sacrifice shalt thou receive, if as thou seest thine die thou shalt thank the God of love. For how shalt such an one be less than Abraham? He saw not his son stretched out a corpse, but only looked to do so. So if he gain in the comparison by his purpose to slay and his stretching forth his hand to take the knife, (Gen. xxii. 10.) yet doth he lose in that the child is lying dead here. And besides, he had some comfort in the prospect of a good work done, and the thought that this so excellent achievement was the work of his own fortitude, and that the voice he heard came from above made him the readier. But here is

---

[1] γνησίον, i. e, the son of the true wife, as opposed to the son of the bondwoman.
[2] μυριάκις δίκαιος.
[3] τυραννικώτερον.
[4] τί πάθω.
[5] ἐὰν νήφωμεν.

[6] ἀναγαγόντος, see Acts vii. 41.

no such thing. So that he had need have a soul of adamant, who can bear with calmness to see a child, his only one, brought up in affluence, in the dawn[1] of fair promise, lying upon the bier[2] an outstretched corpse. And should such an one, hushing to rest the heavings of nature, be strengthened to say the words of Job without a tear, "The Lord gave, the Lord hath taken away;" (Job. i. 21.) for those words' sake alone, he shall stand with Abraham himself and with Job be proclaimed a victor. And if, staying the wailings of the women and breaking up the bands of mourners, he shall rouse them all to sing glory [to God], he shall receive above, below, rewards unnumbered; men admiring, angels applauding, God crowning him.

[7.] And sayest thou, How is it possible for one that is man not to mourn? I reply, If thou wilt reflect how neither the Patriarch nor Job, who both were men, gave way to any thing of the kind; and this too in either case before the Law, and Grace, and the excellent wisdom of the laws [we have]: if thou wilt account that the deceased has removed into a better country, and bounded away to a happier inheritance, and that thou hast not lost thy son but bestowed him henceforward in an inviolable spot. Say not then, I pray thee, I am no longer called "father," for why art thou no longer called so, when thy son abideth? For surely thou didst not part with thy child nor lose thy son? Rather thou hast gotten him, and hast him in greater safety. Wherefore, no longer shalt thou be called "father" here only, but also in heaven; so that thou hast not lost the title "father," but hast gained it in a nobler sense; for henceforth thou shalt be called father not of a mortal child, but of an immortal; of a noble soldier; on duty continually within [the palace]. For think not because he is not present that therefore he is lost; for had he been absent in a foreign land, the title of thy relationship had not gone from thee with his body. Do not then gaze on the countenance of what lieth there, for so thou dost but kindle afresh thy grief; but away with thy thought from him that lieth there, up to heaven. That is not thy child which is lying there, but he who hath flown away and sprung aloft into boundless height. When then thou seest the eyes closed, the lips locked together, the body motionless, Oh be not these thy thoughts, "These lips no longer speak, these eyes no longer see, these feet no longer walk, but are all on their way to corruption!" Oh say not so: but say the reverse of this, "These lips shall speak better, and the eyes see greater things, and the feet shall mount upon the clouds; and this body which now rotteth away shall put on immortality, and I shall receive my son back more glorious. But if what thou seest distress thee, say to thyself the while, This is [only] clothing and he has put it off to receive it back more precious; this is an house and it is taken down to be restored in greater splendor. For like as we, when purposing to take houses down, allow not the inmates to stay, that they may escape the dust and noise; but causing them to remove a little while, when we have built up the tenement securely, admit them freely; so also doth God; Who taking down this His decaying tabernacle hath received him the while into His paternal dwelling and unto Himself, that when it hath been taken down and built anew He may then return it to him more glorious.

Say not then, "He is perished and shall no more be;" for these be the words of unbelievers; but say, "He sleepeth and will rise again," "He is gone a journey and will return with the King." Who sayeth this? He[3] that hath Christ speaking in him. "For," saith he, "if we believe that Jesus died and rose again" and revived, "even so them also which sleep in Jesus will God bring with Him." (1 Thess. iv. 14.) If then thou seek thy son, there seek him where the King is, where is the army of the Angels; not in the grave; not in the earth; lest whilst he is so highly exalted, thyself remain grovelling on the ground.

If we have this true wisdom, we shall easily repel all this kind of distress; and "the God of mercies and Father of all comfort" comfort all our hearts, both those who are oppressed with such grief and those held down with any other sorrow; and grant us deliverance from all despair and increase of spiritual joy; and to obtain the good things to come; whereunto may all we attain, through the grace and loving-kindness of our Lord Jesus Christ, with Whom unto the Father, together with the Holy Spirit, be glory, power, honor, now and ever, and world without end. Amen.

---

[1] ὑποφαίνοντα
[2] βάθρον, bench, Ben βόθρου.

[3] e Paul See 2 Cor. xiii. 3.

HOMILY II.

2 COR. i. 6, 7.

Whether we be afflicted, it is for your comfort and salvation, which worketh in the patient enduring of the same sufferings which we also suffer : and our hope for you is steadfast.

HAVING spoken of one, and that the chief ground of comfort and consolation, namely, having fellowship [by sufferings] with Christ : he layeth down as second this which he now mentions, namely, that the salvation of the disciples themselves was procured thereby. " Faint not, therefore, he says, nor be confounded and afraid because we are afflicted ; for this same thing were rather a reason for your being of good cheer : for had we not been afflicted, this had been the ruin of you all." How and wherein ? For if through lack of spirit[1] and fear of danger we had not preached unto you the word whereby ye learned the true knowledge, your situation had been desperate. Seest thou again the vehemence and earnest contention[2] of Paul ? The very things which troubled them he uses for their comfort. For, saith he, the greater the intensity of our persecutions, the greater should be the increase of your good hope ; because the more abundant also in proportion is your salvation and consolation. For what hath equal force of consolation with this of having obtained such good things through the preaching. Then that he may not seem to be bringing[3] the encomium round to himself alone, see how he maketh them too to share these praises. For to the words, " Whether we be afflicted, it is for your comfort and salvation : " he adds, " which worketh in the patient enduring of the same sufferings which we also suffer." (ver. 7.) Afterwards, indeed, he states this more clearly, thus saying, " As ye are partakers of the sufferings, so also are ye of the consolation ; " but here also meanwhile he alludes to it in the words, " the same sufferings," so making[4] what he says include them. For what he saith is this, " Your salvation is not our work alone, but your own as well ; for both we in preaching to you the word endure affliction, and ye in receiv-

ing it endure the very same ; we to impart to you that which we received, ye to receive what is imparted and not to let it go." Now what humility can compare with this, seeing that those who fell so far short of him he raiseth to the same dignity of endurance ? for he saith, " Which worked in the enduring of the same sufferings ; " for not through believing only cometh your salvation, but also through the suffering and enduring the same things with us. For like as a pugilist[5] is an object of admiration, when he doth but show himself and is in good training and hath his skill within himself, but when he is in action[6], enduring blows and striking his adversary, then most of all shineth forth, because that then his good training is most put in action[7], and the proof of his skill evidently shown ; so truly is your salvation also then more especially put into action[8], that is, is displayed, increased, heightened, when it hath endurance, when it suffereth and beareth all things nobly. So then the work[9] of salvation consisteth not in doing evil, but in suffering evil. Moreover he saith not, " which worketh," but, " which is wrought[10]," to show that together with their own willingness of mind, grace also which wrought in them did contribute much.

Ver. 7. " And our hope for you is steadfast."

That is, though ye should suffer ills innumerable, we are confident that ye will not turn round[11], either upon your own trials or upon our persecutions. For so far are we from suspecting you of being confounded on account of our sufferings that even when yourselves are in peril, we are then confident concerning you.

[2.] Seest thou how great had been their advance since the former Epistle ? For he hath here witnessed of them far greater things than of the Macedonians, whom throughout that Epistle he extolleth and commendeth. For on their [the Macedonians'] account he feared

---

[1] μαλακισθέντες.
[2] φιλονείκια.
[3] περιιστᾷν.
[4] κοινώσας τὸν λόγον.

[5] παγκρατιαστής.
[6] ἐνεργῇ.
[7] ἐνεργεῖται.
[8] ἐνεργεῖται.
[9] ἐνεργεία.
[10] οὐ τῆς ἐνεργούσης ἀλλὰ τῆς ἐνεργουμένης. [Nearly all modern interpreters take the participle in the middle sense (showing itself active) which is represented in the Rev. Ver. C.]
[11] ὑμετέροις διωγμοῖς only, Ben. Ed.

277

and saith, "We sent," unto you, "Timothy...to establish you, and to comfort you concerning your faith, that no man be moved by these afflictions, for yourselves know that hereunto we are appointed." (1 Thess. iii. 2, 3.) And again : "For this cause when I could no longer forbear, I sent to know your faith, lest by any means the tempter hath tempted you : and our labor should be in vain." (ver. 5.) But of these [the Corinthians] he saith nothing of this kind, but quite the contrary, "Our hope for you is steadfast."

Ver. 6, 7. "Or whether we be comforted, it is for your consolation and salvation. Knowing that as ye are partakers of the sufferings, so also are ye of the comfort."

That for their sakes the Apostles were afflicted, he showed when he said, "whether we be afflicted, it is for your consolation and salvation : " he wishes also to show that for their sakes also they were comforted. He said this indeed even a little above, although somewhat generally[1], thus ; "Blessed be God, Who comforteth us in all our afflictions, that we may be able to comfort them which are in any affliction." He repeats it here too in other words more clearly and more[2] home to their needs. "For whether we be comforted," says he, "it is for your comfort." What he means is this ; our comfort becometh your refreshment, even though we should not comfort you by word. If we be but a little refreshed, this availeth for encouragement to you ; and if we be ourselves comforted, this becometh your comfort. For as ye consider our sufferings your own, so do ye also make our comfort your own. For surely it cannot be that, when ye share in worse fortune with us, ye will not share in the better. If then ye share in everything, as in tribulation so in comfort, ye will in no wise blame us for this delay and slowness in coming, because that both for your sakes we are in tribulation and for your sakes in comfort. For lest any should think this a hard saying, "for your sakes we thus suffer," he adds, "for your sakes also we are comforted," and "not we alone are in peril ; for ye also," saith he, "are partakers of the same sufferings." Thus then, by admitting them to be partakers in the perils and ascribing to them the cause of their own comfort, he softeneth what he saith. If then we be beset by craft[3], be of good cheer ; we endure this, that your faith may grow in strength. And if we be comforted, glory[4] in this also ; for we enjoy this too for your sakes, that thereby ye may receive some encouragement by sharing in our joy. And that the comfort he here speaks

of is that which they[5] enjoyed not only from being comforted by themselves, (the Apostles) but also from knowing them (the Apostles) to be at rest, hear him declaring in what follows next, "Knowing that as ye are partakers of the sufferings, so also are ye of the comfort." For as when we suffer persecution, ye are in distress as though yourselves so suffering ; so are we sure that when we are comforted, ye think the enjoyment also your own. What more humble-minded than this spirit ? He who so greatly surpasseth in perils, calleth them "partakers," who endured no part of them whatever[6]; whilst of the comfort he ascribeth the whole cause to them, not to his own labors.

[3.] Next, having spoken before only generally of troubles, he now maketh mention of the place too where they (Ben. he) endured them.

Ver. 8. "For we would not, Brethren, have you ignorant concerning our affliction which befell us in Asia."

"These things we speak," saith he, "that ye may not be ignorant of what befell us; for we wish, yea have earnestly endeavored, that ye should know our affairs : " which is a very high proof of love. Of this even in the former Epistle he had before given notice, where he said, "For a great door and effectual is opened to me at Ephesus, and there are many adversaries." (1 Cor. xvi. 8, 9.) Putting them then in mind of this, and recounting how much he suffered, he saith, "I would not have you ignorant of our affliction which befell us in Asia." And in his Epistle to the Ephesians too he said the same. For having sent Tychicus to them, he gives this as the reason of his journey : whence he saith, "But that ye also may know my affairs, and how I do, Tychicus, the beloved brother and faithful minister in the Lord, shall make known to you all things ; whom I have sent unto you for this very purpose, that ye may know our state, and that he may comfort your hearts." (Eph. vi. 21, 22.) And in other Epistles also he doeth the very same. Nor is it superfluous, but even exceedingly necessary : both because of his exceeding affection for the disciples, and because of their continued trials ; wherein the knowledge of each other's fortunes was a very great comfort; so that if these were calamitous, they might be prepared both to be energetic and to be safer against falling ; or if these were good, they might rejoice with them. He here, however, speaketh as well of being delivered from trials as of being assaulted by them, saying,

"We were weighed down exceedingly, beyond

---

[1] ἀδιορίστως ver. 4.
[2] θεραπευτικώτερον.
[3] ἐπιβουλευώμεθα.
[4] ἐναβρύνεσθε.

[5] Ben. ἐκαρποῦτο.
[6] οὐδὲ τὸ πολλοστὸν.

our power." Like a vessel sinking[1] under some mighty burden. He may seem to have said only one thing here "exceedingly" and "beyond our power:" it is, however, not one, but two; for lest one should object, "What then? granting the peril were exceeding, yet it was not great to you;" he added, it both was great and surpassed our strength, yea, so surpassed it,

"That we despaired even of life."

That is, we had no longer any expectation of living. What David calleth "the gates of hell, the pangs" and "the shadow of death," this he expresseth by saying, "We endured peril pregnant with certain death."

Ver. 9. "But we had the answer of death in ourselves, that we should not trust in ourselves, but in God which raiseth the dead."

What is this, "the answer of death?"[2] The vote, the judgment, the expectation. For so spake our affairs; our fortunes gave this answer, "We shall surely die."

To be sure, this did not come to the proof, but only as far as to our anticipations, and stopped there: for the nature of our affairs did so declare, yet the power of God allowed not the declaration to take effect, but permitted it to happen only in our thought and in expectation: wherefore he saith, "We had the answer of death in ourselves," not in fact.[3] And wherefore permitted He peril so great as to take away our hope and cause us to despair? "That we should not trust in ourselves," saith he, "but in God." These words Paul said, not that this was his own temper. Away with such a thought, but as attuning[4] the rest by what he saith of himself, and in his great care to speak modestly. Whence also further on he saith, "There was given to me a thorn in the flesh, (meaning his trials,) lest I should be exalted overmuch." (2 Cor. xii. 7.) And yet God doth not say that

He permitted them for this, but for another reason. What other? That His strength might be the more displayed; "For," saith he, "My grace is sufficient for thee, for My power is made perfect in weakness." (ver. 9.) But, as I said, he no where forgetteth his own peculiar character, classing himself with those who fall short exceedingly and stand in need of much discipline and correction. For if one or two trials suffice to sober even ordinary men, how should he who of all men had most cultivated lowliness of mind his whole life long and had suffered as no other man did, after so many years and a practice of wisdom[5] worthy of the heavens, be in need of this admonition? Whence it is plain that here too, it is from modesty and to calm down those who thought highly of themselves and boasted, that he thus speaks, "That we should not trust in ourselves, but in God."

[4.] And observe how he treateth them tenderly[6] here also. For, saith he, these trials were permitted to come upon us for your sakes; of so great price[7] are ye in God's sight; for "whether we be afflicted," saith he, "it is for your consolation and salvation;" but they were "out of measure" for our sake, lest we should be high minded. "For we were weighed down exceedingly, beyond our power, that we should not trust in ourselves, but in God that raiseth the dead." He again putteth them in mind of the doctrine of the Resurrection whereon he said so much in the former Epistle, and confirmeth it from the present circumstance; whence he added,

Ver. 10. "Who delivered us out of so great deaths.[8]"

He said not, "from so great dangers," at once showing the insupportable severity of the trials, and confirming the doctrine I have mentioned. For whereas the Resurrection was a thing future, he showeth that it happeneth every day: for when [God] lifteth up again a man who is despaired of and hath been brought to the very gates of Hades, He showeth none other thing than a resurrection, snatching out of the very jaws of death him that had fallen into them: whence in the case of those despaired of and then restored either out of grievous sickness or insupportable trials, it is an ordinary way of speaking to say, We have seen a resurrection of the dead in his case.

Ver. 10, 11. "And we have set our hope that He will also still deliver us; ye also helping together on our behalf by your supplication, that for the gift bestowed upon us by the means

---

[1] βαπτιζόμενον.

[2] [This is the rendering of ἀπόκριμα in the Revised Version, but the American Committee prefer to retain "sentence" of the common version, adding in the margin "Gr. answer." But it seems better to adhere to the view of the British Revisers, since this is the natural meaning of the term, (Prof. Thayer in his edition of Grimm gives no other), and besides, adds greatly to the vivacity of the Apostle's utterance. Again and again he was compelled to ask the question what would be the end of the perils by which he was surrounded, but the answer invariably was Death. This being the case he was permanently driven out of any self-trust, and compelled to rely upon God "who raiseth the dead," and who therefore could easily deliver his servants even when at the point to die. It is true that there is no such thing as implicit confidence in God until men renounce all confidence in themselves.

There are different opinions as to the nature of the terrible peril to which the Apostle was exposed in Asia. Some have suggested the uproar in Ephesus mentioned in Acts xix. 23–41, others a severe illness, others a dangerous shipwreck, others (Rev. Jos. Waite in Bible Commentary) his devouring anxiety about Corinthian affairs. It does not seem necessary to be able to determine this matter precisely. The probability is that he refers to trials of different kinds, and especially to plots and attempts against his life. He could hardly use stronger language than he does to set forth the desperate straits in which he was. "Weighed down exceedingly," "beyond our power," "we despaired even of life." Chrysostom well points out and enforces the lessons to be drawn from the extraordinary experience of this eminent servant of God. C.]

[3] τῇ πείρᾳ.

[4] ῥυθμίζων.

[5] φιλοσοφίαν.

[6] θεραπεύει.

[7] τοσούτου τιμᾶται ὑμᾶς.

[8] τηλικούτων θανάτων. τηλικούτου θανάτου, received text.

of many [1], thanks may be given by many persons on our behalf.

Since the words, "that we should not trust in ourselves," might seem to be a common charge and an accusation that pointed to some amongst them; he softeneth [2] again what he said, by calling their prayers a great protection and at the same time showing that [this] our life must be throughout a scene of conflict [3]. For in those words, "And we have set our hope that He will also still deliver us," he predicts a future sleet [4] of many trials: but still no where aught of being forsaken, but of succor again and support. Then, lest on hearing that they were to be continually in perils they should be cast down, he showed before the use of perils; for instance, "that we should not trust in ourselves;" that is, that he may keep us in continual humility, and that their salvation may be wrought; and many other uses besides; the being partakers with Christ; ("for," saith he, "the sufferings of Christ abound in us;") the suffering for the faithful; ("for," saith he, "whether we be afflicted, it is for your comfort and salvation;") the superior lustre this last (i.e., their salvation) should shine with [5]; "which," saith he, "worketh "[in you]" in the patient enduring of the same sufferings;" their being made hardy; and besides all these, that of seeing the resurrection vividly portrayed before their eyes: for, "He hath delivered us out of so great death;" being of an earnest mind and ever looking unto Him, "for," saith he, "we have set our hope that he will deliver" us; its rivetting [6] them to prayers, for he saith, "ye also helping together on our behalf by your supplication." Thus having shown the gain of affliction and then having made them energetic: he anointeth once more their spirits [for the combat], and animates them to virtue by witnessing great things of their prayers, for that to these God had granted [7] Paul; as he saith, "Ye helping together on our behalf by prayer." But what is this : "That for the gift bestowed upon us by means of many [8], thanks may be given by many on our behalf? He delivered us from those deaths," saith he, "ye also helping together by prayer;" that is, praying all of you for us. For "the gift bestowed upon us," that is, our being saved, He was pleased to grant to you all, in order that many persons might give Him thanks, because that many also received the boon.

[5.] And this he said, at once to stir them up to prayer for others, and to accustom them always to give thanks to God for whatever befalleth others, showing that He too willeth this exceedingly. For they that are careful to do both these for others, will much more for themselves show an example of both. And besides this, he both teacheth them humility and leadeth on to more fervent love. For if he who was so high above them owneth himself to have been saved by their prayers: and that to their prayers himself [9] had been granted as a boon of God, think what their modesty and disposition ought to have been. And observe, I pray you, this also; that even if God doeth any thing in mercy, yet prayer doth mightily contribute thereunto. For at the first he attributed his salvation to His mercies; for "The God of mercies," he says, Himself "delivered us," but here to the prayers also. For on him too that owed the ten thousand talents He had mercy after that he fell at His feet; (Mat. xviii. 24, 27.) although it is written, that "being moved with compassion, He loosed him." And again to the "woman of Canaan," it was after that long attendance and importunity [10] of hers, (Mat. xv. 22.) that He finally granted the healing of her daughter, even though of His mercy He healed her. Hereby then we learn that even though we are to receive mercy, we must first make ourselves worthy of the mercy; for though there be mercy, yet it seeketh out those that are worthy. It will not come upon all without distinction ; those even who have no feeling; for He saith, "I will have mercy on whom I have mercy, and I will have compassion on whom I have compassion." (Rom. ix. 15.) Observe at least what he saith here, "Ye also helping together by prayer." He hath neither ascribed the whole of the good work to them lest he should lift them up, nor yet deprived them of all share whatever in it, in order to encourage them and animate their zeal, and bring them together one to another. Whence also he said, "He also granted to you my safety." For ofttimes also God is abashed [11] by a multitude praying with one mind and mouth. Whence also He said to the prophet, "And shall not I spare this city wherein dwell more than six score thousand persons?" (Jonah iv. 11.) Then lest thou think He respecteth the multitude only, He saith, "Though the number of Israel be as the sand of the sea, a remnant shall be saved." (Is. x. 22.) How then saved He the Ninevites? Because in their case, there was not

---

[1] ἐν πολλῷ προσώπῳ. (Rec. text, ἐκ πολλῶν προσώπων.) perhaps "bestowed upon us as representing many." See Hom. xli. §. 8. on 1st. Cor. and the note.
[2] παραμυθεῖται.
[3] ἐναγώνιον.
[4] νιφάδας.
[5] διαλάμπειν μειζόνως. vid. supra.
[6] προσηλῶσθαι.
[7] The marginal reading of Savile, which Mr. Field has received into his text, has been followed. Previous editions read ἐχαρίσαυτο.
[8] Chrysostom reads ἐν πολλῷ προσώπῳ. See above, and on 1 Cor. Hom. xli. 8.
[9] Ben. αὐτῷ, that a gift had been given him through their prayers by God.

[10] προσεδρείαν καὶ καρτερίαν.
[11] δυσωπεῖται.

only a multitude, but a multitude and virtue too. For each one "turned from" his "evil way." (Jonah iii. 10. iv. 11.) And besides, when He saved them, He said that they discerned not "between their right hand and their left hand:" whence it is plain that even before, they sinned more out of simpleness than of wickedness: it is plain too from their being converted, as they were, by hearing a few words. But if their being six score thousand were of itself enough to save them, what hindered even before this that they should be saved? And why saith He not to the Prophet, And shall I not spare this city which so turneth itself? but bringeth forward the score thousands. He produceth this also as a reason over and above. For that they had turned was known to the prophet, but he knew not either their numbers or their simpleness. So by every possible consideration he is desirous to soften them. For even greatness of number hath power, when there is virtue withal. And truly the Scripture elsewhere also showeth this plainly, where it saith, "But prayer was made earnestly of the Church unto God for him:" (Acts xii. 5.) and so great power had it, even when the doors were shut and chains lay on him and keepers were sleeping by on either side, that it led the Apostle forth and delivered him from them all. But as where there is virtue, greatness of number hath mighty power; so where wickedness is, it profiteth nothing. For the Israelites of whom He saith that the number of them was as the sand of the sea, perished every one, and those too in the days of Noe were both many, yea, numberless; and yet this profited them nothing. For greatness of number hath no power of itself, but only as an adjunct[1].

[6.] Let us then be diligent in coming together in supplication; and let us pray for one another, as they did for the Apostles. For [so] we both fulfil a commandment, and are "anointed[2]" unto love: (and when I say love, I speak of every good thing:) and also learn[3] to give thanks with more earnestness: for they that give thanks for the things of others, much more will they for their own. This also was David wont to do, saying, "Magnify the Lord with me, and let us exalt His name together;" (Ps. xxxiv. 3.) this the Apostle too doth every where require. This let us too labor in; and let us show forth unto all the beneficence of God that we may get companions in the act of praise: for if when we have received any good from men, by proclaiming it forth we make them the readier to serve us: much more shall we, by telling abroad the benefits of God, draw

Him on to more good-will. And if when we have received benefits of men we stir up others also to join us in the giving of thanks, much more ought we to bring many unto God who may give thanks for us. For if Paul who had so great confidence [toward God] doth this, much more is it necessary for us to do it. Let us then exhort the saints to give thanks for us; and let us do the same ourselves for one another. To priests especially this good work belongs, since it is an exceeding privilege[4]. For drawing near, we first give thanks for the whole world and the good things common [to all]. For even though the blessings of God be common, yet doth the common preservation[5] include thine own; so that thou both owest common thanksgivings for thine own peculiar[6] blessing, and for the common blessings shouldest of right render up thine own peculiar[7] praise: for He lighted up the sun not for thee alone, but also for all in common; but nevertheless thou for thy part hast it whole[8]. For it was made so large for the common good; and yet thou individually seest it as large as all men have seen it; so that thou owest a thanksgiving as great as all together; and thou oughtest to give thanks for what all have in common and likewise for the virtue of others; for on account of others, too, we receive many blessings: for had there been found in Sodom ten righteous only, they had not suffered what they did. So then let us give thanks also for the confidence of others [toward God]. For this custom is an ancient one, planted in the Church from the beginning. Thus Paul also giveth thanks for the Romans, (Rom. i. 8.) for the Corinthians, (1 Cor. i. 4.) for the whole world, (1 Tim. ii. 1.) And tell me not, "The good work is none of mine;" for though it be none of thine, yet even so oughtest thou to give thanks that thy member is such an one. And besides, by thy acclamation thou makest it thine own, and sharest in the crown, and shalt thyself also receive the gift. On this account it is that the laws of the Church[9] command prayer also to be thus made, and that not for the faithful only, but also for the Catechumens. For the law stirreth up the faithful to make supplication for the uninitiated[10]. For when the Deacon saith[11], "Let us pray earnestly for the Cate-

---

[1] ἐν προσθήκης μέρει.
[2] ἀλειφόμεθα. The metaphor is taken doubtless from the games, but it seemed better to retain it, from its typical connection with the graces of the Holy Spirit.
[3] "And let us learn." Benedict.

[4] μέγιστον ἀγαθὸν
[5] ἀλλὰ καὶ σὺ ἐν τῷ κοινῷ ἐσώθης.
[6] ἰδίας.
[7] ἰδιάζουσαν.
[8] ἐν τῷ μέρει τὸ ὅλον ἔχεις.
[9] See Bingham, *Christian Antiqu.* book xiv. ch. 5. §. 3. Goar, pp. 70. and 161.
[10] ἀμυήτων.
[11] The whole Prayer for the Catechumens, as gathered from the Homily, will stand thus. "Let us pray earnestly for the Catechumens, That the all-pitying and merciful God would listen to their prayers, that He would open the ears of their hearts and instil into them the word of truth, that He would sow His fear in them and confirm His faith in their minds, that He would unveil to them the Gospel of righteousness, that He would grant to them a

chumens," he doth no other than excite the whole multitude of the faithful to pray for them; although the Catechumens are as yet aliens. For they are not yet of the Body of Christ, they have not yet partaken of the Mysteries, but are still divided from the spiritual flock. But if we ought to intercede for these, much more for our own members. And even therefore he saith, "earnestly let us pray," that thou shouldest not disown them as aliens, that thou shouldest not disregard them as strangers. For as yet they have not the appointed[1] prayer, which Christ brought in; as yet they have not confidence, but have need of others' aid who have been initiated. For without the king's courts they stand, far from the sacred precincts[2]. Therefore they are even driven away whilst those awful prayers are being offered. Therefore also he exhorteth thee to pray for them that they may become members of thee, that they may be no longer strangers and aliens. For the words, "Let us pray," are not addressed to the priests alone, but also to those that make up the people: for when he saith, "Let us stand in order[3]: let us pray;" he exhorteth all to the prayer.

[7.] Then beginning the prayer, he saith, "That the all-pitying and merciful God would listen to their prayers." For that thou mayest not say, What shall we pray? they are aliens, not yet united [to the body]. Whereby can I constrain[4] the regard of God? Whence can I prevail with Him to impart unto them mercy and forgiveness? That thou mayest not be perplexed with such questions as these, see how he disentangleth thy perplexity, saying, "that the all-pitying and merciful God." Heardest thou? "All-pitying God." Be perplexed no more. For the All-pitying pitieth all, both sinners and friends. Say not then, "How shall I approach Him for them?" Himself will listen to their

prayers. And the Catechumens' prayer, what can it be but that they may not remain Catechumens? Next, he suggesteth also the manner of the prayer. And what is this? "That He would open the ears of their hearts;" for they are as yet shut and stopped up. "Ears," he saith, not these which be outward, but those of the understanding, "so as to hear 'the things which eye hath not seen, nor ear heard, neither have entered[5] into the heart of man.'" (1 Cor. ii. 9. Is. liv. 4.) For they have not heard the untold mysteries; but they stand somewhere at a distance and far off from them; and even if they should hear, they know not what is said; for those [mysteries] need much understanding, not hearing only: and the inward ears as yet they have not: wherefore also He next invoketh for them a Prophet's gift, for the Prophet spoke on this wise; "God giveth me the tongue of instruction, that I should know how to speak a word in season; for He opened my mouth; He gave to me betimes in the morning; He granted me a hearing ear." (Is. l. 4. Sept.) For as the Prophets heard otherwise than the many, so also do the faithful than the Catechumens. Hereby the Catechumen also is taught not to learn to hear these things of men, (for He saith, "Call no man master upon the earth[6], but from above, from heaven, "For they shall be all taught of God." (Isa. liv. 13.)

Wherefore he says, "And instil[7] into them the word of truth," so that it may be inwardly learned[8]; for as yet they know not the word of truth as they ought to know. "That He would sow His fear in them." But this is not enough; for "some fell by the wayside, and some upon the rock." But we ask not thus; but as on

---

godly mind, sound judgment, and virtuous manner of life ; continually to think those things which be His, to mind those things which be His, to practise those things which be His, to be occupied in His law day and night, to remember His commandments, to keep His judgments.

"Let us beseech for them yet more earnestly, That He would deliver them from every evil and inordinate thing, from every devilish sin, and from every besetment of the adversary, that He would count them worthy in due season of the Regeneration of the Laver, of the remission of sins, of the clothing of incorruption, that He would bless their comings in and goings out, the whole course of their life, their houses and households, that He would increase their children and bless them, and bring them to full age, and teach them wisdom, that He would direct all that is before them unto good.

"Stand up. Pray, ye Catechumens, for the Angel of peace, that all that is before you may be peaceful ; pray that this day and all the days of your life be full of peace, that your ends may be Christian ; commend yourselves to the living God and to His Christ.

"Bow ye the head. All respond aloud, Amen."

A similar Prayer for the Catechumens, with a few variations, is found in the *Apostolic Constitutions*, lib. viii. cap. 6. Mr. Field considers it to be of later date than that given above.

"Pray, ye Catechumens, and all ye faithful, pray for them in heart, saying, Lord have mercy. And let the deacon speak for them according to his office, saying, for the Catechumens let us all beseech God.

"That the Good [God], the Lover of men, would favorably hearken to their supplications and prayers, and accepting their

suppliant addresses would help them, and grant unto them the requests of their hearts as may be expedient for them, and would reveal unto them the Gospel of his Christ, would enlighten them, and give them understanding, would instruct them in the knowledge of God, would teach them His ordinances and judgments, implant in them His pure and saving fear, would open the ears of their hearts to be occupied in His law day and night, and confirm them in godliness, would unite them to, and enrol them in His holy flock counting them worthy of the Laver of Regeneration, the clothing of incorruption, the true life, and would deliver them from all ungodliness, and give none occasion to the enemy* against them, but cleanse them from all filthiness of flesh and spirit, and dwell and walk in them by His Christ, would bless their comings in and goings out, and direct for them all that is before them unto good.

"Let us again earnestly supplicate for them :

"That obtaining remission of their offences by the initiation, they may be counted worthy of the holy mysteries, and of constant communion with the saints.

"Stand up; ye Catechumens. Pray for the peace of God through His Christ, that this day, and all the time of your life, may be peaceful, and without sin, that your ends may be Christian, God merciful and favorable; pray for remission of offences ; commend yourselves unto the only unbegotten God through His Christ.

"Bow, and receive the blessing."

* ἀλλοτρίῳ, literally, the Alien. The word seems to be used in Diodorus and Polybius for hostile, inimical.

[1] νενομισμένην.

[2] περιβόλων.

[3] Στῶμεν καλῶς.

[4] δυσωπῆσαι.

[5] ἀπορρήτων.

[6] rec. text, πατέρα ὑμῶν, (Mat. xxiii. 9.)

[7] κατηχήσῃ.

[8] ἐνηχεῖσθαι.

rich soil the plough openeth the furrows, so we pray it may be here also, that having the fallow ground of their minds[1] tilled deep, they may receive what is dropped upon them and accurately retain everything they have heard. Whence also he adds, "And confirm His faith in their minds;" that is, that it may not lie on the surface, but strike its root deep downwards. "That He would unveil to them the Gospel of Righteousness." He showeth that the veil is two-fold, partly that the eyes of their understanding were shut, partly that the Gospel was hidden from them. Whence he said a little above, "that He would open the ears of their hearts," and here, "that he would unveil unto them the Gospel of Righteousness;" that is, both that He would render them wise and apt for receiving[2] seed, and that He would teach them and drop the seed into them; for though they should be apt, yet if God reveal not, this profiteth nothing; and if God should unveil but they receive not, there resulteth like unprofitableness. Therefore we ask for both: that He would both open their hearts and unveil the Gospel. For neither if kingly ornaments lie underneath a veil, will it profit at all that the eyes be looking; nor yet that they be laid bare, if the eyes be not waking[3]. But both will be granted, if first they[4] themselves desire it. But what then is "the Gospel of Righteousness?" That which maketh righteous. By these words he leadeth them to the desire of Baptism, showing that the Gospel is for the working[5] not only of the remission of sins, but also of righteousness.

[8.] "That He would grant to them a godly mind, sound judgment, and virtuous manner of life[6]." Let such of the faithful attend as are rivetted[7] to the things of [this] life. For if we are bidden to ask these things for the uninitiated: think in what things we ought to be occupied who ask these things for others. For the manner of life ought to keep pace with[8] the Gospel. Whence surely also the order of the prayer[9] shifts from the doctrines [of the Gospel] to the deportment: for to the words, "that He would unveil to them the Gospel of Righteousness;" it hath added, "that He would give unto them a Godly mind." And what is this "Godly?" That God may dwell in it. For He saith, "I will dwell in them, and walk in them;" (Lev. xxvi. 12.) for when the mind is become righteous, when it hath put off its sins,

it becometh God's dwelling. (Rom. vi. 16.) But when God indwelleth, nothing of man will be left. And thus doth the mind become Godly, speaking every word from Him, even as in truth an house of God dwelling in it. Surely then the filthy in speech hath not a Godly mind, nor he who delighteth in jesting and laughter.

"Sound judgment." And what can it be to have "a sound judgment?" To enjoy the health that pertaineth to the soul: for he that is held down by wicked lusts and dazzled[10] with present things, never can be sound, that is, healthy. But as one who is diseased lusteth even after things which are unfit for him, so also doth he. "And a virtuous mode of life," for the doctrines need a mode of life [answerable]. Attend to this, ye who come to baptism at the close of life, for we indeed pray that after baptism ye may have also this deportment, but thou art seeking and doing thy utmost to depart without it. For, what though thou be justified[11]: yet is it of faith only. But we pray that thou shouldest have as well the confidence that cometh of good works.

"Continually to think those things which be His, to mind those things which be His, to practise[12] those things which be His:" for we ask not to have sound judgment and virtuous deportment for one day only, or for two or three, but through the whole tenor and period[13] of our life; and as the foundation of all good things, "to mind those things which be His." For the many "seek their own, not the things which are Jesus Christ's." (Phil. ii. 21.) How then might this be? (For besides prayer, need is that we contribute also our own endeavors.) If we be[14] occupied in His law day and night. Whence he goeth on to ask this also, "to be occupied in His law;" and as he said above, "continually," so here "day and night." Wherefore I even blush for those who scarce once in the year are seen in church. For what excuse can they have who are bidden not simply "day and night" to commune with the law but "to be occupied in," that is, to be for ever holding converse with it[15], and yet scarce do so for the smallest fraction of their life?

"To remember His commandments, to keep His judgments." Seest thou what an excellent chain is here? and how each link hangs by the next compacted with more strength and beauty than any chain of gold? For having asked for a Godly mind, he telleth whereby this may be produced. Whereby? By continually practising[16] it. And how might this be brought about?

---

[1] νεωθέντας ἐν τῷ βάθει τῆς διανοίας.
[2] πρὸς ὑποδοχήν.
[3] μὴ ἐγρηγορότων.
[4] i. e., the Catechumens.
[5] ποιητικόν.
[6] νοῦν ἔνθεον, σώφρονα λογισμὸν καί ἐνάρετον πολιτείαν. It is obvious that "godly" does not come up to the meaning of the original ἔνθεος, "into which God is inspired," see below.
[7] προσηλωμένοι.
[8] ἐφάμιλλον.
[9] ὁ νόμος τῆς εὐχῆς.

[10] ἐπτοημένος.
[11] δίκαιος.
[12] μελετᾶν.
[13] τοῦ βίου καὶ τῆς ζωῆς.
[14] καταγινώμεθα.
[15] προσαδολεσχεῖν.
[16] μελετᾶν.

By constantly giving heed to the Law. And how might men be persuaded to this? If they should keep His Commandments: yea rather, from giving heed to the law cometh also the keeping His Commandments; as likewise from minding the things which be His and from having a Godly mind, cometh the practising the things which be His. For each of the things mentioned jointly [1] procureth and is procured by the next, both linking it and being linked by it.

[9.] "Let us beseech for them yet more earnestly." For since by length of speaking the soul useth to grow drowsy, he again arouseth it up, for he purposeth to ask again certain great and lofty things. Wherefore he saith, "Let us beseech for them yet more earnestly." And what is this? "That He would deliver them from every evil and inordinate [2] thing." Here we ask for them that they may not enter into temptation, but be delivered from every snare, a deliverance as well bodily as spiritual. [3] Wherefore also he goeth on to say, "from every devilish sin and from every [4] besetment of the adversary," meaning, temptations and sins. For sin doth easily beset, taking its stand on every side, before, behind, and so casting down. For, after telling us what ought to be done by us, namely, to be occupied in His law, to remember His Commandments, to keep His judgments, he assures us next that not even is this enough, except Himself stand by and succor. For, "Except the Lord build the house, they labor in vain that build it;" (Ps. cxxvii. 1) and especially in the case of those who are yet exposed to the devil and are under his dominion. And ye that are initiated know this well. For call to mind, for instance, those words wherein ye renounced [5] his usurped [6] rule, and bent the knee and deserted to The King, and uttered those awful [7] words whereby we are taught in nothing whatever to obey him. But he calleth him adversary and accuser, because he both accuseth God to man and us to God, and us again one to another. For at one time he accused Job to God, saying, "Doth Job serve the Lord for nought?" (Job i. 9. LXX. ver. 16.) at another time God to Job, "Fire came down from heaven." And again, God to Adam, (Gen. iii. 5.) when He said their eyes would be opened. And to many men at this day, saying, that God taketh no care for the visible order of things, but hath delegated your affairs to demons [8]. And to many of the Jews he accused Christ, calling Him a deceiver and a sorcerer. But perchance some one wisheth to hear in what manner he worketh. When he findeth not a godly mind, findeth not a sound understanding, then, as into a soul left empty, he leads his revel thither [9]; when one remembereth not the commandments of God nor keepeth His judgments, then he taketh him captive and departeth. Had Adam, for instance, remembered the commandment which said, "Of every tree thou mayest eat:" (Gen. ii.16.) had he kept the judgment which said, "In the day in which ye eat thereof, then [10] shall ye surely die;" it had not fared with him as it did.

"That He would count them worthy in due season of the regeneration of the laver, of the remission of sins." For we ask some things to come now, some to come hereafter; and we expound the doctrine [11] of the laver, and in asking instruct them to know its power. For what is said thenceforth familiarizes them to know already that what is there done is a regeneration, and that we are born again of the waters, just as of the womb; that they say not after Nicodemus, "How [12] can one be born when he is old! Can he enter into his mother's womb, and be born again?" Then, because he had spoken of "remission of sins," he confirmeth this by the words next following, "of the clothing of incorruption;" for he that putteth on sonship plainly becometh incorruptible. But what is that "in due season?" When any is well disposed, when any cometh thereunto with earnestness and faith; for this is the "due season" of the believer.

[10.] "That He would bless their coming in and their going out, the whole course of their life." Here they are directed to ask even for some bodily good, as being yet somewhat weak. "Their houses and their households," that is, if they have servants or kinsfolk or any others belonging to them. For these were the rewards of the old Covenant; and nothing then was feared so much as widowhood, childlessness, untimely mournings, to be visited with famine, to have their affairs go on unprosperously. And hence it is, that he alloweth these also fondly [13] to linger over petitions rather material [14], making them mount by little and little to higher things. For so too doth Christ; so too doth Paul, making mention of the ancient blessings: Christ, when He saith, "Blessed are the meek, for they shall inherit the earth;" Paul, when he saith,

---

[1] συγκατασκευάζει.
[2] ἀτόπου.
[3] The Benedictine Ed. reads σωματικῶν τε ὁμοῦ καὶ πνευματικῶν, every snare both bodily and spiritual.
[4] περιστάσεως.
[5] See Bingham, Antiq. l. xi. c. 8. §. 2. &c.
[6] τυραννίδι.
[7] φρικώδη.
[8] δαίμοσιν.

[9] ὡς εἰς ἐρήμην κωμάζει ψυχήν. This clause is inserted from Mr. Field's text, who gives the authority of three Mss.
[10] LXX. om. τότε.
[11] φιλοσοφοῦμεν.
[12] John iii. 4. rec. text, ἄνθρωπος, not τις, also δεύτερον, not ἄνωθεν.
[13] ἐμφιλοχωρεῖν.
[14] σωματικωτέραις.

" Honor thy father and thy mother.... and thou shalt live long on the earth." "That He would increase their children and bless them, and bring them to full age, and teach [1] them wisdom." Here again is both a bodily and spiritual thing, as for persons yet but too much babes in disposition. Then what follows is altogether spiritual, "that He would direct all that is before them [2] unto good ; " for he saith not simply, "all that is before them," but, "all that is before them unto good." For often a journey is before a man, but it is not good ; or some other such thing, which is not profitable. Here by they are taught in every thing to give thanks to God, as happening for good. After all this, he bids them stand up during what follows. For having before cast them to the ground, when they have asked what they have asked and have been filled with confidence, now the word [3] given raiseth them up, and biddeth them during what follows engage for themselves also in supplication to God. For part we say ourselves, and part we permit them to say, now opening unto them the door of prayer, (exactly as we first teach children [what to say], and then bid them say it of themselves,) saying, "Pray ye, Catechumens, for the angel of peace ; " for there is an angel that punisheth, as when He saith, "A band of evil angels," (Ps. lxxviii. 49) there is that destroyeth. Wherefore we bid them ask for the angel of peace, teaching them to seek that which is the bond of all good things, peace ; so that they may be delivered from all fightings, all wars, all seditions. "That all that is before you may be peaceful ; " for even if a thing be burdensome, if a man have peace, it is light. Wherefore Christ also said, "My peace I give unto you (John xiv. 27) for the devil hath no weapon so strong as fighting, and enmity, and war. "Pray that this day and all the days of your life be full [4] of peace." Seest thou how he again insisteth that the whole life be passed in virtue? "That your ends be Christian ; " your highest good, the honorable and the expedient [5] ; for what is not honorable is not expedient either. For our idea of the nature of expediency is different from that of the many. "Commend yourselves to the living God and to His Christ ; " for as yet we trust them not to pray for others, but

it is sufficient [6] to be able to pray for themselves.

Seest thou the completeness of this prayer, both in regard of doctrine and of behavior? for when we have mentioned the Gospel and the clothing of incorruption and the Laver of Regeneration, we have mentioned all the doctrines: when again we spoke of a Godly mind, a sound understanding, and the rest of what we said, we suggested [7] the mode of life. Then we bid them [8] bow their heads ; regarding it as a proof of their prayers being heard that God blessed them. For surely it is not a man that blesseth ; but by means of his hand and his tongue we bring unto the King Himself the heads of those that are present. And all together shout the "Amen."

Now why have I said all this? To teach you that we ought to seek the things of others, that the faithful may not think it no concern of theirs when these things are said. For not to the walls surely doth the Deacon say, "Let us pray for the Catechumens." But some are so without understanding, so stupid, so depraved [9], as to stand and talk not only during the time of the Catechumens, but also during the time of the faithful. Hence all is perverted ; hence all is utterly lost: for at the very time when we ought most to propitiate God, we go away having provoked Him. So again in [the prayers of] the faithful [10], we are bidden to approach the God that loveth men, for Bishops, for Priests, for Kings, for those in authority, for earth and sea, for the seasons [11], for the whole world. When then we who ought to have such boldness as to pray for others, are scarce awake even whilst praying for ourselves, how can we excuse ourselves? how find pardon? Wherefore I beseech you that laying all this to heart, ye would know the time of prayer, and be lifted up and disengaged from earth, and touch the vault itself of heaven ; so that we may have power to make God propitious and obtain the good things promised, whereunto may we all attain, through the grace and love towards men of our Lord Jesus Christ ; with Whom unto the Father, together with the Holy Ghost, be glory, might, honor, now and for ever, and world without end. Amen.

---

[1] σοφίσῃ.
[2] τὰ προκείμενα.
[3] ὁ λόγος.
[4] εἰρηνικὴν.
[5] Some include the words τὸ καλὸν καὶ τὸ συμφέρον in the form of prayer.

[6] ἀγαπητὸν.
[7] ἠνιξάμεθα.
[8] The same direction was also given to the Energumeni. See de Incomprehens. Nat. Hom. 3. §. 7. and 4. §. 4.
[9] διαλελυμένοι.
[10] ἐπὶ τῶν πιστῶν.
[11] ὑπὲρ ἀέρων.

HOMILY III.

2 COR. i. 12.

For our glorying is this, the testimony of our conscience, that in simplicity and[1] sincerity, not in fleshly wisdom, but in the grace of God, we behaved ourselves in the world.

HERE again he openeth to us yet another ground of comfort, and that not small, yea rather, exceeding great, and well fitted to upraise a mind sinking[2] under perils. For seeing he had said, God comforted us[3], and God delivered us, and had ascribed all to His mercies and their prayers, lest he should thus make the hearer supine, presuming on God's mercy only and the prayers of others, he showeth that they themselves[4] had contributed not a little of their[5] own. And indeed he showed as much even before, when he said, "For as the sufferings of Christ abound [in us,] so our consolation also aboundeth." (ver. 5.) But here he is speaking of a certain other good work, properly their own[6]. What then is this? That, saith he, in a conscience pure and without guile we behave ourselves every where in the world: and this availeth not a little to our encouragement and comfort; yea, rather, not to comfort merely, but even unto somewhat else far greater than comfort, even to our glorying. And this he said, teaching them too not to sink down in their afflictions, but, if so be they have a pure conscience, even to be proud of them; and at the same time quietly though[7] gently hitting at the false Apostles. And as in the former Epistle he saith, " Christ sent me to preach the Gospel, not in wisdom of words, lest the Cross of Christ should be made of none effect:" (1 Cor. i. 17.) and, "that your faith should not stand in the wisdom of men, but in the power of God;" (ib. ii. 5.) so here also, " Not in wisdom, but in the grace of Christ."

And he hinted also something besides, by employing the words, "not in wisdom," that is, ' not in deceit,' here too striking at the heathen discipline[8]. " For our glorying," saith he, " is this, the testimony of our conscience ;"

that is, our conscience not having whereof to condemn us, as if for evil doings we were persecuted. For though we suffer countless horrors, though from every quarter we be shot at and in peril, it is enough for our comfort, yea rather not only for comfort, but even for our crowning, that our conscience is pure and testifieth unto us that for no evil-doing, but for that which is well-pleasing to God, we thus suffer ; for virtue's sake, for heavenly wisdom's, for the salvation of the many. Now that previous consolation was from God : but this was contributed by themselves and from the purity of their life. Wherefore also he calls it their glorying[9], because it was the achievement of their own virtue. What then is this glorying and what doth our conscience testify unto us? " That in sincerity," that is to say, having no deceitful thing, no hypocrisy, no dissimulation, no flattery, no ambush or guile, nor any other such thing, but in all frankness, in simplicity, in truth, in a pure and unmalicious spirit, in a guileless mind, having nothing concealed, no festering sore[10]. " Not in fleshly wisdom ; " that is, not with evil artifice, nor with wickedness, nor with cleverness of words, nor with webs of sophistries, for this he meaneth by ' fleshly wisdom :' and that whereupon they[11] greatly prided themselves, he disclaims and thrusts aside: showing very abundantly[12] that this is no worthy ground for glorying : and that not only he doth not seek it, but he even rejecteth and is ashamed of it.

" But in the grace of God we behaved ourselves in the world."

What is, " in the grace of God?" Displaying the wisdom that is from Him, the power from Him given unto us, by the signs wrought, by overcoming sages, rhetoricians, philosophers, kings, peoples, unlearned as we are and bringing with us nothing of the wisdom that is without. No ordinary comfort and glorying, however, was this, to be conscious to themselves that it was not men's power they had used ; but that by Divine grace they had achieved all success.

---

[1] The rec. text has εἰλικρινείᾳ θεοῦ. Chrysostom omits θεοῦ.
[2] βαπτιζομένην.
[3] The clause " God comforted us," is inserted by Mr. Field on the authority of two ancient MSS.
[4] i. e. the Apostles.
[5] οἴκοθεν.
[6] οἰκεῖον κατόρθωμα.
[7] ἠρέμα καθαπτόμενος.
[8] τὴν ἔξω παίδευσιν.

[9] Or "boast" καύχησις.
[10] ὑπούλον.
[11] i. e. the false Apostles.
[12] ἐκ πολλοῦ τοῦ περιόντος

["In the world[1]."] So not in Corinth only, but also in every part of the world.

"And more abundantly to you-ward." What more abundantly to you-ward? "In the grace of God we behaved ourselves." For we showed both signs and wonders amongst you, and greater strictness[2], and a life unblameable; for he calls these too the grace of God, ascribing his own good works also unto it. For in Corinth he even overleapt the goal[3], making the Gospel without charge, because he spared their weakness.

Ver. 13. "For we write none other things unto you, than what ye read or even acknowledge."

For since he spoke great things of himself and seemed to be bearing witness to himself, an odious thing, he again appeals to them as witnesses of what he says. For, he saith, let no one think that what I say is a boastful flourish of writing; for we declare unto you what yourselves know; and that we lie not ye more than all others can bear us witness. For, when ye read, ye acknowledge that what ye know that we perform in our actions, this we say also in our writings, and your testimony doth not contradict our epistles; but the knowledge which ye had before of us is in harmony with your reading.

Ver. 14. "As also ye did acknowledge us in part."

For your knowledge of us, he saith, is not from hearsay but from actual experience. The words "in part" he added from humility. For this is his wont, when necessity constraineth him to say any highsounding thing, (for he never doth so otherwise,) as desiring quickly to repress again the elation[4] arising from what he had said.

"And I hope ye will acknowledge even to the end."

[2.] Seest thou again how from the past he draws pledges for the future; and not from the past only, but also from the power of God? For he affirmed not absolutely, but cast the whole upon God and his hope in Him.

"That we are your glorying, even as ye also are our's, in the day of our Lord Jesus Christ.[5]"

Here he cuts at the root[6] of the envy that his speech might occasion, by making them sharers and partners in the glory of his good works. 'For these stick not with us, but pass over unto you also, and again from you to us.' For seeing he had extolled himself, and produced proof of the past and given security for the future[7];

lest his hearers should reflect on him for talking proudly, or, as I have said, be hurried to enviousness, he makes the rejoicing a common one and declares that this crown of praises is theirs. For if, he says, we have shown ourselves to be such, our praise is your glory: even as when ye also are approved, we rejoice and leap for joy and are crowned. Here also again he displays his great humility by what he says. For he so levels his expressions, not as a master discoursing to disciples, but as a disciple unto fellow-disciples of his own rank. And observe how he lifts them on high and fills them with philosophy, sending them on to That Day. For, he saith, tell me not of the present things, that is, the reproaches, the revilings, the scoffings of the many, for the things here are no great matter, neither the good nor the painful; nor the scoffings nor the praises which come from men: but remember, I pray, that day of fear and shuddering in the which all things are revealed. For then both we shall glory in you, and ye in us; when ye shall be seen to have such teachers, who teach no doctrine of men nor live in wickedness nor give [men] any handle; and we to have such disciples, neither affected after the manner of men nor shaken, but taking all things with readiness of mind, and unseduced by sophistries[8] from what side soever. For this is plain even now to those that have understanding, but then to all. So that even if we are afflicted now, we have this, and that no light, consolation which the conscience affordeth now, and the manifestation itself then. For now indeed our conscience knoweth that we do all things by the grace of God, as ye also know and shall know: but then, all men as well will learn both our doings and yours: and shall behold us glorified through each other. For that he may not appear himself alone to derive lustre from this glorying, he gives to them also a cause of boasting, and leads them away from their present distresses. And as he did in respect to the consolation when he said, "We are comforted for your sakes," (ver. 6.) so he does here also, saying, 'we glory on your account, as ye also on ours,' every where making them partakers of every thing, of his comfort, his sufferings, his preservation. For this his preservation he ascribes to their prayers. "For God delivered us," he saith, "ye helping together by prayer." In like manner also he makes the gloryings common. For as in that place he says, "Knowing that as ye are partakers of the sufferings, so also of the consolation:" so here too, "we are your glorying, as ye also are ours."

Ver. 15. "And in this confidence I was minded to come before unto you."

What confidence? 'In relying exceedingly on

---

[1] These words are not found in the MSS, though the commentary seems to require them. If they are omitted, there is no stop.
[2] ἀκρίβειαν.
[3] τὰ σκάμματα ὑπερέβη.
[4] συστέγγειν τὸν ὄγκον.
[5] R. T. om. 'our' and 'Christ.' [R. V. omits the latter. C.]
[6] ὑποτέμνεται.
[7] ἐνεγγυήσατο

[8] μηδαμόθεν παραλογιζομένους.

you, glorying over you, being your glorying, loving you exceedingly, being conscious to myself of nothing evil, being confident that all is spiritual with us, and having you as witnesses of this.'

"I was minded to come unto you, and by you to pass into Macedonia."

And yet he promised the contrary in his former Epistle, saying thus : " Now I will come unto you when I shall have passed through Macedonia : for I do pass through Macedonia." (1 Cor. xvi. 5.) How is it then that he here says the contrary? He doth not say the contrary : away with the thought. For it is contrary indeed to what he wrote, but not contrary to what he wished.

Wherefore also here he said not, ' I wrote that I would pass by you into Macedona ; but, ' I was minded.' For though I did not write on that wise,' he says, ' nevertheless I was greatly desirous, and ' was minded,' even before, to have come unto you : so far was I from wishing to be later than my promise that I would gladly have come before it.' " That ye might have a second benefit[1]." What is, a second benefit? ' That ye might have a double benefit, both that from my writings, and that from my presence.' By " benefit " he here means pleasure[2].

Ver. 16, 17. " And by you to pass into Macedonia, and to come again from Macedonia unto you, and of you to be set forward on my journey unto Judæa. When I therefore was thus[3] minded, did I show fickleness?"

[3.] Here in what follows, he directly does away with the charge arising out of his delay and absence. For what he says is of this nature. "I was minded to come unto you." ' Wherefore then did I not come? Is it as light-minded and changeable?' for this is, " did I show fickleness?" By no means. But wherefore? " Because what things I purpose, I purpose not according to the flesh." What is, "not according to the flesh?" I purpose not ' carnally.'

Ver. 17. " That with me there should be the yea yea and the nay nay."

But still even this is obscure. What is it then he says? The carnal man, that is, he that is rivetted to the present things and is continually occupied in them, and is without the sphere of the Spirit's influence, has power to go every where, and to wander whithersoever he will. But he that is the servant of the Spirit, and is led, and led about by Him, cannot everywhere be lord of his own purpose, having made it dependent upon the authority thence given ; but it so fares with him as if a trusty servant, whose motions are always ruled by his lord's biddings and who has no power over himself nor is able

to rest even a little, should make some promise to his fellow-servants, and then because his master would have it otherwise should fail to perform his promise. This then is what he means by, " I purpose not according to the flesh." I am not beyond the Spirit's governance, nor have liberty to go where I will. For I am subject to lordship and commands, the Comforter's, and by His decrees I am led, and led about. For this cause I was unable to come, for it was not the Spirit's will. As happened also frequently in the Acts ; for when he had purposed to come to one place, the Spirit bade him go to another. So that it was not from lightness, that is, fickleness in me that I came not, but that being subject to the Spirit I obeyed Him. Didst mark again his accustomed logic?[4] That by which they thought to prove that " he purposed according to the flesh," namely, the non-fulfilment of his promise, he uses as the special proof that he purposed according to the Spirit, and that the contrary had been purposing according to the flesh. What then? saith one : was it not with the Spirit that he promised what he did? By no means. For I have already said that Paul did not foreknow every thing that was to happen or was expedient. And it is for this reason that he says in the former Epistle, " that ye may set me forward on my journey whithersoever I go ; " (1 Cor. xvi. 6.) entertaining this very fear that after he had said, ' into Judæa,' he might be compelled to go elsewhither ; but now when his intention had been frustrated, he says it, " And of you be set forward on my journey unto Judæa." So much as was of love, he states, namely, the coming to them ; but that which had no reference to them, his going, namely, from them into Judæa, he doth not add definitely. When however he had been proved wrong[5], he afterwards says here boldly, " toward Judæa." And this too befel for good, lest any among them should conceive of them (the Apostles, Acts xiv. 13.) more highly than they deserved. For if in the face of these things they wished to sacrifice bulls to them, upon what impiety would they not have driven, had they not given many instances of human weakness? And why marvel if he knew not all things that were to happen, seeing that ofttimes he even in prayers knoweth not what is expedient.

" For," saith he " we know not what we should pray for as we ought." And that he may not seem to be speaking modestly, he not only saith this, but instances wherein he knew not in prayers what was expedient. Wherein then was it? When he entreated to be delivered from his trials, saying, " There was given to me a

---

[1] χάριν.
[2] χαράν.
[3] Chrysostom, βουλόμενος. Received text, βουλενόμενος.

[4] σύνηθες θεώρημα.
[5] ἐλήκεγκται.

thorn in the flesh, a messenger of Satan to buffet me. Concerning this thing I besought the Lord thrice. And he said unto me, My grace is sufficient for thee: for My power is made perfect in weakness." (2 Cor. xii. 7—9.) Seest thou how he knew not to ask what was expedient, and so although he asked often he obtained not.

Ver. 18. " But as God is faithful, our word toward you was[1] not yea and nay."

He skillfully overturns a rising objection. For one might say, If after having promised, thou hast put off coming, and yea is not yea, and nay nay, with thee, but what thou sayest now thou unsayest afterwards, as thou didst in the case of this journey: woe is unto us, if all this were the case in the Preaching too. Now lest they should have these thoughts and be troubled thereat, he says, " But as God is faithful, our word toward you was not yea and nay." This, saith he, was not the case in the Preaching, but only in our travels and journeyings; whereas whatever things we have said in our preaching, these abide steadfast and unmoveable, (for he calleth his preaching here, " word.") Then he bringeth proof of this that cannot be gainsaid, by referring all to God. What he saith is this; ' the promise of my coming was my own and I gave that promise from myself: but the preaching is not my own, nor of man, but of God, and what is of God it is impossible should lie.' Whereupon also he said, "God is faithful," that is, " true." ' Mistrust not then what is from Him, for there is nought of man in it.'

[4.] And seeing he had said "word," he adds what follows to explain what kind of word he means. Of what kind then is it?

Ver. 19. " For the Son of God," saith he, " Who was preached among you by us, even by me, and Silvanus, and Timothy, was not yea and nay."

For on this account he brings before them the company of the teachers also; as thence too giving credibility to the testimony by those who taught, and not who heard it only. And yet they were disciples; however in his modesty he counts them as in the rank of teachers. But what is, " was not yea and nay?" I have never, he saith, unsaid what before I said in the Preaching. My discourse to you was not now this, now that. For this is not of faith, but of an erring mind.

" But in Him was the yea." That is, just as I said, the word abideth unshaken and steadfast."

Ver. 20. " For how many soever be the promises of God," in Him is the yea, and in Him the Amen, unto the glory of God by us."

What is this, " how many soever the promises of God?" The Preaching promised many things; and these many things they proffered and preached. For they discoursed of being raised again, and of being taken up, and of incorruption, and of those great rewards and unspeakable goods. As to these promises then, he saith that they abide immoveable, and in them is no yea and nay, that is, the things spoken were not now true, and now false, as was the case about my being with you, but always true. And first indeed he contends for the articles[2] of the faith, and the word concerning Christ, saying, " My word " and my preaching, " was not yea and nay;" next, for the promises " for how many soever be the promises, of God, in Him is the yea." But if the things He promised are sure and He will certainly give them, much more is He Himself and the word concerning Him, sure, and it can not be said that He is now, and now is not, but He "always" is, and is the same. But what is, " In Him is the yea, and the Amen." He signifies that which shall certainly be. For in Him, not in man, the promises have their being and fulfilment. Fear not, therefore; for it is not man so that thou shouldest mistrust; but it is God Who both said and fulfilleth. " Unto the glory of God through us." What is, " unto [His] glory through us?" He fulfilleth them by us, that is, and[3] by His benefits towards us unto His glory; for this is " for the glory of God." But if they be for the glory of God, they will certainly come to pass. For His own glory He will not think little of, even did He think little of our salvation. But as it is, He thinketh not little of our salvation either, both because He loveth mankind exceedingly, and because our salvation is bound up with His glory from these things accruing. So that if the promises are for His glory, our salvation also will certainly follow; to which also, in the Epistle to the Ephesians, he reverteth continually, saying, " to the maintenance of His glory[4];" (Eph. i. 14.) and every where he layeth down this, and shows the necessity of this result. And in this regard he here saith, that His promises lie not: for they not only save us, but also glorify Him. Dwell not on this therefore that they were promised by us ; and so doubt. For they are not fulfilled by us, but by Him. Yea, and the promises were by Him; for we spoke not to you our own words, but His.

Ver. 21, 22. " Now He which stablisheth us with you in Christ, and anointed us, is God ; Who also sealed us, and gave us the earnest of the Spirit in our hearts."

Again, from the past He stablisheth the

[2] δογμάτων.
[3] Ben. omits " and."
[4] Rec. text, εἰς ἀπολύτρωσιν τῆς περιποιήσεως, εἰς ἔπαινον τῆς δόξης αὐτοῦ. Chrys. εἰς περιποίησιν τῆς δ. ἀ.

future. For if it is He that establisheth us in Christ; (i. e., who suffereth us not to be shaken from the faith which is in Christ;) and He that anointed us and gave the Spirit in our hearts, how shall He not give us the future things?

For if He gave the principles and the foundations, and the root and the fount, (to wit, the true knowledge of Him, the partaking of the Spirit,) how shall He not give the things that come of these: for if for the sake of these[1] those are given, much more will he[2] supply those. And if to such as were enemies he gave these, much more when now made friends will He " freely give " to them those. Wherefore He said not simply " the Spirit," but named " earnest," that from this thou mightest have a good hope of the whole as well. For did He not purpose to give the whole, He would never have chosen to give " the earnest" and to waste it without object or result. And observe Paul's candor. For why need I say, saith he, that the truth of the promises standeth not in us? The fact of your standing unwavering and fixed is not in us, but this too is of God; " for " saith he, " He who stablisheth us is God." It is not we who strengthen you: for even we also need Him that stablisheth. So then let none imagine that the Preaching is hazardous in us. He hath undertaken the whole, He cared for the whole.

And what is, " anointed," and " sealed ? " Gave the Spirit by Whom He did both these things, making at once prophets and priests and kings, for in old times these three sorts were anointed. But we have now not one of these dignities, but all three preeminently. For we are both to enjoy a kingdom and are made priests by offering our bodies for a sacrifice, (for, saith he, " present your members[3] a living sacrifice unto God ;) and withal we are constituted prophets too: for what things " eye hath not seen, nor ear heard," (1 Cor. ii. 9.) these have been revealed unto us.

[5.] And in another way too we become kings: if we have the mind to get dominion over our unruly thoughts, for that such an one is a king and more than he who weareth the diadem, I will now make plain to you. He hath many armies, but we again have thoughts exceeding them in number; for it is impossible to number the infinite multitude of the thoughts within us. Nor is their multitude all that one is to consider, but also that in this multitude of thoughts, there are many generals, and colonels, and captains, and archers, and slingers. What else makes a king? His apparel? But this

one too is arrayed in a better and braver robe, which neither doth moth devour nor age impair. A crown too he hath of curious workmanship[4], that of glory, that of the tender mercies of God. For saith [the Psalmist], " Bless the Lord, O my soul, that crowneth thee with pity and tender mercies." (Ps. ciii. 2, 4.) Again, that of glory: " For thou hast crowned him with glory and honor." (Ps. viii. 6.) And " with favor Thou hast crowned us with a shield." (Ps. v. 12. LXX.) Again, that of grace: " For thou shalt receive a crown of grace upon thy head." (Prov. i. 9. LXX.) Seest thou this diadem of many wreaths, and surpassing the other in grace. But let us institute anew and from the beginning a stricter inquiry into the condition of these kings. That king hath dominion over his guards, and issues orders to all, and all obey and serve him; but here I show you greater authority. For the number here is as great or even greater: it remains to inquire into their obedience. And bring me not forth those that have ruled amiss[5], since I too bring those that have been driven from their kingdom and murdered by their very body guards. Let us then bring forth these instances, but seek for those of either kind who have ordered well their kingdom. And do thou put forward whom thou wilt. I oppose unto thee the patriarch against all. For when he was commanded to sacrifice his son, consider how many thoughts then rose up against him. Nevertheless, he brought all under submission, and all trembled before him more than before a king his guards; and with a look only he stilled them all and not one of them dared so much as mutter; but down they bowed and as unto a king gave place, one and all, though much exasperated and exceeding relentless. For even the heads of spears raised upright by many soldiers are not as fearful as were then those fearful thoughts, armed not with spears, but what is harder[6] to deal with than many spears, the sympathy of nature! Wherefore they had power to pierce his soul more than sharpened spear point. For never spear could be so sharp as were the goads of those thoughts, which, sharpened and upraised from beneath, from his affections, were piercing through and through the mind of that righteous man. For here there needs time and purpose and a stroke and pain, and then death follows; but there, there needed none of these, so much were the wounds speedier and acuter. But still though so many thoughts were then in arms against him, there was a deep calm, and they stood all in fair array; adorning rather than daunting him. See him at least stretching out the knife, and set forth as many as thou

---

[1] St. Chrysostom plainly means by "these," not what was last mentioned, but what they are to lead to. There are other instances in his writings of similiar inaccuracies.
[2] The Ben. and other Editions insert some words, "much more will He who gave these supply these also."
[3] Rom. 12, 1. where the Rec. text has σώματα, not μέλη, as St. Chrysos. reads.

[4] ποικίλον.
[5] εκπεσόντας.
[6] χαλεπώτερον.

wilt, kings, emperors, Cæsars, yet shalt thou tell of nought like this, have no like mien to point to, so noble, so worthy of the heavens. For that righteous man erected a trophy at that movement over the most arbitrary of tyrannies. For nothing is so tyrannical as nature; and find ten thousand tyrannicides, one like this shalt thou never show us. For it was the triumph in that moment of an angel, not a man. For consider. Nature was dashed to the ground with all her weapons, with all her host: and he stood with outstretched hand, grasping not a crown, but a knife more glorious than any crown, and the throng of angels applauded, and God from heaven proclaimed him conquerer.

For seeing that his citzenship was in heaven, thence also he received that proclamation. (Phil. iii. 20.) What could be more glorious than this? rather, what trophy could ever be equal to it? For if on occasion of a wrestler's success, not a herald below but the king above should have risen up and himself proclaimed the Olympic Victor, would not this have seemed to him more glorious than the crown, and have turned the gaze of the whole theatre upon him? When then no mortal king, but God Himself, not in this theatre but in the theatre of the universe, in the assembly of the angels, the archangels, proclaimeth his name with uplifted voice shouting from heaven, tell me what place shall we assign to this holy man?

[6.] But if you will, let us listen too to the voice itself. What then was the voice? "Abraham, Abraham, lay not thy hand upon Isaac, neither do thou any thing unto him. For now I know that thou fearest God, and hast not spared thy son, thy well-beloved, for My sake." (Gen. xxii. 11, 12.) What is this? He that knoweth all things before they are, did He now know! And yet even to man the Patriarch's[1] fear of God was evident: so many proofs had he given that his heart was right toward God[2], as when He said to him, "Get thee out of thy country, and from thy kindred;" (Gen. xii. 1.) when for His sake and the honor due to Him he relinquished to his sister's son his priority; when He delivered him out of so great perils; when He bade him go into Egypt, and on his wife's being taken from him, he repined not, and more instances besides; and as I said, from these things even man would have learned the Patriarch's fear of God, much more than God Who waiteth not for the acts to know the end. And how too justified he him, if He knew not? For it is written, "Abraham believed, and it was counted unto him for righteousness." (Gen. xv. 6. Rom. iv. 3.)

What then means this, "Now I know?"

The Syriac hath, "Now thou hast made known;" that is, to men. For I knew of old, even before all those commandments. And why, to men even, "now?" for were not those acts enough to prove his mind was right toward God? They were enough indeed, but this one so much greater than them all that they appear nothing beside it. As exalting then this good work and showing its superiority to all, He so spake. For of things which exceed and surpass all that went before, most men are wont to speak so: for instance, if one receive from another a gift greater than any former one, he often says, "Now I know that such an one loves me," not hereby meaning that he knew not in the time past, but as intending to declare what is now given to be greater than all. So also God, speaking after the manner of men, saith, "Now I know," intending only to mark the exceeding greatness of the exploit; not that He "then" came to know either his fear or the greatness of it. For when He saith, "Come, let Us go down and see," (Gen. xi. 7; xviii. 21.) He saith it not as needing to go down, (for He both filleth all things and knoweth all things certainly,) but to teach us not to give sentence lightly. And when He saith, "The Lord looked down from Heaven:" (Ps. xiv. 2.) it describeth His perfect knowledge by a metaphor taken from men. So also here He saith, "Now I know," to declare this to be greater than all which had preceded it. Of this itself too He furnisheth proof by adding, "Because thou sparedst not thy son, thy well-beloved, for My sake; He saith not "thy son" only, but yet more, "thy well-beloved." For it was not nature only, but also parental fondness, which having both by natural disposition and by the great goodness of his child, he yet dared in him to spurn[3]. And if about worthless children parents are not easily indifferent, but mourn even for them; when it is his son, his only-begotten, and his well-beloved, even Isaac, and the father himself is on the point of immolating him; who can describe the excessiveness of such philosophy? This exploit outshineth thousands of diadems and crowns innumerable. For the wearer of that crown, both death ofttimes assaileth and annoyeth, and before death, assaults of circumstances without number; but this diadem shall no one have strength to take from him that weareth it; no not even after death; neither of his own household, nor of strangers. And let me point you out the costliest stone in this diadem. For as a costly stone, so this comes at the end and clasps it. What then is this? the words, "for My sake?" for not herein is the marvel, that he spared not, but that it was "for His sake."

---

[1] τἀνδρός.
[2] τῆς περὶ τὸν Θεὸν εὐνόιας.

[2] κατετόλμησεν.

Oh! blessed right hand, of what a knife was it accounted worthy? oh! wondrous knife, of what a right hand was it accounted worthy? Oh! wondrous knife, for what a purpose was it prepared? to what an office did it serve? to what a type did it minister? How was it bloodied? how was it not bloodied? For I know not what to say, so awful was that mystery. It touched not the neck of the child, nor passed through the throat of that holy one: nor was crimsoned with the blood of the righteous; rather it both touched, and passed through, and was crimsoned, and was bathed in it, yet was not bathed. Perchance I seem to you beside myself, uttering such contradictions. For, in truth, I am beside myself, with the thought of the wondrous deed of that righteous man; but I utter no contradictions. For indeed the righteous man's hand thrust it in the throat of the lad, but God's Hand suffered it not, so thrust, to be stained with blood of the lad. For it was not Abraham alone that held it back, but God also: and he by his purpose gave the stroke, God by His voice restrained it. For the same voice both armed and disarmed[1] that right hand, which, marshalled under God, as if under a leader, performed all things at His beck, and all were ministered at His voice. For observe; He said, "Slay," and straightway it was armed: He said, "Slay not," and straightway it was disarmed: for every thing [before] had been fully prepared.

And now God showed the soldier and general to the whole world; this crowned victor to the theatre of the angels; this priest, this king, crowned with that knife beyond a diadem, this trophy-bearer, this champion, this conqueror without a fight. For as if some general having a most valiant soldier, should use his mastery of his weapons, his bearing, his ordered movements[2] to dismay the adversary; so also God, by the purpose, the attitude, the bearing only of that righteous man, dismayed and routed the common enemy of us all, the Devil. For I deem that even he then shrunk away aghast. But if any one say, 'And why did he not suffer that right hand to be bathed, and then forthwith raise him up after being sacrificed?' Because God might not accept such bloody offerings; such a table were that of avenging demons. But here two things were displayed, both the loving kindness of the Master, and the faithfulness of the servant. And before, indeed, he went out from his country: but then he abandoned even nature. Wherefore also he received his principal with usury: and very reasonably. For he chose to lose the name of father, to show himself a faithful servant.

Wherefore he became not a father only, but also a priest; and because for God's sake he gave up his own, therefore also did God give him with these His own besides. When then enemies devise mischief, He allows it to come even to the trial, and then works miracles; as in the case of the furnace and the lions; (Dan. iii. and vi.) but when Himself biddeth, readiness[3] attained, He stayeth His bidding. What then, I ask, was wanting further in this noble deed? For did Abraham foreknow what would happen? Did he bargain for the mercy of God? For even though he were a prophet, yet the prophet knoweth not all things. So the actual sacrifice afterwards was superfluous and unworthy of God. And if it was fit he should learn that God was able to raise from the dead, by the womb he had learnt this much more marvellously, or rather he learnt it even before that proof, for he had faith.

[7.] Do not then only admire this righteous man, but also imitate him, and when thou seest him amid so great uproar and surge of waves sailing as in a calm, take thou in hand in like way the helm of obedience and fortitude. For look, pray, not only at this that he built up the altar and the wood; but remember too the voice of the lad, and reflect what hosts like snow storms[4] assaulted him to dismay him, when he heard the lad say, "My father, where is the lamb?" Bethink thee how many thoughts were then stirred up armed not with iron, but with darts of flame; and piercing into and cutting him through on every side. If even now many, and those not parents, are broken down[5], and would have wept, did they not know the end: and many, I see, do weep, though they know it; what must it be thought he would feel, who begat, who nurtured him, in old age had him, had him only, him such an one, who sees, who hears him, and is presently about to slay him? What intelligence in the words! What meekness in the question! Who then is here at work? The Devil that he might set nature in a flame? God forbid! but God, the more to prove the golden soul of the righteous man. For when indeed the wife of Job speaks, a Devil is at work. For of such sort the advice is. But this one uttereth nothing blasphemous, but what is both very devout and thoughtful; and great the grace that overspread the words, much the honey that dropped therefrom, flowing from a calm and gentle soul. Even a heart of stone these words were enough to soften. But they turned not aside, nay, shook not that adamant. Nor said he, 'Why callest thou him father, who in a little while will not be thy father, yea, who

---

[1] Ben. "checked."
[2] ῥυθμοῦ Ben. ῥώμης.
[2] μέχρι προθυμίας.
[4] νιφάδες στρατοπέδων.
[5] κατακλῶνται.

hath already lost that title of honor?' And why doth the lad ask the question? Not of impertinence merely, not of curiosity, but as anxious about what was proposed. For he reflected that had his father not meant to make him a partner in what was done, he would not have left the servants below, and taken him only with him. For this reason, too, surely, it is that when they were alone, then he asks him, when none heard what was said. So great was the judgment of the lad. Are ye not all warmed towards him, both men and women? Doth not each one of you mentally infold and kiss the child, and marvel at his judgment; and venerate the piety which, when he was both bound and laid on the wood, made him not be dismayed nor struggle nor accuse his father as mad; but he was even bound and lifted up and laid upon it, and endured all in silence, like a lamb, yea, rather like the common Lord of all. For of Him he both imitated the gentleness, and kept to the type. For "He was led like a lamb to the slaughter, and as a sheep dumb before his shearer." (Is. liii. 7.) And yet Isaac spake; for his Lord spake also. How dumb then? This meaneth, he spake nothing wilful or harsh, but all was sweet and mild, and the words more than the silence manifested his gentleness. For Christ also said, "If I have spoken evil, bear witness of the evil; but if well, why smitest thou Me?"(John xviii. 23) and manifested His gentleness more than if He had help His peace. And as this one speaketh with his father from the altar, so too doth He from the Cross, saying,"Father, forgive them, for they know not what they do." What then said the Patriarch? (ver. 8.) "God will provide Himself a lamb for a burnt-offering, my son." Either uses the names of nature; the former, father; the latter, son; and on either side arduous is the war stirred up, and mighty the storm, and yet wreck no where: for religion [1] triumphed over all. Then after he heard of God, he spoke no further word nor was impertinently curious [2]. Of such judgment was the child even in the very bloom of youth.

Seest thou the king, over how many armies, in how many battles which beset him, he hath been victorious? For the barbarians were not so fearful to the city of Jerusalem when they assaulted her oftentimes, as were to this man the thoughts on every side besieging him: but still he overcame all. Wouldest thou see the priest also? The instance is at hand. For when thou hast seen him with fire and a knife; and standing over an altar, what doubtest thou after as to his priesthood? But if thou wouldest see the sacrifice also, lo, here a twofold one. For he offered a son, he offered also a ram, yea, more and above all, his own will. And with the blood of the lamb he consecrated his right hand [3], with the sacrifice of his son, his soul. Thus was he ordained a priest, by the blood of his only-begotten, by the sacrifice of a lamb; for the priests also were consecrated by the blood of the victims which were offered to God. Wouldest thou see the prophet also? It is written, "Your father Abraham rejoiced to see My day, and he saw it, and was glad." (Levit. viii. John viii. 56.)

So also art thou thyself made king and priest and prophet in the Laver; a king, having dashed to earth all the deeds of wickedness and slain thy sins; a priest, in that thou offerest thyself to God, having sacrificed thy body and being thyself slain also, "for if we died with Him," saith he, "we shall also live with Him;" (2 Tim. ii. 11.) a prophet, knowing what shall be, and being inspired of God [4], and sealed [5]. For as upon soldiers a seal, so is also the Spirit put upon the faithful. And if thou desert, thou art manifest [by it] to all. For the Jews had circumcision for a seal, but we, the earnest of the Spirit. Knowing then all this, and considering our high estate, let us exhibit a life worthy of the grace [6], that we may obtain also the kingdom to come; which may we all obtain through the grace and love towards men of our Lord Jesus Christ, with Whom, to the Father, together with the Holy Spirit, be glory, power, honor, now and for ever, and world without end. Amen.

---

[1] φιλοσοφία.
[2] περιειργάσατο

[3] In Levitical consecrations, the thumb of the priest's right hand was sprinkled with blood. Lev. viii. 23.
[4] ἔνθους.
[5] vid. Hom. iii. on Rom., comment. on v. 11. p. 113. Oxford Transl.
[6] τῆς χάριτος.

HOMILY IV

2 Cor. i. 23.

But I call God for a witness upon my soul, that to spare you I forbare to come unto Corinth.

WHAT sayest thou, O blessed Paul? To spare them thou camest not to Corinth? Surely thou presentest us with something of a contradiction. For a little above thou saidst that thou therefore camest not, because thou purposest not according to the flesh nor art thine own master, but art led about every where by the authority of the Spirit, and didst set forth thine afflictions. But here thou sayest it was thine own act that thou camest not, and not from the authority of the Spirit; for he saith, "To spare you I forbare to come to Corinth." What then is one to say? either, that this too was itself of the Spirit, and that he himself wished to come but the Spirit suggested to him not to do so, urging the motive of sparing them ; or else, that he is speaking of some other coming, and would signify that before he wrote the former Epistle he was minded to come, and for love's sake restrained himself lest he should find them yet unamended. Perhaps also, after the second Epistle though the Spirit no longer forbade him to go, he involuntarily stayed away for this reason. And this suspicion is the more probable, that in the first instance the Spirit forbade him : but afterwards upon his own conviction also that this was more advisable, he stayed away.

And observe, I pray you, how he remembers again his own custom, (which I shall never cease to observe,) of making what seems against him tell in his favor. For since it was natural for them to respect this and say, ' It was because thou hatedst us, thou wouldest not come unto us,' he shows on the contrary, that the cause for which he would not come was that he loved them.

What is the expression, "to spare you ?" I heard, he saith, that some among you had committed fornication ; I would not therefore come and make you sorry : for had I come, I must needs have enquired into the matter, and prosecuted and punished, and exacted justice from many. I judged it then better to be away and to give opportunity for repentance, than to be with you and to prosecute, and be still more incensed. For towards the end of this Epistle he hath plainly declared it, saying, " I fear lest when I come, my God should humble me before you, and that I should mourn for many of them that have sinned heretofore, and repented not of the lasciviousness and uncleanness[1] which they committed." (2 Cor. xii. 20, 21.) This therefore here also he intimates, and he saith it indeed as in his own defence ; yet rebuketh[2] them most severely and putteth them in fear ; for he implied that they were open to punishment, and will also have somewhat to suffer, unless they be quickly reformed. And he says the same thing again at the end of the Epistle thus ; "If I come again, I will not spare." (2 Cor. xiii. 2.) Only there he says it more plainly : but here, as it was the proem, he does not say it so but in a repressed[3] tone ; nor is he content even with this, but he softens it down, applying a corrective. For seeing the expression was that of one asserting great authority, (for a man spares those whom he has also power to punish,) in order to relieve it, and draw a shade over what seems harsh, he saith,

Ver. 24. "Not for that we have lordship over your faith."

That is, I did not therefore say, "To spare you I came not," as lording it over you. Again, he said not you, but "your faith," which was at once gentler and truer. For him that hath no mind to believe, who hath power to compel ?

" But are helpers of your joy."

For since, saith he, your joy is ours, I came not, that I might not plunge you into sorrow and increase my own despondency; but I stayed away that ye being reformed by the threat might be made glad. For we do every thing in order to your joy, and give diligence in this behalf, because we are ourselves partakers of it.

" For by faith ye stand."

Behold him again speaking repressedly. For he was afraid to rebuke them again ; since he had handled them severely in the former Epistle, and they had made some reformation. And if, now that they were reformed, they again re-

---

[1] Rec. text, *"uncleanness, and fornication, and lasciviousness."*
[2] ἐπιστύφει.
[3] ὑπεσταλμένως.

294

ceived the same reproof, this was likely to throw them back. Whence this Epistle is much gentler than the former.

Chap. ii. 1. "But I determined [1] for myself that I would not come again to you with sorrow."

The expression "again" proves that he had already been made sorry from thence, and whilst he seems to be speaking in his own defence he covertly rebukes them. Now if they had both already made him sorry and were about again to make him sorry, consider how great the displeasure was likely to be. But he saith not thus, 'Ye made me sorry,' but turns the expression differently yet implying the very same thing thus, ' For this cause I came not that I might not make you sorry:' which has the same force as what I said, but is more palatable.

[2.] Ver. 2. "For if I make you sorry, who then is he that maketh me glad, but he that is made sorry by me?"

What is this consequence? A very just one indeed. For observe, I would not, he saith, come unto you, lest I should increase your sorrow, rebuking, showing anger and disgust. Then seeing that even this was strong and implied accusation that they so lived as to make Paul sorry, he applies a corrective in the words, "For if I make you sorry, who then is he that maketh me glad, but he that is made sorry by me?"

What he saith is of this kind. 'Even though I were to be in sorrow, being compelled to rebuke you and to see you sorry, still nevertheless this very thing would have made me glad. For this is a proof of the greatest love, that you hold me in such esteem as to be hurt at my being displeased with you.'

Behold too his prudence. Their doing what all disciples do, namely, smarting and feeling it when rebuked, he produces as an instance of their gratifying him; for, saith he, 'No man maketh me so glad as he that giveth heed to my words, and is sorry when he seeth me angry.'

Yet what followed naturally [2] was to say, ' For if I make you sorry, who then is he that can make you glad?' But he doth not say this, but turns his speech back again, dealing tenderly with them, and says, ' Though I make you sorry, even herein ye bestow on me a very great favor in that ye are hurt at what I say.'

Ver. 3. "And I wrote this very thing unto you."

What? That for this cause I came not, to spare you. When wrote he? In the former Epistle when he said, "I do not wish to see you now by the way?" (1 Cor. xvi. 7.) I think not; but in this Epistle when he said, "Lest when I come again, my God should humble me before you." (2 Cor. xii. 21.) I have written then towards the end this same, saith he, "lest when I come, my God will humble me, and I should mourn for many of them that have sinned heretofore."

But why didst thou write? "Lest when I came I should have sorrow from them of whom I ought to rejoice, having confidence in you all, that my joy is the joy of you all?" For whereas he said he was made glad by their sorrow, and this was too arrogant and harsh, again he gave it a different turn and softened it by what he subjoined. For, he saith, I therefore wrote unto you before, that I might not with anguish find you unreformed; and I said this, "lest I should have sorrow," out of regard not to my own interest but yours. For I know that if ye see me rejoicing ye rejoice, and if ye behold me sad ye are sad. Observe therefore again the connection of what he said; for so his words will be more easy to understand. I came not, he says, lest I should cause you sorrow when finding you unreformed. And this I did, not studying my own advantage, but yours. For as to myself, when ye are made sorry I receive no little pleasure, seeing that you care so much about me as to be sorry and distressed at my being displeased. "For who is he that maketh me glad, but he that is made sorry by me." However, though it be so with myself, yet because I study your advantage, I wrote this same thing to you that I might not be made sorry, herein also again studying not my advantage, but yours; for I know, that were ye to see me sad, ye also would be sorry; as also ye are glad when ye see me rejoicing. Observe now his prudence. He said, I came not, that I might not make you sorry; although, saith he, this makes me glad. Then, lest he should seem to take pleasure in their pain, he saith, In this respect I am glad inasmuch as I make you feel, for in another respect I am sorry in that I am compelled to make those sorry who love me so much, not only by this rebuke, but also by being myself in sorrow and by this means causing you fresh sorrow.

But observe how he puts this so as to mingle praise; saying, "from them of whom I ought to rejoice," for these are the words of one testifying kindred and much tender affection; as if one were speaking of sons on whom he had bestowed many benefits and for whom he had toiled. If then for this I write and come not; it is with weighty meaning [3] I come not, and not because I feel hate or aversion, but rather exceeding love.

[3.] Next, whereas he said, he that makes me sorry makes me glad; lest they should say 'this then is what thou studiest, that thou mightest

---

[1] Rec. text, *determined this.* Chrysostom omits τοῦτο.
[2] τὸ ἀκόλουθον.

[3] μέγα τι οἰκονομῶν.

be made glad and mightest exhibit to all the extent of thy power ; ' he added,

Ver. 4. " For out of much affliction and anguish of heart I wrote unto you with many tears, not that ye should be made sorry, but that ye might know the love which I have more abundantly unto you."

What more tenderly affectioned than this man's spirit is ? for he showeth himself to have been not less pained than they who had sinned, but even much more. For he saith not " out of affliction " merely, but " out of much," nor " with tears," but " with many tears " and " anguish of heart," that is, I was suffocated, I was choked with despondency ; and when I could no longer endure the cloud of despondency, " I wrote unto you : not that ye should be grieved, but that ye might know the love," saith he, " which I have more abundantly unto you." And yet what naturally followed was to say, not that ye might be grieved, but that ye might be corrected : (for indeed with this purpose he wrote.) This however he doth not say, but, (more to sweeten his words, and win them to a greater affection,) he puts this for it, showing that he doth all from love. And he saith not simply " the love," but " which I have more abundantly unto you." For hereby also he desires to win them, by showing that he loveth them more than all and feels towards them as to chosen disciples. Whence he saith, " Even if I be not an Apostle unto others, yet at least I am to you;" (1 Cor. ix. 2.) and, " Though ye have many [1] tutors, yet have ye not many fathers; "(1 Cor. iv. 15.) and again, " By the grace of God we behaved ourselves in the world, and more abundantly to youward ; " (2 Cor. i. 12.) and farther on, " Though the more abundantly I love you, the less I be loved ; " and here " Which I have more abundantly unto you ; " (2 Cor. xii. 15.) So that if my words were full of anger, yet out of much love and sadness was the anger ; and whilst writing the Epistle, I suffered, I was pained, not because ye had sinned only, but also because I was compelled to make you sorry. And this itself was out of love. Just as a father whose legitimate [2] son is afflicted with a gangrene, being compelled to use the knife and cautery, is pained on both accounts, that he is diseased and that he is compelled to use the knife to him. So that what ye consider a sign of hating you was indeed a sign of excessive love. And if to have made you sorry was out of love, much more my gladness at that sorrow.

[4.] Having made this defence of himself, (for he frequently defends himself, without being ashamed ; for if God doth so, saying,

" O My people, what have I done unto thee ? " (Mic. vi. 3.) much more might Paul,) having, I say, made this defence of himself, and being now about to pass on to the plea for him who had committed fornication, in order that they might not be distracted as at receiving contradictory commands, nor take to cavilling because he it was who both then was angry and was now commanding ,to forgive him, see how he provided [3] for this beforehand, both by what he has said and what he is going to say. For what saith he ?

Ver. 5. " But if any hath caused sorrow, he hath caused sorrow not to me."

Having first praised them as feeling joy and sorrow for the same things as himself, he then strikes into the subject of this person, having said first, " my joy is the joy of you all." But if my joy is the joy of you all, need is that you should also now feel pleasure with me, as ye then were pained with me : for both in that ye were made sorry, ye made me glad ; and now in that ye rejoice, (if as I suppose ye shall feel pleasure,) ye will do the same. He said not, my sorrow is the sorrow of you all ; but having established this in the rest of what he said, he has now put forward that only which he most desired, namely, the joy : saying, my joy is the joy of you all. Then, he makes mention also of the former matter, saying,

" But if any hath caused sorrow he hath caused sorrow not to me, but in part (that I press not too heavily) to you all."

I know, he saith, that ye shared in my anger and indignation against him that had committed fornication, and that what had taken place grieved in part all of you. And therefore said I " in part," not as though ye were less hurt than I, but that I might not weigh down him that had committed fornication. He did not then grieve me only but you also equally, even though to spare him I said, " in part." Seest thou how at once he moderated their anger, by declaring that they shared also in his indignation.

Ver. 6. " Sufficient to such a one is this punishment which was inflicted by the many."

And he saith not " to him that hath committed fornication," but here again " to such a one," as also in the former Epistle. Not however for the same reason ; but there out of shame, here out of mercy. Wherefore he no where subsequently so much as mentions the crime ; for it was time now to excuse.

Ver. 7. " So that contrariwise ye should rather forgive him and comfort him, lest by any means such a one should be swallowed up with his overmuch sorrow."

He bids them not only take off the censure ;

---

[1] Rec. text μυρίους.
[2] γνήσιος.

[3] προψκονόμησεν.

but, besides, restores him to his former estate; for if one let go him that hath been scourged and heal him not, he hath done nothing. And see how him too he keeps down lest he should be rendered worse by the forgiveness. For though he had both confessed and repented, he makes it manifest that he obtaineth remission not so much by his penitence as by this free gift. Wherefore he saith, "to forgive[1] him and to comfort him," and what follows again makes the same thing plain. ' For ' saith he, ' it is not because he is worthy, not because he has shown sufficient penitence; but because he is weak, it is for this I request[2] it.' Whence also he added, "lest by any means such a one should be swallowed up with overmuch sorrow." And this is both as testifying to his deep repentance and as not allowing him to fall into despair[3].

But what means this, "swallowed up?" Either doing as Judas did, or even in living becoming worse. For, saith he, if he should rush away from longer enduring the anguish of this lengthened censure, perchance also despairing he will either come to hang himself, or fall into greater crimes afterwards. One ought then to take steps beforehand[4], lest the sore become too hard to deal with; and lest what we have well done we lose by want of moderation.

Now this he said, (as I have already observed,) both to keep him low, and to teach him not to be over-listless after this restoration. For, not as one who has washed all quite away; but as fearing lest he should work aught of deeper mischief, I have received him, he saith. Whence we learn that we must determine the penance, not only by the nature of the sins, but by the disposition and habit of them that sin. As the Apostle did in that instance. For he feared his weakness, and therefore said, "lest he be swallowed up," as though by a wild beast, by a storm, by a billow.

Ver. 8. " Wherefore I beseech you."

He no longer commands but beseeches, not as a teacher but as an equal; and having seated them on the judgment seat he placed himself in the rank of an advocate; for having succeeded in his object, for joy he adopts without restraint the tone of supplication. And what can it be that thou beseechest? Tell me.

" To confirm your love toward him."

That is, 'make it strong,' not simply have intercourse with him, nor any how. Herein, again, he bears testimony to their virtue as very great; since they who were so friendly and so applauded him as even to be puffed up, were so estranged that Paul takes such pains to make them confirm their love towards him. Herein is excellence of disciples, herein excellence of teachers; that they should so obey the rein, he so manage their motions[1]. If this were so even now, they who sin would not have transgressed senselessly. For one ought neither to love carelessly, nor to be estranged without some reason.

[5.] Ver. 9. "For to this end also did I write to you[2], that I might know the proof of you, whether ye are obedient in all things;" not only in cutting off, but also in reuniting. Seest thou how here again he brings the danger to their doors. For as when he sinned, he alarmed their minds, except they should cut him off, saying, "A little leaven leaventh the whole lump," (1 Cor. v, 6.) and several other things; so here too again he confronts them with the fear of disobedience, as good as saying, 'As then ye had to consult not for him, but for yourselves too, so now must ye not less for yourselves than for him; lest ye seem to be of such as love contention and have not human sensibilities, and not to be in all things obedient. And hence he saith, " For to this end also did I write to you, that I might know the proof of you, whether ye are obedient in all things."

For the former instance might have seemed to proceed even of envy and malice, but this shows very especially the obedience to be pure, and whether ye are apt unto loving kindness. For this is the test of right minded disciples; if they obey not only when ordered to do certain things, but when the contrary also. Therefore he said, " in all things," showing that if they disobey, they disgrace not him[3] so much as themselves, earning the character of lovers of contention; and he doth this that hence also he may drive them to obey. Whence also he saith, "For to this end did I write to you; " and yet he wrote not for this end, but he saith so in order to win them. For the leading object was the salvation of that person. But where it does no harm, he also gratifies them. And by saying, "In all things," he again praises them, recalling to memory and bringing forth to view their former obedience.

Ver. 10. "To whom ye forgive any thing, I forgive also."

Seest thou how again he assigns the second part to himself, showing them as beginning, himself following. This is the way to soften an exasperated, to compose a contentious spirit. Then lest he should make them careless, as though they were arbiters, and they should refuse forgiveness; he again constrains them

---

[1] χαρίσασθαι.
[2] Or think it fitting.
[3] ἀπονοίαν, which is however seldom used in this sense by St. Chrysostom.
[4] προκαταλαβεῖν

[5] ῥυθμίζειν.
[6] Rec. text omits ὑμιν.
[7] The incestuous person.

unto this, saying, that himself also had forgiven him.

"For what I also have forgiven, if I have forgiven any thing, for your sakes have I forgiven it." For, this very thing I have done for your sakes, he saith. And as when he commanded them to cut him off, he left not with them the power to forgive, saying, "I have judged already to deliver such an one unto Satan," (1 Cor. v. 3, 5.) and again made them partners in his decision saying, "ye being gathered together to deliver him," (ib. 4, 5.) (thereby securing two most important things, viz., that the sentence should be passed ; yet not without their consent, lest herein he might seem to hurt them ;) and neither himself alone pronounces it, lest they should consider him self-willed, and themselves to be overlooked, nor yet leaves all to them, lest when possessed of the power they should deal treacherously with the offender by unseasonably forgiving him: so also doth he here, saying, 'I have already forgiven, who in the former Epistle had already judged.' Then lest they should be hurt, as though overlooked, he adds, "for your sakes." What then? did he for men's sake pardon? No; for on this account he added,

"In the person of Christ."

What is "in the person of Christ ?" Either he means according to [the will of] God, or unto the glory of Christ.[1]

Ver. 11. "That no advantage may be gained over us by Satan: for we are not ignorant of his devices."

Seest thou how he both committeth the power to them and again taketh away that by that he may soften them, by this eradicate their self will. But this is not all that he provides for by this, but shows also that should they be disobedient the harm would reach to all, just as he did at the outset also. For then too he said, "A little leaven leaveneth the whole lump." (1 Cor. v. 6.) And here again, "Lest Satan should get an advantage of us." And throughout, he maketh this forgiveness the joint act of himself and them. Consider it from the first. "But if any," saith he, "have caused sorrow he hath caused sorrow not to me, but in part (that I press not too heavily) to you all." Then again, "Sufficient to such a one is this punishment which was" inflicted by the

"many." This is his own decision and opinion. He rested not however with this decision, but again makes them partners saying, "So that contrariwise ye should rather forgive" him "and comfort" him. "Wherefore I beseech you to confirm your love towards him." Having thus again made the whole their act, he passes to his own authority, saying, "For to this end did I write unto you, that I might know the proof of you, whether ye are obedient in all things." Then, again, he makes the favor theirs, saying, "To whom ye forgive anything." Then, his own, "I" forgive "also :" saying, "if I have forgiven anything, it is for your sakes." Then both theirs and his, "For," saith he, "if I have forgiven any thing, for your sakes forgave I it in the person of Christ," either [that is] for the glory of Christ, or as though Christ commanding this also, which was most effectual to prevail with them. For after this they would have feared not to grant that which tended to His glory and which He willed. Then again he signifieth the common harm should they disobey, when he saith, "Lest Satan should get an advantage of us ;" well naming it, getting advantage. For he no more takes his own, but violently seizeth ours, for he[2] is reformed[3]. And tell me not that this one only becomes the wild beast's prey, but consider this also, that the number of the herd is diminished, and now especially when it might recover what it had lost.

"For we are not ignorant of his devices,"

That he destroys even under the show of piety. For not only by leading into fornication can he destroy, but even by the contrary, the unmeasured sorrow following on the repentance for it. When then besides his own he taketh ours too, when both by bidding to sin, he destroys ; and when we bid repent, violently seizeth ; how is not this case getting "advantage[4] ?" For he is not content with striking down by sin, but even by repentance he doth this except we be vigilant. Wherefore also with reason did he call it getting advantage, when he even conquereth our own weapons. For to take by sin is his proper work ; by repentance, however, is no more his ; for ours, not his, is that weapon. When then even by this he is able to take, think how disgraceful the defeat, how he will laugh at and run us down as weak and pitiful, if he is to subdue us with our own weapons. For it were matter for exceeding scorn and of the last disgrace, that he should inflict wounds on us through our own remedies. Therefore he said, "for we are not

---

[1] [Modern critics understand this phrase otherwise. They take it as meaning either that the Apostle acted as Christ's representative and by his authority (Luther, Wetstein, *et al.*), or that he took the course which he did in the presence of Christ, i. e., as though Christ were looking on. Either sense is good and suits the connection, but the latter has commended itself to most expositors, (Calvin, Meyer, Hodge, Beet, *et al.*), since nothing could be better adapted to secure both fidelity and tenderness in administering the discipline of God's house than the feeling or rather the conviction that the eyes of Christ were fixed upon the judges. Calvin thinks such a sentiment fitted "to incline us to mercy," but it is not easy to see why it is not as well suited to make one firm in adherence to principle. C.]

[2] The incestuous person.
[3] So two MSS. ap. Field.
[4] πλεονεξία.

ignorant of his devices," exposing his versatility, his craftiness, his evil devices, his malice, his capacity to injure under a show of piety.

[6.] These things then having in mind, let us too never despise any one; nor ever, though we fall into sin, despair; on the other hand, again, let us not be easy-minded afterwards, but, when we transgress, afflict our minds and not merely give vent to words. For I know many who say indeed that they bewail their sins, but do nothing of account. They fast and wear rough garments; but after money are more eager than hucksters, are more the prey of anger than wild beasts, and take more pleasure in detraction than others do in commendations. These things are not repentance, these things are the semblance and shadow only of repentance, not repentance itself. Wherefore in the case of these persons too it is well to say, Take heed "lest Satan should get an advantage of us, for we are not ignorant of his devices;" for some he destroys through sins, others through repentance; but these in yet another way, by suffering them to gain no fruit from repentance. For when he found not how he might destroy them by direct [attack,] he came another road, heightening their toils, whilst robbing them of the fruits, and persuading them, as if they had successfully accomplished all they had to do, therefore to be neglectful of what remains.

That we may not then fruitlessly afflict ourselves, let us address a few words to women of this character; for to women this disorder especially belongs. Praiseworthy indeed is even that which now ye do, your fasting and lying on the ground and ashes; but except the rest be added, these are of no avail. God hath showed how He remitteth sins. Why then forsaking that path, do ye carve another for yourselves. In old time the Ninevites sinned, and they did the things which ye too now are doing. Let us see however what it was that availed them. For as in the case of the sick, physicians apply many remedies; howbeit the man of understanding regardeth not that the sick person has tried this and that, but what was of service to him; such must be also our inquiry here. What then was it that availed those barbarians? They applied fasting unto the wounds, yea applied extreme fasting, lying on the ground too, putting on of sackcloth, and ashes, and lamentations; they applied also a change of life. Let us then see which of these things made them whole. And whence, saith one, shall we know? If we come to the Physician, if we ask Him: for He will not hide it from us, but will even eagerly disclose it. Rather that none may be ignorant, nor need to ask, He hath even set down in writing the medicine that restored them. What then is this? "God," saith He, "saw that they

turned every one from his evil way, and He repented of the evil that He had said He would do unto them." (Jonah iii. 10.) He said not, He saw [their] fasting and sackcloth and ashes. And I say not this to overturn fasting, (God forbid!) but to exhort you that with fasting ye do that which is better than fasting, the abstaining from all evil. David also sinned. (2 Sam. xii. 17. &c.) Let us see then how he too repented. Three days he sat on ashes. But this he did not for the sin's sake, but for the child's, being as yet stupefied with that affliction. But the sin by other means did he wipe away, by humbleness, contrition of heart, compunction of soul, by falling into the like no more, by remembering it always, by bearing thankfully every thing that befalls him, by sparing those that grieve him, by forbearing to requite those who conspire against him; yea, even preventing those who desire to do this. For instance, when Shimei was bespattering him with reproaches without number (2 Sam. xvi. 5, 9.) and the captain who was with him was greatly indignant, he said, "Let him curse me, for the Lord hath bidden him:" for he had a contrite and humbled heart, and it was this especially which wiped away his sins. For this is confession, this is repentance. But if whilst we fast we are proud, we have been not only nothing profited but even injured.

[7.] Humble then thine heart, thou too, that thou mayest draw God unto thee. "For the Lord is nigh unto them that are of a contrite heart." (Ps. xxxiii. 19.) Seest thou not in the gorgeous houses those who are in disgrace; how they answer not again when even the lower servants insult them, but put up with it because of the disgrace with which their fault hath surrounded them? So do thou too: and if any one revile thee, wax not fierce, but groan, not for the insult, but for that sin which cast thee into disgrace. Groan when thou hast sinned, not because thou art to be punished, (for this is nothing,) but because thou hast offended thy Master, one so gentle, one so kind, one that so loveth thee and longeth for thy salvation as to have given even His Son for thee. For this groan, and do this continually: for this is confession. Be not to-day cheerful, to-morrow of a sad countenance, then again cheerful; but continue ever in mourning and self contrition. For, "Blessed," saith he, "are they that mourn," that is, that do this perpetually. Continue then to do this perpetually, and to take heed to thyself, and to afflict thine heart; as one who had lost a beloved son might mourn. "Rend," saith he, "your hearts, and not your garments." (Joel ii. 13.) That which is rent will not lift itself on high; that which hath been broken cannot rise up again. Hence one saith, "Rend," and another, "a broken and a contrite heart God will not despise." (Ps. li. 17.) Yea, though thou be wise, or wealthy, or a ruler, rend thine heart. Suffer it not to have high thoughts nor to be inflated. For that which is rent is not inflated, and even if there be something to make it rise, from being rent it cannot retain the inflation. So also do thou be humble-minded. Consider that the publican was justified by one word, although that was not humiliation, but a true confession. Now if this hath power so great, how much more humiliation. Remit offences to those who have transgressed against thee, for this too remitteth sins. And concerning the former He saith, "I saw that he went sorrowful, and I healed his ways;" (Is. lvii. 17. 18. LXX.) and in Ahab's case, this appeased the wrath of God: (1 Kings xxi. 29) concerning the latter, "Remit, and it shall be remitted unto you." There is also again another way which bringeth us this medicine; condemning what we have done amiss; for, "Declare thou first thy transgressions, that thou mayest be justified." (Is. xliii. 26. LXX.) And for one in afflictions to give thanks looseth his sins; and almsgiving, which is greater than all.

Reckon up therefore the medicines which heal thy wounds, and apply all unremittingly [1], humbleness, confession, forgetting wrongs, giving thanks in afflictions, showing mercy both in alms and actions, persevering in prayer. So did the widow propitiate the cruel and unyielding judge. And if she the unjust, much more thou the gentle. There is yet another way along with these, defending the oppressed; "for," He saith, "judge the fatherless, and plead for the widow; and come, and let us reason together, and though your sins be as scarlet, I will make them white as snow." (Is. i. 17, 18.) What excuse then can we deserve if with so many ways leading us up to heaven, and so many medicines to heal our wounds, even after the Laver we continue where we were. Let us then not only continue so, but let those indeed who have never yet fallen abide in their proper loveliness; yea, rather let them cultivate it more and more, (for these good works, where they find not sins, make the beauty greater:) and let us who in many things have done amiss, in order to the correction of our sins use the means mentioned: that we may stand at the tribunal of Christ with much boldness, whereunto may all we at .in through the grace and love towards men of ur Lord Jesus Christ, with Whom to the F th r, together with the Holy Spirit, be glory, u power, and honor, now and ever, world wit out end. Amen.

HOMILY V.

2 COR. ii. 12, 13.

Now when I came to Troas for the gospel of Christ, and when a door was opened unto me in the Lord, I had no relief for my spirit, because I found not Titus my brother.

THESE words seem on the one hand to be unworthy of Paul, if because of a brother's absence he threw away so great an opportunity of saving; and on the other, to hang apart from the context. What then? Will ye that we should first prove that they hang upon the context, or, that he hath said nothing unworthy of himself? As I think, the second [2], for so the other point also will be easier and clearer.

How then do these (words) hang upon those before them? Let us recall to mind what those were, and so we shall perceive this. What then were those before? What he said at the beginning. "I would not have you," saith he, "ig-norant concerning our affliction which befell us in Asia, that we were weighed down exceedingly, beyond our power." (2 Cor. i. 8.) Now having shown the manner of his deliverance, and inserted the intermediate matter, he is of necessity led to teach them again that in yet another way he had been afflicted. How, and in what way? In not finding Titus. (vii. 6; viii. 6, 16, 22, 23, xii. 18.) Fearful indeed, and enough to prostrate the soul, is it even to endure trials; but when there is none to comfort and that can help to bear the burden, the tempest becometh greater. Now Titus is he, whom further on he speaks of as having come to him from them, and of whom he runs through many and great praises, and whom he said he had sent. With the view then of showing that in this point also he had been afflicted for their sakes, he said these things.

That the words then in question hang on what went before is from all this plain. And I will

---

[1] συνεχῶς.
[2] So Chrysostom, referring apparently to the first sentence in the Homily. It is manifest at least, that the preceeding sentence required "the former" here, and not "the second."

attempt to prove also that they are not unworthy of Paul. For He doth not say that the absence of Titus impeded the salvation of those who were about to come over, nor yet that he neglected those that believed on this account, but that he had no relief, that is, 'I was afflicted, I was distressed for the absence of my brother;' showing how great a matter a brother's absence is; and therefore he departed thence. But what means, "when I came to Troas, for the Gospel?" he saith not simply 'I arrived," but 'so as to preach.' But still, though I had both come for that and found very much to do, (for "a door was opened unto me in the Lord,") I had, saith he, "no relief," not that for this he impeded the work. How then saith he,

Ver. 13. "Taking my leave of them, I went from thence?"

That is, 'I spent no longer time, being straitened and distressed.' And perhaps the work was even impeded by his absence. And this was no light consolation to them too. For if when a door was opened there, and for this purpose he had come; yet because he found not the brother, he quickly started away; much more, he saith, ought ye to make allowance for the compulsion of those affairs which lead us and lead us about everywhere, and suffer us not according as we desire either to journey, or to tarry longer amongst those with whom we may wish to remain. Whence also he proceeds in this place again to refer his journeyings to God, as he did above to the Spirit, saying,

Ver. 14. "But thanks be to God, which always causeth us to triumph in Christ, and maketh manifest through us the savor of His knowledge in every place."

For that he may not seem as though in sorrow to be lamenting these things, he sendeth up thanks to God. Now what he saith is this: 'Every where is trouble, every where straitness. I came into Asia, I was burdened beyond strength. I came to Troas, I found not the brother. I came not to you; this too bred in me no slight, yea rather, exceeding great dejection, both because many among you had sinned, and because on this account I see you not. For, "To spare you," he saith, "I came not as yet unto Corinth."

That then he may not seem to be complaining in so speaking, he adds, 'We not only do not grieve in these afflictions, but we even rejoice; and, what is still greater, not for the sake of the rewards to come only, but those too even which are present. For even here we are by these things made glorious and conspicuous. So far then are we from lamenting, that we even call the thing a triumph[1]; and glory in what

happeneth.' For which cause also he said, "Now thanks be unto God, Which always causeth us to triumph," that is, 'Who maketh us renowned unto all. For what seemeth to be matter of disgrace, being persecuted from every quarter, this appeareth to us to be matter of very great honor.' Wherefore he said not, "Which maketh us seen of all," but, "Which causeth us to triumph:" showing that these persecutions set up a series[2] of trophies against the devil in every part of the world. Then having mentioned along with the author, the subject also of the triumph, he thereby also raiseth up the hearer. 'For not only are we made to triumph by God, but also "in Christ;"' that is, on account of Christ and the Gospel. 'For seeing it behooveth to triumph, all need is that we also who carry the trophy are seen of all, because we bear Him. For this reason we become observed and conspicuous.'

[2.] Ver. 14. "And which maketh manifest through us the savor of His knowledge in every place."

He said above, "Which always causeth us to triumph." Here he saith "in every place," showing that every place and every time is full of the Apostles' labors. And he uses yet another metaphor, that of the sweet savor. For 'like as those who bear ointment, so are we,' saith he, 'manifest to all'; calling the knowledge a very precious ointment. Moreover, he said not, 'the knowledge;' but "the savor of the knowledge;" for such is the nature of the present knowledge, not very clear nor uncovered. Whence also he said in the former Epistle, "For now we see in a mirror darkly." (1 Cor. xiii. 12.) And here he calls that which is such a "savor." Now he that perceiveth the savor knoweth that there is ointment lying somewhere; but of what nature it is he knows not yet, unless he happens before to have seen it. 'So also we. That God is, we know, but what in substance we know not yet. We are then, as it were, a Royal censer, breathing whithersoever we go of the heavenly ointment and the spiritual sweet savor.' Now he said this, at once both to set forth the power of the Preaching, in that by the very designs formed against them, they shine more than those who prosecute them and who cause the whole world to know both their trophies and their sweet savor: and to exhort them in regard to their afflictions and trials to bear all nobly, seeing that even before the Recompense they reap this glory inexpressible.

Ver. 15. "For we are a sweet savor of Christ

---

[1] [The Rev. Vers. renders this clause "leadeth us in triumph," in accordance with Meyer, Beet, _et al._ The principal reason is that the causative sense of the A. V. is against all Hellenistic and New Testament usage, while on the other hand the _neuter_ sense of the verb to "triumph over us" easily passes into the _transitive_, to lead us in triumph. C.]

[2] συνεχῆ.

unto God, in them that are saved and in them that perish."

Whether, saith he, one be saved or be lost, the Gospel continues to have its proper virtue : and as the light, although it blindeth the weakly, is still light, though causing blindness ; and as honey, though it be bitter to those who are diseased, is in its nature sweet ; so also is the Gospel of sweet savor, even though some should be lost who believe it not. For not It, but their own perverseness, worketh the perdition. And by this most of all is its sweet savor manifested, by which the corrupt and vicious perish ; so that not only by the salvation of the good, but also by the perdition of the wicked is its excellence declared. Since both the sun, for this reason most especially that he is exceeding bright, doth wound the eyes of the weak : and the Saviour is " for the fall and rising again of many,"(Luke ii. 34.) but still He continueth to be a Saviour, though ten thousand fall ; and His coming brought a sorer punishment upon them that believe not, but still it continueth to be full of healing [1]. Whence also he saith, "We are unto God a sweet savor ; " that is, 'even though some be lost we continue to be that which we are.' Moreover he said not simply " a sweet savor," but " unto God." And when we are a sweet savor unto God, and He decreeth these things, who shall henceforth gainsay?

The expression also, " sweet savor of Christ," appears to me to admit of a double interpretation : for he means either that in dying they offered themselves a sacrifice : or that they were a sweet savor of the death of Christ, as if one should say, this incense is a sweet savor of this victim. The expression then, sweet savor, either signifieth this, or, as I first said, that they are daily sacrificed for Christ's sake.[2]

[3.] Seest thou to what a height he hath advanced the trials, terming them a triumph and a sweet savor and a sacrifice offered unto God. Then, whereas he said, " we are a sweet savor, even in them that perish," lest thou shouldest think that these too are acceptable, he added,

Ver. 16. " To the one a savor from death unto death, to the other a savor from life unto life."

For this sweet savor some so receive that they are saved, others so that they perish. So that should any one be lost, the fault is from hismelf : for both ointment is said to suffoctae swine, and light (as I before observed,) to blind the weak. And such is the nature of good things ; they not only correct what is akin to them, but also destroy the opposite : and in this way is their power most displayed. For so both fire, not only when it giveth light and when it purifieth gold, but even when it consumeth thorns, doth very greatly display its proper power, and so show itself to be fire : and Christ too herein also doth discover His own majesty when He " shall consume " Antichrist " with the breath of His mouth, and bring him to nought with the manifestation of His coming." (2 Thess. ii. 8.)

" And who is sufficient for these things ? "

Seeing he had uttered great things, that ' we are a sacrifice of Christ and a sweet savor, and are every where made to triumph,' he again useth moderation, referring all to God. Whence also he saith, "and who is sufficient for these things ? " ' for all,' saith he, ' is Christ's, nothing our own.' Seest thou how opposite his language to the false Apostles' ? For they indeed glory, as contributing somewhat from themselves unto the message : he, on the contrary, saith, he therefore glorieth, because he saith that nothing is his own. " For our glorying is this, the testimony of our conscience, that not in fleshly wisdom, but in the grace of God, we behaved ourselves in the world." And that which they considered it a glory to acquire, I mean the wisdom from without, he makes it his to take away. Whence also he here saith, " And who is sufficient for these things ? " But if none are sufficient, that which is done is of grace.

Ver. 17. " For we are not as the rest, which corrupt the word of God."

' For even if we use great sounding words, yet we declared nothing to be our own that we achieved, but all Christ's. For we will not imitate the false apostles ; the men who say that most is of themselves.' For this is " to corrupt," when one adulterates the wine ; when one sells for money what he ought to give freely. For he seems to me to be here both taunting them in respect to money, and again hinting at the very thing I have said, as that they mingle their own things with God's ; which is the charge Isaiah brings when he said, " Thy vintners mingle wine with water : " (Is. i. 22, LXX.) for even if this was said of wine, yet one would not err in expounding it of doctrine too. ' But we,' saith he, ' do not so : but such as we have been entrusted with, such do we offer you, pouring out the word undiluted.' Whence he

---

[1] σωτήριος.

[2] [Rather the sense is a sweet-smelling savor of Christ, something revealing, as perfumes do, the nature of that from which it proceeds, and so a means of diffusing the knowledge of Christ. There does not seem to be any reference to *sacrifice*, as Chrysostom conceives, nor to the incense of the sanctuary, but simply to the grateful and pervasive influence of a perfume. It cannot be hid. It cannot be resisted. Wherever Paul went he diffused abroad the fragrance of the name of Christ, and thus he pleased God. The "savor of Christ," therefore, is not the savor of which he is the author but that of which he is the subject. A savor respecting Christ. The Gospel and those who preach it are well-pleasing to God, as grateful to Him as the purest and most fragrant incense, whether men receive it and are saved, or whether they reject it and are lost. Chrysostom well brings out the solemn and affecting truth that the sweet savor is manifested in both classes, in them that perish as well as in them that are saved. C.]

added, " But as of sincerity, but as of God, in the sight of God speak we in Christ."

'We do not,' saith he 'beguile you and so preach, as conferring a gift on you, or as bringing in and mingling somewhat from ourselves, " but as of God ; " that is, we do not say that we confer any thing of our own, but that God hath given all.' For " of God " means this ; To glory in nothing as if we had it of our own, but to refer every thing to Him.

" Speak we in Christ."

Not by our own wisdom, but instructed by the power that cometh from Him. Those who glory speak not in this way, but as bringing in something from themselves. Whence he elsewhere also turns them into ridicule[1], saying, " For what hast thou that thou didst not receive ? but if thou didst receive it, why dost thou glory as if thou hadst not received it." (1 Cor. iv. 7.) This is the highest virtue, to refer every thing to God, to consider nothing to be our own, to do nothing out of regard to men's opinion, but to what God willeth. For He it is that requireth the account. Now however this order is reversed : and of Him that shall sit upon the tribunal and require the account, we have no exceeding fear, yet tremble at those who stand and are judged with us.

[4.] Whence then is this disease? Whence hath it broken out in our souls? From not meditating continually on the things of that world, but being rivetted to present things. Hence we both easily fall into wicked doings, and even if we do any good thing we do it for display, so that thence also loss cometh to us. For instance, one has looked on a person often with unbridled eyes, unseen of her or of those who walk with her[2], yet of the Eye that never sleeps was not unseen. For even before the commission of the sin, It saw the unbridled soul, and that madness within, and the thoughts that were whirled about in storm and surge ; for no need hath He of witnesses and proofs Who knoweth all things. Look not then to thy fellow-servants : for though man praise, it availeth not if God accept not ; and though man condemn, it harmeth not if God do not condemn. Oh ! provoke not so thy Judge ; of thy fellow-servants making great account, yet when Himself is angry, not in fear and trembling at Him. Let us then despise the praise that cometh of men. How long shall we be low-minded and grovelling ? How long, when God lifteth us to heaven, take we pains to be trailed[3] along the ground ? The brethren of Joseph, had they had the fear of God before their eyes, as men ought to have, would not have taken their brother in a lonely

place and killed him. (Gen. xxxvii.) Cain again, had he feared that sentence as he should have feared, would not have said, " Come, and let us go into the field :" (Gen. iv. 8, LXX.) for to what end, O miserable and wretched! dost thou take him apart from him that begat him, and leadest him out into a lonely place? For doth not God see the daring deed even in the field ? Hath thou not been taught by what befel thy father that He knoweth all things, and is present at all things that are done ? And why, when he denied, said not God this unto him : ' Hidest thou from Me Who am present every where, and know the things that are secret ?' Because as yet he knew not aright to comprehend these high truths[4]. But what saith he ? " The voice of thy brother's blood crieth unto Me." Not as though blood had a voice; but like as we say when things are plain and clear, " the matter speaketh for itself[5]."

Wherefore surely it behoveth to have before our eyes the sentence of God, and all terrors are extinguished. So too in prayers we can keep awake, if we bear in mind with whom we are conversing, if we reflect that we are offering sacrifice and have in our hands a knife and fire and wood ; if in thought we throw wide the gates of heaven, if we transport ourselves thither and taking the sword of the Spirit infix it in the throat of the victim : make watchfulness the sacrifice and tears the libation to Him. For such is the blood of this victim. Such the slaughter that crimsons that altar. Suffer not then aught of worldly thoughts to occupy thy soul then. Bethink thee that Abraham also, when offering sacrifice, suffered nor wife nor servant nor any other to be present. Neither then do thou suffer any of the slavish and ignoble passions to be present unto thee, but go up alone into the mountain where he went up, where no second person is permitted to go up. And should any such thoughts attempt to go up with thee, command them with authority, and say, " Sit ye there, and I and the lad will worship and return to you ;" (Gen. xxii. 5. LXX.) and leaving the ass and the servants below, and whatever is void of reason and sense, go up, taking with thee whatever is reasonable, as he took Isaac. And build thine altar so as he, as having nothing human, but having outstepped nature. For he too, had he not outstepped nature, would not have slain his child. And let nothing disturb thee then, but be lift up above the very heavens. Groan bitterly, sacrifice confession, (for, saith he, " Declare thou first thy transgressions that thou mayest be justified," Is. xliii. 26. LXX.), sacrifice contrition of heart. These victims turn not to ashes nor

---

[1] κωμωδεῖ.
[2] Or, him.
[3] σύρεσθαι.

[4] ταῦτα φιλοσοφεῖν.
[5] βοᾷ.

dissolve into smoke nor melt into air; neither need they wood and fire, but only a deep-pricked heart. This is wood, this is fire to burn, yet not consume them. For he that prayeth with warmth is burnt, yet not consumed; but like gold that is tried by fire becometh brighter.

[5.] And withal observe heedfully one thing more, in praying to say none of those things that provoke thy Master; neither draw near [to pray] against enemies. For if to have enemies be a reproach, consider how great the evil to pray against 'them. For need is that thou defend thyself and show why thou hast enemies: but thou even accusest[1] them. And what forgiveness shalt thou obtain, when thou both revilest, and at such a time when thyself needest much mercy. For thou drewest near to supplicate for thine own sins: make not mention then of those of others, lest thou recall the memory of thine own. For if thou say, 'Smite mine enemy,' thou hast stopped thy mouth, thou hast cut off boldness from thy tongue; first, indeed, because thou hast angered the Judge at once in beginning; next, because thou asketh things at variance with the character of thy prayer. For if thou comest near for forgiveness of sins, how discoursest thou of punishment? The contrary surely was there need to do, and to pray for them in order that we may with boldness beseech this for ourselves also. But now thou hast forestalled the Judge's sentence by thine own, demanding that He punish them that sin: for this depriveth of all pardon. But if thou pray for them, even if thou say nothing in thine own sins' behalf, thou hast achieved all[2]. Consider how many sacrifices there are in the law; a sacrifice of praise, a sacrifice of acknowledgment, a sacrifice of peace[3], a sacrifice of purifications, and numberless others, and not one of them against enemies, but all in behalf of either one's own sins or one's own successes. For comest thou to another God? To him thou comest that said, "Pray for your enemies." (Luke vi. 27, 35. Rom. xii. 14.) How then dost thou cry against them? How dost thou beseech God to break his own law? This is not the guise of a suppliant. None supplicates the destruction of another, but the safety of himself. Why then wearest thou the guise of a suppliant, but hast the words of an accuser? Yet when we pray for ourselves, we scratch ourselves and yawn, and fall into ten thousand thoughts; but when against our enemies, we do so wakefully. For since the devil knows that we are thrusting the sword against ourselves, he doth not distract nor call us off then, that he may work us the greater harm.

But, saith one, 'I have been wronged and am afflicted.' Why not then pray against the devil, who injureth us most of all. This thou hast also been commanded to say, "Deliver us from the evil one." He is thy irreconcileable foe, but man, do whatsoever he will, is a friend and brother. With him then let us all be angry; against him let us beseech God, saying, "Bruise Satan under our feet;" (Rom. xvi. 20.) for he it is that breedeth also the enemies [we have]. But if thou pray against enemies, thou prayest so as he would have thee pray, just as if for thine enemies, then against him. Why then letting him go who is thine enemy indeed, dost thou tear thine own members, more cruel in this than wild beasts. 'But,' saith one, 'he insulted me and robbed me of money;' and which hath need to grieve, he that suffered injury, or he that inflicted injury? Plainly he that inflicted injury, since whilst he gained money he cast himself out of the favor of God, and lost more than he gained: so that he is the injured party. Surely then need is not that one pray against, but for him, that God would be merciful to him. See how many things the three children suffered, though they had done no harm. They lost country, liberty, were taken captive and made slaves; and when carried away into a foreign and barbarous land, were even on the point of being slain on account of the dream, without cause or object[4]. (Dan. ii. 13.) What then? When they had entered in with Daniel, what prayed they? What said they? Dash down Nabuchodonosor, pull down his diadem, hurl him from the throne? Nothing of this sort; but they desired "mercies of God." (Dan. ii. 18. LXX.) And when they were in the furnace, likewise. But not so ye: but when ye suffer far less than they, and oftentimes justly, ye cease not to vent ten thousand imprecations. And one saith, 'Strike down my enemy as Thou overwhelmedst the chariot of Pharaoh;' another, 'Blast his flesh;' another again, 'Requite it on his children.' Recognize ye not these words? Whence then is this your laughter? Seest thou how laughable this is, when it is uttered without passion. And so all sin then discovereth how vile it is, when thou strippest it of the state of mind of the perpetrator. Shouldest thou remind one who has been angered of the words which he said in his passion, he will sink for shame and scorn himself and wish he had suffered a thousand punishments rather than those words to be his. And shouldest thou, when the embrace is over, bring the unchaste to the woman he sinned with, he too will turn away from her as disgusting. And so do ye, because ye are not under the influence of the passion, laugh now.

---

[1] Some Mss. have κακηγορεῖς, revilest.
[2] τὸ πᾶν ἤνυσας.
[3] θυσία σωτηρίου, the rendering of the LXX, for the peace-offering, Lev. iii. 1. &c.

[4] εἰκῆ καὶ μάτην.

For worthy to be laughed at are they, and the words of drunken old gossips; and springing from a womanish littleness of soul. And yet Joseph, though he had been sold and made a slave, and had tenanted a prison, uttered not even then a bitter word against the authors of his sorrows. But what saith he? "Indeed I was stolen away out of the land of the Hebrews;" (Gen. xl. 15.) and addeth not by whom. For he feels more ashamed for the wickedness of his brethren, than they who wrought them. Such too ought to be our disposition, to grieve for them who wrong us more than they themselves do. For the hurt passeth on to them. As then they who kick against nails, yet are proud of it, are fit objects of pity and lamentation on account of this madness; so they who wrong those that do them no evil, inasmuch as they wound their own souls, are fit objects for many moans and lamentations, not for curses. For nothing is more polluted than a soul that curseth, or more impure than a tongue that offereth such sacrifices. Thou art a man; vomit not forth the poison of asps. Thou art a man; become not a wild beast.

For this was thy mouth made, not that thou shouldest bite but that thou shouldest heal the wounds of others. 'Remember the charge I have given thee,' saith God, 'to pardon and forgive. But thou beseechest Me also to be a party to the overthrow of my own commandments, and devourest thy brother, and reddenest thy tongue, as madmen do their teeth on their own members.' How, thinkest thou, the devil is pleased and laughs, when he hears such a prayer? and how, God is provoked, and turneth from and abhorreth thee, when thou beseechest things like these? Than which, what can be more dangerous? For if none should approach the mysteries that hath enemies: how must not he, that not only hath, but also prayeth against them, be excluded even from the outer courts themselves? Thinking then on these things, and considering the Subject[1] of the Sacrifice, that He was sacrificed for enemies; let us not have an enemy: and if we have, let us pray for him; that we too having obtained forgiveness of the sins we have committed, may stand with boldness at the tribunal of Christ; to whom be glory for ever. Amen[2].

HOMILY VI.

2 Cor. iii. 1.

Are we beginning, again to commend ourselves? or need we, as do some, epistles of commendation to you or letters of commendation from you?

He anticipates and puts himself an objection which others would have urged against him, 'Thou vauntest thyself;' and this though he had before employed so strong a corrective in the expressions, "Who is sufficient for these things?" and, "of sincerity . . . speak we." (2 Cor. ii. 16, 17.) Howbeit he is not satisfied with these. For such is his character. From appearing to say any thing great of himself he is far removed, and avoids it even to great superfluity and excess. And mark, I pray thee, by this instance also, the abundance of his wisdom. For a thing of woeful aspect, I mean tribulations, he so much exalted and showed to be bright and lustrous, that out of what he said the present objection rose up against him. And he does so also towards the end. For after having enumerated numberless perils, insults, straits, necessities, and as many such like things as be, he added, "We commend not ourselves, but speak as giving you occasion to glory.,, (2 Cor. v. 12.) And he expresses this again with vehe-

mence in that place, and with more of encouragement. For here the words are those of love, "Need we, as do some, epistles of commendation?" but there what he says is full of a kind of pride even, necessarily and properly so, of pride, I say, and anger. "For we commend not ourselves again," saith he, "but speak as giving you occasion to glory;" (2 Cor. v. 12.) and, "Again, think ye that we excuse ourselves unto you? For[3] in the sight of God speak we in Christ. For I fear lest by any means when I come I should not find you such as I would, and should myself be found of you such as ye would not." (ib. xii. 19, 20.) For to prevent all appearance of a wish to flatter, as though he desired honor from them, he speaketh thus, "I fear lest by any means when I come I should not find you such as I would, and should myself be found of you such as ye would not." This however comes after many accusations[4]; But in the beginning he speaketh not so, but

---

[1] ὑπόθεσιν.
[2] Ben. Ed. 'to Whom be glory, power, and honor, now and ever, and world without end. Amen.'
[3] ὅτι, which is not found in the Received Text.
[4] Others read, "with much accusation."

more gently. And what is it he saith? He
spoke of his trials and his perils, and that every
where he is conducted as in procession [1] by God
in Christ, and that the whole world knoweth of
these triumphs. Since then he has uttered great
things of himself, he urges this objection against
himself, " Are we beginning again to commend
ourselves?" Now what he saith is this: Perchance some one will object, 'What is this, O
Paul? Sayest thou these things of thyself, and
exaltest thyself?' To do away then with this
suspicion, he saith, We desire not this, that is,
to boast and exalt ourselves; yea, so far are we
from needing epistles of commendation to you
that ye are to us instead of an epistle. "For,"
saith he,

Ver. 2. " Ye are our epistle."

What means this, " ye are?" ' Did we need
to be commended to others, we should have produced you before them instead of an epistle.'
And this he said in the former Epistle. " For
the seal of mine Apostleship are ye." (1 Cor.
ix. 2.) But he doth not here say it in this manner, but in irony so as to make his question,
" Do we need epistles of commendation?" more
cutting. And in allusion to the false apostles,
he added, " as do some, [epistles of commen-
dation] to you, or letters of commendation from
you" to others. Then because what he had said
was severe, he softens it by adding, " Ye are
our epistle, written in our hearts, known of all,"

Ver. 3. " Being made manifest that ye are an
epistle of Christ."

Here he testifieth not only to their love, but
also to their good works: since they are able to
show unto all men by their own virtue the high
worth of their teacher, for this is the meaning
of, " Ye are our epistle."

What letters would have done to commend
and gain respect for us, that ye do both as seen
and heard of; for the virtue of the disciples is
wont to adorn and to commend the teacher
more than any letter.

Ver. 3. " Written in our hearts."

That is, which all know; we so bear you
about every where and have you in mind. As
though he said, Ye are our commendation to
others, for we both have you continually in our
heart and proclaim to all your good works.
Because then that even to others yourselves are
our commendation, we need no epistles from
you; but further, because we love you exceedingly, we need no commendation to you. For
to those who are strangers one hath need of letters, but ye are in our mind. Yet he said not
merely, " ye are [in it]," but "written in [it],"
that is, ye cannot slide out of it. For just as
from letters by reading, so from our heart by

perceiving, all are acquainted with the love we
bear you. If then the object of a letter be to
certify, " such an one is my friend and let him
have free intercourse [with you]," your love is
sufficient to secure all this. For should we go
to you, we have no need of others to commend
us, seeing your love anticipateth this; and
should we go to others, again we need no letters,
the same love again sufficing unto us in their
stead, for we carry about the epistle in our
hearts.

[2.] Then exalting them still higher, he even
calleth them the epistle of Christ, saying,

Ver. 3. " Being made manifest that ye are an
epistle of Christ."

And having said this, he afterwards hence
takes ground and occasion for a discussion on
the Law. And there is another[2] aim in his
here styling them His epistle. For above as
commending him, he called them an epistle;
but here an epistle of Christ, as having the Law
of God written in them. For what things God
wished to declare to all and to you, these are
written in your hearts. But it was we who prepared you to receive the writing. For just as
Moses hewed the stones and tables, so we, your
souls. Whence he saith,

" Ministered by us."

Yet in this they were on an equality; for the
former were written on by God, and these by
the Spirit. Where then is the difference?

"Written not with ink, but with the Spirit
of the living God; not in tables of stone, but
in tables that are hearts of flesh."

Wide as the difference between the Spirit and
ink, and a stony table and a fleshy, so wide is
that between these and those; consequently between themselves[3] who ministered, and him[4]
who ministered to them. Yet because it was a
great thing he had uttered, he therefore quickly checks himself, saying,

Ver. 4. " And such confidence have we
through Christ to Godward,"

And again refers all to God: for it is Christ,
saith he, Who is the Author of these things to
us.

Ver. 5. " Not that we are sufficient of ourselves to account any thing as from ourselves."

See again, yet another corrective. For he
possesses this virtue, humility I mean, in singular
perfection. Wherefore whenever he saith any
thing great of himself, he maketh all diligence
to soften down extremely and by every means,
what he has said. And so he does in this place
also, saying, " Not that we are sufficient of ourselves to account any thing as from ourselves:"
that is, I said not, " We have confidence," as

---

[1] πομπεύεται.

[2] Or, perhaps, a special aim, ἄλλως.
[3] i. e. the Apostles.
[4] Moses.

though part were ours and part God's; but I refer and ascribe the whole to Him.

Ver. 5, 6. "For[1] our sufficiency is from God; who also made us sufficient as ministers of a new covenant."

What means, "made us sufficient?" Made us able and fitting. And it is not a little thing to be the bearer to the world of such tables and letters, greater far than the former. Whence also he added,

"Not of the letter, but of the spirit." See again another difference. What then? was not that Law spiritual? How then saith he, "We know that the Law is spiritual?" (Rom. vii. 14.) Spiritual indeed, but it bestowed not a spirit. For Moses bare not a spirit, but letters; but we have been entrusted with the giving of a spirit. Whence also in further completion of this [contrast,] he saith,

"For the letter killeth, but the spirit giveth life."

Yet these things he saith not absolutely[2]; but in allusion to those who prided themselves upon the things of Judaism. And by "letter" here he meaneth the Law which punisheth them that transgress; but by "spirit" the grace which through Baptism giveth life to them who by sins were made dead. For having mentioned the difference arising from the nature of the tables, he doth not dwell upon it, but rapidly passing it by, bestows more labor upon this, which most enabled him to lay hold on his hearer from considerations of what was advantageous and easy; for, saith he, it is not laborious, and the gift it offers is greater. For if when discoursing of Christ, he puts especially forward those things which are of His lovingkindness, more than of our merit, and which are mutually connected, much greater necessity is there for his doing so when treating of the covenant. What then is the meaning of "the letter killeth?" He had said tables of stone and hearts of flesh: so far he seemed to mention no great difference. He added that the former [covenant] was written with letters or ink, but this with the Spirit. Neither did this rouse them thoroughly. He says at last what is indeed enough to give them wings[1]; the one "killeth," the other "giveth life." And what doth this mean? In the Law, he that hath sin is punished; here, he that hath sins cometh and is baptized and is made righteous, and being made righteous, he liveth, being delivered from the death of sin. The Law, if it lay hold on a murderer, putteth him to death; the Gospel, if it lay hold on a murderer, enlighteneth, and giveth him life. And why do I instance a murderer? The Law laid hold on one that gathered sticks on a sabbath day,

and stoned him. (Num. xv. 32, 36.) This is the meaning of, "the letter killeth." The Gospel takes hold on thousands of homicides and robbers, and baptizing delivereth them from their former vices. This is the meaning of, "the Spirit giveth life." The former maketh its captive dead from being alive, the latter rendereth the man it hath convicted alive from being dead. For, "come unto me, ye that labor and are heavy laden," (Matt. xi. 28.) and, He said not, 'I will punish you,' but, "I will give you rest." For in Baptism the sins are buried, the former things are blotted out, the man is made alive, the entire grace written upon his heart as it were a table. Consider then how high is the dignity of the Spirit, seeing that His tables are better than those former ones; seeing that even a greater thing is shown forth than the resurrection itself. For indeed, that state of death from which He delivers, is more irremediable than the former one: as much more so, as soul is of more value than the body: and this life is conferred by that, by that which the Spirit giveth. But if It be able to bestow this, much more then that which is less. For, that prophets wrought, but this they could not: for none can remit sins but God only; nor did the prophets bestow that life without the Spirit. But this is not the marvel only, that it giveth life, but that it enabled others also to do this. For He saith, "Receive ye the Holy Ghost." (John xx. 22.) Wherefore? Because without the Spirit it might not be? [Yes,] but God, as showing that It is of supreme authority, and of that Kingly Essence, and hath the same power [with Himself,] saith this too. Whence also He adds, "Whosoever sins ye remit, they are remitted; and whosoever sins ye retain, they are retained." (ibid. 23.)

[3.] Since then It hath given us life, let us remain living and not return again to the former deadness: for "Christ dieth no more; for the death that He died, He died unto sin once:" (Rom. vi. 9, 10.) and He will not have us always saved by grace: for so we shall be empty of all things. Wherefore He will have us contribute something also from ourselves. Let us then contribute, and preserve to the soul its life. And what is life in a soul, learn from the body. For the body too we then affirm to live, when it moves with a healthy kind of motion; but when it lies prostrate and powerless, or its motions are disorderly, though it retain the semblance of life or motion, such a life is more grievous than any death: and should it utter nothing sane but words of the crazy, and see one object instead of another, such a man again is more pitiable than those who are dead. So also the soul when

---

[1] γὰρ, Rec. text, ἀλλά, [which is retained by all critics. C.]
[2] ἁπλῶς

[3] πτερῶσαι

it hath no healthiness, though it retain a semblance of life, is dead : when it doth not see gold as gold but as something great and precious ; when it thinketh not of the future but crawleth upon the ground ; when it doth one thing in place of another. For whence is it clear that we have a soul? Is it not from its operations? When then it doth not perform the things proper to it, is it not dead? when, for instance, it hath no care for virtue, but is rapacious and transgresseth the law ; whence can I tell that thou hast a soul? Because thou walkest? But this belongs to the irrational creatures as well. Because thou eatest and drinkest? But this too belongeth to wild beasts. Well then, because thou standest upright on two feet? This convinceth me rather that thou art a beast in human form. For when thou resemblest one in all other respects, but not in its manner of erecting itself, thou dost the more disturb and terrify me ; and I the more consider that which I see to be a monster. For did I see a beast speaking with the voice of a man, I should not for that reason say it was a man, but even for that very reason a beast more monstrous than a beast. Whence then can I learn that thou hast the soul of a man, when thou kickest like the ass, when thou bearest malice like the camel, when thou bitest like the bear, when thou ravenest like the wolf, when thou stealest like the fox, when thou art wily as the serpent, when thou art shameless as the dog? Whence can I learn that thou hast the soul of a man? Will ye that I show you a dead soul and a living? Let us turn the discourse back to those men of old ; and, if you will, let us set before us the rich man [in the story] of Lazarus, and we shall know what is death in a soul ; for he had a dead soul, and it is plain from what he did. For, of the works of the soul he did not one, but ate and drank and lived in pleasure only. Such are even now the unmerciful and cruel, for these too have a dead soul as he had. For all its warmth that floweth out of the love of our neighbor hath been spent, and it is deader than a lifeless body. But the poor man was not such, but standing on the very summit of heavenly wisdom shone out ; and though wrestling with continual hunger, and not even supplied with the food that was necessary, neither so spake he aught of blasphemy against God, but endured all nobly. Now this is no trifling work of the soul ; but a very high proof that it is well-strung and healthful. And when there are not these qualities, it is plainly because the soul is dead that they have perished. Or, tell me, shall we not pronounce that soul dead which the Devil falls upon, striking, biting, spurning it, yet hath it no sense of any of these things, but lieth dead-

ened nor grieveth when being robbed of its wealth ; but he even leapeth upon it, yet it remaineth unmoved, like a body when the soul is departed, nor even feeleth it? For when the fear of God is not present with strictness, such must the soul needs be, and then the dead more miserable. For the soul is not dissolved into corruption and ashes and dust, but into things of fouler odor than these, into drunkenness and anger and covetousness, into improper loves and unseasonable desires. But if thou wouldest know more exactly how foul an odor it hath, give me a soul that is pure, and then thou wilt see clearly how foul the odor of this filthy and impure one. For at present thou wilt not be able to perceive it. For so long as we are in contact habitually with a foul odor, we are not sensible of it. But when we are fed with spiritual words, then shall we be cognizant of that evil. And yet to many this seemeth of no importance[1]. And I say nothing as yet of hell ; but let us, if you will, examine what is present, and how worthy of derision is he, not that practiseth, but that uttereth filthiness ; how first he loadeth himself with contumely ; just as one that sputtereth any filth from the mouth, so he defiles himself. For if the stream is so impure, think what must be the fountain of this filth ! "for out of the abundance of the heart the mouth speaketh." (Mat. xii. 34.) Yet not for this alone do I grieve, but because that to some this doth not even seem to be reckoned amongst improper things. Hence the evils are all made worse, when we both sin, and do not think we even do amiss.[2]

[4.] Wilt thou then learn how great an evil is filthy talking? See how the hearers blush at thy indecency. For what is viler than a filthy talker? what more infamous? For such thrust themselves into the rank of buffoons and of prostituted women, yea rather these have more shame than you. How canst thou teach a wife to be modest when by such language thou art training her to proceed unto lasciviousness? Better vent rottenness from the mouth than a filthy word. Now if thy mouth have an ill-odor, thou partakest not even of the common meats ; when then thou hadst so foul a stink in thy soul, tell me, dost thou dare to partake of

---

[1] ἀδιάφορον.

[2] [Chrysostom's view of this verse is correct as far as it goes. But a fuller statement is that the *letter* kills by demanding perfect obedience which none can render, by producing the knowledge of sin and guilt, and by exasperating the soul in holding forth to it a high standard of duty which it neither can nor wishes to obey. The *spirit*, on the other hand, gives life by revealing a perfect and gratuitous righteousness, by exhibiting God's love and awakening hope instead of fear, and by transforming the soul through the Holy Ghost so that it bears the image of God. The letter is equivalent to the Law ; the spirit to the Gospel. The contrast is not between the Old covenant and the New, considered as successive dispensations of the one system of grace, but between the Mosaic economy as conditioning acceptance upon works ("Do this and live"), and the Christian as offering salvation to every one that believeth. C.]

mysteries? Did any one take a dirty vessel and set it upon the table, thou wouldest have beaten him with clubs and driven him out: yet God at His own table, (for His table our mouth is when filled with thanksgiving,) when thou pourest out words more disgusting than any unclean vessel, tell me, dost thou think that thou provokest not? And how is this possible? For nothing doth so exasperate the holy and pure as do such words; nothing makes men so impudent[1] and shameless as to say and listen to such; nothing doth so unstring the sinews of modesty as the flame which these kindle. God hath set perfumes in thy mouth, but thou storest up words of fouler odor than a corpse, and destroyest the soul itself and makest it incapable of motion. For when thou insultest, this is not the voice of the soul, but of anger; when thou talkest filthily, it is lewdness, and not she that spake; when thou detractest, it is envy; when thou schemest, covetousness. These are not her works, but those of the affections[2] and the diseases belonging to her. As then corruption cometh not simply of the body, but of the death and the passion which is thus in the body; so also, in truth, these things come of the passions which grow upon the soul. For

if thou wilt hear a voice from a living soul, hear Paul saying, "Having food and covering, we shall be therewith content:" (1 Tim. vi. 8.) and "Godliness is great gain:" (ib. 6.) and, "The world is crucified unto me, and I unto the world." (Gal. vi. 14.) Hear Peter saying, "Silver and gold have I none, but such as I have, give I thee." (Acts iii. 6.) Hear Job giving thanks and saying, "The Lord gave, and the Lord hath taken away." (Job i. 21.) These things are the words of a living soul, of a soul discharging the functions proper to it. Thus also Jacob said, "If the Lord will give me bread to eat and raiment to put on." (Gen. xxviii. 20.) Thus also Joseph, "How shall I do this wickedness, and sin before God?" (ib. xxxix. 9.) But not so that barbarian woman; but as one drunken and insane[3], so spake she, saying, "Lie with me." (ibid. 7.) These things then knowing, let us earnestly covet the living soul, let us flee the dead one, that we may also obtain the life to come; of which may all we be made partakers, through the grace and love toward men of our Lord Jesus Christ, though Whom and with Whom, to the Father, together with the Holy Ghost, be glory, might, honor, now and for ever, and world without end. Amen.

HOMILY VII.

2 COR. iii. 7, 8.

But if the ministration of death, written and engraven in stones, came with glory, so that the children of Israel could not look steadfastly upon the face of Moses, for the glory of his face; which glory was passing away: how shall not rather the ministration of the Spirit be with glory?

He said that the tables of Moses were of stone, as [also] they were written with letters; and that these were of flesh, I mean the hearts of the Apostles, and had been written on by the Spirit; and that the letter indeed killeth, but the Spirit giveth life. There was yet wanting to this comparison the addition of a further and not trifling particular, that of the glory of Moses; such as in the case of the New Covenant none saw with the eyes of the body. And even for this cause it appeared a great thing in that the glory was perceived by the senses; (for it was seen by the bodily eyes, even though it might not be approached;) but that of the New Covenant is perceived by the understand-

ing. For to the weaker sort the apprehension of such a superiority is not clear; but the other did more take them, and turn them unto itself. Having then fallen upon this comparison and being set upon showing the superiority [in question], which yet was exceedingly difficult because of the dulness of the hearers; see what he does, and with what method[1] he proceeds in it, first by arguments placing the difference before them, and constructing these out of what he had said before.

For if that ministration were of death, but this of life, doubtless, saith he, the latter glory is also greater than the former. For since he could not exhibit it to the bodily eyes, by this logical inference he established its superiority, saying,

Ver. 8. "But if[4] the ministration of death came with glory, how shall not rather the ministration of the Spirit be with glory?"

Now by "ministration of death" he means

---

[1] ἰταμούς.
[2] παθῶν.

[3] παραπαίουσα.
[4] μεθοδεύει.

the Law. And mark too how great the caution he uses in the comparison so as to give no handle to the heretics; for he said not, 'which causeth death,' but, "the ministration of death;" for it ministereth unto, but was not the parent of, death; for that which caused death was sin; but [the Law] brought in the punishment, and showed the sin, not caused it. For it more distinctly revealed the evil and punished it: it did not impel unto the evil: and it ministered not to the existence of sin or death, but to the suffering of retribution by the sinner. So that in this way it was even destructive of sin. For that which showeth it to be so fearful, it is obvious, maketh it also to be avoided. As then he that taketh the sword in his hands and cutteth off the condemned, ministers to the judge that passeth sentence, and it is not he that is his destruction, although he cutteth him off; nay, nor yet is it he who passeth sentence and condemneth, but the wickedness of him that is punished; so truly here also it is not that[1] destroyeth, but sin. This did both destroy and condemn, but that by punishing undermined its strength, by the fear of the punishment holding it back. But he was not content with this consideration only in order to establish the superiority [in question]; but he addeth yet another, saying, "written, and engraven on stones." See how he again cuts at the root of the Jewish arrogancy. For the Law was nothing else but letters: a certain succor was not found leaping forth from out the letters and inspiring them that combat, as is the case in Baptism; but pillars and writings bearing death to those who transgress the letters. Seest thou how in correcting the Jewish contentiousness, by his very expressions even he lessens its authority, speaking of stone and letters and a ministration of death, and adding that it was engraven? For hereby he declareth nothing else than this, that the Law was fixed in one place; not, as the Spirit, was present everywhere, breathing great might into all; or that the letters breathe much threatening, and threatening too which can not be effaced but remaineth for ever, as being engraved in stone. Then even whilst seeming to praise the old things, he again mixeth up accusation of the Jews. For having said, "written and engraven in stones, came with glory," he added, "so that the children of Israel could not look steadfastly upon the face of Moses;" which was a mark of their great weakness and grovelling spirit. And again he doth not say, 'for the glory of the tables,' but, "for the glory of his countenance, which glory was passing away;" for he showeth that he who beareth them is made glorious, and not they. For he said not, 'because they could not look steadfastly upon the tables,' but, "the face

of Moses;" and again, not, 'for the glory of the tables,' but, "for the glory of his face." Then after he had extolled it, see how again he lowers it, saying, "which was passing away." Not however that this is in accusation, but in diminution; for he did not say, 'which was corrupt, which was evil,' but, 'which ceaseth and hath an end.'

"How shall not rather the ministration of the Spirit be with glory?" for henceforth with confidence he extolleth the things of the New [Covenant] as indisputable. And observe what he doth. He opposed 'stone' to 'heart,' and 'letter' to 'spirit.' Then having shown the results of each, he doth not set down the results of each; but having set down the work of the latter, namely, death and condemnation, he setteth not down that of the spirit, namely, life and righteousness; but the Spirit Itself; which added greatness to the argument. For the New Covenant not only gave life, but supplied also 'The Spirit' Which giveth the life, a far greater thing than the life. Wherefore he said, "the ministration of the Spirit." Then he again reverts to the same thing, saying,

Ver. 9. "For if the ministration of condemnation is glory."

Also, he interprets more clearly the meaning of the words, "The letter killeth," declaring it to be that which we have said above, namely, that the Law showed sin, not caused it.

"Much rather doth the ministration of righteousness exceed in glory."

For those Tables indeed showed the sinners and punished them, but this not only did not punish the sinners, but even made them righteous: for this did Baptism confer.

[2.] Ver. 10. "For verily that which hath been made glorious hath not been made glorious in this respect, by reason of the glory that surpasseth."

Now in what has gone before, indeed, he showed that this also is with glory; and not simply is with glory, but even exceedeth in it: for he did not say, "How shall not the ministration of the Spirit be rather in glory?" but, "exceed in glory;" deriving the proof from the arguments before stated. Here he also shows the superiority, how great it is, saying, 'if I compare this with that, the glory of the Old Covenant is not glory at all;' not absolutely laying down that there was no glory, but in view of the comparison. Wherefore also he added, "in this respect," that is, in respect of the comparison. Not that this doth disparage the Old Covenant, yea rather it highly commendeth it: for comparisons are wont to be made between things which are the same in kind. Next, he sets on foot yet another argument to prove the superiority also from a fresh ground.

---

[1] i. e., the Law.

What then is this argument? That based upon duration, saying,

Ver. 11. "For if that which passeth away was with glory, much more that which remaineth is in glory."

For the one ceased, but the other abideth continually.

Ver. 12. "Having therefore such a hope, we use great boldness of speech."

For since when he had heard so many and so great things concerning the New [Covenant,] the hearer would be desirous of seeing this glory manifested to the eye, mark whither he hurleth him, [even] to the world to come. Wherefore also he brought forward the "hope," saying, "Having therefore such a hope." Such? Of what nature? That we have been counted worthy of greater things than Moses; not we the Apostles only, but also all the faithful. "We use great boldness of speech." Towards whom? tell me. Towards God, or towards the disciples? Towards you who are receiving instruction, he saith; that is, we speak every where with freedom, hiding nothing, withholding nothing, mistrusting nothing, but speaking openly; and we have not feared lest we should wound your eyesight, as Moses did that of the Jews. For that he alluded to this, hear what follows; or rather, it is necessary first to relate the history, for he himself keeps dwelling upon it. What then is the history? When, having received the Tables a second time, Moses came down, a certain glory darting from his countenance shone so much that the Jews were not able to approach and talk with him until he put a veil over his face. And thus it is written in Exodus, (Ex. xxxiv. 29, 34.) "When Moses came down from the Mount, the two Tables [were] in his hands. And Moses wist not that the skin of his countenance was made glorious to behold. And they were afraid to come nigh him. And Moses called them, and spake unto them. And when [1] Moses had done speaking with them, he put a veil over his face. But when he went in before the Lord to speak [with Him], he took the veil off until he came out."

Putting them in mind then of this history, he says,

Ver. 13. "And not as Moses, who put a veil upon his face, so that the children of Israel should not look steadfastly on the end of that which was passing away."

Now what he says is of this nature. There is no need for us to cover ourselves as Moses did; for ye are able to look upon this glory which we are encircled with, although it is far greater and brighter than the other. Seest thou the advance? For he that in the former Epistle said, "I have fed you with milk, not with meat;"

saith here, "We use great boldness of speech." And he produces Moses before them, carrying forward the discourse by means of comparison, and thus leading his hearer upwards.

And for the present he sets them above the Jews, saying that 'we have no need of a veil as he[2] had' with those he governed; ' but in what comes afterwards he advances them even to the dignity itself of the Lawgiver, or even to a much greater.

Mean time, however, let us hear what follows next.

Ver. 14. "But their minds were hardened, for until this day remaineth the same veil in the reading of the Old Covenant, [it] not being revealed to them[3] that it is done away in Christ."

See what he establisheth by this. For what happened then once in the case of Moses, the same happeneth continually in the case of the Law. What is said, therefore, is no accusation of the Law, as neither is it of Moses that he then veiled himself, but only the senseless Jews. For the law hath its proper glory, but they were unable to see it. 'Why therefore are ye perplexed,' he saith, ' if they are unable to see this glory of the Grace, since they saw not that lesser one of Moses, nor were able to look steadfastly upon his countenance? And why are ye troubled that the Jews believe not Christ, seeing at least that they believe not even the Law? For they were therefore ignorant of the Grace also, because they knew not even the Old Covenant nor the glory which was in it. For the glory of the Law is to turn [men] unto Christ.'

[3] Seest thou how from this consideration also he takes down the inflation of the Jews? By that in which they thought they had the advantage, namely, that Moses' face shone, he proves their grossness and groveling nature. Let them not therefore pride themselves on that, for what was that to Jews who enjoyed it not? Wherefore also he keeps on dwelling upon it, saying one while, "The same veil in the reading of the old covenant remaineth," it "not being revealed that it is done away in Christ:" another while, that "unto this day when Moses is read," (v. 15.) the same "veil lieth upon their heart;" showing that the veil lieth both on the reading and on their heart; and above, "So that the children of Israel could not look steadfastly upon the face of Moses for the glory of his countenance; which" (v. 7.) glory "was passing away." Than which what could mark less worth in them? Seeing that even of a glory that is to be done away, or rather is in comparison no glory at all, they are not able to be spectators, but it is covered from

---

[2] i. e., Moses.
[3] So he reads the text.

them, "so that they could not steadfastly look on the end of that which was passing away;" that is, of the law, because it hath an end; "but their minds were hardened." 'And what,' saith one, 'hath this to do with the veil then?' Because it prefigured what would be. For not only did they not then perceive; but they do not even now see the Law. And the fault lies with themselves, for the hardness is that of an unimpressible and perverse judgment. So that it is we who know the law also; but to them not only Grace, but this as well is covered with a shadow; "For until this day the same veil upon the reading of the old covenant remaineth," he saith, it "not being revealed that it is done away in Christ." Now what he saith is this. This very thing they cannot see, that it is brought to an end, because they believe not Christ. For if it be brought to an end by Christ, as in truth it is brought to an end, and this the Law said by anticipation, how will they who receive not Christ that hath done away the Law, be able to see that the Law is done away? And being incapable of seeing this, it is very plain that even of the Law itself which asserted these things, they know not the power nor the full glory. 'And where,' saith one, 'did it say this that it is done away in Christ?' It did not say it merely, but also showed it by what was done. And first indeed by shutting up its sacrifices and its whole ritual[1] in one place, the Temple, and afterwards destroying this. For had He not meant to bring these to an end and the whole of the Law concerning them, He would have done one or other of two things; either not destroyed the Temple, or having destroyed it, not forbidden to sacrifice elsewhere. But, as it is, the whole world and even Jerusalem itself He hath made forbidden ground for such religious rites; having allowed and appointed for them only the Temple. Then having destroyed this itself afterwards, He showed completely even by what was done, that the things of the Law are brought to an end by Christ; for the Temple also Christ destroyed. But if thou wilt see in words as well how the Law is done away in Christ, hear the Lawgiver himself speaking thus; "A Prophet shall the Lord raise up unto you of your brethren, like unto me; (Deut. xvii. 15, 19.) Him shall ye hear in all things whatsoever He shall command you. And it shall come to pass, that every soul which will not hear that Prophet shall be utterly destroyed[2]." (Acts iii. 22, 23.) Seest thou how the Law showed that it is done away in Christ? For this Prophet, that is, Christ according to the flesh, Whom Moses commanded them to hear, made to cease both sabbath and circumcison and all the other things. And David too, showing the very same thing, said concerning Christ, "Thou art a Priest after the order of Melchizedek," (Ps. cx. 4;) not after the order of Aaron. Wherefore also Paul, giving a clear interpretation of this, says, "The priesthood being changed, there is made of necessity a change also of the Law." (Heb. vii. 12.) And in another place also he says again, "Sacrifice and offering thou wouldst not. In whole burnt offerings and sacrifices for sin Thou hadst had no pleasure: then said I, Lo, I come." (Heb. x. 5, 7.) And other testimonies far more numerous than these may be adduced out of the Old Testament, showing how the Law is done away by Christ. So that when thou shalt have forsaken the Law, thou shalt then see the Law clearly; but so long as thou holdest by it and believest not Christ, thou knowest not even the Law itself. Wherefore also he added, to establish this very thing more clearly;

Ver. 15. "But even unto this day, whensoever Moses is read, a veil lieth upon their heart."

For since he said that in the reading of the Old Testament the veil remaineth, lest any should think that this that is said is from the obscurity of the Law, he both by other things showed even before what his meaning was, (for by saying, "their minds were hardened," he shows that the fault was their own,) and, in this place too, again. For he said not, 'The veil remaineth on the writing,' but "in the reading;" (now the reading is the act of those that read;) and again, "When Moses is read." He showed this however with greater clearness in the expression which follows next, saying unreservedly, "The veil lieth upon their heart." For even upon the face of Moses it lay, not because of Moses, but because of the grossness and carnal mind of these.

[4.] Having then suitably[3] accused them, he points out also the manner of their correction. And what is this?

Ver. 16. "Nevertheless when [one] shall turn to the Lord," which is, to forsake the Law, "the veil is taken away[4]."

Seest thou that not over the face of Moses was there that veil, but over the eyesight of the

---

[1] ἁγιστείαν.
[2] So Chrysostom, though the LXX agrees with the E. V.

[3] ἱκανῶς.
[4] [There are various methods of supplying a nominative to the verb "turn" in this sentence. Calvin makes Moses the subject, as representing the law which when it is directed to Christ causes the veil to be removed. Stanley also makes Moses the subject, but as representing the people, and renders, "When Moses turns to the Lord, he strips off the veil." But Chrysostom gives what is the generally accepted view, which is that "the heart of Israel is that which turns," indicating of course a general conversion (cf. Rom. xi. 26) yet including the case of each individual that turns to Christ. As Beet well says, "The Apostle cannot leave his people in their darkness without expressing a hope that they will some day come to the light." C.]

Jews? For it was done, not that the glory of Moses might be hidden, but that the Jews might not see. For they were not capable. So that in them was the deficiency, for it[1] caused not him to be ignorant of any thing, but them. And he did not say indeed, "when thou shalt let go the Law," but he implied it, for "when thou shalt turn to the Lord, the veil is taken away." To the very last he[2] kept to the history. For when Moses talked with the Jews he kept his face covered; but when he turned to God it was uncovered. Now this was a type of that which was to come to pass, that when we have turned to the Lord, then we shall see the glory of the Law, and the face of the Lawgiver bare; yea rather, not this alone, but we shall then be even in the same rank with Moses. Seest thou how he inviteth the Jew unto the faith, by showing, that by coming unto Grace he is able not only to see Moses, but also to stand in the very same rank with the Lawgiver. 'For not only,' he saith, 'shalt thou look on the glory which then thou sawest not, but thou shalt thyself also be included in the same glory; yea rather, in a greater glory, even so great that that other shall not seem glory at all when compared with this.' How and in what manner? 'Because that when thou hast turned to the Lord and art included in the grace, thou wilt enjoy that glory, unto which the glory of Moses, if compared, is so much less as to be no glory at all. But still, small though it be and exceedingly below that other, whilst thou art a Jew, even this will not be vouchsafed thee[3]; but having become a believer, it will then be vouchsafed thee to behold even that which is far greater than it.' And when he was addressing himself to the believers, he said, that "that which was made glorious had no glory;" but here he speaks not so; but how? "When one shall turn to the Lord, the veil is taken away:" leading him up by little and little, and first setting him in Moses' rank, and then making him partake of the greater things. For when thou hast seen Moses in glory, then afterwards thou shalt also turn unto God and enjoy this greater glory.

[5.] See then from the beginning, how many things he has laid down, as constituting the difference and showing the superiority, not the enmity or contradiction, of the New Covenant in respect to the old. That, saith he, is letter, and stone, and a ministration of death, and is done away: and yet the Jews were not even vouchsafed this glory. (Or, the glory of this.) This table is of the flesh, and spirit, and righteousness, and remaineth; and unto all of us is it vouchsafed, not to one only, as to Moses of

the lesser then. (ver. 18.) "For," saith he, "we all with unveiled face reflecting as a mirror the glory of the Lord," not that of Moses. But since some maintain that the expression, "when one shall turn to the Lord," is spoken of the Son, in contradiction to what is quite acknowledged; let us examine the point more accurately, having first stated the ground on which they think to establish this. What then is this? Like, saith one, as it is said, "God is a Spirit;" (John iv. 24.) so also here, 'The Lord is a Spirit.' But he did not say, 'The Lord is a Spirit,' but, "The Spirit is the Lord." And there is a great difference between this construction and that. For when he is desirous of speaking so as you say, he does not join the article to the predicate. And besides, let us review all his discourse from the first, of whom hath he spoken? for instance, when he said, "The letter killeth, but the Spirit giveth life:" (ver. 6.) and again, "Written not with ink, but with the Spirit of the living God;" (ver. 3.) was he speaking of God, or of the Spirit? It is very plain that it was of the Spirit; for unto It he was calling them from the letter. For lest any, hearing of the Spirit, and then reflecting that Moses turned unto the Lord, but himself unto the Spirit, should think himself to have the worse, to correct such a suspicion as this, he says,

Ver. 17. "Now the Spirit is the Lord."

This too is Lord, he says. And that you may know that he is speaking of the Paraclete, he added,

"And where the Spirit of the Lord is, there is liberty."

For surely you will not assert, that he says, 'And where the Lord of the Lord is.' "Liberty," he said, with reference to the former bondage. Then, that you may not think that he is speaking of a time to come, he says,

Ver. 18. "But we all, with unveiled face, reflecting[4] as a mirror the glory of the Lord."

Not that which is brought to an end, but that which remaineth.

"Are transformed into the same image from glory to glory, even as from the Lord the Spirit."

Seest thou how again he places the Spirit in the rank of God, (vide infra)

---

[1] Or, "He."
[2] St. Paul.
[3] Two MSS. insert here, "the Jews of that day therefore saw it not, nor do they now;" but Dr. Field rejects the insertion.

[4] This version of the verb was followed by Luther, Bengel and others, and is found in the Revised Version. It is objected to by Meyer, Hodge, Beet et al., as being at variance with the usage of the language since the middle voice of the verb never has this meaning elsewhere, and at variance with the context which lays the stress on free and unhindered seeing and not upon reflecting. But it is urged in reply that Chrysostom may be trusted to know what Greek usage is, and as to the context the splendor which shone in Moses's face, that which suggested this whole train of thought, was a reflection of what he saw in the Mount. Fortunately whichever way the point is decided, the blessed result remains for all believers of a growing transformation into the image of Christ, from glory to glory (like *from strength to strength* in Ps. lxxxiv. 7), i. e., from one degree of glory to another,—a process going on without intermission under the influence of the Lord, the Spirit. C. J

and raises them up to the rank of the Apostles. For he said before, "Ye are the Epistle of Christ; and here, "But we all with open face." Yet they came, like Moses, bringing a law. But like as we, he says, needed no veil, so neither ye who received it. And yet this glory is far greater, for this is not of our countenance, but of the Spirit; but nevertheless ye are able as well as we to look steadfastly upon it. For they indeed could not even by a mediator, but ye even without a mediator can [look steadfastly on] a greater. They were not able to look upon that of Moses, ye even upon that of the Spirit. Now had the Spirit been at all inferior, He would not have set down these things as greater than those. But what is, "we reflecting as a mirror the glory of the Lord, are transformed into the same image." This indeed was shown more clearly when the gifts of miracles were in operation; howbeit it is not even now difficult to see it, for one who hath believing eyes. For as soon as we are baptized, the soul beameth even more than the sun, being cleansed by the Spirit; and not only do we behold the glory of God, but from it also receive a sort of splendor. Just as if pure silver be turned towards the sun's rays, it will itself also shoot forth rays, not from its own natural property merely but also from the solar lustre; so also doth the soul being cleansed and made brighter than silver, receive a ray from the glory of the Spirit, and send it back. Wherefore also he saith, "Reflecting as a mirror we are transformed into the same image from glory," that of the Spirit, "to glory," our own, that which is generated in us; and that, of such sort, as one might expect from the Lord the Spirit. See how here also he calleth the Spirit, Lord. And in other places too one may see that lordship of His. For, saith he, "As they ministered and fasted unto the Lord, the Spirit said, Separate me Paul and Barnabas." (Acts xiii. 2.) For therefore he said, "as they ministered unto the Lord, Separate me," in order to show the [Spirit's] equality in honor. And again Christ saith, "The servant knoweth not what his lord doeth;" but even as a man knoweth his own things, so doth the Spirit know the things of God; not by being taught [them,] for so the similitude holdeth not good. Also the working as He willeth showeth His authority and lordship. This transformeth us. This suffereth not to be conformed to this world; for such is the creation of which This is the Author. For as he saith, "Created in Christ Jesus," (Ephes. ii. 10.) so saith he, "Create in me a clean heart, O God, and renew a right spirit in my inward parts". (Ps. li. 10, LXX.)

[6.] Wilt thou that I show thee this also from the Apostles more obviously to the sense. Con-sider Paul, whose garments wrought: Peter, whose very shadows were mighty. (Acts xix, 12; v, 15. XX.) For had they not borne a King's image and their radiancy been unapproachable, their garments and shadows had not wrought so mightily. For the garments of a king are terrible even to robbers. Wouldest thou see this beaming even through the body? "Looking steadfastly," said he, "upon the face of Stephen, they saw it as it had been the face of an angel." (Acts vi. 15.) But this was nothing to the glory flashing within. For what Moses had upon his countenance, that did these carry about with them on their souls, yea 'rather' even far more. For that of Moses indeed was more obvious to the senses, but this was incorporeal. And like as fire-bright bodies streaming down from the shining bodies upon those which lie near them, impart to them also somewhat of their own splendor, so truly doth it also happen with the faithful. Therefore surely they with whom it is thus are set free from earth, and have their dreams of the things in the heavens. Woe is me! for well is it that we should here even groan bitterly, for that we who enjoy a birth so noble do not so much as know what is said, because we quickly lose the reality, and are dazzled about the objects of sense. For this glory, the unspeakable and awful, remaineth in us for a day or two, and then we quench it, bringing over it the winter of worldly concerns, and with the thickness of those clouds repelling its rays. For worldly things are a winter, and than winter more lowering. For not frost is engendered thence nor rain, neither doth it produce mire and deep swamps; but, things than all these more grievous, it formeth hell and the miseries of hell. And as in severe frost all the limbs are stiffened and are dead, so truly the soul shuddering in the winter of sins also, performeth none of its proper functions, stiffened, as it were, by a frost, as to conscience. For what cold is to the body, that an evil conscience is to the soul, whence also cometh cowardice. For nothing is more cowardly than the man that is rivetted to worldly things; for such an one lives the life of Cain, trembling every day. And why do I mention deaths, and losses, and offences, and flatteries, and services? for even without these he is in fear of ten thousand vicissitudes. And his coffers indeed are full of gold, but his soul is not freed from the fear of poverty. And very reasonably. For he is moored as it were on rotten and swiftly shifting things, and even though in his own case he experienced not the reverse, yet is he undone by seeing it happen in others; and great is his

---

¹ ἐπτοῆσθαι.

cowardice, great his unmanliness. For not only is such an one spiritless as to danger, but also as to all other things. And if desire of wealth assail him, he doth not like a free man beat off the assault; but like a bought slave, doth all [it bids], serving the love of money as it were a severe mistress. If again he have beheld some comely damsel, down he croucheth at once made captive, and followeth like a raging dog, though it behoveth to do the opposite. For when thou hast beheld a beautiful woman, consider not how thou mayest enjoy thy lust, but but how be delivered from thy lust. 'And how is this possible,' saith one? 'for loving is not my own doing.' Whose then? tell me. It is from the Devil's malice. Thou art quite convinced that that which plotteth against thee is a devil; wrestle then and fight with a distemper. But I cannot, he saith. Come then, let us first teach thee this, that what happeneth is from thine own listlessness, and that thou at the first gavest entrance to the Devil, and now if thou hast a mind, with much ease mayest drive him off. They that commit adultery, is it from lust they commit it, or simply from desire of dangers? Plainly from lust. Do they then therefore obtain forgiveness? Certainly not. Why not? Because the sin is their own. 'But,' saith one, 'why, pray, string syllogisms? For my conscience bears me witness that I wish to repel the passion; and cannot, but it keepeth close, presses me sore, and afflicts me grievously.' O man, thou dost wish to repel it, but thou dost not the things repellers should do; but it is with thee just as with a man in a fever, who drinking of cold streams to the fill, should say, 'How many things I devise with the wish to quench this fever, and I cannot; but they stir up my flame the more.' Let us see then whether at all thou too dost the things that inflame, yet thinkest thou art devising such as quench. 'I do not,' he saith. Tell me then, what hast thou ever essayed to do in order to quench the passion? and what is it, in fine, that will increase the passion? For even supposing we be not all of us obnoxious to these particular charges; (for more may be found who are captivated by the love of money than of beauty;) still the remedy to be proposed will be common to all, both to these and to those. For both that is an unreasonable passion, and this, is keener and fiercer than that. When then we have proved victorious over the greater, it is very plain that we shall easily subdue the less also. 'And how is it,' saith one, 'that if this be keener, all persons are not made captive by the vice, but a greater number are mad after money?' Because in the first place this last desire appears to be unattended with danger: next, although that of beauty be even fiercer, yet it is more

speedily extinguished; for were it to continue like that of money, it would wholly destroy its captive.

[7.] Come then, let us discourse to you on this, the love of beauty, and let us see whereby the mischief is increased; for so we shall know whether the fault be ours, or not ours. And if ours, let us do everything to get the better of it; whereas if not ours, why do we afflict ourselves for nought? And why do we not pardon, but find fault, with those who are made captive by it? Whence then is this love engendered? 'From comeliness of feature,' saith one, 'when she that woundeth one is beautiful and of fair countenance.' It is said idly and in vain. For if it were beauty that attracted lovers, then would the maiden who is such have all men for her lovers; but if she hath not all, this thing cometh not of nature nor from beauty, but from unchaste eyes. For it was when by eyeing too curiously[1], thou didst admire and become enamored, that thou receivedst the shaft. 'And who,' saith one, 'when he sees a beautiful woman, can refrain from commending her he sees? If then admiring such things cometh not of deliberate choice, it follows that love depends not on ourselves.' Stop, O man! Why dost thou crowd all things together, running round and round on every side, and not choosing to see the root of the evil? For I see numbers admiring and commending, who yet are not enamored. 'And how is it possible to admire and not be enamored?' Clamor not, (for this I am coming to speak of,) but wait, and thou shalt hear Moses admiring the son of Jacob, and saying, "And Joseph was a goodly person, and well favored exceedingly." (Gen. xxxix. 6, LXX.) Was he then enamored who speaketh this? By no means. 'For,' saith he, 'he did not even see him whom he commended.' We are affected, however, somewhat similarly towards beauties also which are described to us, not only which are beheld. But that thou cavil not with us on this point:—David, was he not comely exceedingly, and ruddy with beauty of eyes? (So 1 Sam. xvi. 12 & xvii. 42. LXX.) and indeed this beauty of the eyes, is even especially, a component of beauteousness of more despotic power than any. Was then any one enamored of him? By no means. Then to be also enamored cometh not [necessarily] with admiring. For many too have had mothers blooming exceedingly in beauty of person. What then? Were their children enamored of them? Away with the thought! but they admire what they see, yet fall not into a shameful love. 'No, for again this good provision is

---

[1] περιέργως.

Nature's.' How Nature's? Tell me. 'Because they are mothers,' he saith. Then hearest thou not that Persians, and that without any compulsion, have intercourse with their own mothers, and that not one or two individuals, but a whole nation? But independent of these, it is hence also evident that this distemper cometh not from bloom of person nor from beauty merely, but from a listless and wandering soul. Many at least it is certain, oftentimes, having passed over thousands of well-favored women, have given themselves to such as were plainer. Whence it is evident that love depends not on beauty: for otherwise, surely, those would have caught such as fell into it, before these. What then is its cause? 'For,' saith he, 'if it be not beauty that causeth love, whence hath it its beginning and its root? From a wicked Demon?' It hath it indeed, thence also, but this is not what we are inquiring about, but whether we ourselves too be not the cause. For the plot is not theirs only, but along with them our own too in the first place. For from no other source is this wicked distemper so engendered as from habit, and flattering words, and leisure, and idleness, and having nothing to do. For great, great is the tyranny of habit, even so great as to be moulded into[1] a necessity of nature. Now if it be habit's to gender it, it is very evident that it is also [habit's] to extinguish it. Certain it is at least that many have in this way ceased to be enamored, from not seeing those they were enamored of. Now this for a little while indeed appears to be a bitter thing and exceedingly unpleasant; but in time it becometh pleasant, and even were they to wish it, they could not afterwards resume the passion.

[8.] How then, when without habit one is taken captive at first sight? Here also it is indolence of body, or self-indulgence, and not attending to one's duties, nor being occupied in necessary business. For such an one, wandering about like some vagabond, is transfixed by any wickedness; and like a child let loose, any one that liketh maketh such a soul his slave. For since it is its wont to be at work, when thou stoppest its workings in what is good, seeing it cannot be unemployed, it is compelled to engender what is otherwise. For just as the earth, when it is not sown nor planted, sends up simply weeds; so also the soul, when it hath nought of necessary things to do, being desirous by all means to be doing, giveth herself unto wicked deeds. And as the eye never ceaseth from seeing, and therefore will see wicked things, when good things are not set before it; so also doth the thought, when it secludes itself from necessary things, busy itself thereafter

about such as are unprofitable. For that even the first assault occupation and thought are able to beat off, is evident from many things. When then thou hast looked on a beautiful woman, and wert moved towards her, look no more, and thou art delivered. 'And how shall I be able to look no more,' saith he, 'when drawn by that desire?' Give thyself to other things which may distract the soul, to books, to necessary cares, to protecting others, to assisting the injured, to prayers, to the wisdom which considers the things to come: with such things as these bind down thy soul. By these means, not only shalt thou cure a recent wound, but shalt wear away a confirmed and inveterate one easily. For if an insult according to the proverb prevails with the lover to give over his love, how shall not these spiritual charms[2] much rather be victorious over the evil, if only we have a mind to stand aloof. But if we are always conversing and associating with those who shoot such arrows at us, and talking with them and hearing what they say, we cherish the distemper. How then dost thou expect the fire to be quenched, when day by day thou stirrest up the flame?

And let this that we have said about habit be our speech unto the young; since to those who are men and taught in heavenly wisdom, stronger than all is the fear of God, the remembrance of hell, the desire of the kingdom of heaven; for these are able to quench the fire. And along with these take that thought also, that what thou seest is nothing else than rheum, and blood, and juices of decomposed food. 'Yet a gladsome thing is the bloom of the features,' saith one. But nothing is more gladsome than the blossoms of the earth, and these too rot and wither. Do not then in this either give heed to the bloom, but pass on further inward in thy thought, and stripping off that beauteous skin in thy thought, scan curiously what lies beneath it. For even the bodies of the dropsical shine brightly, and the surface hath nothing offensive; but still, shocked with the thought of the humor stored within we cannot love such persons. 'But languishing is the eye and glancing, and beautifully arched the brow, and dark the lashes, and soft the eyeball, and serene the look.' But see how even this itself again is nothing else than nerves, and veins, and membranes, and arteries. Think too, I pray, of this beautiful eye, when diseased and old, wasting with despair, swelling with anger, how hateful to the sight it is, how quickly it perisheth, how sooner even than pictured ones, it is effaced. From these things make thy mind pass to the true beauty. 'But,' saith he, 'I do not see beauty

---

[1] καθίστασθαι. Ben. μεθίστασθαι, to pass into.

[2] ἐπῳδαί.

of soul.' But if thou wilt choose, thou shalt see it: and as the absent beautiful may be with the mind admired, though with one's eyes unseen, so it is possible to see without eyes beauty of soul. Hast thou not often sketched a beauteous form, and felt moved unto the drawing? Image also now beauty of soul, and revel in that loveliness. 'But,' saith he, 'I do not see things incorporeal.' And yet we see these, rather than the corporeal, with the mind. Therefore it is, for instance, that although we see them not, we admire angels also and archangels, and habits of character, and virtue of soul. And if thou seest a man considerate and moderate, thou wilt more admire him than that beautiful countenance. And if thou seest one insulted, yet bearing it; wronged, yet giving way, admire and love such, even though they be striken in age. For such a thing is the beauty of the soul; even in old age it hath many enamored of it, and it never fadeth, but bloometh for ever. In order then that we also may gain this beauty, let us go in quest of those that have it, and be enamored of them. For so shall we too be able, when we have attained this beauty, to obtain the good things eternal, whereof may all we partake, through the grace and love towards men of our Lord Jesus Christ, with Whom to the Father, with the Holy Spirit, be glory and might, for ever and ever. Amen.

HOMILY VIII.

2 Cor. iv. 1, 2.

Therefore seeing we have this ministry, even as we obtained mercy we faint not, but we have renounced the hidden things of shame.

Seeing he had uttered great things and had set himself and all the faithful before Moses, aware of the height [1] and greatness of what he had said, observe how he moderates his tone again. For it was necessary on account of the false Apostles to exalt [2] his hearers also, and again to calm down that swelling; yet not to do it away, since this would be a trifler's part [3]. Wherefore he manages this in another manner, by showing that not of their own merits was it, but all of the loving-kindness of God. Wherefore also he says, "Therefore seeing we have this ministry." For nothing more did we contribute, except that we became ministers, and made ourselves subservient to the things given by God. Wherefore he said not ' largess [4],' nor ' supply [5],' but ' ministry.' Nor was he contented with this even, but added, "as we obtained mercy." For even this itself, he saith, the ministering to these things, is of mercy and loving-kindness. Yet it is mercy's to deliver from evils, not to give so many good things besides: but the mercy of God includes this also.

"We faint not." And this indeed is to be imputed to His loving-kindness. For the clause, "as we obtained mercy," take to be said with reference both to the "ministry," and to the words, "we faint not." And observe how earnestly he endeavors to lower his own things. 'For,' saith he, 'that one who hath been counted worthy of such and so great things, and this from mercy only and loving-kindness, should show forth such labors, and undergo dangers, and endure temptations, is no great matter. Therefore we not only do not sink down, but we even rejoice and speak boldly.' For instance, having said, "we faint not," he added,

Ver. 2. "But we have renounced the hidden things of shame, not walking in craftiness, nor handling the word of God deceitfully."

And what are "the hidden things of shame?" We do not, he saith, profess and promise great things, and in our actions show other things, as they do; wherefore also he said, "Ye look on things after the outward appearance;" but such we are as we appear, not having any duplicity, nor saying and doing such things as we ought to hide and veil over with shame and blushes. And to interpret this, he added, "not walking in craftiness." For what they considered to be praise, that he proves to be shameful and worthy of scorn. But what is, "in craftiness?" They had the reputation of taking nothing,, but they took and kept it secret; they had the character of saints and approved Apostles, but they were full of numberless evil things. But, saith he, "we have renounced" these things: (for these are what he also calls the "hidden things of shame;")

---

[1] ὑπερβολῆς.
[2] ἐπαιρεῖν. The Benedictine Latin translates, "necessary to exalt [himself] both on account of the false Apostles, and his hearers."
[3] παίζοντος.
[4] παροχὴν.
[5] χορηγίαν.

being such as we appear to be, and keeping nothing veiled over. And that not in this [our] life only, but also in the Preaching itself. For this is, " nor handling the word of God deceitfully."

" But by the manifestation of the truth."

Not by the countenance and the outward show, but by the very proof of our actions.

" Commending ourselves to every man's conscience."

For not to believers only, but also to unbelievers, we are manifest; lying open unto all that they may test our actions, as they may choose; and by this we commend ourselves, not by acting a part and carrying about a specious mask. We say then, that we take nothing, and we call you for witnesses; we say that we are conscious of no wickedness, and of this again we derive the testimony from you, not as they (sc. false Apostles) who, veiling over their things, deceive many. But we both set forth our life before all men; and we lay bare [1] the Preaching, so that all comprehend it.

[2.] Then because the unbelievers knew not its power, he added, this is no fault of ours, but of their own insensibility. Wherefore also he saith,

Ver. 3, 4. " But if our Gospel is veiled, it is veiled in them that are lost; in whom the God of this world hath blinded the eyes of the unbelieving."

As he said also before, " To some a savor from death unto death, to others a savor from life unto life," (ch. ii. 16.) so he saith here too. But what is " the God of this world?" Those that are infected with Marcion's notions [2], affirm that this is said of the Creator, the just only, and not good; for they say that there is a certain God, just and not good. But the Manichees [3] say that the devil is here intended, desiring from this passage to introduce another creator of the world besides the True One, very senselessly. For the Scripture useth often to employ the term God, not in regard of the dignity of that so designated, but of the weakness of those in subjection to it; as when it calls Mammon lord, and the belly god. But neither is the belly therefore God, nor Mammon Lord, save only of those who bow down themselves to them. But we assert of this passage that it is spoken neither of the devil nor of another creator, but of the God of the Universe, and that it is to be read thus; " God hath blinded the minds of the unbelievers of this world[4]." For the world to come

hath no unbelievers; but the present only. But if any one should read it even otherwise, as, for instance, " the God of this world;" neither doth this afford any handle, for this doth not show Him to be the God of this world only. For He is called "the God of Heaven," (Ps. cxxxvi. 26. &c.) yet is He not the God of Heaven only; and we say, 'God of the present day;' yet we say this not as limiting His power to it alone. And moreover He is called the " God of Abraham, and the God of Isaac, and the God of Jacob;" (Exod. iii. 6. &c.) and yet He is not the God of them alone. And one may find many other like testimonies in the Scriptures. How then " hath " He " blinded " them? Not by working unto this end; away with the thought! but by suffering and allowing it. For it is usual with the Scripture so to speak, as when it saith, "God gave them up unto a reprobate mind." For when they themselves first disbelieved, and rendered themselves unworthy to see the mysteries; He Himself also thereafter permitted it. But what did it behove Him to do? To draw them by force, and reveal to those who would not see? But so they would have despised the more, and would not have seen either. Wherefore also he added,

" That the light of the Gospel of the glory of Christ should not dawn upon them."

Not that they might disbelieve in God, but that unbelief might not see what are the things within, as also He enjoined us, commanding not to " cast the pearls before the swine." (Matt. vii. 6.) For had He revealed even to those who disbelieve, their disease would have been the rather aggravated. For if one compel a man laboring under ophthalmia to look at the sunbeams, he the rather increases his infirmity. Therefore the physicians[5] even shut them up in darkness, so as not to aggravate their disorder. So then here also we must consider that these persons indeed became unbelievers of themselves, but having become so, they no longer saw the secret things of the Gospel, God thenceforth excluding its beams from them.

[1] ἀπογυμνοῦμεν.

[2] See Epiphanius adv. Hær. lib. i. tom. iii. 33.

[3] For a full account of Manichæism, see Library of the Fathers, St. Augustin's Confessions, Note A.

[4] [This is one of the few instances in which the expositor allowed himself to be diverted by dogmatic considerations from the true meaning of the word. It is exceedingly awkward to make of this

world depend upon unbelievers, and not upon the substantive God which immediately precedes. The natural and legitimate construction is the one given in both the English versions, " the God of this world (or age)." But Chrysostom was led to depart from it, as Augustine was afterwards, and Origen and Tertullian had been before, by a desire to resist the Marcionites and the Manichæans who were accustomed to quote this passage in favor of their doctrine of two eternal principles, the one good, the other evil. But the ordinary rendering of the phrase gives no countenance to the Dualism, which for so many centuries opposed and embarrassed the early Church. It is, alas, too certain that Satan rules this world as if he were a God, and from the multitude he receives the service which is due to the Most High alone, but this fact by no means exalts him to an equality with the maker of all or makes him an original and and co-eternal principle of life and action. It is because men turn away from the glory of God as it shines in the face of Jesus Christ that God permits Satan to destroy, in whole or in part, their capacity for spiritual vision. Such a work is eminently appropriate in him who is prince of " the world-rulers of this darkness (Ephes. vi. 12 Rev. Ver.), and the element of whose being is deceit and falsehood. C.]

[5] Literally " physicians' sons."

As also he said to the disciples, "Therefore I speak unto them in proverbs[1], (Mat. xiii, 13.) because hearing they hear not." But what I say may also become clearer by an example; suppose a Greek, accounting our religion[2] to be fables. This man then, how will he be more advantaged? by going in and seeing the mysteries, or[3] by remaining without? Therefore he says, "That the light should not dawn upon them," still dwelling on the history of Moses. For what happened to the Jews in his case, this happeneth to all unbelievers in the case of the Gospel. And what is that which is overshadowed, and which is not illuminated unto them? Hear him saying, "That the light of the glorious Gospel of Christ who is the Image of God, should not dawn upon them." Namely, that the Cross is the salvation of the world, and His glory; that this Crucified One himself is about to come with much splendor; all the other things, those present, those to come, those seen, those not seen, the unspeakable splendor of the things looked for. Therefore also he said, "dawn," that thou mayest not look for the whole here, for that which is [here] given is only, as it were, a little dawning of the Spirit. Therefore, also above as indicating this, he spoke of "savor;" (c. ii. 16.) and again, "earnest," (c. i. 22.) showing that the greater part remaineth there. But neverthelesss all these things have been hidden from them; but had been hidden because they disbelieved first. Then to show that they are not only ignorant of the Glory of Christ, but of the Father's also, since they know not His, he added, "Who is the Image of God?" For do not halt at Christ only. For as by Him thou seest the Father, so if thou art ignorant of His Glory, neither wilt thou know the Father's.

[3.] Ver. 5. "For we preach not ourselves, but Christ Jesus as Lord, and ourselves as your servants for Jesus' sake."

And what is the nature of the connexion there? What hath this in common with what has been said? He either hints at them[4] as exalting themselves, and persuading the disciples to name themselves after them: as he said in the former Epistle, "I am of Paul and I of Apollos;" or else another thing of the gravest character. What then is this? Seeing that they waged fierce war against them, and plotted against them on every side; ' Is it,' he says, 'with us ye fight and war? [Nay but] with Him that is preached by us, "for we preach not ourselves." I am a servant, I am [but] a minister even of those who receive the Gospel, transacting every thing for Another, and for His glory doing whatsover I do. So that in warring against me thou throwest down what is His. For so far am I from turning to my own personal advantage any part of the Gospel, that I will not refuse to be even your servant for Christ's sake; seeing it seemed good to Him so to honor you, seeing He so loved you and did all things for you.' Wherefore also he saith, "and ourselves your servants for Christ's sake." Seest thou a soul pure from glory? ' For in truth,' saith he, 'we not only do not take to ourselves[5] aught of our Master's, but even to you we submit ourselves for His sake.'

Ver. 6. "Seeing it is God that said, Light shall shine out of darkness, who shined in your[6] hearts."

Seest thou how again to those who were desirous of seeing that surpassing glory, I mean that of Moses, he shows it flashing with added lustre[7]? ' As upon the face of Moses, so also hath it shined unto your hearts,' he saith. And first, he puts them in mind of what was made in the beginning of the Creation, sensible light and darkness sensible, showing that this creation is greater. And where commanded He light to shine out of darkness? In the beginning and in prelude to the Creation; for, saith he, "Darkness was upon the face of the deep. And God said, Let there be light, and there was light." Howbeit then indeed He said, "Let it be, and it was:" but now He said nothing, but Himself became Light for us. For he[8] said not, 'hath also now commanded,' but "hath" Himself "shined." Therefore neither do we see sensible objects by the shining of this Light, but God Himself through Christ. Seest thou the invariableness[9] in the Trinity? For of the Spirit, he says, "But we all with unveiled face reflecting in a mirror the glory of the Lord, are transformed into the same image from glory to glory even as from the Lord the Spirit." (c. iii. 18.) And of the Son; "That the light of the glorious Gospel of Christ, Who is the Image of God, should not dawn upon them." (v. 4.) And of the Father; "He that said Light shall shine out of darkness shined in your hearts, to give the light of the knowledge of the glory of God in the face of Christ." For as when he had said, "Of the Gospel of the glory of Christ," he added, "Who is the Image of God," showing that they were deprived of His[10] glory also; So after saying, "the knowledge of God," he added, "in the face of Christ,' to show that through Him we know

---

[1] Rec. Text "parables."
[2] τὰ ἡμέτερα.
[3] Or "than."
[4] Sc. the false Apostles.

[5] νοσφιζόμεθα.
[6] "Our" Rec. Text, [which is correct. C.]
[7] μετὰ προσθήκης.
[8] The Apostle.
[9] ἀπαράλλακτον
[10] God's.

21

the Father, even as through the Spirit also we are brought unto Him.

Ver. 7. "But we have this treasure in earthen vessels, that the exceeding greatness of the power may be of God, and not from ourselves."

For seeing he had spoken many and great things of the unspeakable glory, lest any should say, 'And how enjoying so great a glory remain we in a mortal body?' he saith, that this very thing is indeed the chiefest marvel and a very great example of the power of God, that an earthen vessel hath been enabled to bear so great a brightness and to keep so high a treasure. And therefore as admiring this, he said, "That the exceeding greatness of the power may be of God, and not from ourselves;" again alluding to those who gloried in themselves. For both the greatness of the things given and the weakness of them that receive show His power; in that He not only gave great things, but also to those who are little. For he used the term "earthen" in allusion to the frailty[1] of our mortal nature, and to declare the weakness of our flesh. For it is nothing better constituted than earthenware; so is it soon damaged, and by death and disease and variations of temperature and ten thousand other things easily dissolved. And he said these things both to take down their inflation, and to show to all that none of the things we hold[2] is human. For then is the power of God chiefly conspicuous, when by vile it worketh mighty things. Wherefore also in another place He said, "For My power is made perfect in weakness." (2 Cor. xii. 9.) And indeed in the Old [Testament] whole hosts of barbarians were turned to flight by gnats and flies, wherefore also He calleth the caterpillar His mighty force[3]; (Joel ii. 25.) and in the beginning, by only confounding tongues, He put a stop to that great tower in Babylon. And in their wars too, at one time, He routed innumerable hosts by three hundred men; at another He overthrew cities by trumpets; and afterwards by a little and poor[4] stripling, David, He turned to flight the whole array of barbarians. So then here also, sending forth twelve only He overcame the world; twelve, and those, persecuted, warred against.

[4.] Let us then be amazed at the Power of God, admire, adore it. Let us ask Jews, let us ask Greeks, who persuaded the whole world to desert from their fathers' usages, and to go over to another way of life? The fisherman, or the tentmaker? the publican, or the unlearned and ignorant? And how can these things stand with reason, except it were Divine Power which achieveth all by their means? And what too did

they say to persuade them? 'Be baptized in the Name of The Crucified.' Of what kind of man[5]? One they had not seen nor looked upon. But nevertheless saying and preaching these things, they persuaded them that they who gave them oracles, and whom they had received by tradition from their forefathers, were no Gods: whilst this Christ, He Who was nailed [to the wood,] drew them all unto Himself. And yet that He was indeed crucified and buried, was manifest in a manner to all; but that He was risen again, none save a few saw. But still of this too they persuaded those who had not beheld; and not that He rose again only, but that He ascended also into Heaven, and cometh to judge quick and dead. Whence then the persuasiveness of these sayings, tell me? From nothing else than the Power of God. For, in the first place, innovation itself[6] was offensive to all; but when too one innovates in such things, the matter becomes more grievous: when one tears up[7] the foundations of ancient custom, when one plucks laws from their seat. And besides all this, neither did the heralds seem worthy of credit, but they were both of a nation hated amongst all men, and were timorous and ignorant. Whence then overcame they the world? Whence cast they out you, and those your forefathers who were reputed to be philosophers, along with their very gods? Is it not quite evident that it was from having God with them? For neither are these successes of human, but of some divine and unspeakable, power. 'No,' saith one, 'but of witchcraft.' Then certainly ought the power of the demons to have increased and the worship of idols to have extended. How then have they been overthrown and have vanished, and our things the reverse of these? So that from this even it is manifest that what was done was the decree of God; and not from the Preaching only, but also from the rule of life itself. For when was virginity so largely planted every where in the world? when contempt of wealth, and of life, and of all things besides? For such as were wicked and wizards, would have effected nothing like this, but the contrary in all respects: whilst these introduced amongst us the life of angels; and not introduced merely, but established it in our own land, in that of the barbarians, in the very extremities of the earth. Whence it is manifest that it was the power of Christ every where that effected all, which every where shineth, and swifter than any lightning illumeth the hearts of men. All these things, then, considering, and accepting what hath been done as a clear proof of the promise

---

[1] τὸ εὔθραυστον.
[2] τῶν καθ ἡμᾶς.
[3] δύναμιν. LXX. A. V. army. Gen. 11.
[4] εὐτελοῦς.

[5] Ποίου.
[6] So one MS. at any rate; Ben. "this innovation."
[7] ἀναμοχλεύῃ.

of the things to come, worship with us the invincible might of The Crucified, that ye may both escape the intolerable punishments, and obtain the everlasting kingdom ; of which may all we partake through the grace and love towards men of our Lord Jesus Christ ; to Whom be glory world without end. Amen.

HOMILY IX.

2 COR. iv. 8, 9.

We are pressed on every side, yet not straitened; perplexed, yet not unto despair; pursued, yet not forsaken.

HE still dwells upon proving that the whole work is to be ascribed to the power of God, repressing the highmindedness of those that glory in themselves. 'For not this only,' saith he, 'is marvelous, that we keep this treasure in earthen vessels, but that even when enduring ten thousand hardships, and battered[1] on every side, we [still] preserve and lose it not. Yet though there were a vessel of adamant, it would neither have been strong enough to carry so vast a treasure, nor have sufficed against so many machinations; yet, as it is, it both bears it and suffers no harm, through God's grace.' For, "we are pressed on every side," saith he, "but not straitened." What is, "on every side?"

'In respect of our foes, in respect of our friends, in respect of necessaries, in respect of other needs, by them which be hostile, by them of our own household.' "Yet not straitened." And see how he speaks contrarieties, that thence also he may show the strength of God. For, "we are pressed on every side, yet not straitened," saith he ; "perplexed, yet not unto despair ;" that is, 'we do not quite fall off. For we are often, indeed, wrong in our calculations[2], and miss our aim, yet not so as to fall away from what is set before us: for these things are permitted by God for our discipline, not for our defeat.'

Ver. 9. " Pursued, yet not forsaken ; smitten down, yet not destroyed."

For these trials do indeed befal, but not the consequences of the trials. And this indeed through the power and Grace of God. In other places indeed he says that these things were permitted in order both to their own[3] humblemindedness, and to the safety of others: for " that I should not be exalted overmuch, there was given to me a thorn," (2 Cor. xii. 7 ; ib. 6.)

he says : and again, " Lest any man should account of me above that which he seeth me to be, or heareth from me ;" and in another place again, "that we should not trust in ourselves :" (2 Cor. i. 9.) here, however, that the power of God might be manifested. Seest thou how great the gain of his trials? For it both showed the power of God, and more disclosed His grace. For, saith He, " My grace is sufficient for thee." (2 Cor. xii. 9.) It also anointed them unto lowliness of mind, and prepared them for keeping down the rest, and made them to be more hardy. " For patience," saith he, " worketh probation, and probation hope." (Rom. v. 4.) For they who had fallen into ten thousand dangers and through the hope they had in God had been recovered[4], were taught to hold by it more and more in all things.

Ver. 10. "Always bearing about in the body the dying of the Lord Jesus, that the life also of Jesus may be manifested in our body."

And what is the " dying of the Lord Jesus," which they bare about? Their daily deaths by which also the resurrection was showed. 'For if any believe not,' he says, 'that Jesus died and rose again, beholding us every day die and rise again, let him believe henceforward in the resurrection.' Seest thou how he has discovered yet another reason for the trials? What then is this reason? " That his life also may be manifested in our body." He says, ' by snatching us out of the perils. So that this which seems a mark of weakness and destitution, this, [I say,] proclaims His resurrection. For His power had not so appeared in our suffering no unpleasantness, as it is now shown in our suffering indeed, but without being overcome.'

Ver. 11. " For we which live are also[5] delivered unto death for Jesus' sake, that the life also of Jesus may be manifested in us in our mortal flesh."

---

[1] περικρουόμενοι, a term especially used of striking upon vessels, to sound them.
[2] ἀλογούμεθα. The Ben. Ed. has ἀλγοῦμεν in defiance of MSS.
[3] i. e., the Apostles',

[4] ἀνενεγκόντες.
[5] So Chrysostom : Rec. text " always," [which is correct. C.] Just below he inserts, as will be seen, " in us," [without authority. C.]

For every where when he has said any thing obscure, he interprets himself again. So he has done here also, giving a clear interpretation of this which I have cited. 'For therefore, "we are delivered,"' he says, 'in other words, we bear about His dying that the power of His life may be made manifest, who permitteth not mortal flesh, though undergoing so great sufferings, to be overcome by the snow-storm of these calamities.' And it may be taken too in another way. How? As he says in another place, "If we die with him, we shall also live with Him." (2 Tim. ii. 11.) 'For as we endure His dying now, and choose whilst living to die for His sake: so also will he choose, when we are dead, to beget us then unto life. For if we from life come into death, He also will from death lead us by the hand into life.'

Ver. 12. "So then death worketh in us, but life in you."

Speaking no more of death in the strict sense[1], but of trials and of rest. 'For we indeed,' he says, 'are in perils and trials, but ye in rest; reaping the life which is the fruit of these perils. And we indeed endure the dangerous, but ye enjoy the good things; for ye undergo not so great trials.'

[2.] Ver. 13. "But having the same spirit of faith, according to that which is written, I believed, and therefore did I speak ; we also believe, and therefore also we speak ; that[2] He which raised up the Lord Jesus, shall raise up us also by Jesus." (Ps. cxvi. 10.)

He has reminded us of a Psalm which abounds in heavenly wisdom[3], and is especially fitted to encourage[4] in dangers. For this saying that just man uttered when he was in great dangers, and from which there was no other possibility of recovery than by the aid of God. Since then kindred circumstances are most effective in comforting, therefore he says, " having the same Spirit;" that is, 'by the same succor by which he was saved, we also are saved; by the Spirit through which he spake, we also speak.' Whence he shows, that between the New and Old Covenants great harmony exists, and that the same Spirit wrought in either ; and that not we alone are in dangers, but all those of old were so too ; and that we must find a remedy[5] through faith and hope, and not seek at once to be released from what is laid upon us. For having showed by arguments the resurrection and the life, and that the danger was not a mark of helplessness or destitution ; he thenceforward brings in faith

also, and to it commits the whole. But still of this also, he furnishes a proof, the resurrection, namely, of Christ, saying, "we also believe, and therefore also we speak." What do we believe ? tell me.

Ver. 14, 15. "That He which raised up Jesus, shall raise up also,[6] and shall present us with you. For all things are for your sakes, that the grace, being multiplied through the many, may cause the thanksgiving to abound unto the glory of God."

Again, he fills them with lofty thoughts[7], that they may not hold themselves indebted to men, I mean to the false Apostles. For the whole is of God Who willeth to bestow upon many, so that the grace may appear the greater. For your sakes, therefore, was the resurrection and all the other things. For He did not these things for the sake of one only, but of all.

Ver. 16. "Wherefore we faint not; but though our outward man is decaying, yet the inward man is renewed day by day."

How does it decay? Being scourged, being persecuted, suffering ten thousand extremities. "Yet the inward man is renewed day by day." How is it renewed? By faith, by hope, by a forward will, finally, by braving those extremities. For in proportion as the body suffers ten thousand things, in the like proportion hath the soul goodlier hopes and becometh brighter, like gold refined in the fire more and more. And see how he brings to nothing the sorrows of this present life.

Ver. 17. 18. "For the [8] light affliction," he saith, "which is for the moment, worketh[9] more and more exceedingly an eternal weight of glory; while we look not at the things which are seen, but at the things which are not seen."

Having closed the question by a reference to hope, (and, as he said in his Epistle to the Romans, "We are saved by hope, but hope that is seen is not hope ;" (Rom. viii. 24.) establishing the same point here also,) he sets side by side the things present with the things to come, the momentary with the eternal, the light with the weighty, the affliction with the glory. And neither is he content with this, but he addeth another expression, doubling it and saying, "more and more exceedingly[10]." Next he also shows the mode how so great afflictions are light. How then light? "While we look not at the things that are seen, but at the things that

---

[1] Literally, *the* death.
[2] *Knowing that* &c. Rec. Text [which is well sustained. C.]
[3] φιλοσοφίαν.
[4] ἀλείφειν.
[5] διορθοῦσθαι.

[6] [It is singular that the preacher in citing this verse omitted a clause of great importance, found in all the chief MSS., viz., *with Jesus*, words which teach that believers are raised up in union with Christ and by virtue of that union, and therefore in his fellowship and likeness. This it is that made the resurrection the one great, all-absorbing object of anticipation and desire to the early Christians. They were to be with their Lord and like him. C.]
[7] φρονήματος.
[8] *Our*, A. V., [the true text.]
[9] *Worketh for us*, A. V., [the true text.]
[10] καθ᾽ ὑπερβολὴν εἰς ὑπερβολήν.

are not seen." So will both this present be light and that future great, if we withdraw ourselves from the things that are seen. "For the things that are seen are temporal." (v. 18.) Therefore the afflictions are so too. "But the things that are not seen are eternal." Therefore the crowns are so also. And he said not the afflictions are so, but "the things that are seen;" all of them, whether punishment or rest, so that we should be neither puffed up by the one nor overborne[1] by the other. And therefore when speaking of the things to come, he said not the kingdom is eternal; but, "the things which are not seen are eternal," whether they be a kingdom, or again punishment; so as both to alarm by the one and to encourage by the other.

[3.] Since then "the things that are seen are temporal, but the things that are not seen are eternal," let us look to them. For what excuse even can we have, if we choose the temporal instead of the eternal? For even if the present be pleasurable, yet it is not abiding; whilst the woe it entails is abiding and irremissible. For what excuse will they have who have been counted worthy of the Spirit and have enjoyed so great a gift, if they become of grovelling mind and fall down to the earth. For I hear many saying these words worthy of all scorn, 'Give me to-day and take to-morrow.' 'For,' saith one, 'if indeed there be such things there as ye affirm, then it is one for one; but if there be no such thing at all, then it is two for nothing.' What can be more lawless than these words[2]? or what more idle prating[2]? We are discoursing about Heaven and those unspeakable good things; and thou bringest forth unto us the terms of the race-course[3], yet art not ashamed nor hidest thy face, whilst uttering such things as befit maniacs? Blushest thou not that art so rivetted to the present things? Wilt thou not cease from being distraught and beside thyself, and in youth a dotard? Were Greeks indeed to talk in this way, it were no marvel: but that believers should vent such dotage, of what forgiveness doth it admit? For dost thou hold those immortal hopes in utter suspicion? Dost thou think these things to be utterly doubtful? And in what are these things deserving of pardon? 'And who hath come,' saith one, 'and brought back word what is there?' Of men indeed not any one, but God, more trustworthy than all, hath declared these things. But thou beholdest not what is there. Neither dost thou see God. Wilt thou then deny that there is a God, because thou seest Him not? 'Yes,' he replies, 'I

firmly believe there is a God.' If then an infidel should ask thee, 'And who came from Heaven and brought back word of this?' what wilt thou answer? Whence dost thou know that there is a God? 'From the things that are seen,' he answers, 'from the fair order existing through the whole creation, from its being manifest to all.' Therefore receive also in the same way the doctrine of the judgment. 'How?' he asks. I will question thee, and do thou answer me. Is this God just, and will He render to each according to his deserving? or, on the contrary, doth He will the wicked, should live happily and in luxury, and the good in the contrary things? 'By no means,' he answers, 'for man even would not feel thus.' Where then shall they who have done virtuously here, enjoy the things that be good? and where the wicked the opposites, except there is to be a life and retribution hereafter? Seest thou that at present it is one for one, and not two for one. But I will show thee, as I proceed, that it is not even one against one, but it shall be for the righteous two for nothing; and for the sinners and those that live here riotously, quite the contrary. For they that have lived riotously here have received not even one for one; but those who pass their life in virtue two for nothing[4]. For who are at in rest, they that have abused this present life, or they that followed heavenly wisdom? Perhaps thou wilt say the former, but I prove it of the latter, summoning for my witnesses those very men that have enjoyed these present things; and they will not be so shameless as to deny what I am going to say. For oftentimes have they imprecated curses upon matchmakers[5] and upon the day that their bridal chamber[6] was wreathed, and have proclaimed them happy who have not married. Many too of the young, even when they might have married, have refused for no other reason than the troublesomeness of the thing. And this I say, not as accusing marriage; for it is "honorable;" (Heb. xiii. 4.) but those who have used it amiss. Now if they who have lived a married life, often considered their life not worth the living; what shall we say of those who have been swept down into whores' deep pits, and are more slavishly and wretchedly treated than any captive? what of those who have grown rotten in luxury and have enveloped their bodies with a thousand diseases? 'But it is a pleasure to be had in honor.' Yea, rather, nothing is bitterer than this slavery. For he that seeketh vain honor is more servile than any slave, and desirous of pleasing any body; but he that treads it under foot is superior to all, who careth

---

[1] βιάζεσθαι.
[2] ληρωδέστερον.
[3] ἱπποδρομίων. Vid. Field Ann.

[4] "For one." Bened., against most MSS.
[5] προμνηστρίαις.
[6] αἱ παστάδες.

not for the glory that cometh from others. 'But the possession of wealth is desirable.' Yet we have often shown that they who are loose from it and have nothing, enjoy greater riches and repose. 'But to be drunken is pleasant.' But who will say this? Surely then if to be without riches is pleasanter than to have them, and not to marry than to marry, and not to seek vainglory than to seek it, and not to live luxuriously than to live so; even in this world they who are not riveted to those present things have the advantage. And as yet I say not how that the former, even though he be racked with ten thousand tortures, hath that good hope to carry him through: whilst the latter, even though he is in the enjoyment of a thousand delights, hath the fear of the future disquieting and confounding his pleasure. For this, too, is no light sort of punishment; nor therefore the contrary, of enjoyment and repose. And besides these there is a third sort. And what is this? In that the things of worldly delight do not even whilst they are present appear such, being refuted[1] both by nature and time; but the others not only are, but also abide immovable. Seest thou that we shall be able to put not two for nothing only, but three even, and five, and ten, and twenty, and ten thousand for nothing? But that thou mayest learn this same truth by an example also,—the rich man and Lazarus,— the one enjoyed the things present, the other those to come. (Luke xvi. 19. &c.) Seems it then to thee to be one and one, to be punished throughout all time, and to be an hungered for a little season? to be diseased in thy corruptible body, and to scorch[2] miserably in an undying one? to be crowned and live in undying delights after that little sickness, and to be endlessly tormented after that short enjoyment of his goods. And who will say this? For what wilt thou we should compare? the quantity? the quality? the rank? the decision of God[3] concerning each? How long will ye utter the words of beetles that are for ever wallowing in·dung! For these are not the words of reasoning men, to throw away a soul which is so precious for nothing, when there needeth little labor to receive heaven. Wilt thou that I teach thee also in another way that there is an awful tribunal there? Open the doors of thy conscience, and behold the judge that sitteth in thine heart. Now if thou condemnest thyself, although a lover of thyself, and canst not refrain from passing a righteous verdict, will not God much rather make great provision for that which is just, and pass that impartial judgment upon all; or will He permit everything to go on loosely

and at random? And who will say this? No one; but both Greeks and barbarians, both poets and philosophers, yea the whole race of men in this agree with us, though differing in particulars[4], and affirm that there are tribunals of some sort in Hades; so manifest and uncontroverted is the thing.

[4.] 'And wherefore,' saith one, 'doth he not punish here?' That He may display that longsuffering of His, and may offer to us the salvation that cometh by repentance, and not make our race to be swept away, nor pluck away those who by an excellent change are able to be saved, before that salvation. For if he instantly punished upon the commission of sins, and destroyed, how should Paul have been saved, how should Peter, the chief teachers of the world? How should David have reaped the salvation that came by his repentance? How the Galatians? How many others? For this reason then He neither exacts the penalty from all here, (but only from some out of all,) nor yet there from all, but from one here, and from another there; that He may both rouse those who are exceedingly insensible by means of those whom He punishes, and may cause them to expect the future things by those whom He punishes not. Or seest thou not many punished here, as those, for instance, who were buried under the ruins of that tower; (Luke xiii. 4, 7.) as those whose blood Pilate mingled with their sacrifices; as those who perished by an untimely death amongst the Corinthians, because they partook unworthily of the mysteries (1 Cor. xi. 30.); as Pharaoh; as those of the Jews who were slain by the barbarians; as many others, both then, and now, and continually? And yet others too, having sinned in many things, departed without suffering the penalty here; as the rich man in the story of Lazarus; as many others. (Luke xvi.) Now these things He does, both to arouse those who quite disbelieve[5] in the things to come, and to make those who do believe and are careless more diligent. "For God is a righteous Judge, and strong, and longsuffering, and visits not with wrath every day." (Ps. vii. 11. LXX.) But if we abuse His longsuffering, there will come a time when He will no more be longsuffering even for a little, but will straightway inflict the penalty.

Let us not then, in order that for a single moment (for such is this present life) we may live luxuriously, draw on ourselves punishment through endless ages: but let us toil for a moment, that we may be crowned for ever. See ye not that even in worldly things most men act in this manner; and choose a brief toil in order to

---

[1] ἐλεγχόμενα.
[2] ἀποτηγανίζεσθαι.
[3] τάξιν. The Ben. translate "ordinem Dei aut sententiam."

[4] εἰ καὶ μὴ ὁμοίως.
[5] διαπιστοῦντας

a long rest, even though the opposite falls out unto them? For in this life indeed there is an equal portion of toils and reward; yea, often, on the contrary, the toil is endless whilst the fruit is little, or not even a little; but in the case of the kingdom conversely, the labor is little whilst the pleasure is great and boundless. For consider: the husbandman wearieth himself the whole year through, and at the very end of his hope ofttimes misses of the fruit[1] of those many toils. The shipmaster again and the soldier, until extreme old age, are occupied with wars and labors; and oftentimes hath each of them departed, the one with the loss of his wealthy cargoes, the other, along with victory, of life itself. What excuse then shall we have, tell me, if in worldly matters indeed we prefer what is laborious in order that we may rest for a little, or not a little even; (for the hope of this is uncertain;) but in spiritual things do the converse of this and draw upon ourselves unutterable punishment for a little sloth? Wherefore I beseech you all, though late, yet still at length to recover from this frenzy. For none shall deliver us in that day; neither brother, nor father, nor child, nor friend, nor neighbor, nor any other: but if our works play us false, all will be over and we must needs[2] perish. How many lamentations did that rich man make, and besought the Patriarch and begged that Lazarus might be sent! But hear what Abraham said unto him: "There is a gulf[3] betwixt us and you, so that they who wish to go forth cannot pass thither." (Luke xvi. 26.) How many petitions did those virgins make to their fellows for a little oil! But hear what they also say; "Peradventure there will not be enough for you and for us;" (Mat. xxv. 9.) and none was able to bring them in to the bridal chamber.

Thinking then on these things let us also be careful of that which is our life. For mention what toils soever and bring forward besides what punishment soever; all these combined will be nothing in comparison of the good things to come. Instance therefore, if thou wilt, fire and steel and wild beasts, and if there be aught sorer than these; but yet these are not even a shadow compared with those torments. For these things when applied in excess become then

especially light, making the release speedy[4]; since the body sufficeth not unto intensity at once and long continuance of suffering; but both meet together, both prolongation and excess, alike in the good and the grievous. Whilst we have time then, "let us come before His presence with confession," (Ps. xcv. 2, LXX.) that in that day we may behold Him gentle and serene, that we may escape altogether those threat-bearing Powers. Seest thou not how this world's soldiers who perform the bidding of those in authority drag men about; how they chain, how they scourge them, how they pierce their sides, how they apply torches to their torments, how they dismember them? Yet all these things are but plays and joke unto those punishments. For these punishments are temporal; but there neither the worm dieth nor is the fire quenched: for that body of all is incorruptible, which is then to be raised up. But God grant that we may never learn these things by experience; but that these fearful things may never be nearer unto us than in the mention of them[5]; and that we be not delivered over to those tormentors, but may be hence made wise[6]. How many things shall we then say in accusation of ourselves! How many lamentations shall we utter! How many groans! But it will thenceforth be of no avail. For neither can sailors, when the ship hath gone to pieces and hath sunk, thereafter be of any service; nor physicians when the patient is departed; but they will often say indeed that so and so ought to have been done; but all is fruitless and in vain. For as long indeed as hopes remain from amendment, one onght both to say and do every thing: but when we have no longer any thing in our power, all being quite ruined, it is to no purpose that all is said and done. For even then Jews will then say, "Blessed is He that cometh in the Name of the Lord:" (Mat. xxiii. 39) but they will be able to reap none advantage of this cry towards escaping their punishment; for when they ought to have said it, they said it not. That then this be not the case with us in respect to our life, let us now and from this time reform that we may stand at the tribunal of Christ with all boldness; whereunto may all of us attain through the grace and love toward men of our Lord Jesus Christ, with Whom to the Father, with the Holy Spirit, be glory and might for ever and ever. Amen.

---

[1] Or, "at the very end ofttimes misses of his hope, the fruit, &c."

[2] Or, 'utterly.'

[3] χάος, Chrys. who varies from the text in other respects. [Not, however, so as to affect the sense of the passage. Perhaps in quoting he took only that portion which suited his purpose. The word he uses for *gulf* or *chasm* is employed in the LXX. in the same sense. C.]

[4] *Si gravis, brevis: si longa, levis:* Cic. *Tusc. Disp.*

[5] μεχρὶ ῥήματος στῆναι.

[6] ἐντεῦθεν σωφρονισθῆναι. Ben. ἐνταῦθα against the MSS.

HOMILY X.

2 COR. v. 1.

For we know, that if the earthly house of our tabernacle be dissolved, we have a building from God, a house not made with hands, eternal, in the heavens.

AGAIN he arouses their zeal because many trials drew on[1]. For it was likely that they, in consequence of his absence, were weaker in respect to this [need]. What then saith he? One ought not to wonder that we suffer affliction; nor to be confounded, for we even reap many gains thereby. And some of these he mentioned before; for instance, that we "bear about the dying of Jesus," and present the greatest proof of His power: for he says, "that the exceeding greatness of the power may be of God:" and we exhibit a clear proof of the Resurrection, for, says he, "that the life of Jesus may be manifested in our mortal flesh." But since along with these things he said that our inward man is thus made better also; for "though our outward man is decaying," saith he, "yet the inward man is renewed day by day;" showing again that this being scourged and persecuted is proportionately useful, he adds, that when this is done thoroughly, then the countless good things will spring up for those who have endured these things. For lest when thou hearest that thy outward man perishes, thou shouldest grieve; he says, that when this is completely effected, then most of all shalt thou rejoice and shalt come unto a better inheritance[2]. So that not only ought not one to grieve at its perishing now in part, but even earnestly to seek for the completion of that destruction, for this most conducts thee to immortality. Wherefore also he added, "For we know, that if the earthly house of our tabernacle be dissolved: we have a building from God, a house not made with hands, eternal in the heavens." For since he is urging[3] again the doctrine of the Resurrection in respect to which they were particularly unsound; he calls in aid the judgment of his hearers also, and so establishes it; not however in the same way as before, but, as it were, arriving at it out of another subject: (for they had been already

corrected:) and says, "We know that if the earthly house of our tabernacle be dissolved, we have a building from God, a house not made with hands, eternal in the heavens." Some indeed say that the 'earthly house' is this world; But I should maintain that he alludes rather to the body.[4] But observe, I pray, how by the terms [he uses,] he shows the superiority of the future things to the present. For having said "earthly" he hath opposed to it "the heavenly;" having said, "house of tabernacle," thereby declaring both that it is easily taken to pieces and is temporary, he hath opposed to it the "eternal," for the name "tabernacle" oftentimes denotes temporariness. Wherefore He saith, "In My Father's house are many abiding places." (John xiv. 2.) But if He anywhere also calls the resting places of the saints tabernacles; He calls them not tabernacles simply, but adds an epithet; for he said not, that "they may receive you" into their tabernacles, but "into the eternal tabernacles." (Luke xvi. 9.) Moreover also in that he said, "not made with hands," he alluded to that which was made with hands. What then? Is the body made with hands? By no means; but he either alludes to the houses here that are made with hands, or if not this, then he called the body which is not made with hands, 'a house of tabernacle.' For he has not used the term in antithesis and contradistinction[5] to this, but to heighten those eulogies and swell those commendations.

[2.] Ver. 2 "For verily in this we groan, longing to be clothed upon with our habitation which is from heaven."

What habitation? tell me. The incorruptible body. And why do we groan now? Because that is far better. And "from heaven" he calls it because of its incorruptibleness. For it is not surely that a body will come down to us from above: but by this expression he

---

[1] ἐπάγεσθαι.
[2] λῆξιν.
[3] γυμνάζει.

[4] [In this view that the building from God is the resurrection body, Chrysostom has the support of nearly all the recent expositors—Hodge indeed contends stoutly and ably that the house not made with hands is heaven itself, yet not with success. For if the earthly house is a body, the heavenly house must be one also, else the comparison fails much in force and point; moreover, a body which is said to be now in heaven and afterwards to come from heaven can hardly be identical with heaven. C.]
[5] πρὸς ἀντιδιαστολήν ἀντέθηκεν.

326

signifies the grace which is sent from thence. So far then ought we to be from grieving at these trials which are in part that we ought to seek even for their fulness,[1] as if he had said : Groanest thou, that thou art persecuted, that this thy man is decaying? Groan that this is not done unto excess and that it perishes not entirely. Seest thou how he hath turned round what was said unto the contrary ; having proved that they ought to groan that those things were not done fully ; for which because they were done partially ; they groaned. Therefore he henceforth calls it not a tabernacle, but a house, and with great reason. For a tabernacle indeed is easily taken to pieces ; but a house abideth continually.

Ver. 3. "If so be that being unclothed[2] we shall not be found naked."

That is, even if we have put off the body, we shall not be presented there without a body, but even with the same one made incorruptible. But some read, and it deserves very much to be adopted, "If so be that being clothed we shall not be found naked." For lest all should be confident because of the Resurrection, he says, "If so be that being clothed," that is, having obtained incorruption and an incorruptible body, "we shall not be found naked " of glory and safety. As he also said in the former Epistle ; " We shall all be raised ; but each in his own order." And, "There are celestial bodies, and bodies terrestial." (1 Cor. xv. 22, 23.) (ib. 40.) For the Resurrection indeed is common to all, but the glory is not common ; but some shall rise in honor and others in dishonor, and some to a kingdom but others to punishment. This surely he signified here also, when he said ; "If so be that being clothed we shall not be found naked."

[3.] Ver. 4. " For indeed we that are in this tabernacle do groan[3], not for that we would be unclothed, but that we would be clothed upon."

Here again he hath utterly and manifestly stopped the mouths of the heretics, showing that he is not speaking absolutely of a body differing in identity[4], but of corruption and incorruption. ' For we do not therefore groan,' saith he, ' that we may be delivered from the body: for of this we do not wish to be unclothed ; but we hasten to be delivered from the corruption that is in it. Wherefore he saith, ' we wish not to be unclothed of the body, but that it should be clothed upon with incorruption.' Then he also interprets it [thus,] " That what is mortal may be swallowed up of life." For since putting off the body appeared to many

a grievous thing ; and he was contradicting the judgments of all, when he said, " we groan," not wishing to be set free from it ; (' for if,' says one, ' the soul in being separated from it so suffers and laments, how sayest thou that we groan because we are not separated from it?') lest then this should be urged against him, he says, ' Neither do I assert that we therefore groan, that we may put it off ; (for no one putteth it off without pain, seeing that Christ says even of Peter, ' They shall " carry thee," and lead thee " whither thou wouldest not ;"—John xxi. 18.) but that we may have it clothed upon with incorruption.' For it is in this respect that we are burdened by the body ; not because it is a body, but because we are encompassed with a corruptible body and liable to suffering[5], for it is this that also causes us pain. But the life when it arriveth destroyeth and useth up the corruption ; the corruption, I say, not the body. ' And how cometh this to pass?' saith one. Inquire not ; God doeth it ; be not too curious. Wherefore also he added,

Ver. 5. " Now he that hath wrought us for this very thing is God."

Hereby he shows that these things were prefigured from the first. For not now was this decreed : but when at the first He fashioned us from earth and created Adam ; for not for this created He him, that he should die, but that He might make him even immortal. Then as showing the credibility of this and furnishing the proof of it, he added,

" Who also gave the earnest of the Spirit."

For even then He fashioned us for this ; and now He hath wrought unto this by baptism, and hath furnished us with no light security thereof, the Holy Spirit. And he continually calls It an earnest, wishing to prove God to be a debtor of the[6] whole, and thereby also to make what he says more credible unto the grosser sort.[7]

[4.] Ver. 6. " Being therefore always of good courage, and knowing."

---

[1] το καθολικὸν.
[2] ἐκδυσάμενοι. This doubtless was what St. Chrysostom wrote, as appears from what follows ; but the MSS. all agree in reading ἐνδυσάμενοι, as the Rec. text of the N. T. reads in the Epistle.
[3] " Being burdened," Rec. text, which St. Chrysostom omits.
[4] ἄλλου καὶ ἄλλου.

[5] παθητὸν.
[6] ὀφειλέτην τοῦ παντὸς.
[7] [The argument of these verses is thus presented by Beet, in lo. " By Christians now death is looked upon without terrible recoil, as being the only entrance into Life. We bow to the inevitable. But in the early Christians the possibility of surviving the coming of Christ woke up with new intensity man's natural love of life, and made death seem very dark. They therefore longed eagerly for Christ's return, hoping thus to clothe themselves with immortal raiment without laying aside their mortal bodies. This yearning for an immortal body, Paul felt to be divinely implanted, and therefore not doomed to disappointment. But the possibility of death was to Paul too real to be ignored. Therefore, in view of it, his yearning for an immortal body assured him that if his present body be removed by death a heavenly body awaits him. For, otherwise, he will stand before Christ as a naked spirit, in utter contradiction to yearnings which he felt to be divine and of whose realization he had a divine pledge. In other words his instinctive clinging to his present body was to him a divine intimation that when Christ comes we shall not be naked spirits, but spirits clothed in bodies ; and was therefore a proof that if our present body be removed by death a heavenly and eternal body awaits us. Thus a purely human instinct, not weakened but intensified by Christianity, and sanctified by the felt presence of the Holy Spirit, is seen to be a prophecy of God's purpose concerning us. Similar argument in Romans viii. 23." C.]

The word "of good courage" is used with reference to the persecutions, the plottings, and the continual deaths: as if he had said, 'Doth any vex and persecute and slay thee? Be not cast down, for thy good all is done. Be not afraid: but of good courage. For that which thou groanest and grievest for, that thou art in bondage to corruption, he removes from henceforward out of the way, and frees thee the sooner from this bondage.' Wherefore also he saith, "Being therefore always of good courage," not in the seasons of rest only, but also in those of tribulation; "and knowing,"

Ver. 7, 8. "That whilst we are at home in the body, we are absent from the Lord (for we walk by faith, not by sight); we are of good courage, I say, and are willing to be absent from the body, and to be at home with the Lord."

That which is greater than all he has put last, for to be with Christ is better, than receiving an incorruptible [body.] But what he means is this: 'He quencheth not our life that warreth against and killeth us; be not afraid; be of good courage even when hewn in pieces. For not only doth he set thee free from corruption and a burden, but he also sendeth thee quickly to the Lord.' Wherefore neither did he say, "whilst we 'are' in the body:" as of those who are in a foreign and strange land. "Knowing therefore that whilst we are at home in the body, we are absent from the Lord: we are of good courage, I say, and willing to be absent from the body, and to be at home with the Lord." Seest thou how keeping back what was painful, the names of death and the end, he has employed instead of them such as excite great longing[1], calling them presence with God; and passing over those things which are accounted to be sweet, the things of life, he hath expressed them by painful names, calling the life here an absence from the Lord? Now this he did, both that no one might fondly linger amongst present things, but rather be aweary of them; and that none when about to die might be disquieted[2], but might even rejoice as departing unto greater goods. Then that none might say on hearing that we are absent from the Lord, 'Why speakest thou thus? Are we then estranged from Him whilst we are here?' he in anticipation corrected[3] such a thought, saying, "For we walk by faith, not by sight." Even here indeed we know Him, but not so clearly. As he says also elsewhere, (1 Cor. xiii. 12.) "in a mirror," and "darkly."

"We are of good courage, I say, and willing." Wonderful! to what hath he brought round the discourse? To an extreme desire of death, having shown the grievous to be pleasurable, and the pleasurable grievous. For by the term, "we are willing" he means, 'we are desirous.' Of what are we desirous? Of being "absent from the body, and at home with the Lord." And thus he does perpetually, (as I showed also before) turning round the objection of his opponents unto the very contrary.

Ver. 9. "Wherefore also we make it our aim whether at home or absent, to be well pleasing unto him."

'For what we seek for is this,' saith he, 'whether we be there or here, to live according to His will; for this is the principal thing. So that by this thou hast the kingdom already in possession without a probation.' For lest when they had arrived at so great a desire of being there, they should again be disquieted at its being so long first, in this he gives them already the chief[4] of those good things. And what is this? To be well "pleasing." For as to depart is not absolutely good, but to do so in [God's] favor, which is what makes departing also become a good; so to remain here is not absolutely grievous, but to remain offending Him. Deem not then that departure from the body is enough; for virtue is always necessary. For as when he spoke of a Resurrection, he allowed [them] not by it alone to be of good courage, saying, "If so be that being clothed we shall not be found naked;" so also having showed a departure, lest thou shouldest think that this is enough to save thee, he added that it is needful that we be well pleasing.

[5.] Seeing then he has persuaded them by many good things, henceforth he alarms them also by those of gloomier aspect[5]. For our interest consists both in the attainment of the good things and the avoidance of the evil things, in other words, hell and the kingdom. But since this, the avoiding of punishment, is the more forcible motive; for where penalty reaches only to the not receiving good things, the most will bear this contentedly; but if it also extend to the suffering of evil, do so no longer: (for they ought, indeed, to consider the former intolerable, but from the weakness and grovelling nature of the many, the latter appears to them more hard to bear:) since then (I say) the giving of the good things doth not so arouse the general hearer as the threat of the punishments, he is obliged to conclude with this, saying,

Ver. 10. "For we must all be made manifest before the judgment-seat."

Then having alarmed and shaken[6] the hearer by the mention of that judgment-seat, he hath

---

[1] τά σφόδρα ποθεινά
[2] ἀλύῃ.
[3] προδιώρθωσε.

[4] τὸ κεφάλαιον.
[5] σκυθρωποτέρων.
[6] κατασείσας.

not even here set down the woful without the good things, but hath mingled something of pleasure, saying,

"That each one may receive the things done in the body," as many[1] as " he hath done, whether" it be "good or bad."

By saying these words, he both reviveth[2] those who have done virtuously and are persecuted with those hopes, and maketh those who have fallen back more earnest by that fear. And he thus confirmed his words touching the resurrection of the body. 'For surely,' sayeth he, ' that which hath ministered to the one and to the other shall not stand excluded from the recompenses : but along with the soul shall in the one case be punished, in the other crowned.' But some of the heretics say, that it is another body that is raised. How so? tell me. Did one sin, and is another punished? Did one do virtuously, and is another crowned? And what will ye answer to Paul, saying, " We would not be unclothed, but clothed upon?" And how is that which is mortal "swallowed up of life?" For he said not, that the mortal or corruptible body should be swallowed up of the incorruptible body ; but that corruption [should be swallowed up] " of life." For then this happeneth when the same body is raised ; but if, giving up that body, He should prepare another, no longer is corruption swallowed up but continueth dominant. Therefore this is not so; but " this corruptible," that is to say the body, " must put on incorruption." For the body is in a middle state[3], being at present in this and hereafter to be in that ; and for this reason in this first, because it is impossible for the incorruption to be dissolved. " For neither doth corruption inherit incorruption," saith he, (for, how is it [then] incorruption?) but on the contrary, " corruption is swallowed up of life: " for this indeed survives the other, but not the other this. For as wax is melted by fire but itself doth not melt the fire : so also doth corruption melt and vanish away under incorruption, but is never able itself to get the better of incorruption.

[6.] Let us then hear the voice of Paul, saying, that " we must stand at the judgment-seat of Christ ; " and let us picture to ourselves that court of justice, and imagine it to be present now and the reckoning to be required[4]. For I will speak of it more at large. For Paul, seeing that he was discoursing on affliction, and he had no mind to afflict them again, did not dwell on the subject; but having in brief expressed its austerity[5], " Each one shall receive according to what he hath done," he quickly passed on. Let

us then imagine it to be present now, and reckon on each one of us with his own conscience, and account the Judge to be already present, and everything to be revealed and brought forth. For we must not merely stand, but also be manifested. Do ye not blush ? Are ye not astonied ? But if now, when the reality is not yet present, but is granted in supposition merely and imaged in thought ; if now [I say] we perish conscience-struck ; what shall we do when [it] shall arrive, when the whole world shall be present, when angels and archangels, when ranks upon ranks, and all hurrying at once, and some caught up[6] on the clouds, and an array full of trembling ; when there shall be the trumpets, one upon another, [when] those unceasing voices ?

For suppose there were no hell, yet in the midst of so great brightness to be rejected and to go away dishonored ;—how great the punishment ! For if even now, when the Emperor rideth in and his train with him, we contemplating each one of us our own poverty, derive not so much pleasure from the spectacle, as we endure dejection at having no share in what is going on about the Emperor, nor being near the Sovereign ; what will it be then ? Or thinkest thou it is a light punishment, not to be ranked in that company, not to be counted worthy of that unutterable glory, from that assemblage and those untold good things, to be cast forth somewither far and distant ? But when there is also darkness, and gnashing of teeth, and chains indissoluble, and an undying worm, and fire unquenchable, and affliction, and straitness, and tongues scorching like the rich man's ; and we wail, and none heareth ; and we groan and gnash our teeth for anguish, and none regardeth ; and we look all round, and nowhere is there any to comfort us ; where shall we rank those that are in this condition? what is there more miserable than are those souls? what more pitiable ? For if, when we enter a prison and see its inmates, some squalid, some chained and famishing, some again shut up in darkness, we are moved with compassion, we shudder, we use all diligence that we may never be cast into that place ; how will it be with us, when we are led and dragged away into the the torture-dungeons[7] themselves of hell? For not of iron are those chains, but of fire that is never quenched ; nor are they that are set over us our fellows whom it is often possible even to mollify ; but angels whom one may not so much as look in the face, exceedingly enraged at our insults to their Master. Nor is it given, as here, to see some bringing in money, some food, some words of comfort, and to meet with consolation ; but all is irremissible there : and though it should be Noah,

---

[1] So Chrysostom here, but below with the Received text, "according to that," &c.
[2] ἀνιστᾷ.
[3] μέσον.
　εὐθύνας ἀπαιτεῖσθαι.
[4] τὸ στῦφον.

[6] ἁρπαγαί.
[7] βασανιστήρια.

or Job, or Daniel, and he should see his own kindred punished, he dares not succor. For even natural sympathy too comes then to be done away. For since it happeneth that there are righteous fathers of wicked children, and [righteous] children of [wicked] fathers; that so their pleasure may be unalloyed, and those who enjoy the good things may not be moved with sorrow through the constraining force of sympathy, even this sympathy, I affirm, is extinguished, and themselves are indignant together with the Master against their own bowels. For if the common run of men, when they see their own children vicious, disown[1] and cut them off from that relationship; much rather will the righteous then. Therefore let no one hope for good things, if he have not wrought any good thing, even though he have ten thousand righteous ancestors. "For each one shall receive the things done in the body according to what he hath done." Here he seems to me to be alluding also to them that commit fornication: and to raise up as a wall[2] unto them the fear of that world, not however to them alone; but also to all that in any wise transgress.

[7.] Let us hear then, us also. And if thou have the fire of lust, set against it that other fire, and this will presently be quenched and gone. And if thou purposest to utter some harsh sounding[3] [speech], think of the gnashing of teeth, and the fear will be a bridle to thee. And if thou purposest to plunder, hear the Judge commanding, and saying, "Bind him hand and foot, and cast him into the outer darkness," (Matt. xxii. 13.) and thou wilt cast out this lust also. And if thou art drunken, and surfeitest continually, hear the rich man saying, 'Send Lazarus, that with the tip of his finger he may cool this scorching tongue;' (Luke xvi. 24.) yet not obtaining this; and thou wilt hold thyself aloof from that distemper[4]. But if thou lovest luxury, think of the affliction and the straitness there, and thou wilt not think at all of this. If again thou art harsh and cruel, bethink thee of those virgins who when their lamps had gone out missed so of the bridal chamber, and thou wilt quickly become humane. Or sluggish art thou, and remiss? Consider him that hid the talent, and thou wilt be more vehement than fire. Or doth desire of thy

neighbor's substance devour thee? Think of the worm that dieth not, and thou wilt easily both put away from thee this disease, and in all other things wilt do virtuously. For He hath enjoined nothing irksome or oppressive. Whence then do His injunctions appear irksome to us? From our own slothfulness. For as if we labor diligently, even what appears intolerable will be light and easy; so if we are slothful, even things tolerable will seem to us difficult.[5]

Considering then all these things, let us think not of the luxurious, but what is their end; here indeed filth and obesity, there the worm and fire: not of the rapacious, but what is their end; cares here, and fears, and anxieties; there chains indissoluble: not of the lovers of glory, but what these things bring forth; here slavery and dissemblings, and there both loss intolerable and perpetual burnings. For if we thus discourse with ourselves, and if with these and such like things we charm perpetually our evil lusts, quickly shall we both cast out the love of the present things, and kindle that of the things to come. Let us therefore kindle it and make it blaze. For if the conception of them, although a faint sort of one, affords so great pleasure; think how great the gladness, the manifest experience itself shall bring us. Blessed, and thrice blessed, yea, thrice blessed many times, are they who enjoy those good things; just as, consequently, pitiable and thrice wretched are they who endure the opposite of these. That then we may be not of these but those, let us choose virtue. For so shall we attain unto the good things to come as well; which may all we attain, through the grace and love towards men of our Lord Jesus Christ; by Whom, and with Whom, to the Father, together with the Holy Spirit, be glory, might, and honor, now and for ever, and world without end. Amen.

---

[5] [Chrysostom appears distinctly to accept the common faith of the church that the things done in the body (literally, "through the body," as the channel by which purposes pass into actions) furnish the basis upon which the last assize proceeds. He makes no reference to any *post mortem* probation, but (on pages 331, 332) asserts the contrary, "Here the opportunities of salvation exist, but there are found no longer." Nor is his view of the retributions of the judgment inconsistent with his repeated assertions of salvation as wholly gratuitous. Entrance into eternal life is God's free gift to all who believe. But the degree of glory will be measured by the faithfulness of service, just as the degree of the punishment of the lost will be by the number and aggravation of their sins. Hence it follows that although the salvation of any is due to God's undeserved favor, still each one that stands at the bar will receive an exact recompense for his entire conduct in the days of his flesh. "A remembrance of this exact recompense," it has well been said, "will make us comparatively indifferent about life or death, and emulous so to act as to please our Judge." C.]

---

[1] αποκηρύττουσιν.
[2] ἐπιτειχίζων.
[3] ἀπηχὲς,
[4] πάθους

HOMILY XI

2 COR. V. II.

Knowing therefore the fear of the Lord, we persuade men :
but we are made manifest unto God ; and I hope
that we are made manifest also in your consciences.

KNOWING therefore, he says, these things, that
terrible seat of judgment, we do every thing so
as not to give you a handle nor offence, nor any
false suspicion of evil practice against us.   Seest
thou the strictness of life, and zeal of a watchful soul ? ' For we are not only open to accusa-
tation,' he saith ' ' if we commit any evil deed ;
but even if we do not commit, yet are suspected,
and having it in our power to repel the suspicion, brave it, we are punished.'

Ver. 12. "We are not again commending ourselves unto you, but speak as giving you occasion of glorying in our behalf."

See how he is continually obviating the suspicion of appearing to praise himself.   For
nothing is so offensive to the hearers as for any
one to say great and marvellous things about
himself.   Since then he was compelled in what
he said to fall upon that subject, he uses a corrective, saying, ' we do this for your sakes, not
for ours, that ye may have somewhat to glory of,
not that we may.'   And not even this absolutely,
but because of the false Apostles.   Wherefore
also he added, " To answer them that glory in
appearance, and not in heart."   Seest thou how
he hath detached them from them, and drawn
them to himself ; having shown that even the
Corinthians themselves are longing to get hold
of some occasion, whereby they may have it in
their power to speak on their[1] behalf and to
defend them unto their accusers.   For, says he,
' we say these things not that we may boast, but
that ye may have wherein to speak freely on
our behalf ;' which is the language of one testifying to their great love : ' and not that ye may
boast merely : but that ye may not be drawn
aside.'   But this he does not say explicitly, but
manages his words otherwise and in a gentler
form, and without dealing them a blow, saying,
" That ye may have somewhat to glory
towards those which glory in appearance."
But neither this does he bid them do absolutely, when no cause exists, but when they[2] extol

themselves ; for in all things he looks out for
the fitting occasion.   He does not then do this
in order to show himself to be illustrious, but
to stop those men who were using the thing[3]
improperly and to the injury of these.   But
what is " in appearance?"   In what is seen, in
what is for display.   For of such sort were
they, doing every thing out of a love of honor,
whilst they were both empty inwardly and wore
indeed an appearance of piety and of venerable
seeming, but of good works were destitute.

[2.] Ver. 13. "For whether we are beside
ourselves, it is to God ; or whether we are
of sober mind, it is unto you."

And if, saith he, we have utttered any great
thing, (for this is what he here calls being beside himself, as therefore in other places also he
calls it folly ;—2 Cor. xi. 1, 17, 21.) for God's
sake we do this, lest ye thinking us to be
worthless should despise us and perish ; or if
again any modest and lowly thing, it is for your
sakes that ye may learn to be lowly-minded.
Or else, again, he means this.   If any one
thinks us to be mad, we seek for our reward
from God, for Whose sake we are of this suspected ; but if he thinks us sober, let him reap
the advantage of our soberness.   And again, in
another way.   Does any one say we are mad ?
For God's sake are we in such sort mad.
Wherefore also he subjoins,

Ver. 14. " For the love of God[4] constraineth
us, because we thus judge."

' For not the fear of things to come only,' he
saith, ' but also those which have already happened allow us not to be slothful nor to slumber ; but stir us up and impel us to these our
labors on your behalf.'   And what are those
things which have already happened ?

"That if one died for all, then all died."
' Surely then it was because all were lost,' saith
he. For except all were dead, He had not died for
all[5].   For here the opportunities[6] of salvation

---

[1] The Apostles'.
[2] The false Apostles.

[3] i. e., self commendation.
[4] Rec. text, Christ, [which is certainly correct.]
[5] [Chrysostom seems to understand this clause in the way given
in the Auth. Vers., but all modern critics take the aorist strictly
and hold the meaning to be, not that all were previously dead, but
that all died in his death (Rom. vi. 8.). Christ's death was the
death of all his people. C.]
[6] ἀφορμαί.

exist; but there are found no longer. Therefore, he says, "The love of God constraineth us," and allows us not to be at rest. For it cometh of extreme wretchedness and is worse than hell itself, that when He hath set forth an act so mighty, any should be found after so great an instance of His provident care reaping no benefit. For great was the excess of that love, both to die for a world of such extent[1], and dying for it when in such a state.

Ver. 15. "That they which live should no longer live unto themselves, but unto Him who for their sakes died and rose again."

If therefore we ought not to live unto ourselves, ' be not troubled,' says he, ' nor be confounded when dangers and deaths assail you.' And he assigns besides an indubitable argument by which he shows that the thing is a debt. For if through Him we live who were dead; to Him we ought to live through Whom we live. And what is said appears indeed to be one thing, but if any one accurately examine it, it is two: one that we live by Him, another that He died for us: either of which even by itself is enough to make us liable; but when even both are united consider how great the debt is. Yea, rather, there are three things here. For the First-fruits also for thy sake He raised up, and led up to heaven: wherefore also he added, "Who for our sakes died and rose again."

[3.] Ver. 16. "Wherefore we henceforth know no man after the flesh."

For if all died and all rose again; and in such sort died as the tyranny of sin condemned them; but rose again "through the laver of regeneration and the renewing of the Holy Ghost;" (Titus iii. 5.) he saith with reason, "we know none" of the faithful "after the flesh." For what if even they be in the flesh? Yet is that fleshly life destroyed, and we are born again[2] by the Spirit, and have learnt another deportment and rule and life and condition[3], that, namely, in the heavens. And again of this itself he shows Christ to be the Author. Wherefore also he added,

"Even though we have known Christ after the flesh, yet now we know Him so no more."

What then? tell me. Did He put away the flesh, and is He now not with that body? Away with the thought, for He is even now clothed in flesh; for "this Jesus Who is taken up from you into Heaven shall so come. So? How? In flesh, with His body. How then doth he say, "Even though we have known Christ after the flesh, yet now henceforth no more?" (Acts i. 11.) For in us indeed "after the

flesh" is being in sins, and "not after the flesh" not being in sins; but in Christ, "after the flesh" is His being subject to the affections of nature, such as to thirst, to hunger, to weariness, to sleep. For "He did no sin, neither was guile found in His mouth." (1 Pet. ii. 22.) Wherefore He also said, "Which of you convicteth Me of sin?" (John viii. 46.) and again, "The prince of this world cometh, and he hath nothing in Me." (ib. xiv. 30.) And "not after the flesh" is being thenceforward freed even from these things, not the being without flesh. For with this also He cometh to judge the world, His being impassible and pure. Whereunto we also shall advance when "our body" hath been "fashioned like unto His glorious body." (Phil. iii. 21.)

[4.] Ver. 17. "Wherefore if any man is in Christ, he is a new creature."

For seeing he had exhorted unto virtue from His love, he now leads them on to this from what has been actually done for them; wherefore also he added, "If any man is in Christ," he is "a new creature." "If any," saith he, "have believed in Him, he has come to another creation, for he hath been born again by the Spirit." So that for this cause also, he says, we ought to live unto Him, not because we are not our own only, nor because He died for us only, nor because He raised up our First-fruits only, but because we have also come unto another life. See how many just grounds he urges for a life of virtue. For on this account he also calls the reformation by a grosser name[4], in order to show the transition and the change to be great. Then following out farther what he had said, and showing how it is "a new creation," he adds, "The old things are passed away, behold, all things are become new."

What old things? He means either sins and impieties, or else all the Judaical observances. Yea rather, he means both the one and the other. "Behold, all things are[5] become new."

Ver. 18. "But all things are of God."

Nothing of ourselves. For remission of sins and adoption and unspeakable glory are given to us by Him. For he exhorts them no longer from the things to come only, but even from those now present. For consider. He said, that we shall be raised again, and go on unto incorruption, and have an eternal house; but since present things have more force to persuade than things to come, with those who believe not in these as they ought to believe, he shows how great things they have even already received, and being themselves what. What then being, received they them? Dead all; (for he saith, "all died;" and, "He

---

[1] τοσαύτης.
[2] ἄνωθεν.
[3] κατάστασιν.

[4] i. e. creation.
[5] ["They are" Rev. Ver., in accordance with the best authorities. C.]

died for all ; " so loved He all alike ;) inveterate all, and grown old in their vices. But behold, both a new soul, (for it was cleansed,) and a new body, and a new worship, and promises new, and covenant, and life, and table, and dress, and all things new absolutely[1]. For instead of the Jerusalem below we have received that mother city which is above (Gal. iv. 26); and instead of a material temple have seen a spiritual temple ; instead of tables of stone, fleshy ones ; instead of circumcision, baptism ; instead of the manna, the Lord's body ; instead of water from a rock, blood from His side ; instead of Moses' or Aaron's rod, the Cross ; instead of the promised [land][2], the kingdom of heaven ; instead of a thousand priests, one High Priest ; instead of a lamb without reason[3], a Spiritual Lamb. With these and such like things in his thought he said, "all things are new." But "all" these "things are of God," by Christ, and His free gift. Wherefore also he added,

"Who reconciled us to Himself through Christ, and gave unto us the ministry of reconciliation."

For from Him are all the good things. For He that made us friends is Himself also the cause of the other things which God hath given to His friends. For He rendered not these things unto us, allowing us to continue enemies, but having made us friends unto Himself. But when I say that Christ is the cause of our reconciliation, I say the Father is so also : when I say that the Father gave, I say the Son gave also. "For all things were made by Him ;" (John i. 3.) and of this too He is the Author. For we ran not unto Him, but He Himself called us. How called He us ? By the sacrifice of Christ.

"And gave unto us the ministry of reconciliation."

Here again he sets forth the dignity of the Apostles; showing how great a thing was committed to their hands, and the surpassing greatness of the love of God. For even when they would not hear the Ambassador that came, He was not exasperated nor left them to themselves, but continueth to exhort them both in His own person and by others. Who can be fittingly amazed at this solicitude ? The Son Who came to reconcile, His True and Only-Begotten, was slain, yet not even so did the Father turn away from His murderers ; nor say, "I sent My Son as an Ambassador, but they not only would not hear Him, but even slew and crucified Him,

it is meet henceforth to leave them to themselves : " but quite the contrary, when the Son departed, He entrusted the business to us ; for he says, "gave unto us the ministry of reconciliation."

[5.] Ver. 19. "To wit, that God was in Christ reconciling the world unto Himself, not reckoning unto them their tresspasses."

Seest thou love surpassing all expression, all conception ? Who was the aggrieved one ? Himself. Who first sought the reconciliation ? Himself. 'And yet,' saith one, ' He sent the Son, He did not come Himself.' The Son indeed it was He sent ; still not He alone besought, but both with Him and by Him the Father ; wherefore he said, that, "God was reconciling the world unto Himself in Christ : " that is, by Christ[4]. For seeing he had said, "Who gave unto us the ministry of reconciliation ; " he here used a corrective, saying, "Think not that we act of our own authority[5] in the business : we are ministers ; and He that doeth the whole is God, Who reconciled the world by the Only-Begotten." And how did He reconcile it unto Himself ? For this is the marvel, not that it was made a friend only, but also by this way a friend. This way ? What way ? Forgiving them their sins ; for in no other way was it possible. Wherefore also he added, "Not reckoning unto them their tresspasses." For had it been His pleasure to require an account of the things we had transgressed in, we should all have perished ; for "all died." But nevertheless though our sins were so great, He not only did not require satisfaction, but even became reconciled ; He not only forgave, but He did not even "reckon." So ought we also to forgive our enemies, that ourselves too may obtain the like forgiveness.

"And having committed unto us the word of reconciliation."

For neither have we come now on any odious office ; but to make all men friends with God. For He saith, 'Since they were not persuaded by Me, do ye continue beseeching until ye have persuaded them .' Wherefore also he added,

Ver. 20. "We are ambassadors therefore on behalf of Christ, as though God were entreating by us ; we beseech you on behalf of Christ, be ye reconciled to God."

Seest thou how he has extolled the thing by introducing Christ thus in the form of a suppliant[6] ; yea rather not Christ only, but even

---

[1] ἁπλῶς.
[2] Literally " the promise." Elsewhere St. Chrysostom uses the expression for the promised land. See Hom. xxxix. on St. Matt. Oxf. Trans. p. 563. " We must not only be delivered out of Egypt, but we must also enter into the promise."
[3] ἀλόγου.

[4] [It is clear that Chrysostom did not favor the view given in the A. V., which connects the substantive verb with the phrase "in Christ," and separates it from the participle. He rather agrees with the Rev. Version which obliterates the comma after Christ, and makes the emphasis to lie on the reconciliation effected in or through Christ, and not on the fact that God was in Christ,—a proposition true enough in itself, but not before the Apostle's mind at this time. C.]
[5] αὐθεντία.
[6] τιθέντα τὴν ἱκετηρίαν ταύτην.

the Father? For what he says is this: 'The Father sent the Son to beseech, and to be His Ambassador unto mankind. When then He was slain and gone, we succeeded to the embassy; and in His stead and the Father's we beseech you. So greatly doth He prize mankind that He gave up even the Son, and that knowing He would be slain, and made us Apostles for your sakes; so that he said with reason, "All things are for your sakes." (2 Cor. iv. 15.) "We are therefore ambassadors on behalf of Christ," that is, instead of Christ; for we have succeeded to His functions.' But if this appears to thee a great thing, hear also what follows wherein he shows that they do this not in His stead only, but also in stead of the Father. For therefore he also added, "As though God were entreating by us." 'For not by the Son Himself only doth He beseech, but also by us who have succeeded to the office of the Son. Think not therefore,' he says, ' that by us you are entreated; Christ Himself, the Father Himself of Christ, beseeches you by us. What can come up to this excess [of goodnes]? He was outraged who had conferred innumerable benefits; having been outraged, He not only exacted not justice, but even gave His son that we might be reconciled. They that received Him were not reconciled, but even slew Him. Again, He sent other ambassadors to beseech, and though these are sent, it is Himself that entreats. And what doth He entreat? "Be ye reconciled unto God." And he said not, ' Reconcile God to yourselves;' for it is not He that beareth enmity, but ye; for God never beareth enmity. Urging moreover his cause, like an ambassador on his mission,[1] he says,

Ver. 21. "For Him who knew no sin He made to be sin on our account."

' I say nothing of what has gone before, that ye have outraged Him, Him that had done you no wrong, Him that had done you good, that He exacted not justice, that He is first to beseech, though first outraged; let none of these things be set down at present. Ought ye not in justice to be reconciled for this one thing only that He hath done to you now?' And what hath He done? "Him that knew no sin He made to be sin for you." For had He achieved nothing but done only this, think how great a thing it were to give His Son for those that had outraged Him. But now He hath both well achieved mighty things, and besides, hath suffered Him that did no wrong to be punished for those who had done wrong. But he did not say this: but mentioned that which is far greater than this. What then is this? " Him that knew no sin," he says, Him that was righteous-

ness itself[2], "He made sin," that is suffered as a sinner to be condemned, as one cursed to die. " For cursed is he that hangeth on a tree." (Gal. iii. 13.) For to die thus was far greater than to die; and this he also elsewhere implying, saith, " Becoming obedient unto death, yea the death of the cross." (Phil. ii. 8.) For this thing carried with it not only punishment, but also disgrace. Reflect therefore how great things He bestowed on thee. For a great thing indeed it were for even a sinner to die for any one whatever; but when He who undergoes this both is righteous and dieth for sinners; and not dieth only, but even as one cursed; and not as cursed [dieth] only, but thereby freely bestoweth upon us those great goods which we never looked for; (for he says, that "we might become the righteousness of God in Him;") what words, what thought shall be adequate to realize these things? 'For the righteous,' saith he, 'He made a sinner; that He might make the sinners righteous.' Yea rather, he said not even so, but what was greater far; for the word he employed is not the habit, but the quality itself. For he said not " made" [Him] a sinner, but " sin;" not, ' Him that had not sinned' only, but " that had not even known sin; that we" also " might become," he did not say ' righteous,' but, " righteousness," and, " the righteousness of God." For this is [the righteousness] " of God" when we are justified not by works, (in which case it were necessary that not a spot even should be found,) but by grace, in which case all sin is done away. And this at the same time that it suffers us not to be lifted up, (seeing the whole is the free gift of God,) teaches us also the greatness of that which is given. For that which was before was a righteousness of the Law and of works, but this is "the righteousness of God."

[6.] Reflecting then on these things, let us fear these words more than hell; let us reverence the things [they express] more than the kingdom, and let us not deem it grievous to be punished, but to sin. For were He not to punish us, we ought to take vengeance on ourselves, who have been so ungrateful towards our Benefactor. Now he that hath an object of affection, hath often even slain himself, when unsuccessful in his love; and though successful, if he hath been guilty of a fault towards her, counts it not fit that he should even live; and shall not we, when we outrage One so loving and gentle, cast ourselves into the fire of hell? Shall I say something strange, and marvellous, and to many perhaps incredible? To one who hath understanding and loveth the Lord as it behoveth to love Him, there will be greater comfort if punished after provoking One so loving, than if

---

[1] δικαιολογούμενος.

[2] αὐτοδικαιοσύνην.

not punished. And this one may see also by the common practice. For he that has wronged his dearest friend feels then the greatest relief, when he has wreaked vengeance on himself and suffered evil. And accordingly David said, " I the shepherd have sinned, and I the shepherd have done amiss; and these the flock, what have they done? Let Thy hand be upon me, and upon my father's house." (2 Sam. xxiv. 17. LXX.) And when he lost Absalom he wreaked the extremest vengeance upon himself, although he was not the injurer but the injured; but nevertheless, because he loved the departed exceedingly, he racked himself with anguish, in this manner comforting himself. Let us therefore also, when we sin against Him Whom we ought not to sin against, take vengeance on ourselves. See you not those who have lost true-born children, that they therefore both beat themselves and tear their hair, because to punish themselves for the sake of those they loved carries comfort with it. But if, when we have caused no harm to those dearest to us, to suffer because of what hath befallen them brings consolation; when we ourselves are the persons who have given provocation and wrong, will it not much rather be a relief to us to suffer the penalty? and will not the being unpunished punish? Every one in a manner will see this. If any love Christ as it behoveth to love Him, he knoweth what I say; how, even when He forgiveth, he will not endure to go unpunished; for thou undergoest the severest punishment in having provoked Him. And I know indeed that I am speaking what will not be believed by the many; but nevertheless it is so as I have said. If then we love Christ as it behoveth to love Him, we shall punish ourselves when we sin. For to those who love any whomsover, not the suffering somewhat because they have provoked the beloved one is unpleasing; but above all, that they have provoked the person loved. And if this last when angered doth not punish, he hath tortured his lover more; but if he exacts satisfaction, he hath comforted him rather. Let us therefore not fear hell, but offending God; for it is more grievous than that when He turns away in wrath: this is worse than all, this heavier than all. And that thou mayest learn what a thing it is, consider this which I say. If one that was himself a king, beholding a robber and malefactor under punishment, gave his well-beloved son, his only-begotten and true, to be slain; and transferred the death and the guilt as well, from him to his son, (who was himself of no such character,) that he might both save the condemned man and clear him from his evil reputation[1]; and then if, having subsequently promoted him to great dignity, he had yet, after thus saving him and advancing him to that glory unspeakable, been outraged by the person that had received such treatment: would not that man, if he had any sense, have chosen ten thousand deaths rather than appear guilty of so great ingratitude? This then let us also now consider with ourselves, and groan bitterly for the provocations we have offered our Benefactor; nor let us therefore presume, because though outraged He bears it with long-suffering; but rather for this very reason be full of remorse[2]. For amongst men too, when one that hath been smitten on the right cheek offers the left also, he more avengeth himself than if he gave ten thousand blows; and when one that hath been reviled, not only revileth not again but even blesseth, he hath stricken [his adversary] more heavily, than if he rained upon him ten thousand reproaches. Now if in the case of men we feel ashamed when offering insults we meet with long-suffering; much rather, in respect to God, ought they to be afraid who go on continually sinning yet suffer no calamity. For, even for evil unto their own heads is the unspeakable punishment treasured up for them. These things then bearing in mind, let us above all things be afraid of sin; for this is punishment, this is hell, this is ten thousand ills. And let us not only be afraid of, but also flee from it, and strive to please God continually; for this is the kingdom, this is life, this is ten thousand goods. So shall we also even here obtain already the kingdom and the good things to come; whereunto may we all attain, through the grace and love towards men of our Lord Jesus Christ; with Whom to the Father, with the Holy Spirit, be glory, might, honor, now and for ever, and world without end. Amen.

---

[1] [The comparison here made shows clearly how the author understood the closing words of the fifth chapter of the Epistle. Indeed his treatment of the weighty 21st verse is very satisfactory. He does not with Augustin and others take ἁμαρτίαν in the sense of a sin-offering, a sense which it is very doubtful if the word ever has, and one that here would be inconsistent with the use of the same word in the clause immediately preceding as well as with the evidently designed antithesis between "sin" and "righteousness." But he regards the abstract as used for the concrete, which is certainly the true view. The phrase is, as Beet says, "practically the same as, but stronger than, *made to be a sinner*. By laying upon Christ the punishment of our sin, God made him to be a visible embodiment of the deadly and far-reaching power of sin." But Chrysostom shows by his comments his acceptance not only of the vicarious atonement, but also of the gratuitous justification, set forth concisely yet distinctly in this pregnant utterance. There are passages in these and other Homilies which look as if the author held to justification by works, but here he is outspoken to the contrary. Justification comes by grace, not merit, and the righteousness required is the free gift of God. C.]

[2] δακνώμεθα.

HOMILY XII.

2 COR. vi. 1, 2.

And working together with Him we intreat also that
ye receive not the grace of God in vain. For he
saith,

At an acceptable time I hearkened unto thee.
And in a day of salvation did I succor thee.

FOR since he said, God beseeches, and we are
ambassadors and suppliants unto you, that ye
be "reconciled unto God:" lest they should
become supine, he hereby again alarms and
arouses them, saying: "We intreat that ye receive not the grace of God in vain." 'For let
us not,' he says, 'therefore be at ease, because
He beseeches and hath sent some to be ambassadors; nay, but for this very reason let us
make haste to please God and to collect spiritual
merchandise;' as also he said above, "The
love of God constraineth us," (ch. v. 14) that is,
presseth, driveth, urgeth us, 'that ye may not
after so much affectionate care, by being supine
and exhibiting no nobleness, miss of such great
blessings. Do not therefore because He hath
sent some to exhort you, deem that this will
always be so. It will be so until His second
coming; until then He beseeches, so long as
we are here; but after that is judgment and
punishment.' Therefore, he says, "we are
constrained."

For not only from the greatness of the blessings and His loving kindness, but also from the
shortness of the time he urgeth them continually.
Wherefore he saith also elsewhere, "For now is
our salvation nearer." (Rom. xiii. 11.) And
again; "The Lord is at hand." (Philipp. iv. 5.)
But here he does something yet more. For not
from the fact that the remainder of the time is
short and little, but also from its being the only
season available for salvation, he incited them.
For, "Behold," he saith, "now is the acceptable time; behold, now is the day of salvation." Let us therefore not let slip the favorable
opportunity but display a zeal worthy of the
grace. For therefore is it that we also press
forward, knowing both the shortness and the
suitableness of the time. Wherefore also he
said; "And working together we intreat also.
Working together" with you; 'for we work
together with you, rather than with God for
Whom we are ambassadors. For He is in need

of nothing, but the salvation all passeth over
to you.' But if it is even with God that he speaks
of working together, he repudiates not even this
[interpretation]; for he says in another place,
"we are God's fellow-workers:" (1 Cor.
iii. 9.) in this way, saith he, to save men.
Again, "We entreat also." For he indeed,
when beseeching, doth not barely beseech, but
sets forth these His just claims; namely, that
He gave His Son, the Righteous One that did
not so much as know sin, and made Him to be
sin for us sinners, that we might become righteous: which claims having, and being God, He
ought not to beseech, and that men, and who
had offended Him, but to be besought by them
every day: but nevertheless He beseecheth.
But we beseech, having no claim of our own to
allege nor benefit; but one thing alone, namely,
that we beseech on behalf of God Who hath also
displayed such goodness. But what we beseech
is that ye would receive the benefit and not reject the gift. Be persuaded therefore by us,
and "receive not the grace in vain." For lest
they should think that this of itself is "reconciliation," believing on Him that calleth; he
adds these words, requiring that earnestness
which respects the life. For, for one who hath
been freed from sins and made a friend to
wallow in the former things, is to return again
unto enmity, and to "receive the grace in vain,"
in respect of the life. For from "the grace"
we reap no benefit towards salvation, if we live
impurely; nay, we are even harmed, having
this greater aggravation even of our sins, in that
after such knowledge and such a gift we have
gone back to our former vices. This however
he does not mention as yet: that he may not
make his work harsh, but says only that we reap
no benefit. Then he also reminds of a prophecy,
urging and compelling them to bestir themselves
in order to lay hold of their own salvation.

"For," saith he, "He saith,

"At an acceptable time I hearkened unto thee,
"And in a day of salvation did I succor thee:

"behold, now is the acceptable time: behold,
now is the day of salvation."

"The acceptable time." What is this? That

of the Gift, that of the Grace, when it is appointed not that an account should be required of our sins nor penalty exacted ; but besides being delivered, that we should also enjoy ten thousand goods, righteousness, sanctification, and and all the rest.   For how much toil would it have behoved us to undergo in order to obtain this " time ! "   But, behold, without our toiling at all it hath come, bringing remission of all that was before.   Wherefore also He calls it "acceptable," because He both accepted those that had transgressed in ten thousand things, and not accepted merely, but advanced them to the highest honor ; just as when a monarch arrives, it is a time not for judgment, but for grace and pardon.   Wherefore also He calleth it acceptable.   Whilst then we are yet in the lists[1], whilst we are at work in the vineyard, whilst the eleventh hour is left [us], let us draw nigh and show forth life ; for it is also easy.   For he that striveth for the mastery[2] at such a time, when so great a gift hath been shed forth, when so great grace, will easily obtain the prizes.   For in the case of monarchs here below also, at the time of their festivals, and when they appear in the dress of Consuls, he who bringeth a small offering receiveth large gifts ; but on the days in which they sit in judgment, much strictness, much sifting is requisite.   Let us too therefore strive for the mastery in the time of this gift.   It is a day of grace, of grace divine ; wherefore with ease even we shall obtain the crown.   For if when laden with so great evils He both received and delivered us : when delivered from all and contributing our part, shall He not rather accept us ?

[2.] Then, as it is his constant wont, namely, to place himself before them and bid them hence to take their example, so he does in this place also.   Wherefore also he addeth,

Ver. 3.   " Giving no occasion of stumbling, that our ministration[3] be not blamed,"

Persuading them not from considering " the time " only, but also those that had successfully labored with them.   And behold with what absence of pride[4].   For he said not, ' Look at us how we are such and such,' but, for the present, it is only to do away accusation that he relates his own conduct.   And he mentions two chief points of a blameless life, " none " in " any " thing.   And he said not ' accusation,' but, what was far less, " occasion of stumbling ; " that is, giving ground against us to none for censure, for condemnation, " that our ministration be not blamed ; " that is,

that none may take hold of it.   And again, he said not, ' that it be not accused,' but that it may not have the least fault, nor any one have it in his power to animadvert upon it in any particular.

Ver. 4.   " But in every thing commending ourselves as ministers of God."

This is far greater.   For it is not the same thing to be free from accusation ; and to exhibit such a character as in everything to appear " ministers of God."   For neither is it the same thing to be quit of accusation, and to be covered[5] with praises.   And he said not appearing, but " commending," that is ' proving.'   Then he mentions also whence they became such.   Whence then was it ?   " In much patience," he says, laying the foundation of those good things.   Wherefore he said not barely " patience," but " much," and he shows also how great it was.   For to bear some one or two things is no great matter.   But he addeth even snow storms of trials in the words, " In afflictions, in necessities."   This is a heightening of affliction, when the evils are unavoidable, and there lies upon one as it were a necessity hardly extricable[6] of misfortune. " In distresses."   Either he means those of hunger and of other necessaries, or else simply those of their trials.

Ver. 5.   " In stripes, in imprisonments, in tossings to and fro[7]."

Yet every one of these by itself was intolerable, the being scourged only, and being bound only, and being unable through persecution to remain fixed[8] any where, (for this is in ' tossings to and fro,') but when both all, and all at once, assail, consider what a soul they need. Then along with the things from without, he mentions those imposed by himself.

Ver. 5, 6.   " In labors, in watchings, in fastings ; in pureness."

In these words he alludes to the labors in which he toiled, as he went about and wrought; (Acts xviii. 3) the nights in which he taught ; or, that even in them he wrought. (1 Thess. ii. 9.) And along with all these he neglected not fasting either, although these might have sufficed instead of ten thousand fasts.   But by " pureness " here, he means either chasteness again, or general purity, or incorruptness, or even his preaching the Gospel freely.

" In knowledge."   What is " in knowledge ? " In wisdom such as is given from God ; that which is truly knowledge ; not as those that seem to be wise and boast of their acquaintance

---

[1] ἐν τῷ σκάμματι.
[2] ἀγωνιζόμενος, as 1 Cor. ix. 25
[3] The ministry.
[4] ἀτύφως.

[5] βρύειν, ' blossom.'
[6] δυσδιεξόδευτος.
[7] ἀκαταστασίαις, so translated in the margin of the Author. Version, which, it will be seen, agrees best with the comment of St. Chrysostom.
[8] στῆναι.

with the heathen discipline, but are deficient in this.

"In long-suffering, in kindness." For this also is a great note of a noble soul, though exasperated and goaded on every side, to bear all with long-suffering. Then to show whence he became such, he added ;

"In the Holy Ghost." 'For in Him,' he saith, 'we do all these good works.' But observe when it is that he has mentioned the aid of the Holy Ghost. After he had set forth what was from himself. Moreover, he seems to me to say another thing herein. What then is this? Namely, 'we have both been filled with abundance of the Spirit and hereby also give a proof of our Apostleship in that we have been counted worthy of spiritual gifts.' For if this be grace also, yet still he himself was the cause who by his good works and his toils[1] attracted that grace. And if any should assert that besides what has been said, he shows that in his use of the gifts of the Spirit also he gave none offence ; he would not miss of his meaning. For they who received the [gift of] tongues amongst them and were lifted up, were blamed. For it is possible for one even in receiving a gift of the Spirit, not to use it aright. 'But not so we,' he saith, 'but in the Spirit also, that is, in the gifts also, we have been blameless.'

"In love unfeigned." This was the cause of all those good things; this made him what he was ; this caused the Spirit also to abide with him, by Whose aid also all things were rightly done of him.

Ver. 7. "In the word of truth."

A thing he says in many places, that 'we continued neither to handle the word of God deceitfully nor to adulterate it.'

"In the power of God." That which he always does ascribing nothing to himself but the whole to God, and imputing whatsoever he hath done aright to Him, this he hath done here also. For since he uttered great things, and affirmed that he had manifested in all things an irreproachable life and exalted wisdom, he ascribes this to the Spirit and to God. For neither were those commonplace things which he had said. For if it be a difficult thing even for one who lives in quiet to do aright and be irreproachable, consider him who was harassed by so great temptations, and yet shone forth through all, what a spirit he was of! And yet he underwent not these alone, but even far more than these, as he mentions next. And what is indeed marvelous is, not that he was irreproachable though sailing in such mighty waves, nor that he endured all nobly, but all with pleasure even. Which things, all, he makes clear to us by the next words, saying,

"By the armor of righteousness on the right and the left."

[3.] Seest thou his self-possession of soul and well-strung spirit? For he shows that afflictions are arms not only which strike not down, but do even fortify and make stronger. And he calls those things 'left,' which seem to be painful; for such those are which bring with them the reward. Wherefore then doth he call them thus? Either in conformity with the conception of the generality, or because God commanded us to pray that we enter not into temptation.

Ver. 8. "By glory and dishonor, by evil report and good report."

What saying thou? That thou enjoyest honor, and setting down this as a great thing? 'Yes,' he saith. Why, forsooth? For to bear dishonor indeed is a great thing, but to partake of honor requires not a vigorous[2] soul. Nay, it needs a vigorous and exceeding great soul, that he who enjoys it may not be thrown and break his neck[3]. Wherefore he glories in this as well as in that, for he shone equally in both. But how is it a weapon of righteousness? Because that the teachers are held in honor induceth many unto godliness. And besides, this is a proof of good works, and this glorifieth God. And this is, further, an instance of the wise contrivance of God, that by things which are opposite He brings in the Preaching. For consider. Was Paul bound? This too was on behalf of the Gospel. For, saith he, "the things which happened unto me have fallen out unto the progress of the Gospel; so that most of the brethren, being confident through my bonds, are more abundantly bold to speak the word without fear." (Phil. i. 12, 14.) Again, did he enjoy honor? This too again rendered them more forward. "By evil report and good report." For not only did he bear those things nobly which happen to the body, the 'afflictions,' and whatever he enumerated, but those also which touch the soul ; for neither are these wont to disturb slightly. Jeremiah at least having borne many temptations, gave in[4] upon these, and when he was reproached, said, "I will not prophesy, neither will I name the Name of the Lord.[5]" (Jer. xx.9.) And David too many places complains of reproach. Isaiah also, after many things, exhorteth concerning this, saying, "Fear ye not the reproach of men, neither be ye overcome by their reviling." (Is. li. 7. LXX.) And again, Christ also to His disciples ; "When they shall speak all manner of evil against you falsely, rejoice and be exceeding glad," (Matt. v. 11, 12.) He saith, "for great is your reward in heaven." Elsewhere too He

---

[1] Literally 'sweats.'

[2] νεανικῆς
[3] ἐκτραχηλισθῆναι.
[4] ἀπηγόρευε.
[5] So Chrys. not exactly agreeing either with the English Version or the LXX.

says, " And leap for joy." (Luke vi. 23.) But He would not have made the reward so great, had not the contest been a great one. For in tortures the body also shareth the anguish with the soul; for the pain is both of the body and of the soul; but here it is of the soul alone. Many at any rate have fallen by these alone, and have lost their own souls. And to Job also the reproaches of his friends appeared more grievous than the worms and the sores. For there is nothing, there is nothing more intolerable to those in affliction than a word capable of stinging the soul. Wherefore along with the perils and the toils he names these also, saying, " By glory and dishonor." At any rate, many of the Jews also on account of glory derived from the many would not believe. For they feared, not lest they should be punished, but lest they should be put out of the synagogue. Wherefore He saith, " How can ye believe which receive glory one of another?" (John v. 44.) And we may see numbers who have indeed despised all dangers, but have been worsted by glory.

[4.] " As deceivers, and yet true."

This is, " by evil report and good report."

Ver. 9. " As unknown, and yet well known."

This is, " by glory and dishonor." For by some they were well known and much sought after, whilst others deigned not to know them at all.

" As dying, and behold, we live."

As under sentence of death and condemned ; which was itself also matter of dishonor. But this he said, to show both the unspeakable power of God and their own patience. For so far as those who plotted against us were concerned, we died ; and this is what all suppose ; but by God's aid we escaped the dangers. Then to manifest also on what account God permits these things, he added,

" As chastened, and not killed."

Showing that the gain accruing to them from their temptations, even before the rewards, was great, and that their enemies against their will did them service.

Ver. 10. " As sorrowful, yet alway rejoicing."

For by those that are without, indeed, we are suspected of being in despair ; but we give no heed to them ; yea, we have our pleasure at the full[1]. And he said not " rejoicing " only, but added also its perpetuity, for he says ? " alway rejoicing." What then can come up to this life ? wherein, although dangers so great assault, the joy becometh greater.

" As poor, yet making many rich."

Some indeed affirm that the spiritual riches are spoken of here ; but I would say that the carnal are so too ; for they were rich in these also, having, after a new kind of manner, the

houses of all opened to them. And this too he signified by what follows, saying,

" As having nothing, and yet possessing all things."

And how can this be ? Yea rather, how can the opposite be ? For he that possesseth many things hath nothing ; and he that hath nothing possesseth the goods of all[2]. And not here only, but also in the other points, contraries were produced by their contraries. But if thou marvellest how it is possible for one that hath nothing to have all things, let us bring forth this man himself into the midst, who commanded the world and was lord not only of their substance, but of their very eyes even. " If possible," he says, " ye would have plucked out your eyes, and have given them to me." (Gal. iv. 15.)

Now these things he says, to instruct us not to be disturbed at the opinions of the many, though they call us deceivers, though they know us not, though they count us condemned[3], and appointed unto death, to be in sorrow, to be in poverty, to have nothing, to be (us, who are in cheerfulness) desponding : because that the sun even is not clear to the blind, nor the pleasure of the sane intelligible[4] to the mad. For the faithful only are right judges of these matters, and are not pleased and pained at the same things as other people. For if any one who knew nothing of the games were to see a boxer, having wounds upon him and wearing a crown ; he would think him in pain on account of the wounds, not understanding the pleasure the crown would give him. And these therefore, because they know what we suffer but do not know for what we suffer them, naturally suspect that there is nought besides these ; for they see indeed the wrestling and the dangers, but not the prizes and the crowns and the subject[5] of the contest. What then were the " all things " which Paul possessed, when he said, " As having nothing, and yet possessing all things?" Things temporal[6], things spiritual. For he whom the cities received as an angel, for whom they would have plucked out their own eyes and have given them to him, (Gal. iv. 14, 15.) he for whom they laid down their own necks, how had he not all things that were theirs? (Rom. xvi. 4.) But if thou desirest to see the spiritual also, thou wilt find him in these things also especially rich. For he that was so dear to the King of all as even to share in unspeakable things with the Lord of the angels, (ch. xii. 4.) how was not he more opulent than all men, and had all things? Devils had not else been so subject to him, suffering and disease had not so fled away[7].

---

[1] ακμάζουσαν.

[2] τά πάντων Ben. τά πάντα
[3] καταδίκους.
[4] δήλη.
[5] ὑπόθεσιν, see below.
[6] βιωτικα.
[7] ἐδραπέτευσε.

[5.] And let us therefore, when we suffer aught for Christ's sake, not merely bear it nobly but also rejoice. If we fast, let us leap for joy as if enjoying luxury; if we be insulted, let us dance as if praised; if we spend, let us feel as if gaining; if we bestow on the poor, let us count ourselves to receive: for he that gives not thus will not give readily. When then thou hast a mind to scatter abroad, look not at this only that thou spendest; but that thou also gainest more; and at this rather than that. And not only in almsgiving, but also in every kind of virtue, compute not alone the severity of the toils, but also the sweetness of the prizes; and before all the subjects of this wrestling, our Lord Jesus; and thou wilt readily enter upon the contest, and wilt live the whole time in pleasure. For nothing is wont so to cause pleasure as a good conscience.

Therefore Paul indeed, though wounded every day, rejoiced and exulted; but the men of this day, although they endure not a shadow even[1] of what he did, grieve and make lamentations from no other cause than that they have not a mind full of heavenly philosophy. For, tell me, wherefore the lamentation? Because thou art poor, and in want of necessaries? Surely for this thou oughtest rather to make lamentation, [not][2] because thou weepest, not because thou art poor, but because thou art mean-spirited; not because thou hast not money, but because thou prizest money so highly. Paul died daily, yet wept not but even rejoiced; he fought with continual hunger, yet grieved not but even gloried in it. And dost thou, because thou hast not all the year's provisions stored up, grieve and beat thyself? 'Yes,' he replies, ' for he had to care only for his own needs, whilst I have besides to care for servants, and children, and wife.' Rather, he alone had not to care for his own needs, but for the whole world's. And thou indeed [hast to care] for one household, but he for those so many poor at Jerusalem, for those in Macedonia, for those everywhere in poverty, for those who give to them no less than for those who receive. For his care for the world was of a twofold nature, both that they might not be destitute of necessaries, and that they might be rich in spiritual things. And thy famishing children distress not thee so much as all the concerns of the faithful did him. Why do I say, of the faithful? For neither was he free from care for the unfaithful, but was so eaten up with it that he wished even to become accursed for their sakes; but thou, were a famine to rage ten thousand times over, wouldest never choose to die for any whomsoever. And

thou indeed carest for one woman, but he for the Churches throughout the world. For he saith, "My anxiety for all the Churches." (ch. xi. 28.) How long then, O man, dost thou trifle, comparing thyself with Paul; and wilt not cease from this thy much meanness of spirit? For it behoveth to weep, not when we are in poverty but when we sin; for this is worthy of lamentations, as all the other things are of ridicule even. 'But,' he saith, ' this is not all that grieves me; but that also such an one is in power, whilst I am unhonored and outcast.' And what is this? for the blessed Paul too appeared to the many to be unhonored and an outcast. 'But,' saith he, ' he was Paul.' Plainly then not the nature of the things, but thy feebleness of spirit causeth thy desponding. Lament not therefore thy poverty, but thyself who art so minded, yea rather, lament not thyself, but reform thee; and seek not for money, but pursue that which maketh men of more cheerful countenance than thousands of money, philosophy and virtue. For where indeed these are, there is no harm in poverty; and where these are not there is no good in money. For tell me, what good is it when men are rich indeed, but have beggarly souls? Thou dost not bewail thyself, so much as that rich man himself, because he hath not the wealth of all. And if he doth not weep as thou dost, yet lay open his conscience, and thou wilt see his wailings and lamentations.

Wilt thou that I show thee thine own riches, that thou mayest cease to count them happy that are rich in money? Seest thou this heaven here, how beautiful, how vast it is, how it is placed on high? This beauty he enjoyeth not more than thou, nor is it in his power to thrust thee aside and make it all his own: for as it was made for him so was it too for thee. What too the sun, this bright and far shining star, and that gladdeneth our eyes, is not this too set out[3] common to all? and do not all enjoy it equally, both poor and rich? And the wreath of the stars and the orb of the moon, are they not left equally to all? Yea, rather, if I must speak somewhat marvellous, we poor enjoy these more than they. For they indeed being for the most part steeped in drunkenness, and passing their time in revellings and deep sleep, do not even perceive these things, being always under cover[4] and reared in the shade[5]: but the poor do more than any enjoy the luxury of these elements. And further, if thou wilt look into the air which is every where diffused, thou wilt see the poor man enjoying it in greater both freshness and abundance. For wayfarers and husbandmen enjoy

---

[1] οὐδὲ ὄναρ.
[2] All the MSS. have the word "not," but the sense seems to require its omission.

[3] πρόκειται..
[4] ὑπωρόφιοι.
[5] σκιατραφούμενοι.

these luxuries more than the inhabitants of the city; and again, of those same inhabitants of the city, the handicraftsmen more than those who are drunken all the day. What too of the earth, is not this left common to all? 'No,' he saith. How sayest thou so? tell me. 'Because the rich man, even in the city, having gotten himself several plethra, raises up long fences round them; and in the country cuts off for himself many portions.' What then? When he cuts them off, does he alone enjoy them? By no means, though he should contend for it ever so earnestly. For the produce he is compelled to distribute amongst all, and for thee he cultivates grain, and wine, and oil, and every where ministers unto thee. And those long fences and buildings, after his untold expense and his toils and drudgery he is preparing for thy use, receiving from thee only a small piece of silver for so great a service. And in baths and every where, one may see the same thing obtaining; the rich put to expense in money and in cares and labors; and the poor for a few oboli reaping the benefit of it all with perfect ease. And his enjoyment of the earth is no more than thine; for sure he filleth not ten stomachs, and thou only one. 'But he partaketh of costlier meats?' Truly, this is no mighty superiority; howbeit, even here, we shall find thee to have the advantage. For this costliness is therefore thought by thee a matter of envy because the pleasure with it is greater. Yet this is greater in the poor man's case; yet not pleasure only, but health also; and in this alone is the advantage with the rich, that he maketh his constitution feebler and collects more abundant fountains of disease. For the poor man's diet is all ordered according to nature, but his through its excess resulteth in corruption and disease.

[6.] But if ye will, let us also look at this same thing in an example. For if it were requisite to light a furnace, and then one man were to throw in silken garments and fine linens, many and numberless, and so kindle it; and another logs of oak and pine, what advantage would this man have over that? None, but even disadvantage. But what? (for there is nothing to prevent our turning the same illustration round after another manner,) if one were to throw in logs, and another were to light his fire under bodies, by which furnace wouldest thou like to stand, that with the logs, or that with the bodies? Very plainly that with the logs. For that burns naturally and is a pleasant spectacle to the beholders: whilst this with the steam, and juices, and smoke, and the stench of the bones would drive every one away. Didst

thou shudder at the hearing, and loathe that furnace? Like it are the bellies of the rich. For in them one would find more rottenness than in that furnace, and stinking vapors, and filthy humors, because that, all over in every part, indigestion abounds in consequence of their surfeiting. For the natural heat not sufficing for the digestion of the whole but being smothered under them, they lie smoking above, and the unpleasantness produced is great. To what then should one compare those stomachs of theirs? Yet do not be offended at what I say, but if I do not say true things, refute me. To what then should one compare them? for even what has been said is not enough to show their wretched plight. I have found another resemblance yet. What then is it? As in the sewers where there is accumulation of refuse, of dung, hay, stubble, stones, clay, frequent stoppages occur; and then the stream of filth overflows at top: so also it happeneth with the stomachs of those people. For these being stopped up below, the greater part of these villainous streams spurts up above. But not so with the poor, but like those fountains which well forth pure streams, and water gardens and pleasure grounds[1], so also are their stomachs pure from such-like superfluities. But not such are the stomachs of the rich, or rather of the luxurious; but they are filled with humors, phlegm, bile, corrupted blood, putrid rheums, and other suchlike matters. Wherefore no one, if he lives always in luxury, can bear it even for a short time; but his life will be spent in continual sicknesses. Wherefore I would gladly ask them, for what end are meats given? that we may be destroyed, or be nourished? that we may be diseased, or be strong? that we may be healthful, or be sickly? Very plainly, for nourishment, and health, and strength. Wherefore then do ye abuse them to the contrary, by their means creating unto the body disease and sickness? But not so the poor man; on the contrary, by his plain diet he purchases to himself health, and vigor, and strength. Weep not then on account of poverty, the mother of health, but even exult in it; and if thou wouldest be rich, despise riches. For this, not the having money but the not wanting to have it, is truly affluence. If we can achieve this, we shall both be here more affluent than all that are rich, and there shall obtain the good things to come, whereunto may all we attain, through the grace and love towards men of our Lord Jesus Christ, with Whom to the Father, with the Holy Ghost, be glory, might, honor, now and ever, and world without end. Amen.

---

[1] παραδείσους.

HOMILY XIII.

2 COR. VI. 11, 12.

Our mouth is open unto you, O ye Corinthians, our heart is enlarged, ye are not straitened in us, but ye are straitened in your own affections.

HAVING detailed his own trials and afflictions, for "in patience," saith he, "in afflictions, in necessities, in distresses, (v. 4, 5.) in stripes, in imprisonments, in tumults, in labors, in watchings;" and having shown that the thing was a great good, for "as sorrowful," saith he, "yet always rejoicing; as poor, yet making many rich; as having nothing, and yet possessing all things;" (v. 10.) and having called those things "armor," for "as chastened," saith he, "and not killed:" and having hereby represented God's abundant care and power, for he saith, "that the exceeding greatness of the power may be of God, and not of us;" (c.iv.7.) and having recounted his labors, for he saith, "we always bear about His dying;" and that this is a clear demonstration of the Resurrection, for he says, "that the life also of Jesus may be manifested in our mortal flesh;" (c. iv.10.) and of what things he was made partaker, and with what he had been entrusted, for "we are ambassadors on behalf of Christ," (c. iii. 20.) saith he, "as though God were entreating by us;" and of what things he is a minister, namely, "not of the letter, but of the Spirit;" (c. iii. 6,) and that he was entitled to reverence not only on this account, but also for his trials, for, "Thanks be to God," saith he, "which always causeth us to triumph:" he purposeth now also to rebuke them as not being too well minded towards himself. But though purposing he does not immediately come upon this, but having first spoken of the love which he had displayed towards them, he then enters also upon his discussion of these things. For if even from his own good deeds he that rebuketh be entitled to reverence; yet still, when he also displayeth the love, which he bears towards those who are censured, he maketh his speech less offensive. Therefore the Apostle also having stepped out of the subject of his own trials and toils and contests, passes on into speaking of his love, and in this way toucheth them to the quick. What then are the indications of his love? "Our mouth is open unto you, O ye Corinthians." And what kind of sign of love is this? or what meaning even have the words at all? 'We cannot endure,' he says, 'to be silent towards you, but are always desiring and longing to speak to and converse with you;' which is the wont of those who love. For what grasping of the hands is to the body, that is interchange of language to the soul. And along with this he implies another thing also. Of what kind then is this? That 'we discourse unto you on all points with freedom as unto persons beloved, and suppressing nothing, reserving nothing.' For since afterwards he proposes to rebuke, he asks forgiveness, using the rebuking them with freedom as itself a proof of his loving them exceedingly. Moreover the addition of their name is a mark of great love and warmth and affection; for we are accustomed to be repeating continually the bare names of those we love.

"Our heart is enlarged." For as that which warmeth is wont to dilate; so also to enlarge is the work of love. For virtue is warm and fervent. This both opened the mouth of Paul and enlarged his heart. For, 'neither do I love with the mouth only,' saith he, 'but I have also a heart in unison. Therefore I speak with openness, with my whole mouth, with my whole mind.' For nothing is wider than was Paul's heart which loved all the faithful with all the vehemence that one might bear towards the object of his affection; this his love not being divided and therefore weakened, but abiding in full entireness with each. And what marvel that this was so in the case of the faithful, seeing that even in that of the unfaithful, the heart of Paul embraced the whole world? Therefore he said not 'I love you,' but with more emphasis, "Our mouth is open, our heart is enlarged," we have you all within it, and not this merely, but with much largeness of room[1]. For he that is beloved walketh with great unrestraint within the heart of him that loveth. Wherefore he saith, "Ye are not straitened in us, but ye are straitened in your own affections." And this reproof, see it administered with forbearance, as is the wont of such as love exceed-

---

[1] εὐρυχωρίας.

342

ingly. He did not say, 'ye do not love us,' but, 'not in the same measure,' for he does not wish to touch them too sensibly. And indeed every where one may see how he is inflamed toward the faithful, by selecting words out of every Epistle. For to the Romans he saith, "I long to see you;" and, "oftentimes I purposed to come unto you;" and, "If by any means now at length I may be prospered to come unto you." (Rom. i. 11, 13, 10.) And to the Galatians, he says, "My little children of whom I am again in travail." (Gal. iv. 19.) To the Ephesians again, "For this cause I bow my knees" for you. (Ephes. iii. 14.) And to the Philippians,[1] "For what is my hope, or joy, or crown of rejoicing? are not even ye?" and he said that he bare them about in his heart, and[2] in his bonds. (Philipp. i. 7.) And to the Colossians, "But I would that ye knew greatly I strive for you, and for as many as have not seen my face in the flesh; that your hearts might be comforted." (Coloss. ii. 1. 2.) And to the Thessalonians, "As when a nurse cherisheth her children, even so being affectionately desirous of you, we were well pleased to impart unto you, not the Gospel only, but also our own souls." (1 Thess. ii. 7. 8.) And to Timothy, "Remembering thy tears, that I may be filled with joy." (2 Tim. i. 4.) And to Titus, "To my beloved[3] son; (Tit. i. 4.) and to Philemon, in like manner. (Philem. 1.) And to the Hebrews too, he writes many other such-like things, and ceaseth not to beseech them, and say, "A very little while, and he that cometh shall come, and shall not tarry:" (Heb. x. 37.) just like a mother to her pettish[4] children. And to themselves[5] he says, "Ye are not straitened in us." But he does not say only that he loves, but also that he is beloved by them, in order that hereby also he may the rather win them. And indeed testifying to this in them, he says, Titus came and "told us your longing, your mourning, your zeal." (2 Cor. vii. 7.) And to the Galatians, "If possible, ye would have plucked out your eyes and given them to me," (Gal. iv. 15.) And to the Thessalonians, "What manner of entering in we had unto you." (1 Thess, i. 9.) And to Timothy also, "Remembering thy tears, that I may be filled with joy." (2 Tim. i. 4.) And also throughout his Epistles one may find him bearing this testimony to the disciples, both that he loved and that he is loved, not however equally. And here he saith, "Though the more abundantly I love you, the less I be loved." (2 Cor. xii. 15.)

This, however, is near the end; but at present more vehemently, "Ye are not straitened in us, but ye are straitened in your own affections," 'You receive one,' he says, 'but I a whole city, and so great a population.' And he said not, 'ye do not receive us,' but, 'ye are straitened;' implying indeed the same thing but with forbearance and without touching them too deeply.

Ver. 13. "Now for a recompense in like kind (I speak as unto my children,) be ye also enlarged."

And yet it is not an equal return, first to be loved, afterwards to love. For even if one were to contribute that which is equal in amount, he is inferior in that he comes to it second. 'But nevertheless I am not going to reckon strictly,[6]' saith he, 'and if ye after having received the first advances[7] from me do but show forth the same amount, I am well-pleased and contented.' Then to show that to do this was even a debt, and that what he said was void of flattery, he saith, "I speak as unto my children." What meaneth, "as unto my children?" 'I ask no great thing, if being your father I wish to be loved by you.' And see wisdom and moderation of mind. He mentions not here his dangers on their behalf, and his labors, and his deaths, although he had many to tell of: (so free from pride is he!) but his love: and on this account he claims to be loved; 'because,' saith he, 'I was your father, because I exceedingly burn for you,' [for] it is often especially offensive to the person beloved when a man sets forth his benefits to him; for he seems to reproach. Wherefore Paul doth not this; but, 'like children, love your father,' saith he, which rather proceeds from instinct[8]; and is the due of every father. Then that he may not seem to speak 'these things for his own sake, he shows that it is for their advantage even that he invites this love from them. And therefore he added,

Ver. 14: "Be ye not unequally yoked together with unbelievers."

He said not, 'Intermix not with unbelievers,' but rather dealing sharply with[9] them, as transgressing what was right, 'Suffer not yourselves to turn aside,' saith he,

"For what fellowship have righteousness and iniquity?" Here in what follows he institutes a comparison, not between his own love and theirs who corrupt them, but between their nobleness and the others' dishonor. For thus his discourse became more dignified and more beseeming himself, and would the rather win them. Just as if one should say to a son that

---

[1] This passage is not in the Epistle to the Philippians, but in the first Epistle to the Thessalonians (ii. 19.) but the same expressions occur in Phil. iv. 1.
[2] Or 'even.'
[3] So Chrys. : Rec. text,"own son." [Rev. Vers."my true child."]
[4] δυσχεραίνοντας.
[5] The Corinthians.

[6] οὐδὲν ἀκριβολογοῦμαι.
[7] τὰς ἀρχὰς
[8] φυσέως
[9] καθαπτόμενος.

despised his parents, and gave himself up to vicious persons, 'What art thou doing, child? Dost thou despise thy father and prefer impure men filled with ten thousand vices? Knowest thou not how much better and more respectable thou art than they?' For so he detaches him more [readily] from their society than if he should express admiration of his father. For were he to say indeed, 'Knowest thou not how much thy father is better than they?' he will not produce so much effect; but if, leaving mention of his father, he bring himself before them, saying, 'Knowest thou not who thou art and what they are? Dost thou not bear in mind thine own high birth and gentle[1] blood, and their infamy? For what communion hast thou with them, those thieves, those adulterers, those impostors?' by elevating him with these praises of himself, he will quickly prepare him to break off from them. For the former address indeed, he will not entertain with overmuch acceptance, because the exalting of his father is an accusation of himself, when he is shown to be not only grieving a father, but such a father; but in this case he will have no such feeling. For none would choose not to be praised, and therefore, along with these praises of him that hears, the rebuke becometh easy of digestion. For the listener is softened, and is filled with high thoughts, and disdains[2] the society of those persons.

But not this only is the point to be admired in him that thus he prosecuted his comparison, but that he imagined another thing also still greater and more astounding; in the first place, prosecuting his speech in the form of interrogation, which is proper to things that are clear and admitted, and then dilating it by the quick succession and multitude of his terms. For he employs not one or two or three only, but several. Add to this that instead of the persons he employs the names of the things, and he delineates here high virtue and there extreme vice; and shows the difference between them to be great and infinite so as not even to need demonstration. "For what fellowship," saith he, "have righteousness and iniquity?"

"And what communion hath light with darkness?" (v. 15, 16.) "And what concord hath Christ with Beliar[3]? Or what portion[4] hath a believer with an unbeliever? Or what agreement hath a. temple of God with idols?"

Seest thou how he uses the bare names, and how adeqately to his purpose of dissuasion. For he did not say, 'neglect of righteousness[5]," [but]

what was stronger [iniquity[6]]; nor did he say those who are of the light, and those who are of the darkness; but he uses opposites themselves which can not admit of their opposites, 'light and darkness.' Nor said he those who are of Christ, with those who are of the devil; but, which was far wider apart, Christ and Beliar, so calling that apostate one, in the Hebrew tongue. "Or what portion hath a believer with an unbeliever?" Here, at length, that he may not seem simply to be going through a censure of vice and an encomium of virtue, he mentions persons also without particularizing. And he said not, 'communion,' but spoke of the rewards, using the term "portion." What agreement hath a temple of God with idols?"

"For ye[7] are a temple of the living God." Now what he says is this. Neither hath your King aught in common with him, "for what concord hath Christ with Beliar?" nor have the things [aught in common], "for what communion hath light with darkness?" Therefore neither should ye. And first he mentions their king and then themselves; by this separating them most effectually. Then having said, "a temple of God with idols," and having declared, "For ye are a temple of the living God," he is necessitated to subjoin also the testimony of this to show that the thing is no flattery. For he that praises except he also exhibit proof, even appears to flatter. What then is his testimony? For,

"I will dwell in them, saith he, "and walk in them. I will dwell in," as in temples, "and walk in them," signifying the more abundant attachment[8] to them.

"And they shall be my people and I will be their God[9]. 'What?' saith he, 'Dost thou bear God within thee, and runnest unto them? God That hath nothing in common with them? And in what can this deserve forgiveness? Bear in mind Who walketh, Who dwelleth in thee.'

Ver. 17. "Wherefore come ye out from among them, and be ye separate, and touch no unclean thing; and I will receive you, saith the Lord.

And He said not, 'Do not unclean things'; but, requiring greater strictness, 'do not even touch,' saith he, nor go near them.' But what is filthiness of the flesh? Adultery, fornication, lasciviousness of every kind. And what of the soul? Unclean thoughts, as gazing with unchaste eyes, malice, deceits, and whatsoever such things there be. He wishes then that they should be clean in both. Seest thou how great the prize? To be delivered from what is evil,

---

[1] ἐλευθερίαν.
[2] διαπτύει.
[3] [This reading, given in the margin of the Rev. Ver., is adopted by all the editors instead of "Belial," for which, as Wetcott and Hort say, there is only Latin authority. C.]
[4] A. V. part.
[5] παρανομία [ἀνομία]

[6] The two words in brackets are not found in the text, but seem required by the context.
[7] [The testimony preponderates in favor of the first person, "we," adopted by the Rev. Vers. C.]
[8] σχέσιν.
[9] The Received Text inverts the order of the two clauses

to be made one with God.   Hear also what follows.

Ver. 18. "And I will be to you a Father, and ye shall be to me sons and daughters, saith the Lord."

Seest thou how from the beginning the Prophet fore-announceth our present high birth, the Regeneration by grace?

Chap. vii. ver. 1. "Having therefore these promises, beloved."

What promises? That we should be temples of God, sons and daughters, have Him indwelling, and walking in us, be His people, have Him for our God and Father.

"Let us cleanse ourselves from all defilement of flesh and spirit."

Let us neither touch unclean things, for this is cleansing of the flesh; nor things which defile the soul, for this is cleansing of the spirit.   Yet he is not content with this only, but adds also,

"Perfecting holiness in the fear of God." For not to touch the unclean thing doth not make clean, but there needeth something else besides to our becoming holy; earnestness, heedfulness, piety.   And he well said, "In the fear of God."   For it is possible to perfect chasteness, not in the fear of God but for vainglory.   And along with this he implies yet another thing, by saying, "In the fear of God;" the manner, namely, whereafter holiness may be perfected.   For if lust be even an imperious thing, still if thou occupy its territory with [1] the fear of God, thou hast stayed its frenzy.

[4.]   Now by holiness here he means not chastity alone, but the freedom from every kind of sin, for he is holy that is pure.   Now one will become pure, not if he be free from fornication only, but if from covetousness also, and envy, and pride [2], and vainglory, yea especially from vainglory which in every thing indeed it behoveth to avoid, but much more in almsgiving; since neither will it be almsgiving, if it have this distemper, but display and cruelty. For when thou dost it not out of mercy, but from parade [3], such deed is not only no alms but even an insult; for thou hast put thy brother to open shame [4].   Not then the giving money, but the giving it out of mercy, is almsgiving. For people too at the theatres give, both to prostitute boys and to others who are on the stage; but such a deed is not almsgiving.   And they too give that abuse the persons of prostitute women; but this is not lovingkindness, but insolent treatment [5].   Like this is the vainglorious also.   For just as he that abuseth the person of the harlot, pays her a price for that

abuse; so too dost thou demand a price of him that receiveth of thee, thine insult of him and thine investing him as well as thyself with an evil notoriety.   And besides this, the loss is unspeakable.   For just as a wild beast and a mad dog springing upon us might, so doth this ill disease and this inhumanity make prey of our good things.   For inhumanity and cruelty such a course is; yea, rather more grievous even than this.   For the cruel indeed would not give to him that asked; but thou dost more than this; thou hinderest those that wish to give. For when thou paradest thy giving, thou hast both lowered the reputation of the receiver, and hast pulled back [6] him that was about to give, if he be of a careless mind.   For he will not give to him thenceforth, on the ground of his having already received, and so not being in want; yea he will often accuse him even, if after having received he should draw near to beg, and will think him impudent.   What sort of almsgiving then is this when thou both shamest thyself and him that receiveth; and also in two ways Him that enjoined it: both because while having Him for a spectator of thine alms, thou seekest the eyes of thy fellow-servants besides Him, and because thou transgressest the law laid down by Him forbidding these things.

I could have wished to carry this out into those other subjects as well, both fasting and prayer, and to show in how many respects vainglory is injurious there also; but I remember that in the discourse before this I left unfinished a certain necessary point.   What was the point?   I was saying, that the poor have the advantage of the rich in the things of this life, when I discoursed concerning health and pleasure; and this was shown indistinctly.   Come then, to-day let us show this, that not in the things of this life only, but also in those that are higher, the advantage is with them.   For what leadeth unto a kingdom, riches or poverty?   Let us hear the Lord Himself of the heavens saying of those, that "it is easier for a camel to go through the eye of a needle than for a rich man to enter into the kingdom of heaven:" (Mat. xix. 24.) but of the poor the contrary, "If thou wilt be perfect, sell that thou hast, and give to the poor; and come, follow Me; and thou shalt have treasure in heaven." (Mat. xix. 21.)   But if ye will, let us see what is said on either side.   "Narrow and straitened is the way," He saith, "that leadeth unto life." (Mat. vii. 14.)   Who then treadeth the narrow way, he that is in luxury, or that is in poverty; that is independent, or that carrieth ten thousand burdens; the lax [7] and dissolute, or the thoughtful and anxious?

---

[1] ἐπιτειχίσῃς.
[2] ἀπονοίας.
[3] ἐκπομπεύων.
[4] παρεδειγμάτισας.
[5] παροινία.

[6] ἀνεχαίτισας.
[7] χαῦνος.

But what need of these arguments, when it is best to betake one's self to the persons themselves. Lazarus was poor, yea very poor ; and he that passed him by as he lay at his gateway was rich. Which then entered into the kingdom, and was in delights in Abraham's bosom? and which of them was scorched, with not even a drop at his command ? But, saith one, 'both many poor will be lost, and [many] rich will enjoy those unspeakable goods.' Nay rather, one may see the contrary, few rich saved, but of the poor far more. For, consider, making accurate measure of the hindrances of riches and the defects of poverty, (or rather, neither of riches nor of poverty are they, but each of those who have riches or poverty ; howbeit,) let us at least see which is the more available weapon. What defect then doth poverty seem to possess? Lying. And what, wealth? Pride, the mother of evils; which also made the devil a devil, who was not such before. Again, "the love of money is a root of all kinds of evil." (1 Tim. vi. 10.) Which then stands near this root, the rich man, or the poor? Is it not very plainly the rich? For the more things anyone surrounds himself with, he desires so much the more. Vainglory again damages tens of thousands of good deeds, and near this too again the rich man hath his dwelling [1]. "But," saith one, "thou mentionest not the [evils] of the poor man, his affliction, his straits." Nay, but this is both common to the rich, and is his more than the poor man's ; so that those indeed which appear to be evils of poverty are common to either: whilst those of riches are riches' only. 'But what,' saith one, 'when for want of necessaries the poor man committeth many horrible things?' But no poor man, no, not one, committeth as many horrible

things from want, as do the rich for the sake of surrounding themselves with more, and of not losing what stores they have [2]. For the poor man doth not so eagerly desire necessaries as the rich doth superfluities ; nor again has he as much strength to put wickedness in practice as the other hath power. If then the rich man is both more willing and able, it is quite plain that he will rather commit such, and more of them. Nor is the poor man so much afraid in respect of hunger, as the rich trembleth and is anxious in respect of the loss of what he has, and because he has not yet gotten all men's possessions. Since then he is near both vainglory and arrogance, and the love of money, the root of all evils, what hope of salvation shall he have except he display much wisdom ? And how shall he walk the narrow way ? Let us not therefore carry about the notions of the many, but examine into the facts. For how is it not absurd that in respect to money, indeed, we do not trust to others, but refer this to figures and calculation ; but in calculating upon facts we are lightly drawn aside by the notions of others ; and that too, though we possess an exact balance[3], and square[4] and rule[5] for all things, the declaration of the divine laws ? Wherefore I exhort and entreat you all, disregard what this man and that man thinks about these things, and inquire from the Scriptures all these things ; and having learnt what are the true riches, let us pursue after them that we may obtain also the eternal good things; which may we all obtain, through the grace and love towards men of our Lord Jesus Christ, with Whom, to the Father and the Holy Spirit, be glory, might, and honor, now and ever, and world without end. Amen.

HOMILY XIV.

2 Cor. vii. 2, 3.

Open your hearts to us : we wronged no man, we corrupted no man, we took advantage of no man. I say it not to condemn you ; for I have said before, [as I have also declared above][6], that ye are in our hearts to die together and live together.

AGAIN he raiseth the discourse about love, mitigating the harshness of his rebuke. For since he had convicted and reproached them as being beloved indeed, yet not loving in an

equal degree, but breaking away from his love and mixing up with other pestilent fellows ; again he softens the vehemence of his rebuke, saying, "Make room for us," that is, "love us ; " and prays to receive a favor involving no burden, and advantaging them that confer above them that receive it. And he said not, 'love,' but with a stronger appeal to their

---

[1] ἐσκήνωται.
[2] τὰ ἔνδον
[3] ζυγόν
[4] γνώμονα
[5] κανόνα
[6] This clause, inserted by St. Chrysostom, is not found in the Received text.

pity[1], "make room for." 'Who expelled us?' saith he : 'Who cast us out of your hearts? How come we to be straitened in you?' for since he said above, "Ye are straitened in your affections;" here declaring it more clearly, he said, "make room for us : " in this way also again winning them to himself. For nothing doth so produce love as for the beloved to know that he that loveth him exceedingly desireth his love.

"We wronged no man." See how again he does not mention the benefits [done by him], but frameth his speech in another way, so as to be both less offensive and more cutting[2]. And at the same time he also alludes to the false apostles, saying, "We wronged no man, we corrupted no man, we defrauded no man."

What is "we corrupted?" That is, we beguiled no man ; as he says elsewhere also. "Lest by any means, as the serpent beguiled Eve, so your minds should be corrupted." (2 Cor. xi. 3.)

"We defrauded no man;" we plundered, plotted against no man. And he for the present forbears to say, 'we benefited you in such and such ways;' but framing his language so as more to shame them, "We wronged no man," he says; as much as saying, 'Even had we in no wise benefited you, not even so ought ye to turn away from us; for ye have nothing to lay to our charge, either small or great.' Then, for he felt the heaviness of his rebuke, he tempers it again. And he was neither silent altogether, for so he would not have aroused them ; nor yet did he let the harshness of his language go unmodified, for so he would have wounded them too much. And what says he?

Ver. 3. "I say it not to condemn you."

How is this evident? "For I have said before," he adds, "that ye are in our hearts to die and live with you." This is the greatest affection, when even though treated with contempt, he chooseth both to die and live with them. 'For neither are ye merely in our hearts,' he says, 'but in such sort as I said. For it is possible both to love and to shun dangers, but we do not thus.' And behold here also wisdom unspeakable. For he spake not of what had been done for them, that he might not seem to be again reproaching them, but he promiseth for the future. 'For should it chance,' saith he, 'that danger should invade, for your sakes I am ready to suffer every thing; and neither death nor life seemeth aught to me in itself, but in whichever ye be, that is to me more desirable, both death than life and life than death.'

Howbeit, dying indeed is manifestly a proof of love; but living, who is there that would not choose, even of those who are not friends? Why then does the Apostle mention it as something great? Because it is even exceeding great. For numbers indeed sympathize with their friends when they are in misfortune, but when they are in honor rejoice not with, but envy, them. 'But not so we; but whether ye be in calamity, we are not afraid to share your ill fortune ; or whether ye be prosperous, we are not wounded with envy.'

[2.] Then after he had continually repeated these things, saying, "Ye are not straitened in us ;" and, "Ye are straitened in your own affections ; " and, "make room for us ; " and, "Be ye also enlarged ; " and, "We wronged no man ; " and all these things seemed to be a condemnation of them : observe how he also in another manner alleviates this severity by saying, "Great is my boldness of speech towards you." 'Therefore I venture upon such things,' he says, 'not to condemn you by what I say, but out of my great boldness of speech,' which also farther signifying, he said, "Great is my glorying on your behalf." 'For think not indeed,' he saith, 'that because I thus speak, I speak as though I had condemned you altogether ; (for I am exceedingly proud of, and glory in, you ;) but both out of tender concern and a desire that you should make greater increase unto virtue.' And so he said to the Hebrews also after much rebuke ; "But we are persuaded better things of you, and things that accompany salvation, though we thus speak : and we desire that each one of you may show the same diligence to the fullness of hope even to the end." (Heb. vi. 9, 11.) So indeed here also, "Great is my glorying on your behalf." 'We glory to others of you,' he says. Seest thou what genuine comfort he has given? 'And,' he saith, 'I do not simply glory, but also, greatly.' Accordingly he added these words ; "I am filled with comfort." What comfort? 'That coming from you ; because that ye, having been reformed, comforted me by your conduct.' This is the test of one that loveth, both to complain of not being loved and to fear lest he should inflict pain by complaining immoderately. Therefore he says, "I am filled with comfort, I overflow with joy." 'But these expressions,' saith one, 'seem to contradict the former.' They do not do so, however, but are even exceedingly in harmony with them. For these procure for the former a favorable reception ; and the praise which they convey makes the benefit of those rebukes more genuine, by quietly abstracting what was painful in them. Wherefore he uses these expressions, but with great genuineness and earnestness[3]. For he did

---

[1] ἐλεεινότερον
[2] πληκτικώτερον.

[2] φιλοτίμως.

not say, 'I am filled with joy;' but, "I abound;" or rather, not "abound" either, but "superabound;" in this way also again showing his yearning, that even though he be so loved as to rejoice and exult, he does not yet think himself loved as he ought to be loved, nor to have received full payment; so insatiable was he out of his exceeding love of them. For the joy it brings to be loved in any degree by those one passionately loves, is great by reason of our loving them exceedingly. So that this again was a proof of his affection. And of the comfort indeed, he saith, "I am filled;" 'I have received what was owing to me;' but of the joy, "I superabound;" that is, 'I was desponding about you; but ye have sufficiently excused yourselves and supplied comfort: for ye have not only removed the ground of my sorrow, but have even increased joy.' Then showing its greatness, he not only declares it by saying, "I superabound in joy," but also by adding, "in all our affliction." 'For so great was the delight arising to us on your account that it was not even dimmed by so great tribulation, but through the excess of its own greatness it overcame the sorrows that had hold of us, and suffered us not to feel the sense of them.'

Ver. 5. "For even when we were come into Macedonia, our flesh had no relief."

For since he said, "our tribulation;" he both explains of what sort it was, and magnifies it by his words, in order to show that the consolation and joy received from them[1] was great, seeing it had repelled so great a sorrow.

"But we were afflicted on every side."

How on every side? for "without were fightings," from the unbelievers; "within were fears;" because of the weak among the believers, lest they should be drawn aside. For not amongst the Corinthians only did these things happen, but elsewhere also.

Ver. 6. "Nevertheless He that comforteth the lowly comforted us by[2] the coming of Titus."

For since he had testified great things of them in what he said, that he may not seem to be flattering them he cites as witness Titus the brother[3], who had come from them to Paul after the first Epistle to declare unto him the particulars of their amendment. But consider, I pray you, how in every place he maketh a great matter of the coming of Titus. For he saith also before, "Furthermore when I came to Troas for the Gospel, I had no relief for my spirit because I found not Titus my brother;" (c. ii. 12, 13.) and in this place again we were comforted," he saith, "by the coming of

Titus." For he is desirous also of establishing the man in their confidence and of making him exceedingly dear to them. And observe how he provides for both these things. For by saying on the one hand, "I had no relief for my spirit," he showeth the greatness of his virtue; and by saying on the other, that, in our tribulation his coming sufficed unto comfort; yet "not by his coming only, but also by the comfort wherewith he was comforted in you," he endeareth[4] the man unto the Corinthians. For nothing doth so produce and cement friendships as the saying something sound and favorable of any one. And such he testifies Titus did; when he says that 'by his coming he hath given us wings with pleasure; such things did he report of you. On this ground his coming made us glad. For we were delighted not "only by his coming, but also for the comfort wherewith he was comforted in you." And how was he comforted? By your virtue, by your good deeds.' Wherefore also he adds,

"While he told us your longing, your mourning, your zeal for me. 'These things made him glad,' he says, 'these things comforted him.' Seest thou how he shows that he also is an earnest lover of theirs, seeing he considers their good report as a consolation to himself; and when he was come, gloried, as though on account of his own good things, unto Paul.

And observe with what warmth of expression he reporteth these things, "Your longing, your mourning, your zeal." For it was likely[5] that they would mourn and grieve why the blessed Paul was so much displeased, why he had kept away from them so long. And therefore he did not say simply tears, but "mourning;" nor desire, but "longing;" nor anger, but "zeal;" and again "zeal toward him," which they displayed both about him that had committed fornication and about those who were accusing him. 'For,' saith he, 'ye were inflamed and blazed out on receiving my letters.' On these accounts he abounds in joy, on these accounts he is filled with consolation, because he made them feel. It seems to me, however, that these things are said not only to soften what has gone before, but also in encouragement of those who had acted in these things virtuously. For although I suppose that some were obnoxious to those former accusations and unworthy of these praises; nevertheless, he doth not distinguish them, but makes both the praises and the accusations common, leaving it to the conscience of his hearers to select that which belongs to them. For so both the one would be void of offence, and the other lead them on to much fervor of mind.

---

[1] i. e., the Corinthians.
[2] ἐν R. T. ἐπὶ St. C. [The former is the true text. C.]
[3] Or 'his brother.'

[4] οἰκειοῖ
[5] Or 'natural.'

[4.] Such also now should be the feelings of those who are reprehended; thus should they lament and mourn; thus yearn after their teachers; thus, more than fathers, seek them. For by those indeed living cometh, but by these good living. Thus ought they to bear the rebukes of their fathers, thus to sympathize with their rulers on account of those that sin. For it does not rest all with them, but with you also. For if he that hath sinned perceives that he was rebuked indeed by his father, but flattered by his brethren; he becometh more easy of mind. But when the father rebukes, be thou too angry as well, whether as concerned for thy brother or as joining in thy father's indignation; only be the earnestness thou showest great; and mourn, not that he was rebuked, but that he sinned. But if I build up and thou pull down, what profit have we had but labor? (Ecclus. xxxiv. 23.) Yea, rather, thy loss stops not here, but thou bringest also punishment on thyself. For he that hindereth the wound from being healed is punished not less than he that inflicted it, but even more. For it is not an equal offence to wound and to hinder that which is wounded from being healed; for this indeed necessarily gendereth death, but that not necessarily. Now I have spoken thus to you; that ye may join in the anger of your rulers whenever they are indignant justly; that when ye see any one rebuked, ye may all shun him more than does the teacher. Let him that hath offended fear you more than his rulers. For if he is afraid of his teacher only, he will readily sin: but if he have to dread so many eyes, so many tongues, he will be in greater safety. For as, if we do not thus act, we shall suffer the extremest punishment; so, if we perform these things, we shall partake of the gain that accrues from his reformation. Thus then let us act; and if any one shall say, ' be humane towards thy brother, this is a Christian's duty; let him be taught, that he is humane who is angry [with him], not he who sets him at ease[1] prematurely and alloweth him not even to come to a sense of his transgression. For which, tell me, pities the man in a fever and laboring under delirium, he that lays him on his bed, and binds him down, and keeps him from meats and drinks that are not fit for him; or he that allows him to glut himself with strong drink, and orders him to have his liberty, and to act in every respect as one that is in health? Does not this person even aggravate the distemper, the man that seemeth to act humanely, whereas the other

amends it? Such truly ought our decision to be in this case also. For it is the part of humanity, not to humor the sick in every thing nor to flatter their unseasonable desires. No one so loved him that committed fornication amongst the Corinthians, as Paul who commandeth to deliver him to Satan; no one so hated him as they that applaud and court him; and the event showed it. For they indeed both puffed him up and increased his inflammation; but [the Apostle] both lowered it and left him not until he brought him to perfect health. And they indeed added to the existing mischief, he eradicated even that which existed from the first. These laws, then, of humanity let us learn also. For if thou seest a horse hurrying down a precipice, thou appliest a bit and holdest him in with violence and lashest him frequently; although this is punishment, yet the punishment itself is the mother of safety. Thus act also in the case of those that sin. Bind him that hath transgressed until he have appeased God; let him not go loose, that he be not bound the faster by the anger of God. If I bind, God doth not chain; if I bind not, the indissoluble chains await him. " For if we judged ourselves, we should not be judged. (1 Cor. xi. 31.) Think not, then, that thus to act cometh of cruelty and inhumanity; nay, but of the highest gentleness and the most skillful leechcraft and of much tender care. But, saith one, they have been punished for a long time. How long? Tell me. A year, and two, and three years? Howbeit, I require not this, length of time, but amendment of soul. This then show, whether they have been pricked to the heart, whether they have reformed, and all is done: since if there be not this, there is no advantage in the time. For neither do we inquire whether the wound has been often bandaged, but whether the bandage has been of any service. If therefore it hath been of service, although in a short time, let it be kept on no longer: but if it hath done no service, even at the end of ten years, let it be still kept on: and let this fix the term of release, the good of him that is bound. If we are thus careful both of ourselves and of others, and regard not honor and dishonor at the hands of men; but bearing in mind the punishment and the disgrace that is there, and above all the provoking of God, apply with energy the medicines of repentance: we shall both presently arrive at the perfect health, and shall obtain the good things to come; which may all we obtain, through the grace and love towards men of our Lord Jesus Christ, with Whom, to the Father, with the Holy Spirit, be glory, might, honor, now and ever, and world without end. Amen.

---

[1] χαλῶν Field. The MSS. have καλῶν, for which παρακαλῶν and κολακεύων have been conjectured. χαλάω is used elsewhere in the same sense by Chrysostom. See above, Hom. XIII. p. 346. line 29, first column, "softened."

HOMILY XV.

2 COR. vii. 8.

So that[1] though I made you sorry with my letter, I do not regret it, though I did regret.

He goes on to apologize for his Epistle, when, (the sin having been corrected,) to treat them tenderly[2] was unattended with danger; and he shows the advantage of the thing. For he did this indeed even before, when he said, "For out of much affliction and anguish of heart, I wrote unto you : not that ye should be made sorry, but that ye might know the love which I have toward you." (c. ii. 4.) And he does it also now, establishing this same point in more words. And he said not, 'I regretted indeed before, but now I do not regret : ' but how ? "I regret not now, though I did regret." 'Even if what I wrote,' he says, 'was such as to overstep the [due] measure of rebuke[3], and to cause me to regret ; still the great advantage which has accrued from them doth not allow me to regret.' And this he said, not as though he had rebuked them beyond due measure, but to heighten his praises of them. 'For the amendment ye manifested was so great,' saith he, 'that even if I did happen to smite you too severely insomuch that I even condemned myself, I praise myself now from the result.' Just as with little children, when they have undergone a painful remedy, such as an incision, or cautery, or bitter physic, afterwards we are not afraid to sooth them ; so also doth Paul.

Ver. 8, 9. "For I see that that epistle made you sorry, though but for a season. Now I rejoice not that ye were made sorry, but that ye were made sorry unto repentance."

Having said, "I do not regret," he tells the reason also; alleging the good that resulted from his letter ; and skillfully excusing himself by saying, "though but for a season." For truly that which was painful was brief, but that which was profitable was perpetual. And what indeed followed naturally was to say, 'even though it grieved you for a season, yet it made you glad and benefited you forever.' But he doth not say this : but before mentioning the gain he passes again to his praises of them, and the proof of his own concern for them, saying, "Now I rejoice, not that ye were made sorry," ('for what gain came to me from you being made sorry ?) "but that ye were made sorry unto repentance," that the sorrow brought some gain.' For a father also when he sees his son under the knife rejoiceth not that he is being pained, but that he is being cured ; so also doth this man. But observe how he transfers all that was well achieved in the matter unto themselves; and lays whatever was painful to the account of the Epistle, saying, "It made you sorry for a season ; " whilst the benefit that resulted from it he speaks of as their own good achieving. For he said not, 'The Epistle corrected you,' although this was the case ; but, "ye sorrowed unto repentance."

"For ye were made sorry after a godly sort, that ye might suffer loss by us in nothing."

Seest thou wisdom unspeakable? 'For had we not done this,' he says, 'we had done you damage.' And he affirms that indeed which was well achieved to be theirs, but the damage his own, if indeed he had been silent. For if they are likely to be corrected by a sharp rebuke, then, if we did not sharply rebuke, we should have done you damage ; and the injury would not be with you alone, but also with us. For just as he that gives not to the merchant what is necessary for his voyage, he it is that causeth the damage ; so also we, if we did not offer you that occasion[4] of repentance, should have wrought you damage. Seest thou that the not rebuking those that sin is a damage both to the master and to the disciple ?

[2.] Ver. 10. "For godly sorrow worketh repentance unto salvation, a repentance which bringeth no regret."

'Therefore,' he says, 'though I did regret before I saw the fruit and the gain, how great they were, I do not regret now.' For such a thing is godly sorrow. And then he philosophizeth about it, showing that sorrow is not in all cases a grievous thing, but when it is worldly. And what is worldly? If thou be in sorrow for

---

[1] ' For,' Rec. Text [which is correct. C.]
[2] θεραπεύειν.
[3] τό μετρόν τῆς ἐπιτιμήσεως.
[4] τὰς ἀφορμάς.

money, for reputation, for him that is departed, all these are worldly. Wherefore also they work death. For he that is in sorrow for reputation's sake feeleth envy and is driven oftentimes to perish: such sorrow was that which Cain sorrowed, such Esau. By this worldly sorrow then he meaneth that which is to the harm of those that sorrow. For only in respect to sins is sorrow a profitable thing; as is evident in this way. He that sorroweth for loss of wealth repaireth not that damage; he that sorroweth for one deceased raiseth not the dead to life again; he that sorroweth for a sickness, not only is not made well but even aggravates the disease: he that sorroweth for sins, he alone attains some advantage from his sorrow, for he maketh his sins wane and disappear. For since the medicine has been prepared for this thing, in this case only is it potent and displays its profitableness; and in the other cases is even injurious. 'And yet Cain,' saith one, 'sorrowed because he was not accepted with God.' It was not for this, but because he saw his brother glorious in honor[1]; for had he grieved for this, it behoved him to emulate and rejoice with him; but, as it was, grieving, he showed that his was a worldly sorrow. But not so did David, nor Peter, nor any of the righteous. Wherefore they were accepted, when grieving either over their own sins or those of others. And yet what is more oppressive than sorrow? Still when it is after a godly sort, it is better than the joy in the world. For this indeed ends in nothing; but that "worketh repentance unto salvation, a salvation that bringeth no regret." For what is admirable in it is this that one who had thus sorrowed would never repent, whilst this is an especial characteristic of worldly sorrow. For what is more regretted than a true born son? And what is a heavier grief than a death of this sort? But yet those fathers who in the height of their grief endure nobody and who wildly beat themselves, after a time repent because they have grieved immoderately; as having thereby nothing benefitted themselves, but even added to their affliction. But not such as this is godly sorrow; but it possesseth two advantages, that of not being condemned in that a man grieves for, and that this sorrow endeth in salvation; of both which that is deprived. For they both sorrow unto harm and after they have sorrowed vehemently condemn themselves, bringing forth this greatest token of having done it unto harm. But godly sorrow is the reverse [of this]: wherefore also he said, "worketh repentance unto salvation, a repentance that bringeth no regret." For no one will condemn himself if he have sorrowed for sin, if he have mourned and afflicted himself. Which also when the blessed

Paul hath said he needeth not to adduce from other sources the proof of what he said, nor to bring forward those in the old histories who sorrowed, but he adduceth the Corinthians themselves; and furnishes his proof from what they had done; that along with praises he might both instruct them and the rather win them to himself.

Ver. 11. "For behold," he saith, "this self-same thing, that ye were made sorry after a godly sort, what earnest care it wrought in you." 'For not only,' he saith, 'did your sorrow not cast you into that condemning of yourselves, as having acted idly in so doing; but it made you even more careful.' Then he speaks of the certain tokens of that carefulness;

"Yea," what "clearing of yourselves," towards me. "Yea, what indignation" against him that had sinned. "Yea, what fear." (ver. 11.) For so great carefulness and very speedy reformation was the part of men who feared exceedingly. And that he might not seem to be exalting himself, see how quickly he softened it by saying,

"Yea, what longing," that towards me. "Yea, what zeal," that on God's behalf. "Yea, what avenging:" for ye also avenged the laws of God that had been outraged.

"In every thing ye approved yourselves to be pure in the matter." Not only by not having perpetrated, for this was evident before, but also by not consenting[2] unto it. For since he said in the former Epistle, "and ye are puffed up;" (1 Cor. v. 2.) he also says here, 'ye have cleared yourselves of this suspicion also; not only by not praising, but also by rebuking and being indignant.'

[3.] Ver. 12. "So although I wrote unto you," I wrote "not for his cause that did the wrong, nor for his cause that suffered the wrong." For that they might not say, Why then dost thou rebuke us if we were "clear in the matter?" setting himself to meet this even further above, and disposing of it beforehand[3], he said what he said, namely, "I do not regret, though I did regret." 'For so far,' says he, 'am I from repenting now of what I wrote then, that I repented then more than I do now when ye have approved[4] yourselves. Seest thou again his vehemence and earnest contention, how he has turned around what was said unto the very opposite. For what they thought would have made him recant[5] in confusion as having rebuked them hastily, by reason of their amendment; that he uses as a proof that it was right in him to speak freely. For neither does he refuse afterwards to humor them fearlessly, when

---

[1] λάμποντα.

[2] συνῄδεσθαι.
[3] προδιοικούμενος.
[4] συνεστήσατε.
[5] διατετράφθαι.

he finds he can do this. For he that said farther above such things as these, " He that is joined to an harlot is one body," (1 Cor. vi. 16.) and, " Deliver such an one to Satan for the destruction of the flesh," (1 Cor. v. 5.) and, " Every sin that a man doeth is without the body," (1 Cor. vi. 18.) and such like things ; how saith he here, "Not for his cause that did the wrong, nor for his cause that suffered the wrong ? " Not contradicting, but being even exceedingly consistent with, himself. How consistent with himself? Because it was a very great point with him to show the affection he bore towards them. He does not therefore discard concern for him[1], but shows at the same time, as I said, the love he had for them, and that a greater fear agitated him, [namely] for the whole Church. For he had feared lest the evil should eat further, and advancing on its way should seize upon the whole Church. Wherefore also he said, " A little leaven leaveneth the whole lump." (1 Cor. v. 6.) This however he said at the time ; but now that they had well done, he no longer puts it so but differently : and implies indeed the same thing, but manages his expressions more agreeably, saying,

" That our care for you might appear unto you.[2] "

That is, ' that ye might know how I love you.' Now this is the same thing as the former, but being differently expressed seemed to convey another meaning. For [to convince thyself] that it is the same, unfold his conception and thou wilt perceive the difference to be nothing. ' For because I love you exceedingly,' saith he, ' I was afraid lest ye should suffer any injury from that quarter, and yourselves succeed to that sorrow.' As therefore when he says, "Doth God take care for oxen? " (1 Cor. ix. 9.) he doth not mean that He careth not, (for it is not possible for any existing thing to consist if deserted by the Providence of God :) but that He did not legislate primarily for oxen, so also here he means to say, ' I wrote first indeed on your account, but secondly on his also. And I had indeed that love in myself,' he says, ' even independently of mine Epistle : but I was desirous of showing it both to you, and in a word to all, by that writing.'

Ver. 13. " Therefore we have been comforted."

Since we both showed our care for you and have been wholly successful. As he said also in another place, " Now we live, if ye stand fast in the Lord;" (1 Thess. iii. 8.) and again, " For what is our hope, or joy, or crown of rejoicing? are not even ye?" (ib. ii. 19.) For

this is life, this comfort, this consolation to a teacher possessed of understanding; the growth[3] of his disciples.

[4.] For nothing doth so declare him that beareth rule as paternal affection for the ruled. For begetting alone constitutes not a father ; but after begetting, also loving. But if where nature is concerned there is so great need of love, much more where grace is concerned. In this way were all the ancients distinguished. As many, for instance, as obtained a good report amongst the Hebrews, by this were made manifest. So was Samuel shown to be great, saying, " But God forbid that I should sin against God in ceasing to pray for you : " (1 Sam. xii. 23.) so was David, so Abraham, so Elijah, and so each one of the righteous, those in the New Testament and those in the Old. For so Moses for the sake of those he ruled left so great riches and treasures untold, " choosing to suffer affliction with the people of God," (Heb. xi. 25.) and before his appointment was leader of the people[4] by his actions. Wherefore also very foolishly did that Hebrew say to him, " Who made thee a ruler and a judge over us? " (Exod. ii. 14.) What sayest thou? Thou seest the actions and doubtest of the title? Just as if one seeing a physician using the knife excellently well, and succoring that limb in the body which was diseased, should say, ' Who made thee a physician and ordered thee to use the knife?' ' Art, my good Sir[5], and thine own ailment.' So too did his knowledge make him (i.e., Moses,) what he claimed to be. For ruling is an art, not merely a dignity, and an art above all arts. For if the rule of those without is an art and science superior to all other, much more this. For this rule is as much better than that, as that than the rest ; yea, rather, even much more. And, if ye will, let us examine this argument more accurately. There is an art of agriculture, of weaving, of building; which are both very necessary and tend greatly to preserve our life. For others surely are but ancillary to these ; the coppersmith's, the carpenter's, the shepherd's. But further, of arts themselves the most necessary of all is the agricultural, which was even that which God first introduced when He had formed man. For without shoes and clothes it is possible to live; but without agriculture it is impossible. And such they say are the Hamaxobii, the Nomads amongst the Scythians, and the Indian Gymnosophists. For these troubled not themselves[6] with the arts of housebuilding, and weaving, and shoemaking, but

---

[1] i. e. the incestuous person.
[9] [The true text of this clause is given in the Rev. Vers. "That your earnest care for us might be made manifest." C.]

[3] ἐπίδοσις.
[4] δημαγωγὸς.
[5] ὦ βέλτιστε.
[6] εἴασαν.

need only that of agriculture. Blush ye that have need of those arts that be superfluous, cooks, confectioners, embroiderers, and ten thousand other such people, that ye may live; blush ye that introduce vain refinements [1] into life; blush ye who are unbelievers, before those barbarians who have no need of art. For God made nature exceedingly independent, needing only a few things [2]. However, I do not compel you nor lay it down for law that ye should live thus; but as Jacob asked. And what did he ask? "If the Lord will give me bread to eat and raiment to put on." (Gen. xxviii. 20.) So also Paul commanded, saying, "And having food and covering let us be therewith content." (1 Tim. vi. 8.) First then comes agriculture; second, weaving; and third after it, building; and shoemaking last of all; for amongst us at any rate there are many both servants and laborers who live without shoes. These, therefore, are the useful and necessary arts. Come, then, let us compare them with that of ruling. For I have therefore brought forward these that are of all most important, that when it shall have been seen to be superior to them, its victory over the rest may be unquestioned. Whereby then shall we show that it is more necessary than all? Because without it there is no advantage in these. And if you think good, let us leave mention of the rest and bring on the stage [3] that one which stands higher and is more important than any, that of agriculture. Where then will be the advantage of the many hands of your laborers. if they are at war with one another and plunder one another's goods? For, as it is, the fear of the ruler restrains them and protects that which is wrought by them; but if thou take this away, in vain is their labor. But if one examine accurately, he will find yet another rule which is the parent and bond of this. What then may this be? That according to which it behoveth each man to control and rule himself, chastising his unworthy passions, but both nourishing and promoting the growth of all the germs of virtue with all care.

For there are [these] species of rule; one, that whereby men rule peoples and states, regulating this the political life; which Paul denoting said, "Let every soul be subject to the higher powers; for there is no power but of God." (Rom. xiii. 1, 4.) Afterwards to show the advantage of this, he went on to say, that the ruler "is a minister of God for good;" and again, "he is a minister of God, and avenger to execute wrath on him that doeth evil."

A second there is whereby every one that hath understanding ruleth himself; and this also the Apostle further denoted [4], saying, "Wouldest thou have no fear of the power? do that which is good;" (Rom. xiii. 3.) speaking of him that ruleth himself.

[5.] Here, however, there is yet another rule, higher than the political rule. And what is this? That in the Church. And this also itself Paul mentions, saying, "Obey them that have the rule over you and submit to them; for they watch in behalf of your souls as they that shall give account." (Heb. xiii. 17.) For this rule is as much better than the political as heaven is than earth; yea rather, even much more. For, in the first place, it considers principally not how it may punish sins committed, but how, they may never be committed at all; next, when committed, not how it may remove the deceased [member], but how they may be blotted out. And of the things of this life indeed it maketh not much account, but all its transactions are about the things in heaven. "For our citizenship [5] is in heaven." (Phil. iii. 20.) And our life is here. "For our life," saith he, "is hid with Christ in God." (Col. iii. 3.) And our prizes are there, and our race is for the crowns that be there. For this life is not dissolved after the end, but then shineth forth the more. And therefore, in truth, they who bear this rule have a greater honor committed to their hands, not only than viceroys but even than those themselves who wear diadems, seeing that they mould men in greater, and for greater, things. But neither he that pursueth political rule nor he that pursueth spiritual, will be able well to administer it, unless they have first ruled themselves as they ought, and have observed with all strictness the respective laws of their polity. For as the rule over the many is in a manner twofold, so also is that which each one exerts over himself. And again, in this point also the spiritual rule transcends the political, as what we have said proved. But one may observe certain also of the arts imitating rule; and in particular, that of agriculture. For just as the tiller of the soil is in a sort a ruler over the plants, clipping and keeping back [6] some, making others grow and fostering them: just so also the best rulers punish and cut off such as are wicked and injure the many; whilst they advance the good and orderly [7]. For this cause also the Scripture likeneth rulers to vine-dressers. For what though plants utter no cry, as in states the injured do? nevertheless they still show the wrong by their appearance, withering, straitened for room by the worthless weeds. And like as

---

[1] ματαιοτεχνίας.
[2] ἐξ ὀλίγων.
[3] εἰς μέσον.
[4] παρεδήλωσεν.
[5] conversation A. V.
[6] κωλύων, others, κολούων.
[7] ἐπιεικεῖς.

wickedness is punished by laws, so truly here also by this art both badness of soil and degeneracy and wildness in plants, are corrected. For all the varieties of human dispositions we shall find here also, roughness, weakness, timidity, forwardness[1], steadiness[2]: and some of them through wealth[3] luxuriating unseasonably, and to the damage of their neighbors, and others impoverished and injured; as, for instance, when hedges are raised to luxuriance at the cost of the neighboring plants; when other barren and wild trees, running up to a great height, hinder the growth of those beneath them. And like as rulers and kings have those that vex their rule with outrage and war; so also hath the tiller of the soil attacks of wild beasts, irregularity of weather, hail, mildew, great rain, drought, and all such things. But these things happen in order that thou mayest constantly look unto the hope of God's aid. For the other arts indeed hold their way[4] through the diligence of men as well; but this getteth the better as God determines the balance, and is throughout almost wholly dependent thereupon; and it needeth rains from above, and the admixture of weathers, and, above all, His Providence. "For neither is he that planteth any thing, nor he that watereth, but God that giveth the increase." (1 Cor. iii. 7.)

Here also there is death and life, and throes and procreation, just as with men. For here happen instances both of being cut off, and of bearing fruit, and of dying, and of being born (the same that was dead) over again, wherein the earth discourseth to us both variously and clearly of a resurrection. For when the root beareth fruit, when the seed shooteth, is not the thing a resurrection? And one might perceive a large measure of God's providence and wisdom involved in this rule, if one go over it point by point. But what I wished to say is that this [rule] is concerned with earth and plants; but ours with care of souls. And great as is the difference between plants and a soul; so great is the superiority of this to that. And the rulers of the present life again are as much inferior to that [rule], as it is better to have mastery over the willing than the unwilling. For this is also a natural rule; for truly in that case every thing is done through fear and by constraint; but here, what is done aright is of choice and purpose. And not in this point alone doth this excel the other, but in that it is not only a rule, but a fatherhood,[5] so to speak; for it has the gentleness of a father; and whilst enjoining greater things, [still] persuades. For

the temporal ruler indeed says, 'If thou committest adultery, thou hast forfeited thy life,' but this, shouldst thou look with unchaste eyes, threatens the highest punishments. For awful is this judgment court, and for the correction of soul, not of body only. As great then as the difference between soul and body, is that which separates this rule again from that. And the one indeed sitteth as judge of things that are open; yea, rather, not of all these even, but of such as can be fully proved; and ofttimes moreover, even in these dealeth treacherously[6], but this court instructeth those that enter it that He that judgeth in our case, will bring forward "all things naked and laid open," (Heb. iv. 13.) before the common theatre of the world, and that to be hidden will be impossible. So that Christianity keeps together this our life far more than temporal[7] laws. For if to tremble about secret sins makes a man safer than to fear for such as are open; and if to call him to account even for those offences which be less doth rather excite him unto virtue, than to punish the graver only; then it is easily seen that this rule, more than all others, welds[8] our life together.

[6.] But, if thou wilt, let us consider also the mode of electing the rulers; for here too thou shalt behold the difference to be great. For it is not possible to gain this authority by giving money, but by having displayed a highly virtuous character; and not as unto glory with men and ease unto himself, but as unto toils and labors and the welfare of the many, thus, (I say,) is he that hath been appointed inducted unto this rule. Wherefore also abundant is the assistance he enjoys from the Spirit. And in that case indeed the rule can go no further than to declare merely what is to be done; but in this it addeth besides the help derived from prayers and from the Spirit. But further; in that case indeed is not a word about philosophy, nor doth any sit to teach what a soul is, and what the world, and what we are to be hereafter, and unto what things we shall depart hence, and how we shall achieve virtue. Howbeit of contracts and bonds and money, there is much speech, but of those things not a thought; whereas in the Church one may see that these are the subjects of every discourse. Wherefore also with justice may one call it by all these names, a court of justice, and a hospital, and a school of philosophy, and a nursery of the soul, and a training course for that race that leadeth unto heaven. Further, that this rule is also the mildest of all, even though requiring greater strictness, is plain from hence. For the temporal ruler if he catch an adulterer

---

[1] προπέτεια.
[2] Or, healthiness.
[3] κομῶντα.
[4] συνίστανται.
[5] πατρότης.

[6] προδότης.
[7] ἔξωθεν.
[8] συγκροτεῖ.

straightway punishes him. And yet what is the advantage of this? For this is not to destroy the passion, but to send away the soul with its wound upon it. But this ruler, when he hath detected, considers not how he shall avenge, but how extirpate the passion. For thou indeed dost the same thing, as if when there was a disease of the head, thou shouldest not stay the disease, but cut off the head. But I do not thus: but I cut off the disease. And I exclude him indeed from mysteries and hallowed precincts; but when I have restored him I receive him back again, at once delivered from that viciousness and amended by his repentance. 'And how is it possible,' saith one, 'to extirpate adultery?' It is possible, yea, very possible, if a man comes under these laws. For the Church is a spiritual bath, which wipeth away not filth of body, but stains of soul, by its many methods of repentance. For thou, indeed, both if thou let a man go unpunished hast made him worse, and if thou punish hast sent him away uncured: but I neither let him go unpunished, nor punish him, as thou, but both exact a satisfaction which becomes me, and set that right which hath been done. Wilt thou learn in yet another way how that thou indeed, though drawing swords and displaying

flames to them that offend, workest not any considerable cure; whilst I, without these things, have conducted them to perfect health? But no need have I of arguments or words, but I bring forth earth and sea, and human nature itself, [for witnesses.] And inquire, before this court held its sittings, what was the condition of human affairs; how, not even the names of the good works which now are done, were ever heard of. For who braved death? who despised money? who was indifferent to glory? who, fleeing from the turmoils of life[1], bade welcome to mountains and solitude, the mother of heavenly wisdom? where was at all the name of virginity? For all these things, and more than these, were the good work of this judgment court, the doings of this rule. Knowing these things then, and well understanding that from this proceedeth every benefit of our life, and the reformation of the world, come frequently unto the hearing of the Divine words, and our assemblies here, and the prayers. For if ye thus order yourselves, ye will be able, having displayed a deportment worthy of heaven, to obtain the promised good things; which may all we obtain, through the grace and love towards men of our Lord Jesus Christ, to Whom be glory for ever and ever. Amen.

HOMILY XVI.

2 Cor. vii. 13.

And in your comfort, we joyed the more exceedingly for the joy of Titus, because his spirit hath been refreshed by you all.

SEE again how he exalts their praises, and showeth their love. For having said, 'I was pleased that my Epistle wrought so much and that ye gained so much,' for "I rejoice," he saith, "not that ye were made sorry, but that ye were made sorry unto repentance;" and having shown his own love, for he saith, "Though I wrote unto you, I wrote not for his cause that did the wrong, nor for his cause that suffered the wrong, but that our care for you might be made manifest to you:" again he mentioneth another sign of their good will, which bringeth them great praise and showeth the genuineness of their affection. For, "in your comfort[2]," he saith, "we joyed the more exceedingly for the joy of Titus." And yet this is no sign of one that loveth them exceedingly; rejoic-

ing rather for Titus than for them. 'Yes,' he replies, 'it is, for I joyed not so much for his cause as for yours.' Therefore also he subjoins the reason, saying, "because his bowels were refreshed by you all." He said not, 'he,' but "his bowels;" that is, 'his love for you.' And how were they refreshed? "By all." For this too is a very great praise.

Ver. 14. "For if in anything I have gloried to him on your behalf."

It is high praise when the teacher boasted, for he saith, "I was not put to shame." I therefore rejoiced, because ye showed yourselves to be amended and proved my words by your deeds. So that the honor accruing to me was twofold; first, in that ye had made progress; next, in that I was not found to fall short of the truth.

Ver. 14. "But as we spake always to you in

---

[1] ἐν μέσῳ.

[2] In the R. T. the words "in your comfort" are connected with what precedes, not what follows them. [The Rev. Vers. adopts Chrysostom's connection but changes the pronoun from the second person to the first, reading "in our comfort". C.]

truth, so our glorying also which I made before Titus was found to be truth."

Here he alludes to something further. As we spake all things among you in truth, (for it is probable that he had also spoken to them much in praise of this man[1],) so also, what we said of you to Titus has been proved true.

Ver. 15. "And his inward affection[2] is more abundant toward you."

What follows is in commendation of him, as exceedingly consumed with love and attached to them. And he said not 'his love.' Then that he may not appear to be flattering, he everywhere mentions the causes of his affection ; in order that he may, as I said, both escape the imputation of flattery and the more encourage them by making the praise redound unto them, and by showing that it was they who had infused into him the beginning and ground of this so great love. For having said, "his inward affection is more abundant toward you ;" he added,

"Whilst he remembereth the obedience of you all." Now this both shows that Titus was grateful to his benefactors, seeing he had returned, having them all in his heart, and continually remembereth them, and beareth them on his lips and in his mind ; and also is a greater distinction to the Corinthians, seeing that so vanquished they sent him away. Then he mentions their obedience also, magnifying their zeal : wherefore also he addeth these words,

"How with fear and trembling ye received him." Not with love only, but also with excessive honor. Seest thou how he bears witness to a twofold virtue in them, both that they loved him as a father and had feared him as a ruler, neither for fear dimming love, nor for love relaxing fear. He expressed this also above, "That ye sorrow after a godly sort, what earnest care it wrought in you ; yea what fear, yea what longing."

Ver. 16. "I rejoice therefore, that in every thing I am of good courage concerning you." Seest thou that he rejoiceth more on their account ; 'because,' he saith, 'ye have in no particular shamed your teacher, nor show yourselves unworthy of my testimony.' So that he joyed not so much for Titus' sake, that he enjoyed so great honor ; as for their own, that they had displayed so much good feeling. For that he may not be imagined to joy rather on Titus' account, observe how in this place also he states the reason. As then he said above, "If in anything I have gloried to him on your behalf I was not put to shame ;" so here also, "In everything I am of good courage concerning you." 'Should need require me to

rebuke, I have no apprehension of your being alienated ; or again to boast, I fear not to be convicted of falsehood ; or to praise you as obeying the rein, or as loving, or as full of zeal, I have confidence in you. I bade you cut off, and ye did cut off ; I bade you receive, and ye did receive ; I said before Titus that ye were great and admirable kind of people and knew to reverence teachers : ye proved these things true by your conduct. And he learnt these things not so much from me as from you. At any rate when he returned, he had become a passionate lover of you : your behavior having surpassed what he had been told.'

[2.] Chap. viii. ver. 1. "Moreover, brethren, we make known to you the grace of God which hath been given in the Churches of Macedonia."

Having encouraged them with these encomiums, he again tries exhortation. For on this account he mingled these praises with his rebuke, that he might not by proceeding from rebuke to exhortation make what he had to say ill received ; but having soothed their ears, might by this means pave the way for his exhortation. For he purposeth to discourse of almsgiving ; wherefore also he saith beforehand, "I rejoice that in everything I am of good courage concerning you ; " by their past good works, making them the more ready to this duty also. And he said not at once, 'Therefore give alms,' but observe his wisdom, how he draws from a distance and from on high the preparation for his discourse. For he says, "I make known to you the grace of God which hath been given in the Churches of Macedonia." For that they might not be uplifted he calleth what they did "grace ; " and whilst relating what others did he worketh greater zeal in them by his encomiums on others. And he mentions together two praises of the Macedonians, or rather three ; namely, that they bear trials nobly ; and that they know how to pity ; and that, though poor, they had displayed profuseness in almsgiving, for their property had been also plundered. And when he wrote his Epistle to them, it was as signifying this that he said, "For ye became imitators of the Churches of God which are in Judæa, for ye also suffered the same things of your own countrymen, even as they did of the Jews." (1 Thess. ii. 14.) Hear what he said afterwards in writing to the Hebrews, "For ye took joyfully the spoiling of your possessions." (Heb. x. 34.) But He calls what they did "grace," not in order to keep them humble merely ; but both to provoke them to emulation and to prevent what he said from proving invidious. Wherefore he also added the name of "brethren" so as to undermine all envious feeling ; for he is about to praise them in high-flown

---

[1] i. e. Titus.
[2] Gr. *bowels*.

terms. Listen, at least, to his praises. For having said, " I make known to you the grace of God," he said not ' which hath been given in this or that city,' but praiseth the entire nation, saying, " in the Churches of Macedonia." Then he details also this same grace.

Ver. 2. " How that in much proof of affliction the abundance of their joy."

Seest thou his wisdom? For he says not first, that which he wishes; but another thing before it, that he may not seem to do this of set purpose[1], but to arrive at it by a different connection. " In much proof of affliction." This was what he said in his Epistle to the Macedonians themselves, " Ye became imitators of the Lord, having received the word in much affliction, with joy of the Holy Ghost;" and again, " From you sounded forth the word of the Lord, not only in Macedonia and Achaia, but also in every place, your faith to God-ward is gone forth." (1 Thess. i. 6, 8.) But what is, " in much proof of affliction the abundance of their joy?" Both, he says, happened to them in excess; both the affliction and the joy. Wherefore also the strangeness was great that so great an excess of pleasure sprang up to them out of affliction. For in truth the affliction not only was not the parent of grief, but it even became unto them an occasion of gladness; and this too, though it was " great." Now this he said, to prepare them to be noble and firm in their trials. For they were not merely afflicted, but so as also to have become approved by their patience: yea rather, he says not by their patience, but what was more than patience, "joy." And neither said he " joy " simply, but " abundance of joy," for it sprang up in them, great and unspeakable.

[3.] " And their deep poverty abounded unto the riches of their liberality."

Again, both these with excessiveness. For as their great affliction gave birth to great joy, yea, "abundance of joy," so their great poverty gave birth to great riches of alms. For this he showed, saying, "abounded unto the riches of their liberality." For munificence is determined not by the measure of what is given, but by the mind of those that bestow it. Wherefore he nowhere says, ' the richness of the gifts,' but " the riches of their liberality." Now what he says is to this effect ; ' their poverty not only was no impediment to their being bountiful, but was even an occasion to them of abounding, just as affliction was of feeling joy. For the poorer they were, the more munificent they were and contributed the more readily.' Wherefore also he admires them exceedingly, for that in the midst of so great poverty they had displayed so great munificence. For " their

deep," that is, ' their great and unspeakable,' "poverty," showed their " liberality." But he said not ' showed,' but " abounded ; " and he said not " liberality," but " riches of liberality ; " that is, an equipoise to the greatness of their poverty, or rather much outweighing it, was the bountifulness they displayed. Then he even explains this more clearly, saying,

Ver. 3. " For according to their power, I bear witness." Trustworthy is the witness. "And beyond their power." That is, it " abounded unto the riches of their liberality." Or rather, he makes this plain, not by this expression alone, but also by all that follows ; for he says, " of their own accord." Lo ! yet another excessiveness.

Ver. 4. "With much intreaty." Lo ! yet a third and a fourth. " Praying us." Lo ! even a fifth. And when they were in affliction and in poverty. Here are a sixth and seventh. And they gave with excessiveness. Then since this is what he most of all wishes to provide for in the Corinthians' case, namely, the giving deliberately, he dwells especially upon it, saying, " with much intreaty," and " praying us." ' We prayed not them, but they us.' Pray us what ? " That the grace[2] and the fellowship in the ministering to the saints." Seest thou how he again exalts the deed, calling it by venerable names. For since they were ambitious[3] of spiritual gifts[4], he calls it by the name grace that they might eagerly pursue it ; and again by that of " fellowship," that they might learn that they receive, not give only. ' This therefore they intreated us,' he says, ' that we would take upon us such a ministry[5].'

Ver. 5. " And " this, " not as we hoped." This he says with reference both to the amount and to their afflictions. ' For we could never have hoped,' he says, ' that whilst in so great affliction and poverty, they would even have urged us and so greatly intreated us.' He showed also their carefulness of life in other respects, by saying,

" But first they gave their own selves to the Lord, and to us by the will of God."

' For in everything their obedience was beyond our expectations ; nor because they showed mercy did they neglect the other virtues,' " but first gave themselves to the Lord." What is, "gave themselves to the Lord?" ' They offered up [themselves] ; they showed themselves approved in faith ; they displayed much fortitude in their trials, order, goodness, love, in all things both readiness and zeal.' What means, " and to us ? " ' They were tractable to the rein, loved, obeyed us ; both

[1] ἐπίτηδες.

[2] χάριν.
[3] ζηλωταί.
[4] Literally, spirits.
[5] [Critical authority is altogether in favor of the text of this clause which is adopted in the Rev. Vers. C.]

fulfilling the laws of God and bound unto us by love.' And observe how here also he again shows their earnestness[1], saying, "gave themselves to the Lord." They did not in some things obey God, and in some the world ; but in all things Him ; and gave themselves wholly unto God. For neither because they showed mercy were they filled up with senseless pride, but displaying much lowlymindedness, much obedience, much reverence, much heavenly wisdom, they so wrought their almsdeeds also. But what is, "by the will of God ?" Since he had said, they "gave themselves to us," yet was it not "to us," after the manner of men, but they did this also according to the mind of God.

[4.] Ver. 6. "Insomuch that we exhorted Titus, that as he made a beginning before, so he would also complete in you this grace also[2]."

And what connexion is there here ? Much ; and closely bearing on what went before. ' For because we saw them vehement,' he says, ' and fervent in all things, in temptations, in almsgiving, in their love toward us, in the purity otherwise of their life : in order that ye too might be made their equals, we sent Titus.' Howbeit he did not say this, though he implied it. Behold excessiveness of love. ' For though intreated and desired by them,' he says, ' we were anxious about your state, lest by any means ye should come short of them. Wherefore also we sent Titus, that by this also being stirred up and put in mind, ye might emulate the Macedonians.' For Titus happened to be there when this Epistle was writing. Yet he shows that he had made a beginning in this matter before Paul's exhortation ; "that as he had made a beginning before," he says. Wherefore also he bestows great praise on him ; for instance, in the beginning [of the Epistle] ; "Because I found not Titus my brother, I had no relief for my spirit : " (chap. ii. 13.) and here all those things which he has said, and this too itself. For this also is no light praise, the having begun before even : for this evinces a warm and fervent spirit. Wherefore also he sent him, infusing[3] amongst them in this also a very great incentive unto giving, the presence of Titus. On this account also he extols him with praises, wishing to endear him more exceedingly to the Corinthians. For this too hath a great weight unto persuading, when he who counsels is upon intimate terms. And well does he both once and twice and thrice, having made mention of almsgiving, call ' it grace,' now indeed saying, "Moreover, brethren, I make known to you

the grace of God bestowed on the Churches of Macedonia ; " and now, "they of their own accord, praying us with much intreaty in regard of this grace and fellowship : " and again, "that as he had begun, so he would also finish in you this grace also."

[5.] For this is a great good and a gift of God ; and rightly done assimilates us, so far as may be, unto God ; for such an one[4] is in the highest sense a man. A certain one, at least, giving a model of a man has mentioned this, for " Man," saith he, " is a great thing ; and a merciful man is an honorable thing." (Prov. xx, 6. LXX.) Greater is this gift than to raise the dead. For far greater is it to feed Christ when an hungered than to raise the dead by the name of Jesus : for in the former case thou doest good to Christ, in the latter He to thee. And the reward surely comes by doing good, not by receiving good. For here indeed, in the case of miracles I mean, thou art God's debtor ; in that of almsgiving, thou hast God for a debtor. Now it is almsgiving, when it is done with willingness, when with bountifulness, when thou deemest thyself not to give but to receive, when done as if thou wert benefitted, as if gaining and not losing ; for so this were not a grace. For he that showeth mercy on another ought to feel joyful, not peevish. For how is it not absurd, if whilst removing another's downheartedness, thou art thyself downhearted? for so thou no longer sufferest it to be alms. For if thou art downhearted because thou hast delivered another from downheartedness, thou furnishest an example of extreme cruelty and inhumanity ; for it were better not to deliver him, than so to deliver him. And why art thou also downhearted at all, O man? for fear thy gold should diminish? If such are thy thoughts, do not give at all : if thou art not quite sure that it is multiplied for thee in heaven, do not bestow. But thou seekest the recompense here. Wherefore? Let thine alms be alms, and not traffic. Now many have indeed received a recompense even here ; but have not so received it, as if they should have an advantage over those who received it not here ; but some of them as being weaker than they ought, because they were not so strongly attracted by the things which are there. And as those who are greedy, and ill-mannered[5], and slaves of their bellies, being invited to a royal banquet, and unable to wait till the proper time, just like little children mar their own enjoyment, by taking food beforehand and stuffing themselves with inferior dishes : even so in truth do these who seek for and receive [recompense]

---

[1] ἐπίτασιν
[2] ἐν ὑμῖν St. C. εἰς ὑμᾶς, R. T., [which is the true text. C.]
[3] ἐντιθεὶς

[4] τοῦτο, in sense equivalent to ὁ τοιοῦτος. See Dr. Field's *Index to Hom. on St. Matt.* on the word οὗτος.
[5] ἀπειρόκαλοι.

here, diminish their reward there. Further, when thou lendest, thou wishest to receive thy principal after a longer interval, and perhaps even not to receive it at all, in order that by the delay thou mayest make the interest greater; but, in this case, dost thou ask back immediately; and that too when thou art about to be not here, but there forever; when thou art about not to be here to be judged, but to render thine account? And if indeed one were building thee mansions where thou wert not going to remain, thou wouldest deem it to be a loss; but now, desirest thou here to be rich, whence possibly thou art to depart even before the evening? Knowest thou not that we live in a foreign land, as though strangers and sojourners? Knowest thou not that it is the lot of sojourners to be ejected when they think not, expect not? which is also our lot. For this reason then, whatsoever things we have prepared, we leave here. For the Lord does not allow us to receive them and depart, if we have built houses, if we have bought fields, if slaves, if gear, if any other such thing. But not only does He not allow us to take them and depart hence, but doth not even account to thee the price of them. For He forwarned thee that thou shouldest not build, nor spend what is other men's but thine own. Why therefore, leaving what is thine own, dost thou work and be at cost in what is another's, so as to lose both thy toil and thy wages and to suffer the extremest punishment? Do not so, I beseech thee; but seeing we are by nature sojourners, let us also be so by choice; that we be not there sojourners and dishonored and cast out. For if we are set upon being citizens here, we shall be so neither here nor there; but if we continue to be sojourners, and live in such wise as sojourners ought to live in, we shall enjoy the freedom of citizens both here and there. For the just, although having nothing, will both dwell here amidst all men's possessions as though they were his own; and also, when he hath departed to heaven, shall see those his eternal habitations. And he shall both here suffer no discomfort, (for none will ever be able to make him a stranger that hath every land for his city;) and when he hath been restored to his own country, shall receive the true riches. In order that we may gain both the things of this life and of that, let us use aright the things we have. For so shall we be citizens of the heavens, and shall enjoy much boldness; whereunto may we all attain, through the grace and love towards men of our Lord Jesus Christ, with Whom to the Father with the Holy Ghost, be glory and power for ever. Amen.

HOMILY XVII.

2 Cor. viii. 7.

Therefore that[1] ye abound[2] in every thing; in faith and utterance, and knowledge, and in all earnestness.

See again his exhortation accompanied with commendations, greater commendations. And he said not, 'that ye give,' but "that ye abound; in faith," namely, of the gifts, and " in utterance," the word of wisdom, and " knowledge," namely, of the doctrines, and " in all earnestness," to the attaining of all other virtue.

"And in your love," that, namely of which I have before spoken, of which I have also made proof.

"That ye may abound in this grace also." Seest thou that for this reason it was that he began by those praises, that advancing forward he might draw them on to the same diligence in these things also.

Ver. 8. "I speak not by way of commandment."

See how constantly he humors them, how he avoids offensiveness, and is not violent nor compulsory; or rather what he says hath both these, with the inoffensiveness of that which is uncompelled. For after he had repeatedly exhorted them and had greatly commended the Macedonians, in order that this might not seem to constitute a necessity, he says,

"I speak not by way of commandment, but as proving through the earnestness of others, the sincerity also of your love."

'Not as doubting it,' (for that is not what he would here imply,) 'but to make it approved, display it and frame it unto greater strength. For I therefore say these things that I may provoke you to the same forwardness. And I

---

[1] ὡς, R. T. ὥσπερ.
[2] περισσεύητε, R. T. περισσεύετε. [There is no reason for following Chrysostom in his variation from the common text. C.]

mention their zeal to brighten, to cheer, to stimulate your inclinations.' Then from this he proceeded to another and a greater point. For he lets slip no mode of persuasion, but moves heaven and earth[1] in handling his argument. For he exhorted them both by other men's praises, saying, Ye know " the grace of God which hath been given in the Churches of Macedonia;" and by their own, "therefore that ye abound in everything, in utterance and knowledge." For this hath power to sting man more that he falls short of himself, than that he does so of others. Then he proceeds afterwards to the head and crown of his persuasion.

Ver. 9. "For ye know the grace of our Lord, that though He was rich, yet for our sakes He became poor, that we through His poverty might become rich."

'For have in mind,' says he, 'ponder and consider the grace of God and do not lightly pass it by, but aim at realizing[2] the greatness of it both as to extent and nature[3], and thou wilt grudge nothing of thine. He emptied Himself of His glory that ye, not through His riches but through His poverty, might be rich. If thou believest not that poverty is productive of riches, have in mind thy Lord and thou wilt doubt no longer. For had He not become poor, thou wouldest not have become rich. For this is the marvel, that poverty hath made riches rich.' And by riches here he meaneth the knowledge of godliness, the cleansing away of sins, justification, sanctification, the countless good things which He bestowed upon us and purposeth to bestow. And all these things accrued to us through His poverty. What poverty? Through His taking flesh on Him and becoming man and suffering what He suffered. And yet he owed not this, but thou dost owe to Him.

Ver. 10. "And herein I give you[4] my advice for your profit."

See how again he is careful to give no offence and softens down what he says, by these two things, by saying, "I give advice," and, "for your profit." 'For, neither do I compel and force you,' says he, 'or demand it from unwilling subjects; nor do I say these things with an eye so much to the receivers' benefit as to yours.' Then the instance also which follows is drawn from themselves, and not from others.

Who were the first to make a beginning a year ago, not only to do, but also to will.

See how he shows both that themselves were willing, and had come to this resolution without persuasion. For since he had borne this

witness to the Thessalonians, that "of their own accord with much intreaty," they had prosecuted this giving of alms; he is desirous of showing of these also that this good work is their own. Wherefore he said, "not only to do, but also to will," and not "begun," but "begun before, a year ago." Unto these things therefore I exhort you, whereunto ye beforehand bestirred yourselves with all forwardness.

Ver. 11. "And now also ye have completed[5] the doing of it."

He said not, ye have done it, but, ye have put a completion to it,

"That as there was the readiness to will, so also [there may be] the completion also out of your ability."

That this good work halt not at readiness but receive also the reward that follows upon deeds.

[2.] Ver. 12. "For if the readiness is there, it is acceptable according as a man hath, not according as he hath not."

See wisdom unspeakable. In that (having pointed out those who were doing beyond their power, I mean the Thessalonians, and having praised them for this and said, "I bear them record that even beyond their power;") he exhorteth the Corinthians to do only "after" their power, leaving the example to do its own work; for he knew that not so much exhortation, as emulation, inciteth unto imitation of the like; wherefore he saith, "For if the readiness is there, it is acceptable according as a man hath, not according as he hath not."

'Fear not,' he means, 'because I have said these things, for what I said was an encomium upon their munificence[6], but God requires things after a man's power,' "according as he hath, not according as he hath not." For the word "is acceptable," here implies 'is required.' And he softens[7] it greatly, in confident reliance upon this example, and as winning them more surely by leaving them at liberty. Wherefore also he added,

Ver. 13. "For I say not this, that others may be eased, and ye distressed."

And yet Christ praised the contrary conduct in the widow's case, that she emptied out all of her living and gave out of her want. (Mark xii. 43.) But because he was discoursing to Corinthians amongst whom he chose to suffer hunger; "for it were good for me rather to die, than that any man should make my glorying void;" (1 Cor. ix. 15.) he therefore uses a tempered exhortation, praising indeed those who had done beyond their power, but not compelling these to do so; not because he

---

[1] πάντα κινεῖ
[2] στοχάσασθε.
[3] ὅση καὶ ἡλίκη
[4] St. Chrysostom inserts ὑμῖν, and for τοῦτο γὰρ ὑμῖν συμφέρει reads, πρὸς τὸ ὑμῶν συμφέρον.

[5] ἐπετελέσατε. The *Textus Receptus* gives ἐπιτελέσατε, which appears to be required in what follows. [The aorist seems to be peculiar to Chrysostom. C.]
[6] φιλοτιμίας.
[7] λιπαίνει.

did not desire it, but because they were somewhat weak. For wherefore doth he praise those, because " in much proof of affliction the abundance of their joy and their deep poverty abounded unto the riches of their liberality: " and because they gave " beyond their power ? " is it not very evident that it is as inducing these also to this conduct ? So that even if he appears to permit a lower standard ; he doth so, that by it he may raise them to this. Consider, for instance, how even in what follows he is covertly preparing the way for this. For having said these things, he added,

Ver. 14. " Your abundance being a supply for their want."

For not only by the words he has before used but by these also, he is desirous of making the commandment light. Nor yet from this consideration alone, but from that of the recompense also, again he maketh it easier ; and uttereth higher things than they deserve, saying, " That there may be equality at this time, and their abundance " a supply " for your want." Now what is it that he saith ? ' Ye are flourishing[1] in money ; they in life[2] and in boldness towards God.' Give ye to them, therefore, of the money which ye abound in but they have not ; that ye may receive of that boldness wherein they are rich and ye are lacking.' See how he hath covertly prepared for their giving beyond their power and of their want. ' For,' he saith, ' if thou desirest to receive of their abundance, give of thine abundance ; but if to win for thyself the whole, thou wilt give of thy want and beyond thy power.' He doth not say this, however, but leaves it to the reasoning of his hearers ; and himself meanwhile works out his object and the exhortation that was meet, adding in keeping with what appeared, the words, that " there may be equality at this time." How equality ? You and they mutually giving your superabundance, and filling up your wants. And what sort of equality is this, giving spiritual things for carnal ? for great is the advantage on that side ; how then doth he call it " equality ? " either in respect of each abounding and wanting, doth he say that this [equality] takes place ; or else in respect of the present life only. And therefore after saying " equality," he added, " at this time." Now this he said, both to subdue the high-mindedness of the rich, and to show that after our departure hence the spiritual possess the greater advantage. For here indeed we all enjoy much equality of honor ; but then there will be a wide distinction and a very great superiority, when the just shine brighter than the sun. Then since he showed that they were to be not only giving, but also receiving, and

more, in return ; he tries by a further consideration to make them forward, showing that if they did not give of their substance to others, they would not gain anything by gathering all together within. And he adduces an ancient story, thus saying,

Ver. 15. " As it is written, He that gathered much had nothing over, and he that gathered little had no lack."

Now this happened in the case of the manna. For both they that gathered more, and they that gathered less, were found to have the same quantity, God in this way punishing insatiableness. And this he said at once both to alarm them by what then happened, and to persuade them never to desire to have more nor to grieve at having less. And this one may see happening now in things of this life not in the manna only. For if we all fill but one belly, and live the same length of time, and clothe one body ; neither will the rich gain aught by his abundance nor the poor lose aught by his poverty.

[3.] Why then tremblest thou at poverty ? and why pursuest thou after wealth ? ' I fear,' saith one, ' lest I be compelled to go to other men's doors and to beg from my neighbor.' And I constantly hear also many praying to this effect, and saying, ' Suffer me not at any time to stand in need of men ?' And I laugh exceedingly when I hear these prayers, for this fear is even childish. For every day and in every thing, so to speak, do we stand in need of one another. So that these are the words of an unthinking and puffed up spirit, and that doth not clearly discern the nature of things. Seest thou not that all of us are in need one of another ? The soldier of the artisan, the artisan of the merchant, the merchant of the husbandman, the slave of the free man, the master of the slave, the poor man of the rich, the rich man of the poor, he that worketh not of him that giveth alms, he that bestoweth of him that receiveth. For he that receiveth alms supplieth a very great want, a want greater than any. For if there were no poor, the greater part of our salvation would be overthrown, in that we should not have where to bestow our wealth. So that even the poor man who appears to be more useless than any is the most useful of any. But if to be in need of another is disgraceful, it remains to die ; for it is not possible for a man to live who is afraid of this. ' But,' saith one, ' I cannot bear brows arched [in scorn.]' Why dost thou in accusing another of arrogance, disgrace thyself by this accusation ? for to be unable to endure the inflation of a proud soul is arrogant. And why fearest thou these things, and tremblest at these things, and on account of these things which are worthy of no account, dreadest poverty also ? For if thou be rich, thou

---

[1] κομᾶτε.
[2] i. e., holiness of life.

wilt stand in need of more, yea of more and meaner. For just in proportion to thy wealth dost thou subject thyself to this curse. So ignorant art thou of what thou prayest when thou askest for wealth in order to be in need of no man ; just as if one having come to a sea, where there is need both of sailors and a ship and endless stores of outfit, should pray that he might be in need of nothing at all. For if thou art desirous of being exceedingly independent of every one, pray for poverty ; and [then] if thou art dependent on any, thou wilt be so only for bread and raiment ; but in the other case thou wilt have need of others, both for lands, and for houses, and for imposts, and for wages, and for rank, and for safety, and for honor, and for magistrates, and those subject to them, both those in the city and those in the country, and for merchants, and for shopkeepers. Do you see that those words are words of extreme carelessness? For, in a word, if to be in need one of another appears to thee a dreadful thing, [know that] it is impossible altogether to escape it ; but if thou wilt avoid the tumult, (for thou mayest take refuge in the waveless haven of poverty,) cut off the great tumult of thy affairs, and deem it not disgraceful to be in need of another ; for this is the doing of God's unspeakable wisdom. For if we stand in need one of another, yet even the compulsion of this need draweth us not together unto love ; had we been independent, should we not have been untamed wild beasts? Perforce and of compulsion God hath subjected us one to another, and every day we are in collision[1] one with another. And had He removed this curb, who is there who would readily have longed after his neighbor's love? Let us then neither deem this to be disgraceful, nor pray against it and say, ' Grant us not to stand in need of any one ; ' but let us pray and say, ' Suffer us not, when we are in need, to refuse those who are able to help us.' It is not the standing in need of others, but seizing the things of others, that is grievous. But now we have never prayed in respect to that nor said, ' Grant me not to covet other men's goods ; ' but to stand in need, this we think a fit subject of deprecation[2]. Yet Paul stood in need many times, and was not ashamed ; nay, even prided himself upon it, and praised those that had ministered to him, saying, " For ye sent once and again to my need ; " (Phil. iv. 16.) and again, " I robbed other Churches, taking wages of them that I might minister unto you." (2 Cor. xi. 8.) It is no mark therefore of a generous temper, but of weakness and of a low minded and senseless spirit, to be ashamed of this. For it is even God's decree that we should

stand in need one of another. Push not therefore thy philosophy beyond the mean. ' But,' saith one, ' I cannot bear a man that is entreated often and complieth not.' And how shall God bear thee who art entreated by Him, and yet obeyest not ; and entreated too in things that advantage thee? " For we are ambassadors on behalf of Christ," (2 Cor. v. 20.) saith he, " as though God were entreating by us ; be ye reconciled unto God." ' And yet, I am His servant,' saith he. And what of that? For when thou, the servant, art drunken, whilst He, the Master, is hungry and hath not even necessary food, how shall thy name of servant stand thee in stead? Nay, this itself will even the more weigh thee down, when thou indeed abidest in a three-storied dwelling whilst He owns not even a decent shelter ; when thou [liest] upon soft couches whilst He hath not even a pillow. ' But,' saith one, ' I have given.' But thou oughtest not to leave off so doing. For then only wilt thou have an excuse, when thou hast not what [to give], when thou possessest nothing ; but so long as thou hast, (though thou have given to ten thousand,) and there be others hungering, there is no excuse for thee. But when thou both shuttest up corn and raisest the price, and devisest other unusual tricks of traffic ; what hope of salvation shalt thou have henceforth? Thou hast been bidden to give freely to the hungry, but thou dost not give at a suitable price even. He emptied Himself of so great glory for thy sake, but thou dost not count Him deserving even of a loaf ; but thy dog is fed to fulness whilst Christ wastes with hunger ; and thy servant bursteth with surfeiting whilst thy Lord and his is in want of necessary food. And how are these the deeds of friends? " Be be reconciled unto God," (2 Cor. v. 20.) for these are [the deeds] of enemies and such as are in hostility.

[4.] Let us then think with shame on the great benefits we have already received, the great benefits we are yet to receive. And if a poor man come to us and beg, let us receive him with much good will, comforting, raising him up with [our] words, that we ourselves also may meet with the like, both from God and from men. " For whatsoever ye would that they should do unto you, do ye also unto them." (Mat. vii. 12.) Nothing burdensome, nothing offensive, doth this law contain. ' What thou wouldest receive, that do,' it saith. The return is equal. And it said not, ' what thou wouldest not receive, that do not,' but what is more. For that indeed is an abstinence from evil things, but this is a doing of good things, in which the other is involved. Also He said not ' that do ye also wish, but do, to them.' And what is the advantage? " This is the Law and

---

[1] συγκρουόμεθα.
[2] ἀπευκταῖον.

the Prophets." Wouldest thou have mercy shown thee? Then show mercy. Wouldest thou obtain forgiveness? Then grant it. Wouldest thou not be evil spoken of? Then speak not evil. Longest thou to receive praise? Then bestow it. Wouldest thou not be wronged? Then do not thou plunder. Seest thou how He shows that virtue is natural, and that we need no external laws nor teachers? For in the things we wish to receive, or not to receive from our neighbors, we legislate unto ourselves. So that if thou wouldest not receive a thing, yet doest it, or if thou wouldest receive it, yet doest it not, thou art become self-con-demned and art henceforth without any excuse, on the ground of ignorance and of not knowing what ought to be done. Wherefore, I beseech you, having set up this law in ourselves for ourselves, and reading this that is written so clearly and succinctly, let us become such to our neighbors, as we would have them be to ourselves; that may we both enjoy present immunity[4], and obtain the future good things, though the grace and love towards men of our Lord Jesus Christ, with Whom to the Father, together with the Holy Spirit, be glory, power, honor, now and for ever, and world without end. Amen.

HOMILY XVIII.

2 COR. viii. 16.

But thanks be to God, Which put[1] the same earnest care for you into the heart of Titus.

AGAIN he praises Titus. For since he had discoursed of almsgiving, he afterwards discourseth also of those who are to receive the money from them and carry it away. For this was of aid[2] towards this collection, and towards increasing the forwardness of the contributors. For he that feels confidence as to him that ministereth[3], and suspects not those who are to be receivers, gives with the fuller bountifulness. And that this might be the case then also, hear how he commends those that had come for this purpose, the first of whom was Titus. Wherefore also he saith, "But thanks be to God, Which put (literally, 'gave') the same earnest care into the heart of Titus." What is "the same?" Which he had also in respect to the Thessalonians, or "the same" with me. And mark here wisdom. Showing this to be the work of God, he also gives thanks to Him that gave, so as to incite by this also. 'For if God stirred him up and sent him to you, He asks through Him. Think not therefore that what has happened is of men.' And whence is it manifest that God incited him? Ver. 17. "For indeed he accepted our exhortation, but being himself very earnest, he went forth of his own accord."

Observe how he also represents him as fulfilling his own part, and needing no prompting from others. And having mentioned the grace of God, he doth not leave the whole to be God's; again, that by this also he may win them unto greater love, having said that he was stirred up from himself[5] also. For, "being very earnest, he went forth of his own accord," 'he seized at the thing, he rushed upon the treasure, he considered your service to be his own advantage; and because he loved you exceedingly, he needed not the exhortation I gave; but though he was exhorted by me also, yet it was not by that he was stirred up; but from himself and by the grace of God.'

Ver. 18. "And we have sent together with him the brother whose praise in the Gospel is spread through all the Churches."

And who is this brother? Some indeed say, Luke, because of the history which he wrote, but some, Barnabas; for he calls the unwritten preaching also Gospel. And for what cause does he not mention their names; whilst he both makes Titus known (vid. also ver. 23.) by name, and praises him for his cooperation in the Gospel, (seeing that he was so useful that by reason of his absence even Paul could do nothing great and noble; for, "because I found not Titus my brother, I had no relief for my spirit,"—c. ii. 13.) and for his love towards them, (for, saith he, "his inward affection is more abundant towards you;"—c. vii. 15.) and for his zeal in this matter ("for," he saith, "of his own accord he went")? But these he neither equally commends, nor mentions by name? What then is one to say? Perhaps

---

[1] [The author here has the aorist, but elsewhere has the present participle which seems to be better sustained, and is adopted in the Rev. Vers. C.]
[2] συνεβάλλετο.
[3] Or, 'in respect to that which is ministered.'

[3] ἀδείας.
[4] οἴκοθεν

they did not know them; wherefore he does not dwell upon their praises because as yet they had had no experience of them, but only says so much as was sufficient for their commendation unto them (i.e. the Corinthians,) and to their escaping all evil suspicion. However, let us see on what score he eulogizes this man himself also. On what score then does he eulogize? First, praising him from his preaching; that he not only preached, but also as he ought, and with the befitting earnestness. For he said not, 'he preaches and proclaims the Gospel,' but, "whose praise is in the Gospel." And that he may not seem to flatter him, he brings not one or two or three men, but whole Churches to testify to him, saying, "through all the churches." Then he makes him respected also from the judgment of those that had chosen him. And this too is no light matter. Therefore after saying, "Whose praise in the Gospel is spread through all the churches," he added,

Ver. 19. "And not only so."

What is, "and not only so?" 'Not only on this account,' he says, 'is respect due to him, that he is approved as a preacher and is praised by all.'

"But he was also appointed by the churches along with us."

Whence it seems to me, that Barnabas is the person intimated. And he signifies his dignity to be great, for he shows also for what office he was appointed. For he saith,

"To travel with us in the matter of this grace which is ministered by us." Seest thou how great are these praises of him? He shone as a preacher of the Gospel and had all the churches testifying to this. He was chosen by us; and unto the same office with Paul, and everywhere was partner with him, both in his trials and in his dangers, for this is implied in the word "travel." But what is, "with this grace which is ministered by us?" So as to proclaim the word, he means, and to preach the Gospel; or to minister also in respect of the money; yea rather, he seems to me to refer to both of these. Then he adds,

"To the glory of the same Lord, and to show your readiness[1]." What he means is this: 'We thought good,' he says, 'that he should be chosen with us and be appointed unto this work, so as to become a dispenser and a minister of the sacred money.' Nor was this a little matter. For, "Look ye out," it saith, "from among you seven men of good report;" (Acts vi. 3.) and he was chosen by the churches, and there was a vote of the whole people taken. What is,

"to the glory of the same Lord, and your readiness?" 'That both God may be glorified and ye may become the readier, they who are to receive this money being of proved character, and no one[2] able to engender any false suspicion against them. Therefore we sought out such persons, and entrusted not the whole to one person only, that he might escape this suspicion also; but we sent both Titus and another with him. Then to interpret this same expression, "to the glory of the Lord and your ready mind:" he added,

Ver. 20. "Avoiding this, that any man should blame us in the matter of this bounty which is ministered by us."

What can this be which is said? A thing worthy of the virtue of Paul; and showing the greatness of his tender care and his condescension. 'For,' he says, 'that none should suspect us, nor have the slightest cavil against us, as though we purloined aught of the money placed in our hands; therefore we send such persons, and not one only, but even two or three. Seest thou how he clears them of all suspicions? Not on account of the Gospel, nor of their having been chosen merely; but also, from their being persons of proved character, (and for this very reason) having been chosen, that they might not be suspected. And he said not 'that ye should not blame,' but 'that no other person should.' And yet it was on their account that he did this; and he implied as much in saying, "to the glory of the same Lord, and your readiness:" however, he does not wish to wound them; and so expresses himself differently,

"Avoiding this." And he is not satisfied with this either, but by what he adds, soothes again, saying,

"In the matter of this bounty which is ministered by us," and mingling his severity with praise. For that they might not feel hurt, and say, 'Is he obliged then to eye us stealthily, and are we so miserable as ever to have been suspected of these things?' Providing a correction against this too, he says, 'the money sent by you is of large amount, and this abundance, that is, the large amount of the money, is enough to afford suspicion to the evil-minded had we not offered that security[3].'

Ver. 21. For "we take thought for things, honorable not only in the sight of the Lord, but also in the sight of men."

What can compare with Paul? For he said not, 'Perdition and woe to him who chooses to suspect anything of the kind: so long as my conscience does not condemn me, I waste not a

---

[1] [The Rev. Vers. adopts a reading which omits *same* before Lord's, and puts *our* for *your*.]

[2] Or 'nothing.'
[3] τὴν ἀσφαλείαν.

thought on those who suspect.' Rather, the weaker they were, the more he condescended. For it is meet not to be angry with, but help, him that is sick. And yet from what sin are we so removed as he was from any such suspicion? For not even a demon could have suspected that blessed saint of this unfaithfulness. But still although so far removed from that evil suspicion, he does everything and resorts to every expedient[1], so as not to leave a shadow even to those who might be desirous in any way[2] of suspecting something wrong; and he avoids not only accusations, but also blame and the slightest censure, even bare suspicion.

[2.] Ver. 22. "And we have sent with them our brother."

Behold, again he adds yet another, and him also with an encomium; both his own judgment, and many other witnesses [to him].

"Whom," saith he, "we have many times proved earnest in many things, but now much more earnest." And having praised him from his own good works, he extols him also from his love towards them; and what he said of Titus, that "being very earnest he went forth of his own accord;" this he says of this person also, saying, "but now much more earnest;" laying up beforehand for them the seeds of [the proof of their] love toward the Corinthians.

And then, after having showed forth their virtue, he exhorts them also on their behalf, saying,

Ver. 23. "Whether any inquire about Titus; he is my partner and my fellow-worker to youward."

What is, "Whether about Titus?" 'If,' says he, 'it be necessary to say any thing, this I have to say,' "that he is my partner and fellow-worker to youward." For he either means this; or, 'if ye will do anything for Titus, ye will do it unto no ordinary person, for he is "my partner."' And whilst appearing to be praising him, he magnifies them, showing them to be so disposed towards himself as that it were sufficient ground of honor amongst them that any one should appear to be his "partner." But, nevertheless, he was not content with this, but he also added another thing, saying, "fellow-worker to youward." Not merely "fellow-worker," 'but in matters concerning you, in your progress, in your growth, in our friendship, in our zeal for you;' which last would avail most especially to endear[3] him unto them.

"Or our brethren:" 'or whether you wish,' he says, 'to hear any thing about the others: they too have great claims to be commended to you. For they also,' he saith, 'are our brethren, and,

"The messengers of the Churches," ' that is, sent by the Churches. Then, which is greater than all,

"The glory of Christ;" for to Him is referred whatever shall be done to them. 'Whether then ye wish to receive them as brethren, or as Apostles of the Churches, or as acting for the glory of Christ; ye have many motives for good will towards them. For on behalf of Titus, I have to say, that he is both "my partner," and a lover of you; on behalf of these, that they are "brethren," that they are "the messengers of the churches," that they are "the glory of Christ." Seest thou that it is plain from hence also, that they were of such as were unknown to them? For otherwise he would have set them off by those things with which he had also set off Titus, namely, his love towards them. But whereas as yet they were not known to them, 'Receive them,' he says, ' as brethren, as messengers of the churches, as acting for the glory of Christ.' On which account he adds;

Ver. 24. "Wherefore show ye unto them, to the person[4] of the churches, the proof of your love, and of our glorying on your behalf."

'Now show,' he saith, 'how ye love us; and how we do not lightly nor vainly boast in you: and this ye will show, if ye show forth love towards them.' Then he also makes his words more solemn, by saying, "unto the person of the churches." He means, to the glory, the honor, of the churches. 'For if ye honor them, ye have honored the churches that sent them. For the honor passeth not to them alone, but also to those that sent them forth, who ordained them, and more than these, unto the glory of God.' For when we honor those that minister to Him, the kind reception[5] passeth unto Him, unto the common body of the churches. Now this too is no light thing, for great is the potency of that assembly.

[3.] Certain it is at least that the prayer of the churches loosed Peter from his chains, opened the mouth of Paul; their voice in no slight degree equips those that arrive unto spiritual rule. Therefore indeed it is that both he who is going to ordain calleth at that time for their prayers also, and that they add their votes and assent by acclamations which the initiated know: for it is not lawful before the uninitiated to unbare all things. But there are occasions in which there is no difference at all between the priest and those under him; for instance, when we are

---

[1] πραγματεύεται.
[2] κἂν ὁπωσοῦν.
[3] οἰκειῶσαι.

[4] εἰς πρόσωπον. A. V. 'before,' but St. Chrysostom seems to understand the words, 'unto the person of.' [Nearly all expositors take the phrase to mean "in the face (or presence) of the churches." C.]
[5] τὰ τῆς εὐφημίας.

to partake[1] of the awful mysteries; for we are all alike counted worthy of the same things: not as under the Old Testament [when] the priest ate some things and those under him others, and it was not lawful for the people to partake of those things whereof the priest partook. But not so now, but before all one body is set and one cup. And in the prayers also, one may observe the people contributing much. For in behalf of the possessed, in behalf of those under penance, the prayers are made in common both by the priest and by them; and all say one prayer, the prayer replete with pity. Again when we exclude from the holy precincts those who are unable to partake of the holy table, it behoveth that another prayer be offered, and we all alike fall upon the ground, and all alike rise up. Again, in the most awful mysteries themselves, the priest prays for the people and the people also pray for the priest; for the words, " with thy spirit," are nothing else than this. The offering of thanksgiving again is common: for neither doth he give thanks alone, but also all the people. For having first taken their voices, next when they assent that it is "meet and right so to do," then he begins the thanksgiving. And why marvellest thou that the people any where utter aught with the priest, when indeed even with the very Cherubim, and the powers above, they send up in common those sacred hymns? Now I have said all this in order that each one of the laity also may be wary[2], that we may understand that we are all one body, having such difference amongst ourselves as members with members; and may not throw the whole upon the priests but ourselves also so care for the whole Church as for a body common to us. For this course will provide for our[3] greater safety, and for your greater growth unto virtue. Here, at least, in the case of the Apostles, how frequently they admitted the laity to share in their decisions. For when they ordained the seven, (Acts vi. 2, 3.) they first communicated with the people; and when Peter ordained Matthias, with all that were then present, both men and women. (Acts i. 15, &c.) For here[4] is no pride of rulers nor slavishness in the ruled; but a spiritual rule, in this particular usurping[5] most, in taking on itself the greater share of the labor and of the care which is on your behalf, not in seeking larger honors. For so ought the Church to dwell as one house; as one body so to be all disposed; just as therefore there is both one Baptism, and one table, and one fountain, and one creation, and one Father. Why then are

we divided, when so great[6] things unite us; why are we torn asunder? For we are compelled again to bewail the same things, which I have lamented often. The state in which we are calls for lamentation; so widely are we severed from each other, when we ought to image the conjunction[7] of one body. For in this way will he that is greater, be able to gain even from him that is less. For if Moses learnt from his father-in-law somewhat expedient which himself had not perceived, (Exod. xviii. 14, &c.) much more in the Church may this happen. And how then came it that what he that was an unbeliever perceived, he that was spiritual perceived not? That all those of that time might understand that he was a man; and though he divide the sea, though he cleave the rock, he needeth the influence of God, and that those acts were not of man's nature, but of God's power. And so let another rise up and speak; and so now, if such and such an one doth not say expedient things, let another rise up and speak; though he be an inferior, yet if he say somewhat to the purpose[8], confirm his opinion; and even if he be of the very meanest, do not show him disrespect. For no one of these is at so great a distance from his neighbor, as Moses' father-in-law was from him, yet he disdained not to listen to him, but even admitted his opinion, and was persuaded, and recorded it; and was not ashamed to hand down the circumstances to history; casting down [so] the pride of the many. Wherefore also he left this story to the world[9] engraven as it were on a pillar, for he knew that it would be useful to many. Let us then not overlook those who give us behoveful counsel, even though they be of the meaner sort, nor insist that those counsels prevail which we have ourselves introduced; but whatever shall appear to be best, let that be approved by all. For many of duller sight have perceived things sooner than those of acute vision, by means of diligence and attention. And say not, " why dost thou call me to council, if thou hearkenest not to what I say?" These accusations are not a counsellor's, but a despot's. For the counsellor hath only power to speak his own opinion; but if something else appear more profitable, and yet he will carry his own opinion into effect, he is no longer a counsellor but a despot, as I said. Let us not, then, act in this manner; but having freed our souls from all arrogancy and pride, let us consider, not how our counsels only may stand, but how that opinion which is best may prevail, even though it may not have been

---

[1] Literally, ' enjoy.'
[2] νήφη
[3] The reading of this passage has for the first time been rendered sound by Mr. Field's labors.
[4] i. e., in the Church.
[5] πλεονεκτοῦσα.

[6] Or, so many.
[7] συνάφειαν
[8] τῶν συντελούντων.
[9] τῷ βίῳ. See Wisdom x. 8. for this use of the word.

brought forward by us. For no light gain will be ours, even though we should not have discovered what behoveth, if ourselves accepted what has been pointed out by others; and abundant is the reward we shall receive from God, and so too shall we best attain to glory. For as he is wise that speaketh that which is behoveful, so shall we that have accepted it, ourselves also reap the praise of prudence and of candor. Thus if both houses and states, thus too if the Church be ordered, she will receive a larger increase[1]; and so too shall we ourselves, having thus best ordered our present lives, receive the good things to come : whereunto may we all attain, through the grace and love towards men of our Lord Jesus Christ, to Whom be glory for ever and ever. Amen.

HOMILY XIX.

2 COR. IX. 1.

For as touching the ministering to the saints, it is superfluous for me to write to you.

THOUGH he had said so much about it, he says here, " It is superfluous for me to write to you." And his wisdom is shown not only in this, that though he had said so much about it, he saith, " it is superfluous for me to write to you," but in that he yet again speaketh of it. For what he said indeed a little above, he said concerning those who received the money, to ensure them the enjoyment of great honor : but what he said before that, (his account of the Macedonians, that "their deep poverty abounded unto the riches of their liberality," and all the rest,) was concerning loving-kindness and almsgiving. But nevertheless even though he had said so much before and was going to speak again, he says, " it is superfluous for me to write to you." And this he does the rather to win them to himself. For a man who has so high a reputation as not to stand in need even of advice, is ashamed to appear inferior to, and come short of, that opinion of him. And he does this often in accusation also, using the rhetorical figure, omission, for this is very effective. For the judge seeing the magnanimity of the accuser entertains no suspicions even. For he argues, ' he who when he might say much, yet saith it not, how should he invent what is not true ? ' And he gives occassion to suspect even more than he says, and invests himself with the presumption of a good disposition. This also in his advice and in his praises he does. For having said, " It is superfluous for me to write to you," observe how he advises them.

" For I know your readiness of which I glory on your behalf to them of Macedonia." Now it was a great thing that he even knew it himself, but much greater, that he also published it to others : for the force it has is greater : for they would not like to be so widely disgraced. Seest thou his wisdom of purpose ? He exhorted them by others' example, the Macedonians, for, he says, " I make known to you the grace of God which hath been given in the Churches of Macedonia." He exhorted them by their own, for he saith, " who were the first to make a beginning a year ago not only to do, but also to will." He exhorted them by the Lord's, for " ye know " he saith, " the grace of our Lord, that though He was rich, yet for our sakes He became poor." (ibid. 9.) Again he retreats upon that strong main point, the conduct of others. For mankind is emulous. And truly the example of the Lord ought to have had most power to draw them over : and next to it, the [consideration] of the recompense : but because they were somewhat weak, this draws them most. For nothing does so much as emulation. But observe how he introduces it in a somewhat novel way. For He did not say, ' Imitate them ; ' but what ?

" And your zeal has stirred up very many." What sayest thou ? A little before thou saidst, [they did it] " of their own accord, beseeching us with much entreaty," how then now, " your zeal ? " ' Yes,' he saith, ' we did not advise, we did not exhort, but we only praised you, we only boasted of you, and this was enough to incite them." Seest thou how he rouses them each by the other, these by those, and those by these, and, along with the emulation, has intermingled also a very high encomium. Then, that he may not elate them, he follows it up in a tempered tone, saying, " Your zeal hath stirred up very many." Now consider what a thing it is that those who have been the occasion to others of this munificence, should be themselves behind hand in this contribution. Therefore he did not say, ' Imitate them,' for it would not have kindled so great an emulation, but how ? ' They

---

[1] οἰκονομουμένη.

have imitated you; see then that ye the teachers appear not inferior to your desciples.'

And see how, whilst stirring up and inflaming them still more, he feigns to be standing by them, as if espousing their party in some rivalry and contention. For, as he said above, "Of their own accord, with much entreaty they came to us, insomuch that we exhorted Titus, that as he had made a beginning before, so he would complete this grace;" so also he says here,

Ver. 3. "For this cause have I sent the brethren that our glorying on your behalf may not be made void."

Seest thou that he is in anxiety and terror, lest he should seem to have said what he said only for exhortation's sake? 'But because so it is,' saith he, "I have sent the brethren;" 'so earnest am I on your behalf,' "that our glorying may not be made void." And he appears to make himself of the Corinthians' party throughout, although caring for all alike. What he says is this; 'I am very proud of you, I glory before all, I boasted even unto them[1], so that if ye be found wanting, I am partner in the shame.' And this indeed he says under limitation, for he added,

"In this respect," not, in all points;

"That even as I said, ye may be prepared." 'For I did not say, 'they are purposing,' but 'all is ready; and nothing is now wanting on their part. This then,' he says, 'I wish to be shown by your deeds.' Then he even heightens the anxiety, saying,

Ver. 4. "Lest by any means if there come with me any from Macedonia, we, (that we say not ye,) should be put to shame in this confidence." The shame is greater when the spectators he has arrayed against them are many, even those same persons who had heard [his boasting.] And he did not say, 'for I am bringing with me Macedonians;' 'for there are Macedonians coming with me;' lest he should seem to do it on purpose; but how [said he?] "Lest by any means, if there come with me any from Macedonia?" 'For this may happen,' he says, 'it is matter of possibility.' For thus he also made what he said unsuspected, but had he expressed himself in that other way, he would have even made them the more contentious. See how he leads them on, not from spiritual motives only, but from human ones as well. 'For,' says he, 'though you make no great account of me, and reckon confidently on my excusing you, yet think of them of Macedonia,' "lest by any means, if they come and find you;" and he did not say 'unwillingly,' but "unprepared," not having got all completed. But if this be a disgrace,

not to contribute quickly; consider how great it were to contribute either not at all, or less than behoved. Then he lays down what would thereupon follow, in terms at once gentle and pungent, thus saying, "We, (that we say not ye,) should be put to shame." And he tempers it again, saying, "in this confidence" not as making them more listless, but as showing that they who were approved in all other respects, ought in this one also to have great fearlessness.

[2.] Ver. 5. "I thought it necessary therefore to entreat the brethren, that they would make up beforehand this your bounty, that the same might be ready, as a matter of bounty and not of extortion.[2]"

Again, he resumed the subject in a different manner: and that he may not seem to be saying these things without object, he asserts that the sole reason for this journey was, that they might not be put to shame. Seest thou how his words, "It is superfluous for me to write," were the beginning of advising? You see, at least, how many things he discourses concerning this ministering. And along with this, one may further remark that, (lest he should seem to contradict himself as having said, "It is superfluous," yet discoursing at length about it,) he passed on unto discourse of quickness and largeness and forwardness [in contributing,] by this means securing that point also. For these three things he requires. And indeed he moved these three main points even at the first, for when he says, "In much proof of affliction the abundance of their joy, and their deep poverty, abounded unto the riches of their liberality," he says nothing else than that they contributed both much and gladly and quickly; and that not only did not giving much pain them, but not even being in trials, which is more grievous than giving. And the words, "they gave themselves to us;" these also show both their forwardness and the greatness of their faith. And here too again he treats of those heads. For since these are opposed to [each other,] munificence and forwardness, and one that has given much is often sorrowful, whilst another, that he may not be sorry, gives less; observe how he takes care for each, and with the wisdom which belongs to him. For he did not say, 'it is better to give a little and of free choice, than much of necessity;' because he wished them to contribute both much and of free choice; but how saith he? "that they might make up beforehand this your bounty, that the same might be ready as a matter of bounty[3], and not extortion. He

---

[1] i. e. them of Macedonia.

[2] This verse, as given by Chrysostom, varies somewhat from the Received Text.

[3] A *blessing*, εὐλογίαν

begins first with that which is pleasantest and lighter; namely, the ' not of necessity,' for, it is "bounty" he says. Observe how in the form of his exhortation he represents at once the fruit as springing up, and the givers as filled with blessing. And by the term employed he won them over, for no one gives a blessing with pain. Yet neither was he content with this; but added, "not as of extortion." 'Think not,' he says, 'that we take it as extortioners, but that we may be the cause of a blessing unto you.' For extortion belongs to the unwilling, so that whoso giveth alms unwillingly giveth of extortion.[1] Then from this he passed on again unto that, the giving munificently.

Ver. 6. "But this I say:" that is, along with this I say also that. What?

"He that soweth sparingly, shall reap also sparingly; and he that soweth bountifully shall reap also bountifully." And he did not say niggardly, but a milder expression, employing the the name of the sparing. And he called the thing sowing; that thou mightest at once look unto the recompense, and having in mind the harvest, mightest feel that thou receivest more than thou givest. Wherefore he did not say, ' He that giveth,' but "He that soweth:" and he said not ' ye, if ye sow,' but made what he said general. Neither did he say, 'largely,' but "bountifully," which is far greater than this. And again, he betakes himself to that former point of gladness; saying,

Ver. 7. "Let each man do according as he hath purposed in his heart." For a man when left to himself, does a thing more readily than when compelled. Wherefore also he dwells upon this: for having said, "according as he is disposed," he added,

"Not grudgingly, nor of necessity." And neither was he content with this, but he adds a testimony from Scripture also, saying,

"For God loveth a cheerful giver." Seest thou how frequently he lays this down? "I speak not by commandment:" and, "Herein I give my advice:" and, "as a matter of bounty, and not as of extortion," and again, "not grudgingly, nor of necessity; for God loveth a cheerful giver." In this passage I am of opinion that a large [giver] is intended; the Apostle however has taken it as giving with readiness. For because the example of the Macedonians and all those other things were enough to produce sumptuousness, he does not say many things on that head, but upon giving without reluctance. For if it is a work of virtue, and yet all that is done of necessity is shorn of its reward[2], with reason also he labors at this point. And he does not advise merely,

but also adds a prayer, as his wont is to do, saying,

Ver. 8. "And may God[3], that is able, fulfill all grace towards you."

By this prayer he takes out the way a thought which lay in wait against[4] this liberality and which is now also an hinderance to many. For many persons are afraid to give alms, saying, 'Lest perchance I become poor,' ' lest perchance I need aid from others.' To do away with this fear then, he adds this prayer, saying, May "He make all grace abound towards you." Not merely fulfil, but "make it abound." And what is "make grace abound?" 'Fill you,' he means, ' with so great things, that ye may be able to abound in this liberality.'

"That ye, having always all sufficiency in every thing, may abound to every good work."

Observe, even in this his prayer, his great philosophy. He prays not for riches nor for abundance, but for all sufficiency. Nor is this all that is admirable in him; but that as he prayed not for superfluity, so he doth not press sore on them nor compel them to give of their want, condescending to their weakness; but asks for a "sufficiency," and shows at the same time that they ought not to abuse the gifts received from God. "That ye may abound," he saith, "to every good work." 'It is therefore,' saith he, 'I ask for this, that ye may bestow on others also.' Yet he did not say, ' bestow,' but ' abound.' For in carnal things he asks for a sufficiency for them, but in spiritual things for abundance even; not in almsgiving only, but in all other things also, "unto every good work." Then he brings forward unto them the prophet for a counsellor, having sought out a testimony inviting them to bountifulness, and says,

Ver. 9. "As it is written,

He hath scattered abroad, he hath given to the poor; His righteousness abideth for ever."

This is the import of "abound;" for the words, "he hath dispersed abroad," signify nothing else but the giving plentifully. For if the things themselves abide not, yet their results abide. For this is the thing to be admired, that when they are kept they are lost; but when dispersed abroad they abide, yea, abide for ever. Now by "righteousness," here, he means love towards men. For this maketh righteous, consuming sins like a fire when it is plentifully poured out.

[3.] Let us not therefore nicely calculate, but sow with a profuse hand. Seest thou not how much others give to players and harlots? Give at any rate the half to Christ, of what they give to dancers. As much as they give of ostenta-

---

[1] Literally, *giveth extortion.*
[2] ὑποτέμνεται.
[3] A. V. "God is able to, &c." [which gives the true text. C.]
[4] ὑφορμοῦντα

tion to those upon the stage, so much at any rate give thou unto the hungry. For they indeed even clothe the persons of wantons[1] with untold gold; but thou not even with a threadbare garment the flesh of Christ, and that though beholding it naked. What forgiveness doth this deserve, yea, how great a punishment doth it not deserve, when he indeed bestoweth so much upon her that ruineth and shameth him, but thou not the least thing on Him that saveth thee and maketh thee brighter? But as long as thou spendest it upon thy belly and on drunkenness and dissipation[2], thou never thinkest of poverty: but when need is to relieve poverty, thou art become poorer than any body. And when feeding parasites and flatterers, thou art as joyous as though thou hadst fountains to spend from[3]; but if thou chance to see a poor man, then the fear of poverty besets thee. Therefore surely we shall in that day be condemned, both by ourselves and by others, both by those that have done well and those that have done amiss. For He will say to thee, 'Wherefore wast thou not thus magnanimous in things where it became thee? But here is a man who, when giving to an harlot, thought not of any of these things; whilst thou, bestowing upon thy Master Who hath bid thee "not be anxious" (Matt. vi. 25.), art full of fear and trembling.' And what forgiveness then shalt thou deserve? For if a man who hath received will not overlook, but will requite the favor, much more will Christ. For He that giveth even without receiving, how will He not give after receiving? 'What then,' saith one, 'when some who have spent much come to need other men's help?' Thou speakest of those that have spent their all; when thou thyself bestowest not a farthing. Promise to strip thyself of every thing and then ask questions about such men; but as long as thou art a niggard and bestowest little of thy substance, why throw me out excuses and pretenses? For neither am I leading thee to the lofty peak of entire poverty[4] but for the present I require thee to cut off superfluities and to desire a sufficiency alone. Now the boundary of sufficiency is the using those things which it is impossible to live without. No one debars thee from these; nor forbids thee thy daily food. I say food, not feasting; raiment, not ornament[5]. Yea rather, if one should enquire accurately, this is in the best sense feasting. For, consider. Which should we say more truly feasted, he whose diet was herbs, and who was in sound health and suffered no uneasi-

ness: or he who had the table of a Sybarite, and was full of ten thousand disorders? Very plainly the former. Therefore let us seek nothing more than this, if we would at once live luxuriously and healthfully: and let us set these boundaries to sufficiency. And let him that can be satisfied with pulse and can keep in good health, seek for nothing more; but let him who is weaker and requires to be dieted with garden herbs, not be hindered of this. But if any be even weaker than this and require the support of flesh in moderation, we will not debar him from this either. For we do not advise these things, to kill and injure men but to cut off what is superfluous; and that is superfluous which is more than we need. For when we are able even without a thing to live healthfully and respectably, certainly the addition of that thing is a superfluity.

[4.] Thus let us think also in regard of clothing and of the table and of a dwelling house and of all our other wants; and in every thing inquire what is necessary. For what is superfluous is also useless. When thou shalt have practised living on what is sufficient; then if thou hast a mind to emulate that widow, we will lead thee on to greater things than these. For thou hast not yet attained to the philosophy of that woman, whilst thou art anxious about what is sufficient. For she soared higher even than this; for what was to have been her support; that she cast in, all of it. Wilt thou then still distress thyself about such things as be necessary; and dost thou not blush to be vanquished by a woman; and not only not to emulate her, but to be left even of her far behind? For she did not say the things we say, 'But what, if when I have spent all I be compelled to beg of another?' but in her munificence stripped herself of all she had. What shall we say of the widow in the Old Testament in the time of the prophet Elias? For the risk she ran was not of poverty, but even of death and extinction, and not her own only, but her children's too. For neither had she any expectation of receiving from others, but of presently dying. 'But,' saith one, 'she saw the prophet, and that made her munificent.' But do not ye see saints without number? And why do I speak of saints? Ye see the Lord of the prophets asking an alms, and yet not even so do ye become humane; but though ye have coffers spewing[6] one into another, do not even impart of your superfluity. What sayest thou? Was he a prophet that came to her, and did this persuade her to so great a magnanimity? This of itself deserves much admiration, that she was persuaded of his being a great and wonderful person. For how was it she did not say, as it would have been

---

[1] ἐταιριζομένων.
[2] ἀσωτίαν.
[3] ἀπὸ πηγῶν δαπανῶν.
[4] ἀκτημοσύνης
[5] Chrys. τροφὴν, οὐ τρυφὴν λέγω. σκεπάσματα, οὐ καλλωπισματα, with a manifest play on the words.

[6] ἐρευγόμενα.

likely that a barbarian woman and a foreigner would have reasoned, ' If he were a prophet, he would not have begged of me. If he were a friend of God, He would not have neglected him. Be it that because of sins the Jews suffer this punishment: but whence, and wherefore, doth this man suffer?' But she entertained none of these thoughts; but opened to him her house, and before her house, her heart; and set before him all she had; and putting nature on one side and disregarding her children, preferred the stranger unto all. Consider then how great punishment will be laid up for us, if we shall come behind [1] and be weaker than a woman, a widow, poor, a foreigner, a barbarian, a mother of children, knowing nothing of these things which we know! For because we have strength of body, we are not therefore manly persons. For he alone hath this virtue, yea though he be laid upon his bed, whose strength is from within; since without this, though a man should tear up a mountain by his strength of body, I would call him nothing stronger than a girl or wretched crone. For the one struggles with incorporeal ills, but the other dares not even look them in the face. And that thou mayest learn that this is the measure of manliness, collect it from this very example. For what could be more manly than that woman who both against the tyranny of nature, and against the force of hunger, and against the threat of death, stood nobly fast, and proved stronger than all? Hear at least how Christ proclaimeth her. For, saith He, " there were many widows in the days of Elias, and to none of them was the prophet sent but to her." (Luke iv. 25, 26.) Shall I say something great and startling? This woman gave more to hospitality, than our father Abraham. For she " ran " not " unto the herd," as he, (Gen. xviii. 7.) but by that " handful " (1 Kings xvii. 12.) outstripped all that have been renowned for hospitality. For in this was his excellence that he set himself to do that office; but hers, in that for the sake of the stranger she spared not her children even, and that too, though she looked not for the things to come. But we, though a

heaven exists, though a hell is threatened, though (which is greater than all) God hath wrought such great things for us and is made glad and rejoiceth over such things, sink back supinely.[2] Not so, I beseech you: but let us " scatter abroad," let us " give to the poor" as we ought to give. For what is much and what little, God defines, not by the measure of what is given, but by the extent of the substance of him that gives. Often surely hast thou who didst cast in an hundred staters of gold offered less than he that offered but one obol, for thou didst cast in of thy superfluity. Howbeit do if but this, and thou wilt come quickly even to greater munificence. Scatter wealth that thou mayest gather righteousness. For along with wealth this refuseth to come to us; yet through it, though not with it, it is made present to us. For it is not possible that lust of wealth and righteousness should dwell together; they have their tents apart. Do not then obstinately strive to bring things together which are incompatible, but banish the usurper covetousness, if thou wouldest obtain the kingdom. For this[3] is the [rightful] queen, and of slaves makes freemen, the contrary of which the other doth. Wherefore with all earnestness let us shun the one and welcome the other, that we may both gain freedom in this life and obtain the kingdom of heaven, through the grace and love towards men of our Lord Jesus Christ, with Whom, to the Father together with the Holy Spirit, be glory, might, honor, now and for ever, and world without end. Amen.

---

[1] ἔλαττον φέρωμεν.

[2] ἀναπεπτώκαμεν

[3] i. e., righteousness. [According to the text which the Apostle quotes from Psalm cxii., the abiding of righteousness forever is God's reward for scattering. Righteousness here appears to mean general excellence or virtue as manifested in beneficence. A parallel use of the term is found in the Sermon on the Mount where (Matth. vi. 1) according to the true text, our Lord in giving general directions about almsgiving, etc., begins with the injunction, " Take heed that ye do not your *righteousness* before men, to be seen of them." When therefore it is said in the Psalm that the liberal man's righteousness or beneficence shall continue forever, the implication is that he shall always have the means to continue his liberality. This is sustained by the tendency of things and by the general course of Divine Providence. But Chrysostom, while enforcing the inculcation of beneficence, carries out the spirit of the Apostle's utterances, and calls attention not only to the frequency and amount of one's gifts but also to the spirit which prompts them. The mere mechanical view which makes a merit of voluntary poverty and praises a gift to others without respect to the motive that prompted it, finds no sanction in the Apostle's words or in those of his expounder. C.]

HOMILY XX.

1 COR. ix. 10.

Now He that supplied seed to the sower, both minister bread for your food, and multiply your seed for sowing and increase the fruits of your righteousness[1].

HEREIN one may particularly admire the wisdom of Paul, that after having exhorted from spiritual considerations and from temporal, in respect of the recompense also he again does the very same, making the returns he mentions of either kind. This, (for instance,) "He hath scattered abroad, he hath given to the poor, his righteousness abideth for ever," belongs to a spiritual return; that again, "multiply your seed for sowing," to a temporal recompense. Still, however, he rests not here, but even again passes back to what is spiritual, placing the two continually side by side; for "increase the fruits of your righteousness," is spiritual. This he does, and gives variety by it to his discourse, tearing up by the roots those their unmanly and faint-hearted reasonings, and using many arguments to dissipate their fear of poverty, as also the example which he now brings. For if even to those that sow the earth God gives, if to those that feed the body He grants abundance; much more will He to those who till the soil[2] of heaven, to those who take care for the soul; for these things He willeth should yet more enjoy His providing care. However, he does not state this in the way of inference nor in the manner I have done, but in the form of a prayer; thus at once making the inference plain, and the rather leading them on to hope, not only from what [commonly] takes place, but also from his own prayer: for, 'May He minister,' saith he, 'and multiply your seed for sowing, and increase the fruits of your righteousness.' Here also again he hints, in an unsuspicious way, at largeness [in giving], for the words, "multiply and increase," are by way of indicating this; and at the same time he allows them to seek for nothing more than necessaries, saying, "bread for food." For this also is particularly worthy of admiration in him, (and it is a point he successfully established[3] even before,)

namely, that in things which be necessary, he allows them to seek for nothing more than need requires; but in spiritual things counsels them to get for themselves a large superabundance. Wherefore he said above also, "that having a sufficiency ye may abound to every good work:" and here, "He that ministereth bread for food, multiply your seed for sowing;" that is to say, the spiritual [seed]. For he asks not almsgiving merely, but with largeness. Wherefore also he continually calls it "seed." For like as the corn cast into the ground showeth luxuriant crops, so also many are the handfuls almsgiving produceth of righteousness, and unspeakable the fruits it showeth. Then having prayed for great affluence unto them, he shows again in what they ought to expend it, saying,

Ver. 11. "That being enriched in every thing to all liberality, which worketh through us thanksgiving to God."

Not that ye may consume it upon things not fitting, but upon such as bring much thanksgiving to God. For God made us to have the disposal of great things, and reserving to Himself that which is less yielded to us that which is greater. For corporeal[4] nourishment is at His sole disposal, but mental[5] He permitted to us; for we have it at our own disposal whether the crops we have to show be luxuriant. For no need is here of rains and of variety of seasons, but of the will only, and they run up to heaven itself. And largeness in giving is what he here calls liberality[6]. "Which worketh through us thanksgiving to God." For neither is that which is done almsgiving merely, but also the ground of much thanksgiving: yea rather, not of thanksgiving only, but of many other things besides. And these as he goes on he mentions, that by showing it to be the cause of many good works, he may make them thereby the forwarder.

[2.] What then are these many good works? Hear him saying:

Ver. 12—14. "For the ministration of this service, not only filleth up the measure of the wants of the saints, but aboundeth also through

---

[1] [The Rev. Version differs from Chrysostom's text, which is the same as the T. R. but is not well sustained. C.]
[2] γεωργοῦσι
[3] κατεσκεύασεν
[4] αἰσθητῆς
[5] νοητὴν.
[6] Gr. *Singleness*.

many thanksgivings unto God; seeing that through the proving[1] of you by this ministration, they glorify God for the obedience of your confession unto the Gospel[2], and for the liberality of your contribution unto them and unto all; while they also with supplication on your behalf, long after you by reason of the exceeding grace of God in you."

What he says is this; 'in the first place ye not only supply the wants of the saints, but ye are abundant even;' that is, 'ye furnish them with even more than they need: next, through them ye send up thanksgiving to God, for they glorify Him for the obedience of your confession.' For that he may not represent them as giving thanks on this account solely, (I mean, because they received somewhat,) see how highminded he makes them, exactly as he himself says to the Philippians, "Not that I desire a gift." (Phil. iv. 17.) 'To them too I bear record of the same thing. For they rejoice indeed that ye supply their wants and alleviate their poverty; but far more, in that ye are so subjected to the Gospel; whereof this is an evidence, your contributing so largely.' For this the Gospel enjoins.

"And for the liberality of your contribution unto them and unto all." 'And on this account,' he says, 'they glorify God that ye are so liberal, not unto them only, but also unto all.' And this again is made a praise unto them that they gave thanks even for that which is bestowed upon others. 'For,' saith he, 'they do honor[3], not to their own concerns only, but also to those of others, and this although they are in the extremest poverty; which is an evidence of their great virtue. For nothing is so full of envy as the whole race of such as are in poverty. But they are pure from this passion; being so far from feeling pained because of the things ye impart to others, that they even rejoice over it no less than over the things themselves receive.'

"While they themselves also with supplication." 'For in respect of these things,' saith he, 'they give thanks to God, but in respect of your love and your coming together, they beseech Him that they may be counted worthy to see you. For they long after this, not for the money's sake, but that they may be witnesses of the grace that hath been bestowed upon you.' Seest thou Paul's wisdom, how after having exalted them, he ascribed the whole to God by calling the thing "grace?" For seeing he had spoken great things of them, in that he called them ministers and exalted them unto a great height, (since they offered service[4] whilst he himself did but administer[5],) and termed

them 'proved[6],' he shows that God was the Author of all these things. And he himself again, along with them, sends up thanksgiving, saying,

Ver. 15. "Thanks be to God for His unspeakable gift."

And here he calls "gift," even those so many good things which are wrought by almsgiving, both to them that receive and them that give; or else, those unspeakable good things which through His advent He gave unto the whole world with great munificence, which one may suspect to be the most probable. For that he may at once both sober, and make them more liberal, he puts them in mind of the benefits they had received from God. For this avails very greatly in inciting unto all virtue; and therefore he concluded his discourse with it. But if His Gift be unspeakable, what can match their frenzy who raise curious questions as to His Essence? But not only is His Gift unspeakable, but that "peace" also "passeth all understanding," (Phil. iv. 7.) whereby He reconciled the things which are above with those which are below.

[3.] Seeing then that we are in the enjoyment of so great grace, let us strive to exhibit a virtue of life worthy of it, and to make much account of almsgiving. And this we shall do, if we shun excess and drunkenness and gluttony.[7] For God gave meat and drink not for excess, but for nourishment. For it is not the wine that produceth drunkenness, for if that were the case, every body would needs be drunken. 'But,' saith one, 'it would be better, if even to drink it largely did not injure.' These are drunkards' words. For if to drink it largely doth injure, and yet not even so thou desistest from thy excess in it; if this is so disgraceful and injurious, and yet thou ceasest not even so from thy depraved longing; if it were possible both to drink largely and be nothing harmed, where wouldest thou have stayed in thine excess? Wouldest thou not have longed that the rivers even might become wine? wouldest thou not have destroyed and ruined every thing? If there is a mean in food which when we overpass we are injured, and yet even so thou canst not bear the curb, but snapping it asunder seizest on what every body else hath, to minister to the wicked tyranny of this gluttony; what wouldest thou not have done, if this natural mean were abolished? wouldest thou not have spent thy whole time upon it? Would it then have been well to strengthen a lust so unreasonable, and not prevent the harm arising from excess? and to how many other harms would not this have given birth?

But O the senseless ones! who wallowing as in mire, in drunkeness and all other debauchery,

---

[1] A. V. experiment.
[2] Rec. Text. *Gospel of Christ.*
[3] κοσμοῦσι.
[4] ἐλειτουργοῦν
[5] διηκονεῖτο

[6] i. e In the word, *proving.*
[7] ἀδδηφαγίαν.

when they have got a little sober again, sit down and do nothing but utter such sort of sayings, 'Why doth this end[1] in this way?' when they ought to be condemning their own transgressions. For instead of what thou now sayest, 'Why hath He set bounds? why do not all things go on without any order?' say, 'Why do we not cease from being drunken? why are we never satiated? why are we more senseless than creatures without reason?' For these things they ought to ask one another, and to hearken to the voice of the Apostle and learn how many good things he witnesseth to the Corinthians proceed from almsgiving, and to seize upon this treasure. For to contemn money maketh men approved, as he said; and provideth that God be glorified; and warmeth love; and worketh in men loftiness of soul; and constituteth them priests, yea of a priesthood that bringeth great reward. For the merciful man is not arrayed in a vest reaching to the feet, nor does he carry about bells, nor wear a crown; but he is wrapped in the robe of loving-kindness, a holier than the sacred vestment, and is anointed with oil, not composed of material elements, but produced[2] by the Spirit, and he beareth a crown of mercies, for it is said, "Who crowneth thee with pity and mercies;" (Ps. ciii. 4.) and instead of wearing a plate bearing the Name of God, is himself like to God. For how? "Ye," saith He, "shall be like[3] unto your Father which is in heaven." (Matt. v. 45.)

Wouldest thou see His altar also? Bezaleel built it not, nor any other but God Himself; not of stones, but of a material brighter than the heaven, of reasonable souls. But the priest entereth into the holy of holies. Into yet more awful places mayest thou enter when thou offerest this sacrifice, where none is present but "thy Father, Which seeth in secret," (Matt. vi. 4.) where no other beholdeth. 'And how,' saith one, 'is it possible that none should behold, when the altar standeth in public view?' Because this it is that is admirable, that in those times double doors and veils made the seclusion: but now, though doing thy sacrifice in public view, thou mayest do it as in the holy of holies, and in a far more awful manner. For when thou doest it not for display before men; though the whole world hath seen, none hath seen, because thou hast so done it. For He said not simply, "Do" it "not before men," but added, "to be seen of them." (Matt. vi. 1.) This altar is composed of the very members of Christ, and the body of the Lord is made thine altar. That then revere; on the flesh of the Lord thou sacrificest the victim. This altar is more awful even than this which we now use, not only than that used of old. Nay, clamor not. For this altar is admirable because of the sacrifice that is laid upon it: but that, the merciful man's, not only on this account, but also because it is even composed of the very sacrifice which maketh the other to be admired. Again, this is but a stone by nature; but become holy because it receiveth Christ's Body: but that is holy because it is itself Christ's Body. So that this beside which thou, the layman, standest, is more awful than that. Whether then does Aaron seem to thee aught in comparison of this, or his crown, or his bells, or the holy of holies? For what need is there henceforth to make our comparison refer to Aaron's altar, when even compared with this, it has been shown to be so glorious? But thou honorest indeed this altar, because it receiveth Christ's body; but him that is himself the body of Christ thou treatest with contumely, and when perishing, neglectest. This altar mayest thou everywhere see lying, both in lanes and in market places, and mayest sacrifice upon it every hour; for on this too is sacrifice performed. And as the priest stands invoking the Spirit, so dost thou too invoke the Spirit, not by speech, but by deeds. For nothing doth so sustain and kindle the fire of the Spirit, as this oil largely poured out. But if thou wouldest see also what becomes of the things laid upon it, come hither, and I will show thee them. What then is the smoke, what the sweet savor of this altar? Praise and thanksgiving. And how far doth it ascend? as far as unto heaven? By no means, but it passeth beyond the heaven itself, and the heaven of heaven, and arriveth even at the throne of the King. For, "Thy prayers," saith he, "and thine alms are come up before God." (Acts x. 4.) And the sweet savor which the sense perceives pierceth not far into the air, but this opened the very vault of heaven. And thou indeed art silent, but thy work speaketh[4]: and a sacrifice of praise is made, no heifer slain nor hide burnt, but a spiritual soul presenting her proper offering. For such a sacrifice is more acceptable than any loving-kindness. When then thou seest a poor believer, think that thou beholdest an altar: when thou seest such an one a beggar, not only insult him not, but even reverence him, and if thou seest another insulting him, prevent, repel it. For so shalt thou thyself be able both to have God propitious to thee, and to obtain the promised good things, whereunto may we all attain, through the grace and love towards men of our Lord Jesus Christ, by Whom and with Whom, to the Father and the Holy Ghost, be glory, might, honor, now and forever, and world without end. Amen.

---

[1] ἀναλίσκεται
[2] γεωργουμένῳ
[3] This is St. Chrysostom's usual reading of the passage. As e. g. in his commentary on the text itself Hom. xviii. on St. Matthew, Oxf. Translation p. 277. [This edition p 126]
[4] βοᾷ

HOMILY XXI.

2 Cor. x. 1. 2.

Now I Paul myself entreat you by the meekness and gentleness of Christ, I who in your presence am lowly among you, but being absent am of good courage toward you: yea, I beseech you, that I may not when present show courage with the confidence, wherewith I count to be bold against some, which count of us as if we walked according to the flesh.

HAVING completed, in such sort as behoved his discourse of almsgiving, and having shown that he loves them more than he is loved, and having recounted the circumstances of his patience and trials, he now opportunely enters upon points involving more of reproof, making allusion to the false apostles, and concluding his discourse with more disagreeable matter, and with commendations of himself. For he makes this his business also throughout the Epistle. Which also perceiving, he hence oftentimes corrects himself, saying in so many words[1]; "Do we begin again to commend ourselves?" (Ch. iii. 1.) and further on; "We commend not ourselves again, but give you occasion to glory:" (Ch. v. 12.) and afterwards; "I am become a fool in glorying; ye have compelled me." (Ch. xii. 11.) And many such correctives doth he use. And one would not be wrong in styling this Epistle an eulogium of Paul; he makes such large mention both of his grace and his patience. For since there were some amongst them who thought great things of themselves, and set themselves above the Apostle, and accused him as a boaster, and as being nothing, and teaching no sound doctrine; (now this was in itself the most certain evidence of their own corruptness;) see how he begins his rebuke of them; "Now I Paul myself." Seest thou what severity, what dignity, is here? For what he would say is this, 'I beseech you do not compel me, nor leave me to use my power against those that hold us cheap, and think of us as carnal.' This is severer than those threats towards them uttered in the former Epistle; "Shall I come unto you with a rod, or in love and a spirit of meekness?" (1 Cor. iv. 21.) and then again; "Now some are puffed up as though I were not coming to you; but I will come, and will know, not

the word of them that are puffed up, but the power." (ib. 18 19.) For in this place he shows both things, both his power, and his philosophy and forbearance; since he so beseeches them, and with such earnestness, that he may not be compelled to come to a display of the avenging power pertaining to him, and to smite and chastise them and exact the extreme penalty. For he implied this in saying, "But I beseech you, that I may not when present show courage with the confidence, wherewith I count to be bold against some which count of us as if we walked according to the flesh." For the present, however, let us speak of the commencement. "Now I Paul myself." Great emphasis, great weight[2] is here. So he says elsewhere, "Behold I Paul say unto you;" (Gal. v. 2.) and again, "As Paul the aged;" (Phile. 9.) and again in another place, "Who hath been a succorer of many, and of me." (Rom. xvi. 2.) So also here, "Now I Paul myself." This even is a great thing, that himself beseecheth; but that other is greater which he added, saying, "by the meekness and gentleness of Christ." For with the wish of greatly shaming them, he puts forward that "meekness and gentleness," making his entreaty in this way more forcible; as if he had said, 'Reverence the gentleness of Christ by which I beseech you.' And this he said, at the same time also showing that although they should lay ever so strong[3] a necessity upon him, he himself is more inclined to this: it is from being meek, not from want of power, that he does not proceed against them: for Christ also did in like manner.

"Who in your presence am lowly among you, but being absent am of good courage toward you." What, pray, is this? Surely he speaks in irony, using their speeches. For they said this, that 'when he is present indeed, he is worthy of no account, but poor and contemptible; but when absent, swells, and brags, and sets himself up against us, and threatens.' This at least he implies also afterwards, saying, "for his letters," say they, "are weighty, but his

---

[1] αὐτὸ τοῦτο.

[2] Or, 'severity.'
[3] μυρίαν.

bodily presence is weak, and his speech of no account." (v. 10.) He either then speaks in irony, manifesting great severity and saying, 'I, the base, I, the mean, when present, (as they say,) and when absent, lofty:' or else meaning that even though he should utter great things, it is not out of pride, but out of his confidence in them.

"But I beseech you, that I may not when present show courage with the confidence, wherewith I count to be bold against some which count of us as if we walked according to the flesh. Seest thou how great his indignation, and how complete his refutation of those sayings of theirs? For he saith, 'I beseech you, do not compel me to show that even present I am strong and have power.' For since they said that 'when absent, he is quite bold against us and exalteth himself,' he uses their very words, 'I beseech therefore that they compel me not to use my power.' For this is the meaning of, "the confidence." And he said not, 'wherewith I am prepared,' but 'wherewith I count.' 'For I have not yet resolved upon this; they however give me reason enough, but not even so do I wish it.' And yet he was doing this not to vindicate himself, but the Gospel. Now if where it was necessary to vindicate the Message, he is not harsh, but draws back and delays, and beseeches that there may be no such necessity; much more would he never have done any thing of the kind in his own vindication. 'Grant me then this favor,' he saith, 'that ye compel me not to show, that even when present I am able to be bold against whomsoever it may be necessary; that is, to chastise and punish them.' Seest thou how free he was from ambition, how he did nothing for display, since even where it was matter of necessity, he hesitates not to call the act, boldness. "For I beseech you," he says, "that I may not when present show courage with the confidence, wherewith I think to be bold" against some. For this especially is the part of a teacher, not to be hasty in taking vengeance, but to work a reformation, and ever to be reluctant and slow in his punishments. How, pray, does he describe those whom he threatens? "Those that count of us as though we walked according to the flesh:" for they accused him as a hypocrite, as wicked, as a boaster.

[2.] Ver. 3. "For though we walk in the flesh, we do not war according to the flesh.

Here he goes on to alarm them also by the figure[1] he uses, 'for,' says he, 'we are indeed encompassed with flesh; I own it, but we do not live by the flesh;' or rather, he said not even this, but for the present reserves it, for it belongs to the encomium on his life: but first discourseth of the Preaching, and shows that it is not of man,

nor needeth aid from beneath. Wherefore he said not, 'we do not live according to the flesh,' but, "we do not war according to the flesh," that is, 'we have undertaken a war and a combat; but we do not war with carnal weapons, nor by help of any human succors.'

Ver. 4. "For our weapons are not of the flesh."

For what sort of weapons are of the flesh? Wealth, glory, power, fluency, cleverness, circumventions[2], flatteries, hypocrisies, whatsoever else is similar to these. But ours are not of this sort: but of what kind are they?

"Mighty before God."

And he said not, 'we are not carnal,' but, "our weapons." For as I said, for the present he discourseth of the Preaching, and refers the whole power to God. And he says not, 'spiritual,' although this was the fitting opposite[3] to "carnal," but "mighty," in this implying the other also, and showing that their[4] weapons are weak and powerless. And mark the absence of pride in him; for he said not, 'we are mighty,' but, "our weapons are mighty before God." 'We did not make them such, but God Himself.' For because they were scourged, were persecuted, and suffered wrongs incurable[5] without number, which things were proofs of weakness: to show the strength of God he says, "but they are mighty before God." For this especially shows His strength, that by these things He gains the victory. So that even though we are encompassed with them, yet it is He that warreth and worketh by them. Then he goes through a long eulogium upon them, saying,

"To the casting down of strong holds." And lest when hearing of strong holds thou shouldest think of aught material[6], he says,

Ver. 5. "Casting down imaginations."

First giving emphasis by the figure, and then by this additional expression declaring the spiritual[7] character of the warfare. For these strongholds besiege souls, not bodies. Whence they are stronger than the others, and therefore also the weapons they require are mightier. But by strongholds he means the Grecian pride, and the strength of their sophisms and their syllogisms. But nevertheless, 'these weapons,' he says, 'confounded every thing that stood up against them; for they cast down imaginations,

'And every high thing that is exalted against the knowledge of God.' He persisted in the metaphor that he might make the emphasis greater. 'For though there should be strongholds,' he saith, 'though fortifications,

---

[1] τροπῇ
[2] περιδρομαί
[3] τὸ πρὸς ἀντιδιαστολὴν
[4] The false Apostles.
[5] ἀνήκεστα
[6] αἰσθητὸν
[7] νοητὸν

though any other thing soever, they yield and give way before these weapons.

"And bringing every thought into captivity to the obedience of Christ." And yet the name, "captivity," hath an ill sound with it ; for it is the destruction of liberty. Wherefore then has he used it ? With a meaning of its own, in regard to another point. For the word "captivity" conveys two ideas, the loss of liberty, and the being so violently overpowered as not to rise up again. It is therefore in respect to this second meaning that he took it. As when he shall say "I robbed other churches," (2 Cor. xi. 8.) he does not intend the taking stealthily, but the stripping and taking their all, so also here in saying, "bringing into captivity." For the fight was not equally maintained, but he conquered with great ease. Wherefore he did not say, 'we conquer and have the better,' only ; but 'we even bring "into captivity ; "' just as above, he did not say, 'we advance engines against the "strongholds : "' but, 'we cast them down, for great is the superiority of our weapons.' 'For we war not with words,' he saith, but with deeds against words, not with fleshly wisdom, but with the spirit of meekness and of power. How was it likely then I should hunt after honor, and boast in words, and threaten by letters ; ' (as they accused him, saying, "his letters are weighty,") 'when our might lay not in these things?' But having said, "bringing every thought into captivity to the obedience of Christ," because the name of "captivity" was unpleasant, he presently afterwards put an end to the metaphor, saying, "unto the obedience of Christ : " from slavery unto liberty, from death unto life, from destruction to salvation. For we came not merely to strike down, but to bring over to the truth those who are opposed to us.

[3.] Ver. 6. "And being in readiness to avenge all disobedience, when your obedience shall be fulfilled."

Here he alarmed these[1] also, not those[2] alone : 'for,' says he, 'we were waiting for you, that when by our exhortations and threatenings we have reformed you, and purged and separated you from their fellowship ; then, when those only are left who are incurably diseased, we may visit with punishment, after we see that you have really[3] separated from them. For even now indeed ye obey, but not perfectly. 'And yet if thou hadst done it now,' saith one, 'thou wouldest have wrought greater gain.' 'By no means, for if I had done it now, I should have involved you also in the punishment. Howbeit it behoved to punish them,

indeed, but to spare you. Yet if I spared, I should have seemed to do it out of favor : now this I do not desire, but first to amend you, and then to proceed against them.' What can be tenderer than the heart of the Apostle ? who because he saw his own mixed up with aliens, desires indeed to inflict the blow, but forbears, and restrains his indignation until those shall have withdrawn, that he may smite these alone; yea rather, not these even. For he therefore threatens this, and says he is desirous to separate unto punishment them alone, that they also being amended by the fear may change, and he let loose his anger against no one. For just like a most excellent physician, and common father, and patron, and guardian[4], so did he all things, so cared he for all, removing impediments, checking the pestilent, running about every whither. For not by fighting did he so achieve the work, but advancing as if to a ready and an easy victory, he planted his trophies, undermining, casting down, overthrowing the strongholds of the devil, and the engines of the demons ; and carried over their whole booty to the camp of Christ. Nor did he even take breath a little, bounding off from these to those, and from those again to others, like some very able general, raising trophies every day, or rather every hour. For having entered into the battle with nothing but a little tunic[5], the tongue of Paul took the cities of his enemies with their men and bows and spears and darts and all.

For he spake only ; and, falling upon his enemies more fiercely than any fire, his words drave out the demons and brought over unto him the men that were possessed of them. For when he cast out that demon, the evil one, fifty thousand sorcerers coming together burnt their books of magic and revolted to the truth. (See Acts xix. 19.) And like as in a war, when a tower has fallen or a tyrant been brought low, all his partizans cast away their arms and run unto the [opposing] general; so truly did it happen then also. For when the demon was cast out, they all having been besieged, and having cast away, yea rather having destroyed, their books, ran unto the feet of Paul. But he setting himself[6] against the world as though against a single army, no where stayed his march, but did all things as if he were some man endued with wings[7] : and now restored a lame, now raised a dead man, now blinded a third, (I mean the sorcerer,) nor even when shut up in a prison indulged in rest, but even there brought over to himself the jailor, effecting the goodly captivity we treat of.

---

[1] The Corinthians.
[2] The False Apostles.
[3] γνησίως.

[4] κηδεμών.
[5] χιτωνίσκου.
[6] παραταττόμενος.
[7] ὑπόπτερος.

[4.] Let us also imitate him after our power. And why do I say, after our power? For he that wills may come even near unto him, and behold his valor, and imitate his heroism. For still he is doing this work, "casting down imaginations, and every high thing that is exalted against the knowledge of God." And although many heretics have attempted to cut him in pieces; yet still, even though dismembered, he displayeth a mighty strength. For both Marcion and Manichæus use him indeed, but after cutting him in pieces; but still even so they are refuted by the several members. For even a hand only of this champion being found among them puts them utterly to the rout; and a foot only, left amongst others, pursues and prostrates them, in order that thou mayest learn the superabundance of his power, and that, although shorn of his limbs even, he is able to destroy all his adversaries. 'This however,' saith one, 'is an instance of perversion, that those who are battling with each other should all use him.' An instance of perversion certainly, but not in Paul, (God forbid,) but in them who use him. For he was not parti-colored[1], but uniform and clear, but they perverted his words to their own notions. 'And wherefore,' saith one, 'were they so spoken as to give handles to those that wished for them?' He did not give handles, but their frenzy used his words not rightly; since this whole world also is both wonderful and great, and a sure proof of the wisdom of God, and "the heavens declare the glory of God, and day unto day uttereth speech, and night unto night declareth knowledge;" (Ps. xix. 1, 2.) but nevertheless, many have stumbled at it and in contrary directions to one another. And some have admired it so much above its worth as to think it God; whilst others have been so insensible of its beauty as to assert it to be unworthy of God's creating hand[2], and to ascribe the greater share in it to a certain evil matter. And yet God provided for both points by making it beautiful and great that it might not be deemed alien from his wisdom; yet defective and not sufficient unto itself that it might not be suspected to be God. But nevertheless those who were blinded by their own reasonings fell away into contradictory notions, refuting one another, and becoming each the other's accuser, and vindicating the wisdom of God even by the very reasonings which led them astray. And why do I speak of the sun and the heaven? The Jews saw so many marvels happen before their eyes, yet straightway worshipped a calf. Again they

saw Christ casting out demons, yet called him one that had a demon. But this was no imputation against him that cast them out, but an accusation of their understanding who were so blinded. Condemn not then Paul on account of their judgment who have used him amiss; but understand well the treasures in him, and develop his riches, so shalt thou make noble stand against all, fenced by his armor. So shalt thou be able to stop the mouths both of Greeks and Jews. 'And how,' saith one, 'seeing they believe him not?' By the things wrought through him, by the reformation effected in the world. For it was not of human power[3] that so great things could be done, but the Might of the Crucified, breathing on him, made him such as he was, and showed him more powerful than orators and philosophers and tyrants and kings and all men. He was not only able to arm himself and to strike down his adversaries, but to make others also such as himself. Therefore in order that we may become useful both to ourselves and to others, let us continually have him in our hands, using his writings for a meadow and garden of delight[4]. For so shall we be able both to be delivered from vice and to choose virtue, and to obtain the promised good things, whereunto may we all attain, through the grace and love towards men of our Lord Jesus Christ, with Whom to the Father with the Holy Spirit, be glory, might, honor, now and for ever, and world without end. Amen.

[3] [Some remarks of Hodge *in loco* are worth quoting here as confirming Chrysostom's view of the passage and showing its permanent application. "The conflict to which the Apostle refers is that between truth and error. When the Gospel was first proclaimed it found itself in conflict with all the forms of religion and philosophy then prevailing among men. To the wise of this world the Gospel appeared as foolishness. It was, however, the wisdom and power of God. The conflict then begun has continued ever since, and is now as deadly as at any former period. Men of science and philosophers are as confident in their conclusions, and as much disposed to exalt themselves, or their opinions, against the knowledge of God as ever. There is no doubt as to the issue of this contest. It is a contest between God and man, in which, of course, God must prevail. The instructive lesson which the Apostle designs here to inculcate is that this warfare must not be conducted on the part of the advocates of the Gospel with carnal weapons. They must not rely upon their own resources and attempt to overcome their enemies by argument. They must not become philosophers and turn the Gospel into a philosophy. This would be to make it a human conflict on both sides. It would be human reason against human reason, the intellect of one man against the intellect of another man. Paul told the Corinthians in his former Epistle that he did not appear among them as a philosopher, but as a witness; he came not with the words of man's wisdom: he did not rely for success on his powers of argument or of persuasion, but on the demonstration of the Spirit. The faith which he labored to secure was not to be founded on the wisdom of men, but on the power of God; not on arguments addressed to the understanding but on the testimony of God. That testimony has the same effect which intuition has. It reveals the truth to the mind and conscience as self-evident: and therefore it cannot be resisted. A rationalistic Christian, a philosophizing theologian, therefore, lays aside the divine for the human, the wisdom of God for the wisdom of man, the infinite and infallible for the finite and the fallible." The whole history of the Church shows that whenever high imaginations were cast down and strongholds overthrown, it was by the simple testimony of the word of God, presented not as something to be proved but as something to be believed. C.]

[4] ἀντὶ λειμῶνος καὶ παραδείσου ἐντρυφῶντες.

---

[1] ποικίλος τις.
[2] δημιουργίας.

HOMILY XXII.

2 COR. X. 7.

Ye look at the things that are before your face. If any man trusteth in himself that he is Christ's, let him consider this again with himself that even as he is Christ's, so also are we.

WHAT one may especially admire in Paul amongst other things is this, that when he has fallen upon an urgent necessity for exalting himself, he manages both to accomplish this point, and also not to appear offensive to the many on account of this egotism; a thing we may see particularly in his Epistle to the Galatians. For having there fallen upon such an argument, he provides for both these points; a matter of the very utmost difficulty and demanding much prudence; he is at once modest and says somewhat great of himself. And observe how in this place also he makes it of great account, "Ye look at the things that are before your face." Behold here also prudence. For having rebuked those that deceived them, he confined not his remarks to them, but he leaps away from them to these too; and he does so constantly. For, in truth, he scourgeth not those only that lead astray[1], but the deceived also. For had he let even them go without calling them to an account[2], they would not so easily have been reformed by what was said to the others; but would have been greatly elated even, as not being amenable to accusations. Therefore he scourgeth them also. And this is not all that is to be admired in him, but this further, that he rebukes either party in a manner suitable to each. Hear at least what he says to these, "Ye look at the things that are before your face." The accusation is no light one; but a mark of men exceedingly easy to be deceived. Now what he says is this, 'ye test by what appear, by things carnal, by things bodily.' What is meant by 'what appear?' If one is rich, if one is puffed up, if one is surrounded by many flatterers, if one says great things of himself, if one is vain-glorious, if one makes a pretence of virtue without having virtue, for this is the meaning of, "ye look at the things that are before your face."

"If any man trust in himself that, he is Christ's, let him consider this again with himself, that even as he is Christ's, even so also are we." For he does not wish to be vehement at the beginning, but he increases and draws to a head[3] by little and little. But observe here how much harshness and covert meaning there is. He shows this by using the words "with himself." For he saith, 'Let him not wait to learn this from us; that is, by our rebuke of himself,' but "let him consider this with himself, that even as he is Christ's, so also are we;" not that he was Christ's in such manner as the other was, but, "that even as he is Christ's, so also am I Christ's. Thus far the community holds good: for it is not surely the case that he indeed is Christ's, but I some other's. Then having laid down this equality between them, he goes on to add wherein he exceeded, saying,

Ver. 8. "For though I should glory somewhat abundantly concerning our authority which the Lord gave for building you up, and not for casting you down, I shall not be put to shame.

For since he was going to say somewhat great, observe how he softens it. For nothing doth so offend the majority of hearers as for any one to praise himself. Wherefore to cut at the root of this offensiveness, he says, ".For though I should glory somewhat abundantly." And he did not say, 'if any man trust that he is Christ's let him think that he is far short of us. For I possess much authority from Him, so as to punish and to kill whomsoever I choose;' but what? "For though I should glory even somewhat abundantly." And yet he possessed more than can be told, but nevertheless he lowers it in his way of speaking. And he said not, 'I glory,' but, "if I should glory," if I should choose to do so: at once both showing modesty, and declaring his superiority. If therefore he says, "I should glory concerning the authority which the Lord gave me." Again, he ascribes the whole to Him, and makes the gift common. "For building up, and not for casting down." Seest thou how again he allays the envy his praises might give rise to, and draws the hearer over to himself by mentioning

---

[1] παρακρουομένων.
[2] ἀνευθύνους.

[3] κορυφοῦται

379

the use for which he received it? Then why doth he say, "Casting down imaginations?" Because this is itself an especial form of building up, the removing of hindrances, and detecting the unsound, and laying the true together in the building. For this end therefore we received it, that we might build up. But if any should spar and battle with us, and be incurable, we will use that other power also, destroying[1] and overthrowing him. Wherefore also he says, "I shall not be put to shame," that is, I shall not be proved a liar or a boaster.

[2.] Ver. 9, 10, 11. "But that I may not seem as if I would terrify you: for his letters, say they, are weighty and strong: but his bodily presence is weak, and his speech of no account. Let such a one reckon this, that what we are in word by letters when we are absent, such are we also in deed when we are present."

What he says is this: 'I could boast indeed, but that they may not say the same things again, to wit, that I boast in my letters, and am contemptible when present, I will say nothing great.' And yet afterwards he did say something great, but not about this power by which he was formidable, but about revelations and at greater lengths about trials. 'Therefore, that I may not seem to be terrifying you, "let such an one reckon this, that what we are by letters when we are absent, such are we also in deed when we are present.'" For since they said, 'he writes great things of himself, but when he is present he is worthy of no consideration,' therefore he says these things, and those again in a moderated form. For he did not say, 'as we write great things, so when we are present we also do great things,' but in more subdued phrase. For when he addressed himself to the others indeed, he stated it with vehemency, saying, "I beseech you that I may not when present show courage with the confidence wherewith I think to be bold against some:" but when to these, he is more subdued. And therefore he says, 'what we are when present, such too when absent, that is, lowly, modest, no where boasting. And it is plain from what follows,

Ver. 12. "For we are not bold to number, or compare in ourselves[2] with some that commend themselves."

Here he both shows that those false Apostles are boasters and say great things of themselves: and ridicules them as commending themselves. 'But we do no such thing: but even if we shall do any thing great, we refer all unto God, and compare ourselves with one another.' Wherefore also he added,

"But they themselves measuring themselves by themselves and comparing themselves among themselves are without understanding." Now what he says is this: 'we do not compare ourselves with them, but with one another.' For further on he says, "in nothing am I behind the very chiefest Apostles;" (Chap. xii. 11.) and in the former Epistle, "I labored more abundantly than they all;" (1 Cor. xv. 10.) and again, "Truly the signs of an Apostle were wrought among you in all patience." (Chap. xii. 12.) 'So that we compare ourselves with ourselves, not with those that have nothing: for such arrogance cometh of folly.' Either then he says this with reference to himself, or with reference to them, that 'we dare not compare ourselves with those who contend with one another and boast great things and do not understand:' that is, do not perceive how ridiculous they are in being thus arrogant, and in exalting themselves amongst one another.

Ver. 13. "But we will not glory beyond our measure:" as they do.

For it is probable that in their boasting they said, 'we have converted the world, we have reached unto the ends of the earth,' and vented many other such like big words. 'But not so we,' he says,

"But according to the measure of the province which God apportioned to us as a measure, to reach even unto you." So that his humility is evident on either hand, both in that he boasted nothing more than he had wrought, and that he refers even this itself to God. For, "according to the measure of the province," saith he, "which God apportioned to us, a measure to reach even unto you." Just as if portioning out a vine to husbandmen, even so He meted out unto us. As far then as we have been counted worthy to attain to, so far we boast.

Ver. 14. "For we stretch not ourselves overmuch, as though we reached not unto you: for we came even as far as unto you in preaching the Gospel of Christ."

Not simply 'we came,' but, 'we announced, we preached, we persuaded, we succeeded.' For it is probable that they having merely come to the disciples of the Apostles, ascribed the whole to themselves, from their bare presence among them. 'But not so we: nor can any one say that we were not able to come as far as to you, and that we stretched our boasting as far as to you in words only; for we also preached the word to you.'

[3.] Ver. 15, 16. "Not glorying beyond" our "measure," that is, "in other men's labors, but having hope that as your faith groweth, we shall be magnified in you according to our province unto further abundance, so as to preach

---

[1] Or, casting down.
[2] R. T. compare ourselves, [which is correct, as there is no MS. authority for the preposition inserted by Chrysostom. C.]

the Gospel even unto the parts beyond you, and not to glory in another's province in regard of things ready to our hand.''

He sets forth a large accusation of them on these grounds, both that they boasted of things without their measure, and of other men's labors; and that whilst the whole of the toil was the Apostles', they plumed themselves upon their labors. ' But we,' says he, ' showed these things in our deeds. We will not imitate those men therefore, but will say such things where our deeds bear us witness. And why,' saith he, ' do I say, you?' ''for I have hope that as your faith groweth;'' for he doth not assert absolutely, preserving his own character, but, 'I hope,' he says, ' if you make progress, that our province will be extended even farther, ''to preach the Gospel in the regions beyond.'' For we shall advance farther yet,' he says, ' so as to preach and labor, not so as to boast in words of what other men have labored.' And well did he call it ''province and measure,'' as though he had come into possession of the world, and a rich inheritance; and showing that the whole was wholly God's. ' Having then such works,' he says, ' and expecting greater, we do not boast as they do who have nothing, nor do we ascribe any part to ourselves, but the whole to God. Wherefore also he adds,

Ver. 17. ''He that glorieth, let him glory in the Lord.''

This also, he saith, accrueth to us from God.

Ver. 18. '' For not he that commendeth himself is approved, but whom the Lord commendeth.''

He did not say, we are so, ''but whom the Lord commendeth. Seest thou how modestly he speaks? But if as he proceeds he stirreth up loftier words, wonder not, for this also cometh of Paul's prudence. For if he had gone on in every part to speak lowly words, he would not have hit these men so effectually, nor have extricated the disciples from their error. For it is possible both by modesty ill-timed to do harm, and by saying something admirable of one's self at a proper time to do good. As therefore he also did. For there was no little danger in the disciples being persuaded into any mean opinion of Paul. Not that Paul sought the glory that cometh of men. For had he sought this, he would not have kept silence so long on those great and marvellous matters of '' fourteen years ago;'' (Chap. xii. 20) nor would he, when necessity was laid upon him, have so shrunk back and hesitated to speak of them; very evidently he would not even then have spoken, had he not been compelled. Certainly then it was not from a desire after the glory which cometh from men that he said these things, but out of tender care for the dis-

ciples. For since they cast reproaches[1] at him as a braggart, and as boastful in words but able to show nothing in deeds, he is compelled subsequently to come to those revelations. Although he had it in his power to convince them by his deeds, at the time when he said these things: yet he still persists, nevertheless, in using menaces in words. For he was most especially free from vain-glory; and this his whole life proves, both before and after this. For instance, it was because of this that he changed all at once; and having changed, confounded the Jews and cast away all that honor he had from them, although he was himself their head and their champion. But he considered none of those things when he had found the truth; but took instead their insults and contumely; for he looked to the salvation of the many, thinking this everything. For he that thinketh nothing of hell nor of heaven nor of ten thousand worlds in regard of his longing after Christ, how should he hunt after the glory which cometh from the many? By no means; but he is even very lowly when he may be so, and brands[2] his former life with infamy when he calls himself, '' a blasphemer, and a persecutor, and injurious.'' (1 Tim. i. 13.) And his disciple Luke too says many things of him, evidently having learnt them from himself, himself displaying fully[3] his former life no less than that after his conversion.

[4.] Now I say these things, not that we may hear merely, but that we may learn also. For if he remembered those transgressions before the Laver, although they were all effaced, what forgiveness can we have who are unmindful of those after the Laver ourselves? What sayest thou, O man? Thou hast offended God, and dost thou forget? This is a second offence, a second enmity. Of what sins then dost thou ask forgiveness? Of those which thou even knowest not thyself? Surely, (for is it not so?) thou art deeply anxious and thoughtful how thou mayest give account of them, thou who dost not so much as care to remember them, but sportest with what is no sporting matter. But there will come a time when our sport can go on no longer. For we must needs die: (for the great insensibility of the many obliges me to speak even of things that are evident:) and must needs rise again, and be judged, and be punished; nay rather this needs not, if we choose. For those other things are not at our own disposal; neither our end, nor our resurrection, nor our judgment, but at our Lord's; but our suffering punishment or not is at our own disposal; for this is of those things that may or may not happen[4]. But if we choose,

---

[1] ἔβαλλον
[2] στηλιτεύει
[3] ἐμπομπεύοντος
[4] τῶν ἐνδεχομένων.

we shall make it of the number of impossible things; just as Paul, as Peter, as all the saints did; for it is even impossible for them to be punished. If therefore we have a mind, it is in like manner impossible also that we should suffer ought. For even if we have offended in ten thousand things, it is possible to recover ourselves so long as we are here. Let us then recover ourselves: and let the old man consider that in a little while hence he will depart, since he took his pleasure long enough in his lifetime; (although what sort of pleasure is this, to live in wickedness? but for the present I so speak in respect to his way of thinking;) let him consider, besides, that it is possible for him in a short time to wash away all. The young man again, let him also consider the uncertainty of death, and that oftentimes, when many older persons continued here, the young were carried off before them. For, for this reason, that we may not make traffic[1] of our death, it is left in uncertainty. Wherefore also a certain wise man adviseth, saying, "Make no tarrying to turn unto the Lord, and put not off from day to day: for thou knowest not what to-morrow shall bring forth." (Ecclus. v. 7; Prov. xxvii. 1) For by putting off there is danger and fear; but by not putting off manifest and secure salvation. Hold fast then by virtue. For so, even if thou have departed young, thou hast departed in safety; and if thou shouldst come to old age, thou shalt arrive [at death] with great provision made, and shalt have a double feast all thy life long; both in that thou abstainest from vice, and layest hold on virtue. Say not, 'there will come a time when it may be well to turn,' for this language provokes God exceedingly. And why so? Because He hath promised thee countless ages, but thou art not even willing to labor during this present life, this short life that dureth but a season; but art so indolent and unmanly as to seek a shorter even than this. Are there not the same revellings daily? Are there not the same tables, the same harlots, the same theatres, the same wealth? How long wilt thou love those things as though they were aught? How long will thy appetite for evil remain insatiate? Consider that as often as thou hast fornicated, so often hast thou condemned thyself. For such is the nature of sin: once committed, the Judge hath also passed his sentence. Hast thou been drunken, been gluttonous, or robbed? Hold now, turn right back, acknowledge it to God as a mercy that He snatched thee not away in the midst of thy sins; seek not yet another set time[2] wherein

to work evil. Many have been snatched away in the midst of their covetousness, and have departed to manifest punishment. Fear lest thou also shouldest suffer this, and without excuse. 'But God gave to many a set time for confession in extreme old age.' What then? Will He give it to thee also? 'Perhaps He will,' says one. Why sayest thou 'perhaps,' and 'sometimes,' and 'often?' Consider that thou art deliberating about thy soul, and put also the contrary case, and calculate, and say, 'But what if He should not give it?' 'But what if He should give it?' saith he. God hath indeed given it; but still this supposition is safer and more profitable than that. For if thou begin now, thou hast gained all, whether thou hast a set time granted thee or not; but if thou art always putting off, for this very cause perhaps thou shalt not have one given thee. When thou goest out to battle, thou dost not say, 'there is no need to make my will, perhaps I shall come back safe;' nor dost thou when deliberating about marriage, say 'suppose I take a poor wife, many have even in this way got rich contrary to expectation;' nor when building a house, 'suppose I lay a rotten foundation, many houses have stood even so;' yet in deliberating about the soul, thou leanest on things more rotten still; urging thy 'perhaps,' and 'often,' and 'sometimes,' and trustest thyself to these uncertainties. 'Nay,' saith one, 'not to an uncertainty, but to the mercy of God, for God is merciful.' I know it too; but still this merciful God snatched those away of whom I spoke. And what if after thou hast had time given thee, thou shalt still continue as thou wert? for this sort of man will be listless even in old age. 'Nay,' he said, 'not so.' For this mode of reasoning even after the eighty years desireth ninety, and after the ninety an hundred, and after the hundred will be yet more indisposed to act. And so the whole of life will have been consumed in vain, and what was spoken of the Jews will happen also to thee; "Their days were consumed in vanity." (Ps. lxxviii. 33.) And would that in vanity only, and not unto evil also. For when we have departed thither bearing the heavy burden of our sins, this will be unto evil also. For we shall carry away fuel for the fire and a plentiful feast for the worm. Wherefore I pray and conjure you to halt at length in noble wise, and to desist from wickedness, that we may also obtain the promised good things: whereunto may we all attain, through the grace and love towards men of our Lord Jesus Christ, with Whom to the Father, together with the Holy Spirit, be glory, might, honor, now and ever, and world without end. Amen.

---

[1] πραγματευώμεθα
[2] προθεσμίαν

HOMILY XXIII.

2 Cor. xi. 1.

Would that ye could bear with me in a little foolishness; and, indeed ye do bear with me.*

BEING about to enter upon his own praises, he uses much previous correction. And he does this not once or twice, although the necessity of the subject, and what he had often said, were sufficient excuse for him. For he that remembereth sins which God remembered not, and who therefore saith that he was unworthy of the very name of the Apostles, even by the most insensate is seen clearly not to be saying what he is now going to say, for the sake of glory. For if one must say something startling, even this would be especially injurious to his glory, his speaking something about himself; and to the more part it is offensive. But nevertheless he regarded not timidly any of these things, but he looked to one thing, the salvation of his hearers. But still in order that he might not cause harm to the unthinking by this, by saying, I mean, great things of himself, he employs out of abundant caution these many preparatory correctives, and says, "Would that ye could bear with me," whilst I play the fool in some little things, yea, rather, "ye do indeed bear with me." Beholdest thou wisdom? For when he says, "would that," it is as putting it at their disposal: but when he even asserts [that they do], it is as confiding greatly in their affection, and as declaring that he both loves and is loved. Yea, rather, not from bare love merely, but from a sort of warm and insane passion he says that they ought to bear with him even when he plays the fool. And therefore he added, "For I am jealous over you with a godly jealousy[1]." He did not say, 'for I love you,' but uses a term far more vehement than this. For those souls are jealous which burn ardently for those they love, and jealousy can in no other way be begotten than out of a vehement affection. Then that they may not think, that it is for the sake of power, or honor, or wealth, or any other such like thing, that he desires their affec-

tion, he added, "with a jealousy of God." For God also is said to be jealous, not that any should suppose[2] passion, (for the Godhead is impassible,) but that all may know that He doeth all things from no other regard than their sakes over whom He is jealous; not that Himself may gain aught, but that He may save them. Among men indeed jealousy ariseth not from this cause, but for the sake of their own repose; not because the beloved ones sustain outrage, but lest those who love them should be wounded, and be outshone in the good graces, and stand lower in the affections, of the beloved. But here it is not so. 'For I care not,' he says, 'for this, lest I should stand lower in your esteem; but lest I should see you corrupted. For such is God's jealousy; and such is mine also, intense at once and pure.' Then there is also this necessary reason;

"For I espoused you to one husband, as a pure virgin." 'Therefore I am jealous, not for myself, but for him to whom I have espoused you.' For the present time is the time of espousal, but the time of the nuptials is another; when they sing, 'the Bridegroom hath risen up.' Oh what things unheard of! In the world they are virgins before the marriage, but after the marriage no longer. But here it is not so: but even though they be not virgins before this marriage, after the marriage they become virgins. So the whole Church is a virgin. For addressing himself even to all, both husbands and wives, he speaks thus. But let us see what he brought and espoused us with, what kind of nuptial gifts. Not gold, not silver, but the kingdom of heaven. Wherefore also he said, "We are ambassadors on behalf of Christ," and beseeches them, when he was about to receive the Bride. What happened in Abraham's case was a type of this. (Gen. xxiv. 4, &c.) For he sent his faithful servant to seek a Gentile maiden in marriage; and in this case God sent His own servants to seek the Church in marriage for His son, and prophets from of old saying, "Hearken, O daughter, and consider, and forget thine own people and thy father's house, and the King

---

* [Most critics, with the A. V. and the R. V., prefer to take the verb here as imperative, and render, "nay indeed bear with me," which is supposed to suit better with what follows. C.]
[1] Gr. *jealousy of God*.

² ὑποπτεύσῃ

25

383

shall desire thy beauty." (Ps. xlv. 10, 11.) Seest thou the prophet also espousing ? seest thou the Apostle too expressing the same thing himself with much boldness, and saying, "I espoused you to one husband that I might present you as a pure virgin to Christ ?" Seest thou wisdom again ? For having said, 'Ye ought to bear with me,' he did not say, ' for I am your teacher and I speak not for mine own sake :' but he uses this expression which invested them with especial dignity, placing himself in the room of her who promotes a match, and them in the rank of the bride ; and he adds these words ;

Ver. 3. "But I fear lest by any means, as the serpent beguiled Eve through his subtlety, so your minds should be corrupted from the simplicity that is toward Christ[1]."

'For although the destruction be yours [alone], yet is the sorrow mine as well.' And consider his wisdom. For he does not assert, although they were corrupted ; and so he showed when he said, "When your obedience is fulfilled," (c. x. 6.) and "I shall bewail many which have sinned already;" (c. xii. 21.) but still he does not leave them to get shameless. And therefore he says, "lest at any time." For this neither condemns nor is silent ; for neither course were safe, whether to speak out plainly or to conceal perpetually. Therefore he employs this middle form, saying, "lest at any time." For this is the language neither of one that entirely distrusts, nor entirely relies on them, but of one who stands between these two. In this way then he palliated, but by his mention of that history threw them into an indescribable terror, and cuts them off from all forgiveness. For even although the serpent was malignant, and she senseless, yet did none of these things snatch the woman from punishment. ' Beware then,' he says, ' lest such be your fate, and there be naught to screen you. For he too promising greater things, so deceived.' Whence it is plain that these[2] too, by boasting and puffing themselves up, deceived. And this may be conjectured not from this place only, but also from what he says afterwards,

Ver. 4. "If he that cometh preacheth

___
[1] Such seems to be St Chrysostom's rendering. See below. [It is not easy to understand this note of the English translator. Chrysostom has the accepted text εἰς τὸν χριστόν, which the Vulgate, Beza and Calvin make equivalent to ἐν χριστῷ. But the proper sense is, as Thayer *sub voce* gives it, "sincerity of mind toward Christ, i. e., single-hearted faith in Christ, as opposed to false wisdom in matters pertaining to Christianity." The allusion to the marriage relation in the previous verse is still kept up. The Apostle's fear was that the Corinthians might be so corrupted as to turn away from the undivided affection and devotion which they owed to the Lord Jesus Christ as much as a bride to her husband. His warning is confirmed by his reference to the one standing example of the inconstancy of the human heart, and of the fearful consequences of forsaking God. In his mind the narrative of the fall was neither a fable nor an allegory, but an historical fact. C.]
[2] i. e. False Apostles.

another Jesus, whom we did not preach, or if ye receive a different Spirit which ye did not receive, or a different Gospel which ye did not accept, ye do well to bear with him."

And he does not say, ' Lest by any means as Adam was deceived :' but shows that those men[3] are but women who are thus abused, for it is the part of woman to be deceived. And he did not say, ' so ye also should be deceived : ' but keeping up the metaphor, he says, "so your minds should be corrupted from the simplicity that is toward Christ." ' From the simplicity, I say, not from wickedness; neither out of wickedness [is it], nor out of your not believing, but out of simplicity.' But, nevertheless, not even under such circumstances are the deceived entitled to forgiveness, as Eve showed. But if this does not entitle to forgiveness, much more will it not do so, when through vain-glory any is so[4].

[2.] "For if he that cometh preacheth another Jesus whom we did not preach : " showing hereby that their deceivers were not Corinthians, but persons from some other quarter previously corrupted : wherefore he saith, " he that cometh."

"If ye receive a different Spirit, if a different Gospel which ye did not accept, ye do well to bear" with him. What sayest thou? Thou that saidst to the Galatians, "If any preach another Gospel to you than that ye have received, let him be anathema ; " dost thou now say, "ye do well to bear" with him? And yet on this account it were meet not to bear with, but to recoil, from them ; but if they say the same things, it is meet to bear with them. How then dost thou say, ' because they say the same things, it is not meet to bear with them ?' for he says, 'if they said other things, it were meet to bear with them.' Let us then give good heed, for the danger is great, and the precipice deep, if men run past this carelessly ; and what is here said giveth an entrance to all the heresies. What then is the sense of these words? Those persons so boasted as if the Apostles taught incompletely, and they were introducing somewhat more than they. For it is probable that with much idle talk, they were bringing in senseless rubbish so as to overlay these doctrines. And therefore he made mention of the serpent and of Eve who was thus deceived by the expectation of acquiring more. And alluding to this in the former Epistle also, he said, "Now ye are become rich, ye have reigned as kings without us; " and again, "we are fools for Christ's sake, but ye are wise in Christ." (1 Cor. iv. 8 ; ib. 10.) Since then it was probable that using the wisdom which is without, they talked much idly,

___
[3] γυναῖκας ὄντας τοὺς.
[4] i. e. Is deceived.

what he says is this : that ' if these persons said any thing more, and preached a different Christ who ought to have been preached, but we omitted it, " ye do well to bear " with them.' For on this account he added, " whom we did not preach." ' But if the chief points of the faith are the same, what have ye the more of them ? for whatsoever things they may say, they will say nothing more than what we have said.' And observe with what precision he states the case. For he did not say, ' if he that cometh saith any thing more ; ' for they did say something more, haranguing with more authority and with much beauty of language ; wherefore he did not say this, but what ? [If] " he that cometh preacheth another Jesus," a thing which had no need of that array of words : " or ye receive a different Spirit," (for neither was there need of words in this case ;) that is to say, ' makes you richer in grace ; ' or " a different Gospel which ye did not accept," (nor did this again stand in need of words,) " ye do well to bear " with him. But consider, I pray thee, how he every where uses such a definition as shows that nothing very great, nor indeed any thing more, had been introduced by them. For when he had said, " If he that cometh preacheth another Jesus," he added, " whom we did not preach ;" and " ye receive a different Spirit," he subjoined, " which ye did not receive ; or a different Gospel," he added, " which ye did not accept," by all these showing that it is meet to attend to them, not simply if they say something more, but if they said any thing more which ought to have been said and was by us omitted. But if it ought not to have been said, and was therefore not said by us ; or if they say only the same things as we, why gape ye so admiringly[1] upon them ? ' And yet if they say the same things,' saith one, ' wherefore dost thou hinder them ? ' Because that using hypocrisy, they introduce strange doctrines. This however for the present he doth not say, but afterwards asserts it, when he says, " They fashion themselves into Apostles of Christ ; " (Ver. 13.) for the present he withdraws the disciples from their authority by less offensive considerations ; and this not out of envy to them, but to secure these. Else why does he not hinder Apollos, who was, however, a " learned man, and mighty in the Scriptures ; " (Acts xviii. 24 ; 1 Cor. xvi. 12) but even beseeches him, and promises he will send him ? Because together with his learning he preserved also the integrity of the doctrines ; but with these it was the reverse. And therefore he wars with them and blames the disciples for gaping admiringly upon them, saying, ' if aught that should have been said we omitted and they supplied, we do not hinder you

from giving heed to them : but if all has been fully completed by us and nothing left deficient, whence is it that they caught you ? ' Wherefore also he adds,

Ver. 5. " For I reckon that I am not a whit behind the very chiefest Apostles," no longer making comparison of himself with them, but with Peter and the rest. ' So that if they know more than I do, [they know more] than they also.' And observe how here also he shows modesty. For he did not say, ' the Apostles said nothing more than I,' but what ? " I reckon," so I deem, " that I am not a whit behind the very chiefest Apostles." For since this also appeared to bespeak an inferiority in him, that those having preceded him were of greater name ; and more respect was entertained for them, and these persons were intending to foist themselves in ; therefore he makes this comparison of himself with them with the dignity[2] that becomes him. Therefore he also mentions them with encomiums, not speaking simply of " the Apostles," but " the very chiefest," meaning Peter and James and John.

[3.] Ver. 6. " But though I be rude in speech, yet am I not in knowledge."

For since those that corrupted the Corinthians had the advantage in this, that they were not rude ; he mentions this also, showing that he was not ashamed of, but even prided himself upon it. And he said not, " But though I be rude in speech," yet so also are they[3], for this would have seemed to be accusing them as well as himself, and exalting these : but he overthrows the thing itself, the wisdom from without. And indeed in his former Epistle he contends even vehemently about this thing, saying that it not only contributes nothing to the Preaching, but it even throws a shadow on the glory of the Cross ; (1 Cor. ii. 1.) for he says, " I came not with excellency of speech or of wisdom unto you, lest the cross of Christ should be made void ; (1 Cor. i. 17.) and many other things of the same kind ; because " in knowledge " they were " rude," which is also the extremest form of rudeness. When therefore it was necessary to institute a comparison in those things which were great, he compares himself with the Apostles : but when to show that which appeared to be a deficiency, he no longer does this, but grapples with the thing itself and shows that it was a superiority. And when indeed no necessity urged him, he says that he is " the least of the Apostles," and not worthy even of the title ; but here again when occasion called, he says that he is " not a whit behind the very chiefest Apostles." For he knew that this would most advantage the disciples. Wherefore also he adds,

---

[1] κεχήνατε.

[2] σχήματος.
[3] i. e. Peter &c.

" Nay, in every thing we have made it manifest among all men to youward." For here again he accuses the false Apostles as " walking in craftiness." (Chap. iv. 2.) And he said this of himself before also, that he did not live after the outward appearance, nor preach " handling the word deceitfully (ibid.) and corrupting it. But those men were one thing and appeared another. But not so he. Wherefore also he every where assumes a high tone, as doing nothing with a view to men's opinion nor concealing aught about himself. As he also said before, " by the manifestation of the truth commending ourselves to every man's conscience," (ibid.) so now again he saith " in every thing we have made it manifest to you." But what does this mean? 'We are rude,' he said, 'and do not conceal it: we receive from some persons and we do not keep it secret. We receive then from you, and we pretend not that we do not receive, as they do when they receive, but we make every thing that we do manifest unto you ; ' which was the conduct of one that both had exceeding confidence in them, and told them every thing truly. Wherefore he also calls them witnesses, saying now, " among all men to youward," and also before, " For we write none other things unto you, than what ye read or even acknowledge." (Chap. i. 13.)

[4.] Then after he had defended his own conduct he goes on next to say with severity,

Ver. 7. " Or did I commit a sin in abasing myself that ye might be exalted ? "

And in explanation of this, he adds,

Ver. 8. " I robbed other churches, taking wages of them that I might minister unto you."

What he says is this ; ' I lived in straitness ;' for this is the force of " abasing myself." ' Can you then lay this to my charge ? and do ye therefore lift up yourselves against me, because I abased myself by begging, by enduring straits, by suffering, by hungering, that ye might be exalted ?' And how were they exalted by his being in straits ? They were more edified and were not offended ; which also might [well] be a very great accusation of them and a reproach of their weakness ; that it was not possible in any other way to lead them on than by first abasing himself. ' Do ye then lay it to my charge that I abased myself ? But thereby ye were exalted.' For since he said even above that they accused him, for that when present he was lowly, and when absent bold, in defending himself he here strikes them again, saying, ' this too was for your sakes.'

" I robbed other churches." Here finally he speaks reproachfully, but his former words prevent these from seeming offensive ; for he said, " Bear with me in a little foolishness : " and before all his other achievements makes this

his first boast. For this worldly men look to especially, and on this also those his adversaries greatly prided themselves. Therefore it is that he does not first enter on the subject of his perils, nor yet of his miracles, but on this of his contempt of money, because they prided themselves on this ; and at the same time he also hints that they were wealthy. But what is to be admired in him is this, that when he was able to say that he was even supported by his own hands, he did not say this ; but says that which especially shamed them and yet was no encomium on himself, namely, ' I took from others.' And he did not say " took," but " robbed," that is, ' I stripped them, and made them poor.' And what surely is greater, that it was not for superfluities, but for his necessities, for when he says 'wages,' he means necessary subsistence. And what is more grievous yet, " to minister unto you." We preach to you ; and when I ought to be supported by you, I have enjoyed this at others' hands. The accusation is twofold, or rather three-fold ; that when both living amongst them and ministering to them, and seeking necessary support, he had others supplying his wants. Great the excess, of the one in negligence, of the other in zeal ! For these sent to him even when at a great distance, and those did not even support him when amongst them.

[5.] Then because he had vehemently scourged them, he quietly again relaxes the vehemence of his rebuke, saying,

Ver. 9. " And when I was present with you, and was in want, I was not a burden on any man."

For he did not say, ' ye did not give to me,' but, ' I did not take,' for as yet he spares them. But nevertheless even in the subduedness of his language he covertly strikes them again, for the word, " present," is exceedingly emphatic, and so is " in want." For that they might not say, ' what matter then, if you had [enough] ?' he added, " and was in want."

" I was not a burden " on you. Here again he hits them gently, as making such contributions reluctantly, as feeling them a burden. Then comes the reason also, full of accusation and fraught with jealousy. Wherefore also he introduced it, not in the way of a leading point[1], but as informing them whence and by whom he was supported, so as to stimulate them again, in an unsuspicious way, as to the point of almsgiving ;

" For the measure of my want," he says, " the brethren which came from Macedonia supplied." Seest thou how he provokes them again, by bringing forward those that had ministered to him ? For inspiring them first

---

[1] οὐ προηγουμένως.

with a desire of knowing who these could be, when he said, "I robbed other churches ;" he then mentions them also by name ; which would incite them also unto almsgiving. For he thus persuades those who had been beaten [by them] in the matter of supporting the Apostle, not to be also beaten in the succor they gave to the poor. And he says this also in his Epistle to the Macedonians themselves, "For in my necessities ye sent unto me once and again, even in the beginning of the Gospel ;" (Philipp. iv. 16, 15.) which point also was a very great commendation of them, that from the very beginning they shone forth. But observe how everywhere he mentions his "necessity," and no where a superfluity. Now therefore by saying "present," and in "want" he showed that he ought to have been supported by the Corinthians ; and by the words, "they supplied the measure of my want," he shows that he did not so much as ask. And he assigns a reason which was not the real one. What then is this? That he had received from others ; "for," says he, "the measure of my want those that came supplied." 'For this reason,' he says, 'I was not a burden ; not because I had no confidence in you.' And yet it is for this latter reason that he so acts, and he shows it in what follows ; but does not say it plainly, but throws it into the shade[1], leaving it to the conscience of his hearers. And he gives proof of it covertly in what follows, by saying,

"And in every" thing "I kept myself from being burdensome, and so will I keep" myself. "For think not," says he, "that I say these things that I may receive." Now the words, "so will I keep myself," are severer, if he has not even yet confidence in them ; but once for all had given up the idea of receiving aught from them. He shows, moreover, that they even considered this to be a burden; wherefore he said, "I have kept myself from being burdensome, and so will I keep myself." He says this in his former Epistle also, "I write not this that it may be so done unto me; for" it were "good for me rather to die, than that any man should make my glorying void." (1 Cor. ix. 15.) And here again, "I have kept myself from being burdensome unto you, and so will I keep" myself.

[6.] Then, that he may not seem to speak these things for the sake of winning them on the better [to do this], he saith,

Ver. 10. "As the truth of Christ is in me."

'Do not think that I therefore have spoken, that I may receive, that I may the rather draw you on: for,' saith he, "as the truth is in me, "No man shall stop me of this glorying in the regions of Achaia." For that none should think again that he is grieved at this, or that he speaks these things in anger, he even calls the thing a "glorying." And in his former Epistle too he dressed it out[2] in like terms. For so that he may not wound them there either, he says, "What then is my reward?" "That when I preach the Gospel, I may make the Gospel of Christ without charge." (1 Cor. ix. 18.) And as he there calls it "reward," so doth he here "glorying," that they may not be excessively ashamed at what he said, as if he were asking and they gave not to him. 'For what, if even ye would give?' saith he, 'Yet I do not accept it.' And the expression, "shall not stop me," is a metaphor taken from rivers, or from the report, as if running every where, of his receiving nothing. 'Ye stop not with your giving this my freedom of speech.' But he said not, 'ye stop not,' which would have been too[3] cutting, but it "no man shall stop me in the regions of Achaia." This again was like giving them a fatal blow, and exceedingly apt to deject and pain them, since they were the only persons he refused [to take from]. 'For if he made that his boast, it were meet to make it so every where: but if he only does so among us, perchance this is owing to our weakness." Lest therefore they should so reason and be dejected, see how he corrects this.

Ver. 11. "Wherefore? because I love you not? God knoweth."

Quickly [is it done], and by an easy method[4]. But still, not even so did he rid them of those charges. For he neither said, 'ye are not weak,' nor yet, 'ye are strong;' but, "I love you," which very greatly aggravated the accusation against them. For the not receiving from them, because they felt it an exceeding grievance, was a proof of special love toward them. So he acted in two contrary ways out of love; he both did receive, and did not receive : but this contrariety was on account of the disposition of the givers. And he did not say, 'I therefore do not take of you, because I exceedingly love you,' for this would have contained an accusation of their weakness and have thrown them into distress; but he turned what he said to another reason. What then is this?

Ver. 12. "That I may cut off occasion from them that desire an occasion; that wherein they glory, they may be found even as we."

For since this they sought earnestly, to find some handle[5] against him, it is necessary to remove this also. For this is the one point on which they pique themselves. Therefore that

---

[1] συσκιάζει
[2] κατεσκεύασεν.
[3] Or, "more."
[4] εὐαπαλλάκτως.
[5] σεμνύνονται.

they might not have any advantage whatever, it was necessary to set this right; for in other things they were inferior. For, as I have said, nothing doth so edify worldly people as the receiving nothing from them. Therefore the devil in his craftiness dropped this bait especially, when desirous to injure them in other respects. But it appears to me that this even was in hypocrisy. And therefore he did not say, 'wherein they have well done,' but what? "wherein they glory;" which also was as jeering at their glorying; for they gloried also of that which they were not. But the man of noble spirit not only ought not to boast of what he has not, but not even of what he possesses; as this blessed saint was wont to do, as the patriarch Abraham did, saying, "But I am earth and ashes." (Gen. xviii. 27.) For since he had no sins to speak of, but shone with good works; having run about in every direction and found no very great handle against himself, he betakes himself to his nature; and since the name of "earth" is in some way or other one of dignity, he added to it that of "ashes." Wherefore also another saith, "Why is earth and ashes proud?" (Ecclus. x. 9.)

[7.] For tell me not of the bloom of the countenance, nor of the uplifted neck, nor of the mantle, and the horse, and the followers; but reflect where all these things do end, and put that to them. But and if thou tell me of what appears to the eye, I too will tell thee of things in pictures, brighter far than these. But as we do not admire those for their appearance, as seeing what their nature is, that all is clay; so therefore let us not these either, for these too are but clay. Yea rather, even before they are dissolved and become dust, show me this uplifted [neck] a prey to fever and gasping out life; and then will I discourse with thee and will ask, What has become of all that profuse ornament? whither has that crowd of flatterers vanished, that attendance of slaves, that abundance of wealth and possessions? What wind hath visited and blown all away? Nay, even stretched upon the bier, he beareth the tokens of that wealth and that pride; a splendid garment thrown over him, poor and rich following him forth, the assembled crowds breathing words of good omen[1]. Surely this also is a very mockery; howbeit even this besides is presently proved naught, like a blossom that perishes. For when we have passed over the threshold of the city gates, and after having delivered over the body to the worms, return, I will ask thee again, where is that vast crowd gone to? What has become of the clamor and uproar? where are the torches? where the bands of women? are not these things, then, a dream?

And what too has become of the shouts? where are those many lips that cried, and bade him 'be of good cheer, for no man is immortal?' These things ought not now to be said to one that heareth not, but when he made prey of others, when he was overreaching, then with a slight change should it have been said to him, 'Be not of good cheer, no man is immortal; hold in thy madness, extinguish thy lust;' but 'Be of good cheer' is for the injured party. For to chant such things over this man now, is but like men exulting over him and speaking irony; for he ought not for this now to be of good cheer, but to fear and tremble.

And if even this advice is now of no use to him since he has run his course, yet at least let those of the rich who labor under the same disease, and follow him to the tomb, hear it. For although beforehand through the intoxication of wealth, they have no such thing in mind, yet at that season when the sight of him that is laid out even confirms what is said, let them be sober, let them be instructed : reflecting that yet a little while and they will come that shall bear them away to that fearful account, and to suffer the penalty of their acts of rapacity and extortion. 'And what is this to the poor?' saith one. Why, to many this also is a satisfaction, to see him that hath wronged them punished. 'But to us it is no satisfaction, but the escaping suffering ourselves.' I praise you exceeedingly and approve of you in that ye exult not over the calamities of others, but seek only your own safety. Come then, I will ensure[2] you this also. For if we suffer evil at the hands of men, we cut off no small part of our debt by bearing what is done to us nobly. We receive therefore no injury; for God reckons the ill-treatment towards our debt, not according to the principle of justice but of His loving-kindness; and because He succored not him that suffered evil. 'Whence doth this appear?' saith one. The Jews once suffered evil at the hand of the Babylonians; and God did not prevent it: but they were carried away, children and women; yet afterwards did this captivity become a consolation to them in respect of[3] their sins. Therefore He saith to Isaiah, "Comfort ye, comfort ye My people, ye priests: speak unto the heart of Jerusalem, for she hath received of the Lord's hand double for sins." (Is. xl. 1, 2.) And again; "Grant us peace, for Thou hast repaid us every thing." (ib. xxvi. 12, LXX.) And David saith; "Behold mine enemies, for they are multiplied; and forgive all my sins." (Ps. xxv. 19, 18.) And when he bore with Shimei cursing him, he said, "Let him alone, that the Lord may see my abasement, and requite me good for this day." (2 Sam. xvi.

---

[1] εὐφημούντων.

[2] ἐγγυήσομαι.

[3] κατὰ ἀναλογίαν

11, 12.) For when He aideth us not when we suffer wrong, then most of all are we advantaged; for He sets it to the account of our sins, if we bear it thankfully.

[8.] So that when thou seest a rich man plundering a poor, leave him that suffereth wrong, and weep for the plunderer. For the one putteth off filth, the other bedaubeth himself with more filth. Such was the fate of Elisha's · servant in the story of Naaman (2 Kings v. 20, &c.) For though he took not by violence, yet he did a wrong; for to get money by deceit is a wrong. What then befel? With the wrong he received also the leprosy; and he that was wronged was benefited, but he that did the wrong received the greatest possible harm. The same happens now also in the case of the soul. And this is of so great force that often by itself it hath propitiated God; yea though he who suffereth evil be unworthy of aid; yet when he so suffers in excess, by this alone he draweth God unto the forgiveness of himself, and to the punishment of him that did the wrong. Wherefore also God said of old to the heathen, " I indeed delivered them over unto a few things, but they have set themselves on together unto evil things;" (Zech. i. 15. LXX.) they shall suffer ills irremediable[1]. For there is nothing, no, nothing, that doth so much exasperate God as rapine and violence and extortion. And why forsooth? Because it is very easy to abstain from this sin. For here it is not any natural desire that perturbeth the mind, but it ariseth from wilful negligence[2]. How then doth the Apostle call it, "a root of evils." (1 Tim. vi. 10.) Why, I say so too, but this root is from us, and not from the nature of the things. And, if ye will, let us make a comparison and see which is the more imperious, the desire of money or of beauty[3]; for that which shall be found to have struck down great men is the more difficult to master. Let us see then what great man the desire of money ever got possession of. Not one; only of exceeding pitiful and abject persons, Gehazi, Ahab, Judas, the priests of the Jews: but the desire for beauty overcame even the great prophet David. And this I say, not as extending forgiveness to those who are conquered by such a lust, but rather, as preparing them to be watchful. For when I have shown the strength of the passion, then, most especially, I show them to be deprived of every claim to forgiveness. For if indeed thou hadst not known the wild beast, thou wouldest have this to take refuge in; but now, having known, yet falling into it, thou wilt have no excuse. After him[4], it took possession of his son still

more completely. And yet there was never man wiser than he, and all other virtue did he attain; still, however, he was seized so violently by this passion, that even in his vitals he received the wound. And the •father indeed rose up again and renewed the struggle, and was crowned again; but the son showed nothing of the kind.

Therefore also Paul said, " It is better to marry than to burn:" (1 Cor. vii. 9.) and Christ, " He that is able to receive it, let him receive it." (Matt. xiv. 12.) But concerning money He spake not so, but, "whoso hath forsaken" his goods "shall receive an hundredfold." (ib. 29.) 'How then,' saith one, 'did He say of the rich, that they shall hardly obtain the kingdom?' Again implying their weakness of character; not the imperiousness of money, but their utter slavery. And this is evident also from the advice which Paul gave. For from that lust he leads men quite away, saying. " But they that desire to be rich fall into temptation;" (1 Tim. vi. 9.) but in the case of the other not so; but having separated them "for a season" only, and that by "consent," he advises to 'come together again' (1 Cor. vii. 5.) For he feared the billows of lust lest they should occasion a grievous shipwreck. This passion is even more vehement[5] than anger. For it is not possible to feel anger when there is nothing[6] provoking it, but a man cannot help desiring even when the face which moveth to it is not seen. Therefore this passion indeed He did not cut off altogether, but added the words, " without a cause." (Matt. v. 22.) Nor again did He abolish all desire, but only that which is unlawful, for he saith, " Nevertheless, because of desires[7], let every man have his own wife." (1 Cor. vii. 2.) But to lay up treasure He allowed not, either with cause or without. For those passions were implanted in our nature for a necessary end; desire, for the procreation of children, and anger, for the succor of the injured, but desire of money not so. Therefore neither is the passion natural to us. So then if thou art made captive by it, thou wilt suffer so much the more the vilest punishment. Therefore surely, it is, that Paul, permitting even a second marriage, demands in the case of money great strictness, saying, " Why not rather take wrong? why not rather be defrauded?" (1 Cor. vi. 7.) And when treating of virginity, he says, " I have no commandment," (ib. vii. 25.) and " I speak this for your profit, not that I may cast a snare upon you;" (ib. 35.) but when his discourse is of money, he says, " Having raiment and

---

[1] ἀνήκεστα.
[2] ῥαθυμίας
[3] σωμάτων.
[4] David.

[5] εὐτονώτερον.
[6] Or, 'no one.'
[7] S. Chrysostom here reads, 'because of desires ἐπιθυμίαις, instead of, 'because of fornication,' πορνείας, with the Rec. Text, [which is correct. C.]

food, let us be therewith content." (1 Tim. vi. 8.) ' How then is it,' saith one, ' that by this, more than the other, are many overcome?' Because they stand not so much on their guard[1] against it as against lasciviousness and fornication; for if they had thought it equally dangerous, they would not, perhaps, have been made its captives. So also were those wretched virgins cast out of the bridechamber, because that, having struck down the great adversary, they were wounded[2] by one weaker, and who was nothing. (Mat. xxv. 1, &c.) Besides this, one may say further, that if any, subduing lust, is overcome by money, often[3] he does not in fact subdue lust, but has received from nature the gift of suffering no great uneasiness of that sort; for all are not equally inclined to it. Knowing

then these things, and revolving frequently with ourselves the example of the virgins, let us shun this evil wild beast. For if virginity profited them nothing, but after countless toils and labors they perished through the love of money, who shall deliver us if we fall into this passion? Wherefore I beseech you to do all you can, both that ye be not taken captive by it, and that if taken, ye continue not in captivity, but break asunder those hard bonds. For so shall we be able to secure a footing in heaven and to obtain the countless good things; whereunto may all we attain, through the grace and love towards men of our Lord Jesus Christ, with Whom to the Father, with the Holy Ghost, be glory, might, honor, now and for ever, and world without end. Amen.

HOMILY XXIV.

2 COR. xi. 13.

For such are false apostles, deceitful workers, fashioning themselves into Apostles of Christ.

WHAT sayest thou? they that preach Christ, they that take not money, they that bring not in a different gospel, "false apostles?" 'Yes,' he saith, and for this very reason most of all, because they make pretense of all these things for the purpose of deceiving. "Deceitful workers," for they do work indeed, but pull up what has been planted. For being well aware that otherwise they would not be well received, they take the mask of truth and so enact the drama of error. ' And yet,' saith one, ' they take no money.' That they may take greater things; that they may destroy the soul. Yea rather, even that was a falsehood; and they took money but did it secretly: and he shows this in what follows. And indeed he already hinted this where he said, " that wherein they glory, they may be found even as we:" (Ver. 12.) in what follows, however, he hinted it more plainly, saying, " If a man devour you, if a man take you captive, if a man exalt himself, ye bear with him."(Ver. 20.) But at present he accuses them on another account, saying, " fashioning themselves." They had only a " fashion;" the skin of the sheep was but outside clothing[4].

Ver. 14, 15. " And no marvel; for if even

Satan fashioneth himself into an angel of light, is it a great thing if his ministers also fashion themselves as ministers of righteousness?"

So that if one ought to marvel, this is what he ought to marvel at, and not at their transformation. For when their teacher dares do any thing, no marvel that the disciples also follow. But what is " an angel of light?" That hath free liberty to speak, that standeth near to God. For there are also angels of darkness; those which be the devil's, those dark and cruel ones. And the devil hath deceived many so, fashioning himself " into," not becoming, " an angel of light." So do also do these bear about them the form of an Apostle, not the power itself, for this they cannot. But nothing is so like the devil[5] as to do things for display. But what is " a ministry of righteousness?" That which we are who preach to you a Gospel having righteousness. For he either means this, or else that they invest themselves with the character of righteous men. How then shall we know them? " By their works," as Christ said. Wherefore he is compelled to place his own good deeds and their wickedness side by side, that the spurious may become evident by the comparison. And when about again to enter upon his own praises, he first accuses them, in order to show that such an argument was forced upon him, lest any should accuse him for speaking about himself, and says,

Ver. 16. " Again I say." For he had even

---

[1] παραταττόμενοι.
[2] Al. thrown.
[3] Or, perhaps.
[4] ἐπίκειται.

[5] διαβολικὸν

already used much preparatory corrective : ' But nevertheless I am not contented with what I have said, but I say yet again, '

"Let no man think me foolish." For this was what they did—boasted without a reason.— But observe, I pray you, how often, when about to enter upon his own praises, he checks himself[1]. 'For indeed it is the act of folly,' he says, 'to boast : but I do it, not as playing the fool, but because compelled. But if ye do not believe me, but though ye see there is a necessity will condemn me ; not even so will I decline the task[2].' Seest thou how he showed that there was great necessity for his speaking. For he that shunned not even this suspicion, consider what violent impulsion to speak he must have undergone, how he travailed and was constrained to speak. But, nevertheless, even so he employs this thing with moderation. For he did not say, ' that I may glory.' And when about to do "a little," again he uses yet another deprecatory expression[3], saying,

Ver. 17. "That which I speak, I speak not after the Lord, but as in foolishness, in this confidence of glorifying."

Seest thou how glorying is not "after the Lord?" For He saith, "When ye shall have done all, say, We are unprofitable servants." (Luke xvii. 10.) Howbeit, by itself indeed it is not "after the Lord," but by the intention it becomes so. And therefore he said, "That which I speak," not accusing the motive, but the words. Since his aim is so admirable as to dignify the words also. For as a manslayer, though his action is of those most strictly forbidden, has often been approved from the intention ; and as circumcision, although it is not ' after the Lord, has become so from the intention, so also glorying. And wherefore then does he not use so great strictness of expression ? Because he is hastening on to another point, and he freely gratifies even to superfluity those who are desirous to find a handle against him, so that he may say only the things that are profitable ; for when said they were enough to extinguish all that suspicion. "But as in foolishness." Before he says, "Would that ye could bear with me in a little foolishness," (Ver. 4.) but now "as in foolishness;" for the farther he proceeds, the more he clears his language. Then that thou mayest not think that he plays the fool on all points, he added, "in this confidence of glorying." In this particular he means : just as in another place he said, "that we be not put to shame," and added, "in this confidence of glorying." (Chap. ix. 4.) And again, in another place, having said, "Or what I purpose do I purpose according to

the flesh, that with me there should be the yea yea, and the nay nay?" (Chap. i. 17.) And having shown that he cannot in all cases even fulfil what he promises, because he does not purpose after the flesh, lest any should make this suspicion stretch to the doctrine also, he adds, "But as God is faithful our word towards you was not yea and nay." (Ibid. 18.)

[2.] And observe how after having said so many things before, he again sets down yet other grounds of excuse, saying further thus,

Ver. 18. "Seeing that many glory after the flesh, I will glory also."

What is, "after the flesh?" Of things external, of high birth, of wealth, of wisdom, of being circumcised, of Hebrew ancestry, of popular renown. And behold wisdom. He sets down those things which he shows to be nothings[4], and then, folly also. For if to glory in what are really good things be folly, much more is it so [to glory in] those that are nothing. And this is what he calls, "not after the Lord." For it is no advantage to be a Hebrew, or any such like things soever. 'Think not, therefore, that I set these down as a virtue ; no ; but because those men boast I also am compelled to institute my comparison on these points.' Which he does also in another place, saying, "If any man thinketh that he may trust in the flesh, I more : " (Phil. iii. 4.) and there, it is on their account that trusted in this. Just as if one who was come of an illustrious race but had chosen a philosophic life, should see others priding themselves greatly on being well-born ; and being desirious of taking down their vanity, should be compelled to speak of his own distinction ; not to adorn himself, but to humble them ; so, truly, does Paul also do. Then leaving those, he empties all his censure upon the Corinthians, saying,

Ver. 19. "For ye bear with the foolish gladly." 'So that ye are to blame for this, and more than they. For if ye had not borne with them, and so far as it lay in them received damage, I would not have spoken a word ; but I do it out of a tender care for your salvation, and in condescension. And behold, how he accompanies even his censure with praise. For having said, "ye bear with the foolish gladly ; " he added,

"Being wise yourselves." For it was a sign of folly to glory, and on such matters. And yet it behoved to rebuke them, and say, ' Do not bear with the foolish ; ' he does this, however, at greater advantage. For in that case he would have seemed to rebuke them because he himself was destitute of these advantages ; but now having showed himself to be their superior

---

[1] ἀνακρούεται
[2] παραιτήσομαι.
[3] παραιτήσει.

[4] οὐδένα

even in these points, and to esteem them to be nothing, he corrects them with greater effect. At present, however, before entering upon his own praises and the comparison, he also reproaches the Corinthians with their great slavishness, because they were extravagantly submissive to them. And observe how he ridicules them.

Ver. 20. "For ye bear with a man," he says, "if he devour you."

How then saidst thou, "that wherein they glory, they may be found even as we?" (Ver. 12.) Seest thou that he shows that they did take of them, and not simply take, but even in excess: for the term "devour" plainly shows this,

"If a man bring you into bondage." 'Ye have given away both your money,' he says, 'and your persons, and your freedom. For this is more than taking of you; to be masters not only of your money, but of yourselves also.' And he makes this plain even before, where he says, "If others partake of this right over you, do not we much more?" (1 Cor. ix. 12.) Then he addeth what is more severe, saying,

"If a man exalt himself." 'For neither is your slavery of a moderate sort, nor are your masters gentle, but burdensome and odious.'

"If a man smite you on the face." Seest thou again a further stretch of tyranny? He said this, not meaning that they were stricken on the face, but that they spat upon and dishonored them; wherefore he added,

Ver. 21. "I speak by way of disparagement," for ye suffer no whit less than men smitten on the face. What now can be stronger than this? What oppression more bitter than this? when having taken from you both your money and your freedom and your honor, they even so are not gentle towards you nor suffer you to abide in the rank of servants, but have used you more insultingly than any bought slave.*

"As though we had been weak." The expression is obscure. For since it was a disagreeable subject he therefore so expressed it as to steal away the offensiveness by the obscurity. For what he wishes to say is this. 'For cannot we also do these things? Yes, but we do them not. Wherefore then do ye bear with these men, as though we could not do these things? Surely it were something to impute to you that ye even bear with men who play the fool; but that ye do this, even when they so despise you, plunder you, exalt themselves, smite you, can admit neither of excuse nor any reason at all. For this is a new fashion of deceiving. For men that deceive both give and flatter; but these both deceive, and take and insult you. Whence ye cannot have a shadow of allowance, seeing that ye spit on those that humble themselves for your sakes that ye may be exalted, but admire those who exalt themselves that ye may be humbled. For could not we too do these things? Yes, but we do not wish it, looking to your advantage. For they indeed sacrificing your interests seek their own, but we sacrificing our own interests seek for yours.' Seest thou how in every instance, whilst speaking plainly to them, he also alarms them by what he says. 'For,' he says, 'if it be on this account that ye honor them, because they smite and insult you, we also can do this, enslave, smite, exalt ourselves against you.'

[3.] Seest thou how he lays upon them the whole blame, both of their senseless pride and of what seems to be folly in himself. 'For not that I may show myself more conspicuous, but that I may set you free from this bitter slavery, am I compelled to glory some little. But it is meet to examine not simply things that are said, but, in addition, the reason also. For Samuel also put together a high panegyric upon himself, when he anointed Saul, saying, "Whose ass have I taken, or calf, or shoes? or have I oppressed any of you?" (1 Sam. xii. 3, LXX.) And yet no one finds fault with him. And the reason is because he did not say it by way of setting off himself; but because he was going to appoint a king, he wishes under the form of a defence [of himself] to instruct him to be meek and gentle. And observe the wisdom of the prophet, or rather the loving kindness of God. For because he wished to turn them from [their design,] bringing together a number of grievous things he asserted them of their future king, as, for instance, that he would make their wives grind at the mill, (1 Sam. viii. 11—18.) the men shepherds and muleteers; for he went through all the service appertaining to the kingdom with minuteness. But when he saw that they would not be hindered by any of these things, but were incurably distempered; he thus both spareth them and composeth their king to gentleness. (1 Sam. xii. 5.) Therefore he also takes him to witness. For indeed no one was then bringing suit or charge against him that he needed to defend himself, but he said those things in order to make him better. And therefore also he added, to take down his pride, "If ye will hearken, ye and your king," (ibid. 14.) such and such good things shall be yours; "but if ye will not hearken, then the reverse of all." Amos also said, "I was no prophet, nor the son of a prophet, but only a herdsman, a gatherer of sycamore fruit. And God took me." (Amos vii. 14, 15.) But he did not say this to exalt himself, but to stop their mouths that suspected him as no prophet, and to show that he is no deceiver, nor says of

---

* Chrysostom takes the clause to refer to the preceding, but most consider it the apostle's transition to his own glorying, vv. 22—28. C.]

his own mind the things which he says. Again, another also, to show the very same thing, said, "But truly I am full of power by the spirit and might of the Lord." (Micah iii. 8.) And David also when he related the matter of the lion and of the bear, (1 Sam. xvii. 34, &c.) spake not to glorify himself, but to bring about a great and admirable end. For since it was not believed possible he could conquer the barbarian unarmed, he that was not able even to bear arms; he was compelled to give proofs of his own valor. And when he cut off Saul's skirt, he said not what he said out of display, but to repel an ill suspicion which they had scattered abroad against him, saying, that he wished to kill him. (1 Sam. xxiv. 4, &c.) It is meet therefore every where to seek for the reason. For he that looks to the advantage of his hearers even though he should praise himself, not only deserves not to be found fault with, but even to be crowned; and if he is silent, then to be found fault with. For if David had then been silent in the matter of Goliath, they would not have allowed him to go out to the battle, nor to have raised that illustrious trophy. On this account then he speaks being compelled; and that not to his brethren, although he was distrusted by them too as well as by the king; but envy stopped their ears. Therefore leaving them alone, he tells his tale to him who was not as yet envious of him.

[4.] For envy is a fearful, a fearful thing, and persuades men to despise their own salvation. In this way did both Cain destroy himself, and again, before his time, the devil who was the destroyer of his father. So did Saul invite an evil demon against his own soul; and when he had invited, he again envied his physician. For such is the nature of envy; he knew that he was saved, yet he would rather have perished than see him that saved him had in honor. What can be more grievous than this passion? One cannot err in calling it the devil's offspring. And in it is contained the fruit of vainglory, or rather its root also; for both these evils are wont mutually to produce each other. And thus in truth it was that Saul even thus envied, when they said, "David smote by ten thousands," (1 Sam. xviii. 7.) than which what can be more senseless? For why dost thou envy? tell me! 'Because such an one praised him?' Yet surely thou oughtest to rejoice; besides, thou dost not know even whether the praise be true. And dost thou therefore grieve because without being admirable he hath been praised as such? And yet thou oughtest to feel pity. For if he be good, thou oughtest not to envy him when praised, but thyself to praise along with those that speak well of him; but if not such, why

art thou galled? why thrust the sword against thyself? 'Because admired by men?' But men to-day are and to-morrow are not. 'But because he enjoys glory?' Of what sort, tell me? That of which the prophet says that it is "the flower of grass." (Isa. xl. 6. LXX.) Art thou then therefore envious because thou bearest no burden, nor carriest about with thee such loads of grass? But if he seems to thee to be enviable on this account, then why not also woodcutters who carry burdens every day and come to the city [with them]? For that burden is nothing better than this, but even worse. For theirs indeed galls the body only, but this hath oftentimes harmed the soul even and occasioned greater solicitude than pleasure. And should one have gained renown through eloquence, the fear he endures is greater than the good report he bears; yea, what is more, the one is short, the other perpetual. 'But he is in favor with those in authority?' In that too again is danger and envy. For as thou feelest towards him, so do many others feel. 'But he is praised continually?' This produces bitter slavery. For he will not dare to do fearlessly aught of what according to his judgment he should, lest he should offend those that extol him, for that distinction is a hard bondage to him. So that the more he is known to, so many the more masters he has, and his slavery becomes the greater, as masters of his are found in every quarter. A servant indeed, when he is released from the eye of his master, both takes breath and lives in all freedom; but this man meets with masters at every turn, for he is the slave of all that appear in the forum. And even should some necessary object press, he dares not set foot in the forum, except it be with his servants following, and his horse, and all his other show set in array, lest his masters condemn him. And if he sees some friend of those who are truly so[1], he has not the boldness to talk with him on an equal footing: for he is afraid of his masters, lest they depose him from his glory. So that the more distinguished he is, so much the more he is enslaved. And if he suffer aught that is disagreeable, the insult is the more annoying, both in that he has more to witness it and it seems to infringe his dignity. It is not only an insult, but a calamity also, for he has also many who exult at it; and in like way if he come to the enjoyment of any good thing, he has more who envy and detract and do their vigilance to destroy him. Is this then a good? tell me. Is this glory? By no means; but ingloriousness, and slavery, and bonds, and every burdensome thing one can say. But if the glory that cometh of men be so greatly to be coveted in thy account, and if

---

[1] Or 'worthy.'

it quite disquiets thee that such and such an one is applauded of the many ; when thou beholdest him in the enjoyment of that applause, pass over in thy thought to the world to come and the glory which is there. And just as when hurrying to escape the onset of a wild beast, thou enterest into a cabin and shuttest to the doors ; so now also flee unto the life to come, and that unspeakable glory.

For so shalt thou both tread this under thy feet, and wilt easily lay hold upon that, and wilt enjoy the true liberty, and the eternal good things ; whereunto may we all attain through the grace and love towards men of our Lord Jesus Christ, with Whom to the Father, with the Holy Spirit, be glory, might, honor, now and ever, and world without end. Amen.

HOMILY XXV.

2 COR. xi. 21.

Yet whereinsoever any is bold, (I speak in foolishness,) I am bold also.

SEE him again drawing back and using depreciation and correctives beforehand, although he has already even said many such things : as, " Would that ye could bear with me in a little foolishness ; "(Ver. 1.) and again, " Let no man think me foolish : if ye do, yet as foolish receive me." (Ver. 16.) " That which I speak, I speak not after the Lord, but as in foolishness." (Ver. 17.) " Seeing that many glory after the flesh, I will glory also ; " (Ver. 18.) and here again, " Whereinsoever any is bold, (I speak in foolishness) I am bold also." Boldness and folly he calls it to speak aught great of himself, and that though there was a necessity, teaching us even to an excess[1] to avoid any thing of the sort. For if after we have done all, we ought to call ourselves unprofitable ; of what forgiveness can he be worthy who, when no reason presses, exalts himself and boasts? Therefore also did the Pharisee meet the fate he did, and even in harbor suffered shipwreck because he struck upon this rock. Therefore also doth Paul, although he sees very ample necessity for it, draw back nevertheless, and keep on observing that such speaking is a mark of foolishness. And then at length he makes the venture[2], putting forward the plea of necessity, and says,

Ver. 22. " Are they Hebrews? so am I. Are they Israelites? so am I."

For it was not all Hebrews that were Israelites, since both the Ammonites and Moabites were Hebrews. Wherefore he added somewhat to clear his nobility of descent, and says,

Ver. 22, 23. " Are they the seed of Abraham? so am I. Are they ministers of Christ. (I speak as one beside himself,) I more."

He is not content with his former deprecation, but uses it again here also. " I speak as one beside himself, I more." I am their superior and their better. And indeed he possessed clear proofs of his superiority, but nevertheless even so he terms the thing a folly[3]. And yet if they were false Apostles, he needed not to have introduced his own superiority by way of comparison, but to have destroyed their claim to "be ministers " at all. Well, he did destroy it, saying, " False Apostles, deceitful workers, fashioning themselves into Apostles of Christ," (Ver. 13.) but now he doth not proceed in that way, for his discourse was about to proceed to strict examination ; and no one when an examination is in hand simply asserts ; but having first stated the case in the way of comparison, he shows it to be negatived by the facts, a very strong negative. But besides, it is their opinion he gives, not his own assertion, when he says, " Are they ministers of Christ ? " And having said, " I more," he proceeds in his comparison, and shows that not by bare assertions, but by furnishing the proof that facts supply, he maintains the impress of the Apostleship. And leaving all his miracles, he begins with his trials ; thus saying,

" In labors more abundantly, in stripes above measure." This latter is greater than the former ; to be both beaten and scourged.

" In prisons more abundantly." Here too again is there an increase. " In deaths oft." (1 Cor. xv. 31.) For, " I die," saith he, " daily." But here, even in reality ; ' for I have oft been delivered into mortal dangers[4].'

Ver. 24. " Of the Jews five times received I forty stripes save one."

Why, " save one ? " There was an ancient law that he who had received more than the

---

[1] ἐκ περιουσίας.
[2] κατατολμᾷ.
[3] παραφροσύνην
[4] Literally, ' dangers having death.'

forty should be held disgraced amongst them. Lest then the vehemence and impetuosity[1] of the executioner by inflicting more than the number should cause a man to be disgraced, they decreed that they should be inflicted, "save one," that even if the executioner should exceed, he might not overpass the forty, but remaining within the prescribed number might not bring degradation on him that was scourged.

Ver. 25. "Thrice was I beaten with rods, once was I stoned, thrice I suffered shipwreck."

And what has this to do with the Gospel? Because he went forth on long journeys; and those by sea.

"A night and a day I have been in the deep." Some say this means out on the open sea, others, swimming upon it, which is also the truer interpretation. There is nothing wonderful, at least, about the former, nor would he have placed it as greater than his shipwrecks.

Ver. 26. "In perils of rivers."

For he was compelled also to cross rivers.

"In perils of robbers, in perils in the city, in perils in the wilderness." 'Everywhere were contests set before me, in places, in countries, in cities, in deserts.'

"In perils from the Gentiles, in perils amongst false brethren."

Behold another kind of warfare. For not only did such as were enemies strike at him, but those also who played the hypocrite; and he had need of much firmness, much prudence.

[2.] Ver. 27. "In labor and travail."

Perils succeed to labors, labors to perils, one upon other and unintermitted, and allowed him not to take breath even for a little.

Ver. 27, 28. "In journeyings often, in hunger and thirst and nakedness, besides those things that are without."

What is left out is more than what is enumerated. Yea rather, one cannot count the number of those even which are enumerated; for he has not set them down specifically, but has mentioned those the number of which was small and easily comprehended, saying, "thrice" and "thrice," (Ver. 25.) and [again] "once;" but of the others he does not mention the number because he had endured them often. And he recounts not their results as that he had converted so many and so many, but only what he suffered on behalf of the Preaching; at once out of modesty, and as showing that even should nothing have been gained but labor, even so his title to wages has been fulfilled.

"That which presseth upon me daily." The tumults, the disturbances, the assaults[2] of mobs, onsets of cities. For the Jews waged war against this man most of all because he most of

all confounded them, and his changing sides all at once was the greatest refutation of their madness. And there breathed a mighty war against him, from his own people, from strangers, from false brethren; and every where were billows and precipices, in the inhabited world, in the uninhabited, by land, by sea, without, within. And he had not even a full supply of necessary food, nor even of thin clothing, but the champion of the world wrestled in nakedness and fought in hunger; so far was he from enriching himself[3]. Yet he murmured not, but was grateful for these things to the Judge of the combat.[4]

"Anxiety for all the Churches." This was the chief thing of all, that his soul too was distracted, and his thoughts divided. For even if nothing from without had assailed him; yet the war within was enough, those waves on waves, that sleet of cares, that war of thoughts. For if one that hath charge of but a single house, and hath servants and superintendents and stewards, often cannot take breath for cares, though there be none that molests him: he that hath the care not of a single house, but of cities and peoples and nations and of the whole world; and in respect to such great concerns, and with so many spitefully entreating him, and singlehanded, and suffering so many things, and so tenderly concerned as not even a father is for his children—consider what he endured. For that thou mayest not say, What if he was anxious, yet the anxiety was slight[5], he added further the intensity of the care, saying,

Ver. 29. "Who is weak, and I am not weak?" He did not say, 'and I share not in his dejection?' but, 'so am I troubled and disturbed, as though I myself were laboring under that very affection, that very infirmity.'

"Who is made to stumble, and I burn not?" See, again, how he places before us the excess of his grief by calling it "burning." 'I am on fire,' 'I am in a flame,' he says, which is surely greater than any thing he has said. For those other things, although violent, yet both pass quickly by, and brought with them that pleasure which is unfading; but this was what afflicted and straightened him, and pierced his mind through and through; the suffering such things for each one of the weak, whosoever he might be. For he did not feel pained for the greater sort only and despise the lesser, but counted even the abject amongst his familiar friends. Wherefore also he said, "who is weak?" whosoever he may be; and as though he were himself the Church throughout the world, so was he distressed for every member.

Ver. 30. "If I must needs glory, I will glory of the things which concern my weakness."

---

[1] ῥύμη καὶ ὁρμή
[2] πολιορκίαι
[3] χρηματίζεσθαι.
[4] ἀγωνοθέτῃ.
[5] ἁπλῶς.

Seest thou that he no where glorieth of miracles, but of his persecutions and his trials? For this is meant by "weaknesses." And he shows that his warfare was of a diversified character[1]. For both the Jews warred upon him, and the Gentiles stood against him, and the false brethren fought with him, and brethren caused him sorrow, through their weakness and by taking offense:—on every side he found trouble and disturbance, from friends and from strangers. This is the especial mark of an Apostle, by these things is the Gospel woven.

Ver. 31, 32. "The God and Father of the Lord Jesus knoweth that I lie not. The Governor under Aretas the king guarded the city of the Damascenes, desiring to apprehend me."

What can be the reason that he here strongly confirms and gives assurance of [his truth], seeing he did not so in respect to any of the former things? Because, perhaps, this was of older date and not so well known[2]; whilst of those other facts, his care for the churches, and all the rest, they were themselves cognisant. See then how great the war [against him] was, since on his account the city was "guarded." And when I say this of the war, I say it of the zeal of Paul; for except this had breathed intensely, it had not kindled the governor to so great madness. These things are the part of an apostolic soul, to suffer so great things and yet in nothing to veer about, but to bear nobly whatever befalls; yet not to go out to meet dangers, nor to rush upon them. See for instance here, how he was content to evade the siege, by being "let down through a window in a basket." For though he were even desirous "to depart hence;" still nevertheless he also passionately affected the salvation of men. And therefore he

ofttimes had recourse even to such devices as these, preserving himself for the Preaching; and he refused not to use even human contrivances when the occasion called for them; so sober and watchful was he. For in cases where evils were inevitable, he needed only grace; but where the trial was of a measured character, he devises many things of himself even, here again ascribing the whole to God. And just as a spark of unquenchable fire, if it fell into the sea, would be merged as many waves swept over it, yet would again rise shining to the surface; even so surely the blessed Paul also would now be overwhelmed by perils, and now again, having dived[3] through them, would come up more radiant, overcoming by suffering evil.

[3.] For this is the brilliant victory, this is the Church's trophy, thus is the Devil overthrown when we suffer injury. For when we suffer, he is taken captive; and himself suffers harm, when he would fain inflict it on us. And this happened in Paul's case also; and the more he plied him with perils, the more was he defeated. Nor did he raise up against him only one kind of trials, but various and diverse. For some involved labor, others sorrow, others fear, others pain, others care, others shame, others all these at once; but yet he was victorious in all. And like as if a single soldier, having the whole world fighting against him, should move through the mid ranks of his enemies, and suffer no harm: even so did Paul, showing himself singly, among barbarians, among Greeks, on every land, on every sea, abide unconquered. And as a spark, falling upon reeds and hay, changes into its own nature the things so kindled; so also did this man setting upon all make things change over unto the truth; like a winter torrent, sweeping over all things and overturning every obstacle. And like some champion who wrestles, runs, and boxes too; or soldier engaged by turns in storming[4], fighting on foot, on shipboard; so did he try by turns every form of fight, and breathed out fire, and was unapproachable by all; with his single body taking possession of the world, with his single tongue putting all to flight. Not with such force did those many trumpets fall upon the stones of Jericho and throw them down, as did the sound of this man's voice both dash to the earth the devil's strong-holds and bring over to himself those that were against him. And when he had collected a multitude of captives, having armed the same, he made them again his own army, and by their means conquered. Wonderful was David who laid Goliah low with a single stone; but if thou wilt examine Paul's achievements, that is a child's exploit, and great

---

[1] ποικίλον.

[2] [The Apostle's mention of this isolated fact of his escape at Damascus, at the conclusion of the narrative of his varied labors and trials, has been variously explained, some considering it an afterthought, others the opening of a statement of details intended to be complete but for some reason interrupted. But it does not seem necessary to view it otherwise than it appears on its face, as a reminiscence of a peculiar peril which befel him at the commencement of his Christian career, and by which he was as it were matriculated in the school of persecution. The furtive method of escape (in the darkness of night, Acts ix. 25) shows the extreme danger and helplessness of his position. He could very well put this among the "weaknesses" in which he ventured to glory (xii. 5), since his deliverance was effected not by the pomp of a supernatural interposition as afterwards at Philippi, but by ordinary human instrumentality, and that certainly not of a very dignified kind. "The name of Damascus, somewhat irregularly repeated here in that of its inhabitants, was deeply graven on the Apostle's memory, being inseparably associated with the great turning point of his life, which is the reason why his experience there is mentioned." (Waite). If the solemn asseveration of the 31st verse is to be considered as referring to what follows, then the explanation given by Chrysostom in the text is satisfactory. The Apostle's later trials were well known to the Corinthians; this one might not have been. Yet to Paul it was of the profoundest interest because it showed that where his ministry began, there also began his "weakness." Then and there the persecutor became the persecuted. There is no greater contrast in all human history than that of Paul on his way to Damascus to bind and deliver to death the Nazarenes, and the same man fleeing that city between two days to escape the plots of his former friends and followers. C]

[3] διαδύς.

[4] τειχομαχῶν.

as is the difference between a shepherd and a general, so great the difference thou shalt see here. For this man brought down no Goliath by the hurling of a stone, but by speaking only he scattered the whole array of the Devil; as a lion roaring and darting out flame from his tongue, so was he found by all irresistible; and bounded everywhere by turns continually; he ran to these, he came to those, he turned about to these, he bounded away to others, swifter in his attack than the wind; governing the whole world, as though a single house or a single ship; rescuing the sinking, steadying the dizzied, cheering the sailors, sitting at the tiller, keeping an eye to the prow, tightening the yards, handling an oar, pulling at the mast, watching the sky; being all things in himself, both sailor, and pilot, and pilot's mate[1], and sail, and ship; and suffering all things in order to relieve the evils of others. For consider. He endured shipwreck that he might stay the shipwreck of the world; "a day and a night he passed in the deep," that he might draw it up[2] from the deep of error; he was "in weariness" that he might refresh the weary; he endured smiting that he might heal those that had been smitten of the devil; he passed his time in prisons that he might lead forth to the light those that were sitting in prison and in darkness; he was "in deaths oft" that he might deliver from grievous deaths; "five times he received forty stripes save one" that he might free those that inflicted them from the scourge of the devil; he was "beaten with rods" that he might bring them under "the rod and the staff" of Christ; (Ps. xxiii. 4.) he "was stoned," that he might deliver them from the senseless stones; he "was in the wilderness[3], that he might take them out of the wilderness; "in journeying," to stay their wanderings and open the way that leadeth to heaven; he "was in perils in the cities," that he might show the city which is above; "in hunger and thirst," to deliver from a more grievous hunger; "in nakedness," to clothe their unseemliness with the robe of Christ; set upon by the mob, to extricate them from the besetment of fiends; he burned, that he might quench the burning darts of the devil:

"through a window was let down from the wall," to send up from below those that lay prostrate upon the ground. Shall we then talk any more, seeing we do not so much as know what Paul suffered? shall we make mention any more of goods, or even of wife, or city, or freedom, when we have seen him ten thousand times despising even life itself? The martyr dies once for all: but that blessed saint in his one body and one soul endured so many perils as were enough to disturb even a soul of adamant; and what things all the saints together have suffered in so many bodies, those all he himself endured in one: he entered into the world as if a race-course, and stripped himself of all, and so made a noble stand. For he knew the fiends that were wrestling with him. Wherefore also he shone forth brightly at once from the beginning, from the very starting-post, and even to the end he continued the same; yea, rather he even increased the intensity of his pursuit as he drew nearer to the prize. And what surely is wonderful is that though suffering and doing such great things, he knew how to maintain an exceeding modesty. For when he was driven upon the necessity of relating his own good deeds, he ran quickly over them all; although he might have filled books without number, had he wished to unfold in detail[4] every thing he mentioned; if he had specified the Churches he was in care for, if his prisons and his achievments in them, if of the other things one by one, the besetments[5], the assaults. But he would not. Knowing then these things, let us also learn to be modest and not to glory at any time in wealth or other worldly things, but in the reproaches we suffer for Christ's sake, and in these, only when need compels; for if there be nothing urging it, let us not mention these even, (lest we be puffed up,) but our sins only. For so shall we both easily be released from them and shall have God propitious to us, and shall attain the life to come; whereunto may we all attain through the grace and love towards men of our Lord Jesus Christ, with Whom to the Father, with the Holy Ghost, be glory, might, honor, now and for ever, and world without end. Amen.

---

[1] πρωρεύς.
[2] ἀνιμήσηται.
[3] Or, 'desolateness.'

[4] ἐξαπλῶσαι.
[5] περιστάσεις.

HOMILY XXVI.

2 COR. xii. 1.

It is not expedient for me doubtless to glory,* [for] I will come to visions and revelations of the Lord.

WHAT is this? Doth he who has spoken such great things say, [It is not expedient] "doubtless to glory?" as if he had said nothing? No; not as if he had said nothing: but because he is going to pass to another species of boasting, which is not intended indeed by so great a reward, but which to the many (though not to careful examiners) seems to set him off in brighter colors[1], he says, "It is not expedient for me doubtless to glory." For truly the great grounds of boasting were those which he had re ounted, those of his trials; he has however other things also to tell of, such as concern the revelations, the unspeakable mysteries. And wherefore, says he, "It is not expedient for me?" he means, 'lest it lift me up to pride.' What sayest thou? For if thou speak not of them, yet dost thou not know of them? But our knowing of them ourselves doth not lift us up so much as our publishing them to others. For it is not the nature of good deeds that useth to lift a man up, but their being witnessed to, and known of, by the many. For this cause therefore he saith, "It is not expedient for me;" and, 'that I may not implant too great an idea of me in those who hear.' For those men indeed, the false apostles, said even what was not true about themselves; but this man hides even what is true, and that too although so great necessity lies upon him, and says, "It is not expedient for me;" teaching one and all even to superfluity[2] to avoid any thing of the sort. For this thing[3] is attended with no advantage, but even with harm, except there be some necessary and useful reason which induceth us thereto. Having then spoken of his perils, trials, snares, dejections, shipwrecks, he passeth to another species of boasting, saying,

Ver. 2, 3. "I knew a man, fourteen years ago (whether in the body, I know not; or out of the body, I know not: God knoweth;) such an one caught up even to the third heaven. And I know how that he was caught up into Paradise, (whether in the body, I know not; or out of the body, I know not;) and heard unspeakable words, which it is not lawful[4] for a man to utter. On behalf of such an one will I glory: but on mine own behalf I will not glory."

Great indeed was this revelation. But this was not the only one: there were many others besides, but he mentions one out of many. For that there were many, hear what he says: "Lest I should be exalted overmuch through the exceeding greatness of the revelations." 'And yet,' a man may say, 'if he wished to conceal them, he ought not to have given any intimation[5] whatever or said any thing of the sort; but if he wished to speak of them, to speak plainly.' Wherefore then is it that he neither spoke plainly nor kept silence? To show by this[6] also that he resorts to the thing unwillingly. And therefore also he has stated the time, "fourteen years." For he does not mention it without an object, but to show that he who had refrained for so long a time would not now have spoken out, except the necessity for doing so had been great. But he would have still kept silence, had he not seen the brethren perishing. Now if Paul from the very beginning was such an one as to be counted worthy of such a revelation, when as yet he had not wrought such good works; consider what he must have grown to in fourteen years. And observe how even in this very matter he shows modesty, by his saying some things, but confessing that of others he is ignorant. For that he was caught up indeed, he declared, but whether "in the body" or "out of the body" he says he does not know. And yet it would have been quite enough, if he had told of his being caught up and had been silent [about the other]; but as it is, in his his modesty he adds this also. What then? Was it the mind that was caught up and the soul, whilst the body remained dead? or was the

---

* [A better text of this verse is given in the Revised Version— "I must needs glory, though it is not expedient." C.]
[1] λαμπρότερον.
[2] ἐκ πολλῆς περιουσίας.
[3] i. e. boasting.

[4] Or, 'possible.'
[5] αἴνιγμα.
[6] Or, 'in this instance.'

398

body caught up? It is impossible to tell. For if Paul who was caught up and whom things unspeakable, so many and so great, had befallen was in ignorance, much more we. For, indeed, that he was in Paradise he knew, and that he was in the third heaven he was not ignorant, but the manner he knew not clearly. And see from yet another consideration how free he is from pride. For in his narrative about "the city of the Damascenes" (2 Cor. xi. 32.) he confirms what he says, but here not; for it was not his aim to establish this fact strongly, but to mention and intimate it only. Wherefore also he goes on to say, "Of such an one will I glory;" not meaning that he who was caught up was some other person, but he so frames his language in the best manner he possibly could, so as at once to mention the fact, and to avoid speaking of himself openly. For what sequence would there be in bringing some one else forward, when discoursing about himself? Wherefore then did he so put it? It was not all one to say, 'I was caught up,' and, "I knew one that was caught up;" and 'I will glory of myself,' and, "I will glory of such an one." Now if any should say, 'And how is it possible to be caught up without a body?' I will ask him, 'How is it possible to be caught up with a body?' for this is even more inexplicable than the other, if you examine by reasonings and do not give place to faith.

[2.] But wherefore was he also caught up? As I think, that he might not seem to be inferior to the rest of the Apostles. For since they had companied with Christ, but Paul had not: He therefore caught up unto glory him also. "Into Paradise." For great was the name of this place, and it was everywhere celebrated. Wherefore also Christ said, "To-day thou shalt be with Me in Paradise." (Luke xxiii. 43.)

"On behalf of such an one will I glory?" wherefore? For if another were caught up, wherefore dost thou glory? Whence it is evident that he said these things of himself. And if he added, "but of myself I will not glory," he says nothing else than this, that, 'when there is no necessity, I will say nothing of that kind fruitlessly and at random;' or else he is again throwing obscurity over[1] what he had said, as best he might. For that the whole discourse was about himself, what follows also clearly shows; for he went on to say,

Ver. 6. "But if I should even desire to glory, I shall not be foolish; for I shall speak the truth."

How then saidst thou before, "Would that ye could bear with me a little in my foolishness;" (Chap. xi. 1.) and, "That which I speak, I

speak not after the Lord, but as it were foolishly;" (Chap. xi. 17.) but here, "Though I should even desire to glory, I shall not be foolish?" Not in regard of glorying, but of lying; for if glorying be foolishness, how much more lying?

It is then with regard to this that he says, "I shall not be foolish." Wherefore also he added,

"For I shall speak the truth; but I forbear, lest any man should account of me above that which he seeth[2], or that he heareth from me." Here you have the acknowledged reason; for they even deemed them to be gods, on account of the greatness of their miracles. As then in the case of the elements, God hath done both things, creating them at once weak and glorious; the one, to proclaim His own power; the other, to prevent the error of mankind[3]: so truly here also were they both wonderful and weak, so that by the facts themselves were the unbelievers instructed. For if whilst continuing to be wonderful only and giving no proof of weakness, they had by words tried to draw away the many from conceiving of them more than the truth; not only would they have nothing succeeded, but they would even have brought about the contrary. For those dissuasions in words would have seemed rather to spring of lowliness of mind, and would have caused them to be the more admired. Therefore in act and by deeds was their weakness disclosed. And one may see this exemplified in the men who lived under the old dispensation. For Elias was wonderful, but on one occasion he stood convicted of faintheartedness; and Moses was great, but he also fled[4] under the influence of the same passion. Now such things befel them, because God stood aloof and permitted their human nature to stand confessed. For if because he led them out they said, 'Where is Moses?' what would they not have said, if he had also led them in? Wherefore also [Paul] himself says, "I forbear, lest any should account of me." He said not, 'say of me,' but, "lest any should even account of me" beyond my desert.' Whence it is evident from this also that the whole discourse relates to himself. Wherefore even when he began, he said, "It is not expedient for me doubtless to glory," which he would not have said, had he been going to speak the things which he said of another man. For wherefore is it "not expedient to glory" about another? But it was himself that was counted worthy of these things; and therefore it is that he goes on to say,

Ver. 7. "And that I should not be exalted overmuch, through the exceeding greatness of

---

[2] Rec. text, 'seeth me.'
[3] i. e., in worshiping them.
[4] ἐδραπέτευσε.

[1] συσκιάζων.

26

the revelations, there was given to me a thorn in the flesh, a messenger of Satan, to buffet me."

What sayest thou? He that counted not the kingdom to be any thing; no, nor yet hell in respect of his longing after Christ; did he deem honor from the many to be any thing, so as both to be lifted up and to need that curb continually? for he did not say, 'that he "might" buffet[1] me,' but "that he" may "buffet[2] me." Yet who is there would say this? What then is the meaning of what is said? When we have explained what is meant at all by the "thorn," and who is this "messenger of Satan," then will we declare this also. There are some then who have said that he means a kind of pain in the head which was inflicted of the devil; but God forbid! For the body of Paul never could have been given over to the hands of the devil, seeing that the devil himself submitted to the same Paul at his mere bidding; and he set him laws and bounds, when he delivered over the fornicator for the destruction of the flesh, and he dared not to transgress them. What then is the meaning of what is said? An adversary is called in the Hebrew, Satan; and in the third Book of Kings the Scripture has so termed such as were adversaries; and speaking of Solomon, says, 'In his days there was no Satan,' that is, no adversary, enemy, or opponent. (1 Kings v, 4.) What he says then is this: God would not permit the Preaching to progress, in order to check our high thoughts; but permitted the adversaries to set upon us. For this indeed was enough to pluck down his high thoughts; not so that, pains in the head. And so by the "messenger of Satan," he means Alexander the coppersmith, the party of Hymenæus and Philetus, all the adversaries of the word; those who contended with and fought against him, those that cast him into a prison, those that beat him, that led him away to death[3]; for they did Satan's business. As then he calls those Jews children of the devil, who were imitating his deeds, so also he calls a "messenger of Satan" every one that opposeth. He says therefore, "There was given to me a thorn to buffet me;" not as if God putteth arms into such men's hands, God forbid! not that He doth chastise or punish, but for the time alloweth and permitteth them.[4]

[3.] Ver. 8. "Concerning this thing I besought the Lord thrice."

That is, oftentimes. This also is a mark of great lowliness of mind, his not concealing that he could not bear those insidious plottings, that he fainted under them and was reduced to pray for deliverance.

Ver. 9. "And He said unto me, My grace is sufficient for thee; for my power is made perfect in weakness."

That is to say, 'It is sufficient for thee that thou raisest the dead, that thou curest the blind, that thou cleansest lepers, that thou workest those other miracles; seek not also exemption from danger and fear and to preach without annoyances. But art thou pained and dejected lest it should seem to be owing to My weakness, that there are many who plot against and beat thee and harass and scourge thee? Why this very thing doth show My power. "For My power," He saith, "is made perfect in weakness," when being persecuted ye overcome your persecutors; when being harassed ye get the better of them that harass you; when being put in bonds ye convert them that put you in bonds. Seek not then more than is needed.' Seest thou how he himself assigns one reason, and God another? For he himself says, "Lest I should be exalted overmuch, there was given to me a thorn;" but he says that God said He permitted it in order to show His power. 'Thou seekest therefore a thing which is not only not needed, but which also obscureth the glory of My power.' For by the words, "is sufficient for thee," He would signify this, that nothing else need be added, but the whole was complete. So that from this also it is plain that he does not intend pains in the head; for in truth they did not preach when they were sick, for they could not preach when ill; but that harassed and persecuted, they overcame all. 'After having heard this then,' he says,

"Most gladly therefore will I glory in my weaknesses." For that they may not sink down, when those false Apostles are glorying over their contrary lot[5] and these are suffering persecution, he shows that he shineth all the brighter for

[1] κολαφίση
[2] κολαφίζη.
[3] ἀπάγοντας.
[4] [Chrysostom's view of this peculiar trial of the Apostle, although held by most of the Greek fathers and by some eminent scholars of later ages (Erasmus, Calvin, Fritzsche, Reiche, etc.) does not seem satisfactory. There was nothing peculiar to Paul in the trials and temptations incident to the Apostolic office, for they were shared by all his companions, nor do they seem to be properly expressed by "a stake *in the flesh*," or as some prefer to render "for the flesh," which naturally suggests that the affliction was a bodily ailment, something that caused pain and made the discharge of his duties burdensome. Bp. Lightfoot (Com. on Galatians, pp. 186, 187) suggests that the circumstances imply that the malady was acute and severe; that it was in some way

humiliating as intended to check spiritual pride; that as a grievous hindrance to the Gospel it was a trial to his constancy and resolution; that it was of such a nature that it could not be concealed from others; and that it was continuous or recurrent. All attempts to define it more closely—Chrysostom on this page mentions one, "pains in the head"—fail as being purely conjectural. But the fullest knowledge on the subject however it might gratify curiosity could add nothing to the instructiveness of the case as it stands. That the most honored of all philanthropists, the chiefest of the twelve, the most distinguished of Christ's followers should require to be buffeted with such a chronic bodily ailment; that the most earnest prayers could not succeed in securing its removal; and yet that grace was bestowed on him to bear it, and bestowed in such measure that he could even rejoice in what was painful and glory in infirmities, is a lesson of Christian experience that has been full of comfort and edification in all ages of the church. To this we owe the noble Christian paradox which to myriads of burdened souls has been a well-spring of comfort and peace, WHEN I AM WEAK, THEN AM I STRONG. C.]
[5] ἐπὶ τοῖς ἐναντίοις

this, and that thus the power of God shines forth the rather, and what happens is just matter for glorying. Wherefore he says, "Most gladly therefore will I glory." 'Not as therefore sorrowing did I speak of the things which I enumerated, or of that which I have just now said, "there was given to me a thorn; " but as priding myself upon them and drawing to myself greater power.' Wherefore also he adds, "That the strength of Christ may rest upon me." Here he hints at another thing also, namely, that in proportion as the trials waxed in intensity, in the same proportion the grace was increased and continued.

Ver. 10. "Wherefore I take pleasure in many weaknesses."[1] Of what sort? tell me. "In injuries, in persecutions, in necessities, in distresses."

Seest thou how he has now revealed it in the clearest manner? For in mentioning the species of the infirmity he spake not of fevers, nor any return[2] of that sort, nor any other bodily ailment, but of "injuries, persecutions, distresses." Seest thou a single-minded soul? He longs to be delivered from those dangers; but when he heard God's answer that this befitteth not, he was not only not sorry that he was disappointed of his prayer, but was even glad. Wherefore he said, "I take pleasure," 'I rejoice, I long, to be injured, persecuted, distressed for Christ's sake.' And he said these things both to check those, and to raise the spirits of these that they might not be ashamed at Paul's sufferings. For that ground[3] was enough to make them shine brighter than all men. Then he mentions another reason also.

"For when I am weak, then am I strong." 'Why marvellest thou that the power of God is then conspicuous? I too am strong "then; " ' for then most of all did grace come upon him. "For as His sufferings abound, so doth our consolation abound also." (Chap. i. 5.)

[4.] Where affliction is, there is also consolation; where consolation, there is grace also. For instance when he was thrown into the prison, then it was he wrought those marvellous things; when he was shipwrecked and cast away upon that barbarous country, then more than ever was he glorified. When he went bound into the judgment-hall, then he overcame even the judge. And so it was too in the Old Testament; by[4] their trials the righteous flourished. So it was with the three children, so with Daniel, with Moses, and Joseph; thence did they all shine and were counted worthy of great crowns. For then the sonl also is purified, when it is afflicted for God's sake: it then enjoys greater

assistance as needing more help and worthy of more grace. And truly, before the reward which is proposed to it by God, it reaps a rich harvest of good things by becoming philosophic. For affliction rends pride away and prunes out all listlessness and exerciseth[5] unto patience: it revealeth the meanness of human things and leads unto much philosophy. For all the passions give way before it, envy, emulation, lust, rule,[6] desire of riches, of beauty[7], boastfulness, pride, anger; and the whole remaining swarm of these distempers. And if thou desirest to see this in actual working, I shall be able to show thee both a single individual and a whole people, as well under affliction as at ease; and so to teach thee how great advantage cometh of the one, and how great listlessness from the other.

For the people of the Hebrews, when they were vexed and persecuted, groaned and besought God, and drew down upon themselves great influences[8] from above: but when they waxed fat, they kicked. The Ninevites again, when they were in the enjoyment of security, so exasperated God that He threatened to pluck up the entire city from its foundations: but after they had been humbled by that preaching, they displayed all virtue[9]. But if thou wouldest see also a single individual, consider Solomon. For he, when deliberating with anxiety and trouble concerning the government of that nation, was vouchsafed that vision: but when he was in the enjoyment of luxury, he slid into the very pit of iniquity. And what did his father? When was he admirable and passing belief? Was it not when he was in trials? And Absalom, was he not sober-minded, whilst still an exile; but after his return, became both tyrannical and a parricide? And what did Job? He indeed shone even in prosperity, but showed yet brighter after his affliction. And why must one speak of the old and ancient things? for if one do but examine our own state at present, he will see how great is the advantage of affliction. For now indeed that we are in the enjoyment of peace, we are become supine, and lax[10] and have filled the Church with countless evils; but when we were persecuted, we were more sober-minded, and kinder, and more earnest, and more ready as to these assemblies and as to hearing. For what fire is to gold, that is affliction unto souls; wiping away filth, rendering men clean, making them bright and shining. It leadeth unto the kingdom, that unto hell. And therefore the one way is broad, the other narrow. Wherefore also, He Himself

---

[1] Rec. text 'in weaknesses.'
[2] περίοδον.
[3] ἡ ὑπόθεσις
[4] Or, amidst.

[5] ἀλείφει
[6] δυναστεία
[7] σωμάτων
[8] ῥοπήν
[9] φιλοσοφίαν
[10] διερρύημεν

said, "In the world ye shall have tribulation," (John xvi. 33.) as though he were leaving some great good behind unto us. If then thou art a disciple, travel thou the straight and narrow way, and be not disgusted nor discouraged.[1] For even if thou be not afflicted in that way; thou must inevitably be afflicted on other grounds, of no advantage to thee. For the envious man also, and the lover of money, and he that burneth for an harlot, and the vainglorious, and each one of the rest that follow whatsoever is evil, endureth many disheartenings and afflictions, and is not less afflicted than they who mourn. And if he doth not weep nor mourn, it is for shame and insensibility: since if thou shouldest look into his soul, thou wilt see it filled with countless waves. Since then whether we follow this way of life or that, we must needs be afflicted: wherefore choose we not this way which along with affliction bringeth crowns innumerable? For thus hath God led all the saints through affliction and distress, at once doing them service, and securing the rest of men against entertaining a higher opinion of them than they deserve. For thus it was that idolatries gained ground at first; men being held in admiration beyond their desert. Thus the Roman senate decreed Alexander[2] to be the thirteenth God, for it possessed the privilege of electing and enrolling Gods. For instance, when all about Christ had been reported, the ruler of the nation[3] sent to inquire, whether they would be pleased to elect Him also a God. They however refused their consent, being angry and indignant that previous to their vote and decree, the Power of the Crucified flashing abroad had won over the whole world to its own worship. But thus it was ordered even against their will that the Divinity of Christ was not proclaimed by man's decree, nor was He counted one of the many that were by them elected. For they counted even boxers to be Gods, and the favorite of Hadrian; after whom the city Antinous is named. For since death testifies against their moral nature, the devil invented another way, that of the soul's immortality; and mingling therewith that excessive flattery, he seduced many into impiety. And observe what wicked artifice. When we advance that doctrine for a good purpose, he overthrows our words; but when he himself is desirous of framing an argument for mischief, he is very zealous in setting it up. And if any one ask, 'How is Alexander a God? Is he not dead? and miserably too?' 'Yes, but the soul is immortal?' he replies. Now thou arguest

and philosophizest for immortality, to detach men from the God Who is over all: but when we declare that this is God's greatest gift, thou persuadest thy dupes that men are low and grovelling, and in no better case than the brutes. And if we say, 'the Crucified lives,' laughter follows immediately: although the whole world proclaims it, both in old time and now; in old time by miracles, now by converts; for truly these successes are not those of a dead man: but if one say, 'Alexander lives,' thou believest, although thou hast no miracle to allege.

[5.] 'Yes,' one replies; 'I have; for when he lived he wrought many and great achievements; for he subdued both nations and cities, and in many wars and battles he conquered, and erected trophies.'

If then I shall show [somewhat] which he when alive never dreamed of, neither he, nor any other man that ever lived, what other proof of the resurrection wilt thou require? For that whilst alive one should win battles and victories, being a king and having armies at his disposal, is nothing marvelous, no, nor startling or novel; but that after a Cross and Tomb one should perform such great things throughout every land and sea, this it is which is most especially replete with such amazement, and proclaims His divine and unutterable Power. And Alexander indeed after his decease never restored again his kingdom which had been rent in pieces and quite abolished: indeed how was it likely he, dead, should do so? but Christ then most of all set up His after He was dead. And why speak I of Christ? seeing that He granted to His disciples also, after their deaths, to shine? For, tell me, where is the tomb of Alexander? show it me and tell me the day on which he died. But of the servants of Christ the very tombs are glorious, seeing they have taken possession of the most loyal city; and their days are well known, making festivals for the world. And his tomb even his own people know not, but this man's[4] the very barbarians know. And the tombs of the servants of the Crucified are more splendid than the palaces of kings; not for the size and beauty of the buildings, (yet even in this they surpass them,) but, what is far more, in the zeal of those who frequent them. For he that wears the purple himself goes to embrace those tombs, and, laying aside his pride, stands begging the saints[5] to be his advocates with God, and he that hath the diadem implores the tentmaker and the fisherman, though dead, to be his patrons. Wilt thou dare then, tell me, to

---

[1] ἀποδυσπέτει
[2] That Alexander the Great had at any rate a temple dedicated to him, is mentioned by Lampridius.
[3] See Tertull. *Apol.* Oxf. Trans. p. 13 and note. Justin Martyr mentions Pilate's Report. Eusebius, *Hist. Eccles.* ii. 2. gives the same account as from Tertullian, which Chrysostom here gives.

[4] St. Paul's as Mr. Field supposes.
[5] This passage should have been mentioned in the note at the end of Hom. vi. on the Statues. Tr. p. 134. See also on Statues, Hom. i Tr. p. 4. and on Rom. xvi. 5. Hom. xxxi. Tr. p. 486. Compare also St Augustine,'*On Care for the Dead*,' where he discusses the question. whether burial at a Martyr's Memorial is preferable.

call the Lord of these dead ; whose servants even after their decease are the patrons of the kings of the world? And this one may see take place not in Rome only, but in Constantinople also. For there also Constantine the Great, his son considered he should be honoring with great honor, if he buried him in the porch of the fisherman ; and what porters are to kings in their palaces, that kings are at the tomb to fisherman. And these indeed as lords of the place occupy the inside, whilst the others as though but sojourners and neighbors were glad to have the gate of the porch assigned them ; showing by what is done in this world, even to the unbelievers, that in the Resurrection the fisherman will be yet more their superiors. For if here it is so in the burial [of each], much more will it in the resurrection. And their rank is interchanged ; kings assume that of servants and ministers, and subjects the dignity of kings, yea rather a brighter still. And that this is no piece of flattery, the truth itself demonstrates; for by those these have become more illustrious. For far greater reverence is paid to these tombs than to the other royal sepulchres ; for there indeed is profound solitude, whilst here there is an immense concourse. But if thou wilt compare these tombs with the royal palaces, here again the palm remains with them. For there indeed there are many who keep off, but here many who invite and draw to them rich, poor, men, women, bond, free ; there, is much fear ; here, pleasure unutterable. 'But,' saith one, 'it is a sweet sight to look on a king covered with gold and crowned, and standing by his side, generals, commanders, captains of horse and foot, lieutenants. Well, but this of ours is so much grander and more awful that that must be judged, compared with it, to be stage scenery[1] and child's play. For the instant thou hast stepped across the threshhold, at once the place sends up thy thoughts to heaven, to the King above, to the army of the Angels, to the lofty throne, to the unapproachable glory. And here indeed He hath put in the ruler's power, of his subjects to loose one, and bind another ; but the bones of the saints possess no such pitiful and mean authority, but that which is far greater. For they summon demons and put them to the torture, and loose from those bitterest of all bonds, them that are bound. What is more fearful than this tribunal ? Though no one is seen, though no one piles the sides of the demon, yet are there cries, and tearings[2], lashes, tortures, burning tongues, because the demon cannot endure that marvellous power. And they that once wore bodies, are victorious over bodiless powers ; [their] dust and bones and ashes rack those invisible natures. And therefore in truth it is that none would ever travel abroad to see the palaces of kings, but many kings and have often traveled to see this spectacle. For the Martyries[3] of the saints exhibit outlines and symbols of the judgment to come : in that demons are scourged, men chastened and delivered. Seest thou the power of saints, even dead ? seest thou the weakness of sinners, even living ? Flee then wickedness, that thou mayest have power over such ; and pursue virtue with all thy might. For if the case be thus here, consider what it will be in the world to come. And as being evermore possessed with this love, lay hold on the life eternal; whereunto may we all attain, through the grace and love towards men of our Lord Jesus Christ, with Whom to the Father together with the Holy Ghost, be glory, might, honor, now and ever, and world without end. Amen.

HOMILY XXVII.

2 COR. xii. 11.

I am become foolish in glorying ; ye compelled me : for I ought to have been commended of you.

HAVING fully completed what he had to say about his own praises, he did not stay at this ; but again excuses himself and asks pardon for for what he said, declaring that his doing so was of necessity and not of choice. Still nevertheless, although there was necessity, he calls himself "a fool." And when he began indeed, he said, "As foolish receive me,"and"as in foolishness ; " but now, leaving out the 'as,' he calls himself "foolish." For after he had established the point he wished by saying what he did, he afterwards boldly and unsparingly grapples with all failing of the sort, teaching all persons that none should ever praise himself where there is no necessity, seeing that even where a reason for it existed, Paul termed himself a fool [for

---

[1] σκηνήν.

[2] σπαραγμοί.

[3] μαρτυρία. See Bingham's *Antiquit.* book viii. ch. 1. p. 8. [The name given to a church erected over the grave of a Martyr.]

so doing]. Then he turns the blame also of his so speaking not upon the false Apostles, but wholly upon the disciples. For " ye," he saith, "compelled me." ' For if they gloried, but were not by doing so leading you astray nor causing your destruction, I should not have been thus led on to descend unto this discussion : but because they were corrupting the whole Church, with a view to your advantage I was compelled to become foolish.' And he did not say, ' For I feared lest if they obtained the highest estimation with you, they should sow their doctrines,' yet this indeed he set down above when he said, "I fear, lest by any means, as the serpent deceived Eve, so your minds should be corrupted." (Chap. xi. 3.) Here however he does not so express himself, but in a more commanding manner and with more authority, having gained boldness from what he had said, " For I ought to have been commended of you." Then he also assigns the reason ; and again he mentions not his revelations nor his miracles only, but his temptations also.

" For in nothing was I behind the chiefest Apostles." See how he here too again speaks out with greater authoritativeness. For, before indeed he said, "I reckon I am not a whit behind," but here, after those proofs, he now boldly speaks out asserting the fact, as I said, thus absolutely. Not that even thus he departs from the mean, nor from his proper character. For as though he had uttered something great and exceeding his deserts, in that he numbered himself with the Apostles, he thus again speaks modestly, and adds,

Ver. 12. " Although I be nothing, the signs of an Apostle were wrought among you."

' Look not thou at this,' he says, ' whether I be mean and little, but whether thou hast not enjoyed those things which from an Apostle it was meet thou shouldest enjoy.' Yet he did not say ' mean,' but what was lower, " nothing." For where is the good of being great, and of use to nobody? even as there is no advantage in a skilful physician if he heals none of those that be sick. ' Do not then,' he says, ' scrutinize this that I am nothing, but consider that, that wherein ye ought to have been benefitted, I have failed in nothing, but have given proof of mine Apostleship. There ought then to have been no need for me to say aught.' Now he thus spoke, not as wanting to be commended, (for how should he, he who counted heaven itself to be a small thing in comparison with his longing after Christ?) but as desiring their salvation. Then lest they should say, ' And what is it to us, even though thou wast not a whit behind the very chiefest Apostles?' he therefore added,

" The signs of an Apostle were wrought

among you in all patience, and by signs and wonders." Amazing ! what a sea of good works hath he traversed in a few words ! And observe what it is he puts first, " patience." For this is the note of an Apostle, bearing all things nobly. This then he expressed shortly by a single word ; but upon the miracles, which were not of his own achieving, he employs more. For consider how many prisons, how many stripes, how many dangers, how many conspiracies, how many sleet-showers of temptations, how many civil, how many foreign wars, how many pains, how many attacks he has implied here in that word, " patience ! " And by " signs " again, how many dead raised, how many blind healed, how many lepers cleansed, how many devils cast out ! Hearing these things, let us learn if we happen upon a necessity for such recitals to cut our good deeds short, as he too did.

[2.] Then lest any should say, ' Well ! if thou be both great, and have wrought many things, still thou hast not wrought such great things, as the Apostles have in the other Churches,' he added,

Ver. 13. " For what is there wherein ye were made inferior to the rest of the Churches? "

' Ye were partakers,' he says, ' of no less grace than the others.' But perhaps some one will say, ' What can be the reason that he turns the discourse upon the Apostles, abandoning the contest against the false Apostles?' Because he is desirous to erect their spirits yet further, and to show that he is not only superior to them, but not even inferior to the great Apostles. Therefore, surely, when he is speaking of those he says, "I am more ;" but when he compares himself with the Apostles, he considers it a great thing[1] not to be " behind," although he labored more than they. And thence he shows that they insult the Apostles, in holding him who is their equal second to these men.

" Except it be that I myself was not a burden to you? " Again he has pronounced their rebuke with great severity. And what follows is of yet more odious import.

" Forgive me this wrong." Still, nevertheless, this severity contains both words of love and a commendation of themselves; if, that is, they consider it a wrong done to them, that the Apostle did not consent to receive aught from them, nor relied on them enough to be supported by them. ' If,' says he, ' ye blame me for this : ' he did not say, ' Ye blame me wrongly,' but with great sweetness, ' I ask your pardon, forgive me this fault.' And observe his prudence. For because the mooting this continually tended to bring disgrace upon them, he continually softens it down ; saying above, for

---

[1] ἀγαπητόν.

instance, "As the truth of Christ is in me, this boasting shall not be stopped in me;" (Chap. xi. 10.) then again, "Because I love you not? God knoweth.....But that I may cut off occasion from them that desire occasion, and that wherein they glory, they may be found even as we." (Chap. xi. 11, 12.) And in the former Epistle; "What is my reward then?" Verily, "that when I preach the Gospel, I may make the Gospel without charge." (1 Cor. ix. 18.) And here; "Forgive me this wrong." For every where he avoids showing that it is on account of their weakness he taketh not [from them]; and here, not to wound them. And therefore here he thus expresses himself; 'If ye think this to be an offense, I ask forgiveness.' Now he spoke thus, at once to wound and to heal. For do not say this, I pray thee; 'If thou meanest to wound, why excuse it? but if thou excusest it, why wound?' For this is wisdom's part, at once to lance, and to bind up the sore. Then that he may not seem, as he also said before, to be continually harping upon this for the sake of receiving from them, he remedies this [suspicion], even in his former Epistle, saying, "But I write not these things that it may be so done in my case; for it were good for me rather to die, than that any man should make my glorying void;" (1 Cor. ix. 15.) but here with more sweetness and gentleness. How, and in what manner?

Ver. 14. "Behold this is the third time I am ready to come to you, and I will not be a burden to you; for I seek not yours, but you: for the children ought not to lay up for the parents, but the parents for the children."

What he says is this; 'It is not because I do not receive of you that I do not come to you; nay, I have already come twice; and I am prepared to come this third time, "and I will not be a burden to you.'" And the reason is a noble one. For he did not say, 'because ye are mean,' 'because ye are hurt at it,' 'because ye are weak:' but what? "For I seek not yours, but you." 'I seek greater things; souls instead of goods; instead of gold, salvation.' Then because there still hung about the matter some suspicion, as if he were displeased at them; he therefore even states an argument. For since it was likely they would say, 'Can you not have both us and ours?' he adds with much grace this excuse for them, saying, "For the children ought not to lay up for the parents, but the parents for the children;" instead of teachers and disciples, employing the term parents and children, and showing that he does as a matter of duty what was not of duty. For Christ did not so command, but he says this to spare them; and therefore he adds also something further. For he did not only say that "the

children ought not to lay up," but also that the parents ought to. Therefore since it is meet to give,

Ver. 15. "I will most gladly spend and be spent for your souls."

'For the law of nature indeed has commanded the parents to lay up for the children; but I do not do this only, but I give myself also besides.' And this lavishness of his, the not only not receiving, but giving also besides, is not in common sort but accompanied with great liberality, and out of his own want; for the words, "I will be spent," are of one who would imply this. 'For should it be necessary to spend my very flesh, I will not spare it for your salvation.' And that which follows contains at once accusation and love, "though the more abundantly I love you, the less I be loved." 'And I do this,' he says, 'for the sake of those who are beloved by me, yet love me not equally.' Observe then, now, how many steps there are in this matter[1]. He had a right to receive, but he did not receive; here is good work the first: and this, though in want; [good work] the second; and though preaching to them, the third; he gives besides, the fourth; and not merely gives, but lavishly[2] too, the fifth; not money only, but himself, the sixth; for those who loved him not greatly, the seventh; and for those whom he greatly loved, the eighth.

[3.] Let us then also emulate this man! For it is a serious charge, the not loving even; but becomes more serious, when although one is loved he loveth not. For if he that loveth one that loveth him be no better than the publicans; (Matt. v. 46.) he that doth not so much as this ranks with the beasts; yea rather, is even below them. What sayest thou, O man? Lovest thou not him that loveth thee? What then dost thou live for? Wherein wilt thou be of use hereafter[3]? in what sort of matters? in public? in private? By no means; for nothing is more useless than a man that knows not to love. This law even robbers have oftentimes respected, and murderers, and housebreakers; and having only taken salt with one, have been made his friends[4], letting the board change their disposition, and thou that sharest not salt only, but words and deeds, and comings in and goings out, with him, dost thou not love? Nay: those that live impurely lavish even whole estates on their strumpets; and thou who hast a worthy love, art thou so cold, and weak, and unmanly, as not to be willing to love, even when it costs thee nothing? 'And who,' one asks, 'would be so vile, who such a wild

---

[1] Or, his conduct.
[2] μετὰ ἐπιτάσεως
[3] λοιπόν
[4] μετεταξαντο

beast, as to turn away from and to hate him that loves him?' Thou dost well indeed to disbelieve it, because of the unnaturalness of the thing; but if I shall show that there are many such persons, how shall we then bear the shame? For when thou speakest ill of him whom thou lovest, when thou hearest another speak ill of him and thou defendest him not, when thou grudgest that he should be well accounted of, what sort of affection is this? And yet it is not sufficient proof of love, not grudging, nor yet again not being at enmity or war with, but only supporting[1] and advancing him that loves thee: but when a man does and says everything to pull down his neighbor even, what can be more wretched than such a spirit? Yesterday and the day before his friend, thou didst both converse and eat with him: then because all at once thou sawest thine own member highly thought of, casting off the mask of friendship, thou didst put on that of enmity, or rather of madness. For glaring madness it is, to be annoyed at the goodness of neighbors; for this is the act of mad and rabid dogs. For like them, these also fly at all men's faces, exasperated with envy. Better to have a serpent twining about one's entrails than envy crawling in us. For that it is often possible to vomit up by means of medicines, or by food to quiet: but envy twineth not in entrails but harboreth in the bosom of the soul, and is a passion hard to be effaced. And indeed if such a serpent were within one, it would not touch men's bodies so long as it had a supply of food; but envy, even though thou spread for it ever so endless a banquet, devoureth the soul itself, gnawing on every side, tearing, tugging, and it is not possible to find any palliative whereby to make it quit its madness, save one only, the adversity of the prosperous; so is it appeased, nay rather, not so even. For even should this man suffer adversity, yet still he sees some other prosperous, and is possessed by the same pangs, and everywhere are wounds, everywhere blows. For it is not possible to live in the world and not see persons well reputed of. And such is the extravagance of this distemper, that even if one should shut its victim up at home, he envies the men of old who are dead.

Now, that men of the world should feel in this way, is indeed a grievous thing, yet it is not so very dreadful; but that those who are freed from the turmoils of busy life should be possessed by this distemper,—this is most grievous of all. And I could have wished indeed to be silent: and if silence took away too the disgrace of those doings, it were a gain to say

nothing: if however, though I should hold my peace the doings will cry out more loudly than my tongue, no harm will accrue from my words, because of their parading[2] these evils before us, but possibly some gain and advantage. For this distemper has infected even the Church, it has turned everything topsy-turvy, and dissevered the connection of the body, and we stand opposed to each other, and envy supplies us arms. Therefore great is the disruption. For if when all build up, it is a great thing if our disciples stand; when all at once are pulling down, what will the end be?

[4.] What doest thou, O man? Thou thinkest to pull down thy neighbor's; but before his thou pullest down thine own. Seest thou not them that are gardeners, that are husbandmen, how they all concur in one object? One hath dug the soil, another planted, a third carefully covered the roots, another watereth what is planted, another hedges it round and fortifies it, another drives off the cattle; and all look to one end, the safety of the plant. Here, however, it is not so: but I plant indeed myself, and another shakes and disturbs [the plant.] At least, allow it to get nicely fixed, that it may be strong enough to resist the assault. Thou destroyest not my work, but abandonest thine own. I planted, thou oughtest to have watered. If then thou shake it it, thou hast torn it up by the roots, and hast not wherein to display thy watering. But thou seest the planter highly esteemed. Fear not: neither am I anything, nor thou. "For neither is he that planteth nor he that watereth any thing;" (1 Cor. iii. 7.) one's is the work, God's. So it is with Him thou fightest and warrest, in plucking up what is planted.

Let us then at length come to our sober senses again, let us watch. For I fear not so much the battle without, as the fight within; for the root also, when it is well fitted into the ground, will suffer no damage from the winds; but if it be itself shaken, a worm gnawing through it from within, the tree will fall, even though none molest it. How long gnaw we the root of the Church like worms? For of earth such imaginings are begotten also, or rather not of earth, but of dung, having corruption for their mother; and they cease not from the detestable flattery that is from women[3]. Let us at length be generous men, let us be champions of philosophy, let us drive back the violent career of these evils. For I behold the mass of the Church prostrate now, as though it were a corpse. And as in a body newly dead, one may see eyes and hands and feet and neck and head, and yet no one limb performing its proper

---

[1] συγκροτεῖν
[2] ἐκπομπευομένων

[3] Old Lat. 'we cease not;' in either case he means, 'preachers cease not to court such flattery.'

office; so, truly, here also, all who are here are of the faithful, but their faith is not active; for we have quenched its warmth and made the body of Christ a corpse. Now if this sounds awful when said, it is much more awful when it appears in actions. For we have indeed the name of brothers, but do the deeds of foes; and whilst all are called members, we are divided against each other like wild beasts. I have said this not from a desire to parade our condition, but to shame you and make you desist. Such and such a man goes into a house; honor is paid to him; thou oughtest to give God thanks because thy member is honored and God is glorified; but thou doest the contrary: thou speakest evil of him to the man that honored him, so that thou trippest up the heels of both, and, besides, disgracest thyself. And wherefore, wretched and miserable one? Hast thou heard thy brother praised, either amongst men or women?[1] Add to his praises, for so thou shalt praise thyself also. But if thou overthrow the praise, first, thou hast spoken evil of thyself, having so acquired an ill character, and thou hast raised him the higher. When thou hearest one praised, become thou a partner in what is said; if not in thy life and virtue, yet still in rejoicing over his excellencies. Hath such an one praised? Do thou too admire: so shall he praise thee also as good and candid. Fear not,

as though thou wast ruining thine own interest by thy praises of another: for this is [rather] the result of accusation of him. For mankind is of a contentious spirit; and when it sees thee speaking ill of any, it heaps on its praises, wishing to mortify by so doing; and reprobates those that are accusers, both in its own mind and to others. Seest thou what disgrace we are the causes of to ourselves? how we destroy and rend the flock? Let us at length be members (of one another), let us become one body. And let him that is praised repudiate the praises, and transfer the encomium to his brother; and let him that hears another praised, feel pleasure in himself. If we thus come together ourselves, we shall also draw unto ourselves the Head; but if we live parted[2] from each other, we shall also put from us the aid which comes from thence; and when that is put aside, the body will receive great damage, not being bound together[3] from above. That this then may not happen, let us, banishing ill will and envy, and despising what the many may think of us, embrace love and concord. For thus we shall obtain both the present good things and those to come; whereunto may we all attain, through the grace and love towards men of our Lord Jesus Christ, with Whom to the Father together with the Holy Ghost, be glory, might, honor, now and forever, and world without end. Amen.

HOMILY XXVIII.

2 COR. XII. 16—18.

But be it so, I myself did not burden you: but being crafty, I caught you with guile. Did I take advantage of you by any one of them whom I have sent unto you? I exhorted Titus, and with him I sent the brother. Did Titus take any advantage of you? Walked we not by the same spirit? walked we not in the same steps?

PAUL has spoken these words very obscurely, but not without a meaning or purpose. For seeing he was speaking about money, and his defence on that score, it is reasonable that what he says must be wrapt in obscureness. What then is the meaning of what he says? He had said, 'I received not, nay I am ready even to give besides, and to spend;' and much discourse is made on this subject both in the former Epistle and in this. Now he says something else, introducing the subject in the form of

an objection and meeting it by anticipation.[4] What he says is something like this; 'I indeed have not made a gain of you: but perhaps some one has it to say that I did not receive [of you] indeed myself, but, being crafty, I procured those who were sent by me to ask for something of you as for themselves[5], and through them I myself received, yet keeping myself clear of seeming to receive, by receiving through others. But none can have this to say either; and you are witnesses.' Wherefore also he proceeds by question, saying, "I exhorted Titus, and with him I sent the brother. Did Titus make a gain of you?" 'walked he not just as I walked.' That is to say, neither did he receive. Seest thou how intense a strictness [is here], in that he

---

[1] Bened inserts, 'and hast been grieved,' but the insertion is not countenanced by the MSS.

[2] διωκισμένοι.
[3] σφιγγόμενον.
[4] προηγουμένως
[5] εἰς οἰκεῖον πρόσωπον.

not only keeps himself clear of that receiving, but so modulates those also who are sent by him that he may not give so much as a slight pretence to those who were desirous of attacking him. For this is far greater than that which the Patriarch did. (Gen. xiv. 24.) For he indeed, when he had returned from his victory, and the king would have given him the 'spoil, refused to accept aught save what the men had eaten ; but this man neither himself enjoyed [from them] his necessary food, nor allowed his partners to partake of such : thus abundantly stopping the mouths of the shameless. Wherefore he makes no assertion, nor does he say that they did not receive either ; but what was far more than this, he cites the Corinthians themselves as witnesses that they had received nothing, that he may not seem to be witnessing in his own person, but by their verdict ; which course we are accustomed to take in matters fully admitted and about which we are confident. 'For tell me,' he says, 'Did any one of those who were sent by us make unfair gain[1] of you ?' He did not say, 'Did any one receive aught from you ?' but he calls the things 'unfair gain ;' attacking them and shaming them exceedingly, and showing that to receive of an unwilling [giver] is 'unfair gain.' And he said not 'did Titus ?' but, "did any ?" 'For ye cannot say this either,' he says,' that such an one certainly did not receive, but another did. No single one of those who came did so.' "I exhorted Titus." This too is severely[2] said. For he did not say, 'I sent Titus,' but, 'I exhorted' him ; showing that if he had received even, he would have done so justly ; but, nevertheless, even so he remained pure. Wherefore he asks them again, saying, "Did Titus take any advantage of you ? Walked we not by the same spirit ?" What means, "by the same spirit ?" He ascribes the whole to grace and shows that the whole of this praise is the good result not of our labors, but of the gift of the Spirit and of Grace. For it was a very great instance of grace that although both in want and hunger they would receive nothing for the edification of the disciples. "Walked we not in the same steps ?" That is to say, they did not depart the least from this strictness, but preserved the same rule entire.

[2.] Ver. 19. "Again, think ye that we are excusing ourselves unto you ?"[3]

Seest thou how he is continually in fear, lest he should incur the suspicion of flattery ? Seest thou an Apostle's prudence, how constantly he mentions this ? For he said before, "We commend not ourselves again, but give you occasion to glory ;" (2 Cor. v. 12.) and in the commencement of the Epistle, "Do we need letters of commendation ?" (ib. iii. 1.)

"But all things are for your edifying." Again he is soothing them. And he does not here either say clearly, 'on this account we receive not, because of your weakness ;' but, 'in order that we may edify you ;' speaking out indeed more clearly than he did before, and revealing that wherewith he travailed ; but yet without severity. For he did not say, 'because of your weakness ;' but, 'that ye may be edified.'

Ver. 20. "For I fear, lest by any means when I come, I should not find you such as I would, and should myself be found of you such as ye would not."

He is going to say something great and offensive. And therefore he also inserts this excuse [for it], both by saying, "All things are for your edifying," and by adding, "I fear," softening the harshness of what was presently going to be said. For it was not here out of arrogance nor the authority of a teacher, but out of a father's tender concern, when he is more fearful and trembling than the sinners themselves at that which is likely to reform them. And not even so does he run them down or make an absolute assertion ; but says doubtingly, "lest by any means when I come, I should not find you such as I would." He did not say, 'not virtuous,' but "not such as I would," everywhere employing the terms of affection. And the words, "I should find," are of one who would express what is out of natural expectation, as are also those, "I shall be found by you." For the thing is not of deliberate choice, but of a necessity originating with you. Wherefore he says, "I should be found such as ye would not." He said not here, "such as I would not," but, with more severity, "such as ye wish not." For it would in that case become his own will, not indeed what he would first have willed, but his will nevertheless. For he might indeed have said again, 'such as I would not,' and so have showed his love : but he wishes not to relax[4] his hearer. Yea rather, his words would in that case have been even harsher ; but now he has at once dealt them a smarter blow and showed himself more gentle. For this is the characteristic of his wisdom ; cutting more deeply, to strike more gently. Then, because he had spoken obscurely, he unveils his meaning, saying,

"Lest there be strife, jealousy, wraths, backbitings, whisperings, swellings."[5]

And what he might well put first, that he

---

[1] ἐπλεονέκτησεν.
[2] πληκτικῶς.
[3] The words in the Rec Text here omitted, 'We speak before God in Christ,' are found above, where this text is quoted Hom vi. p 311 [They are undoubtedly genuine. C]

[4] ἐκλῦσαι
[5] The Received Text has 'factions' after 'wraths,' and 'tumults' after 'swellings,' which Chrysostom omits.

puts last: for they were very proud[1] against him. Therefore, that he may not seem principally to be seeking his own, he first mentions what was common. For all these things were gendered of envy, their slanderings, accusations, dissensions. For just like some evil root, envy produced wrath, accusation, pride, and all those other evils, and by them was increased further,

Ver. 21. And "lest when I come again, my God should humble me among you."

And the word "again," too, is as smiting them. For he means, 'What happened before is enough;' as he said also in the beginning [of the Epistle], "to spare you, I came not as yet to Corinth." (Chap. i. 18, 23.) Seest thou how he shows both indignation and tender affection? But what means, "will humble me?" And yet this is glorious rather, to accuse, to take vengeance, to call to account, to be seated in the place of judge; howbeit he calls it a humbling. So far was he from being ashamed of that [cause of] humbling, because, "his bodily presence was weak, and his speech of no account," that he wished to be even for ever in that case, and deprecated the contrary. And he says this more clearly as he proceeds; and he counts this to be especially humbling, to be involved in such a necessity as the present, of punishing and taking vengeance. And wherefore did he not say, 'lest when I come I shall be humbled,' but, "lest when I come my God will humble me." 'Because had it not been for His sake, I should have paid no attention nor been anxious. For it is not as possessing authority and for my own pleasure, that I demand satisfaction,[2] but because of His commandment.' Now above, indeed, he expressed himself thus, "I shall be found;" here, however, he relaxes and adopts milder and gentler language, saying,

"I shall mourn for many of them who have sinned." Not simply, "who have sinned," but,

"Who have not repented." And he said not, 'all,' but "many;" nor made it clear who these were either, thereby making the return unto repentance easy to them; and to make it plain that a repentance is able to right transgressions, he bewails those that repent not, those who are incurably diseased, those who continue in their wounds. Observe then Apostolic virtue, in that, conscious of no evil in himself, he laments over the evils of others and is humbled for other men's transgressions. For this is the especial mark of a teacher, so to sympathize with the calamities of his disciples, and to mourn over the wounds of those who are under

him. Then he mentions also the specific sin.

"Of the lasciviousness and uncleanness which they committed." Now in these words he alludes indeed to fornication; but if one carefully examine the subject, every kind of sin can be called by this name. For although the fornicator and adulterer is preeminently styled unclean, yet still the other sins also produce uncleanness in the soul. And therefore it is that Christ also calls the Jews unclean, not charging them with fornication only, but with wickedness of other kinds as well. Wherefore also He says that they made the outside clean, and that "not the things which enter in defile the man, but those which come out from him;" (Mat. xv. 11.) and it is said in another place, "Every one that is proud in heart is unclean before the Lord." (Prov. xvi. 5. LXX.)

[3.] For nothing is purer than virtue, nothing uncleaner than vice; for the one is brighter than the sun, the other more stinking than mire. And to this they will themselves bear witness, who are wallowing in that mire and living in that darkness; at any rate, when one prepares them a little to see clearly. For as long as they are by themselves, and inebriate with the passion, just as if living in darkness they lie in unseemly wise to their much infamy, conscious even then where they are, although not fully; but after they have seen any of those who live in virtue reproving them or even showing himself, then they understand their own wretchedness more clearly; and as if a sunbeam had darted upon them, they cover up their own unseemliness and blush before those who know of their doings, yea, though the one be a slave and the other free, though the one be a king and the other a subject. Thus when Ahab saw Elijah, he was ashamed, even when he[3] had as yet said nothing; standing convicted by the mere sight of him; and when his accuser was silent, he pronounced a judgment condemnatory of himself; uttering the language of such as are caught, and saying, "Thou hast found me, O mine enemy!" (1 Kings xxi. 20.) Thus Elijah himself conversed with that tyrant then with great boldness. Thus Herod, unable to bear the shame of those reproofs, (which [shame] the sound of the prophet's tongue with mighty and transparent clearness exposed more evidently,) cast John into the prison: like one who was naked and attempting to put out the light, that he might be in the dark again; or rather he himself dared not put it out, but, as it were, placed it in the house under a bushel; and that wretched and miserable woman compelled it to be done. But not even so could they cover the reproof, nay, they lit it up the more. For both

---

[1] ἀπενοοῦντο
[2] αὐθαδιζόμενος

[3] Elijah.

they that asked, 'Wherefore doth John dwell in prison?' learnt the reason, and all they that since have dwelt on land or sea, who then lived, or now live, and who shall be hereafter, both have known and shall know clearly these wicked tragedies, both that of their lewdness and that of their bloodguiltiness, and no time shall be able to wipe out the remembrance of them.

So great a thing is virtue: so immortal is its memory, so completely even by words only doth it strike down its adversaries. For wherefore did he cast him into the prison? Wherefore did he not despise him? Was he going to drag him before the judgment-seat? Did he demand vengeance upon him for his adultery? Was not what he said then simply a reproof? Why then doth he fear and tremble? Was it not words and talk merely? But they stung him more than deeds. He led him not to any judgment-seat, but he dragged him before that other tribunal of conscience; and he sets as judges upon him all who freely gave their verdicts in their thought. Therefore the tyrant trembled, unable to endure the lustre of virtue. Seest thou how great a thing is philosophy? It made a prisoner more lustrous than a king, and the latter is afraid and trembles before him. He indeed only put him in bonds; but that polluted woman rushed on to his slaughter also, although the rebuke was leveled rather against him, [than herself.] For he did not then meet "her" and say, 'Why cohabitest thou with the king?' not that she was guiltless, (how should she be so?) but he wished by that other means to put all to rights. Wherefore he blamed the king, and yet not him with violence of manner. For he did not say, 'O polluted and all-polluted and lawless and profane one, thou hast trodden under foot the law of God, thou hast despised the commandments, thou hast made thy might law.' None of these things; but even in his rebukings great was the gentleness of the man, great his meekness. For, "It is not lawful for thee," he says, "to have thy brother Philip's wife." The words are those of one who teacheth rather than reproveth, instructeth rather than chasteneth, who composeth to order rather than exposeth, who amendeth rather than trampleth on him. But, as I said, the light is hateful to the thief, and the mere sight of the just man is odious to sinners; "for he is grievous unto us even to behold." (Wisd. ii. 15.) For they cannot bear his radiance, even as diseased eyes cannot bear the sun's. But to many of the wicked he is grievous not to behold only, but even to hear of. And therefore that polluted and all-polluted woman, the procuress of her girl, yea rather her murderess, although she had never seen him nor heard his voice,

rushed on to his slaughter; and prepareth her whom she brought up in lasciviousnss to proceed also to murder, so extravagantly did she fear him.

[4.] And what says she? "Give me here in a charger the head of John the Baptist." (Mat. xiv. 8.) Whither rushest thou over precipices, wretched and miserable one? What? is the accuser before thee? is he in sight and troubleth thee? Others said, "He is grievous unto us even to behold;" but to her, as I said, he was grievous to even hear of. Wherefore she saith, "Give me here in a charger the head of John." And yet because of thee he inhabits a prison, and is laden with chains, and thou art free to wanton over thy love and to say, 'So completely have I subdued the king, that though publicly reproached he yielded not, nor desisted from his passion, nor tore asunder his adulterous connection with me, but even put him that reproached him in bonds.' Why art thou mad and rabid, when even after that reproof of his sin thou retainest thy paramour? Why seekest thou a table of furies, and preparest a banquet of avenging demons? Seest thou how nothing-worth,[1] how cowardly, how unmanly, is vice; how when it shall most succeed, it then beccmes more feeble? For this woman was not so much disturbed before she had cast John into prison, as she is troubled after he is bound, and she is urgent, saying, "Give me here in a charger the head of John." And wherefore so? 'I fear,' she says, 'lest there be any[2] hushing up of his murder, lest any should rescue him from his peril.' And wherefore requirest thou not the whole corpse, but the head? 'The tongue,' she says, 'that pained me, that I long to see silent.' But the contrary will happen, as indeed it also hath done, thou wretched and miserable one! it will cry louder afterwards, when it is cut out. For then indeed it cried in Judæa only, but now it will reach to the ends of the world; and wheresoever thou enterest into a church, whether it be among the Moors, or among the Persians, or even unto the British isles themselves, thou hearest John crying, "It is not lawful for thee to have thy brother Phillip's wife." But she, unknowing to reason in any such way, urges and presses,[3] and thrusts on the senseless tyrant to the murder, fearing lest he change his mind. But from this too learn thou again the power of virtue. Not even when he was shut up and bound and silent, does she bear the righteous man. Seest thou how weak a thing vice is? how unclean? For in the place of meats it bringeth in a human head upon a charger.

What is more polluted, what more accursed,

---

[1] οὐδαμινὸν
[2] συσκιασθῇ ὁ φόνος
[3] ἀγχει

what more immodest, than that damsel? what a voice she uttered in that theatre of the devil, in that banquet of demons! Seest thou this tongue and that; the one bringing healthful medicines, the other one with poison on it, and made the purveyor to a devilish banquet. But wherefore did she not command him to be murdered within there, at the feast, when her pleasure would have been greater? She feared lest if he should come thither and be seen, he should change them all by his look, by his boldness. Therefore surely it is that she demandeth his head, wishing to set up a bright trophy of fornication; and give it to her mother. Seest thou the wages of dancing, seest thou the spoils of that devilish plot? I mean not the head of John, but her paramour himself. For if one examine it carefully, against the king that trophy was set up, and the victress was vanquished, and the beheaded was crowned, and proclaimed victor, even after his death shaking more vehemently the hearts of the offenders. And that what I have said is no [mere] boast, ask of Herod himself; who, when he heard of the miracles of Christ, said, "This is John, he is risen from the dead: and therefore do these powers work in him." (Mat. xiv. 2.) So lively[3] was the fear, so abiding the agony he retained; and none had power to cast down the terror of his conscience, but that incorruptible Judge continued to take him by the throat, and day by day to demand of him satisfaction for the murder. Knowing, then, these things, let us not fear to suffer evil, but to do evil; for that indeed is victory, but this defeat.

Wherefore also Paul said, "Why not rather take wrong, why not rather be defrauded. Nay, ye yourselves do wrong, and defraud, and that your brethren." For by the suffering evil [come] those crowns, those prizes, that proclamation [of victory]. And this may be seen in all the saints. Since then they all were thus crowned, thus proclaimed, let us too travel this road, and let us pray indeed that we enter not into temptation; but if it should come, let us make stand with much manliness and display the proper readiness of mind, that we may obtain the good things to come, through the grace and love towards men of our Lord Jesus Christ, with Whom to the Father, together with the Holy Ghost, be glory, might, honor, now and for ever, and world without end. Amen.

HOMILY XXIX.

2 Cor. XIII. 1.

This is the third time I am coming to you. At the mouth of two witnesses or three shall every word be established.

THE wisdom[1] of Paul and his much tender affection, one may observe in many other circumstances, but especially in this, his being so abundant and vehement in his admonitions, but so tardy and procrastinating in his punishments. For he did not chastise them immediately on their sinning, but warned them once and again; and not even so, upon their paying no attention, does he exact punishment, but warns again, saying, "This is the third time I am coming to you;" and 'before I come I write again.' Then, that his procrastinating may not produce indifference,[2] see how he corrects this result also, by threatening continually and holding the blow suspended over them, and saying, "If I come again I will not spare;" and "lest when I come again I should mourn for many." These things, then, he doeth and speaketh, in this too imitating the Lord of all: because that God also threateneth indeed continually and warneth often, but not often chastiseth and punisheth. And so in truth also doth Paul, and therefore he said also before, "To spare you I came not as yet to Corinth." What is, "to spare you?" Lest finding you to have sinned and to continue unamended, I should visit with chastisement and punishment. And here, "This is the third time I am coming to you. At the mouth of two witnesses or three shall every word be established." He joins the unwritten to the written, as he has done also in another place, saying, "He that is joined to an harlot is one body; for the twain," saith He, "shall become one flesh." (1 Cor. vi. 16.) Howbeit, this was spoken of lawful marriage; but he diverted its application[4] unto this thing[5] conveniently, so as to terrify them the more. And so he doth here also, setting his comings and his warnings in the place of witnesses. And what he says is

---

[1] ἀκμάζοντα
[2] φιλοσοφίαν.
[3] ἄγχει

[4] ἀπεχρήσατο.
[5] i. e Fornication.

this : 'I spoke once and again when I was with you ; I speak also now by letter. And if indeed ye attend to me, what I desired is accomplished ; but if ye pay no attention, it is necessary henceforth to stop speaking, and to inflict the punishment.' Wherefore he says,

Ver. 2. "I have said beforehand, and I do say beforehand when I was present the second time ; so now being absent I write to them that sinned heretofore and to all the rest, that if I come again, I will not spare."

'For if at the mouth of two witnesses or three every word shall be established, and I have come twice and spoken, and speak now also by this Epistle; it follows, I must after this keep my word.¹ For think not, I pray you, that my writing is of less account than my coming ; for as I spoke when present, so now I write also when absent.' Seest thou his fraternal solicitude ? Seest thou forethought becoming a teacher ? He neither kept silence nor punished, but he both foretells often, and continues ever threatening, and puts off the punishment, and if they should continue unamended, then he threatens to bring it to the proof. 'But what didst thou tell them before when present, and when absent writest ? ' "That if I come again, I will not spare." Having showed before that he is unable to do this unless he is compelled, and having called the thing a mourning, and a humbling ; (for he saith, "lest my God should humble me before you, and I should mourn for them that have sinned heretofore, and not repented ;—Chap. xii. 21.) and having made his excuse unto them, namely, that he had told them before, once and twice and thrice, and that he does and contrives all he can so as to hold back the punishment, and by the fear of his words to make them better, he then used this unpleasing and terrifying expression, "If I come again, I will not spare." He did not say, 'I will avenge and punish and exact satisfaction :' but again expresses even punishment itself in paternal language ; showing his tender affection, and his heart to be grieved along with them; because that he always to "spare" them put off. Then that they may not think now also that there will be again a putting off, and merely a threat in words, therefore he both said before, "At the mouth of two witnesses or three shall every word be established ; " and [now], "If I come again, I will not spare." Now what he means is this : 'I will no longer put off, if (which God forbid) I find you unamended ; but will certainly visit it, and make good what I have said.'

[2.] Then with much anger and vehement indignation against those who make a mock of him as weak, and ridicule his presence, and say, " his presence is weak, and his speech of no account ; "

(Chap. x. 10.) aiming his efforts² at these men, he says,

Ver. 3. "Seeing that ye seek a proof of Christ that speaketh in me."

For he said this, dealing at once a blow at these, and at the same time lashing those³ also. Now what he means is this; 'Since ye are desirous of proving whether Christ dwelleth in me, and call me to an account, and on this score make a mock of me as mean and despicable, as I were destitute of that Power ; ye shall know that we are not destitute, if ye give us occasion, which God forbid.' What then ? tell me. Dost thou therefore punish, because they seek a proof ? 'No,' he says ; for had he sought this, he would have punished them at the first on their sinning, and would not have put off. But that he does not seek this, he has shown more clearly as he proceeds, saying, "Now I pray that ye do no evil, not that we may appear approved, but that ye may be approved, though we be as reprobates." (Ver. 7.)

He doth not employ those words then as assigning a reason,⁴ but rather in indignation, rather as attacking those that despise him. 'For,' he says, ' I have no desire indeed to give you such a proof, but if you yourselves should furnish cause and should choose to challenge me, ye shall know by very deeds.' And observe how grievous he makes what he says. For he said not, 'Since ye seek a proof of me,' but " of Christ that speakest in me, showing that it was against Him they sinned." And he did not say merely, 'dwelling in me,' but "speaking in me," showing that his words are spiritual. But if he doth not display His power nor punish, (for thenceforward the Apostle transferred what he said from himself to Christ, thus making his threat more fearful,) it is not from weakness; for He can do it : but from long suffering. Let none then think His forbearance to be weakness. For why marvellest thou that He doth not now proceed against sinners, nor in his forbearance and long suffering exacts satisfaction, seeing that He endured even to be crucified, and though suffering such things punished not ? Wherefore also he added,

Ver. 3, 4. "Who to you-ward is not weak, but is mighty in you. For though He was crucified through weakness, yet He liveth through the Power of God."

These words have much obscurity and give disturbance to the weaker sort. Wherefore it is necessary to unfold them more clearly, and to explain the signification of the expression as to which the obscurity exists, that no one may be offended, even of the simpler sort.

---

¹ ἀληθεῦσαι.

² ἀποτεινόμενος.
³ i. e. the Corinthians themselves.
⁴ αἰτιολογικῶς.

What then, at all, is that which is here said, and what the term "weakness" designates, and in what signification it is used, it is necessary to learn. For the term is indeed one, but it has many meanings. For bodily sickness is termed 'weakness:' whence it is even said in the Gospel, "Behold, he whom Thou lovest is weak,"[1] (John xi. 3, 4.) concerning Lazarus; and He Himself said, "This weakness is not unto death;" and Paul, speaking of Epaphras, "For indeed he was weak nigh unto death, but God had mercy on him;" (Phil. ii. 27.) and of Timothy, "Use a little wine for thy stomach's sake and thine often weaknesses." (1 Tim. v. 23.) For all these denote bodily sickness. Again, the not being established firmly in the faith is called 'weakness;' the not being perfect and complete. And denoting this Paul said, "Him that is weak in the faith receive ye but not to doubtful disputations:" (Rom. xiv. 1, 2.) and again, "One believeth that he may eat all things; another, who is weak, eateth herbs," denoting him who is weak in the faith. Here there are two significations of the term 'weakness;' there is yet a third thing which is called 'weakness.' What then is this? Persecutions, plottings, insults, trials, assaults. And denoting this Paul said, "For this thing I besought the Lord thrice. And He said unto me, My grace is sufficient for thee: for My power is made perfect in weakness." (Chap. xii., 8, 9.) What is "in weakness?" In persecutions, in dangers, in trials, in plottings, in deaths. And denoting this he said, Wherefore, I take pleasure in weakness.[2] Then showing what kind of weakness he means, he spake not of fever, nor of doubt about the faith; but what? "in injuries, in necessities, in distresses, in stripes, in imprisonments, that the power of Christ may rest upon me. For when I am weak, then am I strong." (Chap. xii. 10.) That is to say 'when I am persecuted, when I am driven up and down, when I am plotted against, then am I strong, then the rather I prevail over, and get the better of them that plot against me. because that grace resteth upon[3] me, more largely, It is then in this third sense that Paul useth "weakness;" and this is what he means by it; aiming again, as I said also before, at that point, his seeming to them to be mean and contemptible. For indeed he had no desire to boast, nor to seem to be what he really was, nor yet to display the power which he possessed of punishing and revenging; whence also he was accounted to be mean. When then as so accounting they were going on in great indifference and insensibility, and repented not of

their sins, he seizes a favorable opportunity, discourses with much vigor upon these points also, and shows that it was not from weakness he did nothing, but from long-suffering.

[3.] Then, as I said, by transferring the argument from himself to Christ, he enhances their fear, he increases his threat. And what he says is this; 'for even supposing I should do something and chastise and take vengeance on the guilty ones, is it I that chastise and take vengeance? it is He that dwelleth in me, Christ Himself. But if ye do not believe this, but are desirous of receiving a proof by deeds of Him that dwelleth in me, ye shall know presently; "For he is not weak to you-ward, but is even powerful."' And wherefore added he "to you-ward," seeing He is mighty everywhere? for should He be minded to punish unbelievers, He is able; or demons, or anything whatsoever. What then is the import of the addition? The expression is either as shaming them exceedingly by remembrance of the proofs they have already received; or else as declaring this, that meanwhile He shows His power in you who ought to be corrected. As he said also in another place, "For what have I to do to judge them also that are without?" (1 Cor. v. 12.) 'For those that are without,' he says, 'He will then call to account in the day of judgment, but you even now, so as to rescue you from that punishment.' But nevertheless even this instance of his solicitude, although arising from tender affection, observe how he combines with fear and much anger, saying, "Who to you-ward is not weak, but is powerful in you."

Ver. 4. "For though He was crucified through weakness, yet He liveth through the Power of God."

What is, "though He was crucified through weakness?" 'For though He chose,' he says, 'to endure a thing which seems to carry a notion of weakness, still this in no way breaks in upon[4] His Power. That still remains invincible, and that thing which seemeth to be of weakness, hath nothing harmed it, nay this very thing itself shows His Power most of all, in that He endured even such a thing, and yet His Power was not mutilated.'[5] Let not then the expression "weakness" disturb thee; for elsewhere also he says, "The foolishness of God is wiser than men, and the weakness of God is stronger than men;" (1 Cor. i. 25.) although in God is nothing either foolish or weak: but he called the Cross so, as setting forth the conception of the unbelieving regarding it. Hear him, at least, interpreting himself. "For the preaching of the Cross is to them that perish foolishness, but unto us which are saved it is the pow-

---

[1] ἀσθενεῖ, A. V. is sick.
[2] A. V. infirmities.
[3] ἐνιζανούσης.

[4] διακόπτει.
[5] ἠκρωτηριάσθη.

er of God." (Ib. 18.) And again; "But we preach Christ crucified, unto the Jews a stumbling-block, and unto the Greeks foolishness; but unto them which are called, both Jews and Greeks, Christ the power of God and the wisdom of God." (Ib. 23, 24.) And again; "But the natural man receiveth not the things of the Spirit, for they are foolishness unto him." (1. Cor. ii. 14.) Observe, how in every place he expresseth the conception of the unbelieving, who look upon the Cross as foolishness and weakness. And so, in truth, here also he means not "weakness" really such, but what was suspected to be such with the unbelieving. He doth not then say this, that because He was weak He was crucified. Away with the thought! For that He had it in His power not to have been crucified He showed throughout; when He now cast men down prostrate, now turned back the beams of the sun, and withered a fig-tree, and blinded their eyes that came against Him, and wrought ten thousand other things. What then is this which he says, "through weakness!" That even although He was crucified after enduring peril and treachery, (for we have showed that peril and treachery are called weakness,) yet still He was nothing harmed thereby. And he said this to draw the example unto his own case. For since the Corinthians beheld them persecuted, driven about, despised, and not avenging nor visiting it, in order to teach them that neither do they so suffer from want of power,[1] nor from being unable to visit it, he leads on the argument up to The Master, because 'He too,' saith he, 'was crucified, was bound, suffered ten thousand things, and He visited them not, but continued to endure things which appeared to argue weakness, and in this way displaying His Power, in that although He punishes not nor requites, He is not injured any thing at all. For instance, the Cross did not cut asunder His life, nor yet impeded His resurrection, but He both rose again and liveth.' And when thou hearest of the Cross and of life, expect to find the doctrine concerning the Incarnation,[2] for all that is said here hath reference to that. And if he says "though the Power of God," it is not as though He were Himself void of strength to quicken His flesh; but it was indifferent with him to mention either Father or Son. For when he said, "the Power of God, he said by His own Power. For that both He Himself raised it up and sustains it, hear Him saying, "Destroy this temple, and in three days I will raise it up." (John ii. 19.) But if that which is His, this he[3] saith to be the Father's, be not

disturbed; "For," He saith, "all My Father's things are Mine." (John xvi. 15.) And again, "All Mine are Thine, and Thine are Mine." (Ib. xvii. 10.) 'As then He that was crucified was nothing harmed,' he says, 'so neither are we when persecuted and warred against;' wherefore also he adds,

"For even we also if[4] we are weak in Him, yet we shall live with Him through the Power of God."[5]

What is the meaning of "we are weak in Him?" We are persecuted, are driven here and there, suffer extremity. But what is "with Him?" 'Because of the preaching,' he says, 'and our faith in Him. But if for His sake we undergo what is sad and disagreeable, it is quite plain that we shall what is pleasant also : ' and so he added, "but we are saved with Him by the Power of God."

[4.] Ver. 5, 6. "Try your own selves, whether ye be in the faith, prove your own selves. Know ye not as to your own selves, that Christ is in you, unless indeed ye be reprobate? But I hope that ye shall know that we are not reprobate."

For since by what he has said he hath shown that even if he does not punish, it is not because he hath not Christ in himself, but because he intimates His long-suffering, Who was crucified and yet avenged not Himself; he again, in another manner, produces the same effect, and still more irrefragably,[6] establishing his argument by the disciples. 'For why speak I of myself,' he says 'the teacher, who have so much care upon me and am entrusted with the whole world and have done such great miracles. For if ye will but examine yourselves who are in the rank of disciples, ye will see that Christ is in you also. But if in you, then much more in your teacher. For if ye have faith, Christ is in you also.' For they who then believed wrought miracles. Wherefore also he added, "Try your own selves, prove your own selves, whether ye be in the faith. Know ye not as to your own selves, unless indeed that Christ is in you, ye be reprobate?" 'But if in you, much more in your teacher?' He seems to me here to speak of the "faith" which relates to miracles. 'For if ye have faith,' he says, "Christ is in you, except ye have become reprobates." Seest thou how again he terrifies them, and shows even to superfluity that Christ is with Him. For he seems to me to be here alluding to them, even as to their lives. For since faith is not enough [by itself] to draw down the energy of the Spirit, and he had said that ' "if ye are in the faith" ye have Christ in you,' and it happened that many who had faith

---

[1] ἀτονίαν.
[2] τῆς οἰκονομίας.
[3] i. e. Paul.

[4] εἰ om. R. T.
[5] 'Toward you ' R. T.
[6] ἐκ πλείονος περιουσίας.

were destitute of that energy; in order to solve the difficulty, he says, "except ye be reprobate," except [that is] ye are corrupt in life. "But I hope that ye shall know that we are not reprobate." What followed naturally was to have said, "but if ye have become reprobate, yet we have not." He doth not, however, say so, for fear of wounding them, but he hints it in an obscure manner, without either making the assertion thus, 'ye are reprobate,' or proceeding by question and saying, 'But if ye are reprobate,' but leaving out even this way of putting it by question, he indicates it obscurely by adding, "But I hope that ye shall know that we are not reprobate." Here also again, great is the threat, great the alarm. 'For since ye desire,' he says, 'in this way, by your own punishment to receive the proof, we shall have no difficulty in giving you that demonstration.' But he does not indeed so express himself, but with more weight and threatening. "But I hope that ye shall know that we are not reprobate." 'For ye ought indeed,' he saith, 'to have known even without this what we are,[1] and that we have Christ speaking and working in us; but since ye desire to receive the proof of it by deeds also, ye shall know that we are not reprobate.' Then when he has held the threat suspended over their heads, and brought the punishment now up to their doors, and has set them a trembling, and made them look for vengeance; see how again he sweetens down his words and soothes their fear, and shows his unambitious temper, his tender solicitude towards his disciples, his high-principledness of purpose, his loftiness and freedom from vain-glory. For he exhibits all these qualities in what he adds, saying,

Ver. 7, 8, 9. "Now I pray to God that ye do no evil, not that we may appear approved, but that ye may do that which is honorable, though we be as reprobate. For we can do nothing against the truth but for the truth. For we rejoice when we are weak, and ye are strong. For this also we pray for even your perfecting."

[5.] What can be equal to this soul? He was despised, he was spit upon, he was ridiculed, he was mocked, as mean, as contemptible, as a braggart, as boastful in his words but in his deeds unable to make even a little show; and although seeing so great a necessity for showing his own power, he not only puts off, not only shrinks back, but even prays that he may not fall into such a position. For he says, "I pray that ye do no evil, not that we may appear approved, but that ye may do that which is honorable, though we be as reprobate." What is it he says? 'I entreat God. I beseech Him,' he says, 'that I may find no one unreformed, may find no one that has not repented? yea, rather, not this

alone, but that none may have sinned at all. For,' he says, 'that ye have done no [evil], but if ye have perchance sinned, then that ye may have changed your conduct, and been beforehand with me in reforming, and arresting all wrath. For this is not what I am eager about, that we should be approved in this way, but clean the contrary, that we should not appear approved. For if ye should continue,' he says, 'sinning and not repenting, it will be necessary for us to chastise, to punish, to maim your bodies; (as happened in the case of Sapphira and of Magus;) and we have given proof of our power. But we pray not for this, but the contrary, that we may not be shown to be approved in this way, that we may not in this way exhibit the proof of the power which is in us, by chastising you and punishing you as sinning and as incurably diseased, but what? "That ye should do that which is honorable," we pray for this, that ye should ever live in virtue, ever in amendment; "and we should be as reprobate," not displaying our power of punishing.' And he said not, "reprobate" for he would not "be" reprobate, even though he did not punish, nay rather for this very reason he would be "approved;" 'but even if some suspect us,' he says, 'on account of our not displaying our power, to be contemptible and cast away, we care nothing for this. Better we should be so deemed of by those, than display the power which God hath given to us in those stripes, and in that unreformedness of heart.'

"For we can do nothing against the truth, but for the truth." For that he may not seem [merely] to be gratifying them, (for this is what one who was void of vain-glory might do,) but to be doing what the nature of the thing demanded, he added this, "for we can do nothing against the truth." 'For if we find you,' he says, 'in good repute, having driven away your sins by repentance and having boldness towards God; we shall not be able thereafter, were we never so willing, to punish you, but should we attempt it even, God will not work with us. For to this end gave He us our power that the judgment we give should be true and righteous, not contrary to the truth.' Seest thou how in every way he can, he makes what he says void of offensiveness, and softens the harshness of his menace? Moreover as he has eagerly endeavored this, so is he desirous also to show that his mind was quite joined[1] to them; wherefore also he added, "For we rejoice when we are weak and ye are strong, and this also we pray for even your perfecting." 'For most certainly,' he says, 'we cannot do any thing against the truth, that is, punish you if you are well pleasing [to God]; besides, because we

---

[1] τὰ ἡμέτερα.

[1] ᾠκειωμένην.

cannot, we therefore do not wish it, and even desire the contrary. Nay, we are particularly glad of this very thing, when we find you giving us no occasion to show that power of ours for punishment. For even if the doing of such things shows men glorious and approved and strong; still we desire the contrary, that ye should be approved and unblamable, and that we should never at any time reap the glory thence arising.' Wherefore he says, "For we are glad when we are weak." What is, "are weak?" 'When we may be thought weak.' Not when we are weak, but when we are thought weak; for they were thought so by their enemies, because they displayed not their power of punishing. 'But still we are glad, when your behavior is of such a sort as to give us no pretence for punishing you. And it is a pleasure to us to be in this way considered weak, so that only ye be blameless;' wherefore he adds, "and ye are strong," that is, 'are approved, are virtuous. And we do not only wish for this, but we pray for this, that ye may be blameless, perfect, and afford us no handle.'

[6.] This is paternal affection, to prefer the salvation of the disciples before his own good name. This is the part of a soul free from vainglory; this best releaseth from the bonds of the body and makes one to rise aloft from earth to heaven, the being pure from vain-glory; just as therefore the contrary leadeth unto many sins. For it is impossible that one who is not pure from vain-glory, should be lofty and great and noble; but he must needs grovel on the ground, and do much damage, whilst the slave of a polluted mistress, more cruel than any barbarian. For what can be fiercer than she who, when most courted, is then most savage? Even wild beasts are not this, but are tamed by much attention. But vain-glory is quite the contrary, by being contemned she is made tame, by being honored she is made savage and is armed against her honorer. The Jews honored her and were punished with exceeding severity; the disciples slighted her and were crowned. And why speak I of punishment and crowns? for to this very point of being seen to be glorious, it contributes more than any thing, to spit upon vain-glory. And thou shalt see even in this world that they who honor it are damaged, whilst those who slight it are benefited. For the disciples who slighted it, (for there is no obstacle to our using the same example again,) and preferred the things of God, outshine the sun, having gained themselves an immortal memory even after their death; whilst the Jews who crouched[1] to it are become cityless, heartless, degraded, fugitives, exiles, mean, contemptible. Do thou,

therefore, if thou desirest to receive glory, repel glory; but if thou pursuest glory, thou shalt miss glory. And, if ye will, let us also try this doctrine in worldly matters. For whom do we make sport of in our jests? Is it not of those whose minds are set upon it? Certainly then, these men are the most entirely destitute of it, having countless accusers and being slighted by all. And whom do we admire, tell me; is it not those who despise it? Certainly then, these are they that are glorified. For as he is rich, not who is in need of many things, but who is in need of nothing; so he is glorious, not who loveth glory, but who despiseth it; for this glory is but a shadow of glory. No one having seen a loaf painted, though he should be pressed with hunger ever so much, will attack the picture. Neither then do thou pursue these shadows, for this is a shadow of glory, not glory. And that thou mayest know that this is the manner of it and that it is a shadow, consider this that it must be so, when the thing hath a bad name amongst men, when all consider it a thing to be avoided, they even who desire it; and when he who hath it and he covets it are ashamed to be called after it. 'Whence then is this desire,' saith one, 'and how is the passion engendered?' By littleness of soul, (for one ought not only to accuse it, but also to correct it,) by an imperfect mind, by a childish judgment. Let us then cease to be children, and let us become men: and let us every where pursue the reality, not the shadows, both in wealth, and in pleasure, and in luxury, and in glory, and in power; and this disease will cease, and many others also. For to pursue shadows is a madman's part. Wherefore also Paul said, "Awake up righteously and sin not." (1 Cor. xv. 34.) For there is yet another madness, sorer than that caused by devils, than that from frenzy. For that admits of forgiveness, but this is destitute of excuse, seeing the soul itself is corrupted and its right judgment lost; and that of frenzy indeed is an affection of the body, but this madness hath its seat in the artificer mind. As then of fevers those are sorer, yea incurable, which seize upon firm bodies and lurk in the recesses[2] of the nerves and are hidden away in the veins, so truly is this madness also, seeing it lurks in the recesses of the mind itself, perverting and destroying it. For how is it not clear and evident madness, yea, a distemper sorer than any madness, to despise the things which abide forever, and to cling with great eagerness to those which perish? For, tell me, if one were to chase the wind or try to hold it, should we not say that he was mad? And what? if one should grasp a shadow and neglect the reality;[3] if one

---

[1] ὑποκατακλιθέντες.

[2] ἐνδομυχοῦντες
[3] τῶν ἀληθῶν.

should hate his own wife and embrace her shadow; or loathe his son and again love his shadow, wouldest thou seek any other clearer sign in proof of madness? Such are they also who greedily follow the present things. For they are all shadow, yea, whether thou mention glory, or power, or good report, or wealth, or luxury, or any other thing of this life. And therefore truly it is that the prophet said, "Surely man walketh in a shadow, yea, he disquieth himself in vain;" (Ps. xxxix. 6.) and again, "Our days decline like a shadow." (Ps. cii. 11.) And in another place, he calls human things smoke and the flower of grass. But it is not only his good things which are shadow, but his evils also, whether it be death thou mention, or poverty, or disease, or any other thing. What then are those things which abide, both good and evil? The eternal kingdom and the everlasting hell. For "neither shall the worm die, nor shall the fire be quenched:" (Mark ix. 44.) and "these shall rise again to everlasting life: and these to everlasting punishment." (Mat. xxv. 46.) That then we may escape the one and enjoy the other, letting go the shadow, let us cling to the real things with all earnestness, for so shall we obtain the kingdom of heaven, which may we all obtain though the grace and love towards men of our Lord Jesus Christ, to Whom be glory and might for ever and ever Amen.

HOMILY XXX

2 COR. xiii. 10.

For this cause I write these things while absent, that I may not when present deal sharply, according to the authority which the Lord gave me for building up, and not for casting down.

HE was sensible he had spoken more vehemently than his wont, and especially towards the end of the Epistle. For he said before, "Now I Paul myself entreat you by the meekness and gentleness of Christ; I who in your presence am lowly among you, but being absent am of good courage towards you: Yea, I beseech you, that I may not be bold when I am present, with the confidence wherewith I count to be bold against some which count of us as if we walked according to the flesh;" (Chap. x. 1,2.) and, "being in readiness to avenge all disobedience when your obedience shall be fulfilled:" (Ib. 6.) and, "I fear lest when I come, I should find you not such as I would, and should myself be found of you such as ye would not;" (Chap. xii. 20.) and again, "lest when I come my God should humble me before you, and that I should mourn many of them which have sinned heretofore, and repented not of the lasciviousness and uncleanness which they committed:" (Ib. 21.) and afterwards, "I told you before and foretell you, as if I were present the second time, and being absent now I write, that, if I come again, I will not spare; seeing that ye seek a proof of Christ, that speaketh in me." (Chap. xiii. 2,3.) Since then he had said these things and more besides, terrifying, shaming, reproaching, lashing them, he says, in excuse for all, "For this cause I write these things while absent, that I may not when present deal sharply." For I am desirous the sharpness should lie in my letters and not in my deeds. I wish my threats to be vehement, that they may continue threats and never go forth into action. Again even in this his apology he makes what he says more terrible, showing that it is not himself who is to punish, but God; for he added, "according to the authority which the Lord gave me;" and again, to show that he desires not to use his power to their punishment, he added, "not for casting down, but for building up." And he hinted indeed this now, as I said, but he left it to them to draw the conclusion that if they should continue unamended, even this again is building up, to punish those that are of such a mind. For so it is, and he knew it and showed it by his deeds.

Ver. 11. "For the rest,[1] brethren, rejoice, be perfected, be comforted, be of the same mind, live in peace, and the God of love and peace shall be with you."

What means, "for the rest, brethren, rejoice?" Thou hast pained, terrified, thrown them into an agony, made them to tremble and fear, and how biddest thou them rejoice? 'Why, for this very reason I bid them rejoice. For,' he says, 'if what is your part follow·upon mine, there will be nothing to prevent that joy. For all my part has been done; I have suffered long, I have delayed, I have forborne to cut off, I have besought, I have advised, I have alarmed,

[1] Τὸ λοιπὸν, Rec. Text Λοιπὸν.

I have threatened, so as by every means to gather you in unto the fruit of repentance. And now it behoveth that your part be done, and so your joy will be unfading.'

"Be perfected." What is, " be perfected?" ' Be complete, fill up what is deficient.'

"Be comforted." For, since their trials were numerous, and their perils great, he says, ' " be comforted," both by one another, and by us, and by your change unto the better. For if ye should have joy of conscience and become complete, nothing is wanting unto your cheerfulness and comfort. For nothing doth so produce comfort as a pure conscience, yea, though innumerable trials surround.'

"Be of the same mind, live in peace." The request he made in the former Epistle also, at the opening. For it is possible to be of one mind, and yet not to live in peace, [for instance], when people agree in doctrine, but in their dealings with each other are at variance. But Paul requires both.

"And the God of love and peace shall be with you." For truly he not only recommends and advises, but also prays. For either he prays for this,, or else foretells what shall happen ; or rather, both. ' For if ye do these things,' he says, ' for instance, if ye be " of one mind " and " live in peace," God also will be with you, for He is " the God of love and of peace," and in these things He delighteth, He rejoiceth. Hence shall peace also be yours from His love ; hence shall every evil be removed. This saved the world, this ended the long war, this blended together heaven and earth, this made men angels. This then let us also imitate, for love is the mother of countless good things. By this we were saved, by this all those unspeakable good things [come] to us.'

[2.] Then to lead them on unto it, he says,

Ver. 12. "Salute one another with a holy kiss."

What is " holy ? " not hollow,[1] not treacherous, like the kiss which Judas gave to Christ. For therefore is the kiss given, that it may be fuel unto love, that it may kindle the disposition, that we may so love each other, as brothers brothers, as children parents, as parents children ; yea, rather even far more. For those things are a disposition implanted by nature, but these by spiritual grace. Thus our souls bound unto each other. And therefore when we return after an absence we kiss each other, our souls hastening unto mutual intercourse. For this is that member which most of all declares to us the workings of the soul. But about this holy kiss somewhat else may yet be said. To what effect ? We are the temple of Christ ; we kiss then the porch and entrance of the temple when we kiss each other. See ye not how many kiss even the porch of this temple, some stooping down, others grasping it with their hand, and putting their hand to their mouth. And through these gates and doors Christ both had entered into us, and doth enter, whensoever we communicate. Ye who partake of the mysteries understand what I say. For it is in no common manner that our lips are honored, when they receive the Lord's Body. It is for this reason chiefly that we here kiss. Let them give ear who speak filthy things, who utter railing, and let them shudder to think what that mouth is they dishonor ; let those give ear who kiss obscenely. Hear what things God hath proclaimed by thy mouth, and keep it undefiled. He hath discoursed of the life to come, of the resurrection, of immortality, that death is not death, of those other innumerable mysteries. For he that is about to be initiated comes to the priest's mouth as it were an oracle, to hear things full of awe. For he lost his life even from his forefathers, and comes to seek it again, and to ask how he may haply find and get it back. Then God announceth to him how it may be found, and that mouth becomes more awful than the very mercy-seat. For that mercy-seat never sent forth a voice like this, but spake much of lesser things, of wars and such peace as is here below : but this speaks all about heaven and the life to come, and things new and that pass understanding. And having said,

Ver. 13. "Salute one another with an holy kiss," he added, " All the saints salute you."

By this also giving them good hopes. He has added this in the place of the kiss, knitting them together by the salutation, for the words also proceed from the same mouth from which the kiss. Seest thou how he brings them all together, both those who are widely separated in the body and those who are near, these by the kiss and those by the written message?

[3.] Ver. 14. "The grace of our Lord Jesus Christ, and the love of God," and the Father,[2] " and the communion of the Holy Ghost, be with you all." After having united them to one other by the salutations and the kisses, he again closes his speech with prayer, with much carefulness uniting them unto God also. Where now are they who say that because the Holy Spirit is not inserted in the beginnings of the Epistles, He is not of the same substance? For, behold, he hath now enumerated Him with the Father and Son. And besides this, one may remark, that when writing to the Colossians and saying, " Grace to you, and peace from God our Father," he was silent of the Son, and added not, as in all his Epistles, and

---

[1] ὑπούλῳ

[2] καί Πάτρος om. R. T.

from the Lord Jesus Christ.[1] Is then the Son not of the same substance either, because of this? Nay, these reasonings are of extreme folly. For this very thing especially shows Him to be of the same substance, that Paul useth the expression [or not] indifferently. And that what is here said is no conjecture, hear how he mentions Son and Spirit, and is quite silent of the Father. For, writing to the Corinthians, he says, "But ye were washed, but ye were sanctified, but ye were justified in the name of the Lord Jesus Christ, and in the Spirit of our God." (1 Cor. vi. 11.) What then, tell me? were these not baptized into the Father? Then assuredly they were neither washed nor sanctified. But did they baptize them? doubtless then just as also they did baptize. How then did he not say, 'Ye are washed in the name of the Father?' Because it was indifferent in his view, at one time to make mention of this, at another of that Person ; and you may observe this custom in many places of the Epistles. For writing to the Romans he says, "I beseech you therefore by the mercies of God," (Rom. xii. 1.) although those mercies are of the Son; and, "I beseech you by the love of the Spirit," (Rom. xv. 30.) although love is of the Father. Wherefore then mentioned he not the Son in "the mercies," nor the Father in "the love?" Because as being things plain and admitted, he was silent about them. Moreover, he will be found again, to put the gifts also themselves transposedly.[2] For having said here, "The grace of Christ, and the love of God and the Father, and the communion of the Holy Ghost;" he in another place speaks of "the communion of the Son," and of "the love of the Spirit." For, "I beseech you," he says, "by the love of the Spirit." (Rom. xv. 30.) And in his Epistle to the Corinthians, "God is faithful, by Whom ye were called into the communion of His Son." (1 Cor. i. 9.) Thus the things of the Trinity are undivided : and whereas the communion is of the Spirit, it hath been found of the Son; and whereas the grace is of the Son, it is also of the Father and of the Holy Spirit; for [we read], "Grace be to you from God the Father." And in another place, having enumerated many forms of it, he added, "But all these worketh the one and the same Spirit, dividing to each one severally as He will." (1 Cor. xii. 11.) And I say these things, not confounding[3] the Persons, (away with the thought !) but knowing both the individuality and distinctness[4] of These, and the Unity of the Substance.

---

[1] See also Chrys. on Coloss. Oxford Trans. 183. 'From God, saith he, our Father : although he useth not in this place the name of Christ.' Yet the Rec. Text has the words, Col. i. 2.
[2] ἀντιστρόφως
[3] συναλείφων
[4] ἰδιάζον καὶ διῃρημένον

[4.] Let us then continue both to hold these doctrines in their strictness, and to draw to us the love of God. For before indeed He loved us when hating Him, and reconciled us who were His enemies; but henceforth He wishes to love us as loving Him. Let us then continue to love Him, so that we may be also loved by Him. For if when beloved by powerful men we are formidable to all, much more when [beloved] by God. And should it be needful to give wealth, or body, or even life itself for this love, let us not grudge them. For it is not enough to say in words that we love, but we ought to give also the proof of deeds ; for neither did He show love by words only, but by deeds also. Do thou then also show this by thy deeds and do those things which please Him, for so shalt thou thyself reap again the advantage. For He needeth nothing that we have to bestow, and this is also a special proof of a sincere love, when one who needeth nothing and is not in any necessity, doth all for the sake of being loved by us. Wherefore also Moses said, "For what doth the Lord God require of you, but to love Him, and that thou shouldest be ready to walk after Him ?" (Deut. x. 12.) So that when He biddeth thee love Him, He then most of all showeth that He loves thee. For nothing doth so secure our salvation as to love Him. See then, how that all His commandments even tend together to our repose and salvation and good report. For when he says, "Blessed are the merciful, blessed are the pure in heart, blessed are the meek, blessed are the poor in spirit, blessed are the peacemakers ; " (Matt. v. 3-9.) He Himself indeed reaps no advantage from these, but he enjoins them for our adorning and attuning ; and when He says, "I was an hungred," it is not as needing that ministry from us, but as exciting thee to humanity. For He was well able even without thee to feed the poor man ; but as bestowing upon thee an exceeding treasure, he laid these commands upon thee. For if the sun, which is but a creature, needeth not our eyes; for he abideth in his own proper brightness, even though none should look upon him, and we it is who are the gainers when we enjoy his beams; much more is this so with God. But that thou mayest learn this in yet another way ; how great wilt thou have the distance to be between God and us ? as great as between gnats and us, or much greater? Quite plainly it is much greater, yea, infinite. If then we vainglorious creatures need not service nor honor from gnats, much rather the Divine Nature [none from us], seeing It is impassible and needing nothing. The measure of that which He enjoyeth by us is but the greatness of our benefit, and the delight He taketh in our salvation. For this reason He also oftentimes relinquisheth His own, and seeketh thine. " For if any," he saith, " have a wife that believeth not, and she be pleased to dwell with him, let him not put her away ; " (1 Cor. vii. 12.) and, " He that putteth away his wife, saving for the cause of fornication, causeth her to commit adultery." Seest thou what unspeakable goodness ? 'If a wife be a harlot,' He says, 'I do not compel the husband to live with her ; and if she be an unbeliever, I do not forbid him.' Again, 'if thou be grieved against any one, I command him that hath grieved thee to leave My gift and to run to thee.' For He saith, "If thou art offering thy gift, and there remember that thy brother hath aught against thee, leave thy gift before the altar, and go thy way, first be reconciled to thy brother, and then come and offer thy gift." (Matt. v. 23, 24.) And what saith the parable of him that had devoured his all ? (Matt. xviii. 24, &c.) Doth it not show this ? For when he had eaten up those ten thousand talents, He had mercy on him, and let him go ; but when he demanded of his fellowservant an hundred pence, he both called him wicked and delivered him over to the punishment. So great account doth He make of thy ease. The barbarian was about to sin against the wife of the just man, and He says, " I spared thee from sinning against me." (Gen. xx. 6.) Paul persecuted the Apostles, and He saith to him, " Why persecutest thou Me ?" Others are hungry, and He Himself saith He is an hungred, and wanders about naked and a stranger, wishing to shame thee, and so to force thee into the way of almsgiving.

Reflecting then upon the love, how great He hath shown in all things, and still shows it to be, both having vouchsafed to make Himself known to us, (which is the greatest crown of good things, and light to the understanding and instruction in virtue,) and to lay down laws for the best mode of life, and having done all things for our sakes, having given His Son, and promised a kingdom, and invited us to those unspeakable good things, and prepared for us a most blessed life, let us do and say every thing so as both to appear worthy of His love and to obtain the good things to come ; whereunto may we all attain, through the grace and love towards men of our Lord Jesus Christ ; with Whom to the Father, with the Holy Spirit, be glory now and ever, and world without end. Amen.

INDEXES

INDEX OF SUBJECTS

INDEX OF TEXTS